MODERN POLITICAL SYSTEMS: EUROPE

Roy C. Macridis and Robert E. Ward, editors

MODERN POLITICAL

THIRD EDITION

SYSTEMS: EUROPE

Great Britain

SAMUEL E. FINER, University of Manchester, England

France

ROY C. MACRIDIS, Brandeis University

The German Federal Republic

KARL W. DEUTSCH, Harvard University

The Soviet Union

VERNON V. ASPATURIAN, Pennsylvania State University

PRENTICE-HALL, INC., Englewood Cliffs, New Jersey

Library of Congress Catalog No.: 72–075001

Printed in the United States of America

ISBN: 0–13–597161–6

10 9 8 7 6 5 4 3 2 1

PRENTICE-HALL INTERNATIONAL, INC., *London*
PRENTICE-HALL OF AUSTRALIA, PTY. LTD., *Sydney*
PRENTICE-HALL OF CANADA, LTD., *Toronto*
PRENTICE-HALL OF INDIA PRIVATE LIMITED, *New Delhi*
PRENTICE-HALL OF JAPAN, INC., *Tokyo*

contents

FRANCE

FOUR
Parties and Opinion, 192

> The Structure of Public Opinion. Political Parties. The Left. The Center. The Right. The Left and the Gaullists.

FIVE
Elections in the Fifth Republic, 220

> I. THE DE GAULLE YEARS. A Constitutional Referendum and a Gaullist Assembly. The Presidential Election of 1965. The Legislative Elections of 1967. The "Events"of 1968 and the Gaullist Tide. II. AFTER DE GAULLE. The Last Hurrah. The Last Referendum. The Presidential Election Without de Gaulle (June 1969). The Vote in the Municipalities and Towns, 1971.

SIX
The Governmental Institutions, 257

> The President of the Republic. The Cabinet. The Legislature. The Government and the National Assembly. Other Constitutional Organs and Procedures.

SEVEN
The French Administration, 276

> The Chain of Command: From Central Government to Local Mayors. The Council of State (Counseil d'État).

EIGHT
Governmental Performance and Prospects for the Future, 285

> Independence for the Former Colonies. Foreign Policy. A New Defense. The Economy. Education. Prospects for the Future. The Regime. A Return to the Fourth Republic?

Bibliography, 301

THE GERMAN FEDERAL REPUBLIC

THE SOVIET UNION

This third edition is a continuing effort to translate our own versions of some of the recent theorizing and writing in the field of comparative politics into a text for American undergraduates. We have retained the traditional "country by country" format, since this fits best the organization and needs of existing courses. While treating each political system or groups of systems separately, we have tried also to utilize a common framework of exposition and analysis. We conceive of politics as a system for the identification and posing of problems and the making and administering of decisions in the realm of public affairs. Political systems are part of a larger social system which actually generates the conditions, attitudes, and demands that constitute the basic working materials of politics. In this book, therefore, we have made an especial effort to place politics and government in their appropriate historical, social, economic, and ideological setting.

Such an approach makes little sense if it does not also help the student to understand the more general political problems of our time. It is our hope that this volume will stimulate interest in and genuine intellectual curiosity about these problems that will extend beyond the classroom. The fate of parliamentary institutions, the challenge of totalitarianism, the politics of emerging nations, the explosive forces of rising expectations and demands among the new nations, the perennial contradictions between stability and change, the role of expert knowledge and leadership, are problems that influence our lives and shape the kind of world in which we live. If we succeed in introducing such issues to the student and in stimulating some better-informed and more systematic attention to the conditions and forces that underlie them, we shall have achieved our major goal.

preface

Waltham, Mass. R. C. M.
Ann Arbor, Mich. R. E. W.

MODERN POLITICAL SYSTEMS: EUROPE

The study of politics has been going through a period of revaluation. Many believe that it can become a science, like the natural sciences—that is, develop laws that are empirically verifiable for all political systems and for all times. They do not, however, expect that regularities and laws can yet be found, but rather believe that their discovery must be an ultimate intellectual concern. If an overall theory cannot be developed as yet, it is often suggested that correlations between types of political behavior and other manifestations of social behavior—family life, child rearing, class, income, status, etc.—may be established. Thus we may at least arrive at some generalizations—generalizations that apply to a fairly large group of phenomena *and* to a fairly large number of empirical situations. Discovery of correlations, such as "when X (income) goes up, Y (the birth rate) drops," lead to descriptive generalizations. We do not know why Y follows X, and we cannot be sure it always will. But if and when correlations between two discreet variables occur in many systems and over a period of time, then we are close to a descriptive generalization.

This volume is most definitely not concerned with the discovery of "laws" and the verification of hypotheses. What we are concerned with here is empirical generalizations—and then, only with regard to four countries. But even this may be too ambitious. Perhaps all we can do is to identify trends, point to differences, and show their relevance. If the generalizations we make and the trends we identify appear exciting enough, then the reader may try to discover whether they are valid elsewhere.

Each of our authors is concerned with the phenomenon of action (that is, governmental action), with the concerted effort to bring about results, e.g., modernization in the Soviet Union, political consensus in France, constitutional government in Germany, and equality in Great Britain. For each one of these countries, the policy goals of the government are closely examined, its performance assessed, and the conditions under which it operates carefully studied.

We concentrate a great deal on the condition and scope of governmental action, studying its history and analyzing it in terms of the existing alternatives and limitations. This ought

introduction

1

to be quite obvious, since we are studying systems wherein education is widespread and in which the citizens view and demand government action as a means for overcoming obstacles and providing solutions to problems. If there are riots in our cities, we believe that government action will put an end to them; if millions are poor, again we believe that, with the help of the government, there is a way out. Unemployment—a great social blight in the years between the two world wars—called for concerted action, and it seems that governments now have adequate means to cope with it. The Soviet, German, French, and British political leaders are imbued with this voluntaristic aspect of politics—so often disregarded by students of politics. Yet this shows the limitation of our discipline. We can never tell on the basis of verified knowledge what sort of action is desirable and how responsible leaders are likely to act. In all societies, when the problem or the evil has been identified, people disagree about the cure. The doctor, *without* the benefit of laws, has enough empirical data to know how to treat a patient, and how to adjust his empirical knowledge to an individual case. We do not. Take, for instance, the naïve notion that economic aid to underdeveloped societies would lead to stability and democracy. The opposite has often been the case. Or that a majority electoral system would eliminate small parties; or that recruitment of civil servants on the basis of merit would do away with upper-class domination. None of those "political actions" has brought about the desired or expected result. Yet the most ubiquitous political phenomenon in all modern political systems is governmental action—to defend the nation, to plan its economy, to educate its people, to provide welfare, leisure, and security.

THE FOUR COUNTRIES

This book is devoted to four European powers—Great Britain, France, West Germany, and the Soviet Union. All four are today, despite the rapidly changing nature of the world, major powers. They are leaders in science, technology, industry, and art. They account for

one-quarter of the world's total industrial production; their citizens enjoy a standard of living that ranks them among the most prosperous inhabitants of the world. By 1970, the average annual income (at market prices) of an English citizen was $1,976; of a French citizen, $2,783; of a citizen of West Germany, $2,512; and of a Soviet citizen, $1,400. These nations—with the exception of Great Britain—have had among the world's highest rates of industrial growth since the end of World War II, and the highest rates of urbanization of any countries in the world in the last fifty years. Illiteracy is virtually nonexistent, and involvement in politics on the part of the citizenry is widespread. The people in each of these countries are generally articulate about their common purposes and goals, and they share a deep sense of common destiny and nationality with their fellow citizens and abide by common rules through which ideological and social conflicts are settled. In dealing with these four countries, we shall be concerned with "the politics of modernity."

Despite certain common traits, the countries we have chosen differ profoundly in many respects. England, which became the center of the Industrial Revolution that began in the latter part of the eighteenth century, maintained a position of worldwide industrial, political, and naval supremacy almost until World War II. In the name of economic liberalism, she acquired a far-flung empire and used her navy to keep the seas free so her merchant marine could import raw materials and foodstuffs and export manufactured goods to every corner of the earth. But, most important, the representative and parliamentary institutions that originated in feudal times gradually secured wide acceptance first among the British nobility, then among the rising middle class, and finally, in the nineteenth century, among the working class.

By the time the Industrial Revolution arrived in England, Britain had developed a political system that carried all the seeds of a healthy democratic state: respect for individual rights, representative institutions, responsible and limited government, and, above all, the art of compromise and gradual change. Largely because the political system was capable of overcoming sharp social conflicts, Britain is the only country of the four that has not experienced a major revolution since the middle of the seventeenth century. The strains and stresses of the twentieth century and her diminished status as a world power have not affected the strength of her political institutions at home.

Even more remarkable, the British system has been able to cope with the independence movements of her colonies. In the nineteenth century, Britain ruled more than a quarter of the population of the world, in an empire that stretched from New Zealand, Australia, Singapore, Malaya, and India through the Middle East, the Nile Valley, and Africa, and into North America. Some of her colonies were settled by English-speaking peoples who were given their full independence after World War I. In others, colonial rule continued until 1945, and it is only in the last decade and a half that a peaceful "liquidation" of the British empire has been achieved. But here again the British have shown their genius in political adaptability. Most of the colonies, after becoming independent, have joined the British Commonwealth, a community of member states that are linked together by a number of informal ties and in most cases by a common acceptance of the British crown.

In a period of declining power and colonial disengagement, Great Britain has been able to give us, like the Scandinavian countries, a genuine example of democratic socialism. After World War II, the Labour party received a large parliamentary majority and proceeded to overhaul the British economy and social structure: it nationalized a number of key industries, took over the control of the levers of economic activity, established a National Health Service to provide medical care to all as a matter of right, and attempted to narrow income inequalities. This "peaceful revolution" was accomplished without violating parliamentary procedures and individual rights. What is more, after the defeat of the Labour party in 1951, the major reforms were accepted by the Conservatives, thus diminishing party strife and accentuating the broad area of agreement that typifies the British political system.

French democracy has not fared as well. The Industrial Revolution hit France just in time to sharpen the already existing ideological divisions that stemmed from the French Revolution. The Third Republic (1871–1940) was unable to cope with urgent problems of social and economic reform. By 1940, it was ripe for the demise that defeat at the hands of the German army made inevitable. The Fourth Republic, established in 1946 after the liberation of France, was a projection of the Third Republic and perpetuated and reflected ideological and class cleavages. The result was a stalemate on many basic issues that confronted the country. But even more important, long colonial wars in Indochina and later in Algeria gave to the military the opportunity to assume important powers and to defy the authority of the republican state. It was in the wake of a military uprising in Algeria against the government of the Fourth Republic that General de Gaulle was returned to power and given sweeping powers to overhaul the parliamentary institutions. On September 28, 1958, the French people accepted the new constitution—the Fifth Republic—under which the parliamentary supremacy has disappeared in favor of presidential leadership.

Political and constitutional instability has also accounted for the lack of a clearcut policy with regard to the French colonies. Only in the last years of the Fourth Republic were reforms made toward colonial autonomy, but it was only under de Gaulle, and on the basis of his own personal popularity, that the African republics were granted their independence. The army was brought under control and Algeria became independent on July 3, 1962. De Gaulle returned to play the role of Cincinnatus—to settle the Algerian war with which the republican institutions were unable to cope. In November, 1962, in March, 1967, and again in June, 1968 the Gaullist forces won the election and it is likely that the Fifth Republic will continue.

The instability of democratic institutions in France before World War II was symptomatic of a general decline of democracy throughout the whole of Europe in the period between the two world wars. With the exception of the Scandinavian countries and Switzerland, democracy and parliamentary institutions were abandoned or seriously qualified in every country on the Continent. In Germany, the Weimar Republic (1918–33) gave way to a one-party government. Constitutional limitations were set aside, individual rights were abandoned, and the state, controlled by the National Socialists, claimed total control over the minds, conscience, and lives of German citizens. In the name of racial supremacy, Germany set out to conquer Europe, attacked the Soviet Union, and challenged Great Britain and the United States. In the very heart of Europe, the Nazi movement threatened the most cherished traditions of Western European civilization—individual freedom and limitations upon government. It denied the rational assumptions on which democracy rests and came close to destroying Western civilization.

The defeat of Nazism by the Allied powers was followed by the division of Germany into two parts—the German Federal Republic and the German Democratic Republic. The German Federal Republic, commonly called West Germany, reintroduced constitutional and parliamentary government and in the last decade or so has enjoyed an unprecedented prosperity and political stability. The German Democratic Republic (East Germany), under communist rule, has been unable thus far to rival West Germany in economic prosperity, and its existence depends on Soviet support. At this point, the political future of Germany is a burning issue, and one not confined within the borders of the country. Conflict between the two Germanies, subsumed under the broader conflict between the United States and the Soviet Union, may create tensions that will put an end to the democratic experiment of the Federal Republic. As in the past, democracy and parliamentary government retain a tenuous foothold.

The Soviet Union, naturally, presents a special case. Russia was an underdeveloped society governed by a despotic regime until the end of the nineteenth century. In 1917, after some half-hearted reforms had been made in the direction of parliamentary government and democratic freedoms, the Bolsheviks came to power. Inspired by Marxism, they introduced communism to Russia and established a ruthless party dictatorship—under Lenin until 1924 and under Stalin until 1953. The major effort of the Communist party has been devoted to the task of industrializing and modernizing what was primarily an agrarian society. This has meant that the Soviet Union has had to concentrate on building heavy industry, on speeding up the process of urbanization, and on improving its educational system. Under an authoritarian government, the Soviet leaders greatly accelerated industrial development in the USSR, and now claim they will surpass even the United States in the near future. They have thus challenged not only the democratic West, but have provided a new model of development for the former colonial nations of the world.

The Soviet Union provides us with a political system that rivals democratic norms and values. Under Soviet totalitarianism, ultimate authority resides with a small elite within a one-party system, but the whole society is mobilized to attain certain goals. Social and political mobilization is achieved not only through terror but through the manipulation of a number of incentives—income, ideology, social mobility, and others. The Soviet system introduced new political techniques to achieve socialism rapidly, to gain in one generation what the West attained gradually and in the context of democratic values. In accomplishing this rapid modernization, the totalitarian system of the Soviet Union has been a "success," and we are today faced with a number of puzzling questions about the USSR. Is totalitarianism in the Soviet Union a permanent mode of government? Can totalitarianism be considered a transitional system that can lead a backward society rapidly toward modernization? Is totalitarianism likely to evolve gradually into an open society once the country is modernized and has gained prosperity and the comforting benefits of economic security?

Our task in this volume, then, is to analyze four political systems: the highly stable British parliamentary system, the unstable representative institutions of the French Republic, the very recent development of a successful parliamentary democracy in West Germany, and the outright totalitarian system of the Soviet Union. Why and how shall we attempt to compare these four widely divergent political systems?

COMPARISON

The whys of comparative politics are many and persuasive for student and teacher alike. Comparison, to begin with, for any student, and more particularly for the American college student, is like a guided tour of foreign lands. It shows that human beings living in different societies differ in their political behavior. They differ in the political values they hold dear; in the ways in which they apprehend each other and the outside world; in the manner in which they solve similar problems. Thus those who study comparative politics come to realize that health services may be completely nationalized in one country and based on one's ability to pay in another; that trains controlled and run by the government may be just as efficient as trains run by private companies; that individual liberties are highly valued in one system but that the interests of the group or the state are more esteemed in others. The student who reads about the governments of Great Britain, the Soviet Union, Japan, or China begins to gain perspective on his own political system, to reexamine attitudes and practices long taken for granted, and to scrutinize his own political institutions and those of others. Habit and intellectual conformism give place to critical evaluation and appreciation, the mark of an educated man.

Political differences, naturally, raise the question, "Why?" in a variety of contexts: Why did Marxism strike such firm roots in the Soviet Union? Why have so many underdeveloped Asian societies flirted with Marxism or established one-party governments? Why has the parliamentary system brought stability to British politics but not to French politics? Why so many parties still in France but only two in England and, for that matter, in the United States and Japan? Why do certain peoples accept readily the notion of state ownership and management of their economy and hold this compatible with democracy and freedom, while others do not? Finally, why do some

political systems repudiate democracy and representative institutions while others deem them essential? To answer these questions, it is not adequate simply to recognize and list the individual differences that separate one political system from another. Descriptive identification of national differences is important, but we must also explain them. We must search for regularities and differences in political behavior and try to account for them.

The types of explanation we give to the national political differences we note may vary. In some cases, similarities or differences may be explained in terms of the history of the countries involved. For instance, it may well be that parliamentary institutions developed a remarkable viability in England because they were established before the Industrial Revolution. In France and Germany, on the other hand, industrialization came after any very significant experience with parliamentary institutions. This is an essentially *historical* explanation.

Complementing the historical explanation, we have what may be called the *structural-functional* explanation. It views all political systems both in terms of certain common indispensable functions which must be performed —recruitment, communication, the maintenance of order, the adjudication of conflicts, etc.—and in terms of the structures or institutions which perform them. In different political systems, a given function may be associated with quite different structures and institutions. For example, the adjudication of conflicts may be handled by a formal judiciary in one society and by private mediators, village elders, or a priesthood in others. Such differences may in turn be accounted for by variations in social and economic organization or in value systems and prevalent ideologies, or (and this approach is far from incompatible with historical explanations) by specific historical circumstances.

If we were to compare, for instance, the political systems of certain underdeveloped countries that had formerly been colonies, a knowledge of the traditions and institutions implanted in each by their former imperial masters would be indispensable to an understanding of present differences. Thus, present political differences between Malaysia and Indonesia to some extent relate to differences in the histories of the British and Dutch colonial systems. But beyond this they also relate to differences in social structure, population characteristics, levels of literacy, leadership characteristics, and economic circumstances in the two states. Similarly, differences between French and British parliamentary institutions relate to contemporary ideological variances, relative degrees of industrialization, different configurations of interest groups, and a variety of other factors, in addition to "historical" ones.

The structural-functional approach, in other words, strives toward a sophisticated definition in depth of political systems, the identification of the most important institutions in each system, and the classification and explanation of their political differences and similarities. It leads us to formulate hypotheses about political behavior and governmental performance in terms of which we can compare diverse political systems. For instance, it might be posited that in societies lacking serious ideological conflicts with majority electoral systems, a two-party system will tend to develop. Or, it might be said that within a given society industrialization and prosperity will, all other conditions being equal, lead to a decrease in political conflicts over abstract or general issues and the development of a political system primarily concerned with the solution of concrete and specific problems. Again, it might be hypothesized that significant and sizable groups which are systematically denied access to positions of status and influence within a political system will, all other things being equal, eventually seek to gain these by violent means.

Such hypotheses can be tested against historical and contemporary evidence and may be modified or rejected accordingly. Research and empirical observation are indispensable elements of valid comparative political studies, just as they are in all forms of scientific inquiry. It is through empirical observation that we enrich our knowledge of conditioning factors, the presence or absence of which lead to the validation or rejection of our hypotheses. For instance, if we propose that "wherever there is A (e.g., a single-member district majority elec-

toral system), B (a two-party system) will follow," only to find that this is so in one country but not in another, then we must seek empirically the reasons for this disparity. We do so usually through a search for further relevant factors (X, X1, X2, X3, X4, etc.). Once discovered, our hypothesis is then qualified to read that B will follow A, *provided* factors X1, X2, or X3 (e.g., social, religious, or regional factors or others depending upon field observation) also obtain. In this manner, a more comprehensive and refined explanation accounting for differences in party systems can then be formulated.

It is at this point that comparative political analysis becomes particularly challenging, and at the same time frustrating, for the student. He would like to be able to identify quickly the regularities and differences between systems and to come up with a simple explanation for them. But rarely, if ever, can this be achieved in practice. All political systems possess certain characteristics which are unique—which cannot be duplicated. In fact, we will find it virtually impossible to verify any hypothesis or develop definitely any generalization that is valid for *all* political systems at *all* times. Invariably we will be forced to lengthen the chain of conditioning factors (X's) for each and every political system, and note that the generalizations proposed must be carefully qualified in terms of a variety of individual and idiosyncratic factors. Thus, at the very moment when we propose to develop general laws, we seem to bog down in the enumeration of unique situations. In despair, we tend to fall back on the facile explanation that uniqueness is the only rule of politics, that comparative study cannot really explain political differences, and that the degree of indeterminancy in political behavior is so great that no generalizations are possible.

It would be a serious mistake to accept such an attitude. We have been careful to point out that, if one proceeded in the manner suggested, political uniquenesses would be identified and explained. This is a point of crucial importance. We had to start from the general in order to identify and explain the unique. Unless we started with general political concepts and hypotheses, not only would we have been unable to generalize, even in qualified fashion, but we would not even have been able to distinguish among particular political differences, much less try to account for them. After all, how can one tell what is different and unique without first knowing what is general, or without at least first being aware of the existence of a relevant general concept? Power, for example, is a general political concept which is variously manifested in different societies—through, for example, symbols of religion, force, property, or status, to name just a few. But without first grasping the notion of power as a general concept, we would be unable to relate these symbols to power as particular manifestations. This leads to the heart of our problem: deciding which general concepts we shall use in order to compare different political systems and to explain the similarities, differences, and uniquenesses that we observe in them.

FOUNDATIONS: BASIC CONCEPTS

The two basic goals that have guided the authors in this volume are to analyze and study "behavior" and to describe and explain, if possible, "governmental action." The two are related. By *behavior* we mean the large array of social, economic, cultural, psychological, and historical factors within which the government operates—the interests, the beliefs, the aspirations and goals, and the perception of the community itself, and the attitudes about the government that people in any given society have. By *governmental action,* on the other hand, we mean the specific political institutions and structures by means of which decisions are made and carried out. Specifically, we include the parties, the legislature, the executive, the civil service, and the judiciary.

Relevance

Conditions of governmental action are determined by the broad framework of the society as a whole. The family life; the way in which people earn a living; the manner in which income is distributed; the traditions of the past; the training, skills, and values that people get through the family, the school, or other organizations; the way and the manner in which people view the role and functions of government—all these things and many more constitute what we call the foundations of politics. Professor Aspaturian explains, for instance, that Russian dominance over all other ethnic groups in the tsarist empire continues to shape behavior today—it is a "foundation." Professor Macridis points to the most pervasive trait of French political history—lack of agreement on a constitution—and tries to assess the importance of the actions taken by a small group of contemporary political leaders to change this. The gradualist character of British politics, which Professor Finer describes, is based upon a set of behavior patterns; it is a foundation that makes for stability and hinders quick action. And Professor Deutsch shows the ambivalence of past traditions and habits in the German political history that makes it so difficult to predict trends—or even to identify them with any assurance.

It is impossible to encompass *all* the determinants of behavior and relate them to governmental action, even if we knew all about them. There is no doubt that they all have some relevance—but some have greater and others have less. We have to be arbitrary regarding what we choose and what we discard. Most behavior in any given society is apolitical. There is no society in which politics appears to be very exciting or interesting to more than a small minority. People are interested in other forms of self-expression: art, family life, economic production, sex, etc. *Behavior becomes politically relevant only when it is addressed to governmental action*—demanding it or trying to impede it. The French farmers throw their produce in the Rhone River to force the government to do something about prices, and each and every confrontation between "KKK" and "black power" advocates is very much related to competing attitudes and expectations about the government. Any form of behavior can assume at a given time a politically relevant character only to subside into an apolitical stance again. This is another reason why we cannot tell in advance what aspects of the total behavior are politically relevant and which ones are not. The dilemma is obvious. Should we study everything that is *potentially* political? Should we narrow our definition and, if so, how? [1]

We feel that the answer to these questions lies in the fact that while virtually every and any kind of behavior *may* at any given time become politically relevant, some always are, and it is with these that we begin the study of comparative politics. This is what Joseph La-Palombara has called the "rule of parsimony": study those factors we are as sure as we can be are politically relevant.

What are these "factors"? The best we can do is to establish a set of priorities in descending order of importance.

The demand for state action or the demand that a given action cease is the very guts of politics. The most obvious reason why French farmers destroy their produce, the most obvious reason for the establishment of the KKK and of black power groups is to control, to influence, or to oppose state action. Our first priority is therefore the study of organized manifestations, attitudes, and movements that press directly for or against state action—that is, the study of interest groups.

Our second priority is the state and state agencies, by which we mean all the structures and organizations that make decisions and resolve conflicts with the expectation that their decisions will be obeyed: the civil service, the legislature, the executive, the judiciary, the host of public or semipublic corporations and organizations that are called upon to resolve differences and to make decisions. We include also the agencies whose function is to study facts, to deliberate about them, to identify areas of conflict, and to suggest policy decisions. The study of the state—of the organization and performance of such agencies, the scope of their decision-making, the attitudes of the men and women who perform within them, and the major constituencies they serve—has been sadly neglected in the last decade or so. It has been far more fashionable to study the systems in

which there is no state as such, i.e., the so-called developing, emerging, or new nations. As a result, studies of the urgent and nagging empirical situations in the modern and highly industrialized nations in which our fate is to be decided are few.

The "political culture," or what others have called very loosely ideology, is our third priority. Whatever name we give them, the beliefs, norms, and orientations *about the state*—authority, scope of action, legitimacy, sense of participation, and involvement—directly influence political phenomena. Unless we link structure and forms, decisions and policies to attitudes, the specifics of governmental decisions and performance will elude us.

Finally, our fourth and last priority is what may be called the infrastructure of the political world: attitudes and ideas; social, economic, and cultural institutions; norms and values that are prevalent in any given society, national or international. There is no reason why we shouldn't study child-rearing, the patterns of socialization, the degree of concentration of economic power, the identification of personality types and traits, family life patterns, small groups and private associations, religious attitudes, and so on. All of these *may* have relevance to politics.

Thus we begin by pinpointing what is political; we catch it, so to speak, in its most visible, open, and raw manifestation; we begin with the top of the iceberg before we go deep to search for its submerged base. We focus on the state and its agencies, on its types of action and inaction, and on all those organized manifestations that call for action or inaction on its part. We study the forms of decision-making and analyze and evaluate its substance. We explore the impact of the state upon groups, interests, and power elites within the system; we study in turn their reaction to state actions and their counterdemands as they are manifested through various media, from political parties down to voting.

The "Constitution"

The basic political "act" (and for this reason one of the crucial topics in the history of politi-

---

[1] The discussion which follows is based on Roy C. Macridis, "Comparative Politics and the Study of Government: The Search for Focus," *Comparative Politics*, 1, no. 1 (Oct. 1968), 79–90.

cal thought) is the creation of a government. For some, government has been established as a means to protect individual (often called "natural") rights, for others as a means to disarm the individual and establish a single police force to keep order and peace so that citizens might live to a ripe old age while pursuing their interests. For still others, the *raison d'être* of government has been to maximize the welfare of all; while yet another school of thought has seen in government the instrument by means of which a dominant group of persons may maintain their position of control.

The desire to set up a government implies an acceptance of some basic rules and procedures—what we commonly call a *constitution*. We should not take "constitution" in a restrictive literal sense to mean a document signed by those who drafted it, but rather to signify the embodiment, however tentative and fragmentary, of a desire on the part of a society to have some understanding about some rules that affect directly the way in which their government is organized and acts—about *what* their government should do, and *how*. When agreement relates to *what*, we say that this is a *substantive agreement*. For instance, it may be agreed that the government can raise an army and can levy taxes, or that the government cannot interfere with economic or religious freedoms. When we say that there is an agreement on *how*, we say that there is a *procedural agreement*. A constitution usually involves an agreement on *both* what and how. When a government has reached a very comprehensive and stable agreement on both of these, we see this as a sign of a "consensual" society; when agreement appears to be fragile and is not widespread, we talk about "nonconsensus" or "a low level of consensus"; if the conflict over the constitution is sharp, we speak of outright "dissensus." All literature on political culture is about the how and the what—even if it rarely mentions the word "constitution."

Few indeed are the societies that have attained full agreement on the procedures of governmental action and on its substance. Even among the oldest and most developed polities (four of which we discuss in this volume) such a comprehensive agreement is rare. France, West Germany, and the Soviet Union have not fully attained it yet. Only England is a consensual society; the others exhibit either a limited consensus or a low level of consensus, and have often experienced civil war. Professor Aspaturian constantly tries to show the progress made in the direction of consensus building in the Soviet Union, while Professor Macridis indicates the still fragmented character of the French society and tries to identify the factors that may lead to consensus. So long as an answer has not been given to the problem of German reunification, consensus in West Germany is, at best, conditional.

Political Culture: Two "Models"

"Agreement," or lack of it, then, is the most important trait of the political culture. It relates, as we have already pointed out, to attitudes and beliefs—a complex set of psychological orientations, to be sure—about the government. More specifically, these orientations involve the following: (*a*) the degree and extent of individual acceptance and obedience; (*b*) the degree and extent to which the individual values the government as an instrument through which he can satisfy interests and demands; and (*c*) the degree and extent to which the individual considers that he can play an active role in promoting or impeding governmental actions.

Acceptance and obedience. The individual in a consensual society does not entertain the thought of leaving and usually finds the system in which he lives to be the best. Many of the rules limiting or supporting governmental action have become more-or-less part of his own personal life. He knows and *accepts* what he is not supposed to do, and gladly does what he is asked to do. He does not have to be forced to do one and avoid the other. The use of governmental force to exert compliance is almost alien to such a system. It is like an insurance policy people take in case an individual might resort to a private use of force. Constraints and supports are *"internalized."*

Instrumental character. Wherever "problems" develop, internal or external, the individual expects that the government ought to take action. Unemployment, air pollution, urban squalor, low income—for some—are problems that concerted action through the government can settle. This does not mean that government is considered to be the exclusive instrumentality for their solution, but that it is accepted as one—the most important one.

Role of the individual. The individual takes it for granted that he is an active participant in the system. He can demand things from the government and he can, in case it fails, change those that make the decisions.

The perfect model of a consensual society, then, is one in which the people *value, accept,* and *use* the government according to widely accepted and internalized rules. And it follows that the model *non*consensual society has a government which operates either under no rules, or else under rules that are not valued or accepted; one that is not considered an instrumentality for the solution of problems; and finally, one that the individual either does not want to use or is unable to use for the solution of such problems. There is no consensus, and therefore no government except one that relies largely upon force.

Neither of these two models exists in reality. Disagreements about the scope of governmental action (substantive rules) and about the manner of governmental action (procedural rules) are always prevalent. In every society a minimum (even if highly fragile) agreement on certain rules—substantive and procedural—exists. For instance, the Communist party of the Soviet Union is developing some rules guiding the dismissal of its leaders and the appointment of new ones, and the crux of the Fifth Republic is whether de Gaulle's successor will be allowed to use the powers de Gaulle disposed of. No serious disagreements seem to disturb the serene façade of the British constitution, but the discontent with economic policy and the decline of British power indicate potential sources of friction.

This book is directly addressed to the study of consensus and dissensus. The social structure, the ideology, the configuration of interest, and the organization of the economy of each country are discussed at length, not because they have a political character in themselves, but because they relate to major political orientations and governmental action. A number of hypotheses are implicitly, and sometimes explicitly, made by the authors. One can be summed up very crudely as follows: societies with an uneventful history tend to be consensual. That is, in societies that have not experienced invasion of their territory or frequent and immediate threats upon their territorial integrity, the people are likely to have developed habits and attitudes that account for a benevolent attitude toward their government. England, the United States, Switzerland, and some of the Scandinavian countries fit this proposition.

The reader should not rush to the conclusion, however, that all societies that have not been invaded or have not experienced continuing threats upon their territorial integrity are consensual. Other requirements are necessary, and Professor Finer discusses them in pointing out, for example, that the British government and the rules surrounding it show two rather distinct features: they are old and have changed gradually. Parliamentary monarchy is perhaps as old as the Magna Carta, but it came into its own only at the close of the seventeenth century. Within its form, new forces were poured to mould the constitution—but the fundamental dispositions of the individual toward the government were not radically altered. Gradually, through their government, the people began to participate and express their demands and ask for solutions to the problems that began to emerge. Rarely in British history was the government openly defied. When serious economic and social problems emerged, the attitudes of the people crystallized into an acceptance of their government—a willingness to obey, to value, and to use. These attitudes were shared by all, so that they shaped and often overcame the intensity of conflict. When, for instance, the interests of the landowners and the middle classes were sharply at odds, conflict was imminent. One group argued for high agricultural tariffs to protect their produce from imports, and the other for no tariffs so as to import foodstuffs and sell them cheaply—and thus pay low wages. The conflict was settled by Parliament, and the landowners gave in rather than defy the system they valued highly.

Contrast the British situation with those of France, the Soviet Union, and Germany. All three of the latter political societies have been only too frequently invaded; all of them have experienced drastic changes in their rules concerning the actions and limits of government (i.e., their constitutions); in all of them, participation of the citizens to express their interests and satisfy their demands through the government has at times been denied or impeded. In all three of them, the citizens have at one time or another been unable to use the government and rely upon it in order to solve their problems. Only too frequently, conflicts of interest and class, *instead of being settled by the government* within the framework of the constitution, have spilled over into conflicts *about the constitution*. And, as different constitutions have succeeded each other (this has been the case in France, and in part in Germany), or, as people have felt that their interests and demands could not be settled through the government (the case in Russia before and, up to a certain point, after the revolution of 1917), apathy, indifference, or downright hostility have followed.

Conflict and Interest

In all societies at all times, one of the most prevalent phenomena is conflict concerning things people want or value. This is the heart of politics—not because all conflicts become political and invite government action, but because the most important ones do. These latter are generally the ones that relate to the allocations of scarce resources, the distribution of power, the fulfillment of expectations, and the maintenance of things that are highly valued.

CLASS CONFLICT. Because even the wealthiest society will manufacture symbols and goods that cannot be shared by all, conflict is not limited to the area of material resources only. The dream of a classless society may come true, but that of a conflictless one is hard to imagine. Let us limit our discussion to internal conflicts, even though international ones certainly affect very seriously both consensus and governmental action. There are enough illustrations we can use from every political system we examine. To cite a few examples: a tiny minority may own the land, and the great majority labor on it as agricultural workers or tenant farmers. Or a small group may manage to control the production and price of steel when the growth of the population puts heavy demands upon the steel supply for low-rent housing. Or one race may dominate another. In each and every case there will be conflict: the farmers against the landowners; those who own the steel mills against those who want cheap housing; the black against the white. In each of our sections the prevalence of conflict is obvious—serfs against landowners, the middle classes against the landed gentry, industrialists against workers. Such a conflict is one that we usually refer to (without being able to define very accurately the term) as *class* conflict. A class is generally defined in terms of the dominant role it plays in a society usually through control of property or other resources.

GROUP CONFLICT. But we will also find that within a class, and often cutting across classes, there is another prevalent form of conflict: *group* conflict. Groups consist of persons who have *common interests*. This brings up the word *interest*—a word that has preoccupied political scientists and sociologists for a long time. For *interest* can be defined in very narrow terms to mean "material interest," and in a very broad sense to mean "purpose." *We shall understand it to mean a common set of material interests and common goals*. Both are usually present. Material concerns without goals are hardly ever organized, and goals without common material concerns can hardly sustain a group for long. Material concerns account for the organization and action of many groups—such as trade unions, farmers' associations, business groups. But there are groups that do not appear to have immediate material interests: the antivivisection society, a church, a university may be held together without any tangible material interest on the part of its members. Extreme cases omitted, however, common purpose and material concern will induce, in the greatest number of cases, persons to form a group or an association.

However elevated the goals or however sordid the interests on the part of a group, their expression provokes friction with other groups —first, because two may radically clash about the same goals; second, because some groups will give higher priority to their ends as compared to those held by others. The conflict, sometimes highly structured and organized, sometimes totally unstructured, may or may not be contained. It may disrupt a society—this has happened in the cases of tribal conflicts in Africa, and powerful social conflicts in the period of the Industrial Revolution in Europe. Sometimes it may attain a sort of balance—as when competing groups are strong enough to maintain their positions, but not strong enough to overcome those with whom they are in conflict. Sometimes one group may triumph over another. And finally, the conflicting groups may reach a compromise. All four cases are possible.

What concerns the student of politics is not only the source of conflict, but primarily the manner in which it is resolved. To take two illustrations: in Russia, the workers and the farmers, under the leadership of a small group of intellectuals, deposed the landed aristocracy by force. In England, the workers gradually assumed an organization and a style of action that gave them by-and-large what they asked for without having to resort to violence. In France the workers, after resorting to violence, were unable to satisfy their own demands, and for a long time their effort to influence the government proved equally frustrating. As a result, they have been unable *as yet* to choose between revolutionary and democratic methods.

It is not easy to tell when and why a group resorts to force; when and why another compromises; and when and why a third one allows or invites the government to step in and provide for a solution. Generally, the manner in which the conflict will be resolved depends upon the political culture. In a consensual society where the government is valued and the level of participation is high, the solution will come from the government in the form of a decision that is legitimate. Where consensus is low or nonexistent, the government may be unable to solve the conflict, and in fact may become its victim; this was the case with France a number of times, with the tsarist government, and with a number of regimes in Germany.

Interest and, in general, group action are, then, interwoven with the political culture. An interest that accepts its basic values becomes "politicized"—or rather, domesticated—in the sense that it will attempt to realize its goals in a manner compatible with the set of values and procedures we called the political culture. But interest-group behavior as well as the behavior of social classes and status groups help in turn to shape the political culture. By shedding their absolute and rigid demands, they accept and invite the mediation of the government. In England this has been the case over a long period of time. In France, on the contrary, interests have shaped their postures in terms that brook no compromise, and the lack of an agreement on the limits and procedures of governmental action has given them a free hand. Continuity of a stable governmental form in the one case, and sharp discontinuities in the other, account for the different way in which interests act.

But the political culture accounts for more. Participation in and acceptance of the government in England has given to the interest groups—and this is the case with the United States, too—a feeling of effectiveness which has generated a better organization and a greater degree of participation. On the other hand, until recently, recurrent conflicts and distrust of the government created apathy, disinterest, and opposition to government action in France and in the Soviet Union. Professor Finer points to the large membership, strong organization, and effectiveness of the British interest groups, and Professor Macridis to their fragmentation, lack of organization, and relative ineffectiveness (at least until very recently) in France. Professors Deutsch and Aspaturian indicate that there are the beginnings of mutual trust between government and interest groups in both the Soviet Union and West Germany.

The Political Traits of Pluralism

Before we discuss the ultimate purpose of interest-group action—power—it may be well to raise another important question: Does the variety and number of interest groups tell us something about the political culture? No individual has one single preoccupation or goal. Each one of us has in fact many: to keep our church going; to see that our tennis club flourishes; to meet with fellow veterans and students; to see that our air is not polluted and that our insurance companies charge less. The more advanced economically the society, the greater the number of occupations, the greater the congerie of interests, and the broader the horizon of goals that can be attained. If you belong to only one organization—church, party, or interest group—your life is committed to it; you would consider the defense of your group to be your own defense and its success your success; further, you would be prone to develop a state of mind (we can call it an ideology) that fully identifies with the objectives of your own group and tolerates no others. However, if you belong to many groups and associations, you are bound to give to each and all a lower degree of commitment and identification; to balance within your own mind the various manifestations of the interests involved; to consider your attachments a matter of more or less, rather than everything or nothing; and finally, you are likely to establish priorities of loyalty that do not call for one choice to the exclusion of others. A man who belongs to many groups is the best representative of the Aristotelian middle virtue. He is neither a hero nor a scoundrel, but a moderate man who does not like excesses and can balance and compromise his many interests and loyalties. He is also open-minded because, knowing his own many interests and loyalties, he understands and tolerates those of others. Hence he becomes a tolerant man. Such a man is the exact opposite of the man that, according to Professor Macridis, the French Revolution fashioned; he is the exact opposite of the revolutionary envisioned by Lenin, as Professor Aspaturian portrays him, or of a German Nazi. He is fairly close to the tolerant and judicious Britisher who shuns extremes and who since the early days of the nineteenth century has virtually excluded violence as a form of political expression. Even at the risk of being tautological, we shall say this about a society in which there are many interest groups (in the broad sense in which we have defined "interest"): that it is, or at least is likely to be, an open democratic society characterized by a high degree of consensus.

The Configuration of Power

Interest groups and all associations are the dramatis personae of politics. Always "on stage," they act not for applause but for influence, which is their central goal no matter how they couch it. Influence is simply the ability to make somebody else do what you want him to do—and if you have that ability you have power. The tyrant who can order a person over the cliff has power only if he is able to influence his officials to push the man over the cliff. He cannot do it himself, since it is quite likely that at least some of his victims or one of his officials may be stronger physically than he is. A tyrant is strong only if his followers obey—and only if he can make them obey him.[2] He must develop a network of influence through which his command can be made to stick.

The same applies to all groups and government officials. The KKK in the South could not rely upon force (though they did not avoid it) in order to "keep the Negro in his place." It must create a state of mind that will be receptive to its goals. It must influence as many people as possible. But the same thing is true for "black power," the French president, the leaders of the Soviet Union, the British prime minister, and the West German chancellor. Their power is commensurate with their influence. (Even the most "powerful" office in the world, that of the president of the United States, is subject to the

[2] Without attempting to be paradoxical, this is the basic reason why most tyrants are really weak and why they do not live long.

same rule, despite its formidable prerogatives.)

If power, then, is influence over others, what are its most important instruments? Political power, the central phenomenon of politics, stems frequently from extrapolitical sources. Its ingredients throughout the ages have not differed very much. Power stems from *wealth,* from *status,* from control over *the means of coercion,* and from *support.* The first three are easy to identify.

WEALTH. The man of wealth can influence others directly or indirectly. He can "buy" followers, or coerce by threatening deprivations, but more often his influence is indirect: he can play a role behind the stage and tell some of the important actors—the policeman, the judge, the legislator, the civil servant, or even the cabinet ministers, up to the very top—what to do. Very often he will not allow others to get up on the stage and vie for influence. The basic cause of the Bolshevik Revolution was the unwillingness of those who held power (the aristocracy, supported by some other groups), to let the common people (the merchants, workers, and farmers) get up on the political stage.

STATUS. What has made wealth extremely influential is that it "legitimized" itself, both politically and socially. A wealthy man was portrayed as a good man or a superior man. The poor and the many learned to respect him and defer to him. The Protestant ethic in England, in this country, and also in Holland and some of the Scandinavian countries created a mythology that equated wealth with goodness or virtue. Therefore, the wealthy man acceded also to the second ingredient of power: *status.* People deferred to him, or—to put it more mildly—he could influence people because they had been taught to respect him. Status and position in the government went hand-in-hand. Since the wealthy man was competent and wise, who could govern better than he who knew how to take care of his affairs best?

The wealthy man and the government official often became one, and in Great Britain (at least until the turn of the nineteenth century) this was taken for granted. After the Crimean War, for instance, it was argued in England that it was perfectly proper for "gentlemen" to "buy" army commissions because the country could be best defended by those who had a stake in it and therefore a great interest in preserving it—the wealthy. In the Soviet Union this was the accepted arrangement until the Bolshevik Revolution. In France and Germany, however, although seriously defended over a long period of time, the combination of status and wealth was never fully accepted. All our authors take particular pains to find out what are the status groups and what, if any, is the role of wealth in each country that we study. They do so because they are trying to find exactly where the power, in the sense in which we have defined it, lies.

INSTRUMENTS OF COERCION. The holders of status and wealth often managed to control the third ingredient of power—the instruments of coercion. The most important among them have been the police and the army, and in many countries the judiciary. For a long period of time—and again, the political history of the four countries we are studying tells the story—wealth, status groups, and the army were in the same hands. The British "squire" was the judge and the most powerful political boss in the village, and one need only read any nineteenth-century Russian novel to know who really made the decisions: it was the landowner, the aristocrat, and the officer-gentleman. Even in France, despite the revolution of 1789, those who recovered their land and their titles of nobility became mayors or at least controlled the mayors in the rural areas. The army officer corps, recruited from among the wealthy and the status groups, became an effective instrument with which to inculcate obedience and distil deference on the part of the common people to those who held power.

The holders of status and wealth (i.e., power) were able to pass it on from generation to generation. Wealth begets wealth, and status begets status—at least in the vast majority of cases. Leadership remained ascriptive: people usually were born into it. Political competition was for long a sham, for even if new actors were allowed on the stage, they were assigned clearly subordinate roles.

SUPPORT. Status, wealth, the control of the instruments of coercion—the three most common ingredients of power—began to be undermined by the middle of the nineteenth century, and definitely blunted with the turn of the century. The growth of the population and the rise of new occupational groups spurred by the Industrial Revolution began to weaken the control of the landowning aristocracy and the wealthy. The slogan of the French Revolution ("Liberty, Equality, Fraternity") and the success of the American experiment provided important ideological weapons to the new social groups. They demanded access to politics. In some countries they were excluded, but in others they were grudgingly admitted. Soon the mass of industrial workers began to press upon the stage. It was at this juncture (somewhere between 1860 and 1900) that political organization and massive political participation began to delineate the present-day source of political power—*support*. Leadership no longer remained ascriptive, nor could it rely exclusively upon status, wealth, and force; it shifted to those with the ability to command the support of large groups of people.

The transition from the limited and exclusive instrumentalities of power to that of popular support is not only fascinating, but tells us a lot about the political cultures of the systems we study. To put it simply, in Russia the transition took place by violence and has not as yet been fully realized. The wealthy and the status groups, unwilling to make concessions, were challenged by force and ousted, to be replaced by an organization (the Communist party) that claims popular support and solicits it, but has not as yet fully institutionalized it. In England, on the other hand, the transition took place smoothly and gradually. As Professor Finer shows, many symbols of status have been maintained there, but influence and power have shifted to the party that has the majority in Parliament, and to its leaders. In France the violent conflicts of the nineteenth century made the transition difficult. The result was that even when all were given the freedom to organize, form political parties, and support their political leaders, sections of the population demurred—the conservatives rejecting the republic, and the workers distrusting it. In Germany the same has been true. But both Professor Macridis and Professor Deutsch point out that present developments indicate a growing attachment to the logic of popular support. So we can again offer a proposition: *The system in which the transition from the old status groups to popular support took place gradually and without violence has a consensual political culture in which support has become the mainspring and source of power.*

Just as "power" stemming from wealth and status came to be structured and organized in different ways, popular support has come to take different forms and has generated new roles and groups that have replaced the old status groups. For the "people" cannot give or withhold their support without preparation, education, organization, and information. *The dominant institution through which the people give or withhold their support is the party, and the new "influential" groups that have emerged are made up of party leaders, organizers, manipulators.* These are the new "elite" groups that we discuss at some length in this volume.

POLITICAL PARTIES

We have discussed thus far the "foundations" of politics—the political culture, the interest articulation, the configuration of power, and the ingredients of political power. They are directly related to politics because they both invite and shape governmental action. The link between the "political culture" and the "government" is the political party. The party has become a ubiquitous organization, and all four sections of this book devote long chapters to the study of their history, functioning, and role. The reader who covers these sections will have studied *three* major party systems: the British two-party system, the French and to some extent the German multiparty system, and the Soviet one-party system. Although these three do not exhaust the variety and the diversity of party systems, they nonetheless give us adequate material with which to speculate and generalize about parties.

Functions

Political scientists and sociologists provide us with an impressive listing of the functions of political parties, without always the benefit of the discriminating factors under which certain functions can or cannot be efficiently performed, or a satisfactory conceptualization linking function and structure. Thus among the functions most commonly given we find the following: *representation (and brokerage), conversion and aggregation; integration (participation, socialization, and mobilization); persuasion, repression, recruitment and choice of leaders, deliberation, policy formulation, control of the government.*

Interests, we have seen, are demands, and in one or the other manner seek satisfaction in the form of governmental action. The way to gain it is to get power. With the disappearance of the old status groups, or at least with the significant erosion of their position, power has shifted to those who receive support. With the growth and diversification of interests in an industrial society, no single interest has the remotest chance of providing singly the needed support. The use of force is very uneconomical, and persuasion appears to be the most acceptable channel. Thus interests must unite, and must convince as many persons and groups as possible about the validity of their demands. This has become the most general form of political activity, especially in the political systems we are studying here—including the Soviet Union. It takes place through the political party.

The party represents interest, aggregates it, mobilizes it, provides for possibilities of compromise among competing ones, converts it into policy, and, finally, recruits the political leaders who, by assuming control of governmental offices translate it into governmental action. The party is like a train—interests and demands feed its engine; it converts it into energy and drives the government to a predetermined place. The analogy, like all analogies, must, of course, be taken with a grain of salt—very often the place where the party wants to go to is not so definite as Grand Central Station, and quite frequently the party leader takes liberties with the program of the party that no self-respecting conductor would or can afford to take, with regard to the destination of the train.

Representation of Interest

To exert influence, interests must make the government act or not act; they must either control it or greatly influence it. To do this, they must find a way to make the people vote for the candidates for government positions likely to be most in tune with them. To select such a government they must "appeal to the public" and spread their net as wide as possible and persuade as many people as possible that the particular candidates for governmental position are the best possible candidates for the country as a whole. It is at this stage that the party steps in. The party men become a critically important link between the government and the interests—solidly planted in both, or at least carefully looking in both directions; it bridges the two. The party assumes the function of a spokesman for one, or rather, for many interests—the farmers, the trade unions, the pacifists, the veterans, etc. It speaks for each of them, but in order to be fairly successful, it must also speak for many of them. Thus the representative function is not to be construed in literal terms—otherwise there would be a party for every interest and a single interest for every party.

Aggregation and Brokerage

The party attempts to bring together and represent as many interests as possible—but it is not a mere piling up or juxtaposition of interests. It would be hard, for instance, for the party to advocate at one and the same time racial equality (as a spokesman of the blacks) and racial supremacy (as a spokesman of the Southern or perhaps the suburban white). It would be hard for the British Labour party to speak for both free enterprise and welfare benefits for all workers. It would be also difficult

for a party that wishes to win popular support to take a very rigid ideological position on any given issue; even in the Soviet Union, where there is only one party, the Communist party is unwilling to adhere to a rigid ideological position, and the French parties are finding it increasingly difficult both to maintain ideological orthodoxy and to gain popular support. The party must find an area—as large as possible—where there is a congruence of interests: better housing, higher wages, urban renewal, improved education, increased welfare benefits, for instance. The party, in other words, must compromise in order to represent. It acts as a broker. It takes more from one and less from another to give each as much as possible without alienating any. It not only aggregates, but synthesizes the various interests and demands into one product that the greatest possible number of consumers will buy at the political supermarket—the election. The product is the program, a set of promises of what the government will do and what the government will not do.

Mobilization

But interest, at least in the narrow sense of the term (economic interest), is not always as aggressive as people think. And interest in its broadest sense (purpose) may slumber for a long time. The party, under the appropriate conditions and circumstances, mobilizes and awakens both. Interest and purpose, thanks to the party, move from a state of latency into actualization. We shall see how a small movement in France crystallized what was a diffuse discontent among the small merchants and artisans into a party that gained over 2 million votes. Professor Finer shows how the interests of the workers in the trade unions were mobilized thanks to the socialist intellectuals— whose purpose was the construction of a new society—to form the Labour party. Thus the party plays a creative role: it evokes response to demands or goals that have not as yet fully developed. In so doing, the party also restructures support and invites new forms of governmental action.

Clarification of Issues and Selection of the Government

It is the platform that provides the ultimate synthesis and evokes participation and support. But this depends upon the party system. Under a multiparty system like the French one, the platform appeared often as an ideological statement rather than a careful compromise among interests. Under two-party systems, the parties appear to be more pragmatic and more comprehensive. The differences stem in part from the underlying motives for which popular support is sought. In a two-party system, like the British one, while clarification of issues is important, perhaps even more important is the election of a government—and at times of one man. An intensely ideological and partisan position will make victory difficult; a comprehensive and pragmatic one will make it easier to produce a larger and more attractive package. In a multiparty system, on the other hand, an election often amounts to selecting only representatives who will in turn attempt, on the basis of their own compromises and agreements, to form a cabinet—i.e., nominate the government. The parties in a multiparty situation, therefore, try to maintain their electoral clientele by the specific appeal to specific interests and ideologies. This was the case with many of the parties in France under the Fourth Republic.

The purpose of the reform which provides for the direct election of the French president by popular vote is precisely to break up the exclusiveness of many of the parties and force them to coalesce around two candidates, so support may be linked directly to the power of the president. This was also the purpose of electoral reform in West Germany. The more the parties are involved in the direct selection of the president or a government (as in the United States, England, and recently in Germany and perhaps France), the more comprehensive is their appeal, and progressively the less ideological are they bound to be over a given period of time. (Occasional ideological flareups cannot, of course, be avoided—in England or in the

United States.) In contrast, the greater the pre-occupation of the parties with securing a representation in the legislature in order to participate with others in the formation of a government, the greater is their commitment to special electoral clientele, and the greater their propensity toward ideological orthodoxy.

Recruitment

The same is true for recruitment. The two-party system trains its members over a long period of time for governmental tasks. From the moment the "backbencher" (the party member with little status and influence) enters the House of Commons, his eye is set upon the Treasury bench—the place reserved for the prime minister and the cabinet members. His performance, his loyalty to the party, his ability to gain the support of his associates, will slowly bring him closer to it. Every member of Parliament is preoccupied with what the government does. Legislation is taken for granted, and deliberation is relatively unimportant. The important thing is to govern, and for the opposition party to replace the government. The Soviet Communist party recruits for the same ultimate purpose. The rules and the criteria of performance differ, but the purpose is to make room for, and finally to select, the men who will gain the top decision-making jobs and govern under the scrutiny of the party.

The same concern with recruitment does not apply to the multiparty systems, notably with France and with Germany under the Weimar Republic—first, because it was and continues to be unlikely for one party to gain a majority and thus make it possible for its leaders to govern; secondly, because the party leader was not allowed to gain ascendency within the party; and thirdly because the legislatures distrusted government leadership, and through rules and procedures not only discouraged but discredited it as well.

The parties of the two-party system recruit and train leaders and finally make it possible for them to gain popular support and govern. In the multiparty system, emphasis is put on representation and deliberation, and not on government.

THE GOVERNMENT

Interests and demands, acting through the political party, try to grab the leverage of power: the government. Even when limits are imposed upon it, even when there are sharp constitutional restrictions upon what it can do, even if its functions are internally divided, the prize is worth having. For, invariably, what the government can do is much more than what it is prevented from doing. This is a generalization that the student must take for granted: *All governments are becoming more comprehensive in their functions, and more powerful in implementing them.*

In the systems we discuss here, government has become increasingly concentrated in the hands of the executive branch. In all of them, there has been a corresponding diminution of legislative powers and functions. The British section may well be the prototype, since the functions of the legislature have become increasingly restricted to criticism on the part of the Opposition. Even the French legislature finds itself become increasingly a forum—indulging in debate between the "majority" and "the opposition"—or more accurately, "the oppositions."

The Executive

The executive arm of the government includes the institutions formally responsible for governing a political community and applying its binding decisions, to the formulation of which the executive institution may themselves contribute a greater or lesser share. The structure, function, and character of the executive have varied widely over time, and no single conceptual framework will disclose all of those changes and their consequences for the present. Yet certain fundamentals are clear, and on these we can concentrate our attention. The two most prevalent structural forms of the executive are the presidential and the cabinet systems. The source of executive power has shifted from hereditary right, co-optation, and the use of force, to support—through election, either direct or indirect. The primary functions of the executive have become increasingly carried out by specialized structures: today representation, leadership, deliberation, decision making, control and supervision of subordinate decision making, and enforcement are the principal functions of the executive.

The executive office (the president's office or the prime minister and his cabinet) is responsible for the overall performance of the functions associated with it. The number of officials is generally small—twenty or at most thirty. If we include top civil service personnel, heads of planning agencies and nationalized industries, top scientists, and defense officials who participate in deliberation and decision making, the number rarely goes beyond one hundred. While the executive is a collective entity, ultimate responsibility for decision making is sometimes lodged in the hands of one man. This is notably the case with presidential systems, and in many of the cabinet systems where a well-disciplined party controls a majority in the legislature. In a totalitarian one-party system like the Soviet one the leader of the party is either in law or in fact (and often in both) in charge of the executive. On the other hand, in a number of multiparty parliamentary democracies, notably in the Scandinavian countries, the coalition cabinets account for a genuine collegiality of decision making and responsibility. In fact, viewed from the perspective of decision making and responsibility, and depending upon the formal constitutional arrangements, the prevalent norms in the society, and adventitious factors such as personality and circumstances, there is a continuum between genuine one-man rule and genuine collegiality. The structures are generally flexible enough to allow for one or the other, and for a movement from the one in the direction of the other within the same political system. (This, incidentally, is true both for cabinet and for presidential systems.)

Despite these formal differences, universal suffrage, the growth of national parties, and the progressive adoption of a majority electoral system account for striking similarities. In presidential or cabinet systems the immediate source of executive power is support—election and party. In the cabinet system, the leader of the majority party becomes prime minister. If the party is disciplined, it is unlikely, as we shall see, that it will overthrow the prime minister. Thus while the prime minister is technically responsible to the legislature, he is just as immune to it as the president. In the one-party totalitarian systems that have adopted the cabinet system—and again we use the Soviet Union as the prototype—it is the party that sustains executive leadership. As long as the leader controls the party (as Stalin did) or is accepted by the higher party echelons (the Central Committee and the Politburo), he also controls, as Professor Aspaturian points out, the legislature, and is technically immune from legislative scrutiny. If there are dissensions within the party or if the leader loses his support in the Politburo and Central Committee, he can no longer hold his position. (This is what happened to Khrushchev.)

Many trends since World War II account for the reinforcement of the political executive. Among them, the most significant ones are the widespread adoption of the majority electoral system and constitutional reforms establishing the ascendency of the executive over the legislature. The two most notable cases are West Germany and France, which we discuss. In West Germany, proportional representation was greatly modified by the requirement that half the members of the legislature be elected by majority vote. Executive stability and independence were strengthened by the provision that the chancellor cannot be removed from office by an adverse vote of the legislature unless it is accompanied by a positive vote in favor of a successor. In France, proportional representation in legislative elections was abandoned in 1958. In the presidential election, if none of the candidates receives an absolute majority on the first ballot, then the contest is narrowed to only two candidates on the second. As for executive-legislative relations,

Parliament was "rationalized": stringent restrictions were placed on the vote of censure by the National Assembly; the executive was given control over legislative business and legislation; the committee system was simplified and the powers of the committees drastically reduced; and the president was given the right to dissolve the National Assembly and call for an election.

The trend has been significantly the same in Great Britain, where the control of the executive over Parliament is made effective through the control of the majority party, and in the United States, where legislative initiative has passed into the hands of the chief executive, and party discipline in Congress has been greatly tightened.

From an organizational viewpoint, all executive structures of the countries we discuss in this volume display striking similarities. The prime minister or president is surrounded by concentric circles of advisers, and staff and line agencies. The first is the immediate circle of personal advisers and liaison agents; the second consists of specialized coordinating agencies with functions that cut across departmental or ministerial responsibilities (economic planning, national security, atomic energy, space programs, administrative reorganization); the third is the cabinet, consisting of top officials responsible for policy making and administration of functionally defined governmental activities (foreign affairs, trade, labor, welfare, defense); a fourth circle consists of an increasing number of independent or semiindependent agencies with regulatory and supervisory responsibilities, some of which operate or control economic services.

Functions of the Political Executive

The political system, as we have pointed out, is a mechanism through which interests and demands are translated into decisions. Since the political executive plays an important role in transforming interests and demands into decisions, it has, first and foremost, decision-making functions. It is the most important organ within the government. However, since it also represents and accommodates major social and interest groupings, it plays an integrative role as well. And in addition to being the central policy-making organ, it also supervises and controls all the subordinate deliberative and enforcement organs.

DECISION MAKING AND DELIBERATION. Political theory has long distinguished between legislative and executive acts. This formal distinction is no longer adequate. First, the political executive at the head of the party dominates the legislature. Secondly, it possesses independent powers—for instance, in foreign policy and defense. Thirdly, the practice of delegated legislation has given vast, albeit subordinate, legislative powers to the executive. Finally, the law enacted by the legislature is initiated, prepared, and drafted by the political executive; policy initiation has become an executive prerogative. In the totalitarian systems that have adopted cabinet government, legislative scrutiny is of no significance. Generally, this is virtually the case with all cabinet systems that have a strongly disciplined party system. Only in the United States does the legislature continue to have genuinely independent power of legislative scrutiny and initiative.

In order to initiate, decide, and act, the executive must deliberate. As a result intelligence, fact-finding, liaison, and staff agencies have mushroomed. This has been the case particularly with new governmental activities that do not fit the traditional organization of the executive into departments and ministries: problems of economic planning and supervision; coordinating the preparation of budgetary policy; providing administrative reform to create new structures that can cope with new functions; and considering national security matters from a variety of governmental points of view. Thus, new layers of agencies and offices have developed to constitute what is now called the office of the president or the office of the prime minister. The trend is universal, but it is especially clear in developed societies where industrialization has created the imperative of regulation, and international conflict has emphasized coordination and preparedness for quick action. It also reflects a concomitant trend in favor of developing new procedures to provide for deliberation prior to a decision. Given the sheer bulk of matters that call for a decision, and the need for specific knowledge and information in order to make one, decision making becomes a matter of following deliberative and consultative processes.

SUPERVISION AND ENFORCEMENT. While the classic distinction between deliberation (legislature) and execution (executive) is no longer tenable, it is still true that the political executive is the agency of execution in the narrow sense. It supervises and controls all subordinate organs. However, execution, properly speaking, is within the purview of the bureaucracy. Executive decisions are general and comprehensive in scope, and their detailed implementation is in the hands of the civil service and the various subordinate agencies. The political executive remains, however, responsible for the organization and reorganization of the machinery of government. It can create and reorganize departments and agencies, establish the rules of advancement and recruitment within the civil service, and set down procedures for making subordinate decisions. Ultimate responsibility for lack of efficient execution will be focused upon the political executive.

Executive Restraints and Responsibility

The growth of executive power and the increasing scope of initiative and decision making calls for a discussion of the existing restraints and of the manner in which responsibility is institutionalized.

The restraints appear to be relatively few: first, there is the burden of persuading the elite, common to all political executives, including totalitarian ones. Secondly, there are systemic restraints: no leader can attempt a synthesis of policy objectives and goals that does not reflect up to a certain point the existing demands and aspirations of the community. To go too far in suggesting policy goals is to become separated from supporters; to stand still is to alienate the interests and the demands that could provide for support. To be effective and to gain approbation and support, the executive must gear its actions to the interests and demands within the system. As was pointed out earlier, the limits of initiative and freedom of action may be wide, and it is the task of leadership to discover them. But failure to do so, or miscalculation, may lead to disapproval and rejection. Third, there are various types of constitutional and procedural limitations that trace the contours of executive power and provide for executive responsibility. We already mentioned the formal responsibility of the cabinet to the legislature. In presidential systems (e.g., in the United States) and to a certain degree in France, where the chief executive is not responsible to the legislature, a system of checks and balances (separation of powers, judicial review, legislative scrutiny, and, in some instances, the direct association of one or the other of the houses of legislature in the exercise of executive prerogatives) imposes restraints.

The substance of executive responsibility, however, lies in the party system and in periodic elections through which it gains support. The party is both an instrument at the disposal of the leader to attain power and carry out policies, and a device that controls him, since without the support of the party, he is invariably helpless. As long as the party acquiesces or agrees, the political executive is omnipotent in virtually all political systems, despite procedural limitations. In democratic societies, where basic freedoms are respected, an election is the most effective instrument of control, and ultimately of executive responsibility. It gives the electorate the opportunity to approve or disapprove of the policies of the incumbent and to choose among competing parties and leaderships.

As we shall see, the burden of decision making thrust upon the political executive has grown immensely. The effective performance of executive leadership calls for an unprecedented balance between leadership and technical knowhow, information and evaluation, specialization and coordination. Political structures must adjust to new environmental demands. How well have they managed to do it?

Our special chapters on the performance of government give to the reader an appreciation of the problems involved and of the manner in which the various governments have coped with them.

PERFORMANCE

It is not easy to evaluate the performance of government. From a general point of view, performance correlates with responsiveness: the more the decision-making machinery responds to the demands and the interests articulated within the system, the higher the level of performance. By the same token, the more the government allows new socioeconomic groups to participate in the system and make their interests heard and their demands satisfied, the greater the legitimacy and stability of the system. But since governmental decisions are made about the allocation of scarce resources or benefits, priorities must be established. Some may get more and others less. Thus, some demands are likely to be fully met, others only in part, and some not at all. The greater the number of demands satisfied, the greater the rate of governmental performance. Thus, if defense is the highest demand, failure to be prepared against aggression would be an indicator of nonperformance. Prolonged unemployment (i.e., failure to meet the demand for full employment) would amount to nonperformance. Prolonged nonperformance would lower the attachment of many groups to the government and ultimately to the system, thus providing for instability that takes the form of a widespread rejection, not only of the government but of the system itself. Thus, failure to heed the interests and demands of a minority may account for its disaffection and the ultimate rejection of the political system on its part.

It is possible, therefore, to set up as criteria of performance and nonperformance the following questions:

(a) Does the system allow for the open participation of all groups? Is the government responsive to their demands?

(b) Does the government translate, within limits, demands into policy? Has it failed to do so over a prolonged period of time for some groups rather than others?

(c) In making decisions, does the government attempt to provide for a balanced allocation of scarce resources to as many groups as possible, or has it consistently favored some to the exclusion of others?

(d) Has prolonged performance on the basis of the above resulted in growing legitimization and stability of the system, or has continued nonperformance accounted for the reverse?

Examination of the four systems leads us only to tentative conclusions. The British system satisfies the criteria of performance and stability. Ever since the Industrial Revolution the new groups spawned by it have found access into the system, thus gaining participation, pressing for the realization of their demands, and in general getting satisfaction, thanks to the action of the government. Thus, the historical legitimacy of the British political system has been enhanced by the performance of the government.

In France, performance has alternated with nonperformance. A number of issues were not readily settled by the government; a number of groups did not gain access into the system without having to resort to violence; groups with conflicting points of view did not find in the government a ready vehicle of a balanced allocation of resources, and as a result either remained locked in conflict or, having developed a deep distrust for the government, rejected it as an instrument of reconciliation and compromise, thus undermining the legitimacy of the system. Lack of government responsiveness often undermined the thin thread of historical legitimacy only to produce serious constitutional instability. Only in the period of the Third Republic was there some consensus on the institutions—at least until the beginning of World War I. The same is generally the case for Germany, as so well shown in Professor Deutsch's discussion of the ambivalences of the German national character and political culture.

The Russian system suffered until the revolution both from instability and nonperformance virtually on the basis of all the criteria we have discussed: new groups were not allowed access; the government remained unresponsive to all interests except those that had status and wealth, and hence its performance from the standpoint of all other groups was pitifully inadequate. Disaffection or outright violence was the rule, and it culminated in the Bolshevik Revolution. Professor Aspaturian shows that whatever the difficulties encountered by the Communist party, and whatever its shortcomings, Russia under the Soviet regime, and thanks to the party, has attempted to restructure and legitimize the new political system it established. While using outright force against some groups that were literally eliminated, it has progressively opened the door to increased participation and has attempted to become increasingly responsive and representative. The discussion of the interplay of new groups and their vying for benefits and influence within the Communist party is adequate evidence that interests are being heard and that the governmental performance is becoming increasingly a test of legitimization. Although there is no conclusive evidence that the test has been met, there is enough to allow us to say that every effort is being made to meet it.

From an overall point of view, governmental performance relates to the manner in which over a given period of time the government meets and copes with specific social and environmental problems and also anticipates them. Planning, technical expertise, the development of research and information-gathering agencies become, as we noted in our discussion of the executive, the preconditions of performance. It is not unlikely, however, that careful study might indicate that interests and individual pressures for a given decision may be difficult or impossible or even "unwise" to heed. This is the perennial philosophic problem of evaluating and distinguishing what appears to be asked by all and what is proper. It is a difficult question which we shall not attempt to answer. But the point is obvious: most of the groups and interests may demand a means of transportation for instance, which in the long run may be socially very expensive or undesirable; the vast majority of groups and interests may be in favor of massive social expenditures when outside threats jeopardize the very survival of the system. Excessive responsiveness—performance geared to meeting interest demands—may very well defeat, in the long run, the very meaning of the term. This may, for instance, be the predicament of the British political system, as Professor Finer intimates. The governing elites, trained over a long period of time to respond to specific and broad interest and constituency demands, and the tendency of the governmental machinery to adjust to them in order to provide for compromises, have accounted for a situation in which only marginal and incremental decisions are being made while important issues or demands are being evaded. As with the French political system under the Fourth Republic, and perhaps even more so than with the French, there has been a marked *immobilisme* on the part of each and all of the British cabinets that have succeeded each other since World War II.

Political Leadership

While it is easy to identify *immobilisme,* it is far more difficult to specify the conditions—if they can ever be clearly identified—under which the government overcomes the constellation of group interests and their demands, to make decisions that are based upon considerations that transcend them. The crux is political leadership, and the necessary condition is its ability to convince the existing interests and the public, and seek new supports. Leadership has therefore a dynamic and positive role to play. But in anticipating or in making decisions, a leader cannot evade the rule of political power that we discussed earlier—that is, he needs to find supports. He must create new supports by restructuring opinion and group attitudes, by presenting the issues in advance, and by suggesting solutions on the basis of which opinion and group supports may be elicited. This was, as Professor Macridis notes, de Gaulle's great merit with regard to the Algerian war. Despite the ambiguities and equivocations, he gradually moved opinion to support Algerian independence.

When does political leadership emerge? How, and under what conditions, can it manage to restructure opinion? What techniques does it use to gain supports without strongly antagonizing or alienating powerful interests? Frankly, we do not know. Highly stable and responsive systems may become the victims of their success and equate performance with mere responsiveness. Under certain terms, leadership in heretofore highly unstable and inefficient political systems may provide levels of performance that will generate supports and gradually legitimize the system.

The distinction between developed and underdeveloped political systems is often based upon these criteria of stability and performance. In the developed system, governmental capabilities are great; in the underdeveloped ones, small. In the first, supports exist or can be easily mobilized; in the second, they are virtually nonexistent and the communication mechanisms through which they can be mobilized are poor. In the developed societies the governmental institutions are differentiated on the basis of concrete and clearly understood functions that relate to tasks that ought to be performed; in the underdeveloped ones the tasks remain undifferentiated, with a resulting confusion of roles and confusion in the performance of tasks. In the developed societies the individual generally values and uses his government; in the developing ones legitimacy is low, and people have not learned yet to use their governments.

CONCLUSION

The central focus of politics, therefore, and of the study of comparative politics remains the governmental institutions and political elites, their role, their levels of performance and nonperformance. It is the starting point and focus of investigation. Any such investigation, we know today, will inevitably lead us, as it should, far and wide in search of the contextual factors (rather than determinants) within the framework of which a government operates and

to which its action, its performance, and its policies may often be attributed. We have to probe the infrastructure, but without losing sight of either our focus or the relevant question with which we began our investigation.

In the manner of Machiavelli and Montesquieu and Tocqueville we can suggest a number of relevant questions, all of which we tend to evade either because they are "difficult" or because they are not amenable to "scientific inquiry" or because they involve "value judgments": What accounts for a well organized civil service? What is the impact of large-scale organizations—parties, bureaucracy, and so on —upon the citizen? Under what conditions does public opinion exercise its influence on the government? What accounts for political instability? Is an executive who is responsible to the people more restrained than one responsible to the legislature? How and under what conditions does representation degenerate into an expression of particular interests? Under what conditions do the young people maintain political attitudes different from those of their fathers, and at what point do they revolt? Why does a ruling class become amenable to reform? Under what conditions do ruling groups become responsive to popular demands?

We can multiply these questions, but we think they illustrate our point. None of them can lead to hard hypotheses and proof (or disproof). Some cannot be easily answered. But this is not too important. In fact, the questions we suggest lead to a comparative survey, both historical and contemporaneous, of some of the most crucial political phenomena: responsiveness, performance, change, development, and a host of others. Such a survey will inevitably produce inductive generalizations, perhaps in the manner of Machiavelli, but with far more sophisticated tools and greater access to data than was ever the case before. It will inevitably help us to qualify our questions and to reformulate them as hypotheses that will suggest other qualifications—new variables, if you wish—and lead to further investigation— testing if you wish—and the reformulation of the questions—the gradual development of theory.

In the study of governmental institutions

and political elites, we are concerned with fundamental problems of politics. The first symptoms and indicators of all pervasive political phenomena—revolution, authority and stability, legitimacy, participation—are registered in the composition, organization, and performance of the government. We begin with these, moving next to a study of the policies pursued by various governments in differing political systems—to highlight the conditions of performance or nonperformance, as the case may be. This is precisely what we undertake in this volume.

We must be prepared, in the light of the experience we have studied and accumulated, to move forward and offer policies. In doing so we do not enter the forbidden territory of "political action" nor, as it is so naïvely argued so often, do we simply leave our scientific hat in the office to don the activist hat. We remain at the level of problem identification and problem-solving, and we *suggest* remedies to the policymakers. The more detached our suggestions, the better based upon political experience (in the broad sense), the more plausible they are likely to be. And if we evaluate the same problem differently and suggest different solutions and reach different conclusions, this is only an indication, provided all canons of objectivity and reasoning are respected, that ours is an art.

"Government," in the last analysis, is a learning process. Within the systems we are studying here, despite many conflicts and disagreements, the people communicate with and support the system; the government in turn communicates with them and mobilizes their support and responds to their needs. In all of them the government is an organization to translate interest into decision and purpose into action. Relying upon the requirements for supports and the need for performance, contemporary governments, after thousands and thousands of years of societal life, still strive to find ways to maximize both. Their histories and practices of internal evolution, of alternation between stability and instability, of legitimacy and revolution, of immobility and dynamic leadership and action, continue to challenge all who seek to identify regularities and find an explanation.

R.C.M.
R.E.W.

Samuel E. Finer

Michael Steed

GREAT
BRITAIN

Britain is a tiny country. Taking up a mere 0.2% of the earth's land area, it ranks seventy-fifth in area among nations. With a population of 56 million, she is one of the twelve largest in total population. She imports one-fifth of the world's output of raw materials and, in return, exports one-twelfth of the world's manufactured goods that are shipped in international trade. She is the third largest trading nation in the world. Her people are comparatively rich: they enjoy an annual per capita income that is among the top fifteen among the wealthiest countries in the world. Economically, therefore, Britain is a considerable nation. Diplomatically, Britain sits alongside the United States, the USSR, France, and China as one of the permanent members of the U.N. Security Council, but, militarily, her capacities are dwarfed by those of the United States and the Soviet Union, although she is the only country besides these to possess operational H-bombs.

Up to 1947, Britain ruled a world-girdling empire of some 15 million square miles. Today, almost all the former dependencies have become self-governing states, and the remainder consist mainly of tiny territories too small to stand as sovereign states; almost all of them, however, have chosen to remain linked with the United Kingdom as members of the British Commonwealth. Britain's cultural achievements at least equal those of any of her European neighbors. A French poet has celebrated France as the "mother of the arts, of arms and of the law," but Britain fills the description just as well. Newton and Faraday bear witness to her scientific achievements; Chaucer and Shakespeare and Milton to her literature; Wren and Gainsborough to her role among the arts; Locke, Berkeley, and Hume to her contributions to philosophy.

In the long perspective of history, however, Britain's preeminent contribution to civilization may well come to be listed as the common law and the invention of parliamentary democracy. Except possibly in Sweden, every such system in the world today has been modeled directly or indirectly on the British pattern. This even includes the American presidential system, which was derived from the British

ONE

introduction

constitution as it was understood in the eighteenth century.

Britain began her rapid economic ascent after the political "Settlement" of 1689, which established parliamentary supremacy and secured the position of the mercantile interests and later of the industrial middle class. Cheap credit, maritime enterprise, and a vigorous trade, themselves the reflection of secure internal conditions and a benevolent government, began to enrich the country. A century later came the quick succession of agricultural advances, improved internal communications, and mechanical inventions that go under the name of the Industrial Revolution. Between 1815 and 1911, Britain's population leaped from 11 million to 45 million. Between 1832 and 1913, her exports soared from £36 million ($86,000,000) to £525 million ($1,260,000,000), her iron production from 0.7 million to 10 million tons, her coal production from 26 million to 287 million tons. And the country became increasingly urbanized; in 1851, one male in every six still worked on the land, but by 1911 the ratio had increased to become one male in every twenty.

The acme of British industrial supremacy came between 1815 and 1870. Britain was then the most highly industrialized power in the world. After this period, although she became richer and more urbanized with every decade, other countries began to catch up. In 1880, she still produced more coal than all the rest of the world put together; by 1900, the United States had equaled her in coal output and has since forged ahead. In pig-iron production, by 1900 the United States equaled Britain's output and Germany almost did, but now both have surpassed her. And the same is true in steel. As Britain slipped in relative production, however, she turned to the export of capital and became the greatest investor in the world. Today, Britain is economically comparable with West Germany and France, while the United States and the Soviet Union have far outstripped her in gross industrial production and population. But she is still a formidable industrial and commercial power and, in terms of gross national product and per capita income, she is richer than ever before.

Britain's political and military power paralleled her economic ascent. Although threatened by the larger and more populous powers of France and Spain in the sixteenth and seventeenth centuries, Britain was easily able to preserve her independence. As her economic power waxed in the eighteenth century, she became a major European power and intervened in Continental affairs whenever any single state seemed likely to dominate Europe. She made up for her lack of military manpower by the gold she used to finance her allies. After the defeat of Napoleon in 1815, the *pax Britannica* settled over the globe until about 1870. The only world rival to Britain's power was imperial Russia, and the nineteenth century was essentially a conflict between Russia, the great land power pressing down to the Balkans, to the Persian Gulf, the Indian Ocean, and the Yellow Sea, and the great British sea power pressing up to meet the challenge wherever shore and water touched. Britain was so strong that she lived in "glorious isolation," and had no need for permanent alliances.

This phase, like her industrial supremacy, also began to pass away after 1870. By her triumph over France in that year, Germany became the dominant power on the European mainland, and Britain was gradually forced into ententes with Germany's enemies, France and Russia. By 1914, then, Britain had to share her power with several other European nations. Today, following two devastating world wars, Britain's relative strength has declined even further. She is in the process of liquidating her last extra-European military commitments, and in diplomatic and military terms is a medium power, alongside France and the German Federal Republic.

THE BRITISH EMPIRE AND COMMONWEALTH

Britain's rise to imperial status was both the cause and effect of her economic and military advances. Always a maritime nation, she challenged the Spanish and then the Dutch claims to empire in the Americas and in the East Indies, but her aim was to trade with these territories, not to acquire them. She colonized North America herself, and the "first" British

empire consisted of the American colonies, then the areas won in battle from the French (Canada and India) and, later, Australia, New Zealand, and a foothold in South Africa. After 1782, in the period of the so-called second British empire, she exported millions of settlers to Canada, Australia, New Zealand, and South Africa, endowing these countries with representative institutions; at the same time, she consolidated her hold on India, which she governed efficiently but autocratically. The third great wave of expansion, into Africa and Southeast Asia, occurred after 1870. By 1914, the British empire comprised $14\frac{1}{2}$ million square miles of the earth's surface, and by 1919, it was even larger, as "mandated territories" were entrusted to the British government by the League of Nations.

This vast empire has today, for the most part, become a free association of completely independent sovereign states—the Commonwealth. (The basic law defining the terms of this independence is the 1931 Statute of Westminister.) It includes (in order of their adherence) the United Kingdom itself, Canada, Australia, and New Zealand (the last three being sometimes referred to as "the Old Dominions"), and India, Pakistan, Ceylon, Ghana, Malaysia, Nigeria, Cyprus, Sierra Leone, Tanzania, West Samoa, Jamaica, Trinidad and Tobago, Uganda, Kenya, Malawi, Malta, Zambia, Gambia, Singapore, Guyana, Botswana, Lesotho, Barbados, Naurur, Mauritius, Swaziland, and Fiji.

These states are linked, if at all, by cultural, technological, and economic ties rather than constitutional ones. Excepting Canada, all the members are inside the sterling area and maintain their balances with the Bank of England. Their products enter Britain duty-free, or, if they do not, receive preferential tariff treatment as compared with products of other lands. (In some cases certain members give Britain reciprocal preferences; but these "Commonwealth preferences" are of declining importance.) One-fifth of Britain's imports come from the Commonwealth and one-fifth of her exports go to its members. Nearly all Britain's bilateral economic aid, and more than half of her current private investment, goes to the Commonwealth, also. So, too, does most of her technical assis-

tance. Britain sends member states technicians, teachers, and administrators. She provides military missions and training programs, and exchanges staff officers with many of the Commonwealth countries also. Most of these appoint high commissioners (similar to ambassadors) to Britain, and the written and personal communications between them and British ministries on matters of trade, services, finance, and labor are of very great importance in keeping the Commonwealth together. These high commissioners meet periodically with the secretary of state for Commonwealth relations and a Foreign Office minister in London, as well as arranging ad hoc meetings with them.

But the common institutions that existed in 1931 when the Commonwealth numbered only five states have all but disappeared, as it has come to encompass 31. Not all members owe allegiance to the British sovereign, for most of them are republics, and three even have sovereigns of their own. In all these countries the queen is simply "the Head of the Commonwealth." Nor is there a common nationality: each member state defines its own citizens by its own laws and almost all restrict the entry of citizens of other member states. While a few of the members choose to recognize a British court (the Judicial Committee of the Privy Council) as a final court of appeal in constitutional issues, the great majority do not. There is no common line on foreign policy. Indeed, member states have fought one another (India and Pakistan, for example, in 1971); yet the bitter dispute between the British government and almost all the other member states in 1971 over British supply of arms to South Africa did not, for all the threats of some African governments, break up the Commonwealth. The most important common institution is the customary Conference of Commonwealth Prime Ministers.

THE EVOLUTION
OF THE UNITED KINGDOM

Three factors have contributed to making Britain one of the most successful democracies of the world: geography, the continuity of her history, and industrialization (the latter will be discussed in the next chapter).

Geography

Geographically, Britain [1] is a group of islands, cut off from the Continent at the nearest point by 22 miles of sea—the English Channel. The last foreign occupation of British soil was the Norman invasion of 1066. Since then, the British have successfully staved off would-be European conquerors: the Spanish Armada of Philip II in 1588, Napoleon in 1804, Hitler in 1940. Britain is the only nation of Europe that has been unconquered for so many centuries. Her institutions have been developed over nine hundred years by her own peoples behind the ocean moat.

Being a set of islands, Britain has not, till recent years, required a large standing army. The only British experience of military revolution and despotism occurred during the Great Rebellion (1642–60) and the dictatorship of Oliver Cromwell. This encounter with military rule proved so odious it created a prejudice against standing armies that endured as a live factor in politics almost to the present day. Her monarchs were thus deprived of the instrument by which the despots of the Continent were able to centralize administrative machinery and crush political opposition. The absence of an army prevented political dissidents from taking it over and subverting the country by violence.

The sea not only closed the enemy out, but shut the various nationalities of the United Kingdom in. The kings of England, the most wealthy and populous of its four nations (Wales, Ireland, Scotland, and England), were able to extend their dominion throughout all the British Isles. Wales was conquered by the fourteenth century. Scotland united with England-and-Wales in 1706 to form "Great Britain" through a freely negotiated treaty by which both states agreed to be represented in a single Parliament.

The Scots, as citizens of a former sovereign state, retained, as they do to this day, their own legal system, their own educational and local government systems, and, above all, their own national church—the Presbyterian Church of Scotland. Significantly, for the sea lay between, Ireland was never culturally absorbed. Conquered, colonized, and (in 1800) annexed to the political structure of Great Britain, she remained partly alien. (Here the fact that the bulk of the population is Catholic, while most of the population of England, Wales, and Scotland is Protestant, was of great significance.) The rulers of Great Britain could never decide whether Ireland was the farthest bit of Britain or her nearest colony. Although incorporated into the United Kingdom, Ireland was never assimilated. The break came with the rebellion of 1919 and the subsequent secession of the southern counties to form the Irish Free State in 1922.

The Continuity of History

Long united under the English crown, the nationalities of Britain gradually adjusted to one another. The fact that Henry VII, the founder of the Tudor dynasty, was himself a Welshman played a large part in reconciling the Welsh people to becoming a mere region in a unitary state. Scotland remained a separate kingdom even after she was united with England and Wales, in the person of her own king, James VI, who became, in 1603, the king of both countries. She retained her laws and her church even after the union of 1706. Not till the nineteenth century was cultural assimilation advanced. Only the Irish Catholics remained outside the British "community" that developed in the nineteenth century, although the Protestant Ulstermen of Northern Ireland were always and still are an integral part of it.

Time has likewise bound up the wounds of religious intolerance. Henry VIII's break with Rome, in 1534, cast the Catholic faithful into a persecuted minority. The national church (the Anglican communion) established by Henry VIII and his successors, however, proved too

[1] *Britain* is the popular name for what is officially "The United Kingdom of Great Britain and Northern Ireland." "Great Britain" itself is an official expression: it means the Union (1706) of Scotland and England-and-Wales.

Roman for the more thoroughgoing Protestant sects. These religious differences added bitterness to the fierce political struggles of the Great Rebellion of 1642–60 and the "Glorious Revolution" of 1688–89 that put an end to the king's absolutism and that established parliamentary supremacy. In the eighteenth century, therefore, both Catholics and nonconformist Protestants (that is, those who did not accept the Established Church of England) were discriminated against politically as well as socially. The nineteenth century saw the successive removals of restrictions on religious freedom. The chief political disabilities imposed on the nonconformist religious minorities were removed in 1828 and those on Catholics in 1829. In the nineteenth century, there occurred a great revival of Roman Catholicism, as well as a revival of Protestant dissident groups, which was accompanied by an increasing measure of religious tolerance.

THE BRITISH CONSTITUTION

The British constitution is a democratic one, but poured into an antique medieval mold. It is still full of official titles, terminology, and procedures that originated in the Middle Ages. The government is called the "Queen's government"; ministers are the "Ministers of the Crown"; the armed forces are the "Armed Forces of the Crown"; and officers in any branch hold their rank by virtue of a "Royal Commission." The courts and the judges are "Her Majesty's Courts" and "Her Majesty's Judges." High officials still bear titles like "Lord Chancellor," "Lord Privy Seal," and "Chancellor of the Exchequer," which all go back over 600 years.

The importance of this tradition is that it has preserved not only the medieval form, but the medieval *essence,* which in sum said: the king governs—but conditionally, not absolutely. At the heart of the British political system, there has always been a group of officials who formulated policy and saw that it was carried out. Except during the rule of the Long Parliament (1640–49), the opponents of the government have never sought to destroy this group, only to *control* it. British constitutional history

is, simply, the story of the struggle for the control of this administrative machinery. Originally, it was the king and his officials versus the barons in the Great Council or Magnum Concilium. Today, it is the prime minister and his ministers in the cabinet on one side and the Commons (or, more realistically, the opposition party) on the other. The form of an act of Parliament links the present to the remote past and attests to the underlying continuity of the medieval conception of government. An act always begins with these words: "Be it enacted by the Queen's Most Excellent Majesty, by and with the consent of the Lords Spiritual and Temporal and Commons in this present Parliament assembled and by authority of the same. . . ." In present-day Britain, it is the prime minister and other ministers, the cabinet, that really enact, but "by and with the consent" of the Commons.

The evolution of the constitution took place in two stages. First came the long and persistent effort of the more powerful of the king's subjects to control and direct his officers, and thus his policy. In the "Settlement" of 1689 and 1701, the age-old power of the monarch to govern on his own responsibility was terminated. Henceforward, he could act only through an official who could be impeached or dismissed by the Parliament and who could not plead the royal command as an excuse for his actions. The second stage, which began with the loss of the American War of Independence and has continued through the years ever since, has been the struggle to democratize the Parliament, which in 1689 had emerged triumphant from its contest with the crown.

The "Settlement" of 1689 determined that Parliament and not the king would be preeminent. But Parliament at that time was not a very democratic institution. The House of Lords, by definition, was composed of the great landlords. The House of Commons consisted largely of the nominees of these great lords, or of wealthy men who had bought themselves a seat, or of members who sat owing to the ministers' manipulation of the votes (although there were always a great number of independents sitting also). The great landmark in the development of the British system toward democracy was the Reform Act of 1832. It increased the electorate from half a million to some three-quarters of a million people, allowed many of the members of the growing middle class to vote, eliminated many of the "rotten boroughs" (boroughs entitled to send one or two members to Parliament despite the fact that in the course of the years their population had been drastically reduced), and created additional electoral districts in the new urban centers. This weakened the hold of the nobility and the landed gentry over Parliament and paved the way to the representation of the new industrial centers from which the country was beginning to derive most of its wealth.

After 1832, the extension of the franchise to wider sections of the population continued. The 1832 act enfranchised 7 percent of the population over 20 years of age. The 1867 Reform Act, enfranchising chiefly the artisans of the towns, extended the vote to 16 percent of the population over 20 years old. The third Reform Act, in 1884, extended the franchise to the rural workers, enabling 28 percent of the population over 20 to vote. In 1918, the Representation of the People Act extended male suffrage still further and gave the vote to women aged 30 and above. With this, 78 percent of the population over 20 was entitled to vote. In 1928, the voting age for women was reduced to 21, the same as for men; and finally, in 1970, the voting age for both men and women was reduced to 18.

This century-long movement to expand the franchise changed the constitution in three important ways. First, it divested the sovereign of all real political power. Today she retains certain personal prerogatives, but she "reigns but does not govern." Next, it made the House of Commons predominant over the House of Lords, whose veto power over bills was terminated in the case of financial bills and reduced to two years for other bills in 1911. Since then, its power to delay nonfinancial bills has been reduced (by the Parliament Act of 1949) to only one year, and if it used this right in a serious conflict with the Commons it would in all probability see its delaying power curtailed still further or entirely removed. Finally, from about 1885, the expansion of the franchise caused the political parties to become more and more organized and disciplined. Since the power of the cabinet depends on the discipline of its supporters in the Commons, this tendency led in turn to the supremacy of the cabinet over its own parliamentary supporters, and today to the prime minister's increasing dominance over his cabinet ministers.

The Salient Features of the Modern British Constitution

The modern British constitution is characterized by six features:

1. *It is uncodified.* There is no single document in Britain, as there is in France, Germany, and the United States, which purports to prescribe all the most important rules relating to the government. To find out the constitutional position on any particular point in Britain, one must consult all or any of five particular sources. First, there are Acts of Parliament, such as the Parliament Act of 1911 which limits the life of any one Parliament to five years. Next there are the decisions of the courts of law. Thirdly, there are certain principles of the common law; for instance, the basic freedoms—e.g., of speech or of association—are derived from the common law. Fourthly, there is the law and custom of Parliament (*lex et consuetudo Parliamenti*); among other things, this prescribes the special privileges attaching to Parliament and to an individual member. Finally, there is an entirely unwritten element, the *conventions* of the constitution.

    The conventions are rules of practice. The constitution depends very largely upon the conventions. Examples of some of the more important of them are: (1) Parliament must meet at least once a year; (2) the monarch does not attend cabinet meetings; (3) ministers who lose the support of the Commons on a major policy issue must either resign or seek to reverse the opinion of the Commons by advising the monarch to dissolve Parliament and so permit a general election in which the electorate can be called upon to make a decision; and (4) the cabinet is *collectively* responsible to Parliament on matters of policy.

Conventions are *not* laws. They could be broken without incurring a legal penalty. Sometimes they are, but this is most infrequent. The conventions are one of the most conservatively regarded elements of the constitution.

2. *It is flexible.* No greater legislative sanctity attaches to a law of constitutional significance than to any other law. Laws altering the succession to the crown or the status of political parties would be passed in exactly the same manner as a wild birds protection act.

3. *Britain is a unitary, not a federal state.* Parliament is supreme over the whole of the United Kingdom. No localities exist whose governments have coequal legal status with that of Parliament. Local authorities such as county councils or borough councils can be altered or abolished altogether by an act of Parliament.

4. *Parliament is sovereign.* The law courts recognize that Parliament's acts are law and that they therefore must apply them as such. The Parliament is therefore the supreme organ of authority. No authority in the kingdom is competent to override it or to set it aside, but Parliament can override or set aside any other authority in the kingdom. It can legislate on any matter it chooses. It can repeal or amend any act of any former Parliament. It can pass acts of attainder and ex post facto laws. It can legalize past illegalities. It can illegalize past legalities.

5. *The separation of powers.* In the American sense, this principle does *not* operate in Britain. Parliament unites the executive and legislature and it itself is the "High Court" of Parliament. In another sense, the principle *does* operate; the legislature does not interfere with the day-to-day workings of either the judiciary or of the civil servants. And only ministers, not the civil servants in the ministries, are responsible to the Houses of Parliament. The tenure of judges is guaranteed during "good behavior," and the crown (effectively, the government) can remove them only on a joint address from both houses. In practice, this has guaranteed them immunity from political pressure. In addition, the judges enjoy considerable judicial immunities for the things they say or do in their official capacity.

6. *A Cabinet system.* The late L. S. Amery has said that the constitution still consists, as in medieval days, of "a continuous parley or conference in Parliament between the Crown, i.e., the directing and energizing element, and the representatives of the nation." Today, the essential parley or conference occurs between the prime minister in his cabinet on the one side, and the Commons, chiefly the opposition side, on the other. This forms the subject of Chapter 5 and will be discussed there in more detail.

TWO

foundations

of

British politics

THE CLIMATE
OF BRITISH POLITICS:
AN ABSENCE OF IDEOLOGY

Pluralism

Underlying British political behavior is the acceptance of pluralism—that many different viewpoints are reflected in the community, and that each has a right to exist and to be heard. These various sections of the community, as long as they are not breaking the law, or planning to do so, enjoy the common law rights of all British subjects to speak, publish, and associate freely, even if their cause is considered odious by the majority of the public. Democracy is seen as a set of procedures to get things done.

British politics is emphatically not the politics of all or nothing; it is the politics of *less or more.* Few wish to exterminate the capitalist class, but many wish to see more public ownership or control of industry, heavier taxation on high incomes, and the like. Few wish to destroy the trade unions, but many would like to see restrictions imposed on their power to strike in vital industries. In the last decade, politics has even become a matter of a *little* less and a *little* more: Should a greater or a lesser share of the national income go to the workers, the middle classes, the old-age pensioners? Should there be a greater or a lesser pace in the emancipation of the colonies? And so forth.

This pragmatic attitude toward political issues is reflected in a third feature of British politics: the virtual absence of effectual ideological conflict. Ideologists are in evidence in the country, as is attested by the popularity of the left-wing weeklies, the *New Statesman* and *Tribune,* and by the emergence of the group of young men and women who publish the *New Left Review,* but the existence of these factions merely highlights the empirical viewpoint of the Labour party as a whole. On the right, there are hoodlums of the fascist or Nazi type, but they have neither a mass following nor do they make any ideological contributions. The right is, in Britain, the powerful Conservative party, which is even more pragmatic and empirical in its attitude than the Labour party. In short, then, there are no serious ideological cleavages to sunder the nation into procapitalist and anticapitalist factions or into prochurch and antichurch groups, as there are in so many other countries.

Politics of this sort still leaves plenty of room for passionate dispute. There is bitter disagreement over the distribution of the national income; the Labour party and the trade unions press for a larger share for the manual wage earners at the expense of other sections of the community, while the Conservatives argue that the claims of the other sections are equally worthy. There is bitter disagreement over nationalization and public control of industry. Disagreement once smoldered over the pace and extent of the liquidation of the colonial empire, but this has proceeded so fast and so far that the margin of disagreement between the parties has been almost eliminated and now only British relations with southern Africa arouse furious controversy. In foreign policy again, there have been times, especially when Britain and France forcibly intervened in the Suez Canal zone during the fighting between Israel and Egypt (1956), when the country was most bitterly divided; though since then it has become increasingly bipartisan.

The Symbol of British Unity: The Sovereign

Whatever the political system, the greater the sense of corporate unity, the less acrimonious and desperate is political dispute likely to be. Such a sense of unity is a matter of emotion rather than of intellect—in sociologists' terms, it is *affective* rather than *cognitive,* and it is therefore best expressed by a symbol rather than by an intellectual proposition. Britain has its flag, but unlike the United States and indeed nearly all the countries of Europe, the Union Jack is not much seen outside gala days, while the flag-saluting ceremony of the American public school is in Britain entirely unknown. True, Britain has its national anthem, another common national symbol; but this anthem is in fact a royal anthem, "God Save the Queen." For in Britain the unique symbol of the nation is the sovereign, and the sovereign has most powerfully assisted in giving British politics the distinctive quality of forbearance. Not only does the queen never express a political position of her own, but she is seen manifestly as above politics, representing the apex of the *national* family. At least two consequences have followed. In the first place, the sovereign gives the system a greater sense of permanence than is in fact the case. The Commonwealth is a far, far different arrangement from the prewar British empire. Yet the queen, in her frequent state visits to member countries, in her receptions of Commonwealth prime ministers, in her annual Christmas Day broadcast to the peoples of the Commonwealth, makes the Commonwealth appear a natural evolution from the old empire instead of what in fact it is—an abdication from empire. Again, the annual program of a cabinet is announced to Parliament through the mouth of the queen or her commissioners in what is known as "the Queen's Speech." This suggests to the public that nothing in that program can be seriously regarded as antinational; it may be perverse, but it is not unpatriotic.

Antimonarchical sentiment unquestionably exists in Britain, but it is not serious. A scattering of left-wing ideologues are critical of the monarchy, to be sure; but they feel far too strongly about capitalism or racism to initiate a republican movement. The real point in dispute—if *dispute* is the right term—is not whether the monarchy should remain, but whether it should or should not become more "democratic," to evolve in some elusive way into a "classless court."

Citizen Attitudes: The Political Culture

In their remarkable cross-polity survey, *The Civic Culture* (covering Britain as well as the United States, the German Federal Republic, Italy, and Mexico), Gabriel Almond and Sidney Verba significantly add to what has been said about the climate of British politics.

Partisanship, Almond and Verba say, is more pronounced in Britain than in the United States. In America, (according to them) the proportions of supporters willing to say kind words about the opposing party were 70% (where Republicans described Democrats) and 63% (where Democrats described Republicans), but in Britain a mere 32% of Conservative supporters could find anything positive to say about the Labour party, and only 41% of the Labour supporters were prepared to say something positive about the Conservative party. But this difference between the two countries is hardly surprising in view of the coherent, tight-knit characteristics and well-spelled-out platforms of the British parties as compared with those of the United States.

British partisanship, like that of the United States, exists within a deep and widespread support for the political system as such. To begin with, the British *admire* their political arrangements. To the question "What aspects of national life do you take most pride in?" 46 out of 148 replies named the political and governmental arrangements. The corresponding American response was much higher: 85 replies out of a total of 158. Both of these responses form a stark contrast to West Germany and Italy, where only 4% and 2½% of the responses, respectively, named the political system as the aspect of national life in which respondents took most pride!

Furthermore, the British, again like the Americans but even more so, have confidence in their governmental arrangements. In the United States, 83% of the respondents said they expected fair play from the civil service, and 85% likewise expected it from the police; in Britain, 83% expected fair play from the civil service, and no less than 89% from the police. The British people also feel, even more strongly than do Americans, that the civil service and police will take their problems seriously. Respondents were asked: "If you explained your point of view to the officials, what effect do you think it would have? Would they give your point of view serious consideration, would they pay only a little attention, or would they ignore your point of view?" In Britain, 54%

replied that the civil servants would give them "serious consideration" while as many as 74% thought that the police would also do so. In the United States, the proportions were 48% and 59% respectively.

At the same time, the British feel almost as free as the Americans: 50% compared with an American proportion of 54% said they felt "free to discuss politics and talk to anyone or most people about politics"; another 20% (22% in the United States) felt they could discuss politics with a restricted circle. The percentage who said they never discussed their political opinions with anybody was 29% in Britain and 24% in the United States. (In the German Federal Republic, 39% said they never discussed their politics; in Mexico, 61%; and in Italy, no less than 66%.)

It is not surprising, then, to find that a very high proportion of Britons feel that they can do something about unjust local or national legislation: 78% of them replied that they could do something about an unfair local regulation (77% in the United States), and no less than 62% said that they could affect the course of a national regulation—as against 65% who said they could do so in the United States, but only 38% in both Germany and Mexico, and a mere 28% in Italy.

Political Participation

Election statistics are a misleading guide to citizen participation in Britain because elections, as compared with those in the United States, are comparatively rare: general elections take place every four years on the average, and elections for local councils take place every year (usually) for the urban areas, and every three years for the rural ones. Furthermore, the number of elective offices is minute when compared with the number involved in American elections: only the 630 members of Parliament and approximately 30,000 local councillors are elected. Then, too, much of what passes as the responsibility of the public authorities in other lands is in Britain a matter for private bodies, so that it is possible to participate in the running of the country without standing for public office—that is, as a member or officer of a private association. Consequently, British democracy is characterized by an amalgamation of public and private sectors and elected and appointed officers.

Because public officers who are appointed and controlled by elected public authorities draw into their work the interest groups who are also controlled by their own elected officers, three ways of political participation lie open to the citizen. First, he may affect public issues by participating in such private organizations as the British Medical Association or the Transport and General Workers' Union, all of which in certain sectors are assisting to carry out (or to influence) matters of public concern. According to Almond and Verba, 47% of their British respondents stated that they belonged to one voluntary association or another. This compares with a figure of 57% in the United States. The difference lies in the types of associations frequented in these two countries, and the different role played by women. In Britain, for instance, membership in trade unions is considerably greater than it is in the United States, but membership in "religious, civic, and political" bodies is less, and the "fraternal" associations which are common in the United States hardly exist in Britain. At the same time, American women are joiners on a much larger scale than are British women.

The second way of participating in politics is by being co-opted by, associated with, or consulted by the public authorities—and these are the principal means by which the interest groups are involved in policy-making and administrative processes (see Chapter 3).

Finally, the citizen can participate in a strictly "political" way by standing as a candidate, by being active in a party supporting a candidate, by being a dues-paying member of such a party, or, finally, just by voting for a candidate. Membership in political parties is high, but the proportion of party militants, as is to be expected, is low.

Voting turnout has been very high in British general elections, attaining a record high of 84% in 1950. But it has tended to de-

cline since then and was only 72% in 1970. These figures underestimate the true degree of participation, since the register of people entitled to vote is only drawn up once a year (each October to come into force the following February) and a number of the electorate, varying from about 5% to 15%, at any given election represents deaths or removals. Adjusting the figures, some 80–90% of the British population able and eligible to vote do so. However, participation is much lower at local elections; 40% is a modal figure, and this has also declined since 1950.

With the assistance of the invaluable tables in Almond and Verba's *The Civic Culture* and of various estimates made by British scholars, it is possible to indicate some of the dimensions of participation, as shown in Table 2-1.

TABLE 2-1. *Interest and Participation in Goverment in the United Kingdom*

Total electorate	100%
Total voting in general election (1970)	72
Interested in politics *	68/70
Members of voluntary associations	47
Knowledgeable †	42
Party membership (estimated)	25
Activists in voluntary associations ‡	13
Local party activists (estimated) §	0.5
Influential elected and nominated officers —local and central government ‖	0.12

SOURCE: Italicized entries are from Gabriel Almond and Sidney Verba, *The Civic Culture* (Princeton: Princeton University Press, 1965).

* "Sometimes talk politics with others"—70 percent; "Follow politics regularly or from time to time"—68 percent.

† By the (low) standard of their ability to name four or more party leaders.

‡ I.e., those claiming to be or to have been officers in such organizations.

§ Assuming about 150 apiece in the Labour and Conservative local constituency organizations, and about 50 apiece for the Liberal ones.

‖ For breakdown, see Table 2-2.

FACTORS
THAT ASSIST CONSENSUS

The Nature of
Regional Differences

Only 17% of the British population live outside England: 5% in Wales, 9% in Scotland, and 3% in Northern Ireland.

For some time English regional differences have been slight and not electorally significant. After a survey at mid-century, Geoffrey Gorer concluded:

In the three years during which I have been occupied with the data on which my study has been founded I have been increasingly more impressed with the basic unity of the people of England. The upper-middle and lower working classes, the mother-centered North West and father-centered North East depart to a somewhat marked extent from the habits and attitudes of the rest of the country: but in the main, the English are a truly unified people, more unified, I would hazard, than at any previous period of their history.[1]

But in the last four general elections small variations in the movement of opinion have occurred, and following the 1970 election Labour is stronger in northern England than it was in 1955 while in the Midlands and the southern region it is the Conservatives who are stronger than in 1955.

Scotland and Wales, on the other hand, are each ethnically, culturally, and historically very different indeed from England, and these differences do manifest themselves politically. Both Scotland and Wales have a vital sense of nationhood. Scotland joined the United Kingdom of Great Britain voluntarily as an independent state and retained her own native legal, educational, and (above all) religious institutions. Wales was conquered by the English seven centuries ago and has been partly anglicized; but the survival of the Welsh language

among a quarter of the people and a rich indigenous culture of literature and music shared by all have provided the basis for a strong cultural nationalism in Wales.

Since World War I, there has been a marked contrast between the more populous and more prosperous southern and Midlands

TABLE 2-2. *Top Local and Central Decision Makers in the United Kingdom*

I	Elected Personnel	
	M.P.'s	630
	Local councillors (approx.)	30,000
II	Appointed Personnel—Local (approx. 50 senior officers per major local authority) (approx.)	6,500
III	Appointed, Co-opted, and Consulted Personnel—National *	
	Highest civil service	169
	Judiciary	77
	Military leaders	319
	Boards of nationalized industries	345
	Industrial directorate:	
	(a) Top companies— capital £1 million and over	245
	(b) Medium companies—capital £200,000–1 million	6,100
	Boards of major banks and insurance companies	340
	Governors of major autonomous and semiautonomous agencies	150
	Principal government advisory committees	330
	Leaders of science and learning	200
	Leaders of major economic pressure groups	53
	Trade union leadership	60
	Spokesmen of the professions	40
	Heads of churches	70
	Total	45,628

[1] *Exploring English Character* (London: Cresset Press, 1952).

* Derived from W. L. Guttsman, *The British Political Elite* (London: Allen & Unwin, 1963), p. 328.

regions of England, on the one hand, and Scotland, Wales, and the northern and small southwestern regions of England on the other. The latter half of Britain has suffered from the decline of old staple industries, high unemployment rates, and the drift of its population toward jobs in the southeast. This persistent and growing economic grievance has fed a general resentment at Whitehall centralism, especially as the state has expanded its say in the running of society. In England this has nurtured a movement for devolution of power to regional councils—but it is as yet not a strong movement. In Scotland and Wales the regionalist grievance has combined with the sense of nationhood to produce nationalist parties and to give them a wide audience.

Plaid Cymru (in Wales) and the Scottish National party have both been contesting elections without much success for nearly fifty years. But in the late 1960s there was an explosion of support for the two parties in some parliamentary by-elections and in the Scottish municipal elections. In 1967–68 they were polling between 25% and 40% of votes cast in such elections. By the 1970 general election this had subsided to 11½% of the votes cast in both countries, with the highest Nationalist votes occurring in the rural areas of western Wales and northern Scotland. But it had shown the major parties that underneath the normal similarity of voting movements in England, Scotland, and Wales there was a sympathy for nationalism in Scotland and Wales which could one day upset the British political applecart if Scottish and Welsh grievances are not met by the government in London.

Since 1945, only twice has there been a Labour majority of seats in England—in 1945 and in 1966; however, there has always been a Labour majority of seats in Wales. The Conservatives have only once won a majority of seats in Scotland—in 1955. The movements of voting between 1955 and 1970 have made Labour stronger and the Conservatives much weaker in Scotland, whereas in England the two parties won exactly the same number of seats in these two general elections. In the 1950 and 1964 elections Labour depended for its parlia-

mentary majority on this built-in strength in Wales, and to a lesser degree in Scotland.

Northern Ireland

There is, however, one sharp regional difference within the United Kingdom which produces locally sharp dissensus—that between Great Britain and Northern Ireland. Northern Ireland is the product of a conflict which has lasted on in the province. The conflict revolves around the historical experience of the Irish and of their relations with the British, in particular springing out of the history of settlement of the northeastern corner of Ireland by the British in the seventeenth century. The conflict thus engendered between settler and indigenous populations lived on as an historic clash between the supporters of the Orange and Stuart dynasties in 1689 and as a tension between Protestants and Roman Catholics. In the earlier twentieth century it became a constitutional conflict between those who supported the British connection and those who identified with Irish nationalism.

The province of Northern Ireland was created in the interests of its Protestant, or loyalist (to the crown), majority. It has been ruled continuously by one party—the Unionist party (linked to the British Conservatives), which represents exclusively that majority. The Catholic, or republican (i.e., wishing to join the Republic of Ireland) minority never accepted the legitimacy of the border between Northern Ireland and the Republic of Ireland. Accordingly, the latter have been condemned to perpetual opposition within the Northern Irish political system and have complained of systematic political, social, and economic discrimination. Their grievances and irredentism have fed periodic outbreaks of violence, such as the Belfast riots of the 1930s and the campaign of organized violence launched by the Irish Republican Army from 1956 to 1962. But with the failure of the latter it was hoped in Britain that Northern Ireland could forget its bitter past and adapt to the political mores of the rest of the United Kingdom.

In 1968 a civil rights campaign started marches in support of the minority's grievances. This movement rapidly escalated via police violence, splits in the governing Unionist party, acceptance of many of the reforms demanded, a general election, the shattering of the old Irish Nationalist party, and the resignation of Northern Ireland's prime minister, Captain O'Neill, to widespread street riots in Belfast and Londonderry in the summer of 1969. At this point the British army was brought in to restore order and the British government took responsibility for the reform program.

Northern Ireland is both geographically and politically isolated from Great Britain, although Irish political conflicts have played a part in the local politics of two large British cities—Glasgow and Liverpool. But the fact that law and order broke down so completely in a part of the United Kingdom in 1969 and at the time of writing has not been fully restored, together with the responsibility taken for changing politics of Northern Ireland by the British government, ensure that the problem is an internal British one. It is quite insoluble by the methods normally in use for political problems in Britain. The search for different appropriate methods helps to keep the problem out of the mainstream of British politics; but it may nevertheless end up there.

Ethnic Differences

Historically, the British are a mixture of Celtic, Anglo-Saxon, Viking, and Norman immigrants. But the lack of any major immigration from outside the British Isles between the eleventh and the twentieth centuries meant that the British were not fully prepared for the problems of assimilating immigrants of a different ethnic background to themselves. Minor problems were associated with small waves of refugees from eastern and central Europe at the end of the nineteenth century and during the first half of the twentieth. In particular, there was agitation against the immigration of Jews around the turn of the century and some anti-Semitism flourished among extremist groups in the 1930s. But today Jews are fully assimilated

into British political life, well represented inside the Labour and Liberal parties and more recently in the Conservative party.

A similar experience could await the colored immigrants from the Commonwealth countries who flocked to Britain in search of work between 1955 and 1965. But their numbers (already well over a million) and the difference of appearance between them and the host population has meant the growth of some racial tension. So far, in political terms, this has produced a small fringe white racist party, the National Front, and some black power groups. But there has, as yet, been little progress toward the integration of colored Britons into political activity, except in direct defence of their own interests. Whether or not this ethnic difference is assimilated to contribute toward consensus or whether it becomes a source of dissensus will probably be decided in the coming decade.

Religious Differences

Religion no longer drives divisive wedges into British society, nor does it emphasize political differences as it did up to World War I. In the last fifty years, the coincidence of party allegiance and religious affiliation has continually declined. Estimates of the numbers within religious denominations differ, but the following is probably an accurate count of the membership of the largest ones: the Church of England, the Church of Wales, and the Church of Ireland (total 28 million); the Roman Catholic church (5 million baptized members); Presbyterians (1¼ million); Methodists (1 million full members); Congregationalists and Baptists (each with about a quarter of a million). About one-fifth of the adult population belongs to a religious association of some kind. Evidence indicates that, with the exception of the Roman Catholics, there has been a decline in church-going over the last half century. Of all the marriages celebrated in England and Wales in 1967, some 45% were in the Anglican communion, 21% in churches and chapels of other denominations, and 34% were civil marriages in a registry office. In Scotland in 1968, the proportions were: Presbyterian, 50%; Roman Catholic, 16%; other churches, 8%, and registry office, 26%.

The Mass Media

Local, regional, and religious differences, such as they are, are increasingly eroded by the mass media—notably the press, radio, and television. Despite regional editions of newspapers, a flourishing provincial press, and regional radio and television broadcasts that emphasize the interests of Scotland, Ireland, and Wales (including many Welsh-language items), the effect of the mass media is overwhelmingly to standardize tastes, outlooks, and even accents—and accents, whether lilting Scots, singsong Welsh, nasal Cockney, or broad Midlands, are the most obvious way, in Britain, of distinguishing between natives of one region and another.

THE PRESS. The salient facts about the British press are (1) that the country has more newspapers per head than any other country in the world, and (2) that circulation is dominated by the great London newspapers. They all purvey a type of national, as opposed to regional, news, but they differ in character from "popular" or "tabloid" to "quality" papers, and they also differ politically. Table 2-3 lists them, with the most recent circulation figures (1969–70), according to their political attitudes.

RADIO. Radio is organized quite differently from the way it is in the United States. One single corporation (the British Broadcasting Corporation) is responsible for all radio broadcasting, although provision is made for regional variations in programs. The BBC is a public corporation whose directors are nominated by the government, and its charter stipulates that it must use its services to disseminate information, education, and entertainment. It is forbidden to accept commercial advertisements, must refrain from expressing any editorial opinion, and is expected to be impartial in presenting current affairs and politics. From time to time, each political party is given facilities for a "Party Political Broadcast," the proportion accorded to each party being decided after consultation among them. Politically and socially, the effect of the BBC is prodigious, especially since it is a monopoly and is neutral, for practically every household has a receiving set.

TELEVISION. Until 1954, the BBC enjoyed a monopoly of television as well as of radio broadcasting. Since then, it has had to share the field with a second body, the Independent Television Authority (ITA). The ITA owns and operates television stations for programs

TABLE 2-3. *Circulations and Political Affinities of the British National Dailies, July–December 1970*

Labour and Independent Labour		Conservative and Independent Conservative		Liberal/Labour		Independent	
Daily Mirror	4,444,000	Daily Express	3,519,000	Guardian	304,000	Times	374,000
Sun	1,722,000	Daily Mail *	1,814,000			Financial Times	165,000
		Daily Telegraph	1,416,000				
		Daily Sketch *	764,000				
Total	6,166,000	Total	7,513,000	Total	304,000	Total	539,000

* The *Daily Mail* and *Daily Sketch* amalgamated in 1971 as the *Daily Mail*.

which are provided by outside companies. The programs are not sponsored as in the United States, but the program companies sell time for spot announcements at intervals throughout their broadcasts. The ITA is responsible for regulating the system and for securing proper standards in the programs. It must see, for example, that the companies are impartial in presenting matters of political controversy, and accurate in news reporting. Political advertising is forbidden, a provision which the ITA has been extremely strict in interpreting. For instance, it refused to sanction an advertisement for the Communist *Daily Worker* on the ground that it was a political rather than a commercial advertisement.

Today, over 90% of the families in Britain have television sets. Special provision is made for regional variations of programs—notably for Scotland, Wales, and Northern Ireland (ITA goes further in this respect than the BBC does). Yet the main effect of television is to emphasize and to create uniformities. It brings national leaders rather than local ones into the home. By excellent documentary features such as "24 Hours" and "Panorama" (both BBC), it focuses wide attention on national issues. Television has thus become one of the most potent instruments of "nationalization" in British society.

Urbanization and Wealth

The Industrial Revolution, which made Britain "the workshop of the world" in the mid-nineteenth century, both brought about the most profound transformation of her formerly mercantile and agricultural economy, and effected revolutionary changes in her social structure. These changes have worked in two directions, some provoking conflict, others promoting consensus. Among those that have done the latter stands urbanization. The Industrial Revolution turned the British into a society of town-dwellers and town-workers, thus consolidating social attitudes and greatly narrowing the range of social problems with which government had to deal. Today Britain is more urbanized than any other country in the world. This can be seen from Table 2-4, which takes on added significance

TABLE 2-4. *Percentage of Population in Towns of over 100,000 in Five Countries*

U.K.	51.0%
Germany	30.7
U.S.	28.4
USSR	23.5
France	16.8

SOURCE: Compiled from UN Statistical Yearbook 1969; UN Demographic Yearbook 1969.

when we realize that 40% of the entire population live in seven urban centers that account for less than 4% of the country's area. Also, industrialization made Britain wealthy—and wealth makes it easier to close the gap between extreme poverty and extreme riches by equalizing income through taxation and social services, and by providing additional benefits for the masses. Although the British standard of living falls woefully short of that of the United States, it is rich by European standards, and fabulously wealthy by Asian or Latin American standards.

Furthermore, in the last twenty years the living standard has risen visibly. Consumer income per capita rose by 40% between 1951 and 1964, which was more than for the entire previous half-century. Moreover, redistributive taxation and social services spread this income somewhat more equally than before the war. Too, the postwar relaxation of consumers' credit controls allowed working people to spend their swollen earnings on consumer durables—washing machines, television sets, cars, houses (see Table 2-5). The proportion of householders owning the homes they lived in has risen from under one-third in 1951 to about one-half today; the proportion of homes with central heating shot up from 7% in 1964 to 25% in 1969.

Like that of the United States, British society has been called "the affluent society," and informed observers wonder aloud whether the capitalism of the nineteenth century, the capitalism that divided Britain into "two nations, rich and poor," still exists or whether it has

TABLE 2-5. *British Standard of Living, 1956–1969*

Percentage of Households Owning	1956	1969
Automobile	25%	51%
Telephone	16	32
Television set	40	91
Refrigerator	7	60
Washing machine	19	63

TABLE 2-6. *Proportion of Labor Force in British Manufacturing Industries, 1891–1969*

	1891	1951	1969
Textiles & clothing	53.0%	19.5%	14.4%
Metals, machinery, & vehicles	4.3	45.5	51.6
Food, drink & tobacco	4.1	8.7	9.6
Chemicals	1.7	5.1	5.8
Others	36.7	21.2	19.6

not in fact transformed itself into something else which has not yet received a name. Perhaps, they submit, the current phase in British society ought to be termed "postcapitalist." The very fact that such a question can be widely raised is a sign that one legacy of the Industrial Revolution—the sharp cleavage of society into the wealthy and the indigent, the owners and the industrial proletariat—is beginning to disappear and is certainly no longer what it was even twenty years ago. The transformation of the labor force also points in this direction.

The Transformation of the Labor Force

There has been a long-term trend away from heavy manual labor and toward organizational, clerical, and distributive occupations, and from wage earning to salary earning. The primary sector, mainly coal mining and agriculture, has lost labor heavily in the last two decades. In the manufacturing sector there is a striking movement from textiles and clothing to the metals, machinery, and vehicles group which has been under way since the beginning of the century and is a continuing trend over the last twenty years; the growth of employment in the food, drink, and tobacco group and the chemical industry is also notable (see Table 2-6). But the biggest growth is in tertiary-sector occupations—transport, distribution, administration, professional and personal services.

These changes are paralleled by changes in the type of work done within each sector. In 1961 already almost one-quarter of the total labor force in mining and manufacturing were administrative and clerical workers, and this proportion is increasing by 0.5% annually.

Between 1951 and 1961 the most striking increases among male workers lay in the professional and technical occupations (especially the latter): the number of mechanical engineers rose from 25,000 to 46,000; of electrical engineers from 20,000 to 40,000; of chemists and other natural scientists from 9,000 to 20,000; and of male clerical workers from 862,000 to 1,045,000. Similar trends occurred in the female labor force. Reflecting a worldwide trend, the most striking increases lay in the numbers of clerks and typists (from 1,270,000 to 1,780,000) and of those in the professional and technical occupations (from 523,000 to 707,000).

In short, the labor force is becoming more "technical" and more "white-collar." This can be seen from the 1961 census breakdown of the population into sixteen socioeconomic groups (Table 2-7—note that the figures relate to England and Wales only, not to the whole of the United Kingdom).

The first seven groups represent the nonmanual proportion of the labor force; it totals 30.3%. It is likely that the 1971 census returns will show that this proportion has increased to at least one-third. The British labor force is today more white-collar and perhaps more "middle-class" than at any time in the past,

TABLE 2-7. *Socioeconomic Groups in England and Wales, 1961*

Group	Proportion of Work Force
1. Employers and managers—large establishments	3.6%
2. Employers and managers—small establishments	5.9
3. Professional workers, self-employed	0.8
4. Professional workers, employees	2.8
5. Intermediate nonmanual workers (ancillary to professions)	3.8
6. Junior nonmanual (e.g., clerical, sales, communications)	12.5
7. Personal service (food, drink, and clothing; occupations; etc.)	0.9
8. Foremen and supervisors—manual	3.3
9. Skilled manual workers	30.4
10. Semiskilled manual workers	14.7
11. Unskilled manual workers	8.6
12. Own account workers (not professional)	3.6
13. Farmers—employers and managers	1.0
14. Farmers—own account	1.0
15. Agricultural workers	2.3
16. Armed Forces	1.9
Unclassified	2.9

SOURCE: Census of England and Wales, 1961.

and is becoming more so. It is reckoned that by the late 1980s over half the entire labor force of the economy will be engaged in white-collar occupations.

This process blurs the sharp polarization between "capitalist" and "the industrial proletariat." Yet it has also been accompanied by the spreading among nonmanual workers of some "proletarian" methods and attitudes toward their work. Trade unions for technical, administrative, supervisory, and teaching staffs have grown apace in the 1960s and have been adopting militant attitudes toward salary demands hitherto more characteristic of the demands of manual workers' unions for higher wages. Several white-collar unions have become affiliated with the Trade Union Congress, more than making up for the decline in numbers of traditional unions such as the mine workers or railwaymen, and are steadily transforming the character of that body. Whether this process is more significant as a "proletarianization" of nonmanual workers or as a dilution of the once essentially manual worker trade union movement remains to be seen.

FACTORS MAKING FOR CONFLICT

"Socialism," so it is widely repeated in Britain, "is about equality." So is British politics. Britain is still in many ways an unequal society.

Distribution of the National Income

Britain's national income grew from nearly £5 billion in 1938 to nearly £12 billion in 1950 and £38 billion in 1969; since the value of the pound was halved between 1938 and 1951 and again between 1951 and 1969, this represents a doubling of the total national income in real terms.

Together with these developments have gone various leveling factors. For one thing, a greater share of the national income now goes to those who are employed, and a lesser share to those collecting rents, dividends, and interest: the former took 60% of the total in 1938 and 72% in 1959, while the latter, which took 22½% in 1938, took only 10½% in 1959. But this redistribution has not continued: the 1969 figures were, respectively, 70½% and 11½%. Secondly, particularly since the war the wages and salaries of the less-well-paid have risen proportionately more than those of the better-paid, and even more than professional earnings. These two factors are reflected in Table 2-8, which shows the proportion of the national income taken by various classes of persons in 1938 as compared with 1955. As can be seen, the richer had become less rich, the poor had become better off. For example, the top 100,000 per-

TABLE 2-8. *Distribution of Personal Income before Taxes, Prewar and Postwar*

Population, in Order of Income	Proportion of Total National Income before Taxes	
	1938	1955
First 100,000	11.7%	5.3%
First 500,000	21.5	12.3
First 1,000,000	27.8	17.4
First 5,000,000	51.6	42.6
Remainder	48.4	57.4

SOURCE: Carr-Saunders, Jones, and Moser, *Social Conditions in England and Wales* (London: Oxford University Press, 1958), p. 181.

sons in income in 1938 received 11.7% of the nation's income, but in 1955 they received only 5.3%. In 1957 this trend ceased. (See Table 2-9; although this table is not entirely comparable to Table 2-8, the pattern is clear enough.) Indeed, the only significant change shown between 1957 and 1963 is a *reduction* in the share of the national income going to the poorest 30% of the population.

TABLE 2-9. *Distribution of Income before Taxes, Postwar (1949–1963)*

Group of Income Recipients	Proportion of Total National Income before Taxes		
	1949	1957	1963
Top 1%	11.2%	8.2%	7.9%
2–5%	12.6	10.9	11.2
6–10%	9.4	9.0	9.6
11–40%	34.9	37.6	39.0
41–70%	19.2	23.1	22.6
Bottom 30%	12.7	11.3	9.7

SOURCE: R. J. Nicholson, "The Distribution of Personal Incomes," *Lloyd's Bank Review*, January, 1967.

Thus in Britain today income is shared more equally between the classes than it was before the war; but this leveling had been achieved by the mid-fifties, and the trend has, if anything, been very slightly reversed since then. In any case, sharp inequalities of income remain, as also marked differences between the rates at which the income of different groups has risen. Table 2-10 illustrates these for a number of occupations.

SOCIAL MOBILITY AND EDUCATION. In Britain one of the principal hallmarks of "class" is occupation. The 1951 census divides the population into five main classes (see Table 2-11). Class I explains itself. Class II consists largely of lesser professional, administrative, and managerial ocupations, and of farmers, shopkeepers, and small employers. Class III consists of skilled

TABLE 2-10. *Job Salaries or Wages in The United Kingdom, 1970*

Job Description	Salary or Wage Earnings	Purchasing Power as a Percentage of 1938 Salary
Airline pilot (captain)	£5,900	119%
University professor	£5,095	91
Higher civil servant	£4,747	74
Doctor (general practice)	£4,000	86
Accountant (age 30)	£2,200	114
Graduate-school teacher (with 10-yrs service)	£1,585	90
Engine driver	£1,500	139
Miner	£1,391	195
Factory worker	£1,328	158
Bank clerk	£1,270	106
Railway porter	£1,040	183
Agricultural worker	£906	180
Shop assistant	£812	111

SOURCE: *The Economist Diary*, 1971, p. 18.

TABLE 2-11. *Census Classification of Males by Occupation in England and Wales, 1931–1961*

Social Class	1931	1951	1961
I Professional occupations	2%	3%	4%
II Intermediate occupations	13	14	15
III Skilled occupations	49	52	51
IV Partly skilled occupations	18	16	21
V Unskilled occupations	18	15	9

SOURCES: Censuses of England and Wales for corresponding years.

manual workers, shop assistants, typists, foremen, and the like. The last two classes comprise, for the most part, the operatives and workmen in field, factory, and workshop—all "manual working class."

In 1950, Prof. D. V. Glass and his associates completed an extensive survey into the degree of social mobility in Britain.[2] He used a scale based on the census, but with seven divisions instead of five. His investigations showed that in the two top classes, 54% stayed in the same class as their parents, and 46% fell to a lower class. In the two bottom classes, 53% rose and 47% stayed in their parents' class. Thus there was extensive mobility, but it produced a similar structure, since the movements largely balanced one another. In Britain, social class and status is strongly influenced by one's occupation, and occupation very largely depends on education. Current arrangements afford far greater educational opportunities than at any time in the past, and yet in a measure they reflect the present stratification of society and help to perpetuate it.

In England and Wales, which contain some nine-tenths of the school population (the

2 D. V. Glass, ed., *Social Mobility in Britain* (Routledge, 1954).

Scottish school system is different), the present arrangements are these. (1) Some 6% of the school population go to independent fee-paying schools; among these are the prestigious "public schools." The social importance of this sector is out of all proportion to its size. (2) The state provides free and compulsory education from the age of 5 up to the age of 15. But pupils may stay on after that date. (3) Children at state primary schools have hitherto had to undergo some test of ability at the age of 10 or 11 to determine the type of secondary school for which they seem suited. But a beginning has been made toward abolishing this arrangement and in 1969 26% of the state school population went to "comprehensive" schools at the age of 11. (4) At the age of 15 or 16, pupils may take the "ordinary" General Certificate of Education, an important qualification for skilled occupations and a necessary one for certain professional ones, especially for university entrance. At ages 17, 18, and even 19, pupils may take the advanced-level General Certificate, an essential (in all but exceptional cases) for university entrance. (5) In Great Britain there are now 44 universities. Although these are independent corporations, they receive 70 percent of their funds from the central government via the University Grants Committee, on which the universities are strongly represented. The universities lay down their own standards for admitting students, usually based on the students' results according to the advanced-level General Certificate, school reports, and (often) a personal interview. Competition is so severe that at least one in two applicants are turned away. In short, there is an unofficial "17+ or 18+" test, (as well as the "11+" test,) to determine entrance to a university. Once students are admitted, however, they can apply for scholarships which provide not only tuition but also full maintenance. The amount awarded depends on parents' means. In practice, over 90 percent receive grants, of which some 90 percent are in the full amount.

The expansion of educational opportunity is evidenced by the 1961 census: of those born before 1897, only 10.8% had received education beyond the age of 15, while among those born between 1931 and 1941 the proportion was 31.8%. Of the pre-1897 generation, only 2.8% had received education beyond the age of 20, while among the 1931–1941 generation no less than 8.1% had done so. Table 2-12, while not exact because changes in the educational system make comparisons difficult, illustrates the trend.

This educational opportunity is not equally shared among all classes of the population, however. To some extent it follows existing inequalities, and to some extent it even perpetuates them.

To begin with, the private sector—which is confined to the wealthier minority of the population—is a far better avenue for social advancement than the state sector is. Included in this private sector are the so-called public schools, which in fact are private. These are the most prestigious and offer the best education. The greatest of them (Eton, Harrow, Winchester, and the like) enjoy national reputations. They inculcate their pupils with an intense group loyalty so that the "old school tie" and the "old-boy network" proves a significant factor in their later careers. Only about 4% of the school population attend these schools, yet they supplied *one-fifth* of the entrants to uni-

versities in 1961–62 and, in 1960, 51% of the officer cadets admitted to Sandhurst, as compared with only 23% supplied from state schools. They provided 31% of the entrants to the top (i.e., the "Administrative" grade) of the domestic civil service in the 1948–56 period, and 37% in the 1957–63 period. They provide about half of the M.P.'s in the House of Commons; since 1918 the proportion has never dropped below 42.5% and once (1931) reached 65%. The fluctuations reflect mainly the fortunes of the Conservative party, since most enter through that party. The 1970 Parliament has 49% of its members from these schools, but 75% of its Conservative M.P.'s are among them. However, around one in five of Labour M.P.'s (in 1970, 21%) has also come from the "public" schools.

The explanation lies in the social character and academic excellence of the schools. They are socially selective, but they also demand good academic standards from the pupil. Their teaching lays stress on character building, leadership, and corporate loyalty; and the success of their graduates in public life stems from the inculcation of these qualities. Very often, therefore, the positions which graduates hold are the result of excellence. But the fact remains that this excellence is produced by an education to which all but a small minority are too poor to have access, and this has generated bitter egalitarian resentment against the system. These schools, born of the Victorian cleavage between what were then called "the classes and the masses," are seen over a century later as perpetuating it, and are therefore widely regarded as so many "islands of privilege."

A second source of inequality arises from the arrangements for public secondary education. Until recently almost all children were assigned to a secondary school of a distinctive type according to a test of their ability at the age of 10 or 11. The majority—popularly regarded as those who had "failed" this test— were assigned to so-called secondary modern schools (for instance, 55% of the total in 1964 wound up there). In the same year 3% were assigned to technical schools, another 24% to regular secondary grammar schools, and yet another 4% to a special and prestigious type of

TABLE 2-12. *Proportions of the Population Attending School Full-time in England and Wales, 1921–1964*

| Age Group | Number per 1,000 | | |
	1921	1951	1964
10–14 (roughly, "elementary")	809	984	996
15–19 (roughly, "secondary")	62	148	200
19+ (university students)	10	26	36

SOURCES: D. C. Jones, A. M. Carr-Saunders and C. A. Moser, *Social Conditions in England and Wales* (London: Oxford University Press, 1958); and British Department of Education and Science, *Statistics of Education*, 1965.

grammar school. Unlike the others, this latter-most institution charges fees for its pupils but makes a proportion of free places available to pupils from the local primary schools; and again unlike the others, it is not maintained and controlled by the local education authority but receives its grants directly from the Department of Education and Science in London. For this reason it is known as a "direct-grant school."

Now, whether the child goes to a grammar school rather than a "modern," and how long he stays there after the age of 15, both relate to his family background (see Table 2-13). In the first place, the higher the occupational background of the parent, the more likely it is that the child will pass his "11+" and be assigned to the grammar school.

So it is less likely that the child of manual working-class parents will get to the grammar school than the child of nonmanual working-class parents. And it is in the same way that those children of manual working-class parents are less likely to stay on at a grammar school, even if they have managed to be assigned there, than are the children of parents in nonmanual occupations. According to the latest survey, of those continuing at school after age 15, 26% were from professional and managerial families, and only 8% from unskilled manual working-

class background. Only 15% of the children from managerial and professional families left school to take up skilled manual work, and only 18% of those whose parents were in other nonmanual occupations; but 28% of the children of a skilled manual worker did so, and 36% of those whose fathers were unskilled manual workers.

The same social selectivity works upon the passage from school to university. There has been a vast expansion in university student numbers—from 63,000 in 1939 to 120,000 in 1959 and to a quarter of a million today, and this trend is continuing. But this has been shown to be highly correlated with attendance at grammar school; and less so, but still very positively, to the father's occupation and education.

How far the social selectivity we have been discussing operates on university entrance is seen first of all by the proportion of those who enter a university from schools of the types discussed. In 1961–62, no less than 22% of the entire university intake came from the independent schools (overwhelmingly, "public schools" among these); another 15% came from the "direct-grant" schools (with a school population of only 4% of the entire state school population); and 62% came from the grammar schools. This factor can be seen again in a breakdown of the occupations of parents of university entrants (1961–62): higher professional family background accounted for 18%; other professional and managerial family background for 41%; clerical occupational background for 12%. Thus the nonmanual-class families, making up some 30% of the total working population, accounted for 71% of the university entrants. In contrast, only 18% of the entrants came from a skilled manual occupational background, and only 6% from semi-skilled, while the children of unskilled manual working-class parents accounted for a mere 1% of the total.[3] Thus, students whose parents were manual working-class made up only 25% of the total. This is almost identical with the propor-

TABLE 2-13. *Occupations of Fathers of Children in Grammar/Technical Schools and in Modern Schools, 1960*

Father's Occupation	Gram./Tech. School	Modern School
Professional and managerial	18%	4%
Clerical and other nonmanual	19	11
Skilled manual	41	49
Semi- and unskilled manual	10	23
Dead, or retired, or occupation not known	12	13

SOURCE: *15 to 18*, Vol. 2 (Her Majesty's Stationery Office (H.M.S.O.), 1960).

[3] Four percent were of unknown occupational background. See Committe on Higher Education, Cmmd. 2154.

tion for the years 1928–1947, which was 23%.

As we have said, the educational system is closely tied in with the social divisions of English life, and does little to alter them. It is small wonder therefore that the cry of "unequal opportunity" should have been raised and that the system has become a political issue between the Labour and Conservative parties. With the victory of the Labour party in 1964, confirmed by its sweeping majority in 1966, emphasis was put on providing for equal opportunities. One committee of inquiry has investigated the status of the "public schools," and another the anomalous status of the "direct-grant schools." The Labour government decided that all local authorities should change from the system of distinct types of secondary school to the "comprehensive" system (a few local authorities had been making the change in the previous decade voluntarily). Comprehensives are all-embracing schools to which all children go; provision for differing abilities and aptitudes is made by arrangements within the school. In 1964 only 8% of English children went to such comprehensive schools; by 1969 this was raised to 26%. But the 1970 Conservative government's emphasis of local education authorities' autonomy in this field will doubtless slow down the switch from selective to comprehensive secondary education.

SOCIAL CLASS. Thus far we have talked about wealth and education and occupation but these are all related to a fourth factor, social class. The essence of social class lies in the notion of superiority-inferiority, in the idea that some people are considered to rank (by some criterion or other) higher or lower than other people. There are two elements in establishing the rank-order of social class. The first is the *objective* element: granted that certain people are more esteemed than others, by what external characteristics (wealth, dress, speech, etc.) are they recognised as such? The second is the *subjective* element: given that certain people are, say, wealthier or pursue a certain type of occupation, how does society view them?

WEALTH. It should be remembered that social groupings differ from each other in a number of ways, not just in occupation. *Wealth* is extremely unequally distributed in Britain, and much more markedly than *income* (see Table 2-14). Figures subsequent to 1956 are not available; but in that year net assets varied from about $28,000 in the first and second of these classes, to about $2,000 in class 4 and $850 in class 5. While the money values of these sums would have changed (upward, due to inflation) in the last ten years, the relative values of highest and lowest are unlikely to have altered much, if at all. Thus, among the 12% who consti-

TABLE 2-14. *Classes in Britain (Those aged 16 and above)*

Class	Occupations	Percentage of Population
1. Upper middle	Doctors, company directors, senior university teachers, research scientists	4%
2. Middle	Factory managers, headmasters, technicians with professional qualifications, etc.	8
3. Lower middle	Schoolteachers, junior civil servants, small shopkeepers, skilled clerical workers, medical auxiliaries, etc.	18
4. Skilled working	Foremen, skilled workmen, shop assistants, etc.	35
5. Working	Unskilled laborers, agricultural workers, railway porters, cleaners, etc.	25
6. Very poor	Lowest-paid workers, state pensioners, widows, etc.	10

SOURCE: *Readership Survey* (London: Institute of Practitioners in Advertising, 1966).

tute the two top classes, the average wealth is some 30 times that of the working-class families of class 5, despite death duties of great severity for large estates.

DURABLE CONSUMER GOODS. There is a marked correlation between class and the possession of the most expensive consumer durables, that is, automobiles and houses (see Table 2-15).

EDUCATION. Despite the extended facilities under the 1944 Education Act and the figures already quoted, it was still true in 1965 that although 70% of the children of solid middle-class families stayed at school beyond the age of 15, only 7% of those of the lower working-class remained at school after that age.

There are, however, certain important *similarities* between the classes. The educational difference stated above should not be overstressed. Looking at the educational statistics another way, we see that 35% of the solid middle class and 68% of the lower middle class had a similar educational experience to that of the working class; i.e., they, too, left school at age 15.

POPULAR ENJOYMENTS AND TASTES. To a marked extent the middle classes and the working classes share the same tastes in newspapers, in films, and in television shows. "In at least one sense," wrote Richard Hoggart, "we are becoming classless—that is, the majority of us are being merged into one class. We are becoming culturally classless." [4]

Whereas the public as a whole agree on the existence of social classes, and on which occupations "belong" to which classes, individuals differ considerably when asked to which class they assign *themselves*. When members of the public are asked to assign themselves to a class, the procedure is called *self-rating;* and all opinion surveys demonstrate that the numbers in classes as self-rated differ importantly from the numbers as rated objectively by the census or by sociologists. For instance, the middle classes in Table 2-14 and 2-15 represent 30% of the total population, and the working classes, including the "very poor," represent 70%. Using a different breakdown as ascertained by the British Institute of Public Opinion, the "well-to-do" and "middle" classes combined amount to 27% of the total population, and the working classes plus the very poor constitute the remaining 73%. Yet, according to the British Institute polls, the self-rating of individuals is markedly different from this. In 1955, only 53% of the respondents assigned themselves to the working class; in March, 1959, only 49%; and later in that year (on the eve of a general election), not more than 52%. Just before the general election of 1964, only 51% assigned themselves to the working class.

Social class is perhaps the most important factor in British *political* behavior. The class to which the voter is objectively assigned, and even more importantly the class to which he assigns *himself,* is the most significant single indicator of whether he will vote Labour or Conservative.

The Political Role of Social Class

Table 2-16 shows how the votes were cast in the general elections of 1966 and 1970, broken down

TABLE 2-15. *Ownership of Automobiles and Houses by Social Class, 1964*

Class	Proportion Owning Houses	Proportion Owning Automobiles
Upper middle	88%	89%
Middle	80	78
Lower middle	60	55
Skilled working	38	42
Working	24	22
Very poor	26	3

SOURCE: Information supplied by the Institute of Practitioners of Advertising, London.

[4] *The Uses of Literacy* (London: Pelican, 1961), p. 284.

TABLE 2-16. *Profile of Voters, 1966 and 1970 General Elections*

Party	All	Men	Women	Social Class *			
				Middle (12%)	*Lower Middle (22%)*	*Skilled Working (37%)*	*Unskilled Working and Very Poor (29%)*
Conservative	46.2(41.4)	42.2(37.7)	49.9(44.7)	79.1(72.2)	59.2(58.8)	34.6(32.4)	33.6(26.3)
Labour	43.8(48.7)	47.3(52.4)	40.6(45.4)	10.4(15.5)	30.5(29.9)	55.4(58.5)	57.3(65.2)
Liberal & Others	10.0(9.9)	10.5(9.9)	9.5(9.9)	10.5(12.3)	10.3(11.3)	10.0(9.0)	9.5(8.4)

Party	Age					
	18–24 †	*25–34*	*35–44*	*45–54*	*55–64*	*Over 65*
Conservative	42.3(40.6)	41.0(37.1)	46.1(37.9)	43.3(41.8)	47.5(44.8)	56.2(47.4)
Labour	47.2(51.2)	45.8(54.6)	40.6(51.2)	49.1(47.0)	43.7(45.9)	37.1(43.2)
Liberal & Others	10.5(8.2)	13.2(8.3)	13.3(11.0)	7.6(11.2)	8.8(9.4)	6.7(9.4)

SOURCE: National Opinion Poll surveys quoted in D. Butler and A. King, *The British General Election of 1966* (Macmillan, 1966), p. 284; and D. Butler and M. Pinto-Duschinsky, *The British General Election of 1970* (Macmillan, 1971), p. 342.

NOTE: 1970 figures first; 1966 figures are in parentheses. Both are expressed as percentages of the total who said they voted.

* Percentages in parentheses represent proportion of those who said they voted in 1966.

† 21–24 in 1966.

according to age, sex, and class. It is apparent that age and sex make some difference to party support: the Conservatives are stronger among women voters and old people. But these differences are minimal compared with the stark contrast between the vote of middle-class and working-class voters. However, although class is the major determinant of whether a Briton votes Conservative or Labour, it makes little difference regarding whether he joins the one in ten (or so) who at each election opt out of the two-party system to vote Liberal, nationalist, or independent. The minor parties are just as strikingly *not* based on class as the two-party nine-tenths *are* divided on class lines.

But these figures show also that the two main British parties are by no means based ex-clusively on objective class differences. Some very-well-off upper-middle-class voters support the Labour party, and many more working-class voters are Conservative. Indeed, since the large majority of the electorate is working-class, the Conservative party could never win a general election without substantial working-class support. Working-class voters comprise more than half the total Conservative vote, and from that point of view the Conservative party can justify its frequent claim to being more "national" and less class-based than the Labour party (whose total vote is overwhelmingly working-class). But viewed in terms of how large a proportion of its natural class support it receives, the Conservative party is more middle-class-bound than the Labour party is working-class-bound. The Conservatives have polled as much as 90% of the votes of the upper middle class, and in no election since the war have dropped below three-quarters of this class; by contrast, even in its best years the Labour party has barely topped two-thirds of the votes of even the very poorest class.

These figures are all based on assigning voters to social classes on objective criteria of occupation backed up by evidence of income, appearance, and other matters which can be judged externally by an interviewer. When we look at how voters describe themselves, the pattern becomes much clearer still. The study by David Butler and Donald Stokes of political behavior in Britain in the 1960s (Table 2-17) shows this very clearly. Thus, in their sample the top class defined in strictly occupational terms ("higher managerial") divided 86:14 between the two main parties, but among those who chose to describe *themselves* as "upper class" the proportions were 100:0. Table 2-17 shows just how "class self-image" (the authors' term) reinforces and extends the division of voting in occupational terms.

Within each occupational group, there is a difference of about 30% between the votes of those who think of themselves as middle-class and the votes of those who think of themselves as working-class. Much of the Conservative working-class vote (defined in terms of occupation) likes to think of itself as middle-class; the white-collar employee who votes Labour is far more likely to think of himself as working-class than a fellow employee, of equal status and

income, who votes Conservative. Table 2-17 shows, moreover, that the lower-paid white-collar workers (those whom Butler and Stokes call "lower nonmanual"), whose income level is not too dissimilar from the more skilled manual workers, nevertheless votes in much the same way as their managers or supervisors. The class division is by status at work (manual and nonmanual in a firm are usually discriminated between as workers and staff and as wage-earners and salary-earners) rather than simply by size of income.

One reason why self-assigned class status is a much better indicator of voting behavior than objectively assigned class is that, for many people, voting Conservative or Labour is a way of asserting their attitudes toward the social divisions of Britain and their place in them. Thus, a workingman with ambitions to better himself may vote Conservative; a professional man with humble origins may find a Labour vote helps to keep him close to his family and childhood friends. Class voting can thus reflect social aspirations as well as social position. But we can also assume that many people in assigning themselves to a class are doing so more accurately than an interviewer might; almost everyone in Britain knows how his education, his material possessions (especially whether he owns his house), his family background, in many parts of the country his accent, and in fact his general style of life fit him into the social scale, in addition to his occupation. When we take into account social class in all its ramifications, it is clear that it is even more closely related to vot-

TABLE 2-17. *Class Voting by Occupation and Self-assessment*

Class Self-Image	Higher Managerial	Lower Managerial	Supervisory Nonmanual	Lower Nonmanual	Skilled Manual	Unskilled Manual
Middle	90:10	89:11	91:9	83:17	54.46	45:55
Working	57:43	58:42	57:43	52:48	24:76	21:79

SOURCE: David Butler and Donald Stokes, *Political Change in Britain* (New York: St. Martin's, 1969), p. 78.
NOTE: Entries indicate how voters divided between Conservative and Labour (Liberals, others, and "don't knows" ignored). The survey was made in 1963.

ing than a set of figures based on only one measure of class status can show.

In short, whereas religion and the Roman Catholic church play an important part in French and German politics, and nationalities play an important part in Canadian politics, and region is very significant in American politics, in Great Britain (but not Northern Ireland) social-class divisions alone play this role.

This was not always so. In her long history, Britain has experienced nearly all the catastrophic social cleavages that make democracy so precarious in the emergent nations of today. The commingling of Scots, Welsh, Irish, and English into one peaceful political community was neither natural nor inevitable, nor did it occur peacefully and all at once. Scotland and England were at war for some five hundred years before they joined together in the Treaty of Union; and in the case of the Catholic southern Irish, their integration into the British political community never succeeded at all. Again, not much more than three hundred years ago the peoples of the islands were killing one another for the sake of religion, and even sixty years ago party affiliation was based as much on religious denomination as on class or other factors. The English language did not become the majority language in Wales, or the common tongue of the Irish, until the second half of the last century. Tribe, nationality, language, religion—all have struggled against one another; yet today these "lateral" divisions that tended to split the society into a number of watertight compartments have been all but erased. Today the only cleavage of political significance is the "horizontal" division into social and economic classes. Perhaps this is the principal reason why British academics and intellectuals, not to speak of visiting Americans, are so obsessed by the "class" nature of British society: in an otherwise homogeneous—and rather humdrum—society, this one signal difference sticks out like a sore thumb.

Professor R. R. Alford has elegantly demonstrated the factual basis of this impression by quantitative methods. His work, comparing voting characteristics in four "Anglo-Saxon" democracies—Britain, Canada, Australia, and the United States—shows that "Great Britain not only has the highest level of class voting of any of the four . . . but class factors appear to be the only significant ones. . . . Regional and religious loyalties tend not to be expressed through political parties but in a sense may become demands upon the whole system. . . ."[5]

As we stated earlier, British politics are emphatically about equality—and hence about inequality; and British society is still unequal. The top 1% of the population still draw over 5% of the national income, even after taxes, and the top 10% of the population draw (post-tax) 25% of the national income. Wealth is far more unequally distributed: some 80% of the personal wealth is owned by 9% of the population. Since the "public schools" charge fairly stiff fees (in the order of £500 per year), the wealthy can and usually do buy a better education, which also carries greater prestige for their children than the rest of the community can afford. Educational opportunities are, therefore, still unequal; and even in the state system where, in the matter of qualifying for the state grammar schools, opportunity is now based strictly on intellectual quality, family background can adversely affect the child's chances as well as the likelihood that he will stay at school long enough to take the increasingly important General Certificates of Education examinations.

To both summarize and repeat ourselves somewhat: education, skewed in favor of the wealthier, is the key to occupation, which is in turn the key to social and economic class. Consequently, the higher ranks of industry, the armed forces, the public services, and the benches of the House of Commons are still disproportionately manned by the products of the public schools. At the other end of the social scale the inhabitants of certain manual occupations, such as the dockers and miners, are so fiercely aloof from the rest of the society that their occupational loyalty is almost tribal. In between these two poles, however, is to be found the new phenomenon: the "rising working class"—the manual wage-earners who regard themselves as moving up the social scale into

[5] *Party and Society* (London: John Murray, 1964), p. 290.

the middle class. Shifts in occupation, and the partial equalization of wealth and educational opportunity, have produced this group. Its emergence indicates that a less hierarchical and unequal society is on the way. But it is, as we have seen, slow to emerge—which is why at election time the various classes call in the aid of politics to "give history a shove."

The electoral process and the political parties provide one channel of popular representation, and the pressure groups provide another. The first provides political representation, the second functional. The first, by way of a solid party majority in the House of Commons, provides, for possibly five years, the general program of the government. The second, however, qualifies it. Without a disciplined majority to aggregate group demands, and a powerful cabinet able to override them if necessary, policy would be incoherent. Without the pressure groups to influence or resist the cabinet's program, government would be tyrannical. In any case, it is erroneous to consider parties and pressure groups to be mutually isolated. They interpenetrate each other. They may be distinguishable, but they are interconnected. Pressure groups interact with all parts of the machinery of government: with the ministers, with the civil servants, with the parties, with Parliament. It is difficult to overestimate their importance in the actual working constitution of today. They are, in short, a second or auxiliary circuit of representation (the parties and elections being the first). Each circuit would be infinitely poorer and ineffective without the other. The British political system requires both.

It has already been noted that 47 percent of a British national sample replied that they belonged to some private association or other. By no means will all of these, or even a majority of them, normally have the slightest concern in what the government is up to; but at any point of time they *might* be so concerned, and *might* wish to try to influence its policy. Any organized group (and this includes firms and businesses) which tries to influence the policy of public authorities in its own chosen direction (though, unlike the political parties, never themselves prepared to undertake the direct government of the country) can be considered a pressure group.

Pressure groups in the United Kingdom fall into two main types with a hybrid in between. Some—like business groups, cooperatives, and trade unions—defend economic interests, while others promote special causes such as pacifism, nuclear disarmament, the protection of children or animals. In the one case

THREE

pressure groups

it is the protection of material interest that counts; in the other the defense or promotion of a cause.

Certain hybrid groups combine the features of both interest groups and promotional groups. A good example is the Roads Campaign Council, which advocates more and better highways. It is overtly financed by organizations that have a material interest in roads—for instance, the Automobile Association and the Royal Automobile Club—and also by such bodies as the Society of Motor Manufacturers and Traders. It is, therefore, the propagandist spokesman of certain interest groups. In addition, many interest groups (for instance, the National Union of Teachers) have a promotional side to their activities. The NUT believes that education should be improved, but the group also enhances its own interests by promoting this worthy goal.

THE MAJOR PRESSURE GROUPS

Employers

There are at least twenty-five hundred organizations in Britain that serve the many needs of commerce and industry. In a special category is the powerful National Farmers' Union (NFU), with 200,000 members, some 75–80 percent of all the farmers of England and Wales. Another special association is the Institute of Directors, with a membership of over 40,000, whose object is to ease legal and financial restrictions on business executives—e.g., to reduce corporate taxes and death duties. It has jokingly described itself as the "bosses' trade union."

The main organization serving industry is the Confederation of British Industry (CBI). This was formed in 1965 through the amalgamation of three bodies—the British Employers' Confederation, which consisted of employers' negotiating bodies, and the Federation of British Industries and the National Union of British Manufacturers, both of which covered individual firms and trade associations. The immense amalgamated body, with 180 trade associations and 12,500 individual firms and a highly professional bureaucracy of some three hundred officials, is the largest employers' association in the world.

Whereas the CBI represents manufacturers, we find that merchants, insurance houses, shippers, truckers, and the like are associated locally in chambers of commerce, of which there are one hundred in the country, and nationally in the Association of the British Chambers of Commerce (ABCC), which is a very influential body representing about 60,000 firms.

The Trade Unions

Excluding the armed forces, approximately $25\frac{3}{4}$ million persons are at work in Britain. Ten million belong to trade unions, and, in 1969, of these almost $9\frac{1}{2}$ million were affiliated with the Trade Union Congress. Although the constituent unions are autonomous, the congress has developed an important headquarters staff that draws up policy, and acts on mandates received from the congress. The congress does not negotiate wages: that is the concern of the individual unions. In response to the Labour government efforts in 1967–69 to control wages and salaries, the TUC took on the role of vetting its members' claims. But with the disappearance of that pressure under the Conservative government in 1970, it looks unlikely that the TUC has acquired any real power in this respect.

The Co-operative Movement

In 1969 there were 565 retail distributive societies in Britain, with a total membership of over 12 million. In 1969 the sales turnover of the distribution societies amounted to 9 percent of the national total. Almost all the societies were affiliated with the Co-operative Union, the principal organization of this movement. The Co-operative party, supported by 503 of the societies (representing 90 percent of the total membership of the union), fights the political battles for the movement.

The Professions

Another group of interests consists of the professions. Three large professional organizations are often in the news: the British Medical Association (BMA), the National Union of Teachers, and the National and Local Government Officers' Association (none of them affiliated with the TUC). Although the BMA is not the only body representing the interests of doctors, it is by law the negotiating body for the profession, representing as it does some 84 percent of the general practitioners. The NUT does not have a monopoly of representation either, but it does include in its membership about 85 percent of the teachers in state schools.

The National and Local Government Officers' Association, which recently celebrated its fiftieth anniversary, caters to the clerical and administrative grades of the local government service, but not to the manual workers. It counts in its membership about 200,000 out of some 338,000 such employees.

Civic Groups

Among the interests that may be styled "civic groups" are charities (temperance societies, societies for the prevention of cruelty to children or to animals, family case-work agencies, and the like), various bodies that defend particular groups in government (the Magistrates Association, the Association of Municipal Corporations), and large organizations that advocate specific public policies and aspire to a mass following.

In the 1960s there has been a growth in the number and importance of this last type of civic group. At the beginning of the decade the Campaign for Nuclear Disarmament (CND), advocating the unilateral renunciation by Britain of any defense system based on nuclear weapons, was able to attract a great deal of attention and came close to capturing the Labour party. Since then, foreign policy issues have inspired several successors, such as the campaigns regarding Vietnam and Biafra. Most successful were the Stop-the-Seventies-Tour (STST) and Fair Cricket Campaign (FCC), which in 1970 were able to secure the cancellation of the proposed tour of the (white) South African cricket team. The STST, which worked by mass demonstrations with mainly youth and student support and which was often on the fringe of the law, and the FCC, which enlisted prominent people to make representations to the government and cricketing authorities in private, illustrate well the different methods used by such campaigns. Other campaigning civic groups have tackled the plight of less-privileged groups in society; typical have been Shelter, which has raised public consciousness about bad housing conditions, and the Homosexual Law Reform Society, which has seen most laws penalizing homosexuals repealed. Another type have been the groups campaigning to improve or protect the environment; a notable success was scored in 1968 by the campaign to stop a third London airport being built in the countryside at Stanstead.

PRESSURE GROUPS IN ACTION

The groups or associations that habitually work closely with the government or with local authorities can exert pressure simply by breaking off relations, although this recourse is used only rarely. Pressure groups direct their fire at the executive, the legislature, and the general public.

The Executive Level—
Government Departments

Government departments and private associations generally cooperate with one another, since both sides stand to gain through such activities as the exchange of information and the sharing of each other's goodwill. When the Department of Economic Affairs wanted to control the level of wages (1964–1970), it needed the advice and goodwill of the trade unions. Likewise, it could not clamp down on prices without the advice and active cooperation of thousands of firms, and therefore sought it from their trade associations and the CBI.

Between government administrators and private associations there is an extensive system of both formal and informal contact. The formal arrangements comprise three chief methods:

1. *By official inquiry*—such as royal commissions, departmental inquiries, courts of arbitration, and the like. All interested parties put their views before such bodies.

2. *By special advisory committees.* Over five hundred of these committees are attached to their appropriate ministries and bring together civil servants and representatives of all the interested associations. They have meetings throughout the year, at which relevant matters are discussed.

3. *By the method of prior consultation.* Ministries sometimes consult associations in advance of action. Bodies such as the Association of Municipal Corporations and the County Councils' Association have become almost official revising bodies for the administrative departments that make rules and orders affecting local government.

The formal contacts, however, are not nearly as important as the extensive informal contacts that continuously take place. Many of the arrangements are like those in a soccer match, where each player picks a particular man on the other side to attack. The director or secretary of a trade association "works to" certain civil servants in the various departments he frequents over a period of years, and is often on the best of personal terms with them.

Pressure can be, and often is, generated at the departmental level. To pursue a certain program, a director of a trade association might first go to his "opposite number" in the department and give "advice." If noncontroversial, this might be acted on. But if it is not adopted, the association might send a more-high-powered delegation, and its "advice" would become open advocacy. If this also failed to move the civil servants or the minister, the association

might decide upon even more drastic action: it might sever relations with the governmental department, and withdraw cooperation. But this would be most abnormal; its usual alternative would be to go to the top and try to influence Parliament.

The Parliamentary Level

Members of Parliament frequently are representatives of special "interests" themselves. They may belong to an outside association, such as the Institute of Directors; they may be approached by some interest—e.g., the textile or pottery industry—that is prominent in their constituency; they may be asked by an outside interest to sit on its "parliamentary panel" (i.e., to act as its spokesman in Parliament).

More importantly, the two great parties themselves incorporate many important interests. As we shall see later, seventy-nine trade unions are affiliated with the Labour party; they provide it with much if not most of its money, they finance individual candidates, and they command an overwhelming majority of votes at the party conference. All of 112 of the Labour party's 287 seats in the present Parliament are held by trade union-sponsored candidates. Similarly, 17 are held by Co-operative-sponsored candidates. No interest groups are affiliated with the Conservatives, although most of the organizations of employers, industry, trade, and commerce must be regarded as being aligned with the Conservative party. The link is not, as in the case of the Labour party, by organizations qua organization; it is a personal linkage. Members of these organizations are often members of, or give support to (by money or assistance), the Conservative party.

A group that has failed to get satisfaction from the minister or the civil servants (i.e., the executive) may try to exert pressure by raising the matter in the House of Commons. Pressure of this sort is usually checked by the very firm discipline exerted on each party by the whips, but sometimes a particular interest may win enough sympathy in the Commons, with both the majority party and the Opposition, to force a minister to change his mind. The legislative influence of pressure groups is often focused on the committee and report stages of bills, when detailed amendments are introduced. It is here, particularly, that little "caves" of government backbenchers and/or opposition members come together and try to secure specific changes.

It is impossible to emphasize too strongly that the effectiveness of the Opposition, in the comparatively rare instances of its securing substantial concessions from the government, is nearly always a function of the effectiveness of pressure groups which have already made their representations to ministers and are exerting further pressure through the Opposition. This organizes and deploys their representations more-or-less effectively; but persuasive argument achieves little unless it is known by the government to represent strongly held views of influential outside interests. This was most strikingly demonstrated in the passage of the Finance Bill of 1965, in the course of which the government made 440 amendments to its measure. The Opposition (the Conservatives) secured their greatest successes where important outside interests stood behind the amendments. In cases of this kind, the "Esau" phenomenon operates—the party is speaking for outside groups, and it is they, not the Opposition as such, which the government is seeking to conciliate: "The voice is Jacob's voice, but the hands are the hands of Esau."

The Constituency Level

The third and widest area of political pressure is at the level of the constituency. In Britain (unlike in the United States), pressure groups operate comparatively rarely at this level. Such activity is most effective at election time, but in British elections party candidates stick to the party line laid down by the party headquarters. Individual promises to local groups are discouraged by the central headquarters of both the Labour and the Conservative parties. It is therefore unknown for pressure groups to operate at the constituency level to the degree that occurs in America or France, where party structures are so different.

Pressure groups conduct two kinds of publicity campaigns: the *selective* type and the *saturation* type. The selective campaign is directed at the individuals who are the "opinion makers" in their field: local journalists, churchmen, schoolteachers, university teachers, doctors, members of Rotary Clubs, chambers of commerce, trades councils. Both the NUT and the National Farmers' Union carry on sustained activities of this kind. The saturation campaign (or "grass-roots lobby") is comparatively rare and (apparently) relatively ineffective. Most of the saturation campaigns have been those used by capitalist interests against nationalization, but there is increasing evidence that these campaigns were quite unsuccessful (see page 64). One reason may be that one does not get very far in Britain by simply advertising in the press, and, as we have seen, neither radio nor television can be used to transmit political propaganda in Britain.

Sometimes a pressure group will operate at the executive, the parliamentary, and the constituency levels simultaneously. For instance, when the Conservative government introduced a bill to subject agreements to impose fixed retail prices to court jurisdiction (the Resale Price Maintenance Bill), pharmacists were particularly anxious to secure exemption. Their associations sent a joint memorandum to the minister in charge of the bill (Mr. Edward Heath, later prime minister); they published protests; individual pharmacists brought pressure upon their M.P.'s; and they mounted a formidable pressure in the Commons, where they brought the government's majority of one hundred down to one vote only. Most pressure groups, however, concentrate on the administrative level, chiefly because the cabinet is preeminent in Parliament. If the cabinet is prepared to espouse a policy, it usually is adopted. Even if only an individual minister or the civil servants favor a program, it is likely to be put into effect.

A second reason for the importance of the administrative level is that the ministries are in an excellent position to evaluate differing viewpoints. They consult with committees of inquiry, which are set up to enable interested parties to an issue to present their arguments, and with permanent advisory committees, on which civil servants and their opposite numbers in the pressure groups sit together. One of the first things a pressure group tries to do is to acquire "consultative status"—that is, to get the ministry to recognize that it is widely representative of a point of view, and therefore worthy to be brought in for "advice and consent." This relationship is eagerly coveted, and organizations work hard to achieve it. It is regarded in Britain as the ideal tie between government departments and outside bodies.

An informal code governs this relationship. As the director of one trade association described it:

> The recognition which government departments give to any particular association depends primarily on the statesmanlike way with which the association handles its problems and on the confidence inspired by the staff in their dealings with government officials. Under such conditions mutual cooperation and understanding can be established on a basis which is not only satisfactory to both parties but can be very beneficial to the industry; the government officials will trust the staff sufficiently to inform and consult them on matters which are still highly confidential, without prejudice to the ultimate action of either party, but if there is the slightest suspicion that the association's staff had failed to maintain the confidential nature of the information imparted to it, the government officials will shut up like clams and it will be a very long time before the association's staff is entrusted with inside information. . . .[1]

Not surprisingly, therefore, the most influential pressure groups tend to be the ones that are most silent. The Confederation of British Industries or the County Councils Association or the Trade Union Congress usually achieve their results by consultation and discussion with the civil servants and ministers. Bodies like the CND, however, since they have no "foot in the door," must resort to public clamor. Nearly always, the noisier an interest group, the less effective it is!

[1] *Industrial Trade Associations* (London: Allen & Unwin, for P.E.P. [Political and Economic Planning], 1957), pp. 75–76.

THE VALUE OF PRESSURE GROUPS

In pursuing their own goals, the pressure groups actually perform several vital services in the functioning of British democracy:

1. They provide both Parliament and the administrators with technical information they would ordinarily not possess—for example, the exact dimensions of tires, or the permissible width of trucks. Opposing pressure groups challange inaccurate information.

2. They often challenge the government's policy and, conversely, give the government an idea of what the various groups, and through them the people, will accept in the way of new programs and legislation. The only other way a citizen could contact the government would be through the more restricted channel of approaching his M.P. or his local party organizations.

3. They sometimes provide administrative assistance or facilities to the government departments.

4. Because they represent so many points of view, their power to disavow the government policy to their members serves as a check and a balance to the power of the government.

In the absence of pressure groups, new policy presented to Parliament would have to be formulated exclusively by the parties' research departments and the civil service, both of which would be unrepresentative and incompetent without the information and advice supplied them by the associations.

Well-Organized vs. Poorly Organized Groups

Industrial producers are very well organized in Britain, but consumers are not. The Institute for Consumer Research's influence is not equal to that of a railway or dock strike. Generally, organizations that are well organized and mobilized have a clear advantage over those that are not. *Les absents ont toujours tort*—"Those who are absent are always in the wrong." The larger organizations frequently wield more power than the small ones. Great attention is paid to the big British Medical Association, which can marshal a large following, but not to the diminutive Fellowship for Freedom in Medicine, which cannot.

Those in a position to affect the country by direct action have a clear advantage over those who are not. Railwaymen on strike will inhibit the whole economy, not so a strike by those in the cosmetics industry. Those who have the power to harm (even though they do not exercise it) are better able to influence the government than those who have no such power at all. The British system of pressure groups does not consist of a set of evenly matched organizations, but of a series of groups of varying strengths, from the very powerful to the weak and innocuous. The system is biased toward industrial producers; it favors capital and labor over the rest of the community.

The pressure groups play a major part in the British political process. Yet, by and large, they are not a corrupting influence in British public life: they do not result in erratic and grossly inconsistent policy, and they do not lead to the oppression of minorities—or indeed of majorities. Whether Britain is or is not in fact the justly governed country she is usually represented to be, this is how she is regarded by the vast majority of her citizens. This was amply borne out by the findings of Almond and Verba (pp. 35 and 36, above).

The most significant effects of the pressure-group system upon British political life are twofold. First, no matter what the party complexion of the government, the pressure-group system cloys, clogs, enmeshes, and slows down the conduct and decisiveness of the administration's operations. Secondly, it gives the party governments a distinctive bias: they lean toward one set of interest groups or another according to whether the party's complexion is Conservative or Labour: toward trade unions when Labour is in power, and toward middle-

class and business groups when the Conservatives are in office. But this bias is somewhat moderated by the factors set out below, so that in the end, British governments tend to be like the renowned Irish judge: "neither partial nor impartial."

The three checks against undue distortion of government policies by pressure groups are: (1) certain ancient and respected *institutions;* (2) well-defined governmental *processes;* and (3) public *beliefs.*

First among the *institutions* is the civil service. Composed of well-trained and permanent career men, each department in the course of its long and intimate dealings with the pressure groups has formed some kind of "departmental view" about them, and a pressure group has to have a strong case to win over the department to its side. Another institutional check on the pressure groups is the political parties themselves. Each party must strike a balance between conflicting interests, and in the process of modifying the extreme positions of the contenders, the parties tend to reduce the warring factions into two more moderately opposed sides. Parliament and the press also help check the excesses of pressure groups. Both turn pitiless publicity on any deal they regard as "shady." But they are not always in a position to do so. In the late 1960s, cases were discovered of "secret" campaigns mounted by firms of public relations consultants on behalf of clients whose identities were scrupulously hidden, and even one or two instances of "front" organizations, supposedly of disinterested persons, which in reality were being used to promote the interests of some hidden group. These cases are exceptional, but abuses of this kind will always be possible until and unless something like the U.S. Regulation of Lobbying Act is passed by the British Parliament.

In addition to regulation by the political institutions of Britain, pressure groups must abide by the well-established *processes,* or procedures, that govern the way the public interest is conducted. As we shall see when we consider the genesis of a bill and its consideration by Parliament (Chap. 5), the whole process is based, from beginning to end, on maximum consultation with the affected interests at every stage.

The political correspondent of the *Times* of London has written:

How many bills get published without the responsible Minister spending cautious months in sounding every organization with any possible vested interest to ensure that the bill will command broad agreement? Very few, if any; and it ought to surprise nobody that the average bill should read like the compromise made in advance that it almost certainly is.

The Land Drainage Bill brought forward by the Government this session [1960] is an example. Nine years have passed since the Heneage Committee reported, and much of the interval was spent by successive Ministers of Agriculture in striking bargains with the river board interests, the farming interests, and the local authorities. The Licensing Bill is another case in point. Consistent with doing anything at all to alter licensing law, it is the product of consultations, we may take it, with the brewers, the licensed trade, and any union which represents barmen and barmaids. . . .

Of course the preparation of the ground for government action in this way is no new thing. But the practice has increased and is increasing as the isolated voices of a thousand and one sectional interests have been organized into protection associations and pressure groups to which Ministers and governments may with more and more facility apply to smooth their path in carrying out a policy; and the consequence is that today many new bills are more a form of administration than of government, and positively hundreds of sectional associations with the T.U.C., the N.F.U., and the F.B.I., at the head of the list have a built-in relationship with any government that may happen along in office.[2]

For all its advantages, this close collaboration also contains dangers. These understandings between outside interests and the civil service may become *closed* relationships. The *interested* publics are brought into the circle of government—but at the expense of shutting out the *general* public, and notably Parliament. In many instances the arangements represent complicated package deals, and once the minister announces them to the House of Commons, there is little that even his own backbenchers

can do to modify them. Party solidarity, and if needs be party discipline, can be and are invoked to rally them behind the minister.

Secondly, the information on which the agreements have been reached, and the arguments that justify them, have been discussed behind closed doors, not in public hearings.

Finally, some of the deals are so complicated that no single important item could be altered without changing the nature of the whole compromise, thus forfeiting the agreement of the outside parties to it. The annual review of farm prices which takes place between the NFU and the Ministry of Agriculture and the Treasury is of this highly complicated kind; so are such negotiations as have occurred between the Ministry of Health and the BMA about a new "Doctors' Charter" to redefine the status and conditions of doctors in the National Health Service; and so too are such negotiations of extreme delicacy as those conducted between the Department of Economic Affairs and the TUC and CBI over the future of the national prices and incomes policy. Where such deals are put before it, the House finds itself without a role. In the (picturesque but true) words of the *Times'* political correspondent, "The legislature is already in some danger of becoming more like a pianola than a pianist, mechanically rendering tunes composed jointly by departments of state and whatever organized interests happen to be affected." [3] Nothing better justifies the opening words of this chapter, which said that the pressure-group system ought to be regarded as a second and alternative circuit of representation which exists side-by-side with the party-*cum*-electoral system (which is the one traditionally associated with the working of a parliamentary democracy).

Extreme policies of the pressure groups are modified, finally, by the shared *beliefs* of the British community. These beliefs—for instance, that it is the duty of government to promote full employment—are broadly held by all sections of the nation, and pressure groups whose claims conflict with these deep-seated views will invariably be thwarted in their goals. No pressure group can afford to argue that its policy

---

2 *The Times,* November 14, 1960.

3 *The Times,* January 29, 1963.

is "good for the trade." It must show that it is "good for the country," for most Britons believe there is a "public interest" that must be respected, and feel a sense of outrage when it is not. In his essay, "In England, Your England," George Orwell, that pitiless but discerning critic, pointed out the essence of this characteristic:

Here one comes upon an all-important English trait: the respect for constitutionalism and legality, the belief in "the law" as something above the State and above the individual, something which is cruel and stupid, of course, but at any rate, incorruptible. . . . The totalitarians' notion that there is no such thing as law, there is only power, has never taken root.[4]

BIG BUSINESS IN POLITICS

Some observers, while agreeing that the producers' organizations are more influential than other groups in Britain, would go on to argue that those representing business are far more influential than those representing labor. One common complaint is that the business groups claim to be nonpolitical but really do, in fact, enter the arena of political controversy. What about this issue of political participation? Who is "political" and who "nonpolitical" in British public life?

The only bodies that belong organically to a political party and that contribute to its policy making are the seventy-nine individual trade unions affiliated with the Labour party, and the cooperative societies that are affiliated with the Co-operative party. Outside these, no particular groups belong to, or participate formally in, the policy making of any political party. In this respect, the CBI and the Institute of Directors are in exactly the same position as the TUC. The TUC is not affiliated with the Labour party and has made it quite plain in public pronouncements that it does not regard itself as a politically motivated body. Nevertheless, it does discuss matters of public controversy; it undoubtedly espouses the cause of nationalization and social welfare benefits; and it advises its members to vote Labour. Yet strictly speak-

4 In *Selected Essays* (London: Penguin, 1957).

ing, since it is not party-affiliated, it is in exactly the same position as any business group.

The term *political* can also be used to mean that a particular group is habitually aligned with one party or another. The business groups certainly tend to be aligned, through personal connections, with the Conservative party. Yet the groups representing the owners or entrepreneurs in a particular industry sometimes make common cause with the trade unions representing the workers in that industry. They form a faction by banding together against the rest of the sectors of the economy. There have been several recent examples of this in the aircraft industry, such as the responses to the Labour government's cancellation of the TSR-2 airplane in 1964–65 and to the Conservative government's handling of the collapse of Rolls-Royce in 1971.

A more serious criticism is that "business," through its wealth, has an unfair advantage in industry and politics. Business groups and certain publicity organizations that they support (such as the "Aims of Industry" or the "Economic League") do, indisputably, spend much more than labor organizations. But the effect of such expenditure is grotesquely overrated. Certain bodies like the NUT have had much success with successive postwar governments, but have done little spending to achieve it. The medium open to the capitalist groups is limited to the press, for neither radio nor television is available for political purposes in Britain. And, since these latter, more influential media are barred from presenting political advertising, Britain is assured that those with the longest purse do not invariably win.

In any case, it is doubtful whether radio and television would tip the balance. There have been several studies of the effects of the mass media on general election campaigns. It was once believed that it was possible to "sell political policies as one would sell soap." These studies demonstrate that this was precisely what was not possible. Personal political prejudices create a barrier, and are of such a nature that the individual selects what he wants to. The only appreciable effect of the mass media is to reinforce or to crystallize political attitudes, not to alter them.

As to the effects of *press* advertising, it is possible to be more categorical still, for the massive campaign against steel nationalization in 1963–64, the pre-election year, constitutes a case study. During this period the steel companies and a public relations agency, acting in the same interest, spent the massive sum of £1½ million to persuade electors not to support the nationalization of steel as the Labour party made it clear it intended to do. The British Institute of Public Opinion asked a standard set of questions on nationalization at regular six-month intervals for two years preceding this election, and the results are as shown in Table 3-1.

It will be noticed that the mammoth expenditure not only failed to dissuade the public, but it ended with more people favoring nationalization than at the beginning of the campaign!

Although business groups and firms are economically very powerful (employers and managers by and large direct the strategy of industry in the country), labor is not without the influence of power. It has weapons it can and does use—and, as a last resort, it can go on strike. Industrial *economic* power, therefore, rests on *both* sides of the economic fence.

The charge that business, and business alone, is politically powerful is a "power elite" theory (according to which power resides in the hands of a small, close-knit clique). True, the capitalist groups were politically significant between 1951 and 1964, but that was only to be expected because they were aligned with the Conservative party, which was in power. *This alignment was the result, and not the cause, of the popular verdict rendered at the general elections.* Nevertheless, left-wing critics tirelessly repeated that there was an improperly close personal link between the Conservative party, including the Conservative ministers who formed the government, and outside business interests. They even complained about business influence in government during 1945–51, when not the Conservatives, but Labour was in power, and there was an organic bond of sorts between the Labour party, the Labour government, and the trade unions and cooperatives. And, true to tradition (if not to habit), they still objected in the same vein when Labour was returned to govern in 1964 (having suffered a thirteen-year lapse from power).

The fact of course is that the influence of business on even Conservative governments is not absolute, but conditional. It is qualified by the voting power of the working class, for the Conservative party has to keep the support of some 7 million working-class voters (including about 1½ million trade unionists) in order to stay in power.

Because of the inherent "veto" power of business and labor groups—their power, by noncooperation, to thwart the government—these groups always exercise some influence over the government of the day. Generally speaking, labor *does* have more influence with a Labour government, and business with a Conservative government, but neither frame the policy of the government, but only qualify it. We repeat: neither business nor labor groups

TABLE 3-1. *Public Opinion on Nationalization of the British Steel Industry, 1963–64*

Opinion	March 1963	September 1963	March 1964	September 1964
For more nationalization	18%	16%	17%	22%
For more denationalization	26	28	29	24
For "leaving things as they are"	43	40	43	43
Don't know what to think	13	16	11	11

SOURCE: Gallup Political Index, 45:51–54.

can impose policies on the government that would not be tolerated by the electorate. The parties must "sell" their programs to the people, and thus what they can adopt from their pressure groups is always qualified by this central feature of British politics.

The influence of business or of labor waxes and wanes according to the complexion of the government, and this is decided by the electorate. If business is influential with a Conservative government, or if the unions are influential with a Labour government, it is so by the verdict of a free election. And it is the parties, not the pressure groups, that mobilize the electors, fight the election, and organize the House of Commons. To these we must now turn.

FOUR

political parties

and

elections

The General Election, that is to say, an election in which all 630 seats in the House of Commons are simultaneously open to contest, is the pivotal political act in the British parliamentary system of government. This is because, by a convention of the constitution, it is the leader of the majority party in the Commons whom the Sovereign calls upon to act as prime minister. Having accepted this charge, he then nominates for the formal approval of the Sovereign the names of those he wishes for the ministers of his Cabinet, and next the less important or "junior" ministers—in brief, the entire ministerial team, collectively known as "the government." Thus the party that succeeds in winning a majority of parliamentary seats in a general election is the party whose leaders are invested with the plenitude of executive power—headed by the prime minister. By the Parliament Act, 1911, the legal term of a Parliament is limited to five years, so that in the normal way, general elections must be held at least once every five years. Exceptionally however—as in 1939, on the outbreak of World War II—the Parliament may prolong its powers by amending the Parliament Act. This is why there was no general election in Britain between 1935 and 1945. But although the law provides that elections must be held *at least* every five years, a prime minister may ask and receive permission from the sovereign for the dissolution of Parliament at shorter intervals. Thus Mr. Wilson, having narrowly won the election of 1964, seized a favorable opportunity in 1966 to call another, which he won by a much larger majority. Sometimes a prime minister has resigned and been succeeded by another member of his party as prime minister before the legal term of the Parliament has expired; the new prime minister may wish to have Parliament dissolved right away so that he personally can lead his party into electoral battle, on the ground that if he succeeds in this, he has a much freer hand over the choice of his ministerial colleague and much more prestige with his party members than if he had merely "succeeded" to the post of prime minister.

During the lifetime of a Parliament, some MP's die, others resign and so forth. These vacancies are filled by a separate election for each vacated seat. Such elections are known as *by-elections*. These are important as providing tests of the swings of public opinion, and both government and opposition parties contest them keenly. One effect of this is to keep the major party organizations permanently on the alert.

Today, although individual candidates often stand for election in any electoral district (providing they comply with the electoral laws for nomination), it is *political parties* which fight the election; and since 1945 this has increasingly meant the two very large parties, the Labour and Conservative parties. Today (given the insignificant numbers of the Parliamentary Liberal Party) Britain is, overwhelmingly, a two-party state.

The two major parties in Britain are both highly disciplined, and they both enjoy a hard core of electoral support that since 1945 has never sunk below 40 percent of the total electoral vote. The candidates of both parties must agree to support their party's platform, and they must be accepted by their party headquarters if they are to enjoy the help of the national party machine at election time—and without it they are most unlikely to win. In the House of Commons, the party members act, for the most part, with iron discipline; abstention from voting with the party is not common, and cross-voting is almost unknown.

The two-party system is the key to understanding the present operation of the British government. This system is responsible for the following factors:

1. the near-certainty that one party or the other will be returned with a clear and working majority in Parliament
2. the formation of a cabinet drawn from the majority party
3. the stability of the cabinet, since its party majority is disciplined
4. the assurance that the cabinet can last out the full term of Parliament's life
5. the unambiguous responsibility of the cabinet for all that has happened during its period of office
6. the presentation to the electorate of a clear choice between the government party, running on its performance, and the opposition party, running on its promise

The importance of the two-party system in British government cannot be overstressed. British government is government by the cabinet. The Houses of Parliament act as a checking and controlling force, but the directing and energizing element is the cabinet, which is collectively responsible for its policy to Parliament, and beyond Parliament to the people. This collective responsibility for policy is based on the monolithic nature of the party majority that supports it. In France, until the coming of the Fifth Republic, the cabinet was never really a collective unit (although the constitutions of the Third and Fourth Republics said that it had to behave like one) because its parliamentary support fluctuated. If cabinets in Britain were regularly overthrown by temporary combinations of various parliamentary groups, as indeed they were between 1851 and 1868, the legislature would, in effect, formulate policy. Legislative initiative would prevail and not, as at present, cabinet initiative. Such was the character of the French parliamentary system under the Third and Fourth Republics. And such was the character of British government in 1923–24 and in 1929–31, when minority Labour cabinets held office and were liable at any time to be defeated by a combination of their Conservative and Liberal opponents. The short lives of those two cabinets, compared with the usual duration of some four-and-a-half years, tell their own story.

THE HISTORY OF THE PARTIES

Today the two main parties are the Conservative and Labour parties. The Liberal party is a remnant left over from earlier days of power and responsibility. The nationalist parties are small, and the strength of the Communist party is negligible.

Emergence of the Conservative and Liberal Parties

The Conservative and Liberal parties became established as modern political parties in the second half of the nineteenth century. Both were emerging as the traditional Tory and Whig parties were breaking up and adapting to the new political forces unleashed in mid-century by the Industrial Revolution and by the 1832 Reform Act. In turn, the Tory and Whig parliamentary factions were rooted in the conflicts over king and Parliament and church and dissent of the latter seventeenth century.

The 1832 Reform Act extended voting power to the new growing middle class; the Whigs, traditionally an alliance of some landed magnates with the commercial interest, were reinforced by the new manufacturing interest. But a number of left-wing radicals and the increasingly self-conscious Irish M.P.'s made the Whig side of Parliament more of a loose coalition. On the Tory side, Sir Robert Peel, prime minister from 1841 to 1846 and widely regarded as the first leader of the Conservative party, began to move his party of lesser landholders (squires) to the side of the manufacturers; in 1846, however, his Conservative government split into two factions when he decided to bow to the free-trade view of the manufacturers and repeal the protective duties on corn. The minority of his own followers, the Peelites, included William Gladstone; the majority was a rabble of inarticulate squires led by the young Benjamin Disraeli.

For two decades Britain operated on a loose four- or even five-party system—old Whigs, radicals, Peelites, and the Irish increasingly drawing together as the Liberal party on the one side, and the Conservatives regaining strength on the other side. This was a period—the only one in British parliamentary history—of coalition and minority governments that were often brought down by votes in the House of Commons. The consolidation into two disciplined parliamentary groups, the Disraeli-led Conservatives and the Gladstone-led Liberals,

coincided with the second Reform Act (1867), which enfranchised the artisan class of the towns and more than doubled the electorate of 2¼ million. The parties had to find new and popular issues to involve the new electors; the numbers of potential voters in each constituency was now such that local organizations were required to mobilize support instead of using the older informal electioneering methods. With these changes taking place around 1870, contemporary party structure may be said to have begun.

1886–1915: Conservative vs. Liberal

Governments now became stable and long-lived, strengthened as they were by somewhat more disciplined party majorities. Both parties had mass popular followings, the Liberals rather more urban and working-class than the Conservatives (especially after 1885, when the third Reform Act expanded the electorate again). But this socioeconomic cleavage was less important than the denominational and regional difference: the Conservatives were the party of the Anglican Church and of England, especially southeastern England, while the Liberals dominated the north, the West Country, and East Anglia, and Scotland and Wales (respectively Presbyterian and nonconformist each by a large majority). In 1886 a split in the Liberal party over Irish home rule led to an alliance of most of the remaining old Whig landed families, and a radical group led by Chamberlain and based on the industrial west Midlands, with the Conservatives as the Liberal Unionists. In due course the Liberal Unionists merged with the Conservatives—the official title of the party today is "Conservative and Unionist." By the end of the century the Conservatives, in power, were the party of empire, of union with Ireland, and, increasingly, of tariffs; the Liberals, in opposition, stood for Irish home rule, free trade and, increasingly, the trade unions.

In 1906 the Liberals won a crushing victory over the Conservatives and formed one of the great reforming governments of British history;

the foundations of the welfare state were laid by this government. But in retrospect, the most significant result of the 1906 election was the entry of some twenty-nine M.P.'s elected in electoral pacts between the Liberal party and the newly formed Labour Representation Committee. The trade unions had secured direct representation in the Commons and were breaking away from their attachment to the Liberals in order to ally themselves with new political groups whose socialist ideas cut them off sharply from the more conventional economic policies of the Liberal party. The nascent Labour party supported the Liberal government up to World War I, but was growing more restive in both its industrial and political wings as war broke out and brought a truce to internal political strife.

1915–1945: The Rise of Labour

World War I brought the Liberals and the Conservatives together in an uneasy coalition in 1915. The coalition fought and won the "khaki" election (1918), but the Liberal prime minister, David Lloyd George, in his electoral arrangements with his Conservative allies, decided not to endorse a number of Liberal candidates, among them the leader of the Liberal party and former prime minister, Herbert Asquith. This maneuver widened a split in the Liberal party which had opened during the war, one group being led by Lloyd George, the other by Asquith. In 1922, the Conservative backbenchers decided to quit the Coalition. Lloyd George, having no majority behind him, resigned, and a general election took place.

The Conservatives won and formed the new government. Contesting the election as a divided party, the Liberals fared so badly that the new Labour party was established as the second largest party and supplanted the Liberals as the official Opposition. In the 1923 election, the Conservatives lost their absolute majority and were defeated in the House. The king called on Labour leader Ramsey MacDonald to form a cabinet. Since this first Labour government was a minority one that rested on tacit Liberal support, when this support was with-

drawn in 1924 the Labour government was defeated in the House, and the prime minister, getting the king's consent for a dissolution of Parliament, called for a general election. The Conservatives were returned with an absolute majority; the Labour party lost some seats; but the Liberals sank from 159 seats to 40. Its annihilation as a major political force dates from 1924.

In 1929, Labour came back as the largest of the three parties and formed the second (minority) Labour government. Caught almost immediately in the Great Depression, the government foundered in 1931, and another coalition of Conservatives and Liberals, and a few Labour members, called the National Government, was formed, with MacDonald as prime minister. Some Labour and half the Liberals left in 1932 when the Conservative-dominated cabinet decided to introduce protective tariffs. From then on, the so-called National Government was really the Conservative party—especially after 1935, when MacDonald quit the prime ministership, and the prime ministers were Conservatives. From 1940 Winston Churchill presided over a coalition government of Conservatives, Labour, and Liberals, until the end of World War II. (See Fig. 4-1.)

1945–1970: Conservative vs. Labour

Labour was returned in 1945 with an enormous majority (see Table 4-1). In the 1950 election, however, the Conservatives staged a powerful revival, and the Labour party had an absolute majority of only six seats. Nevertheless, it managed to endure for 18 months. In the election of 1951, although it polled more popular votes than the Conservatives, it was defeated, and the Conservatives ended up with an absolute majority of 16 seats. Despite this slender majority, they maintained office and soon began to gather strength, a development that was much assisted by the division in Labour ranks, between the bulk of the party led by Clement Attlee (the former prime minister) and the rebellious left wing led by the late Aneurin Bevan. In 1955, Churchill resigned the premiership to Anthony

TABLE 4-1. *British General Elections since 1945*

Year	Total Electorate	Total Voting	Per- centage Voting	Con- servative and Allied Vote	Per- centage of Votes Cast	Labour and Allied Vote	Per- centage of Votes Cast	Liberal Votes	Per- centage of Votes Cast	Other Votes	Per- centage of Votes Cast
1945	32,836,419	24,082,612	73.5%	9,577,667	39.8%	11,632,891	48.3%	2,197,191	9.1%	674,863	2.8%
1950	34,269,764	28,769,477	84.0	12,101,983	43.5	13,295,736	46.4	2,621,489	9.1	350,269	1.9
1951	34,645,573	28,595,668	82.5	13,717,538	48.0	13,948,605	48.8	730,556	2.5	198,969	0.7
1955	34,858,263	26,760,493	76.8	13,286,564	49.7	12,404,970	46.4	722,405	2.7	346,554	1.2
1959	35,397,080	27,859,241	78.7	13,749,830	49.4	12,215,538	43.8	1,638,571	5.9	255,302	0.9
1964	35,892,572	27,655,374	77.1	12,001,396	43.4	12,205,814	44.1	3,092,878	11.2	374,914	1.1
1966	35,964,684	27,263,606	75.8	11,418,433	41.9	13,064,951	47.9	2,327,533	8.5	452,689	1.7
1970	39,384,364	28,344,807	72.0	13,144,692	46.4	12,179,166	42.9	2,117,638	7.5	903,311	3.2

Eden. In the election of 1955, the Conservatives triumphed again, their majority rising to 61, a good working majority. In January, 1957, Eden resigned and Harold Macmillan became prime minister in his place. In the election of 1959, the Conservatives did what no party since 1832 had ever done—won their third election in a row. This time they increased their majority to 101.

From 1961, however, the Conservatives became increasingly unpopular, the voters at first showing their discontent by voting Liberal in by-elections. From 1963 onward, the Labour party became the main beneficiary of voters' approval; and in October 1964, led by Harold Wilson, it narrowly won the election, with 317 seats to the Conservatives' 304 and the Liberals' 9: its overall majority was only 4. But seizing a moment when the opinion polls favored him, Prime Minister Wilson dissolved Parliament in March 1966, and was returned with an absolute majority of 96. Yet within a few months the Wilson government was establishing new records for unpopularity in local elections, parliamentary by-elections, and the polls; astonishingly, Wilson still seemed to have seized another favorable moment in the opinion polls when he called an early election in June 1970. The "surprise" Conservative victory at this election by an overall majority of 30 was as bad an upset for the reputation of the opinion polls as the Truman victory in 1948, but is less sur-

prising in view of the Labour losses in public esteem during the preceding Parliament.

THE CONSERVATIVE PARTY

The Conservative party can trace its pedigree back to the seventeenth century. Deeply conscious of its long heritage, the party regards itself as a national institution, yet it is remarkably skillful in adapting itself to new political conditions. The Whigs' Reform Act of 1832 appeared to have destroyed forever the basis of Conservative electoral support; but within two years a Conservative government was in office again, and within nine years the party had overwhelmingly defeated its Whig rivals at the polls. Shatteringly defeated in 1945 by the Labour party, it drew almost level by 1950, and governed the country for 13 years, from the general election of 1951 until that of October 1964.

The party has the advantage of broad support from all classes of society—rich and poor, dustmen and duchesses—and its empirical approach to politics has enabled it to appeal to all these classes at once. Historically, the party still is associated with the crown and the aristocracy, and also (though this is of minor importance today) the Church of England. Again, it once used to be the party of imperial expansion,

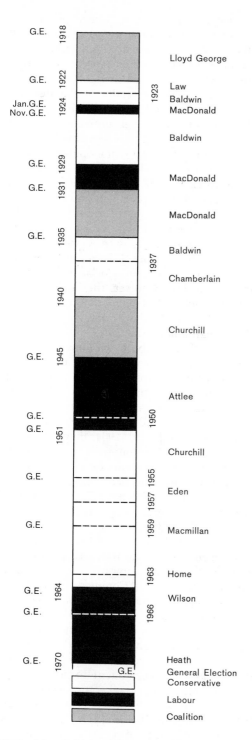

FIG. 4-1. *British cabinets since 1918.*

and still *is* the party of national self-assertion and self-interest. It continues to be associated with the landed interest; but it is preeminently the businessman's own party. And at the same time it is the party of paternalistic concern for the lower middle class and the working class, and it is remarkably adept at altering the emphases of its tradition to catch the moods of the moment. Its principles are broad, its tactics highly pragmatic.

The Conservative party was swept away at the polls in 1945, but made a remarkable recovery. Thrown back upon itself, it reorganized its structure, reexamined its principles, and came up with a program that created the impression of a progressive party and appealed particularly to "the rising working-class" that is in a hurry to "get on in the world." This formula enabled it to win three successive elections. Its period in opposition again from 1964–70 was once more a period of intensive reexamination of its "image" and organization.

"Ideology"

Conservatives are not guided by ideology but by a set of traditional attitudes, and by principles that are highly elastic. In any predominantly two-party system, such as exists in Britain today, each of the two main parties is bound to be so comprehensive that it includes a wide spectrum of individual interpretations of these broad basic principles and attitudes; and so it is with the Conservative party. Few Conservatives profess complete laissez faire, but none favor a fully planned economy. Few if any nowadays regard war with equanimity, but none are pacifists. Few wish to dismantle the welfare state, but none wish to get rid of voluntary service and private self-help. Few openly advocate "privilege and property," but none are egalitarians. The bulk of the party takes a line midway between the leveling, socializing, and pacifistic pressures arising out of the British class structure and politically expressed by the Labour party, and the defense of the existing social order. There is and in the past there always has been tension inside the party between its "ultras" and its moderates, and there is today. Except for the period 1906–14, the moderates have won. But both wings can and do coexist within the very broad traditional principles of this historic party, as a glance at these reveals.

The core of Conservative belief is the unity of the nation. To Conservatives, social classes are both necessary and natural, given the differing abilities of men, but these classes ought not to be founded on the accidents of wealth or birth, but on ability. To this end, they seek an equal opportunity for all to move forward and upward. They are—and never more so than today, when the titled aristocracy have quite lost their hold on national admiration—the *meritocratic* party. The classes, founded on quality, are, in their view, essential organs of the nation that transcend all personal differences. Hence they deplore appeals to class warfare, which they consider a wanton attack on national unity, and they challenge the assumption that there is a basic enmity between employer and employed, holding that both are partners in industry. They accuse the Labour party of favoring one class above all others. They themselves claim that they are the party of all classes, of the whole nation.

According to the Conservative point of view, the development of character is founded on the individual's freedom to choose. The wider the choice, the greater the development of self-reliance. From their preference for voluntary effort over public assistance stems their insistence on free enterprise in industry, their hostility to nationalization, their defense of the profit motive, and their advocacy of indirect rather than direct taxation, the latter in their eyes reducing individual incentive. Favoring giving local authorities responsibility wherever they can be substituted for the central government, the Conservatives tried to decentralize the nationalized industries and to introduce competition from the outside wherever possible. Their slogan, "a property-owning democracy," reflects their faith that private property is both a safeguard of the individual's independence and an incentive to his personal effort.

This is not to deny the state any part in the conduct of industry. Conservatives will even nationalize an industry if they think the circumstances warrant it—e.g., the Central Electricity Board (1926) was a Conservative creation, and in 1971 another Conservative government nationalized Rolls-Royce when it went bankrupt. But they bitterly opposed any further nationalization after 1951, especially of the steel industry. On the whole, they maintain that detailed physical controls encumber rather than help the economy. And they feel that the state ought certainly to prevent monopolies and restrictive practices, to safeguard individuals and firms against calamitous occupational risks, and to act to ensure full employment and the proper geographical distribution of industry. Lastly, nothing in the Conservative tradition bars them from providing social welfare services. In the nineteenth century, the Conservatives championed the factory acts and workmen's compensation for injuries. However, they believe such services must be a "springboard rather than a sofa," a "ladder rather than a net."

In foreign affairs, the Conservative party is as cool toward the U.N. as circumstances will permit. It regards this world body as ancillary to, not a substitute for, a policy of national strength, military preparedness, and defensive alliances. The Conservatives used to be the advocates of empire and imperialist expansion—yet between 1951 and 1964 they conceded independence to the colonies even faster than did the Labour governments of 1945–51. Since the former empire has been liquidated, and since the Commonwealth has to an overwhelming extent become an association of former dependencies largely inhabited by colored peoples, the mass of the party has become increasingly disenchanted with overseas possessions. Instead, it has turned toward the European Economic Community ("Common Market") as a realistic means of maintaining Britain's economic and diplomatic power. In 1961 the Macmillan government opened negotiations to join the EEC and, although these failed (owing to General de Gaulle's veto in early 1963), the party retained its commitment to accession to Europe and was able to take the opportunity to complete successfully the negotiations for British entry to the EEC in 1971. Though this was never to the taste of a few traditionalists, it commanded the overwhelming assent of the annual party conferences and the bulk of the membership.

At home, the Conservatives accept the state's duty to provide full employment and to exercise a general regulation of the economy in the public interest. They have accepted the duty to provide social services, also, but differ with the Labour party over the mode of administering them. These services are still largely based on the Labour reorganization of 1945–51, and provide for a flat rate of benefit for each recipient. Conservatives regard this as wasteful of the limited resources available, and would prefer to vary the payments to each individual by some test of personal need.

In industrial matters, the Conservative governments of 1951–64 abolished Labour's physical controls on prices and output, denationalized the steel and trucking industries, and encouraged competition from the outside against nationalized industries wherever possible—as, for instance, in the television and air transportation industries. They broke up price fixing in industry with the Restrictive Practices Act of 1956, and challenged, by means of the Resale Price Maintenance Act of 1964, the right of manufacturers to fix prices for their retail products. Reluctant to act against the trade unions while in office, since 1964 they have demanded that the courts offer individual members some protection against their unions, and that steps be taken to abolish restrictive union practices in industry. This is not the same thing as demanding an end to the unions. To the contrary: the Conservatives oppose the Labour government's efforts to take collective bargaining over wages and conditions out of the hands of employers and trade unions and impose their own settlements.

The quest for incentive and opportunity, the stress on rewarding ability, is also to be seen in the party's educational policy. Unlike the Labour party, which is taking steps to curtail or even destroy the "direct-grant" schools, the Conservative party wants to have more of these. Against a great wash of intellectual opinion and the professed actions of the Labour government, it equivocates over "comprehensive" neighborhood schools, and favors the policy of sending the ablest children to the grammar schools where, it holds, they will "get on" faster and better. These rival policies in education well point up the differences between the two parties on the meaning of "equality," and illustrate what Conservatives mean when they talk of the "opportunity state."

Structure

The organization of the Conservative party reflects its historical development and is tighter than a superficial look would suggest. The party is composed of three different organizations (see Fig. 4-2). The first is the National Union of Conservative and Unionist Associations. A federation of the constituency parties, it was established in 1867 and was reshaped between 1884 and 1886. The second component is the party in the Houses of Parliament, the parliamentary party, an autonomous body. The third is the Central Office, which was formed in 1870 as the secretariat of the leader of the party, a role it has retained.

The National Union, as the name suggests, is a union of the constituency associations; there is one association for every constituency (electoral district). Its governing body, the Central Council, consists of 3,600 persons and meets once a year, in a sort of annual semiconference. This Central Council has an Executive Committee of 150 persons, which meets every two months, but is so unwieldy that the General Purposes Committee of 56 persons, which meets frequently, makes most of the executive decisions. The most important duty of the General Purposes Committee, perhaps, is to compile the agenda for the annual meeting of the Central Council of the Conference and of the National Union.

But it would be naïve to think that the National Union is run just by its council or its Executive Committee or its General Purposes Committee, for a number of advisory committees help the union to chart policy: the Women's, the Young Conservatives', the Trade Unionists', and those of the Local Government, and the Political Education and Publicity committees. Among the advisory bodies that are not responsible to the union, the most important are the Advisory Committee on Policy, the Central Board of Finance, and the Advisory Committee on Candidates. In theory, no candidate may be endorsed by a constituency association until this committee is satisfied as to the candidate's personal character, party loyalty, past record and experience, political knowledge, speaking ability, and financial integrity. In practice, constituency parties enjoy extremely wide latitude. More significantly, the committee maintains a list of approved candidates that is available to the constituency organizations. The effective decisions on candidates are in practice largely in the hands of one of the vice-chairmen of the party organization, who reports to this committee. This vice-chairman is especially responsible, in the Central Office, for the candidates' file. He is appointed by and responsible to the leader, but by tradition is a respected backbencher of the parliamentary party.

THE CONSTITUENCY ASSOCIATIONS. In both the Conservative and Labour parties, constituency associations are a vital element and, indeed, play a significant role in the political life of the country. The functions laid down for them in the Conservative party's "Model Rules" show why: the associations are expected to provide an efficient organization for the Conservative party in each constituency; to spread knowledge of the party's principles and policy; to promote the interests of the party in the constituency; to support, in local government elections, those candidates for the council chosen by the party; and to watch over the revision of the constituency register of voters.

The constituency party also has the important function of choosing the parliamentary candidate. The executive committee of the constituency association appoints a selection committee. Before a candidate is recommended for

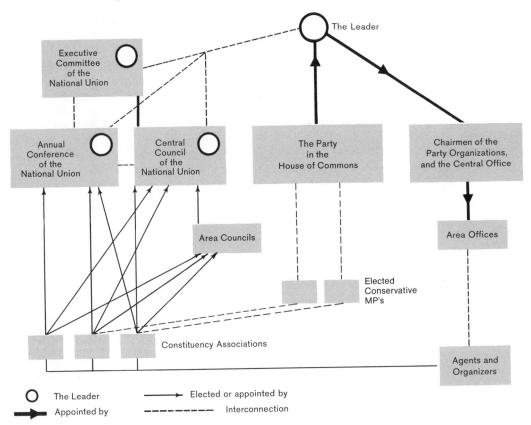

FIG. 4-2. *The organization of the Conservative party.*

adoption, his name must be submitted to the National Union Standing Advisory Committee on Candidates, but it is extremely rare for this to withhold approval. Nevertheless, the procedure ensures that the people who are permitted to stand as candidates (and this is true also in the Labour party) are "seeded"—that is, they have already pledged themselves to support the party's policy and its election manifesto.

Since 1950, the constituency's selection committee has been forbidden to ask intending candidates for financial contributions, and a maximum scale for these is laid down. The most a candidate may contribute to the general running expenses of the association is £25 per year; and the most to the asociation's election-fighting fund also is £25; so £50 in all. When contesting the seat, however, he may also be asked to contribute £100 for "personal expenses." Nevertheless, the local associations have been just as keen as before to pick their candidates from the higher professions and from business rather than from the working class, and have continued to prefer candidates with a public-school and Oxford or Cambridge education. The most marked effect of the reform has been its encouragement to young men to come forward in much larger numbers than before.

THE LEADER AND THE CENTRAL OFFICE. The *leader* of the party is the nominee of the parliamentary party and, once chosen, falls heir to the Central Office. He appoints the chairman of the party organization and (since 1964) its full-time deputy chairman, who is also secretary to the "shadow cabinet"[1]; its two vice-chairmen; and the treasurers, chairman, and vice-chairman of the Policy Committee. The Central Office, which is virtually his personal secretariat, consists of several sections which handle constituency organization and finance, publicity and propaganda, and speakers. The Central Office also includes (since 1965) the Conservative Political Centre—a propaganda and education organization—and the highly influential Research Department. The Central Office ap-

points the regional officials of the party, and these (the regional agent, the regional women's organizer, and so forth) represent the Central Office in the constituencies. Constituency associations appoint their own election agents and officials, who are Central Office-trained and have direct access to headquarters in London but are encouraged to deal with the regional staff as much as possible.

The Central Office must therefore be regarded as a national organization of highly skilled professional partisans. Their duty is to assist the party leadership in the formulation of policy, to carry out decisions, and to act as an intelligence network, advising the constituency associations on the views of the leadership, and in turn advising the leadership on the outlook, morale, and preparedness of the voluntary workers in the constituencies. This party machine is kept in an advanced state of readiness at all times. Local elections and constant by-elections keep it on the alert, and every defeat provokes a reassessment of the party's preparedness for the object of the entire enterprise: to fight and win the next general election.

THE CONFERENCE. The National Union and its associated organs, and the leader and his headquarters, meet together at the annual conference. Each constituency association is entitled to send seven persons, irrespective of its size (unlike the Labour party, wherein representation is proportionate to membership). Furthermore, the persons sent are representatives, not (as in the Labour party) mandated delegates. In addition, the parliamentary party, the official candidates, election agents, and certain members of the Central Office, also attend. About 6,000 are entitled to attend, but only about 4,500 turn up—still too many for effective policy making. This group is by no means the supreme policy-making body of the party; in its advisory capacity, it can pass resolutions, but they are not binding. They are "conveyed" to the leader (as the phrase goes), and if he does not want to adopt them, he need not, for the party's rules clearly state that policy is the responsibility of the leader. Mr. Heath has upgraded the importance of the conference by attending all its sessions. Previously, the leader

---

[1] A "shadow cabinet" consists of those men likely to serve as ministers if the party were to form a government.

came after the conference had concluded, his speech being its closing feature. At best a sounding-board, the conference is usually listened to by the leader, for it would be very unwise of him to ignore its views altogether.

THE PARLIAMENTARY PARTY. Now let us turn to the truer policy-making mechanism of the Conservative party, the parliamentary party, consisting of the Conservative members of Parliament. In February, 1965, the Conservative party adopted a formal election procedure for selecting its leader. (Hitherto, informal "soundings" had been the custom.) This specifies that to win on the first ballot, the candidate must receive an absolute majority of the votes of the Conservative M.P.'s, and 15% more votes than the runner-up. If he does not, provision is made for a second ballot (51% of the vote sufficing), and at this point, new candidates may come forward. And finally, this procedure provides for a third ballot with preferential voting. In July 1965 Sir Alec Douglas-Home resigned as leader, and in the ballot that followed Mr. Heath, though obtaining an absolute majority of votes, was certainly not 15% ahead of his rival, Mr. Reginald Maudling. But the latter immediately withdrew.

The leader is appointed for an indefinite period. There is no annual election of the leader, as in the Labour party, but the leader does not automatically serve for the rest of his life. He has to live with his party and give it good (i.e., successful) service. If he does not, he is liable to face intolerable pressures that will force him to resign. The Conservative party can be very tough on its leaders and has, in the past, removed many of them. It got rid of Arthur Balfour before World War I, Austen Chamberlain immediately after it, and Sir Alec Douglas-Home in 1965.

The leader has, nonetheless, formidable powers. If he is prime minister, he of course selects his cabinet. In opposition, unlike his own Labour counterpart, he selects his own "shadow cabinet." He appoints his chief whip and the junior whips, who serve as his right-hand men in the House of Commons. And it is the leader who ultimately fixes policy. These powers give him a much stronger constitutional position vis-à-vis the rank-and-file members of the parliamentary party, the backbenchers, than the leader of the Labour party in opposition. Yet this authority is by no means absolute. It is qualified by the other party members of Parliament, who are highly organized. A full meeting of the backbenchers, called the "1922 Committee," convenes every Thursday for about an hour or more. The chief whip is always present, and reports the results of the meeting directly to the prime minister (or, when in opposition, to the leader).

In addition to the 1922 Committee, there are several specialized committees, about thirty in number. They have their honorary officers and any member may attend, but, when the party is in power, ministers are not members. In opposition, these bodies play an important role, for attached to each of them is a special secretary who is a member of the Conservative Research Department. The Research Department prepares briefs (sometimes from information supplied by outside bodies) and passes them on to the appropriate backbenchers' committee. When the party is in power, a different kind of situation tends to occur. It is then that, for instance, a minister tends to encounter backbencher opposition on a particular bill. The appropriate backbencher committee might then invite him to explain to them his position. The minister might have to decide to moderate his policy, or he might be able to persuade the backbenchers to come around to his viewpoint.

Crucial in the organization and work of the parliamentary party are the whips. The whips' office is the party's nervous system. Through the whips, the leader knows just what the mood of the party is, and he can transmit back through them his own reactions. He must rely on the whips' techniques of cajolery and persuasion to keep the party loyal to him.

Do not suppose that the backbenchers on the Conservative side are a flock of sheep, for they can be very touchy and very fractious, and need careful handling. This is true even when the party is in power and discipline is normally tighter than in opposition, as examples from the previous Conservative spell in office will show. In December 1961, when the government had agreed to meet a U.N. request for 1,000-

pound bombs to supply its forces in Katanga, the backbenchers forced it to reverse its decision. On July 27, 1963, when Mr. Macmillan, the prime minister himself, was trying to justify his conduct in the protracted, involved, sordid Profumo affair, and when his very continuance as prime minister was at stake, no less than twenty-seven of his backbenchers refused to give him their confidence, and abstained from voting. In March 1964, on the second reading of the resale price maintenance bill, some twenty backbenchers abstained, and twenty actually voted *against* the government—the most serious revolt in the party during its thirteen years of office. And later, in the committee stage, so many voted against one particular item that the government's majority, which was nominally ninety, fell to one.

POLITICAL ATTITUDES IN THE PARLIAMENTARY PARTY. Among the Conservative party members of the House of Commons, professional men and businessmen predominate. In 1970, if classified according to their first and hence formative occupation, 38% were from the professions, 31% were businessmen, 9% were farmers, 9% were in publishing or journalism, 7% were from the armed services, and under 1% were skilled workers (5% were others). But this and similar reckoning grossly underestimates the proportion of businessmen, since many lawyers, in particular, have business interests. In addition, the party draws very largely from the more exclusive public schools. In 1966 no less than 82 of the 330 Conservative members came from Eton, Harrow, or Winchester, and 242 came from some kind of public school. Just over half the parliamentary party had been to Oxford or Cambridge. In short, the party is composed of businessmen and professional people, with almost no representation from the manual working class.

A study of the parliamentary party of 1955–59 discovered a close relationship between the backgrounds of M.P.'s, and the attitudes they assumed.[2] The age of the candidate and the

[2] S. E. Finer, H. B. Berrington, and D. J. Bartholomew, *Backbench Opinion in the House of Commons, 1955–1959* (Pergamon Press, 1961).

year he entered Parliament appeared to be decisive factors in his attitude toward Europe and the Commonwealth. The younger the member and the more recently he entered Parliament, the less disposed he was to put the needs of the Commonwealth before those of Europe. Again, interestingly, the younger the candidate and the more recent his election, the more humane he was likely to be on penal matters.

Conservative Opposition and Return to Power

THE DEFEAT OF 1964. After thirteen years in office, the Conservatives' defeat in 1964, which was decisively confirmed in 1966, obliged the party to rethink and reorganize. No simple explanations can cover the complex movements of opinion which turn one party out of office and put in another, but four reasons were widely given in Britain at this time.

First, the Conservative success in the first decade following their return to power in 1951 had been founded on economic success; the increased majority in 1959 was seen as the response of a grateful nation for rapidly increasing living standards. After mid-1961, a sterling crisis, a mild slump in economic activity, and increasing unemployment (aggravated by the severe winter of 1962) together with the government's response offended both its supporters and opponents.

Secondly, the party's famed adaptability went to unexpected lengths. This ex-imperial party decolonized faster than the Labour party had done; this pro-Commonwealth party sought to enter the European Economic Community in 1961; this free-enterprise party in 1962 established the National Economic Development Council and tried to negotiate a national incomes policy as parts of what it chose to call "Conservative planning"; and this on-the-whole traditionalist party adopted in 1964 a slogan of "modernization." These new moves divided the party, muddling its traditional supporters and bewildering the electorate. On the eve of the election of 1964, the party seemed to be governed by no intelligible principle.

Thirdly, the hitherto respectable party enveloped itself in public scandal and discord. The Vassall spy case of 1962 and the Profumo affair in 1963 both suggested that security was lax and the way each developed implied incompetency, with hints of worse, on the part of Prime Minister Macmillan and his government. Because the inquiry into the Vassall case trod on the sensitive toes of the press, Mr. Macmillan received no mercy from the press when the Profumo scandal broke. Four months later Macmillan resigned and Sir Alec Douglas-Home emerged as his successor amid confusion and disagreement about the methods of his selection. Two prominent members of the Macmillan cabinet, Messrs. Macleod and Powell, ostentatiously refused to serve under him.

All this happened at the same time that the Labour party, which from early 1963 had elected as its leader Mr. Harold Wilson (in succession to Mr. Gaitskell, who had died), was finding an impressive unity, and was renovating its organization and its public relations.

PARTY REORGANIZATION. In July 1965 Sir Alec Douglas-Home retired as party leader, having first ensured that there was an agreed procedure for the election of his successor by the parliamentary party. Mr. Edward Heath was elected, and the leadership crisis which had lasted since mid-1963 was settled for the time being. Mr. Heath set about imposing his stamp on both the organization and the policy of the party.

Reorganization of the Conservative Central Office had started in 1964, with a view to integrating the policy research and publishing activities of the party into the headquarters of the organization. The Conservative Research Department and the Conservative Political Centre ceased to be independent; the director of the Research Department was made deputy chairman of the party organization. The Political Centre's "Contact Programme," a system of local study groups which both educated the party's rank-and-file and communicated its feelings to the leadership, was given fresh emphasis.

Finances caused much concern. All three British parties experienced a decline in voluntary giving as a source of income in the mid-1960s. In 1966 the Conservative party streamlined its employment of personnel and made savings, especially at the regional level, of some $480,000 a year. Modern fund-raising techniques were enlisted in aid of the "National Appeal" in 1967; over the eighteen-month period for which this ran it raised some $5½ million, about three times the party's normal income for such a period.

Steps were taken to upgrade the status and quality of recruitment of constituency election agents. Changes in salary levels in 1965 and 1969 raised their starting salary by 50 percent and almost doubled the maximum salary; with this went an attempt to give them more of a role of "managing directors" of local branches of the party.

Traditionally, a party's organization has been a main channel of communications from those of its supporters who are enrolled as members to the leadership. From 1965, the Conservative party began to use and to rely on a very different way of assessing the attitudes and demands of its supporters—and more important, of potential supporters. Between 1966 and 1970 some $70,000 a year was being spent by the party on an elaborate set of private surveys of opinion. Regular surveys to establish the sections of the population most likely to respond to the party, special issue surveys, and local surveys in selected constituencies all played a part in determining the way the party pitched its appeal and allocated its resources prior to the general election. High-speed campaign surveys fed instantly into the strategy-making machinery during the 1970 election campaign contributed to the way in which the party fought, and won, that campaign.

PROBLEMS OF OPPOSITION. The party organization was improved, and the techniques of securing the information upon which the leadership could base its decisions were vastly improved. Yet efforts to increase membership, and particularly to broaden the social base of the party's recruitment of candidates and workers, signally failed. There was no upsurge of Conservative party confidence and activity such as had occurred during the 1945–51 Labour government. Instead, Mr. Heath tended to look increasingly like a man with problems.

Labour's emphatic victory in 1966 fed a nagging fear in many Conservative hearts: that the Labour party under Mr. Wilson might achieve his objective of becoming the natural majority party. In the half-century up to 1964, the Conservative party had been the majority party—with a plurality of votes in three out of every four elections and in office (alone or in coalition) for four out of every five years. Certain demographic trends favored Mr. Wilson's hopes of reversing this for the remainder of the twentieth century; the Conservatives had been steadily losing their built-in advantage of a substantial section of the electorate which formed its anti-Labour views in youth before World War I. The Conservative's private polls seemed to reinforce this fear. Even at periods when the Conservative party had a record plurality over Labour in *voting intention,* these showed that Labour led the Conservatives in *party identification.*

At the same time, all polls, private or public, showed that Mr. Heath had failed badly to come over to the electorate. Able and resolute, with a vast capacity for work, Mr. Heath is nevertheless diminished by television while Mr. Wilson is one of the finest television "naturals" known to British politics. For the first time in forty years a Conservative leader in opposition lacked the authority that comes from having previously been prime minister; after a heavy defeat at the 1966 election, Mr. Heath found that his lack of authority deriving from his record became worse. Coupled with the knowledge of his low standing in the eyes of the public, and the fact that he has a middle-class background rather than the patrician heritage of his predecessors, Mr. Heath experienced increasing difficulty in holding his party together and maintaining his personal position at the head of it.

The last two factors contributed to a third: the growth of an unorganized movement of right-wing dissent. Right-wing Conservative elements tried to force the pace over such issues as Rhodesia, immigration, and economic philosophy, convinced both that they represented the views of the party's rank and file better than did the party leadership and that a more distinctively anti-Labour stance would reap electoral rewards. Mr. Enoch Powell, who was dismissed from the Conservative shadow cabinet in 1968 because of an inflammatory speech on colored immigration, became the focus of much of this dissent. In the two years prior to the 1970 election Mr. Powell secured a public audience far greater than that of any Conservative front-bench spokesman, and went about making a series of speeches which seemed deliberately designed to embarrass his leader. There was no organized Powellite movement; Mr. Powell himself would have been unacceptable as leader to many right-wing Conservatives. But "Powellism," as it was dubbed, became a constant additional challenge to Mr. Heath's authority.

Against these problems, Mr. Heath could set two facts which pointed to his becoming the next prime minister: the Labour government's sorry performance in the economic field seemed to guarantee defeat for Mr. Wilson, and Conservative victories in local government elections and parliamentary by-elections during the 1967–69 period were enormous and totally unprecedented.

CONSERVATIVE POLICY, 1966–70. An opposition party "making policy" is doing so in a vacuum. But it devotes energy to elaborating policy for three reasons: (1) to satisfy the demands of its own members, (2) to provide the image and appeal on which it will fight the coming election, and (3) to prepare the detailed proposals, backed up by the necessary expertise, which it will implement when in office. These purposes may conflict. The demands of members, expressed through the party's internal structure, can differ from the judgment of its leaders (backed by private polls) about what will win new votes. The issues of the day in opposition, to which the party has to react, may give a different picture to the issues on which the party has proposals for new legislation. The circumstances in which a policy is prepared in opposition may have altered materially by the time the party comes to power. Conservative policy making in opposition in 1966–70, the way the 1970 election was fought, and the first year in power of the new Conservative government illustrate these dilemmas abundantly.

In opposition, Mr. Heath responded to the internal demands of his party by giving increasing emphasis to what he termed "the great divide," painting the picture of an enormous gulf between how the Labour government was handling Britain's problems and how the Conservatives would have done so. In some respects, elaborated below, it is certainly true that the Conservatives were working out policies radically different from those of the government. But concerning the major fields of the management of the economy—maintenance of the exchange value of sterling, measures to stem wage inflation and to cut the growth in public expenditure, for instance—it was difficult not to interpret Mr. Heath as saying, "We will do the same but do it better." In response to this type of criticism, he committed the Conservative party to not reintroducing an incomes control policy, which idea the Labour government had only developed from Conservative experiments in the same direction in 1961–64. In office, the Conservatives found that this pledge became an embarrassment. Another example of a policy made to suit the needs of an opposition which has caused problems for a party in government was Mr. Heath's policy of assimilating Commonwealth immigrants to alien status (a clear response to Powellism), which was more easily announced than put into legislative form.

The justification of the Conservative party's claim to present radically different policies lies mainly in three fields—industrial relations, taxation, and social welfare. Each of these policies worked out in opposition reflected a philosophy farther to the right than either Labour's or those of Conservative governments from 1951 to 1964. They reflected a Conservative emphasis on the individual's responsibility for providing his own security and welfare and on the individual's right to maximize his earnings, in contrast to the Labour emphasis on a collective responsibility for welfare financed out of taxa-

tion of those earning most. The proposals for regulating the powers of the trade unions by law went against the grain of the strictest laissez-faire Conservatives (such as Mr. Powell) but were clearly, nevertheless, a sharp shift to the right compared with the concilliatory policy toward unions held by Conservative ministers of Labour between 1951 and 1964.

For some Conservatives these measures should have been part of a general philosophy of a "freer economy," a marked move away from state intervention in economic matters. For many this should have included measures of denationalization and substantial reductions in government expenditure. But Mr. Heath knew that, however much this might appeal to much of the Conservative party, taken too far it could have been electorally disastrous. So, while he made some play with this theme, Mr. Heath preferred to talk in terms of these policies as part of a more efficient way of managing the country, making the contrast with the shambling, gimmicky way in which he thought Mr. Wilson had mismanaged things. "A new style of government" became the most coherent theme linking diverse Conservative policies. Believing that this involved thorough preparation of intended legislation, Mr. Heath ensured that these policies had been thoroughly worked over in opposition.

On industrial relations, Conservative plans, published in April 1968 in the pamphlet entitled "Fair Deal at Work," were (1) to make collective agreements legally enforceable; (2) to set up a system of industrial courts; (3) to introduce a code of good industrial relations practices; (4) to establish a system of registration and recognition of unions, involving approval of their rules by a registrar; (5) to redefine trade disputes (which have certain privileges in law) in order to exclude certain types of strikes such as sympathy strikes or strikes resulting from interunion disputes; (6) to allow the government to enforce a cooling-off period and a secret ballot before a strike may commence; and (7) to limit the "closed shop" and protect individual workers against it. The Conservative party argued that these proposals would tackle the harm done to the economy by the existing chaotic state of industrial relations. The Industrial Relations Act of 1971 implements the proposals made in opposition.

On taxation, the Conservatives set themselves to find ways of shifting the burden of taxation from direct to indirect taxes. Abolition of the selective employment tax—a tax on those employed in services (as opposed to those in manufacturing)—and a substantial reduction in income tax had to be met by new forms of indirect tax. Study of what these should be was carried out, to use the words of the "shadow chancellor," Mr. Iain Macleod, "in a more detailed and sophisticated way than has ever been done before by an Opposition, or indeed a Government"—contrasted with the precipitous way in which the Labour government had sprung the selective employment tax on the public in 1966. This research, and the feedback within the Conservative party to some earlier proposals, meant that the proposals were altered as time went on. By June 1970, the party had avoided committing itself too clearly to a value-added tax (VAT) to replace the revenue lost in income taxes and the selective employment tax, but had amassed expertise on how it might work. Mr. Wilson tried to make the alleged ill-effects of a VAT an election issue but failed. In this field the opposition party's policy for its supporters and the election campaign was, "cut direct taxation." In government, the relevant policy making became the ability of the new chancellor, Mr. Barber, to introduce very major tax reforms (including the introduction in due course of VAT) in his first budget despite the known reluctance of the tax-gathering Inland Revenue Department to tackle such reforms.

Conservative policy for the social services was not worked out with such coherence or detail. On secondary education the party was split between the views of its education spokesman, Sir Edward Boyle (backed by the findings of opinion polls), who favored the new integrated comprehensive schools, and the desire of many local Conservative parties to campaign for the retention of selective grammar schools. On public housing, Conservative-controlled local authorities tried to allow municipal tenants to buy their houses (against Labour government opposition), and the party advocated a more selective form of housing subsidy. Regarding the National Health Service the Conservative party favored increased use of charges. But although many Conservatives wanted a comprehensive policy of introducing into the welfare state the principles of selectivity (variation of benefits by assessed need), and charging for services, the party leadership, aware that anything looking like an attack on the welfare state would lose electoral support, resisted this pressure. Nevertheless, a majority of Conservative candidates in the 1970 election advocated making welfare benefits more selective.

There was one other area in which events produced the major divergence of policy between government and opposition which Mr. Heath looked for: defense policy in the Indian Ocean. Conservatives had disagreed strongly with the Labour government's decision in 1964 to cease selling arms to South Africa for defense of the route around the Cape of Good Hope. The area of disagreement was considerably widened when the Labour government reversed its previous policy and decided to withdraw British troops from the Persian Gulf and Southeast Asia. For the first time since World War II, there was a major issue in British overseas policy over which the two main parties clearly disagreed at election time. But another potential divisive factor between the two parties was removed when the Labour government also reversed its attitude on the European Economic community and applied for British entry in 1967.

CONSERVATIVE VICTORY, 1970. The policies that keep a party's active members happy or that prepare a party for government need not be those that win an election. Such was clearly the strategy of the Conservative leadership in 1970. Mr. Heath chose to fight the election on Labour's economic record and on Conservative promises to do better. An analysis of the content of his election speeches [3] shows that he

[3] See D. E. Butler and M. Pinto-Duschinsky, *The British General Election of 1970* (London: Macmillan, 1971), p. 444.

took up 17 percent of his time on the three areas (industrial relations, taxation, welfare) where the Conservative party had its most distinctive policies, but no less than 47 percent on the economic situation in general—inflation, the balance of payments, and unemployment. Eight percent went to other issues and 28 percent was so general that it could not be assigned to any one area of policy. Other Conservative candidates followed suit; more of them mentioned inflation in their election addresses than any other specific Conservative policies so painstakingly prepared. In the final week of the campaign there is much evidence that it was the Conservative emphasis on rising prices coupled with fear of another balance-of-payments crisis which tipped the scales in favor of Mr. Heath.

Yet the Conservative government elected as a result could claim—rightly by British political convention—a mandate from the electorate for such actions as its Industrial Relations Bill and its decision to resume arms sales to South Africa. The policies had been clearly put to the electorate; but in what sense had they been approved? The election did resolve a few of the dilemmas which the Conservative party had faced in opposition, and Mr. Heath's personal status was overnight changed. But whether or not a Conservative government elected through dissatisfaction with the previous government's failures in the economic field—rather than through converting electors to Conservative policies or a Conservative partisanship—can maintain public support for whatever measures it has to take remains to be seen. Equally, the 1970 election left entirely open the question of whether demographic trends were really draining away Conservative support or social ones were reinforcing it.

THE LABOUR PARTY

Although the Labour party was officially founded in 1900, it had antecedents in such organizations as the Independent Labour party (founded in 1893), the Fabian Society (founded in 1883), the Social Democratic Federation (founded in 1881); in the ideals of the trade unions, whose history goes back still further into the nineteenth century; in the cooperative movement, founded in 1844; and in the working-class political tradition spanning the years of Owenism in the 1830s and chartism in the 1840s to the mass strikes and the new trade unionism of the 1880s. At its inception the Labour party was not avowedly socialist, but merely an amalgam of socialist and trade union elements; it was not a unitary body, but a federation of societies and trade unions which individuals could join only through membership in one of the component organizations. There was no doctrine except the goal of establishing a distinct Labour group in the House of Commons.

The Labour Representation Committee (as it called itself until 1906) was transformed into a socialist party in 1918, with the adoption of a constitution that is still in effect today. Individual members were allowed to join directly, and the party headquarters organized constituency Labour parties that systematically covered the whole country. The new constitution declared that the object of the party was to "secure for the producers by hand or by brain the full fruits of their industry and the most equitable distribution thereof that may be possible upon the basis of the common ownership of the means of production and the best obtainable system of popular administration and control of each industry and service. . . ."[4] This statement is from the famous "clause IV" of the party's objectives, which we shall cover later.

Ideology and Image

IDEOLOGY. Although its program is basically socialistic, the Labour party has never been the prisoner of an all-embracing Marxist ideology, as have some of the socialist parties of continental Europe. Many elements have shaped its viewpoint. At an early stage, Hyndman's Social Democratic Federation introduced Marxist ideas, but these were not influential. The Independent Labour party was a much

[4] In 1927 the words, "and exchange," were added following "distribution."

more important component, and its philosophy derived largely from the religious nonconformity of the working classes, embodying a disgust for the class injustices of a competitive society and a plea for a more just and humane society based on fellowship and cooperation. Another ingredient was introduced by the small but extremely influential Fabian Society, which favored gradualism. The Fabians wanted to bring industry under public ownership and control and to redistribute the nation's wealth so as to provide all citizens with the minimum requirements for a decent and civilized life. Another influence, syndicalism (called, in its British form, guild socialism), espoused workers' control of their employers' industries. At different periods in the party's history, different views have been uppermost. In the 1920s, for instance, it was the idealistic desire for fellowship and cooperative living; in the thirties, there was a stronger flavor of Marxism; and throughout the forties the party laid its main stress on the need for economic planning, of which nationalization of the basic industries was an essential part. This latter stress, together with a zeal for social equality, are its driving forces today.

Just as the Conservative party still contains right-wing elements who believe in British imperial supremacy, so the Labour party contains a very small left-wing faction that maintains a strong attachment to orthodox Marxism. This group believes in the class struggle of the workers against the capitalists. It wants to remove the capitalistic order altogether by placing the whole economy under public ownership, and in foreign affairs it advocates the unilateral renunciation of nuclear weapons and a neutralist foreign policy for Britain.

The essential philosophy of the Labour party springs from a belief that man is inherently good and that institutions and society are mostly to blame for making him behave badly and live miserably. Economic institutions are particularly guilty because of the enormous influence they exert over the size of the national income, over the way its rewards are distributed, and over the social priorities that are established as the economy's goal. Democracy must therefore be extended from politics into

economic affairs. Using the processes of parliamentary and local democracy, in which the party fervently believes, the electorate should bring firms and enterprises under the ownership or control of the people. The objective, therefore, is to create a cooperative fellowship in place of the scramble for private competitive gain.

In home affairs, therefore, the party has four major objectives: the "democratization" of the economy by means of the nationalization of key industries, and public regulation of the rest; a more nearly equal distribution of wealth, by means of death duties, taxation of unearned incomes, and sharply progressive income taxes on earned incomes; universal social welfare services; and the elimination of class differences. It sees the public schools as a privilege of the wealthy, it deplores the academic segregation of children at the age of 11, and it favors large, comprehensive schools for all.

In the field of foreign affairs, the Labour party would like to see collective cooperation among the nations replace national sovereignty and self-interest. To this end, it is far warmer toward the United Nations than is the Conservative party. Also, its members have a pronounced aversion to the threat or use of force in world affairs, unless employed to support the U.N. The Labour party opposed the Conservative government's landings in the Suez Canal zone in 1956, and the British air drop in Jordan in 1958, but supported the U.N. action in Korea and, later, in the Congo.

The advent of nuclear weapons caused a sharp conflict of conscience inside the Labour party. Since 1955, when the British government first contemplated making an H-bomb, a minority in the party has protested against the manufacture, then the testing, and finally the stockpiling of British nuclear weapons. The "unilateralists" wish to renounce the manufacture and use of nuclear weapons unconditionally without international agreement. Up to 1963, this was a matter of bitter controversy inside the party; since then it has caused much less concern.

Finally, the Labour party has been strenuously anticolonialist; today, with the former empire liquidated, corresponding attitudes of opposition to the racist regimes in southern Africa and of support for aid from Britain to the newly independent states are strongly held in the Labour party.

IMAGE. By 1959–60 the public image of the Labour party was increasingly that of a humorless and aging party of zealots and puritans clinging to the old-fashioned, home-spun virtues, and more and more given over to nostalgia for the epics of its past. It had lost three elections in a row. It was demoralized. And for the next two years it tore itself apart in fruitless controversy over the precise meaning to be attached to "socialism" and over the question of nuclear weapons. The first controversy took the form of a debate over the meaning of the aforementioned clause IV of the constitution of the Labour party: was this to be taken literally or did it permit a mixed, public-*cum*-private economy? The question was never really settled. The second controversy led to the 1960 party conference vote calling for the unconditional and unilateral renunciation of Britain's nuclear armory. This in turn led to internal strife in which the party leader, Mr. Gaitskell, refused to abide by the conference's resolution.

Then all changed. The 1961 conference abandoned its unilateralist stance, and by the time Gaitskell suddenly died in January 1963, the Labour party was united and in the lead in the public opinion polls. Mr. Wilson as his successor consolidated and built on what Mr. Gaitskell had achieved. The Labour party concentrated its electoral fire on ways to achieve greater economic growth, on regional and urban development, on the crisis in education, and on the need for the state to harness the new opportunities given by science and technology. The party adopted the Conservatives' tactic of using public relations and advertising. By the 1964 election, Labour was seen as a vigorous and young party of modernization.

Structure

Basic to the structure of the Labour party is the difference between *individual party members*, who are organized in the constituency Labour parties (CLPs), and the *affiliated members,* mostly trade unionists from the unions that have affiliated with the party (see Fig. 4-3). These unions collect a political levy from their members, part of which goes into the party's coffers. Both types of membership are represented at the annual conference. The trade unions and local constituency Labour parties both send one delegate for every five thousand members. Also entitled to be present, ex officio, are the National Executive Committee, the whole of the parliamentary party, and all the candidates. But these ex officio members have no votes. Usually some one thousand to fifteen hundred persons attend. Resolutions are introduced by the delegates, and then are debated and voted on by the conference. Since inevitably too many resolutions are presented for the conference to discuss adequately, the "platform" tries to have them boiled down into "composite" motions. Of some thirty possible resolutions about the prices and incomes policy for instance, three might reach the conference: one right-wing, one middle-of-the-road, and one left-wing.

The next function of the conference is to elect the National Executive Committee. In addition to acting as the keeper of the party's conscience, the NEC runs the party between the annual meetings of the conference. To prevent the $5\frac{1}{2}$ million trade union–affiliated members from overriding the fewer than 1 million individual members and choosing their own men for the NEC, the latter is divided into four groups: (1) twelve members of the committee are nominated by the trade unions and voted on by them alone; (2) seven members are nominated and elected by the constituency parties alone; (3) a third group consists of five women—and since they are not elected solely by the women (as one might expect) but by the whole conference, they must, clearly, secure the backing of the trade unions; (4) the fourth group consists of only one member, who is elected by the socialist and the cooperative societies represented at the conference. To these twenty-five members are added the leader of the parliamentary party and the deputy leader, who are ex officio members, and the

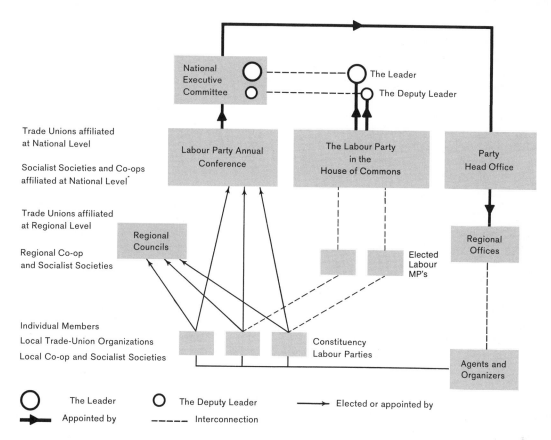

FIG. 4-3. *The organization of the Labour party.*

treasurer, who is elected by the whole conference, for a total of twenty-eight in all. With the parliamentary Labour party, the formal Labour party structure is complete.

How is policy decided in the Labour party, and who is most influential in formulating it? We shall discuss this under three headings: (1) the role of the Conference vis-à-vis the parliamentary Labour party; (2) the role within the party of the constituency parties and of the trade unions; and (3) the role of the parliamentary Labour party itself.

THE CONFERENCE AND THE PARLIAMENTARY LABOUR PARTY. The Labour party conference and parliamentary Labour party are supposedly independent of one another, yet both are responsible for establishing the policy of the

party. Before 1952, the parliamentary party dominated the National Executive Committee because (1) many of the leaders of the parliamentary party belonged to the committee, and (2) the committee was able to rely on the vote of the largest trade unions. In addition, since the Labour party was in power from 1945 to 1951, the leaders of the parliamentary party who formed the cabinet enjoyed a high degree of prestige. But in 1951–52 the constituency parties represented in the conference revolted against the leadership of the parliamentary party and elected to the National Executive Committee a large number of leftist M.P.'s—the so-called Bevanites, named after the late Aneurin Bevan, the fiery Welshman who strove to infuse the party with its old radical zeal. Later there was a shift to the left in the largest of the trade unions, the Transport and General Workers Union, which disposes of one-sixth of the votes in the conference. This further weakened the hold of the leaders of the parliamentary party in the Executive Committee and the conference.

In 1960 a serious cleavage sundered the party when, as described, the conference rejected the platform's resolution on defense and, instead, passed one calling for "a complete rejection of any defense policy based on the threat of the use of strategic or tactical nuclear weapons."

Hugh Gaitskell, the leader of the party, refused to change his own standpoint, and stated that the parliamentary party was not constitutionally obliged to do so either. When Parliament reconvened, the parliamentary party reelected Mr. Gaitskell as its leader by a 2-to-1 majority, and elected a parliamentary committee of antiunilateralists, thus also indicating that it intended to go its own way.

Mr. Morgan Phillips, the party's general secretary, summed up the constitutional question in this way:

1. The annual conference does *not* instruct the parliamentary party. It can instruct only the National Executive Committee.

2. The parliamentary Labour party is unquestionably an autonomous political body, owing ultimate responsibility only to the electorate.

3. The parliamentary Labour party cannot maintain its position in the country if it can be demonstrated that it is at any time and in any way subject to dictation from an outside body, which, however representative of the *party*, could not be regarded as representative of the country.

For some months after the conference, the struggle between the two factions was envenomed. When the party conference met again in October 1961, Mr. Gaitskell's multilateralist policy was carried by a huge majority. Thus, after an embittered period of strife between the conference and the parliamentary party, unity was restored—on the parliamentary party's terms.

THE CONSTITUENCY LABOUR PARTIES AND THE TRADE UNIONS. The role of the unions in the Labour party is enormously important in respect to (1) money, (2) votes, (3) the National Executive Committee, and (4) the sponsorship of candidates.

Financing. The unions contributed £100,-000 to the Labour party's election fund in 1955; £326,000 in 1959; and £598,000 in 1964. Since 1945, they have never contributed less than 80% of the general election fund. Of the current annual revenue of the party organization (1969 figures), of a £367,000 total, £272,000 comes from the unions and only £34,000 from the constituency parties.

Voting. At the conference, there are some 5½ million trade union votes to ⅔ million constituency party votes. Furthermore, the two largest trade unions control more than one-third of that huge trade union vote and the five next largest another third, and it is the practice of each trade union delegation to vote as a single bloc. (In 1960, for example, the Executive Committee of the National Union of Railwaymen decided, by a margin of *one* vote, to support the unilateral renunciation of nuclear weapons; thus, at the Labour party conference in October, the *whole* of the union's 294,000 votes were cast for this resolution.)

The National Executive Committee. As we have seen, the committee has twelve trade union members, and five women and a treasurer elected by a majority of the whole conference. Thus, as many as eighteen out of the twenty-eight places can be held by people who are either trade unionists or favorable to them.

Sponsoring candidates. Certain trade unions have "panels" of candidates, and when any of these candidates is adopted by a constituency, the trade union is prepared to contribute to that candidate's election expenses and also to make a certain annual contribution to the running of his constituency party. How much they actually give depends on the circumstances and on the individual union. A union may pay up to £350 or half a full-time agent's salary (whichever is the larger) to a borough constituency, and £420 per year or half the salary of a full-time agent (whichever is the larger) to a county constituency. These figures must be contrasted with the very small sums a Conservative candidate is permitted to contribute to his constituency association.

In addition, unions pay a sizable proportion of the election expenses for their own candidates when they are adopted: the maximum is 80 percent and the average sum paid out is £550. This has increased the gulf between the constituencies that adopt ordinary candidates and those that are tempted by the allure of a trade union candidate or a candidate sponsored by the Cooperative Party (who also will bring money with him). The trade unions tend to adopt candidates for the safer seats. Of their 138 candidates in 1966, 132 were elected; of 137 in 1970, 112 were elected. Both are very high proportions.

Militants in the constituency parties have tried to demonstrate that the constituency parties raise and spend more money than the trade unions contribute. An independent scholar, however, estimated the annual income for the 1960–64 period thus: [5]

Trade unions' donations to local parties and to Central Headquarters	£ 797,000
Autonomous Central and Regional income	35,000
Co-operative donation to local parties and Central Headquarters	125,000
Autonomous local Labour Party income	500,000
Total annual income	£ 1,457,000

Thus 55% of the total is provided by the trade unions—representing 56% of the sum the unions raise from their members by the "political levy." Only 34% of the total is raised by the local parties by their subscriptions, lotteries, etc.

The Parliamentary Labour Party

In opposition, the parliamentary Labour party is, in certain important respects, organized in

[5] Richard Rose, *Influencing Voters* (London: Faber, 1967), pp. 252–55.

ways widely different from those of the Conservative party. The Labour party's traditional passion for equality and for democratic leadership has handicapped the parliamentary party. The leader is annually elected and then is saddled with a group of people (known as the Parliamentary Committee), who may be personally obnoxious to him, by a vote of the whole parliamentary party. The leader does have the right (and this gives him some patronage) to choose which area of policy he will assign to each man. In office, however, matters are quite different. The "leader" is the prime minister, and as such he "hires and fires" all members of the government, senior and junior.

Both in opposition and in office, the parliamentary party meets as a body once every week, on Thursday afternoons. In principle, what is decided at such meetings is binding on the entire party, under its "Standing Orders." Unlike its Conservative counterpart (the "1922 Committee"), this meeting is attended by ministers. When Labour was in office in 1964–70, a Liaison Committee was also set up, consisting of the elected chairman of the parliamentary party (a backbencher), two other backbenchers as vice-chairmen, the leader of the House of Commons and the chief whip (both prominent ministers, of course), a Labour peer, and the secretary to the parliamentary party. This committee arranged meetings of the full party caucus, prepared the agenda, and represented the views of the rank-and-file to the ministers. Additionally, the party, both in opposition and in office, has a network of "subject" committees of backbenchers, each electing their own chairman, but (under a revision of the Standing Orders in 1966) notified and approved by the chief whip. There are twenty-five such committees. The trade union–sponsored members also meet from time to time as a group.

DISCIPLINE. The theory of the parliamentary Labour party is that it forms its policy democratically, and indeed, in opposition this is true. The majority selects the leader, elects the Parliamentary Committee, which acts as the "shadow cabinet," and chooses the chief whip. Policy is made in the caucus, where the majority decision is binding on the minority. But, obviously, matters are very different in office.

To enforce this majority viewpoint, the party has a set of Standing Orders. Among other things, these require that a member vote along with his party on the floor of the House except in a matter of conscience, when he may abstain. If he disobeys, he must answer to the leadership; if his explanation is unsatisfactory and he continues to disobey, he may be excluded from the parliamentary party. He may also be expelled from the party by its National Executive Committee. As a result, the NEC of the extraparliamentary party would not endorse his candidature at the next election, and so he would stand to lose his seat.

But the parliamentary party has a long history of indiscipline, and the rule has had a checkered career. In the 1945–51 period of Labour rule, the Standing Orders were suspended—the government's majority was so large as to make such tolerance possible. Between 1951 and 1959, however, while in opposition, the left-wingers frequently broke ranks, and the rule was invoked against them. Following the 1959 defeat, the Standing Orders were again suspended, only to be reimposed in 1961 and actually used against six members, who were excluded from the parliamentary party (and only readmitted after some time). The Standing Orders were left in force during the 1964–66 Wilson government, but there was no need to invoke them, as solidarity guaranteed that the backbenchers, with a majority of only four, would not turn out their own government.

The Standing Orders were not imposed in the 1966 parliament, where the government started with a majority of ninety-seven. Backbench unrest in late 1966 led to a pact by which the backbenchers agreed not to set up any unofficial "study groups," while the whips for their part agreed to widen the meaning of a "matter of conscience." But starting in early 1967 a series of revolts by backbenchers, culminating in the successes of backbench pressure in securing the withdrawal both of the House of Lords Reform Bill and of the proposed Trade Union legislation in 1969 produced far worse problems for the leadership. Although disciplinary sanctions were imposed on rebels in

a Common Market vote in 1967 and on abstainers in a vital confidence vote on the government's economic measures in 1968, neither these nor the replacement of a "lax" chief whip by the supposedly tougher Mr. Mellish in 1969 could avoid the massive successful revolts of 1969.

SOCIAL COMPOSITION. Though the Labour vote is overwhelmingly manual working-class, the candidates they elect are overwhelmingly nonmanual-class. Only the trade union practice of sponsoring candidates gives the nonmanual workers a foothold in the parliamentary party. It is possible to classify candidates according to their original or formative occupation, or the one they practiced when elected; the former is the one used below. This overrates the working-class component: many of working-class origin have taken up some white-collar occupation by the time they are elected.

The Labour members are of four main types. The professions, a category which in this party includes a vastly greater number of schoolteachers and university teachers than it does in the Conservative party, made up 43% of the parliamentary Labour party in 1966, and 47% in 1970. Businessmen—again vastly different from the Conservative contingent, which is largely composed of company directors, of whom there are only *four* in the parliamentary Labour party—made up 9% of the latter in 1966, and 10% in 1970. They consist mostly of small shopkeepers, accountants, and executives, rather than directors of large concerns. The next group, the "minor professions," is made up of a miscellany of journalists, organizers, public lecturers, insurance salesmen, and the like: they made up 17% of the party in 1966 and 16% in 1970. Lastly, those of working-class occupations formed only 26% in 1970, having declined to this figure from 37% in 1951 and 32% in 1964. Thus, three-quarters of the parliamentary party is now nonmanual, and this majority is increasing.

Education provides a somewhat better picture of "class" origin when it is remembered that, given the date at which most of the members received their education, "elementary" education and the "elementary+" would tend to denote working-class origin, "secondary" and "secondary+" would denote lower-middle-class, and "university," while it would include elements of both of these (the very bright minds), would mostly indicate a middle-class origin. Those receiving only elementary education formed 9% of the party in 1966, and 19% in 1970. Those receiving secondary education formed only 14% of the party in 1966, and 16% in 1970. The members who started out with elementary or secondary education and then went on, either to night school or to teachers' training or similar types of courses, formed 21% in 1966, and 12% in 1970. Individuals who had been to a university, however, formed 51% of the 1966 party and 54% of the party in 1970.

The parliamentary Labour party likes to boast that it is more socially representative than the Conservatives—and this is obviously true. But for this reason it is much more socially and occupationally heterogeneous. Research on the correlation between social background and political attitudes carried out by the author for the 1955–59 Parliament suggests that this largely accounts for the party's internal schisms and convulsions as compared with the greater solidarity of the Conservative party. In particular, there was a tension between the working-class, trade union–sponsored candidates and the remainder—especially the miscellaneous professions—on "ideological" issues such as nuclear arms and the cold war. Similar research on the 1964 Parliament and beyond has been undertaken at Southampton University, and has yielded similar results. A spot check by the author on two issues—namely, the defense estimates for 1967 and the war in Vietnam—indicates this.

In February 1967, sixty-four Labour M.P.'s abstained from voting with the government at the close of a debate on the defense estimates. In March 1967, a number of Labour members signed a statement in *The Times* calling on their government to dissociate itself from the bombing of North Vietnam and to endorse the peace proposals of U Thant, the secretary general of the U.N. In theory, the signatories should have been from all occupational groups in the party; but as Table 4-4 shows, they were not. The proportion of professional members is

TABLE 4-4. *Occupation and Attitude in the Labour Party, 1967*

Occupational Group	Proportion of Labour Party	Proportion Abstaining in Defense Debate	Proportion Signing in The Times
Professions	43%	39%	40%
Business	9	15	12
Minor professions	17	20	26
Workers	32	25	22

roughly the same as the proportion they bear to the whole party. The "business" group showed a somewhat higher propensity to act than their numbers in the party would warrant. The minor professions also showed a greater propensity to abstain in the defense debate than their party proportion warrants, and a markedly higher propensity to sign the Vietnam document. The workers, on the other hand, are underrepresented among the defense abstainers, and even more markedly underrepresented among the signatories of the Vietnam statement.

Problems of the Labour Party

The problems of the Labour party in opposition since 1970 spring primarily from the failure of the Labour government of 1964–70 to achieve what it set out to do. In the main this means the failure of its economic policy.

THE ECONOMIC PERFORMANCE, 1964–70. Labour had made economic revival the centerpiece of its program in 1964 and in 1966. The specific pledge was given, "In the next five years living standards . . . will rise by 25 percent." The party believed that a series of measures, from the institution of a Department of Economic Affairs to the introduction of a corporation tax, could stimulate an increased growth rate. It was never given a serious chance to try. On taking office in 1964 the new government committed itself to maintaining the exchange parity of the pound sterling; to do this it had to postpone much of its economic proposals in order to deal with recurrent balance-of-payments crises. Then a much more severe crisis in July 1966 precipitated a package of stringent measures, freezing wages and prices. Nevertheless, the following year, the government was obliged to devalue the pound, and shortly afterward announced a series of sharp cuts in intended government expenditure.

The net result was that during this period of Labour government, economic growth was less, but inflation (partly resulting from the currency devaluation) was worse than it had been under the six years of previous Conservative rule. To make things worse, Labour presided over the increase of unemployment, especially in certain less prosperous regions, to record postwar levels. The policies designed to meet these problems, which Labour worked out in office, deeply offended the interests and views of Labour supporters—the statutory incomes policy of 1966–69 and then, still worse, the abortive attempt in 1969 to introduce legal curbs on trade union powers.

As if this was not enough for Labour party members, their government was obliged, by the priority it chose to give to the balance of payments and the parity of sterling, to abandon many of the targets in the field of social welfare. The raising of the school-leaving age was postponed; the public house-building program was cut severely; health service changes, abolished in 1964, were reintroduced in 1968; and research by erstwhile Labour sympathizers on poverty among low-wage-earning large families showed that the net result of Labour policies had been to make the poor relatively poorer.

Thus by 1970 Labour had failed to meet its central economic pledge; had deeply offended its trade union connection, and had bitterly disappointed those who wanted to increase resources devoted to social welfare. Yet in 1970, it became apparent that, whether through government policies or not, Britain's balance-of-payment position was improving markedly. Many Labour supporters believe that their own government destroyed their hopes in 1964–70 only to hand over to the Conservatives a much

healthier economy from which the latter will in due course benefit electorally.

DISSENSION IN THE PARTY. It is hardly surprising that Mr. Wilson found it extremely hard to carry his colleagues with him along this path. The government suffered a series of resignations of prominent ministers; Deputy Prime Minister Brown (over the general running of the government); Mr. Gunter (much the same issue); Lord Longford (the postponement of raising the school-leaving age); Mr. Cousins (incomes policy); Miss Herbison (pensions policy); and Mr. Mayhew (defense expenditure). But these ministers went separately and never formed an opposition bloc inside the party. A series of rebellions in the parliamentary party included a nucleus of left-wingers who were in permanent disagreement with the government over several aspects of economic policy, defense expenditure, the government's support of the United States in Vietnam, and British entry into the Common Market. But joined by a different larger group on each the number of permanent rebels was small, issue.

By 1969 the government's hold on its backbenchers had broken down badly. A filibuster on the House of Lords Reform Bill conducted by backbenchers of both parties was causing so much embarrassment to the government's legislative timetable that the bill was withdrawn—the most serious rebuff over a piece of government legislation delivered by government backbenchers for many years. Encouraged by this success, the rebels planned to defeat the government over the procedure for handling the trade union bill in the Commons. When it became evident that the government whips simply could not undertake to ensure success for the government over the crucial procedural vote, Mr. Wilson and Mrs. Castle were obliged to come to a face-saving agreement with the Trade Union Congress and withdraw their proposals. The government's authority was at an all-time nadir.

In the light of this record, it is perhaps surprising that Labour came as close to winning the 1970 election as it did and that Mr. Wilson had recovered most of his personal authority by then. But the government's difficulties were evident in the essentially negative way in which Mr. Wilson conducted the campaign: 75 percent of his speech material consisted simply of attacks on the Opposition, and the remaining 25 percent rarely contained any word about Labour's future intentions.

LABOUR PARTY ORGANIZATION. Although Labour regained most of the electoral support it had lost in by-elections at the general election, Mr. Wilson could not repair the havoc reaped to the party's organization. Labour was crushed in the municipal elections in 1967–69. In 1964 local Labour parties had controlled twenty-four out of Britain's twenty-five largest city councils; between then and 1970 control was lost in every one of them. Thousands of Labour councillors lost their seats. Membership of the Labour party showed a drastic drop. The official figure for individual membership in 1969 was 680,656 (compared with 816,765 in 1965 and over 1 million at the peak in 1952); but as each local party, however small, is credited with one thousand members, the real figure is more like a third of a million. The extent of the real drop in membership can be seen in the decline of members in local parties claiming over one thousand members: in 1966, 255 such parties claimed a total of 380,920 members, but in 1969 only 111 of them claimed 175,218.

This drastic decline in the Labour party's grass-roots strength accompanied, of course, a similar decline in both the party's morale and in the health of the central organization. The fact that Labour's loss of votes between 1966 and 1970 was much less than its loss of party workers and members only goes to show how communication from the prime minister to voter via the television screen is much more important than communication from party leaders to voters via local candidates and local party workers. And in opposition, it will be much more difficult to rebuild Labour's strength from such a low organizational point.

THE LABOUR PARTY IN OPPOSITION. The Labour leadership's position was immediately helped by the Conservative government. Conservative measures on industrial relations, on South Africa, on taxation and many other matters together with rising unemployment in 1971, felt by Labour to have been the result of Conservative callousness, gave Labour in opposition a unity it had not felt for many years. So instead of dissension over where it had gone wrong, the Labour party has refound some spirit in pursuing what it regards as a particularly right-wing government. This had overlaid thought about the future, although some leading members of the party have published views about where the party should direct itself. But at the time of writing, it is difficult to discern any strategy, either of the leadership as a whole or of any major section of the party, concerning how it should seek to regain office, other than a simple "wait and hope."

THE DILEMMA OF THE LIBERAL PARTY

Since it has only six M.P.'s in the Commons, the Liberal party might be ignored in a description of the British party system. But in the 1970 election, the party put up 332 candidates—roughly one candidate in every other constituency—and polled 7.5% of the total vote. Thus, the effect of increased Liberal candidatures at the next election might well be to draw off more Labour votes than Conservative ones, or vice-versa—and thereby affect the major parties' prospects. Conversely, if Liberal candidatures decline, the former Liberal vote, which is by no means negligible in size (it is one-twelfth of the total) may go more to the Conservatives than to Labour, or vice-versa—again affecting their electoral prospects. The future of the Liberal party, therefore, is of considerable importance.

As we saw in our sketch of the history of the parties, the Liberal party, an offspring of the former Whig party, has a tradition as long as that of the Tory-Conservative party. Throughout the nineteenth century it was the natural alternative to the Conservatives, and government alternated between these two until 1915, when the wartime coalition was formed. From that date to this, the party has been in decline.

In the nineteenth century, the Liberal party

was the party of free trade, of individualism, of radical attack on the landed aristocracy. In the later years of the century, it took the nascent working-class movement into a sort of junior partnership, and in its great administration of 1906 became the champion of wide-sweeping social reforms and social welfare services. In foreign affairs, its attitude was less consistently expansionist than was that of the Conservatives; indeed, its left-wing was militantly anticolonial. It favored self-government (home rule) for the constituent nations of the United Kingdom, notably for Ireland; and it was over home rule for Ireland that the Liberal party split in 1886. In 1912–14, it embarked on a ferocious battle with the Conservatives that might have led to civil war in Ireland.

The Liberal party has stuck to its principles down to the present, but has adapted them to changed circumstances. It sees the Labour party as preaching an obsolete doctrine, and thinks Labour is too closely tied to the trade unions to be capable of independence. It sees the Conservatives as a reactionary party, with strong associations with big business.

The Liberal party favors free trade and is committed to entering the European Common Market. It is hostile to all forms of monopoly or price fixing; it does not except the restrictive practices and privileged legal position of the trade unions. But it also puts forward a quite distinctive policy of "copartnership" between capital and labor in industry. It stresses individualism more unrestrainedly than do the Conservatives. In the economic order it opposes nationalization and public control of private enterprises, and in the political order it champions civil liberties. It supports the welfare state, although with reservations about present methods of administering it, and is particularly keen on extending educational opportunities, which it believes are the guarantee of social mobility. It opposed colonialism and opposes racism. For instance, it is bitterly opposed to the Smith regime in Rhodesia. On defense, the Liberal party many years ago took the view that Britain could not and should not compete in the nuclear race with the United States and the USSR. It recommended that Britain scrap its own H-bombs, rely on American nuclear support or on a common NATO deterrent, and concentrate on developing its conventional arms as part of the Western alliance.

Many of the Liberal party's views once regarded as extremist have later become fashionable. When the Liberals pressed for free trade in 1945, they were considered completely out-of-date. Not so today. The Liberals were the first party to advocate British entry into the European Common Market. The Liberal opposition to the British H-bomb was very unpopular when first announced; today, a number of responsible military thinkers concur with this policy.

However, after the 1951 election, when the Liberal party polled a pitiful 2.5% and went on to lose more votes still in the rare by-elections it was able to fight, it looked as if the party was going to dwindle away. Ten years later Liberalism had experienced a remarkable electoral revival. At their peak in early 1962, Liberals were polling nearly a third of the votes cast in municipal elections and in parliamentary by-elections, and momentarily appeared to be making a breakthrough back to major-party status. Soon afterward half of this support melted away, but left the party with electoral support of from one in six to one in ten of the votes cast in the seats it fights; a handful of M.P.'s who obstinately cling to their seats; and a rather larger foothold in local government. In Mr. Jo Grimond, its leader from 1956 to 1967, it has one of the most respected of British political leaders, and the party's role as a promoter of new ideas in British politics is widely acknowledged.

But the dilemma for the Liberal party is that few of its members want to go on being in a permanently small party, permanently out of office. Mr. Grimond set it the target of replacing the Labour party as the radical party in British politics, but the 1964 Labour victory killed the expectation that the Labour party would conveniently decline. Since an alliance with either major party would split the Liberals down the middle, it is difficult to discern now any role for the Liberal party in British government. But it has played a useful role in gathering support from sources disaffected with the politics of the two main parties. In the 1960s its sources of new recruits have included the new suburban middle classes, neglected rural regions on the fringe of Great Britain, youthful direct-action protesters, and the decaying slum centers of large cities. Its ability to attract such diverse recruits has helped to keep some of them in the mainstream of conventional British politics and has helped to keep alive Liberal hopes of going on to greater things.

ELECTIONS

The object of political parties is to win elections, and we must now discuss the election procedure in Britain that decides which party will govern the country. The Parliament Act of 1911 limits the life of a Parliament to five years. A prime minister, however, for a number of reasons sometimes calls an election before the time limit expires. He may seek a mandate from the electorate to make some radical change in the program on which his party was originally elected; perhaps he has just succeeded to the office and wishes to win an election in his own name; or he may judge that he can improve his party's position in the House of Commons through a new election.

Parliament can only be dissolved by the queen, and only on the request of the prime minister. It is a disputed point whether the queen has the constitutional right to refuse the request. In practice in this century, no prime minister has ever been refused a dissolution.

To vote, in Britain, one must be 18 or over, be a British subject or a citizen of the Republic of Ireland (a curious, but deliberate anomaly of the UK's laws), and have one's name inscribed in the voting register. Excluded from the franchise are aliens, peers, lunatics (unless they have lucid intervals), felons, and persons convicted of past election offenses. The register (voting lists) is made up once a year. A form is sent to every house in the nation by the returning officer (usually the town clerk), and householders must state the eligible persons living at the residence. After the rolls are compiled by the returning officer, an announcement appears that the register is being prepared, and all are invited to check to see if their names are on it.

Elections in Britain are short affairs com-

pared with those in the United States. The first step in the procedure is an announcement by the prime minister that on a certain date—usually in about ten days' time—the queen will dissolve Parliament. As soon as she has done so, a royal proclamation is published, summoning a new Parliament. The elections, by law, must be held within three weeks of the proclamation. Thus from the time of the prime minister's announcement to the election itself, only about four-and-a-half weeks elapse.

Writs are issued to all the constituencies, commanding them to return a representative to Parliament. The very next day, the local returning officer (the town or county clerk) must put up an announcement that there is to be an election; and within eight days of the summons to the new Parliament, the nominations of candidates must be complete. Parliamentary candidates require nomination by two voters, and support by another eight. Also, the candidate must put down a deposit of £150. This provision, dating from the 1918 election, was introduced to discourage freak and frivolous candidates. Candidates get their deposit back if they poll more than one-eighth of the total votes cast; otherwise, it goes to the state to help pay the election expenses.

Nine days after the last day for nominations, the polling takes place, from 7 A.M. to 10 P.M., usually on a Thursday. About a week before the poll, the voter will have received a "poll card," which bears the voter's "number" assigned by the electoral register. It also tells him where he should vote. Until 1970 only the names of the candidates appeared on the ballot, but the law was changed so that each candidate may include a political description of not more than six words. The previous absence of party labels meant that much party effort had to be spent during the election to connect the candidate with his party, through posters and signs such as "Berrington—Conservative," or "Blondel—Labour." At 10 P.M. the ballot boxes are sealed. The votes are counted at one central point, in the presence of the candidates and party officials. By about midnight, unless an election is very close (as it was in 1964), one usually knows how the election has gone.

The expenditure by candidates and by parties within the constituencies is limited by law. In 1970 the total reported expenditure was $3,342,700, or $1,826 per candidate, or 9¢ per elector. Conservative candidates spent the most ($2,278 per candidate), followed by Labour ($1,987), Scottish Nationalist ($1,546), Welsh Nationalist ($1,443), Liberal ($1,260), and Communist ($646); the average for all candidates represented 63 percent of the permitted maximum, though this rose to 79 percent for Conservative and 68 percent for Labour candidates.

This, it must be repeated, simply accounts for the *candidates'* campaign expenditures. In addition, the arrangements cost the state something—in 1964, £1,850,000. Furthermore, no legal limit is imposed on preelection expenditures, and in 1959 and 1964 these reached considerable heights. In 1959, the Conservative party spent an estimated $1,310,000 on preelection advertising, against a mere $288,000 by the Labour party. Spending was even more lavish in 1963–64 when the Conservative party spent an estimated $2,778,000, and this time the Labour party raised its own spending to $879,-000. The steel companies also advertised: the total cost is estimated at $5,309,000. In 1966, with an election coming so soon after the previous one, the amounts spent by the parties were far less.

The Electoral System

Each constituency elects one M.P. (and is thus known as a single-member constituency). Voters cast one ballot only. The candidate with the most votes wins, which means that in a field of more than two candidates, the winner might have captured less than half the total vote. This system usually produces a discrepancy between the proportion of votes cast for a party in the country and the proportion of seats it wins in the House of Commons.

The British electoral system has two important consequences for the parties: it strengthens the predominant two parties against smaller parties, and it keeps the parties internally united. The weakest of the three main parties could poll up to one-third of the national vote and still run third to the other two parties in

all the constituencies. Once a party tends to fall to third place, the electors desert it to vote for one of the two predominant parties, rather than "waste their vote" on a candidate who appears to stand no chance of success. This reduces the weak party's vote still further and drives even more of its supporters to vote for one of the two major parties. In this way, a new party finds it hard to challenge the old established ones, and weak parties become weaker and are eventually "squeezed out."

Only in special circumstances have third parties been able to maintain themselves in Britain. If its vote is heavily concentrated in certain constituencies, it can win seats there. In the nineteenth and early twentieth centuries, the Irish Nationalist party had a very small proportion of the total vote, but it was almost entirely concentrated in Ireland, where it was, therefore, able to win most of the seats. (Too, a third party may make electoral arrangements with one of the two major parties. It was thus in 1906, when the newly founded Labour party concluded agreements with the Liberals, by which the Liberals supported the Labour candidates in certain constituencies and Labour did the same for the Liberals in others, so that the anti-Conservative vote would not be split.) But where a weak third party like that of the Liberals stands aloof from the other major parties and its vote is evenly distributed over the whole country, it will have to poll about one-third of the vote to win a sizable number of seats. The Liberal party won 7½% of the vote in the 1970 election, but won only 1% of the seats. Thus, again, the electoral system confirms the advantage held by the two major parties. As a result, neither the Conservatives nor the Labour party favors proportional representation, which is strongly advocated by the Liberals.

The electoral system also unifies the parties because it imposes a heavy electoral handicap on parties that break up. This can be seen from a simple example. Suppose a constituency has split its vote 60% Labour and 40% Conservative. If the Labour party divided into two roughly equal factions, the result of the next election might well be: European Labour 30%, Non-European Labour 30%, Conservative 40%. Since the Conservative candidate comes at the top of the poll, he would gain the seat from Labour. Parties are deeply conscious of the need to contest the elections as one single body. In the past, the parties that have split—the Conservatives in 1846, the Liberals in 1886, and the Labour party in 1931—have always lost at the ensuing election.

"Swing"

The lack of proportion between the seats won and the votes cast does not mean that the results of an election are unpredictable. On election night in 1966 an electronic computer was able to say, on the basis of the first hour's results, that the Labour majority would be about 100, indicating that there must be some kind of mathematical relationship between votes cast and seats won in the House of Commons. This brings us to the phenomenon known as "swing."

If in 1966, say, the votes in a constituency had been divided 51% Conservative and 49% Labour, but in 1970 changed to Conservative 52%, Labour 48%, we would say there had been a "swing" of 1%. The result is *as if* 1% of the voters had transferred their allegiance from Labour to Conservative. In a normal constituency (which has between 50,000 and 60,000 voters), given the normal turnout of about 80% of the electorate, a 1% swing represents about 500 votes, which we subtract from the Labour candidate and add to the Conservative candidate.

Projected onto the national stage, a small-percentage swing will shift a disproportionate number of seats in the House of Commons from one party to the other: roughly, for every 1% of swing nationally, about sixteen seats will change hands, making twice that difference— i.e., thirty-two—to the majority. In the 1966 election, for instance, a swing of a mere 0.1% would have increased the Labour lead over the Conservatives from twelve seats to twenty; a full 1% swing would have increased it to fifty-eight. There was actually a 3.5% swing in Labour's favor, giving it a lead of 110 seats over the Conservatives. But if there had been a swing of only 0.4% against Labour, the Conservatives

would have led Labour by four seats in the House; and with a swing of 1% it would have led by twenty-two seats, and, assuming that the Liberals had retained all their previous seats, this would have given it a tiny but manageable majority. Clearly then, any government is based on a knife-edge of popular support.

The Election Campaign

The parties employ three main techniques to increase their mass support: political gatherings, propaganda campaigns, and (at elections) drives to get out the vote. Such mobilization and propaganda campaigns go on all the time, for the parties must keep alert between elections. All this effort is for one purpose: to get out the vote and see that it is for the "proper" candidate. To this end, both parties utilize their complete organizations. The constituencies are the front-line groups. Behind them stand regional organizations—the country is divided into regions, each managed by regional party organizers, and each central headquarters has a staff ready to give financial and legal assistance and political advice to the constituency parties. There are never as many professionals on hand as either party would like, although the Conservative party has more full-time workers than does the Labour party.

Table 4-5 shows party staffs as they were in 1963. The number of Labour party election agents declined to 141 in 1970, the Conservatives to 386, and the Liberals to 18. Evidence from the public opinion polls shows that in 1970 more voters recalled being visited by a Conservative canvasser; in 1964 and 1966 there was not much to choose between the attention voters received from the two parties in this respect.

Voting Behavior

Most voting is habitual. In 1959 a *Daily Telegraph* poll asked: "What did you vote last time?" and "Do you intend to vote the same way again?" It found that 92% of prospective Conservative voters and 91% of prospective

TABLE 4-5. *Party Staffs by Function, 1963*

	Conservative (England and Wales only)	*Labour (Britain)*	*Liberal (England and Wales only)*
General headquarters	39	12	5
Agents:			
National and headquarters	9	7	3
Regional	60	38	10
Constituency	520	208	64
Research	25	12	4
Publicity	24	9	3
Totals	677	286	89

SOURCE: Richard Rose, *Politics in England* (Boston: Little, Brown, 1964), p. 147.

Labour voters had voted that same way in the last election. A similar result appears from a reply to the Gallup Poll in 1964. Of those Conservatives who *had* voted in the past, the proportion about to vote Conservative again was 87%, and among the Labour again was 88%. However, 12% of the prospective Conservative voters and 15% of the Labour ones had never before cast a ballot in favor of their prospective party—and the way such "new" voters vote often determines the outcome of an election. For the swing from one party to the other may be caused by former Conservatives voting Labour, or vice-versa; by more voters abstaining from voting in one party than in the other, and thus giving the *illusion* that voters have switched their allegiance from one party to the other; by voters who could have voted before but did not; and by those who were too young to vote before. (Or, by any combination of these.)

In 1959 the swing to the Conservatives could largely be acounted for by many Labour supporters neglecting to vote, while Conservative supporters came to the polls. In 1964, 1966, and 1970, although abstention was on the increase at each election, it does not seem to have affected the swing since both parties were losing voters at about the same rate. However, detailed research on the 1959–64 swing to Labour has shown that a significant proportion was caused by the greater loss to the Conservatives of their more elderly voters dying. If the same factor was operating between 1966 and 1970, then the swing of 4.7% to Conservatives in 1970 understates the conversion of ex-Labour voters.

In Britain "the executive" is *not* a separate organ of the power structure set apart from and over against "the legislature." Instead, the *top echelon* of the British executive—that is to say, the part which corresponds to the American president and his cabinet—is itself a group of parliamentarians, mostly members of the Commons, who command a solid and permanent majority in that House. A general election is a contest between two major teams of Labour and Conservative candidates for the purpose of commanding the House of Commons, on the implied condition that when elected, the winners will support and sustain a government, selected by their party leader from among themselves, for the duration of the Parliament. Fortunately (for their party, at least), once elected as M.P.'s, this is precisely what the majority do; and because they do, no government so formed ever loses a vote in the Commons, except by some temporary mismanagement (which it always can, and usually will, reverse). For the vote only *registers* policy; policy is *made* elsewhere, *before* the voting takes place—in the ministries, where the ministers negotiate arrangements with outside interests, and "upstairs," in the committee rooms of the House of Commons, where they argue with their own party supporters.

Opening a Commons debate on its own procedure, one leader of the House (the minister charged by the prime minister with the overseeing of Parliamentary business)—Mr. Richard Crossman—gave this view of the relationship between government and Parliament:

Procedurally we still behave as though we were a sovereign body which really shared with the Government in the initiation of legislation, and which exercised a real control not only of finance but of the administration of the Departments. But today not only the House of Lords has been shorn of most of its authority. The House of Commons, too, has surrendered most of its effective powers to the Executive and has become in the main the passive forum in which the struggle is fought out between the modern usurpers of parliamentary power, the great political machines.

In this transformation of the parliamentary scene the House of Commons has largely lost the three

FIVE

government and Parliament

functions for which its procedures were evolved and to which they are relevant: the making of Ministries, initiation of legislation shared with the Cabinet, and the watchdog control of finance and administration.

. . . I know that there are some of my honourable friends who dream of a time when the secret negotiations of the Government with outside interests, which precede all modern legislation, and the secret decisions in the Committee Room upstairs, which largely determine party attitudes, will be rendered insignificant because the House of Commons will once again become sovereign and make decisions for itself. I think they are crying for the moon. . . .

Today, for example, it must be the electorate, not the Commons, who normally make and unmake Governments. It must be the Cabinet that runs the Executive and initiates and controls legislation, and it must be the party machines that manage most of our business, through the usual channels, as well as organizing what was once a congeries of independent backbenchers into two disciplined political parties. . . .[1]

For these reasons and more, a discussion of the prime minister and his cabinet must precede the consideration of Parliament.

THE CABINET

Composition

Following the result of the general election, the queen appoints the leader of the majority party as her prime minister, and he then selects (for her formal approval) the remainder of the ministers. Altogether, this sizable group is known as "the government" or "the ministry" or even "the administration." Then a small group, usually numbering from sixteen to twenty-three and including the prime minister himself, are appointed by him to an inner, policy-directing body—the *cabinet*, the keystone of the governmental arch.

Most ministers head up departments, and nearly all are assisted by junior ministers also appointed by the prime minister. Most of the

departmental ministers also appoint "parliamentary private secretaries"—M.P.'s who volunteer to assist them in their parliamentary duties without compensation. In addition, the prime minister must also appoint a number of party whips to certain paid posts, which are nominal offices in either the Treasury or in Her Majesty's Household. All these together comprise "the government."

According to law, a minister need not be a member of *either* House of Parliament, but in practice the qualification is regarded as indispensable precisely because all ministers are answerable to Parliament. Therefore, when, as infrequently happens, the prime minister selects for a ministerial post a person who is not a parliamentarian, steps are immediately taken either to get him to run (or "stand") for a seat in the House of Commons which is "safe" (i.e., which he is sure to win), or to have him nominated for a peerage with the right to sit as a member of the House of Lords. But the overwhelming majority of ministerial appointments are already parliamentarians.

The bulk of the appointees sit as M.P.'s in the Commons, but for various reasons (some legal) a number must sit in the House of Lords. The number of these "ministerialists" (those holding office and expected to conform to the Cabinet's policy by voice and vote) is on the increase, and nowadays is very large (Table 5-1).

To the total of eighty-eight in 1970 must be added some forty unpaid whips and parliamentary private secretaries (P.P.S.'s): so that the number of M.P.'s who were "ministerialists" was some 110—that is to say, one out of every three of the government members in the House! Nevertheless, the previous, 1966 government was much larger—about two out of every five government members of the House of Commons were ministerialists. Mr. Heath, on taking office in 1970, made a serious effort to cut back the growth in the size of governments, as Table 5-1 shows.

The essential difference between the cabinet ministers and those not in the cabinet lies in the fact that the former have the right (possibly the obligation?) to attend every cabinet meeting and to receive in full all the memoranda and minutes circulated by the cabinet secre-

[1] *Parliamentary Debates,* Commons, vol. 738, no. 117, cols. 479–80.

TABLE 5-1. *Growth in Size of British Governments, 1900–70*

	1900	1910	1920	1960	1966	1970
Cabinet Ministers	9	19	19	19	23	17
Noncabinet Ministers	10	7	15	20	31	26
Junior Ministers	31	36	46	44	63	46
Total	50	62	80	83	117	89
No. of M.P.'s in Government	33	43	58	65	99	71
No. of Peers in Government	27	19	22	18	18	18

cabinet ranking departments had become two by 1968. At the same time, the expansion of government responsibilities in economic and social fields was reflected in the growth of the number and size of the relevant departments up to 1960. Since then, as Table 5-2 shows, there has been a considerable reorganization and streamlining of departmental responsibilities.

Function

Each minister is individually responsible to Parliament for the conduct of his duties, but the cabinet is *collectively* responsible to Parliament; it stands or falls as a corporate unity on matters of general policy. Formally, this corporate body is responsible for

1. the final determination of the policy to be submitted to Parliament;
2. the supreme control of the national executive in accordance with this policy, as modified by and consented to by Parliament; and
3. the continuous coordination and delimitation of the activities of the various departments.

But, in practice, much of this formal authority is exercised, outside the plenary meetings of the cabinet, by the prime minister and the ministers concerned, or by committees of the cabinet. To understand how and why this is so, it is first necessary to understand the way the cabinet is organized.

The cabinet is the *prime minister's* cabinet: he summons it, makes up its agenda, and presides over its meetings. Normally, there are two meetings a week, each lasting about two hours. What goes on inside them is kept secret.

As the supreme authority over policy and the machinery of government, the cabinet faces three major problems. First, how are twenty-odd ambitious and able men, constitutionally equals, most with a departmental view to press, to reach a collective decision? They must achieve this through discussion, yet how can they do it in the limited time available? Secondly, with the amount of cabinet work con-

tariat, while the noncabinet ministers are summoned to attend cabinet meetings only when business affecting them is being transacted. Mention of the cabinet as an institution almost never appears in British constitutional law, being recognized indirectly only in the Ministers of the Crown Act of 1937 (an act which is concerned principally with the regulation of ministerial salaries).

In forming his cabinet, his intimate team, the prime minister must be guided by four considerations: (1) the members' personal compatability with himself and possibly with one another; (2) the need to satisfy the various and often conflicting wings of his party (in Labour cabinets, for instance, it is always necessary to balance the trade unionists against the non–trade unionists, and to give at least one post to the Co-operators); (3) the need to have three or four cabinet ministers in the House of Lords to look after government business there; and (4) the special qualifications required by certain specific departments.

The composition of the cabinet in terms of government departments has changed considerably over the years. In 1930 almost half of the departments whose ministerial heads sat in the cabinet were concerned with overseas affairs or defense policy. With the shrinkage of Britain's worldwide responsibilities and the integration of her defense services, these seven

TABLE 5-2. *British Government Departments, 1930–70*

1930	1960	1970
FOREIGN AFFAIRS DOMINIONS INDIA COLONIES	FOREIGN AFFAIRS COMMONWEALTH RELATIONS COLONIES	FOREIGN & COMMONWEALTH AFFAIRS
	DEFENCE	DEFENCE
WAR (ARMY) AIR ADMIRALTY	War Air Admiralty	
EXCHEQUER (FINANCE) HOME AFFAIRS SCOTLAND	EXCHEQUER HOME AFFAIRS SCOTLAND	EXCHEQUER HOME AFFAIRS SCOTLAND WALES
TRADE	TRADE AVIATION POWER	TRADE & INDUSTRY

AGRICULTURE &
  FISHERIES
	AGRICULTURE, FISHERIES,
	  & FOOD
		AGRICULTURE, FISHERIES,
		  & FOOD

EDUCATION	EDUCATION	EDUCATION & SCIENCE
LABOUR	LABOUR & NATIONAL-SERVICE	EMPLOYMENT
WORKS Transport	Works TRANSPORT HOUSING & LOCAL-GOVERNMENT	ENVIRONMENT
HEALTH Pensions	HEALTH Pensions & National Insurance	SOCIAL SERVICES
Post Office	Post Office	Posts & Telecommunications

NOTE: Capital letters indicate a department whose head sat in the cabinet.

tinually multiplying, how can the members of the cabinet address themselves to all the issues they must consider? Thirdly, how are all these men, meeting but twice a week for two-hour meetings, to maintain consistency between one meeting and another in what they decide?

These three problems have been attacked by three institutions:

1. the cabinet secretariat, which acts as a collective memory

2. the agenda, which sifts out the less important matters

3. the committee system, which weeds out the less crucial matters, too, but also reduces the time needed for the cabinet's collective discussions

Institutions

THE SECRETARIAT. Established under the stress of wartime conditions in 1916, the cabinet secretariat has become increasingly useful as a recording agency. It takes the minutes of all cabinet discussions and cabinet committee meetings and circulates them to the cabinet members, and sends appropriate daily extracts to the noncabinet ministers. Thus, each member of the government is acquainted with the work of the entire membership, and is notified of any action for which he is responsible. Since all these records are meticulously indexed, the secretariat serves as the memory of the cabinet, and thereby provides for its self-consistency.

THE AGENDA. Much of the cabinet business, like that of any well-run committee, is based on the advance circulation of papers. Before a department can put an item on the agenda, for example, it must first send a draft paper around to all interested departments for their comments.

THE COMMITTEES. The cabinet agenda is relatively formal, for most of the preliminary work will already have been done by committees. The development of a committee system serviced by a secretariat is one of the most important changes in cabinet procedure in the last quarter-century. There are two kinds of committees: the temporary ad hoc ones that study particular problems, and the standing committees. We know little of these committees, because the cabinet is a secret body, with no "organization chart." Its members take the privy councillors' oath of secrecy on all official matters. This secrecy is a necessary condition for their collective responsibility for policy, since no rumors—let alone information—of any differences of opinion must leak out.

Consequently, all we know of these committees is derived from the memoirs and analyses of ex-ministers—such as P. Gordon-Walker's *The Cabinet* (the most revealing book on the subject)—which are inevitably out-of-date, and

from incidental disclosures of the work being done by the various committees. It is impossible to name or number the ad hoc committees. Between the world wars there were perhaps as many as twenty at any one time, and between 1945 and 1950 as many as thirty, each comprising only three or four ministers. But if the definition of "cabinet committee" is taken to be "all committees of ministers serviced by the cabinet secretariat," then today there are as many as one hundred, and they ramify out and down into the various departments. The standing cabinet committees known to exist today are the *Future Legislation Committee,* which, as will be seen, decides the priorities for government legislation; the *Legislation Committee,* which steers it through the current Parliamentary session; and the *Defence and External Affairs Committee,* which is chaired by the prime minister himself and has the minister of defence as its vice-chairman. This powerful and widely ramifying committee, with the assistance of the chiefs of staff, advises the minister of defence and the service ministers of each of the three branches of the armed services. In 1969 for a period, Mr. Wilson publicly announced the composition of an "inner cabinet," consisting of six or seven of the most senior ministers. But the experiment does not seem to have been a success, for he abandoned it in due course. Nevertheless, in his cabinet the prime minister so overshadows his colleagues that some observers have talked of "prime ministerial" government (or even "presidential" government) as having superseded "cabinet government."

Cabinet and Prime Minister

THE PREEMINENCE OF THE PRIME MINISTER. Whereas a minister has only one role—that of being a minister—the prime minister has *four. First,* he is the leader and representative of the nation. The general election has become a gladiatorial combat between two party leaders: the two teams of candidates for whom the electorate cast their votes are like two electoral colleges whose votes are committed in advance to making their leader the prime minister. Once in office, the prime minister uses the mass media to appeal directly to the nation. Furthermore, the opinion polls nowadays provide a kind of monthly plebiscite on his popularity.

Secondly, he is a leader of a national party, which means that he disposes of a network of professional politicians at the headquarters, regional, and constituency levels to publicize and disseminate his views, as well as the local activists who come to hear them at party rallies. Additionally, he is (ideally, at any rate) the master strategist and tactician of his party: he chooses the date of the election and has the decisive voice in the party's manifesto plans, the tactics of the campaign.

Thirdly, he is the leader of the parliamentary party. This is his power base. Unlike the American president, a British prime minister has no fixed tenure guaranteed by the constitution; instead, his tenure depends on the House of Commons—that is to say, on retaining his party majority there. In principle, if dissatisfied with him, it can even depose him. However, in practice the majority is fairly well limited because he wields very real and impressive powers over it. He hires and he fires, and, as has been seen, about 100 posts are involved with him. And he recommends the faithful for honors and awards. As to party policy, even when he is not its architect (though often he is), in the last resort he is the manager and conciliator of the often restive factions in the rank and file. In like manner he is the ultimate judge as to whether a recalcitrant member shall be denied membership in the parliamentary party—a decision which would probably cause the rebel to lose his seat at the next general election.

Fourthly, he makes and breaks a cabinet; as we have said, he hires and fires its members.

THE PRIME MINISTER AND CABINET PROCEDURES. One aspect of the prodigious power that the prime minister can wield over his handpicked cabinet was dramatically illustrated in July 1962, when Mr. Macmillan removed seven of his colleagues from the cabinet—a third of its numbers—in one swoop. He had hired them, and he fired them. (Indeed, the cabinet is so much the prime minister's cabinet that if he resigns, all ministers must also resign.)

As the chairman of the cabinet, the prime minister convenes it and settles its agenda, not only deciding what is to be included but, more importantly, what is to be left out. He also arranges the order of business—an important matter, since the twice-weekly meeting lasts only two hours. He calls on ministers to speak, decides at what point discussion shall cease, sums up the sense of the meeting (no formal votes are taken in cabinet), and defines the decision for inclusion in the minutes. Most of the matters are formal: reports from the various committees and subcommittees which he has established in order to have the interested ministers reach preliminary agreement. The prime minister nominates the members of these committees and presides over the key ones.

For a long time, prime ministers have exercised direct control over foreign affairs. All prime ministers from 1937 (when Neville Chamberlain was prime minister) to the present day have tended to overshadow their foreign secretaries, representing the country in summit conferences and receiving important foreign heads of state.

Nor is this all. The cabinet secretariat, which services the cabinet meetings and those of its committees, and which prepares the agenda for the prime minister to approve, is the prime minister's *own* secretariat. The prime minister, through the cabinet secretariat, therefore knows —or can know—all that is going on in all the committees at any point of time, and intervenes if he wants to. This aside, he is constantly engaged in person-to-person discussion with any minister who wishes to have a matter put on the agenda, or who finds himself in some perplexity.

In recent years prime ministers have expanded the cabinet office, and so also the power they can exercise through their personal control of it. Mr. Wilson brought in a number of outside advisors. Mr. Heath set up a high-powered unit with the "task of evaluating as objectively as possible the alternative policy options and priorities" open to the government. With the reforms of the civil service bringing the permanent head of the civil service more closely under direct prime ministerial control, the prime minister has now acquired additional tools with which to control the determination and coordination of government policy.

The cabinet, we may sum up, is the supreme leader and coordinator of the entire government machine. But today this body itself is coordinated, led, and personified by the prime minister, partly through the multiplicity of the political roles he nowadays assumes, and partly through the mechanism of the cabinet secretariat, which gives him a synoptic view of the entire field of developing departmental policies.

Cabinet and Commons

The cabinet, the powerhouse of the entire British constitutional system, derives its unique authority from the fact that its members combine in themselves three kinds of status. Like the American cabinet, the British cabinet constitutes the executive branch of the government because its members are ministers—that is, the heads of governmental departments. But, unlike the American cabinet, it is also the steering committee of the legislature; virtually all its members are M.P.'s. Finally—again, unlike the American cabinet—it is a committee of the majority party, since it is composed for the most part of the trusted and tried party chiefs. The executive is thus a committee of the legislature and acts by and with its consent; it gains such consent precisely because it consists of the leaders of the party that controls the House of Commons. Thus the peculiarly dominating role of the cabinet is an outcome of its party's solidarity. As long as the cabinet and its party hang together, they will never hang separately.

Unlike the American cabinet, the British cabinet is no mere aggregation of ministers. It is a corporate unity. Each minister is personally responsible to the Commons for the day-by-day administration of his duties, and it is the minister who stands up in the House of Commons to explain, justify, and answer awkward questions about the way he has carried out these duties. In practice, of course, nearly all the things done in his name are performed by civil servants; but he, not they, must take the responsibility for acts of omission or commission carried out in his name. If he fails to give a

convincing explanation, M.P.'s may demand his resignation. Most commonly, the cabinet regards an attack on a minister as directed against itself, and expects its party to support it. But occasionally ministers *are* forced to resign—when their fault is so grave that even their own backbenchers feel too uneasy to support them. In 1954, for instance, a Conservative minister of agriculture, Sir Thomas Dugdale, was compelled to resign because he had failed to control the activities of some of his civil servants.

But although each minister is personally responsible to Parliament for the good conduct of his department, on matters of *general policy* all members of the cabinet (and indeed of the whole ministerial group, i.e., "the government") take equal responsibility and stand or fall together. Every member of the cabinet is deemed to have acquiesced in the policy of his colleagues. If he disagrees with his colleagues, his proper course is to resign. He is then entitled, by convention, to make a speech to Parliament, explaining his reasons for resignation. Lord Salisbury, a most influential Conservative peer, resigned from Mr. Macmillan's first cabinet because he disagreed with its policy of independence for Cyprus. In 1968 Lord Longford resigned from Mr. Wilson's cabinet because he could not accept the decision to postpone the raising of the school-leaving age. Both these ministers had no departmental responsibility for the decisions concerned; but as they were unwilling to stand by the decision in public, and more especially as leading government spokesmen in the House of Lords, they felt obliged to resign.

The cabinet and the cabinet alone, then, is answerable to Parliament, and beyond it to the country for all acts of policy during its term of office. How does it maintain its position in the House of Commons? It does so only as it retains the support of a united party. How then does it retain this support? Most of the common explanations are misleading. For instance, it is said that the cabinet can expel rebel M.P.'s from the parliamentary party. This could be effective if the rebels were few in number. Movements of backbench protest numbering forty or more M.P.'s—such as are not uncommon—could not be disciplined in this way without breaking the party up. In any case, rebel M.P.'s are not frequently disciplined.

It is also argued that since the prime minister can get the queen to dissolve Parliament and plunge his party into a general election, this makes his backbenchers more compliant, since they do not care to face more election campaigns than are necessary. But for a prime minister to seek a general election at a time when his party was divided would be to court disaster, for, as we have seen, the electoral system works heavily against a disunited party.

In practice, the cabinet controls its supporters for four main reasons:

1. The government as a whole (including the junior ministers) includes almost all of the party leadership. Its senior members are particularly influential party men. And, additionally, it forms a high proportion of the total government seats in the Commons.

2. A fair proportion of the backbenchers strive manfully to become ministers, even junior ones; they do not wantonly incur the displeasure of the prime minister.

3. There is constant consultation between the government and its supporters, and in the normal way both make concessions to one another. The Conservatives practice such consultation more than the Labour party, however, and, as has been seen, in 1967–69 the Labour ministers seriously lost touch with their backbenchers.

4. On many matters a majority of the backbenchers are content to let ministers run things their own way; for in the British political system, the cabinet and its party supporters are elected simultaneously, on the same platform, and believe in the same principles. The party's successes at the next election are entirely bound up with the successes of its cabinet.

THE HOUSE OF COMMONS

Parliament consists of the Crown and the House of Lords, as well as of the House of Commons, but the first two components can be set aside for the present for these reasons: first,

while it is true that all legislation must receive the assent of the sovereign, the last time she vetoed a bill was in 1707, and it is generally agreed that this particular prerogative is obsolete. Secondly, as far as the House of Lords is concerned, this chamber can only impose a month's delay on money bills sent up to it from the Commons, can merely delay for the period of one year other kinds of bills sent to it from the lower house, and very rarely uses this power —for reasons discussed later. Its primary function today is to revise the details of bills from the House of Commons.

Composition, Basic Organization, and Primary Function

At present the House of Commons consists of 635 elected members of Parliament—the familiar M.P.'s. Some citizens are disqualified from sitting as members: they include clergy of certain denominations (namely, those of the Church of England, the Church of Scotland, and the Church of Ireland, and priests of the Roman Catholic church), persons under 21, lunatics, bankrupts, and felons. Peers also are excluded: but the Peerage Act of 1963 permits a peer to renounce his peerage and sit, if duly elected, as an M.P.[2] Except when the Act was first passed

[2] British titles of nobility are highly confusing, even to the natives of the islands themselves. All that need be understood here is that knights and baronets, addressed as "Sir Samuel" or "Sir Edward", are *not* "Peers of the Realm" and do *not* sit in the House of Lords; they are eligible for election to the Commons. The higher nobility, whose ranks in ascending order are baron, viscount, earl, marquess, and duke are all Peers. But the Peers of Irish creation do not sit in the House of Lords though they *are* eligible for election to the Commons. English and Scottish Peers on the other hand all receive a writ of summons to the House of Lords. They may renounce their rank, and so become eligible for election to the Commons. Their rank descends to their heirs. At any time the Sovereign may create new Peers; today this is done on the nomination of the Prime Minister. In addition to these "hereditary" peers, there exists, since 1958 the category of life peers. These, created by the Sovereign on the nomination of the Prime Minister, sit in the House of Lords like the hereditary peers; but their rank is not passed on to their heirs; it dies with them. Peers would be addressed as either "Lord Finer," or—in full—by their rank, such as "Baron Finer of Islington," or (according to their degree) "The Earl of Islington."

(when the Earl of Home was thereby enabled to enter the House of Commons as Sir Alec Douglas-Home to take up the leadership of the Conservative party), this only allows a peer to take this option at the time he succeeds to the title; once he has accepted the title, a peer can never enter the Commons. Once duly elected and sworn in, the member remains a member for the term of the Parliament, though he can be expelled by the House itself, as occurred in 1947 and again in 1954. An M.P.'s membership cannot be revoked by any outside body, not even his constituency. The independence of the M.P. from outside pressures is protected by the hallowed "privileges" of the member, including freedom from arrest in civil actions (save bankruptcy), and freedom from proceedings or from harassment (described by the elastic term, "molestation") for speeches and activities carried out in Parliament in the course of his duties. M.P.'s are paid an annual salary of £3,250. After tax deduction, this is only a little more than twice the average wage in Britain.

The *primary function* of the House is to sustain a government; its secondary function is to criticize it. These two functions are reflected in its physical shape and its party organization. The chamber is a rectangular room with long, padded benches (not chairs or seats) on three of its sides, and the speaker's throne at the "top" end. On the benches to the speaker's right sit the majority party members, the front benches occupied by the ministers. The opposition party or parties sit on his left, with the leader of the Opposition (i.e., the leader of the largest of the of the opposition parties) and his "shadow cabinet" taking the front benches, eyeball-to-eyeball with the ministers. The term "backbencher" applies to those M.P.'s who do not hold any ministerial office; or any post as a spokesman on a particular topic for the *opposition* party. They occupy the benches behind the front ones which are reserved, on the government side, for the ministers, and on the opposition side for the principal spokesmen, i.e. members of the "shadow" cabinet. (The prime minister draws a salary of £14,000 of which £4,000 is tax-free; the leader of the Opposition draws a salary also —£4,500 per annum—for discharging his particular functions; both in addition receive

£1,250 annually for parliamentary expenses.)

The speaker is elected by all the M.P.'s from among their number at the beginning of the new session of Parliament and is customarily reelected thereafter until he expresses a wish to resign. Both sides make every effort to agree on a candidate, though this is not always successful; but once a speaker is elected he sheds all party ties and must preside with complete impartiality in his judgments, in accordance with the precedents of the "law and custom of Parliament." He never votes except to break a tie, in which case he must vote for the existing situation. His rulings may be challenged—but only by a formal motion put to the House, not from the floor; and such motions are very rare.

Standing orders, which can be modified from time to time by the government's majority power, allocate the great bulk of the time of the House to government business, and relatively little to the backbenchers—or "private members," as they are known. "Private members' time" includes the opportunities for introducing bills and motions for debate. The remainder subdivides broadly into the time when the government "has the floor" (i.e., for its legislation, and administrative orders), and the time put at the disposal of the opposition front bench for criticizing the government. The standing orders allow of various types of closure, but most of the closure arrangements are made, amicably, by the chief whips of either side. This is known as "the usual channels." If the Opposition feel cheated, they can obstruct; if the government feel thwarted, they can enforce a closure by their majority. Such upsets do occur, but are relatively rare: Government control and opposition opportunity for debate are mutually accepted objectives. Table 5-3 shows the broad allocation of time spent annually in the House before World War II and after (up to 1959).

How Important Is the House of Commons?

The power of the House is undercut by several factors: (1) It is not a law-initiating assembly. Backbenchers do indeed have opportunities to introduce legislation (known as "private mem-

TABLE 5-3. *Yearly Allocation of Time Spent by Commons Members*

	Prewar		Postwar	
	Days	Proportion	Days	Proportion
Private members	25	18%	29	18%
Opposition	34	23	41	26
Government	69	46	75	48
Remainder	21	13	13	8
Total	*149*		*158*	

The Role of the Opposition

All constitutional governments must somehow reconcile the rights of opposing interests with the necessity for the government to continue functioning. Some systems—the American system is one—seek to achieve this by dividing authority among a number of constitutionally equal and independent bodies; the decision makers are thus checked and balanced by *outside* organs. In contrast, the ultimately supreme power in the British system, the House of Commons, contains an *internal* check and balance, in the form of the opposition party, or "Opposition."

The notion of a neat pyramid by which the cabinet commands the Commons, the Commons the Parliament, and the Parliament the nation, is inadequate and misleading. It omits one of the major characteristics of the system: the integral status of the Opposition. The parliamentary opposition has five characteristics and five functions. Its *characteristics* are the following:

1. It is *organized*. It presents a united challenge to the government on all issues it chooses to contest. We have already noted its organization—its leadership, its nervous system (the whips), its intelligence system (the backbenchers' committees).

2. It is *permanent*. It does not band and disband but is a permanent corporation.

3. It is *representative*. It is the leader of a group of dedicated party followers throughout the country, with whom it is organically connected.

4. It is the *alternative*. If the government falls, the Opposition succeeds it. If the government is beaten in an election, the Opposition takes over. This possibility forces the Opposition to be more moderate in what it condemns and what it promises.

5. It is a *participant*. It helps the government shape the program of the House and participates in the decisions made in each session.

bers' bills"), but they are limited. Their bills do not usually deal with important matters, must not involve public taxation or expenditure, and, in any case, could be debated and enacted only if the government were favorable, or at least neutral. Moreover private members' time is normally confined to Fridays, when the House is thinly attended, since many members have left for their constituencies. Not infrequently, the House is then "counted out" for lack of a quorum of forty members. The government itself initiates all the major legislation, controls the timetable, and receives exactly the appropriations it demands. (2) The parties vote on predetermined lines, with almost no crossvoting, and, although occasionally there are abstentions, these almost never occur on a dangerous scale. If a government forces a vote of confidence, it is certain to get a majority vote. (3) Governments have tended to make all issues matters of confidence—i.e., they will resign on a defeat. Yet the outward show of a cabinet triumphing all along the line and never being overturned by a hostile vote of the Commons is deceptive. The mechanics of control are much more subtle. Cabinets avoid being overturned because they take steps to meet the mood of the House, which means taking into account first their own backbenchers, and secondly the Opposition.

The *functions* of the Opposition are

1. to participate in the deliberations of the House of Commons;

2. to oppose objectionable policies by its voice and vote;

3. to compel the government, by all acceptable methods, to modify its policy;

4. to create by its voice and vote a public revulsion against the government and public sympathy for itself, as the precondition for winning the next election (since, as we have already seen, a relatively small swing of votes in any election can mean the difference between victory and defeat, this is not as difficult as it sounds); and

5. to pose an alternative program. (Perhaps this is the most important of all the Opposition's functions. The mere fact that the Opposition makes promises to, say, the old-age pensioners or the farmers, advocates a particular view about the draft or the European Economic Community, forces the government party to counter or outbid such promises. Students who compare the manifestos of the two main parties will find a surprisingly large measure of agreement. The reason is that both parties are out to attract the votes of relatively uncommitted groups. A long time ago Benjamin Disraeli, before he became Conservative prime minister, talked of the Conservatives as "catching the Whigs bathing and running off with their clothes." He also characterized the conservatism of Sir Robert Peel as being "Tory men and Whig Measures." Both the major parties play this game of borrowing their opponent's most popular measures and adapting them to their own use. In the early 1950s, when R. A. Butler was the Conservative chancellor of the exchequer, the public could detect so little difference between his policies and those of his Labour predecessor, Hugh Gaitskell, that it coined the name "Mr. Butskell.")

The fact remains that the Opposition cannot expect to defeat the government in a floor vote and turn it out of office. The last time that an adverse vote overthrew a government which had a nominal majority in the House was in 1895. No Opposition would count on repeating that nowadays. The most it can hope for is to shame so many of the government's supporters into abstention that the government's stand is morally condemned in the eyes of the nation; and it may well have to wait till the next election to reap the fruits.

In crisis conditions, however, such massive abstention might produce the resignation of the government. The last time this happened was in 1940, when Prime Minister Neville Chamberlain's handling of the war had already provoked serious criticism from both sides of the House. When Hitler seized Norway and defeated the woefully equipped and badly handled British forces at the port of Narvik, unrest boiled over. At the close of a two-day debate, the House voted, giving Chamberlain a majority of eighty-one. Its full majority should have been over double that figure, but some sixty Conservatives abstained and over thirty voted against their government. Mr. Chamberlain thereupon resigned, and the king called on Winston Churchill to form a new cabinet—which became the wartime coalition cabinet.

Such a dramatic success for the Opposition could scarcely be expected in peacetime, for the Opposition can expect to do only three things. *First,* it can (and often does) wring amendments to legislation from the government; and on rare occasions these are substantial in number and importance. For instance, the Conservative Opposition fought the Finance Bill of 1965 for a total of 211 hours, introduced 680 amendments, and had the bill materially changed in certain important particulars. But successes on this scale are rare and can be attributed to the existence of a strong public opinion or outside pressures that induce the government to yield.

Next, the Opposition can expose the weaknesses or injustices of government policies, and sometimes get them modified or even cancelled. In early 1967 for instance, the secretary for education announced that tuition fees for overseas students studying in British universities were to be raised from £50 to £250. This aroused a storm of protest from the universities and was taken up by the Opposition, who pressed it to a debate. At the end, no less than thirty-five Labour M.P.'s abstained; and later, administrative action was taken to modify the policy.

Finally, the attacks of the Opposition can create a mood among the electorate. Its speeches bring many tears, but never turn a vote—though it *can* capture voters *outside* the House of Commons. It is to the electorate that its criticism is directed. For though the cabinet has power, the power is contingent: it faces a dedicated enemy which is armed with procedural privileges and commands an organized national following. And all the government says and does is staked on the hazard of the few votes—three or four in every hundred—that can turn it out.

The Role of the Government's Backbenchers

We have already seen (in Chap. 4) that both parliamentary parties organize themselves into committees. The influence of these on ministers is hard to measure because they hold private meetings, and often great care is taken to see that the content of their proceedings does not leak out. But the pressures they can generate are well documented. Professor H. H. Wilson's *Pressure Group,* for instance, tells how, in 1951–53, a small group of Conservative backbench advocates of commercial television were able to win substantial support in the parliamentary party, and finally to thrust their plans upon an initially hostile cabinet.[3]

Although Labour governments are more resistant to backbench pressures, in 1946, when Mr. Attlee was prime minister, the combination of seventy-two Labour M.P.'s voting against the government, with a similar number of abstentions, led the government to cut conscription from eighteen months to twelve. And in 1966, Mr. Wilson sensed that any deal with Rhodesia which appeared to be a sellout would arouse widespread resistance, and adjusted his

policy accordingly. And it is widely believed that his withdrawal of British approval of American bombing of Hanoi and Haiphong was due to the widespread feeling among his supporters. But even backbench influence is qualified. In the first place, as we have seen, the number of ministerialists is quite large compared with the number of backbenchers, and the appetite for office of the backbenchers also dampens their rebel ardor. Again, to rebel too far and too seriously might risk the overturn of the cabinet itself and destroy the party as a force, not only in the House but in the election as well, and most backbenchers are sufficiently partisan to feel that their own government could not possibly be worse than the Opposition, under any circumstances.

Finally, the backbenchers may be short-circuited by outside groups on legislation. As we pointed out when discussing pressure groups, the proposals brought to the House increasingly represent complicated compromises and package deals made between ministers and the outside interests. Even if the backbenchers had the information with which to base an attack on such deals, they could not alter any substantial part without damaging or perhaps destroying the government's policy.

The Legislative Cycle

In Britain, the *text* of a proposed law is called a *bill.* Only when such a text has been approved by both Houses of Parliament and received the (formal) Royal approval does it become law; and it is then known as an *Act* of Parliament. Whereas the U. S. Congress enacts between five hundred and one thousand bills into law every session, the British Parliament enacts only about one hundred. About forty are "private acts," which do not affect the general population or classes of the general population, and can be put aside until later. Of the remaining "public acts," averaging about sixty or seventy per session, about one-tenth are private members' acts. These, which usually concern minor matters, and are prohibited by the orders of the House from imposing any charge on the public revenue (for this always

[3] H. H. Wilson, *Pressure Groups* (London: Secke & Warburg, 1961).

demands a government resolution), are made on the initiative of the backbenchers, and very often on behalf of outside interests which supply drafting assistance. But 90 percent of the public general acts of Parliament, which averaged forty-nine acts per session between 1959 and today, consist of government bills, put forward by ministers. This is another and very striking indicator of the supreme characteristic of the British governmental system—the fusion of executive and legislature. The legislative cycle cannot be considered as starting on the floor of the House of Commons, or House of Lords, but way back in the offices of a ministry. And the same holds true, as will be seen, of financial legislation.

In legislating, the government is inspired by four considerations, either separately or in some combination: (1) the promises made to the electorate in its manifesto; (2) the desire of the civil servants to introduce or amend legislation, arising out of the performance of their duties; (3) the wishes of outside interest groups; and (4) sudden emergency. For instance, the Unilateral Declaration of Independence by Rhodesia, in 1965, demanded immediate legislation, and such was put to the Parliament, and enacted.

A bill will originate inside a department, as a result of policy discussions between the minister and his senior civil servants. Once it is clear that the policy will require legislation, a memorandum is prepared and sent to the cabinet secretariat, which in turn circulates it to all interested ministers, and always to the Treasury. Since this is routine, it is in the originating department's own interest to have cleared policy with these other ministries and the Treasury beforehand, and this is always done. Thereupon, the general policy is discussed by a cabinet committee, and then in the cabinet. In the normal course of events—i.e., barring some sudden emergency requiring legislation—this bill preparation by departments has become routinized, thanks to the cabinet secretariat.

A parliamentary session usually begins in October or November, and six weeks after it opens the cabinet office asks all the departments to send in lists of the bills they are likely to require in the next session (in twelve months' time) with estimates of how long and controversial they are likely to be, and a forecast of the date at which the department would be ready to give instructions to the counsel who draft the bills—assuming they had permission to go ahead. For this is the crux; parliamentary time is far too limited for the number of bills that departments would like to bring forward. Therefore, once the cabinet office has all its information, its next step is to forward this to one of the cabinet's standing committees, the *Future Legislation Committee,* which will always include the government's leader of the House of Commons and of the House of Lords, and the chief whip.

After the Christmas recess, the Future Legislation Committee examines the list and draws up a tentative short list of bills for discussion with the sponsoring ministers. It meets with them, and finally establishes a provisional list for the session to come, putting the bills in order of priority. This list is put to, and finalized by, the cabinet. Once a proposed bill has a place on such a list, the department may ask for the help of the Office of Parliamentary Counsel to draft the bill.

The moment the new session of Parliament opens, the care of this bill passes from the Future Legislation Committee to the Legislation Committee, whose meetings are attended by the lord chancellor, the leaders of the two Houses of Parliament, the law officers, the chief whip, and any of the ministers involved with the bill. This committee (which prepares the "Queen's Speech," a list of legislative proposals) meets weekly to look in detail at any draft bills submitted. Often these bills are amended, not once but many times, before they are approved. Not until the Legislation Committee gives the word may the minister present the bill to Parliament.

Technically, a bill may be initiated in either the House of Lords or the House of Commons (the cabinet's Legislation Committee decides which); in practice, only about one in five bills are introduced in the House of Lords, the rest in the Commons. At any rate, a bill must receive three readings in both Houses and, for a bill to be passed, both Houses must approve an identical text of it. It then goes forward to receive royal assent, an essential formality. But, it must be repeated, in the case of bills certified by the speaker of the House of Commons to be money bills, the approval of the House of Lords is not required.

Two points must be realized in order to understand the nature of the parliamentary discussion of a bill. First, in sharp contrast to the practice in the United States, the bill receives its floor vote in the Commons *before* going on to a committee stage. Second, the role and operation of these committees is far different from those in the United States and in France.

The first step for a bill in the Commons is taken when the bill is about to receive a "first reading." This is usually just a formality, for only the title of the bill is read by the clerk of the House, from a printed sheet called a "dummy bill," which is then laid on the desk of the House. Publication follows soon after. Usually some two or three weeks elapse between the first reading and the "second reading," allowing time for the Opposition to decide on its line of attack, and for outside interests to make their views known.

The second reading ordinarily lasts a day or two (an unusually long three days will be allocated for very important bills like the Transport Bill of 1946–47), and it is at this time that the general principles of the bill are debated between the government ministers who are in charge of the bill and the opposition "shadow ministers" who are keeping tabs on, or "marking," them. The ministers open the debate; then the backbenchers follow, often speaking to a nearly empty House. As the evening wears on, the other ministers reappear and the frontbenchers on both sides reenter the debate.

Next comes the committee stage—*after* the floor vote. The government may take this stage either on the floor of the House—in the "Committee of the Whole House," which is simply the membership of the House debating in the chamber under relaxed rules of debate; or it may take the bill in one of the standing committees ("upstairs"). Matters of signal or constitutional importance alone are taken on the floor of the House. The rest go to the standing committees of the Commons.

Standing Committees

All but one of the standing committees of the Commons, of which at present six are operating, are symbolized by the letters of the alphabet—A, B, C, etc. That one is called the Scottish Committee because it contains all the Scottish members and deals with all Scottish business; it is the only standing committee that is in any sense specialized. The others each consist of from twenty to fifty members, drawn proportionately from the parties in the House, and empaneled by the speaker, assisted by his Committee of Selection, from names submitted by the party whips. These committees meet in rooms which are small replicas of the House itself. The opposing members range themselves on each side, with the chairman presiding on a cross-bench at the top. The party whips are always present on each side of the committee.

Standing committees must be sharply distinguished from the "Select" Committees of the Commons which it establishes—some of them from time to time as occasion arises, sometimes on a regular footing. Select Committees, consisting of members of both the government and opposition parties, are set up to investigate, hear evidence, and to report to the House on any matter which the Government wishes to be treated in this way. For instance, Select Committees are set up from time to time to look into alleged breaches of the "privileges" of an M.P. or of the House collectively; others are set up every session to look into such matters as the annual estimates of expenditure, or the public accounts, and (more recently) into the conduct of the nationalized industries. But the *Standing* Committees are concerned only with current legislative proposals, i.e., with parliamentary bills that are under discussion. These committees play an entirely different part from that played by the committees of the United States Congress or, indeed, by the committees in the various legislatures of continental Europe. First, they are unspecialized: they are allocated bills as soon as they are free to consider them. Secondly, they never conduct hearings from outside witnesses, nor from civil servants; they do nothing but discuss the bill before them according to strict committee procedures. Thirdly, their proceedings are printed in an official record which is placed on sale. Fourthly, it is not their function to report to the House their views about the policy of the bills, nor is there any way in which they can suppress bills or hold them up indefinitely. The House of Commons, in its second reading of a bill—not the committee—is the body that pronounces judgment on whether its policy is good or bad. Likewise, the cabinet—not the committee—decides whether to hold back or expedite a bill. The function of the standing committee is to take the bill after the House of Commons has approved its policy in a second reading, and to work through it in detail. The committee considers the bill word-by-word and line-by-line, considering new clauses and amendments as it does so.

These standing committees act in the same way as the Committee of the Whole House does when it is taking the committee stage of a bill. They are established simply to save time. While a Committee of the Whole House is considering merely the one bill before it, six standing committees can be considering six bills.

The task of the standing committee is to examine the bill very carefully and to consider amendments. Now is the supremely opportune time for outside interest to influence the bill. Working through their friends on the committee, such interests often greatly change legislation through the amendments they submit that are accepted.

When a bill comes out of committee, it enters the report stage: the bill "as amended in committee" is circulated to all members, and then debated in the House. If additional clauses are found to be necessary, they are added, and further amendments can also be considered, at that time. These are not the same amendments that were discussed in committee and rejected, but "new" amendments. It is the speaker who has the power to decide which amendments are substantially "new" and allow them.

One other important feature of the report stage must be noted. During the committee stage, the minister may tell a member (either one of his own backbenchers or an opposition member) that although he cannot promise to accept the members' amendment, he will consider it. The report stage gives the minister the opportunity to bring forward amendments he wanted time to consider during the committee stage.

When the report stage is over, the bill goes forward for its third (and final) reading, which is, once more, a general debate, this time on the final version of the bill. Third readings do not last more than a day. If a majority of the members vote for the bill, it has passed the House of Commons. But it is still not a law, for it must then be voted on by the House of Lords. If approved by the Lords, the royal assent is then given and the bill has become an act.

Although few bills come out of the House of Commons just as they went in, by and large the government's general policy is upheld. A bill is often altered in one or two important particulars, and usually greatly changed in its less important details. And sometimes (but very rarely) a bill meets such a hostile reception that it is dropped altogether.

Private Bills

When private individuals or corporations seek particular powers and benefits not granted by the ordinary law of the land, bills passed to embody such powers and benefits are known as "private bills." Ordinarily introduced on behalf of local authorities and other statutory bodies, such as public corporations, private bills rarely meet any opposition, since objections are usually warded off by compromises before the petition is framed. If, however, the bill is opposed, it runs a double hazard: it may have to stand up to a grueling examination in specially constituted committees, each consisting of four M.P.'s; and, even if approved by the committee, it may face a debate on the floor of the House of Commons or the House of Lords.

Subordinate Legislation

Yet another type of legislation is known as "delegated" or "subordinate" legislation. This legislation is made by a public (or, much more rarely, a private) body under the authority of an act of Parliament, which is called the "parent act." There is an enormous amount of this kind of legislation. In 1952, for instance, the public acts of Parliament numbered sixty-four, but the number of "instruments"—i.e., the delegated legislation made under acts of Parliament —totaled 2,312. There are five reasons for the growth of delegated legislation: (1) the pressure on parliamentary time; (2) the technical nature of many acts; (3) the likelihood of unforeseen contingencies arising during the administration of a complicated act; (4) the need for legislative flexibility; and (5) the occasional development of emergency conditions that require speedy action. The need for delegated legislation is generally conceded today, but the adequacy of control over it is more widely disputed.

Since instruments are so numerous and technical, for every one that a member detects as objectionable, scores probably escape his notice. Consequently, in 1944 the House created the Select Committee on Statutory Instruments, usually known as the "Scrutiny Committee" (consisting of eleven members, with an opposition member as its chairman), to bring to the attention of the House of Commons any statutory instrument it thinks should be reviewed by Parliament.

The committee may not consider or report on the merits or the policy of any of the instruments. Its duty is to draw the attention of the House to whether it imposes a tax, excludes an appeal to a court, or purports without authority of the parent act to have retroactive effect; or whether there has been unjustifiable delay in its publication or "laying before" Parliament; or, more generally still, whether its language should be clarified, or whether it seems to make some unusual or unexpected use of the powers conferred by the parent act. Between 1944 and 1952, the committee examined 6,900 instru-

ments and reported only ninety-three of these to the House.

Controlling the Government

Once the government makes up its mind on major policy matters, it is not likely to be influenced to change it. (And furthermore, the government *always* gets its vote.) It is only on matters of subpolicy and administrative detail that the government may be induced to alter its thinking. This sort of alteration can be accomplished in one of two ways: either by trying to withhold money, or by direct challenge. It is carried out either through regular channels (general procedures) or with the aid of certain specialized subcommittees. Table 5-4 helps to illustrate how this all happens, as described in the following sections.

TABLE 5-4. *The House of Commons and Its Control over Administration*

By General Procedures	By Subcommittees
Via Finance	
1. Budgetary: the finance bill ("Ways and Means")	1. The Public Accounts Committee
2. The estimates and appropriations ("Supply")—i.e., the 26 "supply days" debates	2. The Select Committee on Estimates
Via Direct Challenge	
1. Questions	The select committee on specific area of policy
2. Adjournment motions	
3. Queen's speech debates and the like	
4. Censure motions	

Financial Scrutiny

THE CONSTITUTIONAL PRINCIPLES. According to the Parliament Act of 1911, in matters of finance the House of Commons is supreme. A bill that the speaker of the House of Commons certifies to be a money bill cannot be amended by the Lords, nor does it need to receive the assent of the Lords to become law. If the House of Lords refuses assent, the bill is merely delayed a month.

A motion to expend public revenue can come only from a minister of the Crown. This rule was established in Standing Order 63, one of the oldest of the standing orders, dating from the reign of Queen Anne. The Opposition, therefore, cannot suggest *increases* in expenditure. In order to combat the government, it is forced to move for reductions—even if it favors increases; this is its paradoxical way of drawing attention to the inadequacy of the grant. There are two financial committees of the whole House: one, the Committee of Supply, appropriates money to the various services that need it; the other, the Committee of Ways and Means, raises money.

THE TAXATION CYCLE. A budget is introduced every year early in April, which is the beginning of the financial year. The House then, on certain days from April through July, goes into the Committee of Ways and Means and discusses what are known as "budget resolutions." When all the resolutions have been debated, they are collected together into a bill which, when passed, is known as the Finance Act. It embodies the government's taxation program for the year.

"SUPPLY." Parliament must also "supply" the government with money—that is, grant it the right to spend for certain approved purposes. The Treasury collects and revises the estimates presented to it by the different departments, and these are introduced in the Commons before April. (It might be noted here that *estimates* is a term that, like *bill*, *resolution,* and various others, often is capitalized in its more formal usages.) The House then discusses these estimates over the next four months, after which, in July, they are incorporated in the appropriation bill. This bill, when passed as the Appropriation Act, permits the various departments to spend on the purposes detailed in the estimates, and on *nothing else.*

Two points must be noticed. First, the House has no effective control over the "timing" of discussion on the estimates. The twenty-six days scheduled for the discussion of these—the "supply days"—must be taken advantage of when they fall, no matter how inconvenient their arrival to the House as a whole. Furthermore, the choice of which estimates are to be debated lies with the Opposition—which, taking full advantage of its prerogatives, and then some, does not use the occasion to probe the details of the estimates, but for a general debate on the broad policy of the department whose estimate is up for discussion. Thus, the supposed "control" of the House over government expenditure is lost in a labyrinth of meandering policy debates initiated by the Opposition. And, on the last day, all the estimates that have not been debated are simply put to the vote *without* discussion!

On the other hand, the House exercises minute control over the *spending* of all money granted—to make sure that it has been spent only as Parliament has authorized, and in no other way (save in very exceptional and justifiable cases). In the process, it investigates and checks details of maladministration. It does this by specialized machinery: through its officer (the comptroller and auditor general) and its select committee (the Public Accounts Committee). The comptroller and auditor general audits the accounts of every department and presents a report to the Public Accounts Committee, which draws attention to discrepancies between what Parliament authorized and what the department actually spent its money on, to cases of unwise or wasteful administration of the sums granted, and to other irregularities. The committee summons the accounting officers of the departments to its hearings to justify any departures mentioned in the report. Chaired by an opposition member, it consists of fifteen M.P.'s, and is exceedingly influential.

The Commons' Control over Finance

We have seen that although the Commons can partly affect the modes of taxation, it has no control over estimates. It relies on the Treasury and the cabinet for the formulation of the estimates, and has neither the time nor the machinery to control them in detail. As long ago as 1912, the Commons set up a Select Committee on Estimates. This committee and the Public Accounts Committee can, at best, examine details after the estimates have been voted and the money is spent. This provides a second specialized piece of machinery to investigate and criticize maladministration. But although this committee (of forty-three M.P.'s subdivided into subcommittees) is becoming increasingly influential, the government is still getting exactly the sums it asks for and for the purposes it has approved. Furthermore, both the government and the Select Committee on Estimates know in advance that the government gets its way. It is therefore impossible for any department to rely on its friends in Parliament to get its estimate altered or improved.

Three important results follow. First, all departments are strictly subordinated to the cabinet's general financial plan. Second, the budget is a coherent document representing the financial aspect of the government's policy. Third, lobbyist pressures are kept in firm check.

Scrutiny and Control of General Administration

It will be seen that although the House devotes much attention to the finance of government, it is no longer so much concerned with finance as such as with the uses to which the government puts finances—that is to say, either with the high policy of the government (insofar as this is expressed through the appropriations which it seeks) or with the details of administrative machinery. It will be noted, also, that Commons devotes its attention to these two classes of matter in two different ways: the challenge on high policy is made through the twenty-six days of *general debate* on topics initiated by the Opposition, which were originally supposed to scrutinize the government's detailed appropriations; while the control over administrative detail is exercised through two *specialized committees,* the Public Accounts Committee and the Select Committee on Estimates.

As we shall now see, these two broad methods of challenging the government's general or detailed administration also apply outside the financial field.

SELECT COMMITTEES TO CONTROL ADMINISTRATIVE DETAIL. In 1956 a Select Committee on Nationalized Industries was set up, with powers to send for "persons, papers, and records." It investigated and reported to the House on the Hydro-Electric Board, the National Coal Board, the airlines, the railroads, and the gas and electricity supply industries. The committee has behaved very independently in its relations with the government of the day; in fact, its reports have often criticized the ministers responsible for the nationalized industries. It is the practice for the boards concerned to make public replies to committee strictures, and the committee has not hesitated to retort to those it has regarded as unsatisfactory. Furthermore, the information elicited has served as ammunition for critical M.P.'s in general debate, thus generating even more pressure. Of course, the committee has no way of forcing the government to act, but, on the whole, governments have proved responsive.

The effectiveness of this committee so reinforced the impression made by the Public Accounts Committee and the Estimates Committee that a Select Committee on Procedure recommended the establishment of additional committees, each supervising the administration of a sphere of government policy. Accordingly, in January, 1967, the House set up, experimentally and only for that session, two new select committees: one a subject committee on science and technology, and the other the first committee to study a government department (the Department of Agriculture). These committees also have the power to send for persons (including ministers), papers, and records; their meetings are public; and they publish a verbatim account of their proceedings.

These two committees were followed by select committees on race relations and immigration, education, Scottish affairs, and overseas aid.

With the new 1970 Parliament, the new government made further proposals for reform of the select committee system. In a "green paper" in October 1970, the government suggested that a Select Committee on Government Expenditure (with forty-five members and a set of subcommittees) take over and expand the activities of the old Estimates Committee. At the same time, only three others (science and technology, race relations and immigration, and Scottish affairs) would be retained. At the time of writing these proposals have yet to be implemented.

Parliamentary Questions

The parliamentary question addressed to a minister (to elicit information or to register criticism) and the daily "question time" are distinctive and vital features of the parliamentary system in Britain. Every member has the right to ask questions of a minister. He may, however, "star" (qualify or mark for special attention, as with an asterisk) his (written) question, by way of asking for an oral answer. He must give at least two days' notice for such an answer, and he may not request more than two such questions for any one day. The chief reason for demanding an oral answer is that it entitles the questioning member—and other members, too—to ask supplementary questions, and these are used to entrap the minister into damaging admissions.

Question time runs from 2:45 P.M., to 3:30 P.M. every day except Friday (but the prime minister can be questioned only on Tuesdays and Thursdays). The turn of each ministry comes up at intervals of about ten days; but, owing to the popularity of question time, the number of questions, and particularly of supplementary questions, has grown enormously. Consequently, it may turn out that a member's question is not reached on the day the minister is down to answer. In that case, it is postponed until the ministry's next turn on the rota (roster)—and so, for an important ministry it may be a month before the M.P. gets an answer to his question. It is up to the clerks to decide which minister is constitutionally responsible for an answer, and they will, if necessary, transfer the question from the minister queried by a member to the constitutionally appropriate one. (It should be noted that not all questions are admissible, for there are twenty-nine conditions to be met for admissibility, such as: the purpose must be to gain information or press for action, and not just an excuse to make a speech; the government must, in some way, be responsible for the matter questioned; questions to which answers have been refused cannot be repeated.)

The questions are numbered and printed on the "order paper." At question time the member rises and, addressing the speaker, says "number 63, Sir"—upon which he resumes his seat while the minister rises and reads his reply. (He has been known to read the wrong reply, with side-splitting results.) On answering, the minister may expect a veritable drumfire of supplementary questions. Where the issue is controversial, the process turns into a cross-examination of the minister by all the House. And sometimes the question or answer is veritable dynamite.

Question time is important because it enables the Opposition to probe weak points in the government's handling of affairs, because it permits this immediately, and because this probing occurs by cross-examination in the presence of the House (which is always crowded for question time). For instance, in February 1967 a daily newspaper stated that outgoing and incoming cables were being scrutinized by the security services. The prime minister, who made a statement on this matter, alleged that the story was sensationalized, and that the practice was standard—and that, in any case, the newspaper had defied a "D notice" (a request that a story be suppressed in the interests of national security). A chain of questions followed, on that day and successive days, until it appeared that the issues were by no means as clear as the premier had at first suggested; and in the end he had to concede an impartial inquiry into the whole matter and the constitutional issues it raised.

The questions always range over an enormously wide area. In one afternoon, for instance, the minister of labour can be asked to provide answers to queries on a list of topics ranging from "actions being taken to offset redundancy in the motor car industry in Scotland," and "racial discrimination in employment practiced by foreign firms," to a pointed personal query as to why a civil servant employed by the statistics department of the ministry allegedly threatened the director of a company with fines of £50 and £200.

As soon as the question is received in a minister's department, it is given priority over all other business. Many departments have a special parliamentary branch, part of whose business is to take responsibility for getting the question answered. A single sheet of text is prepared for the minister, embodying the answer, background data, and suggested answers to possible supplementaries. A well-briefed minister often can defend himself even if he has a bad case, though it is much more likely that his weak position will be exposed. The House may not always discover the truth, but it infallibly recognizes a cheat.

Adjournment Motions

An adjournment motion enables a member to start a debate unrelated to the motion itself. Adjournment motions can take place at the close of a day's business, and also when the House disbands for a vacation or holiday. Thus, members who are dissatisfied with a minister's reply to their questions can seek to raise the matter again "on the adjournment." If successful, they can force the minister into an additional half-hour debate on the issue. Although no vote is taken on such debates, they can be a useful check on ministerial action. For instance,

a Conservative M.P. once raised at question time a complaint from a constituent who charged that the local police had beaten his son. Failing to get a satisfactory reply, the M.P. raised the matter on the adjournment. His case raised such wide sympathy from both sides of the House that the government had to institute a public inquiry.

The "Urgency" Adjournment Motion

For business that brooks no delay, standing orders provide for an "urgency" adjournment motion, under which a debate can take place at 7:00 P.M. that very night, usually amid great excitement. Confidence in the government is often at stake, and since the whips on both sides have to take crash action, by telephone, telegram, and runners, to collect their scattered members, the occasion is generally one of high drama. A debate under this procedure arose, for instance, from the decision of a U.N. mission to quit Aden after a brief and fruitless five-day sojurn there, instead of completing its task of consulting all shades of political opinion. To a restless and indignant House the foreign secretary stated that he had dispatched a resident minister to Aden—but, under questioning, gave no clear indication of what that minister's duties were to be. Thereupon, an opposition "shadow minister" moved the "urgency motion," and the foreign secretary had to do his best to reassure the House that very evening. But such occasions are rare, for the issue has to be one of "immediate, urgent, and public" importance, and speakers have interpreted each of these three modifiers very conservatively. In the last two years, it has been agreed that speakers should adopt a slightly more liberal interpretation of these words, and such debates are now a little more frequent.

Queen's Speech Debates

Every session of Parliament is opened by the "Speech from the Throne," which is either read by the queen in person or by her commissioner, in a ceremony of antique grandeur and dignity. But the speech has actually been drafted by the cabinet, and it sets out the government's legislative program for the session. Six days of debate follow, with the Opposition usually mounting a sustained attack on the government that ranges over foreign affairs, defense, colonial affairs, the state of the economy, and other matters of pressing interest to the Opposition.

Votes of Censure

The Opposition, which is always given time for debate on the queen's address and on the estimates, invariably can persuade the government to "give" it days to debate certain urgent topics. The government, being miserly of its time since it has a program of its own to get through, is of course reluctant to turn the floor over to the Opposition. But the Opposition always has a potent weapon in reserve: it can call for a discussion of a motion expressing lack of confidence in the government—a "vote of censure," as it is called. Strictly an emergency move, the "vote" must be used with discretion; but by convention the government never fails to accede to a demand from the leader of the Opposition for a vote of confidence. For this is a convention based on the fact that the leaders of the Opposition are responsible members who form a potential alternative government—a position of power and trust that not only warrants but guarantees the legitimacy of such an interruption of the normal course of business. And for their part, the government ordinarily has everything to gain by confidently meeting such a direct challenge to its authority at the earliest possible moment.

Is the House of Commons a Legislature?

For some time, considerable concern has been voiced about the "decline" of the Commons: in books with titles like *The Passing of Parliament*

and *Is Parliament in Decline?*; in the informed criticisms of the members of the "Study of Parliament Group" (mostly academics); and during the period of the last Labour government, by Labour backbenchers. Newcomers to the House, mostly young and full of crusading zeal, these backbenchers have found themselves deprived of the opportunity to initiate reforms, and with much less influence on the government than they had anticipated. The House, for its part, has set up a Select Committee on Procedure, to examine what can be done to renovate itself.

Some critics still hope to restore to the House a greater initiative in the making of law. They would like to see bills referred to select committees with powers to send for "persons, papers, and records," and with the capacity to amend the draft bills sent to them—something along the lines of the American or Continental legislative committees. Governments have made it clear, however, that they will not agree to such reforms. Instead, they have conceded some ground to the critics by allowing the growth of select committees whose function is limited to putting more information at the disposal of the House, thus giving it better machinery for reviewing and criticizing the activities of the executive.

The assumption behind this line of thought is precisely that the dominance of the government over Parliament is here to stay: that the House of Commons is ancillary. The following excerpts from the Study of Parliament Group's testimony to the Select Committee of the House of Commons on Procedure, published in 1965, expresses this assumption:

". . . Parliamentary scrutiny of the Executive is fundamental to the whole question of parliamentary reform. *For though it is the business of the Government to govern,* it is also their business to give a running account of their stewardship to the House of Commons which was elected to support them and to submit their action or inaction in any particular instance to the judgment of that House. . . . [emphasis added]" [4]

[4] *Fourth Report of the Select Committee on Procedure,* Session 1964–65, HC303 (1965), p. 135.

THE HOUSE OF LORDS

The House of Lords is a survivor from the very earliest days of the English monarchy, when power lay with the king in his Great Council. That body was the lineal ancestor of the House of Lords, and the House of Commons was a subsequent outgrowth from it. The enduring consequences of these facts are that (1) until 1911, the powers of the House of Lords were coequal with those of the Commons, and (2) to this day it is still largely composed of the hereditary aristocracy.

Powers

We must clear our minds of the fact that the highest court of the United Kingdom is also called the House of Lords. In theory, this court and the current House of Lords are indeed identical; in practice, no *lay* peers ever sit with the court, and no appeal may be held by that court unless three qualified legal personages are present. Such personages are the nine lords of appeal and the lord chancellor; should an insufficient number of such persons be available, then any other of the duly qualified peers may be invited to sit. For all practical purposes, then, the House of Lords, as the highest court in the kingdom, is a separate body from the House of Lords, as a political body and upper House of Parliament.

The powers of the House of Lords, as the upper house, are to initiate legislation and to revise and if necessary to delay bills sent up to it by the House of Commons—money bills excepted. By the Parliament Act of 1911, as amended by the Parliament Act of 1949, any other bill (except a private bill) which is passed by the Commons in two successive sessions within a period of one year can become law *without* the assent of the Lords.

INITIATION OF BILLS. As we have seen, about one-quarter of the government bills in the 1959–63 period were initiated in the House of Lords, thus relieving pressure on the Commons. In recent years private members bills proposing controversial social reforms have sometimes been introduced first in the House of Lords to test opinion there and, through the publicity attaching to Lords' debates, public opinion in general.

REVISION. With much more time at its disposal than the House of Commons, and containing a nucleus of highly qualified lawyers, professional men, and business executives, the Lords is a valuable revising chamber. The author, analyzing the Labour government's transport bill of 1947 in detail, found that the Lords discussed 450 amendments and passed 210: of these, 177 were substantive amendments, of which 80 were introduced by the government itself. Fifty-three amendments of the 177 were designed to meet points raised by the Opposition in the Commons, and 91 were introduced by the Conservative Opposition in the House of Lords itself. There was no doubt that without the help of the Lords, the bill would either have been a very muddled affair, or alternatively, that the Commons would have had to spend a great deal more time in discussing and amending it. The Lords has helped clarify the details of the present government's complicated companies bill and land commission bill in a similar workmanlike manner. Nor does the House of Lords revise only Labour legislation: for instance, it made important qualifications to the Conservative government's television bill in 1953.

DELAY. Although the Lords' functions of initiation and revision rouse no controversy, their delaying powers do, because delay, which is supposed to be a barrier against hasty legislation, can also be used as a barrier to hold up well-thought-out legislation. During the Labour governments of 1945–51, the Lords passed nearly all Labour measures. However, it did hold up for two years the Parliament bill of 1947, which cut down its own delaying powers from two years to one (though this was only to be expected), and rejected a clause in a bill which provided for the abolition of capital punishment. But most importantly—and for this the Labour party have never forgiven it—in the Labour government's last year of its first term office, in 1949, the Lords used its threat of delay to make the government promise that the nationalization of steel, provided for by an act of Parliament, should not commence until after the general election. The government was returned with too flimsy a majority to carry through effective nationalization of the industry, and when the Conservatives came back to power in 1951 they denationalized it.

COMPOSITION. At present, the House of Lords has a membership of over one thousand. These include a small number of special categories—royal dukes (who now number five and do not normally take part), the bishops, and the law lords. All twenty-six bishops are from the Church of England—the other English churches are not represented, nor are any churches in Scotland, Wales, or Northern Ireland—and they sit only for the period for which they hold their bishopric. There are currently eighteen law lords, who sit for life and who exercise the judicial function which formally belongs to the House of Lords as a whole, that of the court of highest appeal. The remainder are, as of 1971, 838 hereditary peers together with nineteen hereditary peeresses in their own right, and 157 life peers together with twenty-three life peeresses.

Until 1958, all peerages except the law lords were hereditary. This does not mean that they were all descendants of feudal aristocrats. Every year some seven to ten new peerages were created, so that the hereditary peerage was an expanding body, constantly adding new blood. An analysis of the peerages created between 1911 and 1956 shows that half were former M.P.'s, and most of the remainder were leading public servants or came from the ranks of industry or the professions. With the Life Peerage Act of 1958, this process of constantly adding new members to the Lords was speeded up and the proportion coming from outside the ranks of politicians increased. Since 1964, no further hereditary peerages have been created; in 1963 it had been made possible for hereditary

peers to renounce their titles on succession (ten have since done so—one of them, Lord Hailsham, only to return as a life peer seven years later).

Reform of the House of Lords

Changes in both the composition and the powers of the Lords have been regularly debated ever since the Parliament Act of 1911 reduced it to its present role. But no agreement was reached between the parties, and both parties were reluctant to face the charge of amending the constitutional position of the upper chamber to suit themselves. In 1947, however, when interparty talks broke down over the problem of linking changes in composition with changes in powers, the Labour government enacted its own proposal of reducing the delaying power to one year. In due course, the Life Peerages Act of 1958 and the suspension of the creation of hereditary peerages in 1964 altered the composition and standing of the Lords.

In 1966 the Labour government reopened negotiations with the leaders of both opposition parties. The result was an agreement which was acceptable to all three party leaderships but which was rejected by so many of their supporters that it was not enacted. The agreement was that the House of Lords should cease to include hereditary peers; its members would be nominated for life by the leaders of the three main parties according to a formula which would ensure that its political composition kept in step with national election results. The power of delay was to become even more limited. The main argument against this agreement among the three party leaderships was that it extended an already important power of patronage which they held (with the introduction of life peerages it had become normal for the leaders of the two opposition parties to nominate in addition to the government). Virtually no one today defends the hereditary principle upon which the bulk of the membership of the upper house is still based, but in the absence of an agreed alternative, it has remained.

THE CROWN

The social and symbolic importance of the queen has already been discussed. What is her political role?

Every act of government is carried out in the queen's name, although the queen's personal discretion is very limited, indeed, in law, she has the right to dismiss her ministers at her own discretion; but this right was last exercised in 1834, and even then with the acquiescence of the prime minister. Again, she has the legal right to veto a bill passed by both Houses of Parliament; but the last time this was exercised was when Queen Anne vetoed the Scotch militia bill in 1707. Again, the queen convenes and dissolves Parliament. May she, at her personal discretion, withhold her consent to a dissolution of Parliament when this is asked for by her prime minister? For more than a century, no sovereign has rejected such advice to dissolve (though examples have occurred in other countries of the Commonwealth). Whether the queen can refuse today is still a contested question.

Those areas of personal prerogatives of the crown which the sovereign still exercises at her own discretion today are two. In the first place, she has the right to "be consulted," the right to encourage, and the right to warn her ministers. She has the right to see all cabinet agenda in advance; to receive copies of all the important Foreign Office telegrams; and to receive the reports of the cabinet's Defence Committee and its important subcommittees. In constant touch with what is happening, she becomes increasingly well informed as her reign lengthens. This may well make her influential; but this influence is advisory only. If her cabinet insists, she must give way.

Secondly and finally, in certain circumstances the sovereign may exercise discretion as to the choice of prime minister—but only if a party has no clear majority and/or no recognized leader.

We have seen how the cabinet stands at the intersection of "party, Parliament, and civil service." Having discussed the cabinet's relationship with party and with Parliament, we now move on to its tie-in with the civil service. And this is a case of "last but not least," because in Britain the senior ranks of the civil service play a cardinal role in shaping government policies.

We should mention, however, before going on, that besides the civil service there are two other types of administrative organs responsible for executing the policies set by the cabinet and Parliament, and that thus play some part in determining government policies: the public corporations (such as the BBC and the nationalized industries) and the elected councils that constitute the local governments of the country. Neither of these is regarded as part of the "executive," although they are certainly administrative agencies. But the spinal column of the whole administrative system is undoubtedly the departments of the central government which are manned by the civil service, and so we shall devote most of our time to them.

THE CENTRAL EXECUTIVE

The so-called executive in Britain consists of the important government departments, with their associated boards and other powerful public agencies. At the head of each department is a political appointee, the minister, who is assisted by a varying number of junior ministers (also political appointees). Apart from fleeting appearances before select committees of the Commons, the civil servants in each department are answerable to Parliament only through their minister—who, for his part, is answerable to Parliament for the actions of his civil servants. It is this relationship that produces "the individual responsibility of ministers for their departments" which we have already discussed.

The minister, the political head of the department, is temporary; he is an amateur; the source of his strength is the popular mandate; and his view is highly colored by immediate political needs. The civil service, on the other

SIX

the executive

hand, is a skilled, permanent, and dispassionate (since it is not elected) body of public servants that keeps its eye on the future, since it will be left with the consequences of a minister's policies long after he has departed. As the duties of government have increased, much work that used to be done by ministers and Parliament has been delegated to the civil service. Today, acts of Parliament do not usually aim at doing more than laying down the essential principles of the law, leaving the details to be filled in by statutory rules, orders, and regulations—which are drawn up by the civil service, with the knowledge of the minister, who has the final say. These regulations vastly exceed the acts of Parliament both in number and in bulk. Many acts now establish special arrangements for adjudicating breaches of these statutory rules and orders through administrative tribunals, and in many cases the jurisdiction of the ordinary courts is excluded.

In addition to these two relatively new functions of the civil service, its ancient one of giving assistance and advice to the minister has enormously expanded. The work of a department is so complex today that on all but the most vital or politically controversial subjects the minister is bound to lean heavily on his civil servants to execute his policy.

Structure

The central executive has three main characteristics: (1) it is organized into a number of departments and their dependent boards and agencies; (2) it is more highly integrated than in, say, the United States; and (3) the senior ranks of the civil service that make up these departments are highly influential in the shaping of policy. The organization of a typical government department is shown in Fig. 6-1.

In striking contrast to the typical American governmental department, in Britain an entire department is the responsibility of a single civil servant, the permanent secretary (except in the Treasury, which now has two permanent secretaries). Although the permanent secretary concentrates on particular aspects of the department, he is charged with overseeing all the operations of the department and is assisted in this by one or more deputy secretaries. Under this central direction come the under secretaries, each in charge of a section, and, below them, the assistant secretaries who head up the lower-echelon divisions of the department. Within these divisions, smaller units are administered by principals and assistant principals.

The lower-echelon divisions correspond roughly to the "bureaus" in an American federal department. Two very important differences from American practice must be noted here. First, the ranks between the equivalents of "bureau chief" and the political head of the department are in Britain filled by permanent career men who have spent a lifetime in the service. In the United States, the equivalent ranks are usually filled by political appointees who may be fairly rapidly and regu-

FIG. 6-1. *The organization of a typical British Government Department.*

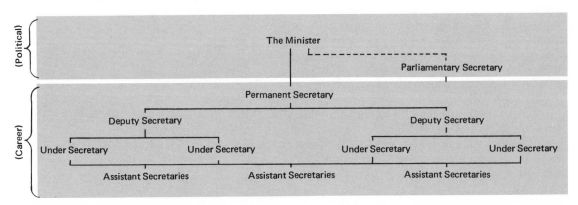

larly replaced. The chief advice given to the incoming political head of a British department thus comes from the tried and trusted top civil servant of the department, not from the party appointees who are brought in together with him. Nor do British incoming ministers follow the French practice of bringing with them their own "cabinet" of advisers.

Further, the fact that the higher ranks consist of career men who have usually spent many years in that particular department helps to make the department a real unity instead of a collection of separate bureaus. All controversies between the different divisions of the department gradually work their way to the top, where they can receive a final decision from the permanent secretary if necessary.

Attached to most of the departments are several boards or commissions for which the departmental minister takes parliamentary responsibility, but which have structures of their own. Against the twenty-four departments that existed in 1967, there were about one hundred boards or commissions of this kind.

Coordination

How are the competing policies of so many departments and agencies brought together into a coherent whole? The institution of the cabinet is one answer. Since it consists of the heads of departments, any disputes can be cleared at its level through the committees, the cabinet secretariat, and the cabinet agenda (as described in Chap. 5). And we have already seen, for instance, how a department must consult all other interested departments, especially the Treasury and the law officers, before bringing the draft of a bill to the cabinet.

In practice, of course, only the most serious of departmental collisions are brought up to the cabinet. Below the cabinet level, the Treasury establishes many of the administrative procedures and minor policies common to all the departments, and there is also a network of consultation and cooperation among departments that buffers any very serious collisions between them.

THE TREASURY. The preeminence of the British Treasury, which is often called "the department of departments," is recognized by all other departments. As its name suggests, the Treasury is concerned (as is the United States Treasury) with all the financial transactions of government; but it does much more besides. It is charged with the responsibility for economic policy—and this gives it a degree of control over what the departments concerned with industry and commerce are doing. Furthermore, it is responsible for the estimates of the various departments. This control of the finances of the other departments gives it a unique insight into their outlook and into the policies they are pursuing and wish to pursue.

The Treasury certainly never tells departments what their policy must be. A department's policy, as we know, is in the hands of its ministers, who must answer for it in the cabinet and in the House of Commons. But the Treasury can and does influence to some degree the policies of the other departments. It has the right to say no to a department's estimates. The minister of the department may fight the decision up to the cabinet, but at least the result will be clearly understood by all and not cloaked in secrecy, or subject to breaking out suddenly in full view. However, although the Treasury can say no, it cannot and does not seek to tell other departments how they ought to spend their money. Actually, the great bulk of spending today follows automatically from some previous policy decision (e.g., a decision to raise the school-leaving age to 16), and all that the Treasury can do is to process the estimates accordingly.

In the course of the Treasury's "review" of departments' spending, it is in the unique position of knowing the direction in which their policies are moving. It is, therefore, able to detect divergencies from the government's policies at an early stage, and can point these out to the departments themselves, or, if the issues are too serious for the departments to settle, to the ministers in charge. Furthermore, in getting the departments to work together, it stands in a very strong position. It is bound to be represented on every important interdepartmental committee. And it has the right and the duty to make trouble over the financing and staffing of all other departments.

The Treasury's coordinating role used to be even greater, for it was once responsible for negotiating all pay, recruitment, promotion, and training policies in the civil service. But following the Fulton committee report in 1968, a separate Civil Service Department, under the direct charge of the prime minister, has been set up.

Interdepartmental Consultation

Most governmental disputes and frictions occur in the actual carrying out of government policy —i.e., at the departmental level rather than at the Treasury, or, still more rarely, at the cabinet level—because the principal interest of one department tends to be a secondary interest of other departments. For instance, housing conditions are a principal interest of the Department of the Environment, but a secondary interest of the Department of Health and Social Security. Nevertheless, the two departments try to hammer out a coherent policy between them as best as possible. They succeed largely because of the habit of mind of the highest class of the civil service, the former administrative class (which we shall discuss more fully later). This class, which consists of no more than thirty-five hundred civil servants, now is drawn from a wider social class than ever before, though it still derives much of its strength from the fee-paying "public" schools, and comes predominantly from Oxford and Cambridge. This common educational background is reinforced by the nature of recruitment, which is by a general, not a technical, examination, thus heavily emphasizing the humanities, especially classics and history. The slow turnover of civil servants brings in recruits in such small doses that they become absorbed into the traditions of the civil service. Many if not most senior civil servants belong to the same half-dozen men's clubs in and around Whitehall, and thus regularly meet one another informally. The long-term effect of this informal collaboration—telephoning one's opposite number, chatting at

lunch, "dropping in to see" a colleague in his office—is very far-reaching.

But formal methods of collaboration are also essential, of course, and the most common and most influential of these is the interdepartmental committee or conference. In fact, the whole of the higher civil service is continuously involved in transient interdepartmental committees that arise in the course of executing policy. Many are not established by any regular process but are created on the initiative of a particular civil servant with a specific problem to solve.

If a department already has a policy it will, of course, try to stick to it. But many interdepartmental committees are convened at an earlier stage, when the departments have not so much policies as *views*. The committee will consist of representatives of the departments, trained in committee work and anxious to find a solution. In the end, somehow, a policy is arrived at which, if important enough, will be considered by a top-level official committee, by a committee of ministers, or even by the cabinet where the matter is most grave. But most of the matters discussed will never go that far. Thus, policy—some might prefer to call it subpolicy—is being made all the time. Within limits set by the governing party and the ministers, the interdepartmental committees make the bulk of governmental policy; and it is in these committees that the presence of the Treasury representative is at its most influential.

THE CIVIL SERVICE

There are at present about 500,000 full-time nonindustrial civil servants in Britain. (Industrial civil servants are such persons as Admiralty dockyard workers.) Following are the main characteristics of the nonindustrial civil service:

1.   Excepting only the few "temporaries" brought in from outside on contract, it is entirely made up of "career" personnel. Once a civil servant has passed his probationary period, he holds a permanent ap-

pointment and will not be discharged except in the very rare cases of personal misbehavior or dishonesty. Resignations are infrequent and the turnover is extremely small.

2. It is recruited by open competitive examination (or, in the appropriate cases, open competitive interview). Examinations for other than technical, scientific, and professional staff test for general aptitude and not special skills; they are similar to the examinations administered to students when they leave school, or university examinations, according to the class of civil servant involved.

3. For purposes of pay, working conditions, and promotion, the civil service is treated as one service. Most civil servants used to be divided into three classes: the clerical class carried out general clerical duties; the middle-rung executive class was concerned with the details of government operations and contained most of the highly trained semiprofessional staff, such as auditors; and the administrative class contained the top thirty-five hundred or so civil servants. Just under half of the civil servants in the administrative class used to be recruited from the executive class by special examination; the rest were recruited from outside, most of them directly upon graduation from a university.

    In 1971 this hierarchy was abolished and a single, open structure substituted. This followed the recommendations of the Fulton committee and was aimed both at promoting better management practices and at providing more opportunities for advancement inside the service. But the habits of mind—in particular, the sense of cohesion among the members of the former administrative class—derived from the old class system will take many years to disappear.

4. The nonindustrial civil service is politically neutral. Neither appointment nor dismissal takes place for political reasons. Although the senior civil servants may not take part

in any partisan activities, the lower ranks are freer; some (providing their departments approve) even become candidates for election.

5. The service is almost totally free from corruption, and in the senior ranks it is completely so.

The work and outlook of the civil service are geared to the prime fact that the minister is the head of his department and that the minister takes responsibility before Parliament for everything the civil servant does or does not do. The only contact between Legislature and civil servants is through a minister. The minister is the civil servant's chief, and the civil servant must serve him, not merely with political neutrality, but with loyalty and enthusiasm. His first task, therefore, is to keep his minister out of trouble with Parliament and, more widely, with public opinion. Consequently, all decisions in the department are made in the knowledge that the minister may be called on to defend them in Parliament, either at question time or in the course of a debate.

For his part, the minister, who often changes more than once in the lifetime of a single cabinet, inevitably turns to his senior civil servant, the officials from the rank of permanent secretary down to the assistant secretaries, for advice and help in running the department and developing its policies. The minister brings, or should bring, to his department his own special political skills, his knowledge of party and cabinet policy, his keen scent for what will be popular and what the public will not stand for, a sense of urgency, and his own conception of what should be the department's policy. The senior civil servant in turn impresses on the minister what may be called "the departmental view." Most departments, out of their own past relationships with their clients and their own internal workings, have evolved a collective view of their own responsibilities and have developed certain rules of thumb to guide them.

Higher civil servants are not passive agents carrying out the policies set by Parliament and cabinet. They are an integral part of the policy-making process, and, although Parliament and the cabinet necessarily have the last word, the civil servants usually have the first one—and often the two are the same.

The responsibilities of a civil servant of the former administrative class are

1. to oversee the day-by-day work of his particular branch of the department;
2. to put forward his own views for advancement of the department's policy;
3. to help prepare legislation;
4. to brief his minister for discussions in the Commons and in committee; and
5. to prepare parliamentary answers for his minister and to supply him with material for speeches, committees, and the like.

THE PUBLIC CORPORATION

In Britain, the government has long participated in the economic activities of the nation. This intervention into the economy did not begin with the Labour government of 1945–51, for the Conservatives, by 1939, had set up six government corporations while they were in power: the Central Electricity Board, which nationalized the generation of electric power in 1926; the British Broadcasting Corporation in 1927; the Electricity Board of Northern Ireland in 1931; the London Passenger Transport Board, which operates the entire Metropolitan Transport system, in 1933; the Northern Ireland Road Transport Board in 1935; and the British Overseas Airways Corporation in 1939. All of these were run by government-appointed boards, and subject to little or no parliamentary control.

The Labour party at the time was much influenced by these models, notably by the London Passenger Transport Board, the brainchild of Herbert (later Lord) Morrison. As early as the mid-1930s, the party had decided to nationalize key industries into public corporations when its had the opportunity to form a government. Elected to power in 1945, the Labour party proceeded to nationalize the Bank of England (1946), the coal mines (1946), civil aviation (1946), inland transport (1947), electricity supply and distribution (1947), and gas supply and distribution (1948), as well as iron and steel (1949). The latter were subsequently denationalized in 1952.

The Labour party, when returned to power in 1964, resumed its program of nationalization. Iron and steel were once more taken into public ownership in 1967. In 1967 an Industrial Reorganization Corporation, designed to stimulate streamlining and mergers in private industry, was set up. A Land Commission was created to buy and hold stocks of land for public building purposes. The Post Office was transformed from a government department into a public corporation. But the Conservative government of 1970 abolished both the IRC and the Land Commission.

The public corporation has four characteristics:

1. Parliament may not inquire into its day-to-day management. Ministers are empowered to give general directions to the corporations on matters affecting the national interest; they appoint the directors of the corporation; they control the corporation's investment plans; and they can set specific goals for each individual industry. In addition, most of the corporations are required to report on their activities annually to Parliament, and the report is subject to debate. To the extent that a minister establishes the policies for a corporation, he is answerable to Parliament for what these policies are. But he need not answer questions on the details of a corporation's operations. This system caused considerable dissatisfaction among both parties in the House of Commons, which in 1957 established a Select Committee on the Nationalized Industries to provide it with more information. The experiment proved highly successful.
2. The personnel of the public corporations are not civil servants, and so neither the Civil Service Department nor Parliament can regulate their remuneration or conditions of service.
3. Their funds are not derived from public taxation. Either the corporations raise most

of their own money on the market, or the Treasury raises it for them.

4. The directors and the chairman of a corporation are appointed by the appropriate minister for a fixed term; thus they do not enjoy the permanent status of civil servants.

Electricity supply and distribution may serve as an example of the way a nationalized industry works. The generation of electricity was nationalized as long ago as 1927, by a Conservative government. The principal reason was the technical desirability of providing one national "grid" to supply the whole nation. Distribution was nationalized in 1947, with the government taking over the private and municipal concerns. Today, the control of the industry vests in two central bodies, the Electricity Council and the Electricity Generating Board. The council is the central body of the whole industry.

Consisting of a number of directors appointed by the minister of trade and industry, together with the chairmen of twelve area boards, the council is responsible for general policy and, more specifically, for capital financing and research. The Electricity Generating Board, consisting of a chairman and other directors, also appointed by the minister, has the technical duty of generating the electricity and supplying it to the area boards, which distribute and sell the electricity. Each area board is composed of a chairman, a deputy chairman, and a number of part-time directors, all appointed by the minister. In each area, area consultative councils represent the interests of consumers. Each council consists of from twenty to thirty members, about half of whom are appointed by the minister from lists nominated by the local authorities. The minister's responsibilities in all this are to appoint the directors, to approve the capital development plans of each area board and of the research program, and to approve the boards' borrowing arrangements. He also has the power to issue general directions in the general interest where he thinks it necessary. Under the 1957 Electricity Act, each area board, and not just the industry as a whole, must pay its own way over a period of time. The industry has been prosperous: up to and including the fiscal year 1964–65, its surpluses amounted to over £374 million.

THE SOCIAL SERVICES

Any setback to economic growth in Britain will seriously affect its social services. This extensive system is administered either by the recently created Department of Health and Social Security (which in 1968 brought together services administered by several different ministries), or by local authorities in partnership with the ministry, and it is reckoned that it costs some $21 billion per annum to run.

The "welfare state" was not invented by the Labour party, but they systematized it. A limited form of National Health Service existed before the war, as well as state unemployment and sickness payments, and old-age pensions. But the Labour party, when it took office in 1945, acted on two documents—a "white paper" entitled "A National Health Service," and the "Beveridge Report" of 1942. The latter, an exhaustive survey of the administration of the social services carried out under the chairmanship of the distinguished sociologist Lord Beveridge, became the basis of the Labour party's policy. The report reflected the problems of the prewar period, with its heavy unemployment. It rested on two main principles: that benefits should be sufficient for subsistence without any other resources, and that there should be a single flat rate of benefit for everyone and for every case of cessation of earnings—whether from sickness, unemployment, or old age.

Both of these principles are under attack. First, "subsistence" at the flat rate is too low a standard. Yet to increase all old-age pensions to a tolerable level would cost far too much. And so the "flat-rate" principle comes under attack also, since it might be better to discriminate, giving more to some and less to others.

The National Health Service

The National Health Service provides free medical advice, drugs, and treatment for every person resident in the United Kingdom; it also provides free hospital care and treatment by specialists; and it carries on a wide range of miscellaneous activities, called the "personal health services"—child clinics, the ambulance service, and the midwife and health visitor service, to mention just a few. These personal health services are the responsibility of the local authorities, under the supervision of the Department of Health and Social Security; but the hospitals, under the National Health Service Act of 1946, are a national responsibility. They are grouped together under twenty regional hospital boards, which are composed of doctors, local government authorities, and members of the general public, all appointed by the minister of health. Finally, the General Practitioner Service is left in the hands of the medical and allied professions themselves, under the control of the minister of health. They work from their own premises. The administration is in the hands of 160 medical executive councils, each consisting of doctors, dentists, and pharmacists, all appointed by the minister.

From the patient's point of view, the system could hardly be simpler. He chooses the general practitioner he wants, and has his name put on that doctor's list. (He can change if he wants to.) From then on, he and his family go to that doctor, who treats them or summons the other services—ambulance, health visitor, specialist, midwife, hospital—as and when he decides they are required. Many criitcisms may be leveled at the National Health Service, as at any administrative agency, but the charge, often made in the United States, that the patient is regimented, is totally without basis.

PROBLEMS OF THE NATIONAL HEALTH SERVICE. Family doctors are dissatisfied with the National Health Service: they complain that there are not enough of their numbers in Britain. Furthermore, many have emigrated, and so, as population has increased the workload for those who have remained has grown. In 1965 a crisis arose between the British Medical Association and the minister over pay and conditions. The doctors threatened to resign in a body from the NHS. In the end the minister

gave way, and an entirely new contract between family doctors and the state was negotiated. Meanwhile the old-fashioned concept of the family doctor working on his own has been changing. With official encouragement, three-quarters of the nation's general practitioners are now in partnership practices based in local health centers.

In addition to doctors' complaints about pay and conditions, the organization of the service has long given rise to problems. Relating the local authority services for maternity and child welfare to the hospital service has proved difficult, and there is a similar lack of relationship between the hospitals and the family doctor. For although the hospitals form part of local society, they are run by the nominees of the minister. It is argued that if they were handed back to enlarged elected regional councils, their interrelationship with the local authority's part of the health services could be greatly improved. On the whole, however, doctors do not like this suggestion: they dislike being controlled by local councillors.

Meanwhile, a more radical school of critics attacks the entire philosophy of the National Health Service. It argues that as long as this has to be financed by general taxation, too little money will be spent upon health. It has been stated, perhaps on doubtful evidence, that perhaps as much as half the population is prepared to accept a scheme based upon private health insurance schemes, with massive government subsidization of the participants. It is unlikely that such a scheme would be adopted. For all its shortcomings, the NHS is very popular and highly prized, as public opinion polls invariably show.

Although the National Health Service was originally totally free, limited charges were introduced soon after its inception. In 1971 the Conservative government announced considerable extension of these charges for drugs and for dental or optical treatment, which met with bitter opposition from the Labour party (although it was a Labour chancellor who first introduced charges); Labour nevertheless went some way toward the views of this school of critics.

Social Security

In 1967–68, $7 billion was spent on social security in Britain, and the sum is rising constantly. Between 1949 and 1969 the sum had multiplied four-and-a-half times, of which only a part represented inflation, since prices as a whole had only doubled during that period. The major payments in 1967–68 were on old-age pensions ($3.4 billion), sickness benefits ($800 million), family allowances ($400 million), unemployment benefits ($312 million) industrial injuries $240 million), and additional sums paid out in special cases ($960 million).

Where does all this money come from? Practically the whole of it comes from the pockets of the employer and the employee. All employed and self-employed persons over the age of 16 must contribute to a national insurance fund. The payments vary according to one's age, and the employer must contribute an amount equal to that of his employee. Wives are insured with their husbands unless they work themselves and choose to be insured separately. This system of compulsory insurance entitles the insured and his family to benefits for sickness and consequent loss of earnings, and for unemployment or industrial injury. Wives receive a maternity grant upon the birth of a child, and a widow a payment upon the death of her husband. If both husband and wife survive, he to the age of 65 and she to the age of 60, they receive an old-age pension. A death grant is also payable on the death of any adult or child. But many persons for one reason or other have not paid their full insurance, or are in such poverty that the insurance benefits are not enough to maintain them and their families; some persons are not covered by the insurance provisions; others are made destitute by some calamity like fire or flood. In such cases the citizen is assisted by a special branch within the Department of Health and Social Security, responsible for relieving extraordinary distress and for supplementing the benefits due under the insurance scheme where this is necessary. Such supplementation varies not only with the need, but also with the *means* of the applicant.

On top of the scheme as described, there has been grafted the beginnings of a *graduated* system. In 1961 the Conservatives introduced a graduated set of contributions, to provide for benefits related to one's earnings. Those earning low wages do not need to contribute, nor do those whose job carries a pension with it, provided steps are taken by the firm to "contract out." The contributor who does come into the scheme pays a percentage of his earnings (over and above what he is paying for the flat-rate scheme) and in return, when he retires, is entitled to receive an addition to his flat-rate pension, suitably adjusted to his earnings at retirement. The Labour party intended to extend and amplify this graduated principle to the entire range of social security benefits, but its far-reaching plans for a new pension system on this basis had not been enacted by the time it lost office.

Grave difficulties arise in the administration of the social security system owing to its flat-rate and subsistence basis. The system takes little account of large families which have small incomes, where the husband is in regular but ill-paid work. It is here that a significant area of child poverty has been exposed. Some have argued for wage supplementation according to the size of family; others for juggling with the present child allowances so as (in effect) to take the money from the bachelor and pay it out to the married man—or, alternatively, to take it from the better-off married man to give to the poorly paid one. Since all these solutions are for a variety of reasons objectionable, it is necessary to consider increasing payments to the poorest families after a test of their means. The Conservatives find no difficulty at all in suggesting something of this kind; but it sticks in the throats of the Labour party.

The old-age pension also arouses controversy. The alternative to raising the pension rate all-round is, once more, that selectivity based on a test of means which is anathema to the Labour party. Yet five new pence (12¢) on the pension requires £20 million ($44 million) in national taxation. The Conservative solution is to make greater use of private occupational pension schemes to finance old age. Nearly two-thirds of the employed population are *already* in such schemes, and four-fifths of the entire labor force work for firms which offer such schemes. The Conservatives urge that these schemes should be generally extended to cover the whole labor force, so that they would be able to draw a pension from the firm *on top of* the flat-rate old age pension, which would continue as it is now.

As long as the national income was likely to increase by 25 percent by (1964/1970), it was possible to ignore all possibilities other than an all-round increase. But since the increase has been little more than half that "planned" in 1964, there is not enough money to service the intended increases in the social services. In that case, it is very likely that the government will be forced into making some payments on a basis of personal means, instead of by a general flat-rate increase. Thus the Beveridge principles of subsistence and the flat rate, already eroded by the beginnings of the graduated-pension scheme, are likely to be much more seriously under attack in the near future.

THE PERFORMANCE
OF THE GOVERNMENTAL
SYSTEM

A Power Pyramid?

In formal terms, public policy is made by a collective council of ministers in which the decisive view (assuming he has one) is the prime minister's. The power of the elected House of Commons to modify this policy is on the decline, the House of Lords' is marginal, and that of the sovereign is negligible. In short, the British system is one of government by the executive branch, tempered by periodical elections. But at a behavioral level this description is quite misleading. It conveys the impression that the government (including the bureaucracy) stand above and away from the life of the nation, freely imposing their policies on it; that secure in its parliamentary majority, it is restrained only at the end of the parliamentary term by a desire to win the next election. But in practice the government is under constant popular constraint, and its freedom of action is limited.

Democratic Constraints

No governments are entirely free to act. A British government is limited, to begin with, by what the administrative machine can manage. It has been a constant source of complaint since at least 1962, for instance, that there have been too few economists in the public service to make economic planning effective. Again, before the 1964 Labour government's intentions to set up a sort of "land bank" (a holding of land by the government for the use of public authorities) could be carried out, it was necessary to establish an entirely new ministry. The government's latitude is confined, again, by the impact of unforeseen emergencies. The entire domestic program has been permanently distorted by the sterling crisis of 1966–67. Of course, in the field of foreign relations, the powers with which it deals, such as the United States, the USSR, or the NATO powers of

SEVEN

Britain today and tomorrow

Europe, often prove entirely intractable. But in addition to constraints like these a British government is subjected to democratic ones reflecting public opinion.

The first of these is the influence of its parliamentary majority. Certainly, where a government regards a parliamentary vote as vital to its survival, it can always rely on a majority. But the parliamentary party is not an artifact of the prime minister and cabinet. It shares distinctively national values, such as sentiments relating to the Commonwealth; and it takes sides, as the general public does, on such disputed matters as industrial relations, economic incentives, taxation levels, and so forth. In addition, it is in constant communion with the public on issues of the day.

Members of Parliament are highly responsive to local anxieties such as unemployment, bad housing, child poverty, and the like. A member is expected to intercede with civil servants and ministers on behalf of individuals and groups in his constituency. He is sensitive to his daily mailbag, and is expected to run weekly or monthly clinics (called "surgeries") for his constituents, wherein he can give them advice and help. Consequently, the parliamentary party can and does become highly disturbed over such unpleasant matters as unemployment and the wage freeze, and ministers, who have to live and work in constant touch with their parliamentary supporters, are inevitably influenced by these expressions of the public's concern. If they are not, they can find a revolt on their hands, such as occurred in 1964 over a bill to limit resale price maintenance. This bill appeared to damage the interests of the small shopkeepers, a highly influential political group, and under their pressure the Conservative cabinet faced the most serious floor revolt that it had met with since taking office in 1951. Though it overrode this revolt in the end, it was not an experience it would willingly court for a second time.

Governments do in fact bear in mind the anxieties of their backbenchers and do what they can to meet these: and indeed, since the backbenchers are a sensitive antenna of the government, in touch with grass-roots opinion,

they find it in their interest to do so. If this appears to contradict what had earlier been said about the limited role which the backbench of the majority party can play in influencing their government, let the reader imagine that Parliament were suspended for a year and the cabinet given power to govern by decree: there can be no doubt that it would act more dictatorially, and with far less concern for public opinion, than it does under the present arrangements.

Secondly, the government is extremely sensitive to unpopularity, and this is why the Opposition is significant. For under the British electoral system the unpopularity of one party is the popularity of the other. The system operates like those little weather-house gadgets whereon one figure, often called "Dry," pops into a doorway while the other, in this case called "Wet," pops out. Governments (and their parliamentary supporters, who fear to lose their seats) watch their unpopularity and the popularity of the Opposition, as measured in public opinion polls, by-elections, and local elections, with the morbid attention of a hypochondriac who keeps taking his own temperature. If the government has sinned by omission, it acts to prevent the Opposition from out-promising it. In the last years, for instance, much public concern has been expressed over child poverty —the plight of low-income families with large numbers of children. When the government failed to legislate for these in its 1967 budget, the Opposition stepped in with a vote of censure. As a result, the government was quick to hint that the matter was "under review." On the other hand, where the government's unpopularity is caused by its act of *commission* (as has been the case with the freezing of wages), it begins to modify its policy.

Obviously, a government is more sensitive to unpopularity at the end of its parliamentary term than at the beginning. But this does not mean that it is unconstrained at the beginning of its term. Throughout its entire period in office it is subject to the administrative or political need to defer to organized group pressures. The importance of this cannot be overemphasized: as has already been said, the interest groups form, as it were, a second circuit of public representation. If parties and elections represent the public at large, the interest groups represent particular and limited publics. Sometimes their pressures reinforce party pressures in the Commons. At other times, the House is presented by the government with the package deals it has negotiated with these groups, and is called on to endorse them—which it does, willy-nilly, since it has neither the time, the information, nor the appropriate procedure to unravel the tangled compromises and begin again. The annual farm price review, the contract of service for doctors in the National Health Service negotiated in 1966–67, and the ill-fated economic "plan" of 1965 provide examples.

Thirdly, however, interest groups sometimes act as "veto" groups, slowing down or actually halting a government's policy. Nowhere is this clearer than in the so-called "prices and incomes policy"—the attempt to find a policy to relate increases in prices, profits, and other forms of incomes to increases in national productivity. In 1962 the Conservatives established a National Incomes Commission, but their policy broke down because the trade unions refused to come before it to present evidence. Further efforts in 1963 and 1964 also broke down, owing to the intransigence of the TUC. With the advent of the Labour government in October 1964, the unions changed their tune and agreed to exercise restraint over wage claims, while for its part the government established the Prices and Incomes Board, giving it the duty of reporting on all changes in these and declaring whether or how far they were consistent with the health of the economy. It was assumed that public opinion would be enough to make employers and employees comply. But by the middle of 1965 this arrangement proved useless, so the government introduced a bill to force employees and employers to give the Prices and Incomes Board advance notification of their intentions. A number of the unions opposed this, and their foremost representative in the cabinet, Mr. Frank Cousins (of the mammoth Transport and General Workers Union) resigned on the issue.

The bill was dropped at the election of March 1966. When reintroduced, it was overtaken by the sterling crisis of July—in response to which the government went much further and tacked a fourth part to the bill. This move gave the government the power to veto any price or wage rises of which it disapproved, and decreed a freeze on wages for the next six months, followed by a six-month period of "severe restraint." It was with the utmost difficulty that the government was able to get the TUC to accept this, and in 1967, when the government sought to make these powers permanent, it had to accept that it could not do so against the opposition of both sides of industry. A limited statutory right remained to refer price rises and wage settlements to the Prices and Incomes Board and to hold these up for up to seven months while the board reported. But as wage settlements could be back-paid when the board reported, this had little effect. This power was later abandoned in face of its inefficiency and continued union opposition.

Then in 1969 the power of the TUC became even more apparent when the Labour government was obliged by the combination of TUC and backbench opposition to withdraw its proposals for legal restrictions on unions. But the success of the Conservative government only two years later in passing an act which included some of the provisions which had formed part of the Labour proposals showed that the veto power of the TUC had been limited.

These interest groups constitute a great "subsystem" in British political life, and it is remarkably stable. When in 1966 the author was revising a book on the interest groups ten years after its previous edition, the most striking feature of the exercise was that, with minor exceptions, the same groups played out the same roles and pursued the same policies, by similar techniques and on similar occasions. The "government" (i.e., the prime minister, the cabinet, and the civil service) is so involved with this political subsystem—partly by the machinery of inquiries and of the six hundred or so advisory committees that serve the various ministries, and partly by the established tradition of mutual consultation and negotiation—

that, irrespective of its party complexion, it finds its discretion trammeled and confined, and its operations slowed down.

Stability—or Immobilism?

Why, then, the surface *appearance* of massive strength and wide discretion on the part of the government? First, because of the mistake of equating the passage of legislation with effective power over the nation. In the Labour party conference of 1965, Mr. Wilson boasted that, despite its majority of only four seats in the Commons, his government had passed more bills than its Conservative predecessors, and would have carried out almost all its pledges within two years. But the object of these pledges was to increase the gross national product and to improve the welfare services. Undeniably, the government had not done either.

Legislation is pointless if the powers conferred are irrelevant to the aims sought—or if, supposing that they are relevant, they prove ineffectual. Whatever the long-term economic results of the nationalization of the steel industry or the establishment of a Land Commission to acquire land for public authorities' building programs, neither of them were of the slightest immediate relevance. And fiscal measures such as the selective employment tax and the capital gains tax, which were immediately relevant to the country's economic plight and the Labour government's desire to equalize incomes when it was in power, were counterproductive. The selective employment tax imposed a levy on each employee engaged in a service industry, and distributed a bonus to each employee engaged in a manufacturing industry. The intention was to cause a drift of employment out of service trades and into manufacture. However, the tax had an exactly contrary effect, while the capital gains tax, a "measure of social justice," which was intended to raise some £80 million per annum, realized only £4½ million in its first year (though considerably more in subsequent years).

In the second place, a great deal of legislation and administration is of no concern to the general public; it affects only special, interested publics, and in these cases the government has far more freedom to maneuver. In matters like the annual farm price review (matters of this kind form the great numerical majority of government bills and regulations), the arrangements are settled by a rather small number of ministers, civil servants, and interest groups; Parliament plays a marginal role, and the general public almost none at all.

But where opinion is genuinely *public* and where it expresses itself, it is arguable that British governments, far from commanding it, surrender to it. The vexed issue of Commonwealth immigration—a euphemism in Britain for *colored* Commonwealth immigration—provides a sad example of this. When the Conservative party introduced a bill in 1961 to refuse entry to Commonwealth immigrants who could not support themselves and did not possess a labor permit (exception was made for students and visitors), the Labour Opposition opposed it bitterly and pledged themselves to repeal it. This commitment grew cloudier as the 1964 election approached, and in their election manifesto Labour merely promised that they would restrict entry until or unless they could negotiate a satisfactory agreement with the Commonwealth countries. The election showed that the policy of restriction was popular, and was dramatically illustrated by the defeat of Mr. Patrick Gordon Walker by a "restrictionist" in the Midlands town of Smethwick. Six months later, in August 1965, the Labour government went much further even than the Conservatives, under whose administration some 20,000 immigrants had entered each year: it announced its intention to restrict the number henceforth to only 8,500.

An even sadder development came two-and-a-half years later. When British citizens of Asian descent (who as citizens had not been affected by the earlier act) began to be expelled from their homes in East Africa in large numbers and to find refuge in Britain, some Conservative politicians raised fears about this immigration and, in a frightened response, the Labour government introduced and had passed through Parliament within one week the Commonwealth Immigration Act of 1968. This act was in defiance of the conscience of most Labour (and some Conservative) M.P.'s, broke Britain's obligation to these Asians, and was opposed by most people who knew anything about the particular problem. But it reflected public opinion.

An even more striking example is provided by economic policy. Ever since 1947, every time a government has intervened to restrain credit and incomes in order to relieve the strain on the balance of payments, it has become profoundly unpopular, and faced the alternative of pursuing inflationary policies or courting electoral defeat: and it has always preferred the former.

At least one former Labour minister (Mr. Benn, minister of technology) once nourished the expectation that the government could stand over and above group pressures, in precisely the way the British government is so often claimed to do. Commenting on the influence of pressure groups, he wrote: "The remedy lies in strengthening those elements that derive their power from the nation as a whole. If the State machine—including Parliament and the Civil Service—can really acquire an impetus of its own . . . then there is hope."[1] Governments are too involved with interest groups and public opinion to acquire any such "impetus of their own." On the contrary, a British government is part of the entire social system, embodying its values, prejudices, aspirations, and interests. It is this remarkably close identification of the two, and the way in which government and people are involved with one another, that makes the system (as opposed to individual governments) so stable and durable. But this characteristic has its corresponding defects: where public sentiment or prejudice is widely involved, governments find it hard to make headway, and in such cases stability has its counterpart in immobilism. One example of this is to be found in economic policy. Another

is in foreign affairs, where widespread notions of great power status, sentiments relating to the Commonwealth, and the noted insularity of the British people all have led governments to undertake far heavier commitments than the country can adequately support.

THE ECONOMY

The economy plays a central role in linking domestic politics with foreign affairs. Domestically, British politics revolve about inequalities, and elections are fought on the issues of increasing the national income and redistributing it. But the strength of the economy also decides the number of troops overseas, the extent to which Britain can assist the rest of the Commonwealth economically (an important factor in its cohesion), and her relationship to the six Common Market powers.

The central features of the economy have been its mediocre growth rate and its instability—the latter arising largely from Britain's position as a vast importer and world banker, a position which exaggerates any balance-of-payments problem and has led to the "stop-go" cycles (i.e., an economy that moves into boom, then into recession). It is important to note, however, that the economic problem is *not* that the economy fails to satisfy rising expectations. Indeed, had it been less successful in this respect, action to improve it might have come much sooner. It is hard to convince the nation that it is badly off when over a recent fifteen-year period the standard of living rose more than over the whole previous half-century. The problem is that this performance, though it satisfies at home, is poor compared with that of Britain's competitors abroad.

One excuse, often alleged, is that such countries have been able to increase their manufacturing labor force in a way Britain cannot —by drawing surplus agricultural labor from the land. But even if adjustment is made for this (as laid out in the OECD booklet, *Economic Growth, 1960–70: A Mid-Decade Review of Prospects*), Britain has lagged far behind.

[1] A. Wedgwood-Benn: *Public Administration*, Vol. 36, (1958) p. 402.

Between 1960 and 1965 (years of exceptionally high growth rate in Britain) the annual percentage increase in output per employed person ran: Japan, 7.2%; France, 4.0%; Italy, 3.8%; Germany, 3.7%; Belgium, 3.5%; Netherlands, 3.2%; United States, 2.9%; and Britain, only 2.5%. At the same time, Britain has been losing her share of world trade: in 1958 her share of world exports was 18%; in 1966 is was only 13%.

The Labour party made the mediocrity of Britain's growth-rate performance and of Conservative "stop-go" policies the central features of its 1964 election campaign, and loudly boasted of the curative powers of its own program involving a new Department of Economic Affairs, a National Economic Plan, and a prices-and-incomes policy. The plan was published in 1965, setting an annual growth rate of 3.8%; and the Labour manifesto of March 1966 foresaw in the next five years a rise in living standards of 25 percent. The sterling crisis of July 1966, which was itself a product of mismanagement during the previous two years, ended this hope. During 1965 wages had soared but prices had lagged behind them, and productivity was almost stagnant. The price paid was the sterling crisis, to which the government responded by wage freeze, deflation, and unemployment (all traditional weapons of the previous Conservative governments). The "National Plan" was dead.

During the next three years the aim of improving Britain's economic growth rate was completely abandoned in the fight to put right Britain's balance-of-payments position. By autumn 1969 the trade returns began to show a better picture. But in the process the government had built up such resistance, in the unions and among its own supporters, to any government policy of controlling incomes that, faced with an impending election, it felt it necessary to allow a free-for-all in wage negotiations. The result in 1970, both before and after the election, was a round of negotiated increases in wage rates averaging 14 percent. Although unemployment was still relatively high and there was little evidence of pressure of demand, this produced a parallel inflation of prices—the clearest instance in Britain of a wage-cost inflation. Mr. Heath's Conservative government took office in June 1970 amid evidence of an accelerating inflation which, if unchecked, could undo the fairly healthy balance-of-payments position which Britain by then enjoyed.

Mr. Heath also took office with two very specific commitments in the economic field which appeared increasingly contradictory as time went on. First, he had promised dramatic and effective action to stop inflation—"reduce prices at a stroke" was his much-quoted election pledge. Secondly, the Conservatives were committed to not reintroducing a Labour government policy of controlling incomes on the lines of the policies tried between 1961 and 1969. The second commitment was maintained —at any rate up to the time of writing—but the government found enormous difficulty in meeting the first. Indeed, the government's own policies, which involved higher protected prices for some food products and introducing or increasing charges for such public services as museums or school meals, were to contribute to price increases.

In 1970 there was a wage inflation of 14 percent and a price inflation of 8 percent— making it by far the worst year ever in Britain's history for inflation. Yet at the same time that inflation was thus accelerating, and impressing both government and public opinion as Britain's most pressing economic problem, industrial output was rising only slowly. Economic growth in 1969 and 1970 was even less than the low rate which had caused such concern some five years earlier. Unemployment in the spring of 1971 reached a postwar record of over 800,-000. In part, this reflected better social security facilities for redundant workers, but it also followed from deliberate government policies of maintaining a fairly tight monetary policy and of refusing financial aid to firms in difficulties. The combined problem of economic stagation and inflation earned the nickname "stagflation"; it gave rise to conflicting demands for government action.

The Conservative government pursued its commitment to stimulate competition, to reduce direct taxation, and to reduce public expenditure. This, in Conservative eyes, should stimulate a better economic performance by privately owned industry.

The government kept a tight hold over its own expenditures; as a result, and also because of the policy of higher direct charges for public services, it was possible in 1971 both to reduce personal taxation and to halve the selective employment tax. The government hoped that the first measure would satisfy some of the demand for higher incomes and that the second, by reducing costs, would reduce prices. At the same time, although eschewing any statutory incomes policy, the government attempted to persuade private employers to resist wage demands of over 10 percent. In the public sector it was able to influence more directly the course of wage negotiations, and consequently over the winter of 1970–71 there were prolonged strikes of municipal workers and of postmen, together with a slowdown action by electric-power workers, who as public employees resisted what they saw as deliberate discrimination against them.

There was also increasing public criticism of what seemed little more than a policy of restricting government expenditure and of exhorting employers and unions not to negotiate too high wage increases. The Labour opposition focused on the increase of unemployment as the most pressing issue and urged a change of economic strategy to combat it. But an increasing body of opinion from both the right and the left in politics, and including several leading academics and public figures, urged that a statutorily enforced incomes policy was the only way of both fairly and effectively stopping wage-cost inflation. Several ingenious variants of an incomes policy, designed to meet the problems which earlier ones had encountered, were being put forward. Others prophesied that the government would shortly be forced to resort to a full wages freeze during which it might be possible for government, employers, and unions to agree on a framework for wage negotiations which would avoid a repeat of the 1970–71 scale of wage inflation. In the background for all was the fear that if "stagflation" continued, Britain's trading position could again deteriorate and her balance-of-payments position yet again become the overriding problem.

BRITAIN AND THE WORLD

Habituation to playing a world role; feelings of kinship with the peoples of such countries as Australia, New Zealand, and Canada; the hangover of the prewar imperial tradition as represented in the new concept of the "multiracial Commonwealth"—all these have played a prominent part in the shaping of Britain's external relations since the end of the war. They have sustained governments which flattered these sentiments, while governments, as part and parcel of the British Commonwealth, have fostered these attitudes in their turn. Though the reasons are more complex than just the mutual interplay of opinion between rulers and ruled, this does go a long way toward explaining why not until May 1967 were all three British political parties united in choosing entry into the European Common Market from among the many alternatives open to them, and were supported there by 57 percent of the population.

Dean Acheson said: "Britain has lost an Empire and not yet found a role." He was right—but on one thing the bulk of the British people *have* concurred since 1945: that whatever the role, it must be a *world* role. The far left has seen this in terms of moral guidance and material aid to the emerging nations; the far right has hankered after a "go-it-alone" policy, based on nuclear capability. The majority have refused to choose between these and so both have been pursued simultaneously.

That Britain should seek to become a nuclear power alongside the United States and the USSR made sense in the 1940s and early 1950s, but has become more and more illusory since then. But the commitment to the Western alliance, and the maintaining of troops in West Germany, is completely understandable, since Europe is Britain's front-line defense. Again, the continuation of world policing made sense as long as great tracts of what is now the Commonwealth remained as dependencies of Britain—but as these became independent, the doctrine lost its logic, at the same time as domestic economics sapped its viability. That this role and the quest for nuclear independence persisted so long is due more than anything else to the lingering imperial vocation of Great Britain.

The British empire was liquidated in the two decades following 1947 with surprisingly little fuss, no bitterness, and no savage rearguard actions such as the French fought in Indochina and Algeria, or the Dutch in Indonesia. The exceptions—the messy withdrawals from Palestine (1948), Cyprus (1957), and Aden (1968), were due, significantly, to the value of these territories as *bases*—not because they were rich territories. That the liquidation of the empire occurred so rapidly and with decency owed much to the "Commonwealth" doctrine. For "empire" was to be substituted a chain of free and independent nations, looking (it was assumed) to Britain for guidance and economic support. This has not happened, and the Commonwealth as a political institution is in an advanced state of dissolution. Unhappily, the myth, while sweetening the end of the empire for the British public, helped perpetuate the illusion that Britain was still a world power, and contributed to her confusion about her defense policy and foreign relations. And it played a major part in restraining the two major parties from closer association with Europe in the fifties.

In 1958 the diminutive Liberal party demanded accession to the European Common Market. In 1961 the Conservatives followed suit—but at the cost of much dissidence in their own ranks, and the opposition of the Labour party, which espoused the cause of the Commonwealth. The Labour party persisted in this role in its 1964 election manifesto. On May 2, 1967, however, eating all his former words, Prime Minister Wilson announced his government's decision to seek admission to the European Common Market. This policy was later endorsed by a nine-to-one majority in the Commons and, according to the public opinion polls, by 57 percent of the population at that time. May 2, 1967 is an historic date, not because this was the first effort to negotiate entry into the EEC (it was the second), nor because it was likely to succeed (it wasn't). It is historic because it marks the moment of truth—when all three parties and most of the population saw that Britain could no longer sustain three world strategies but must make a choice (i.e., from among the United States, Commonwealth, and European attachments); and that of existing alternatives the European choice was the best one.

Defense

Since 1945, Britain has tried to do three things simultaneously: to assist, through NATO, in the defense of Western Europe against the USSR; to possess an independent nuclear deterrent; and to maintain garrisons across the globe.

The first of these follows logically from the desire to keep war from her own shores. Western Europe, to repeat, is Britain's front line.

The second goal made some sense immediately after the war, ran into problems in the fifties and sixties, and is difficult if not impossible to sustain today. The initial decisions, taken in 1946–48, really continued war time trends. The United States had unilaterally broken off the wartime collaboration in nuclear weaponry that had enabled her to build the atomic bomb. But British research was still continuing vigorously, and to continue it did not at that time impose any serious strain on her scientific knowledge or industrial capacity. And the V-bombers, her strike force, could act as carriers.

Britain exploded her atomic bomb in 1952, and her hydrogen bomb in 1957, and the white paper on defense of that year envisaged the new weapons as the chief mode of restraining Soviet attack on Western Europe. But at that very point the policy was rapidly undermined. Britain relied on aircraft; but when the Soviets launched Sputnik in 1957 they made an aircraft delivery system obsolete. Britain therefore decided to build the Blue Streak rocket: but just as this reached its advanced stage in 1959, the Soviets made their moonshot. Now, Blue Streak could only be fired from fixed sites, and the pinpoint accuracy of Soviet rocketry suggested that these would be useless with Soviet missiles zeroed in on to them. So Blue Streak was abandoned and Britain ordered the projected Skybolt missile from the United States. This weapon, fitted to a plane, could be carried for some distance before being released—thus giving it a greatly extended range. But with this, the British deterrent ceased to be entirely independent—since it depended on a component from the United States.

Then in 1962 the United States decided not to develop Skybolt after all, and in return offered Polaris to Britain, which promptly began to build a fleet of four nuclear submarines to take these missiles; and with this the nuclear deterrent became even more reliant on American technology. Despite his acrid criticism of the Polaris fleet while in opposition, Mr. Wilson showed no hesitation in continuing to develop it when he came to office. But advanced technology is eroding its credibility. Soviet antimissile systems make Polaris increasingly unreliable. The substitute is the American advanced missile Poseidon. But these and the cost of converting the nuclear fleet to take them can only be had at a prohibitive price. Advanced technology has priced Britain out of the market as long as she goes it alone.

The third role—that of world policeman—also made sense in the aftermath of the war. Some of the new Commonwealth states (India, for instance) adopted a stance of neutrality; but others, like Pakistan and Malaysia, did not, and arrangements were made to help defend them. Still others, like the sheikdoms of the southern Arabian peninsula and the Persian Gulf, already had defense treaties with Britain which had to be honored. The result was a string of bases encircling the globe, and garrisons in the Mediterranean, the southern Arabian peninsula, and Malaysia.

The more the empire shrank, the greater the difficulty of defending these bases became since, geographically, one "covered" another. Furthermore, the expense of doing so mounted. For these (and other) reasons, in 1947 Britain welcomed the Truman doctrine proclaiming the intention of the United States to defend unilaterally Greece and Turkey, and in 1949

raised no serious objections when Australia and New Zealand entered into a pact with the United States which did not include Britain. Indeed, by the late 1960s, when the "empire" was little more than a string of islands, the chain of bases was being maintained—and even supplemented in the Indian Ocean—less as a moral commitment to the Commonwealth than as part of a deliberate design to continue to play a world role. (This policy was actively encouraged by the United States, which otherwise saw itself relegated to bearing the full cost and responsibility alone; the British government's decision in 1968 to withdraw from its Indian Ocean bases found no favor with the Johnson administration.)

Although the Labour government had committed itself to continue to police the Indian Ocean, both financial and internal political pressures mounted against the policy. Not only did it involve expenditures on defense when the government was trying to reduce the defense budget's proportion of national expenditures, but it involved expenditures in foreign currencies which accentuated the balance-of-payments problem. The policy also came under fire for political reasons from some people in all sections of opinion at home, but most of all from the left wing of the parliamentary Labour party. The final decision to withdraw fully from the Persian Gulf and Singapore bases by 1971 came in January 1968. Devaluation had forced the issue: a decision to withdraw both cut public expenditures and was attractive to the left at a time when the government was asking its left-wing supporters to swallow some very unattractive cuts at home.

But the withdrawal decision was also seen in Britain as part of a deliberate retrenchment from her former world role to a more limited European role. Although the Conservative government decided in 1970 to keep some commitments in Southeast Asia, it confirmed the withdrawal from the Persian Gulf bases, and the somewhat limited commitment to Malaysia and Singapore was seen more as an exception to this retrenchment than as a reversal of it. The historic decision made in the defense field in January 1968 reinforced the historic decision to seek to enter the European Economic Community made in May 1967.

Britain and the European Economic Community

In the immediate aftermath of World War II, British governments (both Labour and Conservative) wanted to keep a foot in the movement toward integration in Western Europe but to avoid becoming too committed to it. Britain helped found the Council of Europe and NATO, but refused to take part in the successful European Coal and Steel Community (ECSC) or the abortive European Defence Community (EDC). When the latter collapsed because of France's failure to ratify the treaty, the British government agreed to help from the West European Union, consisting of Britain and the six states of the ECSC and the proposed EDC. The WEU was to coordinate national defense policies, but in fact only again played a role in Britain's relations with Europe during some diplomatic maneuvering in 1968–69. But when the same six nations of the Continent proposed to set up the European Economic Community (the "Common Market"), Britain did not want to know. In 1957, as the EEC was about to commence, Britain tried to come to terms with it by proposing an Industrial Free Trade Area, which the French scuttled. At this stage, entry into the EEC seemed to the government to conflict too much with Britain's other two circles—the Commonwealth and the special relationship with the United States.

By 1961, when the Conservative government decided to apply for entry to the EEC, both these other ties were declining. But they were still felt too strongly to allow the negotiations to be successful. The actual breakdown of the negotiations was caused by General de Gaulle, who announced that Britain's "special relationship" with the United States disqualified her from entry. Mr. Macmillan had just reinforced that relationship through his agreement with President Kennedy to make Britain's nuclear defense dependent on U.S.-supplied polaris submarines. But the course of negotiations had shown just how difficult it was

to reconcile both Britain's economic and sentimental ties to the Commonwealth with its newfound European enthusiasm. The British negotiators had tried to arrange special conditions to replace the system of Commonwealth trade preferences (free entry of most Commonwealth exports to the British market). Commonwealth sentiment in 1962 was far too strong to permit them to make the best deal for Britain and to let the Commonwealth fend for itself.

Between then and 1967 the Commonwealth relationship had turned sour. In view of the feeling that the Commonwealth had been a handicap to Britain in 1962; of the abandonment, by the new Commonwealth states of Africa, of British political and legal institutions; of the problems associated with Commonwealth immigration; of the proof time and again at the United Nations that the Commonwealth states had no political unity; of the strains created by Britain's failure to deal successfully with the Rhodesian unilateral declaration of independence; of the decline of the proportion of British trade with the Commonwealth and the increasing tendency of Commonwealth countries (including some who had made the most noise about their British trade connection in 1962) to expand their trade with other markets—in view of all these factors, there existed in Britain a general feeling that the Commonwealth must not prove an obstacle to British entry into Europe. In the event, the 1970–71 negotiations have shown that only two very isolated Commonwealth problems remained: New Zealand's dependence on agricultural exports to the British market and the Commonwealth sugar agreement. And at the 1971 Commonwealth prime ministers' conference Mr. Heath made it clear that he was prepared to see the breakup of the Commonwealth rather than have his government's policy toward South Africa dictated by considerations of the feelings of Commonwealth countries.

The "special relationship" with the United States was also losing its attractions. Increasingly, Britain realized that it was, at best, a special dependency—militarily, economically, and diplomatically. The temporary and unlooked-for alliance of the United States and the

USSR at the U.N. against Britain's Suez enterprise in 1956 revealed this dependence in a singularly crude form. And, in 1962, Britain stood helplessly by while the United States and the USSR confronted each other over Cuba. The British government declined to participate in the war in Vietnam (incidentally, thus causing a further diplomatic separation between itself and Australia and New Zealand, both of which had entered into military alliance with the United States). Public opinion found the Vietnam War even more distasteful, and several opinion polls indicated that a majority were against even the moral support for the U.S. government in Vietnam which Mr. Wilson offered. A frequent argument used by supporters of British entry to the EEC was that the only alternative was becoming in effect the fifty-first state.

So, by 1967 there was widespread agreement in Britain that, strategically and politically, Britain's place ought to be in the Common Market. More was to be gained by becoming a partner in an extremely powerful confederation of European nations, with an inevitably strong influence on its common policies, than by staying out. At the same time, the economic arguments for entry—which had played a big part in persuading the Conservative government, backed by most of Britain's industry, to seek entry in 1961—seemed less strong. But the Gaullist veto in 1967 came before negotiations could get under way, so that Mr. Wilson's commitment to entry was never put to a full test.

Between 1967 and 1970, both Britain and the EEC played a waiting game. The weakening of President de Gaulle's position and then his resignation made it clear that, with patience, the door might be reopened for Britain. But neither side wanted to commence serious negotiations until the 1970 general election had decided the composition of the Parliament and government that would take Britain in. The new Conservative government decided to go ahead, and in the autumn of 1970 negotiations started in earnest, and, except for a few details (notably over the Common Market's fishing policy), were successfully completed in June 1971. (Fisheries were negotiated, January 1972.)

But one factor, hitherto latent, had become a major impediment by 1971. The 1961 application had been made with a significant—though not overwhelming—majority of public opinion, as measured by the polls, in favor of entry. Support dropped somewhat as negotiations dragged on, but de Gaulle's first veto seemed to renew British determination to get into the EEC: by 1966 polls recorded over two-thirds in favor of a fresh application, with a very few against. At the time of the application approved by all three parties in 1967, the figure in favor had lowered to 57%. Two years later, as de Gaulle's departure opened Britain's chances, opinion seemed fairly evenly divided. But in the summer of 1969 a marked change came over the poll returns; from autumn 1969 until July 1971 they did not record more than 30% in favor and sometimes 20% or lower. In 1970 and early 1971 the various polls showed a consistent and steady picture: something like two-thirds of Britons did not want to enter Europe, around a quarter wanted to, and the rest didn't know.

When the negotiations succeeded and the Government published the agreed terms in July 1971, it therefore faced considerable difficulty in persuading public opinion of their acceptability and in persuading its own more hesitant supporters that it was justified in asking for their support when the public seemed so opposed.

The summer of 1971 was scheduled by the government as a period of "great debate" about the proposed terms. Between two long debates in Parliament in July and at the end of October the Government and the European Movement campaigned vigorously to convince the public of the need for Britain to join Europe. The opponents, with less unity and fewer resources, replied by stressing fears of loss of national sovereignty and most of all of the rise in food prices consequent upon the acceptance of the common agricultural policy. The two main party conferences were held and showed overwhelming support (by a ten-to-one majority) among Conservatives for entry and only a slightly smaller majority (by five-to-one) in the Labour Party against. The Labour Party's opposition reflected two quite distinct positions.

Firstly an opposition of principle to what many of its Left-wing members regarded as a Capitalist cartel. Secondly, this being Mr. Wilson's position, an opposition to the precise details of the terms of entry negotiated. Mr. Wilson was much criticized for a position which both avoided the fundamental issue and which was inconsistent with the commitments he had made when Prime Minister. But as leader of a party which found itself so opposed to entry he had little alternative and his change of face almost certainly avoided worse tensions inside the party than were actually experienced. His position illustrates exigencies of the British party system and the fact that when the October 1971 vote was taken in Parliament, the Common Market had become for the first time a matter of clear dispute between the two main parties. The Liberal Party remained the most enthusiastic and united in favor of the EEC while the Scots and Welsh Nationalists were both clearly opposed. Northern Irish parties, including the Conservatives' allies the Ulster Unionists, tended to be hostile. Public opinion moved towards favoring entry but the movement was almost exclusively among Conservative voters and left a majority of around three-to-two against entry in early autumn 1971.

When the House of Commons voted to approve British entry on the terms negotiated on 28 October 1971, it had become therefore mainly a party vote. Suggestions that the issue should go to a referendum, as in the other three applicant countries (Denmark, Ireland and Norway), were unitedly dismissed by established political leaders as contrary to British practice.

Suggestions that the Commons should decide on a free vote (i.e., a vote without any instructions on how to vote from the Party Whip) seemed equally unheeded until at the last minute the Government announced a free vote for its own supporters—too late for the Labour leadership to follow suit. In the event the Conservative M.P.'s split 280 to 33 in favor of entry (or 282 to 39 including the Ulster Unionists) with three abstentions. But only 198 Labour M.P.'s obeyed the Whip to vote against entry; 69 voted for entry and twenty more (pro-entry but unwilling to vote against their party) abstained. The Labour rebels included all those who had held office as Foreign Secretary or as Minister for relations with the European Communities during the 1964–70 Labour Government, and half the members of the Cabinet which had applied for entry in 1967. The Labour Party was opposed but its collective leadership remained more than half convinced of the need for Britain to join the EEC.

The Commons majority of 356 to 244 in favor of the Common Market in October 1971 was a considerable reduction from the May 1967 vote which approved the decision to seek entry. It reflected widespread doubt in the country and the fact that the issue had become one of interparty dispute. But in these circumstances, the size and composition of the majority showed that most political leaders were convinced that Britain's future lay in European integration.

The Treaty of Accession was signed—with no Labour members attending this ceremony—on January 22, 1972. History had been made.

bibliography

CHAPTER 1

An excellent geography of the United Kingdom is S. H. Beaver and L. D. Stamp, *The British Isles* (Longmans, 1963).[1] The history of the country may be followed in G. M. Trevelyan, *History of England* (Longmans, 1944), and in the recent *English History: a Survey* by Sir George Clark (Oxford, Clarendon Press, 1971). For recent economic and social history, see G. D. H. Cole and R. Postgate, *The Common People, 1745–1945* (Methuen, 1961), and C. L. Mowat *Britain between the Wars, 1918–1940* (University of Chicago Press, 1955). For the last half century, see the brilliant and controversial A. J. P. Taylor, *English History, 1914–1945* (Oxford University Press, 1968). Constitutional law is outlined in H. Phillips, *Constitution Law* (Sweet and Maxwell, 1957); G. Wilson, *Cases and Materials on Constitutional and Administrative Law* (Cambridge University Press, 1960) is most imaginative and highly recommended. H. Street, *Freedom, the individual and the Law* (Pelican, 1963) is a concise and illuminating introduction to the "liberties of Englishmen." See also S. A. de Street, *Constitutional and Administrative Law* (Penguin Books, 1971).

CHAPTER 2

This chapter deals with a variety of topics, and so the bibliography tends to range widely. The essential statistics are to be found in *Britain—An Official Handbook* [Her Majesty's Stationery Office (H.M.S.O.), 1972]; D. C. Marsh *The Changing Social Structure of England and Wales* (Routledge, 1965); The Annual Abstract of Statistics (H.M.S.O., 1972) and *National Income and Expenditure* (H.M.S.O.).

Much behavioral work is now coming forward including R. Rose's *Politics in England* (Faber, 1965); J. Blondel's excellent *Voters, Parties and Leaders* (Pelican, 1968); and G. A. Almond and S. Verba's superlative *The Civic Culture* (Princeton, 1963). But to get the "feel" of English public life, consult also A. Sampson's *Anatomy of Britain Today* (Hodder and Stoughton, 1965)—a John Guntheresque account.

[1] All titles listed in this bibliography were published in England unless otherwise noted.

He has followed this up by a substantial revision, *The New Anatomy of Britain Today* (Hodder & Stoughton, 1971).

For the educational system generally, see L. Smith, *Education in Great Britain* (Oxford, 1958), and his *Education: an Introductory Survey* (Pelican, 1962). For the press, see A. P. Robinson, *Newspapers Today* (Oxford, 1956), and the *Report of the Royal Commission on the Press* (1961–62), H.M.S.O., *cmnd.*, 1811. For radio and television broadcasting, see B. Paulu, *British Broadcasting* (Minneapolis: University of Minnesota Press, 1956), and his *British Broadcasting in Transmission* (Macmillan, 1961). The relationship between television and electoral behavior has been investigated in: J. Trenamen and D. McQuail, *Television and the Political Image* (Methuen, 1961) and its follow-up study, J. G. Blumler and D. McQuail, *Television in Politics* (Faber, 1968).

The relationship between voting and social class can be followed in J. Bonham, *The Middle Class Vote* (Faber, 1954); in M. Abrams and R. Rose, *Must Labour Lose?* (Penguin, 1960); and in R. R. Alford, *Party and Society* (Rand McNally, 1963). The topic is also dealt with in the final chapter of Sir Ivor Jennings, *Party Politics*, vol. 1, *Appeal to the People* (Cambridge University Press, 1960), which is a history of electioneering and voting patterns up to the present day. The phenomenon of the "working-class Tory" which baffles observers of the British Political scene (because of the unstated assumption that "working class" men would, if rational, vote Labour) has been studied by E. A. Nordlinger, *The Working Class Tories* (MacGibbon & Key, 1967) and by R. T. Mackenzie and A. Silver in *Angels in Marble* (Heinemann, 1968). But the most exhaustive and profound study of the variables making for changes in electoral attitudes is D. Butler and D. Stokes, *Political Change in Britain* (Macmillan, 1969). The notion of the "power elite" is outlined by P. Shore in *In the Room at the Top,* and by N. Mackenzie (ed.), in *Conviction* (MacGibbon & Kee, 1958). Some of the political *facts* are given in W. L. Guttsman, *The British Political Elite* (McGibbon and Kee, 1963).

CHAPTER 3

On pressure groups, consult S. E. Finer, *Anonymous Empire,* 2nd ed. (Pall Mall Press, 1966), and A. Potter, *Organised Groups in British National Politics* (Faber, 1961). Much has been written about the trade unions. E. L. Wigham, *Trade Unions* (Oxford, 1956), is a brief introduction to the subject. J. Goldstein, *The Government of British Trade Unions* (Allen & Unwin, 1952) is a detailed study of a branch of the T.G.W.U. V. L. Allen, *Trade Unions and the Government* (Longmans, 1960) contains much useful information but is disappointing. Much the most illuminating survey of the practice, as well as the "theory" of current industrial relations (prior to the Industrial Relations Act, 1971) is the *Report of the Royal Commission on Trade Unions,* known as the "Donovan" Report, whose references number is H.M.S.O., 1968, *cmnd.* 3623. There are now several full-length studies of British pressure groups. H. Eckstein, *Pressure Group Politics* (Allen & Unwin, 1960) is a study of the British Medical Association; P. Self and H. Storing, *The State and the Farmer* (Allen & Unwin, 1962) is a study of the National Farmers' Union; J. B. Christoph, *Capital Punishment and British Politics* (Faber, 1962), is a case study of the effort to abolish capital punishment and of the work of the Howard League for Penal Reform in trying to bring this about; and H. H. Wilson, *Pressure Groups* (Secker and Warburg, 1961) is a case study of the campaign which succeeded in getting the Conservative government to adopt commercial television. G. Wootton, *The Politics of Influence* (Routledge, 1963) deals with Veterans' Associations.

CHAPTER 4

For the parties in general, see first R. T. McKenzie, *British Political Parties* (Heineman, 1964); S. H. Beer, *British Politics in the Collective Age* (New York: Knopf, 1965); and Sir Ivor Jennings, *Party Politics*, vol. 1, *Appeal to the People* (Cambridge, 1960), and its sequel, vol. 2, *The Growth of the Parties* (Cambridge, 1961). For the Conservatives see G. Block, *A Source Book of Conservatism* (London, Conservative Political Centre, 1964), and the *Campaign Guide 1971* (Conservative and Unionist Central Office, Smith Square, London, S.W.1.). For its history, see Sir Robert Blake, *The Conservative Party: From Peel to Churchill* (Eyre & Spottiswoode, 1969).

Considerably more has been written about the Labour Party. G. D. H. Cole has left his *Working*

Class Politics, 1832–1914 (Routledge, 1942) and his *History of the Labour Party from 1914* (Routledge, 1948). Three books throw light on its diverse "tendencies": A. C. Crosland, *The Future of Socialism* (Cape, 1956), a penetrating and scholarly work representing the right-wing Labour attitude; the special Labour Party edition of *The Political Quarterly*, (Stevens, July–Sept., 1960), which canvassed current difficulties, again from a right-wing point of view; and L. Hunter, *The Road to Brighton Pier* (Barker, 1959), a journalist's account of the "Bevanite" movement between 1950 and 1956. For a "view from the top," ex-Prime Minister Harold Wilson's *The Labour Government 1964–1970*, is, of course, unique. For the Communist Party, see H. M. Pelling, *History of the Communist Party of Great Britain* (Black, 1958). A truly excellent study of the role of the trade unions in the Labour Party is M. Harrison, *Trade Unions and the Labour Party since 1945* (Allen & Unwin, 1960). R. Rose's *Influencing Voters* (Faber, 1967) is a study of the importance of money and mass media; A. Howard and R. West's *The Making of the Prime Minister* (Cape, 1965) describes the parties' run-up to the election of 1964. A. Ranney's *Pathways to Parliament* is a fine study of candidate selection. See also Michael Rush's *The Selection of Parliamentary Candidates* (Nelson, 1969) on the same subject; this study includes case histories. For the Liberal Party, consult J. Rasmussen, *The Liberal Party* (Constable, 1965).

The general electoral system and its consequences are analyzed, statistically and otherwise, in a brilliant volume: D. S. Butler, *The Electoral System in Britain* (Oxford, 1963). The course of all the elections since 1945 can be followed in the "Nuffield" election series: McCallum and Readman, *The British General Election of 1945* (Oxford, 1946), and the subsequent studies, with the same general title, by H. G. Nicholas for the election of 1950, and D. S. Butler for the elections of 1951, 1955, 1959, 1964, 1966 and 1970 (all published by Macmillan). All contain valuable statistical analyses of the results, as well as descriptions of campaign issues, techniques and so forth.

CHAPTER 5

The procedure of Parliament finds its classic exposition in "Erskine May," the colloquial descrip-

tion of the great manual called *Treatise on The Law, Privileges, Proceedings and Usage of Parliament* (Butterworth, 1967) first produced by Sir Thomas Erskine May in 1844, and subsequently revised by successive Clerks to the House of Commons. Lord Campion's introduction to *The Procedure of the House of Commons* (Macmillan, 1958), is an abbreviated manual by the former Clerk to the House; and E. Taylor, *The House of Commons at Work* (Pelican Books, 1963) is a first-class elementary introduction. The place of Parliament in the British system of government is systematically treated in Sir Ivor Jennings' second classic, *Parliament*, 3rd ed. (Cambridge, 1957). This not only describes its practice and procedure, but also treats of the M.P.'s, the Parliamentary Parties, the Whigs, and the sources of legislation. A. H. Hanson and H. V. Wiseman have produced a casebook of examples in *Parliament at Work* (Stevens, 1962). R. Young, *The British Parliament* (Faber, 1962) is a very perceptive study of Parliament with certain key cases being analyzed in detail. B. Crick, *The Reform of Parliament* (New York: Doubleday, 1965) is a brilliant analysis of its current weaknesses. See also the reader by A. H. Hanson and B. Crick, *The Commons in Transition* (Collins, 1970) and the full-scale study of its influence relative to the executive in R. Butt, *The Power of Parliament* (Constable, 1969).

There are many works on particular aspects of Parliament. The House of Lords is dealt with in P. A. Brodmhead, *The House of Lords and Contemporary Politics 1911–1957* (Routledge, 1958). In his *Elections and Electors* (Eyre and Spottiswoode, 1955), J. F. S. Ross has explored the backgrounds of M.P.'s in respect to their age, education, occupation, and the like. S. E. Finer, H. B. Berrington, and D. Bartholomew, in their *Backbench Opinion in the House of Commons 1955–1959* (Pergamon, 1961), have pioneered the technique of examining backbenchers' signatures on the motions on the Order Paper in order to relate these to the social background of the M.P.'s who have signed such motions. The role of the backbencher has recently been explored in P. G. Richards, *Honourable Members* (Faber, 1959). An interesting and provoking book, describing the relationship of the Member to his constituents and to the Parliamentary Party, is Nigel Nicholson, *People and Parliament* (Weidenfeld and Nicolson, 1958). Finally, D. N. Chester and N. Bowring's *Questions in Parliament* (Oxford, 1962) is a full-length and definitive study of the parliamentary question and its effects on the Civil Service and Parliament.

The working of the Monarchy can be followed in D. Laird, *How the Queen Reigns* (Hodder, 1959), and D. Morrah, *The Work of the Queen* (Kimber, 1958). It is necessary to supplement these with biographies such as H. Nicolson's classic *George V* (Constable, 1952), and J. W. Wheeler-Bennett's *George VI* (Macmillan, 1958). For the mystique of the Monarchy see the critical volume, Lord Altrincham, (ed.), *Is the Monarchy Perfect?* (Calder, 1958).

CHAPTER 6

The classic work on the Cabinet is Sir Ivor Jennings, *Cabinet Government* (Cambridge, 1959). An interesting text is H. Morrison, *Government and Parliament* (Oxford, 1960), which gives an inside view by a former Leader of the House of Commons. Reference should certainly be made to the new history of the Cabinet, J. P. Mackintosh's *The British Cabinet* (Stevens, 1968), which is the source of the controversial "Prime Ministerial" thesis which is carried to typically brilliant but extravagant lengths by R. H. S. Crossman in his *Introduction to Bagehot's English Constitution* (Fontana ed., 1963). The two preceding works have generated a controversy which can be followed in A. King (ed.), *The British Prime Minister* (Macmillan, 1969), H. Berkeley, *The Power of the Prime Minister* (Allen & Unwin, 1968), and P. Gordon-Walker, *The Cabinet* (Cape, 1970). These should be checked against the previously mentioned H. Wilson, *The Labour Government 1964–1970* which provides, in the way of political memoirs, the first "day-by-day and blow-by-blow" account of what it is to be a prime minister.

For a general introduction to the British administration, consult S. E. Finer, *A Primer of Public Administration* (Mullers, 1957), and for a comprehensive text, W. J. M. Mackenzie and J. W. Grove, *Central Administration in Great Britain* (Longmans, 1957). The Civil Service is described in F. Dunnill, *The Civil Service* (Allen & Unwin, 1956). R. G. S. Brown, *The Administrative Process in Britain* (Methuen, 1971) is an excellent account of its subject, while G. K. Fry, *Statesmen in Disguise* (Macmillan, 1969) is best described by its subtitle, *viz.,* "The

Changing Role of the Administrative Class of the British Home Civil Service, 1853–1966." The individual Departments are described in the New Whitehall Series, published by Allen & Unwin, as follows: Sir C. J. Jeffries, *The Colonial Office* (1956); Lord Strang, *The Foreign Office* (1955); Sir Frank Newman, *The Home Office* (1954); Sir Geoffrey King, *The Ministry of Pensions and National Insurance* (1958); Sir Gilmor Jenkins, *The Ministry of Transport and Civil Aviation* (1959); Sir Harold Emmerson, *The Ministry of Works* (1956); Sir David Milne, *The Scottish Office* (1957); Sir J. Winnifrith, *The Ministry of Agriculture, Fisheries and Food* (1962); Sir J. Crombie, *H. M. Customs and Excise* (1962); Sir A. Johnson, *The Inland Revenue* (1965); and L. O. Bridges, *The Treasury* (1964).

The important and unique position of the Treasury is described in S. H. Beer's *Treasury Control* (Oxford, 1957); S. Brittan's *The Treasury Under the Tories* (Penguin, 1964) is a vivid account of its internal workings, and its relationship to economic planning. This work has been expanded and revised in the same author's *Steering the Economy: the Role of the Treasury* (Secker & Warburg, 1969). The latter's pamphlet, "Inquest on Planning" (P.E.P., 1967), is an incisive criticism of the way this has been handled. Other works relating to the relationship between the civil service and the other organs of government include: D. Coombes, *The Member of Parliament and the Administration* (Allen & Unwin, 1966), and I. Gilmour, *The Body Politic* (Hutchinson, 1969). See also W. J. Stankiewicz, *Crisis in British Government* (Macmillan, N.Y., 1967). On nationalized industries, see A. H. Hanson, *Parliament and Public Ownership* (Allen & Unwin, 1960), and J. Grove, *Government and Industry in Britain* (Longmans, 1962).

For the Social Services, see M. Brown, *Introduction to Social Administration* (Hutchinson, 1969); Penelope Hall's *The Social Services of Modern England* (Routledge, 1969). For critical appraisals, see the following works on particular aspects of the welfare services: R. Titmuss, *Essays on the Welfare State* (Allen & Unwin, 1958); B. S. Shenfield, *Social Policies for Old Age* (Routledge, 1957); H. Eckstein, *The English Health Service* (Cambridge: Harvard U.P., 1959); A. Lindsey, *Socialized Medicine in England and Wales* (Chapel Hill: University of North Carolina Press, 1962); and Sir P. Abercrombie,

Town & Country Planning (Oxford, 1960). Reference should also be made to R. Titmuss, *Commitment to Welfare* (Allen & Unwin, 1968); J. B. Cullingworth, *Housing and Local Government* (Allen & Unwin, 1966); D. Donnison, *The Government of Housing* (Penguin, 1967).

Roy C. Macridis

FRANCE

France is a relatively small country—smaller in area than Texas. It has approximately 51 million inhabitants. Despite certain backward sectors in her economy, France is a highly industrialized and prosperous nation. The average Frenchman enjoys an individual income that ranks him sixth in wealth in the world. Progress made since World War II in the production of energy, chemicals, aeronautics, aluminum, and automobiles place France in the same industrial rank with England and West Germany, second only to the United States, the Soviet Union, and Japan.

Located in the western part of Europe on the Atlantic Ocean and, to the south, on the Mediterranean Sea, France has been both a Continental and a maritime power. Until World War II, she had the second largest colonial empire, stretching into the heart of Africa, the Middle East, and the Far East. More than 100 million people lived under the French flag, and the great majority still remain linked to France by economic and cultural ties.

France has long been considered the crucible of what we loosely call "Western civilization." Her name carries a special, even if not always the same, message to every educated person in the world. She is the "oldest daughter" of the Roman Catholic church, and her missionaries and religious orders worked to restore the unity of the church against the Reformation and later helped to diffuse the teaching of the church. It is the land where monarchy became associated with national greatness, but also the land of the Revolution of 1789, in which all privileges were swept aside in the name of popular sovereignty, freedom, and equality. Napoleon spread the doctrine of the Revolution and established his dominion over the greater part of Europe. It is a land of people who have constantly experimented with ideas, who take nothing for granted, especially in politics. No other nation has radiated its influence for so long a period and so profoundly affected the world's thoughts and ways of life.

Regime Instability

It is precisely the richness and the diversity of the French past that has accounted for one of

ONE

introduction

the most characteristic features of the French political system—instability. Without any ethnic minorities to speak of (only after the turn of the century and more particularly since World War II has there been an appreciable immigration of Italian, Spanish, and Polish workers and more recently of Algerians); without any significant religious minorities (there are less than 1 million Protestants); and with a strong feeling of national unity forged by a thousand years of national existence, the French have been unable to come to terms with any political regime.

Since the Revolution of 1789 that overthrew the Monarchy (*l'ancien régime*) and proclaimed a republic, France has had sixteen different constitutions that have created many forms of government. The Revolution led to a constitutional monarchy (1789–91), which became a republic (1792–95), which in turn gave place to the directorate and the consulate (1799), with Napoleon as the first consul. In 1804 France was transformed into an "empire," and Napoleon became the "emperor," governing by proclamations and executive orders. In 1814 the empire was brought down by an alliance of most of the other major countries of Europe, and the Bourbon kings were restored. But they gave way after the Revolution of 1830 to the "July Monarchy," the Orleanist branch of the Bourbon dynasty that ruled until 1848. The Revolution of 1848 again discarded the monarchy in favor of a new Republic (the Second Republic) based on universal male suffrage and a presidential system containing checks and balances between the legislature and the presidency. The president, Louis Napoleon (Napoleon III), abolished the republic in 1851, to introduce the "Second Empire," in which he governed, as his uncle had done, by executive proclamations, although he did seek popular support through plebiscites.

The defeat of Napoleon III in the Franco-Prussian War (1870) spawned another crisis, and a new republican constitution (the Third Republic) was introduced in 1875. It was destined to have the longest life in French political history. It weathered many crises, including World War I, which ravaged the economy and decimated France's population, but collapsed when France was overrun by the Nazi armies at

the beginning of World War II (1940). The unoccupied part of France, and later the whole of the country, was then ruled by the so-called Vichy regime (1940–44), in which all powers were concentrated in one man, Marshal Pétain, who was granted broad authority by the constitutional convention that met on July 10, 1940, in the wake of the French defeat. After the Liberation, France returned to a republican form of government—the Fourth Republic—whose constitution was approved by the people in a special referendum on October 21, 1946. It lasted for only twelve years and was radically overhauled in the summer of 1958. On September 28, 1958, the French voted overwhelmingly in favor of a new republican constitution—the Fifth Republic—in which very broad powers are invested in the president.

This turnover of political regimes is not an historical accident. To understand these fluctuations, we must keep in mind that whenever compromise between conflicting groups is not possible, the dominant one will impose its views, often by force. Thus, political changes frequently reflect, as Aristotle pointed out, profound shifts in the balance of power between various social forces. The Revolution of 1789 struck a heavy blow at the landed aristocracy and the monarchy. It also affected adversely the rights of the higher clergy and thus the overall position of the Catholic church. From then on, throughout the whole of the nineteenth century, the nobility and the church looked for revenge at every opportunity. They worked and sometimes conspired against all republics. The restoration of a monarchy in 1814 meant their return to power and influence. They were opposed by the middle and lower-middle classes, many of the farmers, and, after the first half of the nineteenth century, by the workers.

"Bonapartism" is a more difficult phenomenon to define. It borrowed both from the Revolution of 1789—it extolled equality and maintained the symbols of the Revolution—and from the *l'ancien régime*—it reintroduced titles of nobility, was in essence a one-man rule, relied on the army and the bureaucracy, and found it convenient to come to terms with the church. Bonapartism secured the support of the middle class, and its appeal to national unity and greatness found a ready ear among all groups of the population, including even the workers. Both Napeoleons tried to forge national unity and reduce the various social conflicts, but in vain. By the middle of the nineteenth century, the working class began to grow in numbers and to develop political consciousness. This class sought political participation, but twice found itself—in 1848 and in 1871—rejected or suppressed. The universal suffrage granted in 1848 became a mockery under the rule of Louis Napoleon, and the Third Republic was inaugurated in the wake of an uprising of the workers of Paris—the Paris Commune—and a bloody repression in which more than 10,000 workers were killed. It was not that the French ruling classes were by disposition hostile to the workers, but rather that the prevailing climate of opinion made compromise difficult. The workers themselves were unwilling to accept the ways of democracy and use the ballot to further their claims. They favored violent and revolutionary schemes to destroy or to take control of the state.

At the turn of the century, the appeal of the monarchy showed unmistakable signs of decline, while the republic was clearly on the ascendancy. Bonapartism, however, characterized by an appeal to personal government and leadership, continued to be a part of the French political tradition. It emerged twice in the twentieth century when the republic, and especially the parliamentary institutions, appeared hopelessly deadlocked over the issues confronting the nation, and when disaster threatened from abroad—after France's defeat in 1940 and more particularly during the repeated setbacks in the colonial wars between 1945 and 1958.

Every constitutional change in France since 1789, therefore, has resulted from a change in the equilibrium of social forces, from a shift in the alliances between workers, farmers, the lower and middle classes, business, and the professions. Important social and interest groups like the church, the army, the bureaucracy, business, the trade unions, intellectuals, and often students and teachers frequently became deeply involved in these power struggles. It is not accidental, for instance, that three out

of the four republics that preceded the Fifth Republic were toppled by a combination of a military setback and a military coup and that in all cases they were replaced by a political regime which, whatever its form, was headed by a general.

The French since the Revolution of 1789 have not agreed on the political regime they want (see Table 1-1). They have alternated between a monarchy, a republic, and a third type that for a lack of a better term we call Bonapartism, in which broad powers are delegated to one man. France thus has experienced a continuous "crisis of legitimacy." It has experimented with many forms of government, but none of them developed the respect and deference that the British pay their parliamentary system and their monarch. At the most, the various governments in France have known only a low degree of legitimacy. Many have been overthrown by violence. Uprisings and revolutions have been an integral part of French history. Without an awareness of these past cleavages, one can hardly understand the present French society or governments. Past divisions continue to be registered among the French today, coloring their emotions and actions and shaping their political goals.

The "Events" of May–June 1968

The discrepancy between the "political culture" on the one hand and the political regime—any regime—on the other was clearly evidenced in May–June 1968. The French now refer to the virtual social, economic, and political chaos that gripped the country as *les évenements*—the "Events." Whatever the characterization, it was one of the most explosive occurrences that brought the government, the educational system, the civil service, the economy to a virtual standstill. It was directed in a diffuse way, not only against the government and the political regime, but also against the "establishment" at all levels of the economic, political, and social order. In the name of equality and participation, an attempt was made to break down every hierarchical structure, every superior-subordinate relationship. Only the

TABLE 1-1. *The Instability of the French Political System*

Republic	Monarchy	"Bonapartism"
	L'ancien régime (to 1789) ended by revolution	
The First Republic (1792–1795) ended by military coup	Constitutional Monarchy (1789–1791)	Napoleonic dictatorship (1799–1814) ended by military defeat
The Second Republic (1848–1851) ended by military coup	The Bourbon Restoration (1814–1830) ended by revolution	The Second Empire: Napoleon III (1851–1870) ended by military defeat and revolution
The Third Republic (1870–1940) ended by military defeat	The Orleanist "July Monarchy" (1830–1848) ended by revolution	
The Fourth Republic (1946–1958) ended by military uprising		The Vichy Régime: Marshal Pétain (1940–1944) ended by military defeat of the Axis powers
The Fifth Republic ← (1958–)	⟶	The Fifth Republic (1958–)

army remained unaffected. "Communes" and "states general" were formed not only in the universities and sometimes in the high schools, but also in cities and frequently in various civil service, cultural, industrial, business, and even athletic organizations—even some of the most unlikely ones like the football associations and the movie industry! The theme was to replace the boss, the "patron," everywhere with committees and to subject every decision to discussion and consent.

The Events were initiated by the students —not an uncommon practice these days, even elsewhere than France. But in France the student uprising spread to affect the workers, the civil servants, and many professional activities that are strictly middle-class in character.[1]

The Events began with a meeting held at Nanterre (University of Paris) to protest the arrest of students that had been active on behalf of the Vietcong and who had committed a number of acts of violence, many in protest also against the existing restrictions in the university and the dormitories. The "March 22 movement" was thus founded. Its members occupied a lecture hall in the university, an occupation that was condemned by the more representative student union, the National Union of the Students of France (UNEF). The student uprisings and occupations spread. The police were ultimately called in to dislodge the students

[1] The sequence of the events is succinctly described by Professor Bernard E. Brown in *The French Revolt:*

May 1968 (New York: McCaleb-Seiler, 1971), upon which this discussion draws extensively. A good account will be found in the *Année politique,* 1968. A general interpretation of the events and their causes appears in Jean Touchard and Philippe Bénéton, "Les Evenements du Mai–Juin 1968: Une Interpretation," *Revue française de science politique* 20, no. 3 (June 1970), 503–43.

from the Sorbonne, where a number of them had gathered. A strike was immediately called in protest of the arrest of students that followed, arrests that were generally condemned by the public. For two weeks Paris witnessed some of the bloodiest riots it had known in a long history of violence. Barricades were built and pitched battles with the police took place. Not only Trotskyites, Maoists, and anarchists, but also many middle-of-the-road students, joined forces to build barricades and confront the police.

By the middle of May the "revolt" began spreading to involve other elements of the population, particularly the workers. They moved spontaneously to occupy small factories and throw out the management. The Communist-led General Confederation of Labor (CGT) reacted by ordering the occupation of larger plants in the Paris region. They did not want to leave the initiative to the rank and file. Other trade unions, including the Socialist and Catholic, joined in—in fact, with aspirations far more drastic and revolutionary than those advanced by the Communist-led unions. But the revolt spread beyond the workers. Within days lawyers, accountants, midwives, nurses, newspapermen, actors, veterinarians, and salesgirls joined the strike movement. Paralysis followed. There was literally no way to control the situation, and it was not improved when the National Assembly, after a sharp debate, failed, by eleven votes, to pass a motion censuring the government. The Gaullist discipline held, but soon the equivocations of the major ally of the Gaullist party, the leader of the Independent Republicans, made it clear that the government's position was precarious.

De Gaulle hastened his return from Rumania, where he was loftily lecturing on international affairs, and on May 24 proposed a referendum to endorse policies that would introduce "participation" among the various interested parties within the university, the factory, and presumably the civil service and other social and economic units. Fundamentally, the purpose of the referendum was a demand for confidence in the national leader. The reaction of the public and of political leaders to the proposal was negative. The government was forced to make major concessions to the workers in the form of wage increases and social benefits. These concessions were impressive—at least a 10 percent increase in wages across the board. The Communist leaders, in their efforts to channel the revolt into trade union lines and obtain the maximum economic benefits for the workers, were fully behind these arrangements. Not so the many revolutionary groups that began to attack the Communist party leaders of "trade unionism" and "capitulation." The Communists retorted by branding the extreme left of "adventurism," "opportunism," "anarchism," and "counterrevolutionary" practices. Left-wing leaders expected the government to fall momentarily and de Gaulle to withdraw; after ten years in the wilderness, they were beginning to taste once more the "delights and poisons" of political power. The Communists remained cautious. The political acumen of their experienced leaders clearly showed to them that they had nothing to gain and everything to lose from a situation for which they were not responsible but for which they might well be blamed—as well proved to be the case. Reluctantly, they were forced to assume the leadership of strikes and of the occupation of factories, in order not to allow their left flank to be turned. But every day and at every turn of the events they tried desperately to stir the movement into social and economic demands from which the workers, and, of course, the party, could gain. They feared that the right-wing reaction was to come, as it had come throughout French history.

They were right. The late president spoke again on May 30. He laid the idea of a referendum to rest. Instead, he dissolved the National Assembly and called for national elections on June 23–30. He spoke firmly, leaving no doubt that he would not retreat or resign, and that if need be he would call in the army. Within twenty-four hours a huge demonstration on his behalf was organized and the barricades began slowly to come down. The promise of elections diverted most political leaders and groups—except the diehard revolutionaries—to political action, hoping to capitalize from the apparent predicament of the Gaullist regime. In 1967 the Gaullists had managed to win a very slim majority that had been further reduced by some by-elections and rendered precarious by the possible defection of the Independent Republicans, the Gaullist allies. The stability of the Gaullist regime appeared shattered, and the left expected to reap electoral benefits.

A number of interpretations have been given to account for the explosive events of May–June 1968. One is that it was provoked by the tremendous rise in the number of university students to 600,000, with about one-fourth huddled in Paris, and the discrepancy between educational facilities and student needs. Furthermore, many of the students continued to get their degrees in letters and law at a time when corresponding job opportunities were declining. It was also pointed out that the University maintained its archaic administrative structure, providing for little experimentation and innovation in many of the new disciplines and, above all, keeping all decisions in the hands of senior professors and elite academic organizations. Student reaction against this highly authoritarian, elitist, and disciplinarian structure had been brewing for some time, and when it came, it took the most violent form.

But what about the other groups? The workers, it has been pointed out, had become extremely sensitive to the relative declining fortunes of the French economy, partly due to the deflationary measures attempted by the government in preceding years. For the first time since 1945, workers—as many as 75,000—were unemployed; available job opportunities declined; and part-time labor was on the rise, hiding additional real unemployment generally estimated to be in the neighborhood of 150,000. This was a small percentage—hardly over 2.0 percent of the labor force. But the workers feared that the worst was yet to come. This, together with the relative drop in real wages, had created widespread anxiety and unrest. For instance, in April 1968, 50 percent of the people felt that their economic situation was likely to deteriorate. Even the trade union leaders, including the most powerful and disciplined Communist-controlled CGT, could not cope with the unrest when it broke out into the open. The workers, more than 10 million strong, joined the students not by aligning themselves with the students but rather by rising spontaneously against not only the bosses but also against their own leaders. They occupied the factories and ignored the trade union officers. Everything was shut down.

The extent of the movement of rebellion against each and every constituted authority structure gave rise to a third explanation, that of alienation. For a long time the political regime had been associated with one man—de Gaulle—and for a long time decisions were lodged in the hands of the aloof and paternal—if not authoritarian—president. Parliament and the intermediary representative organs had been bypassed. Despite all efforts to decentralize and to set up a dialogue between the decision-making units of government and those concerned with the substance of these decisions at the national, regional, and local levels, the dialogue had not materialized. An aloof president, a cabinet subordinate to him rather than to Parliament, and a highly centralized civil service continued to rule. The divergence between the concerns of the president and the average citizen was well illustrated by the president's decision to go to Rumania when the uprisings were in progress to preach the gospel of European independence, under the leadership of France, vis-à-vis both the Soviet Union and the United States. The average Frenchman, fretting about his own income and future, constantly distrusting state authority, yet unable to channel his demands and anxieties through existing representative organs or through his own associations and ad hoc committees into the government and civil service, simply exploded. The Events were in the nature of a psychological release; they provided a catharsis for the long period of submissiveness to the state and a compensation for the deep resentment that springs from an impotence to act jointly. The explosion took the character of a festival or a national celebration against authority—political authority and every other form of authority. It gave the illusion but not the reality of participation; it provided an ephemeral "togetherness," a feeling of common destiny such as only the French Revolution, the Paris Commune, and World War I in its first months had provided. But it was a togetherness and a participation that in the name of social and communal values was totally indifferent—indeed, quite hostile—to the very fabric of social and communal life. It directed itself against each and every rule. It was highly individualistic and anarchic. Nothing illustrates better the antinomy between individualism that verges on anarchy and the administrative authority of the state that often verges on the authoritarian.

Within three weeks after the Events had subsided, the French returned to their jobs and the students to their universities after the French electorate had given an overwhelming victory to the Gaullists—and to de Gaulle—in the name of "law and order." The "revolution" was over—a revolution without a theory, policy recommendations, leaders, or even real plans to "take over" the state. The political culture had spoken for five weeks and the administrative state was back fully entrenched. But it had underlined once more the fragility of the political regime—indeed, of all French political regimes.

Cabinet Instability

A different and better-known form of instability has been cabinet instability—the high turnover rate of the cabinets under both the Third and Fourth Republics. When France seemed to have become reconciled, even if reluctantly, to the republican regime and had adopted a parliamentary system, the prime minister and his cabinet were unable to stay in office for long and exercise effective leadership. Under the Third Republic (1870–1940), there were more than one hundred cabinets. Under the Fourth Republic (1946–58), there were twenty cabinets and seventeen prime ministers. Thus, while in England the life of the cabinet, which is in charge of the most important activities of government, averages about four years, that of the French cabinet had been seven to eight months. This instability illustrates that within the framework of republican institutions the French have been unable to provide themselves with stable and positive leadership. French society under the Third and Fourth Republics seemed to be caught inextricably in the contradictions of conflicting groups, and political parties and could not resolve them. In the end, they reached a standstill—*immobilisme,* as some French commentators put it.

Constitutional and cabinet instability are only two aspects of the same pervasive phenomenon of the French political culture: the search for authority, and the deep distrust of it. French constitutional history shows recurrent patterns or cycles in which a constitutional arrangement consecrating authority and executive leadership alternates with assembly or direct popular government. For instance, during the Revolution of 1789, France moved from absolute monarchy, through to a phase of a limited monarchy, to a parliamentary republic, which gave place in turn to an authoritarian system led by Napoleon. This arrangement lasted through to the monarchy (1814), which again became a limited monarchy (1830–48), to give place to a Republic. But within a short time the pendulum swung to the second Bonapartist empire, and that was itself followed by another republic. From then on the cyclical pattern became limited to alternation between the republic and a Bonapartist solution (Third Republic—Vichy—Fourth Republic—de Gaulle's presidential Fifth Republic).

Cabinet instability, and in general the history of parliamentary institution, exhibit something of the same cyclical pattern of an alternation between strong leadership and assembly government. Strong prime ministers attempted to impose, sometimes successfully, their leadership over a divided and defensive Parliament. Their efforts often coincided with the confrontation and the solution of serious external or domestic problems: the clerical question; the reorganization of the army; national defense; social and economic reforms; decolonization. But the Assembly invariably found a way to reassert its supremacy by overthrowing them at the very time when their success and popularity gave cause for satisfaction and opened the way for them to assume party leadership. Even within the parliamentary system the quest for authority and leadership alternated between executive leadership and parliamentary supremacy.

The argument was put forth in the last years of the Fourth Republic that cabinet instability, providing for rapid alternations of cabinet and prime ministers, was in itself a way to provide for quick decision on specific problems.

Ad hoc majorities among otherwise competing parties and factions would support a cabinet and a prime minister to cope with a particular problem, only to disintegrate after it had provided a solution for it. Thus, for some policy questions a flexible and extremely rapid mechanism for reconciling cabinet and parliamentary government with the need of decision making was provided.

France is now going through a phase of strong executive leadership. In the last decade, de Gaulle, his constitution, his government, and his leadership dominated the French political scene. His resignation in April 1969 and death a year-and-a-half later raises serious questions about the future of the Fifth Republic under his successor, George Pompidou. It would be relatively easy to concentrate exhaustively on the current presidential regime, to analyze its mainspring, to discuss the constitution—the Fifth Republic—as if it embodied a lasting arrange-

ment. It would be equally easy to consider the Fifth Republic a transient phenomenon and assume that with de Gaulle's disappearance from the scene, the pendulum will again swing to the assembly government and that the old parties, institutions, and practices will return. Neither proposition is correct. The "Gaullist polity"—even after de Gaulle—embodies a number of traits that are likely to last, but it includes also many that are likely to disappear. How shall we tell what is lasting and what is transient? How can we assess at this stage what will be the political system five years hence? We cannot. The best we can do is outline some of the old forces and evaluate the character and significance of their transformation. At this stage, both the political values and the institutional arrangements appear to be fluid, and our task will be to discern and discuss what *may* be lasting, discard what is transient.

The set of memories that people have; the way they pattern their various personal relations; the ideas and values they hold about a number of things (such as work, poverty, cooperation, conflict); the roles they play and the manner in which they view them—all constitute what we call *culture*. The term in its specifically political sense, however, must be confined to a much narrower definition. It refers only to those individual and collective practices, attitudes, and beliefs that relate to such human phenomena as the state, authority, participation, obedience, rebelliousness, and the like. We shall attempt here to give a brief account of the political culture that exists in present-day France.

THE FRENCH POLITICAL CULTURE

The most generalized trait of the French political culture is its ambivalence—but even more, the antinomy between authority and freedom that exists within it. In every Frenchman there is a quest for authority and unity, and yet an attachment to individual liberty that induces him to resist authority. Thus, authority is both valued as a symbol and instrument of national unity, and feared as a vehicle of power that may oppress or enslave the individual.

Since authority is embodied in the state, the French have consistently quarreled about the nature, form, and organization of the state. The state as a symbol of French greatness and national unity has been an object of veneration and sacrifice—but it has also evoked strong opposition and hostility.

What has been lacking in French tradition is an organic linkage, between the individual on the one hand and the state on the other, to reconcile and temper the opposition between the two. This, and not the proverbial and highly distorted accounts of French individualism, is the real reason for the lack of political activity in France as a process of cooperation, bargaining, and compromise. No institutions have developed to bridge the gulf between the individual and the state and make the first a full-fledged participant and the second an instrument for the realization of the demands and

TWO

the foundations of French politics

interests of the citizens. Voluntary associations, political parties, trade unions, and, in general, intermediary associations that allow for participation and provide for compromise have been weak.

It is hard to account for this. Perhaps the reason lies in the legacy of the *Ancien Régime* with its strong centralized authority, nourished by the Bonapartist regimes of the nineteenth century and sustained by a strong, well-organized and centralized civil service. The Revolution and the republican regimes of the nineteenth and twentieth centuries did not change the structure of centralized government but provided for ways and means to control and limit it. The average citizen continues to expect initiative and action from the state (i.e., the civil service) while denying it the right to intervene in the reserved domain—generously interpreted—of individual liberties and individual property rights. Thus, parliamentary and representative institutions were considered, and still are, primarily as fences or restraints against the state, as the embodiment of the national will against the administration.

Throughout the nineteenth century, political parties remained weak and diffuse organizations that represented class, parochial, or ideological interests against the state, rather than becoming vehicles of compromise and action. Participation in political life, except for balloting, remained at a very low ebb.

This situation accounts for another trait. While political participation and sustained political activity remained at a very low level, it alternated with manifestation of extreme and often violent activity. The lack of voluntary associations and well-organized political parties or interest groups to provide for a permanent dialogue between the individual through such organizations and the state left no other form of political expression open except the streets and the barricades. As a result, most French men and women shared, and continue to have, a low opinion of political activity, considering it by-and-large ineffective—whether it be carried out by representatives or through demonstrations and violence that by their very nature are bound to be ephemeral and unproductive.

The distinction between the authority and the individual and the perennial distrust of the first by the second is also related to the sharp distinction between Paris, the seat of the government, and the rest of France. The centralized administration of France (located in Paris) made decisions that affected all. Through the Ministry of the Interior, the *préfet,* and the mayor, Paris made itself known to all and imposed the burdens, and at times provided the benefits, that affected all. But there was no well-structured and institutionalized way for the citizen to act upon the administration. The individual in the provinces, after erecting parliamentary institutions to defend himself against Paris, did not create any permanent institutions to influence the government and participate continuously in the decisions made. To repeat, there was no continuing dialogue between the citizen and the central authority. The citizen had set up (as it were) dikes and dams and fences around authority, but he shunned the establishment of permanent maintenance and communication lines to help make them the means of realizing his demands. "One governs against Paris not through Paris" was an adage that reflects clearly the lack of dialogue.

The image of the state and of state authority—distant, austere, and impersonal—persists even today despite the fact that there appears to be a reconsideration of the role of the state. In a recently conducted survey dealing with relations between the state and the citizens,[1] 41% of the respondents felt that the state was rather close to them, while 51% considered it still something rather remote. Over 70% thought that the affairs of the state were very complicated and that only an expert could understand them. Yet at the same time 69% felt that the work and action of the state had a "very great" or "rather great" influence on their daily lives, and almost the same number of people thought the same about the impact of economic planning upon their standard of living. Only 23% of the people surveyed believed that they had some influence over the decisions of the state; 73% said they did not—a remarkably high percentage. Furthermore, 80% felt

[1] See **SOFRES** [Société Française d'Enquêtes par Sondages], *Les Français et l'État,* Spring, 1970.

that in their dealings with the state they were treated like an IBM card, and only 14% felt that they were given personal attention. Further, a whopping 72% claimed that there were "two standards and measures" in the state's dealings with the citizen, and only 19% felt that everybody was treated in the same manner. Contrary to all the allegations about the *incivisme* of the French, a good citizen is considered to be one who (a) obeys the law (58%), pays his taxes (42%), and votes regularly (50%); (b) is interested in the affairs of the state (39%), is a member of a trade union (12%), and is a member of a political party (but only 9%); and (c) brings up his children well (52%), takes care of his affairs without making trouble (43%), and minds his own business (26%). Thus, respect for the law, participation in election, and political information rate almost as high as individual attachments and preoccupations. Indeed, this is only obvious when it is reported that 64% felt that young people should perform their military obligation and only 30% disagreed—and more particularly, when we consider the reasons given for obeying the law: 40% felt that the laws "serve the general interest."

When it comes to crucial policy questions, there was a widespread sentiment in favor of state action and state initiative and control. Almost 50% felt that the role of the state will be more important in the future and 40% that its role is to "reform the society." In fact, the notion of the welfare state is beginning to be widely accepted: of the major functions of the state, protection against risks such as illness, unemployment, and old age comes first (64%); defense and protection of the underprivileged, third (39%); economic well-being, fourth (36%); and education, fifth (29%). The maintenance of order and defense rank second and sixth (42% and 27%), respectively. Despite the relatively wide scope of economic planning, nationalization, and the growth of public corporations, 40% feel that the state does not intervene far enough in economic affairs. The old liberal aphorism that the state must intervene only to eliminate abuses and inequalities and to "hinder the hindrances" is espoused by 33% as opposed to 36% who believe that the state must *direct* the economy. Demand for economic controls,

attesting to the French widespread acceptance of socialism and economic planning, is carried at times into other areas of social life. For instance, 24% and 32% respectively believe that "morality" should be the preoccupation of the state "wholly" or "in great part." Almost 50% prefer the state to control the dissemination of films and periodicals, with 44% considering this to be a matter that should be left to individual choice.

THE HISTORICAL FOUNDATIONS OF FRENCH POLITICS

The history of a nation, Aldous Huxley once remarked, is very much like the history of a family. It keeps alive traditions and symbols that give its members a sense of unity and continuity and provides a vocabulary with which they can communicate clearly and rapidly. The Declaration of Independence, the Boston Tea Party, Lincoln's refusal to consider the dissolution of the Union, the Western frontier, Pearl Harbor—these are all rich with meaning for Americans. They symbolize common efforts and evoke common memories.

But every country does not have a national memory that serves to unify its citizens. For some nations, the past is a source of discord that divides rather than unites. Traditions and symbols are differently shared by different groups. To evoke the past is to raise clouds that cast shadows across the present and the future. New differences are added to old ones, piling up obstacles to reconciliation and common action. This has been the case with France; understanding this is the key to understanding its political system. But the job is just as difficult as comprehending the personal and sometimes very subtle quarrels that divide a family.

France became a national state under the monarchy. It was one of the first countries in Europe to overcome the various regional and personal loyalties of feudalism and develop a sense of national unity, which was enhanced by the growth of a strong central political organization. France rose to its peak of power during the reigns of Louis XIII and Louis XIV in the seventeenth century, under the direction of the great Cardinals Richelieu and Mazarin, who presided over the king's councils. By the time the long reign of Louis XIV came to an end in 1715, foreign enemies—particularly Spain and Austria—had been neutralized, a strong army had been mobilized, a network of highways had been constructed, the nobility and religious minorities—especially the Huguenots—had been brought under control, and even more important to the future of the nation, a well-organized and efficient central administrative service had been established.

The subsequent overthrow of the monarchy by the Revolution of 1789 did not affect one of the vital pillars of national unity—the administrative departments, which continued to collect taxes, provide services, raise armies, and quell dissidence throughout the nation. The Revolution, and later Napoleon, in fact improved the centralized administration that had been built up during *l'ancien régime,* and the republic inherited and made full use of it. The conception and institutions of an administrative state remained side-by-side with the republican regimes, ushered in by the Revolution of 1789.

The republican tradition of the Revolution of 1789 stressed the claims of the citizens for representation in the government. The state, it was proclaimed, was a creature of the people, vested with no powers other than those delegated to it. The sovereignty of the people resided in the elected representative assemblies. All orders and privileges were abolished; equality and individualism were emphasized. This democratic conception, stemming from Rousseau's idea of the general will, clashed with all the privileged orders of *l'ancien régime*—particularly the nobility and the clergy—and with the tradition of the administrative state. The contradiction was never resolved. The proponents of the republic used the power of the state and its central bureaucracy to crush the privileged orders, while Napoleon used it to buttress the rule of equality and to advance his military designs. The republican theory of popular representation and sovereignty of the people conflicted with the idea of a one-man government and a centralized administration that had been developed under the monarchy and perfected by Napoleon.

During the nineteenth century, many new forces came to divide the community. Representative institutions never took root, and the people often resorted to civil disobedience and revolution. In 1830, in 1848, and again in 1870 the people of Paris, joined sometimes by those of the provinces, overthrew the government and sought to establish a new republican regime. The privileged orders, on the other hand—the Catholic church, the nobility, and very often the army and the administration—advocated the return of the monarchy or the restoration of Bonapartism.

In the latter part of the nineteenth century, these divisions were further intensified. The first president of the Third Republic, Marshal MacMahon, was suspected of trying to institute a constitutional monarchy, and, indeed, there is evidence that he worked for the restoration of a king. But the republic survived. Within two decades, republican leaders launched a direct attack against the Catholic schools and religious orders. Many of the schools were closed, the orders were disbanded, their property confiscated. The conflict between the church and the republic flared anew, and the old wounds of the Revolution of 1789 were re-opened.

After the repression of the workers' government—the Paris Commune—in 1870, the workers formed militant trade unions that advocated the overthrow of capitalism, thus frightening the middle class, who began to waver in their attachment to the republic. Having persecuted the clergy, disappointed the conservatives by failing to restore a king and establish a constitutional monarchy, lost the loyalty of many in the middle class, and alienated the workers, the republic began to weaken.

The wave of nationalism accompanying World War I (1914–18) brought a temporary unity, but after the final victory, which was attained at tremendous cost, the differences broke into the open even more sharply than before. The church claimed subsidies for its schools; the workers demanded social reforms and many joined the newly formed Communist party; the farmers asked for increased protection and price supports; the proponents of the administrative tradition wished to curtail the powers of the representative assembly; while many conservatives and, later, "Fascists" urged the overthrow of the republic in favor of a totalitarian regime. Caught in these contradictory interests, the representative assemblies were unable to make policy decisions, and the civil service performed only the routine functions of government. A weak state and a divided nation were unable to withstand the German attack in 1940.

Defeat in World War II brought about the expected reaction against the Third Republic in the form of the Vichy government, in which all powers were concentrated in the hands of Marshal Pétain, who governed with the support of the army, the civil service, and conservative Catholics. But their rule was short-lived. After the Liberation, the Fourth Republic, very similar to the Third, returned the republican forces to power. But the divisions continued.

A serious rift developed between the advocates of a strong state and the proponents of the representative tradition. The former did not reject the republic but wished to greatly increase the power of the executive, the president or the prime minister—to give him, for instance, the right to dissolve the representative assembly and call for elections, to prepare the budget, and to control the agenda of the legislative assemblies. The defenders of representative government remained steadfastly in favor of legislative supremacy and wanted to keep the president and prime minister and his cabinet subservient to the legislature. The quarrel about constitutional reform was in a subtle sense the old quarrel of the two political traditions—the monarchists and Bonapartists against the republicans.[2]

The historical foundations of the French political system are thus built upon historical layers that underline divisions. National unity is undermined by the existence of many conflicting conceptions of government and authority. Catholics still remember the years of repression under the Third Republic; some of the workers retain a revolutionary posture, even

though they have long had the right to vote and to organize; and there are still some right-wing extremists who bide their time to scuttle the republic at the slightest provocation. History has dealt France a series of blows that have become part of the living memory that divides the French and impedes the creation of an integrated political community and a smoothly functioning government.

THE IDEOLOGICAL FOUNDATIONS OF FRENCH POLITICS

To the extent that historical events live in the minds of a people, they are more than "history"—they become ideas that fashion beliefs and shape conduct. And ideas, as a French writer has said, "are politics." Ideas that impregnate groups and motivate them to action are political ideologies. They are both the lenses through which people look at their society and the world at large and a set of beliefs that makes them act in one way or another. There have been numerous political ideologies in France, and many of them trace their origin back to the French Revolution, to the regime of Napoleon Bonaparte, and to the restoration of the Bourbon kings, when, in the words of the poet, France hovered "between two worlds, one dead, the other powerless to be born."

One French author, writing in 1932, identified six "ideological families" in France: traditionalism, liberalism, Christian democracy, industrialism, socialism, and radicalism. To these we can add two more: Communism, which has emerged as a distinct ideology, and "Gaullism," which has revived the old Bonapartist symbolisms.

Traditionalism, it must be said, is more a state of mind than a coherent political philosophy. It accepts and respects the status quo and is, in general, averse to anything but very gradual change. It is characterized by a marked respect for the past, more specifically, for the traditions of the monarchy and the church, and also for the privileged groups and the instruments of order in the society—the army, the civil service, the propertied groups. *Liberalism*

[2] For a fuller discussion, see Roy C. Macridis and Bernard E. Brown, *The De Gaulle Republic: Quest for Unity,* Part II (Homewood, Ill.: Dorsey, 1960).

favors limitations upon the state; advocates a laissez-faire economy, individual rights, and political freedoms; and remains attached to parliamentary democracy. *Radicalism* claims to be the proper heir of the Revolution. It retains a deep faith in government by the people and their representatives and is suspicious of all vested interests. Like liberalism, it distrusts the state and all its instrumentalities, notably the civil service and the executive, is anticlerical, and invariably supports the supremacy of the legislature. *Christian democracy* accepts the separation between church and state (although it favors public subsidies to Catholic schools), but encourages the active participation of lay Catholics and priests in solving concrete social and economic problems. It urges social welfare programs, economic controls, and the equitable distribution of income.

Industrialism takes its cue from the early nineteenth-century utopian writer, the comte de Saint-Simon, and extols the application of rational techniques to questions of economic production and distribution. It defers to the expert and the administrator and often favors authoritarian solutions. Its contemporary variant is often referred to as "technocracy"—government by the expert and the technicians. *Socialism* has traditionally advocated the control of the means of production by the state, but has espoused the republic and its representative institutions, while *communism* continues to pronounce its intent to overthrow the government and forcefully expropriate private property.

Finally, *Gaullism* is not basically different from Bonapartism. It is the belief that one man can break through the contradictions of the political system and bypass the political parties and the various representative groups, and establish direct contact through referendums and plebiscites with the people. Based on loyalty to one individual, it rejects the properly constituted republican organs in favor of personal rule by a strong leader. Since the end of World War II, de Gaulle claimed, very much as Napoleon I and Napoleon III had done before him, to incarnate the nation in his person. Whether his successor will make the same claim remains to be seen.

The Left and the Right

A commonly accepted way to look at the ideological families in France is to divide them into two large groups: the left and the right. The left, which has traditionally included the radical ideology, has been joined by the Socialists, Communists, and, on a number of issues, by Christian democrats. The right, on the other hand, consists of the traditionalists, the advocates of "industrialism"—the technocrats—many of the "liberals" who advocate economic freedoms, the Gaullists, the outright authoritarians, and a few monarchists.

"Left" and "right" have had changing political connotations throughout French history. The location of the line between them depends on the criteria used to distinguish them, whether it be the attitude toward the church, toward private property, toward business or the privileged groups, toward the republic or constitutional reforms, toward foreign policy, toward atomic rearmament, toward the state, etc. The line of division, in fact, has become so blurred that many argue that the distinction between left and right is only a historical residue and does not correspond to reality.

The multiplicity of ideologies has had a profound effect on the French political system. In the first place, political ideologies are (or at least have been until recently) intensely held by the citizens. They are taken very seriously and are more than mere political slogans. This intensity often has made the ideological differences irreconcilable. People tend to agree more readily on conflicts over material interests than on clashes between deeply felt principles. Those who think that the curé is an enemy will never willingly agree to allow their tax money to be used to support parochial schools, while, on the other hand, a compromise can usually be reached between those who believe in a 2% sales tax and those who oppose any sales tax.

The multiple and contradictory ideologies of France naturally result in a weak state. The government is immobilized by the divisions that split the nation, and the various factions work to perpetuate an ineffectual government, for each group fears that opposing forces will prevail if the state is allowed strong control over the country. This paralysis of government in turn had produced until recently a negative opinion toward the state—a certain degree of alienation or *apolitisme*. The French continue to refer to the government as "they"—something alien, remote, and perhaps hostile. Their attitude is apolitical not because they do not care or think strongly about politics but because, being so much at odds with each other, they finish by rejecting politics as an activity that can solve national problems through common effort.

The end result of this condition is an extreme form of individualism. Having denied to the nation the means of effective action and having splintered into many irreconcilable divisions, the French finally come to reject collective programs and to rely only on individual action. In the words of Voltaire in *Candide*, they demand to be left alone to cultivate their own gardens. The ideological foundation of the French system, then, like the historical tradition, is a fragmented one that provides an uncertain base for the erection of a responsible and effective government.

THE HERITAGE OF THE FRENCH REVOLUTION

Nothing illustrates better the historical and ideological content of the French political culture than the legacy of the French Revolution. Political ideas, tactics, and style trace their origins to it. Political families—to say nothing of the basic distinction between left and right—still associate with that monumental political upheaval which, in a period of less than ten years, moved the country from a monarchy ruled virtually by divine right, to a republican monarchy, to a republic, to a government by one party controlled in effect by a small directorate (under Robespierre) known as the Committee of Public Safety, to a collegial dictatorship—the Directorate—and finally, to a consulate and an empire with the young Napoleon at its head. Within a decade at least four

major constitutions were drafted. Constitutional development throughout most of the nineteenth century was often a reenactment of what had occurred in that fateful decade. Further, the intensity of the struggle, the deadly dedication with which different political ideas were supported, and the universality of the aspirations of the various protagonists and their ideologies, influenced the political style of the generations to come.

The Revolution bequeathed the spirit of total commitment and total solutions. With the shaky compromise between the king and the republican forces broken after 1792, what ensued was a free-for-all conflict to the bitter end. No compromises were to be tolerated, no leniency was to be expected. Every participant, every leader propounded his view for truth and victory with the foreknowledge that failure meant death. Politics was the art of heroes and death the supreme vindication of one's beliefs. By the same token, an appeal to violence to defend political beliefs and to promote political ideas became not a necessity or a tactical expedient but a value in itself. The result was the injection of styles and attitudes that brooked no compromise. As they spread among the citizens they divided villagers, townsmen, and families against each other, and split the nation asunder.

To the king's absolute rule, the Revolution countered with the notion of absolute popular sovereignty—supreme, inalienable, pure, and always right. The old maxim, "The king can do no wrong," was replaced by the new one, "The people are always right." This, again, inculcated a distrust for any and all officeholders and governments, a deep uneasiness with all forms of "personal government," and a tendency to equate democracy with legislative supremacy. The threat that the people are ready to rise has been a repeated theme ever since 1789. As late as 1956, Pierre Poujade, a right-wing radical, promised to set up an assembly of "states general," and the French colonels in Algeria established "committees of public safety" during their uprising against the Republic in May, 1958. The strident uprising of May–June 1968 used many of the same symbolic trappings.

Yet, while the Revolution had injected these divisions, it sought desperately to preserve the national unity of France. Never before and perhaps never since has the idea of the French nationality been so exalted. In the name of freedom and equality the French nation was portrayed as a cohesive and unified force embracing all citizens. Hence the contradiction between authority as the embodiment of the nation and the republic as the expression of individual freedom and equality.

While constitutions and leaders toppled as fast as the guillotine could function, Law was revered as a general and abstract principle expressing the sovereign will of the nation. Legality rather than abiding by the law became the rule, and one law after another was feverishly passed through the legislature with the belief that they would settle all issues and fashion morality for all. The result has been that the French, somewhat like the Americans, will legislate at length to cope with all problems, and will be the first to disregard the laws made. Concern with the letter of the law is accompanied by disregard for its substance.

The question of who incarnates national sovereignty has bedeviled French political thought and action since the Revolution. Who speaks for France? Sometimes the legislature, sometimes the army, sometimes one man has claimed to do it. National sovereignty, an abstract entity, has been claimed on behalf of the people by divergent and conflicting political forces. De Gaulle, like Napoleon, claimed to incarnate it—first when he defied the state, then as its head. In the name of one and the same France, different political regimes have been proposed and espoused by different groups. The greater the disagreements, the greater the quest for unity and stability. The Revolution combined, in the form of ethical imperatives, contradictory political attitudes: the notions of violence and legality, unity and individualism, authority and freedom.

THE REPUBLICAN SYNTHESIS AND THE FOURTH REPUBLIC

It was not until the end of the nineteenth century that a synthesis appeared to have been reached among the various ideological families. The Third Republic, established formally in 1875, provided a broad formula of agreement—a common denominator. The authority of the state was carefully circumscribed: the president of the republic became a figurehead, while the cabinet and the prime minister were deprived of many of the prerogatives they enjoy in England. They could not control the business of the legislature; they could not dissolve it and call for new elections; and they remained constantly at the mercy of the shifting majorities in the legislature. The provincial and rural interests found protection in the second chamber, the Senate, which gradually became equal to the lower house in its power to control and overthrow the cabinet and to pass or reject the budget. The political parties remained, until the turn of the century, electoral alliances of provincial bosses and notables. Essentially, this was a republic in the hands of a divided bourgeoisie that equated good government with the least government. The only cohesive force remained the civil service, whose tasks and efforts gradually became limited to caretaking activities. No dynamic leadership and no initiative was expected of it.

This was a "stalemated republic." As long as extremist movements did not develop from the left or the right—as they occasionally did—it was remarkably stable. National unity and the existing social arrangements were overwhelmingly accepted, while political authority remained suspect. The people voted but did not participate; the parties designated candidates but did not develop programs on the basis of which they could receive a mandate for action; interest groups were on the defensive, unable or unwilling to promote participation and generate political action; the countryside remained remote from the center.

It was after the turn of the century, especially after World War I, that this republican synthesis began to be undermined. The need for social legislation and state controls, the urgent demand for modernization, the growing burdens imposed upon the system by its relations with its colonies and the outside world, and above all the international conflicts that broke out anew, even before the ink on the Versailles treaty was dry—and the renewed menace of Germany—called for decision and firm execution. Even more so, sharp conflicts at home between the left-wing forces, led by the socialists and the more uncompromising Communists, and some of the conservatives and extremists, could no longer be easily compromised within the system. The republican synthesis began definitely to break down.

Yet when the French were ready to refashion their institutions after World War II, the past continued to cast a long shadow. A combination of the old parties and the Communists prepared a constitutional document that in its broad outlines copied that of the Third Republic. The electorate endorsed it, even if by a slim majority. The old practices reasserted themselves. We shall describe them briefly, simply because their tenacity indicates how deeply they are embedded in the French political culture. One or two decades of Gaullism are not enough to efface deeply rooted practices and institutional arrangements unless new factors have entered the system to bring about its transformation.

The Governmental Machinery of the Fourth Republic

The constitution of October 1946 that ushered in the Fourth Republic was sharply criticized throughout its short life, even by those who helped create it. Known as "the system," the governmental machinery of the Fourth Republic was portrayed as being dominated by lobbies, incapable of making needed decisions, and unresponsive to its leaders, who, by and large, were not commanding figures. The constitution vested supreme power in Parliament—notably in the lower house, the National Assembly. The prime minister and his cabinet governed as long as they had majority support in the National Assembly. The president of the republic was elected by Parliament (the National Assembly and the Senate meeting together), and, like the British monarch, was only the titular head of state. Prime ministers came and went with disturbing frequency as the majorities shifted back and forth in the Assembly. The

twelve years of the Fourth Republic saw twenty Cabinets form and dissolve, an average of one every seven months (Fig. 2-1).

MULTIPARTISM

In our discussion of Great Britain we have seen an example of a two-party system in which the parties are disciplined and support the government on the basis of pledges formulated at election time. In France the party system has been—at least until very recently—vastly different. There have been eight or ten parties, most of them without discipline, leadership, or platforms. This multiparty system was projected upon the legislature when a number of parliamentary groups, more-or-less corresponding to the political parties, formed weak and ephemeral coalitions behind a government which therefore was short-lived. The multiparty system led to a fragmented Assembly which in turn accounted for cabinet instability (see Figs. 2-2 and 2-3).

Compounding the lack of focus of the multiparty system has been the fact that most of the parties have been internally divided. After national elections, the elected representatives of a party often formed small groups and thereafter acted independently of the party under whose label they ran. Under the Fourth Republic, any fourteen deputies could organize one of these "parliamentary groups" in the National Assembly, and it was not uncommon for fifteen or more of these groups to exist at one time. When individual parliamentarians "seceded" to form a minuscule group with a new name, they often elected a president and were granted representation in the various parliamentary committees and given a voice in organizing the business of the legislature.

Fragmentation results from weak party discipline. It is easy to point out the factors that account for this. First, it was very difficult for the prime minister or the president under the Third and Fourth Republics to dissolve the legislature and call for elections. A representative, once elected, was secure in his seat, no matter how he voted and acted, for the length of the legislative term. He could oppose the cabinet with virtual impunity, even when the prime minister happened to be from his own party—a practice, as we know, that is very rare in Great Britain. Secondly, many of the French deputies became, like many United States senators, strongly entrenched in their local constituency: they remained as mayors of important or strategically located cities and towns, and frequently as spokesmen for the lobbies prominent in their constituency. Thirdly, with the exception of the parties of the left, particularly the Communists and the socialists, the parties were loose affiliations of notables, political bosses, and leaders. The party organization, in other words, reflected and encouraged a lack of discipline. The nomination of a candidate was mostly a local matter; the control of funds was highly decentralized so that the candidate, once elected, owed little to the party, and the central organization could not penalize him for his actions. Finally, the underlying social and historical factors we have already discussed—the multiplicity of ideologies, and their incompatibility—not only accounted for multipartism but also for the internal fragmentation of parties and for their lack of discipline and central organization. The conflicts about subsidies to parochial schools, the division between the proponents of a welfare state and of economic individualism, the perennial problem of constitutional and electoral reform, and the quarrels over the many pressing issues of the

day—such as foreign policy, European integration, colonial disengagement, and Algeria —merged with uncompromising ideological attitudes to splinter the parties. Virtually every issue that confronted the Fourth Republic was fought within the parties, not between them.

The multiparty system made it difficult, under the Fourth Republic, for national political leaders to emerge. When by chance, as occasionally happened under the Third and Fourth Republics, a man of great quality attempted to speak directly to the nation about pressing problems and to suggest solutions, the various party leaders united against him to thwart his efforts. No leadership was allowed to develop, or centralized party machinery to grow, that would enforce discipline and initiate collective action. Lack of leadership thus has been both the result and the cause of undisciplined political parties.

Because of their multiplicity and internal divisions, the parties in France have not performed two vital functions that parties in other countries ordinarily provide. First, they have not been able to debate and clarify issues for the public. Members of the same party (excepting the Communists and possibly the socialists) often advocated different things in different parts of the country, and in their party congresses their differences have not been resolved. Secondly, the parties could not, under the Fourth Republic, provide for a stable govern-

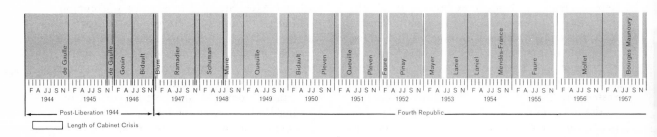

FIG. 2-1. *Cabinet instability under the Fourth and Fifth Republics.*

ment that was committed to certain policy objectives. Unlike elections in Britain and the United States, an election in France under the Fourth Republic did not determine the national government. The electorate voted, as a rule, for the members of the lower house of the Legislature—the Chamber of Deputies under the Third Republic and the National Assembly under the Fourth and Fifth—which in turn endorses a prime minister and supports his cabinet. It was impossible to tell which combinations among parliamentary groups could provide temporary support for a prime minister, and which new combinations would bring about his downfall, and subsequently that of his successors.

The structure of the parties under the Fourth Republic was responsible for another unfortunate development: the widening gap that grew up between the people and the government. To survive, the government had to rely on the support of a coalition of groups that was called the "government majority." But since the coalition was the creature of the party leaders in Parliament and was never itself approved by the electorate, the public became increasingly alienated from a system that did not give it an opportunity to select its government and hold it accountable. As we shall see, the reform of October 28, 1962, allows the people to participate directly in the selection of their national leader, the president.

Electoral Trends and Shifts

The Fourth Republic was not only characterized by multipartism but also by large electoral shifts—usually of 15–20% of the vote—in every national election. In 1946 a new political party, Mouvement Républicain Populaire (MRP), won over 5 million votes, the first important shift (see Table 2-1). In 1951 another new political party, the Rassemblement du Peuple Français (RPF or Gaullists), won over 4 million votes, many of which came directly from the MRP, a second radical shift. A third switch occurred in 1956; the RPF collapsed, but a number of its votes were captured by a new formation, the Poujadists, who received almost $2\frac{1}{2}$ million votes. In another changeover in the same election, almost 2 million votes went to a new electoral alliance, the Republican Front, formed between the Radicals and the Socialists. A fifth shift took place, as we shall soon see, in 1958, in favor of the Union pour la Nouvelle République (UNR)—the new Gaullist party. Elections were thus characterized by a "floating vote" that moved from one formation to another, or occasionally supported a new party or movement. These shifts did not, of course, all come from the same voters, though in each election they were roughly of the same size.

Was this floating vote a protest vote? Or

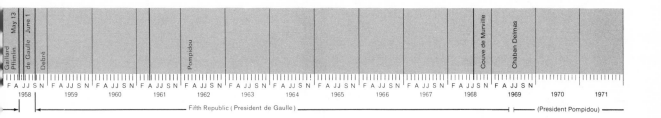

simply a personal vote for de Gaulle, Poujade, or some other leader? Was it directed against parliamentary immobility, or perhaps even against the republic? Did it grow out of the profound social and economic changes sweeping France, particularly economic modernization? These are difficult questions to answer. But the conclusion was inescapable: new forces were troubling the political life of France throughout the period of the Fourth Republic. And, as we shall see, they are still operative in the Fifth Republic.

Cabinet Instability

Cabinet instability throughout the Fourth Republic was fundamentally the result of multipartism. But the cabinets' difficulties were aggravated by the fact that the prime minister could not dissolve the National Assembly unless two consecutive cabinet crises had occurred within a period of 18 months. A cabinet "crisis" was constitutionally defined as the overthrow of the cabinet by an absolute majority on certain occasions—when the prime minister asked for a vote of confidence, as the British prime minister can do, or when the Assembly voted

a motion of censure. Cabinets suffered defeat after defeat by *relative majorities* and were forced to withdraw without being allowed to retaliate by dissolving and calling for a new election. Only once were the conditions for dissolution fulfilled and the right exercised (in December 1955).

Other procedural devices further subordinated the cabinet to the Assembly. The legislative committees in the National Assembly were miniature Parliaments with sweeping prerogatives similar to those of congressional committees in the United States (whose powers, however, in the American system are offset by a stable and powerful presidency). They could pigeonhole bills, amend them at will, or rewrite them. It was their version of a bill (not that of the government) that came on the floor for debate. The agenda of the National Assembly was prepared by the presidents of the various parliamentary groups, not by the prime minister and his cabinet. These powerful parliamentarians established the legislative calendar by sidetracking important governmental measures with which they disagreed. Wrangles over the "order of business" became sharp political conflicts, and the cabinet was reduced to appealing to the National Assembly to restore some of its

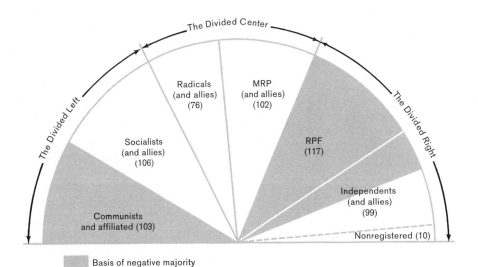

FIG. 2-2. *Major parties and parliamentary groups in the Second Legislature, Fourth Republic (1951–56): "The Hexagonal Assembly."*

own items on the agenda. Often it had to risk a vote of confidence on this purely procedural question.

Cabinet Crises

Since there was no majority party at any time during the Fourth Republic, all cabinets were coalition cabinets, composed of the leaders of many parliamentary groups and parties. Divisions in the Assembly were so sharp that forming a cabinet was like trying to sign a treaty among warring nations, and, indeed, the formation of the cabinet became known as the "contract of the majority." When a cabinet fell, the president of the republic asked a political leader to "scan the political horizon" (*tour d'horizon* or *tour de piste*) to determine the willingness of the various political leaders to participate in a new cabinet and the conditions under which they would join it. If his report were encouraging, he would probably be asked to form a cabinet. He would then appear before the National Assembly to deliver his "investiture speech," which would spell out what he proposed to do and quite frequently, in order to placate certain groups, what he proposed

not to do. If he were "invested"—that is, if he received majority approval—he would become the prime minister, presiding over a coalition cabinet. If he failed to receive the approval of a majority, the whole process would have to be repeated.

In a prolonged crisis, the president of the republic would call a gathering of all former prime ministers and all the presidents of the various parliamentary groups. At this "round-table" conference, the leaders would seek to reach enough agreement to form a cabinet. If the crises lengthened, these meetings would be held more frequently until some consensus was established and a new cabinet created. Within a matter of months, if not weeks, after the formation of a cabinet, small parliamentary groups would usually detach themselves from the government majority. It was estimated that the defection of forty or so members of the National Assembly was ordinarily sufficient to bring down the cabinets of the Fourth Republic. Since a small group of parliamentarians constituted a powerful veto bloc, they were able—because the life of the government depended on them—to exact concessions from the cabinet and impose conditions far disproportionate to their numerical strength.

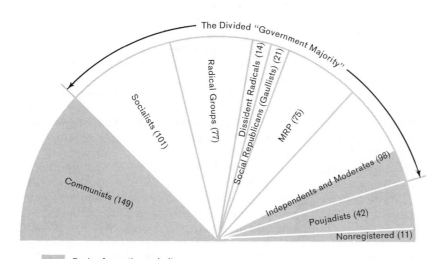

Basis of negative majority

FIG. 2-3. *Parties and parliamentary groups in the last legislature of the Fourth Republic (1956–58).*

TABLE 2-1. *Legislative Election Results in the Fourth Republic and in 1958*

	1946	*1951*	*1956*	*1958*
Communists and Progressives	5,489,288	5,057,305	5,514,403	3,882,204
Socialists	3,431,954	2,744,842	3,247,431	3,167,354
Radical Socialists and allied groups	2,831,834	1,887,583	2,834,265	2,695,287
MRP	5,058,307	2,369,778	2,366,321	2,378,788
Gaullists: RPF, 1951; Social Republicans, 1956; UNR, 1958	—	4,125,492	842,351	3,605,958
Independents and moderates	2,565,526	2,656,995	3,257,782	4,092,600
Poujadists	—	—	2,483,813	669,518
Extreme right	—	—	260,749	—
Other parties	63,976	87,346	98,600	—
Total votes cast	*19,203,070*	*19,129,064*	*21,298,934*	*20,489,709*
Number of registered voters	25,052,233	24,530,523	26,774,899	27,236,491

MRP, Mouvement Républicain Populaire; RPF, Rassemblement du Peuple Français; UNR, Union pour la Nouvelle République.

The Search for a Majority

The French political system under the Fourth Republic was, in a word, paralyzed. The numerous parties prevented any one of them from gaining a majority, and the legislature so hobbled the executive branch that leadership was virtually impossible. Out of the 627 seats in the National Assembly during the Fourth Republic, the Communist strength averaged 125 deputies. From 1947 until roughly 1954, they were in a permanent state of opposition. They voted against all governments, and, with the exception of some tactical votes, against most policy measures. After 1954, they began to urge the formation of alliances and to vote for the endorsement of prime ministers; no prime minister and cabinet, however, were willing to govern if they had to count on Communist support. Hence the *true* number of deputies from which a majority had to be found to counter the Communist vote ranged from 425 to a maximum of 500.

If all the non-Communist parties had been in agreement, the Communist strength could easily have been neutralized. But they were not. The parties of the center and the right cooperated to form the so-called Third Force, which lasted from May 1947 to the middle of 1952. But internal disagreements on price controls, social welfare legislation, increased governmental investments, economic modernization, wage increases, subsidies to Catholic schools, the war in Indochina, colonial policy, and many other issues were sharp. The Third Force disintegrated every time these questions came up.

When the Third Force came to an end in 1952, these disagreements flared up, further paralyzing the center parties. The Communist strength was reduced to about one hundred deputies, but the Gaullists, against whose electoral comeback the Third Force had been fashioned, emerged to the right with almost 120 members. Since the combined Gaullist-Communist group totaled at least 220 deputies, as long as the two voted together against all cabinets, the Assembly was literally ungovernable, faced as it was with a classic case of a "negative majority"—a majority *against* but never *for*. No stable majority could be formed from among the some 370 deputies of the other parliamentary groups to counter the combined Communist-Gaullist opposition.

The Search
for Strong Personal Leadership

Since the parties were thus stalemated on so many vital issues, the Assembly began to search for strong political leaders to solve particular problems. In 1952, Antoine Pinay, a popular parliamentary leader of the independents, was invested as prime minister with authority to launch a new economic policy. In 1954, another popular radical leader, Pierre Mendès-France, was approved as prime minister on his pledge to end the war in Indochina in a month's time, to undertake extensive economic and social reforms, and to cope with the independence movements in Morocco, Tunisia, and Algeria. When fighting in Indochina did cease within the month, Mendès-France received an overwhelming vote of confidence from all the parties. But when he began to initiate economic reforms, he found his majority dwindling, and when he promised "internal sovereignty" to Tunisia, his former supporters, including members of his own party, but also the Communists and the Gaullists, joined forces to bring him down—another case of a "negative majority."

In December 1955, the National Assembly was dissolved, and the ensuing elections, on January 2, 1956, ushered in the third, and what proved to be the last, legislature of the Fourth Republic. As Fig. 2-3 shows, this was again a case of an unmanageable legislature—unable to provide continuing support to any cabinet.

ALGERIA AND THE LAST CRISIS

It was the Algerian war that caused the last crisis and brought an end to the Fourth Republic. Algeria was conquered by France in 1830 and administered as a French department —as a part of France. There were until 1962 roughly 1 million Europeans (all of whom were French citizens) in Algeria, and some 9 million Algerian Moslems. The Europeans, or *colons* ("colonists"), had much higher incomes than did the Moslems, and dominated them politically and economically. After World War II, many Algerian leaders demanded political emancipation and full political and economic integration with metropolitan France. This was rejected. Only after 1952 did they begin to demand independence, and, in 1954, small rebel bands began to harass French detachments and commit acts of terrorism. The threat of losing Algeria, considered by Frenchmen to be an integral part of their country, provoked strong reaction in France. Troops were dispatched across the Mediterranean, and by 1957 more than 400,000 soldiers were combating the rebellion.

Supported by powerful patriotic and rightwing organizations, the army and the *colons* refused to obey the last government of the Fourth Republic, formed by Prime Minister Pierre Pflimlin on May 13, 1958. They called for a government of "public safety." Army units in Algeria and elsewhere were alerted and prepared for a show of strength against metropolitan France, involving, if necessary, a military invasion. The Gaullist groups, fearing a military coup, called for the return of General Charles de Gaulle, who emerged from his long silence to declare his readiness to assume the government of the republic. Pflimlin's cabinet resigned two weeks after it was formed. On June 1, the National Assembly endorsed General de Gaulle and his cabinet and the next day amended the constitution to empower de Gaulle to draft a new one. A military coup had been narrowly averted. De Gaulle was granted full powers to govern and to prepare a new constitution. The breakdown of parliamentary government, the military stalemate in Algeria, the rebellious attitude of the army, the economic difficulties at home—all eventually led the French to return to the tradition of Bonapartism, the personal leadership of one man to solve their problems.

THE DEMAND FOR REFORM

Throughout the whole period of the Fourth Republic, the demand for reform was pervasive. First, there was a strong and persistent dissatisfaction with the parliamentary institutions—not with representative government as such. As early as 1947, when asked the question, "Do you believe that things would be better or worse if there were no Parliament?" only 33% of Frenchmen surveyed felt that things would be worse, 21% better, and 27% the same (17% did not answer). By 1955 nobody seemed satisfied with Parliament: more than two-thirds were either "dissatisfied" or "very dissatisfied." Characteristically, dissatisfaction was due to the following reasons: (a) governments changed too often (95%); (b) there were too many parties (88%); (c) the parliamentary practices were bad (75%). The rate of cabinet turnover was a particular source of dissatisfaction, and the demand for stable and continuing executive power persistent. As early as 1945, 50% of the people favored the election of the president of the republic by direct popular vote. But there was an equally growing desire for greater participation in national politics. In 1945, 66% of the people favored a referendum on constitutional issues. Many had begun to equate a stable government with executive leadership. In 1946, almost half the people wanted to see the president of the republic play a more important role instead of limiting himself only to honorific functions—and their number has grown steadily since the return of General de Gaulle to power. While the parties have continued to be viewed as necessary for democratic government, both their numbers and their ideological commitments came under criticism. They were blamed for the frequent governmental crises, and the average Frenchman began to view the parliamentary game as something that concerned a small group of politicians and had nothing to do with his interests and demands. They seemed to be reconciled to a Parliament with fewer powers.

There were other straws in the wind. First, many of the economic and interests groups became better organized on a national basis, and seemed more willing to undertake cooperation with other groups and with the state. Secondly, economic modernization initiated by a group of intellectuals and technicians in the form of economic planning began to inculcate new demands and a new awareness that politics could satisfy them. Thirdly, the legacy of the wartime Resistance—the assurance that cooperation and participation could accomplish a lot—was much in evidence among a number of young political and professional leaders. The Resistance had bridged the distance between different classes and groups of the social hierarchy—it had a leveling impact that made a dialogue among individuals and groups easier. And finally, the world was changing fast, and the challenge of American wealth and of the German revival could not but affect directly the pride and incentive of the French elites.

The issue of new political institutions was constantly in the air, with many favoring better organized political parties and executive leadership. There was a new attitude toward the state, a greater demand for participation, a dissatisfaction with parliamentary institutions, a demand for greater stability and continuity. For the first time, perhaps, the French were willing to consider a political system in pragmatic terms as an instrument embodying procedures through which action can take place and decisions can be made.

But the Fourth Republic failed where all previous regimes had failed: it failed to develop political institutions that were legitimized and acceptable. While consensus on social and economic questions was growing, political consensus—the development of an acceptable procedure for the solution of problems—had not taken shape. France remained deadlocked on the vital issues of politics: What kind of constitution? What kind of government?

ECONOMIC FOUNDATIONS

Until a few years ago, the dominant characteristic of the French economy was relative underdevelopment. While industrialization rapidly advanced in the last hundred years in England, Germany, Japan, the United States, and, more recently, in the Soviet Union, France's economy grew at a relatively slower pace. In some decades it did not grow at all. Yet France began with a marked advantage over *all* the other countries. During the Napoleonic era and on through till the middle of the nineteenth century, France was one of the more developed nations of the world. From then on, however, despite her wealth of resources (though lack of coal and other sources of energy was an important deficit) and skilled labor, her economy declined in comparison with almost all the countries of Western Europe. Her national income between 1870 and 1940 rose by about 80%, while that of Germany increased five times and that of Great Britain three-and-a-half times. After a rise in economic production and investment between 1924 and 1931, net investment declined in the thirties to a point below zero—that is, France was living on her capital, using her factories and equipment without replacing them in full. She was going through a period of disinvestment. The destruction of World War II, estimated at approximately $50 billion, was an additional blow. With her in-

Note: In preparing the various tables and estimates of the French economy, a certain degree of simplification was unavoidable. The following sources were used: *United Nations Economic Survey for Europe* (1965); *Tableaux de l'économie française,* 1960, 1963, 1966, 1968, and 1970; *Mouvement économique en France de 1944 à 1957;* and *l'Espace économique français* (1955). The last three publications were prepared under the auspices of the official *Institut national de la statistique et des études économiques* (Paris). Also: the *Année politique,* 1969 and 1970; *Le Budget de 1970* and *Le Budget de 1971* (Ministère de l'Économie et des Finances, Paris); and the Reports on France of the OECD (Organization of European Cooperation and Development). I have also used the publications of the Information Services of the French Embassy and for the most recent developments the excellent Paris daily, *Le Monde.*

THREE

*social
and economic
foundations:
the mainsprings
of change*

dustrial equipment destroyed or dilapidated and her transportation network paralyzed, the French economy was in a state of collapse at the end of the war.

What were the major factors behind France's long economic stagnation? First, the slow growth rate of population; second, a backward agriculture; third, the protectionist policies of the state; and finally, business attitudes.

POPULATION. In 1800, France had a larger population than any other country in Europe or the Americas, with the exception of Russia. The Napoleonic armies were recruited and supported from among 26 million French citizens; England at the time had only 11 million inhabitants, the United States 5½ million, and Germany, including Austria, about 23 million. France maintained her population advantage until around 1860, when she numbered 38 million inhabitants. After that, the population level remained virtually static, despite a sharp decline in the mortality rate (see Table 3-1). In 1940, for instance, her population was almost exactly 40 million, while the United States numbered close to 150 million, Great Britain 50 million, and Germany (but without Austria) 65 million. Between 1930 and 1940, the French

population actually declined. Some Italian and Spanish immigrants returned to their homes, and there was an excess of deaths over births. The two world wars took their heaviest toll from among the young and most economically productive, leaving a disproportionate number of older people, which contributed to the economic stagnation.

AGRICULTURE AND THE STATE. A quick review of France's agriculture between 1870 and 1940 reveals that she had a high percentage (35–40%) of farmers, that the productivity of French farmers was low, and that the many small marginal farms were divided and subdivided into minute parcels that were unsuitable for mechanization and new techniques. Until 1940, France used only a small amount of chemical fertilizers, and the number of tractors on the farms was insignificant.

Unfortunately, the unproductive farms were encouraged by the tariff policies of the state. Agricultural interests, and also manufacturing groups, formed powerful lobbies that demanded and got high protectionist tariffs, special subsidies, and guaranteed price supports, all of which sheltered French business and agriculture from foreign competition. The state was thus helping to perpetuate the antiquated economic system.

BUSINESS ATTITUDES. Industrialists and businessmen in France did not show in many cases the initiative and willingness to take risks that we generally associate with a capitalist system. Many business affairs were family enterprises. Managers tended to keep production geared to a limited demand instead of seeking new markets, and profits were often "saved" instead of being reinvested in the business.

The system of distribution was particularly faulty, although there were some large chain stores. The economy was encumbered with too many small merchants and shopkeepers who eked out livings through limited volumes of trade. As a result, costs remained high because efficient techniques of distribution were not developed. Retail prices were disproportionately high when compared to wholesale prices, and the small profits extracted by the numerous

TABLE 3-1. *Growth of French Population in the Twentieth Century*

Year	Population (in millions)
1900	38.9
1913	39.8
1929	42.0
1949	41.4
1962	47.0
1967	50.0 *
1970	51.0
1978 †	55.2 (est.)

* The greater increase between 1962 and 1967 is due to the influx of the French from Algeria.
† Projected.

middlemen who handled the products unduly inflated the price to the consumer. Although a relatively unproductive segment in the economy, the middlemen were organized into strong pressure groups who demanded and received protection, and, to top it off, the sturdy virtues of the storekeepers were extolled as much as was the diligence and stamina of the farmers.

The Beginning of Economic Modernization

The task facing the country immediately after the Liberation in 1944, when industrial production was not even 40% of the level in 1938, was twofold: to replace the industrial equipment that had been damaged or destroyed in the war and to eliminate the weak elements in the economy. This was the objective of the first "Monnet Plan" for 1947–50 (actually extended to 1952), named after Jean Monnet, who was its architect in economic planning and modernization.

This plan, known as the "plan for modernization and equipment," had the following goals:

1. to assure a rapid rise in the living conditions of the population, and particularly an improvement in their diet;
2. to modernize and reequip the basic industries—coal mining, electric power, iron, cement, farm machinery, and transportation;
3. to bring agricultural methods and machinery up to date;
4. to devote the maximum resources possible to reconstruction, keeping in mind the needs of the basic industries, and to modernize the construction-material trades, the building trades, and public works; and
5. to modernize and develop the export industries to assure equilibrium in the balance of payments by 1950.

These targets were set for the year 1950: the production of 65 million tons of coal; the generation of 25 billion kilowatt-hours of electricity; the production of about 12 million tons of steel; the production of 50,000 tractors. Many of these targets were not achieved by 1950, partly because they were too ambitious, partly because the plan often lacked vigorous administration, and partly because of social unrest and strikes. But a beginning had been made. Three more "plans" ensued, and their cumulative impact began to be felt by 1955–56. Despite the weaknesses of the Fourth Republic and the vacillations of the various governments, business and public investment in the economy soared, and the rate of growth began to accelerate.

Several key economic activities were nationalized immediately after the Liberation. Not only the political leaders of the left, but also General de Gaulle believed that public ownership of certain industries was superior to private enterprise. Nationalization had been advocated by many resistance groups and endorsed by the National Council of the Resistance. In many speeches General de Gaulle had implied the need for state control and planning. Sometimes nationalization was urged as a punitive measure against companies that had collaborated with the Germans, sometimes as a necessary step to curb the monopolies, sometimes as an indispensable instrument for intelligent state planning, and almost always as a way to ensure social justice and improve the living conditions of the poor, particularly of the workers.

In 1946, electricity, gas, and some automobile plants, notably the Renault Automobile Company, were nationalized, and the Bank of France and Air France (the most important airline) came under state direction. These nationalizations greatly increased the scope of state ownership, which already had included rail transportation and the production and sale of cigarettes and matches. A sizable part of the economic activity of France thus came under state direction. Massive subsidies, both for state-controlled activities and for private enterprises, were necessary after the war.

Contrary to popular opinion about the French not paying their taxes, taxation—both direct and indirect—reached high levels in the postwar period. The total tax receipts in France in the sixties, for instance, amounted to about

TABLE 3-2. *French Industrial Production in the Twentieth Century (approximate annual averages)*

	1892–1902	1909–13	1925–29	1934–38	1948–52	1955–59	1965–66	1967–70
Steel (millions of tons)	1.5	4.6	9.7	6.2	9.1	15.2	19.0	22.5
Aluminum (thousands of tons)	1.0	13.5	29.1	50.8	74.6	217.5	340.0	370.8
Automobiles (in thousands)	2	45	254	227	286	1,283	1,602	2,100
Tractors	—	—	—	1,750	17,290	77,940	89,500	—
Iron (millions of tons)	5.4	22.0	50	33	31	60.0	59.5	55.4
Bauxite (thousands of tons)	59	309	666	649	767	1,746	2,652	2,773
Merchant Marine (thousands of tons)	1,597	2,319	3,303	2,881	2,710	4,461	4,878	5,962
Electricity (billions of kWhr)	—	—	15.6	20.8	40.6	70.0+	101.2	131.5

18% of the gross national product—considerably higher than in the United States. And they have continued to increase. It is true that indirect taxation accounts for more than half the total, but this is because there are still many small entrepreneurs and independent workers, for whom tax collection is more difficult and evasion easier, rather than because the French are more reluctant than the citizens of other countries to pay their taxes.

An extensive program of social legislation has been adopted. It includes old-age insurance, accident and unemployment compensation, maternity benefits, medical care (a very large part of the patient's expenses for medical treatment, hospitalization, and drugs comes from the national insurance fund), and family allowances that provide supplementary income to families with two children or more.

By 1956–57, the impact of the expanded economic activity became clearly discernible. France's economy (except in housing) was growing at a rate that compared favorably with that of Germany in the years of 1952–56. The decline in the total volume of coal production was fully compensated for by the increased use of gas and electricity. By 1958, agricultural production was 30–35% higher than in 1949. Chemical fertilizers were finally beginning to be widely used, and the annual production of tractors increased rapidly. The prewar national income almost doubled and the population began to grow. France today, therefore, is quite similar to other industralized nations. Of her labor force of about 20 million people, about 17% work in agriculture, 42% in industry, and 41% in so-called tertiary employment—merchants, teachers, members of the professions, in services, etc.

Both the agricultural and the industrial sectors, however, exhibit certain peculiarities. The concentration of industry is not yet as marked as it is in Great Britain, West Germany, or the United States. The great majority of the industrial firms employ between five and fifty workers. There are 1¼ million self-employed (*patrons*) in industry and commerce. But again, the larger part of production is in the hands of corporations and firms that employ thousands of workers. In commerce, however, the predominance of individual units continues to be high, and the number of persons employed in agriculture is inordinately large—about 17%—compared to that in Great Britain, where about 5% of the work force is on farms, and in the United States, where the figure is 7%. The agricultural population, however, is decreasing and so is the number of small marginal farms. The process of urbanization has been slower in France than elsewhere. There are only six cities in France with over a quarter of a million people. About 30% continue to live in small hamlets of less than two thousand population. The Paris urban agglomeration alone, however, accounts for about 9 million—18% of the French population.

The distribution of income is somewhat uneven. The wages of the industrial workers have usually lagged behind the income of other groups, partly because of inflation but also because of their inability to unite in a common front against employers. Now that tax favors and social benefits, particularly family allowances, add, in effect, about 50% to the average worker's wages, the standard of living of the working class today compares favorably with that of workers in Great Britain and West Germany. Pockets of underdevelopment persist in France. Housing construction fell far behind that in England and West Germany, and only in the last few years has France been able to build as many as 1 million units a year.

Not all of the various regions of the country share equally in her wealth. France was traditionally divided into two areas: a "static" region, composed of some sixty-four departments, accounting for less than the national average in economic production, and a "dynamic" region (twenty-six departments, mostly in the Paris region, the north, along the Mediterranean coast, and around the cities of Lyon, Grenoble, and Bordeaux), in which production was above the average. But even this has been changing. The areas of the southwest are being modernized rapidly, thanks to the discovery of natural gas, and the areas of the southeast and south are benefiting from the construction of dams and the production of electric energy. Some industries—oil refineries, aircraft and aluminum factories, and atomic energy plants—have

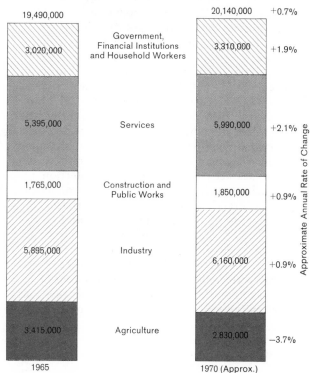

FIG. 3-1. *Profile of the actively employed population, by sector.*

been shifting to the "static" regions, bringing them welcome prosperity.[1]

The increasing number of radio and television sets and the increasingly widespread ownership of automobiles, motorscooters, and motorcycles have brought the farms closer to the towns and broken through the old parochial barriers of the village that were so well described in books such as Laurence Wylie's *Village in the Vaucluse* some years ago. Although there are still some rural departments in which individual income remains abominably low and in which life is not much different from what it was at the end of the nineteenth century, the number of people living under preindustrial conditions is becoming progressively smaller. The poorer sections of France are certainly no worse off than the rural areas of Mississippi or

---

[1] For a more detailed discussion, see Chapter 7.

the depressed mining areas of West Virginia and of South Wales in England, or the ghettos of our cities where millions of Americans live.

Two long-range trends should help boost France's economy tremendously: the increase in population and the benefits of the European Common Market. The elimination of the tariffs between France and West Germany, Italy, Luxembourg, Belgium, and Holland will greatly stimulate the flow of goods, labor, and capital among the participating countries. At the same time, the common external tariff for the Common Market countries provides protection for French agricultural products. Thus, all sectors of the French economy, including agriculture, will be forced to step up modernization in order to meet the competition and the demands of her rising population and her European partners. What is the impact of modernization? How will it affect the political attitudes and actions of the average Frenchman? To these crucial questions we shall return at the end of our discussion.

SOCIAL STRUCTURE

The political analyst ordinarily classifies individual citizens of a country into groups with similar interests or backgrounds. These social groups—workers, farmers, intellectuals, businessmen, the Catholic church, the army, and so on—vie with each other for positions of political influence. In many countries, these groups are relatively homogeneous blocs that tend to operate as a unit. Not so in France, where these groups are splintered internally along political and ideological lines. The workers are divided into many factions holding differing political attitudes; so are the Catholics, the intellectuals, the farmers, and the veterans. The failure of the French to create a political system that is an instrument of compromise perpetuates, and even tends to exacerbate the deep divisions that sunder these social groups into quarreling factions.

One striking phenomenon of the French social structure, as Professor John E. Sawyer pointed out in a very illuminating essay, has been the existence of overlapping social orders. The first is the *traditional order,* mostly in rural

areas, characterized by an attachment to the status quo and to the authority of the church and the old nobility—more recently the landowners. The second is the *liberal order,* represented by the middle class—merchants, artisans, small entrepreneurs—which is essentially egalitarian and individualistic; and the third is the *industrial order,* which borrows some of the elements of liberalism—individualism, equality, mobility—but emphasizes mass production, social discipline, and social organization.

In France, the traditional and liberal orders clashed all through the nineteenth century, largely in the struggle between the nobility, the army, and the church, on one hand, and the republic, on the other. Just when these two "orders" were learning to live side-by-side, during the best years of the Third Republic, between 1905 and 1914, the impact of industrialization was being strongly felt in some regions of France. The "traditional order" survives in some rural areas and among conservative Catholic groups. The "liberal order" is still very much alive among the merchants, artisans, lawyers, shopkeepers, and small entrepreneurs, while the "industrial order," until recently restricted largely to Paris and the north, is gaining ground.

The French attachment to individualism, the stubborn survival of small firms and family-controlled enterprises, the characteristic enthusiasm for smallness, for a sense of balance, and for craftsmanship reflect the heritage of the liberal nineteenth-century tradition and have tended to slow down industrialization. The workers themselves have been influenced by the liberal tradition in both their ideological and economic thinking. Many factories continue to employ only a few workers, making it difficult for them to organize. The workers, exhibiting the individualistic traits associated with the middle class and even the peasants, often reject the discipline and organization required by industrialization. Romantic ideas favoring the destruction of industrial capitalism through the general strike and revolution permeate their ranks. But the industrial order has also been deeply influenced by the liberal order. Industrial managers frequently shied away from modernization and mass production in order to stay small and secure and avoid risks. It was not until the end of World War II that what we have called the "industrial order" began to assert itself among civil servants, some managerial and business groups, and the intellectuals.

SOCIAL CLASSES

The Workers

Out of some 20 million gainfully employed persons in France 6½ million are considered to be workers. Although it is difficult to generalize about such a large group of people, they do have certain common traits that put them in an identifiable socioeconomic category. In the first place, the worker is relatively poor, and his standard of living improved little even in the years of prosperity. As of 1950, for instance, the real wage of the industrial worker remained somewhat below the 1938 figure.

Even now, despite the progress made, the average monthly salary for workers is about $200 for men and less than $150 for women. A qualified worker makes about $170 a month; a specialized (skilled) worker about $180 a month and unskilled workers average not more than $155. With $230 a month, coal miners are among the highest paid. An apprentice earns $80 a month. Service personnel average about $185 a month. For all salaried categories, including engineers, administrative cadres, and technicians—amounting to over 14 million men and women (about three-fourths of the gainfully employed total)—the average salary for men is $280 a month and for almost 3 million women about $175. Only one out of four of all salaried personnel makes more than $300 a month.

More important than the economic conditions of the workers in characterizing them as a social group are their ideology and political attitudes. About two-thirds of the workers vote Communist or Socialist; one out of five of the industrial workers believes, in a romantic sort of way, that "revolution" rather than reform will better his condition. In the parts where the workers live together in the same residential sections—as in the Paris area, in the north, and

in other industrialized centers—there is a sharp division between the workers and other groups—the middle class, members of professions, and even the lower middle class. Differences in manners, dress, entertainment, education, income, housing, summer camps, and vacations have separated the workers from these other classes until very recently.

The workers are divided into a number of trade union organizations: the CGT (General Confederation of Labor) under the control of the Communist party; the CGT-FO (General Confederation of Labor–Force Ouvrière) which split with the Communist-controlled Confederation in 1947 and remains attached to the Socialist party; and the Catholic trade union now called the General Confederation of Democratic Labor (CGDT). In addition there are a number of "independent" organizations. The CGT has about 1¼ million members, the FO fewer than half a million, and the CGDT not more than 750,000. The total represents a considerable drop in trade union membership since the Liberation. The unions have become weakened through political division, and workers seem inable to pursue a united front to improve their conditions.

In the last fifteen years, the lot of the workers has improved, and this has tended to mitigate their revolutionary spirit. Real wages have risen, except for the period between 1966 and 1968; there is full employment; specialized industries have grown up that attract workers with ability and give them the chance to attend technical schools and improve their earnings rapidly (a specialized worker may earn more than three times the wages of a semiskilled one); opportunities for promotion have increased. Internal mobility within a class or sometimes even mobility between status groups is on the rise. Better wages and living conditions have started to eliminate the sharp difference of dress, habits, and manners. Those workers with higher wages can move to better housing facilities and can buy a motorscooter or even a small car.

But many of the French workers remain attached to old habits and ideas. Real wages for many of them—perhaps as many as one-quarter—are not much higher than during the best years of economic prosperity in the 1920s—20% receive less than $1,000 a year. The feeling of exploitation and separateness persists. Workers continue to consider themselves inferior and dream of a revolution that will square accounts with history. This attitude, spearheaded by a strong Communist party, makes the workers an unstable element in French society and a constant danger to a democratic society.

The Farmers

There are some 3 million "farmers" in France (individual owners, tenant farmers, sharecroppers, and agricultural workers), and they constitute approximately 17% of those gainfully employed. About half a million are agricultural workers, who earn less than $95 a month. The rest own their land or lease it. Small farms held by individual owners continue to be prevalent.

More than half a million farmers own such small holdings that they are unable to utilize modern techniques for increasing their productivity. As a result, the productivity of French agriculture was until very recently low compared to that of American, British, and Danish farmers. The authors of the Monnet Plan complained immediately after the Liberation that a French farmer produced only enough to feed three persons, while an American farmer could feed sixteen, a British farmer seven, and a Danish farmer nine.

Foreign observers have described French farmers as a homogeneous group, characterized by their courage against adversity, their moderate political outlook, their sacrifices and patriotism, their labor and wisdom. French authors also have extolled the rural virtues of stoicism and courage, patience and moderation. These impressions were accurate to a great extent for the nineteenth century and the time before World War I. The farmers provided two of the nation's most precious commodities, in addition to their agricultural produce: their sons for the army, and their savings. But the devastation of World War I brought to the fore the farmers' sense of individualism and their suspicion of

the state. This spirit, coupled with the increasingly antiquated machinery and procedures used on the farm, and the constant fragmentation of the land, has resulted in open defiance in a number of regions against agents of the central government.

"Ideologies" that have had the most appeal for the farmers are radicalism and Catholicism. The elements of radicalism—individualism and antistate philosophy—are rooted in the thinking of many farmers. Catholicism, on the other hand, accounts for much of the conservative attitude of farmers. But after World War II, the farmers and their organizations adopted views all across the political spectrum, which increased the political instability of the country. For instance, if we take for purposes of illustration five departments of France with the greatest percentage of farmers—Creuse (85% of the population), Côtes du Nord (81.5%), Gers (80%), Vendée (80%), and Haute-Savoie (80%)—we find that in the election of 1967, the Communists and the leftists groups received over 50% in Côtes du Nord and Creuse, dropped slightly below half in Gers, to receive less than one-fourth in Vendée and one-third in Haute-Savoie. The Gaullists and the centrists together were below 50% in Côtes du Nord and Creuse, gained over half in Gers, and reached 65% in Haute-Savoie and almost 70% in Vendée.

The political orientation of a farm region largely depends on its types of agriculture, on its level of income, its historical experience, and the intensity of religious practices. Wherever landholdings are small and the church weak, the general political orientation is to the Left, ranging from radicalism to Communism. In areas where there are small landholdings and where religious practices are prevalent, the farmers usually vote conservative and sometimes for the liberal Catholics. Where farms range from medium to large in size, the crucial determining factor is religion. In the areas where religious practices are strong, the farmers tend to vote conservative or moderate; where religious practices are weak, they vote for the center or the left.

Catholicism is thus, generally speaking, a conservative force in French politics. But the fact that a farmer owns property, particularly in some of the southern and southeastern regions, does not guarantee that he will not adopt radical ideas. In fact, in one department like Creuse, where private ownership is both widespread and widely parceled, the Communist party is particularly strong.

The Middle Class

The "middle class" instigated the Revolution of 1789 against the nobility and the crown. Its economic power had increased greatly in the eighteenth century, and it was anxious to augment its political power by establishing a representative government. After the Revolution, it was generally the champion of the republic against the nobility, the church, and the army. Thanks to it, the doctrine of the separation of church and state became well established, the army came under the control of the state, the representative institutions became supreme, and vested interests have been subordinated to the legislature.

The term "middle class," however, covers many heterogeneous elements. Do we define it according to occupation, income, or status? One French political scientist uses these three basic criteria for categorizing French citizens as members of the middle class: (*a*) the nature of their jobs, (*b*) their way of life and the manner in which they spend their income, and (*c*) the common situation with reference to their income tax. On the basis of these criteria, the French middle class consists of the following groups: among the salaried are engineers, office personnel, the bulk of the civil servants, judges, teachers, professors, and noncommissioned officers (*sous-officiers*) in the armed services; among the nonsalaried are members of the professions, small merchants, small businessmen, small entrepreneurs, and artisans. They are roughly estimated to total 8½ million people, or approximately 37% of those gainfully employed. This large figure is what many authors have in mind when they refer to France as a "bourgeois"—middle-class—country, a land of small entrepreneurs, independent artisans, small family enterprises, and small shops where

the nineteenth-century values of individualism and quality, moderation and balance, reign.

From the natural affinities that exist within the middle class, one might assume that the group exhibits a unified and constant attitude in matters of politics. But this is hardly the case in France, where the middle class has often changed its political orientation and is today split into many different viewpoints.

HISTORICAL SHIFTS. Until about the end of the nineteenth century, the middle class was generally anticlerical and prorepublican. Since the turn of the century, however, the middle class has slowly turned back to the church and toward a more conservative political attitude. Their distrust of the state, very much like the emphasis on states' rights in the United States, often led them to block social and economic reforms, while the advocacy of socialism by the emerging working class put them increasingly on the defensive. One segment of the middle class, the so-called radicals, continue to pay lip service to anticlericalism and reform, but they are not very strong about them in practice and end up oscillating between the left and the right.

The lower middle class, the artisans and shopkeepers, retained their attachment to the republic until the end of World War II. Since 1945, the "small man" has begun to rise against the income tax and the financial burdens imposed upon him by the state. Conscious that the tide of history is sweeping France toward greater industrialization and is eroding his very existence (the chain stores are driving out the small shopkeeper, the big factories are eliminating the artisan, mechanized farms are squeezing out the small independent farmer, etc.), the "small men" have attempted to arrest this development. Through powerful lobbies, they pressured Parliament for increasing protection and subsidies. In the 1950s, they began to repudiate the republican parliamentary system they had supported for so long and to join extreme-right-wing nationalist groups.

DIVERSITY AND FRAGMENTATION. In the last twenty-five years, the middle class has become divided in its political views among all political parties. Regional, historical, religious, and economic factors account for this wide dispersion of political orientation. In a number of instances, middle-class groups have even supported the Communists. It has been estimated, for instance, that as many as 750,000 to 1 million of the Communist party votes have come from the middle class. The bulk of middle-class votes, however, goes to the center groups and the Gaullists, and a small percentage to the socialists. All political parties in turn make a concerted effort to appeal to the various segments of the middle class and to organize them into a number of professional front associations.

The diversity in political outlook divides and weakens the middle class. Further, the majority is not particularly active or interested in politics and is susceptible to the unifying appeal of a "strong" man; it has succumbed at different times to Bonapartism. Generally, the middle class has supported the republic as the best instrument for accommodating its interests, but in time of crisis it has swung to the right. During the Second Empire (1852–70), with Marshal Pétain in 1940, and, finally, with General de Gaulle, the middle class has opted for what amounts to a one-man government. It has not displayed in the realm of politics the moderation and tolerance that Aristotle and later John Stuart Mill associated with it.

The Church

France is a predominantly Catholic nation. There are only a little more than a million Protestants and Jews and three to four hundred thousand resident Algerian Moslems in France. Yet of the 50 million Catholics, not more than about 25%, a maximum of around 12 million, can be classed as practicing believers. The great majority are "indifferent"; they observe only the basic sacraments prescribed by the church—baptism, communion, marriage, and extreme unction—and perhaps conform outwardly to some of the most important religious ceremonies and rites. A minority, about 6 million, is anticlerical and agnostic. Many densely populated urban centers are virtually "de-Christianized"—without churches, priests, or practicing Catholics. Much of the urban population, especially in the working-class districts, is militantly atheistic. In some areas, even burial is a civil affair. A close correlation exists between conservatism and attachment to the church, and between Communism and socialism and hostility to the church. The right, generally speaking, is religious; the left is overtly anticlerical and very often atheistic.

The degree of religious participation in the various parts of France is largely the result of historical factors. There is both *more* and *less* religious practice in the rural areas. For instance, in the regions of the northwest (Brittany and Normandy), about 80% of the population are devout Catholics, while in some 30 departments of central and southern France, the figure drops to about 20% (see Fig. 3-2). In the towns, generally only about half the population is religious, and in urban centers like Paris, Marseille, Lyon, Toulouse, and Grenoble, the number is even less. In some of the suburban centers of the larger towns, areas dense with working-class settlements, religious practices are almost nonexistent. In the Paris working-class districts, not more than 2% of the people "practice."

History has produced strange things on the religious map of France. The American Catholic tourist who decides to drive from, say, Luçon to Bayeux in Normandy will find that to his left the churches are usually well kept, regular services are held, and priests are readily available, for some 85% of the people to his left "practice." Only a few miles away to his right, however, the situation is exactly the reverse. Only about 20% of the people practice, and priests are difficult to find. Often the tourist will discover a rivulet that divides a village in two, with one part intensely Catholic and the other intensely anticlerical and nonreligious!

The correlation between social groups and religion is fairly precise, but, as with any generalization, there are exceptions. Many farmers, especially in the northwest and northeast, the upper middle class, the bigger landowners, and part of the middle class itself have a high proportion of practicing believers. The workers, many of the farmers of the south, teachers, intellectuals, and some of the lower middle class show a low percentage of practice.

ORGANIZATION. The Catholic church in France is technically separated from the state. Until recently, this separation has also applied to education. The church receives no subsidies, and its schools—grammar schools, nurseries, and technical and high schools—are strictly "private." [2] Matters of religious dogma and practical administration are decided by a loose organization headed by the Assembly of Cardinals and Archbishops. The country is divided into dioceses that correspond to the departments, and these in turn are subdivided into parishes. A total of some forty thousand priests and about one hundred thousand auxiliaries belonging to various religious orders perform the services and administer the many activities of the church—charity, education, relief, hospitals, and so forth. The state intervenes only when a bishop is nominated by the pope, for it must approve the choice for the appointment to be valid.

What is the political orientation of the practicing Catholics? As with other groups we have examined, there is great diversity in the political behavior of Catholics. Some follow the church's dogma and believe the state to be subordinate to the church. Many remain extremely conservative. In the thirties, this group was represented by a militant antirepublican organization, the National Federation of Catholics. On the other end of the spectrum, the "progressive" Catholics are actively concerned with social and economic reform and are more interested in social action than in proselytizing and maintaining the dogma. This group, since the Liberation, has been moving toward the left and has been responsible for establishing new reformist Catholic groups, parties, and trade unions. Between the left and the right are the majority of believers, who generally vote for the center parties.

In the last decades, many Catholic youth organizations composed of lay believers have

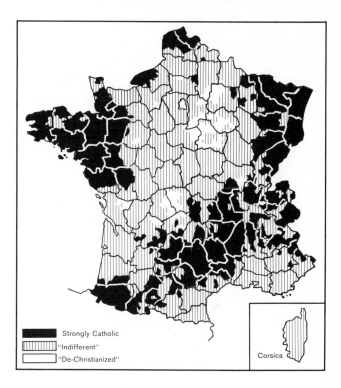

FIG. 3-2. *Religious practice in France [Adapted from François Goguel,* Géographie des Élections Françaises, de 1870 à 1951 *(Paris: Armand Colin, 1952) with the kind permission of the* Foundation Nationale des Sciences Politiques *and the* Librarie Armand Colin.]

been particularly active in social, economic, and political matters. The most significant among them have been the JAC (*Jeunesse Agricole Catholique*—Catholic Agricultural Youth), the JOC (*Jeunesse Ouvrière Catholique*—Catholic Workers Youth), and the JEC (*Jeunesse Étudiante Chrétienne*—Christian Student Youth). They have to spread a new progressive philosophy among the workers and farmers. Often looked upon with suspicion by the Catholic hierarchy and frequently in sharp disagreement with other parareligious organizations of the church, these groups have been quite successful in organizing Catholic workers, farmers, and students, and in bringing about progressive reforms. They have not been able to reduce

---

[2] Except for Alsace-Lorraine, where the church and Catholic schools have been subsidized since 1918.

appreciably Communist influence, but they have succeeded in reaching those who might otherwise have succumbed to it.

In 1944, Catholic action organizations spurred the creation of a large liberal Catholic party, the Republican Popular Movement (MRP); in the fifties, they successfully rebuilt the Christian trade union, the French Confederation of Christian Workers (CFTC). Today they are trying to penetrate the countryside, by sparking a desire for reform among the farmers and villagers, by encouraging economic and technical reforms that are so much needed in French agriculture, and by supporting enlightened candidates at the local level for the offices of mayor, municipal councilor, and, more recently, senators and deputies. They are also beginning actively to enter politics in an effort to restructure the political parties—especially those of the left.

The Army

As in England and all other European countries, the army in France—except for brief periods during the Revolution, the reign of Napoleon, and since World War II—has been characterized by officers of aristocratic and upper-middle-class background. After the Bourbon restoration of 1814, the officer corps became almost a caste—hierarchically organized, antirepublican, and, until the turn of the century, predominantly royalist. The young officers received their "high school" training in exclusive Jesuit schools where they faced rigorous examinations and then were sent to the few select military schools, later to be assigned to regimental or divisional commands or to the various staff organizations in Paris. Family, social, religious, and school ties made them a well-knit group, whose autonomy was assured by the frequent appointment of a general as minister of war. Time after time, the army virtually imposed a veto on the regularly constituted governmental authorities. When the Third Republic was introduced, army officers attempted on two occasions to subvert it in favor of the monarchy. It was the Dreyfus affair at the turn of the century—a landmark in the political history of France—that broke the political autonomy of the army and changed its social composition.

The real issue in the Dreyfus affair (1894–1906) was whether the army could continue to be a state within a state, immune from political scrutiny and able to impose its own will upon the civil government. The army court-martialed Alfred Dreyfus, a Jewish captain, for treason, and, when confronted with evidence that the documents used to convict Dreyfus had been forged by another officer of the general staff, the army protested that any interference with its own jurisdiction and rules would destroy its morale and ultimately undermine the unity of the nation. A wave of nationalism, anti-Semitism, and antirepublicanism swept across the country as Émile Zola and others insisted that Dreyfus was innocent and demanded a new trial for him. After some ten years of unremitting social and political strife, the republican forces won when Dreyfus was exonerated; civil control over the army was asserted, and the hold of the church and the aristocracy on the army was broken.

The end of the Dreyfus affair virtually coincided with the establishment of separation of church and state in France and the dissolution of a number of religious congregations and the confiscation of their property. These developments marked, in a real sense, the culmination of the Revolution of 1789: they weakened the ultraconservative elements of the church, virtually wiped out the influence of the aristocracy, and paved the way for the democratic reorganization of the army under the supremacy of the republican government.

From the turn of the century until 1940, the bulk of the army officers adopted an attitude of political neutrality. The army was referred to as the *"grande muette"*—the "great deaf and dumb." It did not interfere in politics. However, few high-ranking officers were genuinely republican. The army was not attuned to the world of politics, to the need for give and take, negotiation, and compromise, and it thus tended to stand aloof from the arena of political bargaining.

The defeat of the French forces in World War II shook the army to its foundations. It weakened its loyalty to the state, shattered its internal discipline and cohesiveness, and radically changed its social composition; it also led the army to search for a scapegoat to blame for the disaster. When the armistice was signed between the French and the Germans in 1940, the republic was set aside and one man, Marshal Philippe Pétain, established an authoritarian system. He was supported by the bulk of the army. Following the army's tradition of political neutrality, virtually all the officers commanding colonial garrisons obeyed Pétain. In Senegal, Madagascar, Morocco, and Algeria, discipline held. But one general, de Gaulle, did not obey. With a small group of followers, he decided to reject the legitimacy of Marshal Pétain's government and to continue the war. De Gaulle's rebelliousness was not a unique phenomenon, but it was remarkable that he was able to win over to his side more and more officers and colonial garrisons and eventually to march into liberated France as the country's legitimate spokesman. The logic of the situation carried dangerous seeds for the future. If one general could do it, why not another? The dissidence split the ranks of the army. Some officers had sided with de Gaulle, others with Pétain. "Pétainists" and "Gaullists" became expressions conveying two political tendencies and two orientations in the army. Even if the passage of time could temper the hostility between the two blocs, mutual suspicion was inevitable. The hierarchy and discipline of the army was therefore rudely shaken.

Defeat makes any army unpopular. It took a long time, for instance, for the German army to recover from the debacle of World War I, and it has not quite yet recovered from defeat in World War II. Disgraced, useless, and frustrated, the defeated soldiers, and especially the officers, realize that they are something of a pariah in a country that only shortly before had heaped glory and distinction upon them. With the French officer corps, the situation was even more discouraging. The collapse of 1940 was followed by a series of colonial wars in which the French army continuously had to withdraw. The war in Indochina that lasted from 1946 to 1954 took a heavy toll among the officers, while few at home seemed to care what was going on halfway around the globe. In 1956 France pulled out of Morocco and Tunisia; in 1954 the Algerian rebellion erupted and raged intermittently for almost eight years.

Years of defeat and neglect embittered the French army, and the officers no longer had wealth or social position to help siphon off their frustration. The French army in the 1950s contained only a few hundred wealthy officers, compared to some thirty thousand in the latter part of the nineteenth century. The twentieth-century officers were mostly from the lower middle class, and many rose from the ranks. Their parents were frequently military officers or civil servants, members of the professions, small landowners. The officers shared the anxieties and fears of the lower middle class, who were frightened of a world that was changing too rapidly and of a future that carried unknown threats to their security. They thus considered that status and prestige were inordinately important, but found themselves ignored, underpaid, and criticized for losing battles the country itself did not seem to want to win. The officers found their scapegoat in the republic, which they believed had badly let them, and France, down. They formed dissident organizations and sought allies among right-wing, antirepublican forces in an attempt to impose their view on the Fourth Republic. The army thus reentered politics in a rebellious mood.

Algeria was the breaking point. Some half a million recruits and their officers were confronted with a far-from-orthodox war. It was a battle involving ambushes, street fighting, and terrorist attacks. The rebels had the support of the overwhelming Moslem majority, who surrounded the French settlers and the army at every turn. There could be no retreat. Yet victory in the traditional military sense was impossible, since the enemy consisted of elusive bands of guerrillas. In an attempt to "win," the army embarked on a broad-scale campaign that ranged far beyond just firing weapons. They utilized censorships, propaganda, coercion, and torture. They were given the power to censor newspapers, to control the schools, to administer new schools for the Moslems, to set up "resettlement camps" in which Algerians were screened and indoctrinated, and to move hundreds of thousands of Algerians into barracks and new villages where they could be closely watched. But back in Paris, political leaders criticized the war and urged negotiations with the rebels. The army was prevented from "solving" the problem in its customary way—by victory. More and more army leaders came to see that the only way out was to assume political control and eliminate the republic.

Thus the army had come full circle since the Dreyfus affair. Before 1890, it could, in effect, veto actions of the government, but after the Dreyfus case and the victory of World War I, it was assimilated into the republic. It adopted a neutral stand in politics, but not for long. In the late thirties, it began to question the weak and vacillating policies of the republic, and in 1940 most of the officers supported the authoritarian system that emerged from the armistice. General de Gaulle's call emboldened many officers to set their own goals ahead of those of the legally constituted government. All pretense to neutrality was abandoned. At the same time, the army's social character had changed. The army began to recruit its officers extensively from the middle class and the lower middle class. Slowly the insecurities and anxieties of this class crept into the ranks, especially into the officer corps. Algeria spurred the officers, fired by years of isolation and defeat, to become the spokesmen of a new nationalism, and a political regime that would support them. Hoping de Gaulle would do this, they backed him in May 1958. But even their allegiance to the Fifth Republic was conditional; and it took almost a decade and two uprisings before they acquiesced to the authority of the state.

Intellectuals

Intellectuals are people who work with ideas and manipulate symbols and words. Broadly speaking, we can include in this category teachers, lawyers, doctors, higher civil servants, writers, artists, editors, radio commentators, newspaper columnists. If we apply this very general definition of the term, there are about 1 million intellectuals in France, but, for

purposes of political analysis, we need a more limited, a more functional, definition of intellectual. Here, then, we will consider an intellectual to be a person of some education and sophistication who, by using various media of communication, consciously attempts to influence the course of events.

To understand the intellectual's role in politics, we must go back again to the Dreyfus affair. The trial of Captain Dreyfus not only brought sharp conflict over his personal fate, but also generated more profound discussions about the nature of justice, the power of the state, and the rights of the individual. Émile Zola's famous newspaper article, "I Accuse," in which he levied a bitter attack against the army and its officers for framing a fellow officer in the name of the rights of the state, crystallized the deeper issues in the case and awakened in the intellectuals a desire to enter the arena of political dispute. Intellectuals thus became "engaged" in politics, but, like the other groups we have examined, they have been fragmented into many ideological camps that support Catholics, anticlerics, nationalists, republicans, communists, militarists, antimilitarists, etc. They began to reflect the divisions of the society.

Instead of objectively analyzing and clarifying issues, therefore, the intellectuals became protagonists of political causes. The Jesuit schools produced, until the end of the nineteenth century, intellectuals for the army and the bureaucracy, while the teachers' schools (écoles normales) graduated teachers and intellectuals deeply committed to a lay republic, to the separation of church and state, and often to socialism. The League of the French Fatherland (Ligue de la Patrie Française) consisted of conservative, nationalist proarmy intellectuals, while the League of the Rights of Man (Ligue des Droits de l'Homme) included those who were attached to the republic, to individual rights, and to the separation of church and state. Numerous intellectual groups in the thirties took an overtly proroyalist and authoritarian stance. The sympathy of some university professors with Communism provoked, in turn, many conservative intellectuals to favor peace with Germany and later to support Pétain's authoritarian regime. After the Liberation, a sharp debate arose between those who were sympathetic to the Soviet Union and the cause of socialism and those who opposed the totalitarian means the Soviets imposed to accomplish their goal of socialism. The old question of whether the end justifies the means split the intellectuals into bitterly opposed pro-Soviet and anti-Soviet camps.

The intellectuals speak through organizations that constitute important pressure groups, but they speak with so many different voices that they tend to cancel one another out. By often exaggerating and distorting their arguments, the intellectuals end up by aggravating the differences that divide the community. The lively discussions of ideas that continuously take place in France are one of the glories of French culture. But they put a great strain on the nation's political system, and, by mounting ideas as weapons in political battles, make the compromises necessary for effective political action even more difficult to achieve.

INTEREST GROUPS

Economic, social, intellectual, and religious interests are solidly organized in France. For every conceivable interest group, there seems to be an association or a spokesman. If we look at the Paris telephone directory under *"association"* or *"union"* or *"syndicat,"* we shall quickly realize that there is no possible interest that does not have an office or organization in France. What is more, for each single interest there are *many* different associations. We cannot hope to discuss all the interest groups in France, but we will try to examine their general characteristics and study the mode of action of the more important ones.

Types of Interest Groups

At the risk of oversimplification, the interest groups can be divided into two broad categories. First are the *representative groups,* organizations that speak for the most important activities and interests at a national level. Their voice is that of a great number of members and

often a large number of affiliated groups and subgroups. Most important among them are the CNPF, *Conseil National du Patronat Français* (National Council of French Employers), which represents a great assortment of business enterprises and roughly corresponds to our National Association of Manufacturers and chambers of commerce combined; the CNPME, *Conseil National des Petits et Moyens Entreprises* (National Council of Small and Medium-sized Businesses), which is affiliated with the CNPF and represents a vast number of smaller-sized enterprises; the FNSEA, *Fédération Nationale des Syndicats des Exploitants Agricoles* (National Federation of Farmers), speaking for farmers; the three major trade union organizations—CGT, FO, and CGTD; the FEN, *Fédération de l'Éducation Nationale* (Federation of National Education), an "independent" union representing most of the grade-school, high-school, college, and technical-school teachers, and the UNEF, *Union Nationale des Étudiants de France* (National Student Union), representing university students. All these affiliations are nationally organized. They have branches all over France. Their members usually, but not always, agree on a particular means of action, so that their leaders can speak on any given issue with considerable authority and weight.

Second, there are organizations that have a *distinctly economic and corporative character.* Some of them act independently, although most belong to the organizations mentioned under the first category. Some have such a mass membership that their effectiveness is primarily "electoral"—that is, they urge their members to vote for or against a particular party or a candidate. Here is just a partial listing of this type of group: high-school teachers; Catholic families who receive subsidies for the education of their children in Catholic schools; the organizations that belong to the so-called "highway lobby"—motel owners, gas-station owners, car producers, truck and moving companies, gas producers, oil companies, etc.; tavern and bistro owners backed by the powerful alcohol lobby; war widows; and invalids. Other groups occupy critical areas in the country's economy whose temporary suspension may paralyze a good part of the nation: mailmen, electrical workers, railroad employees, miners, dockworkers.

MEANS OF ACTION. In general, French lobbies are quite similar in their methods of action to American lobbies. They give financial support to candidates; they place their spokesmen in the legislature and in the civil service; they have their own journals and hand out news releases in an attempt to sway public opinion to their point of view; they often exact pledges from the candidates they support and sponsor "study committees" in the legislature to promote their own interests.

French lobbies are also directly active in the legislative process. Through their spokesmen, they introduce bills and see to it that the proper amendments are inserted in pending legislation or that prejudicial amendments are blocked. Their influence even spills over into the executive branch. When a bill is passed, the interested lobby tries to prevent the release of any executive order that might be prejudicial to their interest or, conversely, attempts to see that the proper executive orders will be issued. To do this, spokesmen are often planted in certain crucial administrative services—the Ministries of Public Works, Agriculture, Veterans, Finance, and Industrial Production. With the growing participation of the state in economic matters, lobbying at the ministerial level has greatly increased. Every interest attempts to "colonize" the government in a number of ways: by influencing administrators, by offering them important jobs in their own organizations, by presenting them with facts and figures that appear to be convincing.

The Articulation of Interest

Each of the major social groups we have discussed is represented by several associations.

LABOR INTEREST-GROUPS. Less than one-third of the workers belong to unions. They are represented by at least five organizations. The General Confederation of Labor (CGT), the largest of all, includes both industrial unions—i.e., those with members from an entire industry (for example, steel workers, construction workers, automobile workers)—and craft unions. Its directive medium is the National Confederal Committee, which is elected by the delegates to the annual national congress. The leaders have been Communists since World War II, and they often use the union for political purposes. They have called strikes to protest the establishment of both NATO and the European Defense Community and the continuation of the wars in Indochina and Algeria, and they generally pursue the political objectives of the Communist party.

The CFDT—the French Confederation of Democratic Labor—is organized very much like the CGT. Half its members are salaried workers, and it is committed to social reform and to increasing the standard of living and wages of the workers. It has collaborated quite closely with the CGT on economic issues but it is usually unwilling to strike for political purposes. Despite its present name, the bulk of its forces continue to come from the CFTC—the French Confederation of Christian Workers, an old liberal Catholic movement.

The predominantly Socialist CGT-FO, General Confederation of Labor-Force Ouvrière seceded from the CGT in 1947 rather than accept the pro-Soviet political directives of the Communist-controlled CGT. The FO is primarily composed of low-ranking civil servants and workers in nationalized industries. It, too, says its goals are "apolitical," but in practice it has followed the policies of the Socialist party.

There is a small anarchist union, the CNT (National Confederation of Labor), which consists of unions not affiliated with any of the three larger unions. Nonaffiliated unions serve the needs of other employees. The National Federation of Education, for instance, has a membership of more than a quarter of a million grade-school, high-school, technical-school, and university teachers. Although claiming to be apolitical, it has consistently taken political positions on a number of issues. The Socialists and Communists have vied for its control, and the resolutions of the members often reflect sharp political divisions.

FARM INTEREST GROUPS. About seven hundred thousand farmers belong to the National Federation of Farmers. Nationwide in scope, it includes farmers who deal in such products as wheat, wine, beets, milk, and poultry. Although the avowed purpose of the organization is to "represent and defend on the national plane the interests of the agricultural profession in the economic, social, moral, and legislative domain," the federation represents only a small percentage of farmers and is generally dominated by the wealthier ones, notably the beet growers, the so-called alcohol lobby, the dairy interests, and meat producers. In the last few years a dynamic small group of agricultural experts, technicians, and intellectuals has organized the National Council of Young Farmers—concerned with the development of cooperation and understanding among farmers. They have gradually infiltrated the National Federation of Farmers and have contributed to the improvement of agricultural methods and the betterment of the standard of living of the small farms. The federation today, like many other interest groups, is actively participating, in cooperation with the administration, in the overall reorientation of French agriculture.

Almost all the political parties have tried to woo the farmers by setting up their own farm organization or by demonstrating favorable actions within the National Federation of Farmers. The Socialists established the General Confederation of Agriculture, which was quite powerful immediately after the Liberation; the Communists ran the General Confederation of Farm Workers, which is influential in central France and in the southwest, where the farms are parceled into small private holdings; the Catholics and the MRP work through various agricultural Catholic action groups, particularly the Catholic youth farm organizations; the right wing has a number of farm associations; and the Radical Socialist party has become the spokesman for middle-income farmers in a number of areas. Thus, extreme diversity and fragmentation have been the rule with farm organizations, which is clearly reflected by the voting behavior of farmers.

When political-action and pressure-group methods have failed to achieve the farmers' goals, they have borrowed the tactics of the working class and staged demonstrations and strikes, complete with roadblocks and acts of violence. This form of direct action has, of course, precedents that go back to the farmers' uprisings under the *Ancien Régime,* especially in the south; but even as recently as the thirties, farmers were organized into a rural Fascist militia known as the "green shirts." The postwar infiltration into farm groups of both the extreme left (the Communists) and the extreme right (the Poujadists) intensified the farmers' rebelliousness.

The political unrest of the farmers has been exacerbated by economic developments. Since the end of World War II, modernization has increased farm productivity to such an extent that prices of agricultural products have sagged. Although the costs of goods that the farmer buys have dropped, the decrease has not been enough to prevent a relative decline in farm income and a consequent exodus from the farm to the city. Every year about forty thousand persons move from agricultural areas to the larger towns. The farmers have demanded and received increased aid in the form of subsidies, tax exemptions, and price supports. Help of a sort has also come from those who preach that the farmer is the backbone of the nation's moral character. Former Minister of Industrial Production J. M. Jeanneney, for instance, has written that agriculture has a "civilizing mission" and that the stability of a people derives from a sufficient number of farmers.[3]

But the process of modernization cannot be easily arrested. In most mature societies, people are moving off the farms into towns, from agriculture into industry, leaving in their wake severe dislocations in the life of the countryside, especially in France, where intense resentments and political divisions already existed. Efforts to ameliorate the French farmer's condition, to teach him new techniques, to provide him with fertilizers and tractors, to develop cooperatives, and to show him what and how to plant have

[3] *Forces et faiblesses de l'économie française* (Paris: Armand Colin, 1957), p. 65.

been undertaken by the state and a number of voluntary associations. The farmers' situation is on the upswing.

MIDDLE-CLASS INTEREST GROUPS. As we have seen, the middle class is badly divided politically. However, one large organization, the National Council of Small and Middle-sized Businesses, claims to include some three thousand associations representing a total of eight-hundred thousand firms, the great majority of members being shopkeepers and merchants. Dedicated to preserving the interests of the "small" and "medium-sized" firm and store, it has spokesmen in the legislature who influence legislation on tariffs, subsidies, prices, taxation, and means of modernizing the distribution of goods. The council gives financial support to political candidates and has occasionally run its own men in national elections. But the "unity" of the small and middle-sized businessmen is a myth. Their loyalties are divided among all political parties. The Communists, for instance, have set up a number of "front" organizations in commerce and industry—among grocers, artisans, holders of liquor licenses, and small businessmen—and act as the protector of the "small man" against the big corporations.

THE ARMY AND VETERANS. Like any other professional organization, the army has a number of associations closely tied to it. The officers, noncommissioned officers, and graduates of the different military schools all have their own organizations. In addition, France's veterans are organized into several groups that concentrate largely on obtaining pensions and other economic privileges for their members. These veterans' associations are affiliated with various political organizations. The National Union of Veterans supports the moderate political groups of the center; the Republican Association of Veterans is linked with the Communists, the National Federation of Republican Veterans with the Radical Socialists, the Federation of Worker and Peasant Veterans with the Socialists. There are also specialized veterans' groups: veterans of the Algerian war and the

Indochinese war and veterans of specific military branches and divisions.

An effort to unite all these associations into one apolitical organization that would speak on behalf of the veterans' common economic interests and thus become an effective pressure group resulted in the formation right after World War II of the French Union of the Associations of Veterans and War Victims. It was a powerful organization, probably representing more than 5 million members. However, disagreement over the colonial policy of the government and the war in Algeria led to the inevitable fragmentation of the group. By 1956, a special committee was established to support the continuation of the war in Algeria and to assure that France would never allow independence for Algeria. By attracting very nationalistic and often extremely antirepublican support, this committee caused the estrangement of more liberal members of the union and the formation of rival factions.

INTEREST GROUPS OF INTELLECTUALS. The only genuine professional association among what we may call the "intellectuals" is the Confederation of Intellectual Workers of France. A very loosely knit organization of some four-hundred thousand members representing about eighty thousand associations, it includes painters, writers, members of professions, and many others. Although it professes to represent the material interests of the intellectuals, this claim of unity around economic themes is illusory. The intellectuals, as we have seen, are divided into all the political families of the nation, and are deeply "engaged" in the political issues of the day.

Among the political organizations of the intellectuals, the League of the Rights of Man has been one of the most powerful. Founded at the time of the Dreyfus affair, it grew in the thirties to a membership of over two-hundred thousand. Since then it has been on the decline, but continues to represent the forces of the left and champions such causes as individual and political freedom and freedom of the press, and opposes all forms of authoritarianism. It considers itself the guardian of the rights secured by the French Revolution and is a stanch believer in the separation of church and state. Its support comes from all the elements of the left, including civil servants, teachers, university professors, and, at times, even the liberal Catholics.

Students should perhaps also be listed under the category of "intellectuals." They are specifically concerned with advancing their own status and well-being, in the form of scholarships, living quarters, loans, and the like, but, as is the case with all the groups we have discussed, it is impossible for students to maintain an apolitical posture. Their organization, the UNEF (National Union for the Students of France), has branches at all the universities in France and includes in its membership around 15 to 20 percent of registered university students —about one-hundred thousand. It is a very active lobby, constantly sending letters to deputies and parliamentary leaders, either supporting or criticizing government projects.

BUSINESS INTEREST GROUPS. Probably the most solidly organized professional group in France are the businessmen: industrialists, corporation managers, bankers, and merchants. Their strongest organization is the CNPF (National Council of French Employers). Founded after World War I, it includes, according to its own statement, almost a million firms, which employ about 6 million wage-earners and salaried personnel. Besides individual firms, it also includes other business associations, of which the National Council of Small and Middle-sized Businesses is one, together with organizations representing particular industries, such as chemicals, steel, and shipbuilding.

The functions of the CNPF are: (*a*) to establish a liaison between industry and commerce; (*b*) to represent business firms before the public authorities; (*c*) to undertake studies for the purpose of improving the economic and social conditions of the country; and (*d*) to provide information for its members. The council thus speaks on behalf of many powerful interests. Its "representative" character and its huge size render it somewhat inflexible and immobile, and its highly diversified membership makes it difficult to arrive at a common attitude on particular issues. On the other hand, the council is more effective than most other interest groups. It is prudent in its lobbying tactics, for fear of antagonizing the many groups that are traditionally hostile to business. Most of its pressures are exercised secretly, through a network of personal contacts, particularly between the "businessmen" and the legislators and administrators. Whenever it takes a position on specific policies that are of direct interest to the business world—on say, the Common Market, plant and equipment modernization, or fiscal policies—it does so more discreetly than the other interest groups. By successfully avoiding direct identification with political causes, the council has been able to maintain its cohesiveness and prevent the splintering that has plagued other groups. Consequently, it has been strong enough to resist attack and to block policies that are prejudicial to the interests of its members.

FOUR

parties
and
opinion

THE STRUCTURE
OF PUBLIC OPINION

The structure of French public opinion exhibits marked similarities with that of other industrialized democratic societies. Interest in politics in France, measured in terms of the standard criteria—listening to political commentaries on radio and TV, reading about political topics in newspapers, discussing politics with friends, neighbors, and associates—is relatively low. About 8%, as indicated by a nationwide survey, are "deeply interested" and 29% "a little," while 28% claim "very little" interest, and more than a third—35%—none at all. The public level of information at times is abysmally low. Between 1949 and 1960, more than 40% of the French did not know what NATO was. By the end of January 1967, five weeks before a legislative election, 30% did not know when elections were to take place, and 61% could not give the name of a single candidate running in his district. Among those who mentioned a name, 66% did not know the political party to which he belonged. About 40% did not know the groups that were included in the four major political formations that had entered the electoral campaign. A very small number engage in political activity, again measured on the basis of standard criteria: party membership, attendance at meetings, regular letter-writing, distributing leaflets, organized talks and meetings, helping bring out the vote. Political activists—what the French call "militants"—are only a tiny fraction of the electorate. Even at the peak of political activity, right after the Liberation, not more than 2 million were regular party members. Today, out of some 28 million voters, not more than 1 million are regular party members. Of these, not more than 100,000 are *activists*. Yet the French

Note: In writing parts of this chapter I have drawn from Deutsch, Lindon and Weill, *Les familles politiques en France* (Paris: Les Editions de Minuit, 1966), and from the excellent survey of **SOFRES** and **IFOP** (Institut Français de l'Opinion Publique). I am particularly indebted to the directors of **SOFRES** and **IFOP**, M. Pierre Weill and G. Sadoun, respectively, for their help.

voting rate has been among the highest compared with other European nations, Great Britain, and the United States. Since 1958, there have been five referendums, four legislative elections, and two presidential elections. Only once did voting drop below 70% of the registered voters. On the first ballot of the presidential election of 1965, and again in 1969, it was as high as 84%, and in the legislative election of 1967, and 1968 it reached 80%.

Interest and activity correspond to certain standard variables. Men are more interested and more active than women. While 48% of men are "deeply" or "a little" interested, the corresponding figure for women is 26%; 74% of the women are either "very little" interested or "not at all." Age does not seem to be an important variable, though there is a tendency for those between 30 and 55 to show relatively greater interest than the younger or older groups. Farmers show the least interest and corresponding political activity: only 6% are "very much" and 21% "a little" interested. The small merchants and shopkeepers come next: only 4% are "deeply" and 21% "a little" interested. The managerial and professional groups show a relatively high interest, with 20% indicating "deep" interest and 42% "a little"; the salaried groups —civil servants, clerical staff, high-school teachers, etc.—indicate greater interest: 13% are "deeply" interested, and 33% "a little." Workers are almost as low in their interest as the farmers: 4% declare to be "much" interested and 32% "a little," while the "retired" indicate an appreciable interest—10% "deep" and 29% "a little."

The size of the community and the level of education also are significant determinants of interest. Those living in small communities (twenty-five hundred inhabitants and under) are the least interested—"very little" or "not at all" accounting for 70%. But interest generally progresses as the size of the community increases, reaching as much as 50% for the towns of about fifty thousand (it declines again in the larger urban centers, except for Paris, where 50% are "deeply" or "a little" interested). Interest also correlates in the same manner with education. Those with grade-school education are the least interested (69%), but 38% to 52%

of the holders of high-school or technical-school and gymnasium degrees are "deeply" or "a little" interested. Among those with university education, interest is astonishingly high, with 32% indicating "deep" interest and 35% "a little."

How do the citizens view the various ideological families in France, and how do they relate with political parties? Where shall we place and how shall we analyze the attitudes and voting patterns of the very large group that is totally disinterested in politics? We shall turn to these questions in the following section.

Opinion and Ideology

In the last two decades, but perhaps ever since the Liberation, there has been increasing (though by no means conclusive) evidence that the sharpness and intensity of ideological positions and the corresponding identification of the average citizen with ideological families has been on the decline. Frenchmen are more (but by no means definitely) reconciled today with the need for a strong and effective state, and are more likely to identify problems and issues as amenable to solution through cooperative political effort, rather than to place them into an ideological continuum that would produce division. As we noted, there has been a disenchantment with many of the political parties that continue to mirror ideological conflicts of the past, and a growing demand for larger national parties to channel interest. A strong and stable government supported by such a party or parties is generally desired, and governmental stability and effectiveness are beginning to be valued as such. The parties themselves, despite their attachment to ideological themes, are beginning to be oriented towards ad hoc compromises and concrete issues. Even the old conflict between church and state seems to have disappeared, though it flares up occasionally, and the state subsidies to Catholic schools, responsible today for the education of about one out of seven children, is taken for granted by all except the Communists and some militant Socialists. Free enterprise has been considerably qualified by nationalization, state subsidies, indirect state controls, and overall flexible economic planning. Though planning continues to have significant ideological anticapitalist overtones, the old quarrels between "capitalism" and "socialism" as alternate ways of life have been virtually set aside.

Still, residual categories remain, and one of them is the traditional distinction between left and right. The electorate situates itself in the left-right spectrum, but appears to be quite confused as to what the terms mean. The left-right continuum can be broken down into six groupings: extreme left, moderate left, center, moderate right, extreme right, and apolitical. (A very sizable portion of those belonging to the center express such a total disaffection with politics, and exhibit such a profound lack of interest and information, that they may be called downright apolitical, and so constitute a distinct group—see Table 4-1.)

The apolitical constitute the largest group— yet they vote! They come from among those that have the least education, live in smallest towns, and belong to marginal and threatened occupational groups: farmers, artisans, unskilled workers, shopkeepers, veterans, and older people living on pensions. They have no strong attachment to political parties, and hardly ever identify with any political ideology. They have been responsible for the floating vote that swings from one to another party. They account to a large extent for the emergence of a new party (the MRP) after the Liberation; the resurgence of Gaullism in 1951; the strong showing of the right-wing Poujadists in 1956; and the massive votes for de Gaulle and the Independents in 1958. (They deserted de Gaulle on the first ballot of the presidential election, only to return on the second.) Finally, the voting strength of the Communist party comes from a fraction of this group.

While it is relatively easy to identify the "apoliticals," it is extremely hard to identify clearly in the left-right spectrum, to which the rest of the electorate belongs, their attitudes on various issues. There is not a single issue on which a minimum of 75% of the persons who claimed to belong to the left, or 75% of those who claimed to belong to the right, give respectively the same opinion. On the four issues that appear the most critical—attitudes toward the power of the state, aid to parochial (Catholic) schools, nationalization of the large private industries, and the implementation of socialism—a representative cross-section of French voters responded as shown in Tables 4-2, 4-3, 4-4 and 4-5. It appears that only the attitude toward the "power" of the state continues to have some residual ideological significance and to reflect a difference between those who claim to belong to the left and those claiming attachment to the right.

On the basis of these critical questions, only political orientations that are vague and inconclusive can be discerned. But there is a certain

TABLE 4-1. *Ideological Orientations*

Extreme Left	Moderate Left	Center	Moderate Right	Extreme Right
16%	19%	9%	17%	7%

		Apolitical		
		32%		

TABLE 4-2. *Attitude Toward the Power of the State*

	Extreme Left	Moderate Left	Moderate Right	Extreme Right
Must maintain power of the state	19%	30%	54%	62%
Power must be lessened	73	58	30	26
No opinion	8	12	16	12

TABLE 4-3. *Attitude Toward Aid to Parochial Schools*

	Extreme Left	Moderate Left	Moderate Right	Extreme Right
Should be abolished	63%	31%	8%	12%
Should be maintained	33	54	82	82
No opinion	4	15	10	6

TABLE 4-5. *Attitude Toward Socialism*

	Extreme Left	Moderate Left	Moderate Right	Extreme Right
Should be implemented	84%	69%	38%	32%
Should not be implemented	6	11	21	31
No opinion	10	20	41	37

correspondence between "left," "center," or "right," to which a person claims to belong, and the party with which he identifies. The extreme left identifies largely with the Communist party and the Federation of the Socialist and Democratic Left (FGDS),[1] and rejects the Democratic Center, Gaullists, and the independent republicans. The moderate left identifies with the FGDS (Socialists and Radicals), and to a much lesser degree with the Communists. But there is a certain sympathy and tolerance for both the Democratic Center and the Gaullists. The center overwhelmingly identifies itself with

TABLE 4-4. *Attitude Toward Large Private Industries*

	Extreme Left	Moderate Left	Moderate Right	Extreme Right
Should be nationalized	58%	34%	25%	29%
Should not be nationalized	22	42	50	47
No opinion	20	24	25	24

[1] The status of the Federation or FGDS, which varied from day to day until its virtual demise will be discussed below.

the Democratic Center and the Gaullists, and rejects the Communists and the FGDS, in that order. The moderate right favors overwhelmingly the Gaullists, and to a lesser extent the Democratic Center and the Independent Republicans. Their rejection of the Communists is overwhelming, and that of the FGDS very strong. The extreme right identifies, but not strongly, with the Gaullists, whom they tolerate, but not with great sympathy. It rejects the Communists and the FGDS, but not as overwhelmingly as the moderate center or the center does. Finally, the apoliticals, by definition, show a very low level of involvement and identification with any party.

Thus, while it is hard to find tangible correlations between ideological issues (or even policy issues) and the left-right spectrum, there is a residual correlation between left and right and political parties. Only the apoliticals in great numbers appear to be detached until the day of voting, eschewing stable party affiliations. As we noted, they are a source of instability that renders difficult the effort of the political parties to create national organizations and discipline. It is perhaps no longer the ideological conflicts that jeopardize the development of a homogeneous and effective political system in France, although they should not yet be disregarded. It is, rather, the existence of a very large fraction of unorganized and disinterested voters, extremely prone to accept or reject presidential government, attracted in turn by personal and authoritarian solutions, heeding indiscriminately all appeals that are most likely to satisfy their immediate grievances.

POLITICAL PARTIES

The most pervasive trait of the republican regimes has been, as we indicated, multipartism. However, since the inception of the Fifth Republic there has been an opposite trend. Some parties have literally disappeared or have become skeletons of their former selves; others are in the process of combining under a single name and are preparing to amalgamate their organizations into one. The result has been that in the last two legislative elections of 1967 and 1968, virtually only four major party formations confronted each other—an unprecedented phenomenon in the political history of France. A number of factors account for this trend. First, the Gaullist party managed to swallow (but not yet digest) many of the conservative and center groups, thus beginning to create what many French conservatives have dreamed of for a long time: a formation like the British Conservative party. Some center groups found that the only way to resist the Gaullists was to unite, and today the Democratic Center is a formation that comprises some four or five former political parties or groups. The Gaullist strength has also forced the left both to unite and to cooperate. Two of the oldest parties—the Socialists and the Radicals—attempted to form a federation, the Federation of the Socialist and Democratic Left (*Fédération de la Gauche Démocrate et Socialliste* or FGDS). A number of new men, mostly among the intellectuals, formed a small political group known as the Convention of Republican Institutions, and they too joined the FGDS. Finally, the Communists to the left remain strong and independent, and solicit cooperation with the non-Communist left.

Electoral considerations, primarily stemming from the upsurge of Gaullist strength, in both the presidential and legislative elections ever since 1965, forced many groups together. But there were institutional reasons as well. The direct election of the president under conditions of universal suffrage, and the require-ment that only two candidates confront each other on the second ballot, was an important factor. Presidential elections gave also to the parties a new taste for leadership. New men appeared to challenge de Gaulle and lead the opposition. This meant organization and discipline. De Gaulle could impose discipline upon his supporters, but also curb the opposition in the National Assembly by the ever-present threat of dissolution, a power that the new constitution gave him. New rules in the National Assembly helped develop unity. A party now needs thirty deputies to form a parliamentary group in the National Assembly; splinter groups are forced to cooperate, and many learn how to do it. The electoral law stipulates that a candidate who fails to receive 10% of the registered voters in his district has to withdraw from the second ballot or lose his deposit of $200 if he fails to receive at least 5% of the second-ballot votes. This discourages frivolous candidates and reduces automatically their number. Other factors have accentuated the trend toward party simplification. The multiparty system had led to an alienation of the public from the parties. The latter had to combine and show strength if they were to gain credibility. Finally, ideological differences among the parties appeared to be not as strong as the vocabulary used suggested.

Whether there is a permanent trend away from multipartism to a three- or four-party system with party leadership and discipline remains to be seen. On the one hand, it is likely that the Gaullist party may continue, thus forcing the other groups to coalesce, and that the political parties of the non-Communist left may finally unite and cooperate with the Communists. On the other hand, it should be kept in mind that the Gaullist party may break up into a number of formations, and if so, make discipline and unity for the center and for the left less compelling. In discussing, therefore, the party configuration, we pay equal attention to the individual parties and to the broader and more integrative formations that have developed. We shall give a general account of the parties by using, for the sake of convenience, the traditional spectrum of French party configuration: left, center, and right. The following formations belong to the left, which we shall discuss first. They share attitudes and policies traditionally identified with it. They are the Communist party, the Socialists, the Radicals, and the Convention of the Republican Institutions—all three of which sometimes act separately and sometimes within the "Federation"—and the PSU (Unified Socialist party) —which, despite its name, is only a splinter Socialist group.

THE LEFT

The Communist Party

One of the most remarkable phenomena in the political history of France has been the strength of the Communist party, especially since the end of World War II. The country that has been portrayed as a haven of individualism has had, as its largest party, a totalitarian and authoritarian one. Since the Liberation, with the exception of the legislative elections of 1958 and 1962, more than 5 million French men and women (22% or more of the electorate) have voted Communist.

HISTORY. The French Communist party was founded in 1920, when almost three-fourths of the delegates to the Socialist Congress of Tours split off from the Socialists and followed the Boshevik leadership from Moscow. The new party joined the Third International, accepted Soviet leadership, endorsed the revolutionary philosophy of Lenin, and openly advocated the overthrow of French capitalism. It organized the General Confederation of United Labor (*Confederation General du Travail Unitaire,* or CGTU) in an appeal for broad working-class support. Its membership at first, however, did not exceed 100,000, its voters did not number more than 1 million, and its parliamentary representation was small (ten to twenty-six members).

The party gradually increased its popularity and strength by cooperating with the Socialists and the democratic parties of the center in a "popular front"—a broad political alliance directed against the right-wing forces. In the election of 1936, the Communists formed an electoral alliance, the Popular Front, with the Socialists and Radicals. They received a million-and-a-half votes, and their representation in the legislature jumped to seventy-two deputies, a sixfold increase. A Socialist government was formed with the participation of the Radicals and the support of the Communist party, which soft-pedaled its revolutionary posture in order to cooperate with the democratic parties.

When the Nazi-Soviet military pact was signed in 1939, the French Communist party did an about-face overnight. It declared that the war against Nazi Germany was unnecessary, reasserted its support of the USSR (the fatherland of revolutionary socialism), and called for a world revolution of workers to take the place of the "imperialist" war against the Axis powers. The government could not accept this reversal of policy, outlawed the Communist party, and imprisoned many of its leaders. Stunned by the Soviet pact with Hitler, many Communists dropped out of the party, and its membership fell off sharply. The shock of 1939 lasted only until the Nazis attacked the Soviet Union in 1941. For the French Communists, the war then became a holy war against Fascism. They joined the underground to harass the occupying Germans, organized guerrillas in many areas, collaborated with all anti-Nazi groups, and generally were the most effective leaders of the wartime Resistance movement. During the German occupation their membership grew, and their efforts earned them the respect and the support of the people. Capitalizing on their strength, the Communists captured control of the trade unions from the Socialists. By 1945 they emerged as the strongest party of postwar France. They supported General de Gaulle and, in line with the spirit of the Resistance, cooperated with him in 1944 and 1945, and Communist leaders participated in the cabinet.

As soon as the cold war opened a rift between the Soviet Union and the United States, the Communists took the Soviet side. They refused to collaborate with any French government, led the workers into long and crippling strikes against American aid, the Marshall Plan, and NATO, and intensified their attacks in Parliament against every cabinet, thus contributing to cabinet instability.

Between 1947 and 1954—the height of the cold war—the Communists remained in virtual isolation, both within the National Assembly and in the various elections. It was not until 1956 that their efforts to cooperate with other "republican" parties began to bear fruit. They, however, remained virtually alone in their opposition to de Gaulle's return to power, and they were the only party to oppose the new constitution that the Gaullists introduced in 1958. They have been its only consistent critics ever since.

The Gaullist electoral victories and the changing attitude of the Soviet Union brought about not only a reconsideration of the Socialist position vis-à-vis the Communists, but also a more cooperative attitude on the part of the Communists. In the legislative election of 1962, electoral agreements with the Communists were made in a number of departments, and the "dialogue" between the two parties has since led to a search for a common program and a common basis for cooperation against the Gaullist majority. By 1965, almost thirty years since the Popular Front had successfully, even if temporarily, brought Communists, Socialists, and Radicals together, a similar alliance was about to be formed.

Under the Fifth Republic, despite electoral setbacks, the Communists found themselves in a good tactical position. They had led the opposition to de Gaulle's return and, together with some splinter formations and individual leaders, had taken a firm stand against its constitution. It was with a note of optimism, therefore, that the party held its fifteenth party congress in Ivry, late in June 1959. Maurice Thorez presented the report of the party:

Since our Fourteenth Congress [in 1956] we have witnessed the destruction of the democratic institutions and the establishment of personal power. Our party has been the principal force to resist the reaction. . . . The Communist Party predicted the Fascist danger, but the leaders of the Socialist Party continued to divide the working class.

His successor, Waldeck Rochet, speaking at the eighteenth party congress in January 1967, reiterated Thorez's fears but pointed with satisfaction to the cooperation with the Socialists. The Communist party was ready to proceed with the dialogue with the Socialists; it committed itself to a peaceful passage (without revolution) from capitalism to socialism, and endorsed fully the notion of a plurality of parties and rejected the single-party system of some of the Communist states. However, it remained faithful to the basic Marxist notion that socialism cannot be realized without the struggle of classes, and without the full mobilization of the working class and its allies. He asked that the Socialists abandon their collaboration with the bourgeoisie and join forces with the Communists. He repeated the criticisms against the nature of the Gaullists' system: it was a personal Bonapartist system that should be reformed, and it represented the interests of the monopolies and the capitalists that should be done away with.

The Czechoslovakian crisis, the student and worker uprising of May–June 1968, constant criticism from other segments of the left, and internal dissension—especially from those who argued for a reformist and independent party line—began to tax heavily the party's discipline. The dialogue with other left-wing forces, especially the Socialists, has continued under the present leadership of the new party secretary general, Georges Marchais. But at the same time a number of leading Communist members were expelled and every effort has been made to recapture the support of the young and the students. Despite the revolutionary vocabulary, the party begins to sound more and more like the Socialists did some thirty years ago. For instance, late in April 1971 the Central Committee of the French Communist party proclaimed the following major national goals: (a) increased construction of new low-cost and low-rent housing units, (b) double the investments in transportation facilities, (c) open educational facilities to all, (d) proportional representation in all elected assemblies, (e) nationalization of the large pharmaceutical firms, (f) nationalization of the armaments industry, (g) unilateral nuclear disarmament, and (h) increase in the minimum wage. The program on its face appeared more timid than the one advanced by the British Labour party in 1945.

Regarding fundamental doctrinal questions, Georges Marchais assured the remainder of the left that the Communists were not planning to impose socialism through a small minority. On the other hand, once the party came to power he could not see how there could be a question of alternating with others in the exercise of power. Socialism was to be established with majority support, but "if the left when in power takes the measures that satisfy the working segments of the population, the prospect of changing those in power is meaningless. There can be no turning back." [2]

ORGANIZATION. The structure of the French Communist party resembles that of the Communist party of the Soviet Union: it is like a pyramid, in which the base represents the rank-and-file members, and the apex the leaders. The image of a pyramid also conveys the principle on which the party is founded: "democratic centralism." By democratic centralism, the Communists mean that the superior organs of the party make the decisions, after discussions among all the members, but that once a course of action is set by the majority, it is binding upon the minority. There can be no dissension, no divergent "tendencies," within the Communist party, even in France. Open opposition usually brings swift reprisals and frequently expulsion from the party.

The unit of the lowest echelon of the Communist party is the *cell*, which consists of from fifteen to twenty party members, including a secretary. There are three types of cells: *factory cells*, composed of members working in the same plant; *rural cells*, composed of farmers from the same farm or village; and *local cells*, composed of persons living in the same neighborhood. Thirty-five percent of the cells are factory cells, 18% are rural cells, and the remaining 47% are local cells, an indication that the party is not doing so well in the factories and is losing, but only a little, on the farms.

Above the cells are the *sections*, consisting of the elected delegates of the cells. They, too, have a secretariat or a governing committee—a *bureau*. Like the cells, they are primarily agencies of information, propaganda, and action.

[2] Quoted in *Le Monde* (Paris), April 24, 1971.

The *federation* is composed of delegates chosen by the sections. There is one federation for each French department. They are ultimately responsible for the party's activities and electioneering tactics at the departmental level. Their bureaus and secretariats are in the hands of loyal party members who are often on their way to higher positions. The cells, sections, and federations are under the control of the national organs: the National Congress, the Central Committee, the Politbureau, and the Secretariat—the last headed by the secretary general, who is the leader of the party.

The *National Congress* is composed of delegates from the membership at large. It is supposed to meet once every three years, and passes on all resolutions and policy reports submitted by the party leaders. Although, in theory, debates are free and open, the members rarely question the proposals that come from above—i.e., from the Central Committee. The slate of candidates submitted by the top leadership is invariably elected. The congress elects the *Central Committee*, a body composed of seventy-four members and twenty-two substitutes, with mostly deliberative functions, which in turn elects a small group of seventeen members to the *Politbureau*, which selects the Secretariat, consisting of five persons and headed by the secretary general. The *Politbureau* and the secretary general are the true powers of the party. They decide what the party will do in Parliament, among the workers, in the trade unions, during elections, and in connection with whatever other issues come up. For a long period of time this body was under the domination of Maurice Thorez and two or three of his staunchest supporters. It was not until his death in 1964 that the tight leadership control he had imposed began to open up, with new men coming in and many of the old guard gradually·phasing out.

STRENGTH. While the French Communist party organization can be viewed as a pyramid in which control flows from top to bottom, the "strength" of the party is better studied in terms of a series of concentric circles (Fig. 4–1). At the very center is the leadership, while the wider circles represent diminishing degrees of

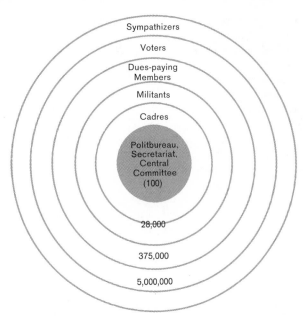

FIG. 4-1. *The organization of the French Communist party.*

support. The first two outer circles are the *cadres* and *militants,* a hard core of organizers and believers; the circles farther from the center are, respectively, *members, voters,* and *sympathizers.*

Members and militants. In the last thirty years, the membership of the party has fluctuated considerably. From the early thirties, when there were not more than 50,000 members, the membership rose in the years of the Popular Front (1936–38) to over 300,000. After the decline following the Nazi-Soviet pact, the party enjoyed a phenomenal growth during the Nazi occupation. In 1946–47, membership exceeded 1 million, the highest point it has ever reached. Since then, it has been sinking. In 1969, the figure given officially by the party was 473,-800, but there is good reason to believe that it was less than that. About sixty percent of the members are workers, 18% are farmers, 7% are salaried employees, 9% are intellectuals, and 6% belong to other groups.

The distinction between members and militants is largely based on the degree of commit-ment to the party. Whereas members simply pay their dues and perhaps participate in party meetings, militants actively work for the party, and often aspire to rise through the party hierarchy. Of the present membership, not more than 7% are militants. The militants who have jobs as administrators, secretaries, members of the bureaus, editors of Communist newspapers, and leaders of trade unions are called *cadres.* Forming a small core of not more than 10,000 men and women, they are the nervous system of the party.

The party membership continues to show a preponderance of men (about 75%) despite the efforts to attract women. However, the party remains remarkably young: about half are under 40, 10% are under 25, and one-third are between 26 and 40. Forty percent are between 41 and 60, and only 17% are over 61. But what is equally remarkable (if we are to believe the official figures) is the high rate of renewal in the party —that is to say, the rate at which new members have come into the party over a given period of time. Only some 13% of the present members joined before World War II, and 22% during or immediately after the war. Almost one-fourth joined the party in the years between 1948 and 1958, and an astonishingly high 42% between 1959 and 1966. Thus the party does not consist of well-disciplined and well-trained old Marxists but of persons who apparently for one reason or another come and go. The rate of turnover in membership is around 50%—which means that one of two Communists quits the party— say, every five years—to be replaced by a new-comer. Almost half of the present members joined during the Gaullist decade—a fact that refutes those who claim that Communism in France is an "old," "outdated" ideology and movement.

IDEOLOGY. The party continues to accept Marxism-Leninism, and preaches the evils of capitalism and the inevitability of its over-throw or demise. It is dedicated to ushering in a new socialist world, founded on equality and social justice, in which the economy will be harnessed to collective goals. It borrows from the vocabulary of the French Revolution in em-phasizing equality and individualism and in echoing the old anticlericalism of the nineteenth century. It also portrays itself as the champion of the underprivileged—the small farmer, the artisan, the widow, the veteran—against the inequities of the social order. It was opposed to de Gaulle's executive leadership and personal government and favors republican institutions that give predominance to a popularly elected legislative assembly. By exploiting many of the historical myths of the French Revolution—anticlericalism, republicanism, and equality—it has given the revolutionary tradition of the nineteenth century a new Marxist twist.

Perhaps we can best explain the strength of the party if we dissociate the two roles it plays. For a few, it is still a revolutionary party dedicated to the cause of communism. These supporters have never found themselves at home with democratic institutions and principles. For them, the working class is the midwife of the revolution that will bring about utopia, and the party is something like a church that demands unqualified loyalty and support. We must quickly point out, however, that the number of such Communists in France today is small, being limited mostly to the cadres and the militants. They have their own schools, their own vacation resorts, their own holidays, their own social life, their own newspapers. They live in a political world that is insulated from the rest of the community. But their number is steadily declining.

The second role of the party is to provide an outlet for the expression of protest on the part of French voters. The party's program has become broad enough to encompass many different and some seemingly inconsistent views. It is both a revolutionary and a reformist party in the eyes of the voters. It advocates economic modernization but also supports many of the marginal groups that impede it; it is for the socialization of basic industries but favors the retention of individual private property. It is the party of the "revolution" in terms that satisfy both the past (the Revolution of 1789) and the future (the Communist revolution). It encourages the national goal of emphasizing the greatness and the civilizing mission of France, and, at the same time, it advances the international ideology of Communism. It is proletarian

but also the stanchest supporter of the small farmer in the South; it is against the curé but usually stands ready to cooperate with liberal Catholics. With an uncanny perception of the basic predispositions of the French voters, it has used effective themes and slogans to attract them to the party. This accounts for both the wide support it receives among so many socioeconomic groups (a fact that continues to baffle all observers) and for the strength it commands in regions that are so different—in both industrialized and rural France.

Today the program of the Communist party reflects a shrewd combination of political tactics and ideological goals: first, to bring down the Gaullist regime; second, to establish a "real democracy"; and third, to implement socialism. A "real democracy" can stem only from the combination of the party that reflects the working-class interests (the Communists) and their "allies"—Socialists, Radicals, and other left-wing groups, including many of the liberal Catholic forces. In such a combination of forces the Communists hope to play the dominant role and move to the realization of their third objective: the establishment of their own political power for the purpose of implementing socialism.

Thus, nothing as yet persuasively indicates that the French Communists are searching new horizons either in domestic or international affairs. They have continued to align themselves with Soviet foreign policy on each and every issue—and to seek the same support and alliances on the domestic front. They have rejected the Gaullist constitution, continue to favor parliamentary supremacy, and oppose direct popular election of the president. Their most significant tactical shift has been to seek closer cooperation and ties with the other parties of the left, notably the Socialists and the Radicals. It is precisely this effort, together with the decreasing military threat from the Soviet Union, that has changed the image of the party in the eyes of the French. Though the party has not explicitly abandoned the theory of the dictatorship of the working class or that of the class struggle, it has qualified its stand enough to evoke no longer the image of a real threat to the republic. Today four out of ten Frenchmen would not object to seeing the leaders of the party participate in a cabinet.

THE COMMUNIST VOTERS.[3] Who are the Communist voters and how does the public view the Communist party? To begin with, the Communist party vote continues to be in great part a working-class vote. About 50% of the Communist vote comes from the workers—accounting, however, for less than one-third of the total number of workers in France. Tables 4-6 and 4-7 indicate Communist voting strength and the percentage of the vote that comes from various occupational groups since roughly the end of World War II.

The history of the Communist vote profile seems to correspond by and large to the socio-professional evolution of the population as a whole. Thus, the diminution of the Communist vote among farmers corresponds to the reduction of farmers among those gainfully employed. The drop in the farm vote, however, has been compensated by a relative increase in the Communist votes among workers—from 38% to 46% at a time when the proportion of workers as a

whole rose from 34% to about 37%. A similar increase seems to have occurred among the white-collar and tertiary and middle groups—again, however, corresponding roughly to the overall increase of the socioeconomic groups involved. Thus, contrary to all expectations, the changes that modernization and economic development have brought in the socioeconomic structure of the population do not seem to have affected seriously the Communist vote. Its geography appears also to be by-and-large quite stable. The electoral bastions of the Communists remain the same—in the north from the Paris region to the Belgian frontier; the southwest center; and in the south, especially in the eastern Mediterranean littoral. In contrast, the party remains weak in the west and the east, the Massif Central, and in parts of the southeast.

A large majority of the French Communist voters, in contrast to the Italian Communist vote, are "dechristianized," i.e., do not believe in or practice Catholicism. Seventy-seven percent of the French Communist electorate has "no religion" as compared to 46% for the Socialist voters, 40% for the Radicals, and 12% for the Gaullists. A majority of the Communist voters (75%) has a strong sentiment of belonging to a class. Finally, the Communist electorate is politically the most active: they give money to the party, they work for the party, they believe in the party and its candidates to a far greater degree than the voters of all other parties, including the Gaullists. There is a strong army of faithful voters who will vote for the party. Communists have their minds made up as to how they will vote long before an electoral campaign begins.

The stability of the Communist vote, the party's efforts to cooperate with the rest of the left, the remarkable turnout in 1969 for the Communist presidential candidate, Jacques Duclos (who received more than 21% of the vote), coupled with the specific efforts of the leadership to avoid revolutionary themes account for the fact that the Communist party is widely accepted in France today. The image of the party has been changing. Only some 40% of the electorate affirmed in 1970 that they would not vote Communist under any circumstances, as

TABLE 4-6. *The French Communist Vote*

Election Year	Number of Votes	Percentage of Registered Voters
1945	5,005,336	20.3%
1946	5,119,111	20.7
1946	5,489,288	21.9
1951	5,056,605	20.6
1956	5,514,403	20.3
1958	3,907,403	14.3
1962	4,003,533	14.5
1967	5,029,808	17.8
1968	4,435,357	15.7

SOURCE: Lavau et al., *Le Communisme en France.*

[3] In writing this section I have relied greatly upon the excellent study by Georges Lavau and his associates, *Le Communisme en France,* Cahiers de la Foundations des Sciences Politiques (Paris: Azmand Colin, 1969).

TABLE 4-7. *Socioeconomic Profile of the Communist Electorate (from opinion surveys)*

	1958	1962	1965	1966	1968
Farmers	13%	6%	5%	8%	9%
Merchants, industrialists, liberal professionals *	9	14	6	7	9
Civil servants, salaried white collar	13	20	13	17	21
Workers	38	43	51	51	46
Retired, pensioned	3	—	7	17	15
Other	24	13	18	—	—

SOURCE: Lavau et al., *Le Communisme en France.*
* Doctors, lawyers, journalists, etc.

opposed to 55% who in 1955 declared the Communist party to be a real enemy of France. More than half the electorate believes that the role of the Communist party has been useful since the end of World War II, as opposed to only 38% in 1964. Fifty-four percent of the electorate has praise for the manner in which the party has dealt with its local responsibilities (through Communist mayors, municipal councillors, etc.). As we noted, 40% of the French would not mind having Communist leaders participate in the cabinet. Surprisingly, 42% do not think that they are likely either to lose or to gain if a Communist regime were established in France (19% believe they would gain and 26% fear they would lose). In general, the party is not perceived as a revolutionary party—indeed, less than 9% of the electorate considers it as such. The party is, however, considered to be the party of the "little man," the party that defends the interests of the poor and the weak: 43% of all people queried said that the party protects wage-earners; 21% the young; 19% the equitable distribution of taxes; and 11% the farmers and the small merchants. Forty-one percent consider it to be the party of the workers and another 27% the party of the dissatisfied. More than half state that the party has changed in the last ten years—that it is more open to discussion (61%) or closer to the concerns or preoccupations of the average Frenchman (51%).

The party itself, as indicated, seems to have done everything possible to reinforce the new image. They no longer preach revolution, but advocate "advanced democracy" involving the nationalization of some industries, the banks, and credit. The electorate has responded accordingly: 51% do not believe that, if it came to power, the Communist party would suppress religious freedom; only 30% believe that the party would suppress the other parties (36% do not think so and the rest "have no opinion").

The Non-Communist Left

No other French political party has managed to emulate the discipline, the organization, and the stability of the voting strength shown by the Communists. Ever since the formation of the Communist party in 1919–20, the non-Communist left found itself facing three choices: to form a "labor party" that included as many groups as possible, and become a center of gravity that might attract Communist voters; to cooperate closely with the Communists at the risk of coming slowly under their domination; or to remain fragmented. Three political parties, two of which had a long history and memory—the *Socialists* and the *Radical Socialists*—continued as separate and often warring entities, while in 1958 a militant splinter—the Unified Socialist party—seceded from the Socialists to form an independent group. Meanwhile, many intellectuals, civil servants, students, and leaders of professional groups launched a new formation: the *Convention des Institutions Republicaines*—the Convention of Republican Institutions. They came from various "political clubs" in Paris and in the provinces that discussed political issues and undertook a critical examination of the nature of the Gaullist institutions. Ever since 1964 an effort has been made to group the non-Communist left under a one-party organization—the Federation of the Democratic and Socialist Left—an effort that, as we shall see, has so far failed.

THE OLD SOCIALIST PARTY. Three conflicting points of views prevalent in the French labor movement have vied with each other for the allegiance of the French Socialists. The first is *syndicalism,* which advocates strong unions and strikes rather than political action as the best way to achieve social justice. The second is *Marxism,* which encourages political action but only as a subsidiary tool in the revolutionary struggle of the workers against the capitalistic class. The third is the *reformism* inspired by French and German intellectual socialists which endorses political action in Parliament and elsewhere as a legitimate means in the struggle to nationalize the means of production and to establish a welfare state.

The French Socialist party was founded before the turn of the century, but did not succeed in unifying its internal factions until 1905, just in time to ride the mounting wave of socialism that swept Europe in the early part of the twentieth century. It and the German Social Democratic party were the two most powerful national parties associated with the Workers' Second International, which was organized in 1889 and was committed to socialism.

Right after World War I, the Socialist leader Léon Blum followed the reformist tradition and, after overcoming a number of quarrels and splits within the party, attempted to adapt socialism to the multiparty system that characterized French democracy. In the elections of 1936, which the "Popular Front" won, the Socialists received 19% of the electoral

vote (approximately 2 million votes), captured 149 seats in the legislature, and proceeded to head a coalition cabinet. But the victory was short-lived. Attacked from the left by the Communists, and abandoned on the right by the Radicals, the Socialist prime minister resigned.

The onset of World War II and France's defeat found the Socialists divided. Eighty of their deputies voted to invest Marshal Pétain with absolute powers in 1940, and during the German occupation they were unable to match the leadership provided by the Communists, who succeeded in wresting control of the Socialists' last bastion of strength, the General Confederation of Labor.

Immediately after the Liberation, the Socialists cooperated with the Communists and the center. The Communists, however, soon moved into the opposition, and the Socialists then became the pivot of centrist coalitions. A Socialist prime minister governed from January 1956 until June 1957, but gave way to the Radicals and ultimately to the return of General de Gaulle to power. De Gaulle's return found the party in a difficult position, demoralized by the tactics of its leader, Guy Mollet, who supported de Gaulle while urging "constructive opposition" to his cabinet in the National Assembly. A number of its members and federations were beginning to look to the splinter Unified Socialist party and to entertain thoughts of cooperating even with the Communists.

The Socialists began to oppose de Gaulle. They objected to his economic and social policies at home, alleging that national wealth was not being equitably divided and that the working class was being discriminated against; they opposed his personal government and disputed his interpretation of the constitution of the Fifth Republic; they took strong exception to the practice of referendums that overshadowed Parliament and reinforced personal government; they vowed to abrogate the legislation giving subsidies to the Catholic schools, and pledged to work for a genuine European unity. They gradually accepted closer cooperation both with centrist groups and with the Communists in an effort to undermine the position of the president and his majority in Parliament.

Together with all the other parties, they voted against the reform of the constitution allowing for the direct election of the president by popular vote, and it was only thanks to the support—sometimes of the Communists and sometimes of some centrists—that they were able to maintain their strength in the National Assembly while seeing their popular vote decline.

Organization. Like the Communists, the Socialists purport to be a "mass party," and emphasize internal discipline, both for members of the party and its parliamentarians. This discipline, however, is tempered by a tolerance for "tendencies" which often makes it impossible for the leaders to enforce party discipline. As a result, the Socialist party has been prey to sharp division and dissensions.

The basic unit of the party is the *section,* a group of party members from a given city, town, or village. In each department there is a *federation,* composed of sections, with a secretary who is its spokesman and executive. The federations control the departmental finances and make decisions about political action not only in local matters but often in national elections. They enjoy considerable autonomy, especially with regard to electoral tactics. The supreme organ of the party is the *National Congress,* composed of delegates chosen by the party federations.

The National Congress elects a *Directing Committee* of forty-five members (though the number has varied), which must include a maximum of twenty parliamentarians and twenty-five members drawn from among the cadres or leaders who are not members of Parliament. The Directing Committee elects a *Bureau* composed of ten members: the general secretary, the assistant general secretary, the treasurer, and seven others. A body comparable to the National Executive Committee of the British Labour party, it makes all the interim decisions on policy, propaganda, parliamentary tactics, discipline, and sanctions.

Strength. As with the Communists, the "strength" of the Socialists must be studied with reference to voters and members. Since the end of World War II the Socialists have lost over half their voters (see Table 4-8): their strength has dropped from about 22% of the electorate to less than 10%.

Many of the strongholds of the Socialists have been lost to the Communists. The socioeconomic character of Socialist support has also undergone a considerable transformation. The working-class vote has diminished, but there has been a gain among the salaried groups: members of the lower middle class, civil servants, school teachers, and pensioners. It has been estimated that among the Socialist voters, 25% are civil servants (particularly schoolteachers), a little over 30% are workers, 11% are salaried, and the rest come from lower-middle-class groups: artisans, merchants, pensioners, shopkeepers, and others. Support for the party is becoming increasingly diversified to include many of the socioeconomic groups. But the Socialist electorate have the least education: 66% have had only what amounts to grade school. They are also in the lowest income bracket: only a quarter earn more than $250 a month. And they are becoming a party of older people: two-thirds of those who vote are 45 years of age or older, and the average age of their parliamentarians has been the highest in the National Assembly.

Membership in the party has also decreased sharply since World War II. In 1946 it boasted 354,000 members; in 1952 the figure was down to 90,000. In the 60s this membership had dwindled to less than 50,000.

TABLE 4-8. *The Decline of the Socialist Vote*

Election Year	Number of Voters	Number of Parliamentary Seats
1945	4,561,000	134
1946	4,187,000	115
1946	3,431,000	90
1951	2,744,842	77
1956	2,240,000	56
1958	3,176,000	40
1962	2,319,000	65

Program. The party continues to use Marxist vocabulary and slogans, yet both its internal composition and its policy pronouncements have revealed it to be a moderately progressive party dedicated to social legislation and welfare measures. It has been opposed, but with considerable qualifications, to colonial war, and has shown a great readiness to modify its program to participate in a coalition cabinet.

The presidential election by popular direct vote—to which the party was opposed—found the Socialists caught in internal rivalries and contradictions. It was a non-Socialist, Mitterrand, who assumed the leadership of the non-Communist left in 1965–66 and slowly brought the Socialists into a cooperative framework of the Federation of the Democratic and Socialist Left. The Socialists ran in the 1967 election as Federation candidates, and for the first time in this century did not form a parliamentary group as such. But even in defeat, and despite the depletion of their strength, the Socialists jealously guarded their independence within the Federation, and have resisted all effort to allow it to become a genuine party with its own independent organization, structure, and leadership.

THE RADICAL SOCIALISTS AND "ALLIED" CENTER FORMATIONS. The Radical Socialist party—Republican Radical and Radical Socialist party—(*Parti Républicain Radical et Radical Socialiste*), to be exact—has been a party without a program, an organization, leadership, and without any membership to speak of. Yet this "party," under different labels and thanks to many shifting alliances, played a controlling role in the formation and life of virtually all the governments under the Third and Fourth Republics. It participated in right-wing electoral alliances only to abandon them and move to the left, but more frequently it managed to do exactly the reverse. Its internal instability both reflected and caused the instability of the cabinet and the divisions of the republic. It has had its own left (closely anchored to the Socialists and even to the Communists), its own center, and its own right (which has often been affiliated with extreme right-wing groups).

History. As a political formation, the Radical Socialists (or simply "Radicals") date from 1901, the year the party was officially founded. But its heritage goes much further back, perhaps to the years of the French Revolution. Its roots have grown out of the traditions of anticlericalism, individualism, economic liberalism, and republicanism. In 1869 it advocated public education, separation of church and state, democratization of the military service, and modification of the tax structure in favor of a progressive income-tax. This was a program that had great appeal to the lower middle class, farmers, artisans, storekeepers, teachers, and above all the professional men of the small towns—the lawyers, public notaries, doctors, engineers. It expressed the interests of groups that were still striving to dislodge the church, the army, and the remnants of the aristocracy from political power.

To win elections, the Radicals soon found that they needed some sort of organization, and Radical committees were established in most departments. Since they were allowed considerable autonomy, diversity among the local formations developed. Until 1910 and perhaps through World War I, the party was no more than a powerful electoral organization. In 1906, it gained a victory that was unprecedented—for any political party: 260 Radical deputies were returned to Parliament. But with the end of World War I, the party became increasingly divided when confronted with the economic and social problems that the Industrial Revolution was belatedly thrusting upon the country. The agitation of the workers and the gains of the Socialists and the Communists both attracted and repelled many of its members and voters dividing the party between left and right. The hearts of the Radicals, it has been said, remain always with the left, but their pocketbooks tightly sewn to the right. With most of the demands for economic and individual liberties and the separation of church and state realized by the end of World War I, their ideology and electoral program was becoming exhausted.

In 1940, many of the Radicals turned their backs on the republic. As a result, the Liberation found them very seriously weakened, and they have continued to decline sharply in the last two decades.

Strength. The strength of the Radical Socialist party has been primarily electoral—it should be gauged in terms of the votes it receives and the number of its representatives that are elected. According to even the most optimistic accounts, its membership has never exceeded 200,000. Today it is doubtful if there are more than 10,000 members.

Since the Liberation, the party's voting strength has ranged from 2 million to a little over 2½ million. Where do these votes come from? The party had strong support from some specific regions. The town of Lyon, the department of Vaucluse, and the southwest part of France have sent a great number of Radical deputies to Parliament. The party's main strength began to come from the small towns and the rural sections. The "urban radicalism" of the nineteenth century is being replaced by a "rural radicalism," largely supported by small-town doctors and lawyers, artisans, and some teachers and civil servants. The supporters of the party come, therefore, mostly from the groups and classes that were in the ascendancy in the nineteenth century but that have definitely declined after 1930.

It is no wonder, then, that the party has gone through a period of severe conflicts in the last twenty years that may end in its permanent disintegration. A minority of its members, led by the young and dynamic Pierre Mendès-France, argued in the 1950s for a renovated radicalism, for a strong and disciplined party dedicated to economic expansion and welfare, with a program that would appeal to many groups: white-collar workers, engineers, civil servants, intellectuals, and workers. Others, however, contended that the strength of the party lay in its "pluralism" (another name for its internal divisions). According to them, the party was not a mass party with a program and discipline, but a government party that thrived on electoral alliances, deals, and coalitions which gave it a power disproportionate to its actual numerical strength.

Internal divisions and personal rivalries, a total lack of a program in the name of pluralism (meaning freedom to play the electoral and parliamentary game), and the resurgence of Gaullist power have virtually wiped out the party. Since 1956 it has split and resplit into many miniscule groups, and its members have formed alliances which have proved to be more profitable than their allegiance to the party.

With the waning of the significance of anticlericalism and the general acceptance of economic planning and state social and economic controls, the Radicals have found themselves not only without men, but also without ideas. Some moved to the Gaullist camp, others reluctantly to the left, while yet a third group found itself anchored in dead center. One group of leaders joined the short-lived Federation as one of its constituent parties, and in the name of this federation were represented in Parliament, about twenty-five strong. Many who remained in the center became part of the Democratic Center, together with other centrists, moderates, and even "Catholic" groups; and many others now find themselves within the Gaullist majority.

A last effort to "revive" the Radical Socialist party has been underway since 1969. Jean Jacques Servan Schreiber, former editor of the successful weekly *L'Express*, a "European" preaching close economic and political cooperation among European nations, was a firm believer in rapid modernization and technological progress, without which he claimed France and Western Europe could never rival the United States. He took over the leadership of the Radical Socialist party and produced a new program committed to modernization and restructuring of the French society. His "Radical manifesto" is calculated to appeal not only to the new technical and managerial groups of the French society, and to many Gaullists for whom independence cannot be realized without industrial strength and without solid European cooperation, but also to the left-wing groups, especially the Socialists. Whatever the success of this new effort is, the Radicals, like the Socialists, are in the process of pouring new wine into old bottles, without as yet managing to find a framework of genuine cooperation.

THE CONVENTION OF REPUBLICAN INSTITU-
TIONS. A notable development during the first
years of the Fifth Republic was the flowering of
"political clubs" composed of students, intellectuals, and leaders of student and professional
associations and organized for the purpose of
debating the future of the country. The clubs
attempted to do what most of the parties appeared to be totally unable to do: think critically of policies and institutions and take a
stand against the Gaullists. At least six such
clubs in Lyon, Grenoble, Marseille, Paris, and
Tours took steps to bring them all together into
a meeting.

The Convention of Republican Institutions (*Convention des Institutions Républi-
caines*) was thus established in 1964, in an effort
to bring the non-Communist left together
against de Gaulle. It was explicitly dedicated to
economic and social planning, to a democratic
government (which meant opposition to the
personal government of General de Gaulle),
and to European unity—all in all, to what was
considered to be the only constructive way to
build French resources in Europe and to create
a strong bloc to offset American influence, if not
outright domination. Not more than eight
thousand—at most ten thousand—made up the
various clubs that sent delegates and observers
to the first congress. But they were all influential
young men, and not only attracted attention,
but began to exercise influence upon the political parties of the left. They offered to act as a
catalyst in the constant dialogue among the
Radicals, the Socialists, the Socialist Unified
party, and even the liberal Catholics and the
Communists, in order to set the foundations
from which a coherent opposition to de Gaulle
would emerge and a coherent democratic force
would develop. They played an important role
in the designation of but *one* candidate of the
left in the presidential election—even if he were
not their first choice—and they worked hard to
create the Federation of the Democratic and
Socialist Left. As a recompense for their efforts,
they became a part of it, as the third constituent
group. Their political strength in terms of number and vote is negligible.

THE PSU (SOCIALIST UNIFIED PARTY).
Nothing exemplifies better the tenacity of
ideology and the continuing tendency toward
fragmentation than the Socialist Unified party
(*Partie Socialiste Unifie* or PSU), a small splinter group that separated from the Socialist
Party in 1958 to oppose the Gaullist constitution. It has fewer than eight thousand members.
It has refused steadfastly to join with either the
Communist party to the left, or the Socialists
to its right, while continuing to favor a regrouping of all the parties of the left on the
basis of a common, well-defined program dedicated to socialism and planning and "revival"
of democratic institutions. Only two PSU deputies adorned the National Assembly between
1958 and 1968. In the presidential election of
1969 its present leader, Rocard, received less
than 4% of the vote but was able to defeat a
Gaullist candidate in a by-election held later in
the year to become the only deputy in the party.

The Search for
Left-Wing Unity: The "Federation"

The presidential election of 1965—France's
first presidential election by direct popular vote
—provided the impetus for the parties of the
non-Communist left to unite, for to face de
Gaulle with any hope of victory, unity was required. It was under these circumstances that
the Federation of the Democratic and Socialist
Left (*La Federation de la Gauche Démocrate et
Socialiste* or FGDS) was born. Its charter, formally publicized a few weeks before the presidential election, provided for both a program
and a skeleton organization.

The FGDS consisted of an "alliance" of
three parties: Radicals, Socialists, and the Convention of Republican Institutions. Each party
would maintain its autonomy and the exclusive
right to admit members. Each would continue
to hold its own congresses; each would be in
charge of its own organizations and platforms.
But provisions for cooperation and overall direction were also made. The FGDS established
a National Bureau consisting of fifty-four members—eighteen from each formation—and a

directing Committee consisting of twelve (four from each). The Committee would designate candidates for legislative elections. The Federation developed its program and proceeded to establish a common platform with the Communist party, which was not reached until 1968.

With regard to institutions, the basic difference between the FGDS and the Communists relates to the role of the president of the republic. The Communist party is anxious to deprive the president of virtually all powers inherent in the office, except that of communicating messages to Parliament and designating the prime minister; all other presidential acts and decisions would be taken only with the consent of the prime minister or the responsible minister. That is, the Communists advocate a return to the classical form of parliamentarism. The FGDS agrees with this position in substance, but differs in degree. While they are willing to allow the president the right to dissolve the National Assembly, they seem anxious to take all other powers away from him—notably his rights to use exceptional powers in case of emergency, to revise the constitution through referendums, and to dismiss the prime minister. Further, they insist that dissolution of Parliament become automatic in the event of a cabinet crisis and that a "contract of the majority" be formulated between Parliament and the cabinet before a cabinet is designated. In summary, both the Communists and the FGDS —in other words, virtually the entire left—demand a constitutional revision, but disagree on the extent of the reforms to be made.

Their disagreements are also a matter of degree when it comes to economic and social policy. Both demand nationalization of credit and of some monopolies; a speedup in the construction of low-cost housing; more comprehensive, more democratic economic planning; raises in minimum wages; fiscal exoneration for low-income families; more investments and subsidies for the "social" sector (education, transportation, telecommunications, vacations, public health, etc.).

Both Communists and the FGDS agreed on the elimination of the *force de frappe*. Otherwise they disagreed on many aspects of foreign policy, with the Communist party closer to the Gaullists, notably with regard to European integration, Israel, recognition of Eastern Germany, and the Atlantic alliance, whose renewal the Communists oppose outright. Major doctrinal questions were left unresolved—how, for instance, the left should take power. If the left does come to power, will it relinquish it if elections return a different party or political formation? Do the Communists adhere to the dictatorship of the proletariat? Will they allow other parties to exist if ever they assume power? Will they exploit propitious conditions to take over power, even though a minority? Will they respect political individual and religious freedoms? Only minor concessions were made by the Communists to the non-Communist left. They are not willing to abandon *formally* their commitment to class struggle and the dictatorship of the proletariat. Despite their concessions that in France the "road to socialism" would be different and that there was no question of following the Soviet model, Socialists and Communists argued throughout their intermittent dialogue over the same issues that have traditionally separated them. The Communists went as far as they could without in effect abdicating their revolutionary tradition, especially in the eyes of the small left-wing revolutionary groups that began to attack the party from the left. The Communists could not and would not allow their left flank to be turned. But precisely for this reason they could not satisfy their associates to their right. The common program underlined the doctrinal and often Byzantine divergences between two families of the left. The quarrels were subtle but pervasive and passionate. The result is a lack of unity.

This was underscored, as we shall see in the next chapter, in the presidential election of 1969, in which the parties of the left failed to agree on a single candidate. Each constituent party of the FGDS nominated its own candidate, and on the second ballot they failed to join forces with the Communists and the PSU, the latter parties calling for abstention. Without common leadership or a national organization, the FGDS began to disintegrate into its component parts. At present, the left appears to be as fragmented and disunited as it was at the beginning of the Fifth Republic. Only the future will tell if the experience of cooperation will provide a framework of unity.

THE CENTER

The Democratic Center

At least 50% of the French, when asked where they belong politically, say to the center. Yet, though many political parties have claimed a centrist vocation (especially the Gaullists), no political party has deliberately called itself a centrist party. Instead, the center has consisted of splinter formations: moderates, unaffiliated independents, peasants, republicans, etc. Only in the years immediately after the Liberation did one large political party—the liberal Catholic MRP—manage to form a coherent political formation, develop a program, and attract more than 25% of the voters. All other groups changed names and leaders, shifted from one political alliance to another—sometimes to the left, and sometimes to the right—in a manner that makes futile any effort to describe them in detail. For instance, the center between 1945 and 1962 consisted of the following: the MRP, the Left Republicans, some of the Moderates and Peasants, dissident Radicals, and "left-center" groups. Among them, they commanded as many as 6 million votes and as many as two hundred deputies, only to drop in 1962 to less than 2 million votes and not more than forty deputies (see Table 4-9). Since 1962, none of these parties have been able to elect an adequate number of deputies to form a political group in the National Assembly, so that they have had to combine forces, sometimes with the right-wing groups and sometimes with the left.

As with the FGDS, it was the presidential election of 1965 that forced the center groups to unite behind a single candidate and formation that was explicitly given the name of *Democratic Center*. Jean Lecanuet declared his candidacy as their spokesman. His showing in the election made it possible for him to announce the formation of a new party, the Democratic Center, to include a number of splinter groups. Its organization is yet to be clearly es-

TABLE 4-9. *The Rise and Fall of the Center (MRP and other Center Formations)*

Election Year	Voters (in millions)	Number of Parliamentary Seats
1945	6.9	176
1946	7.7	199
1946	7.8	213
1951	2.6	82
1956	2.3	71
1958	2.4	57
1962	1.6	36

tablished, and the support it received in the legislative election of 1967 gave little hope of continuity. As long as the left is represented by a cooperative arrangement between the Communists and the Federation, and the right is overwhelmingly preempted by the Gaullists, the center becomes tightly compressed and hope for the future is dim. But if the Federation breaks up (and many claim that this has already happened), and if the Gaullists disintegrate, the hunting to the left and the right might prove extremely rewarding (see Fig. 4-2). The hope for the center, in other words, lies in the disintegration of the left and right, and the revival of multipartism.

In 1969 MRP and centrist leaders could not reach an agreement on the presidential candidate they would support. Some went over to Pompidou while others remained faithful to the centrist candidate. Today MRP members and other centrist leaders have joined forces to constitute the Progress and Modern Democracy (*Progrès et Démocratie Moderne*, or PDM), which in effect is hardly more than a parliamentary group of some thirty-three members. Even this group, however, is disunited. Some support the Gaullist government while others oppose it.

THE RIGHT

Since the end of World War II, few have been the formations that have advocated the outright overthrow of the republic and its

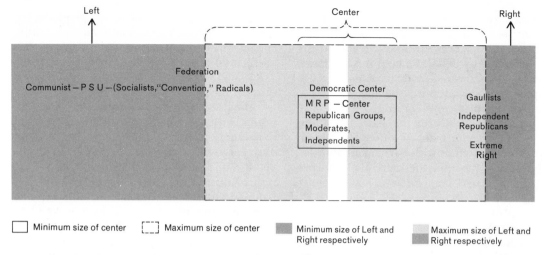

FIG. 4-2. *The "Elastic Center." The revival of the center vote can take place only at the expense of the left and right (Federation and Gaullists) and can be triggered only by serious dissensions within the two.*

replacement with an authoritarian regime. The colonial wars, and more particularly the exacerbation of the fighting in Algeria, both before and after the return of General de Gaulle to power, together with social discontent, accounted for two such formations. The first was the so-called Poujadist movement, and the second an extremist antirepublican movement led by army groups and supported by some activist formations.

The Antirepublican Right

THE "POUJADISTS." In 1954, a curious movement emerged from groups that had been traditionally most loyal to the republic and to parliamentary government—one made up of shopkeepers, artisans, small farmers, and many small-town political leaders. They became known as Poujadists, after the movement's leader, Pierre Poujade. Beginning as a powerful pressure bloc called the UDCA (Union for the Defense of Merchants and Artisans), whose aim was to lighten the tax burden on small businessmen, the movement later became a party, the Union and French Fraternity (UFF). It demanded the complete overhaul of political in-

stitutions; Parliament was to be closed down and the Estates General convoked (last convened in 1789 and composed then of the aristocracy, the clergy, and the bourgeoisie—the three social orders that existed in the *Ancien Régime*); and the leaders of the Fourth Republic tried before a "high court." By 1955, Poujade was able to organize local and departmental federations throughout France. His slogan was "throw out the rascals" (the "rascals" being the deputies of the National Assembly). In the national elections of January 2, 1956, Poujade nominated candidates in many departments, refused to ally himself with any other political formations, and called for a massive vote for his movement. He received 2½ million votes, 12.5% of the total, and 52 seats in the National Assembly—some of which were subsequently contested and lost.

This phenomenal success was followed by an equally remarkable collapse. No subsequent by-election ever gave Poujade or his candidates more than 7% of the vote. In most cases, they received less. With the return of de Gaulle in 1958, the Poujadist movement literally disappeared, having enjoyed a spectacular, albeit short-lived, success.

Besides appealing to the artisans, shopkeepers, small farmers, and those in the backward departments plagued by declining personal incomes, Poujade's clever evocation of the "little man"—crushed by taxes, the civil service, large industrial corporations, and parliamentarians corrupted by the pressures of big lobbies—triggered the frustrations embedded in the history of France: distrust of the state, contempt for the politician (a man who does no honest work), disenchantment with Parliament and the republic, fierce pride in the individual and his rights.

THE ACTIVISTS. As in the last years of the Fourth Republic, some army officers attempted in the course of the war in Algeria to rise against the Fifth Republic and de Gaulle. They were supported in Algeria by the majority of the French populace there—the *colons*—and in France proper by small, secret groups that attracted veterans, a few of the remaining disciples of the authoritarian ideology, and some outright Fascists and extremists, into the so-called OAS—the *Organization de l'Armée Secrète*. The OAS indulged in indiscriminate acts of terrorism and assassination in which many innocent victims perished in both Algeria and France.

Both the organization and its objectives appear to have been laid to rest after the declaration of Algerian independence. Diehard extreme right-wingers are few today: in the presidental election of 1965, Tixier-Vignancourt, one of their spokesmen, campaigned under the program of European unification, maintenance of the Atlantic alliance, and expanded housing and welfare measures—which hardly appears extremist. He received 5% of the vote.

The Republican Right

There are only two formations that we can associate by and large with the republican right: the Independents and the Gaullists. The first appear to be on the way out, like the Radicals and the MRP, while the second are in the process of attempting to become a well-organized political party.

THE INDEPENDENTS. The Independents, like the Radicals, have had virtually no organization and membership, but only alliance among departmental and local political leaders. Like the MRP, their fortunes have varied inversely with those of the Gaullists.

The Independents welcomed the Fifth Republic with great complacency. The party did remarkably well in the elections of 1958—but only because it supported de Gaulle. It gained about a million votes and at least twenty deputies, to bring its strength in the National Assembly to 120. Without mass membership or a coherent program, it exploited the wave of nationalism for its own electoral ends. The Independents became the conservative group in the National Assembly in matters of economic and social reform, and in regard to Algeria. They joined the Gaullists in the cabinet, and one of their leaders, former Prime Minister Antoine Pinay, became minister of finance and was responsible for the formulation of financial and economic policy.

Complacency, however, was transformed into feverish political activity when it became clear that President de Gaulle threatened both the policies and the future electoral chances of the Independents. In the first week of 1960, Pinay was unceremoniously dismissed by the president of the republic. The policy of self-determination for Algeria began to divide the Independents, while the presidential style of government undermined seriously their role in Parliament. They began to move increasingly into the opposition, as more than half their members began to vote against the government on a number of issues.

The more Independents moved into opposition to de Gaulle, the greater became their internal division. In 1962 their opposition to the referendum on the constitutional amendment to allow the president to be elected directly by the people, which carried, and the legislative elections that followed in the same year provoked sharp internal dissensions. One faction, the Independent Republicans as they are called, split from the party to join hands with the Gaullist majority. The bulk of the Independent voters abandoned the party, whose vote went down to less than 1½ million. They hardly managed to survive as a parliamentary group and were forced to join with other centrist formations. Some of them are now participating in the PDM, while others continue to be attracted by the spell of the Gaullist party, and few have struck out on their own as unaffiliated. Their disintegration (and very likely their disappearance) carries the same general message that we mentioned with regard to the disintegration of the Radicals. Yet at this stage, their fate, as with that of the MRP, may well depend on the future of the Gaullists. The Independent Republicans, while maintaining their autonomy within the Gaullist majority, may become a Trojan horse, to split the Gaullists or to attempt with the support of the Democratic Center a larger centrist reformist group.

THE GAULLISTS. Since the Revolution, strong political leaders—often army generals —have occasionally assumed personal rule. The last was General de Gaulle, a career officer who in 1940 refused to accept defeat at the hands of the German army and led a small core of followers to London to proclaim from there his determination to continue the war in the name of France. From then until his death, de Gaulle's towering personal stature overshadowed the course of public events, even when he was in political retirement.

History. In 1944, de Gaulle returned to France at the head of a provisional government and a small, well-equipped army. He favored a strong presidential government, the overhaul of the nation's stagnant economy, and broad social welfare measures. Within eighteen months, on January 20, 1946, he resigned.

De Gaulle saw in the constitution of the Fourth Republic the same defects that had plagued preceding republics: a weak executive, a legislature divided into many groups unable to generate policy, cabinet instability, lack of leadership. He decided to reenter politics in 1946–47, this time the head of a large political movement—the Rally of the French People (RPF)—and outlined his program: a new constitution embodying strong executive leadership; stern measures against the Communists, whom he called "separatists"; the reassertion of French independence from both the Soviet Union and the United States; the dissolution of the National Assembly; and new elections. This was the beginning of the "Gaullist" movement. It has since taken many forms, shapes, and names.

By the end of 1947 the RPF reportedly had some 800,000 members, and had won a sweeping victory in the 1947 municipal election. It subsequently gained more than one-third of the seats in the upper chamber. The Gaullists, sensing victory, pressed hard for dissolution and elections, but in the legislative elections of 1951, the center parties, with the support of the Socialists to the left and the Independents to the right, managed to stave them off. Nonetheless, the Gaullists won 22% of the vote—second only to the Communists—and elected 117 deputies. But the movement had reached its climax. The parliamentary group of the RPF began to disintegrate, and soon de Gaulle freed his deputies from their pledge to follow him. He himself retired shortly from political activity to write his memoirs. In the election of 1956, the Gaullists were reduced to a handful of deputies—the Social Republicans —who received only 4% of the national vote. But a select group of de Gaulle's followers remained active, biding their time until internal and external difficulties would again give them the opportunity to work for their leader's return.

There was no need to wait long. The deterioration of the war in Algeria, and the inability of the government of the Fourth Republic to maintain its control over the French army, gave them the opportunity. De Gaulle returned—first as prime minister, and later, after his constitution was fashioned, as president of the new Fifth Republic. A sweeping movement to recreate the Gaullist party was set in motion, combining many of the old faithful and a number of new men. In the election of 1958, the Gaullists ran under the label of UNR—the Union of the New Republic. It received less than 20% of the vote—a remarkable showing, however, in view of the fact that virtually all other parties, excepting the Communists, ran with the express commitment also to support General de Gaulle. They elected 189 deputies, and were joined by a number of other deputies, bringing their total up to 210 and making them the largest parliamentary group. They soon claimed to be the majority party—a claim that was not, however, vindicated until the election of 1962 when they won over 30% of the vote and, with the support of the Independent Republicans and some other deputies, commanded a majority of at least 275 deputies out of a total of 482.

Organization. Whatever the names of the Gaullist party, and whatever its alliances and reorganizations, its traits have been remarkably the same. First, it is not a party in the proper sense of the term, but a "movement." This means a fluid and changing organization, in support of general objectives rather than specific policy programs. Secondly, it is a personal party attached to the leadership of one man. For instance, the UNR deputies took the following oath of fealty:

Elected Deputy of the UNR, I confirm in a solemn manner my adherence to the Union for the New Republic, and to its parliamentary group. Respectful of the mandate which was given to me by the electors, I will abstain during the period of the legislature from participating in or becoming a member of any other group. I take the following engagement: to remain faithful to the objective of the UNR; to support in Parliament and in my electoral district the action of General de Gaulle; to accept the discipline of voting as decided by the majority of the group for all the important questions relating to the life of the nation and of the French community, in order to maintain the cohesion of our group and the general spirit of our movement.

Thirdly, while the party supported de Gaulle and ran in his name, he maintained a singular aloofness toward it. In 1958 he refused to give it his support, and denied its members the right to use his name—which, needless to say, they ignored. Although he modified his stand in the elections that followed, asking the people to vote against the opposition and for his supporters, he still remained extremely reluctant to allow the party to become well-organized and disciplined, and to develop a strong leadership that he himself was unwilling to assume. He preferred to have a rather loose organization of supporters that he could use at his discretion, instead of a coherent party that might challenge him. As a result, the party, despite its electoral successes, did not develop a strong organization and membership. Both its annual congresses and its Directing Committee were overshadowed by General de Gaulle and by the implicit and explicit loyalty to his person. Though a number of policies have been outlined and debated within the party, the essence of the Gaullists has been General de Gaulle.

Strength. The strength of the party must be measured in terms of its electoral appeal. De Gaulle, in the presidential elections, received 44% on the first ballot, and 55% on the second. In the referendum on the constitutional reform of 1962 to provide for the direct election of the president by universal suffrage (to which all the political parties were opposed), de Gaulle—who had asked specifically for a vote of confidence—received 62%. The Gaullist party, on the other hand, has not managed to exceed 40% in any legislative election since 1958, and has never attained more than 44% on the second ballot. Thus, its strength ran well behind de Gaulle's popularity, though it borrowed to a large extent from it.

Who are the "Gaullist" voters? Their strength corresponds to the weakening of the center and Independent vote. Thus, they have derived most of their strength from the right and the center—especially the Catholic vote that went to the MRP. This is corroborated by the composition of their electorate. It is a party supported by more women (52%) than men. And it is a party that has failed to appeal to the young voters: only 24% of its voters are under 35, and 12%, the largest percentage of all parties, are 65 years old and over. Thirteen percent are farmers, and an appreciable number (27%) are workers. Employed and managerial groups, executives, industrialists, and merchants largely vote for the Gaullists. A great part of the Gaullists' voters (31%) has an income that is above $250 a month. It is a fairly well-educated electorate, urban and rather evenly distributed (with some notable exceptions) throughout the country.

THE INDEPENDENT REPUBLICANS. Allied to the Gaulists, this group of Independents continues to display considerable vitality. Their leader, Giscard d'Estaign, remains influential. In the past few years he has made consistent efforts to establish contacts with the center, the leaders of the Independents, and many moderates, and to organize departmental committees. More pro-European and pro-Atlantic than de Gaulle was, d'Estaign claims to be more progressive in matters of social legislation than the old Independents, and favors economic planning. However, his conservative deflationary policy during the period he was minister of finance (1962–65) secured him the support of financial circles. In the election of 1962, the Independent Republicans won over a million votes and elected an adequate number of deputies to form their own parliamentary group, while allied with the Gaullists.

Will the Gaulists, with the support and in collaboration with the Independent Republicans, manage to realize the dream of many political leaders, and as some political analysts predict, set up a Conservative party like the British one? If they survive de Gaulle, and establish a viable organization with discipline and leadership, then they may succeed. But as we note below, the difficulties are many.

As yet, for the reasons we have indicated, the Gaullists have been unable to organize a new party with departmental and local committees. Their membership does not exceed 75,000, and the political activity of their various branches become relatively active only in the months preceding an election. The party has remained one of political leaders and notables coming from the old formations of the center and the right, bound together primarily by electoral consideration and loyalty to one man. The mass of members and the program are lacking. On the other hand, it may be argued that the Gaullists have had time to develop their local and departmental attachments and that they are better prepared to continue with-

out de Gaulle. Realization that internal splits will deprive them of the status of the majority party that they have held since 1962 is an additional incentive that promotes unity. Much of the political future of France depends therefore on the ability of the Gaullists to maintain unity.

The Gaullist Voters.[4] Since 1968 the Gaullists and their allies the Independent Republicans have found themselves with a firm and unassailable majority in the National Assembly. What is more, de Gaulle's departure in April 1969 was followed by the victory of the heir presumed, Georges Pompidou, the former prime minister under de Gaulle. The Gaullists have controlled the executive and the legislature as no party had ever done in the political history of France. Contrary to general expectations, the party seems to have survived de Gaulle, and the majority in the National Assembly appears to be, despite certain internal conflicts relating often to personal rivalries, just as cohesive and disciplined as under de Gaulle. For instance, in March of 1966, 46% of the French public (as reflected in a poll) thought that the Gaullist party would have no importance and presumably no political future without de Gaulle, as opposed to 31% who thought that the opposite would be true. Most political commentators agreed that the party was "nothing" without de Gaulle—that it was just a number of deputies who supported him. Yet electoral returns began to provide evidence that cast serious doubts on these speculations. From a little over 4 million votes in 1958 (about 15% of all registered voters), the Gaullist vote moved upward in succeeding elections to reach a little over 9½ million in June 1968 (over 34% of the registered voters—see Table 4-10). From some 120 deputies in the first legislature of the Fifth Republic (1958–62), Gaullist representation moved to an astonishing 285 in 1968. With the Independent Republicans they controlled almost 70% of the membership of the National Assembly. To be sure, de Gaulle was still president. But after he stepped down from office in 1969, Pompidou was elected with over

[4] I am indebted, to the excellent analysis of Jean Charlot in *Le phénomène gaulliste* (Paris: Fayard, 1970).

TABLE 4-10.	*The Gaullist Party Vote*	
Election Year	*Number of Votes*	*Percentage of Registered Voters*
1958	4,010,787	14.7%
1962	6,580,606	23.6
1967	8,448,982	29.9
1968	9,663,605	34.3

SOURCE: Charlot, *Le phénomène gaulliste*, p. 75.

43% of the votes on the first ballot and a comfortable 56% of the vote on the second. The Gaullists seemed to be not only the majority party but indeed the "dominant" party. All the opposition parties fell short of the electoral strength of the Gaullists and way below the Gaullist majority in the National Assembly.

There are many reasons for the continuing success of the Gaullists. The party became synonymous with the institutions of the Fifth Republic. The public at large continued to be favorably disposed to the new political and governmental institutions that derived from the constitution of 1958. For instance, 81% of the public consulted in 1969 favored the election of the president by direct popular vote, though only 45% favored the referendum of 1962. Yet 75% favored the power of the president to dissolve the National Assembly. A majority favored the constitution's definition of the powers and role of the president of the republic (60%), but there was disagreement on the role and powers of the National Assembly, 36% favoring existing arrangements and another 36% wishing it to display a more important role. Such support for these institutions, despite some equivocations, implies approval of the party that had launched and sustained them. Last but not least, the party began to organize and to develop departmental and regional organizations and membership. By 1969 it claimed at least 100,000 members, less than 25% of what the Communist party claimed, but far more than all other parties. It began to develop a national organization and structure with five national secretaries—in charge of (a) relations with other parties and groups, (b) public relations, (c) elections, (d) finances, and (e) "implantation" (organization at departmental and local levels).

The party, unfettered by past ideological commitments, was becoming increasingly a "catchall" party appealing to virtually all segments of the French population and all sections of France. It began to attract increasingly all groups for whom ideological commitment had lost its appeal and for whom decision making to solve specific problems had become more important. Thus, the party began to draw votes from all socioeconomic groups, with over 30% coming from among the workers (see Table 4-11, and compare with the Communist electorate, Table 4-7).

THE LEFT AND THE GAULLISTS

Despite the internal dissensions of the left-wing parties and the potential disintegrative forces that may disrupt the unity, cohesiveness, and discipline of the Gaullists, the political map of France continues to show the same basic bifurcation between left and right. The center at this time is squeezed between the two and cannot be resurrected except at the expense of either. Nor can it come to power except with the support of one or the other, as the presidential elections of 1969 clearly showed: the center candidate, Poher, lost the moment the Communist party decided to abstain rather than support him. As we noted, it is not impossible for the Center to regain its lost strength but rather that it is unlikely to do so unless either the Gaullists disintegrate or the Communists decline sharply. All efforts made thus far to bring about the former or to accomplish the latter seem to have failed and Centrist leaders have thus finished by joining the Gaullists rather than by trying to dislocate them.

Although the distinction between the present-day "left" and the "Gaullists" roughly corresponds to the classic one between "left" and "right," the content and substance of their

TABLE 4-11. *Socioeconomic Profile of the Gaullist Party Electorate, 1967–69*

		Percentage of Total Vote	
By Profession	Percentage of Gaullist Vote	Legislature Election, 1967	Presidential Election, 1969
Farmers	17%	45%	47%
Liberal professions	5	44	44
Industrialists and merchants	10	35	43
Employed, white collar	15	35	35
Workers	31	30	32
Retired, without profession	22	43	51
By Sex and Age			
Men	48%	35%	35%
Women	52	41	46
21–34 years	30	37	36
35–49 years	26		38
50–64 years	26	40	41
65 and over	18		54

SOURCE: Charlot, *Le phénomène gaulliste*, p. 75.

political differences (on economic and social matters, governmental institutions, and foreign policy) are no longer so clearcut (as reflected by the socioeconomic profile of their respective electorates—see Tables 4-7 and 4-11). The Gaullists have been the advocates of modernization and continue to practice economic planning. They have introduced and have insisted upon, with varying degrees of success, close participation of the workers in the management of the firm and the sharing of the profits. Over the decade the Gaullists have been in office the real wages of the workers have climbed; and pockets of underdevelopment have been attacked—by the amalgamation of small unproductive farms into larger and more manageable units and the establishment of industries in relatively underdeveloped regions. Despite student unrest—or perhaps in response to it—an immense effort has been made to create new universities, and that part of the budget going into education exceeds that allotted to defense. The words *socialism,*

state controls, and *public corporations* no longer seem to be questioned among the Gaullists.

The left is not united on economic policy issues, but the divergences are a matter of degree. The non-Communist left favors more aggressive and more comprehensive economic planning, socialization of added sectors of the economy, greater benefits for the workers and the poor, and, of course, the diversion of military expenditures into social programs. The Communists would move faster in this direction. Curiously enough, the Communists and the rest of the left are more reticent with regard to structural changes that may affect—at least, temporarily—the small merchants, artisans, shopkeepers, and farmers, but it must be remembered that a large proportion of the Communist vote comes from such groups. By defending them they may swing those among them who voted for Gaullists back to the left.

Foreign policy is a line that divides the Communists not so much from the Gaullists than from the rest of the left. The Communists are, of course, opposed to the Atlantic Alliance, continuation of the Common Market, the Franco-German rapprochement, the *force de frappe,* and large military credits. They favor the Franco-Soviet rapprochement and the Gaullists' embargo on arms to Israel, and approve the posture of French independence that de Gaulle pioneered. The non-Communist left favor European integration and Franco-German rapprochement and are far more sympathetic to the Atlantic alliance, but not to NATO. They question the French policy of arms embargo to Israel. With the Communists they favor reduction of military credits, are opposed to the *force de frappe,* but are suspicious of the Soviet presence and intention in Europe. They opposed vocally and forcefully the military invasion of Czechoslovakia, which the Gaullists deplored and the Communists found in the last analysis a necessary evil. The Communists, while attacking de Gaulle for his personal government and his regime as the embodiment of the trusts and finance capital, began to change their position after 1961 when they detected progressive elements in Gaullism, particularly with regard to foreign policy. Indeed, many thought that their unwillingness to support the anti-Gaullist candidate in the 1969 presidential elections was inspired, among other factors, by foreign policy considerations—namely, that Pompidou was likely to follow de Gaulle's foreign policy guidelines.

There are also notable disagreements among the parties of the left with regard to government institutions. The Communists continue to decry presidential government, remain committed to parliamentary supremacy, are opposed to referendums and emergency powers for the president, and wish to take away the presidential prerogative to dissolve the National Assembly. The other left-wing parties are more circumspect. They favor presidential elections by popular vote, but would agree to deprive the president of his right to hold referendums, of his exceptional powers in case of emergency, and his discretionary right to dissolve Parliament at will. They do not favor parliamentary supremacy; instead, they are urging for minor reforms to restore to the National Assembly some of the legislative initiative and control it has lost and to provide for greater balance between it and the cabinet. For instance, they would deprive the prime minister of the right to demand a vote on the cabinet's legislative text, which forces the National Assembly either to vote for the whole or to introduce a motion of censure. Generally, they would like to see some of the powers used now by the president devolve to the prime minister. They would like to move the regime away from presidentialism in the direction of parliamentarianism—but not to the point of parliamentary supremacy.

The Gaullists are solidly aligned, of course, behind the institutions of the Fifth Republic. In a number of announcements since he took office in 1969, Pompidou, the new president, has reasserted in terms reminiscent of de Gaulle the thesis that the president incorporates the republic and sets the broad lines of policy to be followed, which are delegated to the prime minister for execution. But he too was willing to consider an "opening" or a "dialogue" so that a better relationship between the executive and Parliament may be instituted and so that the National Assembly may have more freedom to scrutinize legislation and participate in its elaboration. He also appeared, at least by inference, to exclude the use of the referendum when the constitution does not specifically authorize it, and to rule out using it as a plebiscite, as de Gaulle had done. The "majority" in the National Assembly, consisting of Gaullists, Independent Republicans, and some centrists, has now designated a "delegation," consisting of representatives from all three groups, that is in touch with the prime minister and through him with the president.

We might say then that the distinctions between the left and the Gaullists when it comes to economic and social questions, foreign policy, and governmental institutions is blurred. Areas of agreement are perhaps more significant and more frequent than areas of disagreement in terms of which sharp policy distinctions can be made. What is even more interesting is that there is no sharp distinction in the profiles of the Left and Gaullist electorates, as Table 4-12 shows.

TABLE 4-12.   *The Left and the Gaullists Electorates: Socioeconomic Profile of Convergence*

	Left (Communist and FGDS)	Gaullist (and Independent Republican)
Sex		
Men	45%	46%
Women	35	54
Age		
21–49	41	40
50+	39	51
Profession		
Farmers	32	48
Liberal professions	28	47
Industrialists and merchants	29	50
Employed and middle ranks	31	39
Workers	53	39
Retired, no profession	40	46
Income		
Very high	36	41
High	49	38
Medium	49	37
Low	49	40
Very low	39	48
Religion		
Regularly practicing Catholics	18	53
Irregularly practicing Catholics	41	41
Nonpracticing Catholics	60	32
No religion	73	18

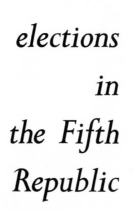

FIVE

elections

in

the Fifth

Republic

Between the time General de Gaulle returned to office in 1958 and his departure eleven years later, there were frequent electoral consultations. In addition to municipal elections and the renewal of one-third of the Senate every three years, there were five referendums (see Table 5-1), legislative elections (see Table 5-2), and two presidential elections by direct popular vote. There was a national consultation of one kind or another on the average of once a year. The French electorate invariably rose to the occasion, showing a marked interest in the voting booth (see Fig. 5-1).

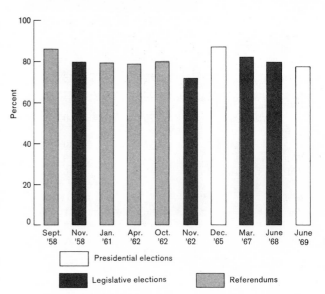

FIG. 5-1. *Voter participation since 1958.*

Note: In preparing the various electoral tables and election figures for the first part of this chapter, some degree of simplification was unavoidable. I relied upon the following: *Les élections legislatives,* 1958 and 1962, Republic of France, Ministry of the Interior; *Année politique,* 1958, 1962, 1965, and 1968, *L'élection presidentielle du décembre,* 1965, Constitutional Council, *Notes et documents,* 1966; *Sondages* [surveys] of the French Institute of Public Opinion, and Sofres; the remarkably good electoral statistics and electoral maps given in *Le Monde;* M. Duverger, *Constitutions et documents politiques* (Paris: Presses Universitaires de France, 1967).

I. THE DE GAULLE YEARS

A CONSTITUTIONAL REFERENDUM AND A GAULLIST ASSEMBLY

Constitutional Reform

The watershed of the Fifth Republic may well have been the constitutional reform of 1962 and the presidential election of December 1965. The constitution of the Fifth Republic was approved by 80% of the voters—a majority in which many commentators saw a massive vote for de Gaulle himself. Only the Communists dared oppose it,

and they lost heavily. Subsequently, two other referendums, addressed to the questions of Algerian self-determination (1961) and Algerian independence (1962) were both approved overwhelmingly. With Algerian independence finally granted on July 3, 1962, many felt that the reasons for de Gaulle's holding power and for the overwhelming confidence that the French had continued to give him had ceased to exist. The system seemed likely to return to "normalcy"—which to the leaders of many of the political parties meant the inevitable efface-ment of General de Gaulle and the ascendancy of Parliament. In other words, they viewed the Gaullist system as a "crisis government" caused by the war in Algeria.

TABLE 5-1. *The Five Referendums under de Gaulle*

	Sept. 28, 1958	Jan. 8, 1961	April 8, 1962	Oct. 28, 1962	April 27, 1969
Registered voters	26,603,446	27,184,408	26,999,745	27,582,113	28,656,494
Abstentions	4,006,614	6,939,162	6,589,837	6,280,297	5,565,475
	15.06%	*23.51%*	*24.41%*	*22.76%*	*19.42%*
Voting	22,596,850	20,791,246	20,401,906	21,301,816	23,091,019
	84.93%	*76.48%*	*75.58%*	*77.23%*	*80.57%*
Invalid	303,549	594,699	1,098,238	559,758	632,131
	1.14%	*2.18%*	*4.06%*	*2.02%*	*2.20%*
Votes cast	22,293,301	20,196,547	19,303,668	20,742,058	22,458,888
Yes	17,668,790	15,200,073	17,508,607	12,809,363	10,515,655
No	4,624,511	4,996,474	1,795,061	7,932,695	11,943,233
Proportion of registered voters					
Yes	66.41%	55.91%	64.86%	46.44%	36.69%
No	17.38	18.37	6.65	28.76	41.67
Proportion of votes					
Yes	79.25%	75.26%	90.70%	61.75%	46.82%
No	20.74	24.73	9.29	38.24	53.17

TABLE 5-2. *Legislative Elections in the Fifth Republic*

	November 1958				November 1962			
	Registered 27,736,491				Registered 27,535,019			
	Voting 20,994,797				Voting 18,931,733			
	Abstentions 6,241,694 (22.9%)				Abstentions 8,603,286 (31.3%)			
	Null and Void 652,889 (2.3%)				Null and Void 601,747 (2.1%)			
	1st ballot	*% of voters*	*2nd ballot*	*% of voters*	*1st ballot*	*% of voters*	*2nd ballot*	*% of voters*
Communists	3,888,204	19.0	3,883,418	20.5	3,992,431	21.7	3,833,418	20.5
Extreme left (includes PSU)	347,298	2.01	146,046	0.8	449,743	2.4	183,844	1.2
Socialists	3,176,557	15.5	2,574,606	13.8	2,319,662	12.6	2,304,330	15.2
Radicals and allied centrist formations	2,347,989	11.2	1,511,111	8.1	1,466,625	8.0	686,876	6.5
MRP	2,378,788	11.4	1,941,021	9.1	1,635,452	8.9	806,908	5.3
Independents and moderates	4,092,958	19.9	3,439,948	18.5	1,742,523	9.6	1,125,988	9.1
Gaullists (UNR)	3,603,958	17.7	5,249,746	28.1	5,847,403	31.9	6,165,929	40.5
					798,092 *	4.4 *	241,853 *	1.6 *
					6,645,495	36.3	6,407,782	42.1
Extreme right	669,518	3.1	172,361	1.0	159,682	0.9		

* Independent Republicans allied to Gaullists.

General de Gaulle put an end to these speculations. He proposed to amend the constitution and provide for the direct election of the president of the republic by popular vote, and not as had been the case in 1958 when a special electoral body had elected him. What is more, de Gaulle proposed that this amendment to the constitution be submitted directly to the people for their approval or rejection, without being debated by two chambers of the Legislature—the National Assembly and the Senate—as the constitution provides. For the first time the political parties that were opposed to this procedure and to the substance of this constitutional reform were able to join forces in a motion of censure against de Gaulle's cabinet. The motion against the cabinet was carried by 280 votes. De Gaulle promptly dissolved the National Assembly and proceeded with his plan to hold the referendum to be followed by a legislative election.

Opposition to de Gaulle's proposal came

TABLE 5-2. *(cont.)*

	March 1967				June 1968			
	Registered 28,291,838				Registered 28,300,936			
	Voting 22,887,151				Voting 22,539,743			
	Abstentions 5,404,687 (19.1%)				Abstentions 5,631,892 (19.99%)			
	Null and Void 494,834 (2.16%)				Null and Void 401,086 (1.42%)			
	1st ballot	*% of voters*	*2nd ballot*	*% of voters*	*1st ballot*	*% of voters*	*2nd ballot*	*% of voters*
Communists	5,029,808	22.46	3,998,790	21.37	4,435,357	20.03	2,935,775	20.14
Extreme Left (includes PSU)	506,592	2.26	173,466	0.93	874,212	3.94	83,777	0.57
Federation of Democratic and Socialist Left	4,207,166	18.79	4,505,329	24.08	3,817,682	17.23	3,214,920	21.7
Democratic Center	2,864,272	12.79	1,328,777	7.1	2,290,165	10.34	1,141,305	7.83
Centrists, moderates and Independents	1,136,191	5.08	702,352	3.73	917,532	4.14	496,463	3.41
Fifth Republic: (Gaullists and Independent Republicans)	8,453,512	37.75	7,972,908	42.60	9,663,605	43.65	6,762,170	46.39
	159,429	.87	28,437	0.15	140,127	0.62	—	—

from all sides and parties: Communists and Socialists stood with the Independents and with some of the extreme-right-wing deputies. It was a classic case of a negative coalition of forces, for it was unlikely that these parties and groups could unite either to provide an alternative to de Gaulle or to form a harmonious coalition in the legislative elections that were scheduled to follow. The opposition to de Gaulle was massive. In the legislative election of 1958, all the parties that now opposed de Gaulle had received more than 75% of the national vote.

They now seemed determined and ready to carry their fight to the people.

De Gaulle had no alternative but to throw his immense popularity onto the scales. He appeared four times on national television to urge a "Yes" vote. He attacked the political factions that were agitating against him and reminded the French of the record of his regime as compared with that of the Fourth Republic. He asked for unity and left no doubt that if the majority of "Yes" votes was "small and uncertain," he would withdraw for good from poli-

TABLE 5.3. *Parliamentary Groups—The Trend Toward Simplifications, 1958–73*

	Fourth Republic Last Legislature—Last Session (1958)	Fifth Republic First Legislature (1958–62) Jan. '59	Fifth Republic First Legislature (1958–62) Oct. '62	Fifth Republic Second Legislature (1962–67)	Fifth Republic Third Legislature (1967–68)	Fifth Republic Fourth Legislature (1968–73)
Communists	143			41	71 (2) of whom one Progressist	34
"Progressists"	5 (1)					
PSU		1	1	1	4 (affiliated with Socialists)	44
Socialist	96 (1)	43 (4)	40 (3)	64		
RDA/UDSR [a] (Dem. Afr. Rally Union of Dem. & Soc. Resist.)	18 (3)				[f] Federation of Democratic and Socialist Left 116 (1)	
Radical Socialists	42 (1)	41 (6)	31 (4)			
Dissident Radicals	14			[b] Democratic Rally 35 (4)		
					[a] Progress and Democracy 38 (3) (Democratic Center)	Center (PDM) 34
RGR (Rally of Repub. Left)	12 (4)					
MRP	81 (4)	49 (15)	51 (6)	[c] Democratic Center 51 (4)		
Independents	86 (12)	107 (11)	121	32 (3) [e] (Independent Republicans allied with Gaullists)	41 (3) (Independent Republicans allied with Gaullists)	60
Gaullists [d]	19 (2)	201 (9)	168 (9)	216 (17)	179 (22)	284
French Union and Fraternity (Poujade)	30					
Nonaffiliated	11	92 (Splinter Algerian Formation)	33	14	7	31
Independent from [a] overseas territories	7					
African Socialists [a] Movement	3 (1)					
Total	596	589	480	482	487	487

224

NOTES: All figures in parentheses indicate number of affiliated members with parliamentary group in question.

Until the new constitution and the new bylaws of the National Assembly, any fourteen deputies could form a parliamentary group. Thereafter, a minimum of thirty were required.

a. After 1959, deputies elected from African possessions of France no longer sat in the National Assembly. After July 4, 1962, Algeria became independent, and the deputies elected there were withdrawn. The total number of deputies was 482, and was increased in 1967 to 487: 470 from metropolitan France, and 17 from the overseas departments and territories.

b & c. After the election of 1962, most of the RGR and MRP, with some Independents, formed the Democratic Center, while some RGR, some UDSR, some Independents, and most of the Radicals formed the Democratic Rally.

d. "Gaullists" is a general term we give for the various Gaullist labels— Rally of the French People in 1951, Social Republicans between 1953 and 1958, Union for the New Republic in 1959, Union for the New Republic and Union of Democratic Labor (UNR-UDT) in 1962, and finally, Action Committee for the Fifth Republic-Democratic Union and Union for the Defense of the Republic.

e. These are the groups of Independents who, under the leadership of Giscard d'Estaign, separated from the National Center of Independents, to affiliate and cooperate with the Gaullists while maintaining an autonomous group.

f. The "Federation" (Federation of Democratic and Socialist Left) groups, Socialists, and a number of Radicals from the Democratic Rally. Members of a number of political clubs participate as a separate body called the Convention of Republican Institutions. Thus, Socialists, the Radical parties, and the Convention, while maintaining their respective autonomy, have formed a single and parliamentary group.

g. Progress and Democracy combines the old MRP, together with some Independent, some centrist, and some moderate groups.

tics. "For me," he declared, "each 'Yes' vote given to me by each of you . . . will be the direct proof of his or her confidence and encouragement. Believe me, I am in need of this for what I may still do, just as I needed it in the past, for what I have already done. It is therefore your answer which, on October 28, will tell me if I can and if I should pursue my task in the service of France." Thus, the referendum on a constitutional question became in effect a vote of confidence—a plebiscite.

The Text of the Referendum of October 28, 1962
Do you approve of the bill submitted to the French people by the President of the Republic concerning the election of the President of the Republic by universal suffrage?

Principal Parts of the Text of the Submitted Bill
Article 6: The President of the Republic shall be elected for seven years by direct universal suffrage.
Article 7: The President of the Republic shall be elected by an absolute majority of the votes cast. If this is not obtained on the first ballot, there shall be a second ballot on the second Sunday following. Only the two candidates who have received the greatest number of votes on the first ballot shall present themselves, taking into account the possible withdrawal of more favored candidates.

The results of the referendum were that out of 27½ million registered voters, almost 13 million voted "Yes," 8 million "No," and over 6 million abstained. The "Yes" vote represented 61.75% of the votes, but only about 46.5% of the registered voters. In 1958, de Gaulle's constitution had been endorsed by almost 80% of the voters and 66.5% of the registered voters. The number of "No" voters to the constitution and to de Gaulle had increased from 20.7% of the voters in 1958 to a little over 38% in 1962. But when we consider the fact that all the political parties with the exception of the Gaullists were against the constitutional amendment, this was an overwhelming personal victory for de Gaulle. Once more—despite the relative drop of the "Yes" vote—he was able to break through the political parties and reach directly to the voter. Only in twelve out of the ninety departments was his reform rejected. He bit deeply into the electoral bastions of the Com-

munists and the non-Communist left, which together accounted for over 45% of the electorate. It put all the political parties into a serious predicament that they were unable to overcome in the legislative elections that followed.

The Legislative Election of 1962

Fresh from the victory on the referendum, the president of the republic proceeded to do what no other president had done since the very beginning of the Third Republic. In a televised address he appealed directly to the people and asked them to vote for his candidates—the Gaullist party. Victory in the referendum, he asserted, had clearly shown that the old parties no longer represented the nation. If the Parliament, "which holds the legislative power and controls the government," is to be dominated again by the "fractions" of yesterday, de Gaulle charged, then it would be unable to govern; the country would once more be confronted with political chaos and paralysis.

"Men and women of France," said de Gaulle, "you sealed the condemnation of the disastrous regime of the political parties on October 28, 1962, and expressed your will to see the new Republic continue its task of progress, development, and reconstruction. But on November 18 and 25 you will choose the deputies. Ah! I hope you will do it in such a manner that this second vote will not go against the first. In spite of local habits and particular considerations, I hope you will now confirm by the choice of men the choice of our destiny you made by voting 'yes.'"

The electoral contest became once more transformed into a plebiscite, and de Gaulle's immense popularity was again thrown into the balance.

The opposition remained divided. Communists, Socialists, MRP, Radicals, and Independents, despite the equivocation of some of them, seemed united in an effort to block the UNR and to return a "republican majority." But, as we have seen, there was no unity among these parties. "Anti-Gaullism," therefore, did not embody any specific program that could be translated into action. This was made abundantly clear in the early efforts to make alliances and to agree on a common candidate to run against the Gaullists. Agreement with the Communists on the first ballot was avoided almost everywhere. But agreements even among the four genuinely republican parties—Socialists, MRP, Radicals, and Independents—proved to be equally difficult: they ran against each other as well as against the Communists and the Gaullists. The contrast with the apparent unity of the Gaullists was obvious. An Association for the Support of the Fifth Republic was formed on October 17, 1962, under the direction of the secretary of state for cultural affairs, André Malraux. It managed to split the ranks of the Independents and, to some extent, of the MRP. The program of the Gaullists was unambiguous: support of General de Gaulle, the maintenance of the institutions of the Fifth Republic, and the continuation of de Gaulle's policies.

Before we discuss the results of this contest, let us very briefly discuss the electoral system used. It was the system that had been used throughout most of the period of the Third Republic. The country was divided into a number of constituencies—482 for France proper and the overseas departments and territories. Each district, despite some notable discrepancies, represented about 90,000 inhabitants. The candidate who won an absolute majority of the votes won the seat. If no absolute majority for any candidate was forthcoming, then a second ballot was to take place a week later in which a plurality was all that was needed to win. However, between the first and the second ballot, candidates were free to withdraw in favor of a "better-placed" one— thus allowing for shrewd bargains and alliances among political leaders, parties, and candidates. It is the second ballot that counts. For under a multiparty system such as the French one, few candidates ever manage to get an absolute majority of the voters (and be elected) on the first ballot. The decision in almost 85% of the constituencies was made on the second ballot.

THE RESULTS. The first ballot of November 18 demonstrated once more de Gaulle's overwhelming impact on the French political

scene: the election was in essence a second referendum. The UNR won an unprecedented 31.9% of the vote, almost doubling its vote throughout the country, and all the other parties, with the notable exception of the Communists, lost. The extreme-right-wing groups were virtually eliminated.

Yet, though "old parties," singled out for de Gaulle's scorn, received a serious setback even on the first ballot, the Communists and the PSU, together with the Socialists and the Radicals, accounted for 44.7% of the vote. The left-wing forces held their own, but the independents and the MRP, together with the extreme rightists, lost 3½ million votes. As in previous elections, a new "shift" of votes occurred. Part of them went to the UNR, and a smaller part into abstention. The vote for the anti-Gaullist parties exceeded appreciably the "No" vote cast in the referendum of October.

The Communist party showed remarkable strength in the Paris region—perhaps the most modernized and richest area of France—capturing 31% of the vote, as opposed to 26% in 1958. In the suburbs of Paris, the Communists received over 38% of the vote, as opposed to 32% in 1958—in some cases managing to surpass in absolute and relative terms the strength they had shown in the period of the Fourth Republic. Thus, after France had experienced a decade of economic modernization and unprecedented prosperity, the Communists not only held their own in the agricultural areas and in many of the provincial towns, but improved considerably their position in the industrialized areas and the Paris region.

As was expected, the UNR transformed the electoral sweep into a sizable gain of seats. It won a total of 229. This figure, when added to about 45 or so Independent Republicans and MRP candidates who were pledged to support General de Gaulle, gave to the Gaullists a stable majority. Never before in the political history of France had one party controlled so many seats. The Communists, second in the popular vote, benefited this time from some of the anti-UNR sentiment, the "popular front" arrangements, and the inability of the other political parties to unite against them as they had done in 1958. The Communist party returned thirty-one candidates, bringing its total to forty-one. The Socialists, thanks to Communist support, became the largest party of the opposition: they won sixty-six seats. The Radicals showed remarkable staying power; supported both by the Communists and the Socialists in certain districts against a UNR candidate, they were also supported in other districts by the UNR, the independents, and often the MRP against a Communist. Thus, with only 8.3% of the popular vote and 7% of the vote cast on the second ballot, they managed to return forty-two deputies to the National Assembly. The MRP, independents, and extreme rightists lost more than 110 seats.

Many observers saw in the election a radical transformation of the French political scene, while others saw in it only a proof of de Gaulle's undiminished popularity. It was not so much the UNR that won, but the Gaullist party. It was de Gaulle himself who had urged the voters to vote for the men who had supported him. The UNR victory underscored the personal element of the Gaullist regime, this time even at the electoral party level.

But of course there was another side to the Gaullist victory. For the first time since 1947, the Communists moved out of their political isolation and cooperated with the Socialists and the Radicals. In many departments the Radicals, Communists, and Socialists (including the left-wing Socialists) formed open or tacit "popular front" alliances to support each other on the second ballot (see Table 5-4). In thirty departments, these alliances accounted for the victory of at least one popular front candidate. When the candidate was a Radical or, more particularly, a Socialist, the popular front al-

TABLE 5-4. *Communist Support and the Beginning of a Popular Front*

Influence of the Communist Vote				How "Popular Front" Alliances Worked in the Department of Hérault *			
First Ballot		Second Ballot		First Ballot		Second Ballot	
				FIRST ELECTORAL DISTRICT			
Dhotel, *Gaullist*	14,233	Dhotel	21,810	Carrié, *Gaullist*	11,991	Carrié	16,630
Mollet, *Leader of*				Grasset-Morel,			
Socialists	12,994	GUY MOLLET	24,375	*Independent*	10,044		
Coquel, *Communist*	11,362			Ville, *Communist*	9,075	POINSELLÉ	18,805
Pouchrison, *MRP*	5,960			Ponseillé, *Radical*	6,773		
				Chaulliac, *Socialist*	5,959		
Debré, *Leading*				THIRD ELECTORAL DISTRICT			
Gaullist	15,588	Debré	20,712	Lurie, *Gaullist*	12,042	Lurie	16,836
Berthouin, *Radical*	9,579			Calas, *Communist*	13,581	MOCH	24,281
Mme. Boutard,				Moch, *Socialist*	11,313		
Communist	7,576	BERTHOUIN	23,667	Thiery, *Independent*	3,026		
Le Garec, *PSU*	2,962						
Courteggiani,				FOURTH ELECTORAL DISTRICT			
Moderate	1,066			Valbrigue, *Gaullist*	13,004	Valbrigue	20,291
				Balmigére, *Communist*	12,298	BALMIGÉRE	21,747
				Crouzet, *Socialist*	6,707		
				de Seriége, *Independent*	2,839		

* Communists, Socialists, and Radicals supported each other in the Hérault Department and won one seat each.

liance worked better. When the candidate was a Communist, the "anti-Communist" reflexes of the public tended to decrease the size of his vote. Would the lesson of cooperation be learned? Were the Gaullists and the left to confront each other in the future over the dying body of the center? Was the political scene to become polarized? The Gaullist victory that produced a majority in the legislature raised some crucial questions about future political alignments.

THE PRESIDENTIAL ELECTION OF 1965

The constitutional reform of 1962 providing for the election of the president of the republic by direct popular vote was implemented by ordinances that simplified the electoral process. A candidate could be designated simply by securing the signed endorsement of one hundred "notables"—members of Parliament or of the Social and the Economic Council, or general departmental councillors and mayors (ten of whom would have to be elected representatives of overseas departments and territories)—and by making a deposit of $2,000, to be forfeited if he failed to receive 5% of the votes. All candidates who managed to receive 5% or more of the votes were now reimbursed for all their overall expenses (other than mailing expenses and those incurred in the printing of circulars and posters—these are normally paid for by the state) by receiving a lump sum of $20,000. All candidates were also given equal free time on radio and TV: two hours for each. The candidate with an absolute majority of the votes would be proclaimed president of the republic, but if there was no absolute majority, a second ballot would be taken within two weeks, in which the number of contestants would have to be narrowed down to two. (The wording of this provision did not necessarily limit the second ballot to the two *first*-placed candidates; it was conceivable that the top candidate might withdraw. But whatever the first-ballot standing of the candidates, the number permitted to run in the second ballot was cut to only two.)

The Parties and the Candidates

De Gaulle's reluctance to announce his candidacy thwarted all activity on the part of the Gaullist party—the UNR. Yet the mere fact that de Gaulle *might* be a candidate paralyzed the opposition, since it was a foregone conclusion that the president, whose popularity had been consistently high, could not be defeated. The presidential election scheduled in December 1965, many thought, would be a repeat performance of the constitution referendum or the election of 1962.

The first concerted effort on the part of the anti-Gaullists was made by the Socialist mayor of Marseille, Gaston Deferre. He suggested the formation of a large federation consisting of all parties and groups, with the exception of the Communists to the left and the Gaullists to the right, with himself as their candidate. The idea of this "grand federation," as it came to be known, was based upon a shrewd tactical calculation. It would force the Communists to go along and vote for its candidate on either the first ballot or (more likely) the second. With the Communist party accounting for a very minimum of 20% of the votes, and with all the non-Gaullists providing a minimum of another 40%, there was a prospect of preventing de Gaulle from getting an absolute majority on the first ballot, and defeating him on the second. All that was needed was the cooperation of all the center parties and the Socialists behind a single candidate on the first ballot, and the support of the Communists on the second.

After a year's efforts, Deferre withdrew. The Communists opposed the "grand federation" since it was designed to isolate them at the very time when they were hoping to set up an alliance with the Socialists and the rest of the left. But the Socialists were also restive since the coalition suggested by Deferre would throw them into an intimate alliance with the center forces. The Radicals were, as usual, divided.

As we have seen, a smaller federation (*La Fédération de la Gauche Démocrate et Socialiste*—the Federation of the Democratic and Socialist Left, or FGDS), limited mostly to the

Socialists and the Radicals, developed instead. It was acceptable to the Communists, and they were willing to support its candidate. But there was no candidate! It was only in September, just three months before the election, that François Mitterrand, a Radical and former leader of a miniscule party, and the spokesman of the Convention of Republican Institutions (see Chapter 4) announced his decision to run. He received the support of the Federation and of the Communists. Mitterrand soon began to represent the "classic" left, and the support of the Communists gave to his candidacy both the character and the substance of a "popular front" alliance.

A number of other candidates appeared on the scene—not all at the last minute. Long before the fall of 1965, Tixier-Vignancourt—an old-time right-winger, the defense lawyer for Marshal Pétain, and a fervent opponent of Algerian independence—had announced his decision to run, and had been stumping the country. He attacked de Gaulle for his personal government, and asked for amnesty for all those serving sentences for their uprisings against de Gaulle and for the acts of violence committed in France by the right-wing activists during the war in Algeria. He appealed to the hard-right-wing groups, and particularly to French refugees from Algeria, who had not forgiven de Gaulle for granting Algeria its independence and forcing them out of their homes.

In addition to Tixier-Vignancourt, a relatively unknown senator, Pierre Marcilhacy, who opposed the personal, presidential government of de Gaulle and who favored a return to cabinet government, announced his candidacy in April 1965.

The candidacy of Mitterrand left the center group, and particularly the MRP, without their own candidate. They had made a number of efforts to establish a new political formation—the Democratic Center. In October 1964, one of the major promoters of this movement, Jean Lecanuet, announced his candidacy. A young and dynamic speaker, a strong advocate of a United Europe and NATO, he hoped to attract the support not only of the center and the conservative groups, but also of Federation voters from among the Radicals and even the

Socialists. If de Gaulle failed to get an absolute majority on the first ballot, and if Mitterrand's showing was weak, he expected to force a contest between himself and the president, in which he hoped to receive the support of the left and the center against de Gaulle, thus in effect reconstructing the "grand federation" idea on the second ballot. The Communists, he thought, would have to vote for him in order to defeat de Gaulle.

The campaign opened on November 19, sixteen days before the first ballot. It was the first time that television brought into the French homes the candidates and "nationalized," so to speak, the presidential election. The aging president contrasted sharply with the forceful Mitterrand and with the dynamic Lecanuet, whom many began to compare with John F. Kennedy. President de Gaulle in his opening address attacked again the old parties, indicated that the opposition was a heterogeneous one from which no genuine leadership could emerge, and stated haughtily that his defeat would lead to chaos. He identified himself with history and his Fifth Republic with the destiny of France. Thereafter he fell into complete silence and refused to stoop so low as to campaign. He refused to use his allotted radio and TV time. He again seemed to consider the forthcoming election a vote of confidence. Only when the opinion polls began to indicate a decline in his strength did he make a second appearance—and that on the eve of the election. He intimated at that time that he might withdraw if the vote was not strongly in his favor.

The themes of the campaign were relatively simple. De Gaulle spoke of the record: the resurgence of France as a great and independent power, the economic and social reforms that had been undertaken, and, above all, the stability of the government and the leadership of the executive, thanks to the constitution of the Fifth Republic. Neither of his two main protagonists directly criticized the Fifth Republic, though both argued that de Gaulle had not respected his own constitution. They deplored personal government, the diminution of the role of Parliament, the use of referendums, and the lack of a genuine dialogue between the government and Parliament. They promised to reform the constitution accordingly. They also criticized sharply de Gaulle's social and economic policies, arguing in favor of stepping up reforms in education, housing construction, and welfare measures. Lecanuet took a stanchly pro-European position, favoring a supranational European arrangement, and close links with the United States under NATO. Both he and Mitterrand were critical of the French atomic force. Of all parties that were active throughout the campaign, the Communists provided, as always in the past, the best organization and financial support. They organized a number of meetings in favor of Mitterrand, both in the provinces and in Paris. Lecanuet counted on his television appeal, and began to make serious inroads into the centrist and conservative electorate. De Gaulle's silence forced the Gaullists to remain inactive.

The First Ballot

The results of the election (see Table 5-5) surprised most of the commentators—though not the opinion analysts, who had detected in the two weeks preceding the elections a movement away from de Gaulle and in favor of his two major opponents. De Gaulle failed to receive an absolute majority. What surprised even more was the high level of electoral participation. Abstentions were the lowest ever recorded in the history of France—only 15%. Many drew from this the inference that presidential election by direct popular vote appealed to the French, and concluded that presidential government was becoming widely accepted. The election returns indicated several things with regard to the three main candidates, which we shall now discuss briefly.

De Gaulle received an absolute majority in only thirteen of the ninety departments, and came in first with a plurality in seventy; Mitterrand managed to win an absolute majority in only two departments, and a plurality in eighteen. Lecanuet was third in all departments except five where he came second.

The geographical distribution of votes among the three candidates indicated a return to the traditional voting patterns. General de Gaulle received overwhelming support in the western and eastern parts of the country, and

TABLE 5-5. *The Presidential Election of December 5 and 19, 1965*

	First Ballot			Second Ballot		
	Totals	Percentage of Voters	Percentage of Registered Voters	Totals	Percentage of Voters	Percentage of Registered Voters
Registered voters	28,913,422	—	—	28,902,704	—	—
Voting	24,502,957	—	—	24,371,647	—	—
Abstentions	4,410,465	—	15.2	4,531,057	—	15.6
Blank and void	248,403	—	0.8	668,213	—	2.3
Valid ballots cast	24,254,554	—	84.0	23,703,434	—	82.1
De Gaulle	10,828,523	44.6	37.4	13,083,699	55.1	45.2
Mitterrand	7,694,003	34.7	26.6	10,619,735	44.8	36.7
Lecanuet	3,777,119	15.5	13.0	—	—	—
Tixier-Vignancour	1,260,208	5.1	4.3	—	—	—
Marcilhacy	415,018	1.7	1.4	—	—	—
Barbu	279,683	1.1	0.9	—	—	—

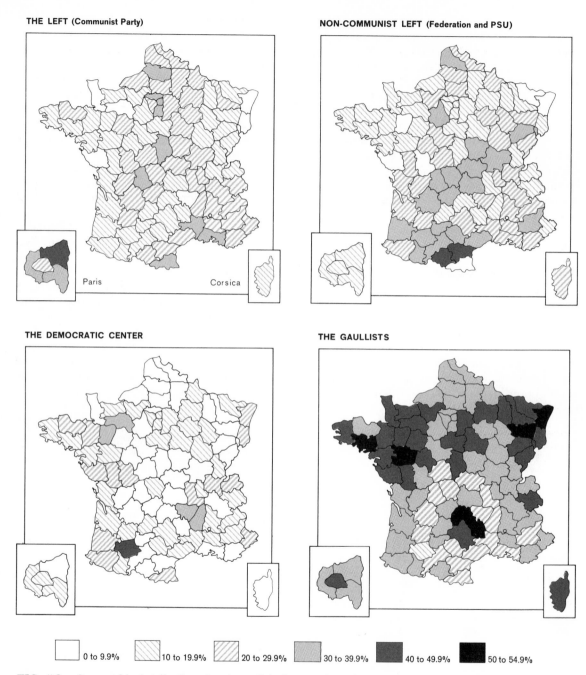

FIG. 5-2. *Geographic distribution of major political formations, first ballot, March 5, 1967 (in percentages of registered voters). [Adapted from the study of Professor François Goguel, "Les Élections Legislatives de Mars, 1967,"* Revue Française de Science Politique, *no. 3 (June 1967): 429–67.]*

in parts of the center where his strength corresponded with the "Yes" votes in all the preceding referendums. The strength of Mitterrand came from the traditional regions and strongholds of the left and of the Communists in parts of the center, in the south, and in the Paris region. The only exception was his relative weak showing in the industrialized departments of northern France. As for Lecanuet, despite his good showing (15.5% of the voters) he was hopelessly outmatched. His strength came from the more backward and rural departments that had traditionally voted conservative.

Lecanuet's vote invited speculation on the significance of the foreign policy issues. It is doubtful that the votes cast for him indicate or reflect the extent of pro-European and pro-Atlantic alliance sentiment. His electoral clientele came from groups that were primarily concerned with domestic and economic problems rather than foreign policy considerations. This is even more obvious since at least 60% of his votes went to General de Gaulle on the second ballot.

Despite the indication of the stability of voting attitudes, the election illustrated once more the personal appeal de Gaulle had among the voters. His personal vote, even if far below that of the four preceding referendums, was much higher than the one the Gaullist party received on the first ballot of the 1962 legislative elections: 44.6% as compared to approximately 37.5%, or about 2 million more votes. Conversely, Mitterrand received considerably below the total number of votes that were cast for the Communist party, the Socialist party, and the Radical Socialist party in the legislative elections of the same year: 34.7% as compared to about 44%. Since Lecanuet's vote was somewhat higher than that of the centrist parties in the election, the inescapable conclusion is that de Gaulle continued to appeal to left-wing voters and managed to detach them from their parties when his own person or his policy were at stake in an election.

The Second Ballot

De Gaulle was thus scheduled to run on the second ballot against Mitterrand. Lecanuet, who had to withdraw, asked his followers not to vote for de Gaulle, thus indirectly counseling either abstention or a vote for Mitterrand. The same was the attitude of Marcilhacy. On the other hand, Tixier-Vignancourt expressly asked his voters to vote for Mitterrand.

On the second ballot, de Gaulle received 55.1% and Mitterrand 44.8% of the vote. This in essence meant that at least 60% of the Lecanuet votes went to de Gaulle and about 30% to Mitterrand, the rest abstaining. The majority of the extreme-right-wing voters who had voted for Tixier-Vignancourt went to the Communist-supported candidate.

Except for the support given to Mitterrand by the extreme-right-wingers and centrists (which was offset by the support given to de Gaulle by left-wing voters), the basic historical voting patterns that we discussed earlier remained in evidence. For instance, as Professor Goguel shows in his analysis [1] (from which I have drawn heavily), the vote for Mitterrand was virtually identical to the vote of May 5, 1946, on the first draft of the constitution of the Fourth Republic sponsored by the Communists, Socialists, and Radicals, and remarkably similar in its geographic distribution. In its broad contours, the geographic distribution of Mitterrand's vote also resembles that of the popular front of 1936—a combination of Communist, Socialist, and Radical strength. The vote for Mitterrand thus represented the traditional ideological families of the left.

THE LEGISLATIVE ELECTIONS OF 1967

As soon as the victory of General de Gaulle had been announced, the preparations for the elections of the National Assembly began in earnest. The electoral system remained fundamentally the same. The only serious modification provided that all candidates who failed to receive 10% of the registered votes on the first ballot were to be automatically eliminated from the second. The electoral districts represented

---

[1] See F. Goguel, "L'élection présidentielle française du décembre 1965," *Revue Française de Science Politique* (April 1966).

about 93,000 inhabitants each, but gross discrepancies were allowed to remain: in some districts the population was as high as 175,000, while in others it was not more than 75,000. Each department continued to be entitled to two deputies, irrespective of its population, so that agricultural areas remained overrepresented. To the 482 districts (465 for metropolitan France and 17 for the overseas departments and territories), five more were added in the Paris region, bringing the grand total to 487. Each candidate was required to deposit $200, which would be forfeited if he failed to receive 5% of the ballots cast. Campaigning expenses were borne by the state, and the parties were given free time on radio and TV. Three hours in all were allotted for this purpose, divided evenly among the "majority" party—the Gaullists—and all the opposition groups represented in the National Assembly. All other political formations were to be given seven minutes, on condition that they nominate more than seventy-five candidates.[2] The campaign was officially declared open three weeks before the polling day, March 5.

The Communist party prepared for the election with two objectives in mind. The first was to demonstrate that it continued to be the most popular party in France—a distinction it had lost since the 1962 election to the Gaullists. The party designated candidates in virtually every electoral district (478). Their second and perhaps more important objective (from a tactical point of view) was to cooperate closely with the members of the left-wing forces that were grouped under the Federation of the Democratic and Socialist Left. There was to be no question of outright Communist support to a non-Communist leftist candidate on the second ballot, as had happened in some cases in 1962. On December 21, 1966, a formal electoral agreement between the Communists and the Federation was reached. Their candidates would compete freely against each other on the first ballot, but on the second ballot they would

undertake to withdraw to support the "better-placed" candidate. It was further agreed that immediately after the first ballot, the top leaders of both formations would meet to make reciprocal withdrawals according to this formula, and to examine special cases that might arise calling for exceptions.

The Federation entered the electoral contest in a mood of optimism. It had managed to remain united and make progress since the strong showing of François Mitterrand in the Presidential election. It had managed to withstand many internal conflicts and to resist the attraction to move to the center and seek alliances there rather than on the left. It designated candidates in the great majority of electoral districts (418). These candidates were carefully apportioned among the three constituent parties in the order of their strength: Socialists, Radicals, and Convention of Republican Institutions. Almost all Socialist and Radical members of the National Assembly were designated as candidates—many in safe seats—while the candidates of the Convention often found themselves running in districts where the odds against them were heavy.

Between the Communist party and the Federation stood the small and militant Unified Socialist Party (PSU). It came into prominence again when its titular head, Pierre Mendès-France, decided to run as its candidate in Grenoble. The PSU managed to designate a little over one hundred candidates—enough to give it a few minutes on radio and TV. After many hesitations and equivocations, it signed the same agreement that had been made between the Federation and the Communists regarding withdrawals and support on the second ballot.

The Democratic Center found itself in a precarious situation. Shut out to the left by the agreement of the Federation, the Communists, and the PSU, it found the door to the Gaullist camp tightly locked by the dislike of the Gaullist leaders for Lecanuet and by the independent republicans, who collaborated with the Gaullists and appealed to the moderate center. There was little room to maneuver. The party designated candidates in 371 districts and its leader, Lecanuet, put all his hopes in strong showings on the first ballot and in the defection of Federa-

---

[2] For the second ballot the time allowed was forty-five minutes for the majority, forty-five minutes for the "opposition," and five minutes for other political formations.

tion voters to his candidates, rather than to Communists, on the second ballot. There was also the threat of maintaining a Democratic Center candidate on the second ballot, thus forcing a triangular contest with a Communist (or a Federation) candidate and a Gaullist. Such a threat could force the left and the Gaullists to withdraw and vote in favor of the centrists—the first to stave off a Gaullist victory and the second to thwart a Communist one!

The Gaullists and the independent republicans expected to repeat their 1962 performance. An "Action Committee for the Fifth Republic" was formed to assume the direction of the campaign. It imposed a tight control on the nomination of all Gaullist candidates in all 487 districts. Designation meant endorsement by the leadership of the party—in many cases, by the prime minister himself. Twenty-five ministers, many of whom had never held or sought a parliamentary mandate before, were asked to run. Discipline was respected. One serious attempt to form a rival organization under the name of "Dissident Gaullists" failed. A number of smaller groups—the right-wing Republican Alliance and the Rally for European Liberation —managed to put up only 68 candidates, the Dissident Gaullists only 35, and unaffiliated candidates, dispersed throughout the country, accounted for another 195.

The Platforms

The platforms of the political parties presented little that was original. There seemed to be, as we noted earlier, a decline of ideological differences. The parties addressed themselves to many immediate problems and avoided others. The Communists, while paying lip service to their revolutionary verbiage, seemed to be at best a reformist party. Their electoral agreement with the Federation emphasized the points in common with the Socialists and the Radicals: Gaullism should be "eliminated," political liberties protected, a coherent economic and social policy set forth, and world peace and disarmament arranged. They urged massive construction of low-income housing and the improvement of public health, national educa-

tion, and scientific research; and proposed a vigorous policy of economic expansion, a new comprehensive economic plan, the nationalization of all armaments industries and commercial banks, full employment, higher wages and social security benefits, better old-age pensions, comprehensive legislation for the aged, and the improvement of living conditions on the farm. They opposed the United States bombings in North Vietnam and favored the application of the Geneva accords; were against the proliferation of atomic weapons; and expressed their "profound opposition" to the French atomic force. The agreement seemed to be so comprehensive as to overshadow the differences. The Federation remained generally pro-European and continued to be oriented toward the Atlantic alliance. Not so the Communists. The Communists favored a profound reform of the constitution and the reestablishment of parliamentary supremacy. Not so the Federation. It seemed willing to accept the letter of the constitution, but considered modifications regarding the power of the president and of parliament. The Communists favored extensive and profound nationalizations; the Federation remained selective, narrowly reformist, and more pragmatic in its approach. But otherwise there was substantial agreement on policy and goals.

Opposed to the Communists and the Federation, the Gaullists' single overriding theme was the continuation of the work of General de Gaulle: stability at home, independence abroad, and continuation of the economic and social reforms. They defended vigorously their record —decolonization, full employment, prosperity, and stability—and asked the voters to provide a majority to make it possible for General de Gaulle to continue his task.

The Democratic Center proposed some kind of Europeanization of the atomic force, the entry of England into the Common Market, European supranational institutions, and continuing attachment to NATO. It accepted by and large the constitution, but proposed the establishment of a supreme court similar to that of the United States. Beyond this the center emphasized what the other parties also stressed: better economic planning; rapid construction of low-cost housing; rapid increase of educational facilities; subsidies for regional planning and aid to the farmers.

The Electorate

On March 5, some 28 million registered voters were called upon to cast their ballots. About 15 million were women, and 13.7 million men— a fact that favored the Gaullists, since a greater proportion of women than men voted for de Gaulle in the presidential election. This was also the oldest group of voters in France (over half were between 40 and 61, 25% were over 61, and about a quarter were between 21 and 40)—again a situation favorable to the Gaullists since a greater proportion of those over 50 voted for de Gaulle in the presidential election.

The Campaign

While a number of issues were aired on radio and TV and in some large meetings, the real electoral battle took place at the level of the electoral district. Each candidate endeavored to establish an intimate and direct contact with the voter. In the school halls and small chemistry laboratories, the candidate—accompanied by his "substitute," the person who would replace him in the National Assembly were he to accept a cabinet post after being elected a deputy—met small groups ranging from a handful to three or four hundred. The topics most often emphasized were the state of the economy and of the welfare measures taken by the government, and the constitution and its future.

The economic situation was discussed in detail by both the Gaullists and the opposition parties. It may be summed up as a battle of statistics. The Gaullists claimed progress in every sector. The opposition often conceded it, but claimed it was inadequate and that relative to the other Common Market countries, France was falling behind. How many miles of highway? How many clinics? How many schools? How many tons of steel and coal? What was the exact rate in the increase of production? What were the provisions made for summer classes

and vacations for children? How many housing units had been constructed? The Gaullists conceded to the Federation and the Communists a certain lag in housing construction and in the development of education facilities, but the reason, they argued, was the rapid growth of population and the correspondingly unprecedented demand for these services. Communist and Federation spokesmen attacked the Gaullists for relying on "free enterprise," castigated the government for lack of positive economic planning, and urged for measures of control and socialization. The leader of the Federation, François Mitterrand, in one of the few large preelection gatherings, demanded more schools, more highways, greater benefits for the sick and the unskilled workers, higher old-age pension rates, better-paid vacations, and increased wages. "When Pompidou [the prime minister, leader of the Gaullists, and an ex-banker] asks me who is going to pay, I answer: '*You,* Monsieur Pompidou.'"

Regarding the second topic, the future of the constitution, debate often became acrimonious and took at least two directions. One involved what might be called the "title of ownership": to whom did the constitution of the Fifth Republic belong? While the Communists proudly rejected any share of the title— they were the only ones that campaigned and voted against the constitution—the Gaullists claimed it all for themselves. It was *their* constitution and it had given leadership and stability to the country. This was refuted indignantly by the leaders of the center and the Federation. They too had shared in the preparation of the constitution and had voted for it. The Fifth Republic belonged to all; executive leadership was desired by all; stability was the result of common efforts. But at this point the debate took off in a different direction. The Federation, the center, and many others argued that the constitution of the Fifth Republic was not respected by de Gaulle and his prime minister. They demanded that the system return to it; that the prime minister and the cabinet become the effective vehicles of executive leadership under the overall control of the National Assembly. The personal power of the president should be curtailed. Similarly, the prerogatives of the National Assembly to exercise control, to scrutinize the government, and to initiate legislation ought to be broadened.

General de Gaulle had opened the electoral campaign with a speech in which he asked for a return of his majority to support the task that history, the constitution, and the voters had invested him with, and claimed that the "partisan" groups that opposed him were "able to unite only in order to destroy but never to construct." Again, forty-eight hours before the balloting, he appealed in a nationally televised address in favor of the Gaullist party. Asserting that a great deal had been accomplished, he conceded that there was still a great deal to do. It would be impossible to do it if the "parties" had the numerical strength in the National Assembly to thwart his task. But, "there is every reason to hope if the Fifth Republic majority wins," he concluded. The president had personally injected himself again into the electoral campaign, asking for the reelection of *his* majority to support him in accomplishing *his* task.

For the 470 seats for metropolitan France, a total of 2,190 candidates entered the competition—about the same number as in the previous election. But despite numerous labels and the number of unaffiliated, the contest involved now four parties—or perhaps three-and-a-half: the Communists, the Federation, the Gaullists, and the Democratic Center.

The Results of the First Ballot

More than 22 million out of some 28 million voted, for a participation of almost 81% of the voters (as opposed to 69% in 1962). The small parties, the nonaffiliated candidates, and those who dissented from their national parties and opposed their leadership were literally wiped out. Even the Democratic Center appeared to have been squeezed between the three large formations and to have suffered irreparable political loss.

Otherwise, hardly any major fluctuation of voting can be detected. As Table 5-2 shows, the Communists improved their strength by a total

of 1 million votes, but in view of the higher rate of participation, by only 1%. The combination of the Communist and the PSU vote indicates a strength for both 1962 and 1967 of slightly over 25% of the total. The Federation lost about 1.5% as compared with the votes cast for two of its major constituent bodies (Socialists and Radicals) in 1962. The Gaullists, including the Independent Republicans, improved their strength in absolute figures but remained at approximately 37.5% of the vote. The decline of all other formations is noticeable and corresponds to a trend that had been established in 1962. The Democratic Center (but with only 371 candidates) lost 4% of its vote (from about 17%, that its constituent groups—MRP and independents—won in 1962, to 13%), and the extreme-right-wing formations remained below 1%.

This stability of balloting accounts for what was widely anticipated: only eighty-one candidates—mostly the Gaullists, and eight Communists—received an absolute majority and were elected on the first ballot. In the thirty-one districts of Paris nobody was elected, though the UNR was ahead in every district.

The vote also showed remarkable stability in its geographic distribution. Gaullists continued to be strong in the east and the west, and in some of the central regions. The Communists maintained their strength in Paris, and improved it in the Paris region, where the Federation also made progress. Both maintained their traditional strength in the south, the southeast and the southwest, and in the industrial departments of the north. If the student were to draw a somewhat arbitrary line between the right (Gaullists) and the left (Communists, the PSU, and the Federation), concede the votes received by the unaffiliated candidates to the right, and give 40% of the Democratic Center to the left and 60% to the right, then the division between right and left would be as follows:

Left: about 49% of the vote, with a total of about 10.5 million.
Right: about 51% of the vote, with a total of about 11.5 million.

The Second Ballot

Over four hundred deputies remained to be chosen on the second ballot. With the collapse of the splinter groups, the candidates that could technically represent their parties with a fair chance of winning came almost exclusively from the Communists, the Federation, and the Gaullists, and a few from the Democratic Center. The issue therefore narrowed to the following: Would the electoral agreement between the Communist party and the Federation be respected; and if so, would it be followed by the voters? Would the Democratic Center maintain its candidates—not more than about 170 were eligible—against both the left and the right, or would it rather throw its support behind the Gaullists on the basis of some last-minute arrangements calling for reciprocity in some selected districts? Whatever the arrangements, would the voters of the Democratic Center follow the instruction of their candidates on how to vote on the second ballot?

Each district had its own tradition and memory, and in each the personality of the candidates was likely to play an important role. Further, the way in which the voters would vote on the second ballot depended on whether there was to be a straight fight between a Communist and a Gaullist, or between a Federation candidate and a Gaullist. While the Communist voters were expected to go all the way for a Federation candidate on the second ballot, the reverse was not likely. It was also taken almost as axiomatic that more than 60% of the Democratic Center vote would go to a Gaullist rather than a Federation candidate, and as much as 80% to a Gaullist rather than a Communist.

The alliance between the Communists and the Federation was effectively implemented. The Federation withdrew its candidates in favor of Communists whenever the latter had received higher numbers of votes, and the Communists reciprocated scrupulously. In fact, they went beyond this. In fifteen so-called "special cases" they withdrew in favor of the Federation candidate even when the Communist candidate had come out ahead of the latter. These special cases involved contests in which either the other candidate was a Gaullist minister, or the Federation candidate was an important political leader, or the Federation candidate had a wider local electoral appeal than the Communist. On the second ballot the Communists, the PSU, and the Federation presented a single candidate in every pertinent district against the Gaullists, who maintained their candidates virtually everywhere. Only some eighty Democratic Center candidates actually ran, and a mere thirty from other formations or from among the unaffiliated. In metropolitan France on the second ballot there were fewer than 880 candidates. In 335 districts, electoral competition was limited to a straight fight between two candidates. In 62 there was a "triangular" conflict, and only in one did four candidates compete for election. The Gaullists were pitted in a straight fight almost everywhere: in 125 districts against the Communists, in 144 against the Federation; in 18 against the Democratic Center; in six against the PSU; and in eight against the right-wing candidates and unaffiliated. Thus, the Democratic Center candidates ran in 18 districts against a candidate of the left, hoping and often expecting to receive Gaullist support, and in 18 districts against the Gaullists, hoping, without necessarily expecting, leftist support. The dominant aspect of the election was the contest between the Gaullists and the single candidate of the left—Communist, Federation, and occasionally PSU.

The Results of the Second Ballot

On the second ballot participation was almost as high as on the first: there was a drop of only 2%. The parties on the left showed a remarkable discipline and were largely followed by their voters—more so for the Communists than the Federation. Generally, the single candidate of the left received a greater number of votes on the second ballot than did all the candidates of the left put together on the first. The Gaullists continued to show remarkable strength, their total percentage going up from 37% in the first ballot to about 45% on the second. In the eighteen contests that pitted the Democratic Center against the Gaullists, the left-wing vote went for the center; in the eighteen that pitted the center against the left, the Gaullist voters supported the center. The electoral strategy of the Democratic Center, in other words, worked—and helped them gain about 20 seats on the second ballot. The election was very close, 55 seats being decided by less than a thousand-vote margin. The Gaullists barely managed to stave off defeat. They *and* the Independent Republicans finally finished with 245 seats—a loss of 37 seats. In contrast, the left improved its position greatly. The Communists moved from 41 to 73 seats—a gain of 32, and the Federation from 89 to 116—a gain of 27. The center lost 9 seats, from 38 to 27, but it managed to recruit some of the "unaffiliated" candidates, while the extreme right failed to gain a single seat.

What accounted ultimately for the loss of Gaullist seats was the transfer of votes from the first to the second ballot. The Federation and the Communists gained more than expected, and the Gaullists simply did not gain all that was expected. In the first ballot the Democratic Center and various centrists and moderates received some 3.8 million votes. Over half of this went back to the centrist candidates that remained on the second ballot—in some 80 districts. The other 1.8 million votes were free on the second ballot to go to a Gaullist, a Federation, or a Communist candidate, or into abstention. Only about 45% went to the Gaullists, another 40% to the candidate of the left, and the rest into abstention. In the Paris districts, in the eighteen cases that pitted a Communist against a Gaullist in a straight fight, 25% of the centrist vote went to a Communist, another 45% to a Gaullist, and the rest into abstention. A part of the center (and at times the extreme right) vote simply went to the left—even to vote for a Communist —in order to defeat a Gaullist. Finally the centrist vote was heavier in favor of the left when the candidate was a Federation man.

Equally unanticipated was the massive transfer of the Federation and the PSU votes to a Communist candidate on the second ballot. Sometimes 80%, and even 90% of the Federation voters were transferred to a Communist.

The Communist voters rarely faltered. They transferred their votes massively to a Federation candidate, often assuring him of his election. Thus, the "popular front" alliance worked —not only at the higher party echelons where the agreements had been made, but even more significantly it was effective among the voters.

The second ballot confirmed the tenacity of the geographical distribution of the vote. In the Paris region, the left continued to show strength, while in the city of Paris itself the Gaullists lost a total of 10 of their 31 seats. The Communists and the Federation maintained their position in the southeast and southwest, and in general south of the Loire, while showing renewed strength in parts of the center and eastern-central regions and in the industrial departments of the Nord and Pas de Calais. The Gaullists made some gains in what was considered to be some of the left-wing strongholds—especially in some departments of the south and southwest, but they were unable to make up for their losses in Paris and the industrial departments of the north and in the southeast.

The election had produced a remarkable voting concentration in three political families (see Table 5-3). But each family was easily recognizable in the political map of France, and within each one old parties could still be identified. The election had given the semblance of unity, but how and when it would overcome the potential sources of disunity remained to be seen. France appeared on the way to becoming a three-party system. But large political formations like the Gaullists or the Federation were only broad alliances that included different groups and rival leaders.

The new National Assembly resembled more that of 1958, though the Gaullists maintained a tenuous majority: 245 out of 487 seats. But in the Gaullist majority the independent republicans that formed an autonomous parliamentary group had 44 members. To the left, the Communists had 73 deputies, an increase of 32; the Federation 121, an increase of 27; the PSU 4, an increase of 3; and the Democratic Center—after combining forces with a number of the moderates and unaffiliated under the name of "Progress and Modern De-

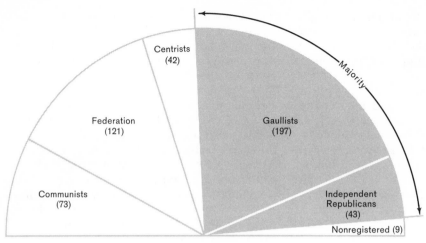

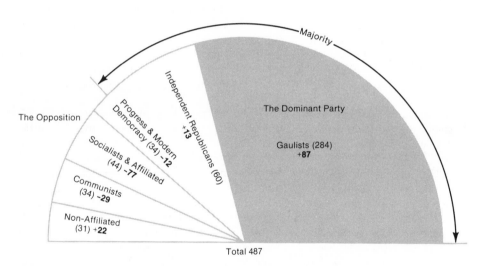

FIG. 5-3. *The Third Legislature of the National Assembly before* (above) *and the Fourth Legislature after* (below) *the election of June 1968. (Boldface indicates the approximate number of seats gained or lost.)*

mocracy," 41. Some seven candidates remained unaffiliated.

THE "EVENTS" OF 1968 AND THE GAULLIST TIDE

The analysis of the election results of March 1967 helps us to understand what hap-

pened fifteen months later when de Gaulle dissolved the National Assembly and called for new elections. They were held on June 23 and 30, 1968. As we saw in the introductory chapter, the students attacked the personal government of General de Gaulle and called for a radical overhaul of the social and political institutions. The workers followed with a widespread strike. In a matter of weeks the country was plunged into one of the worst crises it had ever known. The Gaullist ranks began to falter when two Gaullist ministers resigned and when the Independent Republicans, allied thus far with the Gaullists, threatened to join the opposition. All eyes turned toward the aged president. This was precisely the situation that the powers and independence of the presidency under the constitution of the Fifth Republic were designed to meet. In 1958 de Gaulle was called in to save the republic against the military. Now de Gaulle was president with all the tools that he had fashioned to face this new threat. After some equivocations the president moved. He met with top army officers to secure their support, dissolved the Parliament on whose majority he could no longer rely, called for new elections, and prepared for a show of force.

It was in this climate of crisis, with the political parties unprepared and with the theme of law and order and return to normalcy predominating, that the electoral campaign took place and the election was held. The Gaullists, led again by the prime minister, Georges Pompidou, and fully supported by the president, united under a new label—the UDR (*Union pour la Défense de la République*— Union for the Defense of the Republic). But it was the same Gaullist party, purged of all dissidence—actual or potential. Pompidou again personally supervised the designation of Gaullist candidates with an eye to their loyalty and their ability to defeat the opposition. The Independent Republicans, whose leader had flirted with dissidence and threatened to vote against the government, returned again into the Gaullist fold and his party run under the banner of the UDR. Dissolution had tightened discipline and nipped dissension in the bud. The center groups—especially the PDM (*Progress and Modern Democracy*), many of whose members had voted against the government, found themselves in disarray. They had counted on time and on defections from either the Federation or the Gaullists in order to rebuild their forces. Now there was no time and those who had voted the motion of censure could expect nothing but a difficult campaign against both the left and the Gaullists. A strong showing

from either would just about wipe them out as a viable political force.

But the prospects were no brighter for the left—the Communists, the PSU, and the Federation. Again they formed an electoral alliance providing for independent action on the first ballot and, as in 1967, for a close alliance on the second ballot, where they would withdraw their candidates in favor of the better-placed one and rally behind him. But their flank—especially the Communist flank—had been turned on their left. The support they had received on the second ballot in 1967 from the center and moderate voters was very much in doubt. Even some of their faithful followers from the extreme left couldn't be counted upon. For while the Gaullists accused the left of instigating the rebellion, many die-hard left-wingers claimed that the Communist party had not gone far enough in leading it!

The Gaullists increased their popular vote on the first ballot. Using the theme of law and order and exploiting the fears that the rebellion had created among the middle and lower-middle classes, plus the remarkable prestige of General de Gaulle, the Gaullists alone—not counting their allies, the Independent Republicans— emerged for the first time with an uncontested majority in the National Assembly. Together with the Independent Republicans they won 43.65% of the popular vote on the first ballot gaining over 9.5 million votes as compared to a little less than 8.5 million in 1967. The swing in their favor amounted to about 6% of the voters. They won on the first ballot by an absolute majority 142 seats—almost one-third of all the seats of the National Assembly. All the other political formations lost. The combined vote of the left (Communists, Federation, and PSU) went down by about 4%—the Communists and the Federation losing about 2.5% each, while the PSU, which took the most militant stand in support of the student rebellion, showed a gain of a little over 1%. The center lost about 2% of its vote (see Table 5-2).

The swing to the Gaullists left little doubt about the outcome of the second ballot. A total of some 2,270 candidates had entered the election. One hundred and fifty-four seats had been won on the first ballot in as many electoral districts, settling the issue for some 600 hopefuls. Another 600 failed to receive the requisite 10% of the registered voters and were automatically eliminated. About 900 candidates were therefore free to run on the second ballot in the remaining 345 districts. Only about 650 decided to stay on to the bitter end. In most cases the electoral confrontation involved straight fights between Gaullists and other party candidates: 107 with the Communists, 121 with the Federation, 14 with the centrists. There were only about 45 "triangular elections" and only in about 20 districts were the Gaullists absent.

The Gaullists and the Independent Republicans together won 206 of the remaining 321 seats for a grand total of 358 seats. The Communists, the Federation, and the center lost heavily, while the PSU, the dissident groups, and some new formations were eliminated (see Fig. 5-3).

What had happened on the second ballot was due to a reversal of the trend that had emerged in the preceding election. This is easily discernible in Table 5-6, each section of which gives an approximate idea of the general pattern.

Every one of the examples given was repeated many times, thus accounting for the defeat of the left-wing parties on the second ballot and the victory of the Gaullists in the National Assembly. The Communists barely managed to elect more than 30 deputies and constitute a "parliamentary group"; the Federation got only 57 members as compared to 121 in 1967; the center survived as a parliamentary group thanks only to Gaullist support in some electoral districts, while the Gaullists and their allies—the Independent Republicans—swelled their combined strength from a bare majority of 244 to a total of over 350: 292 to the Gaullists and 61 to the Independent Republicans. The Gaullists alone hold an absolute majority in the National Assembly. The "opposition" comprises no more than about 100 deputies, while the center, under the label of Progress and Modern Democracy (PDM), has dwindled to about 30.

These observations tell the story as clearly as it can be told pending more detailed analysis and opinion studies. The three major forma-tions—Gaullists, Communists, and Federation seem to have solidified their positions, allowing for a floating vote of about 1 million that went from the left to the Gaullists. The center still has some 3.5 million voters, most of whom, however, had nowhere to go on the second ballot except over to the left or to the Gaullists. Yet it holds the balance of power. If in future elections the left discipline fails and the center moves to the Gaullists on the second ballot—as happened in 1968—the result will be a Gaullist landslide. If the left discipline holds and the center divides—as was the case in 1967—then the balance will be very much in doubt. One of the crucial questions for the future, therefore, is the discipline of the left and the voting trends of the center. Moreover, the election of 1967 is likely to prove more typical, for the outcome of the 1968 election was due to a "swing" of about 6% of the voters on the first ballot. The Gaullist landslide in terms of parliamentary seats resulted from the relative failure of left-wing voters to vote for their candidates on the first ballot and from the massive move of the centrist voters to the Gaullists on the second ballot.

II. AFTER DE GAULLE

THE LAST HURRAH, THE LAST REFERENDUM

With a terse statement issued on April 28, 1969, de Gaulle ceased to perform the functions of the presidency. After ten years, ten months, and twenty-nine days in office, first as prime minister and, since January 1959, as president, he withdrew from public life. The immediate reason was the defeat of his proposal in the fifth referendum he had held, on April 27, 1969, in which 53.18% of the voters voted "No" as against 46.81% voting "Yes." For the first time the French had failed to heed his passionate appeal to follow him. This defeat and his subsequent resignation appeared to throw the French political situation into turmoil. Would the system survive without its hero and founder? Would the institutions function? Immediately after de Gaulle's resignation, the

TABLE 5-6.

1. The Communist voting discipline from the first to the second ballot held remarkably well.

A. *Isère   (3rd Electoral District)*

Registered 83,240		Voting 61,995	
1st Ballot		2nd Ballot	
Jenneney		JEANNENEY	31,059
Gaull.	22,707	Mendès-France	30,927
Mendès-France			
Fed.-PSU	19,577		
Giard (PC)	10,715		
Vanier (ex-			
Gaull.)	6,549		
Boissenot (Ind.)	2,071		

B. *Pas-de-Calais   (1st Electoral District)*

Registered 61,507		Voting 51,854	
1st Ballot		2nd Ballot	
Theeten		Theeten	24,796
(Gaull.)	20,869	MOLLET	27,058
Mollet (Fed.)	13,698		
Coquel (PC)	11,956		
Virel (Cent.)	3,887		
Garbe (PSU)	1,533		

2. But the Federation voters did not reciprocate. In a great number of cases they did not vote for a Communist. They went into abstention or voted for a centrist or even a Gaullist.

C. *Gironde   (Third District)*

Registered Voters 63,495		Voting 48,812	
1st Ballot		2nd Ballot	
Collière (Gaull.)	21,920	COLLIÈRE	26,176
Arraut (PC)	16,177	Arraut	22,636
Allier (Fed.)	10,824		

D. *Nord   (17th District)*

Registered 58,930		Voting 40,649	
1st Ballot		2nd Ballot	
Durieux		DURIEUX	20,162
(Gaull.)	16,639	Leloir	18,728
Leloir (PC)	10,926		
Mauroy (Fed.)	10,884		
Wende (PSU)	775		

Nord   (22nd District)

Registered 51,564		Voting 42,168	
1st Ballot		2nd Ballot	
Lebas (Gaull.)	15,076	LEBAS	21,331
Maton (PC)	13,913	Maton	20,837
Forest (Fed.)	12,251		
Baffont (PSU)	1,752		

3. The centrist vote went overwhelmingly to the Gaullists on the second ballot thus repeating the pattern of the 1965 Presidential election rather than that of the legislative election of 1967.

Isère   (3rd District)

Registered 56,963		Voting 44,367	
1st Ballot		2nd Ballot	
Maisonnat		Maisonnat	21,116
(PC)	15,621	AYMAR	23,241
Aymar			
(Gaull.)	15,041		
Villard			
(Cent.)	7,145		
LeRoy			
(PSU)	3,460		
Lacolte (Fed.)	2,886		

Gaull., Gaullist; Fed., Federation; PSU, Socialist Unified party; PC, Communist party; Ind., Independent; Cent., Centrist.

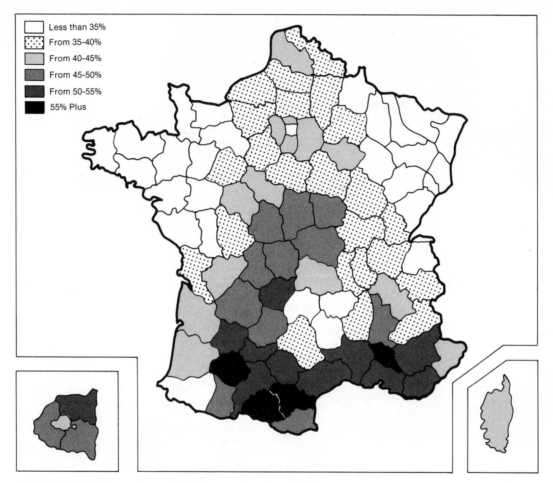

FIG. 5-4. *The referendum of 1962. Percentages shown represent the "no" vote by departments.*

president of the Senate, Alain Poher, a rather obscure centrist politician, assumed, as the constitution prescribes, the functions of interim president and scheduled new presidential elections for June 1. The political parties feverishly entered the campaign. Again, the left and the anti-Gaullists envisaged seriously the prospects of victory.

The Referendum of April 27, 1969

No referendum had been held since 1962. De Gaulle's 1965 election to the presidency had

been won by a relatively narrow margin. Thus, while the ostensible purpose of the 1969 referendum was to gain approval for two important reforms that had been debated and discussed for some time, its underlying objective was to obtain from the French people a reaffirmation of their loyalty to and confidence in their president.

The first proposed reform on the slate of the referendum was *regionalization*—divesting the central government in Paris of many of its powers, especially with regard to economic planning, investments, urban development, regional development, etc. and giving them to

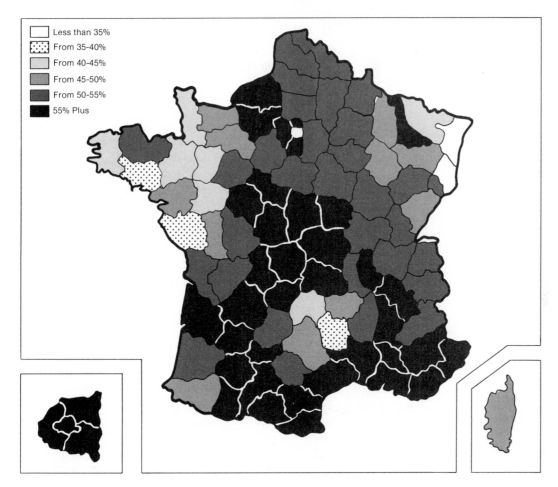

FIG. 5-5. *The referendum of 1969. Percentages shown represent the "no" vote by departments.*

regional units, larger than the departments, that have certain common problems and concerns which they could deal with on their own initiative and through new regional representative assemblies. The second proposal was for the reform of the Senate. De Gaulle proposed a radical transformation of this body in line with a number of proposals he had made after World War II, the essence of which was to merge the Senate with the Economic and Social Council.

Regional reform seemed acceptable to the public. One month before the referendum, over 58% of those polled favored it. Complex and complicated as it was, it nonetheless paved the way to some decentralization from Paris and to regional consolidation of the miniscule departments. The names of the new regions evoked some of the old historical landscape of France: names such as Aquitaine, Bourgogne, Franch-Compté, Languedoc-Rousillon, and Picardie brought nostalgic memories to all those who knew their history—and all French schoolchildren do.

It was the reform of the Senate that created political difficulties. For almost one hundred years the "republican Senate" had been the bastion of the departments and the municipalities of France against the central government. Furthermore, it had been a conservative force representing the rural interests and the mayors, the councillors, and the local elites from which it was elected. Diminished in power under the Fifth Republic, it had nonetheless become the body from which the most eloquent and at times most cogent criticisms against de Gaulle had come. On two occasions it had voted down the *force de frappe;* and the president of the Senate had contested openly the validity of many of the acts of the president of the republic. The latter refused to see him and forbade his ministers to attend the debates in the Senate. The proposal aimed at drastically changing both the composition of this body and its powers. According to the text, 323 senators would be elected: 187 by region—a minimum of 3 per region but with special provisions for the more populated ones, especially Paris—and 146 from the various socioprofessional groups—42 from the workers, 8 from the liberal professions, 30 from the farmers, 10 from family associations, 8 from higher education, 12 from various social and cultural activities, 36 from industrial, commercial, and artisan enterprises, and so forth. Thus, the Senate was to be transformed at least in part into a functional representative assembly. Its powers were also to be drastically reduced. It would have only consultative power though, upon the demand of the government and/or the National Assembly, a legislative text could be sent to the Senate for its concurrence.

Both the diminution of powers of the Senate and the radical restructuring of the composition and mode of election created opposition. Also, the length of the text—together with the proposal for regional reformation it ran fifteen pages—and its many disparate proposals aroused suspicions. Many argued that most of the proposals could have been handled by the Parliament. Some of de Gaulle's associates, notably from among the independent republicans and the center, turned against him. The Communists and the Socialists—in fact, the entire left—saw again an opportunity to succeed where they had so dismally failed in the past. All efforts to divide the referendum into two parts—one dealing with regions (fa-

vorably received) and the other with the Senate (which seemed likely to be defeated)—failed. De Gaulle insisted on the whole package, making it a matter of confidence. He lost.

A comparison of the geographical vote distributions in the referendums of 1962 and 1969 is revealing. In 1962 (Fig. 5-4) de Gaulle lost only in the Mediterranean littoral and southwestern parts of central France—in not more than fourteen departments. The 1969 map (Fig. 5-5) clearly shows the radical change, indicating a swing of at least 15% of the voters from "Yes" to "No." Whereas in 1962 the "Yes" votes had swept Paris, in 1969 the "No" vote carried the city. In sixteen out of the twenty-two projected regions outside the greater Paris area, the "No" vote showed a substantial majority. The "Yes" vote carried only the traditional bastions of Gaullism clearly outlined in the map in white or dotted white.

THE PRESIDENTIAL ELECTION WITHOUT DE GAULLE (JUNE 1969) [3]

The elections for the presidency that followed revealed a number of trends about the regime and the political parties. There was no "chaos" that many Gaullists predicted would follow de Gaulle's demise. The institutions functioned smoothly in the moment of crisis. Never did Paris seem so peaceful and serene, especially for those who remembered the uprisings only a year ago. The president of the Senate assumed the office of the presidency, set the date of the elections, and waited for the nominations of the candidates, among whom he was to become one. Prominent individuals and parties moved rapidly onto the electoral stage. Seven candidates ran for the office of the presidency in June 1969.

First and foremost was the Gaullist former prime minister, Georges Pompidou, who declared himself a candidate as soon as de Gaulle resigned. There was no surprise since Pompidou

[3] In writing this section I have drawn from my article "Pompidou and the Communists," *Virginia Quarterly* (Fall 1969).

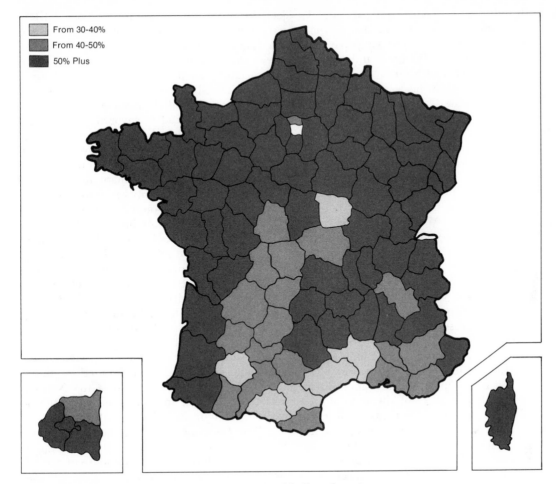

FIG. 5-6. *The presidential election of 1965, second ballot: the vote for de Gaulle in percentages.*

had been holding himself back for that post. The Gaullists rallied behind him—including the leaders of the independent republicans, who had displayed a "yes . . . but" attitude for some time in the past. The Gaullist flanks seemed well covered, and Pompidou was to receive ultimately the support of a number of moderates who had taken issue with de Gaulle both during the May–June "Events," when some had voted to censure the government, and during the referendum, when they had come out for a "No."

Alain Poher, the interim president, found —much to his surprise and to that of almost all political analysts—that he was popular. His fight against the referendum on behalf of the Senate had gained him national notoriety. Now he discovered that public opinion polls gave him a good chance: 37% of those polled declared early in May their intention to vote for him. While Pompidou, in the best Gaullist style, "declared" himself a candidate, Poher, after a number of deliberations and consultations, "consented" to run. He hoped to get not only all the votes that Lecanuet and the other two center candidates had received in 1965—about 20%—but also the votes of the left—if he managed to survive the first ballot as the polls indicated he would. This, of course, depended on what the left would do on the second ballot. In 1965 the left-wing parties threw all their votes behind one candidate—Mitterand. Mitterand had won over 44% in the second ballot in 1965; he was likely to do better in 1969, with de Gaulle out of the picture.

Poher's logic was impeccable. Confronted in 1965 with a choice between a leftist (fully supported by the Communist party) and de Gaulle, the electorate had given de Gaulle 55% of the votes, some $2\frac{1}{4}$ million votes more than he had received on the first ballot, as opposed to 45% for Mitterand. More than half of de Gaulle's votes on the second ballot had come from the center. In 1969 it was likely that Poher would freeze all the centrist votes behind him on the second ballot and receive the full support of the anti-Gaullist left—including, of course, the Communists.

So much for the strategy. It was aimed at reviving the moderate center as a political force. It required an electoral coalition of all the old parties against the Gaullists on the first ballot and the support of the Communists on the second. The capture of the presidency might well lead to the reconstitution in the National Assembly of a large centrist coalition that would include Gaullist deputies, thus provoking the breakup of the Gaullist party, which many took for granted. In fact, the centrist forces hoped to recreate a "Third Force," lying somewhere between the Communists and the extreme right and consisting of Socialists, Radicals, MRP members, some of the independents who had opposed de Gaulle, the Independent Republicans who had been allied to the Gaullists, and many wavering Gaullists. This became apparent when the centrist candidate, Poher, declared that he would not dissolve the Gaullist-dominated National Assembly if he were elected. How would he govern and what kind of government would he be able to fashion? Obviously, one that would have the support of the Gaullist majority that he hoped first to entice and then to disrupt.

But now the left split. The old Socialist party, caught in the crossfire, had no program and no leadership. It had already gone through a number of internal dissensions, and had re-

jected the previous cooperation among all left-wing forces and an alliance between them and the Communist party. What emerged was the "new" Socialist party—which many said was not socialist, not a party, and not at all new! By rejecting all cooperative arrangements with the left it was definitely moving to the center, and some of its leaders favored the outright endorsement of Poher. In a rather confused and confusing party congress, the mayor of Marseilles, Gaston Defferre, was nominated as a presidential candidate. But many departmental delegations refused to support him while still others moved virtually out of the party. Defferre quickly decided to boost his candidacy by co-opting Pierre Mendès-France, whom he designated as his prime minister-to-be. The two of them made a number of joint appearances, attracting little attention, except when Mendès-France, alone, confronted some of the Gaullist leaders, displaying his verve and wit in fighting, as so often in the past, for a lost cause. Aside from the novelty of presenting a candidate for the presidency and one for the premiership—a questionable constitutional practice—and of promising, if elected, to dissolve the National Assembly and call for a new election, the Socialist candidate had little to offer.

The Communists, when their negotiations with the Socialists and other left-wing groups failed to produce a single candidate of the left, nominated their own man, Jacques Duclos—one of the hard-line Stalinists of the party, but one whose rotund figure and southern accent provided a front of *bonhomie* calculated to please and reassure. Duclos never mentioned the word *communism;* he derided his opponents to his left—and there were two of them—for their utopian commitment to socialism and/or revolution. He campaigned for freedom, representative democracy, the unity of the democratic and working-class forces, and for the establishment of what he called "advanced democracy." He promised to maintain "French independence" and favored good relations with all foreign countries, including the United States.

There were three other candidates, but they were given no chance of gaining more than 2 or 3% of the vote each. The Left-wing Socialist Rocard argued for a socialist commonwealth on behalf of the intensely ideological splinter of the Socialist party—the PSU. But he was beginning to embarrass the Communists, who wanted to avoid doctrinal and ideological pronouncements and arguments. The other leftist, the champion and spokesman of the May–June Events, Krivine, was even more of a headache for the Communists. He argued for revolution, the destruction of capitalist society, the elimination of the establishment and of all bourgeois liberal values and practices. "If you vote for me it will be the last time you vote," epitomized his utter contempt for liberal democracy. Rounding the list was a moderate, Ducatel, a former member of the Municipal Council of Paris, totally unknown to the public and totally ineffective. He argued in favor of housing construction and many pointed out that he was simply using the occasion to advertise his business and engineering interests.

What did the major candidates stand for? (See Table 5-7) Pompidou presented himself as

TABLE 5-7. *The Platforms of the Major Presidential Candidates, 1969*

	Pompidou	*Poher*	*Defferre*	*Duclos*
INSTITUTIONS	Presidential government	Qualified presidential government	Reforms of constitution	Parliamentarianism amounting to return to 4th Republic
	Dialogue with Parliament	Greater powers to Parliament & cabinet & prime minister	Five-year president	
	Greater initiative to Parliament	No referendums	Automatic dissolution of National Assembly	
		No blocked vote	Greater power to prime minister and Parliament	
ECONOMIC & SOCIAL POLICY	Industrial modernization	Welfare	Planned economy	Advanced democracy
		Housing	Participation in decisions of trade unions	Nationalizations
	Modernization of agriculture and commerce	Continuation of planning		Investments in social sector
			Investment bank	
	State investment for social changes and regional development		Broader welfare measures	Higher wages and welfare benefits
			Modernization	
FOREIGN POLICY	Against NATO but for Atlantic alliance	European integration	European integration	Against European integration
	For embargo on arms to Israel	Against *force de frappe*	No military alliance like NATO	Against Atlantic alliance
	Independence	Atlantic alliance	Against *force de frappe*	Good relations with all countries, including the U.S.A.
	Enlarged European community	No arms embargo on any "one country"	Against embargo of arms to Israel	
	For *force de frappe*			Against *force de frappe*

the candidate of continuity and "dialogue" (*ouverture*). He was not de Gaulle and would not govern as de Gaulle did by virtue of his historical mission and popularity. Pompidou cast himself more in the role of the political leader and the compromiser. Hence the "dialogue" with many of the centrist leaders: he promised not to use the harsh measure at the disposal of the president but also of his prime minister, for instance, to block debate and initiative in Parliament. Pompidou also promised to reconsider everything from the foreign policy in the Middle East to the *force de frappe*, from educational reform to the role of women in the society. While attracting the centrists, Pompidou was beginning to irritate some of the diehard Gaullists for whom fidelity to the departed leader had been the rule. His willingness to compromise disenchanted many of the left-wing Gaullists who began to agitate within the party in behalf of the social and economic policies—especially planning and participation—that they had advocated. All in all, Pompidou was running as a catchall candidate appealing to all groups and sections, hoping to gain from the de Gaulle mystique and his Gaullist associations while making concessions to new men, promising new channels of communications, and suggesting policy compromises.

Poher's position was far more difficult. He had really no political base, other than the disparate centrist groups. There was not time, assuming it were possible, to weld them into a whole. His only chance was to discredit Gaullism-without-de Gaulle while attracting the left. Like Pompidou, he made few explicit pronouncements. But he spoke firmly against the *force de frappe*—calculated to please the left; against the control of the media of communications by the Gaullists; against some of the police practices and the alleged existence of secret police groups in the hands of the Gaullists. He also came out strongly in favor of the Common Market, European political integration, and the Atlantic alliance to please everybody but the Gaullists and the Communists.

The Results

The only surprise in the returns of the first ballot was the spectacular strength of the Communist candidate, Jacques Duclos. With 21.52% of the votes, he did as well as the Communists had ever done under the Fifth Republic, recovering the ground they lost in 1968. His percentage together with those for the other leftists—Defferre, Rocard, and Krivine—gave to the left almost 32% of the votes—almost the same as with Mitterand in 1965 (see Table 5-5). Poher, whose popularity had been dwindling, just barely managed to come second with 23.42%, thus making it possible to stay for the runoff. The Socialists went down to ignominious defeat, barely squeezing over 5% and managing not to forfeit their electoral deposit and to cover their electoral expenses. Pompidou, with slightly over 44% of the vote, did better than de Gaulle had done in 1965, but with about 700,000 votes less; *All* his opponents put together outdistanced him on the first ballot by 6%. Could they unite against him behind Poher? The traditional families—left, center, and right (Gaullists)—seemed to be as evenly distributed as in the past, but this time there was no reason to believe that Pompidou could break through the non-Gaullist votes, especially to the left, as de Gaulle had done on the second ballot in 1965. As we noted, de Gaulle's vote in 1965 went up from the first to the second ballot, from approximately 10,828,000 votes to 13,080,000, gaining almost 2¼ million votes from one ballot to the next. The major part of these votes came from the center. It was unlikely that this would happen again, with most of the center votes likely to go to Poher. The latter, therefore, stood a good chance, if the Communists threw their support behind him. Table 5-8 indicates that, even assuming Ducatel's votes would go to Pompidou, if all the other left-wing voters and those of the Communists were to go to Poher, Pompidou was likely to lose. In fact, opinion polls before the first ballot indicated a 52–54% margin in favor of Poher for the second ballot.

What upset all calculations and gave Pompidou the victory was the decisions of the Communists to abstain. Instead of using their strength and their remarkable organization in order to dislodge the Gaullists, they now proclaimed that both Poher and Pompidou were the "candidates of reaction," "Tweedledee and Tweedledum," and instructed the Communist

TABLE 5-8. *The Presidential Election, 1969*

	First Ballot June 1			Second Ballot June 15		
Registered	28,775,876			28,747,988		
Voting	22,500,644			19,851,728		
Abstaining	6,275,232 (21.80%)			8,896,260 (30.94%)		
Invalid	289,922 (1%)			1,294,629 (4.50%)		
Votes ent.	22,210,722 (77.18%)			18,557,099 (64.55%)		

	Votes	Percentage of Vote	Percentage of Voters Registered	Votes	Percentage of Vote	Percentage of Voters Registered
Pompidou	9,763,428	43.95%	33.92%	10,686,498	57.58%	37.17%
Poher	5,202,271	23.42	18.07	7,870,601	42.41	27.37
Duclos	4,781,838	21.52	16.61	—	—	—
Defferre	1,128,049	5.07	3.92	—	—	—
Rocard	814,053	3.66	2.82	—	—	—
Ducatel	284,820	1.28	0.98	—	—	—
Krivine	236,263	1.06	0.82	—	—	—

voters to stay home. According to a survey conducted a week before the second ballot, 51% of those who had voted for Duclos planned to abstain, another 15% had not made up their minds, and only 26% said they would vote for Poher.

The issue was closed. Pompidou, although he increased his strength by only 900,000 votes (as compared to 2¼ million for de Gaulle in 1965) while Poher increased his by 2½ million, received 57.58% of the votes cast (2 million votes below de Gaulle's 1965 strength). Despite the abstentions of a majority of the Communists, Poher received a vote that fell only 2¾ million behind that of Mitterand.

Why did the Communists abstain? For over ten years the Communist party had formed and spearheaded the most relentless opposition to the Gaullist regime, to the personal power of the president, and to presidential government in general. Politically, they derived every benefit from playing this role. It helped them move out of their political ghetto; they cooperated with the Socialists and the Radicals in the legislative elections; they gave the weight of their remarkably powerful party organization in support of a single candidate of the left—François Mitterand—in the presidential election of 1965. Unable to dislodge de Gaulle, who continued to draw working-class votes, they were in 1969 in an admirable position to defeat Pompidou and bring about the inevitable opening of the system that would have given them the influence that de Gaulle had denied them. Yet they decided to abstain on the crucial runoff ballot, thus making Pompidou's victory a foregone conclusion. Was it a move that sacrificed the interests of the party to foreign policy considerations on the dubious assumption that Pompidou would follow a Gaullist foreign policy with regard to the United States, Europe, England, and NATO? Or was it rather motivated by fears that the election of the centrist candidate—Alain Poher—would be followed by the establishment of a broad if amorphous majority at the center—ranging from the Socialists to right center, which included many Gaullists, thus again isolating the Communists to the left? The fact remains that the most determined enemies of Gaullism played a crucial, perhaps the critical, role in the election of Pompidou.

The Gaullists won; the left remained disunited; the Socialists suffered a severe setback; the Communists even in abstention were strong and had proved to all the anti-Gaullist forces that no coalition of parties, no electoral arrangement could work against the Gaullists without the full support and cooperation of the Communists. The center was likely to take the lesson of the election. The Charybdis of Pompidou and the Gaullists was likely to scare them far less than the Scylla of the Communist

reality. The dominant party was likely to remain so as long as the Communists to the left allowed no alternative and permitted no alliance that they could not dictate. Their dominance upon the left underlined—perhaps explained—the dominance of the Gaullists over the electorate.

Our remarks regarding the Communist abstention notwithstanding, Pompidou's victory was impressive. Again, the electoral maps (Figs. 5-6 and 5-7) show that, though behind de Gaulle's 1965 showing in the total vote, he held onto the Gaullist positions and in places showed progress—especially in some of the less prosperous departments. What the maps do

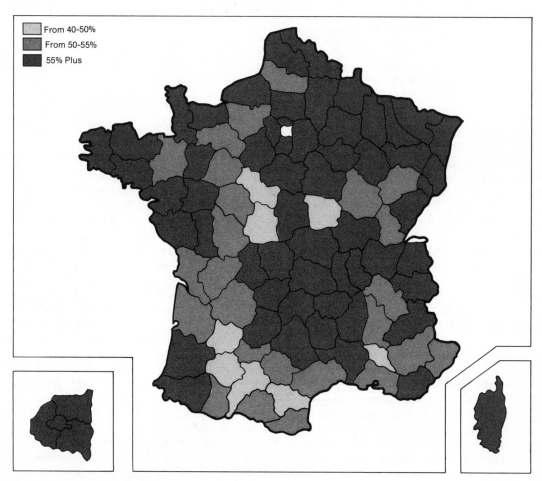

From 40-50%

From 50-55%

55% Plus

FIG. 5-7. *The presidential election of 1969, first ballot: the vote for Pompidou in percentages.*

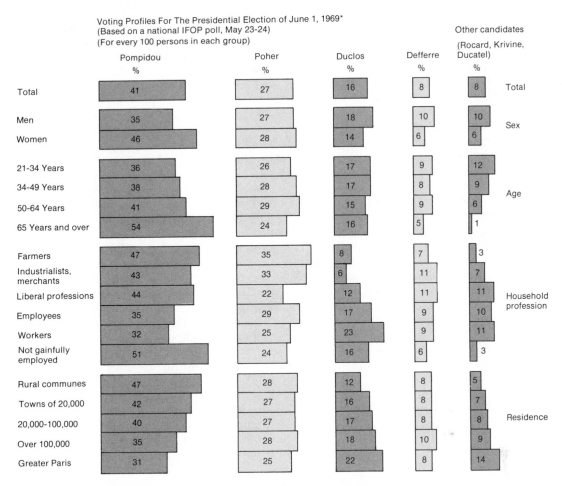

Voting Profiles For The Presidential Election of June 1, 1969*
(Based on a national IFOP poll, May 23-24)
(For every 100 persons in each group)

	Pompidou %	Poher %	Duclos %	Defferre %	Other candidates (Rocard, Krivine, Ducatel) %	
Total	41	27	16	8	8	Total
Men	35	27	18	10	10	Sex
Women	46	28	14	6	6	
21-34 Years	36	26	17	9	12	
34-49 Years	38	28	17	8	9	Age
50-64 Years	41	29	15	9	6	
65 Years and over	54	24	16	5	1	
Farmers	47	35	8	7	3	
Industrialists, merchants	43	33	6	11	7	
Liberal professions	44	22	12	11	11	Household profession
Employees	35	29	17	9	10	
Workers	32	25	23	9	11	
Not gainfully employed	51	24	16	6	3	
Rural communes	47	28	12	8	5	
Towns of 20,000	42	27	16	8	7	
20,000-100,000	40	27	17	8	8	Residence
Over 100,000	35	28	18	10	9	
Greater Paris	31	25	22	8	14	

FIG. 5-8. *Voting profiles for the presidential election of June 1, 1969. (Figures based on a national IFOP poll, May 23–24. Because the survey was conducted before the election, the data provide an approximate profile of the electorate, but do not correspond exactly to voting strength.)*

not show, however, is that he fell behind de Gaulle in the industrial areas and in the towns. Also, he improved on the Gaullist vote in the Mediterranean littoral—an obvious indication that many of the Algerian refugees who had voted against de Gaulle in 1965 now supported Pompidou. In general, the Pompidou vote looks somewhat like the vote of the traditional classic right—more votes coming from small towns, underdeveloped departments, and rural areas, and fewer from the industrialized departments and the bigger towns.

More detailed analyses of the vote (based on surveys) confirm the waning dynamism of Gaullism or (which is perhaps the same thing) its absorption by the right-wing forces and often the extreme right. A larger percentage of Pompidou's voters were old; he received 47% of the farmers' vote, 32% of the workers, 47% of those living in small communes and 42% of those in towns of less than 20,000. He got only 35% of the men's votes as against 46% of the women's. (See Fig. 5-8.)

Over and beyond electoral statistics and evaluation, the most salient feature of the elections for a new president was that it was carried out peacefully; that despite equivocations, some of which were serious of course, the major candidates seemed willing to run within the framework of the new constitution and that the candidate who ultimately won was the man whose interpretation of the functioning of the institutions and the role of the presidency was the closest to the Gaullist interpretation and practice. As Table 5-7 shows, the differences between the candidates were differences of degree, especially with regard to economic and social policies. When it came to the institutions and the interpretation of the constitution, the differences appear fairly important—even if they did not become a source of serious contention and confrontation during the election. The legitimacy of the new constitution was not directly attacked, but had the parties of the left—or even Poher—won, the modifications they intended to bring about would seriously undermine the Gaullist structure of presidentialism with a diminished Parliament. Pompidou's victory gave the Gaullist constitution a new lease on life by making the legitimization of presidential leadership more likely for the future.

THE VOTE IN THE MUNICIPALITIES AND TOWNS, 1971

A further possible indication of electoral trends can be gleaned from the municipal elections held in March 1971. They, too, are decided—with the exception of Paris, where a proportional system applies—by majority vote and a runoff if no one wins on the first ballot. They involve some 34,000 municipalities, who elect almost half a million municipal councillors, who in turn elect their mayor. The major interest of these elections is that they may have provided an answer to one critical question we raised earlier—namely, the extent to which the Gaullist "majority" had managed to organize itself in the countryside, in the small villages and smaller towns, and the extent to which the Communist party was in retreat. It is not easy to give an answer. Generally, municipal elections—particularly for small communes but also for small towns—involve considerations other than political labels, especially the electorate's

evaluation of the outgoing mayor and his municipal councillors. The number of municipal councillors and mayors reelected often is as high as 80%. Continuity is generally the rule.

Despite these difficulties, a qualified answer can be given to the questions we raised: the Gaullists did not make any significant gains. They managed to get some 49,000 municipal councillors, just a little bit over 10%, and their avowed allies, the Independent Republicans, a little bit over 5% for a total of about 16%. The left and center opposition to the Gaullists—Communists, Socialists, Radicals, PSU, and Democratic Center groups—accounted for the other 84%—but a considerable part was favorably disposed to the Gaullists. The left and all opposition groups maintained their strength, and even if we add some of the moderates claimed by the Gaullists, the conclusion is that the latter remain weak in the countryside.

More revealing, however, is the analysis of the returns of some 192 towns (excluding Paris) with more than 30,000 inhabitants (see Table 5-10). They comprise one-third of the population of France. Here, though the accent continues to be on municipal affairs and the record of the outgoing mayor, political considerations are important and political labels often account for the vote. But here again continuity was the rule. Over one hundred elections were decided on the first ballot, with the Communist party getting 37, the PSU 1, the Socialists 20, other left-wing candidates 6, center candidates 22, Independent Republicans 5, Gaullists 16, and 4 going to diverse groups. The remaining 69 towns were to be decided on the second ballot. The Communists made the most significant gains, winning 6 new towns. The total for the "opposition groups" amounted to 119 towns out of a total of 192. The traditional parties held their strength, and the Communists won in Calais, in Amiens, in Nimes, and swept the Paris suburbs. They even took some towns from the Gaullists. It was only in Paris proper that the Gaullists managed to get a clear majority of 56 out of the 90 municipal seats on the Council of Paris.

The traditional forces had held when the reorganization of the Senate was involved in the referendum of April 1969. They seem to be holding their own in the municipal elections. The Gaullists had not yet been able to dislodge the left and the center groups. Their organization had not penetrated the regions and departments of France. Even their victory in Paris was precarious, and a look at the map (Fig. 5-9) shows why: Paris looks like an island besieged by Communist, left-wing, and opposition city halls, and the routes of escape to the not-so-secure countryside are few.

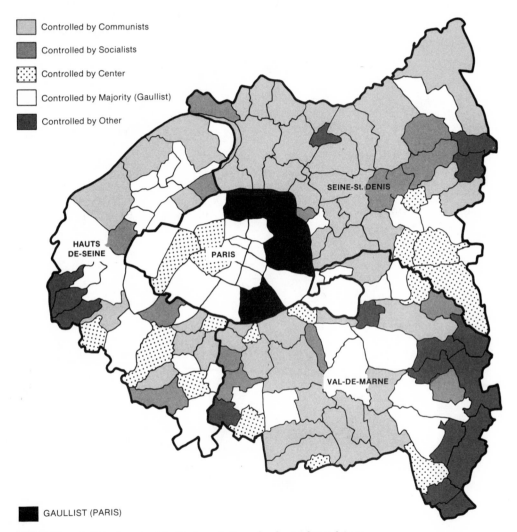

- ☐ Controlled by Communists
- ▨ Controlled by Socialists
- ▨ Controlled by Center
- ☐ Controlled by Majority (Gaullist)
- ■ Controlled by Other

■ GAULLIST (PARIS)

FIG. 5-9. *Political control in Paris and the suburbs. (Adapted from* Le Monde, *March 23, 1971.)*

TABLE 5-9. *Municipal Elections in Towns of More Than 30,000 (March 1971)*

	First Ballot					Second Ballot				Grand Total	Gains or Loss
	Incum-bents	Reelected	Won	Lost	Total	Reelected	Won	Lost	Total	Grand Total	Gains or Loss
Communist party	39	37	1	0	38	2	5	—	7	45	(+6)
Socialist party	40	20	2	—	22	16	2	4	18	40	0
Other "opposition groups"	35	13	2	3	15	14	5	5	19	34	(−1)
Gaullists	28	16	4	3	20	5	5	4	10	30	(+2)
Other "majority groups"	50	27	1	4	28	12	3	7	15	43	(−7)
Total	192	113	10	10	123	49	20	20	69	192	—

The constitution of the Fifth Republic originated with the enabling act of June 3, 1958, in which the National Assembly provided, by the requisite majority of three-fifths, that "the Constitution will be revised by the government formed on June 1, 1958"—that is, General de Gaulle's government. A small group of ministers and experts, headed by the minister of justice and later prime minister, Michel Debré, prepared the new constitution in two months. A special consultative committee, composed of thirty-nine members (two-thirds elected by Parliament and one-third nominated by General de Gaulle), endorsed the proposed new text after suggesting only minor modifications. Submitted to the people in a referendum held on September 28, 1958, it was ratified by an overwhelming majority of 79.25% of the voters.

Although the new constitution (see Fig. 6-1) was written in a short period of time under the stress and strains of the Algerian war, it institutionalized a number of revisionist ideas that had been uttered by General de Gaulle and many political leaders throughout the period of the Third and Fourth Republics. Without entering into the details of the various schemes and ideas of constitutional reform, we ought to single out two major themes that dominated the thinking of the framers: first, the reconstitution of the authority of the state under the leadership of a strong executive; and second, the establishment of what came to be known as a "rationalized" Parliament—a Parliament with limited political and legislative powers. The new constitution was to establish a "parliamentary system," but one in which Parliament was no longer in a position to dominate the executive as it did in the period of the preceding republics.

Both General de Gaulle and his close associate and later Prime Minister, the aforementioned Michel Debré, expressed clearly in a number of their pronouncements the purpose of the projected constitutional reform. The most important landmark was the speech made

Note: For a more detailed discussion of the constitution, see Roy Macridis and Bernard Brown, *The De Gaulle Republic: Quest for Unity* (Homewood, Ill.: The Dorsey Press, 1960), chap. 10 from which I have drawn, with the permission of the publisher.

SIX

the

governmental

institutions

Legislative

NATIONAL ASSEMBLY

487 members—470 from metropolitan France and 17 from overseas territories and Departments.

Mandate: five years. Elected directly by equal and universal suffrage.

Limited Legislative Powers: Legislates on civil rights, nationality, status and legal competence of persons, penal law and procedure, taxation, electoral system, organization of national defense, administration of local government units, education, employment, unions, social security, and economic programs. Authorizes declaration of war. Can initiate constitutional revision. Can delegate above powers to Cabinet—votes organic laws. Can question Cabinet one day a week. Meets in regular sessions for a total that does not exceed six months. Votes budget submitted by government. If budget is not decided with Senate within 70 days, may be issued by decree. *(All other matters fall within rule-making power.)*

SENATE

283 members

Mandate: nine years. Renewable by thirds every three years.

Elected indirectly by municipal and general councillors and members of National Assembly. Approximate size of electoral college: 110,000. Majority system, but PR for seven Departments with largest population.

Functions: Full legislative powers jointly with Assembly. Bills must be approved in identical terms by both Houses unless Prime Minister, in case of discord, asks Lower House to vote "definitive" text overruling Senate.

THE ECONOMIC AND SOCIAL COUNCIL

Elected by professional organizations. Designated by government for five years as specified by "organic law."

Composed of representatives of professional groups (approx. 195 members).

Gives "opinion" on bills referred to it by government. "Consulted" on overall government economic plans.

Executive

PRESIDENT OF THE REPUBLIC

Elected for 7-year term by direct popular election.

Personal Powers: Nominates Prime Minister; dissolves Assembly; refers bills to Constitutional Council for examination of constitutionality; calls referendum; issues decrees with force of law; nominates three of nine members to Constitutional Council; can send messages to legislature; invokes state of emergency and rule by decree; not responsible to Parliament.

PRIME MINISTER AND CABINET

Prime Minister proposes Cabinet members to President for nomination; "guides policies of nation"; directs actions of government and is responsible for national defense; presides over Cabinet meetings; proposes referendum; has law-initiating power. Prime Minister is responsible before Assembly.

Judiciary

CONSTITUTIONAL COUNCIL

Composed of nine justices and all ex-Presidents of Republic. Presidents of Republic, Senate, and Assembly appoints three justices each.

Functions: Supervises Presidential elections and declares returns. Supervises referendums and proclaims results. Examines and decides on contested legislative elections. On request of Prime Minister or Presidents of Republic, Assembly, or Senate examines and decides on constitutionality of pending bills, treaties, and legislative competence of Assembly. Examines all organic laws.

HIGH COURT OF JUSTICE

HIGH COUNCIL OF THE JUDICIARY

ORDINARY COURTS

ADMINISTRATIVE COURT [CONSEIL D'ÉTAT]

FIG. 6-1. *Major features of the constitution of the Fifth Republic.*

by General de Gaulle at Bayeux on June 16, 1946, wherein he outlined the ideas that were to serve as the foundations of the new constitution:

The rivalry of the parties takes, in our country, a fundamental character, which leaves everything in doubt and which very often wrecks its superior interests. This is an obvious fact that . . . our institutions must take into consideration in order to preserve our respect for laws, the cohesion of governments, the efficiency of the administration and the prestige and authority of the State. The difficulties of the State result in the inevitable alienation of the citizen from his institutions. . . . All that is needed then is an occasion for the appearance of the menace of dictatorship.

To avoid this menace, de Gaulle outlined the following institutional arrangements:

1. The legislature, executive, and judiciary must be clearly separated and balanced.

2. Over and above political contingencies there must be a national "mediation" [*arbitrage*].

3. The voting of the laws and the budget belongs to a National Assembly elected by direct and universal suffrage.

4. A second assembly, elected in a different manner, is needed to examine carefully the decisions taken by the first, to suggest amendments and propose bills.

5. The executive power should not emanate from the Parliament. Otherwise the cohesion and authority of the government would suffer, the balance between the two powers vitiated, and the members of the executive would be merely agents of the political parties.

6. A president of the republic [*Chef d'État*], embodying the executive power above political parties, should be elected by a College, which includes the Parliament but is much broader than Parliament . . . to direct the work and the policy of the government; promulgate the laws and issue decrees; preside over the meetings of the Council of Ministers; serve as mediator above the political contingencies; invite the country to express its sovereign decisions in an election; be the custodian of national independence and the treaties made by France, and appoint a prime minister in accord with the political orientation of Parliament and the national interest.[1]

Debré himself pointed out that the object of constitutional reform was to "reconstruct state power."[2] He advocated a rationalized Parliament that involved shorter sessions, a division between legislation and rule making, the right of the executive to legislate by decree, and reorganization of the legislative and the budgetary procedure in a manner to give the government a controlling position. Certain rules that normally were part of the standing orders of the Parliament were also put into the constitution: the personal vote of the deputies, the length of time for which the presidents of the National Assembly and the Senate were elected, the preparation of the order of business of the National Assembly, and so on. But why all these detailed provisions? Debré's answer underlined the perennial dilemma of the French body politic. He insisted that all these provisions were necessary because there was no majority in France and because multipartism made effective government impossible:

Ah! if only we had the possibility of seeing tomorrow a constant and clear majority, it would not have been necessary to establish an Upper Chamber whose role it is to support the government against an Assembly which attempts, because it is so divided, to invade its sphere of action. . . . There would be no attempt to establish order and stability by cutting the ties that united the parties with the government.[3]

Thus, the crucial task was to create a strong and stable government to succeed a parliamentary system that could not produce stable majorities.

The new constitution, however, respects the French republican tradition. The preamble solemnly affirms the attachment of the French

[1] The entire text of the Bayeux speech is in de Gaulle, *Discours et Messages* (Paris, 1946) pp. 721–27.
[2] Michel Debré, *La Novelle Constitution* (Tours, 1958).
[3] Ibid.

people to the Declaration of the Rights of Man of 1789 and to individual and social rights that were affirmed, after France's Liberation, by the constitution of 1946. Article 1 proclaims that "France is a Republic, indivisible, secular, democratic, and social." It insures the rights of all citizens and respect for all beliefs. Article 2 affirms that "all sovereignty stems from the people." But this sovereignty is not to be exercised solely through the representatives of the people but also through referendums. Respect for the freedom of the political parties is reiterated in article 4, where, however, it is stated that the parties "must respect the principles of national sovereignty and democracy"—a provision that many thought was aimed at the powerful Communist party.

The constitution establishes the familiar organs of a parliamentary system: a bicameral legislature; a politically irresponsible chief of state; a cabinet and a prime minister in charge of the direction of the policies of the government and responsible to the lower chamber (the National Assembly); the right of the lower chamber to censure and overthrow the prime minister and the cabinet. But, in contrast to the Fourth Republic, it delegates broad powers to the chief of state (the president) and places serious limitations on the legislature. There is a new principle—that of the incompatibility between a parliamentary seat and a ministerial portfolio, requiring a member of Parliament who becomes a minister to be replaced by the "substitute" who runs on the same ticket at the legislative election. The constitution reproduces many time-hallowed provisions of a democratic government—tenure of judges, immunity of parliamentarians from arrest and prosecution without prior permission of the chamber to which they belong, freedom of speech and press, freedom of association, protection against the arbitrary detention of an individual. Finally, a long section (section 12) organized the relations between France and former colonies that had become semi-independent republics. They were all grouped into the "French Community," a loosely federated organization in which important powers were lodged in the hands of the president of the community, who is also the president of the French republic. This struc-

ture was abandoned after 1960 in favor of complete independence for all the former colonies. The only ties that bind them to France are individual treaties and agreements that can be renegotiated or revoked in the future. The real novelty of the constitution lies, then, in the establishment of a strong executive and a limited Parliament.

THE PRESIDENT
OF THE REPUBLIC

In 1958, the framers wished to give to the president the prestige and prerogatives that would enable him to provide for the continuity of the state, to cement the bonds between France and the former colonies of the French Union, and to supervise the functioning of the constitution. The president is the "keystone of the arch" of the new republic—he is both the symbol and the instrument of reinforced executive authority. To accomplish this, the framers modified the manner in which he is elected and strengthened his powers.

The president was at first elected by an electoral college, which, in addition to the members of the Parliament, included the municipal councillors, the general councillors, and the members of the assemblies and the municipalities of the overseas territories and republics. It was a restricted electoral college favoring rural municipalities and small towns and discriminating against the large urban centers. As a result, it was widely criticized at the time it was introduced by many political leaders and constitutional lawyers who saw in it the perpetuation of the old political forces of the Fourth Republic.

In the middle of September 1962 and again early in October, President de Gaulle proposed to modify the manner in which the election of the president was to take place. He suggested that after the end of his own first term (early in 1966), or in the event of his death in office, the president be elected by direct popular vote. In a message to Parliament on October 2, 1962, he put the matter very succinctly: "When my seven years term is completed or if something happens that makes it impossible for me to continue my functions, I am convinced that a popular vote will be necessary in order to give . . . to those who will succeed me the possibility and the duty to assume the supreme task." On October 28, 1962, in a referendum the people endorsed, as we have seen, de Gaulle's proposal. The heart of the proposal is that the runoff election is limited to two candidates, thus forcing the parties to combine for or against the two and enabling the people to make a clearcut choice.

The constitution of the Fifth Republic maintains the political irresponsibility of the president but at the same time gives him personal powers that he can exercise solely at his discretion:

1. The president designates the prime minister. Although the president presumably makes the designation with an eye to the relative strengths of the various parties in the National Assembly, it is a personal political act.

2. The president can dissolve the National Assembly at any time, on any issue, and for any reason solely at his discretion. There is only one limitation—he cannot dissolve it twice within the same year; and one formality—he must "consult" with the prime minister and the presidents of the two legislative assemblies.

3. When the institutions of the republic, the independence of the nation, the integrity of its territory, or the execution of international engagements are menaced in a grave and immediate manner and the regular functioning of the public powers is interrupted, the president may take whatever measures are required by the circumstances (article 16). Again, this is a personal and discretionary act. The president needs only to inform the nation by a message and to "consult" the Constitutional Council. The National Assembly, however, convenes automatically and cannot be dissolved during the emergency period.

4. Finally, the president can bring certain issues before the people in a referendum:

The President of the Republic on the proposal of the government . . . or on joint resolution by the two legislative assemblies . . . *may* submit to a referendum any bill dealing with the organization of the public powers, the approval of an agreement of the Community or the authorization to ratify a treaty, that without being contrary to the Constitution would affect the functioning of existing institutions. [Article 11—emphasis added]

The calling of a referendum is, however, a personal act of the president of the republic. He may elicit or refuse it depending on the circumstances. Constitutional provisions to the contrary notwithstanding, the president claimed in October 1962, that this article empowered him to submit directly to the people amendments to the constitution.

The constitution also vests explicitly in the president other powers that he can exercise at his discretion. He has the nominating power for all civil and military posts, and, unless otherwise provided by an organic law (a law passed by absolute majority of the legislative branches), he signs all decrees and ordinances prepared by the Council of Ministers. He can raise questions of unconstitutionality on a bill or on a law before a new special constitutional court—the Constitutional Council.

The president continues to enjoy the prerogatives that were vested in the office in the past. He presides over the meetings of the Council of Ministers, receives ambassadors, and sends messages to Parliament. He may ask for the reexamination of a bill or some of its articles, which cannot be refused; he promulgates laws within fifteen days after their enactment; he negotiates and ratifies treaties and is kept informed of all negotiations leading to the conclusion of international agreements; and he is commander in chief of the armed services and presides over the Committee of National Defense.

Special Presidential Powers

To strengthen his position, President de Gaulle made full use of the special powers provided by the constitution. Immediately after the uprising of the Algerian settlers in January 1960, the prime minister and his cabinet asked and received from the French Parliament broad powers to legislate by decree under the signature of President de Gaulle for a period of one year. Thus, the executive assumed full legislative powers, on condition that all measures taken in the course of the year were to be submitted for ratification to Parliament by April 1, 1961, and with the proviso that while the exceptional powers were in force Parliament could not be dissolved.

Hardly has this special delegation of legislative powers come to an end when a new and even broader assumption of powers, this time by the president of the republic alone, came into force, under article 16 of the constitution.[4] Following the military putsch in Algeria on April 22, 1961, President de Gaulle declared: "Beginning today I shall take directly . . . the measures that appear to me necessary by the circumstances." A prolonged state of emergency was declared; a number of persons were arrested or held at their homes without court order; many organizations were dissolved and several publications were forbidden. A number of officers who participated or were associated with the military putsch were expelled from the army, and special military tribunals were formed to try them and their presumed accomplices, whether military or civilian. Finally, the president of the republic was allowed to remove civil servants and judges in Algeria from office.

---

[4] Article 16 provides: "When the institutions of the Republic, the independence of the nation, the integrity of its territory or the fulfillment of its international commitments are threatened in a grave and immediate manner and when the regular functioning of the constitutional governmental authorities is interrupted, the President of the Republic shall take the measures commanded by these circumstances, after official consultation with the Premier, the Presidents of the assemblies and the Constitutional Council.

"He shall inform the nation of those measures in a message.

"These measures must be prompted by the desire to ensure to the constitutional governmental authorities, in the shortest possible time, the means of fulfilling their assigned functions. The Constitutional Council shall be consulted with regard to such measures.

"Parliament shall meet by right."

The powers of the president came to an end on September 30, 1961, by virtue of a special presidential declaration, but the application of some of the decisions continued until the summer of 1962. Again by virtue of the referendum of April 8, 1962, the president enjoyed, until Algeria emerged as an independent "political organization," full legislative powers to deal with any matter that related to the Evian accords (the agreements leading to Algerian independence).

In his second term of office, which began in January 1966, de Gaulle decided, without consulting the legislative organs, and perhaps without the full knowledge of his cabinet, to ask for the withdrawal of the United States forces from France, in effect withdrawing France from NATO. Again he demanded, through his prime minister, in the spring of 1967, for delegation of broad legislative powers to deal with certain economic and social matters—particularly social security—to enable him and his cabinet to legislate for a period of six months on a subject matter reserved to Parliament. In his various trips abroad, he forcefully advocated his own foreign policy, invariably catching many of his ministers—and perhaps, when he advocated the "liberation" and "independence" of Quebec in the summer of 1967, even his own foreign minister—by surprise.

The President as Mediator (*Arbitre*)

The constitution explicitly charges the president with guaranteeing the functioning of the institutions of the government:

The President of the Republic shall see that the Constitution is respected. He shall ensure, by his arbitration, the regular functioning of the governmental authorities, as well as the continuance of the State.

He shall be the guarantor of national independence, of the integrity of the territory, and of respect for Community agreements and treaties. [Article 5]

Mediation is a personal act involving the exercise of judgment. As a result, the president is given an implicit veto power on almost every conceivable aspect of policy. Thus, the list of presidential prerogatives is a very impressive one. In matters of war, foreign policy, the preservation of internal peace, and the functioning of governmental institutions, his powers are overriding. He is deeply involved in politics and can no longer be considered as an "irresponsible head of the state" like the British crown.

Speaking one week after his election in 1958, de Gaulle reaffirmed his conception of the office and his own personal role: "The national task that I have assumed for the past eighteen years is confirmed. Guide of France and chief of the republican state, I exercise supreme power to the full extent allowed and in accord with the new spirit to which I owe it." This view of the office stems directly from French monarchical traditions. De Gaulle claimed to be the custodian of a national unity that has been forged through some thousand years of history — a unity that is "real" and therefore assumed by him to be perceived by every French man and woman, despite the vicissitudes and squabbles of the republican regimes. He was "invested" by history and was responsible to the people only in a vague fashion. He stood above the everyday party conflicts and quarrels, intervening in order to lead and to "arbitrate."

De Gaulle divided the task of government into two not very clearly distinguished categories. The first, *la Politique* (loosely, "statecraft"), concerns France's position in the world and thus involves matters of defense, foreign policy, and relations with the former colonies. In this area, de Gaulle alone apparently initiated policy and made decisions.

The second category of responsibility consists of economic and social matters—the means for the realization of overall national objectives. Problems in this area may be delegated at the discretion of the president to "subordinate" organs—the prime minister or the cabinet and Parliament. It is for them to make appropriate decisions, subject, of course, in the case of conflicts among ministers or between the cabinet and Parliament, to the president's "arbitration."

On three important occasions, President de Gaulle interpreted the constitution in a way to limit the power of Parliament, and in each case his decision was accepted. In the first instance, an absolute majority of the deputies (as the constitution prescribes) demanded the convocation of an extraordinary parliamentary session. It was generally assumed that such a convocation, once the existence of a majority had been ascertained, was automatic. The president, however, claimed that it was only up to him to decide whether it was opportune or not to convene Parliament. In this case, he refused to convene it.

On the second occasion, the constitutional question was more complex. In the summer of 1961, article 16, empowering the president to take whatever measures he deemed necessary, was in force, which meant that Parliament was also in session and could not be dissolved. Parliament had adjourned for the summer vacation, but remained technically in session. Given the unrest among the farmers because of falling farm prices, the parliamentarians decided to convene and consider appropriate legislation. Since they were still in session, it was up to the presidents of the two chambers to convene them. Yet President de Gaulle was opposed to this, arguing that the agricultural problems were totally unrelated to the exercise of his powers under article 16. He could not, in a strict sense, oppose the convening of the Parliament, but he announced that he would not permit Parliament to pass any legislative measures.

In the third instance, as we have seen, de Gaulle decided to submit directly to the people, on October 28, 1962, a bill modifying the constitutional provision for the election of the president of the republic. The overwhelming opinion of the jurists is that a specific bill to be proposed to the people for a constitutional amendment must be submitted to and voted by the two legislative assemblies.

The President as a "Guide"

Gradually, from a conception of "mediator," de Gaulle vested the presidency with broad leadership functions. He now claimed to be "the guide." De Gaulle described in a nutshell the new conception of the office when he stated in 1964 that "the President elected by the nation is the source and holder of the power of the state"—the only man to "hold and to delegate the authority of the state." This ultimately means that, according to de Gaulle—and his successor, Georges Pompidou, who seems to share his "broad construction"—the president can concentrate in his hands the powers of the state. The office of the presidency has become the center of policy making—not only in foreign affairs, something that is taken for granted, but also in domestic issues. Specialized bureaus and offices virtually "second" the ministries. Policy alternatives are thrashed out there, and the minister, or even the prime minister, may be totally unaware of what is happening at the *Elysée,* the French White House. There are a number of presidential policy advisers. The president's staff has the following functions: (*a*) to maintain close liaison with the cabinet ministers and the civil service; (*b*) to prepare drafts embodying policy suggestions; (*c*) to take over from the cabinet and a given ministry the deliberation and the drafting of policy suggestions on matters that come technically under ministerial jurisdiction; (*d*) to prepare on its own, or more likely at the specific request of the president, policy suggestions based on detailed studies; and finally (*e*) to provide the president with information whenever he so requests. In contrast to the past, the presidential staff consists primarily of career civil servants who have been appointed on the basis of competence.

The system has become presidential. The president has emerged as the key policy-making organ, while the prime minister and his cabinet, which are responsible to Parliament and, according to article 20 of the constitution, are in charge of determining and directing the policy of the nation, are bypassed. Even the highly contested notion of "reserved" powers has been abandoned in favor of the thesis that all powers stem from an elected president, who can choose to delegate them or not.

The constitutional power of the president,

under the interpretation given by de Gaulle, is vast. But the political role of the president is just as great. In the legislative elections of both 1962 and 1967, de Gaulle appealed to the people to vote for his supporters. Pompidou is very likely to play the same role—the leader of the Gaullist party. Hence, docility of the Gaullist deputies toward the president and his immediate associates stems directly from the realization that they owe their election directly to him, and that disobedience will be severely punished by the collective threat of dissolution of Parliament—far more potent now in France than it has been in England since the turn of the century—or by withdrawal of support in a future election. In the last analysis, it is political rather than constitutional considerations that count. The overwhelming trait of the Fifth Republic is not the powers the constitution gives to the president, but his popularity. As Fig. 6-2 shows, with the exception of 1963 (and the presidential election of 1965) de Gaulle's popularity never dropped below 50% at any time. Pompidou's popularity since he succeeded de Gaulle as president has been also consistently above the 50% mark.

Because a sense of unity is one of the first requirements of a strong nation, de Gaulle was anxious to impart his view of France's historical mission to the people (which was also one of his prime concerns right after the Liberation). He sought to renew his contact with the people, by frequent tours through the country, in order to create a common national purpose. Thus, General de Gaulle gave to the Fifth Republic a strong personal orientation. He controlled and shaped French foreign policy, with the aid of his foreign minister. He was responsible for all decisions concerning colonial policy, and the sole spokesman for the settlement of the war in Algeria. He was the architect of the new organization for defense and the modernization of the armed forces. The office of the presidency is thus no longer a mere symbol; it has become the seat of political power in France. Pompidou has followed the same general pattern with trips to the provinces and abroad, most notably with trips to the former African colonies in an

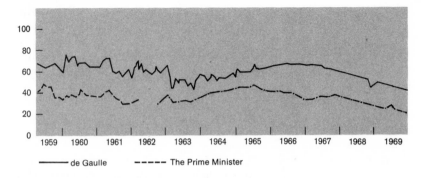

FIG. 6-2. *The popularity of de Gaulle and his prime ministers (percentage of those who declared themselves satisfied).*

effort to maintain France's cultural, political, economic, and strategic presence there.

THE CABINET

In the language of the constitution, the cabinet, composed of the prime minister and his ministers, "determines and conducts the policy of the nation" and is "responsible before the Parliament." Special recognition is accorded to the prime minister. He "directs" the action of the government and is "responsible" for national defense. He "assures the execution of the laws and exercises the rule-making power" —but on condition that all decrees and ordinances are signed by the president of the republic (articles 20 and 21). He determines the composition of his cabinet, presides over its meetings, and directs the administrative services. He defends his policy before the Parliament, answers questions addressed to him by the members of Parliament, states the overall program of the government in special declarations, and puts the question of confidence before the National Assembly. Thus, the constitution establishes a parliamentary government side-by-side with a strong presidency.

The functions of the cabinet became drastically modified under de Gaulle. To begin with, it is no longer composed of parliamen-

tarians who simply resign their electoral mandate—as the constitution requires—in order to assume a cabinet post. Since 1958, more than one-third of the cabinet members have been civil servants, technicians, professors or intellectuals who have never been in Parliament and who never had any desire to do so. The most significant areas of *la Politique* were entrusted to technicians who were presumably able to implement the policies of the president of the republic. Both they and the parliamentarians who renounce their parliamentary mandate are therefore presumed to be independent of immediate political and electoral considerations— only, however, to become increasingly dependent upon the president, to whom they owe their ministerial positions. Under Pompidou this trend appears to have been reversed. Having promised a continuing dialogue with the Parliament, the new president took almost all his cabinet members from the Parliament and included in it a number of non-Gaullists.

While de Gaulle was president, there were only three prime ministers over the period of nine years: Michel Debré (1959–62), Georges Pompidou, (1962–68), and Maurice Couve de Murville (1968–69). When Pompidou took office in June 1969, he designated the fourth prime minister of the Fifth Republic—Chaban-Delmas, who has held office ever since. The cabinet has shown, therefore, a great stability.

Although there have been numerous cabinet reshufflings, most of them have been minor, and on only three occasions have there been important cabinet reorganizations. The major posts—foreign affairs, army, and interior—have been in the hands of the same minister over a long period of time. The Minister of Foreign Affairs held office for almost ten years before he became prime minister, while the Ministries of the Interior and Army were each headed by the same minister for over six years. In contrast, the Ministry of Information and Education and, to a lesser extent, the Ministry of Finance have had a higher rate of turnover. The number who constitute what we may call the "ministerial roster"—the *ministrables* of the Fifth Republic—has been relatively small: about seventy-five persons became ministers, but only some twenty held key ministerial positions, over five years or more. This is a remarkable stability that compares favorably, if not more so, with the stability of the British or American cabinet posts.

The political composition of the cabinet has progressively reflected the strength of the Gaullists in the National Assembly. With the exception of the first Debré cabinet, which was a coalition one, and the first short-lived cabinet under Pompidou in the spring of 1962, all have been controlled by the Gaullists. The presence of a few Independents or Centrists today indicates the efforts made by the Gaullists to co-opt new notables. The ministerial jobs offered to their closest allies, the Independent Republicans, are the only political debt they have to pay. For the first time, France has a cabinet and a president that are in tune with a legislative majority. This enhances executive leadership and stability more than all the constitutional provisions put together.

The meetings of the Council of Ministers under the president are frequent and prolonged. Reports prepared by the ministers or their aides are debated, but generally the discussion revolves around the suggestions and directives of the president. In contrast, the cabinet meetings under the prime minister are becoming rare. Instead, several small interministerial committees have been set up to implement the decisions reached in the Council of Ministers by the president. The cabinet has become a mere instrument for the execution of policy and in some matters—especially defense and foreign policy—is, as we have noted, simply bypassed.

THE LEGISLATURE

The Parliament of the Fifth Republic is, as in previous republics, bicameral, consisting of a National Assembly and a Senate—the lower and upper chambers, respectively. The National Assembly, elected for five years by universal suffrage, is now composed of 487 deputies. The Senate, elected for nine years, is composed of 283 members (264 from metropolitan France, 13 from the overseas departments and territories, and six from among the French citizenry living abroad). The Senate is elected indirectly by the municipal councillors, the department councillors, and the members of the National Assembly. One-third of its membership is renewed every three years.

The two chambers have equal powers except in three extremely important respects. First, the traditional prerogative of the lower chamber to examine the budget first is maintained, and the Senate cannot introduce a motion of censure. Second, the cabinet is responsible only before the National Assembly. Article 45 specifies that every bill "is examined successively in the two assemblies with a view to the adoption of an identical text." But if there is continuing disagreement on the text of a bill after two readings by each assembly, the prime minister can convene a joint conference committee, consisting of an equal number of members of the two chambers, and ask it to propose a compromise text, which is then submitted by the government for the approval of the two assemblies. In case of a persistent discord between the two assemblies, the prime minister may (but does not always) ask the National Assembly to rule "definitively." If the government and the Senate are in accord, the senatorial veto is ironclad. The Senate can be overruled only if there is an agreement between the government and the National Assembly, something which has been the rule ever since 1962, as we shall see.

A "Rationalized" Parliament

The new constitution establishes a "rationalized" Parliament—a Parliament whose powers are limited in the following ways:

1. Only two sessions of the two assemblies are allowed—the first begins October 2 and lasts for eighty days, and the second on April 2, and cannot last more than ninety days—a maximum of five months and twenty days. Extraordinary sessions may take place at the request of the prime minister or of a majority of the members of the National Assembly "on a specific agenda." They are convened and closed by a decree of the president of the republic, who, it appears now, seems also to have the last word on whether to convene an extraordinary session or not, despite the terms of the constitution.

2. The Parliament can legislate only on matters defined in the Constitution. The government (i.e., members of the cabinet) can legislate on all other matters by simple decree.

3. The government now fixes the order of business.

4. The president of the National Assembly is elected for the whole legislative term, thus avoiding the annual elections that in the past placed him at the mercy of the various parliamentary groups. The Senate elects its president every three years.

5. The Parliament is no longer free to establish its own standing orders. Such orders must be found to be in accord with the constitution by the Constitutional Council before they become effective.

6. The number of parliamentary committees is reduced (only six are allowed), and their functions are carefully circumscribed.

7. The government bill, not the committees' amendments and counterproposals as under the Fourth Republic, come before the floor.

8. The government has the right to reject all amendments and to demand a single vote on its own text with only those amendments that it accepts—a procedure known as the "blocked" vote.

All these provisions are directed against "assembly government." By putting rules into the constitution that are essentially of a procedural character, the framers hoped to limit Parliament to the performance of its proper function of deliberation and to protect the executive from legislative encroachments. Many of the new rules reflect a genuine desire to correct some of the more flagrant abuses of the past and are consistent with the strengthening of the executives in modern democracies. Others, however, are designed to weaken Parliament beyond this level.

Relations between Parliament and the Government

Four major provisions in the constitution determine the nature of the relations between Parliament and the government. They concern (1) the incompatibility between a parliamentary mandate and a cabinet post; (2) the manner in which the responsibility of the cabinet before the Parliament comes into play; (3) the distinction between "legislation" and "rule making"; and (4) the introduction of the "executive budget."

THE RULE OF INCOMPATIBILITY. Article 23 of the constitution is explicit:

The "office" of a member of government is incompatible with the exercise of any parliamentary mandate.

Thus, a member of Parliament who joins the cabinet must resign his seat for the balance of the legislative term. He is replaced in Parliament by his substitute (*suppléant*)—the person whose name appeared together with his on the electoral ballot. Despite the rule of incompatibility, however, cabinet members are allowed to sit in Parliament and defend their measures. They are not allowed, of course, to vote.

The purpose of the rule was to introduce a genuine separation of powers and to discourage parliamentarians from trying to become ministers, which was one of the major causes for the high rate of cabinet turnovers under the Fourth Republic. It was also the intention of the framers to establish a government that would be better able to resist pressures emanating from parliamentary groups and thus be in a position to give its undivided attention to its duties.

RESPONSIBILITY OF THE CABINET BEFORE THE LEGISLATURE. The responsibility of the cabinet to the legislature comes into play in a specific and limited manner. After the prime minister has been nominated by the president of the republic, he presents his program before the National Assembly and, through a minister, before the Senate. If this program is accepted by the National Assembly, the cabinet is "invested"; if defeated, the prime minister must submit his resignation to the president of the republic.

The Parliament can bring down the cabinet in the following manner: The National Assembly (but not the Senate) has the right to introduce a motion of censure, which must be signed by one-tenth of its members. The vote on the motion is lost unless it receives an absolute majority of the members composing the National Assembly. In other words, blank ballots and abstentions count for the government. If the motion is carried, the government must resign; if the motion is lost, then its signatories cannot enter another one in the course of the same legislative session.

The prime minister may also, after consultation with the cabinet, stake the life of his government on any general issue of policy or on any given legislative bill. Although the constitution does not use the term, this is equivalent to putting the "question of confidence." A declaration of general policy is presumed to be accepted unless there is a motion of censure voted under the conditions mentioned previously. A specific bill on which the prime minister puts the question of confidence becomes law unless a motion of censure is introduced and voted according to the same conditions, but with one difference: the same signatories may introduce a motion of censure as many times as the prime minister stakes his government's responsibility. If the motion is carried by an absolute majority, the bill does not become law and the government must resign. If, however, the motion of censure is lost, the bill automatically becomes law and the government stays in office; thus, bills may become laws even if there is no majority for them.

"LAW" AND "RULE MAKING." The constitution provides that "law is voted by Parliament." Members of Parliament and of the government can introduce bills and amendments. The scope of Parliament's law-making ability, however, is limited. It is defined in the constitution (article 34) to include

. . . the regulations concerning:
civil rights and the fundamental guarantees granted to the citizens for the exercise of their public liberties; . . .

nationality, status and legal capacity of persons, marriage contracts, inheritance and gifts;

determination of crimes and misdemeanors as well as the penalties imposed therefor; criminal procedure; . . .

the basis, the rate and the methods of collecting taxes of all types; the issuance of currency; . . .

the electoral system of the Parliamentary assemblies and the local assemblies; . . .

the nationalization of enterprises and the transfer of the property of enterprises from the public to the private sector; . . .

[and the] fundamental principles of:

the general organization of national defense;

the free administration of local communities, the extent of their jurisdiction and their resources;

education;

property rights, civil and commercial obligations;

legislation pertaining to employment, unions and social security.

This enumeration of legislative power cannot be enlarged except by an organic law (a law passed by an absolute majority of the members of both houses). Article 37 makes this point clear: "All other matters," it states, "than those which are in the domain of law fall within the rule-making sphere." It goes even further: "Legislative texts pertaining to such matters may be modified by decree." Thus, laws made under the Fourth Republic dealing with matters that are declared by the new constitution to be beyond the powers of the legislature can be modified by simple decree. They are "de-legalized."

The constitution also allows Parliament to delegate law-making power to the executive: "The government may for the execution of its program ask Parliament to authorize it to take by ordinances, within a limited period of time, measures which are normally reserved to the domain of law" (article 38). Such ordinances come into force as soon as they are promulgated, but they are null and void if a bill for their ratification is not submitted by the government before Parliament within a prescribed time, or if the ratification of the bill is rejected.

THE BUDGET. The constitution establishes the "executive budget." The budget is submitted by the government to Parliament. Proposals stemming from members of Parliament "are not receivable if their adoption entails either a diminution of public resources or an increase in public expenditures" (article 47). No bill entailing diminution of resources or additional expenditures is receivable at any time. If "Parliament has not decided within seventy days" after the introduction of the budget, then "the budget bill can be promulgated and put into effect by simple ordinance"

(article 47). Thus, the government may be able to bypass Parliament in case the latter has failed to reach an agreement.

THE LEGISLATIVE COMMITTEES. Until the new constitution, the legislative committees of the legislature resembled those of the committees of the American Congress—they were numerous and powerful. They could decide the fate of virtually any bill by amending it, pigeonholing it, or failing to report it. Only the amended text of a bill could come from the committee to the floor of the legislative assembly. The situation has been drastically altered. Only six committees are allowed: foreign affairs; finance; national defense; constitutional laws, legislation, and general administration; production and trade; and cultural, social, and family affairs. Their composition ranges from 60 to 120 members, nominated to represent proportionately the political parties. They receive the bills, examine them, hear the minister provide for amendments—but the government has the last word on bringing the bills before the floor and on accepting or rejecting the amendments made. Thus, legislative work has been expedited and improved in many respects, while the government no longer remains at the mercy of committees that were often inspired by parochial interests, and even more usually by political considerations. The fact that a Gaullist majority exists in each and every committee further streamlines their work under party discipline.

THE GOVERNMENT AND THE NATIONAL ASSEMBLY

Relations between the cabinet and the National Assembly have varied depending upon the strength of the opposition. The first prime minister under the Fifth Republic, Michel Debré, after being endorsed by an overwhelming vote of 453 to 56, faced six motions of censure, most of them directed against the policy of the president of the republic. As his opposition grew to as many as 210 votes out of an absolute majority of 277, he resorted increasingly to the instruments of control that the constitution made available to him: he used the procedure of the blocked vote; put the question of confidence; refused debates; invoked the limitation of the legislative functions of the National Assembly. The continuation of the war in Algeria and the widespread popularity of General de Gaulle made an open revolt against him impossible, especially when the president could retaliate with dissolution. With the settlement of the Algerian crisis in April 1962, Debré urged the president to dissolve and call for an election at the very height of his popularity, believing that there would be a Gaullist sweep. But disagreements between Debré and de Gaulle apparently crept in with regard to the attribution of their respective functions and roles. The prime minister believed that a cabinet supported by a majority should assume the major responsibilities for policy making, leaving to the president a discretion limited only to the specific constitutional provisions, some of which were to be exercised only upon the advice of the prime minister. With a majority, a French cabinet system could emerge similar to the British one. All that was needed was an election. He also wished to introduce a majority electoral system similar to the British and American one. Such a system, he believed, would discriminate against the Communists in the election, and provide for a Gaullist majority.

All of Debré's arguments were contrary, as we have seen, to the conception of the presidency held by de Gaulle. For him, the executive power is the president. The prime minister and the cabinet are his subordinate organs, while the Parliament remains a deliberative forum. To have accepted Debré's suggestions would have undermined the presidency in favor of a strong prime minister and a strong legislative majority. What Debré was asking appeared to de Gaulle to come perilously close to a return of legislative supremacy. And if a Gaullist majority were in fact returned to the National Assembly, what guarantees were there that it would remain behind the president rather than the prime minister? Debré had to withdraw.

The new prime minister, Georges Pompidou, had served General de Gaulle in many capacities in the past. He had been a close personal adviser, had served for a short period on the Constitutional Council, and had been the director of the Rothschild Bank. He had never sat in Parliament and had never been a political leader. He was the "president's man." Loyal to the conception of strong presidential power, he outlined before the National Assembly a governmental policy dealing almost exclusively with domestic, social, and economic problems and formed a cabinet that differed little in its political composition and its membership from the preceding one.

The National Assembly expressed its discontent by giving to Pompidou only a very slim endorsement. He received 259 votes against 128, with about 155 members abstaining. Speaking in the National Assembly, the veteran political leader Paul Reynaud expressed the sentiments of many deputies and underlined the personal character of the institutions of the Fifth Republic when he confronted Pompidou with the same objection that a deputy had once raised against a prime minister named by King Louis-Philippe: "The proof that we do not live under a parliamentary regime is that you are here." Pompidou, Reynaud claimed, was a political unknown; as with Louis-Philippe's prime minister, he had only the "king's" confidence!

But the restiveness of the National Assembly and the political parties came to a head in a rather explosive manner when de Gaulle proposed a referendum to modify the manner in which the president of the republic was to be elected.

On October 5, 1962 the National Assembly, expressing its hostility to the manner in which de Gaulle proposed to amend the constitution, introduced a motion of censure:

The National Assembly, . . . considering that democracy presupposes the respect of law and above all the respect of the supreme law—the Constitution; . . . considering that the Constitution prepared by General de Gaulle and approved by the French people provides formally that a revision must be voted by the Parliament; . . . considering that by bypassing the vote of the two houses the President of the Republic is violating the Constitution of which he is the guardian; considering that the President of the Republic cannot act except on the proposal of the government, hereby censures the government. . . .

This was a stinging indictment of de Gaulle's action. The censure motion against the government was the only way open to the National Assembly to express its disapproval of the president of the republic. All the political parties with the exception of the Gaullists voted in favor of the motion and against the government and de Gaulle—280 deputies, well above the requisite majority.

Acting in accordance with the constitution, de Gaulle dissolved the National Assembly, and called for elections. The Gaullists won, as we saw, an absolute majority in the second legislature (1962–67). The prime minister, in contrast with Debré, accepted a subordinate role as long as de Gaulle was president—in fact, assumed that he could not but play such a role. His main task was to keep his supporters together, and to act on behalf of the president. There could be no possible friction between the two, and no serious likelihood of serious frictions between Pompidou and his Gaullist supporters in the National Assembly. *But,* the "fiction" that the regime was both presidential and parliamentary—as de Gaulle claimed— was maintained.

A Gaullist Legislature

An overall view of the work of the legislature, especially during the years 1962 to 1971, indicates marked similarities with the practices that developed in England, partly because of the limitations imposed by the constitution, but to a great extent because of the existence of a disciplined majority. Parliament was "productive," passing more than four hundred laws, some of major import: it modified the electoral law, decreed amnesty for a number of political prisoners, ratified the Franco-German treaty, debated and adopted the Fifth Economic Plan, undertook fiscal reforms, reorganized the Paris region, established a new administrative organization for regional development, and overhauled the educational system. The reforms undertaken were important enough to provoke

divisions, but the majority held. In the same period the budget, the perennial graveyard of the government in the past, was voted on ministry by ministry, and then as a whole, without occasioning any serious crisis.

If this legislaitve work appeared to be orderly, it should be kept in mind that most of it was initiated by the government. Only about 15 percent of the laws originated with individual members. The prime minister was able to exert pressure upon his majority. In many instances, the procedure of the blocked or global vote was used, forcing the National Assembly to vote on—as it invariably did—the definitive text of a bill that was acceptable to the government. This did not mean that amendments were not permitted and often incorporated into a bill. In fact, very few bills remained without changes. The government often accepted modifications from its own members, and frequently from the opposition. But it always retained the last word and was able to make its decisions stick.

The existence of a majority behind the prime minister blunted the weapons of a divided opposition. Only twice in the five years of the second legislature was a motion of censure introduced (whereas it had been introduced nine times before). The prime minister did not have to resort to the question of confidence—except once, upon presenting his program—a remarkable phenomenon in view of the fact that during the Fourth Republic, prime ministers had to put the question of confidence and court defeat on the average sixteen times a year.

The opposition was given many opportunities to oppose. There were a number of long and serious debates on policy questions, some leading to a vote but more often not. The military reorganization of the country and its reliance upon atomic weapons was thoroughly debated; the policy of withdrawing from NATO was the object of a long discussion in the National Assembly; the economic plan and the budget were carefully deliberated upon; foreign policy questions were a number of times discussed in committee and brought before the floor. Debate was often of high quality, perhaps because the overthrow of the government was rarely the issue. On the other hand, the question period and the motion of censure proved to be limited instruments of control. The first led frequently to a debate but not a vote, and thus became a way to get information from the government or to air grievances; and the latter proved limited because the chances of success against the Gaullist majority were few. This was evident after the elections of 1967, when the Gaullists commanded a very tenuous majority. The last two motions of censure during the Events of May–June failed by eight and eleven votes respectively, and dissolution became necessary when some of the Gaullist allies began to waver. With the Gaullist majority as commanding as it has been after the subsequent election, the motion of censure becomes a mere formality. Not more than 95 votes were cast in favor of the last censure motion in April 1971—149 short of the requisite absolute majority to topple the government.

The formidable powers of the president and the cabinet, when they are in agreement, are not offset by legislative scrutiny and control that ultimately exist in all parliamentary and even presidential systems. Bills become laws unless there is an absolute majority against the cabinet that initiates them. In every case wherein the prime minister puts the question of confidence, the legislative competence of Parliament is narrowed and its ability to scrutinize and control the executive is curtailed. The direct election of the president of the republic by popular vote further enhances the prerogatives of the executive to the detriment of the legislature. The president, elected for a period of seven years, disposes of powers that are in the last analysis qualified only by his own sense of self-restraint. In general, Parliament has been belittled, and it is very likely that it will seek to regain some of its powers in the future.

The Logic of a
Parliamentary Majority

The legislative elections of the Fifth Republic have all returned a Gaullist majority. In full control of the committees, with their own speaker, and with a majority showing exemplary discipline, the National Assembly has provided the required support. But it has also shown certain signs of complacency. Absenteeism has remained high (sometimes there have been not more than twenty deputies attending the debates), a practice that the Fifth Republic was supposed to have put to an end. As in the past, a few individuals, designated by their colleagues, have held onto keys that operate the voting machines, to vote on behalf of their colleagues. The legislators found it more expedient and profitable to work in their districts and departments rather than remain in Paris, where they felt impotent.

But the presence of a majority began to produce the proper response for unity and combativeness on the part of the opposition. First, in the wake of the governmental crisis of 1962, all non-Gaullists began to refer to themselves as "the opposition." Efforts were made to form a "shadow cabinet" (*contre-gouvernement*)—as in Britain—consisting primarily of the non-Communist left-wing parties. This in turn produced an effort in the direction of the amalgamation of parliamentary groups into larger formations. As opposed to fifteen different groups in the past there are now only five. The opposition came into its own, however, for the brief period following the election of 1967. Grouped into two larger formations—the Communists and the Federation—with the frequent support of the Democratic Center (the "PDM"), they waged a war of attrition against the Gaullists and their immediate allies, the independent republicans. The slightest equivocation on the part of the latter opened the way to censure of the government, and hence to new legislative elections—as it happened in 1968 with disastrous results, however, for the opposition parties.

If and when the opposition overthrows and wins an election, the government system will enter a crisis that will test its future. The president may be unable to throw his weight on the scale of political forces, and may find himself confronted by a new majority unwilling to support him and his government. It is at this juncture that the real test of the system will come. Will the Gaullist majority follow the logic of democracy? Or will it attempt to use the constitutional powers of the president to thwart it or stifle it? In the former case, the Fifth Republic may well survive. Otherwise, it will not.

The Senate

The Senate was conceived as the chamber whose detachment and wisdom would provide for a balance against the National Assembly. While deprived of the right to overthrow the cabinet, the senators were given, as we saw, an ironclad veto over legislation if the prime minister and the government desired it. When a bill is vetoed by the Senate, it is up to the prime minister to call a conference committee of the two houses to iron out the differences. (If he does not do so, the bill dies.) It turned out that the Senate—whether displaying wisdom or not—proved to offer the most stubborn, if ineffective, opposition to the Gaullist majority. On more than forty-five occasions, involving major bills, the Senate refused to go along with the National Assembly. The conference committees failed to reach agreement, and the bills had to be voted two consecutive times by the National Assembly before they became laws.

Conflict between the Senate and the majority in the National Assembly made the Gaullists increasingly hostile to the upper chamber. The ministers simply stopped attending the debates of the Senate—as they have the right to—and refused to answer written or oral questions. Many prominent senators found themselves excluded even from informal contacts with the ministers and the president. As hostility between the government and the Senate increased, speculation about its reform grew. Many claimed that the Senate is an antiquated body that should be transformed into a representative professional body rather than a political one.

The reasons for the intransigence of the Senate lie in its mode of election. Two hundred and fourteen out of the 283 senators are elected by the departmental and municipal councillors. Cities with more than 30,000 inhabitants received one extra elector for each additional

thousand inhabitants. Despite this provision, the small towns and villages continued to play a dominant role. Those with less than 3,000 inhabitants have a majority in the senatorial electoral college: they represent only 33% of the population, but 53% of the senatorial electors. The larger towns, those with more than 10,000 inhabitants, which represent more than 40% of the population, have only 21.5% of the senatorial electors. Only about 60 in the seven largest departments are elected by proportional representation.

On four occasions (in 1962, 1965, 1968, and 1971) since it was first chosen in 1959, the Senate has been renewed by a third of its membership, so that one would expect its composition to correspond with that of the National Assembly. But this is not so: the Senate is almost a replica of what it was when it was first chosen. The electoral college, consisting of notables and local representatives, has shown a great aversity to change. On the other hand, the inability of the Gaullists to capture the local assemblies and the municipalities is a reflection of their weak organization. As Table 6-1 shows, they have not gained much strength in the Senate at the very time when they succeeded in capturing a majority of the National Assembly.

TABLE 6-1. *Approximate Composition of the Senate, 1971–74*

Communists		18	67
Socialists		49	
Center	Radical PDM Democratic center and others	106	106
Gaullists and affiliates	UDR Independent Rep. Moderates	39 60 5	104
Unaffiliated		6	6

But as long as the Gaullists hold a disciplined majority, they can overcome the senatorial vote. When their majority disappears, or when it becomes precarious, the veto of the Senate may strengthen the opposition in the National Assembly. Then the conflict between the government and the Senate may become a source of instability.

OTHER CONSTITUTIONAL ORGANS AND PROCEDURES

The constitution reestablished an Economic and Social Council. Representing the most important professional interests in France, it has consultative and advisory powers regarding proposed economic and social legislation, particularly on measures related to economic planning. If the Senate were to be reformed along the lines indicated, then it could replace, in essence, the Economic and Social Council, with limitative consultative functions only.

As under the Fourth Republic, a High Court of Justice, whose members are elected by the National Assembly and the Senate, may try the president of the republic for high treason and the members of the government for criminal offenses committed in the exercise of their functions. A High Council of the Judiciary, presided over by the president of the republic, nominates judges to the higher judicial posts, is consulted about pardons by the president, and rules on disciplinary matters involving the judiciary. The same section of the constitution (article 66) provides what purports to be a writ of habeas corpus clause: "No one may be arbitrarily detained. The judicial authority, guardian of individual liberty, assures the respect of this principle under conditions provided by law."

A most striking innovation is a Constitutional Council, composed of nine members who serve for a period of nine years. Three are nominated by the president of the republic, three by the president of the National Assembly, and three by the president of the Senate. They are renewed by a third every three years. In addition, all former presidents of the republic are members ex officio. A variety of powers has de-

volved on the Constitutional Council. It supervises the presidential elections and the referendums and proclaims the results; it judges the validity of all contested legislative elections, thus avoiding bitter and long controversies in the legislative assemblies. It is the ultimate court of appeal on the interpretation of the constitution on a specified number of matters. All bills, including treaties, may be referred to it, before their promulgation, by the president of the republic, the prime minister, or one of the presidents of the two assemblies. A declaration of unconstitutionality suspends the promulgation of the bill or the application of the treaty. The council determines the constitutionality of the standing orders of the National Assembly and the Senate which go before it automatically. It is, finally, the guardian of legislative-executive relations; it decides on all claims made by the government as to whether the legislature has exceeded its competence.

The constitutional review provided by the constitution of the Fifth Republic differs from the American practice in two important respects. First, it is almost exclusively limited to certain specified categories of cases involving the relationship between the legislature and the executive; and second, it is brought into play only upon the request of four officers of the Fifth Republic—the president of the republic, the prime minister, and the two presidents of the legislative assemblies. Review applies only to pending bills. A law cannot be attacked for "unconstitutionality" except under the specific and very restrictive terms of article 37—that is, only when it is claimed by the government that the legislature exceeded its competence in enacting it. In contrast to the American practice, the Constitutional Council cannot hear cases brought to it by individuals and is not competent to judge matters where individual rights are violated.

The constitution provides two ways to amend the constitution. An amendment proposed by the two legislative assemblies by simple majorities becomes effective only after it is approved in a referendum. A proposal stemming from the president of the republic and approved by the two chambers by simple majorities may go, at the president's discretion, either before the two chambers, meeting jointly in a congress (in which case a three-fifths majority is required), or to the people in a referendum. Thus, amendments that emanate from the government may go before either the joint congress or the people, while a proposal stemming from Parliament must always be submitted to the people in a referendum. As we have seen, President de Gaulle claimed, by invoking article 11, that an amendment can also be submitted directly by the president to the people in a referendum—thus bypassing Parliament.

SEVEN

the French administration

The key to understanding the French administrative tradition is to realize that the political system is unitary, that decision making is highly centralized, and that the state has an all-encompassing role. No Frenchman fully understands the meaning of the term "federalism." For instance, in a number of opinion polls about European union, the French opt for a federal system but are against supranational institutions. This is as if Americans were for the federal government but against giving legislative power to Congress. From the monarchy through to the Revolution, the four republics, the two Napoleons, and down to de Gaulle, France has remained "one and indivisible." What is decided applies to all alike in every department and every hamlet, and until recently, to every colony. Many years ago, a minister of education dumfounded his visitor by telling him, after looking at his watch, that at that precise hour all the children of the same grade in all the schools of France were having Latin classes and were in the process of conjugating the same verb!

There is but one legal authority in France that can make and enforce decisions affecting the comings and goings of every last Frenchman, even down to the exact moment of his wrestling with a particular Latin conjugation. There can be no parallel or independent authorities, no differentiation on the basis of provincial or local situations. This awesome authority is the central government. Its subordinate organs execute its decisions. It can delegate to inferior or local organs, but only under central scrutiny and control. Its authority is all-encompassing: the running of the railroads, the education of the children, radio and TV, the building of highways, the supervision of cultural activities, tourism, the regulation of medical benefits and family allowances, retirement benefits, sports, stadiums, and parks, the collection of taxes, the police, urban redevelopment, the meticulous arrangements for the economic development of the country as a whole, or of diverse regions—all and many more of these matters are decided by the central government.

The French administrative tradition gives to the state a greater role than that of the government in any other democracy. For numerous reasons, some of which we have already mentioned, the French prefer to see an impersonal and higher authority decide many things for them, rather than to be forced to decide themselves on the basis of local committees and voluntary associations or through general face-to-face relations. After all, decisions "from above," if made without the direct participation of the individuals concerned, are easier to disobey than if they are made by the individuals concerned.

THE CHAIN OF COMMAND: FROM CENTRAL GOVERNMENT TO LOCAL MAYORS

Almost all important governmental decisions are made in Paris by the president, the legislature, and the cabinet, and these decisions are enforced by a network of agents throughout the country. The three principal organs in this network are the minister of the interior, the prefects, and the mayors.

The Ministry of the Interior

The Ministry of the Interior is responsible for the execution of all the decisions of the central government and for administering departmental and local units throughout the country. Staffed primarily by permanent civil servants—and assisted by a number of civil servants "loaned" to it from the Council of State—the ministry supervises all national services. It is responsible for the enforcement of the law, for which it has broad police functions and sweeping powers in time of national emergency.

Prefects

The most important instruments of the Ministry of the Interior are the prefects, who are in charge of the departments of France. They are civil servants responsible for the execution and enforcement of laws and executive orders in each department, and they have supervisory

functions over all the local units within the department as well. Assisted by elected departmental councils and by a number of subprefects, they are the true spinal cord of the administrative machinery and serve as a highly centralized and disciplined extension of the central government.

Mayors

Below the prefect and his subprefects are the mayors and the municipal councils. Both are elected. But once elected, the mayor assumes a double role: he represents both the state and his municipality. For certain matters the mayor is the representative of the national authority, and must account for his actions to the prefect and perform a number of functions required by the national government. In many instances—notably in matters concerning the local budget and local taxation—his decisions have to be endorsed by the prefect before they come into force. In other instances, the prefect can command him to perform certain acts and failure to do so may result in his suspension from office for a period of time or, in extreme cases, his dismissal by an executive order of the minister. Thus, local government—more than 36,000 small communes with their municipal councils and mayors—is controlled from Paris. The mayor operates under what French lawyers call the "tutelage" (*tutelle*) of the prefects and the central authority. Uniformity is the rule.

In the last few years, the departments—established in the years of the Revolution and Napoleon—seem to have shrunk in size and importance, in this day when virtually the whole of France can be traveled by car in a matter of twenty-four hours and when the telephone and the radio have brought every part of the country so close to Paris. As a result, an effort is being made to establish superprefects, regional prefects who have been nominated corresponding to twenty "regions" (see Fig. 7-1), with the Paris region as a separate entity. The regional prefect has under his immediate direction all the state services operating within his own region. In the past all these activities came under the direct control of the various minis-

FIG. 7-1. *Regional prefects and regional action.*

tries in Paris, with the prefect being bypassed. This means that in essence he is assured of a wide range of consultations, deliberations, and decisions, under the control of the Ministry of the Interior, for a great number of public matters—construction, public works, education, welfare, etc. As the spokesman for the region, he will take them all into account in an attempt to coordinate effort and plan better policy. To do so, he is assisted by a number of advisory boards, in which the various regional interests are represented, to inform and advise him. A genuine effort to decentralize, even if it comes

from the top, has been made. However, it is not at all certain that it will succeed, since internal regional rivalries and interministerial rivalries are involved. A simpler solution, advocated by many, is to consolidate the departments into twenty or so regions, and provide for genuine deliberative regional representative assemblies, and delegate them a variety of functions that are still tightly held in Paris.

Another step in the direction of better co-ordination is the merging of municipalities into one. They are allowed to make agreements for the joint administration of services that can be rendered more efficiently and economically on a joint basis—electricity, water supply, etc. Subsidies are provided to spur rather than control local effort.

The Central Government

In Paris, a stable bureaucracy is at the disposal of the cabinet. The basic unit, as in Britain, is the ministry, which is responsible for the execution, enforcement, and, at times, policy formulation of matters under its immediate jurisdiction. The ministries, again as in Britain, are divided into bureaus, and the French civil servants, like their British counterparts, form a permanent body of administrators, the top members of which are in close contact with the ministers and, therefore, with policy making. As with the British Treasury, the Ministry of Finance plays a predominant role, since it prepares the budget, formulates the estimates, collects taxes, and, to a lesser degree, controls expenditures.

Who are the French civil servants? If we include manual workers and teachers of grade schools and high schools, their total comes to over 1 million persons. But if we were to add these and also the career military personnel, and those working in the nationalized industries—the railroads, gas, electricity, and other economic actvities controlled by the state—the total would be 2.4 million, 12.5% of the working force. The vast majority are engaged in subordinate tasks. Only a small group of about 10,000 persons participate in the formulation and execution of policy. The top echelon are selected on the basis of competitive examinations and, as in Great Britain, the majority come from certain schools: the law schools, the Ècole National d'Administration, the Ècole Polytechnique, and a few others.

The government has attempted to give all prospective candidates for the civil service a common education and provide for entry on the basis of merit. In 1946 a special school, the National School of Administration, was established for this purpose. The school is open to candidates, and is not only free, but the student is paid a stipend by the government for a period of three years as a trainee civil servant. Common training makes rotation from one job to another and from one ministry to another easier. The prestige of the National School of Administration has to some degree overshadowed the law schools (although most prospective civil servants continue to study law) and the other specialized schools.

The better qualified enter the most important branches of the higher civil service: the diplomatic corps, the inspectors of finance, the prefectorial body, the Court of Accounts, and the Council of State. The great majority—perhaps as many as 90%—come from the upper-middle classes or the middle classes. Many come from families in which the father is a high-level civil servant—indicating a high degree of co-optation, somewhat similar to that existing in the armed forces. They are the only ones having the educational background to pass the stiff written exams. As for the oral examination administered by the civil servants, manners, speech, and social background continue to play an important role. It is these young men that occupy the central position in the central ministries (Interior, Foreign Affairs, and Finance), and play the crucial role in the various other governmental agencies, notably economic planning.

There are a number of ways for the civil servants to exert power and influence. They advise the minister, and execute the ministerial policies in a manner that allows them discretion; they also have independent scrutinizing and controlling functions. This is notably the case with the inspector of finance and the Court of Accounts. The first is intimately associated with the preparation and the execution of the budget, and the second with the overall scrutiny of all government disbursements. The Council of State has both a consultative and judicial role, as we shall see, while the prefectural and diplomatic corps are involved in deliberation, policy making, and execution within a varying range of discretion. The civil servants are actively engaged in legislation—each and every law today tends to be a statement affirming certain broad principles and basic rules (*loi-programme*) or broad objectives (*loi d'orientation*) to be implemented by the minister. This gives to the civil service a broad area of discretion to issue orders and regulations within the spirit and the letter of the law. This means, of course, freedom to act or not to act.

Within the central government, civil servants increasingly exercise influence both in policy making and execution because of the development of interministerial committees to thrash out policy questions and make suggestions on matters concerning them. Similarly, the development of a host of other organizations to promote state intervention in economic and social affairs—planning, construction, regional development, savings, etc.—that do not have a ministerial status are directly headed by civil servants. The top civil servants, like their British counterparts, have grown to know each other (instead of remaining isolated in their ministries) and to develop a common attitude, a common language, and a common *esprit de corps*. The old departmentalization and parochialism of the ministries has given place, through the osmosis of the interministerial committees and the regulatory agencies of the state, to a "national" civil service, not only in law, but in fact.

From "Mandarin" to "Technocrat"

Since the beginning of the Fifth Republic, the role of the civil service has grown—for the general trend has been to put the civil servant right at the top of policy making. As we noted, de Gaulle's staff was almost exclusively composed of civil servants detached from their ministerial or other duties; one-third of the cabinet consisted of experts and top technicians and of civil servants; and the general stability of the cabinet, despite minor reshuffling, also corresponded to the stability of the minister's staff, the *cabinet ministeriel*, which consists of civil servants. In the national services, and at the top of the Economic Planning Commission, civil servants initiate, implement, deliberate, and often decide. Many claim that the present system is a "technocracy"—a government by the expert and the technician (i.e., the civil servant).

But in a peculiar way, as today's "techno-crats" have been gaining influence, the character, and with it the role, of the civil service has been changing in a manner that reduces its legal power. The civil servants are no longer, as the "mandarins" (as they were called) of the past —guardians of the statist administrative tradition: neutral, impersonal, remote, and legal-minded. They have undertaken the "dialogue" with interest groups, with regional groups, and with the professions, both in the performance of their general functions and with regard to economic planning and regional development. The businessman, the industrialist, and the farmer have become their constituency.

This development is due to at least three reasons. First, the weakening of the parliament, and to a great extent of the parliamentary committees and subcommittees, has shifted drastically the thrust of the interest groups. Groups attempt to influence those who have power. In the past, their point of access was the deputy, the committee, or even selected members of the cabinet in a weak coalition cabinet. Now their thrust is almost primarily directed to the civil servant who, on behalf of his minister and a cohesive cabinet, has the ultimate word. The confrontation between a spokesman for an interest group and a civil servant often results in an agreement, a compromise, or a bargain. Secondly, as the state services begin to resemble those of a private firm or a private industry, the civil servant finds himself increasingly at home with the company director, business executive, and banker. The concerns are common, very often the training is not different, and the social status not dissimilar. Nothing illustrates this better (though it suggests more) than the growing *"pantouflage"*—the shift from civil service positions to private jobs. Thirdly, the dialogue has become increasingly institutionalized through the creation of thousands of advisory committees, bringing together interest and professional groups with the civil servants in a deliberative process. This is notably the case with economic planning and regional development, as well as urban redevelopment. From purveyor of authority, the civil servant becomes a link, and from an executor, a deliberator. In the process, the sharp lines that divided what is public and what is private have been not only blurred, but seriously undermined. No wonder that the civil servant has become today one of the most important advocates of a "participant democracy" as opposed to one that juxtaposes state authority and the individual. Some civil servants, organized in political clubs, have been the most articulate spokesmen of a continuing and institutionalized dialogue between the state and the individual, between the civil service and the interest groups. The aversion to face-to-face relations is giving place to a dialogue from which greater participation, more bargaining, and a more pragmatic orientation are likely to emerge. It is something of an irony (but not uncommon in France) that such an important change is initiated from the top: the civil servant, who embodied the impersonal power of the state, is now eroding his legal supremacy to become an instrument of service and cooperative action.

The Changing Role of the Civil Service: Two Illustrations

Nothing illustrates better the role the civil service has played in becoming a bridge between the state and the country than French economic planning and regional development.

ECONOMIC PLANNING. Economic planning was initiated by Jean Monnet, in cooperation with a small group of the higher echelons of the civil service, in order to meet specific needs and demands arising from the war period. The first task, as we saw in Chapter 3, was to modernize and rebuild the equipment of the country devastated by World War II. Thereafter, the Monnet Plan covered many other branches of economic activity and emphasized "productivity." The planners began to rely increasingly upon cooperation and consultation between business and industry and the civil servants. With the second (1954–55), third (1958–61), and fourth plans (1961–65), they set out to modernize by projecting a growth rate of about 5–6% a year. Attention was given to growth of consumption, social reconstruction, and welfare measures. The planners introduced more sophisticated techniques of forecasting economic de-

velopment for each branch of economic activity, began to develop ways to handle problems of regional development, and took comprehensive measures to improve the agricultural situation of the country—caused in part by low income and a great number of marginal farms, but also by falling prices, inadequate processing facilities, and downright lack of information and know-how on the part of many farmers. The fifth plan (1966–70) provided for an annual rate of expansion of 5% in gross domestic production, a sharper rise in private consumption, and a massive expenditure in social programs, foreign aid, and defense. The plans have been successful, as the figures we gave earlier about the rate and degree of French modernization attest. It is, in great part, the work of the General Planning Commission that prepares it, and submits it for approval to the minister, and, through him, to Parliament. The commission consists of about forty specialists, drawn mainly from the civil service, and about five-hundred executive and clerical personnel. The top forty play the key role in preparing the plan, assisted by the National Institute of Statistical and Economic Studies, which prepares the economic forecasts.

A major work is done by the so-called modernization committees. There are twenty-five such committees concerned with various aspects of the economy, and they are invariably headed by members of the commission and civil servants from various ministries. The most important economic and professional interests in business, industry, commerce, agriculture, labor, and banking are represented. To be specific, in the preparation of the fourth plan (1961–65) there were 114 labor representatives, 20 farmers, 198 business managers, 239 executives, 170 "experts" drawn from the professions and the universities, and 200 civil servants. It is at this level that the new important role of the civil service—dialogue—and the new development that we noted—cooperation between civil servants and the professional interests—takes place. At the regional level, representatives of the regional interests and public servants form the Committees of Regional Economic Development to assess the impact of the economic plan upon their region and make suggestions.

What is strikingly novel about French planning then, is that it has generated a constant contact between the civil service and the community at the national and local levels, but not in the form of what Max Weber called "imperative coordination." The powers of the civil service to command are limited: both in its drafting stage and in its implementation, the plan and planning authority relies on cooperation and consultation. It is to the interest of the professional groups (industry, labor, agriculture, etc.) to learn about the indicators and trends of economic activity—and the planners are in a position to tell them. It is to their interest to know something about population trends—and the planners know. It is to their advantage to get a view of price trends for the future; and it is finally to their interest to know where and how much the state plans to spend—since the state is the largest producer, investor, and consumer. The plan gives an overall idea, and frequently a very specific one. Within the context of the plan, then, decisions can be made about such matters as investment, expansion, and the like, by individual firms and persons, and the state can help with low-interest loans, with tax rebates, with subsidies or by writing off taxes in return for an assurance that the firm will reinvest a part of its profits. Both the private and the public sector have to gain if there is cooperation that involves balanced growth. This is what the plan has done, and in doing so it has increasingly altered the nature of the French economy and by modifying the role of the civil service is injecting new habits and values that are beginning to seriously change the political attitudes of the average Frenchman. He is beginning to cooperate with the state and its agents, and to participate in decisions that were made in the past in Paris behind the closed doors of ministerial offices.

REGIONAL DEVELOPMENT. Equally significant are the procedures set up for the regional development and urban redevelopment of France—two problems that, as we know, are currently plaguing our own country. For France the problem has a special interest. If the demographic and industrial trends are left without control, Paris will dominate the rest, and in the process, may well become unlivable. There are about 9 million people in the Paris agglomeration now, accounting for about 18% of the population of France—whereas New York City accounts for not more than 4% of the population of the United States. Paris has one-fourth of all governmental workers—about 600,000—and 54% of all publishing houses and newspapers; it accounts for half of the country's business turnover; and most of the companies have their central offices there. Twenty-five percent of all industrial workers live in the Paris region, and one-third of all industrial jobs are in Paris.

The second problem is the division of France between developed and underdeveloped regions, which, as the map in Fig. 7-2 indicates, corresponds to a rough division between east and west. Both in terms of per capita income, population, and industrial jobs, the east is advanced and the west relatively behind. But the dark area situated in the northeast comprises only nineteen departments, with about 38% of the population and 20% of the territory. These departments account for 45% of French industrial production. Productivity in this area is 25% above the average. Sixty-five percent of the university students and specialized technical schools are located in Paris or the northeast.

Finally, the last problem is that of the rural areas. They have been steadily losing population. While in 1851, 27 million lived in rural areas, about 7 million in towns, and 1.9 million in Paris, by the year 2000 the figures are projected to be 8 million, 50 million, and 14 million respectively. There is no way to arrest this process—but there is a way to organize agriculture in such a manner that it will be able to provide for the food required by the growing city population. There is also every reason to make available to the farmer all the facilities of city life. Thus, the elimination of marginal farms, the development of mechanized agriculture to suit the particular type of crops, the growth of processing and marketing facilities, and above all refrigeration, canning, and transportation become predominant.

One begins to have a view of the enormity of the problem. It is not only a French problem, for it relates to problems that all modern industrializing societies face: slow transportation, water and air pollution, inadequate recreation facilities, the trauma-inducing shift of populations from familiar regions and occupations to new ones. How and what decisions will be made is a political problem. The novelty of the French experiment is that it is undertaken on a nationwide basis with a vision—based upon careful study—not only of what the situation will be thirty years from now, but of how it *ought* to be. Every plan and every target is, in other words, a commitment to the new generations.

Under the overall supervision of the Planning Commission and the cabinet, a National Commission for Integrated Development has been set up. Its job is primarily to forecast and suggest targets and goals. It has eighty members consisting of various professional groups, and headed by a commission of civil servants and other specialists divided into a number of study groups. Implementation is in the hands of a "Delegation of Integrated Development"—an interministerial committee of twenty-seven that cooperates closely with the Planning Commission. It supervises the execution of the plan in the twenty regions. The interministerial committee screens all ministerial expenditures that relate to investment, equipment, and modernization. It can urge outright expenditure in one region rather than another; ask accordingly for modification of the plan at its deliberative stage; and suggest the granting of loans, subsidies, and tax rebates, depending upon where an industry plans to establish itself. Generally, when it comes to economic expansion, priority is given to the underdeveloped areas and to decongestion of the Paris area.

Planned as an interrelated unit, France, without losing geographical diversity—indeed, by cultivating it—will become more alike in the income, skills, and education of its children. But it should be noted again that all decisions are made with the advice and the participation of the interests and regions involved, through the regional committees of development and through the advisory bodies that participate in the final formulation of the plan. The role of the civil service becomes increasingly that of a catalyst, a bargainer, a compromiser. The authoritative traditions give place to a genuinely

FIG. 7-2. *Highly developed (dark gray), developed (light gray), and underdeveloped regions of France.*

political activity, without which the cooperation of the interests involved could not be readily solicited and institutionalized.

THE COUNCIL OF STATE
(*Conseil D'État*)

One of the most remarkable institutions in the government of France is the Council of State, whose parallel cannot be found in Britain or the United States, but which has been widely copied in most other continental countries. Founded by Napoleon, it originally consisted of top-ranking civil servants who screened executive orders and decrees and became the "watchdog" of the administration. All litigation involving civil servants or the state would be heard by it. Today, the Council of State continues to perform important advisory and deliberative functions. A number of government executive orders require its approval before they go into force. It is reputed to consist of the best lawyers in France. Once admitted, the *conseiller d'état* achieves, by custom, permanent tenure in the civil service. Until the Fifth Republic, no *conseiller* had ever been arbitrarily dismissed by the government.

The Council of State has, however, emerged primarily as a court. It hears cases involving acts of civil servants in their official capacity and cases arising between an individual and the state. Instead of being the watchdog over government administration, the council has today become the defender of individual rights—both property and civil rights—against the state. This change has been the result of a jurisprudence developed over the years by the council. It has declared executive orders or acts of the government to be illegal if they are not consistent with the "parent law"—if they are *ultra vires* (i.e., beyond the powers authorized by law) or if the reasons for which an executive order is issued are not clearly set forth. It has obliged the state to pay damages to private individuals whenever negligence on the part of civil servants could be proved. Finally, in some decisions it has held that the government is obligated to compensate the plaintiff even when no negligence has been proven. When, for example, a prefect suspended the publication of a newspaper, a mayor refused to allow a peaceful religious ceremony to be held, and munitions exploded in a state depot, a public officer and, through him, the state were declared liable in each case even though proof of negligence was absent.

Thus, the Council of State has attempted to curb the arbitrary actions that are inherent in any powerful and centralized administrative system and to protect the individual in all the cases where he has no redress before the civil courts. As a result, its jurisprudence has been one of the most progressive in the world.

An evaluation of the performance of the Fifth Republic may well be premature. In operation since January 1959, it has been until recently more the government of one man than a political system. De Gaulle symbolized, as we noted, the Bonapartist tradition in France. He governed, and it was he, rather than the constitution and the governmental institutions we examined in the preceding chapters, who embodied legitimacy. Perhaps the most crucial problem facing the country is: Will the governmental institutions remain the same after de Gaulle? Will the succession to the office of the presidency continue without serious dissension, or will the present governmental machinery, and perhaps the constitution, be radically transformed? With these troubling questions in mind, we shall now attempt to present the balance sheet of the regime and to assess its performance.

INDEPENDENCE FOR THE FORMER COLONIES

During 1956–57, one of the most important steps in French colonial policy was taken when the Parliament of the Fourth Republic endorsed legislation granting Madagascar and the various African territories of France extensive local autonomy. These territories were given the power to legislate their internal affairs and to establish their own responsible governments, while matters concerning finance, defense, foreign policy, higher education, customs, and radio remained under the jurisdiction of the French government.

In 1958, President de Gaulle pledged to all these territories a new political arrangement—the French Community—and at the same time explicitly promised to respect their right to independence, if they opted for it in the referendum of September 28, 1958, by voting "No." All the territories, with the exception of Guinea, voted "Yes," and thus the French Community came into being. The territories became republics "federated" with France. They were governed, however, by the president of the French republic, who was also president of the community (de Gaulle), with the assistance of

EIGHT

governmental performance and prospects for the future

an Executive Council, consisting of a number of French ministers charged with common community affairs and the prime ministers, or their delegates, of the African republics and Malagasy (formerly Madagascar). A community Senate, with mostly consultative powers, was also established, and a community Arbitration Court was created for the purpose of hearing and passing on controversies among the member states.

In the course of 1959–60, the community was abandoned. All African republics and Malagasy have become independent and all of them have become members of the United Nations. France under de Gaulle has thus liquidated her colonial empire. In doing so, she has improved her position in Africa, where she is now assured of a reservoir of goodwill. Large subsidies to the African republics and Malagasy guarantee their economic modernization, which will improve the living standards of the African people and is eventually bound to increase both French trade and investments in Africa.

Algeria

Progress in Algeria, where a powerful French minority and a strong army were well entrenched, was slow. After many hesitations, equivocations, and two uprisings by the military and the French in Africa against de Gaulle, negotiations were concluded in 1962, granting Algeria her independence. The agreements provided for an immediate cease-fire and for the establishment of a provisional caretaker government in Algeria to organize a referendum on self-determination; they gave to the Algerian population an opportunity to express in a referendum a choice between outright independence, independence in cooperation with France, and integration in the French republic. Since it was presumed that the Algerians would opt for independence in cooperation with France, the Evian agreements provided detailed stipulations on the status of the French citizens. They were to remain French citizens. Even if they opted for Algerian citizenship within a period

of three years, they could still retain their French citizenship and return to France; their property and freedoms were guaranteed. They were further guaranteed their own schools and publications. Special rights were to be bestowed upon the French who became Algerian citizens; a number of seats in the future Algerian Parliament were to be allotted to them, and they were to be given special representation in the large municipalities.

France maintained provisionally her rights to test atomic weapons in the Sahara (which became part of Algeria), to maintain the naval base of Mers-El-Kebir for fifteen years, to maintain control of three airports for three years, and to maintain the French army on Algerian soil (but to reduce its numbers progressively) for a period of three years. Special arrangements guaranteeing the French rights over the Sahara oil were inserted, which, however, have given rise to serious disputes recently. In return, France pledged to continue economic assistance to Algeria for at least three years, to maintain Algeria within the franc zone, to allow free transfer of money from and to Algeria (something of capital importance, since there are about 400,000 Algerians working in France), and to continue to provide for cultural and technical aid.

When these accords were ratified by metropolitan France in a second referendum of April 8, 1962, the way was paved for Algerian independence. On July 1, 1962, a referendum took place in Algeria, and 99% of the voters opted for independence in cooperation with France. On July 3, de Gaulle formally granted Algeria independence and dispatched the first French ambassador to Algeria. Thus, a long, bitter war that lasted seven-and-a-half years, at a high cost for France and considerable loss of human life on both sides, came to an end. Even more, the political passions that it had unleashed, which brought down the Fourth Republic and twice endangered the Fifth Republic, were gradually laid to rest. As it was with the policy of colonial disengagement in the rest of Africa, the way was paved for better relations between France and an independent Algeria.

FOREIGN POLICY

On June 1, 1958, when de Gaulle returned to office, the decline of French power in the world was only too obvious. The Suez adventure had swept aside the French cultural, political, and economic influence in the Middle East. In Indochina, the last French soldier had departed long before, leaving a feeling of bitterness and distrust; Morocco and Tunisia had become independent. In Algeria, the rebellion was gaining ground, and a praetorian army was in near revolt against the republic. Elsewhere in Africa, signs of discontent were becoming ominous. In NATO, France's position was weak, especially when compared with the rising strength of West Germany. As in 1940, de Gaulle considered it his task to weave patiently the fabric of national unity and work for the restoration of French power.

De Gaulle had a vision of a renovated and strong France, with global commitments and world responsibilities. He wanted France to weigh heavily in the contemporary balance of forces and to aspire once more to a vocation of world leadership. It was to this task that he devoted all his energies.

NATO

Soon after his return to power, de Gaulle asserted that it was not the purpose of France to limit her foreign policy "within the confines of NATO." On September 24, 1958, he addressed a memorandum, still technically secret, to Belgian Foreign Minister Paul-Henri Spaak, British Prime Minister Macmillan, and President Eisenhower. He proposed the establishment within NATO of a "directorate" of three—England, France, and the United States—with responsibility for elaborating a common military and political strategy for the whole of the planet, for the creation of allied military commands for all theaters of operation, for joint deliberations about strategy, and for joint decision on the use of atomic weapons. "The European states of the continent," he stated publicly on April 11, 1961, ". . . must know exactly with which weapons and under what conditions their overseas allies would join them in battle." [1] There was also a threat in the memorandum: France would reconsider its NATO policy in the light of the response of England and the United States.

Though ostensibly addressing problems related to NATO, de Gaulle was actually attempting to place France on a level to which no other continental power in NATO could aspire. NATO was to remain a broad organization, but with three of its members—France, England and the United States—jointly in charge of global strategy. The three great powers, in the best tradition of the old diplomacy, were to be in charge, at the NATO level, of the Atlantic problems, and jointly in charge of planetary strategy. De Gaulle remained adamant. When his suggestions were rejected, France withdrew her Mediterranean fleet from NATO command; she refused to integrate her air defense with NATO; she prevented the building of launching sites and the stockpiling of atomic warheads over which she could have no control on French soil. But this stand against military integration was to bring France in conflict with West Germany. This became painfully evident during Chancellor Konrad Adenauer's visit in December 1959, and throughout 1960, when de Gaulle and his advisers talked freely about an "independent" Western European strategy and apparently foresaw even the possibility of the withdrawal of American forces.

With the end of the Algerian war, there was no doubt at all as to where de Gaulle stood and what he wanted. First, European problems had better be left to the European nations. This involved even the problem of German reunification. Second, European nations, notably France, had worldwide commitments that transcended the regional limits of NATO, just as did the United States. Hence, the future of the national armed forces and their deployment and

---

[1] News Conference, April 11, 1961, in *Speeches and Press Conferences,* no. 162, pp. 7–8.

posture was a national matter belonging to France. Third, without ever stating it, de Gaulle implied that the presence of American troops in Europe was becoming, at least politically, a liability. Fourth, NATO and its integrative aspects were to be thrust aside and replaced, at most and on the basis of expedience and contingency, by a classic alliance among individual and separate states—an alliance that was to be negotiated and renegotiated as the circumstances demanded. De Gaulle never rejected the desirability of such a classic alliance, but while insisting on its form—a pact between individual sovereign states—he never specified its content. It seemed clear, however, that such an alliance was to be construed narrowly. The partners would be free to differ on everything that did not involve their defense against a specified foreign attack under the stipulated conditions. France would be free to move in her own way in China, in Southeast Asia, and in Latin America, as well as reconsider her relations with the Eastern European countries or the Soviet Union. De Gaulle's revisionist policy with regard to NATO was, in other words, an explicit reformulation of France's full-fledged independence to act as a world power. If and when the interests of the United States and France converged, so much the better; if they diverged, each would be free to act independently of the other. This, in effect, would put an end to NATO.

In March and April of 1966 the French government communicated its decision to withdraw its forces from NATO on July 1, 1966, and demanded the withdrawal, by April 1, 1967, of all United States armed forces and personnel and of all NATO instrumentalities from French soil. The only remaining possibility was that American forces could be stationed in France, and French forces in Germany, on the basis of bilateral arrangements. Here is, in effect, what happened. NATO headquarters were moved to Brussels while American and French forces remained stationed in West Germany—the latter on the basis of a bilateral agreement between West Germany and France. All United States forces and installations, however, were removed from France.

Britain and the Common Market

Since 1960, the political and military reasons that accounted for de Gaulle's acceptance of the economic provisions of the Common Market have become increasingly apparent. The Common Market suggested the possibility that a larger European whole (France, West Germany, Italy, Belgium, Holland, and Luxemborg) could be placed under the leadership of France, armed with atomic weapons that were denied to Germany by virtue of the Paris Accords. Britain's participation was highly desirable, provided Britain was willing to abandon the intimate Atlantic connections that underwrote the dominance of the United States, and provided also that Britain brought into a European pool—under some form of Franco-British control—her nuclear weapons and knowhow: Britain's nuclear power was to be its dowry in the contemplated marriage with the Common Market.[2] Thus, the heart of the matter was and remains political and strategic: Britain, de Gaulle feared, would remain under the domination of the United States, and her entry into the Common Market would reinforce America's influence.

Having vetoed Britain's entry, de Gaulle turned to Germany. A Franco-German alliance providing for frequent consultations, and possibly for the elaboration of common policy on military, foreign, cultural and economic questions, would provide the hard core that would consolidate Western Europe and, given France's military superiority, safeguard French leadership at the same time. In January 1963, a Franco-German treaty, embodying the principle of consultations on matters of defense, foreign policy, and cultural affairs, was signed. However, the very logic of the treaty raised serious

[2] A review of some of the most important recent publications pertinent to this discussion can be found in "Le grand débat nucléaire," *Bulletin Sedeis*, no. 910, supplement (February 10, 1965). Significant articles have also appeared in *La politique étrangère*.

questions. It was again based on the assumption that West Germany would accept French, rather than American, leadership and protection. But in the light of West Germany's military and economic ties with the United States, and especially in the light of the overwhelming military superiority of the United States, it was unlikely that any West German political leader would acquiesce to this.

In the meantime, the Common Market remained a successful economic arrangement. It had, by 1967, reached the stage when increasing commitments to supranationality were to be made, and when some decision could be made by a qualified majority of the participants. In other words, the Common Market had moved to the critical stage when it was about to assume, even to a limited degree, genuine supranationality. However, such a supranationality was contrary to de Gaulle's basic assumptions about the nature of international relations. Alleging the unwillingness of the other five members to accept common agricultural policies (policies quite advantageous to French agriculture), de Gaulle instructed his ministers, in the middle of 1965, to withdraw from the Council of Ministers of the Common Market. He also attacked the supranational character of the Rome treaty that had set up the Common Market, and claimed that the assumption of power by a body of "stateless" functionaries was prejudicial to the independence of the sovereign member states. The Rome treaty, he concluded, had to be revised in order to do away with all supranational clauses. In effect, he urged that the Common Market remain a purely economic arrangement, held together by the will of sovereign and independent states, and subject to the veto power of each and all.

From a purely economic point of view, however, the Common Market continued to progress. All internal tariffs were in effect abolished by the end of 1969, and it was expected that there would also be a common external tariff in force. A common agricultural policy has been endorsed—after prolonged and often highly contentious debates—and internal agricultural tariffs are being rapidly reduced. Trade among the countries in the community has grown three times as fast as the external trade, and French trade with her European partners has more than doubled. Movement of capital and labor has become greatly liberalized, and efforts are being made to equalize welfare measures among the six member nations.

Inevitably, despite de Gaulle's objections, European political institutions began to develop. In the summer of 1967, the various organs of economic cooperation and coordination were all merged into one executive, the Executive Commission, and one legislature (even if it has only consultative powers)—the European Assembly. Though major decisions are still made by the Council of Ministers, consisting of the foreign ministers of the six member nations (wherein each continues to have what amounts to a veto), the direction lies in the development of greater coordination, and, ultimately genuine supranational bodies wherein decision will be made by majority vote.

The "Opening to the East"

With the emergence of the Sino-Soviet split, with the relative weakening of the Soviet Union's expansionist trends, with the growing preoccupation of the Soviets with many internal problems, and, lastly, with the emerging aspirations of many Eastern European nations for independence in the sixties, the time appeared propitious for France to establish friendly relations with Eastern European nations and the Soviet Union. De Gaulle's emphasis upon a "European Europe," his often-repeated statements about a Europe stretching from the Urals to the shores of the Atlantic, were designed to suggest such a development. Its implementation proved to be a much harder problem. One way was to achieve a genuine Franco-German entente within the context of the Common Market, and then to begin a dialogue with the Soviet Union on matters of German reunification. This proved difficult because of the unwillingness of the Germans to substitute French protection for American, and because of the legitimate doubts of American policy makers about the advisability of such a course of action. De Gaulle then made repeated overtures in the direction of the Eastern European satellites. Cultural and economic ties were stressed; visits were exchanged, a number of leaders of Eastern European countries visiting Paris; and France refused to consider any arrangement that would give the Germans a say about nuclear arms. Thus, under de Gaulle, France returned increasingly to the pre-World War II arrangements—in which an understanding with the Soviet Union is indispensable to the maintenance of peace in Europe—and again the more recent visits exchanged between the Communist leader, Brejnier, and President Pompidou. This might well have been the objective of General de Gaulle's visit to the Soviet Union in the summer of 1966 and of Premier Kosygin's return visit to France six months later.

A NEW DEFENSE

On February 13, 1960, France exploded her first atomic device in the Sahara. It was followed by three more atmospheric tests on the same site, the last of which took place in March 1961. Since then there have been a few underground tests while preparations, both physical and diplomatic, have been underway for nuclear testing in the Polynesian possessions of France in the Pacific, where additional tests were conducted in the summer of 1966. The first French H-bomb was exploded there. New legislation has reorganized the French military forces and a new strategy has been evolved, with emphasis on the atomic force—the *force de frappe*. A new system of selective rather than universal military service has been introduced. Military service has been reduced to sixteen months, and total annual recruitment is expected to average about 200,000 men, out of a total of some 350,000 available for service. Two "program laws" for defense (1961–65, and 1965–70) provide, in addition to the existing air force capabilities, for surface-to-surface ballistic missiles with a range of 2,000 miles, and three nuclear submarines (by the

end of 1973) armed with sea-to-ground ballistic missiles with thermonuclear warheads. It is planned that by 1972–73 all three services (air force, army, and navy) will be fully armed with nuclear weapons. The French army will consist of the Strategic Nuclear Force, the Force of Maneuver (six highly mechanized and mobile divisions), the naval forces and air force, and the forces for the Operational Defense of the Territory (DOT), consisting of one Alpine brigade, five combat regiments, and twenty commando infantry regiments. The heart of the military machine will be the nuclear force and the mechanized divisions—the latter presumably operating, if circumstances demand it, in conjunction with NATO (assuming that this organization is still in existence).

After de Gaulle

In his last formal pronouncement on international politics, his New Year's address of December 31, 1968, de Gaulle cast France in the role of a world power. He did not mention the Common Market or Germany or England's entry; he did not refer to the Soviet ruthless military intervention in Czechoslovakia—a "regrettable" incident that he attributed to Yalta and to the division of the world into two blocs; and he said nothing about the U.S.–Soviet confrontation in the Eastern Mediterrean. He lectured on East–West détente, urging the end of the war in Vietnam; withdrawal of Israeli forces from all occupied territories under the proper frontier guarantees; the entry of People's Republic of China in the United Nations; self-determination for Biafra; a free expression of national life for the French in Canada; aid to the underdeveloped areas of the world; and a new international monetary system that does away with the primacy of the dollar. In this grandiloquent peroration the only item missing was France's nuclear strength —conveniently forgotten because economic difficulties had brought about the postponement of French tests, and the hard realities of the situation had called for some reconsideration of French atomic strategy.

It is wrong, however, to assume that, with de Gaulle's death, there will be a radical overhaul of French foreign policy. France is more powerful, has a better sense of its role in the world, has tasted the fruits of independence and the poison of the atomic era, and has regained the posture she had temporarily lost after the shattering defeat of 1940. But it will be also difficult to believe that, in the years to come, France will be in a position to maintain her present intransigent attitude of independence. There will be no return to a position of tutelage and dependence upon the United States, as happened after 1947, but it is unlikely that there will be a full-fledged separation and independence from the Atlantic commitment. It is also unlikely that the development of closer European ties can be thwarted. It is very unlikely, in other words, that there will be a serious crisis of succession—at least with regard to basic foreign policy goals. On the other hand, the new president and the Gaullist leaders may not be able to pursue with the same adroitness all the various and often incompatible options that de Gaulle pursued at high risks and may have to settle for some clear-cut commitments and choices. Lip service will continue to be paid to many of the Gaullist themes, including his solicitude for the fate of the French in Canada. Gradually, however, the Gaullist vocabulary is likely to give place to more realistic and pragmatic pronouncements; ambiguity will be replaced with clear-cut commitments and a European rank in terms of a firmly entrenched European base of power will replace worldwide ambitions. But for the foreseeable future continuity is likely to be the theme.

There are many reasons for this. First, Pompidou had been as close to de Gaulle as anybody could have ever been and served as his prime minister for over six years; secondly, the new president enjoys in the National Assembly a solid majority; thirdly, the combination of the institutions of the Fifth Republic and more particularly of the office of the presidency with the massive Gaullist majority in the National Assembly (indeed the two may have to remain

linked) gives to Pompidou wide latitude for action and effective means to implement it. French foreign policy is very likely to follow the blueprint traced by General de Gaulle.

Yet differences are likely to develop. Some may be due to a greater degree of realism shared by the younger Gaullists; others to a genuine feeling in favor of a European commitment; still others to the realization that nuclear strategy is an expensive proposition and that the Atlantic umbrella should remain intact if France is to maintain both her independence and her security. Finally there is the problem of the Franco-German relations. The increasing independence of German foreign policy under Willy Brandt to pursue an opening to the East, in treaties with the Soviet Union and Poland and more accommodating relations with East Germany, may spring West Germany loose from the Western European entanglement that Adenauer had fashioned and de Gaulle wanted to exploit to his own ends. France is not prepared to allow this.

These considerations indicate one of the major directions towards which French foreign policy is likely to move. It will become more and more concerned with European rather than world-wide problems. It will become regionalized and retrenched, and because of this, perhaps far more effective than under General de Gaulle. Realism calls for a more careful assessment of resources and a better evaluation of means and goals. The uprisings of May–June 1968 revealed France's economic weaknesses when compared to West Germany. Military expenditures had to be deferred or scaled down, and as a result both nuclear and particularly delivery capabilities continue to raise doubts about France's deterrent ability. Furthermore, it is now clearly understood that the rate of technological development in this field is so great among the superpowers that middle-rank nuclear powers like France are left with the realization that obsolescence of their weaponry may well be the pay-off for their efforts! The alternatives are either to scale down the nuclear effort, which means to simply decrease the deterrence of the French weapon and underline her vulnerability; to acquiesce to the Atlantic protection and even to reinforce it through individual agreements with the United States; or to seek a European nuclear military arrangement. It is quite likely that France in the coming decade will seek either or both of the last two alternatives.

The European focus shared by many Gaullists is closely linked with the question of Franco-German relations. The new foreign minister, Maurice Schumann, had been a member of a pro-European party. Both at the summit meeting of Hague in December 1969 and in a number of subsequent addresses later on, Schumann outlined his famous European *triptych* in this order of priority: the completion of the Common Market; its internal strengthening; its enlargement. By *completion* he meant the full development of an agricultural market and the ushering in of the final and definitive stage in all economic arrangements that is irreversible. He further supported fully the proposal to endow the Community with its own resources to be used under the control of a European parliament. While paying lip-service to the Gaullist anti-supranationalist and anti-integrationist themes, Schumann time after time stated that economic union and political union are "two sides of the same coin." By *strengthening* he meant the development of new community cooperative and integrative arrangements in technology, fiscal policies, monetary policy, and investment policy. All differential traits in the economies of the six member nations should be eliminated until a genuine whole has been established—one that would assimilate each of the six countries to the American states. Finally, *enlargement* corresponded to the addition of new members (notably England). In fact, after many and long deliberations agreement was reached to enlarge the Common Market to include England, Denmark, Ireland, and Norway. The treaties have been signed and if they are ratified these four countries will become full members of the Common Market on July 1, 1972.

It is therefore because of the convergence of a number of factors—a growing realism among the political leaders of the Gaullist majority, the mounting expenses of a nuclear strategy, and the increased strength and independence of West Germany—that France now opts for closer European unity. Finally, with British participation and with the enlargement of the Community, they continue to emphasize the strengthening of the Community ties. As the communique issued late in 1969 states "what has been done must be jealously preserved and the completion (of the Community) must become a definite reality." [3]

Such an emphasis inevitably calls for a reconsideration of the role of the United States in the context of the Atlantic alliance. French strategy, based until recently upon massive retaliation against the "aggressor" from East or West, is neither possible nor credible. Further, the notion that France should be prepared to defend herself against any aggressor coming "from any side," in the words of the former chief of staff, the late General Ailleret, could not be reconciled either with international realities or with France's capabilities. Even before de Gaulle had left office the French military thinking began to change. The enemy was likely to come "from the East" and the French deterrent has no meaning, except in extreme cases, outside of the context of the Atlantic alliance and the realities of the United States' overall nuclear strategy and military presence in Europe.

But closer and even integrative political ties among the ten—particularly in close military cooperation with England—cannot be excluded. Indeed, France may now demand such ties in order to offset German power. If they were to develop, then France in Western Europe, in cooperation with England and West Germany, will be a powerful entity within an extremely powerful regional bloc. With de Gaulle's departure France's vocation for rank may become in fact enhanced but only through regional and European entrenchment. The coming decade may indeed be once more the decade of Western Europe with the prospect of its becoming truly

[3] "France at the European Summit Conference," Ambassade de France, The Hague, Dec. 1–2, 1969.

a third force capable of mediating between the two Empires!

THE ECONOMY

As we saw in Chapter 3, economic modernization has been stepped up in the decade of the fifth economic plan. The gross national product has grown by over 50%, and industrial production by the same—sometimes as high as 6.5% per year for industrial products and about 3% for agricultural products. Housing construction has averaged about 300,000 units, and it is expected to be considerably higher in the years of the fifth plan. Inflation—in the past a serious problem—has been controlled, if not stopped. Individual purchasing power has risen by about 30–35%. The balance of payments has been favorable almost without interruption ever since 1959, and today France holds over $7 billion worth of gold and foreign assets. The push from the farm to the city has continued, and with it the signs of modernization have grown; agricultural workers become fewer, the number of industrial workers remains constant, and the tertiary sector of the employment has been growing. The consumer—mainly in the city, and less so on the farm—is better off. There is more leisure, and paid vacations for workers have become more widespread, and lengthened to three weeks. Over a period of twenty to twenty-five years, the number of householders owning cars has grown from 14% to 60%; those owning television from only a few in 1947, when it was introduced, to 73%; refrigerators from 3% to 73%, and washing machines from 2.5% to 55%. The government continues to pour money into the social sector of the economy, with public investments amounting to about 21% of the total. Welfare measures, despite recent changes in the social security laws (they now call for greater individual contributions) continue to expand. Medical expenses, maternity care, a free and expanding educational system, and allowances for families with two children or more, have been maintained and strengthened.

In the last decade, France has been able to absorb about 1 million refugees from Algeria without any serious dislocation in her economy (though subsidies had to be provided for them), saw its school and university population virtually double, and experienced a steady growth of population amounting to a net increase of about 300,000 a year. All these are signs of stability and growth.

EDUCATION

France's growing population, spurred by the increase of births in the years immediately after World War II, has put a great strain on the country's educational system. On top of this, the compulsory school age has been raised to 16. To strengthen the school system, credits have been allocated for the construction of schools and universities, for scholarships and subsidies to students, and for the development of more technical schools to meet the needs of an industrial society. New universities have been established throughout France, or those which had only one school (law or letters) have now been raised to full-fledged ones. Additional funds have been invested in research, and particularly in scientific research. Government expenditures have amounted to $4½ billion—about 18% of the budget. But the skyrocketing of population and the rapid expansion in the ranks of those entering higher education (see Table 8-1) have created a great strain on the economy of France and have also necessitated drastic overhauls in the direction of decentralization and innovation.

PROSPECTS FOR THE FUTURE

We have noted the remarkable strides toward economic modernization that were undertaken in France during the Fourth Republic and that have continued during the Fifth. New socioeconomic groups have been emerging to replace the old; the white-collar worker, the technician,

TABLE 8-1. *Approximate Number of Students and Rate of Expenditure, 1952–70*
Number of Students (in thousands)

Academic Year	Primary	Secondary	University & Higher Education	Total	Expenditures (1952–53 = 100%)
1952–53	4,546	901	142	5,589	100%
1957–58	5,752	1,290	175	7,217	132.5
1961–62	6,177	1,977	246	8,400	170.8
1962–63	6,284	2,092	263	8,639	181.6
1963–64	6,168	2,348	286	8,802	191.5
1964–65	6,308	2,383	323	9,014	209.1
1965–66	6,342	2,564	410	9,316	215.6
1970–71	6,342	3,300	550	10,192	—

the executive, the managers of private companies and nationalized industries are growing more numerous and influential in present-day France. The medium-sized farm is replacing the small one, and all farmers are employing more fertilizers and tractors and availing themselves of the credit insurance and technical assistance opportunities that are now open to them. An extremely competent generation of civil servants—trained by the School of National Administration set up after the Liberation—is gaining access to higher posts in the administration and is making its weight felt in the deliberations and decisions on economic and social matters. France has entered upon the road of full economic development and modernization. Does this mean that the old political structure—the old institutions, parties, and political ideologies—will be transformed in some way? And if so, how?

To answer these questions, we must distinguish between the long-run and short-term effects of modernization and weigh them carefully against the traditions, practices, and institutions of the past. As new socioeconomic groups make new claims on the political system and inject their expectations into the system, they will slowly transform it. The members of these socioeconomic groups are more practical and pragmatic in their outlook. They

demand action and want results—better living conditions and a stable political system. They tend to shed past ideologies. Instead of looking at every issue through the lenses of Communism or socialism, Catholicism or nationalism, they look at them as practical problems to be solved as quickly and efficiently as possible. They tend to believe that a wealthy society should provide better living conditions for the workers and by so doing put an end to the secular conflicts between managers and workers, between the bourgeoisie and the working class. The Catholics among them believe that the task of a good Catholic is to cooperate with others on concrete and specific issues without letting religious differences become divisive.

The trend of modernization is also bound to change the attitude of the workers. They, too, may realize that the traditional arguments about capitalism and socialism are becoming sterile, that a democratic state gives them the opportunity to use their numbers and power in order to satisfy their claims. The more they do so the more pragmatic and practical in their outlook they should become and the more inclined to set aside their ideological quarrels. The British Labour party, the German Social Democratic party, and, from a different point of view, American trade unionism provide working examples of how the laboring class can organize itself politically to gain a strong voice in determining what share of the country's wealth it will receive.

Many of the social-economic groups associated so closely with the Third and Fourth Republics (the shopkeepers, artisans, and small farmers) are now being squeezed out by the inexorable progress of modernization. Businessmen are beginning to understand that mass production and mass consumption lead to higher profits and are abandoning the protectionist mentality that characterized them for so long. They have accepted the European Common Market, the liberalization of trade, and a policy of cooperation with investment is in the former African colonies. The younger civil servants seem increasingly sympathetic to new rules of fiscal policy and to state controls over credit, interest, and public investment.

We have already noted how these socioeconomic changes have begun to affect the political system. We noted that stability and executive leadership are beginning to be valued; that the presidential system itself has created an electoral situation in which two camps are likely to join forces behind two candidates; we pointed out that the emergence of a majority in the National Assembly has forced the opposition groups to increasingly coalesce, and that the party system has become simplified. In our discussion of the Communist party, we indicated that although still anchored to the ideologies and practices of the past, it is showing a reformist spirit, on the basis of which a viable cooperation with the other parties of the left may become possible. Finally, we discussed at some length the new role of the civil service in bringing the citizen and the state together. All these changes are reinforced by the mass media—the newspapers, but more particularly radio and TV—that create a "national constituency" to obliterate the particularisms of the past. The winds of change, in other words, are here, and the likelihood that the French will transform their previous ideological attitudes into pragmatic and cooperative ones is real. If and when this happens, then politics will be transformed from a set of embattled ideological visions and imperatives into a set of accepted rules of how to make decisions, how to agree, and how to disagree. In other words, a constitution will become legitimate.

The difficulties, however, remain equally impressive. The transformation of the political parties has been slow and painful. Indeed, we discussed all along the predicament of the left and their inability to unite. The Federation appeared for a while to offer the best prospects for unity of the left-wing parties other than the Communists, thus reducing inevitably the chances of the center and leading to what might have become a tripartite system—Communists, Federation, and the Gaullists. In the legislative elections of 1967 and again in 1968 the center was ground out literally between the three formations to the point that most electoral contests that had not been won on the first ballot became straight contests either between a Federation candidate (supported by the Communists) and a Gaullist, or between a Communist candidate (supported by the Federation electorate) and a Gaullist. But the Federation began to break up. It was unable to evolve an independent structure, membership, and leadership. Also, the relations between the Federation and the Communists became strained. No alliance was formed for the presidential elections of 1969, from which the left remained out of the picture at least on the ballot that counted most—the second. The left has no chance without the Communists, but also the center and the left may be unable to win without Communist support, as became apparent in the 1969 presidential election. Yet the other parties of the left cannot unite with the Communists without being absorbed by them. Until the latter modify further their position in the direction of reformism and until they fully accept the rules of parliamentary democracy, the left will remain divided. Its divisions will continue to inspire the moderate and center parties with hopes of regaining their former electoral strength. The vocation of the old Radical Socialist party under Jean-Jacques Servan-Schreiber and the efforts of the new titular head of the party and his ambitious program, the "Radical Manifesto," correspond to an effort to find a new political arrangement —somewhere between the Gaullists and the Communists. Modernization, industrialization, and Europeanism are likely to attract now the new socioeconomic groups, many of which have gone to the Gaullists, and Europeanism will obviously appeal to the center and the whole of the left except the Communists. The centrist vocation of Jean-Jacques Servan-Schreiber created serious fears in the Communist camp, which wishes to avoid any and all anti-Gaullist alternatives that are not dominated by the Communist party. But it has also worried the Socialists who see in the Radical Manifesto their own image.

The Gaullists, on the other hand, remain the "dominant" party, but the conflicts within the Gaullist movement are many and the possibilities of internal dissensions ever-present. First, there is what we might call the Epigone syndrome.[4] For unlike Gaul the Gaullists are divided into more than three parts. There are the diehard right-wingers who want order and stability, take a strong nationalist posture, and favor a curtailment of parliamentary government. They represent the unreconstructed French right. Hostile to de Gaulle on the issue of Algerian independence, they have gradually come around to support Pompidou. There are the "orthodox" Gaullists, who followed de Gaulle's leadership out of personal attachment and fidelity. To them support of de Gaulle was the essence of political commitment and action. There are the Gaullist "ideologues" of the left who reconcile Gaullism with the image of a new egalitarian commonwealth to replace liberal capitalism but without slipping into corporatism. There are the "practical" political leaders and "technicians" who joined the ranks out of a sense of urgency and a desire for efficiency; there are the "newcomers"—former Radicals, independents, and Christian Democrats, who simply joined out of a sense of expediency and political ambition;

there are finally the "allies"—the Independent Republicans and, since the election of Pompidou, many centrists.

The Gaullist majority in the National Assembly may provide Pompidou with the opportunity to create a strong "Conservative party." But drastic political surgery is needed. For it is a heterogeneous majority consisting of Europeans and anti-Europeans, liberals and planners, those committed to social and welfare legislation and those adhering to classic economic measures, those favoring the *force de frappe* and those against it, proponents of the Gaullist foreign policy and those wishing a radical change. It cannot last for long. In fact, any effort to maintain it will inevitably imply that Pompidou, like de Gaulle, wants only parliamentary base rather than a party. Unlike de Gaulle, however, whose national popularity remained high and who could count on the fidelity of many of his followers, Pompidou may lose the support on which de Gaulle could invariably count. An effort, on the other hand, to create a party may dislocate and split the majority into many factions.

De Gaulle's France lived for over ten years under a personal presidential system in which the discretion of a man was tempered by individual and public freedoms and by four legislative elections and five referendums. De Gaulle never considered elections a source of legitimacy. And a referendum was essentially a vote of confidence—a confirmation and a reaffirmation of his destiny and role as the national spokesman. As long as the confirmation was forthcoming, he argued that all powers of the state emanated from the president. As long as the French men and women gave him directly their confidence, he governed. When in the last referendum they failed him, de Gaulle, true to his logic, decided to withdraw from the political scene.

It is difficult to envisage Pompidou in such a pure Gaullist role. Neither his personality, nor his "historical role," nor his political image can allow him to aspire to the greatness to which de Gaulle aspired and which he occasionally reached. He is therefore more likely to consider a different course, one far more

[4] The discussion that follows is adapted from Roy C. Macridis, "Pompidou and the Communists," *Virginia Quarterly Review* (Fall 1969), 587–90.

difficult to chart and fashion. It is what may be called the demystification of Gaullism—or, rather, its politicization. It involves the creation of a genuine Gaullist party as an instrument of representation, of broad national synthesis and mobilization, and of government. It may bring about the realization of Tardieu's dream —the creation of a French Conservative party— long before Léon Blum's hope for a French Labor party comes, if ever, to life. Pompidou is eminently qualified to do it. While the general looked with suspicion upon a strong party organization, Pompidou worked for it. He became the leader of the party; he saw to it that Gaullism was slowly elbowing the classic right out of power in favor of new men; he worked to see the Gaullists implant themselves slowly in republican and radical France in the south; he rewarded his political lieutenants and reinforced their regional or local strength; he also reacted swiftly against disloyalty and dissension. In 1967 and again in 1968 he screened all Gaullist candidates for the legislative elections, and his word was needed before the Gaullist imprimatur of orthodoxy could be given; it was withheld with disastrous results for the dissenters. The victory of the Gaullists both in 1967 and again in 1968 was due primarily to his efforts.

What would be the ideology of such a party? The question is irrelevant. Pompidou campaigned on concrete issues and it is quite likely that all his efforts will be devoted to coping with them rather than worrying about abstract formulations. Besides, he knows only too well that ideological themes divide. He favored continuity, stability, dialogue with all forces and groups, and promised reforms where reforms are needed. Throughout his campaign he did not reject a single point of view developed by his opponents. Neither did he develop a single proposition that separated him from them: France would continue her policy of independence but in cooperation with her traditional allies; he would hold a meeting to decide on the future of European unity; he would proceed to discuss again Great Britain's entry into the Common Market; efforts would be made to reimburse the refugees from Al-

geria; educational reform would continue, but without undermining the authority of the teacher; the franc would be defended; economic planning would continue in consultation with all interested groups and parties; every effort would be made to arrest inflation but without disregarding the legitimate demands of the wage earners; and so forth. If Pompidou manages to cope with some of the most urgent policy problems in a manner that satisfies the lowest possible common denominator of the various interests involved while working for the strengthening and reorganization of the Gaullist party, he will be providing the anesthesia that is needed to make the ardent Gaullists forget the glorious past and help the new ones accept the present. But will he be able to do it?

THE REGIME

What will the French political regime be like a few years from now? Obviously, such speculation is very tenuous and the most we can do is simply outline, on the basis of existing conditions, a few developments that may possibly take place.

A Military Dictatorship

Until the war was ended in Algeria, it was widely believed that in the event of de Gaulle's disappearance, the army might have been inclined or obliged to step in and assume governmental powers. It was the only cohesive force in France; it had been increasingly involved in politics; it had been responsible for the overthrow of the Fourth Republic and had been strong enough to defy at times even de Gaulle's authority.

Today the army has been purged of many of the more extremist officers, and the development of a nuclear force is beginning to demand its full attention. The extreme-right-wing forces and the deputies—particularly among the independents—who advocated the maintenance of French rule in Algeria were, as we saw earlier, literally decimated. They are no longer a political force. It is more likely that the army will return to the role it played before 1940—that of a silent observer of the political world. Only a national crisis—such as a war, a rapid dissolution of the authority of the republic, or a resurgence of Communist strength—is likely to impel it to step in. Since 1940, the army has played in one way or another a very active political role. With de Gaulle out of the picture, many of the habits it learned in the last thirty years might return in a time of internal or external stress.

A "Reformed" Fifth Republic

The Fifth Republic was de Gaulle. But a number of institutional arrangements may outlive him. It is possible that the present relationship between government and Parliament may continue, characterized by limited parliamentary sessions, executive leadership, and limited legislative competence. The right of dissolution and the restriction of the censure motion may give the prime minister and his cabinet the control and stability they lacked under the Fourth Republic. But none of these rules can be effective unless there is a majority to support a prime minister (which again raises the question of the political parties) or unless there is a powerful president who can use the right of dissolution, can appeal over the heads of the deputies to the people through a referendum, and who, above all, has the popularity that de Gaulle enjoyed.

It was precisely the purpose of the constitutional amendment of October 28, 1962, providing for the direct popular election of the president, to give to de Gaulle's successor a direct popular mandate, and thus to strengthen his position. The direct popular election of the president will give to the French a sense of immediate participation in politics—something which had been lacking in the past. Thus, it may strengthen the presidency and pave further

the way toward a simplification of the party system.

A RETURN TO THE FOURTH REPUBLIC?

The overwhelming power and prestige of President de Gaulle undermined a serious dialogue between the executive and the legislature. Despite the orderly functioning of the legislature and its participation in the legislative process, it has played primarily the role of a forum. Policy has been generated and directed by the president, not the party leadership. Nor is the constitutional debate over. Disagreements about the role and the powers of the president, the functions of Parliament, the limitations imposed upon it now, relations between prime minister and the National Assembly, the prime minister and the president, the two branches of the legislature, and the role of the Constitutional Council, continue. The constitution and the political parties will now receive their first genuine test.

Is it likely to envisage a gradual return to the institutions and practices of the Fourth Republic, characterized by a weak president and the supremacy of the legislature? The pull in this direction stems from the ideological and political forces we discussed in earlier chapters. They can be summed up, perhaps, in one sentence: The present Gaullist majority may break up. Without a political majority (presidential or parliamentary), there can be no strong executive leadership of the American presidential type or the British cabinet type. Nor will the prime minister and the cabinet fare much better. The prime minister will have to seek parliamentary support, which presents again the problem of finding a partliamentary majority.

But suppose the Gaullist majority continues. Even then, difficulties lie ahead, for the present constitution allows for serious conflicts at the institutional level. A conflict between the president and the prime minister is ever-present, and this conflict may well spill over all the other divisions, ideological and party, that have agitated the French political scene for so long. With de Gaulle in power, the prime minister was only a subordinate. But a prime minister, supported by a majority and (according to the letter of the constitution) in charge of the country's policy is likely to balk against a president. In this case, the conflict between prime minister and president will have to be resolved with the victory of one over the other. Then the system will become either a presidential one—or a cabinet one, like the British. Finally, the French constitution may produce a severe conflict between a president and a prime minister even when there is a majority that supports them both, if there is rivalry between the two.

Three of the by-elections that have taken place since the 1969 presidential election are representative of the fluidity of the party configuration and of the uncertainties about the future—especially with regard to the formation of future majorities. The 1969 election in Yvelines (Table 8-2) represents a classic convergence of the left to defeat Couve de Murville—one of the most powerful lieutenants of de Gaulle, foreign minister for more than nine years and the premier for a little less than a year. It is the Popular Front alliance, with the Communists and Socialists regrouping their forces on the second ballot behind the best-placed leftist candidate—in this case, the leader

of the left-wing socialist splinter group, Rocard. Note that on the second ballot the Gaullist candidate did not manage to get the votes of the two Centrists. The left-wing leader, on the other hand, gained all the votes of the Communists and Socialists and received, in addition, the votes of some who had abstained on the first ballot. He also gained some of the votes from the center. He managed to triple his vote between the first and the second ballot, while the Gaullist deputy barely increased his strength by 25%. Under similar conditions, Popular Front arrangements give to the left a possible edge.

The second case—the 1970 election in Nancy (Table 8-3)—is more complicated. The voters of Nancy were deeply dissatisfied with the Gaullist government for a number of reasons, not the least of which was that it had decided to bypass Nancy in a number of regional development programs in favor of the neighboring city of Metz. Jean-Jacques Servan-Schreiber entered the political scene to become the leader of the Radicals. His overall electoral strategy was not dissimilar from that of Poher's: he wished to regroup all the centrist and left-wing forces behind him, bite into the Gaullist strength, and force the Communists to support him on the second ballot, or, if possible, win without their support, thus throwing them back into political isolation. He succeeded at the local level where Poher had failed at the na-

TABLE 8-2. *The Left-Wing Possibilities—Yvelines by-election, October 1969*

	First Ballot		Second Ballot	
Couve de Murville (Gaullist—former P.M.)	10,225	(40.95%)	13,063	(46.21%)
Rocard (PSU—Left-wing Socialist)	5,116	(20.49%)	**15,200**	**(53.78%)**
Cuguen (Communist)	4,998	(20.01%)		
Sonneville (Democratic Center)	3,196	(12.80%)		
Brissart (Centrist)	958	(3.85%)		
Debarge (Socialist)	475	(1.90%)		

SOURCE: *Le Monde.*

TABLE 8-3. *The Centrist Vocation—Nancy by-election, June 1970*

	First Ballot		Second Ballot	
Souchal (Gaullist)	10,836	(26.8%)	10,075	(24.6%)
Servan-Schreiber (Centrist-Radical)	18,352	(45.4%)	**22,414**	(55.4%)
Antoine (Communist)	7,684	(19.0%)	8,057	(19.9%)
Borella (PSU)	2,079	(5.1%)		
Albrige (Independent)	522	(1.3%)		

tional level. The Communists did not throw their votes behind him on the second ballot but maintained their candidate, thus forcing Servan-Schreiber into a triangular election from which the Gaullist was likely to benefit. In effect, the Communists were countering Servan-Schreiber's blackmail in order to show him that no party and no grouping of forces could defeat a Gaullist without them. Servan-Schreiber won and the Communists lost. The latter failed to receive all the votes of the left. In fact, they barely increased their strength. Servan-Schreiber was supported by all other groups and even managed to bite into the strength of the Gaullists. This election indicates that whenever the fortunes of the Gaullists are bad—and they definitely faced difficulties with the electorate of Nancy—the center will pick up their votes. This may happen at the national level as well— due to a slowdown of the economy, increased unemployment, or any number of other reasons. This situation represents the best chances for the center, especially if led by a dynamic and colorful personality. Typically enough, this is the situation the Communists fear most. In fact, they do not want the Gaullists to disintegrate as a party, for the moment this happens, as it happened in Nancy, they are no longer indispensable to the rest of the left and to the center.

Finally, the 1970 Bordeaux election (Table 8-4) is the typical and sobering case of the dominant party winning easily on the first ballot. Servan-Schreiber, fresh from his victory at Nancy, decided to go into the lion's lair and contest the by-election where the Gaullist prime minister and long-time mayor of Bordeaux, Jacques Chaban-Delmas, was running. The election took the form of a national contest in that Servan-Schreiber claimed that if he won, the Gaullist prime minister should resign. There was no chance: Chaban-Delmas carried the election on the first ballot with over 60% of the votes. The centrist forces managed to get about 18% of the vote, and the leftists, headed by the Communists, about 19%. The Gaullist alternative was clear and unambigous: it continues to represent a dominant reality.

In all political systems, the government is shaped and fashioned by the existing social and ideological forces. In France, the splintering of ideologies, the sharp divisions between major

TABLE 8-4. *The Dominant Party— Bordeaux by-election, September, 1970*

	First (only) Ballot	
Chaban-Delmas (Gaullist)	**14,904**	**(63.55%)**
Servan-Schreiber (Centrist-Radical)	3,891	(16.53%)
Riviere (Communist)	2,024	(8.63%)
Taix (Conv. Inst. Rep.)	1,820	(7.76%)
Lateste (PSU)	320	(1.36%)
Barthelemy (Trotskyite)	150	(0.63%)
Others	341	(1.44%)

social groups, the distrust between social classes and political traditions have not yet been quite laid to rest. The French political system has not been able to provide the wide areas of agreement necessary to weld conflicting interests and ideologies together into national parties that are able to produce working political majorities. We indicated that there is a trend in this direction, but that many forces are still in the way. It will be some time before the student of French politics can be sure of the direction the system will take.

bibliography

The following publications constitute indispensable source material:

1. *Année politique:* published since 1944 by the Presses Universitaires de France. These annual volumes cover domestic politics, foreign relations, and economic trends.

2. *Sondages:* distributed quarterly since 1945 by the Institut Français de l'Opinion Publique, this publication gives results of opinion surveys.

3. Since 1963, the *Revue française de science politique* has regularly published articles, under the title *Les forces politiques,* which give excellent accounts of the development of, and trends within, political parties.

4. *Tableaux de l'économie française,* published by the National Institute of Statistical and Economic Studies, is an excellent compilation of social, demographic, and economic data.

5. *Le budget de la France,* published annually by the Ministère de Finances, gives a comprehensive and clear view of French public finance.

CHAPTER 1

BROGAN, D. W., *France Under the Republic, 1870–1939* (New York: Harper & Row, 1940).

———, *The French Nation from Napoleon to Petain, 1814–1940* (New York: Harper & Row, 1957).

BURY, J. P. T., *France, 1814–1940* (London: Methuen, 1956).

DUGUIT, L., H. MONNIER, and R. BONNARD, *Les constitutions et les principales lois politiques de la France, depuis 1789,* ed. Georges Berlia, 8th ed. (Paris, 1952).

EARLE, EDWARD MEAD (ed.), *Modern France: Problems of the Third and Fourth Republics* (Princeton: Princeton University Press, 1951).

McKAY, DONALD D., *The United States and France* (Cambridge: Harvard University Press, 1951).

SEIGNOBOS, CHARLES, *The Evolution of the French People* (New York: Knopf, 1932).

THOMSON, DAVID, *Two Frenchmen: Pierre Laval and Charles de Gaulle* (London: Cresset, 1951).

WRIGHT, GORDON, *The Reshaping of French Democracy* (New York: Reynal & Hitchcock, 1948).

CHAPTER 2

AMBLER, JOHN S., *The French Army in Politics, 1945–1962* (Columbus: Ohio State University Press, 1966).

BODIN, LOUIS, and JEAN TOUCHARD, *Front populaire 1936* (Paris: Armand Colin, 1961).

BOSWORTH, WILLIAM, *Catholicism and Crisis in Modern France: French Catholic Groups at the Threshold of the Fifth Republic* (Princeton: Princeton University Press, 1961).

VON CAMPENHAUSEN, AXEL, F., *L'Église et l'état en France* (Paris: Edition de l'Epi, 1964).

COUTROT, A., and F. DREYFUS, *Les forces réligieuses dans la société française* (Paris: Armand Colin, 1965).

DANSETTE, ADRIEN, *Histoire réligieuse de la France contemporaine sous la IIIème République* (Paris, 1957).

DARBON, MICHEL, *Le conflit entre la droite et la gauche dans le Catholicisme français, 1830–1953* (Paris: Toulouse-Privat, 1953).

DUVERGER, MAURICE, *The French Political System* (Chicago: University of Chicago Press, 1958).

FAUVET, JACQUES, *The Cockpit of France,* trans. Nancy Pearson (London: Harvill, 1960).

GIRARDET, RAOUL, *La crise militaire française, 1945–1962* (Paris: Armand Colin, 1964).

———, *Le nationalisme français, 1871–1914* (Paris: Armand Colin, 1966).

GOGUEL, FRANÇOIS, *France under the Fourth Republic* (Ithaca, N.Y.: Cornell University Press, 1952).

DE LA GORCE, PAUL-MARIE, *La république et son armée* (Paris: Fayard, 1963).

HOFFMANN, STANLEY, CHARLES KINDLEBERGER, et al., *In Search of France* (Cambridge: Harvard University Press, 1963).

JOLL, JAMES, *Intellectuals in Politics* (London: Weidenfeld & Nicolson, 1960).

KELLY, GEORGE ARMSTRONG, *Lost Soldiers: The French Army and Empire in Crisis, 1947–1962* (Cambridge: M.I.T. Press, 1965).

MACRAE, DUNCAN, JR., *Parliament, Parties and Society in France, 1946–1958* (New York: St. Martin's Press, 1967).

MEISEL, JAMES H., *The Fall of the Republic* (Ann Arbor: University of Michigan Press, 1962).

NOBÉCOURT, JACQUES, and JEAN PLANCHAIS, *Une histoire politique de l'armée,* vols. 1 and 2 (Paris: Editions du Seuil, 1967).

RÉMOND, RENÉ, *La Droite en France* (Paris: Editions Montaigne, 1963).

———, *La Vie Politique en France* (T.1 et 2) (Paris: Armand Colin, 1965, 1969).

SCHRAM, STUART R., *Protestantism and Politics in France* (Alençon: Corbiere & Jugain, 1954).

SIEGFREID, ANDRÉ, *France: A Study in Nationality* (New Haven: Yale University Press, 1930).

SOLTAU, ROGER, *French Political Thought in the Nineteenth Century* (New Haven: Yale University Press, 1931).

TANNENBAUM, EDWARD R., *The Action Française: Die-Hard Reactionaries in Twentieth-Century France* (New York: Wiley, 1962).

WERTH, ALEXANDER, *France, 1940–1956* (New York: Holt, 1956).

WRIGHT, GORDON, *The Reshaping of French Democracy* (Reynal, 1948).

WILLIAMS, PHILIP M., *Crisis and Compromise: Politics in the Fourth Republic* (Hamden, Conn.: Archon Books, 1964).

CHAPTER 3

ADAM, GÉRARD, *La C.F.T.C., 1940–1958* (Paris: Armand Colin, 1964).

———, *La C.G.T.-F.O.* (Paris: Études Syndicales, 1965).

ARON, ROBERT, *De Gaulle Triumphant: the Liberation of France, August 1944–May 1945* (New York: Putnam, 1964).

———, *France, Reborn: The History of the Liberation, June 1944–May 1945,* trans. Humphrey Hare (New York: Scribner's, 1964).

———, and GEORGE ELGEY, *The Vichy Regime, 1940–1944,* trans. Humphrey Hare (New York: Macmillan, 1958).

BEAUJOUR, MICHEL, and JACQUES EHRMANN, *La France contemporaire* (Paris: Armand Colin, 1965).

BODIN, LOUIS, *Les intellectuels* (Paris: Presses Universitaires de France, 1964).

DEBATISSE, MICHEL, *La révolution silencieuse: le combat des paysans* (Paris: Calmann-Levy, 1963).

DUPEUX, GEORGES, *La société française, 1789–1960* (Paris: Armand Colin, 1964).

Duveau, Georges, *Les instituteurs* (Paris: Editions du Seuil, 1957).

Duverger, Maurice, *The French Political System* (Chicago: University of Chicago Press, 1958).

Ehrmann, Henry W., *French Labor from Popular Front to Liberation* (New York: Oxford University Press, 1947).

———, *Organized Business in France* (Princeton: Princeton University Press, 1958).

Faure, Marcel, *Les paysans dans la société française* (Paris: Armand Colin, 1966).

Fauvet, Jacques, and Henri Mendras, *Les paysans et la politique dans la France contemporaine* (Paris: Armand Colin, 1958).

de la Fournière, and F. Borella, *Le syndicalisme étudiant* (1958).

Hamon, Lèo, *Les nouveaux comportements politique de la classe ouvrière* (Paris: Presses Universitaire de France, 1962).

Latreille, André, and André Siegfried, *Les forces réligieuses et la vie politique* (Paris: 1957).

LeBourre, R., *Le syndicalisme français dans la Vième République* (Paris: Calmann-Lévy, 1959).

Lorwin, Val R., *The French Labor Movement* (Cambridge: Harvard University Press, 1954).

Mallet, Serge, *La nouvelle classe ouvrière* (Paris: Editions du Seuil, 1963).

———, *Les paysans contre le passé* (Paris: Editions du Seuil, 1962).

Meynaud, Jean, *Les groups de pression en France* (Paris: Armand Colin, 1959).

———, *Nouvelles études sur les groupes de pression en France* (Paris: Armand Colin, 1962).

Monatte, Pierre, *Trois scissions syndicales* (Paris: Editions Ouvrières, 1958).

Monteil, V., *Les officiers* (Paris: Editions du Seuil, 1958).

Muret, Charlotte T., *French Royalist Doctrine Since the Revolution* (New York: Columbia University Press, 1933).

Paxton, Robert O., *Parades and Politics at Vichy: the French Officer Corps Under Marshal Pétain* (Princeton: Princeton University Press, 1966).

Planchais, Jean, *Le malaise de l'armée* (Paris: Plon, 1958).

Rémond, René, *Les Catholiques, le communism et les crises, 1929–1959* (Paris: Armand Colin, 1960).

Reynaud, Jean-Daniel, *Les syndicats en France* (Paris: Armand Colin, 1963).

Saposs, David J., *The Labor Movement in Post-War France* (New York: Columbia University Press, 1931).

Szokoloczy-Syllaba, Janos, *Les organizations professionnelles françaises et le marché commun* (Paris: Armand Colin, 1965).

Tavernier, Yves, *La F.N.S.E.A.* (Paris: Études Syndicales, 1965).

Wright, Gordon, *Rural Revolution in France* (Stanford, Calif.: Stanford University Press, 1964).

CHAPTER 4

Bardonnet, Daniel, *Evolution de la structure du Parti Radical* (Paris: Montchrétien, 1960).

Blum, Léon, *For All Mankind* (New York: Viking, 1946).

Cahiers de Communisme, *18e congrès du Parti Communiste français*, special issue (Feb.–March, 1967), Paris.

Charlot, Jean, *L'Union pour la nouvelle république* (Paris: Armand Colin, 1967).

Charnay, John Paul, *Les scrutins politiques en France de 1815 à 1962* (Paris: Armand Colin, 1964).

Colton, Joel, *Léon Blum: Humanist in Politics* (New York: Knopf, 1966).

DeTarr, Francis, *The French Radical Party from Herriot to Mendès-France* (New York: Oxford University Press, 1961).

Deutsch, Karl W., et al., *France, Germany and the Western Alliance: A Study of Elite Attitudes on European Integration and World Politics* (New York: Scribner's, 1967).

Dru, Jean, *Le Parti Democratique* (Paris: Juillard, 1962).

Duverger, Maurice (ed.), *Classes sociales et partis politiques* (Paris: Armand Colin, 1956).

———, *Partis politiques et classes sociales en France* (Paris: Armand Colin, 1956).

———, and Jacques Fauvet, *Le bipartisme est-il possible en France?* (Paris: Entretiens du samedi, 1965).

Einaudi, Mario, and François Goguel, *Christian Democracy in Italy and France* (South Bend, Ind.: University of Notre Dame Press, 1952).

Faucher, Jean André, *Les clubs politiques en France* (Paris: Les Editions John Didier, 1965).

Fauvet, Jacques, *Histoire du Parti Communiste français*, Vols. 1 and 2 (Paris: Fayard, 1964).

GODFREY, E. DREXEL, JR., *The Fate of the French Non-Communist Left* (New York: Doubleday, 1955).

HOFFMANN, STANLEY, *Le mouvement Poujade* (Paris: Armand Colin, 1956).

MALLET, SERGE, *Le Gaullisme et la gauche* (Paris: Editions du Seuil, 1965).

MANUEL, FRANK E., *The World of Henri Saint-Simon* (Cambridge: Harvard Univeristy Press, 1956).

MEISEL, JAMES J., *The Fall of the Republic: Military Revolt in France* (Ann Arbor: University of Michigan Press, 1963).

MICAUD, CHARLES A., *Communism and the French Left* (New York: Praeger, 1963).

———, *The French Right and Nazi Germany, 1933–1939* (Durham, N.C.: Duke University Press, 1943).

MOULIN, JEAN, *Un parti pour la gauche* (Paris: Editions du Seuil, 1965).

NICOLET, CLAUDE, *Le Radicalisme* (Paris: Presses Universitaires de France, 1957).

NOLAND, AARON, *The Founding of the French Socialist Party, 1893–1905* (Cambridge: Harvard University Press, 1956).

RÉMOND, RENÉ, *The Right Wing in France, from 1815 to de Gaulle*, trans. James M. Laux (Philadelphia: University of Pennsylvania Press, 1966).

ROSSI, ANGELO, *A Communist Party in Action: An Account of Its Organization and Operations in France* (New Haven: Yale University Press, 1949).

SIEGFRIED, ANDRÉ, *De la IVè à la Vè République* (Paris: Grasset, 1958).

SOLTAU, ROGER H., *French Parties and Politics, 1871–1930* (New York: Oxford University Press, 1930).

SUFFERT, GEORGES, *De Deffère à Mitterrand* (Paris: Editions du Seuil, 1966).

VEDEL, GEORGES, *La dépolitisation: mythe ou réalité?* (Paris: Armand Colin, 1962).

VIANSSON-PONTÉ, PIERRE, *Les Gaullistes* (Paris: Editions du Seuil, 1963).

———, *Les politiques* (Paris: Calmann-Lévy, 1967).

CHAPTER 5

Association Française de la Science Politique, Les élections du 2 janvier 1956 (Paris: Armand Colin, 1957).

CAMPBELL, PETER, *French Electoral Systems and Elections, 1789–1957* (New York: Praeger, 1958).

CHARNAY, JEAN-PAUL, *Le suffrage politique en France* (Paris: Mouton, 1965).

DEUTSCH, EMERIC, LINDON, and WEILL, *Les familles politiques aujourd'hui en France* (Paris: Les Éditions de Minuit, 1966).

GOGUEL, FRANÇOIS, "L'élection presidentielle française de décembre 1965," *Revue française de science politique* 16 (April 1966).

———, *Géography des élections françaises de 1870 à 1951* (Paris: Armand Colin, 1957).

———, *Le référendum du 8 janvier 1961* (Paris: Armand Colin, 1962).

———, *Le référendum d'octobre et les élections de novembre 1962* (Paris: Armand Colin, 1965).

———, *Le référendum de septembre et les élections de novembre 1958* (Paris: Armand Colin, 1961).

ROCHECORBON, G., "Le contrôle de la campagne électorale," *Revue française de science politique* 16 (April 1966).

WILLIAMS, PHILIP, *The French Parliament* (1969).

CHAPTER 6

ANDREWS, WILLIAM, *French Politics and Algeria* (New York: Meredith, 1962).

ARON, ROBERT, *An Explanation of DeGaulle*, trans. Marianne Sinclair (New York: Harper & Row, 1966).

BAUM, WARREN C., *The French Economy and the State* (Princeton: Princeton University Press, 1958).

University of California, Department of Political Science, *The Fifth Republic* [collection of essays and papers] (Berkeley: University of California Press, 1961).

CHAPMAN, BRIAN, *Introduction to French Local Government* (London: Allen & Unwin, 1953).

CHAPSAL, JACQUES, *La vie politique en France depuis 1940* (Paris: Presses Universitaires de France, 1966).

COHEN, STEPHEN, *French Economic Planning* (London: Weidenfeld & Nicolson, 1965).

CROZIER, MICHEL, *The Bureaucratic Phenomenon* (Chicago: University of Chicago Press, 1964).

DEBRÉ, MICHEL, *Au Service de la Nation* (Paris, 1963).

DE GAULLE, CHARLES, *War Memoirs:* Vol. 1, *The Call to Honour* (New York: Viking Press, 1955); Vol. 2, *Unity* (New York: Simon & Schuster, 1959); Vol. 3, *Salvation* (New York: Simon & Schuster, 1960).

DUVERGER, MAURICE, *La Cinquième République* (Paris: Presses Universitaires de France, 1959).

———, *Constitutions et documents politiques* (Paris: Presses Universitaires de France, 1957).

———, *Institutions politiques* (Paris: Presses Universitaires de France, 1965).

GODFREY, E. DREXEL, JR., *The Government of France* (New York: Thomas Y. Crowell, 1963).

GOGUEL, FRANÇOIS, and ALFRED GROSSER, *La politique en France* (Paris: Armand Colin, 1964).

GRÉGOIRE, ROGER, *The French Civil Service,* rev. ed., trans. (Brussels: International Institute of Administrative Science, 1965).

HAURIOU, ANDRÉ, *Droit constitutionnel et institutions politiques* (Paris: Editions Montchréstien, 1966).

MACRIDIS, ROY C., *De Gaulle: Implacable Ally* (New York: Harper & Row, 1966).

MANNONI, EUGÈNE, *Moi, Général De Gaulle* (Paris: Editions du Seuil, 1964).

MOULIN, JEAN, *L'État et le citoyen* (Paris: Editions du Seuil, 1961).

PICKLES, DOROTHY, *The Fifth French Republic* (New York: Praeger, 1962).

PRELOT, MARCEL, *Le parlementarisme peut-il être limité sans être annihilé?* (Paris: Entretiens du samedi, 1965).

RÉMOND, RENÉ, *La vie politique en France* (Paris: Armand Colin, 1965).

REYNAUD, PAUL, *Et après?* (Paris: Librairie Plon, 1964).

RIDLEY, F., and J. BLONDEL, *Public Administration in France* (London: Routledge, 1964).

VEDEL, GEORGES, and FRANÇOIS GOGUEL, *Les institutions politiques de la France* (Paris: Entretiens du samedi, fevrier, 1964).

CHAPTER 7

ARON, RAYMOND, *France Steadfast and Changing* (Cambridge: Harvard University Press, 1960).

AUBY, JEAN-MARIE; and ROBERT DUCOS-ADER, *Institutions administratives* (Paris: Dalloz, 1966).

BELOFF, NORA, *The General Says "No": Britain's Exclusion from Europe* (Baltimore: Penguin, Books, 1964).

CAMPS, MIRIAM, *What Kind of Europe? A Community Since de Gaulle's Veto* (New York: Oxford University Press, 1965).

CHAPMAN, BRIAN, *Introduction to French Local Government* (London: Allen & Unwin, 1953).

———, *The Prefects and Provincial France* (London: Allen & Unwin, 1955).

DEBRÉ, MICHEL, "La nouvelle constitution" (Tours, 1958).

FURNISS, EDGAR, *France, Troubled Ally* (New York: Harper & Row, 1960).

GOURNAY, BERNARD, *Introduction à la science administrative* (Paris: Armand Colin, 1966).

Un Grand débat parlementaire: L'aménagement du territoire (Paris: La Documentation Française, 1964).

GREGOIRE, ROGER, *The French Civil Service* (Brussels: International Institute of Administrative Science, 1964).

GROSSER, ALFRED, *Foreign Policy of the Fifth Republic* (New York: Little, Brown, 1966).

———, *France and the European Community* (London: PEP, 1961).

HOFFMANN, STANLEY, "La constitution de la Ve République," *Revue française de science politique* 9 (March 1959).

DE LANVERSIN, JACQUES, *L'Aménagement du territoire* (Paris: Librairies Techniques, 1965).

LAVAU, GEORGES, and FRANCIS DE BAEQUE, *La région et la réforme administrative* (Paris: Entretiens du samedi, 1964).

LEMERLE, PAUL, *La planification en France* (Paris: Institut d'Études Politiques de l'Université de Paris, 1964–65).

McKAY, DONALD C., *The United States and France* (Cambridge: Harvard University Press, 1951).

MACRIDIS, ROY C., and BERNARD BROWN, *The De Gaulle Republic: Quest for Unity* (Homewood, Ill.: Dorsey, 1960).

REYNAUD, PAUL, *The Foreign Policy of Charles de Gaulle, A Critical Assessment* (New York: Odyssey Press, 1964).

SHEAHAN, JOHN, *Promotion and Control of Industry in Postwar France* (Cambridge: Harvard University Press, 1963).

Viot, Pierre, *L'Aménagement du territoire en France* (Paris: Institut d'Études Politiques de l'Université de Paris, 1964–65).

Williams, Philip, and Martin Harrison, *De Gaulle's Republic* (London: Longmans, Green, 1960).

CHAPTER 8

Aron, Raymond, *Le grand débat* (Paris: Calmann-Lévy, 1963).

Bloch-Morhange, Jacques, *Le Gaullisme* (Paris: Plon, 1963).

Boisde, Raymond, *Pour une modernisation de la politique* (Paris: Plon, 1962).

Duverger, Maurice, *La Vè République et le régime presidentiel* (Paris: Artheme Fayard, 1961).

Grosser, Alfred, *La politique extérieure de la Cinquième République* (Paris: Editions du Seuil, 1965).

Macridis, Roy C. (ed.), *Foreign Policy in World Politics*, 4th ed. (Englewood Cliffs, N.J.: Prentice-Hall, 1972), Chap. 3.

Martin, Marcel (ed.), *Les institutions politiques de la France* (Paris: La Documentation Française, 1959–61).

Massip, Roger, *De Gaulle et l'Europe* (Paris: Flammarion, 1963).

Pickles, Dorothy, *Algeria and France: From Colonialism to Cooperation* (New York: Praeger, 1963).

Schneider, Bertrand, *La Vè République et l'Algérie* (Paris: Editions Temoignage Chrétien, 1959).

Vianson-Ponté, Pierre, *Histoire de la Republique Gaullienne* (2 vols.) (Paris: Fayard, 1971).

Werth, Alex, *De Gaulle* (New York: Simon & Schuster, 1966).

Karl W. Deutsch

THE
GERMAN
FEDERAL
REPUBLIC

1914

1933

LATVIAN SSR

LITHUANIAN
SSR

BALTIC SEA

Memel
(1939)

DENMARK   SWEDEN

Königsberg
(Kaliningrad)

NORTH SEA

Kiel
SCHLESWIG-
HOLSTEIN

Lübeck

HAMBURG

BREMEN

Danzig
(Gdansk)

EAST
PRUSSIA

Present
Russian-
Polish
Border

Stettin
(Szczecin)

GERMAN

LOWER SAXONY

Weser

Hannover

Berlin

Potsdam

Oder

Warsaw

DEMOCRATIC

NETHERLANDS

NORTH RHINE-

Essen

GERMAN

Düsseldorf   Ruhr

WESTPHALIA

Kassel

Leipzig

Elbe

Neisse

Oder

POLAND

Cologne

Bonn   Rhine

HESSE

GIUM

Weimar

Dresden

Breslau
(Vraclav)

REPUBLIC

SILESIA

RHINELAND-
PALATINATE   Frankfurt

LUXEMBOURG

FEDERAL

SUDETENLAND

Prague

SAAR

BAVARIA

CZECHOSLOVAKIA

LORRAINE

Nürnberg

BOHEMIA-MORAVIA   (1939)

BADEN-

ALSACE

Stuttgart   Danube

REPUBLIC   Munich

WUERTEMBERG

Vienna

R. S. F. S. R.

SWITZERLAND

AUSTRIA

HUNGARY

(1938)

RUMANIA

ITALY

YUGOSLAVIA

KEY

astern and Southern Boundaries
f Hitler's Third Reich, 1940

Annexed Areas, 1938-1939

oundary of Weimar Republic

Areas Lost at Versailles, 1919

0   20   60   100

MILES

(French)

EAST

WEST
(British)

(Soviet)

BERLIN
(American)   BERLIN

The Wall

0   5

Miles

Among the great industrial powers of the world, West Germany—the German Federal Republic (G.F.R.)—by the early 1970s seemed very prosperous and stable for the time being, strained by recurrent inner tensions and by uncertainty about its long-run future, and crucial for world peace. In the world, it ranked ninth in population (with over 59 million people), fourth in gross national product (about $112 billion in 1965), and second in exports (about 10% of the world total). Already by the end of the 1950s, the exports of the Federal Republic had overtaken those of the United Kingdom. The Federal Republic had achieved and maintained full employment. It had found shelter and work for more than 13 million German expellees and refugees from Eastern Europe and from Communist-ruled East Germany, called since 1949 the German Democratic Republic (G.D.R.). Between the years 1960 and 1970, the Federal Republic's national income grew at almost 5% a year, in real terms—that is, corrected for the effects of rising prices and money wages. In the 1950s and 1960s the rate of growth had been so rapid that total West German national income had already outstripped the income of France by 1960 and overtook that of Britain in 1964. In terms of per capita income, the German Federal Republic at the start of the 1970s ranked second to the United States among the world's major powers. Only a few smaller nations, such as Canada, Sweden and Switzerland, exceeded the G.F.R. in this respect.

A PICTURE OF STABILITY

Starting in 1950 and continuing down to 1971, prosperity in economics had been accompanied by remarkable stability in politics. Parties catering to political extremes elicited next to no response from the voters. Early in the 1950s, less than 3% of the total vote was cast for the Communists, and less than 5% for the Socialist Reich party (SRP) and other

ONE

introduction

I am indebted to Professor Wolf-Dieter Narr for valuable data and interpretations on a number of points, and to Mr. Horst D. Dornbusch for valuable assistance throughout. The responsibility for any weakness or errors in this text remains, of course, my own. K. W. D.

splinter parties of the extreme right. When the Federal Constitutional Court outlawed the SRP in 1952 and the Communist party (KPD) in 1956, these decisions were accepted with scarcely a ripple of protest by the bulk of the public. In 1967 a Communist successor party, called *Deutsche Kommunistische Partei* (DKP), was permitted to operate legally, but did not run candidates in the 1969 election. Subsequent to the legalization of a Communist party, two more leftist parties emerged and participated in the 1969 election. They were the *Unabhängige Arbeiter Partei,* UAP (Independent Workers party), and the *Aktion Demokratischer Fortschritt,* ADF (Action for Democratic Progress), and their share of the vote was even less than 1%. On the far right, the extreme nationalist National Democratic party of Germany (NPD) in 1966 and 1967 received at most 8% of the votes in some provincial (*"Land"*) elections, but by 1969 their nationwide share had dropped to about 4%, and it continued to decline in 1970 and 1971.

If moderate parties consistently commanded the support of over 90% of the electorate, a single party of moderately conservative leanings, the Christian Democratic Union (CDU), retained at all times between one-third and more than one-half of the popular vote and until 1969 the clear preponderance of effective political power. Its main rival, the Social Democratic party (SPD), concentrated on promoting the interests of labor and policies of social welfare, within the framework of constitutional democracy, and relegated its traditional ideological appeal of socialism and the nationalization of industry to second place. These moderate policies secured for the SPD between one-quarter and over two-fifths of the national vote, a national coalition government with CDU from 1966 to 1969, and the leadership of a coalition government with the smaller Free Democratic party (FDP) from 1969 onward. Below the national level, the same tactics won the SPD a share in the government of several of the states of the Federal Republic, and the control of a number of important municipal governments, including such cities as Hamburg, Bremen, Munich, and Frankfurt.

Between them, the two major parties steadily increased their share of the popular vote, from 60% in 1949 to 89% in 1969, gaining 94% of the seats in the Bundestag (the federal legislature) in the latter year.

No genuine two-party system, however, thus far has become stabilized. The voting strength of the SPD never has been sufficient to carry it into federal office on its own, and the CDU has only once won a popular majority (in 1957). However, until 1966 the strategy of the CDU, together with that of the smaller middle-class parties, such as the Free Democratic Party (FDP), effectively barred the Socialists from any coalition government at the national level. Whether the first two national coalition governments incorporating the SPD— those of the CDU and SPD (1966–69) and of the SPD and FDP (since 1969)—will bring a lasting change in this pattern remains to be seen. From 1949 to 1966, in any case, West Germany was governed by what was called a "one-and-a-half-party" system, under which the CDU dominated the federal executive, but the SPD made its own substantial contributions in the federal legislature, and even more at the state and local government level. Since 1969, however, there has been in effect a "two-and-a-half-party" system even at the national level, and the impact of the SPD on national policies has increased. Accompanying all these developments has been a remarkable degree of social peace and political tranquility which the coalition governments since 1966 have striven to consolidate still further. Strikes have been few, orderly, and relatively easily settled; political riots and violent demonstrations have been conspicuous by their absence; and until 1968 the police had to worry mainly not about political unrest but about the rapidly swelling automobile traffic.

SOME STANDARDS FOR A MORE CRITICAL APPRAISAL

All of this is true. But it is only one part of the truth. From the mid-1960s onward, a tide of criticism has been rising within the Federal Republic, among many of its thinkers and writers and particularly among an important portion of its younger citizens—those who are now under 35 years old, but whose age group is likely to have a major voice in German politics in the mid-1970s and 1980s. From 1968 onward, their discontent has become loudly manifest in the universities and sometimes in the streets. To remain ignorant of their criticisms, to fail to understand what they say and why they say it, would be to ignore an important part of the present and future reality of German politics.

By what yardsticks do these critics measure the conspicuous success story of Western Germany? Certainly, they do not all speak with one voice. Their complaints vary widely, and so do their demands. But three major themes stand out among them.

The Problem of the Past

First, they cannot and will not forget the terrible past of their country. In three great critical periods of our century, they insistently remind us, Germany chose a course of oppression and destruction. In 1914, Germany had its full share in bringing on World War I. In the midst of the Great Depression, in 1933, Germany accepted and supported the dictatorship of Adolf Hitler and the National Socialist party; and in 1939, Hitler's Germany incurred the major responsibility for bringing about World War II and the Nazi acts of genocide committed in its course.

What was it—the young critics ask—what was it in the structure and institutions of German society, in the psychology and culture of the German people, in the personalities of their fathers, that made these things possible? And if there have been some fatal flaws beneath the orderly surface of German life in the past, may not these hidden flaws still be there, ready at the next opportunity to drive the German people into dictatorship, war, and catastrophe once more? Handsome new West German cities have been built out of the rubble of World War II, but are not some old timebombs still ticking in the cellars?

The Test of Social Structure

Related to this theme of the persistent past is the second theme, the theme of structure. The word is used so often that it is worthwhile stopping here and making quite sure that we understand its meaning.

Structure, as we use the word in our everyday language, is something that changes but slowly, or scarcely at all in the period which we study, in contrast to *processes,* which change relatively quickly during our period of observation. In this sense, *structure* is a relative notion, depending on the time perspective of our observation. To the student of street life, the streets and houses are structure, and what people do there is process. To the city planner, the building of streets is a process and the hills beneath them are structure; but to the geologist, the hills are a process which will end with their erosion. Beyond this, structure means something which resists change; it is seen as relatively rigid, and at best it can be changed only with considerable cost and effort. "Structures" are, therefore, in reality a subclass of processes: they are those processes which change relatively slowly and which can be changed only with great difficulty.

There is a further connotation of *structure.* In its meaning as "fundamental" or "basic" structure—*substructure* or *infrastructure*—it refers to something linked *asymmetrically* to some less basic structure, or *superstructure.* The notion is borrowed from the image of a building: a small change in the substructure will produce a large change in the superstructure, while a large change in the superstructure may have only a minor impact on the substructure beneath it.

But why do "structures" behave in these peculiar ways? We can find an answer, if we link all these commonsense meanings of structure to a somewhat more scientific definition of the concept. A *structure,* in this view, is a set of interlocking and mutually reinforcing—and thus self-preserving and self-repairing—processes. It is this interlocking and mutual reinforcement that makes structures so stable, so durable, so resistant to change, and so likely to restore themselves after limited injuries or disturbances, and that permits them to support other, less stable and durable "superstructures" linked to them.

Such interlocking and mutually reinforcing structures exist not only in mechanics (like the girders of a bridge) or in biology (like the skeleton of a body) but they exist also in political and social systems. Laws are expected to last longer than governments which come and go. In this sense, laws may function as a structural framework for the governmental process. A constitution, in turn, is supposed to change less often than the laws built on its framework; if this is so, then the constitution functions as a substructure for the legal system. But the differences between rulers and ruled, elites and masses, rich and poor may be even more persistent than the written constitution of a country; and so may such long-lasting institutions as the family, or private property, or bureaucratic authority—the obedience given habitually to superiors. If this is the case, then these social classes and institutions may form the basic structure of a country, more durable than its changing laws, governments, and constitutions.

During this century, the governments and constitutions of Germany have changed quickly and often. Western Germany, either independently or as part of greater Germany, has been governed by a monarchy (1871–1918), a unitary republic (1918–33), a National Socialist dictatorship (1933–45), Allied military governments (1945–49), and a Federal Republic (since 1949). But big business firms and rich families, such as those of Krupp and Thyssen, have remained prosperous and influential throughout all changes. Do they not form a part, some critics ask, of a social and economic structure, unequal and undemocratic, but more fundamental, durable, and powerful than any change in the forms of law and government? And if so, is not the Federal Republic condemned to obey this underlying structure at future moments of crisis and decision, and so presumably to reenact much of its tragic past? What hope is there for democracy to become truly strong and stable, so long as this basic undemocratic social structure remains undisturbed?

The Yardstick of Democracy

These questions lead us to the third theme of the critics. They measure the Federal Republic not by comparing it to the past—a yardstick which could not fail to highlight its great successes and accomplishments. Rather, they insist on measuring it against their own conception of democracy—a democracy that does not yet exist anywhere in fact but only in their thoughts and aspirations. But they have learned to develop these aspirations in large part in the environment of the Federal Republic where they grew up, as well as from the long history of the democratic aspirations of mankind.[1] Their notion of democracy does not describe any present-day reality, even though some partial aspects of their ideas may be found in reality in the G.F.R. or in some other countries. What it does describe is a sense of direction. It indicates the direction in which they would like their country to go, and in which they would like every industrial country and people to go, since they hold their goal image of democracy to be relevant for all of them.

What, then, is their notion of democracy? According to some of the most thoughtful of the younger scholars and writers, a whole series of tests are essential for *democracy* in the full meaning of the concept.[2] For convenience, we shall put these tests under fourteen headings:

1. Most obviously, democracy means "the rule of the many," and hence *majority rule*. But majority rule alone could degenerate into mere populism—the rule of a blind and conformist majority which easily may disregard reality, the rights of individuals and smaller groups, and the rights of the possible different majority of

[1] For a discussion of this topic, with pertinent opinion data, see Rudolf Wildenmann and Max Kaase, *Die unruhige Generation: Eine Untersuchung zu Politik und Demokratie in der Bundesrepublik* (Mannheim: Lehrstuhl für politische Wissenschaft, Universität Mannheim, 1968).

[2] For a detailed discussion of the concept and problem of democracy in the West German context, see Wolf-Dieter Narr and Frieder Naschold, *Theorie der Demokratie* (Stuttgart: Kohlhammer, 1971).

tomorrow against perhaps the transitory majority of the day.

2. A second test is a far-reaching measure of *equality,* not only of opportunity but also of probable attainment. This includes a considerable degree of equality in wealth; in social status and respect; in influence and power; in health, nutrition, and in chances for health and physical and mental well-being; and in other values relevant to the society and its members.

3. A third test for democracy, therefore, is its treatment of all *individuals and small groups* —including dissenting ones—as valuable in themselves, and also as potential cognitive and moral resources of the society in which they live. Democracy exists to the degree that not only the majority but also all such minorities are accorded freedom, security, respect for their identity and autonomy, and equal and adequate opportunities for social and political participation as well as for autonomous development—and all this not as a matter of tolerance but of fundamental human right.

4. An extension of the preceding principle is the test of the treatment of more or less cohesive *minorities,* such as those of language, ethnic character, religion, culture, philosophy, or political opinion. Some of these minorities of today may become the majorities of tomorrow; others, like some ethnic or religious groups, are likely to remain permanent minorities. The freedom and security of all of them as cohesive groups, as well as in the persons of their individual members, is a major test of democracy.

5. A fifth test is the *position of the poorest and most disadvantaged group or stratum* in the society. What is the bottom of the ladder in the distribution of wealth, freedom, power, health, and other basic human needs and wants in a democracy? This test recalls the biblical saying of Jesus, "What you have done to the least of these, you have done to me." And this test applies even to those of the poor and disadvantaged who may be unorganized, uninformed, or inarticulate, and thus usually pushed aside and forgotten in the push and pull of politics.

6. A sixth test is the *opportunity for direct participation* by individuals in decisions which affect them seriously.

7. The preceding points imply a further test for democracy: *freedom of speech, of information and opinion*—that is, the freedom to know, to read, to learn, to ask questions and seek answers, and to communicate them freely, without stifling barriers of secrecy, censorship, or persecution for unpopular views.

8. A related test is the *freedom to organize:* to join groups, parties, and organizations, and to found new ones, in the pursuit of what one thinks are one's *interests,* that is, the objects of one's attention, one's expectations of reward, and one's goal images—fallible as all these may be, and inconvenient as governments or popular majorities may sometimes find them.

9. All these rights, if they are to be effective and secure, require some framework of laws and procedures, strong and dependable enough not to be bent by the will of the mighty, nor by the excitement of the day. *Constitutionalism and legality,* respect for established procedures, "a government of laws not men"—this, too, is a test of democracy.

10. All these rights and laws may depend in practice very much on the spirit in which they are applied, that is, on the political culture of the community. Here a test of democracy is the *trust in the autonomy and spontaneity of individuals and small groups,* including trust in their efforts at initiative and innovation. Trust implies a decision on which side to take our chances when our information is incomplete. Thus, in Anglo-American law, an accused person is held to be innocent until proved guilty; the first trust is in people and their innocence, the burden of proof is on those who allege guilt. Generally, a democracy is the more genuine the more both the government and the public are willing to take their chances in trusting people.

11. Freedom to speak becomes a farce without the freedom to remain silent. Another crucial aspect of political culture is *respect for a sphere of privacy* in the affairs of individuals and in their relations with each other. Not to have one's mail read, one's telephone tapped, one's lawyer or physician forced to reveal confidential information; not to force children and parents, or husbands and wives to spy on or testify against each other; not to put priests, nuns, or ministers of religion under pressure to reveal information entrusted to them under the secret of the confession, or in situations substantially similar to it—all this is also an essential test of democracy.

12. To be truly democratic, a political system must serve the chief needs and long-run interests of its population. This requires *openness to correction by reality.* A democracy must not be a self-closing system, defending its collective illusions to the bitter end. It must not be a cognitive trap for its people. It must equip them, and its government must be equipped, with adequate facilities to test opinions against facts, expectations against outcomes, once-promising policies against their consequences. It cannot be infallible, but it must have adequate capacities to correct its errors.

13. A democratic government must govern; it must get things done; and it must deliver the goods, or enough of them, if the people are to continue supporting it. This test, then, is once again one of the most obvious—the test of the *performance* of government or of a political system. The most important aspect of this performance is the delivery of other values and opportunities to the people.

14. What matters to people is not only what they get but when and how they get it. The performance of a government can enhance the sense of power and effectiveness of its people—their sense of being in charge of their own lives and of having some control over their own fate and their environment—or it can turn them into diminished passive objects of paternalism. A fourteenth test for every democratic political system, therefore, is its *responsiveness* not only to the major needs, values, and orientations and desires of its population, but also its responsiveness to their messages and initiatives.

No government and no political system ever has met all these tests perfectly. What these tests jointly can tell us is rarely a "yes" or "no," but much more often a "more" or "less." Among them, these fourteen tests permit an estimate of how far a government has moved in this direction, and which way it is currently moving.

To decide whether a government is near to or far from this goal image of genuine democracy, and whether it is moving closer toward it, or is standing still, or moving away from it—all these are no idle speculations. For many of the younger and more critical voters in the German Federal Republic, the answers to these questions have a direct bearing on the legitimacy which they will accord to the government and the political system of their country.

Legitimacy: The Basis of Government When No One Is Watching

When we call a government *legitimate,* we are saying at least three things about it.

First, we say that its commands and prohibitions are in *harmony with our personal notions of right and wrong*—with our feelings as well as with our rational ideas about morality. We feel that the government has a moral right to act as a government, and that its orders, too, are generally good and right. In these regards, we then tend to integrate, or at least to treat as consonant and mutually reinforcing, the personal everyday notions of right and wrong that we learned in childhood and the official norms of civic and political "right" and "wrong," as established by the government and the entire political system, and as applied to the behavior of citizens, public officials, the government, and the nation-state as a whole.

In the second place, accepting a government or a political regime as legitimate means to accord it *authority,* similar to the authority most have learned in childhood to accord to our parents. Such authority means that we tend to accept messages or commands *because they come from a certain source,* an "authoritative" source, more or less irrespective of the content of the message or command. What counts in authority relations is not the merits of the message (such as the evidence for its truth or its morality) but the nature of its source. In the days before World War I, when most Germans considered the Hohenzollern monarchy legitimate, Emperor Wilhelm II in a famous speech told his soldiers that they ought to be ready to shoot down their fathers and mothers, if he, their imperial commander in chief, should order them to do so—and only a minority of Germans protested. In 1914, his untrue statement that Germany had been attacked by France was believed by his people, and thus his commands taking them into World War I were accepted with enthusiasm. In 1918, however, when the war had been lost and the majority of German soldiers and civilians had ceased to consider his rule and policies to be legitimate, the emperor fled quickly to the Netherlands. There he remained in retirement, having lost his authority in the eyes of most of his people, and with it their obedience and support, and hence most of his power.

The third aspect of legitimacy follows from the two preceding ones. To accept a government or regime as legitimate means to obey it because we feel it is right and good to do so, and because we feel that it speaks with authority that deserves to be obeyed even if we cannot ourselves test or judge its commands on their merits. Through the notion of legitimacy, we have linked our civic obedience to our own inner psychic processes, to our deep beliefs of right and wrong, to the structure of our own personality, to our respect and self-respect. If we fail to obey an authority which we have accepted as legitimate, we are likely to feel diminished or divided within ourselves. Legitimacy thus is also maintained by the *automatic penalty of intrapsychic conflict*—of a "bad conscience"—in the event of disobedience.

Conscience, according to the ancient Greek Sophists, is what controls our behavior when nobody is watching us. In modern terms, conscience is that set of rules of behavior which we learned so early in life and internalized so thoroughly that they have become a part of the more-or-less permanent structure of our personality. Legitimacy is thus the crucial link between the commands of the state and the conscience of the individual.

Even an illegitimate government can rule, so long as it can credibly promise and threaten, punish and reward. It may be obeyed out of sheer apathy and habit, out of disgust and despair at the seemingly hopeless prospect of opposition, or out of the weary feeling that any alternative regime would be no better. But no illegitimate government can count on much obedience or support once its supervision falters or its power wanes. Even those who passively obeyed it will not come now to its aid.

To deny legitimacy to a government or to a political system, or to take away the legitimacy it once had, is thus to pose a major threat to its stability and its long-run survival. Governments can destroy their own legitimacy, by misrule or neglect, by catastrophic errors, or by prolonged immobility and unresponsiveness. If they wish to survive, they must ceaselessly maintain and defend their legitimacy, not only against their critics but even more against the changing demands and pressures of their environment and the developing needs and values of their peoples.

Just this has been happening in the late 1960s and early 1970s in the German Federal Republic, as it has been happening in many other advanced industrial countries. The children of the age of industrial growth and technological marvels after 1950 are beginning to question the wisdom, the goodness, and the legitimacy of many social, economic, and political practices and institutions, and with them they have come to question the legitimacy of the government and of the political order of their country.

For this reason, their criticisms will receive a good deal of attention in this study. Many of their questions are confused. Some of their critical yardsticks are not well thought out, or even inappropriate. But since they touch upon the legitimacy of the German Federal Republic in the eyes of a significant portion of its young citizens, they cannot be ignored.

This portion, to be sure, is far from a majority. Less than one-third of a representative sample of young West Germans between 18 and 29 years of age wanted "far-reaching changes" in their country. But nearly the same share (30%) of respondents between 30 and 64 years wanted such changes; and even among voters 65 years and older, one-fourth favored far-reaching change. By contrast, only one-fourth of all voters under 50 years of age felt that "it would not be so bad if everything remained as it is now," and between 40 and 50% in all age groups favored moderate change.

A majority of West Germans want some social change, but only a minority want the changes to be far-reaching. Even fewer, it seems clear, want such social changes to be radical. The same is true of German youth and of German students. The specific changes they want are moderate in character.

The Unconsolidated Foundations of West German Democracy

And yet the questions by the more critical one-third of opinion will not be stilled, and on specific criticisms of structural inequality and undemocratic practices they find majority backing. "Differences in the conditions of life of particular social groups" are seen as "very large" by 60% of students and 51% of nonacademic youth. The proposition that "members of higher social strata receive preferential treatment in courts of law" is believed by 60% of West German students and by a staggering 78% of their nonacademic age-mates.[3]

In contrast to these critical views are the massive aggressive and authoritarian attitudes that live on, like the large fragments of a ruined fortress, in the minds of a large part of the German electorate. Three-fourths of German poll respondents agreed to the statement, "National Socialism also had its good sides—at least there was order and cleanliness."[4] That National Socialism was "a good idea, only badly carried out" was believed by 50% of all voters responding to a 1968 poll and by 42% of respondents in a parallel youth survey of the age group 17–24 years old, but only by 9% of the students. In the same polls, one-third of all voters, as well as of nonacademic youth, but a mere 5% of the students, agreed that "we ought to have again a single strong national party that really represents the interests of all strata of our people." The call for a national leader,

"as it used to be before," who would "rule Germany with a strong hand for the good of all" was endorsed by one-fourth of all voters polled but only by one-eighth of the nonacademic young and by no more than 4% of the students.[5]

Similarly, 53% of the voters would "not tolerate any criticism of our fatherland by foreigners"; 71% believe that "the number of crimes would rise less rapidly if the death penalty would be restored"; and 74% want an end put to all questions of whether someone had a high position under the Nazi regime.[6]

At the same time, according to the same surveys, 60% of the voters and about 50% of the young "see practically no chance to influence the political process in the Federal Republic in any other way than through the formal act of voting, to be repeated every four years." These results confirm the earlier findings of the American political scientists Gabriel Almond and Sidney Verba that the low level of political participation in the Federal Republic and the small faith of many of its citizens in their own political effectiveness leaves a large part of the people with only feeble emotional ties to their political system. Their "system affect," as Almond and Verba call it, is much weaker than in longer-established democracies; and so are perhaps their sense of the legitimacy of their political regime and their loyalty to it.

So long as the Federal Republic is highly prosperous, this may not matter much. But if prosperity should decline under the pressures of inflation or depression, or if international security should give way to acute military threats, the latent strains and weaknesses in the West German political system could have serious effects.[7] In regard to this still incomplete consolidation of West German democracy, and to the potential dangers which it poses, the 1970s may well be an era of decision.

[3] Wildenmann and Kaase, *Die unruhige Generation,* pp. 44–45.

[4] Klaus Liepelt, "Anhänger der neuen Rechtspartei: Ein Beitrag zur Diskussion über das Wählerreservoir der NPD," *Politische Vierteljahresschrift* 8, no. 2 (1967): 263.

[5] Wildenmann and Kaase, *Die unruhige Generation,* p. 71.

[6] Ibid., pp. 71–72.

[7] Ibid., pp. 7, 37–40; see also Gabriel A. Almond and Sidney Verba, *The Civic Culture* (Boston: Little, Brown, 1965).

The Incomplete Consolidation of Territorial Identity

In most states, both the government and the people know clearly what the territory of the state is and who its citizens are, as well as what is foreign territory and who are foreigners. Under constitutional regimes, they usually also know what the constitution of the country is. In the German Federal Republic none of these matters were clear when that state came into being in 1949. All definitions were to be provisional, pending the eventual reunification of West Germany and the Communist-ruled "Eastern Zone," which became the G.D.R. Only by the early 1970s did it seem that the provisional had become more nearly permanent, that a distinct identity of the Federal Republic had emerged, and that the G.F.R. and its allies might be able to negotiate more permanent territorial settlements with the Soviet bloc. This peculiar condition of West Germany deserves to be looked at in slightly more detail.

In a sense, the German Federal Republic is the youngest of the great powers. A German federal government with limited powers was set up in West Germany under the auspices of the occupying powers—the United States, Britain, and France—only in 1949, after four years of foreign military rule. This Federal Republic was given legal sovereignty in 1955, but had not yet attained full military sovereignty by 1971.

Recent in time, the Federal Republic is also incomplete in space. It includes only two-thirds of the area of present-day "Germany," and only three-quarters of its population. One-third of the area and more than 17 million Germans are included in the Communist-ruled German Democratic Republic. A discussion of the institutions and politics of that entity would go far beyond the framework of this section; and they should better be discussed, in any case, among the political institutions of the other Soviet-bloc countries, which the government of the G.D.R. now resembles far more than it does those of the German Federal Republic, or of other Western countries.

It used to be widely believed in the West,

and particularly in West Germany, that the Soviet-dominated government of the G.D.R. lacks popular support; that it would fall as soon as Soviet Russian military backing were withdrawn from it; and that the territory and population of the G.D.R. would then quickly become reunited with those of the Federal Republic under a single national German government. Accordingly, the government of the Federal Republic—like that of the United States and other Western allies—has long denied formal recognition to the G.D.R., but by the same token it has officially considered the Federal Republic only as the forerunner and trustee of the future reunited German national state.

This reunited national state would then comprise nearly 80 million Germans, [8] and it would form by far the strongest power in Europe, and one of the three or four strongest powers in the world. The constitution of that future, reunited Germany would have to be drawn up by the representatives of its entire population. Until that time, according to West German political and legal doctrine, the present Federal Republic with all its laws and institutions is in theory provisional, since nothing must take away the right of the future all-German constitutional convention to change the structure of the government.

Not only the frontiers of the Federal Republic, but even those of a reunited Germany, according to West German doctrine, are provisional. The government of the Federal Republic, backed by the United States and other Western allies, has long refused to recognize the eastern frontiers of the G.D.R.—the so-called Oder-Neisse line—and it used to insist, again in theory, on the full or partial restoration of former German territories east of that frontier, most of which in 1945 were put, with Allied consent, under Polish administration. These lands were then annexed by Poland, with the backing of the USSR, and were settled after 1945 by the Poles, following the expulsion

[8] In 1970, the G.F.R. comprised 59.7 million; the G.D.R., 17.1 million; West Berlin, 2.1 million. By late 1971 the total was approximately 79.3 million. (Statisches Bundesant, *Statistisches Jahrbuch* 1971 (Wiesbaden, 1971), pp. 25, 531.

of almost all their German inhabitants. In the view of many Poles, these proceedings were justified as the only practical way in which Poland could collect from Germany some reparations for the devastation she had suffered as a result of Hitler's invasion in 1939—and as an essential compensation for the loss of certain eastern Polish territories to the Soviet Union as a result of World War II, which Nazi Germany had unleashed. While the Communist-ruled G.D.R. regime has officially accepted the Oder-Neisse frontier as permanent, the West German government, as well as more than 80% of the West German voters, until the late 1960s continued to reject it; and it was thus impossible for anyone in the Federal Republic to say with any authority just where the definite eastern frontiers of a reunited Germany would be.

Since 1969, the coalition government led by Chancellor Willy Brandt has worked energetically toward a settlement of these problems. Brandt reminded his followers that the majority of Poles now living in the Oder-Neisse territories were born there. In 1970, treaties were initialed between the G.F.R. and the Soviet Union, and the G.F.R. and Poland, in which the Oder-Neisse frontier was recognized. Ratification of these treaties was to await an agreement on the status of West Berlin, and of Western rights of unhampered access to that city. The interplay of domestic and interational developments will be discussed more fully in a later chapter.

Some domestic political difficulties, however, are likely to persist for some time to come. A declining portion of the roughly 10 million expellees, even though successfully resettled in the Federal Republic, continue to keep alive the memories of their lost homes and territories to the east, as well as the theoretical claim for their return—or else for generous compensation. Some politicians still are likely either to share these feelings or at least to find it expedient to cater to them.

Moreover, between one-quarter and one-half of all West Germans have close relatives or friends in the German Democratic Republic, while almost all the inhabitants of the latter, owing to the large-scale exodus from East Ger-

many to West Germany between 1945 and 1961, when the Berlin Wall was erected, now have personal friends or relatives in the Federal Republic. The unsolved problem of relations between east and west Germany, between the G.F.R. and the G.D.R., will thus continue to have a great deal of direct personal relevance for a large part of the German people for a considerable period of time. In theory, the Federal Republic is still considered provisional not only in its boundaries, but also in its constitution—the latter has been called officially since its adoption in 1949 not a "constitution" but the "Basic Law," in order to underscore its temporary character.

The French have a proverb which says that nothing lasts as long as the provisional. When more than a decade had passed since the adoption of the Basic Law in 1949, spokesmen for the ruling party, the CDU, in 1960 suggested in the Bundestag that it was hardly good citizenship for the Opposition still to harp on the provisional character of the Federal Republic. Its laws, practices, and institutions, the government spokesmen implied, had been tested by time and had become embodied in the habits of its population. The East German population after reunification, they intimated, would just have to adopt them with few, if any, major changes, for the institutions of the Federal Republic had now acquired a tradition and a past behind them that commanded their retention. Since the Social Democrats joined the coalition government of the country in 1966, references to the provisional character of the Federal Republic's institutions became still rarer, and under the SPD-led coalition government after 1969 they practically ceased.

Some of these arguments may represent bargaining positions from which concessions might be made, if reunification—or more likely, some arrangement between the two German states, G.F.R. and G.D.R.—becomes politically feasible. In the meantime, however, the German Federal Republic is the only state that claims to represent the entire German people, with its history and its traditions. It has backed this claim by a national policy of resettlement and indemnification of German refugees and expellees from Eastern Europe—a policy that has committed the West German taxpayer to aiding millions of persons who had been citizens of the Germany of 1937, or even of the Germany of 1913, solely on the grounds that they could be considered German in terms of language, culture, and political traditions.

The implied appeal to German tradition and the past has had a strange ring for some ears. For interwoven with the long and proud history of a great nation is also a darker German tradition and a less praiseworthy past that stretches for decades and centuries behind the more than twenty peaceful and prosperous years of the Federal Republic.

TWO

the German political heritage

Every national political system is heavily influenced by history. The physical layout of its country with its cities and transportation routes, the major social, economic, legal, and political structures, the language and culture of its people, and even many of their character traits and political memories—all these bear the mark of the past in which they developed, often over a period of many generations. No people can escape its history by pretending that it did not happen; and yet history is not fate. The past always leaves a range of choices for the present. History may load the dice in favor of some particular outcome, but this loading by itself is rarely decisive. It is still up to the living in each generation which choices to take and where to place their bets and their actions.

Each generation of Germans has made its own history, even though they did not make it under conditions of their choosing. They made it in an interplay between the pressures of the past and the decisions of the present, and these decisions then in turn became a part of a new past in the face of which the next generation had to make its own decisions.

In this chapter, we shall glance over the long history of the German people, because it is still relevant today. But we must not forget that the major choices of German politics were made in this century—when Germany entered World War I, when the Weimar Republic was created with its peculiar limitations, when the German people responded to the Great Depression by accepting Hitler's dictatorship and when they followed him into World War II, and perhaps most important for our time, when they accepted and developed the German Federal Republic with its present legal institutions, social and economic structure, and political culture and processes. To each of these choices there were some alternatives, sometimes less likely but not utterly impossible. It is possible to judge at least tentatively which of these decisions were wise ones and which were not; and we may try to see what can be learned from their experience to help us all in making some of the political decisions which are likely to be required from us in the future.

THE BEGINNINGS: HOW MANY TRIBES BECAME ONE PEOPLE

The German Federal Republic is young among states, but it governs a people that is more than a thousand years old. Words like *theutiscus* (which evolved into *deutsch*) for "German" and the tradition of a "German" people go back to the age of Charlemagne. The first German empire, styled the "Holy Roman Empire of the German Nation," goes back at least to the year A.D. 842, when Charlemagne's heirs divided his empire at Strasbourg into three realms and thus gave rise to the beginnings of modern Germany, France, and a third "realm of Lothar," comprising much of today's Netherlands, Belgium, Alsace, and Lorraine.

Every German schoolchild is taught to see the 1,100 years of German history since then as a long search for German unity. He is reminded that the German empire of those early days included a variety of quite different Germanic tribes, speaking distinct dialects, such as the Franks in the Rhineland, the Saxons in Northern Germany, the Alemanni and Swabians in the southwest, and the Bavarians in the southeast. Each of these major tribes extended beyond what eventually became modern Germany. Descendants of the Franks also make up most of today's Dutchmen in the Netherlands and Flemings in Belgium, and others have become part of the French people, to whom they have given their tribal name. The Saxon people and their distinctive forms of speech are found also in some districts of the eastern Netherlands and perhaps of southern Denmark, and Saxon tribes contributed the major element in the Germanic settlement of England. The Alemannic tribes also make up the bulk of what is now the German-speaking part of Switzerland, and descendants of the Bavarians also make up most of the population of present-day Austria and of the German-speaking population of South Tyrol, which now forms part of Italy.

Each of these major tribes could have become a separate nation, and to weld the bulk of these and many lesser tribes into a single and cohesive German people took many cen-turies. The factors that played a part in this long, drawn-out process of integration were many: the centralizing pressure of royal or imperial rule; the network of intertribal trade routes and navigable rivers, and the rewards of interregional trade; the benefits of contacts among the knights, merchants, and artisans of the different "tribal duchies" and regions (all speaking some mutually intelligible variety of German); the unifying educational and administrative influence of the church, particularly from the ninth to the twelfth century; and the silent but cumulative effects of migration, intermarriage, and, in some cases, resettlement. A major element singled out for emphasis in much of German historiography and education is the role of a central government with political and military power, and with the will to use that power to compel national unification.

THE MIDDLE AGES

For something like the first five hundred years, from the ninth to the fourteenth century, the unification of Germany by some powerful ruler seemed inextricably bound up with the political unification of most of Europe under the same ruler, backed mainly by German military power. German unity and European unification appeared as one and the same task to be accomplished by a German emperor. During its three centuries of greatness, from the coronation of Otto the Great at Rome in 962 to the beheading of Emperor Konradin at Naples in 1268, the medieval German empire laid more-or-less effective claim, as the "Holy Roman Empire," to the dominion of all of Western Christendom.

German empire during those centuries implied the claim to world empire. German government claimed to be, and sometimes was in fact, world government within the Western world; the profound appeal of this idea even for some non-Germans is echoed in Dante Alighieri's famous treatise "On Universal Monarchy" (*De Monarchia*), in which the poet proposes world government by the German emperor. The image of some worldwide mission, peculiar to one's own nation, has become a familiar trait in the nationalistic movements of the nineteenth and twentieth centuries, but there hardly exists a great country in the world where the image of such a universal national mission is as deeply rooted in the national past and as vividly present in the background of contemporary history and education as it is in Germany.

Despite its glory and appeal, the medieval German attempt at world empire ended in failure. The German empire of those three centuries lacked the administrative and financial machinery essential for an effective government. What little resources, personnel, and competence in these matters its emperors could command they had to borrow from the church. What amounts of ready money they could lay their hands on, they largely had to get from the Italian cities, which were then largely governed by their bishops. When, after A.D. 1075, the church revolted against the political domination and exploitation by the German emperors, the main material and psychological foundations of German imperial power were eventually destroyed. Losing control of Italy and of the church, the emperors in time lost control of the princes, nobles, and towns of Germany. By the late thirteenth century, Germany was becoming what it was to remain for the next three centuries: a conglomeration of feudal domains and city-states, presided over by a nominal emperor with little or no power.

The causes of this collapse of the medieval German empire were not clearly understood at the time. Few, if any, German historians or laymen saw clearly that this empire under the glamorous Hohenstaufen dynasty had lived politically and economically far beyond its means, and that its rulers had attempted the unification of Germany and of Europe in complete and irresponsible disregard of the narrow limits of their actual resources. Rather, the image conveyed by many popular historians and retained in folk memory was one of heroic and glamorous emperors, thwarted by German disunity, by the insubordination of the German princes, and by the devious machinations of foreigners, mostly Italians and Frenchmen, and including

notably the Roman popes. If the Germans had only been more united and more disciplined, and if the German clergy had listened more to the German emperors and less to foreign popes, this image suggested, the medieval German world empire need never have fallen.

THE BEGINNINGS OF POLITICAL UNITY

Even without any strong central government, however, the German people remained predominant in central Europe during the next three hundred years, from the fourteenth to the sixteenth century. German princes, knights, and cities extended their sway deep into eastern Europe. Far beyond these expanding limits of German political rules, German merchants, knights, artisans, and peasant settlers were welcomed by eastern European rulers as valued immigrants and accorded privileged status. No major invasions of Germany took place from the eleventh through the sixteenth century, with the exception of a brief Mongol attack in 1241, which was stopped by local forces at Liegnitz in Silesia. Without any strong ruler, Germany was safe, while the Hanseatic cities, the Teutonic knights, and the dukes of Austria expanded German power to the north, the east, and the southeast, and German crafts and cities flourished in prosperity.

In the second half of the fifteenth century, however, the foundations of this German prosperity began to crumble, and by the beginning of the seventeenth century Germany was ruined, before the first shots of the Thirty Years' War (1618–48) were fired. Some of the major causes of this economic decline were remote, indirect in operation, difficult to visualize, and yet devastatingly effective. With the fall of Constantinople to the Turks in 1453, the trade of Italy and Germany with the eastern Mediterranean declined, and the subsequent Turkish advance northward across southeastern Europe to the gates of Vienna in 1529 further diminished Italian and German trade with that area. An even more fateful shift in the routes of world trade away from central Europe and to the Atlantic coasts occurred after the discovery of America in 1492 and the opening of a sea route to India in 1498. Germany and most of central Europe became backwaters of international trade; cities stagnated or shrank; and princes found it harder to raise revenues at a time when the costs of warfare and government were rising.

During this same period, more powerful monarchies emerged in western Europe and changed the scale of politics and warfare. Between 1480 and 1610, Spain, England, France, and Sweden all emerged as vigorous national monarchies, dwarfing the resources of the German petty princes and city states with whom they came in competition for territory, trade, or influence.

The only German dynasty that attained major strength during that period was the House of Habsburg, and it did so mainly by strengthening its non-German connections. In this policy, it was eventually supported by the influence of the church, which had repudiated in 1462 a religious compromise peace with the Protestant Hussites of Bohemia and was now interested in the rise of a strong Catholic power in Austria, so as to oppose both the Bohemian Protestants and the Turks to the southeast. By a remarkable series of intermarriages, the Habsburgs, between 1477 and 1526, acquired lands and wealth from Burgundy and Spain, and eventually the succession to Bohemia and Hungary. The wealth of Spain in particular, derived from the conquest of Mexico and Peru, permitted the Habsburgs to play a major role in German politics—but it was not a role that led to German unity.

After 1517, Germany was shaken by the appeal of Martin Luther's Reformation, which was followed by more than a century of religious warfare. From these conflicts there emerged eventually a standard German language, based in large degree on the central German dialect used by Luther for his translation of the Bible; and there remained a lasting religious division of the German people which by the beginning of our century was composed of about two-thirds Protestants and one-third Catholics, with

the latter mostly in the Rhineland, Bavaria, and Silesia.

IN SEARCH OF STATEHOOD

It was in this period that Germany went through the first stages of political modernization. Between 1500 and 1750, each of the German principalities passed through the transition to the modern bureaucratic state, which collected taxes in money, paid a standing armed force, and was administered by professional officials. The bureaucrats themselves were paid in money, and they carried on most of their work in writing, and increasingly in accordance with fixed rules of more-or-less rational procedure. They were organized and disciplined in some hierarchical pattern of command and were effectively subordinated to their immediate superiors, as well as ultimately to the monarch.

Similar developments during the same centuries in England and France were in part counterbalanced in their social and cultural effects by growing economic prosperity, which increased the confidence and power of the merchants and the middle class. It taught them that they could often promote successfully, by their own efforts, their interests as individuals and groups, and that they could often conclude profitable and honorable compromises with other interest groups or individual power holders. Indirectly, commercial and industrial prosperity in France and England increased the values of the lands of many nobles and of the rents derived from them. It also enhanced the opportunities for nobles and gentlemen to take part in profitable business ventures, as in the great companies of English merchants, or to obtain lucrative pensions or payments for nominal offices from the monarch's treasury, without having to perform any serious amounts of administrative work, as in the case of the French court under Louis XIV. The growing bureaucracies of France and England were thus limited by the power of other groups, and the major part of the aristocracies and of the middle classes of those countries did not merge with them.

In the German principalities, economic stagnation in the sixteenth and seventeenth centuries led to the opposite effects. The open pursuit of group interests and the give and take of compromises between groups tended to be less rewarding and less reputable. The middle class stagnated and became weaker and more submissive in relation to the growing strength of the bureaucracies and of the petty monarchs who commanded them. The lesser nobles remained impecunious and their sons increasingly took to the service of the state as officers, or as civilian bureaucrats. The higher bureaucracy in the German states thus was less separate as a class, and less independent as a political force, from nobility and monarchy. Just for this reason, however, it gained by this close association a vicarious share in their prestige. The German terms for the new bureaucratic authorities of the period, *Obrigkeit,* and for their subjects, *Untertanen,* appear strikingly in Luther's injunction to his followers: "Be ye subject (*untertan*) to the authority (*Obrigkeit*) that has power over you." These German terms carry far stronger authoritarian and paternalistic connotations than any comparable terms in common use in France, England, or the United States; and in German history they were heavily underscored by Luther's call for the savage repression of the German peasants' revolt in 1525. In France and England, similar peasant uprisings had occurred and been suppressed a century earlier, but the German "Peasant War" of 1525 was later and larger; it was suppressed more mercilessly and lastingly; and it left nobles, state bureaucracies, and a large part of the urban upper-middle classes united in a common fear and hatred of any possible revolt of the poor, and a common willingness to rely on strong state authorities to prevent its recurrence.

The churches, too, became allies of and often instruments of princely and bureaucratic authority. After the Religious Peace of Augsburg of 1555, each prince retained the sovereign right to determine the religion of his subjects and to suppress or drive out dissenters. Most of the German principalities, in the course of the sixteenth and seventeenth centuries, became officially identified with a single denomination, Protestant or Catholic, and the theological arguments in favor of the particular ecclesiastical regime established in each state served in effect as a political defense of the state, a safeguard of the reliability of its clergy, and a religious exhortation to civic obedience and loyalty.

The universities were the chief sources of the juridically trained administrative officials, which all of the modernizing states needed, as well as of the theologians and ministers, which each Protestant prince required in order to give religious backing to his claim of divine right to absolute political power. Between them, the German states, particularly the Protestant ones, maintained a larger number of universities and devoted a higher proportion of resources to them than was usual at the time elsewhere in Europe. The German universities had relatively great importance and prestige with their respective states. Professors, and eventually to a lesser degree all teachers, were viewed as somehow associated with authority, and were respected not only for their learning but also for their association with the authoritarian order of the bureaucratic and aristocratic princely governments. The results of these developments have added in the long run to the strength and glory of German learning and science, but they have also made a large part of the German universities into ready admirers and pliant servants of authority in periods of tyranny or war. For good or ill, the sixteenth and seventeenth century combination of unusually strong universities and bureaucracies with an unusually weak commercial and industrial economy has marked German politics, society, and culture in the centuries thereafter.

In France and England, the growing wealth of the cities made it possible eventually for some one dynasty and region to defeat all its rivals and to establish a strong national state. The contemporary religious conflicts in those countries, bloody as they were, did not prevent this outcome. Rather, they often helped in the end to justify the defeat or expulsion of the losing parties and the confiscation of their property. In Germany during that period, on the contrary, there was not enough solid prosperity to finance the rise of any one prince or region to paramount power and its consolidation. Prosperous France and England won their national unity in the same centuries of religious wars in which stagnating Germany became more deeply divided to this day. Many Germans, however, blame the religious split on the long political division of their country and retain from these memories a longing for stronger national unity.

Economically impoverished and politically divided, early in the seventeenth century Germany became the scene and the victim of the power conflicts among her more effectively consolidated neighbors. In the Thirty Years' War (1618–48), the great and lesser European powers, such as France, Spain, the Habsburg empire, Sweden, and the Netherlands, fought one another on German soil, with the eager collaboration of the German princes, but with catastrophic consequences for the German people. The war reduced the population of Germany by one-third, and left the country impoverished in comparison to its western neighbors for perhaps as much as 150 years.

The main responses of the survivors of this catastrophe were increased distrust and fear of foreign nations, increased dependence on the protection of familiar authorities, stronger emotional reliance on household, home, and family, a greater acceptance of discipline and of sustained habits of hard work, and, eventually, a greater acceptance of militarism as a means of strengthening their governments and their ability to protect their subjects against the terrors of war and foreign invasion.

At the same time, the paternalism of the German family, the German landed estate, and the German artisan's household tended to mitigate class distinctions. To some extent, paternalism meant privilege, but it often also meant some warmth and care toward those who kept their place within its framework. The speech of the upper and the lower classes in Germany never became as different as it did in England. (Benjamin Disraeli's famous book, *Sybil, or, The Two Nations,* referring to the rich and the poor, could hardly have been written in Germany, and if it had, its author could not have become a conservative prime minister.) To this day, over 60%

of the German voters prefer notions of social and national solidarity to ideas of class conflict; and a majority have remained suspicious of outsiders and foreigners.

Out of all these experiences came the German people of the eighteenth century, with a prevailing national character that was different in some ways from that of their predecessors. If Tacitus had described the members of the ancient Germanic tribes as proud, freedom-loving, and lazy, the eighteenth-century Germans were more often submissive and diligent. If some observers in the late seventeenth century judged the Germans to be timid and peculiarly incapable of discipline, from the eighteenth century onward the German people were to impress foreigners increasingly by their discipline and military virtues.

THE PRUSSIAN STATE

A major agency in this transformation was the Brandenburg-Prussian monarchy, both through its practices and its example. Bureaucracy, austerity, mercantilism, and militarism were the hallmarks of its policy. Starting out from their holdings in the infertile Brandenburg region—"the sandbox of the empire"—the rulers of the Hohenzollern dynasty soon acquired Prussia, a territory in the northeast, where in earlier days the Knights of the Teutonic Order had imported German settlers and imposed German speech and culture on the Baltic and Slavic original inhabitants. By the middle of the seventeenth century, the rulers of Brandenburg-Prussia had managed to acquire a collection of widely scattered territories throughout northern Germany, including strategic holdings on the banks of the Rhine, Weser, Elbe, and Oder rivers.

In the prerailroad age, these rivers carried a very substantial part of the trade of the various German principalities to the Baltic and North seas, to the Atlantic Ocean, and generally to the world of expanding overseas trade. If held by a powerful military force, these territories could be used to collect tolls from this river traffic and to impose a variety of tariffs and other economic regulations in accordance with the mercantilist practices of the time, and thus to divert a significant part of the wealth of the other German territories into the coffers of the Brandenburg-Prussian state. By spending most of its income on its army and bureaucracy, that state could maintain more soldiers, gain more territories, collect more tolls, impose more profitable regulations, and spend the proceeds again and again on more soldiers and conquests, in a slowly expanding spiral of power politics.

Under these particular conditions, militarism could be made to pay for itself, provided only that the tax receipts from foreign transit and domestic trade were not squandered on luxury consumption by the monarchs and the nobles of the country. Ostentatious spending on expensive luxuries was widespread during much of the seventeenth and eighteenth centuries at other German courts, as it was throughout Europe at that time, but Prussia formed a conspicuous exception. By comparison with the rest of Europe, court life at Berlin and later at Potsdam sometimes seemed Spartan in its simplicity. Many of the younger sons of nobles had to depend on military or bureaucratic careers for their income; and they had to make greater efforts than nobles in other countries in order to acquire the academic training and the practical knowledge and skills necessary for the performance of their duties.

Even the peasantry followed a life of frugality and ceaseless diligence. From the middle of the seventeenth century to the early years of the nineteenth, the peasants, and even members of their families, were pressed into compulsory service on the estates of the nobles. During the slack season of the year, between spring planting and harvest, and particularly during the long winters, they had to spin, weave, or perform other duties under the supervision of the landlord and his employees. Similar demands were made on the rural population in other parts of Germany, but in Brandenburg—or, as it was called after 1701, the Kingdom of Prussia —there emerged most clearly a new and disciplined pattern of life. It combined unceasing and diligent labor by the mass of the population with grim frugality on the part of their rulers.

The Prussian state thus functioned as an engine for extracting forced savings from its population. It channeled these savings into an ever-expanding army, and to some degree into the support of industry and education, using all these activities in turn to enhance the future economic resources and political power of the state. A French observer misunderstood the situation when he remarked that other states had armies but that in Prussia the army had a state. For the Prussian army, too, was but one link in this chain of self-expanding power. Though it received funds more readily than other parts of the government, it, too, had to practice rigorous economies; and a German writer hit closer to the mark when he said that between 1640 and 1780 the state of Brandenburg-Prussia had starved itself into greatness.

The Prussian state won the acceptance, and eventually the loyalty, of many of its inhabitants, for it offered them a better chance of security against foreign attack and of predictable legality and honest administration, some educational opportunity, and long-term economic growth. At the same time, however, the austerity and authoritarian discipline of Prussia repelled many Germans, particularly those outside its borders. They saw it as a vast barracks yard, ruled by a royal drill sergeant. They resented its harsh tariff policies, its ruthless methods of recruiting or impressing young men from other territories into its armies; its unscrupulous policies of territorial expansion and aggression—and they thanked their stars that they were not among its subjects. Yet in 1756, when this dreaded and hated Prussian state under Frederick II defeated for the first time in several centuries a French army in open battle at Rossbach, many of these same Germans rejoiced. "We all were pro-Fritzian then," Goethe reported of the people of the free city of Frankfurt at that particular time.

The attitude of the Germans in the southern and western parts of what is present-day Germany toward Prussia was a mixture of dislike and admiration. When and where Prussian power seemed unneeded or menacing, dislike would prevail; but where Prussian strength seemed needed against a foreign threat or where Prussian drive and efficiency might promise a way out of pettiness and stagnation, Prussian leadership could seem attractive.

In the meantime, the rest of eighteenth-century Germany remained divided into many weak and sleepy little states. Yet crafts and industries revived, the ravages of the Thirty Years' War were slowly healed, and the most gifted and skilled men in many of these petty states came to think of themselves as citizens of a wide and vague "republic of letters," in which their works would be appreciated and in which they themselves might find employment at the courts of hospitable princes, regardless of state boundaries. German composers, scientists, and writers in the eighteenth century did indeed move from one German state court or university to another, or else their works or their pupils did so; and a growing network of German theaters, concert orchestras, publishing houses, and periodicals facilitated the dissemination of their works. Philosophers such as Leibniz and Kant, writers such Schiller and Goethe, composers such as Bach and Beethoven made Germany one of the major contributors to world civilization. At the same time, however, none of these men, nor indeed most of the educated Germans before the end of the eighteenth century, felt that the unification of the German people into a single national state was at all urgently needed.

With the Napoleonic wars and the French occupation of Berlin in 1806, this situation changed. Soon a number of German intellectuals, mostly of a younger generation, became bitterly anti-French and wished for more powerful governments—or even one strong government—for Germany. At the same time, the rulers of Prussia, as well as those of Austria, found it expedient to take advantage of this mood, and to appeal not only to the territorial patriotism, but also to the German nationalism of their subjects. In Austria, this policy was abandoned in 1810, but in Prussia it was strengthened by partial but important reforms and carried through to the immensely popular and ultimately victorious war against France in 1813–15. Victory was followed by a temporary swing back to conservatism, but an important beginning had been made toward linking the aspirations of German intellectuals —and of the German middle class generally— with the military prowess of the Prussian aristocracy and the power interests of the Prussian state.

GERMAN UNIFICATION IN THE NINETEENTH CENTURY

In 1815, Prussia acquired the Rhineland, including the Ruhr area, and soon became the main industrial power in Germany. Under Prussian leadership, a customs union, the *Zollverein*, from 1834 onward united the territories of all German states with the exception of Austria. In the half-hearted and short-lived revolution of 1848, German liberal leaders tried to unite Germany in a single empire on a constitutional and middle-class basis, but failed to win either the cooperation of the Prussian court and aristocracy or the sustained support of the mass of the population, which was still predominantly rural and largely conservative. In the following two decades, however, the growth of German industry and banking, the establishment of a German railroad network and postal system, and the acceptance of a unified code of commercial law all served to knit the German states more closely together than ever. Through a skillful combination of political and military moves in three wars in 1864, 1866, and 1870–71, the Prussian statesman Otto von Bismarck succeeded first in greatly enlarging the territory of Prussia and then in establishing a new unified German empire that preserved and indeed enhanced the power of the Prussian monarchy and aristocracy, while winning almost solid middle-class consent and widespread popular support.

THE SECOND GERMAN EMPIRE, 1871–1918

This new German empire was ruled by the Prussian monarch, who now also became the German emperor, with sweeping emergency powers at his disposal under the new constitution. The emperor appointed a chancellor, who was responsible to him rather than to the legislature. The chancellor, in turn, was in control of the ministers of his cabinet; he, rather than the legislature, could appoint or dismiss them.

The imperial legislature had very little power, and was divided into two chambers. One, the *Bundesrat,* consisted of delegates of the twenty-five states, with Prussia furnishing seventeen out of the total of fifty-eight and usually commanding additional votes from several smaller states. Moreover, since fourteen votes sufficed to block any constitutional amendment, Prussia had an effective right of veto on such matters. The Prussian delegates to the Bundesrat were appointed by the Prussian government, which was subservient to the emperor in his role as king of Prussia; and the Prussian legislature was elected by an extremely unequal three-class franchise that insured its effective control by the land-owning nobility, and to a lesser extent by the upper-middle class of industry and commerce, while virtually disfranchising the rest of the population. In contrast to this extreme form of class franchise for the Prussian legislature, Bismarck's constitution for the empire provided for a second legislative chamber, the *Reichstag* (chosen by popular election), which was designed to attract a greater share of popular interest and, in time, loyalties, to the empire. However, while the Reichstag made a good sounding-board for speeches and debates, it had no real power to decide; even the taxes for the imperial budget could be collected and spent by the imperial government without the Reichstag's consent.

The German emperor thus had vast powers and was subject to no effective constitutional control. The first emperor, Wilhelm I, deferred to Bismarck's personal prestige and influence as chancellor, so that the system worked not too differently from the way a British prime minister and cabinet might have functioned. From 1888 onward, however, the weaknesses of Bismarck's constitution were becoming visible. A new and erratic emperor, Wilhelm II, succeeded to the throne; Bismarck himself was soon replaced by a succession of less able but more subservient chancellors; and Germany policy began its fateful drift toward diplomatic isolation, the arms race with Britain, France, and Russia, and the precipice of World War I.

It would be wrong, however, to see the main causes of the German drift into World War I in the personal shortcomings of Wilhelm II, or in the constitutional defects of the "Second Empire." Behind the constitutional forms stood the reality of a social and economic structure dominated by an alliance of the two most powerful interest groups of the country: the land-owning nobility with its strong links to the army and bureaucracy, and the rapidly rising big-business class in industry, commerce, and banking—the big *bourgeoisie,* as its critics sometimes called it—which allied itself with the aristocracy for a series of sustained policies designed to serve their mutual advantage. The policies of high protective tariffs for industry and agriculture; of active efforts at colonial expansion; of a frantic search for international prestige; and of ever-increasing expenditures for armaments—all these were backed by the most powerful interest groups and elites of the empire. In domestic politics, these policies tended to preserve or even enhance the privileges of the industrial and agrarian elites, and to keep the growing numbers of industrial workers (and the smaller numbers of rural laborers and cottagers) firmly in their subordinate positions.

Thus, a policy of domestic conservatism was pursued by means of foreign and military policies which entailed increasing risks of war. Nonetheless, to many this course seemed safe at home, while its long-run recklessness in international affairs remained hidden. Thus, these policies were overwhelmingly supported by the German middle class, and had substantial support throughout the population. Germans, during the years between 1890 and 1914, found themselves in a world of rising tariffs and expanding colonial empires. Coming late upon the scene of colonial expansion, many of them accepted blindly the proposition that was then enunciated by French and British, as well as by German statesmen: that any great industrial country had to win colonies, *Lebensraum* ("living space"), and "a place in the sun" for itself, if it was not to lag behind, and eventually to perish, in the struggle for national survival. The old memories of a hostile foreign environment, retained since the days of the Thirty Years' War and the Napoleonic invasions, now developed into the notion of a Germany encircled by envious and hostile rivals, and eventually into the widespread belief that war would be inevitable—a belief coupled, as we now know, with almost complete ignorance of what such a war would be like.

World War I proved devastating beyond anyone's expectations. About 2 million German soldiers lost their lives in it, and almost another million civilian lives were lost through the hardships of the food blockade imposed by the Allies during the war and prolonged for some time after the armistice of November 11, 1918. By the end of the war, Germany was thoroughly spent and defeated. In the peace that followed, Germany lost all her overseas colonies, and in Europe she had to give up Alsace-Lorraine to France and important territories in the east to a reconstituted Poland. Most of Bismarck's territorial acquisitions were thus lost again. There was left an impoverished and exhausted country, which now became a republic but which remained burdened with a large debt of reparations owed to the victorious Allies.

Despite its end in catastrophic defeat, Bismarck's empire lives on in popular memory. Forty-five percent of German respondents to an opinion poll in 1951 considered the second empire (1871–1918) the best period in recent Germany history, and in repeated polls in the 1950s a plurality of respondents named Bismarck as the man who did more for Germany than any other. Only with the rise of a new generation of voters in the 1960s has this image begun to fade. The stigma of defeat in World War I was largely transferred in the German popular mind from the empire which actually suffered it to the republic that emerged in November 1918 to pick up the pieces.

THE WEIMAR REPUBLIC, 1918–33

The political and military collapse of the empire in 1918 found most German parties and leaders unprepared. The emperor personally, and the regime to a lesser extent, had lost the confidence of the socialists, the conservatives, and many of the army generals. But at the same time the empire collapsed into a vacuum, for prior to 1918 most Germans, including the majority of Social Democrats, were not real republicans. They had hardly given any thought to the possibility of a different Germany—a Germany without a kaiser, much less a Germany without the interlocking complex of noble landowners, high-ranking military officers and bureaucrats, and the concentrated elite of big industry and finance. So far as this part of the German social structure was concerned, the republic became a new façade on an old building, even though in other aspects of German life it had brought important changes.

And since democracy had been presented to Germany because no other alternative presented itself, rather than democracy being the end product of a struggle led by a dedicated and courageous group of men, the new republic found itself without a respected democratic leadership.

About one-quarter of the electorate continued to hold nationalist and militarist views. They would have preferred to see the old empire go on unchanged, with its black, white, and red flag, its army, and its authoritarian institutions. Most of these nationalist voters came from the middle class and the peasantry. They were represented by the conservative German Nationalist People's Party and by the (at first much smaller) National Socialists; they received significant support from a part of big business, of the landed classes, and of the high-ranking bureaucracy, particularly the judiciary and the military; and they never forgave the new republic for representing, in their eyes, a betrayal of all the traditions and aspirations of the army and the empire in World War I. The Communists who split from the SPD in 1918 as well as the Nationalists and the Nazis rejected the liberal constitution. Thus the republic was continuously hated by more than one-third of the population.

The majority of the socialists retained the old party name (Social Democratic party), remained oriented toward more moderate welfare and state reforms, and soon rallied to the active support of the republic. In early 1918, however, most SPD leaders had not thought seriously about anything more radical than a constitutional monarchy, and neither had the leaders and members of the moderate middle-class parties—the nationalist-liberal German People's party, the liberal German Democratic party and the Center party, which represented the particular interests of Roman Catholic voters. Before 1918, none of these groups had advocated a republic for Germany, and when in that year the monarchy suddenly lost so much of its former popular support that only a republic appeared practicable, nobody seemed prepared to draft its constitution or to make it work if practical difficulties should arise.

The republic thus started out as a makeshift type of government—and it did so within almost anarchical conditions. In order to suppress the challenge from the radical left in the tense winter of 1918–19, the SPD and the moderate middle-class parties allied themselves with the German generals and officers who still controlled units of the armies which had returned to Germany after the armistice in November 1918. The military indeed supplied the main force to suppress radical leftist uprisings, such as the "Spartacus" revolt of January 1919, and in return they received a great deal of formal and informal influence over the reduced armed force of the republic—the *Reichswehr,* whose strength the peace treaties eventually were to fix at 100,000 men. This informal but fateful arrangement came into existence long before the formal constitution was drafted and ratified, but it was to exercise a crucial influence over the fate of the republic in later years. For one thing, the Socialist party's turning to the army for use against their former leftist comrades made the party split on the left irrevocable and thus increased the power of the right. For another, it quickly made the army a state within the state, effectively exempted from civilian control; the army soon extended its protection and covert aid to various extreme-right-wing groups and organizations, some of which later contributed to the rise of the Nazi party.

The early agreement of the SPD with the generals was supplemented within a few days by an agreement between the leaders of the major trade unions and the representatives of big-business management to form a Central Cooperative Group (*Zentrale Arbeitsgemeinschaft*) for the purpose of moderating and reducing industrial conflicts and restoring production for peacetime needs. These arrangements kept the number of strikes to a minimum, reduced the influence of radical groups in the factories and in the unions, and tended to preserve or restore the authority of big-business management —which was considered necessary to maintain production, but which also left big business inordinately powerful.

The agreements with the generals and with the big industrialists symbolized a larger fact. The bulk of the social and economic structure of imperial Germany was preserved in the Weimar Republic: the large landed interests, the personnel and organization of the civil-service hierarchy, the class-ridden judiciary, no less than the monopolies, cartels, and near-monopolies of big business and finance and the core of the military, were taken over more-or-less intact and continued to function and exercise their influence in politics and everyday life. Much of this influence was paraconstitutional— it existed outside the constitution and alongside it—but it was nonetheless real. In times of crisis, it was to prove as important as, and sometimes more important than, the wording of the constitution.

The constitution itself was drafted in the small town of Weimar, symbolic as the residence of Goethe and Schiller in the classic period of German literature, and safely removed from the labor unrest and political turmoil of Berlin and the other industrial regions of the country. The main provisions of the constitution were remarkably democratic. In fact, it was the drafters' primary aim to bring into existence a democratic governmental system representative enough of the people to be worthy of the adjective *democratic*. But at the same time many of the drafters recognized that it would be very difficult to transform the political habits of a people overnight. Thus, in order to preserve democracy, the authors of the constitution also tried to balance the democratic features of the constitution with strong executive powers as safeguards. For example, they concluded that the country needed a strong president as a focus for the people's desire for a respected authority figure standing above parties, thereby providing an *Ersatzkaiser*—a substitute for a formerly revered kaiser who had just recently abdicated.

The constitution of Weimar gave first place to the elected legislature, the *Reichstag,* and it gave to that body the power to approve and dismiss the chancellor and his ministers. At the same time, however, it raised a second power to the same level: a popularly elected president was given the power to nominate the chancellor, to dissolve the Reichstag, and, in case of a national emergency, to rule by decree. Much of the power of the republic could thus become concentrated in the hands of two men, or even subservient to the will of one; a strong president with a compliant chancellor, or, as it actually happened, a strong chancellor with a compliant president, could use the vast emergency powers of government to destroy the constitutional regime—a development that took place later in 1932 and 1933.

Compared to this strong centralizing bias, the federal theme was muted. The second legislative chamber, the *Reichsrat,* which included representatives of the state governments, was mentioned last in the Weimar constitution, and its powers were largely limited to minor matters of administration. In addition to this, the huge state of Prussia was preserved, comprising two-thirds of the total population, so that even state government was far more centralized than would be the case in the United States.

The Record of Weimar

Since the early 1920s, many writers have argued that the weaknesses and ultimate fall of the Weimar Republic were due to the fact that the revolution of 1918, which had created it, had been a far less thoroughgoing revolution than had been the English Revolution of 1640–49, the French Revolution of 1789–95, or the American Revolution of 1776–83, not to mention the vast upheaval of the Russian Revolution of 1917–21. Each of these more far-reaching revolutions, so the argument goes, produced eventually a fairly strong government and a stable political regime. The less far-reaching German revolution of 1918, according to this view, went far enough to enrage its conservative enemies, but not far enough to acquire many strong beneficiaries and friends; hence, it could only produce a feeble and unstable political system.

There is some truth in this argument, but it remains one-sided. It overlooks one central fact of the 1918–20 period: the bulk of the German people in 1918 did not want a drastic social revolution, and the majority of German workers and returning soldiers did not want it either. What they did want was peace, food, clothing, work, and a chance to start life again with their families. All these things were obtainable without a social revolution, and none of them seemed obtainable through any such deep and prolonged upheaval. After the armistice of November 11, 1918, the republic was at peace abroad. Weary of war, few workers indeed desired civil war against expectable bitter middle-class resistance, an intact officer corps, and probable Allied intervention. Food and cotton (for clothing) could only come from the Allies; German stocks were exhausted, and the embattled Soviet government had no significant supplies to spare. Even fuel for the cold winter was scarce in Germany; revolutionary disruptions of mining and transport were likely to make it still scarcer.

These material facts and probabilities were reinforced by cultural ones. The outbreak of the war in 1914 had shown how deeply integrated the Social Democratic party, and indeed most of German labor, had become with their national government and social system. Now, in 1918, they wanted equal political, social, and economic rights, more social welfare legislation, and a better share of the good things of the society in which they lived. Looking at the capitalist economy and middle-class culture of their country, most German workers did not want out. They wanted in.

To some extent, and for a time, many of them got some of the things they wanted. The eight-hour working day, greatly improved social security coverage and payments, improved union recognition and collective bargaining, somewhat better treatment at the hands of public authorities, political control of many city and town governments, improved municipal services and facilities, an intermittent share in coalition governments at the state and national levels, and by 1928 the highest real wages on the European continent—all these were achievements to which the SPD leaders could point with pride and which brought their party regularly between two and three times as many votes as were polled by members of the Communist party.

Perhaps most important, after four-and-a-half years of war and regimentation, a large majority of Germans, including German workers, wanted freedom. The idea of a revolutionary dictatorship repelled them, even when it was linked to promises of a more radical democracy, as it was in many of the appeals of the extreme left. The combination seemed to them neither credible nor desirable, and they turned it down. Here, too, they got for a time what most of them preferred. Labor's gains under the Weimar Republic were being won without dictatorship. Freedoms of speech and organization were a visible reality, with only minor exceptions; and the contrast to the increasingly repressive dictatorship in Soviet Russia was not lost on many socialist and labor voters.

Yet within fourteen years this absence of the threat of foreign war, these domestic welfare gains, these democratic rights and liberties all were to prove precarious. The basic rights of individuals were listed in the Weimar constitution and protected by it (in contrast to the second empire, when they had been left to the various states), but far-reaching emergency provisions could be invoked by the federal government with relative ease to suspend these constitutional protections. This actually happened in the last years of the Weimar Republic, and these sweeping emergency powers, together with the extreme concentrations of power in the hands of the president and the chancellor, did much to smooth the way to dictatorship in 1933.

This disastrous outcome, however, cannot be attributed only, or primarily, to technical mistakes in constitution drafting. The Weimar Republic suffered from political and social weaknesses even more dangerous than its legal ones. In the record, seven such weaknesses stand out.

The first weakness was the structural weakness which we have discussed. The Weimar Republic and the parties identified with it left far too much concentrated power in the hands of its potential enemies. By doing so they took a fateful decision, for they could have acted otherwise. Far short of any total social upheaval, they could still have used the political mood and opportunities of 1918–20 to do better. They could have carried out a land reform in Eastern Germany which would have weakened the power of the nobles—the *Junkers,* as they were popularly called. (Land reforms under similar circumstances were carried out successfully in Finland and Czechoslovakia at the time.)

A determined republican leadership with a strong following could have organized Germany's rump army of 100,000 men more as a citizen's militia, on the model of Switzerland and of the United States in the nineteenth century, instead of letting it become a self-contained and uncontrolled power. They could have reduced the concentrated power of economic monopolies by introducing antitrust legislation similar to that in the United States, and they could have nationalized the key industries and monopolistic strongholds of coal and steel, as Britain did after World War II. They could have retired many of the antidemocratic judges and civil-service bureaucrats, and reformed the judicial and civil-service systems, as many countries have done before and since. They could have reformed the inequitable educational system with its built-in class discrimination, at least by providing in principle a common secondary education for all children, similar to the American high school. In short, they could have chosen to do a great many things that would have made democracy stronger and the gap between it and an underlying undemocratic social and economic structure less dangerous.

They did not choose to do them. But in this outcome the radical left had its full share. The Communist party at that time rejected reforms, insisted on total revolution, and believed in the tactic of small *coups* or uprisings. Even if each such *Putsch* were defeated, they thought, it would have an educational effect on the workers, making them more radical. All these uprisings were defeated and they did have an effect, but in the opposite direction. Most German workers, as well as the SPD leaders, refused to be forced into a revolution which they did not want. The violent leftist *Putsch*-tactics pushed them to the right, closer to the conservative groups and structures as allies in the defense of "peace and order," and further away from more far-reaching democratic reforms that might have been possible. After 1933, sincere middle-class democrats, moderate socialists, and radical leftists ended up side by side in Hitler's concentration camps.

The second weakness was at the governmental level. The republic lasted for a mere fourteen years, and within that time a game of musical cabinet-chairs was being played in the French style, these cabinets having an average life span of nine months. In its last years the continual presidential use of emergency powers allowed conservative chancellors to govern without a majority in the legislature. Throughout the republic's existence, the civil service and the army were able to dilute or bypass their constitutional responsibility to the people's elected leaders.

The third weakness was at the level of the political parties. In the Reichstag, the legislative center of gravity continually moved to the right. Until 1922, the democratic parties of the left and center managed to carry on the government without the aid of the rightist deputies, a coalition of the Social Democrats, the Center party, and the Democratic party forming the government. From 1923 to 1930, the democratic coalition was forced to join forces with the moderately rightist German People's party. In 1930 the middle-class parties insisted on meeting the deepening depression by a policy of deflation, wage reductions, and cuts in welfare services. When the Social Democrats and the labor unions remained opposed,

the middle-class parties broke up the coalition, forcing new elections. Then in the elections of September 1930, 107 National Socialist deputies won seats in the legislature, making it impossible for *any* coalition of parties to find a majority. President von Hindenburg used his emergency powers to appoint chancellors responsible to him rather than to the Reichstag. And with each successive chancellor between 1930 and 1932, the government moved more to the right, culminating in the appointment of Hitler as chancellor.

At any one time there were usually a dozen parties represented in the legislature. In and of itself, this does not necessarily point to the failure of democracy. But the multiparty system, in combination with the political styles of the parties, did. They were largely parties of expression rather than of action—that is, each tended to specialize in expressing the special demands and resentments of some particular group in the population, rather than in getting different groups to cooperate to get things done. Even some of the larger parties limited their appeal mainly to a single element of the population, such as the Social Democrats, who spoke for the urban workers, or the German Nationalist People's party, who spoke for the land-owning *Junkers* and their rural followers. Some parties based their appeals on emotionally charged ideologies, breeding hatred and dogmatism. The outcome was that the parties could never transcend their differences, nor form stable coalition governments capable of producing effective legislation. They could not compromise because their narrow appeal virtually turned them into mere pressure groups tied to the particular interests of one section of the population, and their dogmatic *Weltanschauungen* ("world views") allowed no place for bargaining and cooperation.

The fourth weakness was on the level of mass opinion. The republic remained illegitimate in the eyes of roughly one-third of its population. Throughout the 1920s, about 20% of the voters backed the German Nationalist People's party and similar rightist groups, which longed for the restoration of the monarchy and for a victorious war of revenge for the defeat in World War I, and about 10%

voted for the Communists, who urged the replacement of the "bourgeois" Weimar Republic by a Soviet-style "dictatorship of the proletariat," by which they meant essentially that of the Communist party. Both the extreme right and the extreme left saw the republic as a regime of treason. To the right-wing Nationalists, it represented the betrayal of the monarchy and of the supposedly "undefeated" imperial army in 1918, while to the Communists, the same Weimar Republic represented the betrayal of socialism and of the Russian November Revolution.

Such extremist views, and the intense emotions of hatred and contempt that went with them, were not unusual in European politics between 1918 and 1933, but what was unusual was that a large share of the electorate persisted in these attitudes in Germany through one-and-a-half decades. This hostility of 30 to 40% of the voters in turn produced an unusually great risk of "negative majorities" in the federal legislature, since an adverse vote by only a small part of the deputies from the other parties, when added to this large permanent opposition, was sufficient to produce an antigovernment majority—but a majority unable to agree on any positive action. (See Table 6-1 on pages 434–435.)

The fifth weakness was in the executive and in the instruments of law enforcement. Against any violent attempts to overthrow it, the Weimar Republic depended for its defense on groups that were implacably hostile to it. Against the "rightist" Kapp *Putsch* of 1920, the republic had to invoke a general strike of the workers, including the Communists; and against repeated Communist uprisings between 1919 and 1923, the republic depended on the extremely nationalistic officers and judges who remained its bitter enemies. This dependence on profoundly antidemocratic officers and judges, in fact, undermined the entire security of the republic. It permitted the assassination of many of its leading statesmen, as well as of many less prominent liberals and leftists, with virtual impunity, and it left the republic almost paralyzed in the face of the mounting terrorism of the Nazis after 1930.

By 1928, the Weimar Republic seemed to have survived well despite these five weaknesses. The sixth and seventh ones, however, proved fatal. The sixth source of the republic's failure was the relative instability and precariousness of the nation's economic institutions and the succession of disastrous economic experiences which became associated in the mind of many Germans with the Weimar Republic. The first of these experiences was the period of widespread hunger and poverty which followed upon the defeat of Germany in World War I and which was aggravated by the prolongation of the Allied food blockade of Germany in 1919. A second economic disaster was the runaway inflation of 1923, in which the government permitted the value of the mark to drop to less than one-thousandth of a billionth of its value. When the currency was finally stabilized with United States aid in 1924, one new *"Rentenmark"* was worth 4,200,000,000 of the old ones. A large part of the savings and pensions of the German middle class were wiped out, and many in this group and their children blamed, not the deferred costs of the war, but the republic for their ruin, and especially the SPD, which had brought the republic into existence.

After a brief period of spectacular recovery, fueled by a stream of private loans from the United States that spurred the technological reequipment and modernization of German industry, the third disaster struck. After the "Black Friday" of October 1929 on the New York Stock Exchange, the flow of American credits dwindled, and the German economy suffered particularly heavily from the world wide depression. By early 1933, about 6 million workers were unemployed—roughly about one-third of the industrial work force of the country. The unemployed, their families, and particularly the young people who graduated from the schools and universities straight into unemployment blamed the republic for their misery. The first two of these disasters—the hunger of 1919 and the inflation of 1923—would probably have been tolerated by a majority of voters; in fact, after three years of recovery, the elections of 1928 had considerably strengthened the moderate and prodemocratic parties. The third disaster following hard upon the heels of the preceding ones and re-kindling the bitter memories of the previous two economic crises, however, was too much. From 1930 on, an increasing portion of German voters, and soon a majority, cast their votes for extremist and antidemocratic parties: the Nationalists, the Communists, and the hitherto unimportant National Socialist party of Adolf Hitler.

In the face of this growing danger, the seventh weakness of the Weimar Republic was to prove decisive: the lack of imagination, competence, and courage in the economic and political policies of its leaders during its last years. In several other industrial countries, such as the United States after 1933, unemployment and depression were eventually controlled to some extent by programs of public works and various measures of credit expansion and government spending. The statesmen of the Weimar Republic, however, whatever their party, remained fearful of inflation, a recent and unhappy memory; they clung to a policy of "sound money" and deflation, which resulted in mounting unemployment, while doing almost nothing for the unemployed except providing some pitifully meager relief payments for those condemned to months or years of involuntary idleness. Even less help was provided for the small middle-class shopkeepers and businessmen who lost their businesses in the depression.

Between 1930 and 1933, as governments seemed incapable of acting, a feeling of desperation spread among many groups—a feeling that something had to be done, regardless of risk or cost. "If you must shoot," the poet Erich Kästner wrote in his *Address to Suicides,* "please do not aim at yourself." Kästner's own sympathies were liberal and humanitarian, but many of the young men whose desperation he echoed were becoming ready to shoot at any target that a plausible leader might point out. At a time when elder statesmen seemed to equate experience with impotence, and when rational discussion seemed to produce only excuses for inaction and frustration, millions from all classes were getting ready to overthrow the restraints of reason and experience, of curiosity and doubt, of kindness and pity, of tradition and religion, in favor of their blind need for security and certainty, for hate and aggression, and above all for action and for power, regardless of the cost in cruelty and suffering to others, and ultimately to themselves as well.

THE HITLER ERA, 1933–45

In the politics of the German Federal Republic, the years of Hitler's rule are rarely mentioned, but never forgotten. All Germans over 45 years of age have vivid personal memories of that epoch, and these are the age groups that include almost all political leaders, high-ranking government officials, and military personnel, and almost all leaders of interest groups —in short, almost the entire political elite. In order to understand the memories that still shape in one way or another many of their political thoughts and actions, we must look more closely at this unique and crucial period in their past.

Hitler's ideas were basically simple, as was the Nazi ideology derived from them. They offered a primitive but striking explanation for all the troubles of Germany and of the world. The Jews, Hitler asserted, were guilty of everything. They were the rich plutocrats of Wall Street and of all the world's stock exchanges, who were profiting from high interest rates and the misery of debtors and were benefiting from war, inflation, and depression. But the Jews, according to Hitler, were also the agitators for strikes and trade unions, the wirepullers for Communism and subversion. Their conspiracy, as depicted in such pamphlets as the forged but widely disseminated one attributed to Sergei Nilus, *Protocols of the Elders of Zion,* depicted them as the masters of Wall Street and the Kremlin, which were the twin arms of a single plot against the world, and first of all, against the German people. Hitler actually seems to have believed these fantasies, but he also shrewdly noted in his book *Mein Kampf* ("My Struggle") that it was part of the art of the successful political propagandist to present several quite different opponents in the guise of a single enemy, and thus providing a single target for a skillfully aroused and directed popular hatred.

His appeal was aided by the highly visible concentration of Germans of the Jewish faith in journalism, law, and retail trade, including some of the large department stores. As the depression deepened, the law, the established press, and the department stores became more unpopular, particularly among small businessmen to whom Hitler's ranting began to sound more credible.

According to some of his biographers, Hitler was a man who needed to hate, perhaps even more than he needed to belong to a group, to feel important, to believe in his own superiority, to be a member of a superior race, to be a great leader, and indeed to be a genius-inspired artist, molding the German people and, if possible, all of Europe and the world into the obedient shape dictated by his visions. A poor, half-educated man of illegitimate birth, he had been marginal even in the provincial middle-class society in the small town of Braunau where he had been born. He had failed to win a scholarship to art school, and as a young man he had been torn between his longing to rise to the level of the social elite and his fear of sinking down into the class of unskilled workers.

Other observers have read Hitler's mind differently. They point to his undoubtedly extraordinary gifts, particularly as a propagandist, and to the lack of adequate opportunities for such a brilliant talent in the rigid social system of pre-1914 Germany. The rage and hate that he so often demonstrated later may have been engendered by the frustration and rejection of his youthful aspirations. Or he may even have found it profitable to display more hate than he actually felt, in a calculated effort to whip up the emotions of his audience.

Still other writers have stressed Hitler's fear and hatred of change. He hated new styles in painting and music; industry replacing handicraft; joint stock companies replacing owner-managed firms; department stores pushing out small shops; demands for the equality of women and of the nonwhite races, particularly efforts to free the nonwhite colonies and to abolish colonial empires; and especially intellectuals' criticizing accepted habits and ideas. He liked tradition, German peasants, au-

thority, and order—although eventually he did great injury to all of these. According to this view, Hitler was a rigid conservative gone wild. War, mass killings, and tyranny were in his view means to hammer out a German-dominated world order that would at last remain stable.

All observers agree, however, on Hitler's love of the military life and military values. The German army of World War I had offered him, together with physical danger, the psychological and emotional security of its uniform; and when he stayed in service after 1918, it was the German army that first sent him as a political intelligence agent in the heated labor meetings of the early Weimar Republic. It was here that Hitler discovered his gifts not only as an orator but as a master propagandist who was later to put down the principles of his craft quite frankly in *Mein Kampf.* Talk to people at meetings in the evening, he wrote, for then they are tired and less apt to resist your suggestions. Crowds are like women, he added: they like to be dominated. The bigger an untruth, he wrote, the more apt are people to believe it, since it seems incredible to them that anyone should lie so much. People who blindly disbelieve all they read in the papers, Hitler noted, are just as easy marks for propaganda as those who believe all that is printed. Above all, he concluded, successful propaganda is based on endless repetition that varies the form of the message so as to keep up the interest of the audience, but that hammers home the same unvarying content with ceaseless persistence.

Hitler did not hesitate to use every device of propaganda or of violence that would serve his purpose. At bottom, he believed, he stood for a great truth—the truth, so he believed, that all life was a pitiless struggle for existence, that nature was the "cruel queen of wisdom," that war as a social institution was eternal, and indeed good, for it subjugated or exterminated the inferior races while elevating the superior peoples and races to mastery. Only superior persons and races, he felt, were truly human; no others deserved consideration. The German people, as he saw it, had no other choice than that between victorious conquest or contemptible suffering. It was his destiny, he was convinced, to lead them; and if they were worth anything, they would eventually follow.

Hitler's hopes and dreams, just as his barely suppressed fears and rages, were those of millions of his countrymen. He represented much of their own feelings and desires, in heightened form. Many of them vibrated to his message because it was their own tune that was being played. At the same time, it copied some of the appeals of communism: the vision of revolution, the promise of national solidarity and social justice, the emotional security and discipline of a tightly organized party, the heady sense of historical mission. But Hitler's ideology also included many themes borrowed from the ideas and practices of the West. The glorification of colonial empire and of a white master race; the misapplied ideas, borrowed from Robert Malthus and Charles Darwin, about an eternal struggle for survival among human beings; the rejection of mercy, pity, and the traditions and ideas of the New Testament as unsuited to the real world of eternal struggle—all these ideas had been propagated by various writers in England, France, and the United States, many decades before Hitler discovered them at second hand and bent them to his purpose.

In a nutshell, National Socialism was thus German nationalism plus a demogogic social promise, and minus moral inhibitions. Its leader, Adolf Hitler, promised to accomplish what many Germans wanted—from high-ranking officers and industrialists all the way down to many lower-middle-class clerks and small farmers. He promised to make Germany a very great power, with an empire as large and splendid as the British empire was believed to be; to make her formidably armed and universally admired and respected; and he promised also to ensure for the German people within this greater empire the high level of economic security and living standards that befitted a "master race," comparable to the standards that were supposed to be the rightful due of white men in Africa and Asia.

Even before the coming of the Great Depression, between one-quarter and one-third of the German voters might have approved of some such goal, and an ever larger proportion —including a part of the Communist voters— would have agreed that the world was largely ruled by naked power, force, and fraud, so that nothing great could be accomplished in it without extreme ruthlessness.

Like many nationalists and others who confused cynicism with realism, Hitler proclaimed himself a realist, merely because he assumed that the world was inevitably ruled by power and ruthless competition—that the strong and clever were fated to rule, while the weak or gullible were destined to slavery or death— and that in this inexorable struggle, the German people, like all peoples and races, had the choice to be hammer or anvil, victors or victims—in the last analysis of the struggle for biological survival to be killers or to be killed.

To be sure, this was an extravagantly oversimplified picture of the world, with no possible room for basic changes in human nature, culture, and society; no room for international cooperation among equals; no common victories of science over nature for the benefit of all. The important point was, however, that at bottom this was the sort of thing that, in somewhat less extreme and consistent terms, many German nationalists had long believed. Hitler thus seemed to them to voice their own beliefs with extraordinary force and fervor, and without introducing any frustrating inhibitions of traditional morality, or any doubts about the adequacy of his knowledge of international politics, economics, and military matters.

Conservative nationalists had also long been irked by the coolness of German workers, and generally of the broad masses of the German people, to their programs. Hitler promised to arouse just these masses, and to put the hopes and dreams of the poor and the workers behind the drive for a much bigger German empire than that of Bismarck's day. Even though Hitler in fact won far more support among the lower middle classes than he did among the workers, he did seem to offer an alternative to the appeal of organized labor, and it is not surprising that he found at least some sympathy and support throughout most of the 1920s in some military and business circles when his movement was still relatively insignificant and his one attempt at a *coup* in 1923 had remained a comic-opera affair. After the coming of the Great Depression in late 1929, however, the scale of this support grew very large, just at the time when masses of ordinary Germans became more inclined to listen to his message.

Even in 1933, however, the susceptibility to Hitler's appeal was quite unevenly distributed in the population. A German sociologist, Rainer Lepsius, has estimated that in 1933 Hitler gained about one-tenth of the Social Democratic and Communist workers, one-tenth of the practicing Catholics, half of the conservative rural Protestants, and as much as eight-tenths of the urban Protestant middle and lower middle classes. But even among those who did not vote for him, few moved toward active resistance.

In the electoral campaign of 1930 and thereafter, the Nazis had far more money to spend than their competitors—on posters, leaflets, advertisements, political uniforms, a private army of brown shirted storm troopers and black-shirted "elite guards," on trucks to drive their men to mass meetings, for meeting halls, loudspeakers, spotlights, and all the other machinery of political propaganda. Much, perhaps even most, of this money came from the rank and file of Hitler's followers, for the Nazis were experts at collecting contributions, but much of it also came from bank credits extended to the Nazis by big banks whose managers decided to treat this new extremist as a confidence-inspiring borrower. A good deal of money also came from prominent leaders of German industry and finance, such as the steel magnate Fritz Thyssen, who saw in the Nazis not only a counterpoise to Communism but also a tool to force down the high costs of trade union wages and to prevent implementation of the welfare state advocated by the Social Democrats.[1]

A much-publicized meeting of many of the best-known names in German heavy industry and in the German high nobility, which took place in October 1931 at Bad Harzburg,[2] demonstrated the alliance of Hitler and his lieutenants with the old-style German nationalists. The latter were led by the newspaper publisher and film magnate Alfred Hugenberg, whose newsreels and chain of provincial papers had begun to transmit to their large, unsophisticated audience a favorable image of Hitler and his movement. The Harzburg meeting dramatically underscored this new image of Hitler. Within a few months after the conference, which was featured in words and pictures by the press, Hitler lectured in January 1932 to the industrial elite of Germany, at the Industrialists' Union in Düsseldorf, and the results of this "break-through," according to Hitler's press chief, Otto Dietrich, "became manifest in the following difficult months."[3]

During the last two-and-three-quarter years of its existence, the Weimar Republic was governed by political conservatives—President von Hindenburg and a succession of right-of-center chancellors, Heinrich Brüning, Franz von Papen, and Kurt von Schleicher. Their governments were supported mainly by the Roman Catholic Center party and the Social Democrats (SPD), although these parties—and particularly the SPD—had little influence on the deflationary policies that were becoming ever more unpopular with the electorate. Nevertheless, the two moderate parties lost only a few votes and retained the loyalty particularly of their older voters. The old-style Nationalists also changed little in their voting strength.

The popular appeal of Hitler and the Nazi ideology is seen in the spectacular growth of electoral support given to the Nazis between 1928 and 1932, growing from 3% to 33%. This support was mainly derived from members of the lower-middle class who had previously voted for the liberal parties. By 1932 the middle-class liberal parties enjoyed only about one-fifth of the support that they had in 1928. At the same time, a number of small moderately rightist, nationalist, and conservative parties and groups crumbled, and their members and

---

[1] Much later, the disappointed Thyssen wrote a book entitled *I Paid Hitler*.

[2] For an outstanding scholarly work, giving a partial list of those present, see Karl Dietrich Bracher, *Die Auflösung der Weimarer Republik* [The dissolution of the Weimar Republic], 3d ed. (Villingen: Ring Verlag, 1960), pp. 407–14. An English translation of this work is being published by the Yale University Press.

[3] Quoted in Bracher, *Die Auflösung*, p. 441; also see pp. 438–42.

voters went over to the Nazis. There was a mounting protest vote from millions of former habitual nonvoters, including many women, and from young voters and the unemployed, which was shared by the extremist parties—the Communists and the Nazis. After examining the various studies of Hitler's electoral support, one political sociologist offered the following description of the typical Nazi voter in 1932 (although there were, of course, other types as well): "He was a middle-class, self-employed Protestant who lived either on a farm or in a small community, and who had previously voted for a centrist or regionalist political party strongly opposed to the power and influence of big business and big labor." [4]

Hitler was finally appointed chancellor of Germany by old President von Hindenburg on January 30, 1933. Not strong enough to topple the state from without, Hitler entered it by invitation and transformed it from within. Hitler thus came to sit at the head of a cabinet in which a few Nazi ministers were greatly outnumbered by conservatives, including Alfred Hugenberg and Franz von Papen. Elections were called for March 5. Two weeks before that date, the empty building of the Reichstag, the German parliament, was set on fire and a Nazi rule of terror started. According to the preponderance of such evidence as has survived, the fire was set by the Nazis. There is no doubt that they exploited it to perfection. The Communist party was blamed for the fire and suppressed at once. In Prussia—which covered two-thirds of Germany—the Nazi storm troopers were deputized as auxiliary police. Everywhere in Germany the press and the meetings of all parties still opposing the Nazis were drastically curbed; mass arrests, beatings, and acts of torture served to intimidate opponents. Even under these conditions, however, the Nazis got only 43% of the popular vote. Only together with the Nationalists, who had polled another 8%, could they claim to represent a bare majority of the German electorate.

On March 23, 1933, however, a cowed parliament, including the Center party, voted

Hitler an enabling bill with sweeping powers. Only ninety-four Social Democratic votes were cast against it. The suppression of the Social Democrats and the major trade unions came in May; the Nationalists dissolved themselves in June; the Center party—disoriented by a concordat which Hitler had signed with the Vatican—was obliged to follow suit in July; and on July 14, 1933, the National Socialists were declared the only legal political party in Germany. A bloody purge in 1934 eliminated dissident Nazis and some conservatives, and Hitler's power became, for most practical purposes, absolute.

Once entrenched in power, Hitler communicated assurances of moderation to foreign statesmen and promises of extremism to his followers. He talked peace and prepared rapidly for war. At that time, Germany was still largely disarmed. As a result of the restrictions imposed on her by the Treaty of Versailles, her armed forces lacked large trained reserves, any kind of military aircraft, tanks, heavy artillery, submarines, and full-sized battleships. Nor did she have any substantial fortifications in the west. All these deficiencies were overcome step by step, between 1933 and 1939, with the toleration and sometimes the approval of British and French statesmen, whom Hitler soothed with his anticommunist declarations. Occasionally, he also assured the Soviet government of his peaceful intentions toward them and publicly pledged his friendship to the authoritarian government of Poland.

The Nazis in Power

Hitler proclaimed that the empire he was creating would last a thousand years. It lasted twelve. The main events are familiar. During the first six years, Hitler achieved full employment and temporary prosperity, through controlled currency inflation and rearmament, which brought profits to industry and took hundreds of thousands of young men off the labor market by putting them into uniform. Added to this was an expanded program of public works—superhighways, new public buildings, and some low-cost housing—and improvements

---

[4] S. M. Lipset, *Political Man* (New York: Doubleday, 1959), p. 149.

in some social benefits, such as government loans for home repairs and a popular "strength through joy" recreation program. As in most dictatorships, bread was supplemented by circuses. There were political and military parades, songs and martial music, and party congresses that were spectacles for millions. A network of press, film, and radio propaganda under the virtuoso direction of Joseph Goebbels disseminated these spectacles throughout the country and completed the intoxication of the German nation.

During the same six years, the persecution of the Jews and the terror against all political opposition were organized into a system. The Jews were driven from all academic and free professions, from journalism, literature, the arts, from finance and industry—where they had been much less prominent than the Nazis had pretended—and finally from practically all kinds of business and employment. They had to wear yellow stars on their clothing, and their children were barred from ordinary schools and universities. Those who did not succeed in emigrating sold off their possessions piece by piece in order to live, waiting for a tomorrow that seemed to be becoming ever more bleak. Thousands of Jews were imprisoned and brutally mistreated in concentration camps, and so was an even larger number of German critics of Hitler; the annual number of concentration camp inmates in the 1930s has been estimated at between 20,000 and 30,000. In these years, the Nazis became masters of the art of concealing from the German people just enough of the crimes committed against their victims in the concentration camps to avoid arousing any widespread disgust or moral revulsion; yet they revealed enough to intimidate thoroughly most of the potential opposition within Germany.

But while concealing their crimes, the Nazis publicly used their victims as scapegoats for all of Germany's difficulties. A whole series of so-called enemies was discovered or manufactured. There were the perpetrators of the "stab in the back" that had caused Germany's defeat in World War I; the international capitalists who were bleeding Germany of its economic sustenance; the Marxists who wanted to destroy Germany and hand it over to Stalin; the pacifists who bled Germany of the strength to resist, which was crucial since the country was surrounded by foreign enemies on all its borders; and the papist Catholics who gave their first loyalty to Rome. The Jew, however, was all these rolled into one. He was at once a Marxist and an international capitalist, a pacifist and an internationalist, a Freemason and an ally of the clericals. Above all, the Jew was a debaser of the purity of the German race, with his lewd and perverted sexual interests in blond German women.

The success of Nazi propaganda was not due solely to the expertise with which they wielded it. If propaganda is to be deeply infused in a people, it must satisfy the people's preexisting attitudes and emotions. The genius of the Nazi propagandists is seen in their expert exploitation of the Germans' dormant emotions and prejudices. Anti-Semitism had existed for such a long time in Germany that it was part and parcel of the culture. Military defeat in World War I and the humiliation attending it made the Germans hungry for uniforms, which the Nazis were glad to provide for their storm troopers (SA) and elite guards (SS). A nation that had been taught for generations to revere force and strength would have many people willing to see in Naziism's propagandistic and actually successful violence a movement to be respected. And, among a people that had been used to authoritarian governments, many were ready to believe that the masses indeed were incapable of deciding for themselves what they wanted and what was to be done—and that it was a good idea to have the Nazi elite and the *Führer* decide for them.

While "enemies" were persecuted, the German nation was put into a totalitarian straitjacket through the process of *Gleichschaltung* ("coordination") of all aspects of German life according to the Nazi pattern. All the institutions of society—political, cultural, economic, and educational—were subjected to Nazi control and a "cleansing" operation. All those individuals in important positions who were thought to be unreliable were replaced by Nazi party members, and the remainder were fearful enough of losing their jobs to send them into the recruiting arms of the party and its auxiliary organizations. The Nazis then went one step further by creating new youth and labor organizations, and even organized their control down to the level of the party "block," made up of a group of adjacent apartment houses. These organizations went further than controlling the people's nonpolitical activities. They were also used to spy upon the population. Hitler Youth members were ordered to report their parents if they made critical remarks about the Nazis or listened in on foreign radio broadcasts; some of them complied, while others merely kept their parents cowed.

Despite this shadow of fear and terror in the background, Hitler's partial and short-lived but well-publicized benefits made a profound impression: 40% of the respondents to a national opinion poll in 1951 considered the Hitler years of 1933–39 as the time when Germany had been best off. An even larger proportion (45%) names the pre-1914 Hohenzollern empire as Germany's best period, and only 7% were willing to say as much for the Weimar Republic.[5] In a 1948 poll, 41% recalled having approved of the Nazi power seizure in 1933, and 57% agreed with the statement that National Socialism was a good idea which had been badly carried out.[6] According to a 1968 poll, the latter statement was still accepted by 50% of the total population, and by 42% of the young.[7] Earlier, in 1956, among a sample of young men, nearly half called National Socialism a "good idea," either without qualification (16%) or "in part" (33%), while 29% gave no opinion, and only less than one-quarter called it a bad idea.[8] Also in 1956, 42% agreed that "without the war Hitler would have been one of the greatest statesmen," while 38% denied this proposition. Thus, at that time in the German Federal Republic a preponderance

[5] Elisabeth Noelle Neumann and Erich Peter Neumann, *Jahrbuch der öffentlichen Meinung* (Allensbach: Verlag für Demoskopie, 1947–55), 1: 126.

[6] Ibid., 1: 133, 134.

[7] Rudolf Wildenmann and Max Kaase, *Die unruhige Generation: Eine Untersuchung zu Politik und Demokratie in der Bundesrepublik* (Mannheim: Lehrstuhl für politische Wissenschaft, Universität Mannheim, 1968), p. 71.

[8] Neumann and Neumann, *Jahrbuch* (1957), 2:149; from a sample of 1000 men born 1929–39.

of the public were admirers, to some extent at least, of a total nationalistic dictatorship.

The favorable surface image of Hitler's rule in 1933–39 was reinforced by the conspicuous tolerance, if not connivance, of foreign statesmen before World War II. Between 1934 and 1936, Britain accepted the establishment of a German air force, a limited German program of battleship and submarine construction, the introduction of conscription for a new German mass army, and the remilitarization of the Rhineland—all measures explicitly forbidden under the Treaty of Versailles. Only somewhat more reluctantly, France likewise accepted each of these steps in Hitler's rearmament. In those early years of Nazism, either Britain or France —or, of course, both of them together—could easily have halted the creation of that German armed force that a few years later was to be used against their countries and peoples. Yet their governments chose to accept passively the creation of these German forces, hoping either that they would not be used, or that they would only be used against some other country.

The most obvious "other" country among the great powers was the Soviet Union, and Hitler's pose as the protector of Western civilization against Communism won him important sympathies outside Germany. These sympathies, no less than the fear of his conspicuously growing military and air power, kept the British and French from contesting his annexation of Austria in March 1938. At the Munich conference in September of that year, Britain and France agreed to the dismemberment of Czechoslovakia and the annexation of the Sudetenland, and they acquiesced in Hitler's occupation of much of the rest of Czechoslovakia in March 1939. If Hitler's aggression thus seemed to be directed southeastward, the Soviet government found it to its obvious interest to turn Hitler's ambitions elsewhere.

In August 1939, Hitler and Stalin concluded one of the most cold-blooded bargains in the history of power politics: a Nazi-Soviet nonagression pact which left Hitler free to attack Poland and to make war on the West, and assured him of the benevolent neutrality of the Soviet government, which during the preceding four years had loudly called for an international common front against the Nazi menace. Finally, in September 1939, Hitler took the German people into war against Poland, England, and France. But for the preceding six years, his respectability had been attested to at one time or another by the diplomatic collaboration, often including formal treaties of friendship, of all the major European powers, including even Poland and the Vatican.

In the end, Hitler betrayed all the governments and groups who had trusted his regime, or who had attempted to collaborate with him for their own ends. He violated his 1933 concordat with the Vatican and persecuted the lay organizations, and often the priests, of the Roman Catholic church. He made war on Poland, France, England, the Soviet Union, and many other countries. And as a result, between 1939 and 1945, he led the German people into the depths both of degradation and of suffering. His air force started the practice of large-scale bombing of civilian populations, at Warsaw in 1939 and at Rotterdam in 1940. During the first two years of the war, in 1939–41, Hitler ordered five programs of mass extermination: the "euthanasia" (good death) program that killed thousands of inmates of hospitals and mental asylums; the extermination of the Polish intelligentsia; the extermination of all Political Commissars serving with the Soviet army; the extermination of the gypsies; and in August 1941, at the peak of his military triumphs, the extermination of the Jews—men, women, and children—which he called "the final solution" of "the Jewish question." Special camps were built with gas chambers and with crematoriums for the bodies. From then on, manpower, building materials, fuel, and transport were diverted from the German armies to this infamous project of the Nazis. "We could process 2,000 head per hour," the commandant of the death camp at Auschwitz, Franz Hoess, later told the International Court at Nürnberg. By the end of the war in 1945, an estimated 6 million Jews had perished. The shoes of executed children had been sorted into large piles for further disposal; the national bank of Germany had been enriched by a sizable amount of gold melted down from the gold fillings broken from the teeth of the dead; and some Nazi officials had even tried to have some of the corpses used for the manufacture of soap. During the same years, German armies were ground up at the battlefronts while Allied aircraft rained fire and explosives on German cities. In a few nights at Hamburg in 1943, an estimated 200,000 persons lost their lives in a series of Allied air raids that set off uncontrollable firestorms which raged through whole city blocks, baking countless civilians even in the air-raid shelters.

The war became a nightmare, and German defeat ever more certain. Yet the Nazi control of the German people held until the end. No German town or village rose in rebellion; no German factory crew went on strike; no German troops mutinied, or surrendered without authorization. Thousands of Germans were executed during those years for opposing the government, or for daring to say that the war was lost; but the combination of Nazi propaganda and terror remained effective, since it was backed almost everywhere by the Nazis and Nazi sympathizers among the population, who supplied the secret police with support and information. In addition, the compulsory activities of the Nazis took up so much of the free time of the population that any popular needs for collective political activity became oversaturated, and most of the non-Nazi Germans were left with a mere longing for passivity and privacy—which left the Nazis in control until the end.

A desperate attempt at a *coup d'état* by officers and civilian opponents of the Hitler regime on July 20, 1944, was smashed, and was followed by large-scale executions. The population at large remained passive and obedient. Even under the impact of daily Allied bombings and Allied armies pushing farther and farther into German territory, there was not a single group of Germans that rose up to overthrow even local Nazi authorities. In the end, Hitler died by his own command, at the hands of an obedient subordinate, under the ruins of Berlin. Germany was occupied by the American, British, and French troops from the west and Soviet forces from the east. What remained of the German armed forces surrendered on May 7 and 8, 1945, and the Allied military authorities found themselves in charge of Germany's shattered cities and people.

PARTITION AND ALLIED MILITARY GOVERNMENT, 1945–49

After the collapse of Hitler's German empire, Germany was reduced to a territory smaller than that which had been left her by the Treaty of Versailles. The Nazi annexations of 1939 and 1940 were restored to their original owners. Thus, Austria again became independent and the Sudetenland was returned to Czechoslovakia, and Alsace-Lorraine to France. Of the German territories of 1937, those to the east of the rivers Oder and Neisse (the "Oder-Neisse line")—notably including East Prussia and industry-rich Silesia—were detached from the rest of Germany. Being in fact occupied by Soviet troops, these "Oder-Neisse territories" were administratively separated from Germany with the consent of the Western powers at the Yalta Conference. The northern half of East Prussia was put under the "administration" of the USSR; the southern half, together with Silesia and the rest of the Oder-Neisse territories, came under the "administration" of Poland.

In theory, the fate of all these territories was to be finally decided only by a future peace treaty of all the Allies, Western and Eastern, with Germany. In fact, no such peace treaty has come into existence. A German-Soviet treaty, recognizing explicitly the Oder-Neisse line as the western boundary of Poland, and the existence of two German states, the GFR and GDR, was signed in 1970 with the consent of the Western allies. And, at the time this manuscript had to be closed, the Bundestag was expected to vote for its ratification by May 1972. In the meantime, the governments and peoples of both Poland and the Soviet Union consider the Yalta agreement to have been merely a face-saving gesture by the Western powers to mask their actual acceptance of the Polish and Russian annexation of these territories. These areas were quickly incorporated into the Polish and Soviet national territories. Their German population—in a tragic and ironic reversal of the earlier population transfers of the Hitler

THREE

Germany divided between West and East

343

era—was terrorized and expelled into the reduced Germany of 1945, and the territories were resettled by Poles and Russians. Thus, for example, the devastated German city of Breslau was gradually rebuilt and resettled as the Polish city of Vroclav, and Königsberg in former East Prussia became Kaliningrad in the USSR. A similar fate befell the German minorities in the territories that had not belonged to the Germany of 1937 but which Hitler had temporarily elevated to the status of a "master race" among their neighbors, such as the 3 million Sudeten Germans in Czechoslovakia, and the smaller minorities of *Volksdeutsche* in Rumania, Yugoslavia, Hungary, and Poland. Almost all of these, too, were expelled into the reduced Germany of 1945.

This remaining Germany was occupied by the victors and divided into four zones of occupation—Soviet, American, British, and French—in accordance with wartime agreements. The city of Berlin, which had been the capital of Germany since 1871 and the capital of Brandenburg-Prussia since the seventeenth century, was similarly divided into four sectors of occupation and put under a separate regime. In theory, Germany was to be governed as an economic unit under an Allied Control Council, and Berlin similarly was to be under an Allied Kommandatura. In practice, although these joint bodies were in existence, the differences between the Soviet Union and the Western allies proved unbridgeable; each zone was run separately by its controlling power, and the remaining trickle of interzonal trade was carried on much as among different nations.

Within their zones, the Western powers, particularly the United States and Britain, tried to restore gradually some fabric of German administrative effort and political life. After establishing German municipal administration, the Western allies proceeded to set up regional governments, called *Länder* ("lands"), somewhat analogous to the states of the United States. During the same period, the German press and radio were revived, under personnel screened by the Western allies. Political meetings, and parties were permitted, and eventually so were elections to representative bodies at the

municipal level (January 1946) and the *Land*—i.e., regional—level (June 1946).

From Ex-Enemy to Ally

During 1946, Western policies toward Germany went through a major change. In September, the United States secretary of state, James F. Byrnes, in a speech at Stuttgart, called for a unified German economy and the early creation of a provisional German government, and he treated Germany, by implication, as a potential ally of the West. In the same month, Winston Churchill, speaking at Zurich, called for a united Europe, including Germany, to defend Western values and traditions.

Earlier, in July 1946, the United States proposed economic mergers of their zone with any other zone, and Britain accepted the invitation. Also in July, in the first of several amnesties, the American occupation authorities began to allow the return of former Nazis into high levels of public and private employment, from whence they had been ousted in large numbers by procedures of "denazification." These amnesties were intended to ease the recruitment of experienced civil servants and other personnel for the task of reconstructing West Germany, and perhaps also to help reorient the more moderate sectors of German nationalist opinion toward an eventual posture of alliance with the West. These policy changes were followed, in December 1946, by the establishment of joint committees of German representatives from the eight *Länder* comprising the British and American zones, and the Byrnes-Bevin agreement between the United States and Britain merged the economies of their two zones into a "bizone."

During 1947, a German Economic Council was created for the bizone, a revised plan for West German industry set the 1936 level of German production as its aim, and the preparations for the Marshall Plan and the European Recovery Program opened new and increasingly attractive opportunities for German cooperation with the Western family of nations. In 1948, after the Communist takeover of

Czechoslovakia alarmed the West, the unification of West Germany and its merger with the Western coalition of powers were accelerated. At the London Conference of February 1948, the fusion of the three occupation zones of the United States, Britain, and France was clearly envisaged, and so was the early creation of a federal type of German government. In March 1948, a Soviet walkout ended the Allied Control Council for Germany, and on June 16 a similar Soviet move put the four-power Allied Kommandatura in Berlin out of operation. Two days later, a carefully prepared currency reform was put into effect in the three Western zones, greatly spurring their economic revival but severing another of the previously agreed-on links between the Western- and the Soviet-occupied parts of Germany.

On the same day, the Soviet Military Government, taking advantage of the fact that Berlin is a landlocked enclave within East Germany, announced its decision to blockade West Berlin from June 19 onward. This was followed quickly by a currency reform for the Soviet zone and East Berlin and, on June 24, by the interruption of railroad traffic to West Berlin. Thus started the Berlin "blockade." A dramatic Western allied airlift of food and other vital supplies, using most of the transport aircraft at the disposal of Britain and the United States, enabled West Berlin to hold out for over six months, and the unsuccessful Soviet blockade was lifted on May 12, 1949. By that time, three important precedents had been set: the Soviet government had not attempted to dislodge the Western allies from West Berlin by force, the Western allies did not attempt to use force to break the blockade, and no Soviet pressure on West Berlin, short of force, had been able to compel the Western allies to leave the city or to abandon their plans to establish a united and democratic West German state.

The Formation
of the Federal Republic

Western allied steps toward the creation of such a state proceeded throughout the blockade. By

August 1948, travel restrictions were abolished between the French zone and "Bizonia," creating, in effect, a "trizone." On September 1, a West German "parliamentary council," which was, in fact, a constituent assembly, met in Bonn to draft a constitution for Germany—or rather, since Soviet-occupied eastern and central Germany were not represented, the council limited itself to drafting a "Basic Law" for the German Federal Republic, until such time as an all-German constituent assembly could replace it with a constitution agreed on by the entire German people. By the end of May 1949, this Basic Law had been drawn up by the parliamentary council, adopted by most of the eleven *Land* parliaments, and formally promulgated.

After a general election in September 1949, followed by the choice by the Bundestag—the popularly elected chamber—of Dr. Theodor Heuss as federal president and of Dr. Konrad Adenauer as chancellor (by a majority of one vote), the Western allies were willing to see the Federal Republic actually launched. The Western allies had in the meantime worked out three related "instruments": (1) an Occupation Statute, which defined the residual powers of the Western allies in the Federal Republic; (2) a Trizonal Fusion Agreement, which set up an Allied High Commission for (West) Germany; and (3) a charter for this commission, defining its organization and procedure. After the acceptance of these Western allied instruments by the president and chancellor of the German Federal Republic at Petersberg on September 21, 1949, the German Federal Republic, with Bonn as its capital, formally came into existence.

The formal establishment of the German Federal Republic was followed quickly by the creation, on October 7, 1949, of a Communist-dominated German Democratic Republic (G.D.R.) in the Soviet-occupied zone of Germany. The government of the Federal Republic as well as the Western allies, however, long refused to concede this rival creation any legal standing whatever. They insisted on considering the Federal Republic as the sole legal representative of the German people, pending their eventual reunification. Only in the negotiations of the 1969–71 period of the Brandt government with the Soviet Union, and in direct talks with leaders of the G.D.R., was this position abated, with the consent of a majority of West German public opinion.

A CONVALESCENT REPUBLIC, 1949–55

During the first years of the German Federal Republic, its sovereignty was considerably limited under the Occupation Statute of 1949. Step by step, these limitations were reduced, first by the very nature of the Petersberg agreement, then by the Contractual Agreement of 1952, and finally by the Paris agreements of 1955, which made the German Federal Republic in most respects sovereign. It was authorized to form its own national army, subject only to the major remaining restriction that the Federal Republic renounce certain types of heavy military and naval weapons, and particularly so-called ABC weapons—atomic/bacteriological/chemical. The Federal Republic was prohibited from equipping its own armed forces with such weapons or from producing them for any other country.

Between 1949 and 1955, about 13 million German expellees and refugees from Eastern Europe and East Germany were successfully absorbed by the Federal Republic. West German industry was rapidly reconstructed and the country began to experience prosperity. The 1936 level of aggregate gross national product was surpassed in 1950, and that of the 1936 per capita GNP in 1951. By 1955, the net national income was 179% of that of 1936.[1] A good part—20 to 25%—of this income went into new investments, but by 1953 per capita consumption had also reached 114% of the 1936 level. Thus, throughout most of the 1950s the population of the Federal Republic was better off economically than it had been before the war. These conspicuous economic successes had been made possible by massive economic aid from the United States—as well as by more modest economic aid from Britain and by the very efficient use made by the West German industries and government of the American aid.

The total amount of this aid up to June 1956 was given by the West German Ministry of Economic Cooperation as almost $10 billion, of which $6.4 billion had gone to the Federal Republic proper and $3.6 billion to West Berlin.[2] The forms of this aid varied; almost $4 billion were accounted for publicly by the United States government as aid under the Marshall Plan and its several predecessor and successor programs. Some of the rest may have come in the form of commodity surpluses, the spending of American occupation troops, and American payments for the offshore procurement of military supplies, but some of the dollar receipts of Germany in those years, as was the case with the receipts of some other countries, were not publicized and remained in what the United Nations Economic Commission for Europe described as "the twilight zone of quasi-strategic information."[3] There was no doubt, however, about the effectiveness of the American contribution to the "economic miracle" of the Federal Republic: "it was 'dollar therapy,'" said a German official publication, which credited West Germany's economic revival to "the tonic effect of an American blood transfusion. . . . Every Marshall plan dollar spent in Germany has resulted in $10 to $20 worth of goods produced and services rendered."[4]

Although the United States primed the economic pump, other factors markedly contributed to the country's economic recovery.

[1] Wolfgang F. Stolper, *Germany Between East and West* (Washington, D.C.: National Planning Assn., 1960), p. 11, with reference to *Statistisches Jahrbuch für die Bundesrepublik* (Bonn, 1956), p. 520 (hereafter cited as *S.J.B.*).

[2] Federal Republic of Germany, Ministry of Economic Cooperation, *Der Europäische Wirtschaftsrat* (OEEC, Handbuch, 1956), p. 70; see also K. W. Deutsch and L. J. Edinger, *Germany Rejoins the Powers* (Stanford, Calif.: Stanford University Press, 1959), pp. 145–51, for further details and references.

[3] See United Nations Economic Commission for Europe, *Economic Survey of Europe in 1953* (New York, 1954), pp. 19–20.

[4] Federal Republic of Germany, *Germany Reports* (Bonn, 1953), pp. 239–43.

German management and labor had lost none of their traditional efficiency. The trade unions generally avoided strikes because of their belief that it was more important to increase production than to win a better distribution of the national income for the workers. The millions of refugees from the east provided a cheap and plentiful labor force, willing to work especially hard in order to refashion their lives. Moreover, the worldwide Korean War economic boom of 1950 came at just the right time for a Germany eager to recapture her foreign markets, and capable of doing so by 1950. Much credit also has been given to Economics Minister Ludwig Erhard for efficiently combining laissez-faire market economics with governmental incentives for industry and welfare services for labor.

Domestic Conditions and Foreign Policy

Side by side with this rapid economic reconstruction went the gradual recovery of Germany's position in international life. The Federal Republic became a member of the Marshall Plan and the Organization for European Economic Cooperation in 1949, an associate member of the Council of Europe in 1950, and a full member in 1951. In 1951, the Federal Republic also joined the International Labor Organization (ILO), the World Health Organization (WHO), and the United Nations Organization for Educational and Scientific Cooperation (UNESCO). Guided by the prudent and steadfast policy of her government, and aided by the diplomatic support of the United States, the German Federal Republic was regaining for the German people something that many Germans had always deeply desired: a respected and honored place in the international community.

At home and abroad, the government of the Federal Republic strove to establish a reputation for reliability, moderation, and conservatism—well suited to the inclinations of its leading statesmen and to the mood of a majority of the electorate. In the pursuit of these policies, however, the government not only

strengthened Germany's political credit with its major allies, it also established important precedents for the development of German domestic policies and institutions. From the outset, refugees and expellees who were German by virtue of language and culture were accepted on a basis of full political equality, regardless of what citizenship they had held before the war. From the inception of the Federal Republic until 1969, Adenauer's party, the CDU, together with its Bavarian sister party, the CSU, have been the major element in five national coalition governments. From December 1949 onward, with the eventual endorsement of all major parties (after some early objections by the SPD), both the chancellor and the Bundestag put themselves on record as favoring a German military contribution to Western defense—that is, they favored some form of German rearmament, albeit on a modest scale. After the outbreak of the Korean War in 1950, a contribution to European defense was voted by the Bundestag in 1952, and a force of 500,000 men was promised for 1957.

In contrast to post-1945 developments in Britain, France, and Italy, no significant industries or services were nationalized, and the main emphasis of federal economic policy favored private enterprise. Popular referendums in some German Länder (North Rhine-Westphalia and Hessen) favoring the nationalization of certain big industries were overridden by the Western allies' military governments. The social and economic structure of West Germany was restored with many features of its past, familiar from the Weimar Republic and even the empire that had gone before. Property, authority, hierarchy, stability, inequality, and a good deal of monopolistic concentration were part of the package, but fears of communism, the felt need for the aid of the Western powers, and the hope for a speedy restoration of property made this structure increasingly popular.

The exclusion of the Social Democrats from a share in the federal cabinet until 1966 was significant. At the same time, social services by federal *Land* and local authorities were maintained at a relatively high level; an "equalization of burdens law" (*Lastenausgleich*) further helped to improve the lot of expellees, refugees, and bombed-out families from the Federal Republic; and by 1955, unemployment was down to about 4% of the work force, and dwindled still more in the years that followed.[5] In the early 1960s, the West German economy not only reached the level of full employment, but even had to reach into the surplus labor force of the less rapidly developing Mediterranean countries, particularly those of Italy and Spain, to satisfy its ever-increasing demand for workers. By the end of the 1960s, almost 2 million foreign workers were employed by West German industries. The pattern was thus set for a moderately conservative welfare state in politics, combined with a notable willingness on the part of businessmen, politicians, and government officials to promote investment and innovation in the reequipment of industry and commerce—a combination that was to persist with apparent success well up to the present. This expansionary potential of the West German economy allowed it to cope successfully with the most serious economic crisis since the founding of the Federal Republic in 1949—the so-called coal crisis, which became acute during the years 1966 and 1967 and was only finally mastered by mid-1969.

During the reconstruction period in the 1950s, West German industry and West German households had depended for their energy supply largely on coal. This was a natural energy choice for three reasons: (1) Germany is relatively poor in raw materials with the exception of coal. Most other mining products have to be imported. Thus, it was natural for a newly starting economy with an acute scarcity of capital to exploit domestic energy resources as much as possible. (2) This exploitation of coal in the Ruhr valley created badly needed jobs. (3) Since, in the early 1950s, nobody could predict the political future of the Federal Republic with certainty, a prediction of the development of the degree and certainty of West German access to foreign energy resources was equally difficult. At that stage, it

was "safer" for industry and households to rely on domestic energy sources.

With the growing political and economic consolidation of the Federal Republic, both on the domestic and on the international scene, the above three considerations were more and more overruled by mere cost-effectiveness calculations. Imported oil and natural gas, as well as hydroelectrical power, became more and more attractive as coal substitutes in household furnaces and for industrial use. In addition, the West German railroad, an important customer of the coal mines, began to electrify its transportation system. The reasons that German coal became less and less economical lies in its peculiar mining conditions. Most German seams are too small in diameter to warrant the use of highly automated mining equipment. The result was that, in 1966, for instance, the production rate of one miner per day was 2.7 tons in West Germany, whereas an American miner produced an average of 16.8 tons per day. Between 1963 and 1964, the total annual West German coal production decreased by over 7 million tons. Despite this reduction, the mines were forced to stockpile much of their product. By the end of 1965, the stockpile amounted to about 15.4 million tons; by August 1966, this figure was up to about 19 million tons. These figures acquire even greater significance when seen in relation to the total production rate of 135 million tons in 1965.[6]

This decline of the German coal market led to a broad overall economic crisis, with layoffs, rising costs of living, rising interest rates, a decrease in investments and in tax revenues, and ultimately to a resultant serious deficit in governmental spending: 1967 was the only year since the birth of the G.F.R. in which the national income stagnated. The development of the national income in real and in nominal terms for the years 1965 to 1968 was as shown in Table 3-1.

The inaction of Chancellor Erhard's government during this crisis and its corresponding inability to offer feasible programs that would

[5] Arnold J. Heidenheimer, *The Governments of Germany* (New York: Thomas Y. Crowell, 1966), p. 40.

[6] *Der Fischer Weltalmanach '67* (Frankfurt: Fischer, 1967), pp. 321, 322.

TABLE 3-1. *Annual National Income of the G.F.R. (billions of dollars)*

Year	National Income	
	Real	Nominal
1965	109.4	127.2
1966	116.0	135.0
1967	115.3	135.2
1968	127.8	148.0

SOURCE: *S.J.B.*, 1969, p. 490–91.
Rate of exchange in early 1972, approximately $1 = 3.21 DM.

have balanced the federal budget moved the junior partner of the coalition, the FDP, to withdraw from governmental responsibility. This left the CDU with the alternative to either rule with a minority government or to attempt a coalition with the SPD. The necessity for far-reaching economic measures, however, called for a strong majority in the Bundestag to back up these decisions and actions of the federal government. This situation provided the major rationale for the coalition alliance between the CDU and SPD, leaving the FDP alone in opposition. This "grand coalition," as it was soon called, under Kurt Georg Kiesinger (from the CDU) as chancellor and Willy Brandt (from the SPD) as minister of foreign affairs, was perceived by large parts of the population as potentially dangerous for democracy in the Federal Republic, because it deprived the entire system of an effective opposition. With about 10% of the Bundestag seats, the FDP was too weak to exert any substantial influence over and control of the legislative process. Technically, the government was in a position to push through practically any measure it wanted. Due to its command over roughly 90% of the seats in the Bundestag, it even had the power to change the Basic Law—the constitution of the Federal Republic —an action for which a two-thirds majority

is required by law. Thus, the "grand coalition" was largely considered to be a temporary, emergency alliance for the rescue of the troubled ship of state.

It was the economic policies of the SPD minister of the economy, Professor Karl Schiller, which solved the coal crisis by mid-1969. Schiller initiated a state-supervised trust within which all coal mines were united. Furthermore, he ordered more coal mines to be shut down, compensating the companies for their losses out of federal funds. Thus, between 1963 and 1969, the number of coal mines decreased by 24% from 294 to 224, of which about thirty mines were closed in 1967.[7] At the same time, new industries were granted extensive aid if they decided to open a new plant in the troubled mining areas. German automobile and chemical industries in particular responded to this plan. Government-sponsored job-training programs completed this remodeling of the infrastructure, particularly in the Ruhr valley, where most of the mines are located. On a larger scale, the government sponsored and encouraged foreign trade and domestic investment. Simultaneously, a permanent conference, the "concerted action," was instituted, in which representatives of industry, labor, and government cooperated in adjusting wage and price policies to the economic program of the "grand coalition." By 1969, the coal crisis had been successfully overcome and the economy of the G.F.R. had resumed its stable national and international position.

In foreign policy in the 1949–55 period, Bonn concentrated on maintaining close relations with the United States, and also with France. There was noticeably less emphasis put on ties with Italy, and perhaps still less on those with Britain; and there were no diplomatic relations with the Soviet Union, or any other member of the Soviet bloc.

In contrast to this cold war climate toward the East, Adenauer proposed as early as March 1949 a Franco-German economic union. In 1951, the Federal Republic signed the agree-

7 *S.J.B.*, 1965, p. 236; *S.J.B.*, 1967, p. 224; *S.J.B.*, 1968, p. 199; *S.J.B.*, 1970, p. 187.

ment establishing the European Coal and Steel Community (ECSC) with France, Italy, and the Benelux countries. In the same year, after repeated personal interventions of Chancellor Adenauer in its favor, the German-Israeli Reparations Agreement was signed, pledging to Israel $822 million, in goods, over a twelve-year period. Already in 1952, steps were taken to outlaw the Communist party and the extreme nationalistic Socialist Reich party (*Sozialistische Reichspartei,* or SRP); the outlawing of the latter party formally took place in the same year, while the legal proceedings against the Communists reached their culmination only in 1956. An extreme nationalist party similar to the SRP, the NPD, was legally established in the 1960s, winning up to 8% of the vote in state elections but less than 5% nationwide in 1969. A Communist successor party, the DKP, was granted legality in 1967, but all far-left parties polled less than 1% of the national vote in 1969. Germany's old foreign debts were cut in half, from about $7 billion to about $3.4 billion, by the 1953 London agreements on German foreign debts with the Western powers.

In 1954, pursuing the same policy of accommodation with France and close collaboration with the United States, West Germany ratified the EDC agreement which would have created a Western European army. The European Defense Community was rejected by the French Parliament, but West Germany later in the year signed the Paris agreement to become a member of the North Atlantic Treaty Organization (NATO), and signed agreements with France on the Saar territory and on French-German relations. In May 1955, with the ratification of the Paris agreement, the German Federal Republic became sovereign, limited only by the few remaining restrictions on nuclear and other special armaments, noted above. Germany slowly built up its national army, which French statesmen had tried to prevent earlier, and it stood ready to get back the Saar territory from France in the near future—an event which was consummated in 1956 when the attraction of West Germany prosperity had come to reinforce the Saarlanders' sense of German national identity. Adenauer's policy of

German-French friendship had paid off, and it was going to continue.

BONN'S RETURN AMONG THE POWERS, 1955–71

The years after 1955 brought the rapid return of the German Federal Republic to the rank of such powers as Britain and France. It became not only juridically equal, but increasingly able to diverge from the policies of these European powers and to apply pressure in the pursuit of its own preferred goals. At the same time, the Bonn government showed itself increasingly independent from the day-to-day policies of its principal ally, the United States, even though the long-term alliance between Bonn and Washington continued.

Thus, Chancellor Adenauer's government in September 1955 initiated formal diplomatic relations with the Soviet Union. In 1956, West German public opinion favored Egypt against France and Britain in the Suez crisis, and the Bonn government remained friendly to Egypt. In 1958, Bonn was the first Western power to recognize the new government of Iraq which had been installed by an anti-British revolution.

Again, in December 1955, the Bonn government yielded readily to pressure from mass opinion and the Bundestag, and cut back the term of military service from eighteen months—as demanded by the NATO authorities, as well as by the German military—to a mere twelve months; the eighteen-month term of service was not restored until early in 1962. The target of 500,000 German troops, to be placed at the disposal of NATO, which had first been promised for 1957, and then for 1960, was officially postponed, despite some NATO and United States objections. By mid-1970, Germany still only had about 460,000 men in her armed forces; her coalition government was discussing plans for a small reduction.

Throughout most of the 1950s, West German defense expenditures remained in the neighborhood of 4% of national income, and thus at a proportion similar to that of Denmark, and below that of Sweden and Switzerland, which each spent about 5% of their national income on defense, as against 7 to 8% spent in France and Britain, about 12% in the United States, and an estimated 20–25% in the Soviet Union. It was only in 1959 that the defense spending of the Federal Republic approached 5% of its national income. In the 1962 budget, however, this ratio climbed sharply to almost 7%; the $4.1 billion (16.5 billion DM [German Marks]) budgeted for defense amounted to almost one-third of the federal budget.[8] The defense budget rose to a high of $5.25 billion (21.3 billion DM). By mid-1967, when the grand coalition had to draft its first federal budget, a reduction of defense spending was under discussion. Thus, the 1968 defense budget was reduced to the level of $4.4 billion (17.8 billion DM). The defense budget for 1969 (19 billion DM) amounted to 3.0% of the West German national income of that year. Defense spending in 1971 was budgeted at about 22 billion DM, nearly 23% of the total federal budget.

In sum, by putting off its scheduled contribution to NATO, the Federal Republic was able to devote a higher proportion of its manpower and financial resources to its own industrial development than it otherwise could have done. This decision was, in all likelihood, a wise one and in the best interests of both West Germany and her allies. The point here is, however, that it was a decision taken by the executive and legislature of the Federal Republic, and against the advice of the Western powers, and particularly the United States, which for so long had had a major voice in Bonn's decisions.

The Bonn government had been in no hurry to divert a large part of its labor force from industrial development to garrison duties, but its defense minister, Franz Joseph Strauss, and a number of its army generals began in the late 1950s to press for the eventual equipment of the federal army—the *Bundeswehr*—with nu-

clear weapons, either in the form of a European nuclear force or on a national basis. German soldiers, Strauss argued in June 1960, ought to be equipped with every kind of weapon that a potential enemy might use against them. This argument sounded moderate enough, but since the "potential enemy" was clearly the USSR, and since the USSR had long been racing the United States in a contest for leadership in rockets and nuclear weapons, the minister's argument amounted in substance to a demand for qualitative—although not quantitative—German parity with the Soviet Union and the United States.

At the same time, the Bonn government officially expressed its willingness to cooperate in the organization of a NATO nuclear deterrent, that is, some form of a joint force within which German soldiers would be trained in the use of nuclear weapons and presumably have a share in their custody. However, discussions about such a NATO atomic force among the Allies broke down in 1963; France remained opposed, and the bulk of German opinion was unenthusiastic or critical. General de Gaulle's construction of a national French nuclear striking force furnished a conspicuous precedent for an eventual West German demand for a nuclear force of its own, but no such demand was pressed in the mid-1960s. German elite and mass opinion overwhelmingly remained content with a "division of labor" in the Western alliance which left nuclear weapons to the United States, or at most to the five countries possessing them in 1967. On this basis, the Federal Republic ratified in 1971 the Nonproliferation Treaty, an international, multi-lateral treaty to restrict the possession and production of nuclear weapons to the five existing nuclear powers.

The Common Market

From 1962 on, the main seat of West German power was in the field of economics. The Federal Republic was a party to the European Common Market treaty of 1957, together with other members of European Coal and Steel

[8] From figures for 1962 in *Archiv der Gegenwart* (Bonn) 32, no. 4 (January 21–26, 1962): 9636y; for 1959, *S.J.B.*, 1961), p. 426, table 2; for mid-1950s, United Nations, *Economic Survey of Europe* (New York, 1955).

Community, who became known as "the Six." Germany's economic position was both a cause and a consequence of her belonging to "the Six," which as a group established a common external tariff and a free movement of goods among its members by 1969. (The unification of monetary systems, which was to follow, had run into considerable difficulties by 1971.) The Federal Republic's industries were particularly able to compete in the markets of France, Italy, and the Low Countries, which were opened by the gradual tariff reductions stipulated by the treaty (see Table 3-2). Its financial strength enabled the Federal Republic to make a major, perhaps crucial, contribution to an agricultural fund under the Common Market. The fund, which was to be used for the support of agriculture, helped to win the consent of French and German farmers and other agricultural interest groups to the implementation of the Common Market treaty in the field of agriculture.

From 1962 until 1971, the chief remaining question before the six members of the Common Market was the admission of Great Britain, under conditions lenient enough to permit her to retain some of her special trade relations with the Commonwealth, and also to permit her a transition period to allow for a gradual change in the British system of agricultural subsidies. Since the French government under President de Gaulle had seemed rather unwilling to make any substantial concessions to British interests, much hinged on the attitude of Bonn. Both industrial rivalry and Chancellor Adenauer's policy of close cooperation with France tended to range West Germany against Britain on this issue, while the French policy permitted Bonn to remain inconspicuously in the background of the conflict. Early in 1963 a special treaty providing for greater cooperation between France and West Germany was signed, and on January 28, 1963, France vetoed Britain's entry

TABLE 3-2. *German National Income and Foreign Trade Ratios, 1870–1969*

	Years	GNP	National Income	Imports (I)	Exports (E)	Trade (I + E)	Ratio of trade to national income	GNP
			billions of marks, rounded-off, at current prices					
German empire	1870–79	—	14	3.6 *	2.5 *	6.2	45%	—
	1900–1909	—	35	6.7 †	5.5 †	12.2	35	—
Weimar Republic	1928	—	72	14	12	26	36	—
Hitler's Reich	1938	—	80	6	5.6	11.6	15	—
German Federal Republic	1950	98	88	11	8	19	22	19%
	1958	232	211	31	38	69	33	30
	1961	326	297	44	53	97	33	30
	1965	449	402	70	75	145	36	32
	1969	601	537	97	113	211	39	35

SOURCES: For 1870–1938, K.W. Deutsch and A. Eckstein, "National Industrialization and the Decline of the International Economic Sector, 1890–1959," *World Politics*, 13, no. 2 (January 1961); 274–76, 282, with references. For 1950–65, German Federal Republic, *S.J.B.* (Bonn, 1965), p. 24 [compare also K.W. Deutsch, L.J. Edinger, R.C. Macridis, and R.L. Merritt, *France, Germany and the Western Alliance* (New York: Scribners, 1967), Table 13-4, p. 234]. For 1969, *S.J.B.* (Bonn, 1970), pp. 18, 490.

NOTE: Observe the unchanged ratio of foreign trade to national income for 1928 and 1965, and the as yet unattained levels of 1870–79, despite the smaller territories of the G.F.R.

* Average for 1872–79.

† Average for 1900–1908.

into the Common Market. It was generally believed that the Bonn government had not pressed hard enough for Britain's entry.

This situation had changed by 1971, however, when Britain and France, under the leadership of Conservative Prime Minister Edward Heath and de Gaulle's successor, President Georges Pompidou, respectively, negotiated conditions for Britain's entry acceptable to France and all her Common Market partners, and only British parliamentary and popular consent remained to be won.

As the Common Market countries prospered, their economic integration seemed to prosper, too. During 1955–68, the six countries increased their share in world exports and imports, and trade among them increased still more. This however, was only moderately more than would have been expected on the basis of mere chance. Earlier, between 1913 and 1954, there had been a genuine gain in structural integration among "the Six": their mutual trade had grown by about twice as much than would have been expected from mere random probability. From 1955 to 1958, by contrast, the process of structural economic integration among the Common Market countries seems to have stood still but from 1959 through 1967 it grew again at a moderate but steady rate. In early 1971, most of the new automobiles registered in France were still of French manufacture, and three-fourths of those registered in Germany still were German-made. The economic integration of "the Six"—quite apart from the question of Great Britain—was still some decades away from the level of unity normally found within a single country; and for the next decade or so, the economy of the German Federal Republic, like that of France, is likely to remain predominantly national.[9]

The Threat of Soviet Power

American and Soviet policies, too, came to feel the newly strengthened influence of Bonn.

[9] Data from K. W. Deutsch, L. J. Edinger, R. C. Macridis, and R. L. Merritt, *France, Germany, and the Western Alliance* (New York: Scribners, 1967), pp. 218–39 and from more recent unpublished calculations by R. W. Chadwick and Karl W. Deutsch at Harvard University, 1970–71; see also *Die Zeit* (August 13, 1971), p. 25.

From 1958 to 1962, the Soviet government created an intermittent "Berlin crisis" by threatening to conclude a formal peace treaty with East Germany (the G.D.R.) and to hand over to that state the control of the Western allies' access routes to West Berlin, forcing the Western allies to choose between dealing with a new blockade or with the authorities of the G.D.R., which they had thus far so steadfastly refused to recognize. President Kennedy refused to be forced to make such a choice. With the consent of American congressional and public opinion, American troops in Germany were demonstratively strengthened.

Even after the building of the wall around West Berlin, American and other Western allied access rights were respected; and much of late 1961 and early 1962 was filled with American-Soviet negotiations in search for some agreement that might permit both great powers to retain their essential positions, as well as their prestige, but to trade sufficient concessions in nonessentials to bring about a substantial lessening of the potentially dangerous tension between them. These American-Soviet negotiations, however, were more than once subject to thinly disguised criticism from Bonn. Chancellor Adenauer announced that he expected little if any good to come from them, and his government made clear its objections to most of the Western steps toward a possible accommodation with the Soviet Union that were mentioned as considerations for discussion. Bonn's fears, of course, were directed against any possible American concessions to the Soviets at West Germany's political expense, somewhat as the Ulbricht regime in the G.D.R. feared any possible Soviet concessions to the West that might weaken the grip of dictatorship in the G.D.R.

President Kennedy, in turn, made evident his displeasure about the manifestly unhelpful attitude of Bonn. Nevertheless, Chancellor Adenauer stuck to his main position: no recognition for the G.D.R. and no substantial reduction of Western allied and West German anti-Communist activities in West Berlin. On the American side, proposals which came within the limits of what had been indirectly or directly rejected by the chancellor tended to recede in public discussion. Owing to the profound engagement of the United States in Berlin, West

Germany, and Western Europe, the Bonn republic had acquired an informal veto over an important range of American policy decisions.

The settlement of the dramatic Cuban missile crisis that arose between the United States and the Soviet Union in October 1962 also took some pressure off the Berlin situation. American efforts to bring down the Communist regime of Fidel Castro in Cuba died down, and so did Soviet efforts to challenge seriously the American and Western allied presence in West Berlin. Both sides, in effect, accepted the current state of affairs and managed to live with it. A year later, the United States and the USSR became parties to the Limited Nuclear Test Ban Treaty; in 1968 this was followed by the Nuclear Non-Proliferation Treaty, designed to slow down the spread of nuclear weapons to currently nonnuclear powers. The German Federal Republic, like many other countries, eventually became a party to both these treaties.

The relative lessening of international tensions in Europe during the 1960s also tended to reduce somewhat the conflict between the two German states. A climate favoring negotiations developed under the Kiesinger-Brandt coalition government in 1966–69, and talks and negotiations between the G.F.R. and G.D.R., as well as among the "Four Powers" still legally responsible for Berlin—the United States, Britain, France and the USSR—got fully under way after 1969 when the new SPD-FDP coalition government under Chancellor Willy Brandt took office. By the summer of 1971, acceptable compromises on G.F.R.-G.D.R. relations, the international recognition of the G.D.R., appropriate guarantees for unhampered Western allied access to West Berlin, and the status of that city all seemed in sight, but no formal settlements had yet been ratified.

The Problems Ahead

Powerful in diplomacy and economics, powerful even against such victors in World War II as Britain, France, and the United States— such was the international image of the German Federal Republic in 1971, sixteen years after its attainment of sovereignty under the Paris agreements. Yet how much solid political strength—how much dependable civic consensus—stood behind this impressive international position? How was the political system of the Federal Republic likely to function in the face of major decisions, and how well was it likely to deal with a crisis, political or economic?

At least part of the international strength of the German Federal Republic is attributable to situations that have been beyond its control. The rivalry between President de Gaulle's France and Great Britain, for example, enabled Bonn in 1962–63 to exert a seemingly decisive influence on the fate of Britain's application to join the Common Market, and hence on the future of Britain, of the Commonwealth, and of European integration. When, however, the governments of Britain and France arrived at a direct understanding concerning the terms of Britain's Common Market membership, Bonn's influence loomed less large in the matter, and Britain's public and parliamentary opinion became crucially important. Similarly, it was the long-standing tension between the United States and the Soviet Union that made West Germany and her government such key factors in the calculations of both Washington and Moscow. Again, when in mid-1971 a long series of United States payment deficits, aggravated by the Vietnam war, had brought on a crisis in the international value of the dollar, the responses of Bonn, which had a strong currency and international payments position, became very important. But while the Bonn government was speaking in a more independent tone of voice to its Western allies, the Federal Republic remained dependent for its defense on the presence of American and British troops on German soil.

The fundamental dependence of the Federal Republic on the United States remained even greater. Although this dependence was mutual, Bonn's need for friendly relations with the United States remained greater than the need of the United States government for even minimally good relations with Bonn. West German exports, as well as domestic prosperity, continued to depend in good part on American defense, tax, and tariff policies as well as on the continuing confidence of American investors.

An American stock-market decline, such as that of "Blue Monday" (May 28, 1962), had immediate effects on the economy of the Federal Republic. American taxes on the investments of their nationals abroad, or the 10% surcharge on foreign imports into the United States, announced by President Nixon in August 1971, or fears among American and European investors of military or political instability in West Germany, or generally in Western Europe, could influence West German prosperity and the Federal Republic's balance of payments very rapidly indeed. Under these conditions, Bonn's new power was in fact still a good deal less than it seemed, and at best it had to be used with very great caution.

In fact, the international position of the Federal Republic had not been strong enough to sustain the rigid policies of Chancellor Adenauer toward the end of his regime. West German policies became slightly more flexible under his successor, Chancellor Erhard, and noticeably more so under the coalition government of Chancellor Kurt Georg Kiesinger (CDU) and Foreign Minister Willy Brandt (SPD), which undertook diplomatic overtures to several Soviet-bloc countries and opened diplomatic relations with Rumania in 1967. They became still more flexible under the new SPD-FDP coalition government of Chancellor Willy Brandt and Foreign Minister Walter Scheel, when treaties with the USSR and with Poland were initialed in 1970, and when intense negotiations in 1971 pointed to the possibility of their eventual ratification.

In many ways, the end of an era in West German politics seemed to have arrived by the early 1970s. Many of the political and economic gains of the preceding two decades seemed solid enough. Yet to the careful observer at least some of the power positions and aspirations of Bonn still seemed built on precarious foundations. The Federal Republic steadily had been getting stronger, but perhaps it still was not nearly as strong as it seemed on the surface.

Under these conditions, much would depend not only on the changing conditions of world politics, which West Germany for the most part could not control, but also on the underlying political, social, and ideological

strength of the German people and on the wisdom of the political elite.

THE CONTINUING DIVISION OF GERMANY

One dark shadow has fallen across the Federal Republic ever since it was established. The Communist-ruled German Democratic Republic (G.D.R.) has continued to exist and to remind West Germans of the persistent division of their country. This rivalry between two states and two governments, each claiming, in theory, the leadership of the entire German people, did not come into being all at once.[10] The Soviet authorities after 1945 first favored a policy of treating all of Germany as a unit, since they considered their zone of occupation as a potential bridgehead from which to appeal to German national feeling and to extend their influence into the western regions of the country occupied by the Western allies.

Political parties in East Germany—the Communists (KPD), Social Democrats (SPD), Liberals (LDP), and Christian Democrats (CCDN)—all were licensed for organization on a nationwide level in 1945, earlier than in the west, where the Western allies insisted first on a prolonged stage of local political organization and activities. Although the Communists were given key positions in the administration of East Germany, their party limited itself to a relatively moderate policy, promising a multi-party system with free elections and suggesting the possibility of a special German road to socialism. The expropriation of the large factories and the landed estates of the *Junkers* was justified on grounds of Communist ideology, which saw Fascism as the creation of landowners and capitalists, as well as on anti-Fascist grounds, rather than as part of any overt program of social reform. Large landowners and

---

[10] The following account owes much to the illuminating summaries by Arnold J. Heidenheimer, *The Governments of Germany* (New York: Thomas Y. Crowell, 1966), pp. 182–202, and Elmer Plischke, *Contemporary Government of Germany* (Boston: Houghton Mifflin, 1961), pp. 181–211. Both of these should be consulted for further details.

industrialists, it was said with some truth, had often been friendly to the Nazis; hence, their economic power had to be abolished now to prevent a Nazi comeback later. All parties were expected to support this policy through an anti-Fascist bloc that was to assume political monopoly. While some politicians were beginning to withdraw from such Soviet-inspired and Soviet-directed arrangements, the bulk of the non-Communist leaders, particularly in the SPD, accepted these reforms as largely desirable.

Matters, however, did not stop there. It soon became clear that the Communists had overestimated their chances of becoming popular and that they could not hope to win a free election in the Soviet zone, let alone in West Berlin or in West Germany. By the end of 1945, the Communists began to press the East German Social Democrats to join with the Communist party, but in the end only a minority, led by the chairman of the Social Democratic Central Committee, Otto Grotewohl, accepted this proposal as a national policy. In West Berlin, only 12.4% of the Social Democratic party members supported the merger, while 82% opposed it.[11] The pro-merger minority of the Social Democrats did join the Communists, and formed a new party, the *Sozialistische Einheitspartei Deutschlands* (SED), which turned out to be Communistic in substance. The SED was refused a license to operate in West Germany by the Western allies, so the Communists there had to function under their own name as the KPD until their suppression in 1956. In the late 1960s, however, a Communist successor party, the DKP, became legal in the Federal Republic, and a West Berlin version of the SED, the SEW, became legal in that city. Both the DKP and the SEW, however, have remained small. To the east, the SED became, in effect, the sole ruling party of the Soviet zone, reducing the two remaining middle-class parties—the CDU and the LDP—to the role of powerless appendages.

The Creation of the G.D.R.

Following the creation in West Germany of the German Federal Republic in 1949, the German Democratic Republic (G.D.R.) was set up the same year in the Soviet zone; and after the G.F.R. had attained substantial sovereignty through the Paris agreements of 1955, the sovereignty of the G.D.R. was recognized by the Soviet Union in a treaty signed in September 1955. Although former Social Democrats have served in a few conspicuous positions (such as Grotewohl as prime minister from 1950 until his death in 1964, and Friedrich Ebert, son of a president of the Weimar Republic, as mayor of East Berlin), since the 1955 treaty the G.D.R. has been ruled by a Communist dictatorship, exercised through the SED party and dominated until 1971 by the veteran Communist and first secretary of the SED Politburo, Walter Ulbricht. After 1960, Ulbricht also served as chairman of the Council of State, the most powerful body of the formal government of the G.D.R. In 1971, Ulbricht retired and was replaced by an associate with similar views, Erich Honecker, a survivor of ten years in Nazi prisons, who seemed committed to continuing most of Ulbricht's policies. Although the details of the G.D.R. regime would constitute a separate discussion, what mattered for the political development of the Federal Republic were the economic, social, and political changes in the G.D.R. that impinged directly and indirectly on the political realities and expectations of the Bonn Republic and its people.

In 1955, the G.D.R. had about 17 million residents, roughly 2 million more than had inhabited its territories before World War II; and despite heavy emigration, it still had a population of more than 17 million in 1971.[12] Its income had far surpassed the prewar level, but West German estimates still put its per capita output at only about 75% of that of the Federal Republic.[13] If one takes into account the upward valuation of the mark and the relative decline of the dollar in 1971, this figure

---

[11] Heidenheimer, *Governments of Germany*, p. 168.

[12] *Statistisches Jahrbuch 1971 der Deutschen Demokratischen Republik* (East Berlin: Staatsverlag, 1971), p. 15; see also Heidenheimer, *Governments of Germany*, pp. 44–46, which provides a more detailed breakdown of the population.

[13] Hermann Weber, "25 Jahre SED," in Hermann Weber and Fred Oldenburg (eds.), *25 Jahre SED: Chronik einer Partei* (Cologne: Verlag für Wissenschaft und Politik, B. v. Nottbeck, 1971), p. 35.

would suggest a per capita gross national product of about $2,600 for the Bonn Republic and of about $1,950 for the G.D.R. (as against nearly $5,000 for the United States) in late-1971 dollars. To be sure, consumers in the G.D.R. received a much smaller share of the national product than was the case in the Federal Republic. From 1960 to 1970, net national income in "comparable" prices was officially reported to have grown 57%, but the growth of the index of real income of workers and employees was reported by the same source for the same decade as less than 32%.[14] Even so, by the early 1970s considerable economic progress had been made; a majority of G.D.R. households had acquired radios, television sets, electric refrigerators, and washing machines; growing minorities had acquired automobiles or motorcycles; and reports of a new prosperity in the G.D.R.—albeit modest by Western standards—were appearing in the Western press.[15]

CONTRAST WITH WEST GERMANY. This continuing lag behind West German prosperity is attributed by experts to four major causes.[16] First of all, the Soviet government, during the first years after the war, dismantled and removed substantially more productive equipment from its zone of occupation in Germany than the Western powers did from theirs, and the Soviet Union insisted on substantial reparations payments out of the current production in the G.D.R. until at least 1953, amounting, by Western estimates, to about one-quarter of industrial production. While the USSR—which had been devastated by the war—was taking wealth out of central and eastern Germany, the United States—whose economy had flourished during World War II—was pouring relief, Marshall Plan aid, and other forms of economic assistance into West Germany.

In the second place, the Federal Republic had a much larger supply of labor, owing not only to its size and population, but to the 13 million expellees and refugees it had accepted.

Therefore, it had both the capital to employ these people and the labor supply to make the best use of its capital. In this way, it was possible in the Federal Republic to increase output, productivity, and real wages very considerably, while maintaining only moderate wage increases, thereby avoiding inflation.

The third set of conditions holding back the economy of the G.D.R. centered around its own economic institutions. The division of the estates of the landed aristocracy—the old *Junker* class—had been carried through for political as much as for economic considerations, but it left the G.D.R. with many small, inefficient private farms, which absorbed a relatively large proportion of the labor supply and whose owners often were quite unenthusiastic about economic planning or the prospects of farm collectivization. At the same time, the typical Communist emphasis on heavy industry held back the allocation of capital to agriculture. In the G.D.R. in 1955 there were only about 34,000 tractors, and this number rose by 1969 to about 146,000, while agriculture in the Federal Republic already in 1965 employed about 1,113,000 tractors. In other words, in 1965 the G.F.R. employed already four times as many tractors in proportion to the land used for agriculture as the G.D.R. did in 1969 (see Table 3-3). The greater capital investment in West German agriculture seems evident, even if one allows for the concentration of the G.D.R. on a smaller number of much larger tractors, intended for the sizable fields of its collective farms. These handicaps were combined with the difficulties inherent in large-scale economic planning, the low levels of sophistication in East German planning methods, and the lack of experience and competence of East German planning personnel; all these taken together produced a not-inconsiderable amount of waste.

The fourth group of conditions hampering economic growth in the G.D.R. was largely international in character. The Federal Republic was quickly integrated into the trading and credit community of the Western countries—which included the richest countries in the world—during a period of business prosperity. The G.D.R. was integrated—much less smoothly—into the Soviet bloc, whose members were on the whole much poorer, and where in-

[14] *Stat. Jahrbuch 1971 der D.D.R.*, pp. 19, 343.
[15] Ibid., p. 345; and H. W. Schwarzer, *Die D.D.R. ist keine Zone mehr* (Cologne-Berlin: Kiepenheuer and Witsch), 1969, pp. 88–98.
[16] The account that follows here owes much to Stolper, *Germany Between East and West*, pp. 15–17.

TABLE 3-3. *Farm Tractors in Use in the G.F.R. and G.D.R., 1959 and 1969*

	Agricultural areas (thousands of hectares)	Number of tractors (thousands, all types)	Tractors per thousand hectares
G.F.R.	1959: 13,200 *	754	57
	1965: 12,980	1,113 †	85 †
	1969: 12,853	—	—
G.D.R.	1959: 6,400	47	7
	1969: 6,300	146	23

SOURCES: *S.J.B.*, 1961, pp. 163, 165, 574; *S.J.B.*, 1968, pp. 145, 149; *S.J.B.*, 1970, p. 139. *Statistisches Jahrbuch 1959 der DDR*, p. 426, Tables 6 and 7; *Statistisches Jahrbuch 1971 der DDR*, pp. 179, 184, 197, 198, 310, 311, and Appendix, Table 8.

* Figure for 1960.

† Figures after 1965 were no longer collected by *S.J.B.*

ternational economic interchanges were much less well coordinated, although some improvements did start in 1957 and continued throughout the 1960s.[17] Another source of weakness was the partial but long-lasting economic boycott of the G.D.R. by the Federal Republic and by most of its Western allies, and the loss of nearly 3 million *emigrés* to the G.F.R. and West Berlin between 1945 and 1961, most of them of working age and many of them with needed skills or professional training. In 1970, the chairman of the Council of Ministers of the G.D.R., Willi Stoph—that is, in effect its prime minister— estimated the losses of the G.D.R. due to G.F.R. actions at 100 billion marks, or $25 billion dollars at that time. His demand for reparations in that amount from the G.F.R., however, seemed quite unlikely to succeed.[18] In the 1950s, when most of these losses from the conflict with the G.F.R. occurred, they would have amounted, if one uses Stoph's figures, to 15–20% of the national income of the G.D.R., declining to perhaps less than 5% by the end of the 1960s.

[17] For details of the earlier period, see Stolper, *Germany Between East and West*, p. 17.

[18] Hermann Weber and Fred Oldenburg (eds.), *25 Jahre SED: Chronik einer Partei*, op. cit., p. 190.

Unrest in the G.D.R.

During much of the 1950s, life for many of the inhabitants of the G.D.R. was far more harsh and unpleasant than it was for the inhabitants of the Federal Republic. The efforts of the Communist-led government to win popular favor by developing the arts, particularly the theater and music, were none too successful, nor did its use of radio and other instruments of propaganda succeed in convincing the population that they were well off and would soon be much better off. Since much of this propaganda was so obviously at variance with everyday experience, it tended to infuriate many people rather than to convince them; and since no effective legal expressions of opposition were permitted, those who were dissatisfied felt particularly bitter about the claims of the Communist regime to have "liberated" the working people of the G.D.R.

Throughout the 1950s, thousands of people expressed their dissatisfaction with their feet. They walked out of the G.D.R. into the Western-occupied parts of Berlin and claimed asylum; then, after having been screened in West Berlin, they were flown to West Germany for further screening and eventual resettlement. The Soviet military authorities, as well as those of the G.D.R., were powerless to stop this flow, short of cutting off most of the movements of persons between East and West Berlin—a move which the Western powers would have considered illegal and the Soviets inexpedient. The alternative of cutting off the movement of persons between East Berlin and the rest of the G.D.R. was even less attractive, since such a move would have deprived the G.D.R. of its most important city. The flow thus continued, and the government of the Federal Republic, as well as the Western allied authorities in Berlin, more-or-less encouraged it, even though there were also some efforts to urge East Germans to stay in the G.D.R. and hope for eventual reunification. As a result of this migration through West Berlin and into the Federal Republic, the G.D.R. suffered from 1950 through 1961 an average net loss of more than 190,000 persons each year, or a total net loss of nearly 2.3 million, which followed the loss of another 565,000 in 1945–49—more than offsetting her natural population growth. Some details of the ebb and flow of this migration can be seen from the data in Table 3-4.

These net figures are smaller than the ones publicized by the Bonn government, but they tell a story of a serious—though not fatal—drain on the manpower resources of the G.D.R. They also show that the peak period of that drain occurred during 1953–55, and that the peak year was 1953, when the net loss to the G.D.R. rose to 320,000, or almost double the seventeen-year average. On June 17, 1953, strikes and riots in East Germany approached the dimensions of revolt, challenging the dictatorial power of the East German government and the tanks of the Soviet forces backing it. The riots, however, were quickly suppressed. Earlier broadcasts from West Berlin, the Federal Republic, and the American stations in Europe had done much, wittingly or unwittingly, to encourage the spirit of revolt in East Berlin and the G.D.R., and the American station RIAS had been particularly emphatic. At the time of the actual riots, however, the West German broadcasts urged calmness and caution; and the verbal attacks on the Soviet regime and the G.D.R. were not followed by any effective Western action supporting the rebels by force, because of the risk of local defeat by Soviet troops or the start of a new world war.

In fact, United States policy toward Berlin under President Eisenhower in 1953 remained very much the same as it had been under President Truman during the Berlin blockade in 1948 and 1949: the United States pledged to resist any forcible Soviet or East German interference in Western allied-held territory, but it refused to use any substantial military force to interfere in territories held by the Soviet Union or its allies. The same policy was followed later by President Eisenhower during the Hungarian uprising against the Communist regime of that country in 1956, and it was again followed by President Kennedy when the East German authorities built a wall between West and East Berlin in 1961. Throughout the period, neither the United States nor the Soviet governments showed any desire to use their armed forces for fear of initiating a war in Europe that might have incalculable consequences in the age of nuclear weapons.

If the unrest of 1953 in East Germany was thus quickly suppressed, it nevertheless was not without results. In the G.D.R. and in East Berlin, it reminded the Communist rulers of the extent to which they had alienated popular feeling; it hastened the ending of reparations payments to the Soviet Union; and it started the transition to a policy of at least beginning concessions to consumer needs and to creating better living standards.

In the Federal Republic, the East German uprising of June 17 was taken as a promise of the early collapse of the G.D.R., and as a confirmation of the wisdom of Bonn's policy of consistent nonrecognition of its eastern rival. Thereafter, June 17 was celebrated in the Federal Republic as an official holiday—the "Day of German Unity"—but by the early 1960s it seemed that most West Germans were taking it as an occasion for peaceful family outings rather than for attending political rallies and

TABLE 3-4. *Migraton between the G.F.R. and the G.D.R., 1945–61 (in thousands)*

Year(s)	East to West		West to East		Net shift to Federal Republic	
	number	annual average	number	annual average	number	annual average
1945–61	3,177	187	(388) *	(23) *	(2,789) *	(165) *
1950–61	2,612	218	(318)	(27)	(2,294)	(191)
1945–49	565	113	(70)	(14)	(495)	(99)
1950	198		34		164	
1951	166		26		140	
1952	182		15		167	
1950–52	546	182	75	25	471	157
1953	331		11		320	
1954	184		33		151	
1955	253		33		220	
1953–55	768	289	77	26	691	263
1956	279		32		247	
1957	262		38		224	
1958	204		27		177	
1956–58	754	248	97	32	648	216
1959	150		(19)		(131)	
1960	199		(25)		(174)	
1961	204		(25)		(179)	
1959–61	553	184	(69)	(23)	(484)	(161)

SOURCES: for 1945–60—Alfred Grosser, *Die Bonner Demokratie* (Düsseldorf: Rauch Verlag, 1960), p. 402, with reference to *Frankfurter Rundschau,* January 5, 1960; for 1960 and 1961—*Archiv der Gegenwart* (Bonn) 32, no. 1 (January 6, 1962): 9584A, with references.

* Figures in parentheses are estimates, based on the average 8:1 ratio of eastward to westward migration in 1950–58.

official speeches, and in 1967 it was officially abolished.

By the beginning of the 1960s, the annual net outflow of refugees from the G.D.R. into the Federal Republic had fallen back to the level of the early 1950s, averaging about 161,000 per year in 1959–61, as against 151,000 in 1950–52. This flow does not seem, in itself, to have been an intolerable drain on the economy of the G.D.R., which had borne the much heavier outflow during the mid-1950s. If backed by the Soviet authorities, the East German government could have cut off at any time the movement into West Berlin of persons from the territories it controlled, and it could thus have stopped the westward flow of persons whenever such a step seemed worth its probable political cost.

In August 1961, the East German regime and its Soviet backers finally exercised their option. A wall was built which completed the existing Communist system of enclosures around West Berlin; crossings were permitted only at a very few heavily controlled checkpoints; and practically no East Berliners or inhabitants of the G.D.R. were permitted to cross to the West. A few desperate individuals still succeeded in making dramatic escapes to the West, but throughout the 1960s they made up at most a trickle in place of what had been a stream. The United States and its allies strengthened their troops in West Germany, but held to their policy of refusing, as long as their control in the Western-held territories was respected, to interfere by force in the Communist-held territories and thus to risk making Germany a theater of war.

The people of the Federal Republic remained closely connected by ties of family and old friendship, as well as of national sentiment, with the population of the G.D.R. By the mid-1950s, nearly one-quarter of the population of the Federal Republic were natives of East Germany or of former German territories now parts of CSSR, Poland, and USSR. Forty-four percent of the respondents to a poll in 1953 claimed to have relatives or friends in the Soviet zone of Germany; together with those West Germans who had personal acquaintances there, a majority of West Germans had at least some personal contacts with the population of either the G.D.R. or East Berlin.[19]

Nearly two-fifths of West Germans polled in February 1953 claimed to be writing letters sometimes to the Eastern zone, and nearly one-third to have sent Christmas packages there—a claim confirmed by the 24 million packages sent in 1956, which was exceeded by the 30 million packages reported for 1957. In December 1961, after the building of the wall around West Berlin, the number of Christmas packages increased

further, indicating that human relationships were continuing despite political restrictions. By 1967, however, the balance was reversed: more packages were sent from the G.D.R. into the Federal Republic than went from West Germany into the G.D.R.—a way perhaps of saying "thank you" to relatives and friends for earlier thoughtfulness, but also an assertion of newly won pride.[20]

The Future of the G.D.R.

In the face of the political and human desires for unity between the western and eastern parts of Germany, the foreign policy of Bonn in the 1950s had little more to offer than the hope for the eventual collapse of the government of the G.D.R., or for some drastic loss of power or change of policy on the part of its Soviet backers. None of these hopes of the Bonn government came true in the 1950s or 1960s, and the outlook in the early 1970s seemed no more promising in this respect.

During the 1950s, the planned economy of the G.D.R. continued to develop, growing at rates not very different from those of West Germany. In the judgment of an expert Western observer:

It must be recognized that in the course of the 1950's average annual growth rates in East Germany have been not far below those of the Federal Republic, the figures are estimated at about 8.5 and 10.3% respectively for the period 1950–57. On a per capita basis—population having declined in the East and increased in the West—there is probably little difference in East and West German growth rates between 1950 and 1957. Of course, the continuing depressed level of East German living standards should be noted; on the other hand, it is likely that this disparity will lessen and a distinct possibility that East Germany may for a while actually register higher future per capita rates than the Federal Republic.[21]

In the course of the 1960s, some of the factors retarding the economic growth of the

[19] Deutsch and Edinger, *Germany Rejoins the Powers*, pp. 178–79, with references.

[20] H. W. Schwarze, *Die D.D.R. ist keine Zone mehr*, p. 57; see also generally pp. 40–66.

[21] Stolper, *Germany Between East and West*, pp. 11–12.

G.D.R., relative to that of the Federal Republic, continued to weaken. The effects of the Soviet reparations policies of 1945–53 diminished while the flow of American dollars into West Germany declined somewhat—on a per capita basis and in some years even absolutely. The large-scale migration of German-speaking labor, much of it skilled, from Eastern Europe into the Federal Republic likewise had come to an end, and the building of the wall around West Berlin in August 1961 ended the chances of any sizable flow of refugees from the G.D.R. into West Germany. Planning methods and the competence of planners in the G.D.R. improved somewhat with experience, and the partial economic reforms in the G.D.R. and other Soviet-bloc countries, which began to give a freer hand to management and greater attention to sales and prices in the market, worked in the same direction. The average purchasing power of the GDR's Mark (M), in terms of the Federal Republic's Deutsche Mark (DM) rose from 0.76 in 1960 to about 0.83 in 1967 and 0.86 in 1969. The distribution of incomes among workers and clerical employees at various salary levels in the GFR and the GDR, respectively, also became somewhat more similar, but the GFR continued to offer relatively more jobs at the higher salary levels, as shown in Fig. 3-1.[22]

The international environment of the two rival German states also seemed less likely to favor the Federal Republic as strongly as it had in the past. If the Soviet Union and its bloc of Eastern European countries prospered, as they had been doing during the 1950s and 1960s, they would be able—if their governments consented—to offer more rewarding trade opportunities to the G.D.R.; on the other hand, if the economic boom in Western Europe and the United States slid into a business slump, then the pace of West German economic growth would lessen. This possibility materialized in 1962 and 1963, when the annual economic growth rate of the Federal Republic in real terms fell to 4.0%—about average for the non-Communist world in the later 1950s, but well below West Germany's earlier and later performance. In 1964 and 1965, the real growth rate averaged 6%, dropping to zero in 1967, averaging about 7.5% in 1968 and 1969, and dropping again to a little above 3% in 1970 and 1971. Altogether, the real growth of the

22 Willy Brandt, Peter Christian Ludz, *et al. Deutschland 1971* (Bonn: Bundesministerium für innerdeutsche Beziehungen, 1971), pp. 126 and 137.

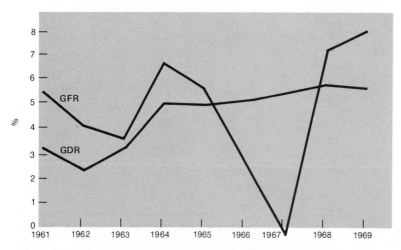

FIG. 3-1. *Distribution of Households of Workers and Clerical Employees by Income Classes in the G.F.R. and G.D.R., 1967. Monthly net income per household in DM (G.F.R.) or M (G.D.R.). (Note, however, the one-sixth lesser purchasing power of the G.D.R. mark in 1967.) From W. Brandt, P. C. Ludz,* et al., Deutschland 1971, *p. 137.*

gross national product in 1960–69 averaged in the GFR 4.8%, against 4.5% in the GDR.

A serious economic depression in the West might, of course, make things much worse for the Federal Republic; and such a possibility seemed less remote after the American stock market decline during the first half of 1962 than it had seemed in earlier years. Even without any more drastic economic troubles, however, a prolonged period of slowed-down growth in the Federal Republic would give the forced-draft planned economy of the G.D.R. a chance to catch up eventually with the per capita income levels of its Western rival. This threat seemed remote in 1970, but if it did materialize, there seemed to be little that Bonn could do about it.

By the beginning of 1971, the G.D.R. was still denied diplomatic recognition by most governments outside the Communist bloc. In accordance with the "Hallstein doctrine"—named after the German diplomat and former professor, State Secretary Walter Hallstein—the Federal Republic had long maintained that it would break off its diplomatic relations with any state that recognized the G.D.R. Only the USSR was exempted from this principle of West German foreign policy. In 1957, when Yugoslavia recognized the G.D.R., Bonn somewhat reluctantly did break off diplomatic—though not trade—relations. But by the beginning of 1971, the Hallstein doctrine had passed into history. Bonn had established diplomatic rela-tions with some Eastern European countries and by 1968 had resumed diplomatic relations with Yugoslavia.

This new diplomatic approach to the So-viet-bloc countries may indicate the hesitant beginnings of a slow but ultimately basic change in West Germany's foreign policy. Prior to 1967, it had appeared as if the only possible way to establish the firm footing of Bonn vis-à-vis her eastern neighbors was through reliance upon American diplomatic and military power, even when this spelled the maintenance of the division of Eastern and Western Europe running through the two Germanies. By early 1971, it looked as if Bonn was interested in establishing a situation of *détente* in the European sphere of the East-West conflict, and thereby hopefully opening up a path to the coexistence of two German states in a manner acceptable to all the parties concerned. These efforts paralleled the efforts of the United States to promote such a *détente* between itself and the Soviet Union. But at the same time, the West German leaders continue to realize that an ultimate solution to the problem rests largely with the Soviet Union and the United States, and that the alliance of the G.F.R. with the United States must also be maintained in this area of policy. More than two decades after its establishment, the German Federal Republic is one of the few countries in the world in which one of its most pressing and emotionally charged national problems remains largely to be decided outside its own borders.

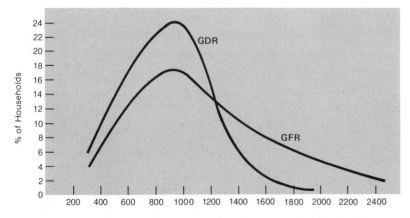

FIG. 3-2. *Real Growth of Gross National Product of the G.F.R. and the G.D.R. at 1967 prices, in percent against the preceding year. From W. Brandt, P. C. Ludz, et al., Deutschland 1971, p. 91.*

FOUR

social structure

and

foundations

Germany has long been predominantly urban and industrial, and it became somewhat more so during the 1950s and 1960s. In 1970, cities and towns contained more than four-fifths of the population of the Federal Republic, including West Berlin. Large cities above 100,000 population accounted for 33%; middle-sized cities with 20,000 to 100,000 inhabitants added another 19%. As many as 30% of West Germans, however, still lived in small towns of between 2,000 and 20,000 people; and the remaining 18% lived in still smaller and for the most part rural communities. No political party stressing mainly rural interests could hope for a majority, but since 48% of the voters lived in communities of less than 20,000 people, the parties could hardly omit making an appeal to rural and small-town voters and their values. However, the right-of-center parties have been significantly more successful in attracting the vote in communities of less than 20,000 people. Whereas 41% of the SPD supporters live in these communities, 55% of the CDU supporters, 51% of the FDP supporters, and 58% of the NPD supporters in the mid-1960s came from these medium-sized and small towns.[1]

World War II still has left its mark on the population. At the beginning of 1968, there were still 53% women to 47% men in West Germany, and in the important age group between 45 and 65 years, from which many men had been killed in the war, women made up 55%. During World War II and the years immediately following it, fewer children were born, so that in 1968 the Federal Republic had more inhabitants aged 65 years and over than it had youngsters between 6 and 14. The somewhat unusual age structure of the population of Germany can be seen from Figure 4-1 and from the comparisons in Table 4-1, which show that the population of the Federal Republic, as well as that of the G.D.R., is old even by Western European standards.

The various political and social attitudes of age groups in the Federal Republic differ

[1] Federal Republic of Germany, *Statistisches Jahrbuch für die Bundesrepublik* (Bonn, 1971), p. 34, Table 6 (hereafter cited as *S.J.B.*); DIVO Institut, *Umfragen*, October 1966.

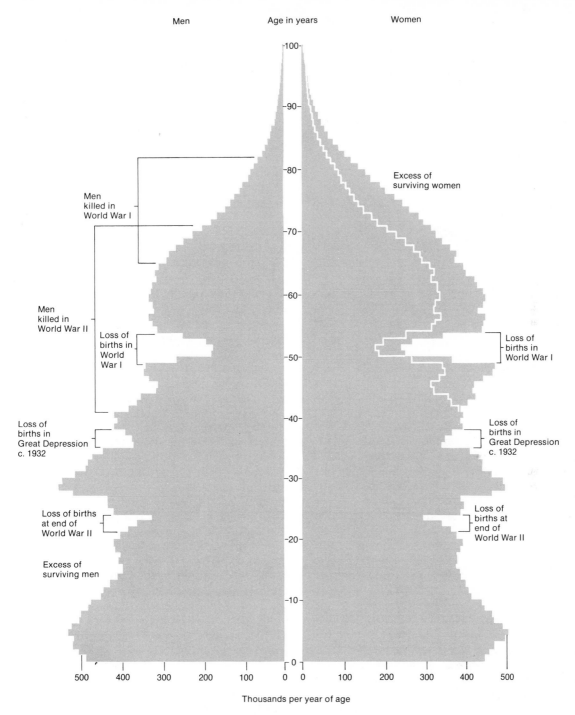

FIG. 4-1. *Age structure of the resident population of the German Federal Republic, December 31, 1968.* [*From the German Federal Republic,* Statistisches Jahrbuch für die Bundesrepublik *(Bonn, 1970), p. 37.*]

TABLE 4-1. *Age Groups in West Germany and Other Countries, 1969*

	Proportion of Total Population			
	under 15	15–45	45–65	over 65
German Democratic Republic	24%	39%	22%	15%
German Federal Republic	23	41	23	13
United Kingdom	24	39	24	13
France	24	42	21	13
Switzerland	24	43	22	12
Italy (1970)	25	43	22	11
United States	30	40	20	10
USSR	(29)	(46)	(21)	(8)
Japan (1969)	24	51	18	7

SOURCE: *S.J.B.*, 1971, p. 29.

considerably. In the 1950s, the younger people were more prosperous than before World War II and tended to be nonpolitical; the oldsters were worse off and more conservative, as is shown in Table 4-2. Instead of leading to any left-of-center radicalism, economic deprivation in the Federal Republic has mainly hit the older people and has left them as conservative, or as moderately right-of-center, as ever, if not more so. Since the mid-1960s, however, the voters under 30 have been more hospitable to change, and somewhat more left-of-center in politics.

Special interest also attaches to two particular age groups. The first, aged in 1966 between 45 and 60, includes many who made their careers first during the Hitler years after 1933; when they were between 12 and 27 years old; the normal retirement of still older men brought the members of this group into many senior positions by 1970. This age group includes relatively more NPD and Nazi sympathizers than does the rest of the population. The second group, aged in 1969 between 30

and 50 years, had to spend a large part of its formative years under Hitler's rule, but it also experienced the failure and collapse of the Nazi dictatorship at an impressionable age; this group is far more critical of extreme nationalism and of the Nazi past, and it is likely to succeed to senior offices in government and private business roughly between 1970 and 1975. The strength of these age groups in the 1969 population of the Federal Republic was 27% for the 30–50-year-old group, 29% for those over 50, 20% for the more liberal age group of 15–30, and 23% for the youngsters under 15 years of age.

In short, the preference of the West Germans for reconstruction over reproduction between 1945 and 1955 made West Germany a country with one of the oldest populations among the large nations. Under these conditions, the appeal of youth in German politics was likely to be slightly weaker, and the appeal of age and experience slightly stronger, than in the United States. These facts may have had something to do with the seemingly perennial popularity of the late Chancellor Konrad Adenauer, known in Germany as *der Alte*—"the old one" (he was 88 when he resigned as chancellor)—and they persisted for a time in the public appeal of white-haired statesmen like Chancellor Kurt Georg Kiesinger, who in 1967 still continued to outshine the more youthful image of his SPD vice-chancellor, Willy Brandt. From 1968 on, however, the picture changed. Young people came to comprise a slightly higher proportion of the population; in 1971 the voting age was lowered to 18; the attitudes of the young began to carry over, at least to a limited extent, into the ranks of people over 30. The election of 1969 showed a markedly less conservative trend, and some of this change in the political climate may persist in the politics of the 1970s and 1980s.

THE STRENGTH OF OCCUPATIONAL GROUPINGS

About 44% of the people of the Federal Republic in 1969 were members of its work force of 26.9 million.[2] The rest are for the most part their dependent children and other family members, but there are also a good many pensioners who make up a substantial 15% of the total population.

The Federal Republic is one of the most highly urbanized and industrialized large countries in the world; less than 10% of its work force is engaged in agriculture. Nevertheless, only a little less than half the work force (48%) is engaged in mining or construction industry or in crafts. The sizable remaining group of 42% is occupied in commerce, transportation, and services, both private and public. There are not enough farmers to bring victory to a traditionalist party, but there are enough to press effectively for special economic and political concessions.

Nor are there quite enough industrial workers to bring success to a straight class appeal. Industry proper accounts for only 48% of the work force; of these about 29% are various kinds of white-collar employees, and only 19%, or about 5 million, are industrial workers of the kind which Karl Marx expected to become a majority of each industrialized nation's

workers. Even if one adds to their number the workers in large enterprises outside industry, such as those in transportation, the proportion of "proletarians," in the Marxist sense of the term, within the West German working population falls far short of a majority. Even by adding to their number all "blue-collar" employees in small business, workshops, and service establishments, as well as the few remaining rural laborers (1%), and the 0.4% registered unemployed, the aggregate proportion of workers of all kinds can be brought to only 47% of the work force. By contrast, the workers in factories with over one thousand employees—whom Lenin considered the best prospects for left-wing radicalism—numbered by 1968 only about 3.1 million, or roughly 11% of the total.[3] Only by adding to the blue-collar workers another 7–8% of the total to include approximately one-half of the pensioners of working-class origin could we arrive at a potential majority of blue-collar working-class voters in the Federal Republic.

After the 47% blue-collar workers, the strongest group consists of white-collar employees, who make up about 35% of the working population and who include about 6% public officials and perhaps 1% of high-level employees

[2] These and the following data are based on figures in *S.J.B.*, 1970, pp. 118–27.

[3] *S.J.B.*, 1970, pp. 190–91.

TABLE 4-2. *Age Groups and Attitudes in West Germany in the Mid-1950s*

Attitude Reported in Polls	18–29	30–44	45–59	60 and Over
Personal economic situation (May 1955):				
Better than prewar	36%	26%	17%	15%
Worse than prewar	21	40	50	57
Talk occasionally about politics (June 1956)	39	57	53	53
Right-of-center in politics (Feb. 1956)	31	39	41	44
Left-of-center	15	22	21	19
Do not know meaning of "right" and "left"	37	25	22	24

SOURCE: Elisabeth Noelle Neumann and Erich Peter Neumann, *Jahrbuch der öffentlichen Meinung* (Allensbach: Verlag für Demoskopie, 1957), 2:35, 46, 48.

and managers. Another 10% consists of the self-employed urban middle class and the members of their families assisting them in their enterprises. The main groups within this middle class are small businessmen in commerce and the service industries (6%), artisans (3%), and the small group of professional men (1%). The remainder are peasants (93%) and family members working on their farms (5%).

These figures show the remarkable strength of the self-employed group. Together with the members of their families working in the family enterprises, they still made up 18% of the total in 1969—10% in the towns and 8% in the country. In 1966, nearly one-fifth of this group were potential supporters of the neo-Nazi NPD party, in contrast to only one-eighth of the general electorate so inclined. Under these conditions, the white-collar employees (35%) are often likely to prove the decisive group in mass politics: without their support, neither labor nor middle-class appeals are likely to be successful. Moreover, two of the subgroups included among them—the same 6% public officials and somewhat more than 1% soldiers—may actually or potentially carry influence well beyond mere numbers.

There is a strong tendency for blue-collar workers to vote for the SPD, and for employers, professional people, and farmers to vote for the CDU (see Table 6-2). Here again, the white-collar employees are a swing group that may well decide an election.

The picture changes somewhat if the occupational differences between men and women are taken into account (see Table 4-3). Among men, there is still a majority of blue-collar workers, 53%; another 15% are self-employed, and many of these are employers. About two-thirds of West German men are thus blue-collar workers or employers, the two groups in whom Karl Marx saw the main classes of industrial society. But among working women, only 36% are blue-collar workers, and only another 2% are self-employed. Nearly two-thirds are white-collar employees or family members assisting their menfolk, and thus they are a far less promising public for a class appeal.

In addition, 5% of the total West German work force are foreigners, most of them re-cruited from Italy, Yugoslavia, Turkey, Greece, or Spain, and employed in unskilled or semi-skilled blue collar work. Perhaps every tenth worker today is such a foreigner who cannot vote. He may join a labor union, receive its benefits, and strengthen it by his support, but the fact that one-tenth of West German workers are voteless foreigners cannot but weaken the potential voting strength of labor and the SPD. By 1970, the number of foreign workers had risen to 1.6 million, or nearly 6% of the work force. If the steady rise in the number of foreign workers from 1965 to 1970 should continue, their share in the total work force by 1977 would be 8–9%, reducing the share of German workers to 35% or less.

INCOME GROUPS, STATUS GROUPS, AND SOCIAL CLASSES

The Distribution of Income

The distribution of income in the Federal Republic is somewhat more unequal than it is in Britain or in the Scandinavian countries, and the leveling effects of postwar taxation have gone somewhat less far.[4] Income distribution in Germany appears to be as unequal as it is in France, but much less unequal than it is in the other Mediterranean countries of Europe.

Among twelve countries for which data are available, as shown in Table 4-4, the German Federal Republic in 1964 ranked first in the share of personal income—41%—going to the richest decile (10%) of its population. It ranked second in the overall index of income inequality; and it ranked first in the stability over time of this unequal distribution; since the 1930s, its index of inequality had hardly changed at all.

The only major mitigating factor in this picture is the Federal Republic's relatively

[4] United Nations, *Economic Survey of Europe in 1956* (New York, 1957); Bruce M. Russett, H. R. Alker, Jr., K. W. Deutsch, and H. D. Lasswell, *World Handbook of Political and Social Indicators* (New Haven: Yale University Press, 1961), pp. 243–47; K. W. Deutsch, *Politics and Government* (Boston: Houghton Mifflin, 1970), pp. 218–20.

TABLE 4-3. *Occupational Structure in the German Federal Republic, 1969 (percentage of total work force)*

	Men	Women	1969 total	Total shift since 1961	projected 1977 total
Self-employed	9%	2%	11%	−3%	8%
Family members assisting them	1	6	7	−2	5
Subtotal: self-employed plus family assistance	*10*	*8*	*18*	*−5*	*13*
Civil servants	5	1	6	+1	7
White-collar employees	15	14	29	+8	37
Subtotal: civil servants plus white-collar employees	*20*	*15*	*35*	*+9*	*44*
Blue-collar workers:					
German	30 *	12 *	42		35
Foreign	4 *	1 *	5		8
Subtotal: all workers	*34*	*13*	*47*	*−4*	*43*
Total	**64**	**36**	**100**	**—**	**100**
Proportion of self-employed in total	15	6	11	−3	8
Proportion of blue-collar workers in total	53	36	47	−4	43
Proportion neither self-employed nor blue-collar workers in total	32	58	42	+7	49
Total	*100*	*100*	*100*	*—*	*100*

SOURCE: Adapted from *S.J.B.*, 1970, pp. 119–23, 127.
* Author's estimate.

more decent treatment of its poor. The poorest decile of the West German population still gets 2.1% of the total personal income, only one-fifth of the average and one-twentieth of the income of the richest decile. But even this meager allotment is proportionately more than what the poorest decile of individual income receivers get in any other non-Communist country for which we have data. (The family data given for the United States in Table 4-4 understate the extent of individual inequality, since in the poorer families more members are likely to work.)

The inequality in the distribution of West German incomes has held steady over time. This seems to have been the result of several conflicting shifts. In 1950, inequality was greater than it had been in the 1930s, and it increased further until 1955. Over the next five years there was some slight leveling of incomes, followed perhaps by another trend toward somewhat greater concentration of incomes in 1960–65. Income inequality decreased somewhat among clerical employees, but it increased considerably among the self-employed.[5]

The higher degree of inequality among the self-employed and generally in the formation of wealth, rather than mere current income, as revealed by a sample survey in 1962–63, is shown in Figure 4-2.

[5] Hans-Jürgen Krupp, "Wandlungen der Einkommensstruktur in der Bundesrepublik," in *Industriegesellschaften im Wandel: Japan und die BRD,* Karl Hax and Willy Kraus (eds.) (Düsseldorf: Bertelsmann Universitätsverlag, 1970), pp. 49–56.

TABLE 4-4. *Distribution of Personal Income Before Taxes in Twelve Countries*

	Year	Percentage of Income Going to			Ratio of Richest to Poorest Decile (rounded off)
		richest decile	middle 8 deciles	poorest decile	
France	1962	36.8%	62.7%	0.5%	74
German Federal Republic	1964	41.4	56.5	2.1	20
Finland	1962	32.5	67.0	0.5	65
The Netherlands	1962	33.8	64.9	1.3	26
United Kingdom	1964	29.3	68.7	2.0	15
Sweden	1963	27.9	70.5	1.6	17
Denmark	1963	27.1	71.2	1.7	16
Israel	1963	27.0	71.6	1.4	19
Norway	1963	24.9	74.1	1.0	25
United States:					
Family incomes	1964	(25.0) *	(72.5) *	(2.5) *	(10) *
Individual incomes	1964 *	33.0 *	65.5 *	1.5 *	22 *
Yugoslavia (households)	1963	(25.4)	(71.3)	(3.3)	(8)
Hungary	1962	21.5	74.0 *	4.5 *	5

SOURCE: Adapted from K. W. Deutsch, *Politics and Government,* Table 4-1, pp. 92–93; S. M. Miller and P. Roby, *The Future of Inequality* (New York: Basic Books, 1970), Table 2-5, pp. 38–39.
* Author's estimate.

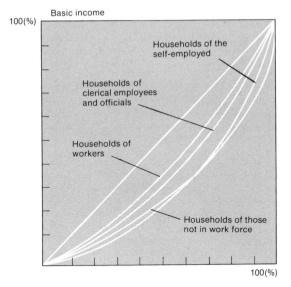

100(%)

Basic income

Households of the
self-employed

Households of
clerical employees
and officials

Households of
workers

Households of those
not in work force

100(%)

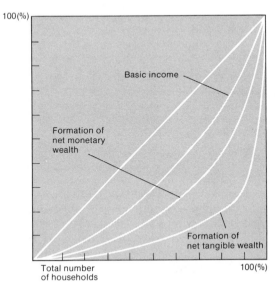

100(%)

Basic income

Formation of
net monetary
wealth

Formation of
net tangible wealth

Total number
of households

100(%)

FIG. 4-2. *The distribution of wealth in the German Federal Republic, 1962–63. [From H. J. Krupp, "Wandlungen der Einkommensstruktur," pp. 51, 54.]*

The Distribution of Wealth

The inequality of incomes is only part of the story. Most people can count on most of their income only when they are young enough and well enough to work. When they are not, they will depend on their savings and other forms of wealth, or else on public welfare. Wealth also contributes to the current income of its possessor, but not all of the increase in a person's—say, a businessman's—assets appear as personal income in official statistics, nor does the increase in economic security and power which wealth entails.

In the Federal Republic, as in most non-Communist countries, the distribution of wealth is still much more unequal than the distribution of income. By 1966, a mere 1.7% of all West German households owned 31% of all private wealth and a staggering 74% of productive wealth. Considerable inequality also applied to much broader strata: between 1950 and 1969, a self-employed person outside of agriculture had accumulated on the average a fortune of 121,000 DM (*Deutsche Mark*)—about $36,000 at late 1971 exchange rates—including the retained profits of his enterprise, twenty times as much as the wealth of 6,000 DM (about $1,800) accumulated by the average worker (see Table 4-5). Changes over time were mutually contradictory. The 1969 data show a slight decrease since 1960 in the concentration of general wealth in the hands of the richest 1.7% of households from 35% to 31% but an increase in the concentration of productive wealth from 70% to 74% in the hands of the same small group. As regards changes among larger groups between 1963 and 1969, the shares of wage- and salary-earners, *rentiers* and pensioners, and of peasants increased, partly in response to the strong growth in the number of white-collar employees, and the share of non-agricultural self-employed decreased. In 1969, this last group owned 36% of the wealth accumulated between 1950 and 1969, while in 1963 their share had been 44%, corresponding to an average decline of more than 1% per year

TABLE 4-5. *Distribution of Private Wealth in West Germany, 1950–69 (including undistributed profits)*

	Income Receivers, 1969 (Millions) Number	Proportion of Total	Share of total Wealth 1969	(1963)	Average Wealth per Income Receiver
Self-employed outside agriculture	2.6	7%	53%	(64%)	121,500 DM
Peasants	2.3	7	4	(3)	9,900
Subtotal: Self-employed	*4.9*	*14%*	*57%*	*(67%)*	*68,700 DM*
Officials	1.9	6	6	(4)	19,100
Clerical Employees	7.3	21	16	(11)	13,000
Workers	12.2	34	12	(10)	6,000
Subtotal: Wage- and Salary-Earners	*21.4*	*61*	*34*	*(25)*	*9,500 DM*
Rentiers and Pensioners	9.1	25	9	(8)	6,000
Subtotal: Non-Self-employed	*30.5*	*86*	*43*	*(33)*	*8,500 DM*
Total	**35.4**	**100**	**100**	**(100)**	**16,700 DM**

SOURCE: Adapted from J. Siebke, "Die Vermögensbildung der privaten Haushalte in der Bundesrepublik Deutschland," as reported in *Frankfurter Rundschau*, no. 180, August 7, 1971.

during the 1960s. If one includes undistributed profits, the share of the self-employed outside agriculture (who make up only 7% of all income receivers) is much larger: 64% in 1963, declining to 53% in 1969 (still more than one-half of the total).

The most frequent form of private wealth in the Federal Republic (see Table 4-6) as of 1966 was nonagricultural real estate (41%); followed by monetary wealth, such as bank deposits and cash (28%); productive wealth, consisting of ownership of enterprises and shares of their capital (26%); and at a great distance, agricultural wealth (4%). These figures tell us something of the great potential power of real estate interests and of financial institutions, and of the declining influence of agriculture.

The German Federal Republic in 1966 had 30,000 DM-millionaires but only about 900 households worth 10 million DM each. A great deal of private wealth was in the hands of households owning between DM 150,000 and 1 million, and a little more belonged to another 130,000 households, with wealth between DM 100,000 and 150,000, leaving 98% of all households unmistakably outside the circle of wealth. Also, as shown in Table 4-7, there was no increase in the total net wealth of DM-millionaires relative to remaining groups from 1960 to 1966, a period in which total German private wealth doubled. At the same time, the

TABLE 4-6. *Types of Private Wealth in West Germany, 1960 and 1966*

	1960		1966		Shift, 1960 to 1966	
	DM bils	*Proportion of Total*	*DM bils*	*Proportion of Total*	*DM bils*	*Proportion of Total*
Nonagricultural real estate	109	36%	248	41%	+139	+5%
Monetary wealth	65	21	173	28	+108	+7
Productive wealth (worth of enterprises and capital shares)	107	35	160	26	+53	−9
Agricultural wealth	23	8	27	4	+4	−4
Total Net Wealth	*304*	*100*	*608*	*100*	*+304*	*0*

SOURCE: Siebke, "Die Vermögensbildung der privaten Haushalte," in *Frankfurter Rundschau*, op. cit., August 7, 1971, Table 3.

DM-millionaires increased substantially their share of productive wealth—the form of wealth with the highest potential for political and social power.

Under the Bonn republic, most Germans have been less interested in the just distribution of a fixed income than they have been in seeing this total income increase, and in having

TABLE 4-7. *Share of Upper Income Groups in the Weath of Private Households, 1960 and 1966*

	1966	1960 *			1966 †		
Total Wealth	*Number of Households (thousands)*	*share of households*	*share of total net wealth*	*share of productive wealth*	*share of households*	*share of total net wealth*	*share of productive wealth*
Over 10 million DM	0.9	0.003%	4.0%	11%	0.004%	3.6%	12.4%
1–10 million DM	30	0.08	13.2	33	0.14	13.6	41.4
150,000–1 million DM	362	—	—	—	1.7	31.0	73.9
100,000–150,000 DM	430	1.7	35.1	70	2.0	32.4	75.4
Under 100,000 DM	20,844	98.3	64.9	30	98	67.6	24.6
All households	*21,274*	*100*	*100*	*100*	*100*	*100*	*100*

SOURCE: Adapted from data in Siebke, "Die Vermögensbildung der privaten Haushalte," in *Frankfurter Rundschau*, op. cit., Tables 3, 4, and 5.
* Total net wealth = 608 billion DM; productive wealth = 160 billion DM.
† Total net wealth = 304 billion DM; productive wealth = 107 billion DM.

their own incomes rise with it. The upward shifts in household incomes are summarized in Table 4-8 and the results in terms of major consumer goods are shown in Figure 4-2.

These rising income figures, and the increase in the number of households in the middle-income bracket—during a period in which German prices did not rise very much—have found tangible expression in the lives of West Germans. There is an impressive list of durable household goods that have become widespread. To cite two examples: the proportion of households with electric refrigerators rose from 10% in 1955 to 83% in 1969, while the proportion owning electric washing machines grew from 23% to 61% between 1958 and 1969.[6]

[6] Elisabeth Noelle Neumann and Erich Peter Neumann, *Jahrbuch der öffentlichen Meinung* (Allensbach: Verlag für Demoskopie, 1970), 1:27–28 (hereafter cited as *Jahrbuch*); Erich Peter Neumann, *Public Opinion in Germany, 1961* (Allensbach and Bonn: Verlag für Demoskopie, 1961), pp. 14–17, 24–25; DIVO, *Pressedienst,* July 1966; and *S.J.B.*, 1970, p. 467.

Status Groups and Social Classes

Germans have long been a highly status-conscious people, and the distribution of status differs in some respects from the distribution of income. Occupations requiring more education, clerical work, and either private or public trust rank more highly in status than the pay that they bring might indicate. A majority of respondents (56%) to a poll in March 1955 said that the population in general would have more respect for a commercial clerk earning 300 DM ($75) a month than for a foundry worker earning 450 DM ($113). In the same month, nearly half (45%) of employed workers in a poll said that they would switch to a clerical job for the same pay, if they were given the opportunity to do so.[7]

In three polls between 1952 and 1955, over two-thirds of the general population expressed

[7] *Jahrbuch,* 1:244.

TABLE 4-8. *Net Incomes of Households in the G.F.R. and G.D.R., 1958–60 and 1969–70, in Marks* *

		Average Household Income per capita of Working Population (in thousands)	Percentage Distribution				
			under 600	600–800	800–1000	1000–1200	over 1200
G.F.R. †	1958	8.2 ‡	93%			7%	
	1969	14.7 §	23%	18%	15%	14%	30%
G.D.R. ‖	1960	9.1 #	34	25	22	11	8
	1970	12.4	15	14	19	22	30

SOURCES: *S.J.B.*, 1970, p. 468, and *Stat. Jahrbusch 1971 der D.D.R.*, p. 350.

* Note that the purchasing power of the G.D.R. Mark ("*Ostmark*") for many consumer goods is less than that of the G.F.R. *Deutsche Mark*. Although the official rate of exchange is 1:1, in terms of average purchasing power 1 DM equaled approximately 1.16 *Ostmark* in 1969, as against 1.32 *Ostmark* in 1960. See p. 362, above.

† Excluding households in agriculture.

‡ 1960.

§ 1968.

‖ Households of wage- and salary-earners only.

Income per household.

their preference for collaboration among the classes, and so did three-fifths of the workers polled. The idea of class conflict was endorsed by only 15% of the general population and by about one-quarter of the workers.[8] Employers in 1955 were considered efficient, rather than merely greedy, by about half the public, but 52% said in December 1956 that employers cared only for their profits, and not for the welfare of their employees. Two-thirds of the workers thought so, and so did 43% of white-collar employees and public officials, as well as 44% of small-business and professional men. A majority of the public (53%) agreed that the employers had to be compelled by law to respond to the wishes of their workers and office employees.[9] The total picture is one of moderate status envy, willingness to cooperate with employers without any great trust in them, and

[8] Ibid., 244–45.
[9] Ibid., 246–47.

a preference for limited but effective governmental regulation.

The West German social structure has remained remarkably stable during the last several decades of political convulsions. The actual distribution of classes and status groups in the Federal Republic has changed only a little from that which prevailed in Hitler's Germany; and Hitler's Reich differed in this respect but little from the Weimar Republic. The relative strength of the differing strata among fathers and sons in a large sample of the German population taken in 1955 is shown in Table 4-9.

The most important fact is the expansion of the upper-middle-class stratum, from about 3% among the fathers of the present generation to nearly 5% among this present generation itself. There are more than three upper-middle-class jobs available to the present generation for every two such jobs that were within reach of their fathers. Near the other end of the scale, the proportion of farmers and

TABLE 4-9. *Social Strata in West Germany, 1955*

Population Sampling	Present Generation (N = 3,385)	Father's Generation (N = 3,385)
Upper-middle stratum: Professionals, managers and proprietors of larger establishments, and high-ranking civil servants	4.6%	3.0%
Lower-middle stratum: Minor officials, clerical and salespersons, small businessmen, and independent artisans	28.0	24.6
Upper-lower stratum: Skilled workers and employed artisans	13.3	12.4
Lower-lower stratum: Semiskilled and unskilled workers	34.9	31.6
Farmers	10.6	22.0
Farm workers	3.7	4.6
Unclassifiable *	4.9	1.8

SOURCE: Morris Janowitz, "Social Stratification and Mobility in West Germany," *American Journal of Sociology* 64, no. 1 (July 1958); 6–24, and Table 3, p. 10; and K. W. Deutsch and L. J. Edinger, *Germany Rejoins the Powers* (Stanford, Calif.: Stanford University Press, 1959), p. 262, and, generally, pp. 36, 260–66.

* Includes those war and social security pensioners to whom no occupational position could be meaningfully assigned.

farm workers has contracted. While many of the children of these groups have entered the ranks of unskilled or semiskilled labor, these lower groups of labor have also shrunk a little.[10] There has been a partial but significant upward movement throughout the society. A summary of more complex tables of social mobility across a generation is shown in Table 4-10.

From these figures, it can be estimated that only about half the West Germans of 1955 still were in the same social stratum in which their fathers had been, while as many as 30% reported that they had risen in the world, and only about 20% said that they had stepped down, by one or more steps. With half the adult population having changed its social class within its own lifetime, any political appeal to permanent class interests was likely to find only very limited support. And with nearly one-third of the voters having stepped up in the social scale, their outlook on the Bonn republic was likely to be at least cautiously optimistic—and perhaps also a little concerned to hold on to the improved social status which they and their families had gained. Appeals to conservatism, moderation, and collaboration among classes

might sound more meaningful to them in times of prosperity; and unless new cleavages should open between the classes, appeals to national solidarity and perhaps to nationalism might well move a great many West Germans in times of crisis.

All these effects of social mobility—as well as of geographic mobility—were reinforced in the case of the expellees and refugees and their West German-born children—totaling altogether about 10 million in 1950, 12 million in 1962, but declining to 9 million in 1969—who made up nearly one-sixth of the population of the Federal Republic in the last of these years. They had more than one-fifth of the jobs in the public service, but less than half of that share among the self-employed, as well as of the jobs in banking, commerce, and in industrial plants. The only activity in which their share exceeded substantially that in the general population was positions as officials of the federal government (22%).[11]

As newcomers, these expellees and refugees cannot but help to break down the differences between regions, classes, and even religious groups, and to strengthen the patterns of national solidarity, nationwide mobility, and—particularly as far as the older generation is concerned—a continuing and lively interest in the revision of the frontiers to the east. The children of the expellees, on the other hand, are most interested in making their homes in West Germany where they now live. Despite the strenuous efforts of such expellee and refugee youth organizations as the *Deutsche Jugend des Ostens* (DJO), the rights and wrongs of Eastern European politics are beginning to sound as remote to most of them as the troubles of the Old World used to sound to the children of American immigrants who were hardly concerned with the political claims and quarrels their parents had left behind them.

TABLE 4-10. *Intergenerational Mobility in West Germany, 1955*

Stratum in Present Generation	Proportion of Present Total	Stratum of Recruitment from Father's Generation		
		lower	same	higher
Upper-middle	4.6%	72%	28%	0%
Lower-middle	28.0	46	51	3
Upper-lower	13.3	46	29	25
Lower-lower	34.9	22	57	21
Farmers and farm workers	14.3	0	77	23
Unclassifiable	4.9	0	0	100

SOURCES: Janowitz, "Social Stratification," 12, Table 7; and Deutsch and Edinger, *Germany Rejoins the Powers*, pp. 262–63.

[10] References are those given in Table 4-9.

LEVELS OF EDUCATION

All West German children must go to school for at least eight years, but four-fifths of

[11] *S.J.B.,* 1961, pp. 54–55; *S.J.B.,* 1970, p. 41.

the students leave school at age 14 when they finish their primary education. Thus, in the early 1960s, only 18% of West German youth in the 15-to-19-year-old age group were full-time students, compared to 31% in France and 66% in the United States.[12] Nearly one-quarter (22%) of the 16-year-olds in 1959 were getting the *Mittlere Reife,* which is the German counterpart to an American nonacademic high-school education.[13] This was a considerable improvement over the education received by their parents. According to polling data from the mid-1950s, only 12% of the general population over 18 years had attained this educational level.[14]

Graduation from a full-fledged German academic high school—the *Abitur,* which is the equivalent of an American junior college—had been achieved by only 4% of the general population in the mid-1950s, but it was being attained by as many as 10% of the 19- and 20-year-olds in 1968—by about 12% of the men and 8% of the women.[15]

There was similar evidence of substantial broader access to university education. Between 1957 and 1969, the number of university students almost trebled, rising from 112,000 to 300,000, when about 9% of the 19-year-olds were entering the universities—13% of the men and 5% of the women.

In 1969, of the total population of all ages, about five out of every thousand were attending some university or technical college, as against the earlier proportion of two per thousand in 1950 and in 1932 at the end of the Weimar Republic, and against only one student per thousand population under Hitler's regime in 1938.[16] Quietly and without much rhetoric, the Bonn republic by the early 1970s opened the gates of the German universities nearly

three times as wide as they had ever been opened. While the West German levels (six per thousand, if students and teachers in colleges are added) are still well below the United States figure of eighteen students per thousand population—and of perhaps twelve American students per thousand above the junior-college level, which corresponds to the German *Abitur* —and while there was no very broad college-educated group in the West German electorate, the proportion of university-educated men and women had grown significantly, and promised to continue to do so.

The widening of opportunities for higher education also has brought with it a broadening of the social composition of the student body. One-fourth of the West German university students now receive more than one-half of their support from public funds, usually from scholarships under a national foundation; and the top students, approximately 1% of the total, get more substantial grants. There are probably still not more than 5–10% sons of workers among the students at West German universities, but even this proportion is larger than it has been under any previous regime, and it seems likely to grow in the future. Together with the absolute increase in the number of students, the increase of the share of students from poorer families has meant that the total opportunities available to students of, say, working-class background have improved appreciably. At the same time, this process is giving to the Federal Republic a substantially larger share of academically educated voters, recruited from a wider variety of backgrounds; and this may well have some effects on the future style and trend of West German politics.

It is more difficult to gauge exactly the potential political implications of this expansion in the share of the better educated among the electorate. In the United States, college education has been on the whole a liberalizing influence; in many surveys and polls, the college-educated have shown a greater interest in facts, a markedly greater tolerance for views other than their own, a greater readiness to compromise on matters of ideology or tradition, and a greater commitment to human rights and civil liberties. In Germany under the

12 Thomas Ellwein, *Politische Verhaltenslehre* (Frankfurt: Europäische Verlagsanstalt, 1963), pp. 131–34.

13 These and the following figures are based on data in *S.J.B.,* 1961, pp. 46, 97, 105, and 108, unless otherwise indicated.

14 *Jahrbuch,* 1958, 2: xliv, 4.

15 *S.J.B.,* 1961, pp. 46, 97, 105, and 108; *S.J.B.,* 1966, pp. 99, 101; and *S.J.B.,* 1970, pp. 35, 74–79.

16 Ibid., and William L. Shirer, *The Rise and Fall of the Third Reich* (New York: Simon & Schuster, 1960), p. 252.

Weimar Republic, on the other hand, students and university graduates were on the average more nationalistic, militaristic, and intolerant than the bulk of their countrymen. After 1933, the Nazi government cut university enrollments in half within six years; the Nazis tended to impose political screening upon the remaining students, and even more upon the university faculties and especially upon new appointees to academic posts. Although these controls were not perfectly efficient, they had their effects. A major survey in 1950 still found pro-Nazi and anti-Western sentiments significantly higher among German holders of academic degrees than among the population at large. The nationalism of German academics, as it appeared in this survey, was exceeded only by that of peasants, and of men with more than six years of military service.[17] The education offered at West German universities in the 1950s and 1960s was permeated with a more moderate and democratic spirit, even though there were still, among the prominent professors in 1971, men with a past record of Nazi sympathies, or party membership, or past public endorsements of Nazi leaders or doctrines. On the other side, there are many German scholars who maintained an honorable record of integrity during the Hitler years, and of opposition to the Nazi tyranny. Quite a few of these men suffered exile, imprisonment, or other persecution. Nevertheless, a survey for the year 1955 did not find among the published biographies of the heads of thirty-eight institutions of higher education a single mention of an anti-Nazi record, and this peculiar tradition of neutrality survived in many universities throughout the 1960s.[18]

Among the students, the traditional, extremely nationalistic student groups of the drinking and dueling type had been for the most part archconservative rather than National Socialist in political outlook. Despite their opposition to the totalitarian claims of the Nazi regime, their past record of hostility to democracy, contempt for Western countries and values, and sympathy for aggressive militarism brought them into discredit and eclipse during the first years after the Nazi collapse in 1945. During the 1950s, however, these dueling fraternities had a partial revival, strongly aided by alumni in high positions in German industry, business, and to a lesser extent the civil service, who made it known that a student's membership in their old and now reconstituted fraternity might greatly benefit his later career. By the beginning of the 1960s, an estimated 5% of university students were Nazi sympathizers, and another 15 to 20% were members of the revived drinking and dueling fraternities—a proportion corresponding roughly to the 25% share of holders of right-wing sentiments found among the general electorate.

A stronger trend among university students and a part of the nontenured junior faculty members of the German universities was to the left. The share of students and academic personnel in the German work force had grown nearly threefold, but their political influence, social status, and economic level had not grown in proportion. In the Federal Republic, as in other countries, a student was still most often a man with the income of a boy. Study was regarded by many nonacademics, and by many older people generally, not as work but as a kind of idleness, play, or children's occupation, or else as a preparation for a lifetime of privilege—just when the large increase in the number of students promised to make an academic degree no longer the possession of a privileged few. At the same time that students became more numerous and more frustrated, many of them became more stirred and enraged by the overload of contradictory knowledge brought to them by their studies and by the mass media, and by the normative and cognitive dissonance between their ideas and aspirations and the realities of the world in which they lived. Some of these realities could well be infuriating. They included the unchanged authoritarian structure of much of German university life (as well as of the homes and families from which most of them had come) and the unresponsive

[17] Friedrich Pollock, ed., *Gruppenexperiment: Ein Studienbericht*, Frankfurter Beiträge zur Soziologie (Frankfurt: Europäische Verlagsanstalt, 1955), 2:236–72; see also Deutsch and Edinger, *Germany Rejoins the Powers*, pp. 40–43.

[18] Deutsch and Edinger, *Germany Rejoins the Powers*, p. 123.

character of many of their country's political and economic institutions. Nothing moderate or legal that young people could do, it seemed to them, would make any difference to the conditions governing their lives; but perhaps, so an increasing number among them began to think, they could make a difference by resorting to more drastic methods.

Such feelings of unrest and dissonance had been growing under the surface during the 1960s, and more quickly so from 1966 onward. In 1967 and 1968, they broke into the open with large student demonstrations, occupations of buildings, disruptions of academic work, and varied demands for university reform, more permissiveness in matters of sex and life style, and more far-reaching political changes.

By 1971, the turbulent and variegated movement had partly succeeded in regard to the first two demands but largely failed in regard to the third. Students and junior faculty members gained significant shares in the governing of many universities, and university reform legislation was passed in several of the *Länder*. Rules of censorship and public order were relaxed, as they were in other countries, and permissiveness increased substantially in many matters. But the social and political structure of the country remained unchanged. Neither the radical Marxist nor the anarchist factions among the students found much sympathy among the factory workers or among the population at large. Only on matters of antiauthoritarianism, more permissive sex mores, and demands for free speech and greater equality did they find an echo among a majority of nonuniversity youth.

Even so, the movement changed the predominant political climate within the universities. Excesses by small extremist groups drove many faculty members into a more conservative position; and in some cases the left-wing student groups proved more dogmatic and intolerant in imposing their views, and in silencing critics and dissenters (including some of Germany's most distinguished liberal scholars), than the old university authorities had been at any time since 1945. The main thrust of the movement, however, despite much confusion, remained radically democratic and antiauthori-

tarian. The great majority of students and junior faculty had no interest in a bureaucratic Communist dictatorship of the sort existing in the G.D.R. or the Soviet Union. For the early 1970s, at least, the main political influences coming from the universities seemed likely to be left-of-center, humanistic, libertarian, and remarkably confused. How long this mood would continue, and where it would eventually lead, no one could foretell.

REGIONAL AND RELIGIOUS FACTORS

It is said that Chancellor Adenauer once described Germany as being divided naturally into three parts—the Germany of wine, the Germany of beer, and the Germany of schnapps, or hard liquor—and that he expressed his love for the first, his sympathy for the second, and his willingness to do his duty for the third. Much has been written by others about the cultural and psychological differences between the wine-drinking Rhineland, beer-drinking Bavaria, and liquor-drinking northern and eastern Germany; and in less picturesque language, the west, the south, the north, and the east-central regions are widely accepted as the main geographic subdivisions of Germany. The first three of these now constitute three informal regions of the Federal Republic. The fourth has been turned into the G.D.R. and the Oder-Neisse territories, but it lives on in West German politics through the memories of one-quarter of its population, who are refugees and expellees, and through the memories of an even larger proportion of some of the crucial elite groups of the Federal Republic. Thus, in a survey of over five hundred members of German foreign policy elites in 1956–57, as many as 41% of the military leaders, 29% of the diplomats, and 41% of the SPD leaders came from the central and east German areas.[19]

The political and administrative structure of the Federal Republic is built upon ten states, or *Länder*. In some instances, these *Länder* con-

[19] Deutsch and Edinger, *Germany Rejoins the Powers*, pp. 126–27, 134.

tinue the traditions of earlier German political units, as in the cases of Bavaria, Hamburg, and Bremen, while others, such as North Rhine-Westphalia, Baden-Württemberg, and Lower Saxony, represent postwar creations in which earlier territorial units have been merged.

By far the largest *Land* is North Rhine-Westphalia. It comprises more than one-fourth of the population of the Federal Republic, and it accounts for almost one-third of the national economic activity. The second most populous state, and the largest in area, is Bavaria, followed by Baden-Württemberg and Lower Saxony. All the remaining *Länder* have less than 6 million population each. Indeed, only Hessen and Rhineland-Palatinate are even middle-sized; the rest each have less than 2.6 million people.

The western part of West Germany, prosperous and densely populated, thus consists of one large state, North Rhine-Westphalia, two middle-sized ones, Hessen and Rhineland-Palatinate, and the small but coal-rich Saarland, which was incorporated into the Federal Republic only in 1957. Southern Germany consists of two large Lands, Bavaria and Baden-Württemberg, while northern Germany is made up of one large state, Lower Saxony, one small and predominantly rural *Land,* Schleswig-Holstein, and two old and prosperous city-states, Hamburg and Bremen.

Religious Composition

Western Germany and southern Germany have Roman Catholic majorities; northern Germany is overwhelmingly Protestant. In the Federal Republic, excluding Berlin, there were in 1969 about 29 million Catholics, who form a strong minority of 49% of the total, while the nearly 28 million Protestants constitute the same proportion of the population. Most of the remaining 3% do not belong to any religious denomination. About 30,000 Jews were left in the Federal Republic in 1969, most of them elderly; fewer than 200 Jewish children were born there in that year. The addition of West Berlin would add 1.5 million Protestants,

300,000 Catholics, and 6,000 Jews to the respective totals.

These figures show a shift from 1955, when among adults a somewhat larger majority of 52% Protestants confronted a minority of only 44% Catholics, while 4% were reported as "other." [20] The slight Protestant majority in the Federal Republic, excluding West Berlin, had disappeared within little more than a decade. Only reunification with the largely Protestant G.D.R. would restore and increase it substantially.[21]

The Protestant share was substantially larger, however, in a sample of the German upper-middle class, where it was as high as 60% in 1955, as against only 31% Catholics, 5% unaffiliated, and 4% other denominations.[22] Since the upward social mobility of Protestants also was found to be somewhat higher than that of Catholics,[23] and since the Catholics generally were represented somewhat more strongly among the less highly skilled and educated strata of the population, the Protestant hold on perhaps three-fifths of the upper-middle-class positions in the Federal Republic seems likely to persist.

All these figures have political significance. There is evidence from polls that Roman Catholics in the Federal Republic go nearly twice as often to church as do Protestants, and that, with much active encouragement from the Catholic church and lay organizations, they tend to furnish three-fifths of the CDU vote, two-thirds of the steadfast CDU voters, and three-quarters of the CDU membership, as well as two-thirds of the CDU members of the Bundestag and a majority of the federal cabinet before the CDU first formed a coalition with the SPD in 1966 and then left the fed-

[20] *Jahrbuch*, 2:3; and *S.J.B.*, 1965, p. 90.

[21] From data in *S.J.B.*, 1961, pp. 59, 94, and *S.J.B.*, 1965, p. 90.

[22] Computed from data in Morris Janowitz, "Social Stratification and Mobility in West Germany," *American Journal of Sociology* 64, no. 1 (July 1958): 10, Table 3, and 15, Table 8; reprinted in Deutsch and Edinger, *Germany Rejoins the Powers*, p. 262, Table 2-3, and p. 264, Table 2-6.

[23] Deutsch and Edinger, *Germany Rejoins the Powers*, p. 264, Table 2-6.

eral government in 1969.[24] In turn, the CDU, the formal functioning of the federal and *Land* governments, and perhaps the informal effects of the regions all contribute something close to majority status upon the Catholic minority. Some aspects of this process are shown in Tables 4-11 and 4-12.

24 See *Jahrbuch*, 2:77, 264; Gerhard Loewenberg, *Parliament in the German Political System* (Ithaca, N.Y.: Cornell University Press, 1967), pp. 100–101; Juan Linz, *The Social Bases of West German Politics* (Ann Arbor, Mich.: University Microfilms, 1959), p. 44 with reference to Arnold J. Heidenheimer, *La Revue française de science politique* 7, no. 3 (July-September 1957): 635; U. W. Kitzinger, *German Electoral Politics* (Oxford: Clarendon Press, 1960), pp. 223–33, and references on p. 223n; Deutsch and Edinger, *Germany Rejoins the Powers*, pp. 131, 135.

The West German States (*Länder*)

The figures in Table 4-11 illustrate, first of all, the considerable differences in population, area, and wealth among the *Länder*. By any account, North Rhine-Westphalia stands out. Together with Bavaria, these two states account for nearly one-half the population of the Federal Republic. The "gross domestic product" figures, technically called economic turnover, show something of the levels of economic development in each *Land*. Very roughly speaking, national turnover data for the G.F.R. tend to amount to perhaps three times the national income. The city-states of Hamburg and Bremen

TABLE 4-11. *Economic Aspects of West German* Länder *and Regions*

Land	Population, 1970 (millions)	Area (thousands of sq. kilometers)	Gross Domestic Product, 1968		
			total (billions of DM)	Proportion of total	per capita (thousands of DM)
North Rhine-Westphalia	17.2	34.0	154	29.0%	9.1
Hessen	5.5	21.1	49	9.3	9.3
Rhineland-Palatinate	3.7	19.8	27	5.1	7.4
Saarland	1.1	0.8	8	1.5	7.1
Subtotal: western region	*27.5*	*75.7*	*238*	*44.9*	*8.7*
Bavaria	10.6	70.5	83	15.8	8.1
Baden-Württemberg	9.0	35.8	77	14.6	9.0
Subtotal: southern region	*19.6*	*106.3*	*160*	*30.4*	*8.2*
Lower Saxony	7.1	47.4	54	10.2	7.7
Schleswig-Holstein	2.6	15.7	19	3.5	7.4
Hamburg	1.8	0.1	28	5.4	15.5
Bremen	0.8	0.1	8	1.6	11.1
Subtotal: northern region	*12.3*	*63.3*	*109*	*20.7*	*8.9*
Totals:					
G.F.R. not including Berlin	59.3	245.3	508	96.0	8.8 *
West Berlin	2.1	0.5	21	3.9	9.6

SOURCE: *S.J.B.*, 1970, p. 495.
* Including West Berlin.

are noteworthy, of course, for their high per capita basis, and also the absolute wealth going through Hamburg is impressive. They are followed by Hessen, North Rhine-Westphalia, and Baden-Würtemberg, with their industries, but all the remaining areas are below the national average, with the rural states of Schleswig-Holstein, Rhineland-Palatinate, Lower Saxony and Saarland at the bottom of the per capita rank order.

As Tables 4-11 and 4-12 suggest, the postwar arrangement of *Länder* and regions has been least favorable to northern Germany. That region is by far the smallest of the three, yet it is divided into four states, and the economic "raisins" of Hamburg and Bremen are separated from the "cake" of their hinterland in Lower Saxony and Schleswig-Holstein. North-

ern Germany is the region of Protestantism, and of relatively least support for the CDU, but it is small, divided, partly poor, underrepresented in most national elites, and generally less influential in national affairs than it was under the Hohenzollern empire and the Weimar Republic.

This does not necessarily mean, however, that the present arrangement is unpopular, even in northern Germany. The continued separate statehood of Hamburg and Bremen appeals to a proud civic tradition, and it has provided the Social Democrats with excellent opportunities for winning and holding control of the government of these city-states, in partial compensation for their long exclusion from federal office. Moreover, the Protestant church, and particularly its main constituent bodies, the

TABLE 4-12. *Social and Political Aspects of West German* Länder *and Regions*

Land	Percentage of Population		Percentage of 1969 Votes for CDU/CSU	Seats in Bundesrat	Governing Party or Coalition, 1971
	expellees and refugees, 1969	Roman Catholics, 1963			
North Rhine-Westphalia	14%	50%	46.1%	5	SPD/FDP
Hessen	16	31	38.4	4	SPD/FDP
Rhineland-Palatinate	7	56	47.8	4	CDU/FDP
Saarland	1	36	46.1	3	CDU/FDP
Subtotal: western region	*12*	*48*	*42.4*	*16*	—
Bavaria	16	66	54.4	5	CSU
Baden-Württemberg	14	43	50.7	5	CDU/SPD
Subtotal: southern region	*15*	*54*	*51.4*	*10*	
Lower Saxony	24	16	45.2	5	SPD/CDU
Schleswig-Holstein	26	5	46.2	4	CDU/FDP
Hamburg	10	8	34.0	3	SPD
Bremen	14	10	32.3	3	SPD/FDP
Subtotal: northern region	*22*	*13*	*41.9*	*15*	
Totals:					
G.F.R. not including Berlin	16	49	43.6	41	SPD/FDP
West Berlin	6	13	—	4	SPD/FDP

SOURCE: *S.J.B.*, 1966, pp. 46, 90, 141, 144.

Lutheran churches, have a tradition of non-political submission to whatever political authorities there be, and of a deep cleavage between the working classes and the somewhat authoritarian Protestant upper-middle classes and their culture—a double tradition that would have reduced the political effectiveness of German Protestants in any case well below the level of their numbers. If the Social Democrats have welcomed their special political opportunities in Hamburg and Bremen, nationalists and conservatives have also welcomed countervailing opportunities for right-of-center politics in Lower Saxony and Schleswig-Holstein. If some well-informed observers have stressed the considerable uniformity of politics in the Federal Republic, and the minor importance of regional differences on many issues,[25] then these views should be qualified in the light of what has just been said, and of such interregional differences in poll data as are shown in Table 4-13.

[25] See Linz, *Social Bases of West German Politics,* pp. 165–66.

The poll results from the mid-1950s in Table 4-13 suggest that northern Germany suffered more than the rest of the country in World War II; and that it was poorer. The results also indicate that its voters were more highly aware of politics, more inclined to be right of center, more nationalistic, and more intensely insistent on German reunification than were the voters of the other two regions, and that there was more potential support in northern Germany for an active military and political policy toward this end. Part—but not all—of the difference could be accounted for in terms of northern Germany's greater share of refugees and expellees, but on several issues the contrast with the attitudes in southern Germany was far greater than would be explainable by this single factor. By 1971, the interregional differences had become weaker. Rural northern Germany still was poorer than most of the south and west. But in 1969, it gave more votes than the national average to the less nationalistic parties, the SPD and the FDP, both of which favored a more concilia-

TABLE 4-13. *Regional Differences in West Germany, 1956 (Percentage of totals for each region)*

Response to Opinion Poll	National Average	Western Germany	Southern Germany	Northern Germany	West Berlin
Home destroyed in World War II (June)	29%	30%	23%	37%	30%
Running water in present home (March)	84	88	86	73	98
"Can manage well" on income (Aug.)	33	35	32	27	40
Favor separate *Land* citizenship in addition to federal (Oct.)	8	5	12	7	3
"Right of center" (Feb.)	38	35	35	47	45
Do not know political meaning of "right" and "left" (Feb.)	27	28	32	20	17
Favor West German army (May 1955)	40	35	39	44	60
Division of Germany "intolerable" (Sept.)	53	56	44	57	84
Demand reunification "again and again" (Sept.)	65	65	59	73	81
Favor moving federal government from Bonn to Berlin (Dec.)	44	45	29	55	88

SOURCE: *Jahrbuch,* 1: pp. 20, 21, 37, 48, 189, 281, 295, 316.

tory policy toward the eastern neighbors of the Federal Republic.

Only West Berlin shared some of the attitudes, but not the poverty, of northern Germany. The West Berlin attitudes were then almost equally far to the right; and in some matters of nationalist or reunification policies, the readiness to take risks for more radical steps seems to be still greater. Together with the West Berlin voters' preference for social welfare policies, it is this intense concern with anti-Communism and German reunification which has set the conditions for the political appeal—economically moderate but nationally militant—which Willy Brandt had to make in order to succeed first of all as the popular mayor of that embattled city before becoming a national leader of the SPD, later vice-chancellor and foreign minister of a national coalition government, and since 1969 chancellor in a second coalition.

The southern German attitudes usually deviate from the national average in the opposite direction. Southern Germany suffered least from the war and can manage tolerably well on its income; in the mid-1950s it had little more than a one-third of its voters describing themselves as right-of-center. Its voters have markedly stronger local attachments, and markedly less interest in the rest of the country. Differently put, social distinctions are more moderate in southern Germany, and a larger share of middle-class voters see the center point of the political scale itself a little farther to the left. While southern German voters favor reunification, they are much less concerned about it; and only less than a third of them have any use for dramatic and risky gestures that might intensify the struggle for Berlin. By 1971, this picture had somewhat changed. Conservative and nationalist views were somewhat stronger in southern Germany, and particularly in rural and small-town Bavaria outside the metropolitan region of Munich, than they were in the rest of the country. This led the leading parties of the region, the CDU/CSU, into an attitude of holding fast to old policies of higher East-West tension, but with no clear positive steps to offer.

The western German region, finally, emerges as the one that is most nearly representative of the political attitudes of the entire country. It is less nationalistic and intense than the North, but less locally preoccupied and non-political than is the South. Even its greater prosperity only represents a state of affairs which the other regions wish to reach as soon as possible; and on the general issues, its attitudes are usually closest to the national average. In addition to the size of its population, economic resources, and higher share in important national elites, it is perhaps this representative character of many Western German attitudes that fitted this region so long for national leadership.

The Importance of the Land Governments. Altogether, the system of *Länder* and regions has had remarkable political results despite its shallow historic roots. These roots are shallow, first of all, in the seven of the ten *Länder*—all except Bavaria, Hamburg and Bremen—that are relatively recent conglomerations with no long and inspiring history of their own. An average of one-quarter of their populations are refugees and expellees and their children, with no old ties to the *Land* in which they happen to reside; and since an average proportion of about 2% of the population of the Federal Republic moved from one *Land* to another in each of the years from 1964 to 1969—and presumably a similar proportion did so in the preceding years—not much more than 50% or at most 60% of the voters in each *Land* are likely to be native to it.[26]

Even so, the *Länder* carry out a large part of the functions of government; their budgets and payrolls are substantial; and by now they have done it for almost a quarter-century. In 1964 the *Länder* received, and then spent, 50 billion DM, or nearly one-third of the 160 billion DM passing through the total government sector—federal, *Land,* and municipal—in that year. Since the 1964 national income of the Federal Republic was 317 billion DM, this

[26] See migration data in *S.J.B.,* 1971, p. 54, and *S.J.B.,* 1961, p. 71.

indicates that about 22% of the national income was spent by the federal government, and 16% by the *Land* governments. Measured by this financial yardstick, the *Land* governments, taken together, are almost two-thirds as important as the federal government, including the latter's control of the federal railroads and the postal, telegraph, and telephone service; and the *Länder* are significantly more important, in terms of income and spending, than

are the total of municipal authorities.[27] These relationships are set forth roughly in Table 4-14. The figures in this table involve technical problems of aggregation and should be used with caution, but the relative orders of magnitude are clear. The public sector consistently takes in 46% or more of national income, with relatively minor fluctuations. Of this share,

[27] See sources cited in Table 4-14.

TABLE 4-14. *Budgetary Stakes of Politics in the German Federal Republic: National, State, and Local, 1959, 1964, and 1968*

	Billions of DM			Percentage of National Income		
	1959	1964	1968	1959	1964	1968
National income	192.2	316.5	415.3	100%	100%	100%
Federal government share of tax revenue	42.5	62.9	83.2	22	20	20
Income from federal railroads, mails, telegraph, etc.	11.9	17.5	19.6	6	6	5
Subtotal receipts: federal-sector	*54.4*	*80.4*	*102.8*	*28*	*26*	*25*
Länder governments' share of tax revenue *†	29.7	50.5	49.7	15	16	12
Tax income, municipal governments	8.6	38.7	36.2	4	12	9
Subtotal receipts: Land *and local sector*	*38.3*	*89.2*	*85.9*	*19*	*28*	*21*
Total: government-sector income	*92.7*	*169.6*	*188.7*	*47*	*54*	*46*
Public expenditures:						
Federal expenditures (direct)	30.9	62.4	69.3	16	20	17
Federal railroad and mail expenditures	11.4	8.4	(19.6)‡	6	3	5
Subtotal: federal sector	*42.3*	*70.8*	*88.9*	*22*	*23*	*22*
Länder †	24.3	50.7	47.3	13	16	11
Municipalities	18.8	39.1	47.1	10	12	11
Subtotal: Land *and local sector*	*43.1*	*89.8*	*94.4*	*23*	*28*	*22*
Total government spending	*85.4*	*160.6*	*183.3*	*45*	*51*	*44*

SOURCE: Figures rounded off from *S.J.B.*, 1961, pp. 340, 372, 427, 434–36, 544; *S.J.B.*, 1966, pp. 359, 386, 442–43, 551; and *S.J.B.*, 1970, pp. 296, 321, 373–75, 496–97.

   * *Länder* include city-states (Hamburg, Bremen, West Berlin).

   † *Land* incomes for 1959 and 1964 included 5.8 billion DM in Federal grants (4.0) and loans (1.8). This tended to overstate the size of the government total sector for these years. The 1968 data are adjusted for transfer payments, so that double counting from this source is avoided.

   ‡ Estimated.

the federal government collects more than one-half, mainly in the form of taxes or as payments for public services, but since it transfers some of its revenues to the *Länder* and municipalities in the form of grants, these lower and more decentralized levels of government spend slightly more than one-half of the total.

In terms of employment, the public sector employs nearly one-eighth of the total work force of the Federal Republic, but it provides more than one-quarter of all the white-collar jobs in the country. Within the government sector, the *Länder* provide about one-third of the official positions, and nearly half the clerical jobs. The majority of the federal officials are employed by the railroads and mails. The number of other federal officials is relatively small. The great bulk of official positions, other than with the railroads or mails, is in the *Land* administrations and subject to the processes of *Land* politics. Some details are shown in Table 4-15.

Regional diversities are thus met by the partial decentralization of politics through the institution of the *Länder;* and this system of *Länder,* in turn, has enhanced the political importance of local and regional politics. The system has helped to adapt government to the inequalities of economic development among the different territories. It has permitted favored regions to retain some of their advantages, while using redistributive taxation to reduce gradually the interregional cleavages. The system has perhaps also served to isolate a part of the Protestant right in northern Germany from the mainstream of national politics, while it has amplified the influence of western Germany, of the Roman Catholic church, and of the CDU/CSU party combination.

At the same time, however, regionalism and the system of *Land* governments have served to protect political diversity and to keep alive a strong and responsible opposition. Excluded from federal office until 1966, the SPD has

TABLE 4-15. *Public Employment in the German Federal Republic: National, State, and Local Levels, 1968*

Source of Employment	Number Employed (thousands)				Percentage of National Work Force
	officials	clerical	workers	total	
Federal	78	95	104	277	
Federal railroads, mails	482	57	253	792	
Other economic institutions	11	75	4	90	
Total federal personnel	*571*	*227*	*361*	*1,159*	*4%*
Länder (including city-states)	651	329	100	1,080	
Land economic institutions	8	70	51	129	
Total Land personnel	*659*	*399*	*151*	*1,209*	5
Municipalities	133	333	251	717	3
Total public employment	*1,363*	*959*	*763*	*3,085*	*12*
Total work force	*1,427*	*7,540*	*12,403*	*26,169* *	*100*
Percentage in public sector	95%	13%	6%	12%	
		26%			

SOURCE: *S.J.B.,* 1970, pp. 118–20, 385–86.

* Including 2,857 self-employed and 1,942 members of families assisting them.

drawn strength and experience from its successes in the government of various *Länder*. In 1967, the SPD governed Hamburg and Hessen, and was the leading partner in the governing coalitions in Lower Saxony, Bremen, and West Berlin. The FDP, which had been excluded from federal office during 1957–61, and, from 1966 to 1969, continued to share in government at the *Land* level as the junior coalition partners in six of the eleven *Land* governments.

Although every party wants to win a share in the federal government, the opportunities in regional and municipal governments seem substantial enough to keep opposition parties alive, if need be, for an indefinite length of time. In these, and other ways, the opportunities of regionalism and *Land* government have contributed substantially to the stability and adaptability of democracy in the German Federal Republic.

FIVE

the

basic law

of the

Federal Republic

The Basic Law of the German Federal Republic is its Constitution, not in name, but in fact. Its language suggests that it is provisional, and its concluding article 146 says: "This Basic Law loses its validity on the day on which a Constitution comes into effect which has been freely decided upon by the German people." Yet its principles were intended to be permanent, and, with the passage of time, its provisions increasingly have come to be accepted as permanent.

The fundamental decision to organize a democratic and federal German government in the three Western zones of occupation, and to have it based on a written constitution, drafted by a constituent assembly and confirmed by popular ratification, was taken by the Foreign Ministers of the Western powers at their meeting in London in February, 1948. Machinery to carry out this decision was set in motion when the three Military Governors of the Western powers met on June 30, 1948. On the following day, they presented the Ministers President of the German *Lands* with documents empowering them to convene a constituent assembly not later than September 1 of that year, and to consider also modifying the boundaries of the then-existing German states. A third document dealt with the powers which the Allies intended to reserve for themselves until the occupation should be terminated.[1]

The Ministers President objected on the grounds that they wanted to avoid any hardening of the division of Germany, and they "requested that the new political organization should not bear the character of a sovereign state, and that the procedures followed in its creation should distinctly evidence its provisional status." Following joint Allied-German discussion, it finally was agreed that the German conclave would be called the "Parliamentary Council" (rather than Constitutional Convention) and that the constitutive act would be

[1] Elmer Plischke, *Contemporary Government of Germany* (Boston: Houghton Mifflin, 1961), pp. 21–22. Despite its conciseness, this is a particularly well-informed account of legal and administrative aspects of the emergence of the Federal Republic.

called the . . . "Basic Law" rather than . . . "Constitution." [2]

Out of such provisional beginnings came a constitutional document embodying an uncommon wealth of dearly bought historical experience and expert skill. The Parliamentary Council and its committees had at their disposal the advice of a number of constitutional and political experts, including distinguished specialists from the United States. Nevertheless, and despite the expressed wishes of the occupying powers—particularly France—in favor of a more strongly decentralized and federative solution, there emerged a document that was essentially German in conception and content, and that bore the clear marks both of professional skill and of successful resistance to outside interference.[3]

One of the primary motivations of the men who drafted the Basic Law was to correct what were considered the constitutional faults of the Weimar constitution, in the hope of preventing a repeat performance. Unlike the Weimer Republic, the new state created by the Basic Law was to be stable; unlike Bismarck's empire and Hitler's Reich, it was to safeguard the liberty of individuals and groups, and to resist any stampede into dictatorship or aggressive war. It was to be federal so as to resist better any drive toward militarism or dictatorship and so as to win the approval of the *Land* legislatures, which had delegated the members of the Parliamentary Council and which had to ratify the final document.

Accordingly, the Basic Law decentralized particularly the means of state power and persuasion. It left the *Länder* with a substantial part of the bureaucratic machinery of administration and left the federal government dependent on the *Länder* for the execution of most of its own legislation. The *Länder* were to be in control of the police, except for very small federal units that were to be used for special purposes. One such unit is the federal border guard (*Bundesgrenzschutz*), a paramilitary force based on volunteers and stationed along the borders of the G.F.R. Article 12a of the Basic Law determines that these volunteers are exempted from the draft. According to article 115f, the command of the *Bundesgrenzschutz* rests with the federal government, which, in cases of emergency, is empowered to use that force in the entire territory of the Federal Republic—if necessary, even against the will of individual *Länder*.

As far as the realm of competence of the *Länder* is concerned, they have charge of all schools and education and of the bulk of radio and television, for the Basic Law restricted the federal power to matters expressly delegated to the federal government, thus leaving—according to some jurists, by implication—all residual powers to the *Länder*.[4]

At the same time, the Federal Republic, as created by the Basic Law, is better equipped than the Weimar Republic to form and maintain a stable political will, that is to say, to formulate and carry out consistent policies and to make specific decisions in accordance with them. The great powers given to the federal chancellor, including his effective control over the membership of his cabinet; the provision that the chancellor can be ousted from his office by the Bundestag only if the latter can agree on a successor for him—the so-called "constructive vote of no-confidence"—thus preventing purely negative majorities from dismissing a chancellor, as in Weimar days; and the narrow limits set to judicial review of federal laws and of acts of the government—all these tend to concentrate and stabilize the power of legitimate decision making on the federal level. The explicit recognition of political parties in the Basic Law, together with the exclusion by the electoral law of splinter parties (those which fail to receive in any one election either 5% of the national popular vote or a majority in at least three single-member constituencies)

[2] Ibid., p. 22.

[3] Sigmund Neumann, "Germany," in *European Political Systems*, ed., Taylor Cole (New York: Knopf, 1954), p. 351; Alfred Grosser, *Die Bonner Demokratie* (Düsseldorf: Rauch, 1960), p. 59.

[4] Theodor Eschenburg, *Staat und Gesellschaft in Deutschland*, 3d ed. (Stuttgart: Schwab, 1956), pp. 563, 765. Some conservative German jurists disagree and would assign some of the residual powers to the federal government.

from the distribution of seats in the legislature (the so-called exclusion clause), likewise tends to encourage the prevalence of large, powerful parties. Small parties are squeezed out or forced to compromise their differences.

A GERMAN TYPE
OF FEDERALISM

The same goal—to avoid any dangerous concentrations of power, but to facilitate the formation and execution of a single national political will—is also served by the peculiar German variety of federalism which the Basic Law has adopted. The classic concept of federalism in American, British, and British Commonwealth doctrine and practice has its essence in the simultaneous existence of two governments—federal and state—over the same territories and persons, both governments impinging directly upon the same individual but with each claiming sovereign power within its sphere of jurisdiction, subject only to judicial review by the highest court.[5]

The type of federalism developed in Switzerland, later adopted in Germany and Austria, and now revived in the Basic Law is quite different. Here, too, the citizen is subject to two governments, federal and *Land,* but the two are much more closely intermingled. In West Germany, the federal authorities in most matters have a clearly superior position. As a matter of general principle, as would be familiar from American experience, the *Länder* retain the residual powers to legislate about all matters in which the Basic Law itself has not explicitly given exclusive or competing legislative powers to the federal authorities (articles 70–72). With regard to legal practices, the federal institutions are also clearly superior. According to article 99, a *Land* court *may* obtain a decision from the Federal Constitutional Court where litigation results in a conflict over the compatibility of the application of a particular *Land* law with the constitution of that *Land.* Where

litigation produces a conflict over the compatibility of a particular *Land* law with the Basic Law, however, the *Land* court *must* suspend the proceedings and *must* obtain a final ruling on this issue from the Federal Constitutional Court (article 100.1). Thus, the explicit federal powers are very great, and on many important subjects the *Land* administrations serve as the executors of federal laws, guided by federal administrative directions, and under federal supervision (articles 72, 74, 75, 84, 85 of the Basic Law). Substantial spheres of "exclusive" legislation are reserved for the federal government, and the *Länder* may legislate only if empowered by specific federal law (articles 71, 73). In other areas of "concurrent" legislation, the *Länder* may legislate only to the extent that the federal government (called the Federation) does not make use of its own legislative powers (article 72). In these matters, federal law overrides *Land* law (article 31).

The Federation is thus clearly predominant in the area of legislation, while the *Länder* retain the greater part of the administrative tasks and personnel. As long as government and politics remain within the confines of legality and legitimacy, the federal authorities have a clear preponderance of power; in situations of crisis, however, any illegal or illegitimate attempts to establish a dictatorship or to stampede public opinion will encounter a major obstacle in the federal dependence on the administrative cooperation of the *Land* bureaucracies and governments, and the *Land* governments' control of the police forces. This arrangement increases the capabilities of the federal government for legitimate decision making, while providing for strong obstacles in the way of any *coup d'état.*

THE GUIDING VALUES:
HUMAN AND CIVIL RIGHTS

The first paragraph of article 1 of the Basic Law proclaims that the dignity of the individual must not be touched; to respect and protect it is the obligation of every state organ and authority. Article 1 has been interpreted broadly in West German legal thought as implying in itself many of the more specific basic

[5] For the best development of this view, see Kenneth C. Wheare, *Federal Government,* 3d ed. (London: Oxford University Press, 1953).

rights. It thus outlaws all torture or corporal punishment or any physical or mental mistreatment of prisoners (a prohibition made explicit in article 104), such as by excessive deprivation of water or sleep; and it bars similarly the use of "truth drugs" or lie detectors and the use of any evidence obtained with their aid, since all such methods tend to reduce or destroy the freedom of the will—and hence the dignity —of the defendant.[6]

Article 1 is also particularly important because it directs that the basic rights listed thereafter are binding upon all executive and judicial authorities "as immediately valid law." The basic rights are many. They begin with the "free development of one's personality," "life and physical integrity," and "freedom of the person" (article 2). The first of these bars, among other things, any prohibition of writing or painting, such as were imposed upon some artists by the Nazi regime. The second outlaws any sterilization or medical experiments with prisoners—even volunteers, since under the circumstances, their will cannot be considered wholly free.[7]

Further basic rights include equality before the law, equal rights for men and women, and nondiscrimination in regard to sex, descent, race, language, home and origin, or religious or political views (article 3). This provision may have had special importance in barring any preference for local or West German residents as against expellees or refugees. Article 4 guarantees freedoms of religion, of conscience, and of the profession of religious or philosophic views, and the right to refuse armed military service on grounds of conscience. Subsequent legislation and court decisions require that conscientious objectors must refuse to bear arms for any cause, not just refuse to bear arms in the service of some particular policy, and legitimate conscientious objectors may be required to render an equivalent period of civilian service (article 12.2).

Article 5 protects the freedom of opinion, research, and teaching, but adds that "the freedom to teach does not absolve from loyalty to the Basic Law." Article 6 protects marriage and the family; it declares that "the care and education of children is the natural right of their parents," gives "every mother" a claim to protection and care by the community, and provides legitimate and illegitimate children with an equal claim to legislative protection of their social position and opportunities for personal development. The entire language of article 6 shows the great interest and influence of religious groups, both Catholic and Protestant, and of the CDU in all matters of the family and education, with some secondary concessions to the more secular viewpoint represented by the SPD and FDP.

A similar distribution of influence appears in the wording of article 7, which puts all schools under the supervision of the state (i.e., the *Länder,* according to article 70.1). Religious instruction, according to article 7, is to be a regular subject in the public schools, except for the "nondenominational" schools. Wherever it is taught in public schools, religion must be taught according to the principles of the respective churches. The parents decide about the participation of their child in such instruction, and no teacher may be obligated to give religious instruction against his will.

In recent years, the Federal Republic has largely abolished its traditional practice of separating Protestant from Catholic children by assigning them to different schools. Even in subjects like mathematics and reading the teachers had to have the same religious affiliation as the pupils. Today, in most *Länder,* pupils of all denominations are educated in mixed classes. The denominational separation of the classroom prevails only during the periods of religious instruction. The right to open private schools (including parochial schools) is guaranteed by the Basic Law, provided they submit to state supervision, do not fall below the standards of the public schools, do not underpay their teachers, and do not promote a separation of pupils according to income.

[6] Eschenburg, *Staat und Gesellschaft,* pp. 417–19, with reference to the Federal Law of Criminal Procedure of 1950, par. 136a, 1 and 2; and to H. J. Abraham et al., *Kommentar zum Bonner Grundgesetz* (Hamburg: Hansischer Gildenverlag, 1950), art. 1, p. 3.

[7] Eschenburg, *Staat und Gesellschaft,* p. 424, with references.

The Basic Law goes on to guarantee the right of unarmed assembly without prior permission or announcement (article 8) and the right to found organizations (article 9). Here the trade unions get their innings. The right to form economic or occupational interest organizations (such as employers' organizations or labor unions) is guaranteed "for everybody and all occupations." Agreements aimed at limiting or hindering this right are void; measures directed to any such purpose are illegal (article 9.3). Exceptions to the right of assembly are provided in the case of outdoor meetings, which may be regulated by law (article 8.2). Organizations whose goals or activities are criminal or "directed against the constitutional order or the idea of international understanding" are prohibited (article 9.2). The constitutional guarantees of free choice of residence and occupation—particularly valuable to refugees and expellees—have been further enhanced in their importance by the prolonged full employment and the great amount of housing construction in the Federal Republic during the 1950s and 1960s.

The possibility of nationalization of enterprises is explicitly provided for in article 15. Land, natural resources, and means of production may be transformed into common property, or into other patterns of a mixed public-private economy, but only by means of a law which regulates the kind and extent of compensation, with the same legal safeguards as in cases of expropriation under article 14. This article, by implication, guarantees the constitutional legitimacy of socialist aspirations within the democratic order, and of socialist programs and measures, such as those advocated by various socialist groupings and by the SPD prior to its Godesberg program of 1959. This article also provided the constitutional basis for the partial nationalization of the coal mines during the economic crisis of 1966–68.

German citizenship may not be withdrawn in any case. Even involuntary loss of citizenship may only occur on the basis of law and only if the person concerned does not become stateless (article 16.1). No German may be extradited abroad. The politically persecuted have the right of asylum (article 16.2). Article 16 thus insures that even Nazi war criminals, if they are Germans, cannot be extradited to the countries demanding their punishment, but must be dealt with by German courts.

Many constitutional rights may be denied to those who misuse them in order to destroy the democratic system. Those who misuse the freedom of speech or of the press, the freedom to teach, the freedom of assembly or of association, the privacy of letters, mails, and telecommunications, the right of property or of asylum will forfeit these basic rights. This forfeiture and its extent will be declared by the Federal Constitutional Court (article 18). The same court may outlaw political parties "which, according to their aims, or according to the behavior of their adherents, tend to harm or abolish the basic libertarian democratic order, or to endanger the existence of the Federal Republic." This broad language makes parties liable not only for their programs but for the probable or expectable behavior of their followers. This clause is influenced by the memory of the disastrous tolerance of Nazi subversion by the Weimar Republic, and by the ever-present shadow of the Communist dictatorship in the neighboring G.D.R. The provision for the banning of political parties acquired practical significance in the outlawing of the neo-Nazi *Sozialistische Reichspartei* (SRP) in 1952, and the Communist party in 1956.

The basic rights listed in articles 1 through 18 are particularly protected by article 19 against any later amendments that might destroy them. No part of the Basic Law may be amended except by a law passed by two-thirds majorities of the Federal Parliament (article 79.2). Article 19 concludes the section labeled "Basic Rights." Rights and values, which are not protected by article 19, are stated in the remaining sections of the Basic Law. Article 20 fixes the character of the German Federal Republic as a "democratic and social federal state"—a phrase that affirms in the connotations of the German word *sozial* the values of social compassion and of social justice, and that gives special constitutional legitimacy to welfare legislation. The Basic Law further establishes popular sovereignty, representative government, and the separation of powers: "All power of government issues from the people. It is exercised by the people in elections and votes, and through separate organs of legislation, of the executive power, and of the judiciary" (article 20.1–3).

The legislative power is bound by the constitutional order, and the executive and the judiciary are bound by law (article 20.4). No change is permissible in the Basic Law that would infringe upon the principles stated in article 20, those in article 1 (the protection of human dignity and human rights), the division of the Federation into *Länder,* or the principle of the cooperation of the latter in the legislative process (article 79.3). Together with the prohibition in article 19.2 of amendments touching the essential content of any basic right, these are striking and somewhat unusual limitations upon the amending power, which testify to the intense concern and commitment of the drafters of the Basic Law to the future preservation of a constitutional and legal order.

Other rights or values are more specifically stated. Peace is specially protected. Actions which are both "apt and intended to disturb the peaceful coexistence of people, particularly to prepare an aggressive war, are contrary to the Basic Law. They are to be made subject to punishment" (article 26.1). There must be no special courts. No one must be denied trial before a legally appointed judge. Courts for particular subject matters may be established only by law (article 101). The death penalty is abolished (article 102). There may be neither retroactive punishments nor double jeopardy: an action may be punished only if it was legally punishable before it was committed (article 103.2), and no one may be punished on the basis of the general criminal laws more than once for the same action (article 103.3). There is an equivalent to the American right of habeas corpus: personal liberty may be limited only on the basis of law; arrested persons may not be mistreated "physically or mentally." The police may not hold anyone beyond the day after his arrest without his appearing before a judge, who must tell him the charge against him, question him, and give him an opportunity to make objections; the judge then must either order him released or issue a retroactive arrest war-

rant, including reasons; with every judicial order of arrest or continuation of custody, notice must be given without delay to a relative of the arrested person, or to "a person whom he trusts"—such as his lawyer (article 104.1–4).

This constitutional protection of individual civil liberties compares well with similar provisions to be found in the constitutions of the major traditional democracies. Only once, in 1969, have there been discussions about a modification of these legal guarantees. In reaction to frequent student unrest during the crisis years of 1966–69, some conservative forces in the CDU/CSU favored a revision of paragraph 2 of article 104, hoping thereby to attract some voters from the far-right NPD. With the beginning of the 1969 election campaign the CDU/CSU announced on the Bundestag floor that it would like to see article 104.2 amended by a preventive-detention clause. This clause would have empowered the police to hold persons in custody for forty-eight hours merely on the basis of an officer's suspicion that these persons were about to commit offenses against the law (such as disorderly conduct or disturbing the peace). It would have relieved the police of the necessity of obtaining arrest warrants confirming probable cause relating to an actually committed crime. The reluctance on the part of the SPD and the liberal FDP to render their support to such dubious "law-and-order" legislation killed the project in the Bundestag, and the electoral payoff to the CDU/CSU from this issue was not impressive. Since the formation of the Social Democratic-Liberal coalition after the election, the CDU/CSU dropped the issue, and the question of preventive detention has not reappeared in Bundestag debates. The incident might be a small indicator of the beginning consolidation of democratic values in the Federal Republic and of their chance to prevail in the future.

The right to citizenship is regulated in the same spirit. A German, according to the Basic Law and other pending legal regulations, is "anyone who has German citizenship, or who has been received in the territory of Germany within the frontiers of 1937 as a refugee or expellee belonging to the German people, or as his or her spouse or descendant" (article

116.1). Former German citizens, who during the Nazi regime of 1933–45 were deprived of their citizenship for political reasons, must have it restored to them if they claim it. They are deemed not to have been deprived of their citizenship at all if they have taken residence in Germany after May 8, 1945, and have not expressed their will to the contrary (article 116.2). The result of these provisions, as well as of legislation in both the Federal Republic and the G.D.R., is that, "although there are at present two German state executives, two state territories, and two state populations, there is only one German citizenship: no German citizen is a foreigner in either of the two presently existing German state formations." [8] Since far more Germans, whenever they had any effective choice, have preferred to live in the Federal Republic, the almost unprecedentedly generous and farsighted provisions of the Basic Law for their reception as citizens with equal rights, backed by the material opportunities created first by Western economic aid and later by West German economic development, have been of the greatest practical and political significance.

The aggregate of all these rights shows a particular concern for protecting individuals and families, largely by restraining the power of the state. There is no catalog of positive rights, such as the right to work or to housing, even though some rights of this kind are mentioned in some *Land* constitutions. In the ruined and impoverished Germany of 1948, when the Basic Law was drafted, such rights might not have sounded realistic; in the prosperous Federal Republic after the early 1950s, they would have seemed to most voters unnecessary. A legal claim to the minimum of material support necessary to sustain an individual's life and dignity—that is, a basic legal claim to welfare support in distress—can be derived indirectly, however, from articles 1 and 2, and from the characterization in article 20 of the Federal Republic as a "social" state. Similarly, although the right to strike is not explicitly provided in the Basic Law, it is held to be implied in the

freedom to form economic and occupational interest organizations—the so-called "freedom of coalition"—guaranteed by article 9. According to the civil service law, however, civil servants are explicitly excluded from the right to strike. If compared to the situation in the United States, for instance, this provision acquires great political and economic importance. Since, in West Germany, all mail, rail, and telephone services are provided for by government corporations, all employees in those fields have civil servant status. Thus, the German economy is relatively safely protected against strikes disrupting its nervous system, the transportation and communication networks. (Recent United States experience indicates that such prohibitions of strikes may not always work.) The extensive West German social security, labor, and welfare legislation thus lacks specific constitutional protection in its details. The laws of which it consists could all be changed or abolished by simple parliamentary majorities, at least in theory, but the fact that workers and salaried employees together form the great majority of the electorate informally, yet effectively, guarantees their endurance.[9]

The limited goals embodied in the Basic Law are politically realistic, and they accommodate the aspirations of the major parties. They specifically meet the interest of the CDU in religious instruction and in greater power for the *Länder;* the interest of the FDP and CDU in safeguards for private property and enterprise; and the interest of the SPD in labor unions and welfare legislation, in the legitimate possibility of nationalization, and in equal rights for unwed mothers and for nonreligious pupils and teachers. Even the many members of a silent political group, the former members of the Nazi party, the SS elite guard, the Gestapo secret police, and similar organizations of the Hitler period, all find substantial protection in the Basic Law and in the civil and human rights it guarantees. The Basic Law forbids all blanket discrimination against former members of political parties or organizations. Its article 131 opened the way to the return of the large ma-

---

[8] Theodor Maunz, *Deutsches Staatsrecht,* 5th ed. (Munich-Berlin, 1956), p. 27, quoted in Eschenburg, *Staat und Gesellschaft,* p. 383.

[9] Eschenburg, *Staat und Gesellschaft,* pp. 406, 419, 487–90, with references.

jority of former Nazi officials into public service, with the result that out of about 53,000 civil servants removed from office in the Western zones by denazification procedures, only about 1,000 remained permanently excluded through German official action, while most of the rest were gradually taken back into various official agencies.[10]

Fanatical Nazis, to be sure, remained hostile to the constitutional order despite its tolerance, but they were few. In opinion polls, only 6% of the electorate in 1956 still rejected the Basic Law as "not good," while the usual 29% of determined democrats endorsed it; as to the rest, 14% were undecided and 51% professed their ignorance.[11] Since the number of former Nazi voters and adherents has been well above 40%, of whom roughly half were still living in 1956, the poll data suggest that perhaps something like two out of three former Nazis have become reconciled, at least passively, to the system of constitutional government that offered dignity and security to themselves. In this manner, the Basic Law was not only a response to the ideological cleavages within the German people, which we shall survey in the next chapter, but was also an instrument for their modification. It aimed at establishing standards of legality and human rights that gradually won the respect and acceptance of a majority of the electorate, and eventually the support of the majority, particularly the younger generation. The Bundestag took a major step in this direction in 1970 when it lowered the voting age from 21 to 18 years and the right to be elected to public office from 25 to 21 years. This is the result of the twenty-seventh bill of constitutional change, which went into effect on July 31, 1970. It thus modified article 38.2 of the Basic Law, creating an odd legal situation in the Federal Republic. The electoral law, which has been unchanged since 1956, still defines the voting age at 21 years (electoral law, article 12.1) and the minimum age of eligibility for election to public office at 25 years (electoral law, article 16.2). But since no law passed in the Federal Republic may stand in contradiction to the Basic Law, these two clauses of the electoral law are successfully superseded by the Basic Law's revised article 38.2.

Part of the reason for the progressive acceptance of the Federal Republic and its institutions by the majority of its citizens has been due also to such extraconstitutional factors as prolonged economic prosperity and peace, or at least a tolerably low level of international tensions. Another factor in this success, however, has been the efficiency and the actual functioning of the constitutional system which the Basic Law created. For the actual operation of parliamentary government is in very close conformity to the Basic Law, which has helped to legitimize parliamentary democracy; if the provisions of the Basic Law were being disregarded, it would obviously lead the citizens to lose a good deal of respect for the governmental system, and for democracy in general. It is these very governmental institutions and the manner in which they operate that we shall now survey.

THE PREDOMINANCE OF FEDERAL POWERS

In the division of powers between the Federation and the *Länder,* the Federation has the most important powers, even though, as we have seen, the *Länder* under some interpretations of the Basic Law have all the legislative and administrative powers of the state, unless they are explicitly assigned to the federal government (articles 30, 70). The areas of exclusive federal legislation are listed in article 73. They include foreign affairs, defense, federal citizenship, freedom of movement and of internal trade, currency, railroads, mails and telecommunications, and the legal status of federal employees.

Further federal powers are in the area of concurrent legislation, listed in article 74.

---

[10] Arnold J. Heidenheimer, *The Governments of Germany* (New York: Thomas Y. Crowell, 1966), p. 132, with reference to Taylor Cole, "The Democratization of the German Civil Service," *Journal of Politics* 14 (February 1952):7.

[11] Elisabeth Noelle Neumann and Erich Peter Neumann, *Jahrbuch der öffentlichen Meinung* (Allensbach: Verlag für Demoskopie, 1958), 2:165 (hereafter cited as *Jahrbuch*).

These include all civil and criminal law and procedure; the regulation of organizations and assemblies; refugees and expellees; public welfare; war damages and restitution; all economic and labor legislation; nuclear energy; social security and unemployment insurance; expropriation and nationalization; prevention of abuses of economic power; agriculture; real estate and housing; health, physicians, and drugs; shipping, automobiles, and road traffic. In these areas, the *Länder* may legislate only until and insofar as the Federation does not make use of its legislative powers (article 72.1). Concurrent federal legislation is permitted, however, only insofar as there is a need for it: if the matter cannot be regulated effectively by the legislation of single *Länder,* or if such a *Land* law might impair the interests of other *Länder* or of the community at large, or if federal regulation is needed to preserve the legal and economic unity of the Federal Republic, particularly the uniformity of living conditions beyond the territory of a *Land* (article 72.2). Under the same conditions, the Federation may issue general rules (*Rahmenvorschriften*), but the details of implementation must be filled in by *Land* legislation for such matters as the legal status of *Land* and municipal employees, the general legal position of the press and motion pictures, the use of land and water resources, and the identification and registration of the population (article 75).

The Federation guarantees the constitutional order in the *Länder* (article 28.3). Federal law overrides *Land* law (article 30). The *Länder* execute federal laws under their own responsibility, except where the Basic Law itself states or permits otherwise (article 83). The *Länder* organize their own administrations and appoint and promote officials, but the federal government may issue general administrative regulations, and it may supervise the legality of the execution of its laws by the *Land* administrations and may send commissioners to the highest *Land* authorities and, with the consent of the Bundesrat, also to the lower-level ones. Similarly, the federal government may be empowered, by a law passed with the consent of the Bundesrat, to give specific directions to *Land* authorities, even in individual cases (articles 84.1–3, 5).

If a *Land* does not fulfill its obligations under the Basic Law, or under any other federal law, the federal government, with the consent of the Bundesrat, may force it to do so by means of "federal coercion." In carrying out this federal coercion, the federal government or its commissioner has the right to issue directives to any *Land* and its authorities (article 37). Whether a *Land* has violated its legal obligations to carry out a federal law is determined by the Bundesrat, subject to appeal to the Federal Constitutional Court (article 84.4). To ward off a threat to the basic democratic order of the Federation, or of a *Land,* a *Land* may request the services of the police forces of other *Länder;* but if the *Land* in which the danger is threatening is either unready or unwilling to combat it, the federal government may put the police forces of this *Land,* as well as those of other *Länder,* under its own direction. This federal takeover of *Land* police forces must terminate with the end of the danger, or whenever the Bundesrat so requests (article 91). In short, the federal government can do little against any single recalcitrant *Land,* unless most of the other *Länder,* through their representatives in the Bundesrat, support it; with such support, however, its powers are overwhelming.

The distribution of financial resources between the federal government and the *Länder* is specified in the Basic Law (articles 105–15). The list of taxes reserved to the Federation and the *Länder,* respectively, appears in articles 105 and 106. The Federal Republic has thus become probably the only country on earth to enshrine the beer tax in its constitution; article 106.2.5 reserves it to the *Länder,* to the joy, presumably, of the Bavarian representatives. The turnover tax is one of the most important sources of tax revenue. It is calculated on the basis of 11.5% of the value added to a good or service at its different stages in the economic exchange process. This turnover tax—popularly called the "added-value" tax (*Mehrwertsteuer*)—is federal, but the local municipalities have claim to a share of that tax proportional to the population under their administration. In 1969, this tax yielded 32% of all federal revenues.

The yield of income and corporation taxes —which totaled only 24% of federal revenues in 1969—has to be divided between the Federation and the *Länder.* Between 1956 and 1969, the ratio had been 38:62, according to article 106.3 of the Basic Law. In May 1969, articles 105–8 were revised. Since then, the federal and *Land* share of those taxes is dependent on the population of each *Land.* This measure ensures a more equitable distribution of tax revenue among both the richer industrial and poorer agricultural *Länder.* The details of the financial arrangements in the Basic Law and related legislation are very complex, but in one respect the rules are relatively simple: the Federation has legal control over all taxes, except local ones.[12] In the general setting of financial policy and in the conduct of the predominant part of financial practice, the federal controls, direct and indirect, are decisive.

The outcome of the system is that taxes are collected in the proportion 60%/25%/15% by the Federation, the *Länder,* and the municipalities, respectively. Since a part of the funds collected by the federal government is transferred for spending to the *Länder* and municipalities, the actual expenditures at these three levels of government approximate the ratio 41%/33%/26%. The federal share in total government revenues is thus significantly lower than in the United States.[13]

THE BUNDESTAG

The main agency of federal legislation is the Federal Parliament, or *Bundestag,* established under articles 38–49 of the Basic Law. According to the Electoral Law of 1957, half its members are elected from 247 single-member

constituencies by simple majorities or pluralities of the "first votes" cast by the voters in each district for the individual candidate of their choice. The other half are elected from party lists of candidates in each *Land,* by proportional representation in accordance with the share of their parties in the "second votes" cast by all voters at the same elections for the party of their preference. The outcome is a distribution of seats in fairly close accordance with proportional representation, but at the same time, the electorate's choice of individual candidates acts to personalize proportional representation, which otherwise usually involves voting for party lists rather than individuals.

In attempting to "democratize" the parties' internal organization by imitating the American primary and convention system, the electoral law provides that list candidates be nominated by assemblies of party members elected for that purpose in each *Land* and individual candidates by similar assemblies in each of the 247 constituencies. Although constituency nominations are subject to an understanding between local and *Land* or federal party organizations, in law as well as in reality the local organization has the last word.[14]

Only those parties may obtain seats from this distribution according to party lists which win at least 5% of the valid votes cast in the entire Federal Republic, or whose candidates win majorities or pluralities in at least three single-member districts. This "exclusion clause" eliminates most splinter and regional parties. Each of the remaining parties is entitled to its proportionate quota of seats. The difference between this proportionate quota and the number of seats a party won directly in the single member constituencies is filled in with candidates from the party list. If a party wins more than its proportionate quota of direct seats, however, it retains these "overhang mandates," so that the final number of Bundestag deputies is usually slightly higher than twice the number of single-member districts. Thus, the Sixth Bundestag, elected in 1969, had 496 members, not counting

[12] Eschenburg, *Staat und Gesellschaft,* p. 630, with references.

[13] Tax collection ratios for the Federal Republic from Heidenheimer, *Governments of Germany,* p. 148; spending ratios computed from data in Table 4-14. Here, as everywhere in this study, the city-states of Hamburg and Bremen have been considered as *Länder,* in accordance with their legal and political position. A somewhat higher federal share in total government spending—60%, including nearly 5% derived from the "equalization of burdens" program—is given in Plischke, *Contemporary Government of Germany,* p. 115, and contrasted with 40% in the empire before 1914, and 70% during the last years of the Weimar Republic.

[14] Gerhard Loewenberg, "Parliamentarism in Western Germany: The Functioning of the Bundestag," *American Political Science Review* 15, no. 1 (March 1961): 88.

the 22 nonvoting members from West Berlin.[15] The size and political composition of the six Bundestags elected between 1949 and 1969 are given in Table 5-1.

A further legal provision that favors the development of large parties is contained in the Party Law of 1967, which was slightly modified in 1969. The Party Law is composed of the legal definitions of the constitutional position of a party (article 1), its legal nature (articles 2–5), its democratic structure and internal functioning (articles 6–17), and its rights and duties in the political process (articles 23–41). The content of the Party Law consists of its formal acceptance and legal protection of the party as an agent mediating between the political electorate and the political decision-making process in the institutions designed for that purpose by the Basic Law.

The politically most important part of the 1967 Party Law, however, is the set of regulations concerning federal funding of general election campaigns (articles 18–22). The impact of this law changed nearly two decades of German politics, for the new law requires that the federal government include in its budget of each general-election year a factor of 2.50 DM (about 70 cents) per citizen of voting age. This sum is then distributed among the competing parties according to the number of votes they received in the previous general election. Thus, a party which did well four years ago has more money to spend this year than a party that did worse, independent of the present popularity of either group. This law reduced greatly the dependence of parties on financing by outside interest groups, such as big business and industry in the case of the CDU/CSU and the FDP, and the labor unions in the case of the SPD. It increased particularly the independence of the FDP, and it may have facilitated in 1969 the decision of the latter to join the SPD in the national government headed by Chancellor Willy Brandt. At the same time, however, critics have pointed out that this form of party financing by public funds prevents change and has a stabilizing,

system-maintaining effect, because it perpetuates the publicity of the bigger parties by providing the financial resources for their public relations activities, whereas, at the same time, it makes it harder for smaller or new parties, which are normally financially weak, to find broad attention among the electorate. The Party Law of 1967 actually reinforces and protects the existing "two-and-a-half-party system," and, by the same token, erects strong barriers against the proliferation of new parties and splinter groups on the basis of mere political propaganda and agitation.

The figures in Table 5-1 show that minor parties have been effectively eliminated, but that—except for the brief period of the "grand Coalition"—no two-thirds majority, required for changes in the Basic Law, can be formed in the Bundestag without the support of members of the Opposition.

Bundestag deputies are elected by general, direct, free, equal, and secret vote, according to article 38 of the Basic Law, but the electoral procedure can be, and has been, changed by ordinary federal law. According to the same article, the deputies are not subject to directions by anyone. In fact, however, the tradition of party discipline, the power of the parties over the placing of candidates in electoral districts and on *Land* lists, together with the need for funds to meet the costs of campaigning, have made the votes and actions of Bundestag members highly predictable.

Cases of defiance of important party orders by a deputy are rare. The exclusion clause would make his reelection as an independent practically impossible, and his chances to found a new party strong enough to surmount its requirements are remote. Moreover, the great majority of voters demand trustworthy party labels more than strong personalities, just as many housewives prefer well-known brand names to the wares of less-well-known individual tradesmen.[16]

All the Bundestag members of each individual party (its parliamentary delegation or *Frak-*

15 For a good account of the various stages of West German electoral legislation, see Plischke, *Contemporary Government of Germany*, pp. 69–71, 157–63.

16 In a 1953 survey, only 4% of all voters mentioned the personality of the district candidate as a reason for their vote. See Wolfgang Hirsch-Weber and Klaus Schütz, *Wähler und Gewählte* (Berlin: Vahlen, 1957), p. 345.

TABLE 5-1. *Party Representation in the Bundestag, 1949–71*

	1949	1953	1957	1961	CDU/ FDP Coalition 1965–66	CDU/ SPD Coalition 1966–68	SPD/ FDP * Coalition 1969–
Small rightist opposition groups	26	3	0	0	0	0	0
Potential government coalition parties:							
DP	17	15	17	0	0	0	0
CDU/CSU	139	243	270	242	245	245	242
Refugee party	0	27	0	0	0	0	0
FDP	52	48	41	67	49	49	30
Potential opposition (1949–71)							
Small center-left groups	22	0	0	0	0	0	0
SPD	131	151	169	190	202	202	224
Communists	15	0	0	0	0	0	0
Total left opposition	*168*	*151*	*169*	*190*	*202*	*0*	*0*
Actual government coalition	*208*	*333*	*328*	*309*	*294*	*447*	*254*
Total voting numbers	402	487	497	499	496	496	496

SOURCE: Plischke, *Contemporary Government of Germany*, p. 71; *Archiv der Gegenwart* (Bonn) 31, no. 40 (October 10, 1961):9371C; Heidenheimer, *Governments of Germany*, p. 113; and Lewis Edinger, "Political Change in Germany," *Comparative Politics* 2, no. 4 (July 1970).

* In 1970, the voting strength of the government coalition decreased by three votes, due to the fact that three deputies of the FDP (among them former party chairman and Vice-Chancellor Erich Mende) left their party in opposition to the coalition with the Social Democrats. All three joined the *Fraktion* of the CDU. Thus, the present ratio of voting strength between government and opposition in the Bundestag is 251:245.

tion) meet frequently, for it is in these meetings that the important decisions regarding voting strategies are taken. The *Fraktionen* determine the general positions that the party deputies will take on pending legislation, going over the Bundestag agenda point by point and taking positions on each one, even going so far as to determine the public arguments and the speakers to be used to express their positions. The decisions taken in these party meetings effectively bind both the words and the votes of the deputies in the Bundestag. Thus, in the First and Second Bundestags, there was 99.8% cohesion among the CDU/CSU deputies, and 94.5% cohesion among the SPD deputies.[17] Which is to say that party discipline is nearly

[17] Loewenberg, "Parliamentarism in Western Germany," p. 95, and the references cited there.

perfect, the overwhelming majority of the deputies voting together as a block on all but a minuscule number of rollcall votes.

The Bundestag determines when to end and reopen its sessions. Its president may call it into session earlier, and he must do so if the federal president, or the chancellor, or one-third of the members demand it (article 39.3). A Permanent Committee is provided by the Basic Law to watch over the interests of the Bundestag during the intervals between two electoral periods (article 45). Two other committees, on foreign affairs and on defense, were provided by constitutional amendment in 1956 (article 45a). The Permanent Committee and the Defense Committee also have the rights of investigating committees; that is, they may gather evidence and proofs, by procedures analogous to those of general criminal procedure, including the power to compel testimony. Special investigating committees, on any matter other than defense, must be set up whenever one-fourth of the members of the Bundestag demand it. These committees have the same rights and procedures in regard to evidence and testimony. Their proceedings are public, unless a majority of the committee members vote to make a session confidential (article 44), which they usually do. Since their composition is proportionate to the strength of the parties in the Bundestag, any strong Opposition—e.g., the CDU—can compel the setting up of an investigating committee, even on a subject embarrassing to the government; but the majority of the members of the government coalition on the committee may control much of the proceedings, as well as the language of the majority report, leaving the Opposition to make its points by bringing out particular items of evidence and perhaps by issuing a minority report.

Most of the work of the Bundestag is done in committee, to a greater extent even than is the case in the United States Congress. There are seventeen regular committees in the Sixth Bundestag, each dedicated to some special subject area, from the immunity of deputies and the verification of their mandates to cultural policy, economic policy, questions of German reunification and Berlin, and "atomic energy questions." [18] Each committee has between fifteen and thirty-one members, many of whom have been selected by their parties with an eye to their expert knowledge in the area of the committee's jurisdiction. Deputies are paid also for their attendance at committee sessions, as well as at sessions of their *Fraktion* (parliamentary party delegation). At the same time, the Bundestag has gone further than the British, French, and United States legislatures in delegating much of its work to committees. It has usually held only about fifty-five plenary meetings, but for every one it also held "no less than twenty committee and nine party meetings." [19]

The power of these committees and their members, however, is weaker vis-à-vis the executive than is the case in the United States. Fixed party positions and tight party discipline rarely leave much scope for individual committee members, except for the influence which these persons gain through their special concern and expertise. Moreover, since committee meetings ordinarily are secret, they cannot be turned easily into instruments for publicity for particular deputies or interests. Each committee may require the presence of any cabinet member at its meetings, and cabinet members and civil servants also have their own right of access to committee meetings at any time (article 43). In contrast to United States congressional committees, the Bundestag committees have neither adequate professional experts and staffs of their own nor the aid of an adequate legislative reference service, so that many committee members, despite their experience and partial specialization, often find it difficult to maintain their views against those of the cabinet ministers, which are bolstered by the expert testimony of the civil servants on their staffs. It is estimated, however, that about half the deputies have some expert help and secretarial assistance available through the offices of interest groups in Bonn.

The chief officer of the Bundestag is its president, who is elected by secret ballot but is taken, in fact, from the strongest party. Three vice-presidents are elected by the chamber in the same manner; they are taken from the remaining parties, more or less in order of their strength. A Council of Elders, composed of these officers, together with other representatives of the parliamentary party delegations, is in theory only an advisory committee to the president of the Bundesrat, but is in practice a very important body, somewhat comparable in its power to the Rules Committee of the House of Representatives in the United States. The

[18] For brief discussions of the committee system, see Eschenburg, *Staat und Gesellschaft*, pp. 549–53, with a list of committees; Grosser, *Die Bonner Demokratie*, pp. 93–95; Heidenheimer, *Governments of Germany*, pp. 111–12.

[19] Gerhard Loewenberg, *Parliament in the German Political System* (Ithaca, N.Y.: Cornell University Press, 1967), pp. 135, 404, with reference to comparative statistics in "Wie die Parlamente tagen," *Das Parlament* (December 12, 1960), p. 11.

chairmen of all other committees are not elected but are appointed in effect by the Council of Elders, which also schedules the debates on particular items of legislation—sometimes only one hour of plenary session for an important law—and allocates the times and order of speaking to the various parties and speakers.

The major sources of power and action in the Bundestag are the aforementioned *Fraktionen,* or parliamentary party delegations, which are recognized by the rules of procedures for every party having at least fifteen deputies— another device to discourage splinter groups and minor parties. Only parties strong enough to form a *Fraktion* are represented on committees, may count on being assigned speaking time in plenary debates, may effectively initiate bills, direct parliamentary inquiries to the government—in short, take an effective part in the work of the Bundestag. After every election since 1961, there have been, as shown in Table 5-1, only three *Fraktionen:* those of the CDU/ CSU, the SPD, and the FDP. The Bavarian Christian Social Union (CSU), however, received separate representation on the committees and study groups within the joint CDU/ CSU *Fraktion.*[20]

Each of these three *Fraktionen* works somewhat like a small parliament. In the meetings of each party delegation, which are similar to the caucuses of parties in the legislatures in the United States, the delegations debate and decide whether to support or oppose some particular bill, or to demand modifications in it. Individual deputies may vote for or against the proposed policies in the closed meeting of their *Fraktion,* but once a policy has been adopted for the entire party delegation by majority vote, all deputies are expected to support it and to vote for it in the plenum. Thus, a bill endorsed originally only by a minority of deputies who form, however, the majority of one or two party delegations could become law through the working of party discipline within each delegation. Since the party delegations themselves are very large, power within them has largely shifted to

their executive committees, composed of about two dozen particularly influential deputies. In the SPD and CDU/CSU, power rests with inner executive committees of four or five deputies.

The leadership groups of each of the *Fraktionen,* and subsequently the entire *Fraktionen,* meet before every major decision or debate of the Bundestag in order to set their policy, usually in concert with the leadership of their party outside the Bundestag. Since the parliamentary leadership group is also, as a rule, heavily represented on the national committee of their party, conflicts between national parties and their parliamentary delegations are rare. Together with the decisions of the cabinet—and primarily of the chancellor—it is the decisions of these leadership groups of the parliamentary and national parties that have the greatest influence on what happens in the Bundestag, even though many details of legislation are still modified by the suggestions of the civil servants and the political give-and-take of the legislative process in the Bundestag committees.

Deputies have the usual privileges and immunities, but they are not exempt from responsibility for "slanderous insults" (article 46.1). They may be arrested or prosecuted only with the permission of the Bundestag or if they are arrested in the act of committing a punishable offense or within a day thereafter; if the Bundestag so requests, however, they must be released at once, and all criminal proceedings against them stopped (article 46.2–4). They may refuse to name or testify about any persons they have received any information from as legislators or about the content of such information; within this area of privileged communication, no documents may be seized (article 47).

Bundestag members are only moderately well paid—far less so than their colleagues in France or the United States, where national legislators are paid roughly on the scale of the top levels of the civil service in each country. Presently, Bundestag deputies receive a basic annual salary of about $11,000, which amounts to exactly one-third of the salary of a cabinet minister. In addition, a Bundestag deputy receives about $11,700 for various expenses, but

[20] For this practice during the 1950s, see Eschenburg, *Staat und Gesellschaft*, p. 534.

GERMANY

as travel and secretarial assistance. From this they have to pay certain amounts to their parties (more heavily so in the case of the deputies of the SPD), leaving them a net income of about $13,600 per year.[21]

By the mid-1960s, the Bundestag and its members had come some distance in establishing themselves as respected members of the political system. On the other hand, the evidence indicates that there is still a good distance to travel before the Bundestag becomes highly valued by the great majority of West Germans. The growing extent to which the population trusts the deputies is seen in the responses to a question asking whether the deputies primarily represent the people or whether there are other interests which are more important to them. Between 1951 and 1958 the proportion of West Germans who said the deputies were primarily concerned with the people's interests rose from 25% to 41%. There has been a similar increase in the proportion of West Germans who believe that individuals must have great competence to become deputies; in 1951, 39% answered in this manner, rising to 61% in 1961. Annual polls were also taken which asked the following question: "What do you think of the Bundestag in Bonn as our representative assembly?" Between 1951 and 1965, the proportion replying that it was doing an excellent or a basically good job increased from 35% to 52%; the proportion who said that it was doing a fair job remained fairly constant at about 34%.[22]

While such trends seem to augur well for the future, it should be noted that this growing respect for the Bundestag has perhaps not struck very deep roots. For one thing, over 85% of the population has not heard anything about the activities of their own deputies—a proportion that has not changed since 1951. Nor are the West Germans likely to try to influence

their deputies—directly or through the press—when they have a grievance. In 1959 only 12% of the West Germans said that they would attempt to influence a national decision through their legislative representatives, compared to 44% of the British and 57% of the Americans. Furthermore, the positive evaluation of the Bundestag has fluctuated as much as 19% from one year to the next. And when it is also noted that there is a close association between such a positive evaluation and the individual's preference for one of the governing parties at the time, it suggests that the West Germans' respect for the Bundestag is not based on deep-seated attachments, as is the case in Britain, for example. Thus, not only democratic values in general, but also respect for the national legislature has yet to strike deep roots, even though the attachments were stronger in the mid-1960s than during the Weimar Republic and the first decade of the Bonn republic.[23]

THE BUNDESRAT

The second branch of the federal legislature—the council of *Länder,* or *Bundesrat*—is even less well known. In repeated polls, the proportion of West Germans who knew at least roughly "what the Bundesrat is here for," inched up slowly from a mere 8% in 1951 to a still feeble 14% in 1956.[24] Nevertheless, the Bundesrat is a coordinate branch of the federal legislature and has a significant share in the legislative process, as well as considerable powers in emergencies.

The Bundesrat is the specific organ through which the *Land* governments cooperate in federal legislation and administration (article 50 of the Basic Law). It is composed of members of the *Land* governments—that is, ordinarily of ministers—even though these in turn are represented at many meetings by high-ranking officials of their ministries. The ministers do not serve, however, as individual deputies, but as members of the delegation of their *Land,* which must vote as a unit (article 51.3). Each

21 Letter from Ernst Paul, member of the Bundestag, to the author, November 14, 1963, and Loewenberg, *Parliament,* pp. 48–52. For rates in 1972, consult *Bundesministergesetz,* article 8, section 11. See also "Vom Segen, Minister zu sein" in *Capital,* October 1971, Hamburg.

22 EMNID, *Informationen,* cited in Loewenberg, *Parliament,* pp. 45, 47, 429.

23 Loewenberg, *Parliament,* pp. 426–30; Gabriel A. Almond and Sidney Verba, *The Civic Culture* (Princeton: Princeton University Press, 1965), pp. 225–27.

24 *Jahrbuch,* 2:280.

Land has at least three votes; *Länder* with more than 2 million inhabitants have four votes, and *Länder* with over 6 million inhabitants have five votes (article 51.2). The 1965 distribution of *Land* votes in the Bundesrat was shown in Table 4-12. If a *Land* is governed by a coalition of several parties, the entire vote of its delegation is cast as a unit in accord with an agreement of the member parties, usually following the views of the strongest party, which usually is also that of the *Land* prime minister. Bundesrat decisions require at least a majority of its constituent votes, so that abstention from voting on a proposal is equivalent to voting to reject it (article 52.3). Most of the Bundesrat's work is done by fourteen committees; on these, other members of *Land* governments, or their deputies, such as civil servants from *Land* administrations, may serve. Members of the federal government have the right and, if requested, the duty to attend any meeting of the Bundesrat or its committees (article 53).

The Bundesrat has a share in all federal legislation. For constitutional amendments, a two-thirds majority of Bundesrat votes is required, just as it is of Bundestag members. About half of the remaining legislation is composed of the "federative" or "consent" laws—perhaps something like sixty bills a year. These are all the laws for which Bundesrat consent is explicitly required by the Basic Law. Thanks to a successful broad interpretation of the Basic Law by the Bundesrat, all federal legislation which is to be carried out by the *Länder* and which thus has implications for their administrative institutions and procedures must also be approved by the Bundesrat. For all other bills, the Bundesrat has a suspensive veto, which the Bundestag may override by simple majority. If the Bundesrat's rejection of the bill was by a two-thirds majority, however, a similar two-thirds majority in the Bundestag is required to override the veto (article 77.4).[25]

For any kind of bill, the Bundesrat may require, within two weeks after its receipt from the Bundestag, that it be submitted to a joint coordinating committee of the two chambers, composed of eleven members of the Bundesrat, one for each *Land*, and an equal number of Bundestag members. In the case of "consent" legislation, the Bundestag itself, as well as the federal government, may also invoke the procedure before the joint coordinating committee (article 77.2).

During the First Bundestag period, 1949–53, when 805 bills were initiated—472 by the federal government, 301 by the Bundestag, and 32 by the Bundesrat—the joint coordinating committee was invoked seventy-five times. Of these seventy-five cases, seventy-three ended by compromise; the Bundesrat cast three suspensive vetoes and was overridden by the Bundestag twice. Of the many bills requiring its consent, the Bundesrat vetoed six; of these, two were passed by it later in amended form, and four failed permanently.[26] The power of the Bundesrat is reflected, not in the few vetoes it cast, but in the many compromises which it forces on the Bundestag in the joint conference committee, and in the extent of substantive changes which it thus imposed on the original draft legislation.

Unlike the Bundestag, the Bundesrat also has considerable powers in the area of administration. Its consent is required for all administrative ordinances of the federal government that are based on "consent" laws, or on the basis of laws which the *Länder* are required to execute as agents of the federal government, or that regulate the tariffs or conditions of use of the federal railroads, mails, and telecommunications.[27]

The role of the Bundesrat is still more significant in emergencies, or in cases of conflict between the federal government and a *Land*, or between different branches of the government. Bundesrat consent is required for the initiation of federal coercion against any *Land* that fails to fulfill its legal obligations (article 37), and the Bundesrat alone is competent to determine in the first place that such a failure on the part of a *Land* to meet its obligations has occurred

25 For details, see Plischke, *Contemporary Governments of Germany*, pp. 82–83; and Eschenburg, *Staat und Gesellschaft*, pp. 562–63, 620–22; Loewenberg, *Parliament*, pp. 266–67, 365–66.

26 From data in Grosser, *Die Bonner Demokratie*, p. 88; and Eschenburg, *Staat und Gesellschaft*, p. 622.

27 Article 80.2; and Eschenburg, *Staat und Gesellschaft*, p. 622.

(article 84.4). The consent of the Bundesrat is also essential for the proclamation of a "legislative emergency" by the federal president, in the case of a deadlock between the chancellor and a negative majority in the Bundestag, and for the enactment of legislation during its duration. The federal government, without the consent of the Bundesrat, may put *Land* police forces under its orders to combat a danger threatening the existence of constitutional order of the Federal Republic or of any of the *Länder;* but any such emergency measure must be rescinded whenever the Bundesrat demands it (article 91.2).

The Bundesrat has important assets to meet its tasks. Its members usually are ministers in the cabinets of their *Länder,* and its president—elected for one year and taken by custom in rotation each time from a different *Land*—is usually the prime minister of his *Land.* They thus have considerable status and prestige, and since the ministers can draw upon the technical advice of the expert staffs of the *Land* bureaucracies, they also command a good deal of technical competence.

These assets have brought their temptations. Over the years, the Bundesrat has become increasingly inclined to play down its political and straight legislative role, and rather to stress the technical and administrative aspects of its activities. In practice, this tactic of disguising political wishes or objections in the cloak of technical concerns is said to have been quite effective. Technical arguments thus seem to lend more strength to a proposed course of action than do political ones; and this fact testifies in its own way to a significant trend throughout West German politics: the increasing weight of administrative and bureaucratic considerations and the growing power of the federal executive.

THE CHANCELLOR

The *federal chancellor* holds the most important office in the Federal Republic. In effect, he appoints and dismisses all members of the federal cabinet, since his proposals are binding on the president of the republic, who has the formal power of their appointment and dismissal (article 64 of the Basic Law). Informally, the political parties whose deputies are to elect him to his office may stipulate in their agreement of coalition that certain ministerial portfolios should be given to certain individuals or to members of certain parties, but once the chancellor is appointed, the parties have no effective control over his appointment policies, short of threatening to bring down the government by electing a new chancellor.

The chancellor has the power and the responsibility to determine the guidelines of public policy (article 65). His virtual subordinate, the federal minister of defense, is commander in chief of the armed forces in peacetime, but as soon as the "case of defense"—that is, war or warlike emergency—is declared, the supreme command of all forces is vested in the chancellor himself (article 65a, added in 1956). This declaration is made by the Bundestag or, in the case of emergency, by the president of the republic, with the countersignature of the chancellor (article 59a). Unlike the president of the republic, the chancellor cannot be impeached; if a law bearing the required signatures of the chancellor and president were found illegal, only the latter would be subject to possible impeachment.[28]

The chancellor has the "competence to determine competence" within the general framework of constitutional provisions—that is, he can assign the jurisdiction of the different ministries, create new ones, or change their organization. He has the main effective control over personnel policies in the federal government.

There are three ways in which a chancellor may be elected by the Bundestag: (1) nomination by the president of the republic and by the votes of the majority of the members of the Bundestag; (2) in case of the failure of the presidential nominee to win such a majority, someone else may be elected chancellor two weeks later by a majority of the Bundestag members; (3) if no candidate has been elected within those two weeks, another Bundestag vote must be taken at once, in which that candidate is elected chancellor who gets the largest number of votes, even short of a majority. If

---

[28] Eschenburg, *Staat und Gesellschaft,* pp. 634–35.

the chancellor has been elected by such a mere plurality, the president of the republic must appoint him within seven days or else dissolve the Bundestag and thus bring about national elections of a new legislature (article 63).

Once elected and appointed, the chancellor is very likely to remain in office for the entire four-year period of the Bundestag. A hostile majority of Bundestag members can oust him only by a "constructive vote of no-confidence" —that is, by electing another chancellor, whom the president of the republic is then obligated to appoint (article 67). If the Bundestag returns a plain vote of no-confidence against the chancellor, without electing a successor, the chancellor may remain in office or else the president of the republic, if the chancellor so requests, may dissolve the Bundestag within twenty-one days and thus bring about new elections (article 68).

As long as a recalcitrant majority of the Bundestag cannot agree on a successor to the chancellor, the latter under certain conditions could govern quite effectively against it. German legislatures traditionally have not had a "power of the purse" comparable to that held by legislators in English-speaking countries. Even if the Bundestag should fail to vote a federal budget for the coming year, the federal tax laws would continue to operate until they are specifically repealed, and the federal government would be entitled to collect taxes and other legal income, to continue to spend public funds in order to meet all obligations, to maintain all institutions based on existing laws, and to continue to perform all tasks for which any amounts have been voted in earlier budgets. In addition to its continuing sources of income, the federal government in such a case also has automatic authority to borrow for such purposes up to one-quarter of the total amount of the last preceding budget (article 111). The Bundestag always retains control, however, over new federal credits and guarantees that are to extend beyond a single fiscal year, for these must always be based on a federal law (article 115).[29]

The chancellor may even bring about the enactment of federal legislation against the will of a hostile but divided Bundestag. If he has been defeated on an important bill, but not removed from office by the election of a successor, and if the Bundestag has not been dissolved by the president, the latter, on the motion of the federal government and with the consent of the Bundesrat, may declare a "state of legislative emergency" and have the bill pass into law in the form proposed by the federal government, insofar as it has been approved by the Bundesrat (article 81.1–2). For a six-month period from the first declaration of such a state of legislative emergency, the chancellor during his term of office may also cause any other legislative proposal of his government to be enacted in this manner, if it has been turned down by the Bundestag. Only the Basic Law may not be changed or suspended, wholly or partly, by such emergency procedures (article 81.3–4).

Together, and under favorable political and economic conditions, all these provisions tend to make even a weak chancellor strong, and a fairly strong chancellor a great deal stronger. His initial strength depends on his position in his own party and on the strength of that party, or on the strength and stability of the coalition of parties that back him. In time, however, if his administration is successful, particularly if it is further aided by economic prosperity and a favorable international climate, then the continuing concentration of power and publicity in his person will tend to make him a commanding figure in the nation.

Thus, Konrad Adenauer, a moderately well-known regional leader of the Catholic Center party in pre-Hitler days and long-time mayor of Cologne, was elected chancellor by a slight margin in the Bundestag of 1949, by 202 votes out of 402, but was re-elected with much larger majorities in 1953, 1957, and 1961. During his early years in office, opinion polls showed his popularity trailing behind that of his party, the CDU, but from 1952 on, Adenauer's popularity began to lead that of the CDU, and the party's 1957 electoral campaign exploited this personal leadership appeal with

[29] On the whole problem of budgetary powers, see ibid., pp. 584–91.

great success.[30] In November 1961, poll results showed that 50% of the voters still preferred that the 85-year-old Adenauer remain as Chancellor, either for a limited period (26%), or indefinitely (24%), at a time when the national vote for the CDU in the September 1961 elections had dropped to 45%.[31]

But in 1963, Adenauer's "mild feudal rule" as a "bourgeois emperor" had become more difficult and after months of expectancy, Adenauer realized that he had lost his firm grip over his CDU disciples, and consequently resigned from the chancellorship. Despite Adenauer's negative feelings toward Minister of Economics and Vice-Chancellor, Professor Ludwig Erhard, and his numerous attempts to prevent him from succeeding to the chancellorship, Erhard took over the reins of government in October 1963. He was elected by a clear majority of the Bundestag, despite the fact that twenty-four of his nominal CDU and FDP supporters abstained.

At the outset, it appeared as if Erhard would retain his position for a long time to come, while continuing to dominate the Bundestag as Adenauer had done. Erhard's preeminent position was based upon his great popularity with the voters, leaving the CDU deputies little choice but to support him. Thus, "chancellor democracy" continued after Adenauer. Erhard sometimes acted without the cabinet's approval, remained beyond the Bundestag's day-to-day control (although he was more cordial to deputies than Adenauer was), and he played the most prominent role in the 1965 Bundestag election—the contest being viewed largely as one between two men, Erhard and Willy Brandt, the leader of the SPD.

Erhard's experience showed that the German political system allows the chancellor to exercise strong and independent leadership, but only as long as the chancellor has the support of the country and his party—a situation that is very close to that of a British prime minister.

Erhard, however, soon was to lose this support. The electorate became somewhat disenchanted with him when it became apparent that he was not as authoritative a figure as Adenauer, which left them with a mild feeling of insecurity and dissatisfaction, allowing rival party leaders and party dissidents (who thought he was not sufficiently "European"—i.e., favorable toward European integration) to assert themselves. Erhard's political style allowed for open competition among competing policies and individuals until a consensus appeared, rather than attempting to force his own views upon the cabinet. Nor did Erhard build up a coterie of supporters in the cabinet and the party that were loyal to him, as Adenauer had done. In the words of one writer: "Possibly no major government leader has taken less advantage of the patronage power inherent in his office." [32] Erhard's popularity was further undermined when, as the German economy began to lose steam in 1965–66 during the early stages of the coal crisis, which we discussed already in Chapter 3, he appeared to be unwilling to take any decisive remedial action, in seeming contrast to his earlier years, when he had built his reputation upon his direction of the "economic miracle." Moreover, Adenauer's direct and indirect public attacks upon him further undermined his position, despite the fact that Adenauer was violating the rules of party solidarity. Thus, between August 1964 and August 1966, the number of Germans who held a positive opinion of Erhard declined from 85% to 48%.[33]

In November 1966, after Erhard's resignation, the CDU/CSU deputies elected Kurt Georg Kiesinger as the new chancellor by an

[30] See the opinion data given in Deutsch and Edinger, *Germany Rejoins the Powers*, pp. 65–66, with references; for important additional data, see Kitzinger, *German Electoral Politics*, pp. 104–5, and E. Faul et al., *Wahlen und Wähler in Westdeutschland* (Villigen, 1960), pp. 89 ff.

[31] DIVO Institut für Wirtschaftsforschung, Sozialforschung und angewandte Mathematik, *Bundestagswahl*, 1961, Repräsentativumfrage 326, Repräsentativerhebung no. 322, July 1961; no. 323, September 1961; no. 326, November-December 1961; Frankfurt, 1961 (henceforth cited as DIVO 322, 323, and 326, respectively). The data cited are from DIVO 326, p. 15, Q.C. 36. The authors are indebted to Prof. Erwin Scheuch of the University of Cologne for making these materials available.

[32] Heidenheimer, *Governments of Germany*, p. 124.
[33] DIVO, *Pressedienst*, November 1966.

absolute majority. Kiesinger had been a member of the Nazi party from 1933 to 1945, and an official in the Nazi government during World War II, responsible for some of its propaganda efforts directed at the Allies. He appears to have become disenchanted with the Nazis, however, since the mid-1930s, and during the war he was accused of "sabotaging" some of the anti-Semitic policies of the regime. After the war, Kiesinger joined the CDU, was elected to the Bundestag, and later became chairman of the Bundestag's Foreign Affairs Committee. He had resigned this post in 1958 in order to become the chief minister of Baden-Württemberg, where he made a good democratic record as leader of a coalition government.

Since the Free Democrats had recently left the federal government, leaving the CDU/CSU without an absolute majority in the Bundestag, Kiesinger's first decisions revolved around the formation of another coalition government. After a month of negotiations with the Free Democrats and the Social Democrats, a broadly based coalition government was formed with the latter. As leader of the SPD, Willy Brandt—a veteran of the anti-Nazi underground who in World War II had fought against Hitler's Germany as a member of the Norwegian armed forces—became vice-chancellor and foreign minister. Even the breach among the "European" and "American" factions of the Christian Democrats seemed at least temporarily resolved, with the leader of the "European" faction, Franz-Joseph Strauss, returning as finance minister.

The resignations of Adenauer and Erhard indicate that the chancellor's powerful position is ultimately dependent upon the electorate's evaluations and the confidence of his party's deputies. But given this support, the chancellor's position is further enhanced by several agencies which are directly subordinated to him. Foremost among these is the Federal Chancellery (*Bundeskanzleramt*). This is, in effect, a superministry, the office of organization and coordination for the entire federal government. It often has decisive influence on the fate of legislative drafts. Such drafts are proposed by some ministry, but they need the approval of

the chancellor and cabinet, and thus the informal approval and guidance of the Federal Chancellery is often sought even in the early stages of drafting. The Federal Chancellery also serves to mediate in conflicts between different ministries, so that only the most important ones have to be decided by the chancellor himself. It is headed by a secretary of state, who is the top administrative aide of the chancellor and who also may be his chief political assistant. Under the secretary there are about twenty high-ranking civil servants, each of whom is charged with reporting on the affairs of one federal ministry. A strong chancellor may concede certain cabinet posts, or even the post of vice-chancellor, to members of other factions within his own party or to members of other parties in the government coalition, but he will seek to keep the Chancellery in the hands of men who are politically and personally close to himself.

Such considerations for a long time continued to focus attention on Secretary of State Hans Globke, for many years the closest collaborator of Chancellor Adenauer and considered at the beginning of the 1960s by a well-informed French observer "the most controversial and perhaps the most powerful man of the Federal Republic." [34] Globke's position was compared with that of Sherman Adams during some years of the Eisenhower administration, but his duties also included the supervision of the secret intelligence organization headed (until 1967) by General R. Gehlen. Since Globke's resignation, his successors have attracted less publicity.

[34] Grosser, *Die Bonner Demokratie*, p. 106. Under the Nazi regime, Dr. Globke had written in 1936 for the infamous Nürnberg racial laws an official commentary, the reading of which he later described as repulsive and detestable. According to some writers, his commentary made these laws still more severe; according to others, it tended to narrow their application and thus saved many individuals. The attacks on Globke were not free from politics, and the chancellor defended his associate to the utmost, taking him everywhere on his major travels. Some observers saw in Globke a steadfast adherent of the Roman Catholic church, who had at all times the confidence of its leaders and who remained in his compromising and distasteful job under the Nazis only in order to preserve a significant channel of information for the church.

Another instrument of the chancellor is the Federal Press and Information Office, which was headed by another close associate of the chancellor, Felix von Eckardt, from 1952 to 1963. The chancellor also has at his disposal a secret fund which was budgeted in 1955–56 at a little less than $3 million and which permits the subsidization of favored periodicals, newspapers, and journalists.[35] The office is particularly effective in influencing the provincial press in rural areas and small towns, but the CDU/SPD coalition of 1966–68 made the fund publicly accountable, larger, and less partisan.

Despite the concentration of powers in the chancellor and the continuing efforts to enlarge them, it is not impossible that a chancellor may be politically weak, without adequate support in his party and in the Bundestag and much in need of cooperation from other factions, parties, and branches of the government. In such a situation, the attitudes and powers of the president of the republic may well prove crucial.

THE PRESIDENT OF THE REPUBLIC

The president is the ceremonial head of the Federal Republic in domestic and international affairs. As such, he has constant opportunities to contribute to the leadership of public opinion and to the setting of the tone and style of politics and culture in the country.

The first president, Theodor Heuss, a distinguished intellectual figure and professor of political science, did much to use these opportunities to elevate the prestige and dignity of republican and constitutional institutions and to anchor them to unambiguously democratic values. His indications of dissent from some of Chancellor Adenauer's foreign and military policies were of little avail, but when he left office after two terms (1949–59), he had won general popularity and high respect not only for himself as a person, but to a significant degree for the republic which he had represented. While Heuss, a long-standing leader of the lib-

eral wing of the Free Democratic party, had been elected president at a time when as yet no single political party or leader dominated the scene, his successor, Dr. Heinrich Lübke, a quiet farm leader who had been imprisoned by the Nazis, was selected for the presidency from Chancellor Adenauer's own party at a time when the chancellor's personal prestige and power had long been commanding. For the ten years of his incumbency, President Lübke fulfilled his functions correctly and with dignity.

The president is elected for a five-year term and may be reelected for a consecutive term only once. He is elected by a special Federal Convention, composed of the members of the Bundestag and of an equal number of members of *Land* legislatures elected on the basis of proportional representation, which brings the total to about one thousand persons. Election is by majority vote of the members of this body. If in two votes no majority has been obtained by any candidate, a plurality in a third vote suffices for election (article 54 of the Basic Law). The rationale for the president's indirect election stems from the Weimar experience, in which a popularly elected president was able to compete with the legislature in claiming to represent the electorate—a situation fraught with potential conflict and the possibility of a stalemated government. In case of the president's incapacity or of the vacancy of his office before the end of his term, his duties devolve upon the president of the Bundesrat (article 57).

All presidential orders and decrees are valid only if countersigned by the chancellor or by the competent federal minister. The Basic Law permits only three exceptions to this requirement: the appointment and dismissal of the chancellor; the dissolution of the Bundestag in the event of its failure to elect a chancellor by majority vote; and the order to a chancellor or federal minister to carry on the affairs of his office until the appointment of a successor (article 58).

The president, nevertheless, has important reserve powers. If the Bundestag cannot be assembled in time, it is he, together with the chancellor, who must decide whether to declare that the "case of defense" has occurred, and

---

[35] Eschenburg, *Staat und Gesellschaft*, p. 749.

thus, in effect, to declare war (article 59.2). He must decide whom to propose first as a candidate for the post of chancellor to the Bundestag and whether to dissolve the Bundestag if no chancellor is elected by a majority vote of the members (article 63). Similarly, he must decide whether to dissolve the Bundestag if it has refused the chancellor a vote of confidence, but has failed to replace him by another (article 68), or whether to back a minority chancellor in such a case by declaring, at the request of the federal government, a state of legislative emergency (article 81). The president thus can lend considerable strength to a weak chancellor, or else he can compel him quickly to resign.

For his actions, the president can be impeached before the Federal Constitutional Court, on the grounds of willful violation of the Basic Law or any other federal law. Impeachment is voted by the Bundestag or by the Bundesrat, by two-thirds of the members of the former, or a majority of the votes of the latter; the motion to impeach, before it can be considered in either of these bodies, requires the backing of one-quarter of the Bundestag members or of the Bundesrat votes, respectively. After impeachment, the court may enjoin the president from exercising his office; if the court finds him guilty, it may deprive him of his office altogether (article 61). These provisions underscore the separate legal responsibility of the president, which is distinct from the political responsibility of the chancellor, and they tend to strengthen the president's hand in his dealings with the federal government by stressing the autonomous character of his decisions, signatures, and actions, even in cases where the government has requested them. During the controversy over the ratification of the European Defense Community treaty, in December 1952, President Heuss came close to setting a precedent when he requested an advisory opinion from the Federal Constitutional Court on the constitutionality of the treaty. After a single interview with Chancellor Adenauer, however, he withdrew the request, a few hours before the court's opinion was to be made public.

On the whole, however, no major conflicts between the chief institutions and officers of the Federal Republic have arisen thus far, and the president's reserve powers have remained largely untested. Indeed, some constitutional experts feel that the legal and political potentialities of the presidency under the Basic Law have been by no means fully utilized. But until now, most of his activities have been taken up by more formal duties of representation and government routine.

In West Berlin, in 1969, the Federal Convention elected to the presidency Dr. Gustav Heinemann, a distinguished politician of high personal esteem and integrity who had a broad range of experience in public office, to succeed Dr. Lübke. Heinemann was a prominent nonpolitical German leader as chairman of the Evangelical Church of Germany (EKD) from 1949 to 1955. His political career began earlier, in 1945, as a cofounder of the CDU, of which he was a member until 1952. Between 1946 and 1949, he was mayor of Essen, a large industrial city in the Ruhr valley. In 1947–48, he also served as minister of justice of North Rhine-Westphalia. In 1949, Adenauer appointed him minister of the interior in the first cabinet of the G.F.R. But one year later, in October 1950, Heinemann, a strong pacifist, resigned from this post in opposition to the chancellor's West German rearmament plans. In 1953, Heinemann founded his own party, the All-German People's party (*Gesamtdeutsche Volkspartei*), which proved unsuccessful, however, and dissolved three years later. In May 1957, Heinemann joined the SPD, of which he was Bundestag deputy since 1957. Representing the SPD, Heinemann served in 1966–69 as minister of justice in Kiesinger's "grand coalition" cabinet.

For many reasons, the election of Heinemann as president was a significant event on the West German political stage. First, with Heinemann the Federal Republic had its first Social Democratic president. This was a valuable gain in prestige for the SPD, particularly in the election year 1969, since the Social Democrats had entered the grand coalition three years earlier to prove to the German people that the SPD was capable of holding responsible public office. Heinemann's election was a confirmation of that position not only in the eyes of the German electorate but—equally important —also in the eyes of the more traditionally oriented, older party members of the SPD, who had followed their leadership somewhat suspiciously into the alliance with the Christian Democrats.

The second important aspect with future implications of the Heinemann election was that it resulted from a voting alliance between the deputies of the SPD and the FDP. This success reinforced the initially cautious cooperation between the two parties, which was to result in a government coalition after the general election in the fall of that year. Thus, the Federal Convention of 1969 was the overture to a shift of the center of gravity in the German party system.

And thirdly, the course of the 1969 presidential election spoiled the only chance of the neo-Nazi NPD to influence the national political composition of the G.F.R. Since neither of the two major parties, the CDU and the SPD, commanded sufficient voting strength of their own to get their respective candidates elected, both depended for their success on the behavior of the two smaller parties, the FDP and the NPD, which did not run candidates of their own. According to article 54.3 of the Basic Law, the NPD, though it was not represented in the Bundestag, had the legal right to send a delegation to the federal convention because it had obtained some 8% of the seats in a few *Land* parliaments during the crisis years of 1966–68. Prior to the presidential election, the NPD had announced that it would cast its vote in favor of the CDU candidate, Dr. Gerhard Schroeder. Thus, the SPD-FDP alliance in the 1969 Federal Convention saved the Federal Republic from the embarrassment of being led by a president who gained office by virtue of the support of neo-Nazis. Such an election would have created a situation with potentially disastrous consequences for the domestic and international reputation and prestige of the Federal Republic and its institutions.

Events like the Heinemann election, the failure of the NPD to satisfy the 5% exclusion clause in the general elections, the rejection of a conservative preventive-detention proposal by the Bundestag, and the smooth shift of governmental power from one party to the other after the election made 1969 a successful year for democracy in West Germany. If seen in proper perspective, these events constitute a hopeful trend pointing toward the consolidation of democratic values of liberty and of due process in the Federal Republic of the 1970s.

THE MECHANICS OF LAW MAKING

It may be convenient at this stage to summarize the roles of the different legislative and executive agencies in the normal process of legislation. The simplified flow diagram in Fig. 5-1 should be largely self-explanatory.

Bills can be initiated by the federal government, the Bundestag, or the Bundesrat. Those initiated by the federal government— more than half the total—first must be submitted to the scrutiny of the Bundesrat, while those few bills originating in the Bundesrat must first be commented on by the federal government. Then, however, all bills—including the nearly one-half that originated in the Bundestag itself—go through the main legislative process in the Bundestag. This starts with a first reading and a vote in the full Bundestag— the "plenum"—on the general principles of the bill, followed by intensive work on its details in one of the standing committees of the Bundestag, which in its report produces a draft version of the bill. This is followed by a second reading and a vote in the plenum on the specific details of the bill, and a third reading and vote to make sure of the cohesion and consistency of the changed bill that may have emerged. (Before a bill goes through each successive stage, however, there are party meetings in which most of the actual decisions are made.)

After adoption by the Bundestag, the bill goes to the Bundesrat, and if not amended there, it passes on directly—as do more than nine-tenths of all bills—to the president of the republic and to the chancellor or the competent federal minister for their signatures, and on to promulgation into law. For the one-tenth or fewer bills that are amended in the Bundesrat, another round of procedures is required,

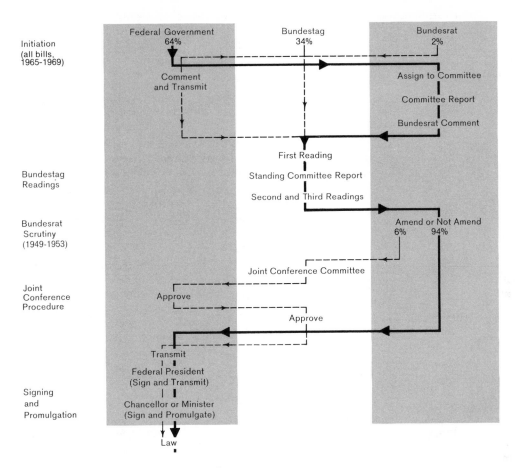

Initiation
(all bills,
1965-1969)

Federal Government
64%

Bundestag
34%

Bundesrat
2%

Comment
and Transmit

Assign to Committee

Committee Report

Bundesrat Comment

First Reading

Bundestag
Readings

Standing Committee Report

Second and Third Readings

Bundesrat
Scrutiny
(1949-1953)

Amend or Not Amend
6%   94%

Joint Conference Committee

Joint
Conference
Procedure

Approve

Approve

Transmit

Federal President
(Sign and Transmit)

Chancellor or Minister
(Sign and Promulgate)

Signing
and
Promulgation

Law

FIG. 5-1. *The passage of ordinary bills in the German Federal Republic. The heavy line indicates the route of most bills.* [*Data from the German Federal Republic,* Statistisches Jahrbuch für die Bundesrepublik *(Bonn, 1970), p. 115.*]

from the working out of a compromise version in a joint conference committee to the approval of the compromise by each of the two chambers, before the approved text is returned to the main track for executive signatures and promulgation.

This formal description understates, however, the true influence on legislation of the federal and *Land* ministries and their officials. Many of the draft bills entered by Bundestag deputies actually have been drawn in some ministry. Preliminary drafts are worked on in interdepartmental committees where both fed-

eral and *Land* officials participate, so that the views of the Bundesrat are often taken into account at this stage. Parliament then may make further corrections in these drafts, particularly if the civil servants have in their draft misjudged the political strength of one or more of the interest groups concerned. In general, however, the Bundestag resembles the British Parliament, rather than the United States Congress, in expecting to receive legislative drafts more nearly ready for enactment.

The system looks somewhat cumbersome on paper, but it has worked well in practice, insuring thorough consideration of most measures within a reasonable time. Even in a smoothly working system, however, some deadlocks and conflicts are likely to occur. To deal with these, another set of agencies is provided in the courts.

THE COURTS

The chief agency for resolving constitutional conflicts is the Federal Constitutional Court, provided for in articles 93 and 94 of the Basic Law. Broadly speaking, the court is competent to deal with six kinds of cases:

1. *The control of the constitutionality of laws.* There is a hierarchy of laws, in which the Basic Law ranks highest, other federal laws next, then *Land* constitutions, and finally other *Land* legislation. Any law thus may have to be scrutinized for its compatibility with a higher one, up to the Basic Law. The Federal Constitutional Court may be invoked for this purpose by any other court of law, where in a pending case a conflict of this kind may have arisen, or by the federal government, or by any *Land* government, or by one-third of the members of the Bundestag.

2. *Interpretations of the Basic Law, occasioned by disagreements about the limits of the rights and duties of any one of the highest organs of the Federal Republic.* Here the court may be invoked by the president of the republic, the Bundestag, the Bundesrat, the Permanent Committee of the Bundestag provided for by article 45 of rules of the Bundestag, the federal government, or certain of the major parts of any of these, such as the one-tenth or one-fourth of the members of the Bundestag who have the right to initiate certain procedures there. In any case, however, the plaintiffs must show their specific legal interest in the case at issue.

3. *Disagreements about the rights and duties of the federal government or of the* Land *governments.* Proceedings may be initiated only by the federal government for the fed-eral authorities, and only by a *Land* government for any *Land* authorities.

4. *Formal deprivations of certain constitutional rights, somewhat analogous to criminal proceedings:*

   a. Forfeiture of basic rights, on grounds of their anticonstitutional misuse, according to article 18 of the Basic Law.

   b. Banning of specific political parties as unconstitutional, according to article 21.2.

   c. Impeachment of the president of the republic by the Bundestag or Bundesrat, according to article 61, on a motion by the federal government, or the Bundestag, or the Bundesrat, or by a *Land* government in the case of parties limited to a single *Land.*

   d. Impeachments of federal judges, on the motion of the Bundestag, according to article 98.2.

5. *Complaints against decisions by the Bundestag in regard to the validity of an election or the acquisition or loss of membership in the Bundestag by a deputy or candidate,* according to article 41.2, on the motion of the rejected candidate, or of 101 voters, or of a Bundestag *Fraktion,* or of one-tenth of the Bundestag members.

6. *All constitutional complaints by individuals against any alleged violation of any of their basic rights, or any of the rights contained in articles 33, 38, 101, 103, or 104 of the Basic Law.* Such complaints may be initiated by any individual, but ordinarily he may appeal to the Federal Constitutional Court only after having exhausted his normal legal remedies in the regular courts. The Federal Constitutional Court, however, may accept and decide such a complaint at once if it deals with a matter of general importance or if the delays of normal legal proceedings through the courts would work serious and unavoidable harm for the plaintiff.

The Constitutional Court, located at Karlsruhe, consists of two chambers or "senates," each composed of eight judges, or sixteen for the entire court. Originally the First Senate was to deal with conflicts between federal or *Land* laws and the Basic Law, or between federal and *Land* laws, while the Second Senate was to deal with conflicts between the highest organs of government. Experience soon showed that legal and constitutional disputes of the first kind were frequent, particularly the individual complaints (see category 6, above), while top-level political conflicts of the second type were rare. The court began to operate in 1951; within the first five years, the First Senate heard nearly 3,000 complaints, while the Second Senate had to deal with about thirty. After the redistribution of the work load in 1956 and 1960, the First Senate now deals mainly with complaints against violations of civil and constitutional rights, leaving most other kinds of cases to the Second Senate, which consequently has somewhat gained in power.

The decisions of each senate of the Constitutional Court are final. The legal interpretations embodied in them in each case are binding for future decisions by the other senate. If that senate wishes to depart from them, the matter must be decided by the full court—the plenum—which requires for a quorum the presence of at least two-thirds of the members of each senate. In this way, the unity of decisions by the two senates of the court is to be preserved. If a senate should wish to reverse its own earlier legal interpretation, the matter presumably also might have to be dealt with by the plenum in a similar manner. The aim seems to be, not to make the legal views of the court immutable, but to make sure that the two senates of the court will at all times function as two organs of a single judicial authority.

At times, there has been a tendency in the Federal Republic to pass difficult political problems to the courts, and particularly to the Constitutional Court, so as to avoid the strains and stresses of handling them through the legislative and executive institutions. As in other countries, this tempting practice has threatened to engage the prestige of the courts in political controversy, but respect for the courts has remained high. In a country that still lacks deep-rooted habits and traditions of constitutionalism and democracy, it has been perhaps more necessary to call on the courts and the respect for law to limit political conflicts, to curb the excessive pragmatism and potential ruthlessness with which interest groups might come to press their claims, and to guard the basic essential rules and procedures of constitutional politics.

In addition to the Federal Constitutional Court, there are six other superior federal courts, each of which has the highest jurisdiction over appeals in its special field. The ordinary system of German civil and criminal courts is arranged in three ascending tiers, from the *Amtsgerichte* through the *Landesgerichte* to the *Oberlandesgerichte*. All these are part of the *Land* jurisdiction, but they apply federal law (the German criminal code of 1871 and the civil code of 1900, as amended, are valid in all states), and their decisions are subject to appeal to the Federal High Court (*Bundesgerichtshof*) at Karlsruhe. This court supersedes the old *Reichsgericht* and is the court of last resort in civil and criminal adjudication, insofar as it does not involve questions of constitutionality. The Federal High Court has three sections of five judges each. These sections deal with civil cases, criminal cases, and treason, respectively; for the last-named, the court's jurisdiction is original.

The five superior administrative courts include:

1. the Federal Finance Court (*Bundesfinanzhof*) at Munich, dealing with taxes and other fiscal matters;

2. the Federal Administrative Court (*Bundesverwaltungsgericht*) at West Berlin, dealing with disputes among or claims against governments not involving constitutional questions;

3. the Federal Labor Court (*Bundesarbeitsgericht*) at Kassel, which deals with labor affairs;

4. the Federal Social Court (*Bundessozialgericht*) at Essen, which is competent to decide cases arising from social security and public welfare questions; and

5. the Federal Court of Discipline (*Bundesdisziplinarhof*) at Frankfurt, which hears

appeals from cases against federal public servants under the disciplinary regulations.

The first four of these are provided for by the Basic Law; the last is implied by it (article 96.1, 3).

The crowning body for this entire judicial edifice is to be the Supreme Federal Court (*Oberstes Bundesgericht*), which is provided for by the Basic Law (article 95) and is charged with the task of safeguarding the unity of the application of the laws. Its judges are to be selected by a panel consisting of the federal minister of justice and a special selection committee composed of the *Land* ministers of justice and an equal number of members elected by the Bundestag. After more than two decades, however, no legislation implementing this complex arrangement has been passed, and the Supreme Federal Court thus far has remained on paper. Even so, the growth in the organization and stature of the West German judiciary has been impressive. In contrast to the imperial and Weimar periods—not to mention the degradation of the Hitler era—the judiciary under the Federal Republic is separated from the executive power. It is constitutionally protected in its separateness, as is the independence of the judges. There is a distinct supreme tribunal to deal with questions of constitutionality, and there is an effective doctrine of judicial review, which has subjected the traditional bureaucratic-authoritarian patterns of German government to a far-reaching control by law. Together, these are in many ways far more profound and thoroughgoing changes than those worked by the 1918 revolution.

The changes in the constitutional role of the judiciary contrast with the remarkable continuity of the judges. The personnel of the highest courts, and particularly of the Federal Constitutional Court, have been selected with conspicuous care with regard to both their high professional qualifications and their clean political records. Elsewhere in the West German judiciary, as well as among prosecutors and attorneys general of the *Länder*, and even of the federal government, cases of jurists with Nazi records kept coming up as late as 1967. Earlier, in 1962, a federal bill offered early and rela-

tively attractive retirement terms to judges who would admit that they had imposed political death sentences under the Nazi regime, or had collaborated in procuring such death sentences for defendants who would not have been sentenced to death by other than Nazi standards.

A number of judges avoided proceedings by accepting this offer, but others continued to forget or conceal their pasts until confronted with evidence which produced startling headlines in the West German press. The bulk of the judges, however, have not been touched by these spectacular happenings. They are traditionalists and conservatives, not right-wing radicals. As a group, they are remarkably tightly knit and closely related to the upper-middle classes. By duty and intention, they are to be impartial appliers of the law. By background, marriage, and associations, they are overwhelmingly tied to a single class, and they are almost completely separated from, and uninformed about, that half of the German people which consists of workers—skilled, semiskilled, and unskilled—who are defendants in their courts.[36] This, however, brings up a matter that goes beyond any problem of legal rules: the crucial question of which persons, elites, and interest groups *actually* operate the West German political system.

THE STATUTE OF LIMITATION AND NAZI CRIMES—THE MORAL AND LEGAL DILEMMA OF 1965

In 1965, the leadership of the Federal Republic had to solve probably the most difficult and serious legal and moral problem facing it since its inception in 1949. The issue evolved around the statutory-limitation clause of the federal criminal law and article 103.2 of the Basic Law. Up to 1965, article 67.1 of the federal criminal law—inherited from the imperial criminal code of 1872—stated: "If a crime is punishable by imprisonment for life, its prosecution is limited to a period of twenty years."

[36] See Ralph Dahrendorf, *Gesellschaft und Freiheit* (Munich: R. Piper, 1961).

In other words, a murderer was immune against prosecution if his crime had not been discovered after twenty years. (This is in contrast to the Anglo-American legal tradition, which recognizes no statute of limitation for murder.) By mid-1965 it was exactly twenty years since the collapse of the Nazi regime in Germany. Thus, this statute of limitation would have freed many of the still-undiscovered Nazi criminals from their legal liability for mass murder and other violations of human rights. Extension or abolition of this statute of limitation, however, conflicted with a particular interpretation of the Basic Law (article 103.2), which states that an action can be punished only if its criminality was defined by law prior to the time it was committed. According to West German legal thinking the Federal Republic is a continuation of the first democratic system in Germany, the Weimar Republic. By the same token, the federal criminal code enacted in 1949 is not viewed as a new set of laws but rather as an organic development of the Weimar legal system. Consequently, crimes deemed to have been committed between 1933 and 1949 were defined by the Weimar criminal code, which is considered to have been in force, though not enforced, during the Nazi dictatorship. Accordingly West German jurisprudence held the prosecution of Nazi crimes to properly fall within the jurisdiction of the Federal Republic.

The Bundestag was in a dilemma. Politically and morally, it would have undermined the democratic credibility of the Federal Republic and its institutions and that of the German people as a whole, if they had decided to tolerate known Nazi criminals in their midst without taking legal steps against them. To continue prosecuting of Nazi crimes, however, would have cast doubt on the commitment of the Federal Republic to protecting civil liberties as outlined in the Basic Law. One of the fundamental values of a democratic system is that justice is administered by rule rather than by political arbitrariness. Thus, it would not have been well-becoming for the Federal Republic to bend its own Basic Law for the purpose of a political consideration—a practice which is quite common in most Communist and Fascist dictatorships. Whichever way the Bundestag

decided—on the basis of moral principles or of formal legal considerations—its decision was bound to have shortcomings. Would the Federal Republic continue to face the consequences and moral burden of an unglorious recent past and thereby bend a fundamental civil right on which its present society was based, or would it decide to institute a cover of silence over an estimated 27,000 major Nazi crimes [37] the perpetrators of which were still unprosecuted?

The Bundestag had basically three options: (1) it could decide to leave the statutory-limitation clause of the federal criminal law unchanged and let known mass murderers go free; (2) it could abolish the statute of limitation completely; (3) it could decide on a new statutory limitation of the period during which capital crimes can be prosecuted. Both the second and third options would necessitate an interpretation of article 103.2 of the Basic Law to the effect that a statute of limitation is not part of the definition of the criminality of a particular conduct.

The particular rationale for the second option was provided for by the fact that article 102 of the Basic Law declares capital punishment abolished. It was thus argued by some members of the Bundestag that the only logical step following from this provision was to exempt all capital crimes which were formerly punishable by death from the statute of limitation. The starting point for a long and heated debate in the *Bundestag* was a bill drafted by CDU deputy Benda and endorsed by the SPD, proposing an amendment of federal criminal law. Article 1 of that bill specifically amended article 67.1 of the federal criminal code to provide a new statutory limitation of 30 years for the prosecution of capital crimes. When the first reading on March 10th 1965 failed to provide a majority, the bill was sent to the Justice Committee for further consideration. That committee acted with unusual speed in developing a compromise satisfying the two major groups in conflict on the Bundestag floor. The resultant proposal left the 20 year statute of limitation

---

[37] Figure from Michael Hereth, ed., *20 Jahre Bundesrepublik Deutschland in Dokumenten* (Munich: List, 1969), p. 11.

unchanged, but argued a new basis for calculating the starting date for the statute. The new formula was justified by claiming that there was no working *German* authority following the collapse of the Nazi regime until the effective institution of the Federal Republic, at the end of 1949. The Justice Committee proposed, therefore, that the period from May 8, 1945 to December 31, 1949, should not be considered a time during which capital crimes could have been prosecuted. Consequently, the 20 year statute was deemed to be in effect only from January 1st, 1950 onwards, expiring at the end of 1969 for Nazi crimes. The committee version of the bill was passed by the Bundestag during the third reading on March 25th, 1965, by a majority of 361 to 96.

After careful consideration of both the formal-legal and the moral standards involved in the problem of criminal prosecution of Nazi crimes, the Bundestag clearly decided to place humanistic moral values above pure formalistic legalism. The revised law implied that due process is no end in itself, but is subordinate to the content of justice which it is to serve. It was a salient feature of the legislation that it simultaneously preserved both high moral principles and the universal administration of justice by application of rule of law. By 1970, it was commonly reasoned, there would be only a few elderly Nazi mass murderers still alive who had not been already tried and convicted, and these few might remain undisturbed.

EMERGENCY LAWS

The stability and maturity of a democratic system is challenged most in situations where the formal and procedural requirements of a democratic order come into conflict with the essential values of democracy. Sometimes, situations arise in which the application of democratic rules and procedures inevitably produces a result that would be intolerable to the moral consensus of the democratic community. Such a conflict was clearly borne out in the discussion about the statute of limitation in the Federal Republic in 1965.

An equally delicate matter for a democratic order is the set of provisions that go into effect in situations where the democratic mechanism cannot be made to work for external reasons, such as wars, mass uprisings, or natural catastrophies. The danger for democracy is greatest at a point when an emergency forces the system to resort for a period of time to a form of government which is essentially undemocratic. Here the shortness of such a period and the machinery for its termination may be crucial. For there is always some chance that those in control of the emergency regime may want to stay in power and not let the system resume is previous democratic functioning. This fear is not unjustified in Germany. It was precisely this mechanism that facilitated in 1930–33 the shift from the unstable democracy of the Weimar Republic to a dictatorship of the Nazis.

Prior to June 6, 1968, the G.F.R. had no emergency provisions in its Basic Law. Despite the fact that the Bundestag has passed twenty-seven bills of constitutional change up to January 1971, the entire Basic Law has remained essentially unaltered. These twenty-seven bills of change required seven deletions, thirty-four insertions, and forty-nine substitutions of articles, paragraphs, or subparagraphs.[38] At first glance these figures appear to be an indication of large constitutional instability. In reality, however, most of these changes were concerned with minor problems of wording and of legal definitions and clarifications. This should not surprise one, since the entire constitution had to be drafted within a few months in 1949. Some of the changes, however, carry important political significance. Among them is, for instance, the previously mentioned redistribution of tax revenue between the federation and the *Länder,* which was enacted in May 1969 (articles 105–8). The other important revision of the Basic Law, the emergency legislation, was the subject of the seventeenth bill of constitutional change passed in June 1968, which effected the insertion of articles 53a and 115a–l.

The legislation of 1968 bears the marks of three political facts: (1) since the early 1960s, civil servants, the military, the CDU/CSU, and West Germany's NATO allies all had pressed

[38] See *Grundgesetz,* 11th ed. (Munich: Beck, 1971), pp. 27–28.

for some legislation of this kind; (2) the SPD insisted on extensive safeguards, and its votes were indispensable for passage; (3) the protest campaign of 1968 of labor unions, students, intellectuals, and part of the press had to be taken into consideration.

In normal circumstances, only the Bundestag can announce a state of emergency or of war, and it can do so only by a two-thirds majority of those present. To provide for cases where the Bundestag is unable to meet, the new article 53a calls for the institution of a permanent "Joint Committee" (*Gemeinsamer Ausschuss*), which is composed to one-third of members of the Bundesrat and to two-thirds of members of the Bundestag. Members of the Joint Committee may not be members of the cabinet. Furthermore, the Joint Committee is not subject to orders from any governmental or administrative body or institution. In cases of emergency or situations requiring national defense, in which the Bundestag cannot convene, the Joint Committee is empowered to announce officially a state of emergency or "case of defense" (i.e., war). It can do so with two-thirds of the votes of its members present if that also constitutes at least a majority of all its members.

Such a declaration of a state of emergency or war automatically makes the chancellor commander in chief of the armed forces (article 115b). Necessary and urgent legislation has to be introduced into both the Bundestag and the Bundesrat at the same time at the earliest opportunity. Both houses have to debate those bills together to prevent any delay (article 115d). If the Joint Committee decides by two-thirds of the votes present, but by at least a majority of its members, that there is not sufficient time for the convening of the Bundestag and Bundesrat, the committee assumes the status of both houses and has to carry out their functions (article 115e.1). The Joint Committee, however, is not empowered to change the Basic Law or suspend its application (article 115e.2). In defense situations, the *Land* governments are subject to federal executive orders (article 115f). Even in a "case of defense," the rights and the position of the Federal Constitutional Court cannot be altered, unless the court itself so decides by a

vote of a majority of its justices. Furthermore, in an emergency situation all elections are suspended. The Bundestag cannot be dismissed during such a situation (article 115h). Article 115i empowers the *Land* governments to assume full legislative and executive power over their territories in cases where the federal organs are unable to order and carry out the necessary defense measures. Article 115k specifies that emergency laws supersede all existing laws that conflict with the emergency measures. And finally, article 115l declares that the Bundestag, in agreement with the Bundesrat, can revoke all legislation passed by the Joint Committee, and can also define the emergency situation as terminated. If the Bundesrat alone proposes such steps, the Bundestag is obligated to take a vote on this matter. After a war, a final peace treaty is subject to subsequent federal law.

With regard to the checks and balances which the above emergency legislation of the Bonn republic entails, it compares very favorably with article 48 of the Weimar constitution of August 1919. The formulation of this article 48 was very broad and thus contained the acute danger of its abuse. It empowered the *Reichspräsident* to order "all measures necessary for the restitution of public security and order," if that "public security and order . . . is significantly disturbed or in danger." It was not specified which circumstances were sufficient for invoking article 48. Furthermore, it was not specified which measures were and which were not permissible as means of restoring "public security and order." This article, then, served as the constitutional basis for Hitler's suspension of all the basic rights in the constitution by means of an executive order on February 28, 1933, four days after he had combined the office of chancellor and president in his person. By virtue of its conspicuously vague wording, article 48 became a convenient constitutional vehicle for making the office of *Reichspräsident* the sole legislative implement in a situation of acute governmental instability during the last two years of the Weimar Republic.

Four decades later, the bitter experience of Weimar, as well as the protest campaigns of 1968, had borne some fruit. In its 1968 emergency legislation, the G.F.R. was very careful to preserve as much of the regular legislative process as possible in cases of emergency. The position of the Bundestag and Bundesrat, and also that of the Federal Constitutional Court, remain practically unrestricted. In fact, given the probable decline of most sources of political influence and pressure during a time of inner disorder and turmoil, it is likely that the weight of the popular representation will even increase.

What articles 115a–l clearly avoid is the concentration of all power of the state into one hand—or even leaving the decision about when to declare a state of emergency in one hand. In comparison to article 48 of the Weimar constitution, the present West German emergency legislation is more democratic and contains many more safeguards against its possible abuse.

When we know an individual well, we know which things he will be likely to do often, and which ones rarely or not at all. We know his likes and dislikes, his patterns of probable attention and inattention. We may know what particular images and memories he carries in his mind, and which among these are particularly important to him; what kinds of messages or experiences will lead to their recall into awareness; and what particular kinds of perceptions this combination of old memories and new messages and impressions is likely to produce. We know what he is apt to notice and what to ignore, what to seek and approach, and what to avoid or reject.

All these are matters not of certainty but of frequency or probability. We infer these probability distributions of his future actions and preferences from his past behavior, and we call them his *predispositions* or his *attitudes*. The particular combination of attitudes found in an individual we call his *character*. Our inferences about it we call our *judgment* of his character; and his subsequent actual behavior may show us whether our judgment was realistic or mistaken.

POLITICAL CULTURE AND NATIONAL CHARACTER

Just as any single individual can be said to have a certain set of political attitudes, so large numbers of people can be said to have typical political attitudes. Such attitudes toward different aspects of politics are characteristic of a nation, and in particular respects they differ significantly from the typical attitudes of many other nations. We call these characteristic political attitudes a country's *political culture*, which is, of course, a part of its general or national culture.

It is also sometimes useful to think of the relation of the national culture to the ensemble of attitudes of many individuals, which we call their *individual character* or *personality*. In relation to the most widespread personality characteristics among its constituent individuals, we sometimes call the national culture of the people of a nation their *national character*. When

SIX

political culture, parties, interest groups, and elites

talking about politics, our use of "national character" often will come close to the meaning of "political culture," but with a slightly different focus of interest on the relevant personality structure of individuals.

"Political attitudes" or "political culture" may refer to any aspect of politics and government, whether it be attitudes toward governmental authority, political participation, partisanship, or the type of government that is desired. These attitudes are made up of a set of images, beliefs, evaluations of political phenomena, and degrees of emotional detachment or involvement. But these political attitudes are embedded in something broader and deeper—in the character of the individuals, groups, and nations that hold them.

Once we are able to describe a country's political culture and national character, we can raise a number of related questions. How does the political culture help us to understand and explain the operating characteristics of a country's government? In what ways does the political culture help or hinder democratic government? What were the origins of the political culture—those events and conditions that led to its formation? How are these typical attitudes transmitted from one generation to the next? Most of these attitudes are taught by the family and schools and by the cumulative effects of many examples in daily life, through which each succeeding generation learns the attitudes of the preceding one. Sometimes a conscious attempt is made to inculcate a new set of attitudes, as in postwar Germany, where the occupying powers reorganized the schools in the hope of developing democratic attitudes among the students. Present-day West German attitudes are thus the outcome of the conflicting influences of events and memories from long-past German history, of recent or current institutions and practices in society and family life, of old and new images and ideas about human relations and politics, and of social and political developments since 1945.

HISTORY
AND POLITICAL CULTURE

The long and often violent history of the German people has left them with deep-seated memories that have colored their political decisions in the past and will continue to do so for years to come. These memories are embedded in German schoolbooks and in learned histories, in words of creative literature and in the minds of individuals. These historic memories recall that for centuries the international environment has not been kind to Germany. From the horrors of the Thirty Years' War to the desperate struggles of Frederick II's Prussia and the Napoleonic wars, foreign economic and military developments are remembered as having threatened or injured Germany, and to this are added memories of the overwhelmingly strong foreign coalitions that united to defeat Germany in two world wars. In such a dangerous world, these memories seem to suggest, Germans should not show any weakness or disunity, or any excessive trust in foreigners or foreign powers. This impression is reinforced by memories of real or imagined exclusion of peaceful German trade from many overseas areas, both before 1914 and between the world wars—and perhaps today, though to a lesser and steadily diminishing extent—through the lingering or continuing effects of colonial administrations, currency blocs, linguistic preferences, formal and informal controls over credit and trade, all of which were believed to have functioned somehow to the disadvantage of Germany.

In the past, many Germans believed that they worked harder and more efficiently than the members of any other great industrial power in Western Europe, and many also believed that for their efforts they received relatively less in terms of real income, domestic living standards, and international prestige. Members of other nations could move about distant parts of the globe and yet feel respected and at home in the colonies of their nation, but Germans at best had to enter as foreigners and always had to adapt themselves to the ways of others.

THE GERMAN
"NATIONAL CHARACTER"

In the face of an environment that thus seemed often less than fair to their aspirations, many Germans felt that they had to hold on to their particular virtues as a people. Outstanding among these virtues was a capacity and liking for hard work. Most people seem to consider the members of their own nation as hard-working, but the Germans do so to a far greater extent. While 68% of American respondents to a UNESCO poll applied this term to their own people in 1948–49, and respondents in six out of seven other countries claimed the same distinction for themselves with lesser majorities or pluralities, the Germans interviewed in the poll proclaimed their faith in the diligence of their own people with a solid 90% majority.[1] Later polls confirmed this image; majorities of 60% in 1955, and 56% in 1956, reiterated in German polls the conviction that their own people were "more efficient and gifted than the other peoples." By 1960, however, this view was no longer held by a majority; in a representative poll of Germans over 18 years of age only 42% of the respondents thought West Germans more "competent" than other peoples.[2]

There is no doubt that these images are based on very real German virtues. Foreign observers, as well as Germans, have attested time and again to the energy, diligence, and thoroughness of Germans in their work, both physical and intellectual. There is a high degree of care and thoughtfulness in German workmanship; there is steadfastness in the face of difficulty, and great courage and discipline in the face of danger. There is a tradition of selflessness, of readiness to sacrifice and suffer, of solidarity with one's group—national, social, or ideological; there is a serious concern for justice and a deep well of imagination. Not all Germans, of course, have all these virtues at all times; but many Germans have shown them often, and under critical conditions. It is these virtues that stand out in the symbols of German literature and poetry; it is these themes that have moved, and still can move, many Germans in political appeals; and it is these qualities that

Germans may often still be expected to show in their actions.

Yet the German "national character"—or those frequent elements and patterns in German culture, traditions, and personality that have relevance for their political behavior—is more complex. Like similar patterns in other countries, it moves often in polarities, that is, in pairs of opposites. Thus, German political and cultural styles have moved between the poles of idealism and materialism. Both German and foreign observers have spoken of a German fascination with abstract doctrines and ideas, and sometimes of the preoccupation of Germans with wealth and material success—as once again today people talk of the "success Germans" of the Bonn republic.

Other polarities exist between the rival images of German profundity and practicality or matter-of-factness (*Sachlichkeit*); and between chivalrous romanticism and pedestrian stolidity. The romantic nobleman Walter Stolzing is counterposed to the obtuse critic Beckmesser in Richard Wagner's opera *Die Meistersinger,* or the romantic, searching scientist Dr. Faust is contrasted with his diligent but uncreative assistant Wagner in Goethe's *Faust.*

German political styles sometimes have been dominated by similar contrasts, or have oscillated between them. Periods of admiration for grandiose or even demonic heroes have been followed by periods of contentment with solid mediocrity; and periods of great resistance to change have been followed by periods of its overacceptance. More than once in German history, dependable moderate courses of action were firmly held for years and decades, until some strain became too much, and a rapid and intense realignment of political sympathies and styles of action followed. Thus the "blood and iron" period of Bismarck followed nearly a half-century of predominantly moderate and peaceful politics. Hitler followed the years of moderation under the Weimar Republic. (Thus, it is vital for the peace of the world that the present period of stability under the Bonn republic should prove to be durable.) In this manner, much of German history has been a history of breaks in political style.

German attitudes toward politics have often oscillated between an insistence on the

---

[1] I. W. Buchanan and H. Cantril, *How Nations See Each Other: A Study in Public Opinion* (Urbana: University of Illinois Press, 1953), pp. 46–47.

[2] Elisabeth Noelle Neumann and Erich Peter Neumann, *Jahrbuch der öffentlichen Meinung* (Allensbach: Verlag für Demoskopie, 1958), 2:139 (hereafter cited as *Jahrbuch*). Lewis J. Edinger, *Politics in Germany* (Boston: Little, Brown, 1968), p. 74.

virtues of being "nonpolitical" or "above the parties" and a willingness to accept the most extreme partisan commitments of totalitarian fanaticism. Both attitudes derive from the same fundamental view of politics, which sees the world of politics as fundamentally evil, governed by the laws and necessities of what St. Augustine described as the city of robbers; which Machiavelli saw as ruled by the pragmatic necessities of force and fraud, rather than by traditional morality; and which Luther saw as a world of princes who had to be obeyed even if they were immoral, since they were set by Providence to rule over subjects corrupted by original sin.

In fact, this was a very naïve version both of actual politics and of the views of Augustine, Machiavelli, and Luther, all of whom had been more complex and subtle thinkers. It was a simplified version, however, which fitted the emotional needs of an educated people who lacked any deep or rich experience of responsible political participation, and who found themselves bewildered by what little of politics they actually saw. To conclude that politics was basically wicked, then, meant that one kept away from it as long as possible, but that—if one had to act in politics at all—one might be quite willing to accept some quite ruthless or extreme political practice or ideology, for that was in any case what politics really was like. By no means have all Germans at any one time been stranded on the poles of this nonpolitical or hyperpolitical dilemma, but a sufficient number of them have been often enough in the past to give to German political attitudes a characteristic cast and potential.

Some of these polarities perhaps can be traced back to the influences of German history, and so can some of the potential political weaknesses which they imply. German history is rich in memories of authoritarian princes and magistrates, and of the dependence of their subjects on them for protection. Eighteenth-century Prussia differed significantly from other European states in the governmental structure and the ideas which served to legitimate it. Prussian government under Frederick I and Frederick the Great was not only archetypically autocratic, but his autocracy was based upon a blending of civil and military affairs, the militarization of social life, and the development of an exceptionally powerful and centralized bureaucratic apparatus. This autocratic bureaucratic government was to a large extent legitimized by the political docility found in orthodox Lutheranism, the German idealistic (and metaphysical) notion that the bureaucracy was the state, and that rights and liberties were to be found within its hierarchical embrace.

Some of this authoritarianism was reinforced by the patriarchal tradition of the pre-industrial western European and German family structure and patterns of bringing up children; and in turn it reinforced this tradition in Germany. In this way, a stronger element of authoritarianism—a willingness to submit to those in authority combined with a tendency to demand obedience from subordinates—has been transmitted from generation to generation, and transferred into the formation of German national character and political attitudes. The extent to which the Germans continue to emphasize the notions of order and authority was brought out by a 1966 survey in which the respondents were asked which qualities should be primarily emphasized in bringing up children. The responses indicate that 18% of all Germans favor "obedience and submission," and another 49% think "love of order and thrift" ought to be primarily emphasized, while only 29% mentioned "self-sufficiency and independence." [3] Not all Germans, by any means, are authoritarian, but more of them seem to be so to a higher degree than are the populations of, say, France, Britain, or the United States.

The Lack of a Strong Commercial Class

Another historic legacy may be the result of the long period of relative weakness of the commercial middle classes in Germany from

---

[3] From an unpublished 1966 national survey conducted by the Zentralarchiv für Empirische Sozialforschung, University of Cologne (hereafter cited as "1966 Survey").

the mid-sixteenth to the mid-nineteenth century—that is, during a period when these classes became relatively strong in England, France, and the United States. And even into the twentieth century the successful entrepreneurs remained highly deferential to the *Junker* aristocracy, seeing as the culmination of their lives admission into aristocratic and military circles, despite the concomitantly required debasement of their commercial professions. Whenever given the opportunity to choose, the *haute bourgeoisie* would gladly accept the disdainful values toward business held by the *Junkers,* at the expense of their own. As a result, some of the characteristic political assets of a mercantile civilization may have become somewhat underrepresented in German culture. In commerce, as in politics, it is important to be able to bargain easily and successfully, without being either duped or angered, and without expecting either to give in or else to have things all one's own way. Merchants learn to accept bargaining and compromise as natural, rational, and honorable, while to aristocrats these practices may seem frustrating and somehow dishonorable. These two contrasting attitudes may carry over into politics, where the word *compromise* has long had a ring of illegitimacy in German ears.

Merchants also need to be capable of some degree of empathy; it helps them greatly to be able to perceive quickly and accurately the moods of their customers, to put themselves in their customers' place. These skills of perceptiveness, sensitivity, and empathy are common ones for the merchant and the politician—and for the types of diplomats, civil servants, and political leaders that England has long been training at Oxford and Cambridge—but they have not often been conspicuous in German politics. German empathy has come more often from imagination than from perception. German rationality has been more often not the rationality of the negotiator but rather that of the soldier, the scholar, and the bureaucrat.

The German lack of a strong mercantile tradition and the German authoritarian heritage do not make it easy for Germans to deal smoothly and effectively with equals, or to feel at ease in relations with them. "It is not easy to come to a strange country," the German author Bertolt Brecht once wrote; "you do not know at whom you may shout, and before whom you must doff your hat."

This difficulty of relating easily to equals, which is characteristic of the so-called authoritarian personality, has been reinforced by German geography and history. For long periods, Germany's western neighbors appeared to be clearly richer and more advanced, and thus potential objects of envy, while the peoples to the east seemed clearly poorer and more backward, and thus potential objects of contempt; but there were few, if any, prolonged periods in the history of the German people during which they could look upon any other large nation as just about their equals. Remembering a highly stratified environment abroad, it was difficult for Germans to think of their domestic and foreign policies in equalitarian terms.

POSTWAR CHANGES
IN POLITICAL ATTITUDES

In the face of this complex heritage of psychological and political assets, liabilities, and contrasts, the Bonn republic has done remarkably well. It has gone far toward making the politics of compromise appear both successful and legitimate. It has increased the degree of equality in German society and politics, through nearly full employment, broader educational opportunities, and a mitigation of class consciousness among the workers, and class exclusiveness among the *bourgeoisie.* It has acted toward the other countries of Western Europe, and particularly toward France, as an equal. More generally, it seems to have lowered the levels of bitterness and tension that could be found in earlier decades in the life and outlook of the German people; and this seems the more remarkable since tensions might have been expected to rise after a defeat in war.

In the early 1930s, the sharp rise in the frequency of suicides among Germans was cited by political spokesmen of various parties as evidence of the increase of such bitterness and desperation. Although it is not easy to say to what extent changes in the suicide rates do, in fact, reflect changes in the level of tensions and frustrations in a country, it may be significant that, under the Bonn republic, suicide rates have fallen 35–45% below their prewar levels, while according to all available evidence they have not done so in the German Democratic Republic under Communist rule.

Most important, perhaps, the Federal Republic has provided time, security, and opportunity for a new generation of young Germans to grow up and to reach the threshold of political life.

The political performance of the Bonn republic has matched this improvement in the general cultural and psychological climate. In contrast to the Weimar Republic, Bonn's governments have been highly stable; not one government has been overthrown by the opposition parties in the Bundestag, whereas Weimar's governments were toppled on the average of once every nine months. For the most part the government has operated in accordance with the rules set down in the Basic Law, unlike Weimar with its political violence and the excessive influence of the military-bureaucratic complex. And both the government and the parties have been fairly responsive to the demands of the voters and their pressure groups, making for a realistically representative democracy. Finally, the governments of the Bonn republic have managed to carry out some consistent long-range policies, and for the most part these policies have been judged to be highly successful by the population. Thus, the Bonn republic has been stable, representative, and effective.

Are there then any changes in the political culture that can help to explain Bonn's success? Given the fact that the Germans lived under a totalitarian regime for twelve years between the collapse of Weimar and the formation of the Bonn republic, it would seem that this intervening experience would have played an important part in the alteration of basic political attitudes. Perhaps the single most important effect of the totalitarian experience is the resulting breakdown of the simple traditional German identification of "freedom" with order and with the capacity to act, and hence in practice with the powerful and authoritarian state.

The tradition which merged the German quest for liberty with the acceptance of authoritarian government has been largely shattered by the experience of a brutal totalitarianism combined with a devastating military defeat. Thus, when asked whether they identify the ideas of freedom and order with democracy or National Socialism, 70% of the Germans interviewed in 1966 identified both freedom and order with democracy.[4]

The revulsion from the unsuccessful totalitarian experience also produced a new basis for evaluating the state: the state would now be judged on the basis of what it could do for the people, and not what the people could do for the state. The purpose of the state was placed squarely in the realm of the purely pragmatic, becoming the utilitarian servant of the people. Emerging from the country's economic and industrial ruin, the Bonn republic was assigned as its chief purpose the job of reconstructing the economy. Even in the late 1950s and early 1960s, after the job of reconstruction had been more than completed and the Bonn republic had entered into a period of previously unrivaled prosperity, West Germans continued to conceive of the state's functions primarily in terms of its success in maintaining a high level of economic affluence. The Germans' support of the Bonn regime, and more generally their attachments to democratic government, thus have primarily grown out of the regime's success in overseeing the "economic miracle."

The "All-Weather" Supporters of Democracy

That the Germans have not deeply rejected democracy—which they may very well have done considering their past history and the fact that democracy was given to them as a "gift" by the victorious Allies—may be more significant than the absence of emotional commitments to democracy. Moreover, there is a large group of Germans who, though they do not constitute a majority of the population, exhibit a continuous and broad-ranging set of

4 Ibid.

democratic attitudes, and a still larger group is conditionally committed to the Bonn republic for as long as their expectations are realized.

For most purposes, consistent defenders of democracy constitute about one-quarter of the West German electorate, and there is some evidence that they have grown in the course of the 1960s to one-third or more. Only on a few issues did the support of the democratic position in the 1950s and 1960s drop to about one-fifth of the total, as it did in 1966 in the case of only 15% approving of differences in customs and religions among Germans. One-fourth of the respondents to polls in 1952 condemned Adolf Hitler without qualification; demanded, in 1954, access to high government offices for members of the anti-Hitler resistance; declared, in 1953 and 1956, that they would do all they could to prevent the return of any Nazi-type movement to power; said, in 1956, that Germany was not better off for having no Jews; and expressed, in the same year, their acceptance of democracy in terms not only of rights but also of duties. A somewhat larger fraction, 29%, expressed approval of the Basic Law of the Federal Republic in 1956; and between 30% and 34%, depending on the wording of the question, endorsed in the same year the Federal Republic's black, red, and gold flag—a clear gain from the 25% who had done so in 1954. And in 1960, 25% approved of naming a public school after one of the heroes of the resistance against Hitler.

On many issues, the hard core of 25% "all-weather" democrats are joined by larger numbers of their countrymen. Already in 1952, as many as 71% demanded that a good political party should be "democratic"; and as already noted, in 1964, 76% approved of democracy for Germany—a substantial increase over the 57% who did so in 1953. Smaller numbers (38%) in 1956 denied that Hitler would have been a great statesman even if there had been no war; 40% in several polls in 1951–54 endorsed peacetime resistance against the Nazi regime; 47% in 1952 recorded a "bad opinion" of Hitler; and the same proportion in 1956 put the main guilt for World War II on Germany—a substantial increase over the 32% who had done so in 1951. When asked if they would vote for or against

"a man like Hitler," the proportion who would vote against such a man increased from 67% in 1953 to 83% in 1967.[5]

A Politically Cautious Pragmatism

These opinion data have provided a description of the attitudes of the committed democrats constituting more than one-quarter of the population. But as we have already noted, the German political culture is primarily characterized by pragmatic attitudes toward the democratic regime. It is to the attitudes of these pragmatists, making up about half the population, that we now turn, although it should be pointed out that this keen concern with security and the material benefits provided by the government is found in a more diluted form among the committed democrats as well.

The hard core of the pragmatists is found in the 15% of the electorate who usually stay at home and the additional 25% who vote only occasionally or who tend to switch their votes from one party to another; they also include most of the 5–15% who say "undecided" or "don't know" in the opinion polls. They seem to have no commitments and no ideology, and they have been called by many names: "fellow travelers of democracy," "success Germans," "the skeptical generation." This group seems larger in Germany than in most other developed countries. As far as many political issues are concerned, the Federal Republic is like a ship with half its cargo not secured—cargo ready in stormy weather to slide in any direction.

Yet this uncommitted section, too, shares to some extent a body of common commitments and a common ideology. They have a lively sense of concrete benefits, which they prefer to abstract slogans. In their reactions to political posters, this group has shown that they prefer an emphasis on jobs and homes to such abstract terms as "socialism" or "free enterprise." They are interested in security and solidarity,

[5] Deutsch and Edinger, *Germany Rejoins the Powers*, pp. 38–41; *Jahrbuch*, 2:126, 145, 165, 173, 279; communication of poll results from EMNID Institut, Bielefeld, 1957, 1964, 1966, and 1967.

and they are willing to accept and support policies and leaders that seem to promote these values.

A manifestation of the uncommitted voters' desire for security is their willingness to follow leaders and elites. The main Christian Democratic poster in the 1957 election showed only the impressive sun-bronzed face of Chancellor Adenauer and the slogan "No Experiments!" It was developed with the advice of experts in public opinion and persuasion, and it was a resounding success. Even apart from such campaigns, elite opinion may safely depart quite far from mass opinion in many matters, including specific measures of foreign policy and armament—since in the end the majority of the voters may be expected to accept, or at least passively support, the policies of their leaders.

The independence of elites may be seen, for example, in the CDU's selection of a successor to Chancellor Erhard in November 1966. When asked whom they would prefer as a successor to Erhard, in August 1966, only 3% of a national sample mentioned Kurt Georg Kiesinger.[6] Yet it was Kiesinger whom the CDU chose as their new leader, and thus as chancellor. In 1965, the debate over the statute of limitation on the Bundestag floor was paralleled by a discussion of this issue among the population. The separate formation of opinions on those two levels, the public and the leadership, resulted in a direct conflict between mass opinion and the government. Even though the public knew that a significant number of war criminals had not yet been apprehended, the majority opposed the suggested extension of the statute of limitations because they no longer wanted to be reminded of the Nazi era. Heidenheimer has aptly summarized the situation:

Especially because the issue arose in an election year, German politicians were placed in a dilemma. Elite opinion in allied countries as well as in the Federal Republic strongly urged the extension, and the Bonn politicians knew that if they did not act it would be grist in the mill of the East German propagandists who always sought to link Bonn to pro-Nazi tendencies. At the same time they knew that most of their constituents opposed the measure.[7]

In the end, the statute of limitations was extended; prosecutions of Nazi personnel for mass murders were pressed somewhat more vigorously; and these measures were accepted by the public.

A further trait is an interest in national power and prestige, not uncommon among the voters in any modern nation-state, but tempered in West Germany since World War II by a sober sense of realism. The great mass of West German voters will back any government measure that promises to increase German prosperity, security, prestige, or power, provided that its risks are moderate. Since 1945, the great majority of the West Germans have had no interest in desperate adventures; they very much want peace, and they have shown no inclination to underrate the strength of other countries, either of the United States or of the Soviet Union. Thus, in 1965, when asked if they thought that Germany would ever become a major world power again, only 17% said "yes." [8] Only 26% of respondents in 1956 favored fighting an atomic war in defense of democratic freedom rather than let Europe fall under Soviet rule; 36% said they preferred to avoid war even at this price, and the rest were undecided. In 1958, 71% had opposed equipping the Bundeswehr with nuclear weapons, and 81% had opposed the installation of launching platforms for nuclear rocket weapons on the territory of the Federal Republic.[9] And in 1966, only 8% of West Germans thought that German reunification should be brought about by more intensive pressures, entailing an increased risk of war. In 1961, a bare majority (52%) favored retaining the Bundeswehr, while 29%

[6] DIVO, *Pressedienst*, November 1966.

[7] Arnold J. Heidenheimer, *The Governments of Germany* (New York: Thomas Y. Crowell, 1966), p. 85.

[8] Unpublished report of the Institut für Demoskopie, June 1965.

[9] *Jahrbuch*, 3 (1959): 258; Erich Peter Neumann, *Public Opinion in Germany* (Allensbach and Bonn: Verlag für Demoskopie, 1961), pp. 52–53; EMNID, *Informationen*, January 31, 1967.

would have preferred to abolish it.[10] Thus, despite their overwhelmingly pro-Western orientation—being pro-American in the cold war and favoring the "Western way of life" to the Communist one—these attitudes suggest the willingness of the bulk of West German voters to accept defense policies at moderate levels of visible risk, but a distinct unwillingness on the part of the voters to go much further.

Unexpected circumstances could strain or shatter this limited consensus on policies of cautious national advance. The long, drawn-out crisis of West Berlin under Soviet pressure has received unceasing publicity throughout the Federal Republic, while the popular sentiment for German reunification seems to have grown somewhat, rather than receded, since the early 1950s. Inflamed by various incidents, these feelings may get out of hand and create situations which the Bonn government may find hard to control, and which may confront its Western allies with agonizing choices. A sharp deterioration of economic conditions, a rapid gain of power and confidence among the West German armed forces if they should acquire nuclear weapons, the consistent demands for reunification on *Western* terms might be other sources of serious instability, as could any sudden major threat or provocation by the Soviet-bloc powers.

How the Federal Republic's leaders will succeed in maintaining democracy, moderation, and the limited consensus among the different ideological elements of its population under the difficult conditions of the future may well test their statesmanship. By early 1972, it seemed that this level of statesmanship had prevailed. Though the economic boom had slackened and financial worries had increased during the crisis period of 1965–68, the Kiesinger-Brandt coalition government and its successor, the Brandt-Scheel government, had maintained economic solvency and civic peace, just like the Adenauer and Erhard cabinets up to 1965. West German democracy thus far has been based largely on the collaboration of a significant number of committed democrats with an even larger number of "fair-weather"

10 Ibid.

democrats whose allegiance is primarily based upon what they expect to get. This purely pragmatic orientation of the latter is by no means the best cultural foundation for democracy, nor is it the worst. It has given democracy in the Federal Republic only few convinced defenders, but it has cut down even more the number of its enemies.

IDEOLOGICAL CLEAVAGES AND GROUPINGS

"Ideology" is a label we sometimes apply to the belief systems of other people. It is a sobering experience to discover that we, too, hold many beliefs that we take for granted; that many of these beliefs are coherent and mutually supporting; that we use this collection of our coherent beliefs as a map of reality, or a frame of reference, on which we enter whatever new information we receive, and by which we try to make sense of it. In particular, we use ideologies as instruments to organize our fragmentary and disjointed knowledge of the world, and to make it look more complete and more consistent than it actually is, sometimes to allay our own anxieties. In short, we, too, may be said to have ideologies which serve us, and inevitably influence us, both in orientation and in action. It would be utterly naïve to deny that ideology exists, and only a little less naïve to claim that it exists exclusively in others. To be more realistic, we must try to assess ideology and its effects critically in each case, both in others and in ourselves.

Germany was a "highly ideological" country between 1930 and 1945, with an intense degree of ideological commitment among the Nazis and most of their opponents. Between 1945 and the present, the situation has been quite different. Intense ideological fanaticism has been rare; even many of those who were deeply committed to political ideas kept them within the limits of pragmatism and moderation. Under this landscape of moderate and practical politics in the Bonn republic, however, many ideological commitments and cleavages have persisted, and some of these may show up again in times of political or economic stress. This is true not merely of some older people in holding on to the attitudes of their past. During the last two decades, younger people in Germany have accepted new political ideas that may again sharpen into more intense ideological commitments under the stimulus of some crisis.

The Popular Rejection of Communism

One earlier ideology, however, has practically disappeared from West German politics. The Communists, who attracted an average of 13% of the votes cast in each of the seven national elections between 1924 and 1933, have dwindled into insignificance in the Bonn republic. This change was complete even before the outlawing of their party in 1956. In the 1949 Bundestag elections, the Communist share dropped to less than 6% of the valid votes cast. In 1953, the Communist strength dropped still further, to about 2%, of the popular vote. In 1969, when Communist parties were allowed again, the two radical leftist parties running candidates attracted even less than 1% of the votes cast.[11]

Poll results consistently show the same picture. Expressions of sympathy for the Communist party, or for the Communist regime in the G.D.R., are down to, or below, the 2% level, while 96% of West German respondents—a staggeringly high proportion—say they are certain that living conditions in the Federal Republic are better than in Communist-ruled East Germany.

In West German politics, Communism is as unpopular as sin—or, if possible, more so. The reasons for this change from the 1920s are

[11] Prewar data from Sydney L. W. Mellen, "The German People and the Post-war World, A Study Based on Election Statistics, 1871–1933," *American Political Science Review* 37, no. 4 (August 1943): Table 2, 612–13; postwar data from Erwin Faul, ed., *Wahlen und Wähler in Westdeutschland* (Villingen-Schwarzwald: Ring, 1960), pp. 321–23. The latter is an outstandingly useful and thoughtful collection of studies on voting behavior in the Federal Republic. Another important study is Erwin Scheuch and Rudolf Wildenmann, eds., *Zur Soziologie der Wahl* (Cologne: Carl Heymanns, 1965); also see *Handbuch des deutschen Bundestages*, 6. Periode, II, p. 2.

complex. The division and occupation of Germany at the end of World War II and the excesses of Soviet troops cannot account for all of it. Communist votes in West Germany were higher in 1946–49, when the memory of any such excesses would have been fresher than at any later time; they even dropped when the events of 1945 were receding into the past. Moreover, in Finland, which was also occupied by Soviet troops and lost important territories to Soviet Russia, the Communist party continued to receive a much higher degree of popular support.[12] Popular revulsion from Communism in West Germany may have been promoted by the continuing stream of expellees and refugees from Communist-ruled areas; by the inflow of these intensely anti-Communist millions into the least-skilled and worst-paid occupations, where the Communists otherwise might have hoped for converts; and most important of all, by the unprecedented rise and spread of economic prosperity after 1948, combined with effective social welfare legislation.

The Changed Emphasis of Democratic Socialism

Even the democratic version of Marxist ideas, traditional for generations in the Social Democratic party, has greatly receded. The Social Democrats have always been implacably opposed to Communist ideas of violent revolution and dictatorship, but they had accepted Karl Marx's belief in the central importance of class conflict and in the necessity of a fundamental change in property relations in industry, banking, and large-scale agriculture, to be brought about by far-reaching policies of nationalization. While some ideas of this kind were still voiced in the early years after 1945 by such SPD leaders as Kurt Schumacher, they did not prove popular in the elections of 1949 and thereafter, since they had become associated in popular memory with the economic

[12] These points are made by Juan Linz, *The Social Bases of West German Politics* (Ann Arbor, Mich.: University Microfilms, 1959), Columbia University Ph.D. Dissertation, pp. 64–65.

shortages, austerity, and rationing of the early postwar years. Since the late 1950s, the SPD has tried to change its public image from that of a "workers' party" to that of a "party of all the people," stressing human rights, welfare policies, full employment, and the guidance of a private enterprise economy through tax and credit policies, somewhat in the style of a large part of the Democratic party in the northeastern United States. The "basic program" of the SPD, voted by a special party congress at Godesberg in 1959, formally expressed this change of emphasis; and in 1962, when it was suggested that the customary socialist form of address, "comrade," be dropped, it was only decided to retain this old salutation "for the sake of long tradition." And at a special meeting of the SPD in December 1967, the hall was not decorated by the red flags that had previously appeared at official party gatherings. These symbolic changes are one manifestation of the impact of the younger generation on West German politics. Many of these men and women feel oversaturated with the trappings of close human community in politics, such as political salutations and the ritual use of the familiar "thou," all of which became discredited through their use by the Nazis.

The "New Left" and the German Students

Communism in terms of the system of government currently practiced in the Soviet Union, the G.D.R., and other Soviet-bloc countries is being rejected as authoritarian, bureaucratic, oppressive, and untrustworthy also by many young people in favor of social justice and equality and fundamental political and social changes. In recent years these young people have been avidly reading the various writings of Marx, Engels, Lenin, Rosa Luxemburg, Antonio Gramsci, Fidel Castro, Che Guevara, and Mao Tse-tung. Other Marxist writers who were held in disfavor by the official Communist parties, such as Nicolai Bucharin, George Lukács, Leszek Kolakowski, and Herbert Marcuse have also been widely read. It is surprising for visitors to see tables displaying writings by all these authors—sometimes with an odd pamphlet by Leon Trotsky, or even by Joseph Stalin—in the main entrance hall of a German university, doing a brisk trade.

Where classic Marxists, like classic capitalists, had stressed the need for higher industrial output, machine technology, gross national product, labor productivity, efficiency, and performance, many of the new student radicals deprecate the "worship of the gross national product" and the "society of high consumption and high performance" which only leads in their view to excessively hard work, unnecessarily high consumption, and the soulless alienation of man from his proper emotional, moral, and intellectual pursuits. The "new humanism" is characterized by individual self-expression, communal and small-group experiments with new styles of living, sexual experimentation, permissiveness, and freedom from all dominance and obedience. Thus, many of the antiauthoritarian and antiindustrial misgivings of the early-nineteenth-century romantics and the anarchists of later decades have returned.

These radical ideologies, and the occasional seizures of research institutes or other buildings, are, however, fringe phenomena. The majority of students do not share this complex of ideologies nor do they support the coercive tactics that go with them.

Nazi Ideology and the Extreme Right

Compared to Communist-inspired ideologies, those of the right have retained greater strength in their extreme versions and even more in their more moderate versions. From the mid-1950s to the early 1970s, about one German in twenty could still be counted as an intense hard-core Nazi, while one in eight professed explicit Nazi sympathies. Thus, in a 1953 poll, 13% said they would welcome the attempt of a new Nazi party to seize power, including 5% who promised their active support.[13] In repeated polls during the years 1949–63, simi-

13 *Jahrbuch*, 2:277, 279.

lar proportions of 7 to 15% said (1) they liked Hitler and his rabid propaganda minister, Joseph Goebbels, (2) professed Nazi race doctrines about the Jews, and (3) blamed foreign powers, and not Germany, for the outbreak of World War II in 1939.[14] Almost the same proportion of explicit Nazi sympathies has been found among the younger generation. In three polls—in 1953, 1954, and 1955—among young people between 15 and 25, an average of 10% professed favorable opinions of Hitler and of National Socialism.[15] In July 1956, in a special poll of young men, 16% declared without qualification that National Socialism had been "a good idea." [16]

Another 10–15% of Germans in the 1955–65 period were unmistakable, though less fervent, sympathizers of National Socialism or extreme nationalism. Together with the 10–15% of professed Nazi sympathizers, they bring up the ideological right wing of the German electorate to about 25% of the total. The same proportion, about one-quarter of poll respondents, expressed "predominantly favorable" opinions of Hitler, his deputy, Rudolf Hess, and the Nazi youth leader Baldur von Schirach; rejected in repeated polls the black, red, and gold flag of the Federal Republic; registered an unfriendly attitude toward democracy; blamed domestic sabotage and treason as the main causes of Germany's defeat in World War II; insisted "unconditionally" that in 1933 Germany had had no choices other than Communism and National Socialism; and wanted to bar from high government positions in the Federal Republic any man who had taken part in the wartime resistance against Hitler.[17]

On many particular issues, a considerably large proportion of Germans agreed with Nazi views. A number of differently worded polls through the mid-1960s consistently found 30–40% of the respondents expressing anti-Semitic views.[18] The reality of the attitudes indicated by these poll results was demonstrated in December 1959 and January 1960, when a Jewish tombstone and a synagogue in Cologne were disfigured with painted anti-Jewish slogans and Nazi swastikas. These acts of vandalism received wide and unfavorable publicity in the West German press, radio, and television, but were promptly followed within about four weeks by 470 similar incidents, at first particularly in North Rhine-Westphalia, but later, in the wake of the mounting publicity, in all *Länder* of the Federal Republic. A journalistic survey of crime waves in Germany later cited this chain reaction of outrages as a typical example of "sequential crimes"—that is, of cases where a predisposition to committing a particular type of crime or psychopathic outrage is triggered by the news of a similar act having been committed elsewhere.[19] The West German authorities, both *Land* and federal, were quick and unequivocal in condemning these outrages, and so were most articulate Germans. Yet the fact that there should be so many latent offenders, ready to commit so many imitative outrages in so short a time, vividly suggests how much tinder still resides beneath the tranquil surface of West German politics.

The 1961 trial in Israel of one of the chief organizers of the mass killing of Jews under Hitler, Adolf Eichmann, seems to have had a distinct impact on German opinion. Eichmann confessed to supervising the organized killings of men, women, and children, but defended himself on the grounds of having only obeyed superior orders. The fact that 6 million Jewish lives were lost as a result of Nazi persecution was established once again by expert testimony at the trial. Earlier, in 1952, about two-fifths of

[14] On these and the following points, see Deutsch and Edinger, *Germany Rejoins the Powers*, pp. 40–42; and poll data in *Jahrbuch*, 1:126, 132, 136, 138, 174, 276; *Jahrbuch*, 2:141, 277–79; *Jahrbuch* (1959), 3:216–17, 233, 297.

[15] From data in Rolf Fröhner, *Wie stark sind die Halbstarken: Dritte* EMNID *Untersuchung zur Situation der deutschen Jugend* (Bielefeld: Stackelberg, 1956), pp. 119–21, 305–10.

[16] *Jahrbuch*, 2:149.

[17] *Jahrbuch* 1:135–37; *Jahrbuch*, 2:144, 170, 172–73; *Jahrbuch*, 3:232–33, 235.

[18] *Jahrbuch*, 2:126; *Jahrbuch*, 3:216–17; Erich Lüth, "Deutsche und Juden heute," *Der Monat* 10, no. 10 (November 1957): 47, 49; *New York Times*, March 28, 1958; Deutsche and Edinger, *Germany Rejoins the Powers*, p. 41.

[19] *Der Spiegel*, 16, no. 27 (July 4, 1962):47–49. According to Heidenheimer, *Governments of Germany*, p. 88, the official count of outrages finally rose to 685.

Germans polled had opposed legal punishment for anti-Semitic propaganda; poll results published in 1957 showed that nearly two-thirds of the respondents had rejected a lower estimate of 5 million Jewish victims of the Nazis as "too high," and that 37% had called it "grossly exaggerated." By January 1960, however, only 7% insisted that the perpetrators of hostile actions against Jews should not be punished by the courts, while another 15% avoided a yes-or-no answer to this question. In April 1961, two-thirds of German poll respondents condemned Eichmann as a criminal and murderer: only 15% wanted a mild judgment for him, another 19% answered "don't know," 35% demanded the death penalty for the Nazi executioner, and another 31% wanted him to get penal servitude for life. Whether the impact of the Eichmann trial on German opinion has been only temporary, or whether it has contributed to a long-run change, only the future can reveal.[20]

Nazi ideas or practices receive support from a broader sector of the German electorate on a variety of other issues, particularly where national solidarity or military considerations are involved. In many such cases, national solidarity seems to outweigh more universal standards of ethics or morality among a sizable group of voters. Thus, in a poll published in 1961, as many as 36% said that even "if after 1933 a person was firmly convinced that wrongs and crimes were being committed under Hitler," he should not have offered any resistance; and when further asked what such a person should have done during the war, the group rejecting any resistance rose to 49%, with 34% advising the moral objector to "wait until after the war," and another 15% saying simply "neither then nor ever." In the 1956–60 period between 40% and 49% opposed the alleged proposal of a city government to name a public school after a well-known hero of the German wartime resistance.[21] Similarly, 39% said in 1954 that anti-Hitler refugees should be barred from high government positions in the Federal Republic; in 1960, 30% declared that "without the war, Hitler would have been one of the greatest German statesmen," accepting apparently within this judgment his concentration camps, mass murders, and dictatorship; more than 50% in 1951 asked for the lifting of the ban on the wearing of the Nazi war decorations, and opposed their being reissued with the swastikas removed; and 55% in 1953 denied that there had been major war crimes by the German military, and insisted that the German soldiers of World War II had no cause for any self-reproach for their behavior in occupied countries.[22]

Most of the potential strength of the extreme-right-wing ideology in Germany rests upon just this partial overlap with the beliefs and attitudes of broader sections of the German people. Ideological hard-core activists have become very few in West Germany, well below 2% of the electorate in the case of the Communists, and about 5% in the case of the Nazis and related right-wing extremists. But while much of the Communist ideology implies a sharp break with many popular German traditions and beliefs, the ideology of the extreme right often represents an extreme exaggeration of more widespread popular habits and beliefs. Where the few remaining Communists in West Germany are isolated within a wall of popular rejection and distrust, the hard core of extreme-right-wing and Nazi adherents can be likened to the central layers of an onion, surrounded by layer upon layer more distant from the core, but with few sharp breaks between them.

Very slowly, some of this right-wing strength is being eroded. The 12% who insisted on a one-party system for Germany in 1959 were the remnant of a larger sector, 22%, who had expressed this view in 1951.[23] The proportion of people who would vote for "a man like Hitler" decreased from 15% in 1954 to 4% in 1967, although 13% in 1967 replied that they do not have any opinion on the subject.[24] However, the recent sudden growth of electoral support for the right-wing National Demo-

20 Data in this paragraph are from *Jahrbuch*, 1:125–137; Erich Lüth, "Deutsche und Juden heute," 47, 49; Erich Peter Neumann, *Public Opinion*, pp. 48–49.

21 Neumann, *Public Opinion*, pp. 44–47; *Jahrbuch*, 2:145; *Jahrbuch*, 3:235.

22 Deutsch and Edinger, *Germany Rejoins the Powers*, p. 42; *Jahrbuch*, 2:278; *Jahrbuch*, 3:233.

23 Neumann, *Public Opinion*, pp. 50–51.

24 EMNID, *Informationen*, March 1967.

cratic party indicates that neo-Nazi supporters continue to exist. The National Democrats only received 2% of the vote in the 1965 Bundestag election. However, in four *Landtag* elections carried out in 1966 and 1967 they polled between 7 and 12% of the vote—in Schleswig-Holstein, Hesse, Bavaria, and Bremen. And in a 1966 national survey, 10% preferred to see the further growth of the NPD, with another 19% replying that they had no opinion on the subject.[25]

Although the leader of the National Democrats does not have a Nazi past, some of the members of the central executive do. And the party's appeal is in some ways reminiscent of Nazi propaganda before 1933. The National Democrats recurrently charge that the federal government is controlled by an "unscrupulous clique" that is undermining "national values." The CDU and the SPD, they say, have "sold out" to foreign interests, allowing the country to be deeply penetrated by foreign capital and workers. The vice-chairman of the party once denied the party's anti-Semitic orientation, but added that "the foreign workers are for us what the Jews were for the Nazis." [26] And the party newspaper carried advertisements for a four-volume edition of Hitler's speeches. The party's neo-Nazi tendencies are also manifested in a 1967 poll which asked whether the respondents would vote for or against "a man like Hitler." Among the NPD's supporters, 36% said that they would, compared to 11% of the NPD's sympathizers, and 3% of the population as a whole.[27]

Despite the fact that the NPD, since its establishment in 1964, succeeded to enter seven *Landtags,* it is likely to remain insignificant in West Germany's national and state legislatures. The election of 1969 was a turning point in the development of this party. With only 4.3% of the popular vote, the NPD was banned from entry into the Bundestag by the exclusion clause of the electoral law. The organizational disintegration of the party became apparent

shortly thereafter when, in October 1969, the party leadership called for a postelection congress in Saarbrücken and only a small fraction of the invited party deputies showed up.[28] This seems to confirm the assumption that the elections have isolated the NPD. Its structural collapse became complete when, in early 1970, the two vice-chairmen of the party and many high-ranking functionaries renounced their membership. Furthermore, by mid 1971, after elections in eight of the ten *Länder,* the NPD lost five of its seven representations. If this trend continues, the NPD is even likely to lose all its representations. Despite the latent danger stemming from a large proportion of neo-Nazi sympathizers, the fate of the NPD indicates that the right extremist trees are not likely to grow into the sky, and during the first twenty years of the Federal Republic a stronger bloc of adherents to the ideology of democracy has had an opportunity to consolidate itself. Here the search of the younger generation for acceptable values may well prove crucial.[29]

The Changing Party System

During the three generations from 1871 to 1967, West Germany has undergone spectacular but uneven changes. Its constitutional arrangements have changed most often and most dramatically. Its political parties have changed somewhat less, and its most influential interest groups have changed relatively least of all. To be sure, the word "relatively" is important here; among the major interest groups, the great landowners and aristocrats who enjoyed such a large share of power and prestige in imperial Germany, and who still wielded such considerable and even fateful influence in the decline of the Weimar Republic, have disappeared. Most of the other large interest groups of the past, however, have reemerged, and they

25 "1966 Survey." There appears to be no relationship between NPD sympathies and age.

26 Quoted in Walter Laqueur, "Bonn Is Not Weimar," *Commentary* (March 1967), p. 37.

27 EMNID, *Informationen,* March 1967.

28 "Thadden's Kämpfer vor verschlossenen Türen vereint," *Frankfurter Allgemeine Zeitung,* November 17, 1969.

29 For a good discussion about the future of German rightist movements, see Steven Warnecke, "The Future of Rightist Extremism in West Germany," *Comparative Politics* 2, no. 4 (July 1970):629–52.

pursue with zeal their social, economic, and political interests through the changed party system of the Federal Republic.

With the demise of the landowners, the second traditional great body of interests—big business and industry—has come into its own. For the first time, the business community has no major rival in its relations with the political parties and in its claims for the solicitude of government. Farmers and labor organizations can and often do exert effective pressure in pursuit of their specific interests; but the very much greater influence and prestige of business in the Federal Republic is conspicuous. When different business groups oppose each other, their influence is weakened, but when business speaks with a united voice, its views, with rare exceptions, weigh heavily in Bonn.[30]

Even the needs and demands of the most powerful interest groups, however, must be translated into political decisions and into administrative and legislative action. They must be made compatible with the interests of other interest groups, so as to secure for them an adequate measure of support, and they may have to be made palatable to potentially opposing interests by a process of political bargaining and mutual concessions. Although the great and persistent interest groups of the country most often get their way, they get it only through the political process, and particularly through the mediation and agency of the political parties.

At the first Reichstag elections in 1871, the parties of the right and center together won the votes of about 49% of the electorate (i.e., of all eligible voters) in Bismarck's Reich.[31] Ninety-four years later, in 1965, the reorganized and renamed parties of the center and the right

won the support of approximately 50% of the electorate of the German Federal Republic. During the intervening decades, the joint share of the right and center parties dropped to a low of 45% in 1919, and rose to a high of 61% in 1933. Through wars and revolutions, monarchies and republics, the regimes of Bismarck, Ebert, Hitler, and Adenauer, this electoral share of the German right and center parties never varied more than eight percentage points from a midpoint of about 53% of the electorate —a point not too far from their actual share of the electorate in 1969.

At that first election in 1871, only 2% of the electorate gave their votes to the Social Democrats, while another 49% made no use of their franchise. During the decades that followed, however, the voting habit spread. By 1912, a solid 29% of the electorate supported the Social Democrats, while only 15% stayed at home. This broad distribution of the pattern of 1912 was to remain characteristic for much of German politics thereafter. In 1965, the Social Democratic share of the electorate of the Federal Republic stood at 33%, and in 1969 it rose to 37%. Throughout the intervening half-century, with all its dramatic changes, the share of the labor and socialist parties of the left had only varied between 38% in 1919 and 26% in 1924 and 1949—with the important modification that this entire share now is concentrated once again in a single party, the SPD, as it was in 1912; in the elections from 1919 to 1953, however, it was split between Social Democrats and Communists, and sometimes also Independent Social Democrats. Finally, the percentage of nonvoters ranged between a high of almost 26% in prosperous 1928 to a low of 12% in the crisis election of 1933, remaining at about 16% after the Bonn republic was launched.

Within the first two of these three broad divisions—center-plus-right, left, and nonvoters —the shifts have been considerably more dramatic. The right, including both Conservatives and National Liberals, started out with 27% of the electorate in 1871. The share of its successor parties dropped to a low of 12% in 1919, to rise again to a spectacular 47% in 1933, and to dwindle to an insignificant 4% of the elec-

---

[30] The nearest thing to such an exception may have been the German-Israeli Reparations Agreement of 1952, which was opposed by some German business interests, but was pushed through by Chancellor Adenauer for reasons of morality, as well as of foreign policy, and which passed the reluctant Bundestag thanks only to the solid support of the chief opposition party, the Social Democrats. See Deutsch and Edinger, *Germany Rejoins the Powers*, pp. 168–76, and Kurt R. Grossman, *Germany's Moral Debt: The German-Israel Agreement* (Washington, D.C.: Public Affairs Press, 1954).

[31] For these and the following data, see Table 6-1.

TABLE 6-1. *Electoral Shares of German Parties and Groupings, 1871–1969*

	1871	1912	Jan. 1919	June 1920	May 1924	May 1928	Sept. 1930
Citizens entitled to vote (in millions)	7.7	14.4	36.8	36.0	38.4	41.2	43.0
Valid votes cast (in millions)	3.9	12.2	30.4	28.2	29.3	30.8	35.0
(approximate percentage of eligible voters)							
Far Right:							
Nazis	—	—	—	—	5	2	15
Conservatives	12	11	8	13	19	14	10
Moderate Right:							
National Liberals	15	12	4 *	11 *	6 *	6 *	3 *
Subtotal RIGHT	*27*	*23*	*12*	*24*	*30*	*22*	*28*
Progressives and Democrats (1928: State party)	8	10	16	7	6	10	9
Center and Bavarian Peoples' party	10	14	16	14	13	11	12
Particularists	4	9	1	1	1	1	1
Subtotal CENTER	*22*	*33*	*33*	*22*	*20*	*22*	*22*
Social Democrats	2	29	32	17	15	22	20
Independent Social Democrats	—	—	6	13	1	—	—
Communists	—	—	—	2	10	8	11
Subtotal LEFT	*2*	*29*	*38*	*32*	*26*	*30*	*31*
Nonvoters	49	15	17	22	25	26	19
Total	*100*	*100*	*100*	*100*		*100*	*100*

SOURCES: Dolf Sternberger et al., *Wahlen und Wähler in Westdeutschland* (Villingen/Schwarzwald: Ring, 1960), pp. 321–23; Sidney Mellen, "The German People and the Postwar World," *American Political Science Review* 37, no. 4 (August 1943), 601–25; Lewis Edinger, "Political Change in Germany," *Comparative Politics* 2, no. 4 (1970):552–53. The elections of December 1924 and July 1932 have been omitted; their inclusion would not change any of the major trends.

* DVP.
† DP and DRP.
‡ NPD.
§ FDP.
\# CDU.

torate in 1969. Nonsocialist parties of the center started with 22% of the electorate in 1871, rose to 33% in both 1912 and 1919, but dropped to a fatally low 14% in 1933. These parties of the center, however, rose spectacularly under the Federal Republic, when they inherited the

Nov. 1932	Mar. 1933	Aug. 1949	Sept. 1953	Sept. 1957	Sept. 1961	Sept. 1965	Sept. 1969
44.4	44.7	31.2	33.1	35.4	37.4	38.5	39.2
35.5	39.3	24.5	28.5	31.1	31.3	32.6	33

(approximate percentage of eligible voters)

Nov. 1932	Mar. 1933	Aug. 1949	Sept. 1953	Sept. 1957	Sept. 1961	Sept. 1965	Sept. 1969
26	39					2 ‡	4 ‡
7	7	4 †	4 †	4 †	1 †	—	—
2 *	1 *						
35	47	4	4	4	1	2	4
2	2	9 §	9 §	6 §	11 §	8 §	5 §
12	12	24 #	36 #	43 #	38 #	40 #	40
2	0	13	7	5	2	—	—
16	14	49	52	54	51	48	45
16	16	22	25	27	31	33	37
—	—	—	—	—	—	—	—
13	11	4	2	—	1	—	—
29	27	26	27	27	32	33	37
20	12	24	17	15	16	16	14
100	100		100	100	100	100	100

votes of most of the politically homeless former supporters of the discredited right. As early as 1949, in the first federal election, 49% of the electorate gave its support to a number of such nonsocialist middle-of-the-road parties. By 1969, a much diminished number of such parties was backed by 45% of the registered voters —the CDU, supported by 40% and the FDP, backed by about 5% of the electorate.

Throughout the days of the empire and the Weimar Republic, the voting strength of the center and the right had been scattered over many parties, with the only exception being in 1933 when the Nazis united a large part of it for their adventure in extremism. Never before the days of the Federal Republic had a moderate party succeeded in uniting under its leadership the bulk of this potential right and center vote, let alone in keeping it together through election after election. All this the CDU has accomplished, and in doing so it has become Germany's first example of a moderate and successful party of political integration.

THE CHRISTIAN DEMOCRATIC UNION (CDU)

The Christian Democratic Union, CDU, together with its Bavarian sister party, the Christian Social Union, CSU, is the successor of the old Catholic Center party, as well as of some small Protestant nonsocialist parties, such as the Christian Social People's Service (*Christlichsozialer Volksdienst*), and of parts of several middle-class and moderately conservative parties, such as the German People's party (*Deutsche Volkspartei*). For the first time in the history of German political parties, one party—the CDU/CSU—has succeeded in uniting strongly committed Catholics and Protestants, together with voters of less intense religious feelings, in a single large party. At the same time, it has united rural and urban voters, farmers and businessmen, artisans and white-collar workers, professionals and housewives, employers and labor union members, into a single broad party, which has succeeded in maintaining its significant appeal to every one of these diverse interests and groups.

All of these groups have, in fact, responded by giving a substantial part of their votes to the CDU, and they have continued to do so through six federal elections and a much larger number of elections in the *Länder*. They have differed significantly, however, in the measure of their support. The extent of these differences in the middle 1960s is shown in Table 6-2.

The figures in Table 6-2, as well as additional survey data, show that the CDU is getting twice as much support from Roman Catholics as from Protestants.[32] It also seems clear that the CDU is geting more of the votes of farmers, professional people, and businessmen, both big and small, than any other party. It gets more of the votes of the wealthy and the well-off, but it does fairly well in every income group. It has a strong appeal for voters over 60 years of age, who, we may recall, are more numerous in Germany than in many other countries. The CDU does least well, but still not too badly, among Protestants, skilled workers, nonskilled workers, and rural laborers.

The sources of the CDU's electoral support are reflected in the composition of the leading bodies of the party. The formal decision-making body of the party, its national executive (*Bundesvorstand*), mirrors the diversity of the party's supporters and its strong local roots, particularly in southern and western Germany. Formal power in this executive is divided between leaders of regional organizations (*Landesverbände*) and the party's chief representatives in the federal government and in the Bundestag, between Protestants and Catholics, and between trade union leaders and representatives of business and industry. More relevant for policy decisions, particularly in regard to foreign policy, has been an inner elite of the CDU. As of mid-1970, this group was composed of the party chairman, ex-Chancellor Kurt Georg Kiesinger, four vice-chairmen of the CDU, General Secretary Bruno Heck, and the party's parliamentary leaders—the chairman of the CDU delegation in the Bundestag, Rainer Barzel, and his two deputies; the chairman of the CSU delegation to the Bundestag, Franz-Josef Strauss, and his deputy; and the chairmen of the eight Bundestag committees, who also were CDU deputies.

A multiplicity of interests are directly and indirectly represented in the councils of the CDU. Among them are such powerful ones as the Roman Catholic church, big business and industry, farm groups, small businessmen's and employers' organizations, Protestant church leaders, and Christian trade unionists. This very multiplicity of interests and the breadth of the party's electoral support, however, give the party and its leaders a measure of independence against any single pressure group. The same facts, however, also increase the importance of the highly visible national leaders, who, after years of successful performance in government, have become unifying symbols for their party and its electorate, or for large parts of it. Chancellor Adenauer's power over his

---

[32] For data from 1953 surveys showing much the same picture, with a minor increase in Catholic preferences for the CDU since 1953, see Linz, *Social Bases of West German Politics*, pp. 181–87, especially p. 185.

TABLE 6-2. *Distribution of Party Preferences in the G.F.R., 1964*

	Proportion of Adult Population, 1961	Preferences Expressed in Opinion Poll, 1964				
		CDU/CSU	SPD	FDP	Others	None indicated
Total	100%	34%	34%	6%	2%	24%
Men	46	30	41	7	2	20
Women	54	38	28	5	2	27
Age cohorts:						
Born before 1933	72	35	32	6	2	25
Born after 1933	28	34	38	4	1	23
Religious identification:						
Protestants	51	28	39	8	2	23
Roman Catholics	45	45	26	4	1	24
Others or none	4	20	46	3	4	27
Educational level:						
Primary (8 years)	82	31	38	4	2	25
Secondary (9–10 years)	13	46	20	13	1	20
Higher (including university)	5	43	20	16	1	20
Occupations:						
Industrial and agricultural workers	50	22	50	2	2	24
Salaried employees	23	37	29	9	1	24
Civil servants and other government employees	7	49	27	7	1	16
Self-employed and professions	12	40	19	12	2	27
Independent farmers	9	62	7	14	2	15
Income level (monthly) *						
Under 400 DM	17	48	46	4	4	—
400–799 DM	61	40	50	5	5	—
Over 800 DM	22	57	30	14	1	—

SOURCES: Noelle and Neumann, *Jahrbuch der öffentlichen Meinung, 1958–1964,* pp. 3ff. EMNID, *Informationen,* Nos. 13 and 26 (1964).

* Income of principal earner in household as a proportion of all respondents reporting income in survey. (For total adult population, 1963 income.)

party was well known, but Chancellors Erhard and Kiesinger, and also such party leaders as Franz-Josef Strauss and Gerhard Schroeder, who served in most CDU governments as cabinet ministers of various departments, have all built up significant reputations.

The unity of the CDU has never been effectively threatened. All interest groups within the party stand to gain little and to lose much if it were lost. Some Protestant members may chafe at the predominance of Catholic politicians in the inner councils, but the CDU provides more patronage for middle-class Protestants than the latter would be likely to secure by any voting strength which they could command by their own unaided efforts. In Gerhard Schroeder as chairman of the Protestant caucus in the CDU, they have an influential representative of their views in the inner circles of the party. Many Protestant workers vote in any case for the SPD; and the CDU policy of allocating national, regional, and local patronage roughly in proportion to the overall strength of the denominations, with only minor deviations in favor of Catholics, also gives the CDU Protestants the benefit of the quota of those Protestants who have been voting for the SPD.

Something similar applies to other groups. Catholic trade unionists have been dissatisfied with the steady rightward drift of the CDU, which has moved from stressing social reform and the acceptance of moderate socialism in the party's *Ahlener Programm* of 1947 to the conservatism and increasing identification with the views of business enterprise during the Adenauer era. Yet, as committed Catholics, these unionists are unlikely to join the SPD, because of the latter's Marxist (i.e. nationalist)

origins in the 19th century, and they have no realistic alternative to staying in the CDU. Farm groups likewise have found that they can get much through the CDU—including substantial farm price supports as well as the prestige of having had a farm leader, Heinrich Lübke, as president of the republic—while any alternative political alignment they might make would offer them much less.

The relative satisfaction of all these groups with the CDU during the years of mounting prosperity has tended to restrict the political chances of the SPD, almost regardless of the policies or skills of its leaders. But the slowing down of prosperity after 1963, and particularly during the coal crisis, together with the demands for a more equitable distribution of some of the gains that are still being made, resulted in a relative loss of popular support for the CDU in the 1969 elections (see Table 6-3).

The CDU has been one of the most successful political parties in the world. Starting from a coalition of diverse elements, it has held them together and led them to many electoral

TABLE 6-3. *Voters' Evaluations of the Political Parties in the G.F.R., 1961–69*

	Pre-election Sept. 1961	Post-election Nov. 1961	CDU/ CSU/FDP Coalition under Erhard July 1964	Post-election Oct. 1965	Formation of CDU/ CSU/SPD Coalition Nov. 1966	Mid-term of CDU/ CSU/SPD Coalition April 1968	Beginning Crisis of CDU/CSU/SPD Coalition			Pre-election September 1969
							Feb. 1969	March 1969	April 1969	
SPD	+108	+108	+191	+137	+178	+154	+193	+213	+210	+249
CDU/CSU	+196	+166	+210	+216	+151	+168	+180	+195	+207	+249
FDP	+ 36	− 41	− 1	− 4	− 70	− 22	− 9	+ 22	+ 14	+ 58
NPD	—	—	—	—	−252	−253	−278	−302	−296	−280

SOURCE: Hans D. Klingemann and Franz Urban Pappi, "The 1969 Bundestag Election in the Federal Republic of Germany: An Analysis of Voting Behavior," *Comparative Politics* 2, no. 4 (July 1970):539.

NOTE: These voter's ratings of political parties were measured with the help of a "scalometer" question. This question was posed at regular intervals to a representative cross section of the population. Use of this scalometer question involved asking the respondents to express the degree of their attraction to a particular party on a scale ranging from +5 to −5. The ranking of a party is shown by an index figure which may reach ratings of +500 to −500. The index figure is computed with the help of relative frequencies such as the arithmetic mean, the difference being merely that the results are not divided by 100. As a result the scale ranges from +500 to −500 instead of from +5 to −5. The closer the index figure comes to the point +500, the more positive were respondents' sympathies for a particular party.

victories; once, in 1957, the party won an absolute majority of the valid votes cast—which amounted to 43% of the total electorate—something never before achieved in German history by a single party in a free election. Although it could not hold its 1957 share of the vote, by 1969 it had consolidated many of its gains at a level of 40% of the electorate or more and seems likely to remain a large West German party for the indefinite future.

Within this spectacularly successful party, however, distinctive elements have persisted. One bloc of voters follows closely the direct and indirect lead of the Roman Catholic church in political affairs; the stability of this group's commitment is strengthened not only by the influence of the clergy, but also by that of many local and community leaders who as youths were influenced by the various Roman Catholic lay organizations, in which many of the leaders are still active. Particularly important elements among these stable Catholic CDU supporters are rural groups and Catholic trade union members. Similar but much smaller groups of strongly committed Protestant voters are also reliable CDU supporters. All these stable groups back the CDU regardless of the party's current electoral propaganda or of its financial resources.

These groups that consistently vote for the CDU are not adequate to maintain a large party and give it a good chance to win each election. Many of the voters who ordinarily cast their ballots for the CDU pay little attention to politics. They must be aroused anew at each election and brought to the polls in just the right kind of mood. All this costs a remarkable amount of money—far more than the CDU can collect from its members. Although the CDU/CSU in 1957 polled over 15 million votes, the party had only about 250,000 members, or one member for every sixty votes. Annual membership fees are estimated to have brought in less than $300,000. About another $400,000 per year came in from levies on Bundestag and *Landtag* deputies of the party, and the remaining $400,000 or $500,000 needed to make up the $1.1–1.2 million necessary to run the party organization even in a nonelection year had to come from private donations.

In the 1957 election, however, private campaign contributions on behalf of the CDU/CSU and expenditures by the party itself and through parallel campaigns—e.g., the special campaign on behalf of Dr. Ludwig Erhard—totaled perhaps $9 million. This was about eight times the amount of off-year spending. By comparison, in Britain, a country with a comparable number of voters, the Conservative party spent about $1.8 million in the 1955 election. In other words, the CDU collected on the average a little more than $1 from each of its members, while spending about $4 per member in an off-year, and about $36 per member—or about 60 cents per vote obtained—in the 1957 election. These per capita figures approach American levels of campaign expenditure, in a country with less than half the American per capita income.[33]

In contrast to the CDU, the SPD, in 1957, with 600,000 members—or one for every sixteen votes—collected about $2 million in dues, or an average of more than $3 per member; it spent less than $2.4 million in the election, corresponding to roughly $4 per party member and 25 cents per vote obtained.[34] In short, the CDU in the 1957 election outspent the SPD by more than 2:1 per vote, by about 4:1 in total campaign expenditures, and by 8:1 per member.

Much of this money is raised from economic interest groups, primarily from those in industry, commerce, and banking; the continuing need for money of this kind makes the CDU, and FDP as well, more dependent on the support of organized business interests, and particularly of big business, than are comparable parties in England and the United States. As we shall see below, business interests in the German Federal Republic have special centralized institutions—the Sponsors' Associations

[33] For detailed figures, see U. W. Kitzinger, *German Electoral Politics* (Oxford: Clarendon Press, 1960), pp. 202–3, 312n. Kitzinger's careful calculations are lower than the off-year figures computed in Arnold J. Heidenheimer, "German Party Finance: The C.D.U.," *American Political Science Review* 51, no. 2 (June 1957), 369–85. The figures given in SPD publications are substantially higher; for details see Kitzinger, *German Electoral Politics*, pp. 304–12.

[34] Kitzinger, *German Electoral Politics*, pp. 202–4.

and the Civic Associations—whose contributions are mostly tax-deductible and who get the most political value for their money.

However, the business associations have not been as reliable in their distribution of funds as the CDU would have liked. For example, they temporarily cut off funds to the party when Adenauer displeased the industrialists by revaluating the currency in 1961.

As we mentioned in the previous chapter, much of the influence of interest groups upon the policy of the major parties by means of granting or withholding badly needed funds has decreased since the enactment of the Party Law of 1967. Its articles 18–22 ensure the parties a steady and reliable flow of governmental subsidies during the election years. The Party Law relieves the parties of their immediate dependence on contributions from sponsor organizations; but since there is no legally prescribed ceiling for campaign expenditures in the Federal Republic, the present regulation still gives the pressure groups vast opportunity to exert influence through additional contributions.

One further source of influence on the CDU should be noted here. The figures for its 1957 campaign expenditures given above do not include any sums spent by the federal government at the time of the electoral campaign to popularize its policies, nor do they include the services of government personnel, who also happened to be chiefly CDU members, loaned to the CDU for campaign purposes. The SPD alleged that government spending in 1957 on what was in effect campaign propaganda for the CDU amounted to another 40 million DM, or $10 million. On this point, the cautious judgment of U. W. Kitzinger deserves citation:

It was generally admitted that Government funds were used on a large scale before and during the election to propagate the Government's foreign, military, and domestic policies among the electorate. The Chancellor's fund of 11 million DM per annum was one of the chief sources of finance for such activity, the Press and Information Office with its annual budget of 20 million DM used a certain proportion of its funds in a similar direction, and the information budgets of the various ministries, particularly that of the Ministry of Defense, which amounted to 6 million DM per annum, were also used in part

for overt and indirect activity of this kind. But no useful purpose would be served by attempting to calculate a wholly arbitrary figure of Government expenditure incurred more or less directly to return the Government parties to power. The line between propaganda for a government and its policies and for the Government parties and their personalities is not easy to draw in a state where the Opposition rejects such important parts of Government policy as was the case in the Federal Republic. This undoubted fact was used (even perhaps abused) by supporters of the Government to defend its information policy; but it is also a source of very real difficulty for any attempt at a breakdown of information accounts for the purposes of political studies.[35]

If, nevertheless, we do try to estimate the size of this indirect government intervention in the campaign, we might perhaps deflate the SPD's estimate about one-half—that is, by the same ratio by which Mr. Kitzinger's careful estimates reduced the SPD allegations of the electoral expenditures by the CDU and parallel campaigns by private groups. This would leave us with another $5 million of effective pro-CDU campaign expenditure by the government, or somewhat more than half of all other campaign spending by or on behalf of that party.

THE SOCIAL DEMOCRATIC PARTY (SPD)

The leaders and many of the members of the Social Democratic Party, SPD, think of it as a grand old party with a great tradition, going back for nearly a century to the days of Ferdinand Lasalle, August Bebel, and even—although this is stressed less often—Karl Marx. They are particularly proud of the party's long record of firm commitment to democracy, maintained in the years of Nazi persecution, as well as against the appeals and threats of Communism, in both West and East Germany and in besieged West Berlin, whose people have been electing SPD majorities for a long time.

Although the party has long since shed much of the vocabulary of Marx, much of its

[35] Kitzinger, *German Electoral Politics*, p. 311.

concern for ideology, and much of its old, sharply focused class appeal to industrial labor, the fact is that many of its old symbols—the red flag, the old labor union songs, and the salutation "comrade"—still remind the members of the hope for a bright and fraternal future. The party has largely deemphasized or dropped its former demands for nationalization of industries and has replaced them with a stress on indirect economic controls, reminiscent of Keynesian economics and the American New Deal and New Frontier ideas. It is trying to become a "people's party," rather than the party of a single class, and to break through the "40% barrier" within which its share of votes in the Federal Republic and in most of the *Länder* was so long confined. This new image of the SPD helped produce its electoral "victory" in the fall of 1969, when the Social Democrats attracted 42.7% of the voters. And by 1970, the ministers president of five *Länder* —half of the total number of *Länder*—came from the SPD.

If the party has achieved this changed image in the eyes of many of its own members, it has not done so in the view of many of its more fundamentalist stalwarts or in the view of a large part of the electorate. To most middle-class voters, the party is still "red." To the Catholic church, the SPD's treatment of religion as a strictly private matter, coupled with the actual religious indifference or heterodoxy of many party leaders, has remained unsatisfactory. To those of a conservative temper, including a great many women voters, the party still appears suspect. While the SPD can change many of the sharp edges of its political style, it cannot shed its character as a party that is advocating more comprehensive reforms than is its counterpart, the CDU. But when, during the coal crisis, a majority of the German electorate became once more interested in economic reforms, the efforts of the SPD to develop a more popular image brought success and enabled it to form its coalition with the FDP. The SPD continues, though to a lesser degree than during the 1950s, to derive its most reliable voting support from trade union members, skilled workers, unskilled workers, nonchurchgoers, men, large-city residents, pensionees and

trainees, and the lower-middle- and low-income groups—in roughly that order.[36]

The party is based on a strong and disciplined membership. In 1932, before the Nazi dictatorship, the SPD had had about 980,000 members; in 1946, the reemerging party in the much smaller Federal Republic already had 710,000 members, or proportionately nearly the same number within the population. This membership then rose to a peak of 840,000 in 1948, to decline to a low of 600,000 by 1957. By 1970, its membership was up again to a figure of 710,500. The membership dues collected amounted to an annual total of about $2.5 million during 1965–70, a clear indication of the consolidation and loyalty of the membership and a guarantee of the substantial financial independence of the party.[37]

The income from membership dues, however, is small when compared to governmental subsidies of campaign expenditures during federal election years, and the proceeds from special donations, fund-raising drives, election contributions, and the like. None of its diverse sources seemed likely to exert effective influence or pressure on the party. The trade unions continue to be the main interest group of whose views the SPD is likely to be mindful. In contrast to the Weimar period, however, the major labor unions united in the German Trade Union Federation (DGB) include not only Social Democrats but also the former Christian trade unions, whose members and functionaries support the CDU and who would oppose any strong partisan commitment by their organization. The somewhat greater pro-SPD activitiy of the DGB in the 1953 elections ended in embarrassing political defeat. For these and other reasons, active trade union support for the SPD in subsequent election campaigns remained peripheral.

36 DIVO Institut, *Umfragen* (October 1966); Blücher, *Der Prozess der Meinungsbildung; Jahrbuch,* 1:264.

37 See Erich Matthias, "Die Sozialdemokratische Partei Deutschlands," in *Das Ende der Parteien 1933* ed. Erich Matthias and Rudolf Morsey (Düsseldorf: Droste, 1960), p. 119n, with references; Grosser, *Die Bonner Demokratie,* p. 139; Kitzinger, *German Electoral Politics,* p. 204; *The Europa Yearbook 1971* (Den Haag, 1971), p. 744.

A major source of strength for the SPD, together with its membership, are its functionaries—the chairmen of local party organizations, the party representatives elected to seats in the local governments, the national and district secretaries of trade unions, of cooperatives, and of the SPD itself. These people are committed to the SPD, sometimes with all their bureaucratic virtues and weaknesses—steadfastness, discipline, and loyalty to a centralized hierarchy and routine. The party frequently insists that newcomers serve long political apprenticeships at low levels in the organization, and is unwilling to let brilliant "young men in a hurry" make dazzling careers in the party.

Since the early 1950s, the party has been tightly governed by its deputy chairman, Herbert Wehner, who is presently also chairman of the SPD delegation in the Bundestag. Next to Chancellor Willy Brandt (who is also party chairman), he plays the role of an energetic whip and organizer to ensure party discipline and unity. His position and his ascetic and implacable personal style make him one of the most powerful figures in the Social Democratic party.

The highest authority of the SPD is its biennial congress, but the real power lies in the party's national executive committee—the *Parteivorstand*—in the chancellor and the cabinet members, and in the leadership group of the SPD delegation in the Bundestag. This executive committee is effectively in control of the party. Regional leaders have far less power than they do in the CDU. The Bundestag delegation has no tradition of open disagreement with the executive committee of the party. The most prominent SPD parliamentarians are members of the party executive as well, and many deputies are also employees of the party, or of some organization under its control. The SPD executive committee forms a fairly homogeneous group.

The SPD has had a more intense interest than the CDU in German reunification and the recovery of the present G.D.R. territories, from which before 1933 much of the SPD strength was traditionally drawn. The party was cool toward the NATO military alliance with the West and would have preferred to buy German reunification at the price of German neutrality and continued disarmament, provided only that reunification should bring genuinely free elections in the G.D.R. areas. This, however, the government of the Soviet Union has never been willing to concede, and thus the SPD's willingness during the 1950s to accept some limited compromises with the Soviets was somewhat unreal. Gradually, the party came to accept all the essentials of Adenauer's foreign policy, including German membership in NATO and in the Common Market and the policy of firm alliance and increasing integration with the West. In June 1960, this acceptance was formally put on record by the national party secretary, Herbert Wehner, speaking for the SPD in the foreign policy debate in the Bundestag.

Chancellor Willy Brandt, the former mayor of West Berlin, who as the leader of the SPD became the foreign minister in the CDU-SPD coalition government of 1966–69, has become the symbol of this new SPD course toward greater stress on national unity. The SPD has remained less enthusiastic, however, about the pace and scope of German rearmament, and has retained a distaste for nuclear armaments on German soil or in the hands of German troops. Although the SPD and the CDU were thus united on basic foreign policy in the middle 1960s, the SPD position continued to be slightly more moderate and flexible than the rigidly uncompromising "hard line" of the CDU. Brandt's preference for diplomacy over power politics as a principle of foreign relations activities culminating in his government's talks with the Soviet Union over the status of Berlin and the Oder-Neisse territories, was instrumental in gaining him the 1971 Nobel Peace Prize.

Within the SPD, there are fewer distinct interest groups than there are in the CDU. Labor unions and consumers' cooperatives, however, are directly represented in the party leadership and in the SPD delegation in the Bundestag, through members who are or have been their paid functionaries. Another interest group is composed of the many SPD functionaries and deputies who are linked to the municipal governments dominated by the party. These include the mayors of traditionally SPD-controlled industrial centers such as Hamburg and Bremen. Finally, there are the expellees and refugees, who are now represented among the deputies of both major parties. Within the SPD, their representation used to be particularly effective, but by the early 1970s, it had declined there, too.

THE FREE DEMOCRATIC PARTY (FDP)

The last of the smaller parties to survive in the Bundestag, the Free Democratic party (FDP), has a somewhat divided character and heritage. It continues from Weimar days the tradition both of the liberal-progressive Democratic party and of the moderate-conservative German Nationalist People's Party (DVP), which in turn had been a successor to the National Liberals of the pre-1914 era. The progressive tradition of the party links the FDP to the liberal, middle-class Protestants of southern Germany, and the conservative tradition ties it to the Protestant and anticlerical business and professional elements in the northern and western regions of the country. Until the grand coalition period, the adherents of other parties regarded the FDP as a party somewhat to the left of center, but most supporters saw it as a party of the right. The latter view was the more realistic. For a time power within the FDP was shifted from the liberal wing represented by the first president of the republic, Dr. Theodor Heuss, to the somewhat more nationalistic and business-oriented views of Erich Mende, who was the party leader until late 1967. (In 1970, Mende renounced his FDP membership and became a deputy of the CDU.) During its time in opposition, from 1966 to 1969, the FDP underwent a remarkable transformation. With support from its younger members, the new leadership, under Chairman Walter Scheel, made headlines with its demand for a new *"Ostpolitik,"* including the formal abolition of the Hallstein doctrine, detente treaties with Germany's eastern neighbors, a possible formal recognition of the G.D.R., and

a denial of any claims of the West German government concerning the restitution of Germany within the borders of 1939. This "soft line" vis-à-vis Communism meant a rather radical departure from the CDU foreign policy of the preceding seventeen years, which the FDP had endorsed by and large. This and the FDP support for antiauthoritarian university reforms led to a renewed reputation of the FDP as a left-liberal and progressive party.

During the early 1960s, when both the CDU and the SPD had succeeded in winning support from a wide range of social groups and strata, the FDP alone, in the words of a contemporary German study, could "still be characterized as a class party." [38] It had the image of a party of the middle classes, of employers and business management. Accordingly, it sharply criticized the economic and social welfare policies of the CDU. While it has agreed with the SPD in favoring the separation of religion and politics and in opposing the extension of the church influence in education, public life, and government administration, in 1969 the FDP was not only able to cooperate with the SPD in economic policy at the national level, but after changes in its leadership and the amelioration of its financial dependence upon the business class thanks to the 1967 Party Law, it could even join a national coalition with the SPD. In Bonn, the FDP had long functioned as a political reserve of the CDU, available for a coalition with the CDU, but unavailable to the latter's SPD rivals. The change of tactics in the FDP of the later 1960s reflects the shift of interests among its members and supporters.

Whether the FDP with its new image as a left-liberal party will be able to survive the 1970s as a third force vis-à-vis the two major catchall parties, the CDU and the SPD, is one of the important structural questions for German democracy of the near future. In case the FDP collapses and West Germany develops a two-party system like that of the United States or Great Britain, it is hard to predict at this point which of the two major parties would benefit more from such a development.

[38] Viggo Graf Blücher, *Der Prozess der Meinungsbildung,* p. 116.

A BROAD AND GROWING CONSENSUS

Whereas the left-wing and right-wing parties under Weimar were separated by a wide chasm of ideologies, the parties of Bonn show a good deal of affinity in their programs. Competing for the more numerous votes near the center of the political spectrum, all the major parties have come to emphasize moderate, middle-of-the-road policies. While the right wing of the CDU and the left wing of the SPD still exercise a good deal of constraint upon their respective party leaders, the center of gravity in both parties definitely resides with the more moderate elements. The relatively smooth formation of the CDU-SPD coalition government in 1966 and the easy shift of power from the CDU to the SPD in 1969 shows how far this consensus has developed.

The three great cleavages that characterized German party competition in the first half of the twentieth century have largely disappeared. The conflict between the supporters of democratic and of dictatorial forms of government has been largely settled, as the CDU, the SPD, and the FDP have all made it crystal clear that they accept the democratic rules of the game, founded upon a free and open society. Unlike the situation in the French Fourth and Fifth Republics, Bonn's parties do not disagree with each other about any procedural (i.e., constitutional) issues. Secondly, church-state issues have receded into the background at the federal level, and have lost most of their bitterness at the *Land* level, where the issue, however, remains a significant one, involving the *Land* governments' responsibility for educational matters— the issue having evolved into a debate about the assistance that the *Land* governments ought, or ought not, to give to the denominational (especially Catholic) schools. The third cleavage that has characterized German politics in the twentieth century—the conflict between nationalization/state control of industry and the free-enterprise system—has also been effectively tamed. On the one hand, the socialists have accepted the idea of a largely free-market economy, and on the other hand, the CDU has accepted some government intervention and antimonopolistic measures that have, in the interests of the consumer, placed limitations upon business competition.

Thus, in 1964, when a sample of German elite members were asked to name "the most important differences between the major political parties," fully 59% replied that such differences either do not exist at all, or are at worst only superficial ones. The comments offered in response to this question further emphasized the broad consensus between the major parties: one of SPD Chairman Willy Brandt's closest associates blandly defined the differences between the parties as "some are in and others are not." An important CDU leader said that it was difficult to find points of controversy with the SPD, quoting a cabaret joke which held the SPD in 1964 to be "the best CDU we ever had." A few of the elite members, especially among the mass-media leaders, regretted the fact that the parties had lost their sharp differences and no longer offer the voters a real choice between alternative policies. But most of the elite sample, including the party leaders themselves, were not troubled by such considerations.[39]

INTEREST GROUPS

Political parties, especially when they are broadly based, as in the case of the CDU and SPD, have "policy umbrellas" (platforms) that cover and protect as many diverse interests as possible so as to maximize their electoral support. It is then the function of interest groups to represent particular policy preferences at a lower level of aggregation than do the parties. They formulate and press for specific demands that parties then aggregate into more-or-less coherent platforms. Interest groups—or pressure groups, as they are often called—thus bring together into an organized form the preferences of like-minded individuals and groups, such as large business firms, for it is by organizing these individuals and groups that they can most effectively influence governmental policy.

39 K. W. Deutsch et al., *France, Germany and the Western Alliance* (New York: Scribners, 1967), p. 129.

Although we cannot reliably rank the democratic countries according to the importance and success of their interest-group activities, it is possible to suggest certain general characteristics that tend to enhance the significance of pressure groups. The first such characteristic is policy consensus. A wide-ranging policy consensus is most conducive to intense pressure-group politics; sharp cleavages reduce its potency, for when fundamental differences of opinion exist, the comparative safety of the political arena is forsaken in favor of self-destructive competition between the parties. When party arguments come to revolve around, say, the legitimate governmental structure, or the relationship between the state and the churches, the conflicts involve too-broad principles and too-large sections of the population —for pressure groups are (or at least should be) concerned with more specific and limited objectives, and involve much smaller groups of people. On the other hand, when there is a general policy consensus, as there is in West Germany, politics revolve around limited and unemotional issues which the pressure groups are most concerned with and are best capable of handling. In short, when party conflicts are not intense—when they are based upon personalities and indistinct policy tendencies—pressure groups come into their own.[40]

The importance of interest groups is also related to the extensiveness of governmental activities in the economic and social spheres. As governmental involvement increases, so does the likelihood that pressure groups will be formed in order to affect governmental policy where it impinges on their interests. Although Bonn's governments have not created a centralized economic planning policy, the government is continually involved in the economic life of the country (as could be seen most clearly during the coal crisis), and it has also developed a vast social service state—two types of governmental activities that have encouraged the creation and active involvement of interest groups in these areas. Since individuals and groups have far more to gain or lose through

governmental action in a welfare state, they will tend to form interest groups and intensify the pressures of existing ones.[41] Moreover, the complex and bureaucratic nature of the welfare state necessitates the cooperation of the chambers of commerce, farmers' organizations, and other associations in the work of advising the civil service on technical matters, and in administering certain regulations that can be handled better by the associations themselves rather than by the governmental bureaucracy.

Thirdly, the characteristics of the interest groups themselves play a decisive role in determining their importance and effectiveness. One of these characteristics is *wealth,* and we have already noted the extensive contributions made by the business associations to the CDU— contributions which still assure them of a significant voice in party councils. Another group characteristic is the *prestige* accorded them by the population; for if interest groups were not accorded this respect, it would be easier for politicians to ignore their appeals. By 1964, only 19% of the Germans interviewed said that pressure groups have more influence than they ought to have, and there was hardly any difference between the views of CDU and SPD supporters.[42] And in the case of German business groups, they indeed enjoy an enormous prestige in a postwar culture that places exceptional emphasis upon material success and industrial production. In contrast, the labor unions are not accorded nearly the same amount of prestige by the middle class as business enjoys among many employees and workers.

Still another characteristic is size and comprehensiveness. When the pressure groups represent nearly the entire section of the population that subscribes to a particular set of interests, and if these pressure groups are effectively organized in order to press their demands upon the government, then again we can expect that they will be both important and successful. In Germany, both business and labor are effectively organized into nationally centralized organizations. Both are organized according to a hierarchical principle by which the

---

[40] Harry Eckstein, *Pressure Group Politics* (Stanford, Calif.: Stanford University Press, 1960), pp. 31–32.

[41] Ibid., pp. 26–27.
[42] EMNID, *Informationen,* no. 11, 1965.

so-called *Spitzenverbände* (the "peak associations") coordinate the activities of the local and regional associations, and then speak with one voice when negotiating with the government. The interest groups are strongly encouraged to organize on a national basis because the rules of procedure that are binding upon all the federal ministries require that civil servants deal only with the representatives of the national or "peak associations"; and these rules also provide that only those associations that have a nationwide membership be consulted in the preparation of legislative drafts.[43] German interest groups are, then, as inclusive (having as members a very high proportion of the people whose interests they speak for) and well-organized as are British pressure groups, and far more inclusive and tightly organized on a national basis than are interest groups in the United States.

Because of these factors, interest groups play a vital role in West German politics. Their influence and acceptance as legitimate parties in the formation of policy is evidenced in the regular consultations that take place between cabinet members and pressure group representatives well before any law is even framed for presentation to the Bundestag—a pattern that also prevails in England. The extensive demands and forceful pressures that the interest groups have directed toward Bonn led Chancellor Erhard, for instance, to complain publicly about the *"Interessentenhaufen"* (the "heap of interest-mongers") into which he saw the West Germans developing. Another indirect indication of the pervasiveness of pressure-group activity may be found in the resignation of a distinguished deputy and industrialist from the chairmanship of the Committee on Finance and Taxation in the early 1960s, partly because of his disgust with the growing influence of pressure groups.[44] However, in a recent sample survey of German elites, only a small minority complained of the excessive influence of pressure groups; the great majority felt that the power of particular groups was balanced by the power of others, without any single interest achieving dominance.[45]

Having noted their importance, we can now ask which "targets" the interest groups aim at in attempting to realize their goals. Clearly, the most important factor that determines through which channels the interest groups will exercise their influence is the governmental structure—or, more specifically, the governmental institutions that have the power to affect their particular interests. The three prime pressure group "targets" in Germany are the cabinet ministers (who are also the party leaders), the Bundestag's specialized committees, and—with the devolution of vast powers to the bureaucracy in a social service state—the civil servants.

Although it is extremely difficult to estimate the frequency with which interest groups seek to influence each of these three centers of power, one piece of evidence underlines the efforts expended vis-à-vis the cabinet. In the annual reports of the Federation of German Industry (BDI) there is a list of the association's "most important memorandums," with the overwhelming number of these petitions being addressed to members of the cabinet.[46] Cabinet ministers are petitioned not only because they are the heads of vast governmental departments, but perhaps more importantly because of their role as leaders of disciplined parties. Considering the great powers of Adenauer, for instance, during his fourteen years as chancellor, combined with his willingness to grant the interest groups access to the office of the federal chancellor, it is not surprising that the pressure groups selected the latter as one of their prime "targets"—a situation which accrued both to the power of Adenauer and the effectiveness of the pressure groups.[47]

[43] Rupert Breitling, *Die Verbände in der Bundesrepublik* (Meisenheim: Hain, 1955), pp. 88–90.

[44] Wolfgang Hirsch-Weber, "Some Remarks on Interest Groups in the German Federal Republic," in *Interest Groups on Four Continents,* ed. Henry W. Ehrmann (Pittsburgh: University of Pittsburgh Press, 1958), p. 111.

[45] Deutsch, et al., *France, Germany and the Western Alliance,* p. 130.

[46] Hirsch-Weber, "Interest Groups in the G.F.R.," p. 111.

[47] Karl Dietrich Bracher, "Germany's Second Democracy—Structures and Problems," in *Democracy in a Changing Society,* ed. Henry W. Ehrmann (New York: Praeger, 1964), p. 135.

Unlike American congressional committees, the Bundestag's committees do not call upon pressure-group leaders to give testimony. Yet their influence on these committees may be all the more effective because deputies who have a direct connection or a personal interest in the area of any committee usually make up about half the committee's membership. Thus, of twenty-one members of the Committee on Foreign Trade in the 1949–52 legislature, almost 50% were leaders of employers' associations or held leading positions in private business; and in the Committee on Refugee Affairs, 70% of the members were refugees from Communist-controlled German lands.[48] The interest groups' connections with the civil service are largely, though not entirely, based upon informal relationships based upon common backgrounds and shared experiences. It is such old friendships and professional contacts, often dating back to the Nazi regime, that appear to play a more-than-usual role in providing certain interest-group representatives with access to, and influence over, civil servants participating in the formulation and execution of policy. Moreover, it is not unusual for civil servants to take leaves of absence in order to work for associations and private businesses, then returning to their civil service posts (without loss of seniority).

Having discussed the broad patterns of interest-group activity, we can now turn to a more detailed description of the organization and activities of the important interest groups in the Federal Republic.

The Business Interests

The business groups in the Federal Republic are organized into three major organizations or *Spitzenverbände:* the Federation of German Industries (BDI), the Diet of German Industry and Commerce (DIH), and the Federal Union of German Employers Associations (BDA). In addition, there are separate associations for banking, insurance, wholesale and foreign trade, retail trade, shipping, transportation, handi-

crafts, and others. Serving as a coordinating committee for all these central associations is the Joint Committee of German Trades and Industries (*Gemeinschaftsausschuss der deutschen gewerblichen Wirtschaft*). This joint committee attempts to iron out difficulties among its member organizations and provide public representation for the business community as a whole.

The wealthiest, most influential, and most active of the three top organizations is the BDI. Its membership consists of thirty-six nationwide industrial trade organizations which in turn are subdivided into more specialized organizations. The BDI has twelve regional offices which coordinate activities of the trade associations at the *Land* level and conduct public relations and lobbying vis-à-vis the *Land* governments. Policy for the BDI is set by its assembly, in which its thirty-six member associations are represented with a voting strength roughly proportional to the total number of employees employed by the member firms of each association. Under this arrangement, the heavy industry of the Rhine-Ruhr area has the greatest voting strength in the assembly.[49]

The BDI is governed by its central committee, which elects a smaller executive committee, and this body in turn elects a presidium of sixteen members which seems to be the most important of the elective bodies for day-to-day decisions and which is empowered to make decisions for the federation in an emergency. Finally, the BDI has a large professional staff, directed by a general manager and the president of the federation. The BDI is thus far more inclusive and more centralized than is its counterpart in the United States, the National Association of Manufacturers. Power in the BDI is concentrated in its central organs, in its permanent bureaucracy, and in its thirty-six constituent trade associations which are themselves highly centralized. Since its formation in 1949, the BDI has been under the control of a moderate leadership, despite a minority which

---

[48] Deutsch and Edinger, *Germany Rejoins the Powers*, pp. 91–92.

[49] For these and the following points, see Gabriel A. Almond, "The Politics of German Business," in *West German Leadership and Foreign Policy*, eds. Hans Speier and W. Philip Davison (Evanston, Ill.: Row, Peterson, 1957), pp. 212–17.

has been demanding a more nationalistic foreign policy and a stronger line toward labor.

The contacts of the BDI with the government have been direct and effective. As one observer has pointed out, the BDI committees and their staff have direct access to their opposite numbers in the Bundestag committees and the ministries:

In the fiscal year 1954–55, around 200 formal communications were submitted to these agencies by the B.D.I. . . . One cannot escape the impression . . . that there is a constant stream of influence from the professional staffs of the B.D.I. and the trade associations directly into the appropriate units in the ministerial bureaucracies charged with the recommendation of legislative policy, the formulation of regulations, and the execution of public policy.[50]

A more specialized organization is the Federal Union of Employers Associations (BDA), which concentrates on matters of labor and welfare policy. This group is also organized on a regional and functional basis. Its units do not themselves carry on collective bargaining, but develop the employer's position for this purpose and mobilize support for industries affected in the event of a strike. As in the BDI, the regional and central organizations of the BDA between them attempt to influence relevant legislation at the federal and *Land* levels.

For major tasks of public relations, the BDI and the BDA collaborate in employing the German Industry Institute (DII). The DII disseminates the view of industry through a large number and variety of publications. These range from books to two semimonthlies, three weeklies, a semiweekly service for the press, and a daily sheet for radio stations. Special publications are directed to the business community itself, such as the "Letters to Entrepreneurs" (*Unternehmerbriefe*) and the "Lecture Series," which have exhorted businessmen to become more active in politics. The DII, like other business organizations, generally favors the CDU. In 1957, the "Letters to Entrepreneurs" urged its readers to "see to it by all permitted and available democratic means that

. . . no party cheats the voter by a pact with Socialism after the election." [51]

The main financial organs of the business community in dealing with political parties are the Sponsors' Associations (*Förderergesellschaften*), and their more modern version, the Civic Associations (*Staatsbürgerliche Vereinigungen*). Sponsors' Associations were founded in 1952 for the purpose of mobilizing the financial resources of business for the 1953 electoral campaign, and to strengthen the position of businessmen against the competing claims of the various nonsocialist parties. Instead of being asked for support by several parties, many businessmen could make their main contributions in a single payment, and perhaps obtain better political conditions for their money. The Sponsors' Associations were in a position to check on the proposed expenditures of each party that asked for their support, to insist that the nonsocialist parties should not waste their money in fighting one another during the campaign, and to demand at least informal assurances that none of these parties would enter a coalition with the SPD on the federal level—a practice which had to be modified, because of the formation of the CDU-SPD coalition government in 1966 and that between SPD and FDP in 1969.[52]

Farmers' Organizations

The chief farm organization in the G.F.R. is the League of German Farmers (*Deutscher Bauernverband*), which in 1952 reported 1.3 million members, comprising 77% of all independent farmers. German farm organizations have considerable political influence, which has been directed effectively toward specific demands such as agricultural subsidies and prices. As a result, German farming has been remarkably well protected and it has been effectively compensated for its high costs. Accordingly, in the fall of 1962, wheat prices in West Germany were almost 30% higher than in the Nether-

---

[50] Almond, "Politics of German Business," p. 214.

[51] *Unternehmerbriefe*, May 23, 1957, quoted in Kitzinger, *German Electoral Politics*, p. 246.

[52] Kitzinger, *German Electoral Politics*, pp. 207–18.

lands, and almost 50% higher than in France. However, France's powerful bargaining position in the Common Market has since led to a significant decrease in the common price for wheat, and under a 1966 Common Market agreement, French, Italian, and Dutch agricultural products have been admitted more freely to the German market since 1967. At the same time, however, German agriculture is likely to continue to be effectively compensated for its high costs through governmental actions.

The Labor Unions

There are three large labor unions in the Federal Republic, which together have enrolled as members approximately 40% of the wage-earners, 20% of the white-collar employees, and a staggering 99% of the civil servants. The most important of these is the German Confederation of Trade Unions (*Deutscher Gewerkschaftsbund,* DGB), with about 6.5 million members in 1969. The DGB includes all wage-earners' unions, and is also the largest organization of white-collar employees and civil servants. About 41% of all wage-earners, 13% of all salaried employees, and 47% of all civil servants belong to the confederation. Since the wage-earners are much more numerous than the other groups, they form more than four-fifths of the DGB membership, with white-collar employees furnishing another 11% and the civil servants the remaining 6%. The DGB is dominated by the large wage-earners' unions, and it tends to stress the similarities between the wage-earners and the white-collar employees and the civil servants in regard to their interests in the labor market. Within the DGB, the large enterprises are most thoroughly organized and most highly represented. The member unions of the DGB follow industrial or craft lines. The strongest industrial union, I. G. Metall, accounts for one-quarter of the membership of the entire confederation.

Second in size to the DGB among white-collar employees is the German Employees Union (*Deutsche Angestelltengewerkschaft,* DAG), with a half-million members, or about 10% of all white-collar employees. This union

has tended to stress the quasi-professional characteristics of white-collar employees—their separate status and their distinct interests—in contrast to those of the wage-earners. Nevertheless, in practice the DAG has found itself often pressing economic demands very similar to those advocated by the DGB.

The German Federation of Civil Servants (*Deutscher Beamtenbund*) is the most nearly professional and nonpolitical of the three great interest organizations. With 718,000 members in 1969, it included about 52% of all civil servants.

The Churches

Other groups besides economic interest groups have contributed major influences to recent German politics; foremost among them have been the churches. Since the role of religious groupings has already been discussed, only a few facts need to be recalled here. Although there are somewhat fewer Roman Catholics than Protestants among the population of the Federal Republic, there are far more Catholics than Protestants in church on most Sundays, and there are far more Catholics effectively organized for political action. Between 50% and 60% of the nominal Catholics attend church once a week, while only about 10% of urban Protestants—and 20% of rural Protestants—attend church at least once a month.[53]

About 11 million Catholics, or one-quarter of the German electorate, can be found at mass on any Sunday in the year. Thus, every week the Catholic clergy can reach a larger audience than all Germany politicians taken together could secure by their own efforts. The 10 million weekly circulation of the Catholic Church press reinforces these possibilities, and the 3–5 million Catholics who are members of Catholic lay organizations or youth groups are ten times as numerous as the total membership of the CDU. During electoral campaigns, these Catholic audiences are vigorously exhorted by bishops, the lower clergy, the church press, and lay organizations to vote, to vote as a duty to

[53] Kitzinger, *German Electoral Politics,* p. 223.

their conscience, to remember the great merits of the CDU government, and not to vote for irreligious parties, such as the SPD and the FDP. Typical of the pastoral letters that Catholic bishops send out, and which are read to a quarter of the electorate on preelection Sundays, is the following: "Do your electoral duty! Vote only for men and women whose basic Christian principles are well known and whose public activity corresponds to these principles." In effect, they are being urged to vote for the CDU, and the evidence for the continuing effectiveness of the appeal seems overwhelming.[54]

Catholic groups in West Germany embrace almost all activities from cradle to grave—from Catholic kindergartens to Catholic young farmers' leagues, traders' associations, a Catholic Woman's League, and many more. Unlike the churches and their organizations in the United States, England, and France, whose financing comes from voluntary contributions, in Germany the churches are financed by the state, which levies a tax on all those individuals who were baptized in a particular denomination and have not officially withdrawn their membership.

Outstanding among church-related groups for their political work—which is thus in part indirectly financed by the state—are the Catholic Workers' Movement and the Kolping Family. The Catholic Workers' Movement (*Katholische Arbeiterbewegung*, KAB) has been directly active in electioneering, particularly in North Rhine-Westphalia, where four-fifths of its 150,000 members are concentrated in the three dioceses of Münster, Paderborn, and Cologne. Thirty members of the KAB were elected to the 1957–61 Bundestag. The German Kolping Family—called before 1933 the "League of Catholic Artisan Journeymen"—is the counterpart of the KAB on the skilled-worker-to-lower-middle-class level. It has about 210,000 members, nearly as many as the CDU. Since half of the Kolping members are unmarried young men, they are able to lend very active support to the CDU; and the ways in which they could and did do so have been discussed in the literature of their movement. In the 1957 campaign, their help appears to have been effective: thirty-two of their members entered the Bundestag. Since eleven of them were at the same time also KAB members, the combined Bundestag strength of these two organizations consisted of fifty-four members.[55]

The Protestant churches are unlikely to be attended by more than 2 million people on any Sunday, and the weekly circulation of their church press is below 5 million. Moreover, no organ of the Evangelical Church government issues statements in support of any of the parties during elections.[56] A relatively large number of the top leaders of the Protestant churches come from eastern or central Germany, and many have strong anti-Nazi records. Their churches have remained far more concerned with the political issues of peace and reunification, because these churches include the Protestants of both West and East Germany—with about 25 million being in the Federal Republic, 1.6 million in West Berlin, and 15.5 million in the G.D.R. Thus, as early as 1965, in the face of the government's inaction on the questions of Germany's eastern frontiers and of her present and future relationship with her eastern neighbors, it was the German Evangelical Church that publicly took its stand in a widely discussed memorandum, favoring more active and accommodating negotiations with the East, and thereby helped bring that issue back into the political arena.

THE BUREAUCRATIC, DIPLOMATIC, AND MILITARY ELITES

There are roughly 1.1 million professional civil servants employed at the national, *Land*, and local levels of government in the German Federal Republic, in addition to another 1.3 million clerical and manual workers in public employment below the formal level of civil servant.[57] These civil servants have a strong, castelike sense of tradition, responsibility, and

---

[54] Ibid., pp. 225–28.

[55] Ibid., pp. 230–31.
[56] Ibid., p. 239.
[57] See Table 4-15.

privilege. Many of them are skeptical of democracy, of popular participation in the government, and of outsiders entering the service.[58] This bureaucracy is the only social group that has retained its substantial share of power without major interruption from the days of the late-nineteenth-century German empire through the two world wars and three changes of political regime. Its members have become more pliable and more willing to serve efficiently and conscientiously whatever regime may be in power. They are less apt to insist on old traditions of monarchist, nationalist, or ultra-conservative ideology than before, but they have retained their sense of role and duty, of separateness as a social group, of revulsion from Communism, and of distrust of Western liberal and democratic innovations.

They are more strongly organized in defense of their immediate interests, such as career security, pensions, salaries, status, and prestige, than any other large social group in the country. As we saw above, fully 99% of their number are organized in two organizations: 52% in the exclusive German Federation of Civil Servants (*Deutscher Beamtenbund*), and another 47% in the German Confederation of Trade Unions (DGB). Beyond this, however, they have demonstrated a good deal of informal but effective solidarity. Thus, they have successfully opposed and eventually rendered ineffective a great part of the Western allied efforts at denazification and civil service reform, and have preserved largely intact their hold on the higher ranks of public employment.

There are some indications that the military and diplomatic elites favor particularly those policies that will preserve for the Federal Republic the shelter of the American, NATO, and Western European alliances, as well as the economic opportunities of the Common Market, as long as these increase the national capabilities of the Federal Republic in economic as well as military matters. In the early 1960s,

the demands of Franz-Josef Strauss, defense minister at that time, for nuclear weapons for the army, either under collective NATO auspices or as an eventual part of West German national military equipment, found some support among the military, even though the much-discussed "generals' memorandum" on this topic actually seems to have represented an effort on the part of the civilian Strauss to bolster his previously expressed views by inducing the generals under his authority to produce the kind of expert memorandum he wanted.[59]

In any case, the political and economic weight of the West German military elite seems likely to grow to the extent that the defense sector grows within the German economy, that the army appproaches its half-million manpower goal planned originally for NATO, and that troops have come to outnumber the American and British forces in the territory of the Federal Republic. At the same time, the bulk of West German mass and elite opinion is likely to remain cool to any great increases in armament; and by 1967, cutbacks in military spending and manpower went into effect, reducing the strength of the *Bundeswehr* from 470,000 men to its current level of 460,000 men.

A Test Case of Elite Conflict: The *Spiegel* Affair

In October 1962, the West German federal police arrested Rudolf Augstein, the publisher of the well-known West German news magazine *Der Spiegel*. This periodical—a kind of stepped-up counterpart to *Time* magazine—was somewhat closer to the views of the FDP than to those of any other party, but it had built up its half-million circulation by sensational though generally well-informed reporting in a hard-boiled and iconoclastic style, well suited to the skeptical and disillusioned mood of many of its readers.[60]

[58] For these and some of the following points, see the revealing study of John H. Herz, "Political Views of the West German Civil Service," in Speier and Davison (eds.), *West German Leadership*, op. cit., pp. 96–135; see also Karl Hochschwender, *German Civil Service Reform after 1945*, Ph.D. thesis, Yale University, 1961.

[59] Helmut Schmidt, *Verteidigung oder Vergeltung: Ein deutscher Beitrag zum strategischen Problem der N.A.T.O.* (Stuttgart: Seewald, 1961), pp. 197–99.

[60] For a critical review, see Hans Magnus Enzensberger, "Die Sprache des Spiegel," in *Einzelheiten* (Frankfurt: Suhrkamp, 1962), pp. 62–87.

The journal had long carried on a feud with Defense Minister Franz-Josef Strauss. In its issue of October 10, 1962, *Der Spiegel* featured a report of instances of inefficiency or unpreparedness in the West German armed forces as allegedly revealed in recent NATO maneuvers. So serious were these faults, the paper claimed, that the *Bundeswehr*—after almost seven years of rearmament, and after six years of tenure in office of its supreme commander, Strauss—still bore the lowest of (four possible) NATO ratings: "conditionally suited for defense." [61]

The response of the federal authorities was spectacular. During the night of October 26— by coincidence, at a time of extreme international tension over the Cuban crisis between the Soviet Union and the United States—agents of the federal police raided and sealed the editorial offices of *Der Spiegel* in Bonn and Hamburg, and arrested Augstein and four other executives of the magazine on charges of treason and bribery. Bail was refused them, on grounds of possible collusion, and thus they faced the prospect of being kept in jail on suspicion until their trial, which might be months away.

The federal prosecutor's office could have treated the charges made by the magazine as untrue, and prosecuted its publisher and editors for slander or for undermining the morale of the armed forces. Instead, the authorities chose to prosecute for violation of state secrets, taking the view that some of the details of the charges must have come from secret West German military documents which the paper could have obtained only by bribery. Judged by American standards, this legal interpretation seemed to admit that there might be some truth to some of the facts alleged by the paper, but it threatened its publisher and staff members with far more severe penalties for treason. [62] Actually, West German law uses the label of "treason" far more loosely than Anglo-American law, including under it also the publication of

any untrue statement which, if it were true, would injure, in the opinion of the federal government, the interests of the Federal Republic. The language of the law is so broad that it could be used to punish many journalistic practices which in the United States would be considered lawful and a legitimate exercise of the freedom of the press. In the case of the German law, much depended on the spirit in which it would be applied, and the *Spiegel* case was expected to become a precedent of far-reaching importance.

The *Spiegel* affair dramatically posed four issues before the public. The first of these, common to all free countries, was the issue of legitimate government secrecy, particularly in matters of defense, as against legitimate journalistic enterprise in getting out the news, and in taking advantage of whatever documents some individuals or factions within the bureaucracy may be "leaking" to the press. This issue would be for the courts to decide, where *Der Spiegel*, with its long record of disrespect for authority and of frequent attacks on members of the judiciary with a Nazi past, could count on very little sympathy from the usually conservative judges.

The second issue was one of the police methods used. Henceforth, "the man who presses our doorbell in the early morning hours," said the *Frankfurter Rundschau*, "is not necessarily the milkman. It might be the political police." [63] In a country where people remembered all too well the night raids of the Nazi Gestapo and were well aware of the continuing police-state methods in the Communist-ruled G.D.R. to the east, these methods seemed "wholly repugnant—and wholly unnecessary—in a democratic society." [64]

The third issue was political, and in the end it helped bring down the Adenauer cabinet. The prosecution had been set in motion, and the raids and arrests had been carried out without the knowledge of the minister of justice, FDP member Wolfgang Stammberger, under whose responsibility the matter ordinarily belonged. Minister of Defense Strauss

[61] *Der Spiegel* 16, no. 41 (October 10, 1962):33.
[62] *New York Times,* November 3, 1962, pp. 1, 2, 3; November 5, 1962, 3:13; *Der Spiegel* 16, no. 45 (November 7, 1962); *Time* 80, no. 19 (November 9, 1962).

[63] Quoted in *Time* 80, no. 19 (November 9, 1962).
[64] Ibid.

had delegated his responsibilities in the matter to his subordinate, State Secretary of Defense Volkmar Hopf, in order to avoid, as he said, an appearance of his personal bias against the magazine that had attacked him. Subsequently, as the *New York Times* reported, State Secretary Hopf "assumed the responsibility for having told" the state secretary of justice, Dr. Walter Strauss (who was not related to the defense minister) that he should not inform his superior, Minister of Justice Stammberger, of the planned raids and arrests.[65]

The minister of justice thus had been bypassed in his own department by his subordinates, and possibly with the knowledge of some cabinet members and perhaps the chancellor. Minister Stammberger thereupon submitted his resignation, the FDP threatened to withdraw its four ministers from the cabinet and to bring down the government coalition which since the 1961 election again depended on the votes of the FDP delegation for its Bundestag majority. The FDP insisted not only on the dismissal of the two state secretaries, Walter Strauss and Wolfgang Hopf, by way of satisfaction for the humiliating treatment meted out to its minister of justice, but it also demanded new guarantees that its voice henceforth "would be heeded in the Cabinet," and that Dr. Stammberger would be placed in charge of the investigation into *Der Spiegel.*[66]

The FDP, in short, saw the issue as a threat to its equality of status as a coalition partner. However, the resulting shakeup of the cabinet, in which Franz-Josef Strauss and Dr. Stammberger were replaced, allowed the FDP to continue in the coalition government—though its position became increasingly tenuous.

The fourth issue posed by the *Spiegel* affair was that of the relative power and prestige of two contending elites—the government bureaucracy, civilian and military, on the one hand, and the press on the other. In the United States, the press is highly respected, not only in terms of its acknowledged power but also in

terms of the status and respect accorded to its publishers and writers. The American division of powers between the legislative, executive, and judicial branches of the government, together with a long tradition of press freedom, further guarantees and enhances this freedom and high status of the press in American politics, society, and culture. In West Germany, by contrast, there is no such long tradition of a free press. Under the parliamentary system of Bonn, there is far less separation of powers between the federal government and the Bundestag dominated by the government parties, and the German judiciary traditionally has regarded itself not so much as a coequal branch of the government, but rather as a subordinate part of the executive power.

Civil servants, military officers, and judges all traditionally had served the same monarch. From this old tradition, many of these groups still derive social status, prestige, and solidarity. Newspapers and journalists, on the contrary, traditionally had been looked down upon in Germany as creatures of the gutter and spokesmen for the mob. Often journalists had been considered failures who lacked the brains, character, or breeding to qualify as civil servants, and who thus had become hack writers in the hire of commercial purveyors of cheap gossip and sensations. This traditional contempt for newsmen has been dying very hard, although it is deeply inimical to the effective functioning of democracy. Despite the American-backed innovation of judicial review and stronger press freedom, these traditions of democracy are still young and weak in Germany. Many judges still see themselves as servants of the executive power, and a large part of the public still looks upon journalists as impudent upstarts who deserve a sharp rebuke.

By the end of 1962, the *Spiegel* affair had already produced a number of changes in West German politics. A wave of popular protest against any revival of high-handed police methods had arisen, cutting across party lines and insisting on greater respect for the freedom of the press. In an opinion poll, 54% of respondents demanded the resignation of Defense Minister Strauss; only 31% wanted him to stay in office; the rest were undecided or unin-

[65] Sidney Gruson, "Adenauer Trying To Save Coalition," *New York Times*, November 5, 1962, 1, 3.

[66] Ibid. Also see Gerhard Loewenberg, *Parliament in the German Political System* (Ithaca, N.Y.: Cornell University Press, 1967), pp. 257–58.

formed.[67] The federal cabinet resigned. Chancellor Adenauer formed a new one, supported by the same coalition, but with one-third of the old ministers dropped, including both Franz-Josef Strauss and Wolfgang Stammberger. Strauss's post as defense minister went to a northern Protestant CDU leader, Kai-Uwe von Hassel, who until then had been prime minister of Schleswig-Holstein and who had a reputation for correctness in his administrative methods and for right-of-center sympathies in politics. Stammberger was replaced as minister of justice by another FDP member, the southern German liberal, Dr. Ewald Bucher, with a reputation of particular concern for civil liberties. Most of the new ministers were a good deal younger than their predecessors. The party and denominational balance of the cabinet was preserved, except that the influence of the Bavarian CSU seemed to have been somewhat weakened.[68]

Before the reorganization of the cabinet, the chancellor and the CDU had negotiated with the Social Democrats concerning a possible "grand coalition" of the two major parties and a possible change in the electoral law which would wipe out the FDP. This threat in turn made the FDP more willing to enter the new cabinet and to accept the continuing predominance of the CDU within it. The results of the entire affair included the temporary eclipse of Franz-Josef Strauss; a slight increase in the political stature of the SPD, which had been treated publicly as a possible partner in the national government; a limited gain in the stature of the FDP, offset in part, however, by the threat of a possible "grand coalition" of the CDU and SPD; and, perhaps most important of all, a definite upsurge of public opinion in favor of press freedom, democracy, and constitutional legality—a striking affirmation of the changes that had occurred in German political culture since 1945.

By early 1968, *Der Spiegel* had won the substance of its case, with far-reaching effects. It sharply illuminated the continuing struggle

between the old and new traditions. If the paper had been squelched, it would have served as a warning to all others. Journalists and publishers would have walked in greater fear, and government officials in greater assurance. With the magazine's success, a free press and the right of citizens and of minority groups and parties were strengthened. The *Spiegel* affair showed once again how much the balance of power between the different West German elites was still in flux, how much the political culture and traditions of the Bonn republic were still the subject of struggle, but also how significantly popular attachment to democratic liberties had grown in strength.

Other confrontations, however, between the opposing political forces were likely to follow. In early 1968, Franz-Josef Strauss had recovered part of his power. As minister of finance in the CDU-SPD coalition government, he continued to lead the CDU's strong Bavarian affiliate, the CSU, and continued to encourage a succession of doubts and objections to West Germany's acceptance of the international treaty against the proliferation of nuclear weapons then being proposed by the United States and the Soviet Union. The nonproliferation treaty was, however, ratified by the Bundestag in 1971, with the support of the great majority of German opinion at all levels, but other struggles concerning the policies and character of the Federal Republic were likely to go on.

The Common Characteristics of Bonn's Elites

The elites that we have surveyed vary widely in their composition, interests, and outlooks. Yet there are a number of significant views which they share with one another, as well as with a majority of mass opinion in the country. No major elite group has any illusion that it alone could run the country, or that Germany alone could have her will prevail in Europe or the world. There is a sober recognition in each group that it must live in an environment of other groups and interests with whom it must make the best terms it can get. No group

[67] *New York Times*, November 24, 1962.

[68] See German press commentaries in *The German Tribune* (Hamburg) 1, no. 39 (December 29, 1962):3–5.

has cut itself off from reality by wrapping itself into some impenetrable private ideology or doctrine. The groups share many of their images of reality. Even those critical of the United States remain mindful, for the most part, of the vast American capabilities. Even the most intense anti-Communists—and almost all West Germans are anti-Communists to some degree—do not ignore or deny the reality of very substantial Soviet strength. All groups are aware of the limitations of their power, both in domestic and international affairs. All feel that they have much to lose, and that changes should be approached with caution.

Yet, all these groups are moving toward change. They are moving toward it, not necessarily by choice, but by the logic of events. In economics, the growth of the West German economy has made it more competitive in world trade, but also more vulnerable to the fluctuations of the business cycle. The institutions of the 1950s, which dealt successfully with the limited foreign-trade problems and the moderate waves of boom and recession of that period proved not to be sufficient for the greater international economic problems and more severe bouts of recession of the late 1960s. By then, the CDU-SPD coalition government and the new SPD-FDP alliance seemed well aware that more powerful institutions of international economic co-operation and of domestic economic guidance and control had to be devised —and that it was the task of the political parties, interest groups, and elites to work out the political consensus needed to devise and sustain these new policies and institutions.

SEVEN

the German Federal Republic today . . . and tomorrow

In the 1970s, West Germany must make basic decisions about its economic and employment policies, its labor relations and welfare services, and it must adapt its economy to a world market that may be more competitive, to the underdeveloped countries that may need more economic aid, and to an international monetary system and a business cycle that may be more severe in their fluctuations. It must also establish a military policy. Will West Germany accept as her share in the common defense effort of the West the provision of moderately strong conventional forces within the limitations of her treaties of the 1950s? Or will she press for a more competitive role toward other Western powers?

A TURN AWAY FROM THE ARMS RACE

In early 1972, the leaders and voters of the West German people seemed to have made such a decision, at least for some time to come. Already in 1964, an overwhelming majority of 93% of West German leaders in an elite survey had expressed their view that a national nuclear deterrent for the Federal Republic would not be worth its cost. Similar high majorities had added that such national nuclear weapons would not increase the Federal Republic's prestige, would not be essential for its independence, and would not be credible to its potential enemies. The proposal for a multilateral nuclear force (MLF) within a NATO framework divided the German leaders down the middle: 34% favored it; the same proportion expressed opposition; and the rest were indifferent or uninformed. A number of the German leaders who backed a NATO-controlled MLF said that they did so because they were willing to go along with the wishes of the United States government, which at that time had seemed to be vigorously promoting the project. Its proponents in Washington at that time had been arguing that the MLF was necessary to head off a supposed strong desire for national nuclear weapons. On closer study, no such German desire was discovered; important United States objections to the MFL subsequently developed, and the project was quietly shelved.[1]

An alternative project of a purely European multilateral nuclear force was turned down in the same survey by 83% of the German leaders. Strong majorities of both elite and mass opinion endorsed the relaxation of tensions between the United States and the Soviet Union. German elite and mass opinion also backed further American-Soviet agreements on arms control and against the spread of nuclear weapons, even if the Federal Republic should not be consulted about them—and still more so, of course, if it were.

These attitudes persisted through the 1969 election, and were deepened in the two years that followed. The West German leaders and masses by 1971 saw the best guarantee for the security of their country in a firm alliance with the United States, and they had come to accept the concept of a "division of labor," in which moderate West German conventional forces would be backed by similar American and British forces on West German soil, and by the great nuclear striking power of the United States. Second to the American alliance, they wanted good relations with France, whose elites —under President Pompidou much as earlier under President de Gaulle—overwhelmingly abhorred any thought of German access to nuclear weapons, in whatever form. Since the foreign policies of France and the United States clearly were not in harmony during most of the 1960s, the most promising area for German-French collaboration in the early 1970s remained in the field of economic policy within the Common Market; and here close collaboration with France and, if possible, the early admission of Britain were endorsed at all levels of opinion, within the limits of preserving the essential sovereignty of the nation-state.

The full restoration of a German national state—that is, national reunification of the populations and territories of the present G.F.R. and G.D.R.—consistently was named in mass-opinion polls as the most urgent single task

before the Federal Republic. In 1965, as during most of the preceding decade, a majority named such national problems as their top concern, either as "national reunification" (47%) or "Berlin" (4%). They outnumbered more than 15:1 the mere 3% who had named as their most urgent political concern unification of Europe.[2] At the same time, majorities of both masses and elites believed that no early gains in these matters could be expected from any policy of threats or violence against the East; and they appeared predisposed to explore new approaches to negotiation and limited accommodation with their eastern neighbors and the Soviet Union, provided that essential German claims and interests could be preserved.

The actual policies of the Kiesinger-Brandt and Brandt-Scheel coalition governments corresponded closely to these mass and elite opinion trends. Already in 1967, the government had made it clear that the Federal Republic did not want nuclear weapons, and that it was more interested in reducing somewhat, rather than increasing, its military manpower contribution and defense expenditure, provided that this could be done within a continuing alliance with the United States and in agreement with its government. Contemporaneously, Bonn had taken some steps to reduce tensions vis-à-vis Eastern Europe. It had opened diplomatic relations with Rumania; it had improved trade relations with other Soviet-bloc countries. Chancellor Kiesinger declared that his government considered as invalid the infamous Munich agreement of 1938, by which, under Hitler's threats of war, the governments of France and Britain had handed over to him Czechoslovakia's Sudetenland on the eve of World War II. This belated gesture from Bonn was meant to go some way toward reassuring the Czechoslovak government, which repeatedly had expressed intense concern about the efforts of some German refugee politicians in the Federal Republic to treat that agreement as a valid basis for political claims in the postwar period. Czechoslovakia, however, had wanted Bonn to agree that the Munich treaty (to which the United States had never been a party) had

[1] For data on the foregoing, see K. W. Deutsch et al., *France, Germany and the Western Alliance* (New York: Scribners, 1967).

[2] Ibid., p. 246.

been invalid from the outset; while the German refugee politicians in 1971 still felt that Kiesinger had gone too far even in accepting that the treaty was invalid now. Efforts to reduce tensions with the Federal Republic's eastern neighbors are likely to be plagued by such conflicting claims and pressures for some time to come.

In regard to its most immediate neighbor, the Communist-ruled German Democratic Republic (G.D.R.), to a limited extent Bonn's policy aimed at reducing conflicts and obtaining humanitarian improvements, while persisting in its basic claims. For the first time, some communications from the G.D.R. were accepted and answered in 1967 at the cabinet level, with careful explanations that this was not to imply any legal recognition. Technical consultations among lower-level officials of the G.F.R. and G.D.R. were somewhat improved; mutual press attacks became slightly less vitriolic; and some works by authors living in the G.D.R. and critical of both parts of Germany (such as Rudolf Friess's East-West beatnik novel, *The Road to Oobliadooh* and Christa Wolf's more sensitive and deep-probing novel, *Erinnerungen an Christa T.*), were published in the Federal Republic and were well received there. When the United States and the Soviet Union in August 1967 submitted identical drafts for an international agreement prohibiting the spread of nuclear weapons to countries which did not then possess them, it seemed clear that this agreement was likely to be accepted, and, indeed, it was ratified by the Bundestag in 1971. As of late 1971, most of the people and the leaders of the German Federal Republic had chosen to stake their future hopes upon a continuing alliance with the United States within a world of peace.

The political course pursued by the voters and leaders of the Federal Republic in 1963–71 however, was not the only one which had been urged upon them. Other policies were and are available to them, and these continue to have their advocates among interest groups and leaders. Though these alternative policies today are only supported by minorities, usually of less than one-third of West German voters and leaders, such political alignments may change once again in the future, as they have done so often in the past; and these West German minority views of the early 1970s still deserve to be borne in mind by the Federal Republic's neighbors and allies.

The first of these possible alternative policies would be for the Federal Republic to strive to gain access to nuclear weapons, to seek eventual qualitative equality with the nuclear superpowers, and to return to a highly competitive, rather than cooperative, course of action in world politics.

A POSSIBLE RETURN TO GREAT-POWER COMPETITION?

One of the most prominent spokesmen in the late 1950s and early 1960s for the nuclear armament of Western Germany, the then-Defense Minister Franz-Josef Strauss, made it clear that this policy did not necessarily imply any inclination toward militaristic adventures, despite repeated charges to that effect from Soviet-bloc sources. All that it implied, Strauss insisted, was a desire to make West Germany so strong as a military and nuclear power that she would become an indispensable partner or party in all future confrontations or negotiations between East and West. In Strauss's words:

A policy of strength in the age of the hydrogen bomb means in no case that one wants to use military pressure, with the risk of a third world war, in order to bring about some territorial changes, if necessary even by force. A policy of strength means rather that one's own freedom of decision cannot be influenced by pressure from hostile or unfriendly quarters. . . . *Germany . . . must become so indispensable to her Western friends and so respectable to her potential adversary that both will value her presence in the negotiations.*[3]

Inevitably, however, the same military strength that would make Germany an indispensable and influential party at all future top-level negotiations would also make her a high-priority target in any atomic war that

[3] "Sicherheit und Wiedervereinigung," *Aussenpolitik* 6, no. 3 (March 1957):140–47. Italics supplied.

might follow upon a failure of negotiations. In practice, most of the likely uses of any increased bargaining power of a strongly rearmed Germany would involve heightened risks to that country, to her neighbors, to world peace, and to the cohesion of her alliance with the West. Strauss, having lost the Defense Ministry as a result of the *Spiegel* affair of 1962 (see Chapter 6), returned to the federal cabinet in 1966 under the Kiesinger-Brandt coalition government as minister of finance. In this new post, his reputation depended primarily on his ability to limit government expenditures, including spending on defense. In this role he continued until 1969 as a member of the government that seemed to have turned its back upon any pursuit of nuclear weapons. After 1969, Strauss continued to play a prominent role in the CDU/CSU party, now in opposition to the government, as leader of the CSU. Outside his Bavarian stronghold, however, his influence appears to have receded.

The foreign policy objectives to which the military and diplomatic power of the Federal Republic might be committed in the early 1970s will most likely have been shaped by the popular expectations formed in the preceding decades. The popular expectations of the 1950s included notably the liberation of Eastern Europe, of the G.D.R., and of East Berlin; the breakdown or abolition of Communist rule in these areas; the eventual recovery of the formerly German Oder-Neisse areas to the east; and the return of the Sudeten Germans and other expellees to their former districts, homes, and properties in Eastern Europe. Since the late 1940s, these hopes have been kept alive by the deeply felt wishes of many Germans and by a succession of specific hopes. The success of the Marshall Plan, it was hoped, would produce in the middle of Europe such a contrast between Western prosperity and Eastern poverty as to make Communist rule untenable. Stalin's death or some other inner crisis, it was hoped, might fatally weaken the Communist grip on the territories under their power.

As these hopes faded, there still remained the firm insistence of the Western allies on treating the Potsdam agreements, and the distribution of governments and territories resulting from them, as merely provisional. The Western allied refusal to accept the post-1945 state of affairs, by means of a peace treaty, as in any way legal or legitimate, came to appear to many West Germans as an implied promise. It seemed a promise that some day, somehow, as West Germany and the entire West grew stronger, this Western strength would be used to sweep away the post-1945 divisions, frontiers, and regimes in Eastern Europe and to restore both German national unity and some of the ancient German positions in Eastern Europe. Until the late 1960s, no West German government or major political leader dared publicly renounce these claims or hopes. Until that time, opinion polls continued to show German reunification as the top-ranking issue in the minds of the young as well as of the old, and they showed very high majorities insisting on a deferred but undiminished German claim to the Oder-Neisse territories.

For two decades, the West German government not only refused to recognize the G.D.R., but under the "Hallstein doctrine" Bonn for a long time even declined to have normal diplomatic relations with the governments of Poland, Yugoslavia, and other Eastern European states which had recognized the East German regime. For the same reason, the Bonn republic avoided entering the United Nations —except for special UN organizations—in order not to offer the G.D.R. an opportunity to enter that world body with the aid of the Soviet Union, which seemed certain to use its veto power to insist on the admission of "two Germanies or none."

These hopes for liberation and reunion, and the policies based on them, could not of course be kept up indefinitely without at least some encouraging sign, now and again, of their eventual fulfillment, and by 1969 no such signs had become discernible. As year after year passed, and as the Berlin Wall continued to stand as a symbol of East German fear and West German frustration, the government and people of the Bonn republic eventually had to decide what to do about a political quest that offered little hope for success through conventional political methods. West Germans had to choose whether to make some reckless bid to attain their goals by a policy of deliberate risk or open force, or whether to accept some unsatisfactory compromise arrangement with the Soviet bloc, leaving the latter with most of its conquests; or whether, finally, to settle down to an indefinite period of frustration in the east, while transferring most of their attention, their hopes, and their dreams to the more promising developments in Western Europe and of Western European integration.

Other possible basic strategies besides the three just sketched might have presented themselves, or there might have been possible combinations among them. But by commission or omission, choices had to be made, and the Brandt-Scheel coalition government began to make them in the 1970s. One choice was soon made by the government and accepted by West German public opinion. The claims to the restoration of formerly German territories and properties in Eastern Europe were renounced; the Hallstein doctrine was quietly buried; the G.D.R. was recognized as a sovereign German state, though not yet given full diplomatic recognition. The latter, however, seemed only a matter of time, and so did the eventual entry of both German states as full members into the United Nations. The crucial compromise concerned the status of West Berlin, and in late 1971 its details were worked out in difficult negotiations between the governments in Bonn and East Berlin. The main principles had already been agreed on by the Four Powers —the United States, Britain, France, and the Soviet Union. West Berlin was guaranteed its continued freedom and unhampered access from the west—not only by air but henceforth also by road, rail, and barge traffic. West Berliners now have easier access to East Berlin and to the G.D.R., where many of them still have relatives. Economic relations will be improved between West Berlin and both German states, so as to enhance the city's viability, and the connections between West Berlin and the German Federal Republic are recognized and protected; but the city is not to be considered part of the G.F.R. and there were to be no further conspicuous sessions of the West German legislature or execu-

tive in West Berlin. All this was prepared by the Four Power Agreement of August 1971.

By September 1971, negotiations had shifted to direct talks between representatives of the G.F.R. and G.D.R., and promptly hit a snag. The word *connections* in English (and its Russian counterpart *svyazi*) is conveniently ambiguous, but the German language is embarrassingly specific. It distinguishes *Verbindungen*—i.e., geographic or technical communications or connections—from *Bindungen* —i.e., bonds, ties, loyalties, or obligations, which may be emotional or political. The East German spokesmen came to insist on the first translation; the West Germans on the second. For West Berlin in many ways has become part of West Germany, but not in all respects, and not in international law. Bonn wants to stress its unity with West Berlin, while the G.D.R. wants to emphasize the city's separate existence. The particular quarrel of September 1971 was resolved by the end of the year, but other quarrels are likely to follow. In Berlin, as well as in the wider relations between the G.D.R. and the G.F.R., the road toward a compromise truly accepted by both German governments and both political elites, East and West, still seems long, bitter, and uncertain. Yet no alternative appeared more promising, and it is expected that this reluctant accommodation contributes to a détente.

In the West, the Brandt-Scheel government was facing another choice: whether to limit the German share in the ongoing process of Western European integration to the point where it might remain compatible with the strongest development of German national capabilities, or whether to throw the resources and institutions of the Bonn republic more fully into the melting pot of the emerging Western European federation, at the price of sacrificing not just the trappings but the substance of German national sovereignty in favor of the new union. Next to the decisions about war and peace, these decisions between partial and full commitment to Western European integration may well be among the most important decisions any Germany government and electorate have ever made.

THE DECISION ABOUT WESTERN EUROPEAN INTEGRATION

All the great steps toward Western European integration during the 1950s and 1960s—the European Coal and Steel Community, the European Atomic Energy Agreement, the European Common Market—still remained in their results at the margins of the national economies of the participating countries. The flow of trade between Germany and France had increased only moderately between 1913 and 1954. It had grown in absolute amounts, as had the national incomes of both countries, and French exports to Germany had risen from 13% of all French exports in 1913 to 22% in 1969, while German exports to France had grown from 7% in 1913 to 12% in 1970.[4]

If we compare the share of each country in the exports of the other with the percentage of world exports which the same country accepted in the same year, we can demonstrate the substantial increase in mutual preference for one another's goods that has occurred. In 1890, for instance, the volume of trade between Germany and France was 35% less than one would have expected it to be on the basis of the amount of trading activities of the two countries with the rest of the world. In other words, the existing political tensions between Germany and France prevented both countries from buying each other's exports in strict proportion to both their total purchases in the world market. By 1959, however, other countries had greatly increased their shares of the world market, while the share of world exports purchased by France and Germany had shrunk. Thus, already in 1954, when the percentages of the *national* exports of each country, sent to the other, were the same as in 1890, they represented a much higher degree of mutual preference. By then Germany bought from France 46% *more* than she would have done on the

basis of mere random foreign trade choices; and France bought 30% *more* goods from Germany than would have corresponded to the general French share of goods accepted from the world market. By 1970, the indices of relative acceptance for the trade between the two countries were still higher. Some further details and references are given in Table 7-1. Here it must suffice to say that the analysis in terms of indices of relative acceptance shows that substantial strides toward limited French-German economic integration have been taken since the end of World War II.

The figures in Table 7-1 show the gains in aspects of integration between Germany and France as the key example of the integration between Germany and all the other Common Market countries. They show that these gains are real but limited. Thus far, these advances are much more limited than the enthusiastic publicity for the integration of Europe would suggest—a publicity that is understandably inclined to take future aspirations for present accomplishments.

The gains appear still more limited if we consider that in large, highly developed countries such as Germany and France, exports represent only a fraction of the gross national product. Trade with France, taking both imports and exports together, amounted in 1970 to less than 6%, and trade with the entire Common Market to about 13%, of the gross national product of the Federal Republic.

To date, the freeing of trade under the Common Market has not affected the ability of the federal authorities to maintain acceptable levels of employment, prices, availability of credit, and general stability and rate of economic growth. In the boom years of the 1950s, relatively little government action was required for these ends, and the powers of the Bonn government—and thus indirectly of the West German electorate—were ample for the purpose. As Western European integration progresses through the 1970s, however, the time may arrive when the powers of the Bonn government and the national institutions of the Federal Republic no longer will suffice to maintain the levels of prices, employment, credit, and

[4] Federal Republic of Germany, *Statistisches Jahrbuch für die Bundesrepublik, 1971* (Bonn, 1971), pp. 299, 302, 77 (hereafter cited as *S.J.B.*).

TABLE 7-1. *German-French Trade Integration, 1890–1970*							

Year	1890	1913	1928	1938	1954	1959	1970
Average percentage of mutual share in each other's mail	15% *	12%	5%	4%	4% †	9% ‡	16% #
Average percentage of national exports:							
France to Germany	9%	13%	11%	7%	9%	14%	22% §
Germany to France	7%	8%	7%	4%	7%	12%	12%
Index of relative acceptance (percentage plus or minus of amount exportable under conditions of indifference):							
France to Germany	−35	−27	+0.008	−27	+46	+78	+114 ‖
Germany to France	−35	−9	+3	−25	+36	+79	+110 ‖

SOURCES: Mail figures from K. W. Deutsch, "Towards Western European Union: An Interim Assessment," *The Journal of International Affairs* 16, no. 1 (January 1962):89–101; trade figures from Richard W. Chadwick, Karl W. Deutsch, and I. Richard Savage, *Regionalism, Trade and Political Community,* forthcoming; and *S.J.B.,* 1971, pp. 370, 374. For the "Index of Relative Acceptance," see also K. W. Deutsch, "Toward an Inventory of Basic Trends and Patterns in Comparative and International Politics," *American Political Science Review* 54, no. 1 (March 1960):34–57, especially 46–48; 1960:551–72.

* 1888.
† 1952.
‡ 1958.
# 1969. See Union Postale Universelle, *Statistique des services postaux, 1969,* Berne, 1971, pp. 6, 7, 8.
§ 1969.
‖ 1968.

value of the national currency in the face of possible fluctuations. By that time, the business cycle may put more severe demands on the capabilities of the federal government to conceive, execute, and maintain effective policies of economic stabilization. But by that time, European integration may have so weakened the powers of national governments, including the powers of the Federal Republic, that only common Western European institutions, supported by the common will of the Western European elites and electorates, would be able to take the necessary action.

How willing are the West German voters to accept such common European institutions and to surrender their national sovereignty to them, both in form and in substance? In 1955, only 32% of poll respondents were willing to cede the ultimate power of decision to a European parliament; a larger number, 42%, insisted on reserving that power to a German parliament, and 26% were indifferent or uninformed. In 1960, a somewhat differently worded question left only 8% undecided. The rest were divided in nearly the same proportion, between 42% adherents of a European government and 50% presumably upholders of national sovereignty. Between 1955 and 1960, the net proportions between the "Europeans" and the defenders of the nation-state had shifted only by about 2%, an insignificant amount in view of the different wording of the question. However, by 1967, fully 78% favored a "United States of Europe." And significantly enough, the young and middle-aged (between 16 and 44 years old) approved of the idea in greater numbers than did those over 60—82% versus 68%. Similarly, some 90% of those with at least a secondary education preferred a united Europe compared to 75% of those with an elementary school education.[5]

In mid-1971, when the international mone-

[5] DIVO Institut, *Umfragen* (Allensbach: Institut für Demoskopie, October, 1967), 3:18, 4:36.

tary situation became critical, both France and West Germany behaved as national states. Each government made a series of sovereign decisions about the value of its national currency. Each informed its partner about its own action but did not wait for the other's consent. They did not negotiate and they made no joint decisions. Each nation still acted for itself—just as the United States did at that time.

Altogether, these figures suggest two conclusions. The idea of actual European integration, here and now or in the near future, has become an important issue in West German politics. Never in German history before World War II has so large a majority of Germans backed it. The second conclusion sounds a caution. For the twin goals of German accommodation with the G.D.R.—if not reunification —and of European integration appear to be singularly hard to reconcile—at least in the foreseeable future.

In the meantime, the Bonn government has moved away from its rather rigid policy of 1961–62 toward the entry of Britain into the Common Market. During these years, the governments at Paris and Bonn insisted that Britain accept in essence their policies and bow to their will. Britain, they seemed to insist, should drop most of her ties to the Commonwealth and to the United States, and she should consider her entry into the Common Market only a prelude to her early surrender of a substantial part of British sovereignty to a European political union, shaped largely in accord with French and West German desires.

These demands of the French and German governments, together with their refusal of any major concessions to special British needs, delayed the entry of Britain into the Common Market through the fall of 1962, and allowed France in early 1963 to veto Britain's entry without arousing strong German opposition. German readers smiled broadly at cartoons showing the German chancellor guarding the raised drawbridge which was keeping the British troubadour out of the castle of Europe. Some of them even felt a thrill of power over Britain, which had been a victor in World War II and one of the occupying powers of Germany until the 1950s. Yet neither the economic nor

the political institutions of the German Federal Republic had as yet shown anything like the stability of their British counterparts, which had stood the tests of boom and depression, of defeats and victories, with unwavering firmness. This contribution of tested and dependable stability—despite labor unrest and the long, bitter conflict in Northern Ireland—even more than Britain's military contributions at Berlin and at the Rhine, still seemed essential for the stability of Europe.[6] In the mid-1960s, West German attitudes toward Britain improved somewhat. Mass opinion, elite opinion, and Bonn's official policy all favored, at least mildly, Britain's entry into the Common Market on more lenient terms—though not at the price of a West German test of wills with France. The 1971 French-British agreement between President Pompidou and Prime Minister Heath, eased the conditions for British entry into the Common Market and opened the way to lengthy but not ultimately unpromising negotiations, made it easier for Bonn to keep on good terms with both countries. But both the French and British governments indicated, in late 1971, growing misgivings about the Federal Republic's increasing independence in working out the details of its diplomatic dealings with the Soviet Union. Chancellor Brandt replied to these criticisms, as well as to the political attacks of his CDU/CSU opposition, by stressing the sovereignty and equal status of his country. The Federal Republic's European policy, like its democracy at home, was still in need of further consolidation.

THE POLITICAL DREAMS OF THE NEW GERMAN LITERATURE

On the surface, and to its critics, the Bonn republic looks prosperous and stolid, enthusiastically dedicated to economic success, to conventional middle-class values, to a fair amount of efficient mediocrity, to a fear of innovation and experiment, to a longing for protection by superior authority, to the solidarity

[6] See Viggo Graf Blücher, *Der Prozess der Meinungsbildung* (Bielefeld: EMNID, 1962), pp. 118–19.

of its national in-group, and to a prudent disinclination to probe or question too deeply its own past, present, or future. But after all these reassuring successes, there recurs the little question: "And then . . .?" What is there to dream about, to remember from the past, or to long for in the future? If men must seek a wider horizon and a deeper meaning for their lives, they must reach out beyond the conventions and taboos that have become installed in much of West German life together with the "economic miracle."

This broadening of perspectives is just what a new generation of West German writers is trying to do. They question the past and insist that it be brought up again for unflinching examination. Writers born in the late 1920s, like Günter Grass, who were adolescents when Hitler's regime fell, now recreate in their writings the years in the early 1930s when the Nazis rose to power. They portray, as in an X-ray picture, the sick culture that produced these events, and they and their readers seem to think that these are relevant things to write and think about amidst the prosperous forgetfulness of Bonn.

Here, again, we encounter the problem of differential rates of change. The economic, political, and military burdens on the Federal Republic, and on the consensus among its citizens, may grow faster than the republic's capabilities to meet them, or faster than its citizens can initiate and carry through needed policies. Since we can at present only guess at the speed with which men learn to act effectively and in concert to attain the goals and values they already seek, so we can also only guess at the speed and direction of their movement toward new goals and new values.

This subtle shift toward new goals and new values may be one of the least conspicuous and yet most important aspects of West German politics. Individuals, groups, and whole nations sometimes change their goals and even their character. When they do so, changes in their actions follow. By the early 1970s, there were some signs of such changes in the German Federal Republic. Her artists and writers had already earlier given some hints of the changes that were going on quietly but started to become manifest later. Theirs were more than

merely private dreams. Their books are very widely read, and thus they also say something about the minds of their countrymen who find their writings relevant.

The images of the new writers usually are not images of Europe or of the Atlantic world. Rarely are they dreams of a reunited Germany. Most often—as in Uwe Johnson's *The Third Book about Achim*—they are poignant visions of the mounting barriers to understanding that are rising between the two parts of one people that are becoming every day more different from one another. Johnson communicates his revulsion at the regimented life under the East German dictatorship, but he insists that a new generation of nonfanatical but committed collectivists is growing up there, and he conveys his longing to understand them and to keep open the last remaining opportunities for communication between them and their neighbors to the West. Johnson's book is more subtle and penetrating than those of the more popular writers on the German East-West problem. Among the latter, Hans Helmut Kirst, author of an earlier best-selling trilogy of war novels, has written, in *The Seventh Day,* an uncomfortably plausible scenario of an East German uprising, followed by a border clash between West German and East German troops and ending in the destruction of Europe by the nuclear weapons of the allies of both sides.[7]

Most often, the new writers deal with West Germany herself and with the people and the spirit that are developing within her borders. They begin with the insistent demand that Germans face the hidden and intolerable past. In *The Tin Drum,* Günter Grass brings back this past, using as his memory-triggering device the persistent drum rhythms of a stunted child who has refused to grow up into the kind of adult world that has confused and frightened him through all the years of Hitler, the war, and postwar Germany. Postwar Germany is portrayed in the image of the elegant "onion bar" at Düsseldorf, where prosperous executives and

[7] See Uwe Johnson, *Das dritte Buch über Achim* (Frankfurt: Suhrkamp, 1961); Hans Helmut Kirst, *Und Keiner kommt davon* (Munich: Desch, 1957)—English translation: *The Seventh Day* (New York: Doubleday and Ace Books, 1959).

intellectuals pay for a serving of breadboards, knives, and large raw onions, and proceed to chop up the onions in order to regain their lost capacity for shedding tears.[8]

A Catholic writer, Heinrich Böll, introduces us to a civil engineer and structural expert who deliberately blew up the great abbey which his father had designed and built, and whose son now in turn hesitates to accept the offer of a job to rebuild the structure. In the same novel, *Billiards at Nine Thirty,* one meets a successful organization man and police torturer of the Nazi era, now once again a high-level executive, offering small favors to those of his victims who happened to survive.[9]

In Gerd Gaiser's *Final Ball,* Soldner, the demobilized veteran and teacher without certificate, observes, in the teeth of the economic miracle of the city of Neu-Spuhl, that "an automobile is a means of transportation; the utterly ignorant consider it a badge of rank." Later, Soldner walks out on teaching and on his love, and prospers in business. "I go along with being rich," he says, "until the next time of poverty comes." [10] And there is Gaiser's final symbol, "the day of the dragonflies":

Suddenly I noticed that something was moving in the morass: unrecognizable dirty life. . . . I suddenly saw that an apparent twig, covered with mud, was in reality a large ugly larva. The larva pushed with an awkward unquenchable force to a dry place and lay there in obvious exhaustion.

Many such larvae are crawling out of the mud. And now something happens to one:

The grey husk burst, and a body, gleaming wetly, arched itself with blue and green rings. Then with a quick pull, it came long and slim out of the tube; a dragonfly was sitting on the stalk and trembling imperceptibly. Its tremendous, rapacious eyes still seemed dead, while from somewhere, perhaps out of the air, substance seemed to flow into the slack body and helped fill it. In the air there also were

hardening the crumpled, finely veined wings; they began to stretch out, taut and brittle. The eyes began to shine, as if some blinding dust was disappearing from them. They became illuminated from within. Finally I saw the first dragonfly hovering above the water. A flash; it stood hovering; it sped away, a blue spark. . . . Wherever we looked, we saw pushing and slipping out. The brown pool seemed a place of transformation. They crawled and rose. Everywhere a straining upward and a slipping out. . . . We saw newly emerged ones laboriously straining, and we saw others spread their wings that had turned hard and glassy, and saw others shoot upward with a whir. *Imago.* This is the way it will be.

The image is compelling and ambiguous. Is it to be once again the emergence of something long and slim, tremendous and rapacious, hard and glassy out of the warm mud of the money-minded city of Neu-Spuhl? Gerd Gaiser is a former fighter pilot of the Luftwaffe of World War II. Does he envision the metamorphosis of an insect which emerges from its husk only as an exact repetition of the pattern of the preceding generation? Is this a poetic way of saying: "The day will come"—*Es kommt der Tag*—when the uniforms, the machine guns, the pistols, and the fighter planes come once again? Or is this meant to be an image of the rebirth of human beings and of a human community, a human spring beyond the fatal repetition of the biological cycle of the seasons and the dragonfly—a truly new birth and a new beginning?

No one inside or outside Germany can tell for certain. The riddle of her future is part of the riddle of our own. At the beginning of the interplanetary age, all the world's nations are unfinished once again. Their past is inescapably real, and yet the meaning and power of that past is in question. Their national institutions are once again being melted and recast. Their political bodies and souls are strained by the pressures for change, and they may yet be born again. More or less, this is true of all the great nations—but perhaps it is most true of Germany, the Germany beneath the surface of its so recently consolidated institutions and behind the highly gifted German people of whom no one, not even they themselves, yet knows what they will become.

Some of mankind's greatest treasures of in-

[8] See Günter Grass, *The Tin Drum* (New York: Pantheon Books, 1963).

[9] See Heinrich Böll, *Billiard um halbzehn* (Köln-Berlin: Kiepenheuer & Witsch, 1959).

[10] See Gerd Gaiser, *Schlussball* (Frankfurt: Fischer, 1961).

tegrity, courage, and kindness have persisted in Germany—among the German prisoners in her concentration camps, among the members and martyrs of her resistance, among those who preferred danger or exile to acquiescence in injustice, and among those, young and old, political and nonpolitical, who throughout the years of trial retained an honest mind, a sensitive heart, and a helping hand for others. In today's Germany, these treasures have increased. Among her people, and most of all among her youth, there is a more sober but profound commitment to spiritual and human values than before.

Some of Germany's successes, however, are beginning to create new elements of crisis. Its symptoms have become most clearly visible in the West German universities. New students, sometimes with weaker academic preparation, are thronging the universities in larger numbers, while the universities in many ways have not kept pace. Lecture rooms, laboratories, and other facilities are badly overcrowded. Many students feel neglected and abandoned, facing subject matter which seems too difficult, or meaningless; and their professors sometimes seem too few and too remote to fulfill their traditional role as authority figures who can serve as models for imitation or as specific targets for revolt, so that frustration seems to come from an anonymous "system."

Another change cuts still deeper, perhaps, and not only in the universities. The young Germans of the early 1970s have grown up in an atmosphere of stronger democratic values and beliefs, and of higher standards and expectations—both material and moral—than any generation before them. The gap between what they have learned to expect and reality seems to many intolerably wide. They have heard again and again about the "crime" of silence and blind obedience, which so many of their elders committed in Hitler's day, and many of the young now feel a sense of personal responsibility and a need to speak out against what they see as wrong or evil.

All these and other conditions may have combined to produce the sense of crisis in the West German universities, which was evident in the late 1960s and early 1970s, and which

seems unlikely to end soon. Some students—perhaps as many as 40%—were responding to alienation and conflicting pressures by seeking once again a sense of security and belonging in the authoritarianism of the traditional dueling fraternities. Many others—though their numbers are hard to estimate—seek to affirm their identity by various forms of protest or sympathy for protest. A few outdo their counterparts in the United States in gestures of rebellion and long-haired defiance of convention and authority; others throw themsleves into more serious varieties of radical protest politics. They demand quick reforms in the German universities, and an end to the United States military effort in Vietnam. They have picketed some meetings of the major parties. They have challenged and debated leaders of the older generation. They also turned out in large numbers in June 1967 to picket the Shah of Iran during his visit to the opera in West Berlin, because they considered him a dictator who had helped destroy constitutional government in his own country. Police repressed them with a violence that smacked of panic. One student, Benno Ohnesorge, was killed in front of the Opera House by a policeman's bullet—the first such student victim in the history of the Bonn republic. About one-third of the students at many West German universities were reported to have taken part in a silent demonstration at the time of Ohnesorge's funeral, and the police chief of West Berlin resigned shortly after "for reasons of health." Most young people in West Berlin and West Germany clearly continue to prefer the Western, democratic way of life to what they have seen of the dictatorial regime in the G.D.R., but by late 1960s and early 1970s the active discontent of many among them had become a factor to be reckoned with in the political and cultural life of the Federal Republic.

Among the young, behind the activism of the few there has been growing a limited but important shift in the attitudes and habits of the many. A longing for more permissiveness and freedom, more imagination and enjoyment, less authority and more friendship, less competition and more equality, less domination and more participation, less privilege and more social justice—all these have been growing not only among a majority of the students but also among a large part of nonacademic youth. These changed attitudes are limited and not always consistent. They come up against the massive inequalities of wealth and power that have persisted in the social structure of the country, and they must face the slow-changing habits of their elders, who constitute a majority of the voters and who dominate the established party organizations. Some of the young will drop their ideas of political and social change as they grow older; others will isolate themselves in the radicalism of some political sect or faction; but many will retain a good part of their aspirations and in time they will claim and gain their share in the voting power and political leadership of their country.

In the meantime, they are hard to govern, hard to administer and teach, hard to integrate into the political parties and other democratic institutions of the G.F.R. Yet their country needs them and their commitment, if its democracy is to grow stronger. "This," said Horst Ehmke, one of the chief advisers of Chancellor Willy Brandt, "is the generation we have been waiting for." [11]

11 *Politik der praktischen Vernunft* (Frankfurt: Fischer, 1969).

Even with the help of this new generation —if it should be forthcoming—the path of the Federal Republic will not be easy. More than other large countries, the Federal Republic depends for its stability upon the actions of foreign powers—East and West—and upon the civic support of its people, particularly its young. The specific attacks of the radical right, the diffuse frustrations of the intellectuals and of the young, and the ever-present possibility of a new international economic or military crisis may well present increasingly serious challenges to the democratic skills, loyalties, and institutions which have been developed during the preceding two decades. But these will be challenges not only to the survival of democracy but to its creativity. During the last quarter-century, West Germany has already pioneered a number of important reforms. More reforms will be needed. If they should be forthcoming, they may be of worldwide importance. For Germany is a test case of modern industrial society. Any future success of democracy and structural reform in the German Federal Republic may be significant for all of us.

bibliography

GENERAL

The following are general accounts of West German politics, or of some of their major aspects. They are relevant for several or all of the chapters, but they will not be repeated in the special bibliographies for each chapter.

BLÜCHER, VIGGO GRAF, *Der Prozess der Meinungsbildung dargestellt am Beispiel der Bundestagswahl, 1961* (Bielefeld: EMNID, 1962).

DEUTSCH, KARL W., *Arms Control and the Atlantic Alliance* (New York: Wiley, 1967).

———, L. J. EDINGER, R. C. MACRIDIS, and R. L. MERRITT, *France, Germany and the Western Alliance* (New York: Scribners, 1967).

———, and L. J. EDINGER, *Germany Rejoins the Powers: Mass Opinion, Interest Groups and Elites in German Foreign Policy* (Stanford, Calif.: Stanford University Press, 1959).

DIVO Institut, Umfragen: Ereignisse und Probleme der Zeit im Urteil der Bevölkerung (Frankfurt: Europäische Verlagsanstalt, 1959–62).

German Democratic Republic, Statistisches Jahrbuch 1971 der Deutschen Demokratischen Republik (East Berlin: Staatsverlag, 1971).

German Federal Government, Facts about Germany (Bonn: Press and Information Office, 1965).

GERMAN FEDERAL REPUBLIC, *Bundesministerium für innerdeutsche Beziehungen, Deutschland 1971: Bericht und Materialien zur Lage der Nation* [Willy Brandt, Egon Franke, Peter Christian Ludz, *et al.*] (Bonn and Köln: Westdeutscher Verlag, 1971). A new source of outstanding importance. The first systematic comparison of the performance of a Communist and a non-Communist political system.

Federal Republic of Germany, Statistisches Jahrbuch für die Bundesrepublik (Bonn, 1963–71).

GROSSER, ALFRED, *Die Bonner Demokratie* (Düsseldorf: Rauch, 1960. Also available in French. The best general treatment available at full length.

———, *The Federal Republic of Germany: A Concise History* (New York: Praeger, 1964).

HEIDENHEIMER, ARNOLD J., *The Governments of Germany* (New York: Thomas Y. Crowell, 1966). An excellent survey.

KITZINGER, U. W., *German Electoral Politics: A Study of the 1957 Campaign* (Oxford: Clarendon Press, 1960). An outstanding election study by a British author that tells much about the background of German politics.

LINZ, JUAN, "The Social Bases of West German Politics," Ph.D. dissertation, Columbia University, 1959; Ann Arbor, Michigan, University of Michigan Microfilms, 1959.

NEUMANN, ERICH PETER, *Public Opinion in Germany, 1961* (Allensbach and Bonn: Verlag für Demoskopie, 1961).

NEUMANN, ELISABETH NOELLE, and ERICH PETER NEUMANN, *Jahrbuch der öffentlichen Meinung (1947–1955), Jahrbuch I, Jahrbuch II,* and *Jahrbuch III* (Allensbach: Verlag für Demoskopie, 1957, et seq.). The most extensive collections of important German poll data that have been published.

PLISCHKE, ELMER, *Contemporary Government of Germany* (Boston: Houghton Mifflin, 1962). The best brief treatment in English of legal and constitutional aspects of German politics, and of the role of the American occupation.

POLLOCK, JAMES K., and HOMER THOMAS, *Germany in Power and Eclipse* (New York: Van Nostrand, 1952).

SPEIER, HANS, and W. P. DAVISON (eds.), *West German Leadership and Foreign Policy* (Evanston, Ill.: Row, Peterson, 1957).

United Nations Economic Commission for Europe, Economic Survey of Europe, 1953, 1955 (Geneva and New York 1956–   ).

CHAPTER 1

ALMOND, GABRIEL A., *The Struggle for Democracy in Germany* (Chapel Hill: University of North Carolina Press, 1949).

———, and SIDNEY VERBA, *The Civic Culture* (Princeton: Princeton University Press, 1965).

Federal Republic of Germany, Ministry for Expellees, Refugees, and War Victims, *Facts* (Bonn, 1961).

LIEPELT, KLAUS, "Anhänger der neuen Rechtspartei: Ein Beitrag zur Diskussion über das Wählerreservior der NPD," *Politische Vierteljahresschrift* 8, no. 2 (1967).

NARR, WOLF-DIETER, and FRIEDER NASCHOLD, *Theorie der Demokratie* (Stuttgart: Kohlhammer, 1971).

United Nations, Yearbook of National Account Statistics (New York, 1961).

WILDENMANN, RUDOLF, and MAX KAASE, *Die unruhige Generation: Eine Untersuchung zu Politik und Demokratie in der Bundesrepublik* (Mannheim: Lehrstuhl für politische Wissenschaft an der Universität Mannheim, 1968). Lithoprinted.

CHAPTER 2

ALLEMAN, FRITZ RENÉ, *Zwischen Stabilität und Krise* (Munich: Piper, 1963).

BARRACLOUGH, G., *Origins of Modern Germany,* 2d ed. (Oxford: Blackwell, 1962).

BRACHER, KARL D., *Die Auflösung der Weimarer Republik* [The dissolution of the Weimar Republic], 4th ed. (Villingen: Ring, 1964).

———, *The German Dictatorship: the Origins, Structure, and Effects of National Socialism* (New York: Praeger, 1970).

———, W. SAUER, and G. SCHULZ, *Die Nationalsozialistische Machtergreifung: Studien zur Errichtung- des totalitären Herrschaftssystems in Deutschland 1933/34,* 2d ed. (Köln and Opladen: Westdeutscher Verlag, 1962). The standard work on the Nazi takeover.

CRAIG, GORDON A., *The Politics of the Prussian Army* (New York: Oxford University Press, 1956). The best and most balanced historical treatment through 1918.

DORPALEN, ANDREAS, *Hindenburg and the Weimar Republic* (Princeton: Princeton University Press, 1964).

ERIKSON, ERIK H., *Young Man Luther* (New York: Norton, 1958).

FAY, SIDNEY BRADSHAW, *The Rise of Brandenburg-Prussia to 1786* (New York: Holt, 1937).

Der Fischer Weltalmanach, '67 (Frankfurt: Fischer, 1967).

FISCHER, FRITZ, *Griff nach der Weltmacht* (Düsseldorf: Droste Verlag, 1967). An outstanding discussion of German war aims in World War I, based on documents.

FRIED, HANS, *The Guilt of the German Army* (New York: Oxford University Press, 1942).

HILDEBRAND, KLAUS, *Deutsche Aussenpolitik, 1933–1945: Kalkül oder Dogma?* (Stuttgart: Kohlhammer, 1971).

HOFER, WALTER, *Der Nationalsozialismus: Dokumente, 1933–1945* (Frankfurt: Fischer, 1957).

HOLBORN, HAJO, *Modern Germany,* Vol. 1, *The Reformation* (New York: Knopf, 1959).

HUGHES, STUART, *Consciousness and Society* (New York: Knopf, 1959). An outstanding discussion of European intellectual development, 1890–1930, notably including Germany.

KOHN, HANS, *German History: Some New German Views* (Boston: Beacon Press, 1954).

———, *The Mind of Modern Germany* (New York: Scribners, 1960).

KRACAUER, SIEGFRIED, *From Caligari to Hitler: A Psychological History of the German Film* (New York: Noonday Press, 1959).

KRIEGER, LEONARD, *The German Idea of Freedom* (Boston: Beacon Press, 1957).

LOWIE, ROBERT H., *The German People: A Social Portrait to 1914* (New York and Toronto: Farrar & Rinehart, 1945).

———, *Toward Understanding Germany* (Chicago: University of Chicago Press, 1954).

MATTHIAS, ERICH, and R. MORSEY (eds.), *Das Ende der Parteien, 1933* (Düsseldorf: Droste, 1960).

NEUMANN, FRANZ, *Behemoth* (New York: Oxford University Press, 1942).

PARSONS, TALCOTT, "Democracy and Social Structure in Pre-Nazi Germany," in *Essays in Sociological Theory,* rev. 2d ed. (Glencoe, Ill.: Free Press, 1954). A brief but important essay.

PINSON, KOPPEL S., *Modern Germany. Its History and Civilization* (New York: Macmillan, 1966).

REINHARDT, KURT, *Germany: 2000 Years,* rev. ed. (New York: Unger, 1961).

RÖHL, J. C. G., *From Bismarck to Hitler* (New York: Barnes & Noble, 1970).

ROTH, GUENTHER, *The Social Democrats in Imperial Germany* (Totowa, N.J.: Bedminster Press, 1964).

ROTHFELS, HANS, *The German Opposition to Hitler,* rev. ed. (Chicago: Regnery, 1962).

———, *Zeitgeschichtliche Betrachtungen* (Göttingen: Vandenhoeck & Ruprecht, 1959).

SCHMERTZING, WOLFGANG P. VON, *Outlawing the Communist Party—A Case History* (New York: The Bookmailer Co., 1957).

SCHOENBAUM, DAVID, *Hitler's Social Revolution* (New York: Doubleday, 1966).

SCHOLL, INGE, *Die Weisse Rose* (Frankfurt: Fischer, 1955). The story of the wartime resistance of Munich students to the Nazi regime.

SCHWARZER, HANS WERNER, *Die DDR ist keine Zone mehr* (Cologne-Berlin: Kiepenheuer und Witsch, 1969).

SHIRER, WILLIAM L., *The Rise and Fall of the Third Reich: A History of Nazi Germany* (New York: Simon & Schuster, 1960).

STERN, FRITZ (ed.), *The Path to Dictatorship* (New York: Doubleday, 1966).

THYSSEN, F., *I Paid Hitler* (New York: Farrar & Rinehart, 1941).

WEBER, HERMANN, and FRED OLDENBURG, *25 Jahre SED: Chronik einer Partei* (Cologne: Verlag für Wissenschaft und Politik, 1971).

WEHLER, HANS-ULRICH, *Bismarck und der Imperialismus* (Köln and Berlin: Kiepenheuer & Witsch, 1969).

ZINK, HAROLD, *The United States in Germany, 1944–1955* (New York: Van Nostrand, 1957).

CHAPTER 3

AGNOLI, JOHANNES, and PETER BRÜCKNER, *Die Transformation der Demokratie* (Frankfurt: Europäische Verlagsanstalt, 1968).

ALTMANN, RÜDIGER, *Das Erbe Adenauers* (Stuttgart: Seewalt, 1960).

———, *Zensuren nach 20 Jahren Bundesrepublik, Erteilt von Rüdiger Altmann* (Cologne: Verlag Wissenschaft und Politik, 1969).

ARNDT, HANS-JOACHIM, *West Germany: The Politics of Non-Planning* (Syracuse, N.Y.: Syracuse University Press, 1966).

BLÜCHER, VICO GRAF, *Die Generation der Unbefangenen* (Stuttgart: Fischer, 1966).

BUCHANAN, J. W., and H. CANTRIL, *How Nations See Each Other: A Study in Public Opinion* (Urbana: University of Illinois Press, 1953).

DEUTSCH, K. W., and A. ECKSTEIN, "National Industrialization and the Decline of the International Economic Sector, 1890–1959," *World Politics* 13, no. 2 (January 1961).

DIVO Institut, Bundestagswahl, 1961, Repräsentativumfrage 326 Nov.-Dec. 1961; 322, July 1961; 323, Sept. 1961. Lithoprint.

FRÖHNER, ROLF, *Wie stark sind die Halbstarken: Dritte E.M.N.I.D. Untersuchung zur Situation der deutschen Jugend* (Bielefeld: Stackelberg, 1956).

Federal Republic of Germany, Ministry for Economic Cooperation, *Der europäische Wirtschaftsrat,* OEEC Handbuch (Bonn, 1956).

————, *Germany Reports* (Bonn, 1953).

GROSSER, ALFRED, *Die Bundesrepublik Deutschland: Bilanz einer Entwicklung* (Tübingen: Wunderlich, 1967).

HERETH, MICHAEL (ed.), *20 Jahre Bundesrepublik Deutschland in Dokumenten* (Munich: List, 1969).

HEUBENER, THEODORE, *The Schools of West Germany* (New York: New York University Press, 1962).

JASPERS, KARL, *Wohin treibt die Bundesrepublik?* (Munich: Piper, 1966).

LANE, JOHN C., and JAMES K. POLLOCK, *Source Materials on the Government and Politics of Germany* (Ann Arbor: Wahrs, 1964).

LOWELL, DITTMER, "The German NPD: A Psycho-Sociological Analysis of 'Neo-Nazism,'" *Comparative Politics* 2, no. 1 (1969).

MELLEN, SYDNEY L. W., "The German People and The Postwar World, A Study Based on Election Statistics, 1871–1933," *American Political Science Review* 37, no. 4 (August 1943).

MERKL, PETER, *The Origin of the West German Republic* (New York: Oxford University Press, 1963).

NEIDHARDT, FRIEDHELM, *Die junge Generation* (Munich: Piper, 1967).

NEUMANN, ELISABETH NOELLE, and ERICH PETER NEUMANN (eds.), *The German Public Opinion Polls, 1947–1966* (Allensbach: Verlag für Demoskopie, 1967).

SCHELSKY, HELMUT, *Die skeptische Generation* (Düsseldorf: Diederichs, 1957).

STAHL, WALTER (ed.), *The Politics of Post-War Germany* (New York: Praeger, 1963).

STOLPER, WOLFGANG, *Germany Between East and West* (Washington, D.C.: National Planning Assn., 1960).

————, *The Structure of the East German Economy* (Cambridge: Harvard University Press, 1960).

UNGERN-STERNBERG, RODERICH VON, "Die Selbstmordhäufigkeit in Verhangenheit und Gegenwart," *Jahrbücher für Nationalökonomie und Statisik* 171, no. 3 (Stuttgart: Fischer, 1959).

VERBA, SIDNEY, "Germany: The Remaking of Political Culture," in *Political Culture and Political Development,* eds. Lucian W. Pye and Sidney Verba (Princeton: Princeton University Press, 1965).

CHAPTER 4

ANGER, HANS, *Probleme der Deutschen Universität* (Tübingen: J. C. B. Mohr [Paul Siebeck], 1960).

HEIDENHEIMER, ARNOLD, "La structure confessionelle, sociale et regionale de la C.D.U.," *Revue Française de Science Politique* 7, no. 3 (July-September 1957).

JANOWITZ, M., "Social Stratification and Mobility in West Germany," *American Journal of Sociology* 64, no. 1 (July 1958).

KRUPP, HANS-JÜRGEN, "Wandlungen der Einkommensstruktur in der Bundesrepublik," in *Industriegesellschaften im Wandel, Japan und die BRD,* eds. Karl Hax and Willy Krauss (Düsseldorf: Bertelsmann Universitätsverlag, 1970), pp. 43–60.

POLLOCK, FRIEDERICH, *Gruppenexperiment: Ein Studienbericht,* Frankfurter Beiträge zur Soziologie, Vol. 2 (Frankfurt: Europäische Verlagsanstalt, 1955).

WILDENMANN, RUDOLF (ed.), *Sozialwissenschaftliches Jahrbuch für Politik,* Vol. 2 (Munich: Günter Olzog Verlag, 1969). See particularly articles by Rudolf Wildenmann, Max Kaase, Hans Klingemann, and Hansjörg Mauch.

CHAPTER 5

Archiv der Gegenwart (Bonn) 32, no. 4 (Jan. 21–26, 1962):9636y; 32, no. 1 (Jan. 6, 1962):9584A; 31, no. 40 (Oct. 10, 1961):9371C.

ABRAHAM, H. J., et al., *Kommentar zum Bonner Grundgesetz* (Hamburg: Hansischer Gildenverlag, 1950).

BOLTE, KARL MARTIN, *Deutsche Gesellschaft im Wandel* (Opladen: Westdeutscher, 1966).

COLE, TAYLOR, "Democratization of the German Civil Service," *Journal of Politics* (February 14, 1952).

ELLWEIN, THOMAS, *Das Regierungssystem der Bundesrepublik Deutschland,* 2nd ed. (Köln and Opladen: Westdeutscher Verlag, 1965). A major source both for facts and analysis.

ESCHENBURG, THEODOR, *Der Sold des Politikers* (Stuttgart: Seewald, 1959).

————, *Staat und Gesellschaft in Deutschland,* 3d ed. (Stuttgart: Schwab, 1956).

GROSSER, ALFRED, and HENRI MÉNUDIER, *La vie politique en Allemagne fédérale* (Paris: Colin, 1970).

GRUNDGESETZ, 2d ed. (Munich: Beck, 1971).

HEIDENHEIMER, ARNOLD J., "Wie die Parlamente tagen," *Das Parlament* (December 12, 1960).

JACOB, HERBERT, *German Administration since Bismarck: Central Authority versus Local Autonomy* (New Haven: Yale University Press, 1963).

LEIBHOLZ, GERHARD, *Strukturprobleme der modernen Demokratie* (Karlsruhe: C. F. Müller, 1958).

LOEWENBERG, GERHARD, *Parliament in the German Political System* (Ithaca, N.Y.: Cornell University Press, 1966).

LOHMAR, ULRICH, *Innerparteiliche Demokratie* (Stuttgart: Enke, 1963).

MAUNZ, THEODOR, *Deutsches Staatsrecht,* 5th ed. (Munich-Berlin: Beck, 1956).

NEUMANN, SIGMUND, "Germany," in *European Political Systems,* ed. Taylor Cole (New York: Knopf, 1954).

SCHOLZ, PETER, *Die Deutsche Demokratie* (Munich: Olzog, 1969).

STAMMER, OTTO, et al., *Verbaende und Gesetzgebung* (Cologne: Rauch, 1965).

WALSER, MARTIN (ed.), *Die Alternative, oder Brauchen wir eine neue Regierung?* (Reinbek bei Hamburg: Rowohlt Taschenbuch, 1961).

WHEARE, KENNETH C., *Federal Government,* 5th ed. (London: Oxford University Press, 1961).

WILDENMANN, RUDOLF, *Macht und Konsensus als Problem der Innen und Aussenpolitik* (Frankfurt: Athenäum, 1963).

CHAPTER 6

BREITLING, RUPERT, *Die Verbaende in der Bundesrepublik* (Meisenheim: Hain, 1955).

BRIEFS, GOETZ (ed.), *Mitbestimmung?* (Stuttgart: Seewald, 1968).

CHALMERS, DOUGLAS A., *The Social Democratic Party of Germany* (New Haven: Yale University Press, 1964).

Comparative Politics, 2, no. 4 (July 1970). Special Issue on the West German Election of 1969.

DAHRENDORF, R., "Deutsche Richter: Ein Beitrag zur Soziologie der Oberschicht," in *Gesellschaft und Freiheit* (Munich: Piper, 1961).

DIVO *Institut, Der Westdeutsche Markt in Zahlen* (Frankfurt: Europäische Verlagsanstalt, 1962).

EDINGER, LEWIS, *Kurt Schumacher* (Stanford, Calif.: Stanford University Press, 1965).

ENZENSBERGER, HANS M., "Die Sprache des Spiegel," in *Einzelheiten* (Frankfurt: Suhrkamp, 1962).

FAUL, ERWIN, and ADOLF STERNBERGER (eds.), *Wahlen und Wähler in Westdeutschland* (Villingen-Schwarzwald: Ring, 1960).

GAUS, GÜNTER, *Staatserhaltende Opposition ode Hat die SPD kapituliert?—Gespräche mit Herbert Wehner* (Reinbek: Rowohlt Verlag 1966).

GROSSMAN, KURT R., *Germany's Moral Debt: The German-Israel Agreement* (Washington, D.C.: Public Affairs Press, 1954).

HARTENSTEIN, WOLFGANG, and GÜNTER SCHUBERT, *Mitlaufen oder Mitbestimmen* (Frankfurt: Europäische Verlagsanstalt, 1961).

HARTMANN, HEINZ, "Die interessante Zahl," *Junge Wirtschaft* (December 1957).

————, *Authority and Organization in German Management* (Princeton: Princeton University Press, 1958).

HEIDENHEIMER, ARNOLD J., "German Party Finance: the C.D.U.," *American Political Science Review* 51, no. 2 (June 1957).

HERETH, MICHAEL, *Die Parlamentarische Opposition in der Bundesrepublik Deutschland* (Munich: Olzog, 1969).

HIRSCH-WEBER, W., and K. SCHUTZ, *Wähler und Gewählte: Eine Untersuchung der Bundestagswahlen 1953* (Berlin: Vahlen, 1957).

HOCHSCHWENDER, K., *German Civil Service Reform after 1945,* Ph.D. thesis, Yale University, 1961.

KIRCHHEIMER, OTTO, "The Vanishing Opposition," in *Political Oppositions in Western Democracies,* ed. Robert Dahl (New Haven: Yale University Press, 1966).

LÜTH, ERICH, "Deutsche und Juden Heute," *Der Monat* 10, no. 110 (November 1957).

MAIER, HANS, *NPD: Struktur und Ideologie einer "nationalen Rechtspartei,"* (Munich: Piper, 1967).

MELLEN, SYDNEY L. W., "The German People and the Postwar World, A Study Based on Election Statistics, 1871–1933," *American Political Science Review* 37, no. 4 (August 1943).

MONTGOMERY, JOHN W., *Forced to be Free* (Chicago: University of Chicago Press, 1957). *New York Times,* Mar. 28, 1958; Nov. 3, 1962; Nov. 5, 1962.

NARR, WOLF-DIETER, *CDU-SPD* (Stuttgart: Kohlhammer, 1966).

PILGERT, HENRY P., *Press, Radio and Film in West Germany,* 1945–1953, Historical Division, Office of the Executive Secretary, Office of the U.S. High Commissioner for Germany (Frankfurt, 1953).

RAUSCHER, ANTON (ed.), *Mitbestimmung* (Cologne: Bacher, 1968).

SCHEUCH, ERWIN, and RUDOLF WILDENMANN (eds.), *Zur Soziologie der Wahl* (Cologne: Rauch, 1965). Contains articles on West German political attitudes, party finance, and campaign studies.

SCHMIDT, H., *Verteidigung oder Vergeltung: Ein deutscher Beitrag zum strategischen Problem der N.A.T.O.* (Stuttgart: Seewald, 1961).

SCHROERS, ROLF (ed.), *Der Demokratische Obrigkeitsstaat* (Bonn: Liberal, 1968).

WILDENMANN, RUDOLF, WERNER KALTEFLEITER, and HANS SCHLETH, "Auswirkungen von Wahlsystemen auf das Parteien—und Regierungssystem der Bundesrepublik," *Kölner Zeitschrift für Soziologie und Sozialpsychologie* 9 (1965).

CHAPTER 7

BÖLL, HEINRICH, *Billiard um halbzehn* (Köln-Berlin: Kiepenheuer & Witsch, 1959).

DIVO Institut, Umfragen, Vols. 3 and 4 (Frankfurt: Europäische Verlagsanstalt, 1962).

DEUTSCH, K. W., "Towards Western European Integration: An Interim Assessment," *Journal of International Affairs,* 16, no. 1 (January 1962).

———, "Toward an Inventory of Basic Trends and Patterns in Comparative and International Politics," *American Political Science Review* 54, no. 1 (March 1960).

———, and R. SAVAGE, "A Statistical Model of the Gross Analysis of Transaction Flows," *Econometrica* 28, no. 3 (July 1960).

GAISER, GERD, *Schlussball* (Frankfurt: Fischer, 1961).

GRASS, GÜNTER, *Die Blechtrommel* [The Tin Drum] (Darmstadt: Luchterhand, 1960; New York: Pantheon Books, 1963).

HALLSTEIN, WALTER, *United Europe: Challenge and Opportunity* (Cambridge: Harvard University Press, 1962).

JOHNSON, UWE, *Das dritte Buch über Achim* (Frankfurt: Suhrkamp, 1961).

KIRST, HANS H., *Und keiner kommt davon* [The seventh day] (Munich: Desch, 1957; New York: Doubleday, Ace Books, 1959).

LEIBHOLZ, GERHARD, *Sovereignty and European Integration: Some Basic Considerations* (Lehden: A. W. Sythoff, 1960).

LOHMAR, ULRICH, *Deutschland 1975* (Munich: Kindler, 1965).

MERKL, PETER, *Germany: Yesterday and Tomorrow* (New York: Oxford University Press, 1965).

Der Spiegel, October 10-November 15, 1962; 16:41, October 10, 1962; 16:45, November 7, 1962; 16: 27, July 4, 1962.

STRAUSS, FRANZ-JOSEF, "Sicherheit und Wiedervereinigung," *Aussenpolitik* 6, no. 3 (March 1957).

Vernon V. Aspaturian

THE
SOVIET
UNION

FR. BELG. NETH. LUX.

GERMANY

NORWAY

ALASKA

ARCTIC OCEAN

DENMARK

SWEDEN

BARENTS SEA

Franz Joseph Land

Wrangel Island

AUSTRIA

CZECHOSLOVAKIA

HUNGARY

POLAND

KALININGRAD OBLAST (TO RSFSR)

FINLAND

KARELIAN ASSR

Murmansk

Severnaya Zemlya

New Siberian Islands

CHUKOT NA

LITHUANIAN SSR

Riga

Tallinn

ESTONIAN SSR

Novaya Zemlya

KORYAK NA

Vilna

LATVIAN SSR

RUMANIA

Lwow

UKRAINIAN SSR

BYELORUSSIAN SSR

Minsk

Leningrad

Archangel

NENETZ NA

Vorkuta

TAYMYR NA

BERING SEA

MOLDAVIAN SSR

Smolensk

MOSCOW

KOMI ASSR

Pechora

YAMALO-NENETZ NA

Kiev

CHUVASH ASSR

Volga

YAKUT ASSR

BLACK SEA

Odessa

Kharkov

Dnieper

MORDVIN ASSR

MARI ASSR

KOMI-PERM NA

KHANTY-MANSY NA

EVENKI NA

Sevastopol

SEA OF AZOV

Rostov

Don

UDMURT ASSR

Perm (Molotov)

TATAR ASSR

Volga

Kuibyshev

BASHKIR ASSR

Sverdlovsk

Lena

Yakutsk

ADYGEI AR

KARACHAI-CHERKESS AR

KABARDINO-BALKAK ASSR

Volgograd (Stalingrad)

Chelyabinsk

Magnitogorsk

SEA OF OKHOTSK

ABKHAZIAN ASSR

Batumi

KALMYK ASSR

N. OSSETIAN ASSR

Astrakhan

KAMCHATKA

ADZHARIAN ASSR

GEORGIAN SSR

S. OSSETIAN AR

Tbilisi

CHECHEN-INGUSH ASSR

Petropavlovsk

ARMENIAN SSR

Yerevan

CASPIAN SEA

DAGHESTAN ASSR

Omsk

Ob

Yenesei

Krasnoyarsk

TRANS SIBERIAN RAILWAY

SAKHALIN

KHICHEVAN ASSR (TO AZERBAIJAN)

Baku

KAZAKH SSR

Novosibirsk

UST-ORDINSK BURYAT MONGOL AR

KHAKASS AR

Lake Baikal

BURYAT ASSR

Kurile Islands

NAGORNO-KARABAKH AR

AZERBAIDZHAN SSR

Krasnovodsk

KARA-KALPAK ASSR

ARAL SEA

Karaganda

Irkutsk

Ulan Ude

Chita

JEWISH AR

Khabarovsk

AGINSK BURYAT-MONGOL NA

Semipalatinsk

GORNO-ALTAI AR

TUVA AR

Amur

TURKMEN SSR

Amu Darya

Balkhash

MONGOLIAN PEOPLE'S REPUBLIC

Vladivostok

Askhabad

UZBEK SSR

Bukhara

Tashkent

Frunze

Alma Ata

SEA OF JAPAN

Samarkand

KIRGIZ SSR

JAPAN

TADZHIK SSR

GORNO-BADAKHSHAN AR

AFGHANISTAN

KOREA

CHINA

KEY

RUSSIAN SOVIET FEDERATED SOCIALIST REPUBLIC

ASSR Autonomous Republic

AR Autonomous Region

NA National Region

SSR UNION REPUBLIC

0 100 200 300 400 500

MILES

In 1848, when two young German intellectuals, Karl Marx and Friedrich Engels, both in their mid-twenties, wrote the *Communist Manifesto,* communism was simply a startling idea, but one which the two youthful authors declared was "a specter haunting Europe," destined to inspire a fundamental reorganization of society which would sweep away the civilization created by capitalism. Within the short space of fifty years, Marxist communism had spawned influential Socialist and Social Democratic parties in western Europe and a multitude of splinter and sectarian political groups. One of them—the radical Bolshevik wing of the Russian Social Democratic party (later renamed the Communist party), led by Vladimir Ilyich Lenin—used the ideas of Marx to shape a revolutionary party that seized power in one of the great nations of the world, the Russian empire. For the first time, the world witnessed the establishment of a social, economic, and political system that was frankly and boldly inspired by the ideas expressed in the *Communist Manifesto.*

The Bolshevik Revolution of 1917 constitutes one of the great watersheds in the evolution of human history. The multiple revolutions and transformations that have taken place throughout the world in the past five decades have been profoundly shaped and influenced by the ideas behind this revolution, and the power of the Soviet state which it brought into being. A little more than 120 years after the appearance of the *Communist Manifesto,* communism is no longer a simple idea, but is a way of life embracing fourteen states with a population of nearly 1 billion people, occupying approximately one-third of the earth's total land surface. Within this bloc of nations are to be found over two hundred different nationalities and ethnic and linguistic groups, most of the races of mankind, and numerous cultures and religions. Furthermore, Communist parties, large and small, exist in more than seventy-five additional countries on five continents, ranging from minuscule illegal groups to large mass parties like those found in France and Italy. All these parties are dedicated to establishing communism as a way of life in their own countries.

ONE

introduction

THE SOVIET CHALLENGE

In fifty years, communism has transformed Russia irrevocably, but in the process the ideas of communism have also been subjected to a profound revision. The communism that haunts or challenges the world in the last quarter of the century is not the utopian vision of Marx and Engels, nor even the modified version conjured up by Lenin, but rather the concrete realities of the new social order forged in the Soviet Union during the past five decades.

The Soviet challenge has a dual character. First of all, the Soviet system emerges as a rival *process* of industrialization and modernization, a process which before the success of the Soviet system was historically the monopoly of capitalism. Secondly, it is a rival *way of life* to that of the West, whose civilization and institutions it seeks to supersede. Thus, the Soviet challenge is simultaneously a promise and a threat. What communism has done for Russia during the past fifty years is to enable it to meet successfully the challenge of rapid modernization, which excites underdeveloped countries eager for quick modernization and industrialization, but repels the advanced and modernized societies, which prefer their own social and political systems to that developed in Russia.

SOVIET RUSSIA AS A FORMER UNDERDEVELOPED COUNTRY

Before 1917, Russia was a giant with feet of clay. Although it was a huge sprawling empire stretched across both Europe and Asia and one of the great powers of Europe, its prestige was in rapid decline because it failed to meet the imperatives of the modern industrial era. The most significant feature of the imperial Russian state was not that it was a despotic autocracy, but that it was a country with a great potential which remained unrealized. In both Germany and Japan, autocratic governments took the initiative in adapting their societies to the industrial age, but not in Russia.

In 1914, Russia ranked last among the great industrial states of the world, but by 1960, the Soviet Union had already surpassed all the great industrial powers of Western Europe (and Japan) in the basic indicators of industrialization, and was second only to the United States, which it avowedly aims to equal and overtake.

In 1914, Russia was militarily weak; she had suffered defeat in one war after another after 1850, and in 1905 was humiliatingly beaten by an upstart Japan. Her rapidly declining military strength was further verified by defeat, occupation, and revolutionary convulsions during World War I. Today, however, the Soviet Union continues to rival the United States for military supremacy, and although it fell behind in recent years, it now threatens to surpass the United States.

In 1914, Russia had a vast unskilled and illiterate population. She produced a few outstanding individual scientists, but in general was lagging far behind the rest of Europe in educational, technological, and scientific advancement. By 1960, the Soviet Union had achieved virtually 100% literacy. Today, the Soviet Union has over three times as many students enrolled in higher education as Great Britain, France, Italy, and West Germany combined. It now annually graduates more than four times as many engineers as the United States. In many respects, it has established an educational system second to none.

The story is virtually identical in the field of social services, particularly in medicine. In 1914, Russian medical science was woefully retarded, and medical care was available only to the very wealthy. The number of physicians and dentists before the Revolution was 28,000. By 1970 it was over 642,000, which gives the Soviet Union today more doctors per capita than any other country (except Israel) in the world. Today, every Soviet citizen is entitled to free medical care. Life expectancy has gone up from an average age of 32 before the Revolution to about 70, which gives the Soviet Union one of the longest average life expectancies in the world. The number of hospital beds has also increased: from 207,300 before the Revolution to over $2\frac{1}{2}$ million in 1970.

As in many preindustrial societies, prerevolutionary Russia did not provide many educational or occupational opportunities for women. Today in the Soviet Union, 53% of all Soviet citizens with some secondary education are women. Before the Revolution, 10% of the medical doctors were women; today, more than 72% of all physicians in the Soviet Union are women. The situation with respect to teachers is almost identical. Women are to be found in all walks and all levels of Soviet cultural, professional, and scientific life in increasing numbers and in higher proportions than in any other country.

These are substantial achievements, and they transcend ideologies and social systems, for industrial power, military strength, literacy and education, scientific and technological progress, medical care, and the emancipation of women are universally desired goals. These are the undeniable marks of a modernized, industrialized, and westernized society. They symbolize power, prestige, and dignity for the communities which bear them. The underdeveloped countries are interested in results, for they have no vested interest in doctrines or dogmas, and they are attracted to that process which promises to accelerate their entry into the modern technological age. In the Soviet experience, they see the concrete fulfillment of the dreams and aspirations of a previously underdeveloped country.

Also significant is the fact that the Soviet achievement was not only spectacularly quick, but was practically a do-it-yourself operation against overwhelming odds. For more than thirty years, Bolshevik Russia was an isolated pariah in a world of antagonistic capitalist states. The Bolsheviks inherited a country ravaged by war, foreign occupation, and economic disorganization. She industrialized herself in the face of severe external impediments and internal convulsions. After 1933, she was the avowed object of conquest by Germany and Japan; she survived the Nazi attack, and, although most of her developed areas (virtually half of European Russia) were occupied and despoiled, she was able to mobilize a counterattack which broke the back of the German army and set the stage for Germany's ultimate defeat.

Soviet communism thus emerges as a process for the accelerated metamorphosis of backward agrarian and semifeudal states into advanced industrial societies. It promises the "quick switch": the rapid transformation of illiterate populations into educated communities, and of raw, unskilled peasants into skilled technicians and workmen; the swift elimination of disease; the early emancipation of women; and rapid improvement in the standard of living. But, above all, it promises the speedy acquisition of power, influence, and dignity for emerging national communities whose aspirations exceed their capacities. The larger the population of a given underdeveloped country and the more diversified and extensive its natural resources, the more applicable the Soviet experience is apt to be. The largest underdeveloped national community in the world, China, has already embarked on the same process. China, under Communist rule, enjoys greater power and prestige in world affairs than at any time in the past two hundred years.

In short, Soviet communism offers a seductive and effective way to meet the demands of the "revolution of rising expectations" that is sweeping the underdeveloped lands.

THE MAIN FEATURES OF THE SOVIET SYSTEM

The Soviet social order, taken as a whole, is unique, but its political system has certain features in common with both modern and ancient autocracies and dictatorships. Undue preoccupation with the political institutions and practices of the Soviet system in isolation from its social institutions and ideological goals serves to place the Soviet dictatorship in the company of the Nazi and Fascist totalitarian systems. While the Soviet Union shares with these two systems certain political practices, the ideological principles and social goals of the Soviet state are sharply divergent from those of the Nazi and Fascist orders. A proper understanding of the Soviet system, therefore, requires that its political system be examined within the context of its ideological goals.

Modern dictatorships that mobilize and manipulate the masses and demand their active support are called "totalitarian dictatorships," to distinguish them from the traditional personal dictatorship or dynastic autocracy which sought to justify or preserve their rule without the active involvement of the masses.

While Soviet spokesmen reject the labels of totalitarianism and personal dictatorship, they accept the notion of a "class" dictatorship and until 1961 defined the Soviet regime as a "dictatorship of the proletariat." But they claim that the dictatorship of the proletariat is essentially democratic, since it embodies a system in which a majority (the workers and their allies) rule over a minority. Indeed, they reject the Western idea of democracy as being a "bourgeois" or capitalist democracy—that is, democracy for the few: the capitalists. In their eyes, then, Western democracy is a dictatorship over the working masses, while Soviet democracy is a dictatorship over the former capitalist ruling class.

Democracy as a symbol has always played an important role in Soviet policy and doctrine because of its obvious appeal. Even at the height of the Stalinist terror, Soviet authorities described the Soviet system as "the most democratic system" in the world. After Stalin's death, however, Khrushchev conceded that the Soviet Union under Stalin, at least from 1934–53, was in fact a personal dictatorship.

The political life of the Soviet Union is monopolized by a single party, the Communist party of the Soviet Union, which is the only legal political organization in the country. Highly centralized in its organization, the party, as the custodian and interpreter of the official ideology, actually governs the country. Its membership currently amounts to only 5% of the total population, but it furnishes or selects the key personnel in all political, economic, military, and cultural institutions. Thus not only is the official ideology "total," but control is total as well, since the party does not permit the appearance of any political or social force that could challenge its monopoly of power in the Soviet system.

The Soviet economy is also "total" in the sense that it is almost entirely public in character. In response to the ideological norms of Marxism, the Soviet state owns outright all the land, water, natural resources, industrial establishments, and financial institutions of the country. None of these can be privately owned. Virtually the entire urban working population is employed by the state or by state-and-party-directed institutions. In the countryside, most of the rural population works on collective farms, which are theoretically cooperative enterprises. The state owns the land, however, and the collective farms are closely governed by state laws and regulations.

Control of the economy is considered to be an indispensable prerequisite to a centrally directed and planned economy. The Soviet state, upon instructions from the party, determines the economic development of the country. The state decides what shall be produced and how much. It sets the market price of commodities as well as the wages and salaries of employees and managers. Collective bargaining and strikes are unknown in the Soviet Union. Everything is determined from the top and at the center.

No less under the control of the Soviet state than the economy is the cultural life of the country. The party and state institutions own or control all the media of communication and distribution, all schools and universities, museums and recreational facilities, libraries, newspapers, printing and publishing establishments, radio and TV stations, motion-picture studios, and theaters. Control over culture and communications ensures that the party and state can condition and manipulate the minds of their citizens by controlling their access to information. In the Soviet Union, it is assumed that the interests of society must prevail against those of the individual and that the latter can find true freedom only as a member of society. The individual, by definition, thus cannot have rights and interests in opposition to those of the state and, in the event of conflict, those of the individual must give way.

The decision of the party under Stalin to modernize and industrialize Soviet Russia quickly collided with the inertia and interests of vast sectors of the population. In order to impose the state's ideological goals upon an unwilling population in the name of building a socialist and Communist society, Stalin resorted to the use of terror and violence. The modernization of Soviet Russia was quickly achieved, but at tremendous cost in human lives and liberty. Soviet Russia became a vast police empire of terrorized citizens, whose main incentive for working was not the prospect of a better life but sheer survival.

Since Stalin's death in 1953, the terroristic aspects of the Soviet system have been largely eliminated. The secret police have been considerably reduced in numbers, many of their veterans have been removed or executed, and the concentration camps have been emptied of their prisoners. Soviet citizens are allowed considerably more freedom of thought and movement, although the basic features of the Soviet dictatorship and the fundamental structure of society remains intact. Most serious observers agree that the Soviet system can no longer be characterized as totalitarian, and many even perceive the progressive development of pluralistic tendencies in Soviet society.

The Soviet system offers, as we have said, a way of quickly overcoming the poverty, illiteracy, and backwardness of the underdeveloped countries—but it is a shortcut which exacts a terrible tribute for its advantages. Nevertheless, Soviet leaders boast that in the twentieth century all roads lead to communism because it has already demonstrated its superiority in achieving rapid and concrete results. Unless the Western world, led by the United States, is able to renovate and export the values and institutions it cherishes, and can demonstrate an alternative that will deliver both the quick results of the Soviet pattern and the freedoms of Western civilization, then the attractiveness of communism, and with it its international impact, may grow.

It is to be admitted, however, that in recent years the diplomatic and economic setbacks of the Soviet Union, the Sino-Soviet dispute, and the generally drab character of everyday Soviet life, to which more and more visitors have been exposed, have tarnished somewhat the luster of the Soviet achievement—which, while impressive, has nevertheless fallen considerably short of official claims, boasts, and promises. Consequently, some of its former appeal to underdeveloped countries has been eroded.

When Lenin and the Bolsheviks overthrew the provisional government under Alexander Kerensky in November 1917, they thought that the umbilical cord with the past had been irrevocably severed. The Soviet system was to begin with a clean slate; Russia's past was to be repudiated, and the future would be inspired by the ideological vision of Karl Marx in which nations would melt into one another to produce an authentic international community.

TWO

the Russian political heritage

THE RUSSIAN "NATIONAL CHARACTER"

Nations, however, cannot dispose of their heritage so easily. The latitude of action permitted to the Bolsheviks was severely limited by the human and physical resources with which they had to work. The Soviet state, territorially, was a truncated version of the Russian empire; it possessed the same geographical location, the same exposed frontier, and the same enemies, who still looked upon her territories with envy. Most important, Soviet Russia inherited Russia's population, most of whom were Russians. The people of Russia, then, with their religions and languages, knowledge and ignorance, skills and superstitions, memories, fears, anxieties, and customs, were the raw human material out of which a Communist sociey was to be fashioned. The Bolsheviks also inherited Russia's potential, and this was enormous in terms of both natural resources and population. The most tenacious element of the legacy the Bolsheviks inherited was that elusive thing called the Russian "national character." Russia presents a unique illustration of both the tenacity and plasticity of national character and traditions. An avowed objective of the Bolsheviks was to transform the people of Russia by radically reorganizing the country's social and economic order. Yet many of the qualities of prerevolutionary Russia persist in contemporary Soviet society. Indeed, the Russian culture has been extended to nearly 100 million *non*-Russians within the Soviet system.

Being the most numerous and influential element in the population, the Russians inevitably became the instruments for disseminating the culture, language, and traditions of the Communist doctrine to the non-Russian nationalities. The Russian language became the *lingua franca* of the Union, while the Cyrillic alphabet (in modified form) became the vehicle for reducing other languages to writing. Of all the nationalities of the USSR, only the three Baltic nations, Georgia, and Armenia (whose numbers total less than 12 million out of 242 million) do not use the Cyrillic alphabet. Russian cultural attainments have become the common treasures of all the peoples of Soviet Russia, and while their own cultures, languages, and traditions have also been permitted to flourish (within definite limits, however), they have been relentlessly exposed to Russian cultural norms for more than five decades. The Soviet Union today is thus simultaneously more *and* less "Russian" than ever before, because, under Soviet rule, Russian culture has been converted from a purely national phenomenon into a multinational civilization. The only conspicuously Russian cultural institution which has not been universalized is the Orthodox church.

THE HISTORICAL BACKGROUND

The Autocratic and Byzantine Legacy

Indigenous Slavic states of a tribal character flourished on the soil of modern Russia as early as the seventh century A.D., but it was the Kievan state of Rus, founded by Norse marauders under Rurik the Red in the ninth century, that marks Russia's formal entry into recorded history. The Kievan state, located in the territory of the present-day Ukraine, was in every way comparable in the development of its civilization to that of the feudal states of western Europe, but its principal outside contacts were with the Byzantine empire, with which it quickly established intimate and fruitful commercial, political, and cultural connections.

The Byzantine influence on Russia was the earliest and most pervasive of all alien influences on Russian political development. Byzantine culture was an amalgam of Roman, Greek, and Near Eastern elements. From Rome, through Byzantium, Russia inherited the imperial title of *tsar,* a corruption of *Caesar;* from the Greeks, the Russian language gained the Cyrillic alphabet; from the Near East, Russia adopted the institution of the god-emperor in its specific Byzantine Christian adaptation known as Caesaro-papism, whereby the authority of the pope and the emperor are amalgamated in the person of the tsar.

A further important Byzantine influence on Russia was the notion of messianic orthodoxy—the idea that the orthodox faith was the one and only vehicle of eternal salvation, to be extended dogmatically and with undiminished fervor. Constantinople was the "second Rome," and its emperors the successors to the Roman empire. Twenty years after the fall of Constantinople to the Turks (1453), the grand dukes of Moscow proclaimed themselves successors to the tsars of Byzantium, arrogated the headship of the Orthodox church, proclaimed Moscow to be the "third Rome," preempted the Byzantine double-headed eagle, and invested themselves with the title, "Tsar, autocrat, chosen by God." As the Russian monk Theophilus wrote shortly after the fall of Constantinople:

The Church of Old Rome fell because of its heresy; the gates of the Second Rome, Constantinople, have been hewn down by the axes of the infidel Turks; but the Church of Moscow, the Church of the New Rome, shines brighter than the sun in the whole Universe. . . . Two Romes have fallen, but the Third Rome stands fast; a fourth there cannot be.[1]

MONGOL-TATAR DOMINATION: THE INSTITUTIONALIZATION OF BARBARISM. The second major alien influence on Russia was that of the Mongols and Tatars. The Kievan state of Rus was easily overwhelmed and destroyed in the thirteenth century by the Mongol conquest, and the Russian lands passed under control of the khans from 1234 to 1460. Mongol-Tatar rule was indirect; native princes and bishops, if they chose to cooperate, were reduced to vassalage but allowed to rule their own subjects and

---

[1] Quoted in Arnold J. Toynbee, *Civilization on Trial* (New York: Oxford University Press, 1948), p. 171.

to maintain their property and serfs. They were forced to deliver annual tribute to the khans, which they exacted from their own subjects with the same cruelty and barbarism they experienced in dealing with their masters.

The two hundred years of Mongol-Tatar domination not only reenforced the despotic qualities borrowed from Byzantium, but also cut Russia off from contact with western Europe, retarding not only her social and economic development, but also insulating her from the liberating currents of the Renaissance and the Reformation which swept through the West.

The chief legacies of Mongol-Tatar domination were essentially psychological and administrative: the refinement of despotic arts; the cultivation of cruel and insensitive methods of rule and rebellion; the premium placed on centralization of power, enforced national unity, and ideological conformity; the tradition of backwardness and the efforts of the rulers to overcome it.

THE LEGACY OF MUSCOVITE ABSOLUTISM. Under the khans, Russia's center of political gravity shifted to the Moscow region, whose princes gradually rose to prominence beginning in the twelfth century. A succession of unusually able but unscrupulous rulers expanded Moscow's power over the other princes and enhanced its influence at the Tatar court. Ivan I (1325–41), known as *Kalita* or "Moneybags," maneuvered himself into the job of collecting the tribute from the other princes for the khans, and his successor, Simeon I (1341–53), managed to be appointed chief prince over the others. As Muscovite absolutism increased, the power of the khans was correspondingly eroded. Ivan III, the Great (1462–1506), finally overthrew the Tatars completely in 1480. (In 1472, Ivan married Sophia, the last Byzantine emperor's niece, thus claiming succession to the Byzantine emperors.)

Centralization of political power and its absolute exercise—two persistent features of contemporary Soviet rule—thus have an ancient legacy. Only through ruthless centralization of power could Moscow overthrow the khans, and subsequent history has demonstrated that when this power was fragmented or seriously challenged by an internal opposition, Russia was exposed to invasion and defeat. The idea that decentralization is tantamount to anarchy and weakness and that dissent is treason is firmly rooted in Russian history. Stalin recognized the importance of this tradition on the occasion of Moscow's eight hundredth anniversary in 1947:

Moscow's service consists first and foremost in the fact that it became the foundation for the unification of a disunited Russia into a single state with a single government, a single leadership. . . . Only a country united in a single centralized state can count on being able to make substantial cultural-economic progress and assert its independence.[2]

The Consolidation of Autocratic Rule

Throughout imperial Russia's history all attempts to limit the absolute power of the tsar failed, and the Russian autocracy was preserved virtually intact down to the 1917 Revolution itself. As in other feudal societies, the monarch could be effectively opposed only by the hereditary nobility, whose members jealously sought to cultivate authority in their own domains, and occasionally to aspire to the throne itself. Sharing power with the tsar was the Duma of Boyars, comparable to the House of Lords in Britain. The boyars struggled against the absolutism of the tsars for their own personal and class advantage, but met their match in Ivan the Terrible (1533–84), a half-mad genius both feared and loved by the common people as their protector against the cruel boyars. He eventually broke the power of the boyars by various stratagems, including the formation of the first Russian secret police organization, the dreaded Oprichnina, which ruthlessly liquidated all opposition to the tsar.

Ivan also introduced, in 1549, an embryonic "House of Commons," the Zemsky Sobor, a quasi-representative assembly made up of the lesser nobility, upper clergy, landed

2 *Pravda,* September 11, 1947.

gentry, and urban bourgeoisie, to counterbalance the strength of the boyars. The Zemsky Sobor successfully limited the power of the boyars, and during the "Time of Troubles" (1584–1613), it played a significant role in governing Russia, when the country was plagued by false pretenders to the throne and threatened with foreign intervention by the Poles. Its most important act was the election of Prince Michael of the Romanov family as tsar in 1613. The Zemsky Sobor was unable to maintain its authority, however, and degenerated in a manner similar to the French Estates General. Both it and the Duma of Boyars gradually deteriorated and were ultimately abolished by Peter the Great.

Subsequent attempts to limit the power of the tsar were either instituted by the tsar himself or forced upon him by revolutionary pressures. Peter the Great (1689–1725), for instance, sought to westernize and modernize the autocracy so as to increase the power of Russia and render its absolute government more efficient. He introduced a bureaucratic system based on merit, wherein faithful service to the state by the landowners or gentry could earn them titles of nobility or promotion to higher status. A hierarchy of fourteen ranks was organized for the armed services, the courts, and the civil service, each with its own distinctive status, with promotion awarded to the most able. The system, eventually corrupted by nepotism, bribery, and favoritism, lasted down to 1917, when it was abolished—only to be resurrected in new and expanded form by Stalin in 1943, when all branches of the Soviet bureaucracy were once again organized into ranks, replete with uniforms and special privileges.

Peter also created the Imperial Governing Senate in 1711 to replace the Duma of Boyars. Officially an advisory body akin to a cabinet (it was made up of nine members, including the royal governors of the provinces, appointed by the tsar to coordinate and direct the administration of the state), it was actually a supine creature of the tsar. Directly under the senate were eight departments of government, each run by a committee of from three to five men, which reduced the possibility that any one person would become too powerful in administer-

ing the country. Peter abolished the Russian patriarchate and placed the church under the direction of the Holy Synod (1721), which was dominated by the "eyes and ears" of the tsar: the procurator, a trusted layman. Many of Peter's reforms served to strengthen both the autocracy and the country as a whole. Under him, Russia continued her expansion in all directions, finally absorbing the future site of St. Petersburg and thus acquiring her long-sought "window" on the Baltic.

Under Catherine the Great (1762–96), elective municipal councils (dumas) were established, although the elections were severely limited to the propertied classes. And, under this former German princess the steady infiltration of German ideas and bureaucrats into Russia was accelerated, and the Romanov dynasty was soon all but Germanized.

During the reign of Alexander I (1801–25), Michael Speransky was commissioned to draw up an elaborate plan of governmental reform providing for the indirect election of local, intermediate, and provincial assemblies, ultimately to be climaxed with a national duma, or parliament. Speransky's efforts led only to the creation of a marginal organ, the Imperial State Council, half the members of which were appointed by the tsar, and the other half elected by special social groups. Virtually all its members were drawn from the nobility, and it merely served as another administrative coordinating body. After 1905, it became the upper house of the Imperial Legislature.

In the middle of the nineteenth century, a system of local self-governing bodies—the zemstvos—based on and authorized by popular elections, was established, but their powers were limited and their authority restricted essentially to such local matters as sanitation, roads, hospitals, and schools. Elections were frequently rigged, and the zemstvos were usually dominated by the local gentry. Under Alexander III (1891–94), the executive committees of the zemstvos were controlled by provincial governors. These organizations, which continued to attract reform-minded and progressive members of the nobility, constituted the only school of local self-government in the entire history of the Russian autocracy.

The Fear and Attraction of Anarchy

Throughout the history of Russia runs an elusive but detectable thread of anarchism. Superficially, this seems to contradict the spirit of absolutism that has animated Russia's rulers, but, in fact, the two may be viewed as complementary. The relaxation of authority has, in the past, threatened to plunge the country into anarchy, so a strong central government has been necessary to keep the people under control. During the nineteenth century, latent anarchistic forces gave rise to various movements designed to destroy the state, in the hope that society would reformulate itself spontaneously into a stateless socialistic community. It is perhaps more than fortuitous that Marxism emerged as an ideology tailor-made to fit the contradictory impulses of both absolute order and anarchy, for Lenin's Bolshevism imposed the necessary order, while Marx's vision of a classless society promised a community in which the state would ultimately "wither away."

The Revolutionary Tradition

The concentration of absolute power in the hands of the tsar meant that change and reform could come about only by initiative from above or revolution from below. Reforms from above were few and far between and usually followed by periods of repression. As the pressure built up for revolution, underground groups increased their violent and terroristic methods. All the accumulated resentments, disappointments, sufferings, and sublimated hopes of nearly a thousand years seemed to explode in the Revolution of 1917.

The Revolution of 1917 did not develop without precedents. Previous revolutions, however, were limited in character, either geographically or socially. Characteristically, down to the twentieth century, revolutions were directed against the harsh social and economic order. The tsar and the autocratic system itself were by-and-large immune, for the tsar was viewed as a benevolent patriarch who would have instantly intervened had he known the miseries and agonies of his people. In times of external crises, the tsar was a powerful symbol around whom all classes of Russians rallied.

The Russian faith in the autocracy was reenforced by a deep and primitive faith in the power and majesty of God, from whom the tsar claimed divine sanction. The Orthodox church had been completely subordinated to the state after a brief and unequal struggle between the patriarchate and the tsar, and it became one of the basic instruments of autocratic rule. The Orthodox priests cultivated in the minds of the Russian peasants a fatalism about their earthly conditions of life and thus increasingly became a principal bulwark of the autocracy, blessing and sanctifying its endeavors and activities, even to the extent of pressuring ordinary priests into the service of the secret police. The ferocity of the Bolshevik reaction against the Orthodox church must always be assessed with this perspective in mind, for the Orthodox church was not a "free church," but an indispensable and willing instrument of the autocracy in its oppressive rule over the people of Russia.

Ivan the Terrible's "Revolution from Above"

The earliest popularly supported "revolution" in Russia was, in fact, a "revolution from above," executed by Ivan the Terrible. In 1564, as a consequence of his conflict with the boyars, led by Prince Kurbsky, Ivan abandoned Moscow for a small village and denounced the boyars and upper clergy as traitorous, corrupt, and evil, at the same time absolving the urban *bourgeoisie* and the common people. Without abdicating, he announced that he had given up his kingdom and would let God determine his future course. When asked to return by a delegation from the middle classes and the common people, he laid down a number of conditions, including the right to establish a special institution called the Oprichnina, over which he would have personal jurisdiction. In effect, the Oprichnina became a vast secret police empire, untrammeled by law and subject only to the jurisdiction of the tsar.

The ultimate objective of the Oprichnina was to destroy the power of the boyars, by arresting and exiling them to remote parts of the country and expropriating their estates. The methods and tortures employed by the Oprichniki were worthy precedents for the subsequent secret police systems in Russia: the Imperial Okhrana, and the Soviet Cheka, GPU, NKVD, MGB, and the current KGB. These measures against the boyars were by no means unpopular among the common people, who saw in the tsar their protector against the hated landlords.

Ivan's assault against the boyars set the stage for the gradual destruction of an independent Russian nobility, whose power and status supposedly stemmed not from the grace of the tsar, but, like the tsar's, from divine right transmitted by heredity from one generation to the next. Many of the boyars were scions of princely families, who considered themselves peers of the dynastic line itself, and who, in fact, challenged the existing dynasty's right to rule. Through the Oprichniki, Ivan inundated the ranks of the boyars by creating a new landed aristocracy and court nobility, the *pomeschiki* and the *dvoriane,* who were obligated to render service to the state in return for their grants of land and serfs, seized either from the boyars or from newly conquered territories. Unlike the boyars, the new nobility owed both its power and status to the tsar. This nobility was further expanded by Peter the Great, who swelled its ranks with recruits who had performed with loyalty and competence either on the field of battle or in the state bureaucracy. Thereafter, the imperial landowning nobility never constituted a threat to the power of the tsar.

THE DECEMBRIST REVOLT. Of much greater significance was the so-called Decembrist Revolt of December 26, 1825, which was a movement directed against the autocracy itself rather than against "abuses" and "corruption." The Decembrist uprising was an attempted palace revolution by the officers among the tsar's own guards. Inspired by the ideas of both the American and French revolutions, and organized into secret societies and conspiracies, these liberal-minded but politically unsophisticated young officers were united in a common determination to sweep away the autocracy as the chief obstacle to progress in Russia. They were not clear about what should replace it, however. Some advocated a constitutional monarchy, others a republic; some wanted to retain a centralized state, others argued for a federation; still others agitated for a democracy, while some demanded a benevolent dictatorship.

THE REVOLUTIONARY INTELLIGENTSIA. The Decembrist Revolt was quickly crushed by the new tsar, Nicholas I, and Russia was subjected to a renewed period of reaction and oppression. The revolt became, however, the inspiration for many revolutionary movements and terrorist groups, all of which had to go underground because political parties and movements were outlawed by the autocracy. Hounded and infiltrated by the tsarist secret police, provoked to premature action by *agents provocateurs,* many of these revolutionary groups were driven to extreme and violent action because of the unhealthy atmosphere in which they were forced to operate. Their agents, in turn, infiltrated the tsarist secret police, and double agents and even triple agents were not unusual. A few individuals did not really know whether they themselves were primarily revolutionaries or agents of the tsarist police.

The most oppressive institution in early nineteenth-century Russian society was that of serfdom, which embraced most of the rural population of Russia. The serfs tilled the soil and were owned by the landed aristocracy. Extensive studies of the condition of the serfs had been commissioned by the tsars, but little had been accomplished to alleviate their virtual slavery.

It was only in 1861 that serfdom was abolished by the liberal-minded Tsar Alexander II. Although its abolition was an important step in the social evolution of Russia, it did little to stem the growing tide of revolutionary sentiment that had gripped the Russian intellectuals and university circles, which became increasingly inspired by the ideas of the French Revolution, the idealistic philosophies of Fichte, Schelling, Kant, and Hegel, and the utopian socialism of the French philosophers.

The revolutionary intelligentsia were drawn from all classes of Russia—the bureaucracy, the gentry, the peasantry and working class, the merchants and professions—but they considered themselves to be without class, irrespective of their social origins. They were united not so much by common ideas of philosophy, but by a common passion to reform the social order, so that Russia might fulfill her physical and spiritual potential. Some thought that Russia's best course would be to adopt the technology, philosophy, and institutions of the West, and they were called "westernizers." Others emphasized the unique spiritual and psychological traditions of Russia and insisted that Russian civilization was superior to Western culture, and that the country's salvation lay in freeing the true Russia which had been all but suffocated by successive layers of foreign ideas and institutions. These members of the intelligentsia were labeled "slavophils." Still others of the intelligentsia maintained a foot in each camp, trying to bridge the two in an endeavor to create a synthesis made up of the best of both worlds. Both groups were essentially utopian in outlook, and the slavophils were also profoundly messianic in their orientation, for some felt that Russia had a mission to emancipate not only herself but the entire world from the materialistic philosophy of the West. Yet, even the westernizers reflected a messianic faith in Russia's destiny.

The same spirit animated Stalin in 1917, before the Revolution, when he argued against the notion that Russia had to take second place to the industrialized countries in blazing the path to socialism:

The possibility is not precluded that Russia will be the country to lay the road to socialism. . . . We must cast aside the obsolete idea that only Europe can show us the way.[3]

[3] J. V. Stalin, *The Road to Power* (New York: International Publishers, 1937), pp. 20–21.

THE NARODNIK MOVEMENT (POPULISTS). Intellectual ferment gave way to political organization after the emancipation of the serfs, principally in the Narodnik movement, whose various sects and factions were influenced by the ideas of both the westernizers and the slavophils. The Narodniki were initially drawn from student and intellectual groups who were motivated by a desire to achieve an agrarian socialist society uncorrupted by Western industrialization, capitalism, and materialism. According to the Narodniki, the Russian peasant, organized in the ancestral *mir,* or village commune, was naturally socialist in his inclinations, and once the oppressive autocratic system and the iniquitous feudal order were destroyed, Russia would spontaneously be reorganized as a vast association of agrarian cooperative communities. The Narodniki favored appealing directly to the people living in their village communes, enlightening and educating them, ministering to their wants, winning their confidence, and inspiring them to revolt against the existing order.

The peasants, however, viewed many of the Narodniki, who settled in the villages as teachers, nurses, and counselors, with deep mistrust and suspicion, often reporting their activities to the tsarist authorities and, in some instances, taking direct action against them. The failure of the peasantry to respond to their good intentions, and the increasingly repressive measures employed by the government, resulted in fragmenting the Narodnik movement into a variety of underground and illegal organizations ranging from pacific anarchism to terroristic nihilism. The more the peasants failed to respond to the Narodnik program, the more convinced were the reform leaders that the revolution could be accomplished only by a militant elite —a view which later powerfully influenced Lenin's brand of Marxism.

REVOLUTIONARY VIOLENCE AND TERRORISM. Broadly speaking, the revolutionary groups emerging out of Narodism tended either toward some brand of anarchism or to the view that some sort of progressive state was necessary to replace the tsarist autocracy. Portions of these groups advocated peaceful measures, but the rest cried for violence and even for terrorism. The peaceful anarchists wanted to dissolve the state in favor of a giant association of peasant communes. The best-known representatives of violence were Peter Tkachev, and Bakunin and his protégé Nechayev, the latter of whose views were grimly set forth in the *Catechism of the Revolutionist:*

The revolutionist is a doomed man. He has no personal interests, no affairs, sentiments, attachments, property, not even a name of his own. . . . He despises and hates the present-day code of morals with all its motivations and manifestations. To him, whatever aids the triumph of the revolution is ethical; all which hinders it is criminal. . . . All tender softening sentiments of kinship, friendship, love, gratitude, and even honor itself must be snuffed out in him by the one cold passion of the revolutionary cause. . . . The Association has no aim other than the complete liberation and happiness of the masses.[4]

The first revolutionary party, *Zemlya i Volya* (Land and Freedom), was oriented toward violence. It in turn split into two factions, the *Narodnaya Volya* (People's Will), which specialized in bombings and assassinations, and the *Chorny Peredyel* (Black Redistribution), which called for the peasants to seize the land from the landlords. Members of the first group were responsible for the assassination of Alexander II in 1881, and to this movement belonged Lenin's older brother Alexander Ulyanov, who was executed in 1887 for complicity in a plot to assassinate Alexander III. The execution of his brother profoundly intensified Lenin's own political fanaticism.

The *Chorny Peredyel* is noteworthy because the first Russian Marxists were among its members. Because Russia was essentially an agrarian society, the ideas of Karl Marx appeared to be largely irrelevant to her social and economic problems. Before 1865, the working class in Russia was virtually nonexistent, and a political movement dedicated to representing the interests of the proletariat would have been an anomaly. After the emancipation of the

[4] Quoted in Max Nomad, *Apostles of Revolution* (Boston: Little, Brown, 1939), pp. 228–33.

serfs, opportunities were created for the development of capitalism in Russia, and by 1890 the new social class of proletarians numbered some 2,400,000 members, as compared to 200,000 in 1865. Mostly concentrated in St. Petersburg, Moscow, Baku, and the Donetz basin, this class was quickly courted by revolutionaries disillusioned by the political inertia of the peasantry.

The Development of Marxism in Russia

The first Russian Marxist organization was founded abroad in 1883 by George Plekhanov, Vera Zasulich, P. B. Axelrod, and L. G. Deutsch, and called itself the Emancipation of Labor. It translated the works of Marx and Engels into Russian, struggled against the views of the Narodniki, repudiated the whole concept of Russian agrarian socialism, and maintained that the industrialization of Russia would soon create a revolutionary proletariat. It wrote off the revolutionary potential of the peasants and advocated instead an alliance between the liberal middle class and the working class to bring about a revolution to establish a middle-class constitutional and representative democracy.

Marxist groups sprang up in the urban centers of Russia between 1883 and 1894, including one in 1895 in St. Petersburg headed by Lenin. During the same period, Joseph Dzhugashvili (Stalin) was active in Tiflis and the Caucasus, while Leon Bronstein (Trotsky) was to become politically active a few years later in St. Petersburg. In 1898, representatives of some of these groups convened a "congress" in Minsk, attended by nine people, which issued a manifesto announcing the formation of the Russian Social Democratic party, modeled after the Social Democratic party in Germany. Although no party was actually organized and no program was issued, the foundations were prepared for active Marxist political organization and agitation.

The growth of industry in Russia and the attraction of Marx's ideas all but obliterated the Narodnik movement. Those who still retained faith in agrarian socialism merged with others in 1901 to form the Social Revolutionary party, one of the largest in the country, whose program of land redistribution represented the interests of the peasantry more than that of any other party. Following this, middle-class intellectuals, members of the professions, and progressive elements of the *bourgeoisie* and nobility supported the formation of an association called the Union of Liberation, under the leadership of Paul Milyukov. Because they favored essentially a renovation of the autocracy in a constitutional monarchy patterned after the British model, they later adopted the name Constitutional Democrats, or Cadets. A middle-class party par excellence, it played a significant role during the decade of the Duma that followed the Revolution of 1905, and in the events leading to the March Revolution of 1917.

BOLSHEVIKS AND MENSHEVIKS. At the second congress of the Russian Social Democratic party, which was convened in Brussels and then moved to London in 1903, the party split into two factions over questions of membership, organization, and principles of action. Lenin managed to secure a small majority as a result of procedural technicalities, and the faction led by him was called the Bolsheviks (majority), as opposed to the Mensheviks (minority). The labels stuck, and the two wings of the Social Democratic party were to be known henceforth as the Bolsheviks and the Mensheviks. Ironically, it was the Bolshevik faction that was subsequently most often in the minority.

Lenin presented a proposal (based on his work *What Is To Be Done?*) that had been published just prior to the meeting. In essence, he called for an entirely new kind of non-parliamentary party, one whose objective was not to win votes at the ballot box (which in any event did not exist in Russia at the time), but to seize power on behalf of the working class and to establish a "dictatorship of the proletariat." The party was to be restricted to a hard-core elite, made up of professional revolutionaries and organized along militant lines rather than as a mass party. Its guiding principle was "democratic centralism," whereby the authority of the party was to be concentrated in the hands of its central committee, in which,

in turn, the minority would bow to the majority. In *What Is To Be Done?* Lenin wrote:

I assert: (1) that no movement can be durable without a stable organization of leaders to maintain continuity; (2) that the more widely the masses are spontaneously drawn into the struggle and form the basis of the movement and participate in it, the more necessary it is to have such an organization, and the more stable must it be (for it is much easier for demagogues to side-track the more backward sections of the masses); (3) that the organization must consist chiefly of persons engaged in revolutionary activities as a profession; (4) that in a country with an autocratic government, the more we *restrict* the membership of this organization to persons who are engaged in revolutionary activities as a profession and who have been professionally trained in the act of combating the political police, the more difficult will it be to catch the organization; (5) the *wider* will be the circle of men and women of the working class or of other classes of society able to join the movement and perform active work in it.[5]

Lenin pressed his views in the newspaper *Iskra* ("The Spark") and in numerous pamphlets. He eventually succeeded in creating just such an organization of dedicated professional revolutionaries, while his rivals in the Menshevik faction continued to emphasize democratic principles of organization and nonviolent principles of action. Although the two factions constituted distinct organizations, both continued to operate within the framework of a single political party. As long as neither was in power, Lenin's principles were restricted only to his group. Many individuals freely migrated from one faction to the other, while some, like Leon Trotsky, remained as it were suspended between the two during the years before 1917. Once the Bolsheviks seized power, however, Lenin's ideas were applied to the entire country, and the foundations of totalitarian politics were firmly laid. The ban on factional opposition was transformed into a prohibition of other political parties and organizations; the principle of the subordination of the minority to the majority was converted into a condemnation of dissenting political views; terrorist

[5] V. I. Lenin, *Selected Works* (New York: International Publishers, n.d.), 2:138–39.

and conspiratorial methods used in pursuing the revolution were transformed into instruments directed against counterrevolution. What were originally the principles governing a small sectarian party were eventually extended to command the lives of millions in a vast empire.

The Revolution of 1905

After 1900, Russia was once again on the verge of revolution. A severe economic crisis stimulated strikes in the cities and rebellions in the countryside. Thousands of real and suspected revolutionaries were imprisoned or exiled either abroad or to Siberia.

The Japanese attack on Port Arthur in 1904 temporarily postponed the inevitable revolutionary outburst, but on January 9 (Bloody Sunday) of the following year, when soldiers fired on a peaceful procession of workers bearing a list of grievances to the "Little Father" (the tsar), killing hundreds and wounding thousands, an amorphous revolt broke out in the capital. The workers went out on a general strike, the sailors on the battleship *Potemkin* mutinied, and peasants rebelled in scattered rural localities. Soviets, or workers' councils, were established in the cities to direct the strike. The most important council was the St. Petersburg Soviet, one of whose leaders was a youthful 26-year-old revolutionary, Leon Trotsky. The St. Petersburg Soviet called for the amelioration of social and economic conditions and for moderate political reforms: a constitution, elections, a national parliament, and freedom for political parties. The aim of the 1905 Revolution was to achieve middle-class political reforms comparable to those that had been won in western Europe.

The Reforms of 1905: the Decade of the Duma. The revolution was easily quashed, but not until after a frightened monarch issued his famous October Manifesto, promising a constitution, political parties, elections, a national Duma, and civil liberties. Although the reforms that followed were more formal than real, differences in political conditions before and after 1905 were substantial and should not

be minimized. The open organization of political parties and national elections in themselves were important achievements, even if the Duma was more a debating society than a lawmaking body and the tsar's absolute power remained virtually intact. The introduction of such civil liberties as freedom of speech, assembly, worship, and movement, the relaxation of censorship, parliamentary immunity, and political agitation, while frequently violated in practice, made Russia after 1905 a less oppressive society than Russia before. Besides the political parties already mentioned, political organizations of the right also materialized, ranging from the conservative Octobrists to the reactionary Union of the Russian People.

In addition to the popularly elected Duma, the tsar established the Council of State as an upper chamber, half of whose members were appointed by the tsar and half by the bureaucracy, upper clergy, and nobility. The Council of Ministers, the bureaucracy, and the armed forces remained under the control of the monarch. All bills, before they could become law, had to have the approval of the Council of State and of the tsar, who retained the power of absolute veto. The tsar kept the exclusive right to initiate modifications of the fundamental law and controlled the Duma through his power to convene or dissolve it at his discretion. He also retained the title of Supreme Autocrat and in this capacity could govern by decree during periods of emergency, which he had the authority to declare.

The first Duma was elected in 1906, but was dissolved after seventy-three days because it outspokenly advocated further and immediate reforms. A limited agrarian reform program, however, was implemented by decree. The government tried to control the elections to the second Duma, but it proved to be even more radical than the first, and it, too, was dissolved, this time after 103 days of existence. A new electoral law, adopted in violation of the constitution, severely limited the suffrage in favor of the propertied classes and served as the basis for the election of the third Duma. The fourth Duma, elected in 1912, demonstrated considerable vitality in spite of its overwhelmingly conservative character. The Constitutional Democrats, particularly, were active far out of proportion to their numbers, and criticism of the government by opposition radical and reform parties was spirited.

The outbreak of war in 1914 once again arrested the eruption of revolutionary violence, for all the parties, with the exception of the Bolsheviks, supported the war against Germany in an outburst of patriotic feeling. The incompetence of the government in prosecuting the war was quickly revealed as Russia suffered severe reverses at the front. The Duma was convened to deal with the situation, but its suggestions for military, economic, and political reforms were disregarded. The imperial court was dominated by the Siberian monk Rasputin through his influence over the tsarina, and his venality infected every agency of the state, including the military. Ministers were appointed and dismissed upon his advice, and even strategic war plans were influenced by his "nocturnal visions." Russia's difficulties, however, had more profound causes, and Rasputin's assassination in 1916 did little to help the deteriorating situation.

The Revolution of 1917

Defeat in war, repressive measures at home, the incompetence and corruption of the court, the ineptitude of the tsar, espionage, bribery and treason in high places, general war weariness, the disaffection of the border nationalities, the breakdown of the transportation system, bread riots and strikes in the cities, demoralization and desertion at the front, and peasant rebellions in the countryside climaxed a millennium of frustration and resentment, which erupted in the violent upheavals of 1917.

The occasion was characteristically inauspicious. When the "Progressive bloc" in the Duma, made up of liberal and moderate elements, demanded that the Duma be given more power in order to restore the confidence of the country in the government, the tsar refused and, instead, ordered the Duma dissolved. Refusing to disband, the leaders of the Duma organized a provisional executive committee. The tsar was advised to abdicate in favor of his brother, who declined to accept the throne. As a consequence, the provisional committee of the Duma became the provisional government of Russia, and the Revolution became an accomplished fact. The Bolsheviks played no direct part in the "overthrow of tsarism," for all their leaders were either in exile or were imprisoned in Siberia, although they were soon allowed to return to the capital by the political amnesty issued by the provisional government.

During the first days of the Revolution, local revolutionary councils, or soviets, sprang up all over Russia, in villages, towns, and in the armed forces. Unlike the soviets of 1905, which were restricted to the workers, those of 1917 also included soldiers and peasants, and accurately reflected the revolutionary mood of the country. The most significant of the soviets was the Petrograd Soviet, controlled by the moderate left. (St. Petersburg, the imperial capital, had been renamed Petrograd in 1914; after Lenin's death in 1924, it was renamed Leningrad; and the Bolsheviks reestablished Moscow as the capital of Russia in 1918.) From the very beginning, the Petrograd Soviet proved to be a formidable rival to the provisional government, an essentially middle-class regime whose goal was political reform and a constitutional monarchy, in contrast to the profound social and economic changes and the creation of a republic demanded by the Petrograd Soviet. The immediate consequence was dual power, a dyarchy in which political power was divided between a legal provisional government and a spontaneous representative institution, the Petrograd Soviet. The provisional government actually enjoyed little popular support, and in an endeavor to eliminate the awkward dyarchy, it invited Alexander Kerensky of the Petrograd Soviet to join the government as minister of justice.

Although the soviet voted confidence in the provisional government, Lenin's return to Russia in April produced an explosive crisis. Lenin issued his famous April Theses, in which he denounced the provisional government, calling for its overthrow and the immediate transformation of the "bourgeois-democratic revolution" into a "proletarian" revolt. His defiance caused great consternation among the other revolutionary parties and even among his own followers in the capital, including Stalin, who had been supporting the provisional government in *Pravda* ("Truth"), the Bolshevik newspaper. Lenin demanded immediate land reforms, and Russia's withdrawal from the "imperialist" war. "Land, peace, and bread" became his social program, and "All power to the soviets" his political objective. Lenin recognized in the soviets the future institutions and organs of the "dictatorship of the proletariat," and exhorted the Bolsheviks to infiltrate and win them over.

The Bolshevik program of land for the peasant, bread for the worker, and peace for the soldier hit a responsive chord in the masses. The provisional government's determination to carry on the war, while popular with Russia's allies, was becoming increasingly unpopular at home. Its ambiguous position on land reform also earned it the distrust of the peasants, who were already seizing the property of the landlords and wanted their expropriations legalized. By July, Kerensky had become minister of war in the provisional government; the influence of the Octobrists had vanished, while that of the Constitutional Democrats was waning. Clearly, the program of moderate, constitutional reform was too little and too late. With the installation of Kerensky as prime minister, the provisional government faced the increasing discontent of the soviets.

The Bolsheviks stepped up their activities, encouraging the soldiers to desert, the workers to strike, and the peasants to expropriate land. In July, Lenin was indirectly implicated in an attempted revolt by unruly and hungry soldiers and workers in Petrograd, and an order went out for his arrest. He fled to Finland and temporarily directed operations from there. The Bolshevik strategy was to use the soviets, which came increasingly under their control, to dislodge the provisional government. The doom of the Kerensky government was sealed in August, when his army commander, General Kornilov, demanded that the soviets be abolished, and attempted to overthrow the government in favor of a right-wing dictatorship. Kerensky had few reliable troops at his disposal and was compelled to ask Lenin's Red Guards to aid

him in suppressing the military coup. Once the Petrograd and Moscow soviets passed to the Bolsheviks, Lenin knew that the time was rapidly approaching when the Bolsheviks could make an open bid for power.

On the night of November 6–7,[6] Lenin ordered the Red Guards to surround all government buildings and arrest the members of the provisional government. The provisional government was dissolved, and Lenin proclaimed that all power had passed to the Soviet and its Central Executive Committee. A Council of People's Commissars, with Lenin as chairman, Trotsky as commissar of foreign affairs, and Stalin as commissar of nationalities, was established, and the Soviet Republic was born. Only the left wing of the Social Revolutionary party supported the Bolsheviks. The elections for a Constituent Assembly took place in the following month. Of the 808 deputies elected in Russia's only democratically organized election, the Bolsheviks had only 168 members. In January 1918, they disbanded it!

The Bolsheviks, contrary to official mythology, displaced, not an oppressive tsardom, but a democratic regime that had allowed the greatest amount of political and civil liberty in the entire history of Russia during its brief period of existence. By postponing reform, the provisional government lost the support of the masses, and it lost the confidence of the Russian nationalists and the army through its inability to prosecute the war successfully. The only realistic alternatives to the Kerensky government appeared to be either a dictatorship of the right or one of the left. The right made its bid for power in August and lost; the Bolsheviks succeeded two months later. There seemed to be no middle ground between the rightists, who promised despotism and order, and the Bolsheviks, who promised despotism and social justice. No strong liberal middle class had developed in Russia.

[6] At the time, Russia was using the old Julian calendar, which differed by thirteen days from the present one. Thus, the Bolshevik Revolution occurred on October 24–25 of the old calendar ("old style") and on November 6–7 of the new ("new style"). Similarly, the first revolution of 1917 took place in either February or March, depending on the calendar employed.

THREE

the foundations
of
Soviet politics

The Soviet Union, like the tsarist empire it superseded, is the largest intercontinental state in the world. Sprawling across two continents, Russia embraces the eastern half of Europe and nearly the entire northern half of Asia. Within the boundaries of some 8½ million square miles (approximately one-sixth of the total land surface of the earth) are to be found more than 241 million people, representing more than one hundred different racial, ethnic, national, and linguistic groups, which range from the most advanced level to the most primitive nomadic tribes. At its widest point, the Soviet Union stretches some 6,000 miles around the Northern Hemisphere, or about twice the distance from New York to San Francisco, while from north to south the maximum points are about 3,000 miles apart. More than a dozen states (including Japan) border on the Soviet Union, whose frontier is the longest and most exposed of that of any state, totaling nearly 38,000 miles in extent.

Inside the Soviet Union are to be found an extraordinary diversity and range of climates, land features, and natural resources, more variegated than those of any other state in the world. In many ways, the Soviet Union is a microcosm of the world.

ECONOMIC FOUNDATIONS

Natural Resources

Russia is one of the richest countries in the world in natural resources and is considered second only to the United States in natural potential; new finds of mineral deposits are discovered virtually every year, and it is not inconceivable that she may soon exceed the United States in known deposits of strategic minerals. Russia possesses deposits of almost every important mineral, and, like the United States, is practically self-sufficient in the production of food.

According to a U.S government report of October 1960, "Russia has nearly twice the conventional energy sources of the entire free world, without considering recent oil discoveries in the Soviet Union."[1] Imperial Russia's

[1] Quoted in the *New York Times*, January 22, 1961.

known coal deposits amounted to only 3% of the world's total, but today the USSR claims 57% of the world's coal deposits and 60% of its peat. Oil discoveries elsewhere have lowered the USSR's share of known oil reserves from a little over half to less than 40% of the world's reserves. She also claims over a quarter of the world's water power and one-third of its timber.

The Soviet Union's reserves of minerals and chemicals are no less impressive. Prerevolutionary Russia's iron ore deposits amounted to less than 4% of the world's total, but today she claims 53.5%, three times as much as the United States, Britain, France, and West Germany together. She claims no less than 88% of the world's manganese, 54% of its potassium salts, and 30% of its phosphates, and claims to be first in the known reserves of copper, lead, zinc, nickel, bauxite, tungsten, mercury, and sulphur. The only major resources that she lacks in quantity are tin and natural rubber. The Soviet Union's vast resources have enabled her to achieve second place only to the United States in the production of steel, pig iron, coal, and oil. Since geological explorations continue on a massive scale, these statistics are subject to constant revision upward. And about 25% of the Soviet territory still remains geologically unexplored, and nearly 250 million acres of rich black soil remains to be taken advantage of.

As Soviet resources are converted into production items, the entire political and economic balance of power in the world may be fundamentally altered. Already, the Soviet Union has invaded the world oil market, backed by her tremendous reserves and accelerated production (3 million barrels per day in 1960, exceeded only by that of the United States), and undersells the prevailing market price by 20–30%. From shipments of only 35,000 barrels a day in 1953, the Soviets exported at the rate of 500,000 barrels per day in 1961.[2] While the Soviets produced 140 million tons of oil in 1960, in 1970 they produced over 350 million tons.[3]

The fact that the Soviet Union possesses

[2] *New York Times,* January 13 and 22, 1961.
[3] *Narodnoye Khozyaistvo S.S.S.R. v 1969 Godu* (Moscow, 1966).

tremendous reserves of raw materials does not mean that she is not plagued with resource problems. As the Soviet economy exploits its natural resources ever more intensively, the prospect of eventual exhaustion manifests itself. Furthermore, Soviet planners and engineers do not always employ the most efficient methods, and problems of wastage are not uncommon. As mines and resources are depleted, the costs of exhaustion and processing mount, and more remote and inaccessible areas must be tapped at greater cost. Furthermore, industrial and technological development brings with it the problems of pollution and conservation which have provided trenchant exchanges between various sectors of the economy, between conservationists and industrial managers, and even a public display of contention at the 24th Party Congress (1971) between the minister of agriculture and the minister of power, with the former rebuking the latter for flooding fertile bottomlands and the latter replying that electrification meant progress. Thus, on January 16, 1967, *Pravda,* the most authoritative Soviet paper, while delighting in the Soviet Union's enormous natural resources, intimated that the asymmetrical distribution of natural resources and population created special problems:

The USSR has approximately 55 percent of the world reserves of coal, 45 percent of the natural gas, more than 60 percent of the peat. It has significant reserves of petroleum. Of the general world quantity of oil-bearing area, 32 million square kilometers, about 11.9 million square kilometers, or 37.1 percent, are on the territory of the Soviet Union. Only 8 percent of our potential hydroelectric power resources have so far been utilized. The European part of the USSR and the Urals have most of the population of our country. In these areas are located also the chief potentials of the national economy. But 87 percent of the mineral fuel reserves are located in Siberia, the Far East and the Central Asian Republics. In the eastern regions are found the basic reserves of the economical types of fuel: gas, oil, and also more than 90 percent of the hydroelectric resources.

Industrial Growth and Power

The foundation of modern national power is industrialization, a fact which Joseph Stalin, the architect of the Soviet Union's power, recognized at an early date. In 1928, soon after he established his control over the Soviet state, Stalin introduced an ambitious Five-Year Plan designed both to socialize and to industrialize the USSR in order to secure national strength and to provide a strong base from which the ideological goals of world communism could be pursued.

The first of the three prewar five-year plans was supposed to concentrate on heavy industry, the second (1933–38) on consolidating the gains of the first and emphasizing quality, while the third (1939–44) was to shift over to light industry and the production of consumer goods. The rise of Hitler in Germany and the designs of Japan in the Far East, however, forced Stalin to alter this program in favor of accelerating the expansion of heavy industry and increasing the military capacity of the Soviet Union. The third plan was disrupted by World War II and was never completed. After the war, Stalin inaugurated a new series of three five-year plans designed, respectively, to repair the war devastation and restore the country to a sound state, to overtake the advanced industrial states of Western Europe, and to close the industrial gap between the Soviet Union and the United States.

By 1951, the Soviet Union had fully recovered from the destruction of the war and had already developed an atomic bomb and was on the verge of producing the H-bomb. Although Soviet recovery was hastened by the $10 billion in reparations exacted from Germany, and by her exploitation of the satellite states of Eastern Europe, the recovery was largely dependent on her own resources. The rapid postwar recovery of the Soviet economy is even more remarkable in light of the damages suffered not only by the economy during the war but by the population as well. The Germans occupied fully half of European Russia, including some of her most important industrial centers and food-producing regions. Judging from the 1959 census (the first in twenty years), the Soviet Union lost more than 25 million persons who were killed during the war, plus 20 million or so who were not born as a result of the deaths and dislocations of the war. These war losses were concealed by Stalin to prevent the exposure of Soviet weakness to the outside world.

Only in 1961 did the Soviet government permit the publication of statistics showing the magnitude of the war damage to the Soviet economy (see Table 3-1). By 1942, the second year of the war, industrial production dropped to a level about equal to that of 1928–32. Steel production dropped from 18.3 million metric tons to 8 million, though by 1944 it rose again to nearly 11 million. The production of iron ore, as vital as steel in modern war, dropped from about 30 million metric tons in 1940 to 22 million in 1942, and to little more than 18 million in 1943–44. Coal production was also cut in half, from 166 million tons to 75, although by 1944 it climbed back up to more than 121 million.[4]

The losses in agriculture were equally severe. Only 60% of the area sown in 1940 was planted in 1942, while livestock suffered a sharp decline in numbers. Pigs were reduced from 27.5 million in 1941 to a low of 5.6 million in 1944; horses from 21 million to less than 8 million; cows from nearly 28 million to less than 14 million in 1943, rising to 16.5 million in 1944. The number of sheep and goats declined from 91.6 million to a low of 62 million in 1943, while cattle dropped from 54.5 million to a low of 28.4 million in 1943. In view of these figures, the $11 billion of lend-lease aid that had been given to the USSR by the United States during the war may well have provided the margin of survival.

By the time of Stalin's death, however, in March 1953, the Soviet Union was well on the road to becoming the second greatest industrial power in the world, and (for a while, at least, if not from time to time) first in space and rocket technology. In 1946, Stalin announced what in retrospect appeared to be modest industrial goals to be achieved by 1961. Steel production was aimed at 60 million tons, pig iron at 50 million, oil at 60 million, and coal at 500 million. These projections were ridiculed by many foreign observers as ambitious and unrealistic, designed primarily for propaganda purposes.

[4] *New York Times*, January 2, 1961.

TABLE 3-1. *Basic Industrial Production in the USSR, 1913–70*

	1913 (Russia)	1928	1940	War Years (annual average)	1950	1955	1959	1965	1970	1975 (planned)
(millions of tons)										
Steel	4.2	4.3	18.3	8.0	27.3	45.3	60.0	91.0	116.0	142–50
Pig iron	4.2	3.3	14.9	—	19.2	33.3	43.0	66.0	81.6 †	101–5
Iron ore	9.2	6.1	29.9	18.0	39.7	71.9	105.0	153.4	186.0 †	—
Rolled steel	3.5	3.4	13.1	—	20.9	35.3	49.0	70.9	87.5 †	101–5
Cement	1.3	1.8	55.7	—	10.2	22.5	38.8	72.4	95.0	122–27
Coke	4.4	4.2	21.1	—	27.7	43.6	56.0	67.5	—	—
Coal	29.1	35.5	165.9	75.0	261.1	391.3	507.0	578.0	624.0	685–95
Peat	1.7	5.3	33.2	—	36.0	50.8	60.5	46.0	44.8 †	—
Oil	9.2	11.6	31.1	—	37.9	70.8	129.6	243.0	349.0	480–500
Gas										
(millions of cubic meters)	17.0	336.0	3,392.0	—	6,181.0	10,356.0	37,200.0	129,200.0	198.0	300–20
Electricity										
(billions of kWh)	1.9	5.0	48.3	—	91.2	170.2	265.0	507.0	740.0	1030–70
Metal-cutting lathes										
(thousands of units)	1.5	2.0	58.4	—	70.6	117.1	150.0	186.1	205.5	—
Gross national product										
Total (billions of dollars)	—	—	—	—	124	174	226	333 *	490	—
Per capita (dollars)	—	—	—	—	688	889	1,081	1,418 *	1,630	—

SOURCE: *Narodnoye Khozyaistov S.S.S.R. v 1969 Godu* (Moscow, 1966); *Pravda,* February 20, 1966, and April 9, 1971.

* 1966 (*New York Times Magazine,* March 19, 1967).

† 1969.

Yet some of these goals were exceeded by 1960: steel production, for instance, was 71.5 million tons. And by only 1959, oil production in the Soviet Union reached 129 million tons, and coal production totaled 507 million tons.

The growth of the national power of the Soviet Union is systematically planned. The equilibrium between production for national power and private consumption is tightly controlled and manipulated by the state. Under Stalin, the public sector of the economy was developed at the expense of the private sector. Consequently, the Soviet standard of living lagged far behind the rate of technological advance. Since the death of Stalin, his successors have devoted more attention to raising the standard of living, although it remains a poor second to the country's capital investment in national power.

Although the total production of goods and services in the United States is more than two times that of the Soviet Union, a substantial proportion is devoted to private consumption, while the amount devoted to maintaining and enhancing national power is only about equal to that of the Soviet Union in absolute terms, and in some key areas has been less. Since 1961, however, the proportion devoted to national power and public services in the United States has been considerably increased.

The standard of living in the Soviet Union has thus been deliberately depressed in favor of other priorities set by the regime. Since Stalin's death, however, successive Soviet leaders—Malenkov, Khrushchev, and the Brezhnev-Kosygin team—have promised the Soviet public to alter the priorities in favor of producing consumer goods, though somehow this promise has always been at least partially subverted by the continued priority for defense requirements. During the Khrushchev decade (1955–65), the Soviet standard of living experienced a substantial rise, but not at the tempo of his exaggerated promise (made at the Twenty-second Party Congress in 1961) to outstrip the United States by 1975. Although consumer goods production increased, real wages for factory and office workers were increased, medical and educational facilities were expanded, the work week was reduced to 41 hours, and the income of collective farmers was raised; since all of this was not accompanied by a parallel increase in productive efficiency, the Soviet economy developed unevenly, and its rate of productive growth actually dropped—by 1963, from about 9% to 3–4% annually. (However, in the heavy-industry sector the 1965 targets of Khrushchev's Seven-Year Plan were in many cases achieved.)

Khrushchev's diplomatic failure during the Berlin crisis of 1961, his retreat from Cuba in October 1962, his demoralizing reorganization of the Communist party in the same year, the growing dispute with China, his mismanagement of the economy, the agricultural failures of 1963, and his tendency to ignore the party's Central Committee culminated in his sudden removal in October 1964. The ills of the Soviet economy were frankly conceded by Brezhnev in March 1966:

In recent years such negative features have become manifest as reduced growth rates in production and in the productivity of labor, lower efficiency in the use of fixed assets and investments. . . . The Central Committee of the C.P.S.U. analyzed the state of affairs in the economy after the October [1964] plenum, and laid bare the causes of these negative manifestations and indicated ways of overcoming them. Defects in management and planning, the underestimation of the methods of running the economy at a profit, and the underuse of material and moral stimuli all contributed to the lowering of economic growth rates. The forms and methods of management, planning, and the use of economic stimuli were not in accordance with the new, higher level of the country's productive forces, and had begun to check their development.

At the same time, however, he promised the patient Soviet consumer that the new regime was even more dedicated to his immediate needs than was Khrushchev:

For that reason, while the preceding 5-year period group A (heavy industry) was increased by 58 percent and group B (consumer and light industry) by 36 percent, in the next five years we plan a 49–52 percent increase in the production of the means of production and a 43–46 percent increase in the output of consumer goods.[5]

Foreign travelers to the Soviet Union consistently report a steady though modest rise in the Soviet standard of living every year, and this increase will continue to be steady and modest. The Soviet leaders no longer boast about how soon they will catch up with and surpass the United States in productivity. In absolute terms, however, Soviet industrial growth remains impressive. On the eve of World War II, the industrial output of the Soviet Union accounted for but 10% of the world's total, whereas by 1965, with only 7% of the world's population, the industrial output of the USSR accounted for 20% of it.

Agriculture and Food Production

Soviet and non-Soviet observers universally agree that agriculture constitutes the Achilles' heel of the Soviet economy. An adequate food supply is just as vital as industrial production in contributing to national power, but agricultural production is not as susceptible to rational planning and control as is industrial production.

The weaknesses of Soviet agriculture are not all due to the vagaries of the climate. The very process of rapid industrialization and urbanization within the span of a single generation was bound to dislocate the equilibrium between town and country life. Top priority was given to industrialization, in accordance with Marxist principles, at the expense of agriculture and the peasants if necessary. Badly needed factory workers were drawn from the farms. Since the Soviet regime could not secure

[5] Quoted in *Pravda*, March 30, 1966.

financial assistance from the capitalist countries in the form of loans or gifts, it had to rely on agricultural exports to accumulate enough capital to import foreign machinery and technicians to start the industrialization of Russia. The diminishing labor supply in the countryside and the drain of agricultural exports reduced the country's food supply to below the subsistence level.

Stalin was thus confronted with a dilemma of serious proportions, a dilemma that inevitably confronts every underdeveloped country wishing to industrialize rapidly. How to resolve it is one of the supreme political problems of the modern age. Stalin's method of increasing agricultural production consisted of three parts: collectivization, mechanization, and state control. Collectivizing the farms satisfied both the Marxist demand for the socialization of agriculture and the demands of efficiency, for small individual farms were replaced by large state-supervised collective farms. Mechanization of farm equipment helped compensate for the reduced labor supply; and the state's retention of the ownership of the land and agricultural machines, together with its exclusive power to set agricultural prices and buy agricultural commodities, insured that the peasants would remain under the thumb of the government.

The net result of Stalin's program was a disaster for rural Russia. The kulaks (the wealthy peasants) ferociously resisted collectivization; they burned their crops, slaughtered their livestock, and destroyed their implements rather than surrender them to the state. The food supply diminished catastrophically. The disaster was magnified by the worldwide economic depression which knocked the bottom out of the market prices for agricultural commodities, causing the Soviets to export more for less return. During the height of the crisis, a severe drought hit the Ukraine, which further reduced agricultural production. Famine stalked rural Russia as millions died of starvation, and vast numbers of kulaks were "liquidated."

Rural Russia has never fully recovered, and Soviet agricultural production has only recently exceeded the production registered in 1916. Per capita production for the total population is still not much better than it was nearly fifty years ago, and lags considerably behind that of the United States. The number of livestock, in particular, dropped tremendously, and only after 1950 did the Soviet Union manage to reach the figures of 1916.

The Soviet government has endeavored to raise agricultural production through the more intensive use of existing farmlands and by an expansion of the acreage under cultivation. In attempting to get more productive use of present farmlands, the Soviet government has steadily enhanced the mechanization of agriculture, fostered greater scientific research, and increased the production of fertilizer, even copying some techniques from the United States.

The most ambitious attempt to expand the area under cultivation was started in 1955, when Krushchev inaugurated the so-called virgin lands project whereby enormous tracts of uncultivated lands in western Siberia and the central Asian Republic of Kazakhstan were plowed up and planted. The program involved enormous risks, because the climate on these plains is so unpredictable. A large amount of capital was invested in the program, and energetic efforts and inducements were made to get farmers to settle in the new lands. Every year hundreds of thousands of Komsomols (members of the Communist youth organization) and university students "volunteered" to spend a year or two working in the area. Life is very hard, and even the modest amenities of ordinary Soviet life are largely absent in the great tent cities that have been erected on the central Asian steppes.

The "virgin lands" program has undoubtedly increased the total production of grain, but whether on balance it has been worth the effort and cost is still debatable. Three crop years out of the first five were adjudged failures, and the careers of important Communist party and government officials have suffered with each failure.

The most conspicuous political victim of the near-disastrous crop failures of 1963–65 was Chairman Khrushchev, who prided himself as being an agricultural expert. One by one, his short-cut attempts to increase Soviet agricultural production failed, and in 1963 the Soviet government was forced to spend hundreds of millions of dollars in scarce gold and hard currency to purchase grain from the United States and other "capitalist" countries in order to satisfy the needs of its own population and to meet its commitments to some underdeveloped countries. Agriculture was thus the most glaring failure: not only did it fall considerably short of the target goals of the plan, but its rate of growth in 1964 was even less than in the preceding five years.

Khrushchev, of course, was blamed for the failures which, according to Brezhnev, resulted from neglecting the role of material incentives for the farmers (who were often paid less for their commodities than their actual cost of production), serious shortcomings in procurement procedures, and insufficient investment of funds and of material and technical resources. Brezhnev and Kosygin introduced new procurement procedures, increased state prices for agricultural commodities, lowered prices of manufactured goods to conform with prices charged in the urban areas, and gave the collective farmers a guaranteed annual income. Although the Soviet Union experienced a severe drought in 1965, there was some improvement as a consequence of the reforms. The 1966–70 plan for an increase of 25% in overall agricultural output over the preceding five-year period, with grain slated for a 30% increase, was substantially achieved. In 1966, with the cooperation of the weather, the Soviet Union harvested a bumper crop—the largest in its history by far (171 million tons). Meat, milk, and egg production also went up, but whether good fortune will continue to smile on Soviet agriculture remains as uncertain as ever. The abandonment of some of the unproductive virgin lands, the increase in income for the farmers, greater investment, and the expansion of fertilizer production all will have a beneficial impact on Soviet agricultural production, but agricultural production still lags behind the rest of the economy and continues to plague the Soviet planners and disappoint the Soviet consumer. The 1971–1975 plan calls for the production of 195 tons of grain in 1975.

POPULATION

A nation's demographic configuration reveals a great deal about its power and potential. If we examine the size and growth of the Soviet population, its territorial distribution, sex and age, skills, talents and literacy rates, social composition, and finally its ethnic diversity, we will learn much about the current capabilities as well as the future prospects of the USSR.

At the outset, perhaps we should outline the general profile of the present Soviet population. As a result of World War II, today there are at least 45 million fewer citizens of the USSR than there might have been had there been no war. Whereas before the war the population of the Soviet Union was 46% larger than that of the United States, presently it is only 18% larger (see Table 3-2). From 1914 to 1970, Russia's population rose from 159 million to 242 million, an increase of only 83 million. During this same period, the population of the United States shot upward from 92 million (census of 1910) to 204 million (census of 1970). World War II left the Soviet Union with 20 million more women than men (the most unbalanced ratio of any country save East Germany), and this has resulted in social, economic, and military problems of an acute character. The age structure of the Soviet Union's population was also drastically affected. In the United States, the war produced a "boom" in babies, but the precise opposite took place in the USSR, which, consequently, faces a diminished supply of workers and soldiers during the years of the immediate future.

Because of advances in science, medicine, and sanitation, the life expectancy of the Soviet citizen has increased to the point where it equals that of the United States and is one of the highest in the world. Much of the Soviet Union's rapid growth in population up to 1960 was thus due to the declining death rate. But this means that the future population of the Soviet Union will continue to show a higher proportion of old people. The Soviet birth rate, in the meantime, has declined sharply since 1959, dropping from 25 per 1,000 to less than 16 in 1970. Industrialization has brought about a revolution in the urban-rural ratio of the Soviet population. Today, 56% of the population is urbanized (that is, lives in towns with over 3,000 population), and the Soviet educational effort has transformed a nation of illiterates into one of the most literate countries in the world. The Soviet Union now has virtually 100% literacy, and all children attend school.

Besides the population movement from country to town, there had been a corresponding movement of population eastward, which has since diminished in recent years. The overall population increase from 1939 to 1959 was only 9.5%, but all the regions east of the Urals registered increases of more than 30%, with the Soviet Far East showing a high of 70%. Some of the western border regions, however, have actually decreased in population, owing to both the war and migrations eastward. One result of this movement eastward has been the spread of the Slavic nationalities among the non-Slavic populations of central Asia. In the Kazakh Republic, for example, the Kazakhs had been reduced to a minority in their own republic already by 1959, and in 1970 accounted for only 32.4% of the total, while the three Slavic nationalities—the Great Russians, Ukrainians, and Byelorussians—accounted for 42.8%, 7.2%, and 1.5% respectively, i.e., for more than 50% of the total. The 1970 census, however, showed that the Slavic proportion of the population in the central Asian republics had been reduced somewhat in comparison to 1959 because of the higher growth rate among the central Asians (almost 50%) as compared to the Slavic groups (almost 12%) and because of a slowdown in the eastward migration of Slavs.

Perhaps the most unique characteristic of the Soviet population is its ethnic diversity. The people of the Soviet Union remain divided among more than one hundred different nationalities, of which the Great Russians account for more than half the total. The language and literacy data of the 1959 and 1970 censuses reveal two important modifications of the ethnic situation in the Soviet Union. The

first is the increasing "russification" of many of the smaller non-Russian nationalities; the second is the virtual establishment of Russian as a second spoken language for all non-Russians. In 1959, an impressive number of small non-Russian nationalities had more than 50% of their members list Russian as their mother tongue. The compulsory teaching of Russian in all non-Russian schools has resulted in a bilingual population, virtually all of whom speak and read Russian in addition to their native language. The Soviet population, in spite of its ethnic diversity, is thus a far more homogenized population than it was some three decades ago.

Size and Growth

For all practical purposes, the Soviet Union and the United States are in the same population class, both being considerably overshadowed by two demographic giants, China and India. Since the gap between the population of the USSR and that of the United States has decreased over the past decades, the competitive struggle and rivalry between the two countries will increasingly turn on which country most effectively marshals and mobilizes its human and natural resources. The population of the United States is not expected to reach the current Soviet size before 1985. With immigration into the United States practically at a standstill, that country must now rely on natural increases to replenish its demographic resources.

According to censuses of 1970, the population of the United States was over 204 million, while that of the Soviet Union was 242 million (Table 3-2). In 1966, the rate of natural increase for the United States was 15.7 per 1,000 per year, as compared with 10.9 per 1,000 for the Soviet Union. When compared with the 1940 rates of 8.6 and 13.4, respectively, we see the remarkable advance chalked up by the United States. The Soviet increases were caused by a rapid decline in the death rate and only a slight decline in the birth rate; the increases for the United States, according to an authori-

TABLE 3-2. *Populations of the U.S. and USSR 1913–70 (millions)*

	1913 (Russia)	1920	1926	1930	1940	1950	1960	1970	Rate of Increase 1913–70
U.S.	96 *	106	—	123	132	151	180	204	112%
USSR	159	—	147 †	—	191	179 ‡	209	242	52%

* Interpolated from 1910 and 1920 census returns.
† Applies to Soviet boundaries existing before September 1939.
‡ Estimated.

tative source, resulted from not only a declining death rate but from a 30% spurt in the birth rate.[6] The rate of the natural increase in the Soviet population has been declining steadily since 1939, when it was 19.2 per 1,000 population, as opposed to 8.9 in 1969. The comparable figures for the United States during these years were 9.2 and 10.3 respectively, although the U.S. growth rate moved from 8.0 per 1,000 in 1935 to 18.1 in 1956, before its recent descent.

Age and Sex

The ratio of men to women in the Soviet population had been steadily decreasing since World War I. In 1926, the number of males per 100 women was 93.4; in 1939, 91.9; and, according to the 1959 census, the percentage had dropped to 81.9. During the same period, the number of males per 100 females in the United States declined from a small surplus of 103.1 to a small deficit of 98. The lack of men in the USSR deprived about 21 million women of husbands and children and forced many women into heavy manual labor and other unskilled work, a situation that often shocks Western observers.

The imbalance between the sexes appeared to be improving and may be wiped out within two decades. The 1970 census showed an in-

[6] See *Joint Economic Committee Studies, Comparison of the United States and Soviet Economics* (Washington, D.C.: G.P.O., 1966), Parts 1-5.

crease in the ratio of women to men (up to 85.5%), but the distribution is highly uneven, with virtually matched proportions in the age groups under 40. The highest degree of imbalance is in the higher age groups. A close examination of the age-sex structure of the Soviet population suggests that these imbalances resulted not only from the disproportionate number of men that perished during World War II, but also because a higher number of males died during the period of the purges, 1934–39. Although the sex ratio in the Soviet population is being rectified, the share of the labor force drawn from the female side of the population continues to grow, with the most menial tasks still performed by women. Declining birth and death rates, combined increasingly with postponed entry into the labor force on the part of young people because of expanded educational opportunities, has seriously affected the share of the able-bodied population that can be channeled into productive labor. As a consequence, women will continue to be drawn in larger numbers into the Soviet working population. Thus, 92.4% of all able-bodied people of both sexes were reported in the 1970 census as fully employed or full-time students, as opposed to only 82% in 1959, but only 85% of the employed were drawn from the able-bodied part of the population (ages 16–59 for men, 16–54 for women). According to the census release itself, "the increase in the number of employed took place through attracting into social production able-bodied people engaged in housekeeping or working on their subsidiary households," of which only 5.9 million remain as contrasted with 17.9 million in 1959.

There is, of course, an obvious relationship between the uneven sex ratios in the population and the declining birth rate, but this has been further aggravated by the engagement of virtually the entire female sex in full-time employment, and Soviet demographers are becoming increasingly concerned with the long-range social, economic, and political implications of this problem. Soviet planners are delighted with the increased labor supply, and the families of the women who are employed are at least momentarily pleased, since family income is often nearly doubled as a consequence—an important factor in a country where the average monthly wage is typically 100–120 rubles ($110–132). But in view of the serious erosion of the birth rate among the European sectors of the population and in the large urban centers, the Soviet regime at some point must make the unhappy choice of either keeping the female part of the population nearly 100% employed or paying serious atten-

tion to the encouragement of larger families rather than playing games like awarding titles of "Heroine Mother" to women who bear many children. This has become a very crucial problem for some nationalities—including small ones like the Estonians—whose growth rates are approaching zero, while that of their fellow citizens in central Asia will more than double their population every two decades.

Equally, if not even more serious, than the uneven distribution of the sexes and the disproportionate growth rates among nationalities is the aging of the Soviet population, which at some point will also affect population growth (see Table 3-3). Not only does this throw a greater burden upon the proportionately shrinking able-bodied age groups, who were reduced to 54% of the population in 1970 as opposed to 57.4% in 1959 because of the decreased birth and death rates and the increasing life span of the Soviet population, but it also threatens to introduce a serious imbalance between the producing and consuming sectors of the population just as the Soviet economy is on the crucial brink of moving into the post-industrial age.

TABLE 3-3. *Age Structure of the Soviet Population, 1939–70*

Age	Number of People (millions) 1939	1959	1970	Percentage of Total 1939	1959	1970
0–9	43,476	46,363	49,986	22.8%	22.2%	18.6%
10–15	28,365	17,133	29,724	14.9	8.2	12.3
16–19	13,030	14,675	17,263	6.8	7.0	7.1
20–24	15,786	20,343	17,105	8.3	9.7	7.1
25–29	18,520	18,190	13,770	9.7	8.7	5.7
30–34	15,598	18,999	21,145	8.2	9.1	8.7
35–39	12,958	11,590	16,594	6.8	5.6	6.9
40–44	9,603	10,408	19,003	5.0	5.0	7.9
45–49	7,776	12,264	12,256	4.1	5.9	5.1
50–59	12,533	19,146	21,091	6.6	9.2	8.8
60–69	8,535	11,736	17,595	4.5	5.6	7.3
Over 70	4,462	7,972	10,919	2.3	3.8	4.5
Able-bodied	102,241	119,822	130,847	53.6	57.4	54.0

SOURCE: *Pravda,* April 17, 1971.

Distribution

The population of neither the United States nor the Soviet Union is distributed equally throughout the country. In the United States, the bulk of the population is found east of the Mississippi; in the USSR, the overwhelming proportion of the population is west of the Urals. In both countries, there has been a steady movement of people from the more densely populated areas to those that are relatively sparse in people. Vast stretches of territory remain virtually unpopulated in both countries. Much of Soviet Asia is inhospitable and incapable of supporting large populations.

Excluding the ancient settled regions of central Asia, Russia east of the Urals, including Kazakhstan, around the turn of the century contained a little more than 8 million people. By 1926, it had more than doubled to 17.4 million. In 1939, it had risen to 22.7 million, jumped to 32 million in 1959, but according to the latest census (1970), the total population of Siberia and Kazakhstan is now approximately 38 million. Until a few years ago, these increases were almost all due to the migrations from the western regions of Russia, but the eastward movement of the Soviet population has apparently slowed down.

Since the Revolution, the Soviet government has sedulously planned the movement of the population eastward, for essentially three reasons: (1) to increase the proportion of European Slavs in Soviet Asia and thus to reduce the possibility that the non-Russian groups in Asia would defect; (2) to more effectively tap the rich natural resources of the region; (3) to protect Soviet Asia against the ambitions of a predatory Japan and against the possibility of population pressures from China. Much of the Soviet Far East was once a nominal part of China, which lost its hold on the area largely because of the activities of various Russian adventurers, beginning in the seventeenth century and continuing down into the nineteeth.

Russian population movements eastward have, by and large, not been voluntary. A substantial part of the shift has resulted from forcible deportations. During the Stalinist era, millions of Russian and Ukrainian peasants were deported to central Asia and the Soviet Far East, and millions were herded into vast concentration camps. When released, most of the ex-prisoners were obliged to remain in the area, or found it convenient to begin life anew in Soviet Asian provinces.

Since Stalin's death, most of the slave-labor camps in the Soviet Union have been disbanded, and compulsory emigration to Soviet Asia has been stopped. Now the government is inducing people to move eastward, especially to the "virgin lands" of the Kazakh Republic and western Siberia, by offering them long-term financial support on generous terms, large and potentially fertile farm lands, wage bonuses, and other rewards.

In spite of these impressive attempts to spread Soviet population to the east, nearly 70% of the Soviet population is still found west of the Urals. Soviet Asia, with 75% of the land area of the Soviet Union, supports only about 25% of the population, or 60 million people (compared with only 14 million in 1897). The Soviet government intended to continue the migration eastward, and allocated substantial capital investments for the development of Soviet Asia, which also reflected the government's anxiety about Communist China's possible designs on the scantily populated regions of the Soviet Union bordering on her territory.

Although the Soviet Union east of the Urals remains sparsely populated and the Chinese threat has escalated rather than diminished, the Soviet regime during the past half-decade has had little success in sustaining the early high levels of migration eastward. With the abandonment of Khrushchev's ambitious "virgin lands" program, there has even been a substantial migration back to European Russia, with most of the recent population increases attributable to natural growth rates, particularly among the highly fertile Moslem nationalities of central Asia. In the new Five Year Plan (1971–76) adopted by the Twenty-fourth Party Congress in 1971, the Asian regions of the USSR will not be particularly favored, as the new emphasis on cost-accounting and efficiency dictates that industrial investment be concentrated near existing population centers and markets rather than in remote areas of sparse settlement. In view of the fact that the Asian regions currently account for only 10% of the iron and steel industry, for example, the decision to expand in the European centers of the USSR, combined with the difficulty in inducing Russians to move eastward and the galloping rate of Moslem population growth, suggests that the Soviet regime may be loath to lessen the dependence of the Asian regions upon the Russian center by supplying them with an independent industrial establishment that might encourage national assertiveness as they grow in numbers.

Urban-Rural Distribution

More dramatic than the movement of the Soviet population from west to east has been the shift of people from country to town. In 1926, the total urban population of the country was only 26 million, which by 1939 had grown to more than 60 million (Table 3-4). In 1970, the urban population of the USSR amounted to nearly 137 million, or 56% of the population. Urbanization has taken place throughout the country, but in the Asian regions it has increased by more than 100%. The Soviet Far East and some of the central Asian republics have registered

increases of 150%, as against an average of 30% for the western areas during this period.

Between 1939 and 1959, 756 new cities and 1,490 new urban-type settlements were created. As an indication of the continuing character of Soviet urbanization, 256 cities and 629 urban-type settlements came into being between 1959 and 1970. Today, the Soviet Union has a larger number of cities with a population of 50,000 or more than has the United States. Of cities with populations in excess of 500,000 in 1960, the USSR had twenty-five (up to thirty-three in 1970), while the United States had only twenty-three by 1970. The United States leads in supercities, however; it has four with 2 million inhabitants or more to the Soviet Union's two, Moscow and Leningrad. It should be emphasized that the Soviet government has, by law and administrative action, prevented the development of overcrowded and swollen city populations. Moscow today has more than 7 million people, Leningrad a little more than 3.5 million, followed by eight other cities, including Kiev and Baku, with over 1 million each.

Thus, while the increase in population from 1939 to 1970 was about 27 per cent, the urban population during the same period more than doubled. Between 1926 and 1959, villages of mud huts and straw-covered houses were transformed into modern towns, and the empty plains and valleys of Soviet Asia saw the erec-

TABLE 3-4. *Urban Growth in the USSR, 1926–70*

Settlement	1926	1939	1941	1951	1956	1959	1966	1970
Cities	709	923	1,241	1,451	1,566	1,679	1,832	1,935
Urban-type settlements	1,216	1,450	1,711	2,320	2,423	2,940	3,418	3,569
Cities								
(50,000–100,000)	60	94	—	—	138	156	183	188
(100,000–500,000)	28	71	—	—	113	123	162	188
(over 500,000)	3	11	—	—	22	25	30	33
Total urban population	26,300,000	60,400,000	60,600,000	71,400,000	86,600,000	99,778,000	124,749,000	136,991,514

SOURCES: *Narodnoye Khozyaistvo . . . v 1959 Godu, v 1965 Godu;* and *Pravda,* April 17, 1971.

tion of giant new cities, whose populations were busily exploiting the natural resources of Siberia. Imposing industrial centers like Karaganda (522,000) and Magnitogorsk (364,000) did not even exist before 1926.

Although the image of the Soviet Union as a vast land populated by peasants has long been outdated, the rural population still accounts for 44% of the population, or about 106 million people.

Ethnic Composition and Distribution

Like imperial Russia before it, the Soviet Union is a country of many nationalities and tribal groups who speak a variety of languages and dialects. The 1970 census tabulates nearly one hundred nationalities, tribes, and linguistic groups. This ethnic heterogeneity renders any purely quantitative analysis of Soviet population based on size, growth, territorial distribution, age structure, sex ratios, etc., grossly misleading unless it is accompanied by an ethnic analysis as well.

The Great Russians occupy the continental interior of Eurasia, and they are fringed on all sides by a belt of non-Russian nationalities that forms a buffer around the borders of the Soviet Union. Most of the Baltic coast is inhabited by Estonians, Latvians, and Lithuanians, while the Byelorussians, Ukrainians, and Moldavians occupy the territories bordering Poland, Czechoslovakia, and Rumania. In the Caucasus, the Georgians, Armenians, and Azerbaidzhani Turks inhabit the regions next to Turkey and Iran. In central Asia, the Turkmen, Uzbeks, Kazakhs, and Kirgiz live in the border areas adjacent to Iran, Afghanistan, and the Sinkiang province of China, and a multitude of Turkic, Mongol, and Tungusic tribes occupy the border regions near Outer Mongolia. Only in the Soviet Far East do Great Russians inhabit territories adjacent to the international frontiers of the USSR, and this is a region remote from the heartland of the Soviet nation.

Of the nearly one hundred nationalities enumerated in the 1970 census, twenty-two consist of more than 1 million each, and these ac-

count for more than 95% of the total population (Table 3-5). The remaining nationalities amount to less than 10 million.

The demographic contours of the Soviet population thus vary widely from one ethnic group to another, and this unevenness is of fundamental significance in assessing Soviet power and political behavior. The mosaic of nationalities in the USSR has had, and continues to have, an important impact on its foreign policy, its internal constitutional structure and political processes, and its social and cultural development. The geographical balance and distribution of the Russian and non-Russian nationalities of the Soviet Union is thus of crucial importance. The Great Russians occupy the continental interior of Eurasia, and they are fringed on all sides by a virtually uninterrupted belt of non-Russian nationalities who form a buffer separating the Russian-inhabited territories from the international borders of the Soviet Union. Because of their strategic location and their relationship to the Russian people, the border nationalities have always been a vital factor in Russian and Soviet security considerations. The failure of the tsars to earn the loyalty of the non-Russian nationalities contributed significantly to the military inefficiency of Russia during World War I, and their dissatisfaction under tsarist rule contributed materially to the Revolution, while Bolshevik promises of national self-determination was an important factor in Lenin's successful seizure and preservation of power. The nature and intensity of the loyalty and political reliability of the various nationalities of the Soviet Union vary from nationality to nationality, with the Russians—as would be expected—being the most intensely loyal and patriotic. During World War II, Stalin retaliated against five of the very small nationalities by dissolving their autonomous republics and deporting their populations to Siberia, on grounds that they had gone over to the Germans. This action was denounced by Khrushchev in 1956, and some of their republics have since been revived and their populations repatriated.

The numerical balance between the Slavic and non-Slavic nationalities in the Soviet Union is shifting in favor of the latter in terms of

TABLE 3-5. *Major Nationalities in the USSR, 1939–70 (thousands)*

	1939	*1959*	*1970*	*Percent increase or decrease, 1959–70*
Great Russians	99,019	114,500	129,015	+13.1
Ukrainians	28,070	36,981	40,753	+9.3
Byelorussians	5,267	7,829	9,052	+14.4
Uzbeks	4,844	6,004	9,195	+52.8
Tatars	4,300	4,969	5,931	+19.3
Kazakhs	3,098	3,581	5,299	+46.3
Azerbaidzhanis	2,275	2,929	4,380	+48.9
Armenians	2,152	2,787	3,559	+27.7
Georgians	2,249	2,650	3,245	+20.5
Moldavians	—	2,214	2,698	+21.8
Lithuanians	—	2,326	2,665	+14.5
Jews	3,020	2,268	2,151	−0.5
Tadzhiks	1,929	1,397	2,136	+52.8
Germans	1,424	1,619	1,846	+13.9
Chuvash	1,368	1,470	1,694	+15.0
Turkmen	812	1,004	1,525	+52.1
Kirgiz	884	974	1,452	+49.8
Latvians	—	1,400	1,430	+2.1
Mordvins	1,451	1,285	1,263	−1.7
Bashkirs	843	983	1,240	+24.5
Poles	627	1,380	1,167	−15.4
Estonians	—	969	1,007	+0.4
Totals	190,700	208,827	241,720	(+15.71)

SOURCE: *Pravda*, April 17, 1971.

natural increases of births over deaths, for behind the overall Soviet average birth rate, it should be noted that birth rates in central Asia and the Caucasus continue to be sustained at a very high rate (over 30 per 1,000), while in the western Slavic parts of the Soviet Union, they have slipped to below 10, just barely above the death rate.

If the current growth rates continue over the next four decades, the Moslem nationalities of the Soviet Union may well constitute a majority of the total population. As Table 3-5 indicates, in 1970 the central Asians and Azerbaidzhanis showed an increase of about 50% over 1959, while the Russian increase was 13.1, the Ukrainian only 9.3, and the two Baltic republics Latvia and Estonia were rapidly approaching the nirvana of birth-control enthusiasts, zero population growth (ZPG). Concurrently with the remarkable demographic vitality of the Moslem nationalities is the phenomenon of increasing "russification"—i.e., assimulation of individual non-Russians into the Russian nation. This apparently accounts for the relatively high growth rate for the Russians among the European nationalities of the Soviet Union. The assimilation process and its rapidity as well as uneven applicability to different nationalities, social groups, and regional location, all of which are reported in the census data, is demonstrated, first by the increasing number of non-Russians who gave Russian as the "mother language"—13 million in 1970 as opposed to only 10 million in 1959—and second, by the virtual establishment of Russian as the "second language" of nearly 42 million non-Russians, who were reported as speaking it fluently, for a grand total of 184 million out of 242 million who are fluent in the Russian language. Already after the 1959 census some enthusiastic Soviet "assimilationists" were exhibiting these data as evidence of "assimilation." Thus, one Soviet nationality specialist noted with obvious satisfaction:

During the period of Socialism . . . a substantial portion of the non-Russian peoples mastered the Russian language to such an extent that they regard it as their native tongue. . . . The increase in the numbers of the Russian nation is occurring not only from among the Russian population, but as a consequence of the voluntary entry therein of persons of non-Russian ancestry. . . . What we have here is a transfer of a particular portion of the population from one national group to another.[7]

This increase of the Russian population through assimilation comes at a time of declining birth rates among the Slavic and other European nationalities, which can seriously alter the nationality composition and balance, first by eroding and weakening the smaller European nationalities vulnerable to assimilation, and second, by contributing to an eventual demographic confrontation between the dominant Russian nationality and the growing Moslem groups. Some nationalities, like the Jews, Poles, and Mordvins, suffered an actual decrease in numbers from 1959 to 1970. The Jews, who were estimated to number about 3 million people in various Soviet sources just prior to the 1970 census, suffered a net loss of 117,000, thus suggesting that some 850,000 Jews reported themselves as "Russians" in the latest census. Since this unexpected decline in the Jewish population comes at a time of increasing dissidence on the part of Soviet Jews who wish to emigrate to Israel, the decrease may reflect both a predisposition on the part of many Jews to avoid Soviet reprisals because of "Zionist" agitation and perhaps even some fudging on the part of the authorities to demonstrate that

the "Jewish problem" is withering away in the Soviet Union. In any event, the procedures of the latest census, which allowed individual citizens to orally report their nationality without supporting documentation, facilitated the "voluntary entry" of many non-Russians into the Russian nation.

LITERACY AND EDUCATION

As of 1970, the Soviet Union had achieved virtually 100% literacy, with fewer than 500,-000 people between the ages of 9 and 49 reported as being unable to read and write. This cultural revolution in the Soviet Union during the past fifty years is one of the most significant transformations achieved in the social history of any nation. "In the organization of a planned society in the USSR," read the report of the first United States official educational mission to the USSR, "education is regarded as one of the chief resources and techniques for achieving social, economic, cultural and scientific objectives in the national interest. . . . They are convinced that time is on their side and that through education and hard work they can win their way to world acceptance of Communist ideology." [8] The Soviet Union has recently established eight years as the minimum schooling for children. Until a few years ago, the government was able to guarantee only a four-year education in many of the rural areas of the country.

Another feature of the Soviet educational effort merits attention: adult classes. An adult-education program, on the job and in the evening, was inaugurated soon after the Revolution to combat illiteracy. That battle having been won, its place has been taken by factory schools, correspondence courses, and evening classes, whose primary purpose is to provide opportunities for working people to learn new skills or improve old ones. It is perhaps worth noting that Nikita Khrushchev could neither read nor write until he was over 20 years old

---

7 M. S. Dzhunosov, "Soviet Autonomy and the Vestiges of Nationalism," in *Istoriya SSSR*, 1963, No. 1.

8 U.S. Department of Health, Education and Welfare, *Soviet Commitment to Education* (Washington, D.C.: G.P.O., 1959), p. 1.

and thus owes his rise to this adult-education program of the Communist party. In 1970, the total Soviet student enrollment in higher educational institutions was over 4½ million, about one-half of that in the United States but about four times that of Great Britain, West Germany, Italy, and France combined. More than half of all Soviet students in institutions of higher education, however, are enrolled in night classes or in correspondence courses (668,000 and 1,742,000, respectively).

Before the Revolution, 76% of the people were illiterate, including 88% of the women. Virtually complete illiteracy prevailed among the indigenous populations of Siberia and Soviet central Asia. Indeed, more than forty languages had not been reduced to writing at all. Prior to the Revolution, only 290,000 Russians possessed any kind of higher education, whereas the 1970 census reported that more than 24 million citizens had some higher or specialized secondary education, and more than 71 million people had 7–10 years of education

Before the Revolution, 80% of the children of Russia were deprived of educational opportunities, and all instruction, with but few exceptions, was in the Russian language. Today, all Soviet children must attend school, and instruction is provided in no less than fifty-nine indigenous languages, although Russian is the universal and virtually obligatory second language where it is not the native tongue. Raising the literacy rate from 24% to almost 100% within the span of less than two generations for

more than 200 million people would be an achievement in itself if only one language were involved, to say nothing of the severe problems posed by a multilingual society.

In 1914, only 127,000 students were enrolled in ninety-five institutions of higher learning; in 1970, there were 4.55 million enrolled in some 800 institutions of higher education, and 4.3 million in 4,302 technicums (nonprofessional technical colleges) and other specialized secondary schools (Table 3-6). Nearly 60 million people were enrolled in all types of schools in 1970, as compared with less than 10 million people in the years 1914–15.

Educational institutions of every level have been established in all the republics and in areas inhabited by other major nationalities (Table 3-7). Instruction in non-Russian schools is offered in both the native language and in Russian. The quality of Soviet educational institutions varies considerably, with the venerable universities of Moscow and Leningrad setting the highest standards of excellence in the country. Although a non-Russian can acquire a higher education in his native language, it is to his advantage to master Russian if he wishes to enter one of the national universities, apply for the diplomatic service, or work outside his native republic.

To indicate the massive character of the Soviet educational effort in central Asia, the Uzbek Republic, which is the most advanced of the central Asian areas today, as it was in prerevolutionary Russia, provides an apt illus-

TABLE 3-6. *School Enrollment in the USSR, 1914–70 (thousands)*

Level	1914–15	1927–28	1940–41	1945–46	1956–57	1960–61	1969–70
General schools	9,656	11,638	35,552	26,808 *	30,127 *	36,186	49,426
(Grades 8–11)	(152)	(170)	(2,571)	(1,091) *	(6,136)	(5,121)	(12,615)
Technical and special secondary schools	54	189	975	1,008	2,107	2,060	4,302
Higher education	127	169	812	730	2,001	2,396	4,550

* Lower figures reflect birth deficits caused by World War II.

TABLE 3-7. *Institutions of Higher Learning in the Non-Russian Soviet Republics, 1914–70*

Republic	1914	1927	1970
Ukraine	27	39	138
Byelorussia	0	4	28
Uzbek	0	3	38
Kazakh	0	1	43
Georgia	1	6	18
Armenia	0	2	12
Azerbaidzhan	0	3	12
Lithuania	—	—	12
Latvia	—	—	10
Estonia	—	—	6
Moldavia	—	—	8
Tadzhik	0	0	7
Kirgiz	0	0	9
Turkmen	0	0	5

SOURCE: *Narodnoye Khozyaistvo . . . v 1959, . . . v 1960 Godu, . . . v 1965 Godu, . . . and . . . v 1969 Godu.*

NOTE: Figures do not include technical or special secondary schools.

tration. Before the Revolution, only 2% of the population was literate. There were no native engineers, doctors, or teachers with a higher education. In short, central Asia was no different in this respect from most of the colonial dependencies of the European powers, and worse off than many.

Today, in the Uzbek Republic alone, there are thirty-eight institutions of higher learning, more than 159 technicums, and special technical schools, over a dozen teachers' colleges, and over 1,500 kindergartens. Over 3 million children attend school, and over 50% of its teachers have had some higher education. In addition, the republic has an Academy of Sciences and an Academy of Agricultural Sciences. The rate of literacy is over 95%. The republic before the Revolution possessed no public libraries; today there are over 7,000. The number of books printed in the Uzbek language in 1913 was 118,000; today it is over 25 million. When this record is compared with that of Iran, Afghanis-

tan, the Arab countries, the states of Southeast Asia, or even Turkey, all of which were at a comparable or more advanced level of educational attainment in 1914, the achievement is impressive.

Not only has the Soviet government assiduously developed the human potential among the non-Russian nationalities, but it has also paid serious attention to the education and training of women. In 1960, 49% of all Soviet citizens with some higher education and 53% of those with some secondary education were women. In 1970, women accounted for 54% of all students in special secondary schools, and 48% of enrollment in higher education. Soviet women are being educated in practically all fields of science, culture, technology, and the professions in rapidly increasing numbers.

It is evident that the Soviet Union has established the basic educational foundation for the creation of a postindustrial, mass-consumption, technetronic society. Emphasis from this point forward must be on the intensification and extension of the qualitative level of education and skills. Compulsory secondary education has been gradually extended to most of the rural areas, and as the Soviet Union approaches the age of universal, compulsory secondary education it must be prepared to contend both with its delights and agonies. Neither the Soviet standard of living, in terms of the quality and amenities of life, nor the Soviet political system, with its reliance on primitive and fraudulent democratic façades and charades, has kept pace with the increasingly large numbers of Soviet citizens who are culturally sensitive, politically sophisticated, highly skilled, imaginative, and intelligent, and are thus able to conceive and visualize better alternatives to the existing archaic political system. And yet the Soviet regime is committed to contribute to the growth of this element in the population, apparently cognizant of the latent, explosive social dynamite that it threatens to become.

Although the longitudinal development of Soviet education will continue—i.e., "longer" as opposed to "higher" education—the most difficult step in the universal education of a mass society is yet to come. Unlike the countries of Western Europe and very much like the United States, the Soviet regime is ultimately committed to universal higher education, not selective higher education, although for the moment existing facilities limit both the dimensions and pace of higher education. But even more quickly than the United States, because its educational development has progressed more rapidly than its economic, the Soviet government may find it impossible to create sufficient jobs suitable for highly educated, ambitious, and energetic youth and thus will unwittingly aggravate an emerging generational confrontation.

Nevertheless, the distance that the Soviet Union must still travel is not to be gleaned from the admittedly impressive quantitative achievements of Soviet higher education, and the Soviet tendency to exaggerate a creditable achievement results in some rather comic and pathetic displays of disproportion. Thus, one recent Soviet textbook seriously intones:

Suffice it to say that the number of students per 1,000 population in Soviet Kirgizia, whose people had no written language, is larger than France, Belgium, or Italy [and] as regards the achievements of Soviet Turkmenia in this sphere, she has overtaken not only the countries of the Middle East, but also Britain, France, and the Federal Republic of Germany.[9]

Clearly some discrimination is necessary to separate the quantitative and qualitative aspects of educational development in order to properly assess the Soviet achievement. Even if the University of Ashkabad turns out four times as many students as Heidelberg, Oxford, or the Sorbonne, Ashkabad will still have a long way to go.

A close examination of Soviet educational levels of attainment demonstrates quite clearly that the major task of educating the Soviet population still lies ahead. Thus, of the 95 million citizens over 10 years of age listed in the 1970 census as having at least an incomplete secondary education, only 8,262,000 had a complete higher education, while only 39,812,000 had a complete secondary education (10 years)

[9] B. Bayanov, Y. Unansky, and M. Shafir, *Soviet Socialist Democracy* (Moscow, 1968), p. 57.

—see Table 3-8. When measured against comparable levels of educational attainment in the United States, even the quantitative aspects of the Soviet educational achievement are somewhat diminished.

COMMUNICATIONS MEDIA

One of the earliest acts of the Bolshevik regime was to abolish the private ownership of newspapers, book-publishing firms, radio stations, and other mass-communications media and subject them to the control of the Soviet state. Although article 125 of the Soviet constitution guarantees the Soviet citizen "freedom of speech, . . . press, . . . assembly, including the holding of mass meetings, . . . street processions and demonstrations," the exercise of these "rights" is severely limited by the constitutional admonition that these rights shall be allowed only "in conformity with the interests of the working people, and in order to strengthen the Socialist system." All media of

TABLE 3-8. *Educational Levels of Achievement in the U.S. and the USSR, 1969/70 (thousands)*

	USSR (1970)	U.S. (1969)
Number of persons with secondary education		
Incomplete	47,368	51,341
Complete	36,811	47,700
Number of persons with higher education		
Incomplete	2,605	14,547
Complete	8,262	12,871
Totals	95,046	126,459

SOURCES: USSR figures from *Pravda*, April 17, 1971; U.S. figures calculated from population survey data in U.S. Bureau of the Census, *The Statistical Abstract of the U.S. 1971* (Washington, D.C.: G.P.O., 1970), p. 111.

public communication in the Soviet Union are thus directly or indirectly owned or controlled by agencies of the government and the Communist party, whether they be national or local in scope.

Soviet Control of Information and Opinion

Within the framework of the Soviet system, communications media, like the educational system, are considered instruments of indoctrination and propaganda rather than vehicles of information and recreation, and they are utilized to reshape the minds of the Soviet people into the mold of communist ideology. All information coming from abroad is rigorously censored by the government, and information originating within the USSR is revised to further the objectives of the system.

As the Soviet system increases in power and stability, the mass media "have been" allowed to relax their drive for indoctrination. Ownership and control, however, remain in the hands of the state and the party, although greater latitude may be permitted individual editors and writers who can be relied on not to publish anything that would consciously injure the Soviet system. But the party remains vigilant and has the last word.

By the time of Stalin's death, the widening gap between an increasingly educated public and a communications system dedicated to propaganda and monotonous indoctrination could no longer be perpetuated without seriously damaging the Soviet system. Stalin's successors have been more lenient because they have greater confidence in the political reliability of the Soviet people and their loyalty to the system. Since 1953, publishers and journalists have been permitted a wider range of discretion, and some have produced works they knew beforehand would not be welcomed by the regime. Errant writers are no longer always expelled to Siberia or executed, although they are still often subjected to harsh criticism and are asked to revise their material and some have been committed to lunatic asylums.

After Khruschev's removal, ideological controls and censorship were intensified somewhat, arousing fears that the liberalization process might be reversed. Liberal writers and poets were subjected to harsh criticism, and in some cases to administrative harassment. Although they continue to travel abroad in response to invitations, it is with less certainty in the expectation of receiving permission from the authorities. On the eve of the Twenty-third Party Congress, which was convened in March 1966, twenty-six prominent Soviet intellectuals addressed a letter to the Central Committee, opposing the possible rehabilitation of Stalin at the congress—an act which was apparently widely feared among Soviet intellectuals. The harsh sentences meted out in 1966 to Andrei Sinyavsky and Yuri Daniel, two Soviet writers who published satirical accounts of Soviet society abroad under pseudonyms, also agitated the Soviet intellectual community, and appeared to many to be little more than an artless attempt to intimidate independently minded authors. And in May 1967, the prominent Soviet writer Solzhenitsyn (*A Day in the Life of Ivan Denisovich*) addressed a letter to the Soviet Writers' Congress, then meeting in Moscow, in which he complained of administrative harassment and persecution, the confiscation of his manuscripts by the secret police, the refusal of publishing houses to publish his material, and the rejection of permission to travel abroad. He called upon the Writers' Congress to defend and protect writers against administrative restrictions, and demanded that it condemn the existing system of bureaucratic censorship for which there was no warrant in the Soviet constitution.

Although Solzhenitsyn's letter was not published in the Soviet union, it was published abroad, and the Writers' Congress did come to his assistance, and his manuscripts were retrieved from the secret police. The situation remains in flux, though the general long-range trend is in the direction of greater freedom and liberalization. Solzhenitsyn's major works have not been published in the USSR although he won a Nobel prize.

Newspapers and Magazines

Newspapers and magazines are the chief printed media for the dissemination of information and propaganda in the Soviet Union. The printed word in the USSR appears in nearly one hundred different languages, sixty of them in languages spoken by Soviet nationalities. In 1969, over 9,000 newspapers were being published, with a combined circulation of over 135 million, or more than one copy for every two Soviet citizens. Since Stalin's death, a calculated effort has been made to infuse greater liveliness and individuality into periodicals, but variety is still depressingly absent.

Of the nearly 8,000 newspapers in the USSR, less than thirty are national in character, and they account for more than one-third of the total circulation. Of these, the most important and well known are *Pravda* (the official organ of the Central Committee of the Communist party) and *Izvestia* (the official journal of the government). *Pravda*'s circulation in 1969 was listed as 8.4 million, *Izvestia*'s as about 8.3 million.[10] The organ of the Young Communist League, *Komsomolskaya Pravda*, under the aggressive editorship of Alexei Adzhubei, Khrushchev's son-in-law, outstripped *Izvestia*'s circulation and hit over 7 million in 1967. (Adzhubei later became editor of *Izvestia*, and was dismissed upon the ouster of his father-in-law.)

Every union republic, national ethnic group, and large city publishes its own newspaper. The overwhelming number of Soviet

[10] *Yezhegodnik Bolshaya Sovetskaya Entsiklopediya,* 1970 (Moscow, 1970), p. 105.

journals are local publications, including nearly 3,000 collective-farm newspapers. National, or all-union, newspapers are essentially organs of various organizations: *Krasnaya Zvezda* is published by the Armed Forces, *Literaturnaya Gazeta* by the Union of Writers, *Trud* by the trade unions. *Pravda,* as we have seen, is the official organ of the Communist party, *Izvestia* of the government. All Soviet newspapers must thus speak for some legally recognized group, since privately owned newspapers are prohibited. Dissident elements are thereby effectively deprived of any opportunity to employ the printed word. Needless to say, the policies of the state are never subject to attack except in the rare instance when the leadership is divided and various newspapers are controlled by contending factions. Once the struggle for power is resolved, conformity is once again imposed.

The Soviet Union is a land not only of newspapers, but of periodicals as well—political, scholarly, and popular. In 1969, Soviet sources reported the publication of 5,552 periodicals (total circulation: nearly 150 million items), of which about 800 were magazines, the others being bulletins, circulars, and throwaways. Soviet magazines are published in nearly sixty languages, of which forty-one are languages of Soviet nationalities. Like the newspapers, magazines in the Soviet Union are printed and published by state-recognized organizations and agencies.

TABLE 3-9. *Radio and TV Sets manufactured and in use in the USSR, 1940–69 (thousands)*

	1928	1940	1945	1950	1955	1958	1960	1965	1969
In use									
Radios	70	1,123	475	3,643	6,097	21,694	27,811	38,228	46,700
Wired speakers	22	5,853	5,589	9,685	19,544	27,000	30,800	35,638	43,400
TV sets	—	0.4	0.2	15	823	3,000	4,800	15,693	30,800
Production									
Radios	—	—	—	—	3,530	3,900	4,165	5,160	7,266
TV sets	—	—	—	—	496	1,000	1,726	3,655	6,596

SOURCE: *Narodnoye Khozyaistvo . . . v 1969 Godu.*

It should be noted, and perhaps emphasized, that the only foreign newspapers and magazines sold in the Soviet Union are those published in other Communist countries (except Albania and China) or by friendly Communist parties in non-Communist countries. Thus, non-Communist newspapers and magazines are not available at Soviet news outlets, and are available in libraries only by special permission. Most of the Communist states of Eastern Europe, however, allow non-Communist foreign newspapers and magazines to be sold on a restrictive basis which varies from one country to another. Thus, aside from the news available through foreign radio broadcasts, Soviet citizens remain essentially a captive audience of the regime.

Radio and Television

From the very inception of the Soviet regime, radio was envisaged as one of the most important instruments of indoctrination and propaganda. The Soviets zealously began to construct broadcasting facilities and to manufacture radios and distribute them to the people. They even devised a method to prevent the Soviet public from hearing foreign radio broadcasts, by creating elaborate systems of wired speakers in central meeting and assembly areas that could receive only official programs. As more people acquired their own sets, however, this system became increasingly inadequate, and the government resorted to "jamming" (rendering inaudible) unwanted foreign broadcasts. But this was an extremely costly and often ineffective procedure, and most foreign radio broadcasts are no longer systematically jammed: the news and other programs of the BBC and the Voice of America can now be tuned in by Soviet citizens without interference—although, ironically, the abusive broadcasts from Peking continue to be jammed.[11] The number of receivers in the Soviet Union now exceeds the number of wired speakers, and by 1966 virtually every urban family had its own receiver, usually capable of receiving foreign broadcasts, which are very popular in the Soviet Union.

Television is still in an infant stage of development in the Soviet Union. As of 1969, there were more than 30 million sets in use, with 120 TV stations in operation. Television transmission is still limited to the large cities, but the government is planning a rapid expansion of television broadcasting, since not only does it offer greater political and educational possibilities than radio, but is less subject to outside intrusion, at least in the present state of electronic technology. Over 8 million TV sets were produced in 1969, and the total of 40 million sets slated for production by 1970 appears to have been met. In March 1965, the Soviet Union signed an agreement with France whereby the Soviets agreed to develop the French color TV system, and thus ultimately enable Soviet citizens to watch foreign TV programs.

11 Voice of America broadcasts were jammed again selectively after the Soviet invasion of Czechoslovakia in August 1968.

THE PHILOSOPHY
OF KARL MARX

The official ideology of the Soviet Union is called Marxism-Leninism to distinguish it from other varieties and interpretations of Marxism. As a philosophical system, Marxism owes its origin not only to the great fund of accumulated Western philosophy, but more immediately to many of the currents and ideas that were prevalent in the nineteenth century. The century that produced Marx also produced Comte, Darwin, J. S. Mill, Spencer, and others, all of whom were preoccupied with the development of comprehensive theories of history and society. Marx and his group of followers imagined that just as Darwin had discovered the "laws" of evolution, Marx had discovered the "laws" governing the development of history and society.

Three ideological strands merged into Marxism: (1) German philosophical idealism, particularly that of Hegel, from whom Marx derived his dialectical method of history; (2) French revolutionary and utopian doctrines, to which Marxism owes its revolutionary militancy and its doctrine of a classless and stateless society; (3) British classical economic theory, especially that of Ricardo, from whom Marx appropriated his labor theory of value. As a comprehensive philosophy, Marxism purports to explain everything. It encompasses theories of human nature, society, history, economics, politics, ethics, esthetics, knowledge, and logic. It simultaneously seeks to explain the world (a theory of analysis or reality) and to change it in conformity with certain preconceived social norms (a normative theory or theory of utopia). Thus Marx boasted before he was 30 years old that "the philosophers have *interpreted* the world in various ways; the point however is to *change* it." [1]

---

[1] Karl Marx, *Selected Works* (New York: International Publishers, n.d.), 1:473.

FOUR

*ideological
foundations*

The Dialectical Process

Dialectics is a process of discovering the truth (intellectual or factual) by revealing the contradictions in an opponent's argument or ideas, or in nature itself. Hegel's dialectic gave primacy to the inner conflict of ideas and their synthesis within the recurrent triadic formula of thesis (idea), antithesis (counteridea), and synthesis (fusion of idea and counteridea), which automatically becomes a new thesis. For Hegel, the conflict of ideas shaped the development of the physical world, which was its reflection, and thus Hegel's system is sometimes called *dialectical idealism* to distinguish it from Marx's *dialectical materialism*. The chief characteristic of the dialectic is its dynamic quality, for the world is viewed as being in a state of constant transformation and motion, in contrast to the normal tendency to view reality as static or evolutionary. Thus, Marx describes the dialectical process as "the science of the general laws of motion—both of the external world and of human thought."[2]

In contrast to Hegel, whose movement was divinely inspired, Marx's dialectic is *naturalistic* in that change is inherent in reality itself and results from the energies released by internal contradictory forces, not from something external, like a prime mover or God.

The Marxist Theory of History

Marx appropriated Hegel's dialectic, but gave it a materialistic content. Claiming that he found Hegel's system standing on its head and restored it right side up, Marx asserted that instead of the earthly world being a reflection of the dialectical development of ideas in conflict and synthesis, the ideas were in fact a reflection of the dialectical process working itself out in the physical world.

The application of Marx's dialectical method to the study of history and society is

[2] Quoted in V. I. Lenin, *Selected Works* (New York: International Publishers, n.d.), 2:17.

called *historical materialism*. For Marx, history moves neither in a straight line nor in a circle nor fortuitously, but rather moves upward through predetermined stages. By apprehending the laws of social development, it is possible, on the basis of the past and present, to predict several stages of development in the future.

Each succeeding stage of history is more progressive than the preceding one, and hence the special meaning of "progress" in Marxist-Leninist terminology must be understood in terms of movement along the historical dialectic. Thus, a slave society is more progressive than primitive communism, a feudal society superior to a slave-based economy, a capitalist society preferable to a feudal order but in turn inferior to a socialist society, which in turn is less progressive than a Communist society. Accordingly, each historical stage contains the seeds of its own destruction and constitutes the womb out of which its successor emerges. Each phase makes its contribution to civilization, a part of which is carried over from one stage to the next, thus giving an organic unity to historical movement and to human civilization.

The Class Struggle

The fuel that powers the historical dialectic is manufactured by the class struggle. The two conflicting classes are those who own the land and the means of production and those who must work and operate them in order to live. Those without property are forced to deliver their labor in return for a bare subsistence living. According to Marx's "surplus labor" theory of value, all value is created by labor, which is expropriated by those who own the means of production, who pay out in wages just enough to keep the workers alive. This is the Marxist meaning of "exploitation of man by man." Thus, an irreconcilable conflict between classes prevails which is resolved by revolution, only to reappear in new form. Capitalism, Marx wrote, is the last historical society in which exploitation of man by man will exist. With the advent of the proletarian revolution, the expropriation of the capitalists, and the establishment of socialism, humanity will finally emancipate itself from exploitation and the class struggle. In the words of the *Communist Manifesto:*

The history of all hitherto existing society is the history of class struggles. Freeman and slave, patrician and plebian, lord and serf, guildmaster and journeyman, in a word oppressor and oppressed stood in constant opposition to one another, carried on an uninterrupted, now hidden, now open fight, a fight that each time ended either in a revolutionary reconstruction of society at large, or in the common ruin of the contending classes. . . . In our epoch . . . society as a whole is more and more splitting up into two great hostile camps, into two great classes directly facing each other—bourgeoisie and proletariat.[3]

Economic Determinism

The specific form of the class struggle is determined by the way in which society organizes the instruments and means of production. Thus, in the Marxist scheme, the given economic order constitutes the foundation of society and determines the character of the social, political, ethical, and legal "superstructure" which it supports. When the economic foundations change, the "superstructure" inevitably crumbles, to be reestablished in conformity with the contours set by the new economic relations. At any stage of history, those who own the instruments of production constitute an exploiting class, which seeks to preserve the given economic order from which it benefits.

But the economic foundations of society are fluid and cannot remain fixed, for, in accordance with the dialectical laws of contradiction, man, in his eternal search for more efficient instruments of production, renders the existing system increasingly obsolete and automatically subverts the prevailing order. Those who stand to gain most from the new methods of production are inevitably shaped into a class hostile to those who benefit from the existing system. The class struggle is thus joined. The old class is overthrown; the new is enthroned, and the en-

tire superstructure of society—social relations, political institutions, morals, etc.—is then automatically adjusted to correspond with the new economic foundations of society. In a famous passage from Marx:

In the social production of their means of existence men enter into definite, necessary relations which are independent of their will, productive relationships which correspond to a definite state of development of their material productive forces. The aggregate of these productive relationships constitutes the economic structure of society, the real basis on which a juridical and political superstructure arises, and to which definite forms of social consciousness correspond. The mode of production of the material means of existence conditions the whole process of social, political and intellectual life. It is not the consciousness of men that determines their existence, but, on the contrary, it is their social existence that determines their consciousness. At a certain stage of their development the material productive forces of society come into contradiction with the existing productive relationships, or, what is but a legal expression for these, with the property relationships within which they had moved before. From forms of development of the productive forces these relationships are transformed into their fetters. Then an epoch of social revolution opens. With the change in the economic foundation the whole vast superstructure is more or less rapidly transformed.[4]

It must be understood that these changes in the fundamental economic structure of society, according to Marx, proceed irrespective of man's will or cognizance and can be determined with scientific accuracy.[5] They are inevitable, and movement from one stage of history to the next cannot be prevented, although man can intervene to speed up or delay the process, providing he has become aware of the dialectical laws governing the movement of history. Marx called his socialism "scientific" because the society he had been anticipating was destined to come inevitably, not because of man's hopes and wishes (as with utopian socialism).

---

[3] Marx, *Selected Works,* 1:205–6.

[4] Quoted in Emil Burns, *A Handbook of Marxism* (New York: Random House, 1935), pp. 371–72.

[5] See Friedrich Engels, *Socialism: Utopian and Scientific* (New York: International Publishers, n.d.).

The Proletarian Revolution

The most relevant aspect of Marxism for us here is, of course, the transition from capitalism to socialism and the processes by which this is accomplished. Under capitalism, according to Marx, society is divided into two great contending classes: the capitalists—owners of factories, business enterprises, financial institutions, and other means of production—who become constantly smaller in numbers as they grow wealthier; and the proletariat, which becomes more impoverished as it grows more numerous. With the increasing concentration of wealth into fewer hands and the increasing misery of the vast majority, the downtrodden proletariat becomes conscious of its historical mission, which is to overthrow the capitalist ruling class, not only in its own interests but in the interests of society as a whole.

The proletarian revolution was thus supposed to take place in an advanced industrialized society, in which "the lower strata of the middle class—the small tradespeople, shopkeepers, and retired tradesmen generally, the handicraftsmen and peasants—all these sink gradually into the proletariat . . . and . . . the proletariat is recruited from all classes of the population." [6] In contrast to "all previous historical movements [which] were movements of minorities, or in the interest of minorities . . . the proletarian movement is the self-conscious, independent movement of the immense majority, in the interest of the immense majority." [7]

The consequence of the revolution is the elevation of the proletariat as the ruling class and the establishment of a "dictatorship of the proletariat," whose primary purpose is to expropriate the capitalists in favor of the state and to suppress the overthrown *bourgeoisie* and eliminate it as a class, as a prelude to the elimination of classes, class struggles, and exploitation generally. Ultimately, the state would "wither away."

[6] Marx, *Selected Works*, 1:213.
[7] Ibid., 217.

The Theory of the State

"The State," wrote Lenin, "inevitably came into being at a definite stage in the development of society, when society had split into irreconcilable classes, . . . ostensibly standing above society," but in fact protecting the interests of the property-owning classes. All states, therefore, are class states; i.e., they are instruments of the ruling economic class, whose interests they serve. The idea that the state is an impartial agent standing above society and classes as a referee or umpire is rejected as a myth inspired and perpetuated by the ruling class as part of the prevailing ideology. A society's legal system and courts, its philosophy, religion, education, morality, and even art all play their role in disguising the class nature of the state by rationalizing, justifying, and sanctifying the existing social order. The state, with its legal monopoly of the instruments of coercion (army, police, law, courts, etc.) preserves that status quo, by force if necessary.

LENIN: THE EMERGENCE OF VOLUNTARISM

The dialectical movement of history was asserted by Marx to be independent of man's will. It is this imperative of inevitability which imparts to Marxism its predictive or scientific quality. For if history indeed moves along a predetermined arc, knowledge of the "laws" governing this movement will enable men to predict the future. But to "predict" human history means also to "control" and manipulate history. It is precisely this manipulative quality of Marxism which was in direct conflict with the scientific theory of inevitability. The idea that events can be shaped and determined by the will of man is called *voluntarism,* which is considered by Marxists to be the diametric opposite of determinism. Voluntarism, however, is more than implicit in Marxism. If determinism was necessary to impart to the system its pseudo-scientific character, voluntarism was just as indispensable to guarantee that the scientifically predicted future would come about.

"Give me an organization of revolutionists," Lenin boasted, "and we shall overturn the whole of Russia." Later, he asserted that "politics cannot but have precedence over economics. To argue differently means forgetting the ABC of Marxism." [8] Under these conditions, Marxism was transformed from a "science" into a self-fulfilling prophecy in which men organize to achieve events which theory postulates to be inevitable!

Lenin's Theory of Party Organization

Nothing illustrates better the influence of voluntarism than Lenin's theory of the Communist party. By 1900, most of the socialist political parties inspired by the ideas of Karl Marx had abandoned active revolutionary objectives in favor of becoming parliamentary parties seeking to win control of the government at the ballot box or by some other legal means. The Marxist notions of a proletarian revolution to smash the "bourgeois bureaucratic state machine," and establish a "dictatorship of the proletariat" had been largely abandoned. Even the idea of the "class struggle" had been considerably deemphasized and had been replaced by political and parliamentary maneuvering.

The mellowing impact that parliamentary institutions had on Marxist parties in the West, however, was notably absent in imperial Russia, where neither a parliament nor legal political parties existed before the Revolution of 1905. Thus, a greater profusion of terroristic and conspiratorial political groups sprang up in nineteenth-century Russia than in the West. It was virtually inevitable that Marxist movements in Russia would in some measure retain the kernel of their terroristic origins.

This was particularly true of the Bolshevik wing of the Russian Social Democratic party, which emerged as a distinct organizational movement under Lenin's leadership after 1903. It was Lenin's view that a proletarian revolution was likely to come about, not spontaneously, but rather through the calculated efforts of a professional and militant organization acting in behalf of the proletariat. The historical mission of the proletarian class was thus to be guided by a revolutionary elite, whose primary purpose was not to express the momentary whims of the masses, or to win votes at ballot boxes, or to engage in parliamentary maneuvering or debates, but rather to execute the preordained mission of the proletariat by mobilizing the masses in a revolutionary assault against the capitalist ruling class. Lenin therefore placed great emphasis on leadership and discipline, on a militant spirit and on effective political organization.

Since the proletariat had a single purpose, the party could have but a single will; it could not be divided into factions and converted into a futile debating society. The minority view would always have to be subordinated to the will of the majority in accordance with what Lenin called the principle of "democratic centralism," which meant that the authority of the party would come to rest in its executive bodies. When Lenin first revealed his ideas on the party in 1903, Leon Trotsky (only 23 years old at the time) subjected it to scathing and prophetic criticism:

The organization of the Party takes the place of the Party itself; the Central Committee takes the place of the organization; and finally the dictator takes the place of the Central Committee.[9]

Although its primary purpose was to maximize the effectiveness of revolutionary action, the principle of "democratic centralism" harbored the germ of what subsequently emerged as Soviet totalitarianism, because after the Revolution the principles of Bolshevik party organization were extended to the whole of society.

Lenin's Theory of Revolution in Russia

Lenin was primarily interested in bringing about a proletarian revolution in Russia. But

[8] Lenin, *Selected Works*, 9:54.

[9] Quoted in Bertram D. Wolfe, *Three Who Made a Revolution* (New York: Dial Press, 1948), p. 253.

whereas Marx had predicted that the proletarian revolution would take place initially in advanced industrial societies like England and Germany, Russia was overwhelmingly backward culturally, had a basically agricultural economy, and was feudal in its political organization and practices.

Lenin, however, argued that since the revolution was inevitable, it was unnecessary to await the full maturation of capitalism. Rather than wait for the proletariat to grow and develop a class consciousness, which might take an intolerably long time, the party could act *for* the proletariat, and thus a proletarian revolution could take place as soon as any society embarked upon the road of capitalist development. This doctrine was little more than a disingenuous rationalization for an anticapitalist revolution in Russia at a time when the country had just entered the phase of capitalism.

In order to compensate for the fact that the Russian proletariat was no less a minority of the population than the *bourgeoisie* and to provide moral justification for a revolution executed on behalf of a minority class, Lenin contrived the formula of an "alliance" between the working class and the peasantry. The Bolsheviks could then carry out a revolution on behalf of the proletariat in alliance with the peasants. In this way, Lenin sought to impart the color of "democracy" to the Revolution. It was not his intention, however, that the peasants would share power with the proletariat or its party, for although a government of workers and peasants would be established, the party would retain a monopoly of power on behalf of the proletariat and would dictate the policies of the government.

Lenin's Theory of Imperialism

One of Lenin's most significant contributions to Marxist doctrine was his theory of imperialism, formulated just prior to the Revolution, while he was in exile in Switzerland. His short book *Imperialism, the Highest Stage of Capitalism,* remains of utmost importance because it not only provided Lenin with a further rationalization of the revolution in Russia, but

it also served to explain why certain of the Marxist predictions about revolutions did not materialize in western Europe. Lenin's *Imperialism* remains one of the basic documents upon which the Soviet perception of the world still rests, and it has become particularly relevant in understanding Soviet policies in the underdeveloped and ex-colonial countries of the world.

According to Lenin's *Imperialism,* Western capitalism had managed temporarily to delay its inevitable doom through revolution by the device of colonial imperialism. By establishing overseas dependencies, the major capitalist powers of Europe were able to invest capital in the colonies and, in return, receive raw materials for processing which were then exported as manufactured goods. In this way, Lenin concluded, new outlets were found for surplus capital, old jobs were preserved for the workers and new ones created, and new markets were found for goods which could not profitably be absorbed in domestic markets.

The transformation of capitalism into imperialism, Lenin wrote, resulted in several important consequences: (1) The standard of living of the upper strata of the working class in the major capitalist countries was raised, thus blunting their class consciousness and diverting them away from revolution and into trade unions and preoccupation with higher wages and better conditions of work. According to Lenin, these elements of the working class had become unwitting allies of the capitalists in exploiting the colonies and could no longer be relied upon to bring about a revolution. (2) The socialist revolution in the advanced countries was temporarily delayed, but new internal strains and stresses were introduced into the capitalist system, which was transformed from a national system in each individual country into an international system, involving the entire world, both backward and advanced areas. In Lenin's view, imperialism was the final, overripe stage of world capitalism, the phase in which all the devices contrived to prolong the existence of capitalism were exhausted, making it ready for revolutionary conflagration. (3) The internationalization of the capitalist system created entirely new revolutionary possibilities completely unforeseen by Marx and Engels. The class struggle, instead of now being the individual affair of each country, was internationalized, and the focus of revolutionary contradictions shifted away from the advanced industrial centers to their periphery in the colonial and semicolonial societies, which were subjected to ruthless exploitation by international capitalism. (4) The division of the world into colonial empires of the various capitalist states not only internationalized the class struggle, but wars as well, which were transformed into worldwide conflicts as the capitalists fought over the division and redistribution of markets and colonies.

In accordance with this analysis, Lenin maintained that prior to the existence of imperialism, the class struggle and the impetus to revolution proceeded more-or-less independently in each country, depending on its economic development. Now, however, capitalism had become worldwide through the formation of international monopolies and cartels, and the advanced countries used their advantage to arrest the development of the less advanced regions of the world. The greatest possibilities of revolution were to be found, not in the industrial countries, but at the "weakest link" in the world capitalist chain, where the "front" of capitalism was exposed and the revolutionary ferment was most intense. Not the size of the proletariat, but its revolutionary consciousness and zeal would determine the location of proletarian revolutions.

Lenin believed that Russia was in 1917 this "weakest link" and that an uprising in Russia could plunge the entire world into a revolutionary convulsion. The "imperialist" war (World War I), he thought, could be transformed into a worldwide civil war in which the proletariat of Europe would join with the colonial populations against their imperialist rulers. The failure of the revolution to spread, however, soon produced a new crisis in the theory of communism.

STALIN: THE HARDENING OF TOTALITARIANISM

Lenin died in 1924, and his successors were confronted with an uncertain future. Neither Marx nor Lenin had provided a precise blueprint for maintaining a revolution in isolation in a predominantly agricultural country. If Lenin converted Marxism into a revolutionary formula for seizing power in virtually any society with a vast dispossessed and discontented population, it was left to Joseph Stalin to further transform Marxism into an instrument of industrialization and modernization of backward societies.

"Socialism in One Country"

The idea of building a socialist society in a backward country like Russia seemed to some of the Bolshevik intellectuals and leaders, particularly to Leon Trotsky, as both impossible and a deviation from Marxism. Stalin, however, was a man endowed with extraordinary talents for organization, administration, and political intrigue. He occupied the post of general secretary of the party, which he quickly converted into a powerful and strategic springboard for seizing control of first the party apparatus, then the party itself, and then the state. Considered by most of his colleagues to be an intellect of mediocre caliber, Stalin possessed a sharp mind with a firm grasp of the situation. He understood power and men and possessed an exceptional ability to size up a situation immediately, reach quick decisions, and implement them with an implacable determination.

To silence his opponents, Stalin contrived the idea of "socialism in one country" and shrewdly ascribed the theory to the dead Lenin, whose loyal and faithful disciple he repeatedly claimed to be. The theory found a responsive echo not only among the Communist rank and file, but among ordinary citizens of the country as well. They preferred constructive promises linked with Russia's national security and national development to the anxieties and turmoil promised by the policy of "permanent revolution" advocated by Trotsky, in which Russia was to spearhead revolution in the name of Communist internationalism. The people of Russia were tired of war and revolution; they wanted peace and an opportunity to reconstruct their homes and country.

Stalin was determined to modernize and industrialize Soviet Russia, not only that it might become a powerful country in its own right, but also that it might serve more effectively as a base for expanding the Communist revolution. Socialism was to be developed through a series of five-year plans, which required a single-minded purpose and concentrated effort for their successful fulfillment. Stalin's modernization program was based on three principles: (1) first priority was to go to the construction of heavy industry, which would enhance the military power of the state; (2) agriculture was to be collectivized and mechanized in order to destroy the capitalist system of private farming in the countryside, to increase agricultural production, and to permit the siphoning off of labor into the cities and factories; (3) a large reservoir of scientific personnel and skilled workers was to be created through a centrally planned and directed program of education. Once the state-owned heavy-industrial base had been constructed and stabilized, the farms collectivized, and an appropriate level of educational and technological achievement reached, Soviet Russia would automatically enter an era of socialism.

Stalin's powerful resolve to impose his program of "socialism in one country" against all opposition, internal and external, profoundly affected the entire theoretical structure of Soviet Marxism, to say nothing of its concrete application. The Marxist-Leninist doctrines on the organization and functions of the party, the nature and role of the state in a socialist society, the destiny of the world revolution, and the delicate balance between Communist internationalism and Russian nationalism were all subjected to radical revision.

From Party Dictatorship to Personal Dictatorship

In 1903, Trotsky had predicted that Lenin's theory of party organization and leadership logically would culminate in the establishment of a personal dictatorship. Under Stalin, this is, in fact, what actually happened. In his secret speech before the Twentieth Party Congress in 1956, Nikita Khrushchev finally conceded what had been widely known and acknowledged both outside and inside the USSR: that the Soviet Union under Stalin was governed by the most brutal and capricious form of personal dictatorship, masquerading as a "dictatorship of the proletariat" under the leadership of the party.

After the party seized power in 1917 and established a monopoly over all political activity and organization, expulsion from the party meant political extinction. Since all rival parties were dissolved and declared illegal, the only opposition to the party line could come from within the party itself, and, as a result, various factional groupings, "oppositions," and deviations developed within the party against that of the majority view. As long as it was expressed before a decision had been taken on a particular question, opposition was considered by Lenin to be legitimate, but once a vote had been taken, the minority was duty-bound to subordinate its views to the majority.

Stalin started out in the same way, but once he had solidly entrenched himself in power, he applied measures, reserved by Lenin for the outside enemies of the system, to his rivals in the party. His major theoretical contribution in this connection, if it can be so described, was the concept of the "enemy of the people," which meant that any person so designated was charged with counterrevolutionary and treasonable activities and then executed, imprisoned, or banished, with or without trial. Thus, according to Nikita Khrushchev's indictment of Stalin before the Twentieth Party Congress:

Stalin originated the concept "enemy of the people." This term automatically rendered it unnecessary that the ideological errors of a man or men engaged in a controversy be proved; this term made possible the usage of the most cruel repression, violating all norms of revolutionary legality, against anyone who in any way disagreed with Stalin, against those who were suspected of hostile intent, against those who had bad reputations.[10]

[10] The full text of Khrushchev's secret speech on "the cult of personality," is reprinted in Bertram D. Wolfe, *Khrushchev and Stalin's Ghost* (New York: Praeger, 1957).

It should be noted, however, that despite what developed in practice, Stalin never repudiated the principle of "collective leadership," but always maintained that he was simply the spokesman for the Central Committee or the Politburo of the party. Nor did he countenance the formulation of a theory of personal rule, although in practice and in ceremony he both fostered and demanded sychophantic adulation, which, in the words of Khrushchev, transformed him "into a superman possessing supernatural characteristics akin to those of a god. Such a man supposedly knows everything, sees everything, thinks for everyone, can do anything, is infallible in his behavior." [11]

Stalin's Theory of the Soviet State

The 1936 proclamation of socialism in the USSR required some fundamental revisions of the basic doctrine of the state. Since, theoretically, the class struggle and exploitation by the ruling classes had been eradicated, what was to be the function of the Soviet state? In 1930, at the Sixteenth Party Congress, Stalin boasted that the Soviet state was the mightiest in all history, and that well before it would, like all other states, inevitably "wither away," it most assuredly would become even more powerful. But the issue of a mighty leviathan in a socialist society continued to haunt the Communist party. Stalin himself raised the problem at the Eighteenth Party Congress in 1939:

It is sometimes asked: We have abolished the exploiting classes; there are no longer any hostile classes in the country; there is nobody to suppress; hence there is no more need for the state; it must die away. . . . Now, the Marxist doctrine of the state says that there is to be no state under Communism. Why then do we not help our Socialist state die away? [12]

Stalin then proceeded to review the Marxist literature on the "withering away" of the state,

and concluded that classical Marxist doctrine is applicable when socialism has been established in a number of countries simultaneously, but it is not applicable when it is being built in just a single country. By 1950, in another major theoretical disquisition, Stalin finally concluded that the Soviet state represented the interests of society as a whole. Indeed, under Stalin major emphasis was put on strengthening the state.

Stalin and World Revolution

Stalin's doctrine of "socialism in one country" was not a repudiation of world revolution. As long as Soviet Russia was weak, Stalin believed, it could not actively promote world revolution. But if Russia were transformed into a strong industrial and military power, it could effectively support revolutionary movements elsewhere, with the assistance of the Red Army if necessary. To ensure that the Soviet Union would be converted into a base for world revolution, the Communist International (Comintern) and Communist parties in all countries were required to give first loyalty to the Soviet Union as the only fatherland of the world proletariat, and were thus forced to submit to the complete discipline of Moscow. Those foreign Communists who resisted the centralization and domination of the Comintern by the Soviet party were expelled, and gradually the Comintern was completely subjugated to the dictates of Stalin; foreign Communist parties became willing instruments of Soviet policy, and acted as fifth columns by engaging in espionage and subversion.

Stalin proclaimed that the world revolution was impossible without the Soviet base and that consequently the interests of the world revolution were identical with the interests of the Soviet Union. Therefore, anything that strengthened the Soviet Union promoted the world revolution; anything that reacted adversely toward Moscow retarded the world revolution. In this way, the interests of the Soviet Union as a state were irrevocably fused with the interests of promoting world revolution, and the interests of all Communists in the world were tied to the preservation of the Soviet nation-state.

11 Ibid.
12 J. V. Stalin, *Leninism: Selected Writings* (New York: International Publishers, 1942), pp. 468–69.

After World War II, when Communist parties were installed in power in Eastern Europe, Stalin insisted that Communist leaders would have to continue to sacrifice the interests of their own countries to the greater glory and power of the Soviet Union, which remained the base of the world revolutionary movement. Marshal Tito of Yugoslavia successfully rebelled against this view in 1948, advocating instead that individual Communist parties owed first loyalty to their own country; otherwise the Stalinist principle of "proletarian internationalism" would be nothing short of Soviet imperialism, with the most powerful Communist country exploiting the weaker and smaller ones. Communist leaders in the other satellite states of Eastern Europe who were suspected of harboring views similar to those of Marshal Tito were removed (many were imprisoned or executed, after the manner of Stalin's earlier victims) under Soviet pressure, even though they were leaders of foreign countries. Between 1948 and 1952, a succession of bloody purges and executions swept the entire satellite world.

Stalinism and the Russian Heritage

Not only did Soviet totalitarianism reach its full flowering under Stalin, but the doctrine of "socialism in one country" also caused the traditional cultural and historical forces of Russia to blend with the new dynamics of Marxism. Marxism profoundly altered Russia, but itself was profoundly altered in turn. Marxism gave order to the primitive anarchical impulses of Russia, while Russian traditionalism succeeded in channeling Marxism into a unique secular religion, at once both terrifying and effective.

Many of the influences of the Russian tradition upon Marxism were inevitable. After all, socialism was not being built in a vacuum but in Russia—in historic Russia, with its cultural traditions, geography, and people. The language of Russia became the language of socialism and communism, and the vanguard of the world proletariat was to become the Russian working class, with its own memories and responses.

A backward country, Russia, was to be transformed into the first country of socialism.

In order to tap the spiritual and physical resources of the Russian people, Stalin, beginning in 1934, systematically resurrected Russia's past glories and grandeur, even to the point of retrospectively refurbishing her tsars and territorial conquests with progressive intentions and consequences. In his characteristically ingenious way, Stalin saw in Russian nationalism the ultimate key to the success of his policies. With the support of the Russian people, his program might succeed; without that support, it was doomed. Russia's past was rewritten as a reflection of the Soviet present, and both Ivan the Terrible and Peter the Great were recreated in Stalin's image. In this way, Stalin was made into a legitimate extension of Russia's long history.

The revival of Russian nationalism reached its zenith during World War II, when the very survival of the Stalinist regime depended on the loyalty and patriotism of the Russians, which could be more effectively exploited by an appeal to Russian nationalism than by Marxist slogans. Virtually all the old Marxist clichés vanished, while Russia's past heroes and their military exploits were resurrected. Traditional ranks and titles were reinstituted in the civil service, diplomatic corps, and military and police forces, and gilt-edged shoulderboards reappeared on tsarist-type uniforms. Numerous medals were struck honoring the generals and admirals of Russia's past, and Stalin himself was appointed first a marshal of the Soviet Union and then generalissimo of the armed forces. The war itself was called the "Second Great Patriotic War of the Soviet Union," the first being the national resistance against Napoleon in 1812. "The war you are waging is a war of liberation," Stalin urged four months after the German attack. "Let the manly images of our great ancestors—Alexander Nevsky, Dmitri Donskoi, Kuzma Minin, Dmitri Pozharsky, Alexander Suvorov, Mikhail Kutuzov—inspire you in this war!" [13]

[13] J. V. Stalin, *The Great Patriotic War of the Soviet Union* (New York: International Publishers, 1945), pp. 37–38.

SOVIET IDEOLOGY
SINCE STALIN

The death of Stalin unleashed new ideological forces in the Soviet Union which cracked the shell of Stalinist dogma. Innovations in both internal and foreign policy took place almost immediately after his death, culminating in the denunciation, at the Twentieth Party Congress in 1956, of the old tyrant himself and of the personal dictatorship and terror which he established (called the "cult of personality" in Soviet jargon).

The Post-Stalin Party
and State

The repudiation of the "cult of personality" and the so-called restoration of collective leadership required no modifications of doctrine, since Stalin had always presented himself as simply the "wisest of the wise" in the executive organs of the party, and claimed that all his policies represented the decisions of the party and its Central Committee rather than his personal whim. Since his death the dictatorship has been continued, but in the form of an ever-rotating and expanding oligarchy rather than an absolute autocracy, and it is no longer appropriate to characterize the Soviet system as totalitarian.

Two important Stalinist doctrines were renounced: the concept of the "enemy of the people" and the theory that class struggle became more intense as Soviet society moved closer to its ultimate objective of communism. Both ideas were important props supporting the Stalinist terror. When the Molotov-Malenkov-Kaganovich faction in the party Presidium failed to oust Khrushchev in June 1957, the plotters were removed from the leading organs of the party, not as "enemies of the people," but as an "antiparty group." The plotters were neither expelled completely from the party, nor imprisoned. All were given important, although demeaning (in view of their past eminence), positions in accordance with their specialties. And the members of the "antiparty group" were given the opportunity to propound their

views before a special meeting of the Central Committee, which issued the order of expulsion.

At the Twenty-second Party Congress in 1961, Khrushchev introduced some new theoretical refinements concerning the nature and destiny of the Soviet state, which can be summarized as follows:

1. The dictatorship of the proletariat has fulfilled its historic mission and is now being gradually transformed into "a state of the entire people . . . expressing the interests and will of the people as a whole."

2. The dictatorship of the proletariat is withering away, but "the state as an organization of the entire people will survive until the complete victory of Communism."

3. The organs and institutions of the state will be gradually converted into "organs of public self-government" as it embarks upon the road to oblivion.

4. In the meantime, government officials will be systematically rotated out of office at every election and at all levels, so that leading officials as a rule will hold office for not more than three consecutive terms, unless they are unusually gifted.

5. The military power of the Soviet state will continue to be strengthened to fulfill "its international duty to guarantee . . . the reliable defense and security of the entire Socialist camp."

Soviet Ideology and the
External World

The most dramatic and immediate modifications were made in Stalinist views of the outside world. Of greatest significance was the abandonment of the Stalinist dogmas of "capitalist encirclement" and of the "inevitability of wars," and of his view that the world is divided into two camps, poised in military readiness for the inevitable Armageddon that would decide for all time the issue of communism versus capitalism.

The doctrine of "capitalist encirclement" was one of the foundations of the Stalinist terror, since the danger of "capitalist attack" justified the brutal and ruthless dictatorship. Although the expansion of Soviet power into Eastern Europe after World War II and the Communist victory in China created a buffer against "capitalist encirclement," Stalin refused to alter his position and, instead, extended the terror to the entire Communist orbit.

Closely related to the idea of "capitalist encirclement" was the Leninist-Stalinist doctrine that wars are inevitable as long as capitalism and imperialism continue to flourish. Stalin insisted on this dogma even when nuclear weapons introduced a factor unforeseen by either Marx or Lenin. As far as Stalin was concerned, nuclear technology was simply another stage in the development of weapons and could not in any way alter the course of historical development, whose direction was irrevocably determined by scientific and objective laws discovered by Marx and Engels.

Wars, according to Stalin, were neither the result of accident nor of human will, but were rooted in the capitalist system itself. They would end only with the elimination of capitalism. Stalin's postwar policy was thus predicated on an inevitable conflict with the West, which was clearly going to be led by the United States.

Both the doctrines of "capitalist encirclement" and the "inevitability of wars" were repudiated at the Twentieth Party Congress. "The period when the Soviet Union was . . . encircled by hostile capitalism now belongs to the past," [14] a reluctant Molotov was forced to say at the congress, and in March 1958, Khrushchev added a new twist to the entire encirclement concept:

At the present it is not known who encircles whom. The Socialist countries cannot be considered as some kind of island in a rough capitalist sea. A billion people are living in the Socialist countries, out of a total of 2.5 billion. . . . Thus, one cannot speak any more about capitalist encirclement in its former aspect.[15]

The Stalinist "two-camp" image was replaced by a "three-camp" image. A third "anti-imperialist" group of powers, which had been released from the decaying colonial empires but had not joined the Communist cause, was recognized by Khrushchev at the Twentieth Party Congress. Stalin's inflexible two-camp image needlessly threatened to alienate these new states and force them back into the bosom of capitalism.

The Soviet leaders hoped to woo the underdeveloped world first into the Soviet diplomatic orbit and then eventually into the Communist ideological camp. Anticipating that the demands of the emerging nations for rapid modernization and industrialization would conflict with the interests of the capitalist powers, the Soviet leaders expected that the hostile or apathetic reaction on the part of the West would drive the poorer countries into their arms. Castro's Cuba is considered to be the prototype of this kind of process. Thus, according to the Soviet view, Cuba moved from being dependent on the United States through a noncapitalist, non-Communist stage, and was finally forced into the Communist orbit because of the hostility of the United States.

The new Soviet leaders have scrapped Stalin's bellicose policy in favor of a formula of "peaceful coexistence" between capitalism and communism, which calls for nonviolent forms of competition between the two forces until communism wins its inevitable victory. Wars are still considered to be possible, because of the instability of the capitalist system and the chance that war might be triggered accidentally, but they are not thought to be inevitable. The Soviet Union still intends to remain strong militarily, and her leaders believe that the development of their rocket and nuclear technology and the psychological impact of their space achievements may have given them an irreversible advantage in the cold war. In Khrushchev's view, the capitalist countries would not resort to war, not because they had become more humanitarian, but because they realized that the Soviet Union was capable of laying waste the entire American landscape. Soviet leaders may still think that victory for them is only a matter of time.

The ultimate objective of Soviet policy theoretically remains the attainment of world communism, by peaceful means or violent, by fair

14 Radio Moscow, February 20, 1956.
15 Interview with Serge Groussard in *Le Figaro* (Paris), March 19, 1958.

methods or foul, although the current official Soviet view is that it can be achieved nonviolently. The intensity with which this goal is pursued appears to have diminished considerably since the Cuban missile crisis in October 1962 and the conclusion of the Limited Nuclear Test Ban Treaty in July 1963. The vigorous pursuit of world communism which tended to provoke periodic confrontations with the United States and maximized the chances of nuclear war has increasingly been viewed by Soviet leaders as suicidal. And the demands of important segments of the Soviet public (elites and nonelites alike) for a reduction in international tensions, friendly relations with the United States and the West, and the diversion of money and resources away from heavy-industry and military expenditures to agriculture and the production of consumer goods have also played an important role in the waning of ideological fervor in Soviet policy. Furthermore, the Sino-Soviet conflict and the progressive dissolution of the Soviet bloc have brought into serious question even the desirability of world communism, particularly if it might fall under the control or influence of China—which has not only challenged Soviet leadership of the world Communist movement, and even questioned her ideological orthodoxy, but also has laid claim to some 500,000 square miles of Soviet territory in the Far East and central Asia. Little wonder that, as the world Communist movement has fallen more and more outside the control of Moscow, both its utility as an instrument of Soviet interests and foreign policy and Soviet enthusiasm to prosecute it have correspondingly diminished.

As a consequence of these developments, Soviet leaders have found it expedient to redefine the role of the Soviet Union in bringing about world communism. Cautiously but methodically, they first abdicated its position as the leader of the movement. Then they relinquished its role as a "center" or "base." Now they offer it merely as a model society to emulate. In order to minimize the ideological disarray which would result therefrom, instead of explicitly disavowing world communism the Soviet leaders have condemned the "export of revolution," maintaining that they can best discharge their ideological commitment to world communism by raising the Soviet standard of living:

It is the internationalist duty of the Communists of the Socialist countries to build the new society well and successfully, to develop the economy, to strengthen defense capability, to consolidate the Socialist camp, and to strive to insure that through practical implementation the ideas of Socialism become increasingly attractive to all working people.[16]

While the contradiction between Soviet security interests and ideological goals in foreign policy has long been recognized by observers of the Soviet scene, the contradiction between enhancing economic prosperity at home and fulfilling international ideological obligations is a new variable in Soviet policy. This new factor has not gone unnoticed by the Chinese, who accused Khrushchev of abandoning Soviet ideological and material obligations to international communism and the national liberation movement in favor of avoiding the risks of nuclear war and building an affluent society to satisfy the appetites of the new Soviet "ruling stratum":

The revisionist Khrushchev clique has usurped the leadership of the Soviet party and state and . . . a privileged bourgeois stratum has emerged in Soviet society. . . . The privileged stratum in contemporary Soviet society is composed of degenerate elements from among the leading cadres of party and government organizations, enterprises, and farms as well as bourgeois intellectuals. . . . Under the signboard of "peaceful coexistence," Khrushchev has been colluding with U.S. imperialism, wrecking the Socialist camp and the international Communist movement, opposing the revolutionary struggles of the oppressed peoples and nations, practicing great-power chauvinism and national egoism, and betraying proletarian internationalism. All this is being done for the protection of the vested interest of a handful of people, which he places above the fundamental interests of the peoples of the Soviet Union, the Socialist camp and the whole world.[17]

The same charge has also been leveled at Khrushchev's successors, who, Peking maintains, are simply practicing "Khrushchevism without Khrushchev." [18]

[16] *Pravda*, April 3, 1964.
[17] *Jen Min Jih Pao* (Peking), July 14, 1964.
[18] For an amplification of the author's views on Soviet ideology and foreign policy, cf. *Process and Power in Soviet Foreign Policy* (Boston: Little, Brown, and Co., 1971).

FIVE

the

Soviet

social order

In the Soviet Union, private ownership of land, of the means of production, and of distribution has been abolished in favor of total and permanent public ownership. Ownership is permanently vested in an institution, the state, or in an abstraction, "society." The state, however, is the executive and administrative arm of the Communist party, which allegedly represents the social will of the working class and is the source of all policy formulation. Control of the party assures control of the state, and through it control of the land, the economy, the coercive instruments of society (the armed forces, police, courts, and legal system), the means of transportation and distribution, and the media of communication. No matter who controls the party, *ownership* of the means of production is never an object of the struggle for power, for it remains permanently vested in the state.

According to article 1 of the Soviet constitution, "the Union of Soviet Socialist Republics is a Socialist state of workers and peasants," which is defined in article 12 as a society in which "work . . . is a duty and a matter of honor for every able-bodied citizen," and which is organized in accordance with two principles: "He who does not work, neither shall he eat," and "From each according to his ability, to each according to his *work*." According to official dogma, the Soviet Union has been a socialist society since 1936 and is now well advanced on the road to communism, in which distinctions between "workers" and "peasants" will cease to exist and society will be governed by the principle of communism according to Marx: "From each according to his ability, to each according to his *needs*."

Contrary to a widespread misconception, the Soviet Union does not claim to be an egalitarian society; social differentiation exists, and definite and often rigid hierarchical lines divide one social group from another. Soviety society is not defined as a *classless* society, but is officially described as a society in which *class conflict* and exploitation of man by man have been eliminated. Two classes are recognized, the workers and peasants, and they are supposed to work together in harmony and peace; the intelligentsia, which is not mentioned in the constitution and is not officially designated as a class, is a part of the upper social layer of the working class. The intelligentsia, however, constitutes the social and political elite of Soviet society and from its ranks spring those who struggle for control of the party, the state, and the economy. Although the state is a "dictatorship of the proletariat," it is defined constitutionally as a "Socialist state of workers and peasants," which, according to article 2, "grew and became strong as a result of the overthrow of the power of the landlords and capitalists."

The initial function of the Soviet "dictatorship of the proletariat" was to establish proletarian control over the former ruling bourgeois class in order to eradicate it as a class and pave the way for a classless society in which the state would ultimately "wither away." This becomes possible only when the proletariat seizes power and nationalizes all means of production. Article 4 of the Soviet constitution states:

The economic foundation of the U.S.S.R. is the Socialist system of economy and the Socialist ownership of the instruments and means of production, firmly established as a result of the liquidation of the capitalist system of economy, the abolition of private ownership of the instruments and means of production, and the elimination of exploitation of man by man.

Article 6 further specifies that

the land, its mineral wealth, waters, forests, mills, factories, mines, soil, water and air transport, banks, communications, large state-organized agricultural enterprises (state farms, machine and tractor stations, and the like), as well as municipal enterprises and the bulk of the dwelling-houses in the cities and industrial localities are state property—that is, belong to the whole people.

Aside from state-owned property, the Soviet constitution recognizes cooperative and collective-farm property as a form of socialist ownership, since it is collectively exploited by groups. All land, however, belongs to the state and is only leased to cooperative and collective groups "in perpetuity." Private property exists only in two forms: (1) individual peasants' and artisans' establishments in which production is based on the owner's labor (hiring others for personal gain is constitutionally defined as "exploitation" and is severely punished as one of the most serious crimes against society), and (2) personal property, including individual homes, articles of personal and household use, and savings.

The current organization of Soviet society, however, is as much an outgrowth of the social realities of Russia at the time of the Revolution as it is of the social theories of Marx and Lenin. "Socialism" in the Soviet Union is the society that emerged as a result of Stalin's industrial and agricultural transformation of a backward rural nation within the span of a single generation. Its characteristics are as unmistakably Russian as they are Marxist.

THE SOCIAL TRANSFORMATION OF RUSSIA

Before the Revolution, Russia was a semifeudal society with rigidly distinct class divisions. At the top was a small stratum composed of the landed gentry, the court nobility, the upper clergy, and the imperial family, which together owned most of the arable lands of the country and controlled the state. At the bottom was a large land-hungry, superstitious, illiterate, and sullen peasant population, only recently emancipated from serfdom, whose ugly moods periodically threatened to disrupt the social order. Sandwiched between the top and bottom was a small middle class, made up of merchants, civil servants, professional people, intellectuals, and students, who, however, did not constitute a true *bourgeoisie* in the Marxist sense (capitalists who owned the means of production), because most of the industrial and financial enterprises in Russia were owned by foreign capitalists. Alongside the small middle class was a slightly larger working-class population, recently uprooted from the countryside, alienated from society, and living in incredible squalor in Moscow, St. Petersburg, Baku, and the Donetz basin.

In 1913, more than 78% of the population was made up of peasants, divided between those with no land or small plots (about 66.7% of the population) and rich peasants, or kulaks (about 11.3%). Of the 367 million hectares of agricultural land (1 hectare = 2.471 acres) owned before the Revolution (within the pre-1939 borders of the USSR), the poor and moderately well-off peasants possessed altogether only 135 million hectares, while the great landlords, the imperial family, and the Orthodox church, amounting to only 3% of the population, owned 152 million hectares. The rich peasants owned the remaining 80 million hectares. Thirty percent of the peasants possessed no land whatsoever, while 34% owned no agricultural implements or livestock. The middle class accounted for about 6% of the population, while the urban workers amounted to about 13% of the total.

"WAR COMMUNISM" AND THE NEP

The original intention of the Bolshevik regime was to establish a Communist society by an executive fiat nationalizing all the land, natural resources, financial institutions, and factories of the country, thus expropriating the landowning and capitalist classes. All class distinctions were abolished, as were the official ranks in the government and the armed forces. Workers and peasants were instructed to seize the factories and lands on behalf of the state, and were ordered to establish direct control over production and distribution. During this initial period of "War Communism," equality was the rule: equality of social status and equality of income, irrespective of the quality and quantity of work performed.

Under these conditions, the economy of the country was reduced to a shambles as the workers proved incompetent to manage factories and other enterprises. They embarked upon a "Roman holiday," voting themselves unrealistic increases in wages and absurdly numerous holidays. The economy in the cities came to a virtual halt; workers threatened riots when the customary payday arrived and the payroll did not materialize. Famine once again stalked the streets of the urban areas as the peasants refused to deliver their produce in return for the worthless printed money of the state and demanded manufactured goods of comparable value, which were being turned out in increasingly diminished quantities.

Lenin called a halt to "War Communism" in 1921, and introduced the "New Economic Policy" (NEP), which authorized the temporary revival of small-scale capitalist enterprises. Small factories and retail establishments, privately operated and based on incentives, quickly sprang up and flourished in the cities. Equally desperate was Lenin's decision to abolish state-imposed prices for agricultural goods in order to spur agricultural production. The peasants were required to deliver a certain amount of grain to the state, but they then could sell whatever they produced in excess of this amount on the open market at whatever price they could exact. This program resulted not only in reviving the economy, but also in the reemergence of a small entrepreneurial class, the "Nepmen," in the cities, and a powerful and numerically significant rich-peasant (kulak) class in the countryside.

The NEP was introduced as a purely temporary measure and was not intended to be permanent. The state retained the "commanding heights" of the economy, from which it subsequently descended upon the hapless Nepmen and kulaks. Banks, large industrial and economic enterprises, communications media and transportation systems, foreign trade, natural resources, and the ownership of land remained in the hands of the state. This guaranteed that the state would at all times be complete master of the situation. But it was becoming increasingly clear that either the NEP would have to become a permanent characteristic of the Soviet system or it would have to be abandoned in favor of socialism. After the death of Lenin in 1924, a "great debate" ensued among his successors as to Soviet Russia's future course, and this issue became an integral part of a complicated struggle for power.

Stalin emerged as the new Soviet leader, outmaneuvered his opposition, and, by 1927, felt sufficiently confident to press for an ambitious Five-Year Plan designed to erect a heavy-industrial foundation for the Soviet economy and to mechanize and collectivize agriculture—in short, to bring about a cultural and technical revolution in the USSR. The scope of his plan, particularly with respect to the peasants, brought him into direct conflict with the more conservative members of the party, who wanted to proceed cautiously in the countryside, even at the expense of delaying industrialization. Stalin had the majority, however, and administrative measures were initiated against the kulaks, who were withholding grain from the market, threatening the cities with famine. Originally, the Five-Year Plan called for the collectivization of only 20% of the country's agriculture, but Stalin changed his mind once the program was under way and decided to destroy all the kulaks.

THE "REVOLUTION FROM ABOVE" (1928–33)

The overall objective of the Five-Year Plan that came into effect in 1928 soon became nothing less than a "second revolution," whose goal was to completely transform Russia from a backward agrarian country into an industrialized and modern socialist society. Stalin had to achieve eight objectives if his ambitious project was to succeed: (1) the elimination of the residual capitalist classes, in particular the kulaks; (2) the collectivization of agriculture; (3) the creation of a large army of industrial workers out of raw, untutored peasants; (4) the creation of a heavy-industrial base; (5) the creation of a corps of cultural and technical specialists out of the working class who would be capable of coping with the demands of an industrialized society; (6) the rapid mechanization of agriculture to make up for the reduced rural labor supply necessitated by the industrialization program; (7) the cultural and educational transformation of Russian society; and (8) the preservation of his own power at all costs.

Stalin realized that this period would not see a rise in the standard of living, for it was to be a period of sacrifice, with the possibility that food, shelter, and clothing would be reduced to a bare subsistence level. The magnitude of Stalin's ambitions was matched only by the

forces that almost overwhelmed him: (1) the hostility of the capitalist world, which hoped and expected him to fail; (2) the opposition of the peasants, particularly the kulaks, to collectivization; (3) the opposition of his rivals within the party; (4) the shortage of foreign exchange, which was required to purchase necessary machinery and to hire foreign technicians and specialists and which could be earned only by selling agricultural commodities on the world market, thus further reducing the home supply; and (5) the fundamental inertia of a backward, illiterate, superstitious, and overwhelmingly agricultural population.

Stalin's plan succeeded, but largely at the expense of the peasant population (which still remains the most exploited and downtrodden of Soviet Russia's social classes). Millions died through starvation, exposure, deportation, and execution so that Russia might be industrialized.

The estimates of the number of people who died during the farm-collectivization program range from 3 million to 15 million, and the Soviet Union's total population deficit for this period is set at about 20 million. The catastrophe was further intensified by a drought which blighted the land during the height of the collectivization drive, and by the world economic crisis which depressed the world market price for grain. The memories of this era are indelibly etched in the minds and psychology of the Soviet population in both town and country, while the physical scars are still evident in lagging production statistics, the depressed living conditions of the peasantry, the decimated livestock population, as well as the sullen and passive resistance of the collective farmer.

By 1934, the kulaks had been destroyed and 90% of the peasants transformed from a class of individual farmers into a collectivized group held in bondage by the state. The transformation was later described as a "second revolution" or a "revolution from above," because it was stimulated by the government against the people rather than generated from below against the regime. With the collectivization of agriculture and the liquidation of the kulaks, the residual manifestations of private ownership over the means of production had been eliminated. Stalin could thus report in 1935:

The landlord class, . . . the capitalist class, . . . the kulak class, . . . and the merchants and profiteers . . . have ceased to exist. Thus all the exploiting classes have now been eliminated. There remains the working class, . . . the peasant class, [and] the intelligentsia.[1]

The "second revolution" introduced a new dynamic quality into what had been essentially a static society. By 1937, the working class was nearly double that of 1928, while the intelligentsia was nearly quadrupled during the same period. The number of the peasantry was reduced by about 20%.

THE STRATIFICATION OF SOVIET SOCIETY

Officially, there are only two classes in present-day Soviet society: the working class and the collective-farm peasantry. The intelligentsia is not called a "class" but a "stratum" and is considered the upper layer of the working class. Yet it is this "stratum" which is the most significant social group in the USSR today and is itself divided into a number of substrata or elites. The relative numerical size and political influence of these three social groups have been in a state of flux since 1928 and are continually changing.

Until the early sixties, it was impermissible for Soviet scholars to tamper with the orthodox Marxist-Leninist approach to social structure, but it was becoming increasingly obvious to many Soviet observers that the oversimplified doctrinaire class division of Soviet society into "workers" and "peasants," along with a "stratum" of intelligentsia, was inadequate to explain the differences and divergencies of interests, attitudes, social outlook, and behavior of various strata of the Soviet population. In order to cope with this problem some Soviet scholars are now emphasizing the importance of "intraclass" differences in Soviet society, hoping in this manner to meet the imperatives of

both the official preconceived doctrine and the demands of empirical social realities, without subverting the former or neglecting the latter. Thus, one Soviet writer points out:

Interest in the problems of the social structure of Soviet society has grown noticeably in recent times. In this connection, literature has been remarking more and more insistently on the need for studying not only the class structure but the intraclass structure as well. It is justly pointed out that class structure does not coincide with social structure; that the latter can exist even in a classless society and that the creation of a socially homogeneous society pursues a twofold course: the elimination of both interclass and intraclass differences. . . . Perhaps the chief shortcoming of our sociological literature is the undervaluation of intraclass differences.[2]

These pioneering Soviet scholars, who refer to their field as "complex sociological research," come perilously close to employing "interest-group" analysis within a "structural-functional" framework, and to that degree their approach has undoubtedly been influenced by the work of American scholars. Thus, another prominent Soviet sociologist argues that whereas *class* structure may be slated for extinction, *social* structure and social stratification are an ineradicable feature of any organized society:

Social structure is an extremely broad concept, embracing the totality of social groups (classes, strata, collectives, nations, etc.) and the sphere of social relations, which have their hierarchy of numerous structure organizations, based on the dissimilarity, the divergence, of people's position in society. The social structure exists and will exist throughout all of man's history. Specific social organisms have systems of structural organization inherent in them, . . . differences in people's socioeconomic position have been of decisive importance in the system of social differences; the highest expression of these differences is the class differentiation of society. Subordinated to class differences (yet possessing relatively independent social importance in themselves) are the socioeconomic differences between city and countryside, between persons engaged in mental

---

[1] Stalin, *Leninism: Selected Writings*, p. 382.

[2] Yu V. Arutyunyan, "The Social Structure of the Rural Population," *Voprosy Filosofii*, no. 5 (May 1967): 51–52.

and physical labor, and finally, intraclass differences. It is these last differences we are singling out from the totality of social differences.[3]

While Soviet sociologists refrain from drawing political implications and conclusions from their emphasis on "intraclass" differences at this point in their investigations, they do suggest that economic interests, social attitudes, and social behavior are shaped by one's socio-functional role and sociostructural status in society:

What then is the dominant, determining factor of intraclass division? In our opinion the nature of the social group within the class and in society as a whole is determined by the nature and quality of the labor performed by members of the given group. The nature of labor lies at the basis of intraclass differentiation.[4]

[3] O. I. Shkaratan, "The Social Structure of the Soviet Working Class," *Voprosy Filosofii,* no. 1 (January 1967): 29.
[4] Arutyunyan, *op. cit.*

And another Soviet scholar warns against "the tendency to deny the existence of significant differences between these social groupings":

The insolvency of such assertions are obvious. The present-day stage in the development of Socialist social relations is still attended by differences between social groupings. The differences can lead to certain nonantagonistic contradictions, which are resolved on the basis of the social, political, and ideological unity of Soviet society.[5]

Since the Revolution, the industrialization of Soviet Russia has increased the size of the working class and proliferated its skills. The cultural, educational, and technological advances have similarly expanded numerically the intelligentsia, which has become the most differentiated social group in Soviet society and actually consists of a constellation of social and political elites, from which the economic and political decision makers are recruited. In the process, the number of peasants has been drastically reduced by more than half (Table 5-1).

[5] M. Rutkevich, "Changes in the Social Structure of Soviet Society," *Pravda,* June 16, 1967.

TABLE 5-1. *Social Structure in the USSR, 1913–69*

Class	Proportion of total population							1969 numerical totals
	1913	1928	1937	1939	1955	1959	1969	
Nobility, upper-class *bourgeoisie*, clergy, military officers etc.	3.0%	—	—	—	—	—	—	0
Kulaks	11.3	4.6%	—	—	—	—	—	0
Middle class ⎰		—	—	—	—	—	—	0
Intelligentsia ⎱	6.0	4.0	14.0%	17.5% ⎰		22.8%	23.91%	57,600,000
				⎱	58.3%			
Workers	13.0	13.6	22.2	32.2 ⎭		45.5 *	54.50 *	131,400,000 *
Collective farmers	—	2.9	57.9	47.9	41.2	31.4	21.56	52,000,000
Individual peasants and artisans	66.7	74.9	5.9	2.6	0.5	0.3	.03	725,000

SOURCES: *Narodnoye Khozyaistvo . . . v 1959 Godu and . . . 1969 Godu; Vestnik Statistiki,* no. 12 (1960), pp. 3–21.
* Includes several million Sovkhoz workers and other "rural working-class" elements.

It has largely gone unnoticed that these socio-economic transformations of Soviet society have not simply upset the balance between town and countryside, but have also drastically restructured Soviet rural society in the process, giving rise to a distinctive rural social structure which is only now attracting the attention of serious Soviet scholars.

Rural Society: The Farms

As of 1970, 44% (105,728,000) of the Soviet population was still rural in character, although only about 22% (52 million) consisted of collective farmers and their families. The remaining 22% that made up the rural population were rural "workers and employees" and their families, which includes workers on the state-owned farms and other state-owned enterprises and institutions, and members of the rural intelligentsia and their families.[6]

The two main rural institutions of Soviet society are the *kolkhoz,* or collective farm, and the *sovkhoz,* or state-owned farm. The kolhkoz is considered by Communists to be a relatively low form of socialist organization in contrast to the more ideal commune and sovkhoz, which the regime originally supported as the more suitable forms for a socialist society.

THE KOLKHOZ. The dominant type of collective farm, the kolkhoz, is neither a genuine cooperative nor a state-owned enterprise. It can be best described as a compulsory cooperative that has been established and is supervised and controlled by the state. Most of the agricultural land is pooled, but the peasant is entitled to retain his own house and a small garden plot, upon which he can grow vegetables and fruits to sell in the open market. The peasant is also authorized to keep small flocks of fowl and a private cow. Under no circumstances can the peasant hire anyone but members of his immediate family to work in his private garden. The existence of these private gardens (which, incidentally, virtually all workers, farmers, and

[6] A. Amvrosov, "The Countryside and the Times," *Izvestia,* August 11, 1967.

intelligentsia in the countryside appear to have) and the time which peasants spend on them have been a source of continuing anxiety and concern to the regime, and have even been responsible for heated ideological controversies in the highest councils of the state and party. The chief worry is that they keep alive feelings of private ownership and capitalist psychology which the regime would like to eradicate.

The kolkhoz is supposed to be governed by its members, who meet in a general assembly that is theoretically empowered to elect an executive committee and a chairman or director to manage the farm. The general meeting, according to the kolkhoz charter, supposedly confirms the farm's production plan, admits and expels members, and establishes the general regulations governing finance and administration. Actually, the director is "elected" after he is appointed by party and state officials. Soon after the replacement of Malenkov as Soviet premier in 1955, some 30,000 new collective-farm chairmen were appointed in accordance with a directive from Moscow, and all were duly "elected" by their respective collective farms. The executive committee is normally selected or confirmed by local party and state officials.

The "voluntary" character of the collective farm and the theoretical control of the general meeting by the peasants are easily refuted by an examination not only of how the system works in practice but also of the freedom allowed it by law. The first legal restriction is that the land is owned by the state. In return for its use, the farms, before 1957, were forced to deliver a certain quota of their output to the state, at prices, fixed by the state, that were well below the prices at which the state resold the commodities on the market. Forced deliveries were abolished in 1957, and the state has warned the farms that they no longer can be assured an automatic market; the state now purchases only what it needs at competitive prices. As long as agricultural commodities are in short supply, however, it is unlikely that collective farms will remain without buyers, and the farms have been receiving higher prices than before.

Before 1958, there was a second restriction on the initiative of the collective farms, in the form of state-owned machine and tractor stations (MTS), which "rented" their heavy agricultural machinery to the farms under "contract," in return for payment in kind. Thus, the state owned not only the land but the principal means of production as well. The power to withhold an MTS contract gave the state an effective instrument of control over the farms, since the state had to be satisfied with a farm's work norms, plan schedules, programs of forced deliveries, and use of scientific techniques before it would grant the farm a contract. The MTS were abolished in 1958 and their equipment sold to the collective farms, but the farms must now first pay installments to the state for the machinery and meet all other financial obligations to the state for loans, technical assistance, and new types of seed before they can distribute the "profit" of the farm among its members.

The peasant receives payment in cash and kind for his services on the collective farm, in accordance with the number of "labor-day" units he has accumulated during the year. The labor-day is an arbitrarily fixed production norm established by law and is based on a complicated formula involving both quantity and quality of work performed. All income is computed in terms of labor-days, which need not correspond to the actual labor performed during a workday, but which provides a basic unit that can be readily divided and multiplied and applied to various types of rural labor. In 1948, nine new different labor-day norms were established, the lowest being rated at one-half a labor day for a whole day of the least skilled work performed on the farm, and the highest being set at 2.5 labor days, or five times that of the lowest.

Since the peasant can make more by intensively working his own tiny garden plot, sometimes illegally expanded by various ingenious devices, the state in 1939 made it compulsory for the peasant to meet his "norm," or suffer criminal and financial penalties, and to accumulate a minimum number of labor-day credits during the year or face exile to Siberia. The criminal penalties were abolished in 1956, but not the financial ones. Even with financial penalties, however, some peasants still find it more profitable to work their own plots, where they can grow whatever they wish to fulfill consumer demand and sell it on the open market for high prices. The peasant cultivates his own plot with great care, and what he produces is often of much higher quality than that produced by the farm, where he grudgingly reports for work. In some categories of agricultural production the tiny plots (which comprise 3% of the arable land and 17% of total production) altogether produce more than the collective farms themselves—for instance in 1966 they accounted for 60% of the potatoes produced, 68% of the eggs, 39% of the milk, and 40% of the meat.

Although the minimum monthly wage in the countryside was raised in 1968 from 40–45 to 60–70 rubles (1 ruble = $1.10) and about 75% of the collective farmer's income is now in cash (up from 42% in 1955), the collective farmer's average annual income is only about 750 rubles, of which about one-fourth is in kind. Half of his cash income is derived from produce raised on his private plot. It should be noted that the income of the collective farmer has increased from about 350 rubles in 1958; this suggests the deplorably low level of life which the collective farmers have had to endure. In an endeavor to provide a subsistence wage for the collective farmers, the regime introduced in 1968 a guaranteed monthly income, integrated them into the state pension system, and now permits them greater flexibility in working their small private plots.

The highest-paid individual on the collective farm is normally the director, who receives a certain number of labor-day units to begin with, based on his experience and on the size and type of farm he manages. Like the factory manager, he can earn bonuses and other financial rewards for exceeding production norms. The rural intelligentsia, "stakhanovites" (workers who habitually exceed their norms by substantial amounts), and other skilled workers are also relatively well paid.

THE SOVKHOZ. The state farm is described as the highest form of socialist agriculture in Soviet society, and is the regime's favored form of agricultural organization—but the peasants hate and fear it even more than they do the collective farm. Whereas the average collective farm embraces about 5,000 acres, the average sovkhoz runs to about 15,000 acres. The tendency is for the collective farms to become larger and the sovkhozes to diminish in size, so that eventually distinctions in size will be rendered irrelevant. In recent years many collective farms have been transformed into state farms, and thus while the number of the latter increases, that of the former decreases (see Table 5-2). Each sovkhoz is managed by a director who is appointed by the minister of agriculture, and his status is comparable to that of a large factory's manager and is usually more important than that of the kolkhoz director. He is also likely to have more experience and formal education than the kolkhoz director. Workers are hired directly by the state, and receive wages. They are not described as peasants in the official literature but are listed among "workers and employees." Several farms may be grouped together in a larger administrative unit, the *trust*.

Many of the sovkhozes are located in remote areas, and most of the new lands brought under cultivation (the "virgin lands") are organized into state farms. Like the collective farm, the sovkhoz is a self-contained rural community with its own recreation centers, schools, medical clinics and laboratories, agricultural machinery, animals, and implements. Many sovkhozes specialize in certain crops and often are centers of agricultural experimentation, with their own scientific and technical personnel. The average annual wage of a sovkhoz worker in 1969 was about 1,130 rubles plus what he grows on his private plot, which is usually smaller than that of the collective farm.

OTHER STATE-OWNED AGENCIES. It is often overlooked that in rural sectors, the state employs some 5.2 million workers and employees in a wide variety of nonagricultural work: education, health, culture, science, industry, constuction, communications, trade, and transportation. About 1.2 million of these employees are members of the intelligentsia, about 2 million are engaged in low-level "mental" labor, and the remainder (2 million) perform some type of physical labor. The precise social status of these nonagricultural workers in the rural areas is difficult to determine, as is their assimilation and accommodation to the state and collective farms, which are often self-contained units.

Rural Social Stratification

Five distinct social strata flourish in Soviet rural society: about 60% of the rural population are ordinary peasants, and the remaining 40% consist of the rural intelligentsia, rural foremen, the rural "working class," and other workers and employees in state-owned enterprises and institutions (Table 5-3).

THE DIRECTORS. The rural social pyramid has at its apex the directors of the collective farms and the sovkhozes, who are invariably not native to the locality in which they serve. The director, whether of the kolkhoz or the

TABLE 5-2. *Kolkhozes, Sovkhozes, and MTS, 1928–69*

	1928	*1940*	*1953*	*1957*	*1959*	*1960*	*1966*	*1969*
Kolkhozes	33,300	236,900	93,300	78,200	54,600	44,900	36,900	34,700
Sovkhozes	1,407	4,159	4,857	5,905	6,496	7,375	11,681	14,310
MTS	6	7,069	8,985	7,903	34	23	0	0

SOURCE: *Narodnoye Khozyaistvo . . . v 1959 Godu and . . . v 1965 Godu.*

TABLE 5-3. *Rural Social Structure in the USSR, 1970*

	Number of Personnel
Intelligentsia	1,743,963
Directors and executives	103,993
Sovkhoz directors	14,426
Kolkhoz directors	33,661
Sovkhoz deputy administrators	39,067
Kolkhoz deputy directors	16,779
Technical intelligentsia	439,970
Sovkhoz	207,170
Kolkhoz	232,800
Other employees and intelligentsia * (estimated)	1,200,000
Rural Foremen	391,610
Sovkhoz	140,860
Kolkhoz	250,750
Rural "Workers"	5,443,000
Sovkhoz	1,401,000
Kolkhoz	2,042,000
Other † (estimated)	2,000,000
Farmers	33,000,000
Sovkhoz	7,000,000
Kolkhoz	16,000,000
Part-time and private sector	10,000,000
Total	*40,578,573*

* Includes military specialists, executives and administrators of other state-owned enterprises, and cultural, educational, health, and other professional personnel in rural areas.

† Includes members of the armed forces and workers, low-level "mental" workers, and service personnel in industrial, construction, communications, and other state-owned enterprises in rural areas.

sovkhoz, represents the interests of the party and the state, to which he is beholden for his position, his salary and bonuses for superior production records, and his professional and political future. His primary goal is thus to satisfy the demands of the party and the state and not the peasants, who often become mere instruments of production. The director usually cultivates the popularity of the peasants and caters to their interests only if it will enhance production and is conducive to efficient management. As an agent of the regime, the director is responsible for seeing that the state receives its proper share of farm produce, that the property of the state is safe from pilferage, and that an indoctrination program is given the peasants (in cooperation with the local party organization) to insure that they faithfully execute all the state and party directives. In the words of one Soviet scholar, because of "the very structure of today's rural society . . . the chairman [kolkhoz director] must combine two utterly different roles in his day-to-day work: organizer of production, and 'leader' of the village society." [7]

The director is often the most powerful administrative and political personage in the rural locality, not excluding the local party secretary and the chairman of the local soviet, with whom he shares local political power. The latter two individuals have powerful inspection and auditing authority, and they are also responsible for the formal transmission of party and state directives—but they are not invested with managerial or administrative authority over the farms. The director himself is frequently the most powerful political individual in a local district by virtue of his long experience and membership in the party. In 1960, for example more than 95% of the directors were party members. The director, party secretary, and chairman of the local soviet often constitute a local "troika" or directorate, and the three together virtually preempt all political power in the rural locality.

In 1959, the number of kolkhoz chairmen and their deputies were given as 102,800, but by April 1970, in conformity with the planned amalgamation of collective farms, the numbers had been reduced to 50,440, of which 33,661 were listed as directors and 16,779 as assistant directors. As the collective farms are increased in size, the complexities of management and the importance of political reliability increase. The amalgamation process, which has been under way since 1950, does much to explain the higher percentages of technically qualified and

[7] *Komsomolskaya Pravda*, June 2, 1967.

politically motivated collective-farm directors. The number of sovkhoz directors in 1970 was 14,420, and, since many of the larger state farms are divided into a number of sectors for administrative purposes, these officials were assisted by 39,067 deputies and assistants.

The Peasants

The ordinary peasantry itself is divided into three groups, the first being those (about 7 million) who work on the sovkhozes and by and large are engaged in agricultural specialization. The second group consists of about 2 million collective farmers who also pursue some type of specialization in crop production. The third group is made up of some 20 million full-time and part-time muzhiks without any type of specialization, who constitute the overwhelming bulk of the collective farmers and private-plot workers and rest at the bottom of the rural social structure, and indeed at the bottom of the Soviet social and economic order as a whole. The sovkhoz farmers enjoy the highest status of the three; their cash income ordinarily is much higher than that of the kolkhoznik, although on some of the rich kolkhozes the collective farmers are better off.

The Soviet peasantry in its entirety, numbering about 65 million people (including families) on both collective and state farms, still rivals the working class as the largest single social class in Soviet society. Although the peasant works longer and harder than his urban counterpart, he receives less than any other class in terms of education, medical care, sanitation, transportation and communication facilities, consumer goods, recreational facilities, and other ordinary amenities of Soviet life. In terms of real income, even Soviet sources reported in 1956 that the income of the Soviet peasant "in cash and kind" was only three times that of the peasant before 1913, which was described as "extremely low." This indicates that millions of peasants earned little more than the subsistence amount represented by the then legal Soviet minimum wage of 27–35 rubles ($30–38) per month. In 1964, the minimum

wage was raised to 40–45 rubles ($44–50) per month and again to 60 rubles in 1968 and has been extended to virtually all sectors of the Soviet economy.

As a political force, the peasantry has little direct influence. As opposed to the workers and various sections of the intelligentsia, who have not only their trade unions but also various guild and professional organizations, the only legal rural organization permitted the Soviet peasants has been (with the exception discussed below) the collective farm—and thus the Soviet peasantry is deprived even of the Soviet version of a "pressure group." Their only recourse is to malinger, refuse to meet quotas, spend more time on their own little garden plots, and in general "drag their feet"—all of which they have been doing very well. The situation had become so serious by mid-1962 that the regime ordered an extraordinary increase in the price of butter and meat. This increase, which represented a 25–30% rise, offered the collective farms higher prices for their commodities as a spur to greater production. After Khrushchev's ouster, further inducements were made in the form of higher prices and the extension of certain minor yet attractive privileges—such as more freedom in using the private plot.

Agricultural production remains a chronic problem in spite of the government's repeated promises to increase investments, introduce new technology and machinery, expand fertilizer production, raise incentives and inducements on the farm, plow new lands, and so forth. While Khrushchev's successors have managed to overcome the specific defects resulting from Khrushchev's energetic but often ill-planned efforts to cope with the problem of agriculture, the Brezhnev-Kosygin regime has returned to familiar methods in the 1971–75 Five-Year Plan: (1) increasing investments—but as usual with too little and too late; (2) improving agricultural management, which often means more party interference and disorganization, rather than improved efficiency; (3) raising the deplorable living standards and improving amenities and facilities in rural areas in an effort to create incentives for greater production and to induce young people to stay on the farm instead of migrating to the cities; and (4) allowing more flexibility in the use of collective-farm land by individual collective farms and small groups, although this runs the danger of eroding the collective farms into "family" or "neighborhood" farms. Another promising but unimplemented avenue was to allow the collective farmers to organize on a national basis so as to allow them to develop more political leverage within the Soviet political system and enable them to "demand" a greater share of investments rather than "beg," as they must do at present. A Third All-Union Kolkhoz Congress was allowed to convene in 1969 (the first since 1930), but the frightening prospects of an organized collective-farm lobby or pressure group apparently led the regime to retreat, allowing the formation of only a Kolkhoz Council with "advisory powers" headed by the minister of agriculture, the very person the proposed Kolkhoz Union was designed to pressure in the first place.

Nevertheless, local collective-farm unions of sorts are being tolerated on an experimental basis, even to the point of allowing them to coordinate their activities and bargain with state planners over state crop purchases and deliveries. Although the Third All-Union Kolkhoz Congress adopted a new model charter for collective farms that calls for the establishment of local, regional, and republican farm councils, culminating in an All-Union Council, the charter is a far cry from the original draft that called for the right of collective farms to join "associations and unions." It represents a forward step, however, and pressures will continue for permission to organize an authentic Soviet-type union network in the countryside similar to that permitted the intelligentsia and working class. Only when the regime takes measures to restore dignity and self-respect in the farms and allows the peasantry to speak from a base of organized social power (within the Soviet context of course) even the material measures taken to improve agricultural production will fail once again to mollify the Soviet peasantry. As Brezhnev himself pointed out, but with an opposite intent of course, "It would be wrong to reduce everything to ma-

terial incentives; this would impoverish the inner world of Soviet man."[8] It should be noted in this connection that farmers on state farms are allowed to join trade unions, since they are classified as "workers" in the Soviet system.

In the meantime, social mobility on the farm has become sluggish. With the end of the era of rapid industrialization, economic and social opportunities have seriously decreased. Peasant youth are no longer encouraged to migrate to the cities; in fact, urban dwellers are urged to move back to the farm. Since educational opportunities for the children of collective farmers are less than those for workers and the intelligentsia, the peasantry is entering a period of social stagnation. Opportunities for direct movement from the peasantry to the intelligentsia within a single generation are few. The ranks of the intelligentsia are being filled increasingly from within itself and from the workers. Since mobility from peasant status to that of worker is itself becoming more difficult, direct movement from peasantry to the intelligentsia is virtually impossible. Although the eight-year school was recently made compulsory for all rural areas, in the cities the ten-year school is the rule, with ample opportunities for attendance at institutions of higher learning, or specialized secondary schools (see Table 5-4).

The Workers

According to the census of 1959, the social category "workers and employees," together with their families, accounted for nearly 143 million people, or more than 68% of the Soviet population. By 1969, however, the percentage had increased to 78.4% (190 million). The 1959 census reported a total of 99 million people actually employed (about 47% of the population), with more than 81% of all employed people being engaged in "productive" work and 19% involved in services and other nonproductive labor. Of the total employed, 78,-635,000 (79.3%) were engaged in physical labor,

[8] Speech delivered in Leningrad, February 16, 1968.

TABLE 5-4. *Urban and Rural Educational Levels in the USSR, 1939–70 (thousands)*

	1959 total	1959 urban	rural	Percentage rural 1939	1959	Per 1,000 1939 urban	rural	Per 1,000 1959 urban	rural	1970 total	Per 1,000 1970 urban	rural
Number of persons with higher education												
Complete	3,778	3,170	608	20%	16%	16	1.7	32	5.6	8,262 }	62	14
Incomplete	1,738	1,332	406		23					2,605 }		
Number of persons with secondary education												
Specialized	7,870	5,446	2,424	30	31	162	37	344	188	13,420 }	530	318
Complete	9,936	7,426	2,510		25					23,391 }		
Incomplete	35,386	20,254	15,132		45					47,368 }		

SOURCE: *Narodnoye Khozyaistvo . . . v 1959 Godu* and *Pravda,* April 17, 1971.

while 20,495,000 (20.7%) were engaged in "mental work." Women accounted for 48% of all those employed and 54% of those engaged in intellectual labor. In the Soviet Union, virtually the entire adult population of the country is gainfully employed, with 54% of all males and 41.5% of all females actively working.

The total Soviet labor force (the able-bodied, working-age sector of the population) in 1970 was about 130.5 million, of which about 115.5 million were actually employed, distributed as follows: (1) approximately 3 million in the armed forces; (2) over 40 million in agriculture; (3) over 31 million in industry; and (4) over 42 million in other nonagricultural sectors of the economy (construction, transportation, communications, education, science, culture, health, and service categories). Of the totally employed in the civilian part of the economy, 88 million were classified as "workers and employees," 27 million were to be found on collective farms, including several million part-time or seasonal workers in private plots and collective farms. Of the 88 million workers and employees, 30 million were classified as "mental workers," leaving 58 million to be categorized as "physical workers."

Of this group, about 8 million were farmers on state farms. Over 3 million equipment operators and maintenance personnel were also to be found on state and collective farms. Thus, we can arrive at an estimated figure of 53.4 million for the entire "working class," including equipment operators and maintenance personnel on the farms.

Soviet data since the 1959 census was not available at the time of this writing so as to provide complete information on the separate classification and statistical breakdowns for "physical labor" and "mental labor," although statistics on the distribution of "workers and employees," including both "physical" and "mental" by sectors of the economy were available. Nevertheless, the growth in the number of "workers and employees," and their changing distribution in the Soviet economy, are significant indicators of Soviet economic development, as Table 5-5 demonstrates.

The general trend in Soviet employment distribution is for the proportion of collective farmers to diminish in relation to state-farm workers, and for agricultural labor to diminish in relation to nonagricultural work. In the latter category, the general trend is for unskilled work to diminish (it has vanished in industry

TABLE 5-5. *Distribution of "Workers and Employees" in the Soviet Economy, 1928–69 (thousands)*						

Economic Sector	1928	1940	1950	1959	1966	1969
Industry	3,773	10,967	14,144	20,207	27,070	31,159
Construction	723	1,563	2,569	4,800	5,620	6,651
Transportation	1,270	3,425	4,082	5,972	7,295	7,797
Communications	95	478	542	691	1,010	1,262
Trade (all forms)	583	3,303	3,325	4,389	6,030	7,287
Public health	399	1,507	2,051	3,245	4,290	4,927
Education/science	807	3,024	4,029	6,030	9,260	10,905
Administration	1,010	1,825	1,831	1,273	1,440	1,834
Housing/communal	147	1,221	1,210	1,713	2,410	2,930
Agriculture	1,735	2,976	3,881	6,190	9,435	9,509
"Other" (residual)	248	903	1,231	1,999	3,040	3,661
Totals	10,790	31,192	38,895	56,509	76,900	87,922

SOURCE: *Narodnoye Khozyaistvo v 1969 Godu.*

and was only about 16% in construction in 1966) as the categories of both skilled and semi-skilled labor increases. In 1925, only 18.5% of the workers in industry were considered skilled; by 1950, the proportion had increased to 49.6%; and in 1961 it was 64.6%. During the same period, semiskilled workers accounted for 41.3%, 47.9% and 35.4% respectively, the remainder being considered unskilled. On the farms, in contrast, 42% of those on state farms and 76.6% on collective farms possessed no skill at all. *It should be particularly noted, however, that the overwhelming proportion of unskilled workers in the Soviet economy is made up of women, who perform much of the arduous and menial labor in the Soviet Union.*

Another important trend in Soviet employment is for the balance between "physical" and "mental" labor to change in favor of the latter as the Soviet economy becomes more sophisticated and moves in the direction of a consumer-oriented "affluent" society. In 1969, 30 million "workers and employees"—about 26% of the totally employed (including members of the armed forces)—were classified as mental workers, an increase of over 9 million since 1959. Eighty-five million were classified as "physical," an increase of 6.5 million over 1959, when 78.5 million were so classified.

TRADE UNIONS AND MANAGEMENT. The Soviet working class is organized into trade unions whose membership currently exceeds 89 million. Unlike workers' organizations in most other countries, these unions are not truly voluntary organizations representing the economic, social, and more often political interests of the workers, but are more-or-less compulsory mass organizations under the complete control and supervision of the state and party. (As a social group, the working class enjoys far greater representation in the party than does the peasantry, and the opportunities for working-class children to move upward socially via higher education are definitely superior to those of the peasant.)

The advantages of union membership are so obvious that it is virtually universal. Actually some of the so-called social and economic rights guaranteed to the Soviet citizen by the constitution can be exercised only after joining a trade union. Also, union members receive twice the sickness and disability benefits paid to other workers; they can apply for special loans and grants from union funds; and their likelihood of spending a vacation at one of the various health resorts on the Crimean or Caucasion shores of the Black Sea is greater. Furthermore, only members can take advantage of the trade unions' elaborate networks of cultural, educational, and recreational facilities in the factories and elsewhere.

All these benefits notwithstanding, of course, members of Soviet labor organizations cannot have a role in political life outside the framework of the Communist party. Although the worker has a formal "pressure group" in the form of a union, he is shorn of any independent political leverage. However, because of his close proximity to the centers of power, and his access to party membership, he does have an opportunity to exert individual pressure through his union, his local party organization, or his local soviet—or simply by writing a letter to the newspapers.

Workers do not strike in the Soviet Union, not because they "own" the factories, as today's Soviet leaders fatuously maintain, but because they would suffer violent repression. Strikes are not technically illegal, but the penalties for "sabotage" and "counterrevolutionary activity" are very severe, and strikes called without the approval of party or trade union authorities would be so designated. However, workers are relatively free to pick their own jobs, unlike in the grim days of the Stalin era when many workers were prevented from leaving their places of work or were assigned to new jobs and locations for trivial infractions such as absenteeism or being late for work.

In spite of changes in the responsibilities and authority of the trade unions, introduced between 1959 and 1965, the paramount objective of the plant union leader remains virtually identical to that of the plant director and the factory party secretary. This factory "troika" encourages the workers to fulfill or exceed production goals established by the regime, so that the workers and the "troika" can collect bonuses and enhance their professional careers. The unions also engage in sham "collective bargaining" and actually sign a "contract" with the director, covering working conditions, individual grievance procedures, and the general administration of their specific plant or enterprise. Under no circumstances are the workers allowed to complain against the established economic or labor policies of the government, but they may "expose" corruption, collusion,

inefficiency, and negligence on the part of management if they feel sufficiently courageous. Since Stalin's death, workers have more often exercised their right to complain about such matters as work norms, promotions, transfers, dismissals, job classifications, application of proper wage scales, overtime pay, sick leave, and severance pay. Dissatisfied employees may now even appeal the decision of a labor-disputes board to a public court for a review of the dispute or grievance.

The administration of the factory is the sole responsibility of the director, and although his performance is watched and checked by both the plant party secretary and the trade union leader, they cannot interfere with his direction unless they wish to make formal charges of mismanagement. The three normally work cooperatively with one another and are not ordinarily in professional competition with each other. The plant director is commonly a technically trained specialist (usually an engineer), though this is not the usual background of the party and union officials.

INCOME AND WAGES. In industry, the quality and number of skills have gradually expanded through on-the-job training and special vocational schools, which continue to train millions of new workers every year. The more skilled, talented, and educated the worker, the greater is his reward. The ideal citizen of the future in the Soviet vision is the worker-engineer who works with both hands and brain.

Like others in Soviet society, workers are paid according to their skill and the amount (and quality) of their work. Each skill has its basic pay scale, based on production norms established by the regime, with extra pay for fulfillment and overfulfillment of the quotas. The minimum wage for urban workers established by law in 1957 was 35 rubles per month, which was raised in 1964 to 45 rubles. About 8 million workers were making less than 35 rubles per month in late 1956, and the 1957 law raised their pay to the new minimum.

Khrushchev's successors, Brezhnev and Kosygin, have continued to periodically boost the income of Soviet workers in an only slightly successful effort to enhance both labor productivity and quality. The minimum wage for workers was once again raised in January 1968 from 40–45 rubles per month to 60–70 rubles, and was extended to collective farmers as well. Wage increases from 1965 to 1969 raised the average monthly wage for "all workers and employees" from about 95 rubles ($105.56) to about 120 rubles ($132.00). If the fifteen-day annual paid vacation which workers and employees receive (up from twelve days in 1968) and social and welfare benefits provided by the state are calculated in the wage, the average would rise to 158–171 rubles per month, not an inconsiderable figure when compared to a decade earlier (see Table 5-6). The five highest paying economic sectors—not occupations, official data for which is not available—and hence the most prestigious have been science, construction, industry, administration, and transportation. Agriculture, art, health services, and communal-housing services remain at the bottom, with the collective farmers, who are not classified as "workers and employees" having the lowest incomes of all.

It should be noted, however, that average family income by per family income is substantially higher than average wages, since almost all families now include two wage-earners, and although this creates other social and demographic problems, it does serve to enhance family income and the standard of living.

The normal Soviet workweek since 1967 has been the 41-hour five-day week, which is a reduction of the 41-hour six-day week, which earlier replaced the 48-hour six-day week, the norm before 1956. When the changeover was made in 1967 in celebration of the fiftieth anniversary of the Bolshevik Revolution, the fervor of some two years of planning, popular discussion, and anticipation of the increased leisure time was reflected in the press, which behaved as if the Soviet Union had invented the five-day workweek and that it was an exclusive right enjoyed only by Soviet workers. Journalists and sociologists waxed ecstatic over the increased use that would be made of educational and cultural facilities—especially those such as libraries and theaters—as a result of the

TABLE 5-6.　*Average Earnings of Workers in the USSR, 1958–69 (rubles)*

Sector	1958 Annual	1958 Monthly	1965 Annual	1965 Monthly	1969 Annual	1969 Monthly	Number Employed, 1969	% Women, 1969
Industry	1,045	87	1,236	103	1,536	128	31,159,000	48
Construction	1,040	87	1,308	109	1,680	140	6,651,000	27
Agriculture	637	53	883	74	1,116	93	9,083,000	43
Transportation	988	82	1,266	106	1,572	131	7,797,000	24
Communications	696	58	886	74	1,128	94	1,262,000	67
Trade	697	58	907	76	1,116	93	7,287,000	75
Housing-communal	665	55	871	73	1,092	91	2,930,000	51
Health	707	59	944	79	1,092	91	4,927,000	85
Education	833	69	1,122	94	1,248	104	7,777,000	72
Science	1,271	106	1,387	116	1,596	133	3,128,000	47
Credit-insurance	865	72	1,030	86	1,284	107	363,000	77
Administration	1,010	84	1,256	105	1,440	120	1,834,000	60
Art	—	—	—	78	1,116	93	403,000	42
Average	934	78	1,144	95	1,440	120	87,922,000 *	50.5

SOURCE: *Narodnoye Khozyaistvo . . . v 1969 Godu*, pp. 538–40.
NOTE: Figures include managers and technical personnel.
* Includes 2,895,000 other workers and employees.

increased leisure time. Instead, when the five-day workweek arrived, citizens instead wanted such things as haircuts, public baths, and meals in restaurants—only to discover to their dismay that those employees were on the same five-day workweek. A survey showed that use of cultural facilities declined while the consumption of alcohol, especially vodka, skyrocketed, prompting the Soviet satirical journal *Krokodil* to suggest that the two-day weekend had created the opportunity to double the consumption of vodka as well as of culture. Soviet planners are still attempting to reconcile the five-day workweek, which they wish to universalize, with expanded availability of leisure, recreational, and cultural facilities.

All workers and employees are now guaranteed a fifteen-day annual paid vacation, provided they meet the qualifications in terms of length of service; and in 1968, all machine-tool operators received a special 15% wage boost, wage differentials were established for workers in the polar regions and the Far East, temporary disability payments were raised to 80–100% of average wages, and minimum pension-eligibility ages of collective farmers were reduced to 55 years for females and 60 years for males, respectively. In the Soviet Union hours of work, working conditions, wages, pensions, retirements, and penalties for violation of labor discipline are set by law and are not subject to dispute or negotiation. Any change in these sectors comes from the top as an "act of grace."

The Soviet wage-earner's take-home pay is not much affected by taxes and other deductions. Taxes on all incomes below 60 rubles per month were abolished in 1960, and those on incomes between 60 and 80 rubles were reduced by 15% in 1968. Income tax rates range from 0.7% to a maximum of 13%, with a special additional bachelor's tax of 6% levied against unmarried men between the ages of 20 and 50 and unmarried women between 20 and 45. There are no deductions for such items as social insurance, retirement, and medical care, all of which are taken care of by the state, although there is no unemployment insurance in the Soviet system, which has created problems for the increasing number of unemployed who have been laid off as a result of economic reforms. The purchasing power of the Soviet worker has been increased in other ways as well, such as the cancellation in 1957 of compulsory state bond purchases and the establishment of new pension rates in 1968, which now range from a minimum of 50% up to 100% (in special cases) of the worker's wage, depending upon length of service and other stipulations.

The Soviet Standard of Living

The worker's standard of living is still appreciably higher than that of the peasant but lower than that of the intelligentsia. In Soviet society, the spread between the few who receive the highest income (about 2,000 rubles per month) and those who receive the lowest (about 50 rubles per month) is very wide, indeed (Table 5-7). The mean Soviet income for all classes seems to be around 120 rubles per month. The maximum Soviet annual income, which is about $26,400, from which about $3,000 is deducted in taxes, allows the highest members of the Soviet elite to live at a level only comparable to that of the American or Western European upper middle class. This income is very modest compared to that for top American executives, and there are no Soviet citizens whose income or standard of living even approaches that of the big executives, the successful performing artists, or the large entrepreneur and investor in the United States.

With the advent of the five-day work week, higher wages, and two breadwinners per family, Soviet citizens have more leisure time, more disposable income, and more opportunity and cause to express grievances and dissatisfaction with the consumer end of the Soviet economy. Although retail prices for essential goods have remained stable since 1955 and have been periodically reduced, this is meaningless for the many commodities that are in great demand and short supply. Thus, the increasingly discriminating Soviet citizen finds it increasingly difficult to spend his money, since either goods are unavailable at the official price or the quality is unacceptable. The ninth Five-Year

TABLE 5-7. *Monthly Incomes of Representative Occupations in Soviet Society, 1960*

Occupation	Rubles *
Intelligentsia	
Top party and state leaders	2,000
Scientist (academician)	800–1,500
Minister or department head	700
Opera star	500–2,000
Professor (science)	600–1,000
Professor (medicine)	400–600
Docent (assistant professor)	300–500
Plant manager	300–1,000
Engineer	100–300
Physician, chief	95–180
Physician, staff	85–100
Teacher (high school)	85–100
Teacher (primary school)	60–90
Technician	80–200
Bookkeeper	110–115
Working Class	
Office clerk	80–90
Skilled worker	100–250
Semiskilled worker	60–90
Unskilled worker (cleaning woman, cook)	33–50
Peasantry	27–50

SOURCE: *Monthly Labor Review* (London), April 1960.

* In "hard rubles" introduced in 1961. Official rate of exchange is 1 ruble = $1.11.

Plan (for 1971–75), adopted by the Twenty-fourth Party Congress, once again promises to raise quickly the Soviet standard of living, but without the vain and fatuous boasts of the Khrushchev era about overtaking the United States. This time, however, when the draft directives for the plan, signed by Brezhnev, were released prior to the congress meeting for examination and discussion, its promises to produce more and better consumer goods were met with widespread skepticism and even derision by some organs of the Soviet press.

Thus, when one planner, N. N. Mirotvortsev, in an interview with a reporter for *Literaturnaya Gazeta,* recited the grandiose figures of the new Five-Year Plan, the reporter said he was impressed with all the statistics, but aggressively demanded to know:

As a consumer, I'm impressed in the following: will the shelves in the stores be bursting with goods and services as a result of the new Five-Year Plan? How close are we to the full satisfaction of demands? [9]

The planner cavalierly replied that the demand for the following items now in short supply would be fully satisfied by 1975: TV sets, washing machines, refrigerators, tape recorders, vacuum cleaners, watches, cameras, tableware, dishes, kitchen utensils, electrical appliances. And then he proudly added: "We will offer the public for sale 800,000 cars" in 1975 as opposed to only 124,000 in 1970, whereupon the reporter wearily responded, "So, the waiting list for cars [up to three years] will still not be ended by this Five-Year Plan." [10]

Another planner, who casually told a newspaper reporter that under the New Five-Year Plan everyday services would increase by 100%, was immediately challenged by the reporter who wanted to know, for example, how the Five-Year Plan would increase the supply of tailors to meet public demand. His reply, typical for a Soviet planning bureaucrat, was that going to a tailor was a waste of time because according to his calculations only 15% of the population had "nonstandard" physiques and only 10% might want "to wear something particularly individual from aesthetic motives," and that therefore 75 percent of the population should be satisfied with the "standard" sizes, colors, and styles projected by the planners. Yet, when the reporter suggested that people resorted to tailors because they were dissatisfied with factory-made clothes not only because of size, color, and style, but because of the poor quality of Soviet made factory clothing, the planner retorted that "people who have 'standard' figures waste their time at tailor shops in long arguments"—although he admitted that

9 *New York Times,* February 18, 1971.
10 *Washington Post,* February 21, 1971.

to adequately meet demands only in terms of size, color, price, material, and styles, a store would have to carry 12,000 suits, and then complained that in all Moscow "there is not a single store that has such a wide assortment," betraying once again the Soviet planning bureaucrat's penchant for hugeness as the only way to deal with economic problems, even in the consumer sphere.

Even the standard litany of how much better the next five years will be as compared to the preceding five, or even fifty, was rudely brushed aside by one reporter, who sarcastically noted:

It seems to me that comparing the rise of consumer goods with the past is no longer convincing. In the past, people frequently had virtually no clothes or shoes.

More deplorable than consumer goods production is the Soviet service industry; indeed, the frightening prospects of even providing more and unforeseen services if all of the consumer goods demanded by the Soviet public were satisfied may be an even greater deterrent to departures from past practice than mere production problems, which after all are largely quantifiable and measurable in character. How can the Soviet economy develop sufficient flexibility and versatility to respond to the myriad of changing demands—whimsical, arbitrary, sudden, ephemeral, and unanticipated? How will it reward or punish producers who make poor guesses in the consumer disposables area? Unless these questions are adequately dealt with, the consumer sector of the Soviet economy will continue to stumble and falter in its clumsy and awkward way. The challenge of mass consumption may prove to be the acid test of the Soviet economic order.

The purchasing power and income of the Soviet citizen is expected to rise even further under the latest Five-Year Plan. Unlike Khrushchev, who made grandiose promises at the Twenty-second Party Congress (1961) which the Soviet economy was incapable of delivering, the Brezhnev-Kosygin regime encouraged more modest and realistic expectations for its first five years and was able to deliver on its promises to raise average monthly earnings of work-

ers and employees to 115 rubles per month, reduce taxes on incomes between 60 and 80 rubles per month, increase the minimum wage to 60 rubles, establish a guaranteed annual income for collective farmers, increase old-age and disability pensions, and lower the retirement age of collective farmers to that of industrial workers.

The new Five-Year Plan is correspondingly modest and realistic in its plan for raising incomes, which still manage to rise faster than the standard of living, since the regime has been unable to deliver on all its promises concerning the production of consumer goods, services, and agricultural commodities. Under the Five-Year Plan for 1971–75, wages and salaries are scheduled to rise another 20–22% to a maximum of 145 rubles per month ($165.00). Real income is again supposed to rise by 30%, but this is contingent on the plan's demand that the Soviet worker increase his productivity by 36–40%, which is far less likely than his increase in income.

A definite ceiling is established on the Soviet standard of living, irrespective of income, for it is limited by the quantity, quality, and diversity of goods, services, and housing that are available—all of which are controlled by the Soviet government. Housing, for example, is quite cheap (4 to 5% of income), but it is in desperately short supply, and accommodations are apt to be very uninviting. The average urban family, for example, would consider itself fortunate if it had two small rooms to itself and shared a kitchen with one or more families. Indeed, according to the 1959 census, the majority of families still lived in one-room apartments. Only 23.5% had private kitchens—36.5% shared kitchens, and 22.3% were without kitchens at all. Some 11% of the families used the kitchen as a dwelling place as well. Average apartments in many crowded metropolitan areas would be considered slums, or at least substandard housing, in the United States or in Western Europe. Maintenance and repair are almost always inadequate or nonexistent.

The occupancy density of Soviet apartments, according to 1965 figures, was 2.33 persons per room—down from 2.78 in 1960 (1.5 person per room is considered excessive by

Western European and U.S. standards). In 1958, there were 5.40 square meters (less than 60 square feet) of dwelling space per urban inhabitant; in 1965, this had been raised to 6.42 square meters (less than 70 square feet, exclusive of kitchen and bath) per occupant, although the official norm is supposed to be 9 square meters. In Moscow alone, 40% of the housing was considered substandard in 1964 by Soviet standards, with tenants forced to share common kitchens and bathrooms. While the space per capita has not shown much improvement, there is more privacy now for Soviet citizens. New apartment rooms are smaller and have fewer people per room and more private baths and kitchens.

Housing usually is assigned in accordance with the individual's status in the economy and social hierarchy. Needless to say, perhaps, the intelligentsia monopolizes the most decent housing in the cities, but even this is quite modest—usually two rooms and a kitchen. Even the best-paid and most noteworthy members of Soviet society rarely have apartments exceeding four or five rooms. The celebrated Yuri Gagarin, the first Soviet cosmonaut, for example, was moved from an old two-room apartment to a new four-room dwelling after his historic venture into space.

The Soviet worker spends about 50 to 70% of his income for food, while the peasant spends virtually none. Food prices for ordinary staples are cheap, but the staples are not always available. Of course the intelligentsia can afford more and better food, not only at home, but in restaurants, where prices are very high.

Although the Soviet standard of living rose appreciably in the 1960s, so has it risen in the United States and Western Europe, and the Soviet Union still lags far behind. In 1966, Soviet per capita consumption of food was about 50% of that in the United States. Health and educational services were about 53% of the level in the United States; and in other services, it was about 24%. In the area of non-food consumer goods, however, it was less than 15%. Even if Soviet output of consumer goods increases rapidly in the 1970s, it must still contend with the complicated network of repair, maintenance, and service facilities that will be required. Furthermore, the accumulated stock of durable consumer goods, which creates a vast used-goods market and results in discounted prices and which exists in the United States, is virtually absent in the Soviet Union. Thus, production figures alone are insufficient to establish proper comparisons and contrasts. A representative selection of durable household goods in stock in the United States and the Soviet Union emphasizes the wide gap that still remains between the two countries (see Table 5-8).

TABLE 5-8. *Stocks of Selected Household Durable Goods in the USSR and the U.S., 1955–66*

	Units per thousand persons				
	USSR			U.S.	
Item	1955	1960	1966	1966	USSR % of U.S., 1966
Sewing machines	31	92	151	136	112%
Refrigerators	4	7	40	293	14
Washing machines	1	10	77	259	30
Radios	66	130	171	1,300	13
Television sets	4	22	82	376	22
Automobiles	2	3	5	398	1

SOURCE: U.S. Congress, Joint Economic Committee, *Soviet Economic Performance, 1966–1967* (Washington, D.C.: G.P.O., 1968), p. 94.

The economic reforms introduced during the past few years and designed to stimulate productivity and quality while simultaneously reducing costs is exacting its toll in a social phenomenon new to Soviet society—unemployment. Unemployment was "abolished" in 1930 and accordingly unemployment insurance is presumably unnecessary and hence does not exist. Since the constitution guarantees every able-bodied citizen employment as a matter of right and in stern puritanical cadence states that "he who does not work, neither shall he eat," the rise of unemployment is socially and ideologically explosive. Several years ago, quite a domestic stir was caused when a Soviet economist noted, in a scholarly article, that labor "surpluses" were being created in isolated areas of the Soviet economy during a period of generally severe labor deficits. The surpluses were caused by newly instituted economic reforms, according to which managers were allowed to lay off unproductive workers in the interests of efficiency and showing a profit; furthermore, workers were leaving certain inhospitable areas of the country for more attractive areas, where labor was not in short supply, thus creating labor shortages and surpluses.[11] Nevertheless, in the interests of improving the Soviet economy, the controversial economic reforms are being extended in accordance with Brezhnev's dictum:

The fundamental question now is not how much you produce, but at what cost. . . . It is in this field that the center of gravity in the competition between the two systems lies in our time.[12]

Two months before this speech, an unpublished decree of February 27, 1970, revealed a year later by the economic journal *Ekonomiki,* had been issued providing up to three months' salary for administrators only who are laid off because of reforms or reorganization and who had to be retrained for jobs in industry.[13] The new decree had been issued to relieve the factories introducing the reforms of the burden of finding new jobs for those laid off, in order that the Soviet constitutional and ideological commitment to full employment not be violated. In December, 1970, it was revealed that 250,000 workers would have to find jobs in the following year. Cutbacks in administrative personnel had accelerated after October 1969, when a decree called for the reduction of swollen staffs in the interest of saving money.

Some Soviet economists are now advocating that the provision for unemployment insurance be extended to other workers and that the burden of finding them new employment be lifted from the factories and shifted to society. The obvious and perhaps ultimate solution, unpalatable though it is, may be to allow enterprises to lay off freely in the interests of production and cost efficiency and to establish a state or trade union system of unemployment insurance. This would, however, be a hard pill for Soviet leaders, whose proudest boast has been that the Soviet system had abolished unemployment.

The Soviet Intelligentsia

The Soviet concept of the intelligentsia embraces not only members of the arts, sciences, and professions, but engineers, lawyers, technicians of various kinds, government officials, doctors, journalists, university students, and a wide spectrum of "white-collar" employees. The intelligentsia are all considered to be "mental workers"—a term we have used several times already.

After the Revolution, the intelligentsia was to be made to serve the new ruling class—the proletariat. Virtually all "nonpolitical" technical and specialist posts were filled with members of the old intelligentsia, pending the creation of a new corps of technicians and specialists from the proletariat. The government bureaucracy, the army, and educational and medical establishments continued to rely on the old intelligentsia for their operations. As the new Soviet intelligentsia grew in numbers, the remnants of the old were gradually retired, purged, or isolated in innocuous enterprises. Surprisingly, however, the suspicions of the working class, the peasantry, and the regime

---

[11] See E. L. Manevich, *U.S.S.R.: Full Employment?* (Moscow: Novosh Agency, 1968).

[12] *Pravda,* April 14, 1970.

[13] *New York Times,* February 21, 1971.

regarding the intelligentsia did not abate completely, and the existence of a privileged stratum in a society that cherishes the cult of equality continues to nag the system.

Between 1939 and 1970 the number of mental workers increased from a little under 10 million to about 30 million, with the greatest increment being registered in the lower ranks (Table 5-9). Of course, it would be absurd to classify all "mental" workers as members of the

TABLE 5-9. *Soviet "Mental Workers," 1939–70*

	1939	*1959*
Totals	9,600,000	20,495,000 †
Executives in state administration, public organizations, and their departments	445,000	392,100
Executives of enterprises and their departments	757,000	955,000
Collective-farm chairmen and their deputies	(278,800) *	(102,800)
Engineering and technical personnel	1,656,500	4,205,900
Engineers (excluding executives)	(247,300)	(834,300)
Designers and draftsmen	(103,900)	(297,100)
Foremen	(267,000)	(753,500)
Technicians	(274,000)	(513,000)
Laboratory assistants	(156,500)	(436,200)
Agronomists, zoo technicians, vets, foresters	294,900	477,200
Scientists and educators in higher education	111,600	316,400
Heads of educational institutions	(73,100)	(114,900)
Other teachers, educators, scientific workers	1,368,400	2,403,700
Senior physicians and medical executives	46,500	44,000
Physicians	122,300	337,900
Dentists	14,000	31,700
Interns, midwives, nurses	332,400	1,058,200
Planning, auditing, accounting personnel	3,102,000	3,501,900
Economists, planners, statisticians	(282,100)	(308,300)
Accountants, bookkeepers	(1,785,400)	(1,816,900)
Cashiers, clerks	(279,300)	(413,500)
Inspection and audit personnel	(755,200)	(963,200)
Literature and publishing	58,000	104,100
Cultural workers	285,000	462,000
Librarians	(87,000)	(239,000)
Arts	143,300	190,600
Lawyers, judges, prosecutors	82,600	101,700
Communications personnel	265,400	476,400
Trade, restaurants, etc.	1,626,000	2,268,220
Directors, etc.	(244,900)	(334,800)
Secretarial personnel	489,400	535,900
Public and social services personnel	202,500	277,100
Agents and expediters	176,400	146,000
Unaccounted for (probably includes military, etc.)		1,875,000

SOURCE: *Vestnik Statistiki,* no. 12 (1960).
* Figures in parentheses are included in the total of the general category.
† The corresponding figure for 1970 was 29,900,000.

Soviet intelligentsia proper, which comprised only about 15 million in 1970. (Table 5-10).

The intelligentsia occupies a crucial and powerful position in the Soviet economy. Virtually all economic and political power is concentrated in this group. Those who control the party and state are automatically part of the intelligentsia. All the managerial, technical, and scientific skills are concentrated in the intelligentsia, for, by definition, any person who possesses these skills is a member of the intelligentsia. The intelligentsia plans production, establishes national goals and purposes, allocates rewards, and makes, executes, and enforces the law. If the intelligentsia were in

permanant control of the economy and other institutions of society and could transmit this control from one generation to the next, it would meet all the formal requirements for being a "ruling class," but it does not have this power. Its individual members have no legal right to their social status, nor can they hope to keep it through material wealth; to belong to the intelligentsia, one must actively perform certain specialized functions *and* demonstrate ideological conformity.

A better index to the size of the Soviet intelligentsia proper would begin with the total number of specialists with higher and specialized secondary education employed in the national economy (see Table 5-10). As of November 15, 1965, these persons numbered 12,066,000 (17,200,000 if the military, pensioners and others not employed in the national economy are included).

TABLE 5-10. *Distribution of Intelligentsia by Specialization, 1965*

Higher Education

Engineers	1,630,800
Agricultural technicians	302,800
Economists, statisticians	301,100
Trade specialists	35,000
Lawyers	84,600
Physicians	500,800
Teachers, librarians, cultural specialists	1,859,500
Total	4,891,000

Specialized Secondary Education

Technicians	2,886,700
Agricultural technicians	465,000
Planners, statisticians	571,000
Trade specialists	291,000
Lawyers	16,400
Medical specialists, including dentists	1,453,600
Teachers, librarians, cultural specialists	1,282,300
Total	7,174,900
Grand Total	12,065,900

WOMEN IN THE INTELLIGENTSIA. In 1959, women made up 54% (11,055,000) of the "mental workers." Within the intelligentsia itself, women are overwhelmingly represented in some sectors, only sparsely in others. Among state, party, and economic executives, the number of women is very small, while in areas like teaching, medicine, and in the offices of economic planning bodies, they dominate. But when these categories are more closely scrutinized, we find that whereas nearly 70% of the teachers are women, only about 22% of the school principals are women; although 38% of the scientific workers in 1969 were of the female sex, their proportion diminished rapidly as the status, prestige, and importance of the position increased. Thus, in 1969, of the 48,400 junior research workers and research assistants, 24,200 (50%) were women; of the 37,300 senior research workers (research associates), 10,200 (28%) were women; of the 64,900 docents (associate professors), 14,000 (22%) were women; but of the 16,900 academicians and professors, only 1,600 (9%) were women. And, although in 1965 women accounted for 73% of the physicians and 92% of all medical specialists, most of the important administrative positions in medical establishments were occupied by the few men in the field. Thus, while individual women can aspire to any social level in Soviet society, from membership in the party politburo or a government ministry to the lowest menial occupations, the more significant the political or power implications of the position, the narrower their opportunities. Furthermore, as in most other societies, women have virtually no access to the main instruments of coercion in Soviet society, the armed forces and the secret police.

NATIONALITY COMPOSITION OF THE INTELLIGENTSIA. Although the Russians account for less than 54% of the total population of the USSR, they made up more than 62% of the intelligentsia in 1965. Of the other nationalities, only the Jews, Georgians, and Armenians reflect a higher ratio in the composition of the intelligentsia than their share of the population.

The other nationalities, in varying degrees, are underrepresented, the most extreme cases being in central Asia. Tremendous progress, however, has been registered in creating a national intelligentsia for each nationality, as is shown in Table 5-11.

Generally speaking, it is the policy of the regime to bring about a numerical correlation between a nationality's proportion in the total population and its share of the intelligentsia. As a consequence, the underrepresented nationalities show a more rapid rate of growth in the size of their intelligentsia, while the overrepresented nationalities (except for the Russians) show a corresponding decrease in their relative share of the intelligentsia. The nationality composition of the Soviet population revealed by the 1970 census suggests that the Soviet formula of proportionate balance, while

TABLE 5-11. *Distribution of Soviet Intelligentsia by Nationality, Level of Educational Attainment and Sex, 1965/70*

| | Population, 1970 | Specialized Secondary Education, 1965 | | Higher Education, 1965 | | Scientists, 1969 |
		Number	Women	Number	Women	Number
Russians	129,015,000 (53.4%)	4,361,400	65%	2,679,400	57%	583,564
Ukrainians	40,753,000 (16.9)	1,067,100	60	667,200	49	95,097
Jews	2,151,000 (0.9)	159,700	54	332,700	48	66,661
Byelorussians	9,052,000 (3.7)	216,400	64	126,200	49	17,850
Georgians	3,245,000 (1.3)	80,700	58	106,900	41	17,100
Armenians	3,559,000 (1.5)	72,300	54	91,400	42	18,708
Tatars	5,931,000 (2.5)	105,800	65	67,200	55	10,899
Azerbaidzhani	4,380,000 (1.3)	68,200	37	61,500	29	12,396
Uzbeks	9,195,000 (3.8)	72,900	28	72,600	26	11,254
Kazakhs	5,299,000 (2.2)	57,000	36	49,800	31	7,132
Lithuanians	2,665,000 (1.1)	59,500	67	40,100	49	7,482
Latvians	1,430,000 (0.6)	47,100	63	31,800	55	5,758
Estonians	1,007,000 (0.4)	36,000	64	24,000	52	4,539
Moldavians	2,698,000 (1.1)	27,600	60	16,700	42	2,213
Tadzhiks	2,136,000 (0.9)	16,600	19	15,500	17	2,206
Turkmen	1,525,000 (0.6)	13,300	18	14,400	15	1,704
Kirgiz	1,452,000 (0.6)	13,800	34	13,100	28	1,640
Total (incl. other nationalities)	241,720,000 (100)	6,702,100	62%	4,547,600	52%	883,420 *

* Women accounted for 38% of the total.

commendable, may inadvertently arouse unappeasable expectations, since the natural population growth of the underrepresented nationalities threatens to wipe out the gains made in the 1960s and thus create pressures for even greater preferential treatment for the more underrepresented nationalities. This, in turn, causes resentment among more highly qualified persons of other nationalities, who must consequently alter their career plans in order to facilitate social justice.[14] On the other hand some of the overrepresented nationalities, particularly the Jews, whose population growth rates are low, find themselves under new pressures since their overrepresentation tends to become more conspicuous simply by virtue of their not growing. Thus, the Russians, whose share in the total population dropped to 53.4% in 1970, have been increasing their proportion in the ranks of the intelligentsia (62.3% in 1966), although some of this may reflect a greater degree of assimilation of non-Russians in the intelligentsia than in other social groups. The Moslem nationalities, on the other hand, while registering about a 50% increase in their share of the population, are even more seriously underrepresented among the Soviet elites as a result. Thus, the Uzbeks, who now rank third in size after the Russians and Ukranians, rank eighth in the ranks of the intelligentsia and scientists, while the Jews, who have dropped to twelfth place among the nationalities in size, remain an impressive third in the ranks of the intelligentsia (see Table 5-11).

These unexpected demographic trends are bound to create problems for the Soviet regime with both the Uzbeks and Jews. While it may be relatively easy to adjust proportions at the political level of participation—this can be done by fiat and depends upon the principles of representation in any event—adjustments in the social system will be much more difficult, since the regime will be contending with two crucial but increasingly contradictory imperatives: the demand for equitable national representation and the demand for competence and achievement, which resurfaces within the

broader context of social justice for different social groups within a system ideologically committed to equalitarianism, but whose continued successful development increasingly depends upon the pragmatic search for quality and excellence.

SOCIAL MOBILITY IN THE SOVIET UNION

Every society develops its own special avenues to higher rewards and status, although as the society "matures" and the opportunities for its evolution and differentiation within the existing sociopolitical framework are narrowed, these roads tend to be blocked by law, custom, and advantages of birth. During the early years of the Soviet Union, when it was struggling for survival, virtually the only conditions for social movement upward were political loyalty and ideological conformity. Access to positions of responsibility and to higher education and training was available only through the party or its preparatory institutions. However, once it was realized that political loyalty and ideological conformity were insufficient to ensure the technical competence and professional knowledge necessary for the economic and cultural transformation of society, political and ideological tests were deemphasized for positions which were relatively nonpolitical in character but which required special ability, knowledge, and skill. It was only demanded that the individual not be actively hostile to the regime. Naturally, the rarer the skill and the knowledge, and the fewer the individuals with special aptitudes, the greater the immunity from political and ideological tests.

Political Conformity and Professional Competence

In due time, two separate but parallel avenues of social advancement were established: those of political loyalty and technical competence. When the two are combined, success is virtually assured in the Soviet system. Competence alone is sufficient to assure high status and rewards,

---

[14] See M. S. Dzhunosov, "Soviet Autonomy and the Vestiges of Nationalism," *Istoriya*, no. 1 (1963).

but not the highest; loyalty alone is rarely sufficient, since, by itself, it is always in plentiful supply. However, whether one embarks on the ideological-political or technical-professional road to success, higher education is the common vestibule through which all must first pass. Access to higher education, and the rewards it promises, is thus fundamental, since upward mobility in Soviet society is almost impossible without it.

The best avenues of social mobility are still through politics, but the risks are correspondingly higher. The more remote one is from politics, the more secure is his status. For this reason, many people eschew "political" careers entirely, immersing themselves in the sciences and mathematics, the study of foreign languages, ancient history, literature, and a host of other fields widely divorced from political reality. High social rewards in Soviet society are thus possible in certain technical and specialized areas even without membership in the Communist party. Large numbers of outstanding scientists, professors, and artists deliberately remain outside the Communist party and consciously avoid involvement in politics, relying only upon their abilities and talents to achieve success.

Even within the sciences, professions, and arts, however, there is the "political" scientist, professor, or artist who may have achieved some distinction in his field but is not of outstanding caliber and who propels his movement upward by joining the party and accepting the inherent risks and corresponding opportunities. Administrative and supervisory positions in bodies like the Soviet Academy of Sciences are likely to be bestowed upon the savant who chooses to become involved in party activities rather than the most eminent personality in the given field of endeavor.

If loyalty and competence are the two primary personal factors involved in social mobility, there are peripheral or secondary considerations which can affect social mobility adversely or advantageously: sex (which we have already discussed), social origins, and nationality.

SOCIAL ORIGINS. Social origin plays a crucial role in affecting accessibility to higher education and one's advancement after its attainment. During the early years of the Soviet Union, social origin played an important negative role, with definite preferences being shown toward those of working-class and peasant parentage. Today, a kulak, clerical, merchant, or even noble ancestry is no longer a social crime, although it is slightly more respectable to be of working-class, peasant, or "toiling intelligentsia" background.

Social origin, once again, is assuming an important influence on the contours of social mobility. All things being equal, the children of members of the intelligentsia will have greater opportunities for remaining in the privileged stratum or advancing upward within it than will children of working-class and peasant parents. As Soviet society becomes more routinized and stabilized, the normal patterns of family connections and favoritism inevitably exact their tribute in gaining admission to schools, acquiring preferred geographical assignments, and gaining promotions. Children of working-class origin still have ample opportunity for higher education, provided they have demonstrated ability, but they labor under the normal disadvantage of not having the superior cultural, environmental, and psychological preparation which the children of the intelligentsia enjoy.[15]

Children of peasant origin, particularly on the collective farms, have fewer and fewer such opportunities. Although compulsory education in rural areas is now eight years, this is insufficient to allow them to compete equally with children in the urban areas, who are now assured of ten years of schooling. Most of the children of peasant parentage are doomed to stay on the farm and can hardly aspire to more than a modest advance into the rural working-class or rural foreman group.

These disturbing trends have been confirmed by sociological studies conducted in the Soviet Union on social mobility. Despite their routinely expressed optimism that these problems will be solved in a socialist society, the underlying tone of the studies gives more cause

[15] For a recent Soviet study of this problem, see M. N. Rutkevich, "The Social Sources of the Replenishment of the Soviet Intelligentsia," *Voprosy Filosofii*, no. 6 (June 1967):15–34.

for pessimism. Most of these studies reveal that social mobility in the Soviet Union is slowing down, and that increasing mass education, while it does not necessarily facilitate social mobility, does arouse greater expectations, intensify competition, and result in alienation among increasing numbers of skilled and educated people who cannot find jobs commensurate with their personal expectations and ambitions. For to a substantial degree the Soviet Union is still a semideveloped country because of a lopsided emphasis on heavy industry in its economic development.

As a consequence, social lines appear to be hardening in the Soviet social system, with the intelligentsia threatening to reproduce itself because of the greater opportunities its children have to replace their own parents in what may soon become a social self-replacement society. The Soviet authorities are well aware of the emerging problem of what is called the "self-production of the intelligentsia": sociological studies have verified this tendency, but most Soviet scholars simply offer explanations which would be considered superficial in other countries. Thus, one study, a 1964 sample survey of five institutions of higher learning in the Sverdlovsk region, discovered that workers or their offspring accounted for 51% of the daytime students, while students of collective-farm origin numbered only 5% and students of "employee" origin accounted for 44%. The more prestigious the institution and the more exacting the department or profession, the higher the proportion of students from intelligentsia families. The author of the study, obviously dismayed at the results, nevertheless claimed that this was "a completely understandable phenomenon," because

such higher-educational institutions as the Medical Institute and the University are attended by larger numbers of children of doctors, teachers, and the like, for among the intelligentsia these occupations are often "hereditary." [16]

And when the "employee" category was further refined to distinguish between "specialists" (those having a higher or specialized secondary education), the children of specialists at Sverdlovsk University accounted for 38% of the students, rising to a high of 60% of those enrolled in the physics department. In 1965, the number of specialists in the total population was 12 million (about 50% of them women).

Another study found that while most Soviet youth desired to continue on to higher education, the chances of their expectations and hopes being fulfilled varied widely from one social class to another,[17] thus suggesting that in spite of the widespread ideological conditioning in Soviet society and socialization in schools, the Soviet educational system has been unsuccessful in overcoming the uneven advantages that accrue to Soviet youth because of family status and conditioning. Among the secondary-school graduates of the Novosibirsk Oblast, the study found, the likelihood of a high-school graduate from an urban nonmanual family background going on to higher education was about 8 times greater than that of a graduate from a peasant family background, although 93% of the first group and 76% of the second expressed the same desire to continue their studies (see Table 5-12). The severe social, psychological, and environmental handicaps that affect rural children are demonstrated by the fact that even among children of the rural intelligentsia the motivation to study was weaker than for children of the urban working class, and identical with that of peasant children, although their hopes were realized in 58% of the cases. It is interesting to note that the children of urban industrial and construction workers (the highest-paying industrial sectors in the Soviet economy) fared better in gaining a higher education than did children of rural nonmanual workers, thus suggesting that Soviet rural life succeeds in blunting both motivation and opportunity. As the author observes:

It is important to bear in mind that the opportunity to enter higher-educational institutions depends sig-

---

[16] L. I. Sennikova, "Higher Education as a Factor in Social Mobility," in *Zhiznennye Plany Molodezhi,* ed. M. N. Rutkevich (Sverdlovsk, 1966).

[17] V. N. Shubkin, "Youth Starts Out," *Voprosy Filosofii,* no. 5 (1965).

TABLE 5-12. *Social Status of Families, Personal Plans of Secondary-School Graduates, and their Realization in Novosibirsk Oblast, 1965*

Occupational Status of Family	Percentage of Graduates who Expressed Desire to Continue Studies	Percentage of Graduates who Succeeded in Continuing Studies
Urban nonmanual	93%	82%
Rural nonmanual	76	58
Manual, industry and construction	83	61
Manual, transport and communications	82	45
Manual, agriculture	76	10
Manual, services	76	59
Others	38	25
All students	83%	61%

nificantly not only upon the demographic situation in the country, but also upon a number of social factors which, in our view, it is impermissible to ignore. The opportunities available today to young people living in large cities to enter higher-educational institutions are considerably higher than in rural localities because the level of preparation in urban schools is, as a general rule, higher. Analysis also shows that their parents' educational level has a serious influence upon the children's interests and strivings. . . . The standards of living, housing conditions, etc. have a major influence upon a child's grades, upon his occupational inclinations, and consequently upon the opportunity to obtain an education. As a result of all this, the social structure of those entering first grade differs markedly from that of those who graduate and, even more, from that of students in higher-educational institutions.[18]

NATIONAL ORIGIN. Even if not officially admitted, national origin does influence the social mobility of an individual. Membership in certain nationalities automatically creates definite limitations, while membership in other nationalities provides better opportunities which are equally accidental in character. All things being equal, a Great Russian is endowed with greater advantages than citizens of other nationalities. Russian is the official language of the party and

[18] Ibid.

state, the medium of instruction in all of its most important institutions of higher learning, the language of the most numerous and powerful nationality, the language of the most influential culture. An absolute command of the Russian language is an indispensable prerequisite for social mobility beyond the purely local national level, and this is a special barrier which the native Russian does not have to overcome. The opportunities for Ukrainians are also fairly abundant. Smaller nationalities, like the Georgians, Armenians, Jews, and Germans, have also enjoyed special advantages because of a relatively higher rate of educational attainment and acquired skills, although both Jews and Germans have suffered discrimination and prejudice for political reasons—namely, suspicions of divided ideological and psychological loyalties. While many Jews are found in the arts, sciences, and professions, they appear to be systematically excluded from sensitive areas like the diplomatic service, and informal quotas have been established limiting their numbers in institutions of higher learning.

The Moslem nationalities have had fewest opportunities of all, not only because of a heritage of backwardness (which was real enough), but also because of suspected political unreliability and the inevitable residual cultural prejudices which continue to divide Christian and Moslem nationalities. With the accelerated educational and cultural transformation of these nationalities, their opportunities have correspondingly increased, and prejudices resulting from national origins will continue to diminish progressively in the future, although the changing nationality mix may serve to complicate matters, as the population explosion in Moslem areas outstrips development and "progress."

Thus, in many respects, the Soviet regime is confronted with a more complicated, latent explosive version of the problems faced by American society in seeking to equalize not only the opportunities but also the achievements among the various social and ethnic minorities. Like American society, Soviet society is partially trapped by its own self-congratulatory rhetoric concerning its formal commitment to social justice and equality, which, while accurately reflecting earlier successes in dealing with injustice, now serve to divert attention from the hard residual problems of social injustice. It is no longer sufficient, even in the Soviet Union, to deal with serious social problems by declaring them either solved or nonexistent. In this category is the so-called national problem, which like unemployment and class conflict was allegedly solved decades ago. Yet the "national problem" refuses to go away, and is now threatening to intersect with the broader problems of social, economic, and political justice and representation.

As the number of secondary-school graduates of all nationalities and social groups increase and the opportunities for upward social mobility decrease, serious problems will arise, first in the scramble and competition for admission to institutions of higher learning, and second, in the contest and rivalry for jobs after graduation. Since the Soviet regime has greater control than do most other countries over the flow of its students through educational institutions and can modify the flow to correspond

with economic development and opportunities, its responsibilities and accountabilities are more conspicuous. The absence of organized dissent and criticism of existing policies intensifies even more the responsibility of the regime for finding solutions. How the Soviet regime will control the social flow in the interests of social stability, simultaneously discharging its commitments to to national and social equality and demanding higher levels of excellence and efficiency in occupational, professional, and scientific performance, will be one of the miracles Soviet leaders are called upon to perform. One Soviet scholar, who clearly recognizes the problem, defines it incisively, rejects earlier solutions based upon preferential quotas as inadequate, and calls essentially for more study—a clear indication that no real solution is perceived on the horizon:

It must be particularly emphasized that the increased competition for admission to higher-educational institutions, combined with the rise in the number of secondary-school graduates, may lead to a diminution in the percentage of workers and peasants entering higher-educational institutions. Therefore, it is necessary to take measures in advance to counteract such trends. This is a rather complicated problem. On the one hand we must strive to provide equal opportunities for all. On the other hand due to [social and environmental differences] . . . young people of equal capacities—but differing in preparation—will actually differ in their opportunities to gain an education. . . . Efforts to establish preferential conditions for admission to higher-educational institutions for particular social groups, regardless of level of preparation, not only will not help to solve the problems but, on the contrary, may reduce the general level of education, which would be equivalent to holding back the progress of science and technology. This is the contradiction. It cannot be solved quickly, but it must be recognized, and specific steps to resolve it must be planned, in accordance with the level of development of the productive forces.[19]

19 Ibid.

The ultimate power in Soviet society is vested in the Communist party of the Soviet Union (CPSU). Political action outside the framework of the party is illegal and thus subject to the harshest penalties. The monopoly position of the party in the Soviet system is given juridical expression in article 126 of the Soviet constitution:

The Communist Party of the Soviet Union . . . is the vanguard of the working people in their struggle to build a Communist society and is the leading core of all organizations of the working people, both public and state.

As the ultimate repository of power in the Soviet system, the symbol of legitimacy, and the organization through which are disseminated the policies of the Soviet leadership, the Communist party of the Soviet Union emerges as the arena in which social, ideological, and political conflicts are resolved into decisions. Although the nature and composition of the party have undergone significant change over the years, there has been little alteration in its formal organization and structure. The membership of the party has been substantially expanded, its institutions and organs periodically rearranged, and qualifications for membership adjusted, but in its outward form and in its basic principles of organization, the party shows remarkable continuity.

Article 19 of the 1961 party statutes outlines the principal characteristics of party organization as follows:

The guiding principle of party organizational structure is democratic centralism, which means:
a. Election of all leading party organs, from the lowest to the highest organ.
b. Periodic accountability of party organs to their party organizations and higher organs.
c. Strict party discipline and subordination of the minority to the majority.
d. The decision of the higher organs are absolutely binding on lower organs.

The principal "democratic" feature of the party organization is the theoretical right of the rank-and-file membership of the party to elect the representatives of the lowest party organs

SIX

the Communist party

directly. Those lower organs in turn select representatives to the next-higher body, and so it goes, on up through the pyramidal structure of the party, culminating in the Central Committee, the Politburo, and the Secretariat.

At the bottom of the party pyramid are the myriad primary party organs, which remain the only party units organized along functional lines (Fig. 6-1). The structure of the party follows the territorial-administrative pattern of the state, which is divided into both territorial-administrative and ethno-administrative units, which frequently overlap. Thus, whereas the primary party units elect delegates to the next higher territorial organizations, the rayon and city organs may send delegates directly to oblast, kray, or party conferences, as the case may be.

In the case of some of the smaller Union Republics, the territory is divided simply into rayons, and the rayon organizations elect delegates directly to the Union Republic Party Congress.[1]

[1] In 1962, Khrushchev reorganized the party at the regional levels, dividing it into agricultural and industrial sectors with twin parallel organizational structures which were merged at the level of the union republic. This doubled the number of regional and local party secretaries and party organs, diluted the power and authority of existing party officials and bodies, and generally disoriented many party workers. Immediately after Khrushchev's removal in October 1964, this double-headed organizational monstrosity, which never functioned properly or effectively, was dissolved and the territorial-administrative principle of organization was restored.

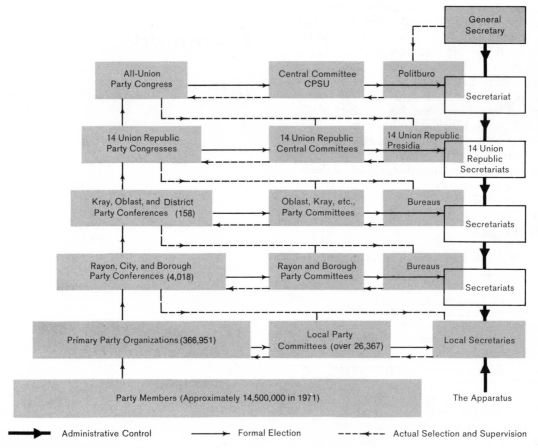

FIG. 6-1. *The organizational structure of the Communist party of the Soviet Union.*

Theoretically, each party organization, at whatever level, elects its own executive officials and secretaries, but they are held to be accountable not only to the organ which elects them but to the next-higher organ as well. Since the party rules read that "the decisions of the higher organs are absolutely binding on lower organs," officials and secretaries of lower organs reflect the will, not of the bodies which elected them, but of the organ directly above them. Accountability of officials to their own party organizations thus amounts to little more than faithful and efficient execution of decisions handed down from above.

The total number of party organizations in 1971 was over 370,000, embracing 13,810,089 party members and 645,232 candidate members, for a total membership of nearly 14.5 million people—an increase of about 2,000,000 since the Twenty-third Party Congress in 1966. The party organizations in 1971 were distributed as shown in Table 6-1.

THE PRIMARY PARTY ORGANIZATIONS

The primary party organizations (PPOs), formerly called "party cells," and still referred

TABLE 6-1. *Communist Party Organizations in the USSR, 1971*

Organizational Level	Number of Party Organizations
Union republic	14
Kray	6
Oblast	142
District	10
City	760
Borough	448
Rayon	2,810
Primary party organizations	366,951

SOURCE: *Partiinaya Zhizn,* no. 10 (May 1966): 8–17; no. 7 (April 1967):7–8; and no. 19 (October 1967):8–20; *Pravda,* March 31, 1971.

to as "cells" informally, are found at every level of Soviet society. Ranging in membership from three to three thousand people, they are formed at a place of work, except in rural areas where they may be organized at a place of residence or in a housing administration. PPOs are found in factories, farms, schools, universities, research institutes, stores, cultural institutions, government bureaus and offices, armed forces and police units. In any Soviet institution or enterprise in which there are at least three party members, a primary organization may be formed.

As the basic unit of party organization, the party cells are in direct contact with the rank-and-file membership of the party and are thus the final organs for the dissemination of party policies and decisions. In the performance of this function, the party cell "carries out mass agitation and propagandist work, educates the masses in the spirit of Communism," and further

organizes workers to implement Communist construction tasks, leads Socialist competition to implement state plans and pledges, mobilizes the masses, . . . and strives to strengthen labor discipline, to achieve a steady increase in labor productivity and improvement of production standards, and to protect and increase communal property in enterprises and on collective and state farms.

Primary party organizations also check to ensure that the enterprises or institutions in which they are located are performing in accordance with party dictates, and the cells are supposed to "promptly inform the party organs of any shortcomings in the work of the establishment or individual workers, regardless of their positions."

Communist party cells thus resemble permanent vigilante committees; they must show more zeal and enthusiasm for the Soviet cause than ordinary citizens, and very often their self-righteous exhortations irritate many sectors of the Soviet population. Since many Soviet citizens become party members for opportunistic reasons, their ideological enthusiasm is often superficial. The meetings, lectures, parades, and cultural programs constantly being organized by party cells to disseminate the party's ideological propaganda are not always well attended, and are far from popular.

REGIONAL AND UNION REPUBLIC PARTY ORGANIZATIONS

All party organizations above the primary units are territorial in character and parallel the territorial-administrative divisions of the Soviet state; they supervise and inspect the work of all Soviet institutions, enterprises, and activities within their territorial unit.

The USSR is divided into fifteen union republics, which are the highest territorial-administrative divisions in the country. The larger republics are divided into *oblasts*—the basic provincial unit—and some also include lesser nationality units called autonomous republics, autonomous oblasts, and national districts, in descending order of importance. The smaller republics and the oblasts are divided into rural units called *rayons* and city administrations. Normally, the administrative chain of control would be from all-union to republic to oblast to rayon and city. The largest republic, the Russian Soviet Federated Socialist Republic (RSFSR), also has six special territorial units called *krays,* which are indistinguishable from the oblast except that five of them contain national autonomous oblasts. Autonomous republics and autonomous oblasts are subordinate directly to the Union Republic or kray in which they are located.

The organizational hierarchy is thus from primary party organization to rayons and city organizations, to oblast, autonomous republic, and kray organizations, then, to the fourteen republic party organizations, one for each of the non-Russian republics. The Russian SFSR does not have a separate party organization; its party affairs were directed by a special bureau of the Central Committee chaired by Nikita Khrushchev when he was in power. The RSFSR Bureau, which was a Khrushchev power base, was abolished at the Twenty-third Party Congress (1966), and its functions transferred to the party Secretariat and Politburo.

All party organizations contain five organs:

1. a constituent body, "the highest governing organ of party organization," which is called the "General Meeting" in the primary party organizations, the "Party Conference" at the rayon, city, oblast, and kray levels, and the "Party Congress" at the Union Republic and all-union levels;

2. a delegated governing body—called a "Committee" at lower levels and the "Central Committee" at republic and all-union levels—which is elected by the constituent body to act for it between its sessions;

3. an executive decision-making organ—called the "Bureau" at all levels except that of the all-union and in the Ukrainian party organization, where it is called the "Politburo"—which is elected by the appropriate delegated governing body, for which it substitutes when that body is not in session;

4. a permanent administrative organ, called the "Secretariat" (elected by the appropriate committee or central committee)—consisting of several secretaries and their staffs, including a first and second secretary at higher levels—which handles the day-to-day work of the party organization and makes up the powerful network of permanent officials called the "party apparatus"; and

5. a body called the "Auditing Commission" at lower levels and the "Central Auditing Commission" at the all-union level, which inspects the work of the party organization itself.

To understand properly the functioning of formal structure of party organization at all levels, the following points should be kept in mind:

1. While constituent bodies are called the "highest governing authority" of party organizations, and theoretically "elect" their committees, the members of the committees are, in effect, selected by the bureaus and secretaries from among the most prominent government, party, cultural, and economic personalities in the area under their jurisdiction.

2. Since constituent bodies and their committees meet only infrequently and are relatively large and cumbersome, they abdicate

their authority to the bureaus and secretaries. The bureaus and secretaries are themselves selected by the next-higher party organization.

3. The members of the bureaus who are not party secretaries normally have other administrative responsibilities which occupy most of their time and efforts. These members thus do not exercise continuous administrative control over their party organization.

4. The party secretaries are full-time party officials and are the most permanent officials in the party. They are frequently members of the committee of the next higher organization and thus constitute a bridge between higher and lower organs.

5. As the permanent official of the party organization, the party secretary speaks and acts for the organization more-or-less continuously.

6. Since the party secretary is selected by the next-higher secretary in the hierarchy, he tends to look up to him for instructions and advice rather than to his own committee, to which he transmits orders from above.

7. As the permanent links between higher and lower organizations, the secretaries make up a chain of power that often becomes the master of the party rather than its servant. This chain of power is called the "apparatus," and its members are called the *apparatchiki*.

8. The decisions of higher organs are absolutely binding on lower organs, which means the decisions of higher secretaries, beginning with the general secretary of the Communist party of the Soviet Union (Leonid Brezhnev since 1964), are absolutely binding on lower party secretaries.

INTRAPARTY DEMOCRACY

Party Elections

All elections within the party are theoretically by secret ballot. Each candidate is supposed to be voted upon separately and is considered elected if he receives at least 50% of the vote. In practice, however, all candidates are approved by officials of the next-higher organization.

The party rules adopted in 1961 included some innovations. To frustrate the revival of "the cult of personality" (dictatorship), the "principle of the systematic renewal of the membership of party organs" was incorporated into the party statutes. At least one-fourth of the all-union Central Committee membership and its Politburo were to be changed at each election. Politburo members "as a rule" were to be elected for not more than three consecutive terms (a total of twelve years), although certain "outstanding" leaders could be elected for more than three consecutive terms if they received not less than three-quarters of the vote. At least one-third of the membership of the central committees of the union republics and of the oblast and kray committees, and at least one-half of the committees of lesser organizations, had to be changed at every regular election. These innovations were, in turn, subjected to significant modifications by Khrushchev's successors at the Twenty-third Party Congress in 1966. The provision calling for the *mandatory* replacement of party officials was abolished.

Criticism and Self-Criticism

The party rules have always stipulated that party members have both rights and duties. The cherished Bolshevik principle of "criticism and self-criticism" is conceived as the self-regulating mechanism that prevents a party with a monopoly of power from degenerating into a static, complacent, and corrupt organization; at the same time, it is supposed to preserve the "democratic" character of the party. As a duty, party members are obliged

to develop criticism and self-criticism; boldly expose shortcomings and work to eliminate them; fight against exhibitionism, conceit, complacency, and localism; decisively rebuff all attempts to suppress criticism; and oppose any activities prejudicial to the party and report them to the party organs, right up to the C.P.S.U. Central Committee.

Under the section on the rights of party members, the party statutes authorize the party member

to discuss freely at party meetings, conferences, congresses, party committee meetings, and in the party press questions regarding party and practical activities; submit proposals; and openly express and defend his opinion before the organization adopts a decision.

Elsewhere, paragraph 27 of the new party rules reads:

Free and businesslike discussion of the questions of party policy in individual party organizations or in the party as a whole is an inalienable right of a party member and an important principle of intraparty democracy. Criticism and self-criticism can be developed, and party discipline . . . strengthened, only on the basis of intraparty democracy.

Beginning with Khrushchev's reforms, the bounds of discussion have been widened considerably. The new rules spell out what rights of criticism the party members have, although a nebulous area of ambiguity still exists between what is permitted and what will not be tolerated.

The incompatibility of democracy and centralism under conditions of a one-party monopoly remains as valid as before; the real difference is not that there has been more democracy since Khrushchev, but rather that centralism is implemented less barbarously and in more humane and rational ways. The Soviet system and party life remain as undemocratic as before, but the terroristic aspects of Bolshevik totalitarianism have been lifted or suspended. The right of those in control to stigmatize undesirable criticism and discussion as "antiparty" in character, while not as grim in its consequences as Stalin's formula of "enemy of the people," preserves for them the ultimate authority to narrow or expand the area of discussion and criticism at will.

THE CENTRAL INSTITUTIONS OF THE PARTY

In the Soviet system, a functional division of labor exists between the institutions of the party and the state, which are interlocked at every level of power and administration. The function of the party is to translate ideological norms into policies and decisions, which are then transmitted to the organs of the state for their execution and administration as formal laws and official acts of the state. The party performs a further function in supervising and checking on the execution of its decisions through corresponding state institutions. The party, however, is warned "not [to] supplant administrative, trade union, cooperative, and other social organizations of working people and not [to] tolerate confusion between the functions of the party and other organs, or superfluous parallelism in work." However, it has not always been easy to separate the functions of the party from government and other institutions, and the relationship between party and state organs has exhibited remarkable fluidity in the past, depending on personalities, problems, and events.

The Communist party's function of translating ideological, policy, and personality conflicts into decisions is performed by the all-union organs of the party, which stand at the pinnacle of the party pyramid. These decisions are then transmitted to the central institutions of the state for their execution and administration as formal acts and laws of the state. The interlocking of state and party organs is traditionally symbolized at the apex by fusing the leadership of the party with the leadership of the government in a single personality. This interlocking relationship at the highest level is periodically and temporarily sundered after each succession crisis. Thus, during the prolonged succession crisis following Lenin's death (1924–34), the two positions were separated and continued to be occupied by different personalities even after Stalin's consolidation of his personal dictatorship. Only in 1941, on the eve of the German attack upon the Soviet Union, did Stalin assume the chairmanship of the Soviet government and fuse it with his authority as general-secretary of the party, a condition which persisted down to his death in March 1953, when the two positions were again separated until Khrushchev reunited them in his person in 1958 after he had defeated and expelled members of the opposition factions from the Soviet hierarchy. With Khrushchev's removal in October 1964, the two positions have been once again separated.

At the summit, the party is divided into the same five functional divisions of responsibility as are the lower party organizations. (see Fig. 6-2). These are (1) a constituent body, the all-union *Party Congress;* (2) a delegated constituent body, the *Central Committee;* (3) an executive decision-making organ, the *Politburo* (called *Presidium* from 1952 to 1966); (4) a permanent administrative body, the central *Secretariat,* headed by the general secretary; and (5) a self-inspecting body, the *Central Auditing* (or *Inspection*) *Commission.*

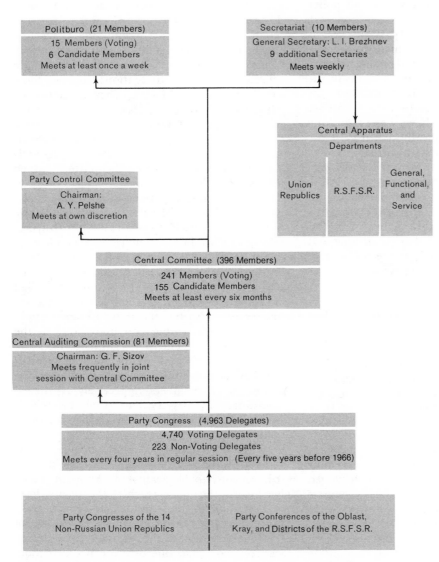

FIG. 6-2. *The central organs of the Communist party of the Soviet Union, April 1971.*

The Party Congress

In theory the most exalted, but in practice the most impotent of the central party institutions is the all-union Party Congress, which is described in the party statutes as "the supreme organ of the Communist Party of the Soviet Union." Traditionally, the most important pronouncements on Soviet ideology and policy are reserved for meetings of the Party Congress, which, according to the party statutes, "determines the party line on questions of domestic and foreign policy and examines and decides on the most important problems in the building of Communism." In actual fact, the Party Congress is little more than a rubber stamp whose delegates have been carefully picked and screened from above through the apparatus of the party, and thus it simply confirms decisions made by the party leadership, adopts resolutions introduced from above, and, in general, provides the ritual of ideological sanctification demanded by the Soviet system.

The formal authority of the Party Congress has remained relatively unchanged throughout the history of the party and is reflected in article 33 of the 1961 party statutes as follows:

The Congress: (a) hears and approves the reports of the Central Committee, the Central Auditing Commission, and other central organizations; (b) reviews, amends, and approves the party program and statutes; (c) determines the party line on questions of domestic and foreign policy and examines and decides on the most important problems in the building of Communism; (d) elects the Central Committee and the Central Auditing Commission.

According to the party statutes, the Party Congress must be convened regularly every four years, but Brezhnev asked that this be changed to every five years in 1971. The Party Congress is considered to possess full authority if at least half the party members are represented in .it. Special sessions of the Party Congress may be convened by the Central Committee on its own initiative or at the request of one-third of the party members represented at the last Party Congress. Convocations of regular congresses must be announced at least six weeks in advance; extraordinary (special) sessions can be convened on two months' notice.

Representation in the Party Congress is based on territorial constituencies. Each party congress of the fourteen non-Russian republics sends a delegation, as do the conferences of oblast and kray, of the Russian SFSR, which does not have a separate party congress. Moscow and Leningrad were authorized to send delegates, elected by borough and rayon conferences, to the Twenty-second (1961), Twenty-third (1966), and Twenty-fourth (1971) Party Congresses. Members of the armed forces are represented through delegations from the territorial constituency in which they are stationed, while those stationed abroad are allowed separate unit representation.

The party statutes read that "the proportion of representation at the Party Congress is established by the Central Committee," which means that the latter body possesses the authority to define the territorial constituencies which shall elect delegates as well as the size of the congress itself. Delegates are of two types: (1) those with full voting rights, representing full members of the party; and (2) those representing candidate members, who have participating rights only (and are hence called "candidate delegates"). As the size of the party has increased, so has the Party Congress itself. Delegates (both voting and nonvoting) to the party congresses held in 1952 (nineteenth) and 1956 (twentieth) were elected on the basis of one seat for every five thousand party members and candidate members, respectively. At the extraordinary Twenty-first Party Congress held in 1959, the ratio was one delegate per six thousand members. The Twenty-second Party Congress (1961) reflected a radical change in the ratio of representation, whose full significance still remains to be evaluated. Although membership in the party reached the record level of nearly 10 million, instead of reducing the ratio of representation so as to keep the size of the congress uniform, the ratio of representation was stepped up to one delegate per two thousand members and one nonvoting delegate per two thousand candidate members. This raised the size of the Party Congress to 4,813 delegates (of which 405 were nonvoting), no less than three-and-one-half times the size of each of the three preceding congresses! This trend has been continued with the twenty-third (1966) and twenty-fourth (1971) congresses, but with one delegate for every twenty-nine hundred party members or candidate members respectively at the last congress. The size of the congress has correspondingly expanded to nearly five thousand delegates as a result.

As the Party Congress has grown in numbers, and hence increasingly unwieldy, its significance and power have correspondingly diminished (Table 6-2).

During the Leninist era (1918–25), the Party Congress met every year, but after 1925 the intervals between each succeeding congress were extended, first to two years, then to three, then four, and finally to five, which remains the current rule. In patent violation of his own rules, Stalin not only shot or arrested a majority of the delegates to the Seventeenth Party Congress, but refused to convene a Party Congress after 1939 (eighteenth) until 1952—an interval of thirteen years—although the party rules still required a session every four years.

In recent years, the main constitutional and reviewing activity of the Party Congress has been to act as a sounding board for the speeches delivered by members of its Central Committee and Politburo, which are duly ratified and approved unanimously. The agenda of the congress is set by the Central Committee, and every regular congress includes a report of the Central Committee (called the main report), which

---

TABLE 6-2. *Party Congress and Party Membership of the CPSU, 1918–71*

Congress	Year	Size of Congress *	Party membership †
Seventh	1918	46 + (58)	145,000
Eighth	1919	301 + (102) ‡	313,766
Ninth	1920	554 + (162)	611,978
Tenth	1921	694 + (296)	732,521
Eleventh	1922	522 + (165)	532,000
Twelfth	1923	408 + (417)	386,000
Thirteenth	1924	748 + (416)	735,811
Fourteenth	1925	665 + (641)	643,000 + (445,000)
Fifteenth	1927	898 + (771)	890,000 + (350,000)
Sixteenth	1930	1,268 + (891)	1,206,874 + (711,609)
Seventeenth	1934	1,225 + (736)	1,874,488 + (935,298)
Eighteenth	1939	1,574 + (466)	1,588,852 + (888,814)
Nineteenth	1952	1,192 + (167)	6,013,259 + (868,886)
Twentieth	1956	1,349 + (81)	6,795,896 + (419,609)
Twenty-first	1959 §	1,269 + (106)	7,622,356 + (616,775)
Twenty-second	1961	4,408 + (405)	8,872,516 + (843,489)
Twenty-third	1966	4,620 + (323)	11,673,676 + (797,403)
Twenty-fourth	1971	4,740 + (223)	13,810,089 + (645,232)

* Candidate delegates in parentheses.

† Candidate members in parentheses.

‡ These are the figures given in J. V. Stalin, *History of the Communist Party of the Soviet Union* (New York: International Publishers, 1939). Another source, N. Popov, *Outline History of the C.P.S.U.*, vol. 2 (New York: International Publishers, n.d.), gives the figures as 286 and 100, respectively.

§ Extraordinary (special) congress.

is usually divided into three areas of concern: (a) the external situation, (b) the internal situation, and (c) the state of the party. This report is normally delivered by the most important figure in the party hierarchy. A second report, which appears regularly, is that of the Central Auditing Commission, which is perfunctory and technical in character. A third regular item is the election of central party organs. Other business on the agenda is determined by the Central Committee and can include virtually anything. The only special Party Congress in the history of the party, the twenty-first, held in 1959, had only one item on its agenda: the goals for the seven-year economic plan (1959–65).

Since 1930, all decisions by the Party Congress have been unanimous. By approving the "reports" and resolutions introduced by the leadership and by confirming all acts performed in the name of the party since the preceding congress, the congress "establishes the line" of the party.

The Party Congress elects the Central Committee and the Central Auditing Commission, supposedly by a secret ballot cast individually for each candidate. Voting is held behind closed doors, and the precise electoral procedure remains a secret. Members of the congress have the right, under party rules, to reject candidates and to criticize them in open discussion. Under the revised rules, the congress determines the size of the Central Committee and the Central Auditing Commission, with all candidates receiving at least a majority of the congress votes being considered elected. The Twenty-second Party Congress established the rule that at least one-fourth of the Central Committee membership be retired at each election and that any person who had been a member for three consecutive terms could be elected only if he received three-quarters of the vote, but this rule was relaxed by the Twenty-third Party Congress.

The Party Congress no longer functions as a constituent body for the party in a real sense. Its present size, nearly five thousand members, clearly precludes that function—as did, indeed, its more modest size of about fourteen hundred members at preceding congresses. Its role has become ritualized as a sounding board for important ideological and policy pronouncements, as a vehicle for disseminating the party line at home and abroad, and as an occasion for formally altering the leadership of the Central Committee and the Politburo. Thus, at the Twentieth Party Congress in 1956, Khrushchev used the occasion to introduce radical innovations in doctrine, such as repudiating the Stalinist concepts of "capitalist encirclement" and the "fatal inevitability of wars." The Twenty-second Party Congress (1961) was also used as a platform for denouncing the leaders of the Albanian Communist party for their adherence to Stalinist positions, for provoking a public ideological dispute between the USSR and Communist China, and for excoriating once again the "antiparty group" led by Molotov. At the Twenty-third Party Congress (1966), Khrushchev's policies were sharply criticized, although his name was not mentioned. The main report to the Twenty-fourth Party Congress, however, was relatively placid.

The Party Congress serves a further function as an institution which imparts formal legitimacy to the acts and decisions of the Central Committee and its Politburo. Thus, at the Twenty-third Party Congress (1966), some rather significant modifications were made in the new party statutes adopted in 1961. Unlike the party statutes of 1961, which were published in draft form and widely discussed some months before they were adopted in revised form by the Twenty-second Congress, the 1966 innovations were revealed only at the congress itself. Before the congress actually convened, rumors were rampant in Soviet circles that the leadership was planning at least a partial rehabilitation of Stalin, which caused considerable anxiety among many Soviet intellectuals and prompted a letter, directed to the Central Committee and signed by twenty-six prominent intellectuals, appealing to the leadership against such a move. Although Stalin was not rehabilitated, it is quite evident that the Stalin "question" continues to agitate the Soviet leadership, which appears to be divided on the issue. Nevertheless, the Twenty-third Party Congress, without protest, unanimously agreed to restore the Stalinist title of "general secretary" in place of "first secretary" (which Khrushchev had coined in 1953), and the pre-1952 term "Politburo" in place of "Presidium" (which Stalin introduced just before his death). The leadership justified the restoration of the old institutions as a revival of Leninist norms, but it was still widely feared that the reappearance of Stalin's title, "general secretary," reflected powerful neo-Stalinist sentiments in the party leadership.

The Twenty-third Party Congress also relaxed the rules on the systematic turnover of party officials; abolished the RSFSR Bureau; reestablished the pre-1934 practice of convening party conferences (made up of party officials who are appointed from above rather than elected) between party congresses; tightened the rules on party membership, making it more difficult to become a member; and introduced provisions making it easier to expel errant members. The title "general secretary" was formally incorporated into the party statutes (which was the case with neither Stalin's general secretaryship nor Khrushchev's first secretaryship).

The status and prestige of the Party Congress has been further diminished since Khrushchev's ouster. In clear violation of the party statutes, the meeting of the Twenty-fourth Party Congress was arbitrarily delayed by the top leadership for an entire year, apparently because it was seriously divided or undecided about several crucial aspects of domestic and foreign policy, particularly economic priorities, defense, and Sino-Soviet and Soviet-American relations. In order to provide retroactive validation to the postponement of the congress, Brezhnev, unwittingly underscoring its diminishing authority, proposed that the congress be convened every five years instead of every four, thus automatically extending his mandate and that of the Central Committee. Ironically, the Twenty-fourth Party Congress was more representative than any before, with a higher proportion of women, educated, and young delegates elected; but as it becomes more representative, and presumably more competent, the congress becomes more dangerous and its latitude for exercising its hypothetical "supreme power" must be more carefully circumscribed.

The Central Committee

With the increasing size of the Party Congress and the diminishing frequency of its meetings, the significance of its delegated body, the Central Committee, increased for a brief period in the late 1920s and early 1930s. As discussion and debate vanished from the congress, it slipped behind the closed doors of the Central Committee, where sharp exchanges continued down to about 1936. They were stifled after Stalin, according to Khrushchev's account, "arrested and shot" 98 of the 139 members and candidate members (70%) of the Central Committee elected by the Seventeenth Party Congress.

According to the party statutes, the Central Committee "during the intervals between Congresses directs all party activities and local party organs," and "directs the work of the central state and social organizations." It also "selects and distributes leading cadres; . . . organizes various organs, establishments, and institutions of the party and directs their activities; appoints the editorial staff of central papers and journals functioning under its control; and . . . represents the C.P.S.U. in its relations with other parties." In actual fact, the Central Committee is invested with virtually the plenary powers of the congress during the five-year intervals between its sessions. The committee is empowered to meet every six months, which it neglected to do in the last years of Stalin's life. The Central Committee has also gradually grown in size until by 1961 its total membership exceeded that of party congresses elected during the early years of the Soviet regime.

As the Central Committee grew in size, so its importance diminished. In 1918, the Central Committee consisted of only fifteen members and eight candidate members; in 1927, of seventy-one full members and sixty-eight candidate members. It was almost doubled in size by the Nineteenth Congress in 1952, and it had a total of 255 full and candidate members. The Twenty-first (special) Party Congress did not elect a Central Committee, but at the

Twenty-second Party Congress (1961), the size of the Central Committee was expanded to 175 full members and 155 candidate members, for a total of 330 members. It was slightly enlarged in 1966 to 195 full members and 165 candidate members, for a total of 360, and again in 1971 to 241 full and 155 candidate members, for a total of 396.

Candidate members are authorized to participate in deliberations of the committee, but do not possess voting rights. According to the party rules, the full members of the committee are replenished from among the candidate members in the event of vacancies caused by expulsion, resignation, or death. Meetings of the Central Committee are called "plenums," and frequently joint meetings are held with the Central Auditing Commission.

As Stalin's grip on the party apparatus tightened, plenary sessions were called infrequently, and during Stalin's later years, meetings were not even held with the regularity required by the party statutes. After 1936, the Central Committee, like the Party Congress, was reduced to a sounding board, and its decisions were in all likelihood unanimous. There is no question but that the Central Committee proved to be as superfluous as the Party Congress for Stalin: between March 1946 and October 1952, this "directing organ" of the party was convened only three times. Since Stalin's death, its role has been enhanced and its power revitalized. While it failed to meet with the regularity required by the party statutes before Stalin's death, since then it has met more often than required. Thus it was convened five times in 1953; twice in 1954, in 1955, and in 1956; four times in 1957; six times in 1958; and twice in 1959 and 1960; and two to four times annually during the past decade. Since Stalin's death, the typical plenum has lasted two days, with the shortest being a single day and the longest lasting eight days. This eight-day plenum, which ousted the "antiparty group" from the Central Committee, the Presidium, and the Government in June 1957, has been the most significant of any during the post-Stalin era, except for the alleged plenum which ousted Khrushchev in October 1964, whose proceedings have never been published even in fragmentary form.

From the evidence of several published records of Central Committee plenums in the post-Stalin period, the proceedings of the Central Committee appear to deviate little from those of other party bodies. The general secretary delivers a report on the main item on the agenda, which is then "discussed" by other members. The "discussions" assume the form of speeches delivered by members, which in his time were freely interrupted by Khrushchev, who affirmed, criticized, warned, and even threatened the speakers, who in return meekly made the appropriate gestures. One lower-ranking member of the Central Committee revealed at the Twentieth Party Congress:

At plenums of the Central Committee . . . its First Secretary, Comrade Khrushchev, and other members of the Presidium . . . corrected errors in a fatherly way when we individual members of the Central Committee have made mistakes, correcting us regardless of our posts or reputations.[2]

At the December, 1958, plenum, seventy-five speakers "discussed" Khrushchev's report, and Bulganin used the opportunity to denounce himself for his complicity in the "antiparty group" conspiracy to oust Khrushchev from power the preceding year, after scathing condemnation by other members of the Central Committee.[3]

The more-or-less placid character of the Central Committee plenums reflected in the published proceedings can be quite misleading, since it is known that many of the post-Stalin plenums have been characterized by stormy controversy and fierce infighting between various cliques and factions. Perhaps the stormiest of the post-Stalin plenums was its longest, held in June 1957, when the "antiparty group" of Molotov, Malenkov, Kaganovich, Bulganin, and Voroshilov, together with Pervukhin and Saburov—a clear majority of the Presidium members—was overruled by the Central Committee in its attempt to oust Khrushchev as

2 Speech of Z. I. Muratov at the Twentieth Party Congress, Radio Moscow broadcast, February 21, 1956.

3 *Plenum Tsentralnovo Komiteta Kommunisticheskoi Partii Sovetskovo Soyuza 15–19 Dekabrya 1958 g.* (Moscow, 1958).

first secretary of the party. It was officially reported that 60 members delivered speeches and 115 filed statements in an authentic and acrimonious debate preceding the vote, whose unanimity was tarnished by a single obstinate abstention cast by Molotov—the first and only publicly admitted dissident vote in a Central Committee meeting in almost thirty years.[4]

Other plenums, such as the one that ousted Malenkov as secretary of the party in March 1953, the one that expelled and ordered the trial of Beria in July 1953, the one that denounced Molotov's foreign policy views in July 1955, and the one that reversed economic policies in December 1956 and February 1957, were also charged with violent conflict and clash of opinion. Since the expulsion of the "antiparty group" in June 1957, the Central Committee meetings have been marred by the expulsion of Marshal Zhukov from the Presidium, by controversy over the pace and tempo of the de-Stalinization program, and by the ideological controversies with China and Albania over foreign policy and the world Communist movement.

Khrushchev's victorious faction in 1957 soon betrayed signs of splitting on a wide range of domestic and foreign policies. The leadership tended to polarize around two main factions: a "moderate" group, led by Khrushchev, and a "conservative" group, whose leaders appeared to be M. A. Suslov and F. R. Kozlov, later apparently supported by traditional elements of the professional military and representatives of heavy industry. Generally speaking, the moderate faction sought a relaxation of international tensions and a détente with the United States, even at the expense of alienating China; the conservative faction saw little value in a détente with the United States, especially at the expense of alienating the Soviet Union's most important ally. Domestically, Khrushchev and the "moderates" were willing to tolerate greater relaxation of controls at home and advocated a change in the economic equilibrium in the direction of producing more consumer goods at the expense of heavy industry. The "conservatives" were opposed to further re-

laxation at home and may have even demanded some retrenchment, and they were virtually dogmatic in their insistence that priority continue to be given to heavy industry over light industry and agriculture. Under these conditions, formalized debate in the Central Committee gave way to a genuine, if largely esoteric, articulation of divergent factional viewpoints, which was also evident from the content of the speeches delivered at the Twenty-first and Twenty-second Party Congresses, in January 1959 and October 1961, respectively.

From the time of the Twenty-second Party Congress until Khrushchev's ouster in October 1964, the Soviet leadership was plagued by constant factional squabbles, and these often found expression in the Central Committee plenums. Khrushchev stayed in power only because the factional balance was extremely delicate, with some leaders supporting him on some issues and opposing him on others. Thus, Soviet factional politics was not only institutionally and functionally oriented but issue-oriented as well, and it was the existence of issue-oriented factionalism which provided Khrushchev with the margins necessary to stay in power. Khrushchev once again narrowly missed being ousted as a consequence of the Cuban missile crisis of October 1962, when his opposition at home and his critics in Peking seemed perilously close to having a common point of view.

Khrushchev's inept handling of the dispute with China, his generally crude and unsophisticated behavior as a politician, and his constant boasting in public apparently finally alienated some of his supporters, who saw in his person an impediment to a reconciliation with China and an obstacle to a rational approach to domestic problems. In October 1964, he was ousted, in a coup engineered largely by his own trusted subordinates, Brezhnev, Kosygin, and Mikoyan. He was indirectly accused of concocting "harebrained schemes," "boasting," and general ineptness. Khrushchev's ouster allegedly took place at a Central Committee plenum, but the proceedings were not made public. The manner and abruptness of his dismissal caused considerable commotion and disturbance in other Communist countries and parties, whose

4 See *New York Times,* July 6, 1957.

leaders demanded and received an explanation in a series of bilateral conferences.

Thus, perhaps the most interesting plenum of all is the one about which the least is known: the October 1964 plenum which removed Khrushchev from his positions of authority. There is even considerable doubt over whether such a plenum in fact was ever convened. The only thing certain is that Khrushchev could not be forced or persuaded into making a public confession of error or to debase himself before the Central Committee and "confess his mistakes." Central Committee proceedings which have been published since Khrushchev's removal reveal a more orderly and sober body, but one still charged with controversy and real discussion.

The most important decisions and policies of the party are issued in the form of resolutions and decisions of the Central Committee. In times of crisis, or on particularly significant occasions, decrees are issued jointly with the Council of Ministers, which have the force of state law. The Central Committee thus remains a potentially powerful institution, and, far more than the Party Congress, constitutes a body with authority and power in its own right. This stems from the fact that those selected for membership came from the most powerful, influential elites and groups in Soviet society. In the Central Committee are to be found the members and candidate members of the Politburo, the members of the Secretariat, the important ministers of the government, the first secretaries of the republic party organizations and second secretaries of important republic party organizations, first secretaries of important oblast, kray, and other regional organizations, the most important government officials of the union republics, marshals, generals, admirals, ambassadors, trade union and Komsomol officials, and leading party ideologists and cultural celebrities. More than any other designation, membership in the Central Committee imparts status and recognition in the Soviet system. While increasing the size of the Central Committee may tend to diminish its power, it also widens the ambit of recognition and status.

Like its two inner organs, the Politburo and the Secretariat, the Central Committee was subjected to a thorough purge during the Khrushchev era. No less than 64% of the members of the 330-member Central Committee elected by the Twenty-second Party Congress in 1961 were new to this body. Over 50% of the members of the 1956 Central Committee and Central Auditing Commission had been dropped.

In contrast to the turnovers in membership during the Khrushchev period, the Central Committee elected by the Twenty-third Party Congress (1966) differed very little from its predecessor. The turnover rate in full members was one out of five, as compared to half in 1961 and about four out of ten in 1956.

The turnover rate at the Twenty-fourth Party Congress was similarly moderate. Of the 241 full members, 153 (63.5%) were full members carried over from the smaller old committee, while 38 (15.8%) were promoted from candidate status. Thus, in the 1971 Central Committee of 241 full members, there were only 50 new faces, and even some of these were promoted from the Central Auditing Commission, while only 42 failed to return for one reason or another. A few were demoted to the Central Auditing Commission—mainly ambitious young politicians associated with Shelepin, whose star has been in decline since 1967. Of the 155 candidate members in the new Central Committee, 71 were old candidate members and 17 were promoted from the Central Auditing Commission. A substantial contingent of the old candidate members, as noted above, were promoted to full membership. Altogether 109 old candidate members were returned as full or candidate members to the 1971 Committee. Thus, 73% of the total membership of the 1966 Central Committee was returned in 1971. Many of the new faces in the 1971 Central Committee were people closely associated with General Secretary Brezhnev, including many of his personal aides and members of his staff.

As the Central Committee stabilizes its membership, its average age increases, and thus threatens to create a generation gap in leadership, and perhaps ultimately a conflict between generations for influence and control. Over 80% of the full members and 66% of the candidate members of the Central Committee elected in 1966 were born before the Revolution. Even more significantly, over 30% of the full members were born before 1907, while less than 3% were born after 1926. Although many of the new faces elected to the Central Committee are relatively young—i.e., in their forties—the retention of 80% of the old membership means that the average age of the 1971 Central Committee member is over 55. The stabilization of the membership of the Central Committee, while undoubtedly having its positive points, does, however, serve to restrict opportunities for the younger element in the party. With the abolition of mandatory systematic rotation of membership, the average age of the leadership will continue to increase. Even the far less exalted delegates elected to the Twenty-fourth Party Congress (1971) were fairly advanced in years, with no less than 68% of its members over 51 years old, and with less than 18% younger than 35. Even more remarkable is the fact that nearly 75% of the delegates were elected to the Party Congress for the first time.

As the Central Committee expands and its membership stabilizes, it, too, seems to be eroding in prestige and authority from its high-water mark in June 1957, when Khrushchev appealed to this body against his rivals in the party Presidium, who apparently had a majority. After 1967, Khrushchev's favorite formulation was "the CPSU Leninist Central Committee with Comrade N. S. Khrushchev at its head," in contrast to the post-Stalinist practice of referring to the "CPSU Central Committee headed by its Presidium," a formula which was revived after Khrushchev's ouster. Khrushchev clearly sought to underscore the preeminence of the Central Committee as the chief source of authority in the party and as the organ from which he derived his authority—thus downgrading both the Presidium (now Politburo) and Secretariat. At the Twenty-third Party Congress in 1966, when Stalin's old post of general secretary (euphemistically described as a title that originated under Lenin) was restored, some delegates further suggested that the Central Committee and the Politburo be "headed by" the general secretary, but this was not considered. Instead, the Politburo was restored to its symbolic position at the apex of the party. It should also be noted in this connection that some party functionaries have suggested the adoption of the phrase, "the Central Committee headed by the Political Bureau and Secretariat." These comic quibbles over phraseology and precedence should not obscure the fact that they conceal a continuing struggle between various Soviet institutions at the apex of the system as they become instruments of contending factions and personalities in the continuing struggle for power and policy.

The ritualistic maneuvering and manipulation of symbols at the Twenty-fourth Party Congress strongly suggest that the Central Committee has suffered a further decline in prestige and authority, and this time to the advantage not only of the Politburo, but also of the new institution of the general secretaryship, which was catapulted even a notch above the Politburo itself, an event whose implications are discussed below.

The Politburo

There is no question but that the most important decision-making organ in the party and state is the Politburo of the party (called, it will be recalled, "Presidium" between 1952 and 1966). The ultimate authority of the party is entrusted to this organ, although its decisions may be overruled by the Central Committee. The party statutes instruct the Politburo to direct the work of the Central Committee. Members are elected by a majority vote of the Central Committee.

COMPOSITION. Membership in the Politburo, however, is largely determined in fact not by the Central Committee, but by the Politburo itself, which is a self-perpetuating body. The Central Committee merely ratifies the candidates offered by the ruling Politburo, the nominees reflecting the equilibrium of power existing within the Politburo itself. This equilibrium is, of course, further reflected in the candidates put forward for election to the Central Committee and selection for the Party Congress. Thus, whenever a change in the distribution of power takes place in the Politburo, this is usually registered downward through the various party echelons.

Like other party bodies, the Politburo has both full members and candidate members. Only full members are entitled to vote; candidate members are entitled to take part in the discussions. The membership of the Politburo has varied considerably. Stalin kept the membership of the Politburo at about a dozen members, but reduced and expanded it at will and appointed and expelled members according to his whim or fancy. At the Nineteenth Party Congress (1952), he unexpectedly abolished the Politburo and replaced it with an enlarged Presidium of twenty-five members and eleven candidate members. According to Khrushchev, this change "was aimed at the removal of the old Political Bureau members . . . and a design for the annihilation of the old Political Bureau members." The post-Stalin Presidium was reduced to ten full members and four candidate members. At the Twentieth Party Congress in 1956, its size was set at eleven full members and six candidate members; after the expulsion of the "antiparty group" in 1957, it was reconstructed at fourteen full and eight candidate members; at the Twenty-second Party Congress, it was once again reduced to eleven full and five candidate members. But by early 1963, membership had been expanded to twelve full members and six candidates, and in 1966 the renamed body had eleven full members and eight candidate members. The Twenty-fourth Party Congress (1971) expanded the Politburo to twenty-one members—fifteen full and six candidates. All sitting members were reelected; of the four new full members, three (Grishin, Kunayev, and Shcherbitsky) were advanced from candidate membership, while the fourth (Kulakov) was moved directly from the Secretariat to full membership, thus extending the overlap between the two bodies. In order to avoid tie votes in the Politburo, it is preferred, but not mandatory, that full membership in the Politburo be in odd numbers. Only three new faces have made their appearance on this body since 1966: Andropov, the security

chief, who was made a candidate member in 1967 and simultaneously dropped from the Secretariat, Kulakov, a party secretary, and M. S. Solomentsev, a party secretary appointed a candidate member in November 1971, thus raising the total membership to twenty-two.

In between regular elections, the size of the Politburo has expanded and contracted in response to the struggle for power. Explusions from and elections to the Politburo are technically made by the Central Committee, but, in fact, the committee often merely ratifies whatever changes have been made by the controlling factions in the Politburo. Removals and appointments, however, are formally announced after Central Committee plenums, the regular election being at the plenum held by the new Central Committee elected by a Party Congress.

The Politburo of the party represents the fusion of party and state authority at the highest level, as reflected in the interlocking character of its membership. Some members are virtually ex officio, like the general secretary, the premier, the chairman of the Presidium of the Supreme Soviet, the first secretary of the Ukrainian party, and the premiers of the Ukraine and the Russian SFSR. Other members are drawn from the Secretariat and the Council of Ministers, or are key republic party and government officials. The precise distribution reflects the equilibrium of power that exists among the various elite groups at any given time. Since the ascendancy of Khrushchev, and particularly since the expulsion of the "antiparty group," the party apparatus has been the dominant elite represented in the Politburo.

During the years since Stalin's death, there has been a remarkable rotation of personalities at the pinnacles of Soviet power, but virtually no alteration in institutional forms (Fig. 6–3). Since 1952, more than sixty individuals have sat on the Politburo, either as full or candidate members. The number of individuals admitted to membership and candidate membership in the Central Committee approaches one thousand. More than thirty Soviet citizens who have experienced the dizzying heights of the Politburo are now in less responsible positions.

One of the ironies of the Khrushchev era is that although he castigated Stalin at the Twentieth Party Congress (1956) for plotting to remove all of the "old members" of the Politburo, by the time of his own ouster he had himself expelled five of the ten surviving members of Stalin's pre-1952 Politburo. His removal in 1964 was accompanied by a further cleansing of the Politburo of the Stalinist holdovers. Aleksei Kosygin, who was removed from the Politburo by Stalin in 1949 and barely escaped execution as an associate of the Leningrad organization, only to return in 1952 as a very junior candidate member of Stalin's enlarged 1952 Presidium, is the only member of Stalin's old Politburo still at the apex of power. No less than six members of Stalin's twelve-man all-powerful Politburo are still alive. Kosygin is premier; Mikoyan is in semiretirement, although still a member of the Central Committee and an ordinary member of the Presidium of the Supreme Soviet; Malenkov (former premier), in disgrace, is presumably still in Kazakhstan as director of a giant hydroelectric plant; and Molotov (ex-premier), Kaganovich, and Bulganin (ex-premier) are vegetating in disgrace. Khrushchev, who had been unceremoniously but generously put out to pasture, Voroshilov, Shvernik, and Andreyev died only recently of advanced age. Only Beria was executed, and that in 1953. Even more remarkable, of the ten full members of the Presidium who arbitrarily took over after Stalin's death in March 1953, seven are out of power and still living: Mikoyan, Molotov, Malenkov, Bulganin, Kaganovich, Pervukhin, and Saburov. Beria, as noted above, was executed, while Voroshilov lived to a ripe old age of 80 nearly a decade after he was ousted in semidisgrace in 1960, and Khrushchev was buried with neither ceremony nor honors in 1971. The survival of so many members of Stalin's dread Politburo after being dethroned is something of a tribute to the way in which Khrushchev "civilized" the Soviet political process. With three ex-presidents and four ex-premiers forced into retirement, the Soviet system finally seems to be firmly on the road to political security and maturity.

How the politburo functions. The post-Stalin Politburo, according to a remark by

Khrushchev in 1957, "meets regularly, not less than once a week"; and according to a more recent remark by Brezhnev in his report to the Twenty-fourth Party Congress, it still meets every week. In its deliberations, it tries to arrive at a consensus by discussion, but in the event of disagreement, questions are resolved by a simple majority decision. Only full members are entitled to vote, although candidate members participate in debate and discussion. According to Khrushchev and Mikoyan, most decisions are adopted unanimously, and this is undoubtedly true, but the revelations of the circumstances surrounding the expulsion of the "antiparty group" in 1957 indicate that many Politburo meetings have been stormy and inconclusive.

As an institution, the Politburo, like the Central Committee, has recovered much of its former prestige and authority and is the symbol of collective leadership. It is no longer a mere façade for a one-man dictatorship, but functions as an institution in its own right. The general secretary, who presides over its meetings as its informal chairman, continues to be the most powerful and influential personality, but he is more likely to represent a particular faction rather than function as an absolute autocrat. The strong representation of the Secretariat in the Politburo since 1957 betrays the continuing dominant role of the party apparatus.

The Politburo's procedure has also been changed considerably since Stalin's death. Present indications are that the Politburo works from an agenda prepared in advance, containing items suggested by members of the Politburo that may have in turn been prompted by subordinates and government ministers. Since all Politburo members have administrative responsibilities in either the government or the party, they must rely on their professional and technical staffs to control the flow of information and problems that reach them from the lower levels of the state and the party. Greater delegation of responsibility to subordinates has also been the rule since Stalin's death, and many problems originating at lower levels of administration are decided before they reach the top.

Specialists and experts, as well as bureau

FIG. 6-3. *Composition of the Party Politburo-Presidium in the Soviet Union, 1952–71.*

		July 1952 (Politburo)	October 1952 (Presidium)	March 1953 (Presidium)	February 1955 (Presidium)
FULL-TIME PARTY FUNCTIONARIES	*Secretariat*	STALIN MALENKOV KHRUSHCHEV Suslov Ponomarenko	STALIN ARISTOV KHRUSHCHEV MALENKOV MIKHAILOV PONOMARENKO SUSLOV *Brezhnev* *Ignatov* *Pegov*	KHRUSHCHEV Ignatyev Pospelov Shatalin Suslov	KHRUSHCHEV Suslov Pospelov
	Provincial Party Secretaries		ANDRIANOV MELNIKOV *Patolichev* *Puzanov*	*Melnikov* *Bagirov*	*Ponomarenko*
	Party Control Committee	ANDREYEV	SHKIRYATOV		
FULL-TIME GOVERNMENT FUNCTIONARIES	*Central Government Officials*	STALIN MOLOTOV BERIA VOROSHILOV KAGANOVICH BULGANIN MIKOYAN KOSYGIN *Shvernik*	STALIN SHVERNIK BERIA BULGANIN IGNATYEV KAGANOVICH MALENKOV MALYSHEV MIKOYAN MOLOTOV PERVUKHIN PONOMARENKO SABUROV VOROSHILOV *Kabanov* *Kosygin* *Tevosyan* *Vyshinsky* *Zverev*	BERIA BULGANIN KAGANOVICH MALENKOV MIKOYAN MOLOTOV PERVUKHIN SABUROV VOROSHILOV *Ponomarenko*	BULGANIN KAGANOVICH MALENKOV MIKOYAN MOLOTOV PERVUKHIN SABUROV VOROSHILOV
	Provincial Government Officials		KOROTCHENKO KUUSINEN		
MISCELLANEOUS			CHESNOKOV KUZNETSOV MIKHAILOV *Yudin*	*Shvernik*	*Shvernik*

SMALL CAPITALS: Full Member, Politburo, Soviet Communist Party.
Italic type.   *Candidate member, Politburo, Soviet Communist Party.*
Roman type: Not Politburo members, Secretariat only.

February 1956 (Presidium)	June 1957 (Presidium)	December 1959 (Presidium)	January 1963 (Presidium)	July 1967 (Politburo)	April 1971 (Politburo)
KHRUSHCHEV	KHRUSHCHEV	KHRUSHCHEV	KHRUSHCHEV	BREZHNEV	BREZHNEV
SUSLOV	SUSLOV	KIRICHENKO	KOZLOV	SUSLOV	SUSLOV
Brezhnev	BELYAYEV	SUSLOV	SUSLOV	KIRILENKO	KIRILENKO
Furtseva	ARISTOV	ARISTOV	KUUSINEN	*Demichev*	KULAKOV
Shepilov	BREZHNEV	BREZHNEV	Demichev	*Ustinov*	*Demichev*
Belyayev	FURTSEVA	FURTSEVA	Ilyichev	Ponomarev	*Ustinov*
Aristov	KUUSINEN	KUUSINEN	Shelepin	Rudakov	Ponomarev
Pospelov	*Pospelov*	MUKHITDINOV	Ponomarev	Kapitonov	Kapitonov
		IGNATOV		Kulakov	Katushev
		Pospelov			Solomentsev *
KIRICHENKO	IGNATOV	BELYAYEV	PODGORNY	SHELEST	SHELEST
Mukhitdinov	KIRICHENKO	*Kirilenko*	VORONOV	*Mzhavanadze*	*Mzhavanadze*
	KOZLOV	*Mazurov*	KIRILENKO	*Rashidov*	*Rashidov*
	Kalnberzin	*Mzhavanadze*	*Mazurov*	*Masherov*	*Masherov*
	Kirilenko	*Podgorny*	*Mzhavanadze*	*Kunayev*	KUNAYEV
	Mazurov		*Rashidov*	*Grishin*	GRISHIN
	Mukhitdinov				
	Mzhavanadze				
Shvernik	SHVERNIK	SHVERNIK	SHVERNIK	PELSHE	PELSHE
BULGANIN	BULGANIN	KHRUSHCHEV	KHRUSHCHEV	KOSYGIN	KOSYGIN
VOROSHILOV	VOROSHILOV	KOZLOV	BREZHNEV	PODGORNY	PODGORNY
KAGANOVICH	MIKOYAN	MIKOYAN	MIKOYAN	POLYANSKY	POLYANSKY
MIKOYAN	ZHUKOV	VOROSHILOV	KOSYGIN	MAZUROV	MAZUROV
MOLOTOV	*Kosygin*	*Kosygin*		*Andropov*	*Andropov*
PERVUKHIN	*Pervukhin*	*Pervukhin*			
SABUROV					
MALENKOV					
Zhukov					
	Korotchenko	*Polyansky*	POLYANSKY	VORONOV	VORONOV *
		Korotchenko	*Shcherbitsky*	*Shcherbitsky*	SHCHERBITSKY
		Kalnberzin			
			Grishin	SHELEPIN	SHELEPIN

* Solomentsev replaced Voronov as R.S.F.S.R. Premier and was elected a candidate member of the Politburo in November 1971.

and department heads, are often invited to Politburo meetings when technical or specialized advice is required by the Politburo. Questions relating to party matters flow up through the party apparatus into the Secretariat, where they are handled by the appropriate sections or dispatched upward to the individual members of the Secretariat, some of whom are also Politburo members. Problems relating to some aspect of state administration similarly move upward through the echelons of the given ministry. Some ministries, like the Foreign Ministry and perhaps the Defense Ministry, report regularly to the Politburo, although in recent years neither minister has been a member of the Politburo.

Another aspect of the Politburo's style of work which distinguishes the present body from those of Stalinist days is the activity of its individual members. During the Stalinist era, neither Stalin nor other members of the Politburo engaged in "grass-roots" politics or barnstormed through the provinces to contact the lower echelons of the bureaucracy or the masses of Soviet citizenry. But now this practice, which was introduced by Khrushchev, is wide-spread, and Brezhnev, Kosygin and other Politburo members are on the move continuously, speaking at local conferences and meetings, collective farms, and professional and cultural assemblies, from one end of the country to the other. There is no question but that all this activity has served to bring both the party and the state closer to the Soviet people, giving them a deeper sense of personal involvement, participation, and commitment to both institutions. Unlike Stalin, but like Khrushchev before them, Brezhnev (general secretary), Kosygin (premier), and Podgorny (chief of state) also make frequent trips abroad, but with Brezhnev restricting himself generally to Major Powers and Communist countries, Kosygin dealing mainly with Western Europe and America, and Podgorny concentrating on the other countries of Europe and Asia. This is not a hard-and-fast division of labor, but it is obvious that three leaders can cover more ground than one and can be dealing simultaneously with various capitals.

The Secretariat and the Central Apparatus

The Secretariat, as an institution, was established in 1919 along with the Politburo and the Orgburo, and with Stalin's appointment as general secretary, in April 1922, he became the only important party leader who was a member of all three bodies. Within the year, Lenin, in his "testament," written on December 25, 1922, warned that Stalin had already used his position to accumulate unprecedented power:

Comrade Stalin, having become General Secretary, has concentrated enormous power in his hand; and I am not sure that he always knows how to use that power with sufficient caution.[5]

In a postscript to the "testament," dated January 4, 1923, Lenin also suggested that Stalin be removed from this post.

The growth of the party was accompanied by an increase in the activities of the central apparatus and in the size of its staff, but the Secretariat typically consisted of the general secretary (Stalin occupied this post until his death in 1953) and three or four other secretaries. As a rule, Stalin's closest and most trusted cronies were to be found in the Secretariat, but because of its pivotal position as a possible springboard to power, they were often transformed, in Stalin's suspicious eyes, into impatient and impudent aspirants to his power who had to be liquidated.

The size of the Secretariat has fluctuated erratically in response to the continuing struggle for power, dropping to a low point of only three members in 1953–54 and reaching its post-Stalinist high point of twelve members in December 1962. At the Twenty-second Party Congress (1961), the number had been reduced to nine. In 1966, it had eleven members. It continues to fluctuate and to reflect the shifting individual fortunes of Soviet leaders in the

5 Full texts of the "testament" and "postscript" are printed in Bertram D. Wolfe, *Khrushchev and Stalin's Ghost* (New York: Praeger, 1957), pp. 260–63.

struggle for power and influence. The Twenty-fourth Party Congress (1971) reduced its size to ten.

According to the party statutes, the members of the Secretariat are elected by the Central Committee "to direct current work, mainly in the selection of cadres and organization and supervision over fulfillment of Party decisions." Brezhnev revealed in his report to the Twenty-fourth Party Congress that the Secretariat meets every week. As the administrative center of the party, the Secretariat supervises a large and variegated central apparatus, which constitutes the staff and technical departments of the Central Committee. Each secretary is in charge of a group of related departments and sections, which are organized along both functional and geographical divisions. Although no formal ranking of the secretaries exists, aside from that of general secretary, there is reason to believe that an informal ranking does apply, comparable to the second and third secretaries at lesser organizational levels. Normally, the second-ranking man in the Secretariat—the informal second secretary, as it were—handles general administrative supervision over the apparatus under the general secretary.

As the chief administrative organ of the party, the Secretariat supervises the execution and fulfillment of the party's policies and decisions in all administrative, economic, military, social, cultural, and professional institutions, organizations, and establishments in all parts of the country and at every level, through the hierarchy of secretaries which makes up the corps of full-time professional party functionaries. What emerges as the de facto policy of the party is in large measure what the party apparatus implements in its day-to-day activities.

The Secretariat thus maintains an organizational and hierarchical network of professional functionaries that constitutes a powerful instrument for usurping and maintaining control of the party, the state, and the entire Soviet system itself. In a real sense, it constitutes an *imperium in imperio,* for, in the words of Stalin, "the party cadres constitute the commanding staff of the party; and since our party is in power, they also constitute the command-ing staff of the leading organs of the state. . . . Party cadres become the decisive force in the work of guiding the party and the state."

In its operations, the party apparatus gives concrete shape to the decisions and policies of the party because it not only implements the decisions of the party but checks on their execution by other organs, institutions, and establishments. In summary, the Secretariat and the apparatus perform the following functions: (1) they determine key appointments in all party, state, economic, social, cultural, professional, and military institutions at every level; (2) they explain and implement the policies of the state and party in all sectors of Soviet life; (3) they check and ensure the fulfillment of party and state directives; (4) they mobilize and manipulate the energies and pressures required for the implementation of the party's will; (5) they accumulate and organize information and prepare reports and recommendations for action, which are transmitted to the Politburo; and (6) they keep a close tab on public moods and sentiments, report their impressions to the central authorities, and maintain an extensive file of dossiers on party members.

Although the formal authority to make policy is vested in the Politburo, this power is clearly shared with the Secretariat, which at times tends to overshadow the Politburo. The balance of power between the two organs is reflected in the degree of interlocking membership between them (see Fig. 8-3). The rise of Khrushchev to primacy was accompanied by an increase in the number of secretaries who were also members of the Presidium. Thus, in 1953–54, Khrushchev was the only secretary in a Presidium of ten full members. After the Twentieth Party Congress (1956), however, the Secretariat was expanded to eight members (five of them new to this body), with five being simultaneously elected to a Presidium of eleven full and five candidate members. With the expulsion of the "antiparty" group in 1957, all eight secretaries were elected to membership in an expanded Presidium of fifteen full and nine candidate members. The ten secretaries appointed at the Twenty-first Party Congress (1959) were also elected members of the Presidium. Even more important, of the fourteen full or voting members of the Presidium, no less than nine were also members of the Secretariat. This meant, in effect, that the policies and decisions of the Presidium were in reality those of the Secretariat, and that the division of function between the two organs had been all but obliterated. This rivalry is sometimes revealed in Soviet commentaries on the two bodies. Thus, in 1968, one source attempted to elevate the Secretariat to a position of equality with the Politburo:

The Central Committee of the CPSU, headed by the Political Bureau and the Secretariat, is the theoretical, political and organizational headquarters of the party. . . . The Politburo and Secretariat adopt many decisions of the CC in its name.[6]

The composition of the Secretariat and its interlocking membership with the Presidium began to change soon after the Twenty-first Party Congress. Having defeated his Stalinist contemporaries, Khrushchev moved to consolidate his power by purging his own supporters, some of whom may have been overly ambitious or whose loyalty was not matched with competence. Between 1959 and 1961, Khrushchev supporters (Kirichenko, Aristov, and others) were dropped from both the Secretariat and Presidium. New faces were introduced to the summit at the Twenty-second Congress—four in the Presidium, five in the Secretariat—but none was appointed to simultaneous membership in both. The interlocking membership between these two bodies was reduced to four veteran leaders (Khrushchev, Kozlov, Suslov, and Kuusinen), leaving Khrushchev formally in charge of both the Presidium and the Council of Ministers but depriving him of control over the Secretariat, which was reduced to its function of executing the policies of the Presidium instead of making them. On the whole, however, leaders who made their way to the summit through the party apparatus continue to dominate the Politburo, and they continue to constitute an absolute majority of its membership.

    [6] D. Yu. Bakhshiev, *Marksistko-Leninskie Osnovy Stroitelstva i Deyatelnosti KPSS* (Moscow, 1968), p. 119.

Powerful as the party apparatus is, its relative strength in the Soviet political structure has diminished in response to the steady growth of the economic and military power of the Soviet Union. This growth has resulted in the creation of several parallel hierarchies and structures of power in the Soviet system that challenge the supremacy of the apparatus in the party and compete with it for control over the party and its symbols of authority and legitimacy. It is within the context of this rivalry that conflicts within the party are institutionalized and resolved into concrete decisions. The increasing complexity in the intersection and collision of party and state institutions as they discharge their respective and parallel but frequently conflicting responsibilities in the Soviet system is discussed more fully in the next two chapters.

The General Secretary

At the Twenty-third Party Congress in 1966, as we have noted, Stalin's old title of "general secretary" was revived to replace the more modest title of "first secretary," which Khrushchev employed. While the suggestion was rejected that the general secretary also be formally named "head" of the Politburo, Secretariat, and Central Committee, which would have transformed it into an institution rather than a mere title, the idea was apparently successfully resurrected and implemented in indirect form at the Twenty-fourth Party Congress five years later. The proceedings and resolutions of the Twenty-fourth Party Congress and the behavior of Brezhnev there strongly suggest that the general secretaryship is now more than a title and more akin to an institution or organ, distinct from and superior to the Secretariat, Central Committee, and Politburo. Its precise position at the top of the Soviet institutional hierarchy has not yet been definitely demarcated, but seems nevertheless destined to be so. At the Twenty-third Party Congress, when Brezhnev first assumed the title of general secretary, it was used simply to identify him as the senior member of the Secretariat, and apparently carried no special significance in his capacity as a member of the Politburo: it was essentially a Secretariat title, not a party, Central Committee, or Politburo title. At the Twenty-fourth Party Congress, however, in full view of television cameras which transmitted his entire address live to Soviet audiences, Brezhnev, in naming the members of the leading organs of the Central Committee, reported first his own election as "general secretary of the Central Committee of CPSU," which, *Pravda* reported, was greeted with "stormy, prolonged applause. All rise." He next listed the membership of the Politburo, beginning with his own name, with the same title, which was greeted with mere "applause," as was everyone else's without exception. He then read off the membership of the Secretariat, beginning again with his own name and title, which was reported in *Pravda* as being met with "stormy, prolonged applause." The information communiqué of the Central Committee plenum reported the elections in the same way as did the press, along with the text of Brezhnev's announcement, but with a significant departure from actuality. On TV, Brezhnev listed the members of the Politburo apparently in accordance with their informal pecking order, listing Kosygin third—after Podgorny—rather than second, which had been his presumed position; in the Soviet press, all members of the Politburo, after Brezhnev, were listed in alphabetical order, with Voronov following immediately after Brezhnev ("v" follows "b" in the Russian alphabet), although in the TV listing he was ranked in ninth place.

Thus, not only was Brezhnev's election as general secretary reported separately from the election of the Politburo and Secretariat, but was reported *first*. The fact that Brezhnev's title was not included when he was listed by the press as a member of the Politburo suggests that the title does not possess any formal significance or invest him with a special status as a Politburo member. Listing the Politburo's membership ahead of the Secretariat's preserved the Politburo's precedence over the Secretariat, but this was earlier dimmed by the naming of the general secretary first. The lower level of applause which reportedly greeted the announcement of Brezhnev's membership in the Politburo further detracted from the Politburo's status in relation to the general secretary and Secretariat. All this suggests that while Brezhnev may be supreme in the Secretariat and dominant in the Central Committee, he is more nearly *primus inter pares* in the Politburo than a chairman or director. This picture was reinforced by his emphasizing internal party democracy and stressing that "the spirit of collective leadership and collective work has been affirmed," thereby suggesting that in the Politburo his views do not always prevail. Thus, although the draft directives of the new Five-Year Plan were issued over Brezhnev's name alone, on behalf of the Central Committee, two months before the Party Congress convened and without benefit of a Central Committee plenum to discuss it, Kosygin delivered the report on the Five-Year Plan to the congress; no debate or discussion ensued, however, presumably because this was a state matter and therefore would be debated and discussed at the next session of the Supreme Soviet. Thus, apparently the only party forum in which the plan was discussed was the Politburo, where the various institutional and functional contenders in the Soviet system meet head-on.

SEVEN

social structure and political power in the Soviet system

In all societies, the social structure has a profound influence on the political dynamics of the system, irrespective of formal institutions and processes. The Soviet Union is no exception to this rule. Since the Communist party is the only legal political organization in the country, the struggle for power in the Soviet system inevitably resolves itself into a struggle for control of the party. During the early years of the Soviet Union, the struggle proceeded from very narrow social foundations, but after Stalin's death the conflicting demands made upon the system by the new social groups created by the great transformations of the preceding four decades erupted into factional strife within the Presidium. Inconclusive struggle in this body led rival factions to seek support in the Central Committee, below which controversy has not been permitted to filter down. If the factional divisions within the Politburo were formalized, they would crack the party pyramid down to its base and perhaps open the way to an eventual evolution toward a two- or even multi-party system operating within the framework of Marxist-Leninist ideology.

Under the Soviet one-party system, factional rivalry at the party summit becomes a crude surrogate for a two-party contest, while the relationship between the Central Committee and its Politburo is, as we have seen, the nearest approximation to a system of institutional responsibility and accountability.

Conflicts within the party arise as a result of both personal ambitions for power and differences over doctrine and policy. Personal rivalries and policy disputes are so intricately interwoven that attempts to isolate the two are bound to be a sterile exercise. The rival cliques within the party hierarchy that were formed during Stalin's later years, and may have indeed been encouraged by him in his efforts to play off subordinates against one another, evolved into factions, each with its own aspirations and social foundations of power outside the party structure.

THE SOCIAL FOUNDATIONS
OF FACTIONALISM
IN SOVIET SOCIETY

Contrary to the official Soviet view that factions within the party do not arise from social conflicts within Soviet society but are rather the deviationary expressions of personalities seeking power, it is obvious that factions could neither arise nor flourish unless they received nourishment from powerful social forces in Soviet society. Just as party factions do not organize themselves into separate political organizations to challenge the supremacy of the party for political power, so social groups with their own interests do not form separate social bodies to demand formal representation in the party, but rather seek to make their demands on other groups in the party.

In Soviet society, where private ownership of the means of livelihood is legally proscribed and where definite limitations are imposed upon the accumulation of any kind of property or material wealth, private property has been eliminated as a social source of power or basis for social stratification. This is also becoming increasingly true of some underdeveloped countries where private ownership of the means of production are severely circumscribed. Under these conditions, other traditional social sources of power assume decisive significance in the struggle for control over the means of livelihood, particularly functional sources of power such as specialized skills, knowledge, and talents.

In the Soviet Union, private ownership of the land and of what Marxists call the means of production, as well as of the media of distribution, communication, transportation, and even recreation, has been legally abolished and forbidden in favor of a system of total, absolute, and permanent public ownership, whether through the state or through state-sponsored societies and organizations. All citizens in Soviet society bear an identical relationship to the instruments of production and the means of livelihood in the sense that they cannot be dis-

tinguished as owners and nonowners. This universal relationship to the means of livelihood provides the legal basis for the ideological assertion that the exploitation of man by man has been eradicated in the Soviet system.

While the Soviet system has for the first time in history ruptured the venerable and durable connection between private ownership of property and the possession and accumulation of power, there still remains a highly unequal distribution of power based upon the relationship of various social groups to the *control* of the means of livelihood. Historically, private ownership emerges as one method of control over the means of livelihood and not as the generic source of social and political power, as was assumed by Marx and some other writers. In the Soviet Union, ownership of the principal means of production is permanently vested in an institution—the state—or an abstraction—"society"; for while the state is (ostensibly) a temporary agent, it is also, in fact, the executive and administrative arm of the Communist party. Control of the party assures control of the state and through it control of the land, the economic establishment, the coercive instruments of society (the armed forces, police, courts, and legal system), and the means of transportation, distribution, and communications.

All Soviet legality is thus bound up with the processes and institutions of the state and remains a somewhat intact and self-contained unit, with no rupture of legal continuity or relations, even though control of the Communist party itself may at any given moment remain an object of strife and struggle. The struggle for power is thus conducted outside the structure of the law, institutions, and processes of the state, although of course the latter may become involved as instruments of the struggle itself. Irrespective of the course and outcome of the struggle, *ownership* of the means of production is never an object of the struggle for power, for ownership remains permanently vested in the state: there is never a redistribution of ownership, but only one of control. While power vacuums are inevitable in the Soviet system, the possibilities of legal vacuums or lapses of authority are reduced to a minimum, and in any event ownership of property cannot become a source of political power in the Soviet order. The state, for example, is not employed for the purpose of transferring ownership of property from one hand to another or from the state to private possession, or for the purpose of facilitating the accumulation of private property by various individuals or social groups through manipulation of the legal system, or for preserving the existing pattern of property distribution among private individuals and groups in society.

Within the context of Marxist-Leninist ideology, a social group with its own distinctive interests is automatically designated a social class that is, by definition, in conflict with the interests of other classes. After the Revolution, the interests of the working class, as determined by the party, were alone considered to be legitimate, and the interests of other classes were suppressed. The Communist party was verbally transformed from a party representing only the interests of the working class into one representing the interests of all Soviet social groups. Consequently, Soviet ideology and party doctrine continue to deny the legitimacy of competing interest groups, and refuse to tolerate their autonomous existence.

In dissecting the political process in the Soviet system, the basic political actors can be isolated as elites within the intelligentsia. Their informal organizational expressions within the organs of the party are *factions,* while divisions and rival groupings within factions can be called *cliques.* In Soviet parlance, however, "factions" are characterized as formalized groupings within the party which engage in cabalistic intrigue, conspire to take concerted action within the party, and offer a program and slate of candidates in opposition to those of the official party line. A faction constitutes, in effect, a "disloyal opposition," since a loyal opposition grouping is not yet recognized as legitimate. True enough, some factions may have very little social support, as is officially maintained, and may represent only the views of individual party leaders.

Institutions as Interest Groups

Social classes and interest groups within them in Soviet society have highly uneven opportunities for articulating their interests inside and outside the party, although all social classes and many subclasses within are reflected in officially approved institutions, associations, and organizations. Political power in the Soviet system remains largely a monopoly of the intelligentsia, but its distribution among various elites within the intelligentsia is also sharply uneven, and favors those elites that largely coincide with political institutions and that are organized into hierarchical structures of power. Unlike the various subclasses within the intelligentsia, none of the subdivisions within the working class or peasantry are permitted separate associational existence. Trade unions are not organized along craft, functional, or horizontal lines, but vertically by enterprise, and include managers as well as unskilled workers in the same organization. The only association permitted the peasantry is the collective farm, which is a rural institution designed to control the peasants rather than to articulate their interests. The working class and peasantry are thus effectively decapitated politically, but they do participate or rather are involved in the political process through ritualized periodic elections to the soviets, in which they are given the privilege of electing to government positions candidates selected for them by the elites who dominate the party. The proliferation and expansion of interest conflict within the intelligentsia, however, could draw the masses more directly into the political process if the latent power of the workers and peasants could be mobilized to good advantage by one faction or another within the party structure. Once the elites openly compete for the "goodwill" of the peasantry and the workers, it will signify their formal entry into the Soviet political system as active rather than passive actors.

Interest groups in the Soviet system do not readily lend themselves to ready-made classifications, and in any case must be related to larger social groupings such as social class. Within the three broad social groupings in Soviet society are to be found three types of interest groups—institutional, associational, and functional—some of which are purely intra-class while others are interclass in character. The party as a whole can no longer be accurately described as an interest group because of its artificial numerical dilution by working-class and peasant members, who have little tangible common interests with the intelligentsia aside from a vague common ideological bond. The members of the intelligentsia within the party clearly have more in common with the intelligentsia outside the party than with the workers and peasants within.

The principal (but by no means only) political actors in the Soviet system are four political institutional groups, all found within the intelligentsia, and identifiable with diminishing institutional precision, as: (1) the party apparatus; (2) the professional military; (3) the state bureaucracy; and (4) the managerial-technical, or economic, bureaucracy. No attempt will be made here to provide detailed descriptions of the groups or their internal divisions and political processes. It should be noted at this point, however, that these four institutional groups vary considerably in size of membership, functional diffusion, and institutional coherence. The party apparatus and the professional military are more clearly defined institutional structures, in terms of function and organization, than either the state bureaucracy or the managerial-technical bureaucracy. The last is perhaps only marginally an institutional group, but because of its pivotal role in the economic establishment and because of the generally uniform training its members receive and the almost deterministic impact of their function in society on their social outlook, it is more institutional than noninstitutional in its behavior. Some institutions, like the party apparatus, because of its small numbers, its key location in the party, and its more clearly defined group spirit, have been more successfully employed as instruments of subgroups and individual leaders, while the military has largely articulated its own interests as an institution

rather than as a vehicle for the specific interests of this or that clique or individual personality.

The principal distinguishing feature of the state bureaucracy, which separates it from the military and economic bureaucracies as a group, is that it is the only institutional group which has custody of important symbols and credentials of legality. The state is the source of all law in the Soviet system; it is in fact the corporate embodiment of the Soviet legal order. Only the state can authorize legal rewards and punishments. To the extent that law and legality are associated with legitimacy, the state bureaucracy possesses a powerful political lever of great potential and long-range significance. Whereas in other political systems legitimacy is embodied in the state, in the Soviet system, legality only is embodied in the state, whereas legitimacy is an ideological concept vested in the party. The Soviet state represents—physically, legally, and psychologically—an extension of the historic Russian state; it possesses a latent force to be ultimately reckoned with.

Stripped of all refinements, the party apparatus represents a structure of legitimacy; the state bureaucracy, a structure of legality; the professional military, a structure of coercion; and the managerial-technical bureaucracy, a structure of production and distribution. While individuals have freely moved from one structure to another, and considerable overlapping and rotation of personnel continues to take place, these four structures represent distinctive and separate avenues of power in the Soviet system.

Although the Soviet intelligentsia consists of a number of elite groups, all its members have a common desire to perpetuate the Soviet system from which they have sprung and in which they benefit as a privileged group. Within this broad common framework of interests, however, these elites are concerned preeminently with the social status of their own group, and they seek to shape doctrine and policy according to their own special interests. They are officially recognized as occupational and professional categories, but they cannot formally organize themselves into political organizations outside the party or as explicit factional groupings within the party. They must exert their influence and make their demands only as amorphous entities inside the Communist party. Since they cannot legitimately articulate a separate interest as such inside or outside the party, they are inevitably forced into competing for control of the party's decision-making organs, and into presenting their interests in terms of the party and the society as a whole.

Because Soviet ideology demands conformity, conflicts among social elites and their representatives in the party's leading organs cannot be permanently resolved within an institutionalized framework of political accommodation and compromise. Rather, one interest group or faction tries to assert its supremacy over the others and impose its interests as those of all of society. If one group is unable to subdue the others, an uneasy and temporary coexistence ensues, and the party, under the pressures of diverse groups seeking political articulation, becomes a cover for a conglomeration of interests whose incompatibilities are only partially and temporarily obscured by a veneer of monolithic "unity." Ultimately, this pattern may give way to a process of genuine accommodation and consensus formation.

Issues and Interest Groups

In recent years factional groupings cutting across institutional and functional lines have also polarized around "issues." High on the list of "issues" that impel forces within the Soviet social system to crystallize into interest-group formations are those concerned with the allocation of resources, investment, and effort to various sectors of the economy for the fulfillment of various purposes, some of them ideologically as well as economically inspired. Increasingly, it is conceded in public that certain policies and decisions affect the fortunes and interests of various social groups and institutions unevenly and that support for or opposition to various policies can often be traced not only to the abstract merits of a given policy but also to the perceptions of different groups and individuals as to how such policies will affect their interests, role, power, and status

in the Soviet system. As early as 1963, this was obliquely intimated by a prominent Soviet ideologist, who conceded the political implications of what on the surface were only economic problems. Directing his attention specifically to problems of allocation and priorities of investment among the various sectors of the economy, he pointed out:

These are not only economic but also political problems since their solution concerns the interests of different social groups—workers, office employees, and collective-farm peasantry, and the interests of the different nations which compose the Soviet Union.[1]

The principal, but by no means exclusive, issues and the social and functional interest-group cleavages they generate can be summarized as follows:

1. Allocation of priorities between ideological and nonideological purposes and interests.
2. Determination of priorities between defense and nondefense demands, interests, and objectives.
3. Allocation of effort and investment to productive as opposed to consumptionist sectors of the economy.
4. Distribution of resources between agricultural and nonagricultural sectors.
5. Allocations of investment within the agricultural sectors as well as within the nonagricultural sector: heavy industry versus light industry; goods versus services; pure science, technology, and research versus hardware.
6. Priorities among various services: education, health, recreation, culture, trade and commerce, communications, transportation, housing, restaurants, amenities, etc.
7. Priorities and investments among the various sectors of heavy industry and light industry: steel versus chemicals; consumer durables versus consumer disposables; etc.

---

[1] G. Glezerman, "V. I. Lenin on the Interrelation of Economics and Politics in Building the New Society," *Kommunist*, no. 7 (1963):32.

For decades, after an equilibrium of sorts between the ideological and nonideological imperatives and purposes of the state had been achieved, the overarching issue around which various groups, institutions, and personalities have polarized into competing constellations has been the relative shares of defense and heavy industry as opposed to agricultural and the civilian sectors of the economy. And within agriculture, the issue was largely whether to develop agriculture by providing incentives for the peasants and raising their standard of living or by catering to the powerful urban classes through the mechanism of lower food prices to the detriment of the farmer. The productionist-consumptionist debate, on the other hand, continues to rage between those who argue that the productive sectors of the economy should be developed to their maximum extent so as to guarantee a later high level of consumption and those who argue that larger amounts of scarce resources should be immediately pumped into the consumptionist sector to meet the increasing and impatient demands of the Soviet consumer. All of this, of course, also feeds back into the debate over defense and foreign policy, with the advocates of continuing the priority of defense and heavy industry more prone to perceive threats to Soviet security and the partisans of the consumptionist sector tending more to perceive the possibilities of détente and a relaxation of international tensions.

For decades now, the continuing postponement of priorities for the consumptionist sector has been officially justified in terms of Soviet foreign policy obligations and security considerations. At the Twenty-fourth Party Congress in 1971, Premier Kosygin revealed that the Soviet military establishment had been absorbing about 25% of all funds available for economic development over the preceding five years, in an endeavor to demonstrate that enhanced development of the consumptionist sector of the economy was being frustrated by the terrible appetites of the Soviet military spokesmen at the congress, like the defense minister, Marshal Grechko, who however, demanded an even larger share of the resources, not less, as they continued to emphasize that the United States and NATO were still plotting aggressive

actions and spending huge sums on armaments in order to dictate to the Soviet Union from "a position of strength."

The undoubted interests that some groups have in a détente and reduction of international tensions in order to force a reordering of priorities is constantly articulated in Soviet speeches and writings. Thus, in 1969, it was pointed out by one source:

Soviet foreign policy has done and is doing everything to find all possible opportunities for lowering international tension and for solving the problems of disarmament or in the initial stages even for the freezing of the arms race. . . . Experience has proven that only under conditions of a relaxation of tensions is it possible to concentrate a maximum of resources for accomplishing the plans for building of communism.[2]

On the other hand, a military spokesman writing in *Krasnaya Zvezda,* the official newspaper of the Soviet Defense Ministry, quoted Lenin, to suggest that no ceiling should be placed on military spending:

"Everyone will agree that an army that does not train itself to master all arms, all means and methods of warfare that the enemy possesses, or may possess, is behaving in an unwise or even in a criminal manner." [3]

The author of the article then emphasized: "Special attention should be given to the words 'may possess,'" thus suggesting that the Soviet Union should develop any and all weapons that the United States may conceivably possess in the future. The proponents of greater investment in the consumptionist sector have articulated a contrary view in a particularly audacious manner for a Soviet position:

There are objective limits to military spending and if they are exceeded this will have a negative effect not only on expanded production, but also on the strengthening of defense. . . . It is essential to observe definite ratios between the output of armaments and producer and consumer goods. . . . An

[2] K. P. Ivanov, *Leninskiye Osnovy Vneshei Politiki SSSR* (Moscow, 1969), p. 50.

[3] Major General A. Lagovsky, in *Krasnaya Zvezda,* September 25, 1969.

expansion of military consumption beyond permissible boundaries does not lead to a strengthening of the military power of a state, but to its weakening and an inevitable breakdown of the economy as a whole and military-economic potential in particular.[4]

And even among the champions of the consumptionist sector of the economy, debate and conflict may rage over precise allocations and priorities—such as between light and heavy industry, between consumer durables and disposables, between goods and services, between quantity production and qualitative performance. One can see that there are myriads of possible conflicts and interest-group and subgroup formations and coalitions along essentially functional or "issue" lines, many of them temporary and ephemeral, as well as along more visible and permanent institutional groupings and subgroupings.

All of these cleavages are provoked by decisions at the top, and in turn they creep upward to affect the behavior of the Politburo as the ferment and conflict below creates opportunities for leaders at the top to mobilize support for their own policies and interests. In the process, leaders and groupings both adjust and accommodate to one another to mutual benefit and advantage as leaders in search of social support often make common cause with groupings in search of advocates and spokesmen in the inner councils of the Soviet system. A symbiotic process is thus induced that has increasingly become the norm in the Soviet political system.

The reports delivered at the Twenty-fourth Party Congress, together with evidence of discussion, controversy, and debate in the Soviet press in the years preceding the congress itself, enables us to associate certain top Soviet personalities with particular institutions and issues in an incomplete and fragmentary way. Premier Kosygin, for example emerges as a subtle and persistent, if not always successful, advocate of shifting greater attention to the consumptionist sector, with particular emphasis on light industry, consumer durables, and

greater efficiency and rational methods of economic management. He shows much less concern for the agricultural sector of the economy, and somewhat less concern for the enhanced production of consumer disposables and services, which can easily engulf the entire Soviet economy in a quagmire of increasingly endless demand without the real possibility of measuring production and performance within the context of socialist norms of efficiency and output.

General Secretary Brezhnev, on the other hand, has demonstrated considerably more partiality to maintaining priority for heavy industry and defense and greater solicitude for enhancing the agricultural branches of the consumptionist sector of the economy, although his behavior at the Twenty-fourth Party Congress strongly suggests that as a pragmatic politician he sees the advantage of allowing a slightly greater share of investment for consumption than in the past. Like Kosygin, he is essentially a man of the center, and while more ambitious and energetic than Kosygin, he is likely to refrain from exhibiting too much zeal for any one grouping. In summary, we can say that Brezhnev tries to meet the demands of heavy industry and defense just sufficiently to keep them from being alienated and allows sufficient increase in the allocation of resources to the consumptionist sector to prevent it from becoming a source of social opposition. Kosygin, similarly, is willing to trim his demands for light industry and consumer goods in the interests of maintaining a centrist coalition.

Among Politburo members, Polyansky and Voronov in recent years have emerged as articulate and energetic spokesmen for the agricultural sector, but here the political payoff is rather slender and both appear to be in trouble for their excessive zeal on behalf of the long-suffering Soviet peasant.

Others in the Soviet leadership, like Shelepin and Shelest, are heavyhanded in their advocacy of greater militancy in foreign policy and hence postponement of raising living standards. In the mid-1960s Shelepin, in particular, apparently hoped to capitalize on Brezhnev's seeming refusal to support the military-industrial complex all the way, and to build a

---

[4] P. V. Sokolov, ed., *Voenno-Ekonomicheskiye Voprosy v Kurse Politekonomii* (Moscow, 1968), p. 254.

sociopolitical base from which to challenge Brezhnev; but he failed, and in the months following the Arab defeat in 1967, which provoked anguished and heated debate among the Soviet leadership, Shelepin and his key supporters were administered a sharp rebuke in the form of demotions and expulsions. Like Polyansky, Voronov, and Shelest, Shelepin's position in the hierarchy appears somewhat tenuous. The others in the Soviet leadership, including such heavyweights as Podgorny and Suslov, are apparently part of the Brezhnev-Kosygin centrist coalition, which has survived since October 1964, although the sociopolitical foundations upon which it rests continue to pull in opposite directions.

THE SOCIAL COMPOSITION OF THE PARTY

The relationship between social structure and political power in the Soviet system is reflected in the social configuration of the Communist party as a whole. It has increasingly become an organization whose membership is overwhelmingly drawn from the intelligentsia (which at times has accounted for more than 70% of its total membership). Representation of the peasantry in the party has virtually disappeared at times. By 1967, party membership was predominantly Great Russian (62%), male (80%), urban (78%), middle-aged (50%), and intelligentsia (46%).

The Shifting Composition of the Party, 1905–71

Before the Revolution, workers consistently accounted for 60% or more of the party, while the intelligentsia, which provided virtually its entire leadership, made up only about one-third of its membership. The peasants, who were neither attracted to the party nor actively recruited, furnished from 5 to 8%. After the Revolution, the balance among these three social groups underwent a substantial shift. From 1917 to 1920, the proportion of the working class was systematically reduced until it

reached a low point of 33% while that of the peasantry rose to nearly 37%, to constitute the largest single social group to be represented. The proportion of the intelligentsia also suffered some reduction. The year 1920 was the high point of peasant representation in the party.

The party experienced its first purge in 1921, when party membership was nearly halved from 732,521 members to 401,000. From 1922 to 1931, the proportion of workers was steadily increased until it reached a high of 66.6%, while that of the peasantry was trimmed to 22.3% and that of the intelligentsia was slashed to less than 10%. During the period of the five-year plans, the role of the intelligentsia in the industrialization and modernization of Soviet Russia was of crucial significance, and, within the complex of incentives and rewards introduced by Stalin, membership in the party assumed cardinal importance. The barriers erected against the intelligentsia were gradually relaxed, and were finally eliminated in 1939. Because of their education and abilities, the members of the intelligentsia easily met the formal qualifications for membership, quickly moved upward in the party hierarchy, and soon monopolized all positions of importance. The proportion of party members drawn from the intelligentsia swelled to well over 50% of the total.

The "proletarian" character of the party was partially restored during World War II, when workers and peasants in uniform were fairly indiscriminately recruited into the party, and the percentage of workers may have risen once again to about one-third of the total membership. Immediately after the war, however, another purge hit the party, and those who were hastily recruited into it during the war were mustered out, most of those expelled being workers and peasants. The intelligentsia in all probability accounted for nearly 70% of the total at this time.

In January 1962, Soviet authorities published the first comprehensive social breakdown of the party in three decades, probably because for the first time since 1933 the proportion of the intelligentsia in the party dropped to below 50% of the total. As of January 1971, according to Brezhnev's report to the Twenty-fourth Party Congress, workers accounted for 40.1% of the total membership and peasants accounted for 15.1% (Table 7-1). "Employees and all others" accounted for 44.8%, a category which includes the intelligentsia and perhaps the members of the armed forces. The statistics for 1956 were also divulged in 1962, and these were 32% workers, 17.1% peasants, and 50.9% "employees and all others." [5] In spite of this influx of workers and peasants in the party, the intelligentsia, which together with their families account for less than 25% of the total population, still provides close to 50% of the membership of the party.

Rural Representation in the Party

The party is predominantly urban in character, with 78% of its membership being drawn from the cities (urban workers and intelligentsia). It has always been weakly organized in the countryside, not only because of built-in ideological biases, but also for the following reasons: (1) the agricultural and rural proportion of the population has been in steady decline since 1938; (2) educational opportunities in rural areas are limited, and the quality of literacy and cultural life is much lower than in the cities—hence most collective farmers can-

[5] *Partiinaya Zhizn*, no. 1 (January 1962):44–54.

not meet the qualifications for membership; (3) incentives on the farms are very low, with the result that most of the ambitious and capable elements of the rural population migrate to the cities; (4) many collective farms have been transformed into state farms. In 1934, more than 50% of the collective farms did not have a single party member, and even by 1939, only 5% of the 243,000 collective farms had primary party organizations, with the membership on these farms accounting for only 153,000 out of almost 2½ million. With the amalgamation of the collective farms, the proportion with party organizations increased, until by 1953, 85% of the farms had party organizations. At the Twentieth Party Congress (1956), further progress was registered, but more than 7,300 collective farms were still without primary party organizations. By 1961, primary party organizations were to be found on 41,387 collective farms, 5,721 of which were large enough to have party committees, while 9,206 primary units were located on state farms, of which 2,718 were large enough to have party committees. By January 1, 1965, the number of primary organizations on collective farms had decreased to 38,251, but with 8,630 large enough to have party committees, while primary organizations on state farms rose to 11,601, of which 3,827 were large enough to have party committees. [6]

The rural population was 106,900,000 in 1966—about 46% of the total Soviet popula-

[6] *Partiinaya Zhizn*, no. 10 (May 1965).

TABLE 7-1. *Social Composition of the Communist Party of the Soviet Union, 1905–71*

	1905	1917	1920	1932	1956	1961	1967	1971
Workers	61.7%	60.2%	33.2%	64.5%	32.0%	34.5%	38.1%	40.1%
Peasants	4.7	7.6	36.9	27.8	17.1	17.5	16.0	15.1
Intelligentsia	33.6	32.2	22.1	7.7	50.9	48.0	45.9	44.8
N =	8,400	23,600	612,000	3,172,215	7,173,521	9,176,005	12,684,133	14,455,321

SOURCE: *Partiinaya Zhizn*, no. 7 (April 1967):7–8, and *Pravda*, March 31, 1971.

tion. Rural party membership, however, accounted for only 22.6% of the total party membership and was spread unevenly among the different social groups in Soviet rural society (Table 7-2). Thus, while more than 95% of the collective-farm chairmen and virtually 100% of the sovkhoz directors were party members, little more than 2% of the ordinary collective farmers were to be found in the party.

As of January 1, 1965, there were 2,164,255 agricultural members in the party: 1,285,077 (59.4%) on collective farms, and 879,178 (40.6%) on state farms and other state agricultural enterprises.[7] Of this number, 520,000 were equipment operators and mechanics (322,535 on kolkhozes and about 197,000 on sovkhozes), while ordinary dirt farmers, including rural foremen, accounted for about 672,000 on kolkhozes and about 500,000 on sovkhozes. The remainder, about 465,000 (21.5%), was drawn from the rural intelligentsia, including farm

[7] Ibid.

TABLE 7-2. *Social Composition of the Communist Party of the Soviet Union in Rural Areas, 1965*

	Number	*Percentage*
Sovkhoz directors and deputies	30,000 *	3.4%
Kolkhoz directors and deputies	45,000 *	
Rural intelligentsia and pensioners	408,000 *	18.5
Sovkhoz foremen, farmers, and workers	687,000 *	32.1
Equipment workers on kolkhozes	322,535	15.0
Collective farmers, including rural foremen	672,065	31.0
Total	2,164,255	100.0%

* Rounded off to nearest thousand.

directors. The leverage that rural society in general, and the peasantry in particular, has in the Soviet political process is thus very slight, and this has been consistently reflected in the low priorities and rewards which have been allocated to the farm areas in Soviet society.

Urban Representation in the Party

As we have seen, the working class has always occupied a significant role in the doctrine and practice of the party. During the period of the great social and economic transformation of the Soviet social order between the two world wars, the party underwent a profound change. The most able and ambitious members of the working class acquired new skills and education, and thus mustered themselves out of the working class and into the "ruling class" in the Soviet system. While expelling them from the party, or erecting barriers to reduce their ratio of membership, might satisfy the official myth, it would effectively destroy the incentive of the workers. The requirements of reality had to be reconciled with the imperatives of ideology, and the intelligentsia was redefined as a "working" or "toiling" intelligentsia, whose social origin was predominantly proletarian or peasant in character. The heavy over-representation of the intelligentsia in the party, however, conveys the impression that the party is an instrument of the intelligentsia rather than the "workers," and gives rise to periodic suggestions that Soviet ideology be revised to meet social and political realities, i.e., that the intelligentsia has replaced the proletariat as the dominant class in Soviet society. Thus, one Soviet ideologist criticized this "erroneous" view as tantamount to supporting the view of "bourgeois" writers who allege that the working class does not constitute the dominant class in the Soviet system:

Unfortunately, erroneous interpretations of the role of the working class are encountered even in certain works published in our own country. I. Zabeln, for example, writes in his book *Man and Mankind* that "the working class took power in order to yield its place in the historical arena to the intelligentsia," that "the intelligentsia . . . has now become the leading revolutionary class," and that the future apparently belongs to it alone.[8]

The ideological guilt feelings aroused by the transformation of the party into a party of the Soviet intelligentsia was clearly betrayed by the nearly three-decade refusal to reveal the social composition of the party. According to the data released in 1967, the working class accounted for more than one-third (38.1%) of the total membership, an increase from 34.5% in 1961. But this category not only included industrial foremen, who make up a substantial proportion of the party membership, but also about 700,000 workers on sovkhozes, who are classified as workers in Soviet data. Of the 43 million urban workers in Soviet society at the time, only about 3.6 million (including foremen) belonged to the Communist party—that is, about 8.3% of the workers in urban areas. This compares with the more than 22% of the mental workers who belonged to the party. In recent years, emphasis has been placed on recruiting party members from "branches of material production," which includes workers, peasants, and intelligentsia occupied in producing goods as distinguished from those in "nonproductive" or service enterprises and occupations. As of 1967, 73.3% of all members were engaged in production, while 26.7% were in nonproductive spheres of the economy.[9]

By 1967, the Communist party was well on the road to becoming a mass party, and while Khrushchev's successors have continued the practice of allowing the party to grow, the anxieties of the leadership have been clearly evident in the relatively large number of members who have been expelled and dropped from membership (203,000 between 1962 and 1964; 86,112 in 1966 alone), the tightening of qualifications for membership, and the fact that new members are increasingly funneled through the Komsomol (45% of the new members in 1971). The expansion of the party membership to

nearly 14.5 million in 1971 apparently prompted Brezhnev's proposal at the Twenty-fourth Party Congress that new party cards be issued in exchange for old ones (the first time in seventeen years), which would presumably be employed as a device for more closely scrutinizing the quality, qualifications, and commitments of party members. It may also be used as a convenient cover for a mild purge of the party membership for purely political and factional purposes. "We would organize this work," Brezhnev recommended, "so that the exchange of Party cards will promote the further strengthening of the Party and will increase the activeness and discipline of Communists." As the party continues to grow in size and becomes more representative, power is simultaneously diffused at the core among the elite interest groups and contracting from the outer periphery of the party as a whole. Thus, we must look not to the party, as such, for the social sources of power within Soviet society, but rather at the constellation of elites within the party—namely, the party intelligentsia.

THE SOCIAL PYRAMID OF POWER

The Distribution of Elites in the Party

As of January 1, 1967, 46% of the Communist party was made up of the category "employees and all others," which encompasses the intelligentsia—including perhaps about 880,000 members of the armed forces (unless they were distributed by occupation)—and university students. In 1967, more than 4,671,000 members of the party were classified as "specialists with higher or specialized secondary education," nearly half of whom were engineers, technicians, or agricultural specialists.

In searching for the ultimate social foundations of power in the Soviet system, it becomes necessary to discover where the lines of social power intersect with the political structure (Fig. 7-1). Specifically, the point at which the 5.8 million members of the party who are in the "employee and other" categories intersects with the twenty-six million Soviet citizens who

[8] Ts. Stepanyan, "All-Conquering Force of Scientific Communism," *Krasnaya Zvezda*, May 21, 1971.

[9] *Partiinaya Zhizn*, no. 7 (April 1967):7–8.

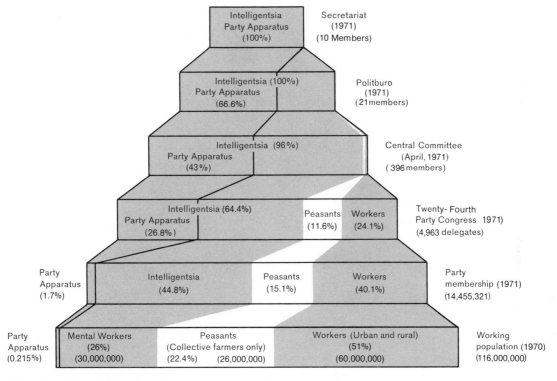

FIG. 7-1. *The social pyramidization of power in the Soviet system. Percentages for the Central Committee are as of 1966.*

are classified as "mental workers" must be defined, with due regard given to the distribution in both aggregates by nationality, sex, and age. Increasingly (except in the case of the estimated 250,000 career party officials), one's authority in the party is defined by one's role, status, function, and influence in the social structure, rather than the other way around—although forces continue to work in both directions.

Within the category of "mental workers," we find an even more elite category, designated as "specialists with a higher or specialized secondary education." There were about 17 million of these in 1965, and of these, some 12 million worked in the national economy, the difference being made up of retired people, members of the armed forces, students, and women not employed. As of January 1965, 4,063,530 (34.6% of party membership; 36.2% of the "specialists" category) were members of

the party. It is within this group, of whom the great majority (80%) are men, together with the army, that the social foundations of power in the Soviet system are to be found. It might be termed the Soviet "ruling elite," because it is from this group that all decision makers in the Soviet system are recruited. Table 7-3 provides in greater detail a social profile of the party and a political profile of the intelligentsia.

The Social Composition of Party Congresses

Throughout the party's history, the largest social groups in the Soviet Union have had the narrowest representation at the top of the party pyramid. Conversely, groups with narrow social bases have dominated the party. Thus, even in 1905, when 62% of the party was made up of

TABLE 7-3. *Distribution of Intelligentsia in the Communist Party of the Soviet Union, 1966*

Social category	Total size of social category employed	Percentage of social category in party	Party membership *	Percentage of party
Mental workers	26,000,000 †	20.9%	5,432,196	46.2%
Intelligentsia	11,249,700 ‡	36.2	4,450,530	37.8
(women)	(6,940,700)	(13.0)	(900,000)	(7.7)
Executives	} 1.200,000	76.0	423,700	8.6
Administrators			586,656	
Engineers, technical §	4,400,000	40.0	1,765,400	15.0
Cultural, professional, and scientific personnel	5,200,000	24.3	1,265,700	10.8
Trade, service, etc. personnel	470,000 }	4.2	510,592	4.3
Other office workers	14,000,000 ‖			
Armed forces personnel (est.)	3,000,000	29.3	880,000 #	7.5
Workers (urban and rural) **	51,000,000	8.6	4,385,700	37.4
Collective farmers	30,000,000	6.5	1,940,160	16.5
Totals	110,000,000		11,758,169	

* As of January 1965.

† As of January 1966.

‡ As of November 15, 1964 (12,065,900 as of November 1965). Includes all "specialists" working in the national economy.

§ Includes agricultural personnel.

‖ Mainly women.

Primarily officers and senior noncoms; calculated on the basis of military representation at the Twenty-third Party Congress (April 1966).

** Includes all foremen and 8 million rural workers on state farms.

workers, 93% of the delegates to the Party Congress were classified as intelligentsia and only 4% were listed as peasants. Of the fifteen members on the Central Committee in 1918, only one was classified as a worker; about 40% of the Party Congress, however, was composed of workers.

In 1952, the percentage of workers, including foremen, in the Party Congress was less than 8%, while the intelligentsia accounted for more than 84% of the delegates (Table 7-4). The situation has improved substantially since Stalin's death. The proportion of workers elected to each of the Twenty-second and Twenty-third Party Congresses (1961 and 1966) was nearly three times that in 1952, but the

number of delegates to the congresses had quadrupled. Considering that the percentage of workers was tripled, the increase in delegates from the intelligentsia was little short of astronomical: in absolute numbers, the increase in the number of delegates from this class was from about 1,114 members in 1952 to 3,248 members in 1966, and down to 3,194 in 1971.

Khrushchev and his successors have tried to give greater representation to workers, peasants, women, and the agricultural sectors of Soviet life. Most of the delegates representing the workers and peasants in the party congresses are foremen or supervisory personnel rather than ordinary workers or collective farmers. Even at the level of the Party Congress, in spite

TABLE 7-4. *Social Composition of Party Congresses of the CPSU, 1952–71 (Voting delegates only)*

	1952 Number	1952 Percent	1956 Number	1956 Percent	1959 Number	1959 Percent	1961 Number	1961 Percent	1966 Number	1966 Percent	1971 Number	1971 Percent
Totals	1,192		1,355		1,269		4,408		4,943[h]		4,963[h]	
Workers		7.8%[a]		12.2%	399	32.0%	984	22.3%	1,141	23.0%	1,195	24.07%
Peasants		7.8[b]		4.9			469	10.6[c]	554	11.2	574	11.56
Intelligentsia	84.4			82.9	870	68.0	2,955	67.1	3,248	65.7	3,194	64.35
Party apparatus			526	37.3[d]	456	36.0	1,262	28.7[e]	1,330[i]	27.0	1,331[l]	26.81
State officials			177	13.1	147	11.5	465	10.5	539	10.9	556	11.20
Managerial-tech.			—	—	126	10.0	667	15.0[f]	756[j]	15.3	666[m]	13.19
Cultural-profess.			—	—	50	4.0	235	5.3	271[k]	5.5	354	7.13
Military			116	8.5	91	7.0	305	7.0[g]	352	7.1	287[o]	5.78
Other							21	0.5	—	—	—	—
Women		12.3	193	14.2	222	17.5	1,073	22.3	1,154	23.3	1,204	24.25

[a] Includes foremen.
[b] Includes farm directors and rural intelligentsia.
[c] Includes farm directors.
[d] Includes 20 trade union and Komsomol officials.
[e] Includes 104 trade union and Komsomol officials.
[f] Includes 260 agricultural specialists.
[g] Includes police officials with military rank.
[h] Includes alternates.
[i] Includes 82 trade union and 44 Komsomol officials.
[j] Includes 320 agricultural executives and technical personnel.
[k] Includes "other."
[l] Includes 126 trade union and Komsomol officials.
[m] Includes 296 agricultural executives and technical personnel.
[n] Includes an estimated 350 military representatives.
[o] Residual; may include a few nonmilitary delegates.

of the ornamental additions of representatives of workers and peasants, imbalance between the size of the class and its power in the party emerges. The intelligentsia as a whole, which accounts for only about 30% of the working population, comprised close to 45% of the party membership in 1971, and accounted for over 64% of the delegates to the Party Congress in 1971 (although the percentage was down, from 84.4% in 1952).

The Distribution of Elites in the Central Committee and Politburo

Although "workers" and "peasants" are sprinkled throughout party committees at lower levels of organization, their numbers thin out progressively as one moves up the party pyra-

mid, and virtually disappear at the level of the all-union Central Committee (Table 7-5). Even at the lowest levels, in 1965, only 36.4% (up to 40% in 1971) of the members of city and borough party committees were "workers" and "peasants," while 24.2% were from the local party and governmental bureaucracies; 18% were engineers, technicians, and professional workers; 12.9% were industrial and farm executives; and 8.5% were from other agencies (probably including the military). Of the total, 21% were women.

At the level of the Central Committee in 1966, the party apparatus accounted for nearly half the total membership, while the state bureaucracy, including both administrative and managerial officials, constituted over one-third. Thus, the state bureaucracy remains the chief rival of the party apparatus for control of the party, and the power struggles since Stalin's

TABLE 7-5. *Social Composition of the Central Committee of the CPSU, 1952–71 (Members and candidates)*

Social category	1952	1956	1961		February 1966		April 1966		April 1971	
Party apparatus	103	117	158	(48.0%) *	107	(34.2%)	155	(43.0%) †	—	
State and economic officials	79	98	112	(34.0)	115	(36.8)	136	(37.9)	—	
Military officers	26	18	31	(9.3)	31	(9.8)	33	(9.7)	31	(7.8%)
Cultural and scientific	—	—	18	(5.4)	—		15	(4.2)	—	
Police	9	3	2		—		2	(0.5)	—	
Workers and peasants	—	—	—		—		10	(2.8)	—	
Others	19‡	19‡	9 §	(3.3)	61	(19.1)	9	(2.5)	—	
Totals	236	255	330		314		360		396	
Women	—	—	—		—		15	(4.2)	15	(3.7)
Over age 40	—	—	—		—		327	(90.8)	—	
New members	—	—	—		—		121	(33.6)	154	(38.8)

* Includes nine trade union and Komsomol officials.
† Includes ten trade union and Komsomol officials.
‡ Includes cultural and scientific personnel.
§ Includes a few "workers" and "peasants."

death can be charted through the changing balance and distribution of the elites in the Central Committee and its Politburo. Under Khrushchev, the state apparatus gained substantially over the party apparatus in the composition of the Central Committee but not in the Presidium (as the Politburo was then termed). The Central Committee elected in 1961 included 48% party officials and only 34% from the state. By February 1966, the proportions had been drastically altered to favor the state apparatus over the party by 36.8% to 34.2%. At the Twenty-third Party Congress (1966), the old balance was restored somewhat, but the state held on to some of its gains, and the proportions emerged as 43% party and 38% state. The Central Committee elected then also betrayed a greater sensitivity to the presence of "workers" and "peasants," if only for ornamental purposes: in this Central Committee there was a grand total of two authentic peasants (brigade leaders, to be sure) and eight genuine workers (foremen and "honored workers").

When we examine the Central Committee that was elected in 1966 more closely, we dis-

cover that the party apparatus is represented by 155 members (127 republic and local secretaries, 18 central officials, and 10 trade union and Komsomol functionaries). Of the 134 state officials, 17 were in diplomatic work, 66 were from the central government (including economic ministries), 43 came from local governmental bodies, and eight were regional economic administrators. The military was represented by 33 generals, admirals, and marshals, and the secret police by two civilian officials. The cultural-scientific-professional groups totaled a meager 15 (the scientists were mainly administrators, and the cultural representatives were party journalists and ideologists). Two veteran retired members of the Politburo, Mikoyan and Shvernik, were also elected, while Voroshilov was also restored to membership.

The composition of the 1971 Central Committee appears to have strengthened the relative position of the party apparatus, mainly because it received a larger share of the expansion in membership. A preliminary and incomplete analysis of its composition shows that all first and second secretaries of the 14 Union Republics were elected full or candidate members, as were the 14 republican premiers. The professional military was represented by 31 members, 20 of them full members and 11 candidates. Thus, the military's representation decreased in absolute numbers as well as proportionately, although its complement of full members was sharply enhanced. Among the state officials, 16 full members and 2 candidate members were drawn from the foreign ministry and the diplomatic service. At least two workers, one on the distaff side, were elected. Altogether, 15 women (3.7%) were elected to the Central Committee, 6 as full members, including the durable Ekaterina Furtseva and the world's first and only woman cosmonaut, V. V. Nikolayeva-Tereshkova, and 9 as candidate members. Eight were elected to the less prestigious Central Auditing Commission.

As the Soviet leadership divides increasingly over policy issues, institutional cleavages become less significant indicators of group interests as various factions seek representation in party, state and other institutional organs and bodies, and different majorities dissolve and congeal in response to policy debates and issues. While institutional groupings remain important as structures, they are by no means monolithic in their outlook on matters of policy and/or ideology.

The Politburo, whose membership can formally be altered by the Central Committee, is peculiarly sensitive to the fluctuations in the balance of power, and is a fairly accurate barometer of changing political fortunes. Changes in the composition of the Politburo now reflect, to some degree, changes in the factional balance in the Central Committee as groups and individuals maneuver for position and advantage—bargaining, negotiating, and accommodating. The Central Committee's authority becomes crucial, and perhaps even decisive, when the factional balance is delicate. Then, rival groups seek to gain wider support and alter their policies to meet the demands of wider constituencies. Thus, while the Politburo is the more accurate gauge of day-to-day politics, the composition of the Central Committee is apt to reflect more durable, long-range trends.

As the Soviet system matures and becomes inextricably identified with the interests of its various privileged elites, the decision makers must give greater consideration in the calculation of policy to factors affecting the internal stability of the regime; and they will show greater sensitivity to the effects of decisions on the vested interests of the various elites in Soviet society. The rise of powerful social and economic elites in the Soviet Union, and their insistent pressure for participation in the exercise of political power could only introduce stresses, strains, conflicts, and hence new restraints into Soviet behavior.

Within the context of an ideology that imposes a single interest representing society as a whole, each interest group will tend to distort ideology and policy in an endeavor to give it the contours of its own interests; the next step is to elevate these to transcendental significance. Under these conditions, Soviet ideology may be constantly threatened with a series of fundamental convulsions if one interest group displaces another in the struggle for the control of the party machinery. Hence, a rational system of accommodating conflicting interests appears to be evolving. As the vested stake of each major group becomes rooted in the Soviet system, the contours of Soviet policy will inexorably tend to be shaped more by the rapidly moving equilibrium or accommodation of interests that develop internally than by abstract ideological imperatives, which may conflict with the concrete interests of specific major elites in Soviet society.

The definite post-Khrushchev composition of the Politburo was made at the Twenty-third Party Congress (1966), when Mikoyan and Shvernik were retired from the Politburo and Pelshe, a Latvian party secretary, was appointed a full member over the heads of all the candidate members. All of these members were reelected in 1971, although four new members were added. Immediately after Khrushchev's ouster, two new candidate members were appointed: Kunayev, a Kazakh party leader, and Masherov, a Byelorussian party secretary who had become a full member of the Central Committee only in November 1964—which suggests that he played a key role in the post-Khrushchev factional maneuvering. The composition of the Secretariat remained unchanged, except that Kirilenko, also a full member of the Politburo, replaced Podgorny, since the latter's new post as chairman of the Presidium of the Supreme Soviet is traditionally disassociated from the Secretariat.

The restructuring of the party summit at the Twenty-third Party Congress strongly suggested that Brezhnev, the general secretary of the party, had strengthened his position and that he enjoyed a factional majority or consensus, but had not assumed the power of a Khrushchev or a Stalin irrespective of the symbolic manipulation of nomenclature at the congress. Of the eleven full members of the Politburo, four were members of the Secretariat, while of the eight candidate members, two were members of the Secretariat. This meant that six members of the eleven-man Secretariat also sat on the Politburo. The clear dominance of the party apparatus in the Politburo was further indicated by the presence of six party secretaries of republics (Ukrainian, Latvian, Georgian, Uzbek, Byelorussian, and Kazakh) as full or candidate members. This broadened its ethnic base to include representation from six of the fourteen major non-Russian nationalities, including two central Asian Moslem nationalities (Uzbeks and Kazakhers), and gave the party apparatus a total of six full members and six candidate members of the Politburo, or twelve voices out of nineteen—a clear majority. In addition to this, career party bureaucrats like Podgorny and Mazurov moved into key state offices.

Changes in the party summit made at the Twenty-fourth Party Congress (1971) reflected even more emphatically the emerging dominance of Brezhnev within the Soviet leadership. Aside from the elevation of the general secretaryship to virtually an institutional role at the apex of the party and symbolically listed ahead of the Politburo, Brezhnev's increasing authority was also indicated by changes in the composition of the Politburo and the interlocking membership between it and the Secretariat. Four new full members were added to the Politburo, while members like Kosygin, Voro-

nov, Polyansky, Shelest, and Shelepin suffered a decline in importance, if the order in which Brezhnev listed them in his televised report is an accurate indication of their relative standing in the Politburo. The unexpected appointment of Kulakov, a close associate of Brezhnev and a relatively junior member of the Secretariat, to full membership on the Politburo over the heads of six sitting candidate members is the clearest indication of Brezhnev's growing authority. All of the candidate members advanced to full membership, Kunayev, Grishin, and Shcherbitsky, have had close relations with Brezhnev in the past, and Kunayev and Kulakov gained in rank soon after Khrushchev's ouster in 1964. Kunayev is a Kazakh and is thus the first Moslem to achieve full membership since Khrushchev's Uzbek protégé, Mukhitdinov, was elevated in 1956 (he was later demoted as Khrushchev's political fortunes waned).

All ten sitting members of the Secretariat were reelected, with six of the ten also sitting on the Politburo, four of them as full members and two as candidate members, thus giving the Secretariat four votes out of fifteen on the Politburo. However, it should be noted that among the full members are four other full-time party functionaries: Pelshe, chairman of the Party Control Committee; Kunayev, first secretary of the Kazakh party; Shelest, first secretary of the Ukrainian party; and Grishin, first secretary of the Moscow city party organization. Thus, of the fifteen full members of the Politburo, no less than eight—a majority—are full-time party functionaries, under the administrative authority of the general secretary. Furthermore, although Shelepin was transferred to trade union work, he is also a career party official. Of the six candidate members of the Politburo, two (Demichev and Ustinov) are central party secretaries, while three are first secretaries of union republic party organizations: Rashidov (Uzbek), Mzhavanadze (Georgia), and Masherov (Byelorussia). The remaining candidate member, Andropov, is also a veteran party functionary who was a member of the Secretariat until his appointment as head of the secret police in 1967. Thus, of the twenty-one members of the Politburo elected at the

Twenty-fourth Party Congress, eight full members and five candidate members were full-time party officials.

In the 1971 reshuffling of Politburo membership, the representatives of state officialdom clearly suffered a setback, with only Podgorny, Kosygin, Mazurov, and Polyansky representing the central state officialdom among the full members, and Voronov (Russian SFSR) and Shcherbitsky (Ukraine) representing republican officials. It is also noteworthy that in Brezhnev's listing of the eleven full members of the Politburo reelected, state officials, as a rule, were at the bottom, and that this listing differed significantly from the ordered-ranking in 1966, as follows:

1971	1966
Brezhnev	Brezhnev
Podgorny *	Kosygin *
Kosygin *	Podgorny *
Suslov	Suslov
Kirilenko	Voronov *
Pelshe	Kirilenko
Mazurov *	Shelepin
Polyansky *	Mazurov *
Shelest	Polyansky *
Voronov *	Shelest
Shelepin	Pelshe
Grishin	
Kunayev	
Shcherbitsky	
Kulakov	

* Government officials.

Voronov was replaced as Russian SFSR Premier by Secretariat member M. S. Solomentsev in November 1971, who was also appointed a candidate member of the Politburo, thus raising the total membership to twenty-two.

It is normal practice to divorce membership in the Secretariat from membership in the Council of Ministers, since the Secretariat is supposed to exercise an independent audit of the government's work and check on the execution and implementation of party directives and resolutions. The only consistent deviation from this practice occurs when the same personality functions as general secretary of the party and chairman of the Council of Ministers, as was the case during the later years of the Stalin and Khrushchev eras. Similarly, the chairmanship of the Presidium of the Supreme Soviet is considered to be incompatible with membership in the Secretariat, and both Brezhnev and Podgorny relinquished their membership in the latter upon their appointment to the former post. It is traditional, however, for the general secretary to be an ordinary member of the Presidium of the Supreme Soviet if he holds no other state post, and it is usual for the Presidium to include several other members of the party Secretariat, thus ensuring party audit and control over its activities. It is also now illegal for membership in the Presidium of the Supreme Soviet to overlap with membership in the Council of Ministers, since the latter is juridically responsible to the former. Since the death of Stalin, it has been normal practice to include high state and party officials of the Russian SFSR and the Ukraine in the Politburo.

The Secretariat, by its very nature, remains the exclusive domain of the party apparatus, and the distribution of power at the summit is reflected in the degree of interlock between state and party officials in the Politburo. Since Stalin's death, the pattern of distribution in the party's highest body has been as shown in Table 7-6.

The Nationality Composition of the Party

The distribution and influence of various nationalities within the party at the "all-union" level has been highly uneven. In sheer numbers, Great Russians have always dominated membership in the party. Whereas Russians accounted for only 53% of the population in 1926, they made up 72% of the party only two

TABLE 7-6. *Distribution of Elites in the Politburo/Presidium of the CPSU, 1952–71*

	October 1952	*March 1953*	*February 1956*	*July 1957*	*July 1961*	*October 1961*	*January 1963*	*April 1966*	*April 1971*
Party apparatus *	13 (5)†	2 (2)	4 (3)	10 (6)	10 (3)	7 (3)	8 (4)	6 (7)	9 (5).
State bureaucracy								5 (1)	6 (0)
Economic	5 (4)	4	4	1 (2)	2 (1)	2	2	—	—
Noneconomic	4 (2)	3 (1)	3 (1)	3	2 (2)	2 (2)	2 (2)	—	—
Professional military	0	0	0 (1)	1	0	0	0	0	0
Police	2	1 (1)	0	0	0	0	0	0	0 (1)
Cultural intelligentsia (ideologists)	1 (1)	0	0 (1)	0 (1)	0 (1)	0	0	0	0
Trade unions	—	—	—	—	—	—	—	—	0
Totals	25 (11)	10 (4)	11 (6)	15 (6)	14 (7)	11 (5)	12 (6)	11 (8)	15 (6)
Women ‡	0	0	0 (1)	1	1	0	0	—	0

    * State and police officials, ideologists, and others who were appointed to government positions from the party apparatus are included in this category rather than in their official position. Main career experience determines classification. Thus, M. A. Suslov is classified with the party apparatus rather than with the cultural intelligentsia, as is Shelepin.

    † Figures in parentheses represent candidate members.

    ‡ Furtseva in all cases.

years earlier. The Ukrainians, in contrast, who provided more than 21% of the population, made up only 6% of the party members. In 1962, the first complete national breakdown of the party in decades was published. Great Russians still accounted for a majority (64% of the total); the decrease in percentage resulted from a determined effort on the part of the regime to increase the representation of other nationalities. More than one hundred nationalities were represented in the party as of January 1965. Nationality distribution is shown in Table 7-7.[10]

    The representation of the non-Russian nationalities in the higher organs of the party has varied considerably over the years. A score or more nationalities have been represented in the Central Committee of the party since 1952. Although the proportion of non-Russians, especially Ukrainians, has been steadily increas-

ing since Stalin's death, the Russian presence has been overwhelming, rising as high as 80% of the total membership. At the apex of the party, the proportion of Russians has been smaller, but only nine non-Russian nationalities have found representation on the party's highest body. Of the more than ninety members or candidate members who have served on the Party Politburo for any length of time between 1917 and 1971, over sixty have been Great Russians. Nationalities have been distributed as shown in Table 7-8.

    Statistics alone, however, do not tell the complete story. Although the Ukrainians constitute the second largest nationality in the Soviet Union, not a single Ukrainian was admitted to the party's highest body between the years 1938 and 1952. The first Moslem to be admitted was an Azerbaidzhani crony of Beria's, who was appointed a candidate member in 1953, only to be executed about a year later. The first central Asian, an Uzbek, was admitted to the Presidium in December 1956, and was

    [10] *Partiinaya Zhizn,* no. 1 (January 1962); and no. 10 (May 1966):8–17.

TABLE 7-7. *Distribution of Nationalities in the CPSU, 1961–67*

	1961		1965		1967	
	Party members	*Percentage*	*Party members*	*Percentage*	*Party members*	*Percentage*
Russian	6,116,700	63.5%	7,335,200	62.4%	7,846,292	61.9%
Ukrainian	1,412,200	14.7	1,813,400	15.4	1,983,090	15.6
Byelorussian	287,000	3.0	386,000	3.3	424,360	3.3
Georgian	170,400	1.8	194,000	1.7	209,196	1.7
Armenian	161,200	1.7	187,900	1.6	200,605	1.6
Kazakh	149,000	1.5	181,300	1.5	199,196	1.6
Uzbek	142,000	1.5	193,600	1.7	219,381	1.7
Azerbaidzhani	106,000	1.1	141,900	1.2	162,181	1.3
Lithuanian	42,000	0.4	61,500	0.5	71,316	.56
Latvian	33,900	0.3	44,300	0.4	49,559	.39
Tadzhik	32,700	0.3	41,900	0.4	46,593	.37
Turkmen	27,300	0.3	32,400	0.3	35,781	.28
Kirgiz	27,300	0.3	35,000	0.3	39,053	.31
Moldavian	26,700	0.3	40,300	0.4	46,562	.37
Estonian	24,100	0.2	33,900	0.3	37,705	.29
Other	866,100	9.0	1,035,300	8.8	1,113,263	8.8
Totals	9,626,700		11,758,200		12,684,133	

TABLE 7-8. *Distribution of Nationalities in the Politburo/Presidium of the CPSU, 1917–71 (Totals)*

	Full members	*Candidate members*	*Total*
Great Russians	41	20	61
Ukrainians	7	3	10
Jews	3	0	3
Georgians	3	1	4
Armenians	1	1	2
Uzbeks	1	1	2
Latvians	2	3	5
Karelo-Finns	1	0	1
Azerbaidzhani	0	1	1
Poles	1	1	2
Kazakhs	1	0	1
Byelorussians	1	1	2
Totals	62	32	94

replaced by another in 1961, who was joined by a Kazakh in 1966. Under Stalin, the Politburo was in fact dominated by the Great Russians and the Caucasian nationalities, the latter typically constituting from one-third to one-fourth of the membership. Since 1956, at least six to eight nationalities have been represented in the Politburo. In 1971, Russians accounted for eight full members (Brezhnev, Kosygin, Suslov, Kirilenko, Voronov, Shelepin, Grishin, and Kulakov) and three candidate members (Ustinov, Demichev, Andropov); Ukrainians were represented by four full members (Podgorny, Polyansky, Shelest, Shcherbitsky); Byelorussians numbered one full member (Mazurov) and one candidate member (Masherov). The Kazakhs (Kunayev) and Latvians (Pelshe) were represented by one full member each, while the Georgians (Mzhvanadze) and the Uzbeks (Rashidov) were each represented by a candidate member.

EIGHT

the

Soviet

constitutional

order

The Soviet system during its more than five decades of existence has operated under three different constitutions. The first constitution, which was restricted only to the Russian Republic—the RSFSR—was promulgated on July 10, 1918; it was superseded by the first constitution of the USSR, which came in force officially on January 3, 1924. The present constitution was promulgated on December 5, 1936, and has remained in force ever since, although it has been amended frequently, especially in recent years. It is virtually impossible to secure an up-to-date text of the Soviet constitution, whose versions now appear almost with the frequency of a periodical. Amendments to the Soviet constitution are not conveniently enumerated, as is the case in American constitutional practice, but rather the alterations are inserted directly into the text, so that amendments can be detected only by examining various versions of the constitution itself.

The situation had become so bewildering by the time that Khrushchev became premier that on more than one occasion he complained vociferously about it, seeing the need for either its drastic overhaul or its replacement with a new document. Eventually (on April 26, 1962), Khrushchev formally proposed before the Supreme Soviet that a new draft of the Soviet constitution be undertaken. A drafting commission was quickly appointed, with Khrushchev serving as its chairman (an additional position which he lost upon his ouster). Trying to patch up the already battered and mutilated Stalin constitution, Khrushchev noted, "would be nothing but adding new wings to an old building." The new constitution would reflect a society in which, in Khrushchev's words, "Socialism had achieved full and final victory [and] . . . has entered the period of full-scale Communist construction," during which time "the state of the dictatorship of the proletariat has evolved into a Socialist state of all the people" and "has emerged from capitalist encirclement," to lead "a great community of Socialist states." [1] Although the drafting commission is now chaired by Brezhnev, little concerning its deliberations has been made public.

[1] Quoted in *Pravda*, April 25, 1962.

THE FUNCTIONS AND PRINCIPLES OF THE CONSTITUTION

The Soviet constitution performs the four universal functions of constitutions everywhere: (1) it legalizes the existing social order and makes explicit its ideological principles; (2) it establishes a framework of government and administration; (3) it regulates social and institutional behavior; (4) it enumerates normative Soviet goals and aspirations. In addition, the Soviet constitution performs another function: (5) it serves as a propaganda document for export abroad.

The constitution gives legal expression to the basic ideological norms of Soviet doctrine that have been concretely implemented. The most important of these are: (1) the abolition of private ownership of the means of production in favor of state or public ownership; (2) the collectivization of agriculture; (3) the nationalization of natural resources; (4) a centrally directed planned economy; (5) mandatory employment, in accordance with the formulas "He who does not work, neither shall he eat" and "From each according to his ability, to each according to his work"; (6) the legal monopoly of the Communist party over political life.

Among the normative goals, which are essentially hortatory in character, are "the aim of increasing wealth, of steadily raising the material and cultural standards of the working people" (article 11) and "the steady growth of the productive forces of Soviet society, the elimination of the possibility of economic crises, and the abolition of unemployment" (article 118). These are general aspirations, expressing hope rather than concrete fulfillment.

Some normative goals in the constitution, however, have been realized to some degree: "the right to rest and leisure," "the right to maintenance in old age and also in case of sickness and disability," and "the right to education." In the same category is the principle that "women in the USSR are accorded equal rights with men" (article 122) and the princi-ple of national and racial equality, which asserts the "equality of rights of citizens . . . irrespective of their nationality or race," violations of which are "punishable by law." The implementation of these doctrines has been extremely uneven, often capricious and unreliable. The government's record concerning the non-Russian nationalities, for instance, has been exemplary in some areas and deplorable in others.

Other principles of the Soviet constitution can be dismissed as transparent propaganda clichés which are essentially meaningless. Among these are the assertions that (1) the Soviet Union "is a socialist state of workers and peasants"; (2) "all power in the USSR belongs to the working people"; (3) the Soviet Union is "a voluntary union of equal . . . Republics"; (4) the republics have "the right to freely secede from the USSR"; (5) "the highest organ of state power in the USSR is the Supreme Soviet."

Another category of unrealized principles are those which are purely declaratory in character. These are the principles dealing with political rights of Soviet citizens and the manner in which they are to be exercised. Thus, article 125 asserts that Soviet citizens "are guaranteed by law . . . freedom of speech . . . of the press . . . of assembly, including the holding of mass meetings . . . of street processions and demonstrations," provided that these freedoms are exercised "in conformity with the interests of the working people, and in order to strengthen the Socialist system." Any other form of expression is likely to be dangerous and a violation of article 70 of the criminal code, which reads:

Agitation or propaganda carried on for the purpose of subverting or weakening Soviet authority . . . is punishable by deprivation of freedom to seven years.

It was under this provision of the criminal code that writers Andrei Sinyavsky and Yuri Daniel were tried and sentenced in 1966 to hard labor in concentration camps. In recent years as dissent has grown inside the Soviet Union, this law has been both repeatedly flaunted as a warning and invoked to convict and imprison dissidents. In the words of a recent Soviet textbook, "Lenin considered it a criminal act even to think of violating the law, no matter what the motive." [2] Under this law, Soviet Jews who wish to emigrate to Israel; many citizens protesting the partial rehabilitation of Stalin; errant writers, poets, historians, and scientists demanding the freedom to exercise their constitutional rights have been arrested, convicted, and imprisoned.

With reservations similar to those applied to the freedom of speech article 126 reads that Soviet citizens "are guaranteed the right to unite in public organizations: trade unions, cooperative societies, youth organizations, sport and defense organizations, cultural, technical and scientific societies"—*but not in political parties or organizations.* Article 126 does not give Soviet citizens even the right to join the Communist party, which is reserved only for "the most active and politically conscious citizens," and "is the core of all organizations . . . both public and state."

Article 124, concerning the exercise of religion, provides for "freedom of religious worship and freedom of antireligious propaganda." This means that freedom of "religious propaganda" is not guaranteed in the constitution; indeed, it constitutes a crime under separate legislation. On the other hand, the full power and apparatus of the state and party are mobilized on behalf of "antireligious propaganda," which is a basic freedom in the Soviet constitution obviously superior to freedom of religion. Since virtually all physical property in the Soviet Union belongs to the state, churches and religious institutions are either nonexistent or in a state of decay and disrepair; clergymen are hounded and persecuted, while "believers" find themselves harassed and insulted and their opportunities in Soviet society severely limited. "Freedom to worship," in effect, means freedom to worship silently, inconspicuously, and in isolation.

The Soviet textbook quoted above treats the constitutional "freedom of conscience" in the following manner:

The bourgeois press sometimes spreads rumors that in the USSR religious believers are suppressed and persecuted. Such claims are either sheer fabrications or the intentional falsification of Soviet laws which merely demand that legislation concerning religious activities be obeyed. It is true there is considerable atheistic propaganda in the Soviet Union, and the law states that religious activities should not disturb public order or infringe upon the rights of others. But this does not mean that religion is suppressed. . . . From what has been said it does not follow that .the Communist Party is indifferent to matters of religion. The Party does not conceal its disapproval of religion as an unscientific, reactionary world outlook. . . . It would be a great mistake to think that freedom of conscience implies the freedom to perform religious rites only. It also includes the freedom to carry on atheistic propaganda, the propagation of a scientific world outlook.[3]

Another group of principles in the Soviet constitution covers "rights" that have been continuously and grossly violated. Article 127 reads that "citizens of the USSR are guaranteed inviolability of the person [and] no person may be placed under arrest except by decision of a court or with the sanction of a prosecutor," while article 128 asserts: "the inviolability of the homes of citizens and privacy of correspondence are protected by law."

These are "rights" that Soviet jurists now acknowledge were systematically outraged during the entire period of the Stalinist regime. Ironically enough, the very moment these "rights" were promulgated as sacred provisions of the "most democratic" constitution in the history of mankind, they were being violated by the secret police, which arrested, tortured, and executed hundreds of thousands of ordinary citizens and state and party officials of the highest rank, without benefit of public trial, legal counsel, or formal arraignment as provided by the constitution and legal codes. Since 1956, Soviet jurists have been actively engaged in disavowing the Stalinist violations of the "norms of Socialist legality," the secret police has been shorn of its powers and dismembered, the concentration camps have been emptied of political prisoners, and the criminal and proce-

[2] B. Bayanov, Y. Umansky, and M. Shafir, *Soviet Socialist Democracy* (Moscow, 1968), p. 151.

[3] Bayanov, Umansky, and Shafir, *Soviet Socialist Democracy*, pp. 191–92.

dural codes have been revised in an effort to provide some concrete fulfillment of these universally cherished human rights. Since 1966, however, the "norms of socialist legality" have once again been under severe strain as the regime moved more militantly against dissidents.

SOVIET FEDERALISM: THEORY AND PRACTICE

The Soviet Union is constitutionally described as "a federal state formed on the basis of a voluntary union of equal Soviet Socialist Republics." Although, juridically, the USSR resembles more a confederation than a federation, in practice it is organized as a tightly centralized system.

The Origins of Soviet Federalism

The Soviet federal system does not spring from Marxist doctrine, but rather has its source in the ethnic legacy left by the collapse of the tsarist system. The Bolsheviks fell heir to a land with more than one hundred races and nationalities, which had been absorbed but never digested by the expanding Russian empire. Long exposed to "russification" and domination, these peoples smoldered with discontent, and their hostility was one of the chief political problems of the imperial system which was never satisfactorily resolved.

Federalism as an idea was anathema to both Marx and Lenin, for it seemed to be incompatible with the imperative of central economic planning. Furthermore, nationalism—and its moral justification, national self-determination—contravened the Marxist emphasis on class solidarity and a unified international proletariat. In spite of these ideological prejudices against nationalism, Lenin demonstrated his flexibility by recognizing that in the light of the experiences of the nations of the Russian empire, no political movement could succeed without allowing for the nationalistic impulses which motivated the non-Russian minorities. In 1903, Lenin espoused the principle of national self-determination in spite of his ideological

reservations. At first, he tried to interpret it in such a way that it would exclude the right of secession and independence, but by 1913, Lenin recognized that national self-determination "cannot be interpreted otherwise than in the sense of *political* self-determination—i.e., the right of secession and formation of an independent state."[4] From that point on, the right of the nations of Russia to secede became a declaratory principle that appears in every Soviet constitutional document.

The Bolshevik stand, it should be made clear, was dictated by tactical expediency, as Lenin frankly admitted:

We, on our part, do not want separation at all. We want as large a state as possible. . . . We want a voluntary amalgamation and that is why we are obliged to recognize the freedom of secession.[5]

Wherever it could, however, the Soviet regime used the power of the Red Army to prevent secession and to reconquer those areas of the former Russian empire which took the Bolshevik position seriously and tried to secede. Those border regions that managed to make good their separation, even in the face of an attempted Soviet conquest (i.e., Poland, the three Baltic states, and Finland), remained outside the Soviet Republic.

The Principles of Soviet Federalism

The federal structure of the Soviet state is dictated more by historical necessity than by ideological inspiration. In general, the trend has been toward greater *juridical decentralization accompanied by tighter ideological and political centralization*. While Soviet federalism reflects a conventional pattern of organization in its purely juridical dimension, it also exhibits five unique characteristics:

4 V. I. Lenin, *Selected Works* (New York: International Publishers, n.d.), 7:123.
5 V. I. Lenin, *Collected Works* (New York: International Publishers, 1945), 16:507. See also V. V. Aspaturian, "The Theory and Practice of Soviet Federalism," *Journal of Politics* 12 (1950):20–51.

1. Soviet federal units are based on nationality rather than on regional, economic, or historical distinctions. All federal units are nationality units; hence the Soviet system is primarily a *multinational* federalism.

2. Not all nationality units possess the same degree of national autonomy, but rather a hierarchy of national units eixsts, with the highest being called *union republics* and the lowest *National Districts* (*okrugs*).

3. The highest federal units, the Union Republics, have a juridical right to secede, as the ultimate symbolic manifestation of their national autonomy.

4. Since February 1, 1944, all Union Republics are constitutionally endowed with the power to engage in diplomatic relations, to sign international agreements, and to maintain separate troop formations. Thus, juridically, foreign affairs and defense are decentralized. Although two republics, the Ukraine and Byelorussia, are members of the United Nations and engage in limited diplomatic activity and all Union Republics have foreign ministries, the diplomatic powers of the republics remain potential rather than real. In the matter of defense, not a single republic has ever established a defense ministry, appointed a defense minister, or organized a separate army.

5. Since December 1958, the collective head of the Soviet state, the Presidium of the Supreme Soviet, must have as many vice-chairmen as there are Union Republics. By custom, the chairmen of the presidiums of the union republics are ex officio vice-chairmen of the Presidium of the Supreme Soviet Union. Similarly, the chairmen of the councils of ministers of the union republics are ex officio members of the all-union Council of Ministers. Thus, in the Soviet pattern, the basic federal units have representation in the central executive and administrative organs of government.[6]

[6] Numbers 1-4 from V. V. Aspaturian, *The Union Republics in Soviet Diplomacy* (Geneva: Librarie Droz, 1960), and "The Union Republics and Soviet Diplomacy: Concepts, Institutions and Practices," *American Political Science Review* (June 1959):383–411.

Aside from the unique departures enumerated above, Soviet federalism in its formal dimensions is quite conventional. It follows the principle of federal supremacy, in that all republic constitutions must be in conformity with that of the USSR, and federal laws take precedence over republic laws.

The Hierarchy of National Units

As the constitution of a federal state, the Soviet constitution establishes a system of multiple jurisdiction and shared sovereignty. In a strictly technical sense, the federal character of the Soviet Union is restricted to the relationship between the Soviet Union and the union republics, of which there are currently fifteen. Lesser national units enjoy narrower degrees of autonomy. The union republics vary in size from the Russian SFSR—which embraces three-quarters of the territory of the USSR, stretches from the Baltic to the Pacific, and includes 55% of the population of the Soviet Union—to Estonia, the smallest in population (1.3 million), and Armenia, the smallest territorially. According to existing Soviet doctrine, first enunciated by Stalin in 1936, a national territory must meet three physical criteria in order to qualify as a union republic:

1. The eponymous population must constitute a majority of the population in the republic.

2. The republic must have a population of at least 1 million.

3. The republic must be located on the international border.

According to Stalin:

Since the Union Republics have a right to secede from the USSR, a republic . . . must be in a position logically and actually to raise the question of secession from the USSR. . . . Of course none of our republics would actually raise the question of seceding from the USSR. But since the right to secede from the USSR is reserved to the Union

Republics, it must be so arranged that this right does not become a meaningless scrap of paper [sic].[7]

The right to secede, of course, is illusory. No republic has ever attempted it, although non-Russian Soviet leaders have been tried and executed allegedly for plotting to take various republics out of the union.

Since the republics are juridically organized as national states, each has a constitution, a government, and a flag, and also a coat of arms that is a variation of that possessed by the Soviet Union. Each republic has a supreme soviet (unicameral instead of bicameral, however), a collective head of state called the presidium of the supreme soviet, a council of ministers with a chairman (premier), a supreme court, a procurator, a foreign ministry, and provisions for a defense ministry. Union republics have thirty-two (up from twenty-five since 1966) deputies in the Soviet of Nationalities—the second "federal" chamber of the all-union Supreme Soviet.

Immediately below the union republic in the Soviet federal hierarchy is the autonomous republic, which is reserved for moderately large nationalities that are "culturally advanced" but cannot meet the criteria for union republic status. Autonomous republics, of which there are twenty, resemble union republics in almost all particulars. They have constitutions and governments virtually indistinguishable from those of the union republics, but they do not have the juridical right to secede, are subject to the jurisdiction of a union republic rather than to that of the Soviet Union directly, are not endowed with international responsibilities, enjoy neither a vice-chairmanship on the all-union Presidium of the Supreme Soviet nor ex officio membership on the all-union Council of Ministers, and are entitled to only eleven deputies in the Council of Nationalities.

7 J. V. Stalin, *Leninism: Selected Writings,* p. 400. In 1955, because it failed to meet these criteria, among other reasons, the Karelo-Finnish Union Republic was reduced to the status of an autonomous republic within the USSR. Thus, with the stroke of a pen, the republic lost its "rights" to secede, to engage in diplomacy, and to maintain its own army. Such is the durability of a union republic's "soveignty."

The autonomous oblasts, of which there were eight in 1971, are populated by smaller nationalities than are the autonomous republics, and their juridical status and powers are considerably inferior to those of the union and autonomous republics. The autonomous oblasts are entitled to five deputies in the Council of Nationalities.

The lowest national units are the national okrugs, all ten of which are located in the RSFSR. These units are populated by very small national, ethnic, or linguistic groups, numbering in the thousands.

Altogether, fifty-three national groups are organized into units. National units can move up or down in the federal hierarchy, but the usual procedure is promotion to higher status: national oblast to autonomous republic, or autonomous republic to union republic.

Soviet Federalism in Perspective

Since Soviet federalism arose neither as a practical device to restrain the power of the central government nor in response to an ideological compulsion, its true significance is not likely to be found in its functional attributes, but rather in its role as a device for organizing many national groups under a uniform ideology. Federalism is still viewed in Soviet doctrine as a transitional device to centralization, although it has undoubtedly influenced Soviet administration in ways not originally intended. Soviet federalism is a very weak restriction against the power of the central authority. Since the constitution itself is not designed as a limiting instrument, it is not likely that the federalism it establishes can become an effective limitation on the central government.

While the Soviet policy on nationalities is deficient in many particulars, the Soviet multinational system is a unique experiment. Western criticism of Soviet nationality policy and Soviet federalism is leveled principally at the uniform ideological content of Soviet life, the totalitarian character of Soviet rule, and the inadequacies of Soviet federalism as a limitation on the state. It remains true, nonetheless, that nationalities were given a modicum of administrative authority and that their cultural self-expression was respected and at times even restored. The party, on the other hand, is anti-federal, and transcends the constitution itself; it is the single thread that weaves together the entire union into a compact political monolith. This unification is enhanced by the centralization of economic planning and by the socialization of the means of production by the Soviet state.

The Soviets under the 1936 Constitution

The 1936 constitution established a pseudo-parliamentary system, although the term *soviet* was retained. All soviets (people's legislative bodies) are elective. All electoral discriminations were abolished in favor of equal, direct, and universal suffrage. Soviets (literally, "councils") exist at all territorial-administrative levels, from the village through the towns and cities, rayons, oblasts, krays, autonomous oblasts, and autonomous republics, union republics, and finally at the union level. The soviets at the union, union republic, and autonomous republic levels are called supreme soviets, while the lesser bodies are called oblast soviets, rayon soviets, etc.

Every soviet elects an executive committee to function as an administrative and supervisory body, with a chairman who in effect functions as the chief administrative officer of the unit concerned. At the union, union republic, and autonomous republic levels, instead of an executive committee, there is an elected presidium and council of ministers, each with a chairman. The soviets are the ultimate repositories of "state power" for the territorial unit which they administer, and in this capacity they exercise control over the courts as well as over the executive, legislative, and administrative branches of local government.

The total number of regional and local soviets in 1971 was nearly 50,000 (a drop of more than 10,000 since 1957 because of the consolidation and shrinkage of rural soviets): kray, 6; oblast, 10; autonomous oblast, 8; national okrug, 10; rayon, 2,926; city, 1,933; borough,

452; settlement, 3,467; and village, 40,907. Altogether, these soviets elected over 2.1 million deputies in 1971 and gave rise to an equal number of executive bodies. These soviets varied in size from 40 to 80 in districts, 70 to 150 in rayons, and 50 to 700 in cities, with as many as 850 in large metropolitan areas. Unwieldy in size and meeting irregularly, they delegate their authority to the smaller executive bodies, whose chairmen are high party officials and whose members are full-time paid officers of local administration. The executive committees exercise the powers of the soviets between sessions and are responsible not only to the soviet but to the executive committee of the next-higher territorial unit. In instances where the executive committee itself is fairly large, a bureau or presidium serves as an inner executive body.

Immediately below the all-union level are the supreme soviets of the fifteen union republics, with a total of 5,879 deputies elected in June 1971; and just below this tier are the supreme soviets of the twenty autonomous republics, with a total of 2,994 deputies.

It should be noted that the soviets parallel and virtually duplicate the party organizations at all levels, and a close and continuing relationship exists between the two (Fig. 8-1). In theory, the soviets represent the "masses," since they are elected by all citizens, whereas the party represents the "vanguard" or leading element in the population. Consequently, at all levels of organization there is an overlapping between party and soviet organizations. Party membership among deputies to local soviets in 1971 ranged from an average of 41.3% in Estonia to over 47% in Moldavia. As a general rule, the higher the administrative level of the soviet, the greater the proportion of party members, which at the all-union Supreme Soviet level in recent years has varied from 70 to 85%. (Since the soviets represent the masses, it is only appropriate that a certain proportion of deputies at all levels be ordinary nonparty citizens.)

Table 8-1 demonstrates that, as one moves up the ladder of the soviets, besides the increase in the proportion of party members there is a corresponding increase in the proportion of men and members of the intelli-

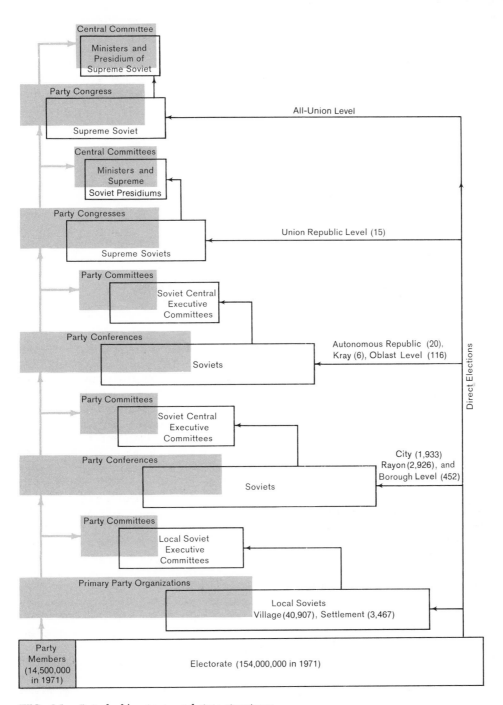

FIG. 8-1. *Interlocking party and state structures.*

TABLE 8-1. *Party and Social Composition of Soviets, 1971*

Level	Total Deputies	Party Members		Men		Intelligentsia		Under Age 30	
		Number	Percentage	Number	Percentage	Number	Percentage	Number	Percentage
All-union (1)	1,517	1,096	72.3%	1,054	69.5%	839	55.5%	281	18.5%
Union republic (15)	5,879	3,994	67.6	3,834	65.2	2,916	49.6	1,012	17.2
Autonomous republic (20)	2,994	1,902	63.5	1,857	62.0	1,560	52.1	554	18.5
Regional and local (49,685)	165,037	963,173	44.5	1,172,401	54.2	751,292	34.7	557,015	25.7
Totals	2,175,427	970,165	44.6	1,179,146	54.2	756,607	34.8	558,862	25.7

SOURCE: *Pravda,* June 20, 1971.

gentsia involved. Thus, we may extend our general rule to say that the more important the function and status, the more it is male-dominated, and the more influential and important the institution, the more it is dominated by male party members of the intelligentsia.

Forgetting for a moment the influences of the intelligentsia on our considerations, let us concentrate on the qualifications "male" and "party member" as they together affect the composition of the soviets. The predominance of males and party members is more than conspicuous in the executive committees and directing organs of the local soviets. In 1961, for example, of the 347,101 members of executive committees, 262,990 (75.6%) were men and 252,328 (72.7%) were party members. And of the 49,824 chairmen of executive committees, 42,136 (84.6%) were men and 45,171 (90.7%) were party members, while the less significant post of secretary, not to be confused with the party secretaryship, which is nearly a male monopoly, was occupied by 29,243 (58.7%) women, and only 18,808 (37.8%) were members of the party.[8] In the local soviets themselves,

[8] Sovety Deputatov Trudyashchikhsya, no. 3 (March, 1963).

the proportion of women varied from 43.6% to 46.3% in 1971.

SOVIET ELECTIONS

Under the 1936 constitution, Soviet elections are direct, universal, equal, and "secret," but since there is only one candidate for each elective position, elections are obviously not designed to provide the electorate with a choice of representatives, but merely a superficial opportunity to ratify and approve the policies of the Communist party. The Soviet electorate of 154,000,000 (1971) is one of the largest in the world, with the minimum voting age set at 18. Even though article 141 of the constitution stipulates that "the right to nominate candidates is secured to public organizations, trade unions, cooperatives, youth organizations, and cultural societies," candidates are, in fact, selected and screened by the appropriate organs of the party, although they may encourage other groups to suggest names as possible candidates.

Elections in the Soviet Union have more the character of a festive occasion than of a serious political event. Since no contest exists, artificial stimulants are required to create a feeling of public participation. Rallies and assemblies are held, "campaigns" are conducted, slogans are coined, speeches are made, banners and pins are distributed, and get-out-the-vote drives are organized. Elections are normally scheduled on a holiday or nonworking day in order to assure maximum turnout. Election commissions consisting of representatives of the party and other organizations are established at all levels, from the precinct to the union; they administer and supervise elections, certify candidates, register voters, examine complaints, check "irregularities," count the votes, and report the results—in a solemn and serious manner. The number of citizens involved in these electoral bodies runs into the millions.

In order to adhere to the constitutional imperative of a "secret" ballot, polling booths are provided for the voters at voting stations, but since only one candidate exists for each position, the normal procedure is simply for the voter to mark his ballot, fold it, and drop it in the ballot box—all in full view of the voting officials. His other choices are not to vote at all or to cross the name off the ballot as a gesture of disapproval. The latter would require that the voter utilize the polling booth. Since use of the booth would arouse suspicion, it is infrequently used; under Stalin, resort to the booth often signified the last election in which the voter would participate for some time. If more than 50% of the voters scratch a candidate's name, he fails election, but rejection by the voters is a rare occurrence and happens only at lower levels and often when officially inspired.

Voter participation in Soviet elections is very high, since the social and political pressures to vote are intense. Failure to vote may provoke social criticism and penalties, although it is not against the law to abstain. In a system that relishes and demands unanimity, deliberate abstention is tantamount to a negative vote. Whereas in earlier years the proportion of eligible voters who participated was less than 50%, it has been more than 95% since 1937, reaching a high point of 99.97% in 1958. In the 1966 elections to the all-union Supreme Soviet, 99.94% of the 144 million eligible voters took part in the elections; of those who voted,

99.71% cast their votes for the single candidate in each district, with 346,000 casting negative votes against candidates running for the Soviet of Union, and 289,000 voting against candidates aspiring to the Soviet of Nationalities. The turnout was slightly better in 1970, with 99.96% of the 153,237,112 eligible voters casting ballots, of which 99.74% approved the candidates for the Soviet of Union and 396,343 voted against. In the balloting for the Soviet of Nationalities, 99.79% approved the official candidates and 320,633 negative votes were cast. The record is virtually identical in elections to the local soviets, except that the 277,000 negative votes out of a total of more than 146 million cast in March 1967 managed to reject 129 candidates (119 village, 5 settlement, 3 city, and 2 rayon) out of the 2,045,419 who were running; in 1969, 145 candidates for local soviets were turned down; and in 1971, 95 were rejected.[9]

Elections to the all-union Supreme Soviet take place every four years (even-numbered), as do those to the supreme soviets of union and autonomous republics (odd-numbered years), while elections at all other levels are conducted every two years (odd-numbered).

Since neither in theory nor in practice is it the purpose of Soviet elections to choose a government, what functions are performed by these elections and why are they held with so much fanfare and expense? Several very useful purposes can be served by even these manipulative and staged elections:

1. The elections provide a façade of legitimacy and legality for the Communist regime. Since the Soviet system claims to be the most "democratic" in the world, some external evidence of democratic "choice" must be demonstrated. And since the regime is controlled by an elite party that makes up but a small fraction of the total population, there is a compulsion to provide unanimity in elections to render emphatic the ratification of the party's policies and identify them with the will of the "masses."

9 *Pravda*, March 26, 1967, March 22, 1969, and June 20, 1971.

2. Soviet elections also impart to the population a feeling of participation and involvement in the political process, and they mobilize the energies and enthusiasms of the people and imbue them with a sense of Communist civic responsibility—i.e., the opportunity to vote for the candidates presented by the regime.

3. Soviet elections can also serve as useful barometers of dissatisfaction for the regime and act as warning devices. While to the uninitiated eye the dreary unanimity of the voting may be unenlightening, the smallest variation from one section of the country to another or from one election to the next in the total number of abstentions and negative votes can be very revealing to the regime.

4. Elections also provide ceremonial occasions for the leaders of the regime to make speeches and pronouncements, to establish contact with the general population, to disseminate and popularize the policies of the regime, and to provide a stage for the announcement of new policies and major shifts of personnel in the government.

5. Finally, Soviet elections perform a valuable external propaganda device by providing a spectacular occasion for disseminating propaganda abroad concerning the Soviet constitution and Soviet electoral procedures and democratic institutions. While these gestures may register little impact on countries that enjoy free and periodic elections, their effect on countries that do not have elections, or whose elections are narrowly restricted or corrupt, may be substantial.

THE SUPREME SOVIET OF THE USSR

According to article 30 of the Soviet constitution, "the highest organ of the state power in the USSR is the Supreme Soviet of the USSR," which means that all the constitutional powers in the Soviet system are vested in this body. Elected for a term of four years, the Supreme Soviet superficially resembles a bicameral legislative body of an ordinary federal state (Fig. 8-2). One chamber—the Soviet of the Union—is elected directly by the people, while the other—the Soviet of Nationalities—includes representatives from the federal units. The constitution specifies that "the legislative power of the USSR is exercised exclusively by the Supreme Soviet of the USSR."

The Supreme Soviet is an institution that formally symbolizes democracy and legality. It transforms the will of the party into laws enacted by the "representatives" of the masses. The Supreme Soviet is in reality the custodian, not of supreme power in Soviet society, but of supreme *state* power. Although it is the highest legal organ, the real source of Soviet power and legitimacy, as we have seen, is to be found within the Communist party. The Supreme Soviet, therefore, is an institution designed to lead the masses into thinking that they participate in government.

The Powers, Functions, and Composition of the Supreme Soviet

Some powers are entrusted exclusively to the Supreme Soviet. Only the Supreme Soviet can pass "laws" or statutes, called zakons; only the Supreme Soviet can "amend" the constitution (article 146); only the Supreme Soviet, in joint session, "elects" the Presidium of the Supreme Soviet, "appoints" the government of the USSR (the Council of Ministers), "elects" the Supreme Court of the USSR (article 105), and "appoints" the Procurator General of the USSR (article 114). It also possesses exclusive authority to enact legislation concerning union citizenship, rights of foreigners, and the determination of the "principles" governing marriage and the family, the judicial system, judicial procedures, and criminal and civil codes.

The constitution, however, is deliberately ambiguous on the precise demarcation of authority between the Supreme Soviet and its Presidium, since article 14 assigns powers not only to the Supreme Soviet, but also to the "higher organs of state power," which also include the Presidium. Thus, the Supreme Soviet

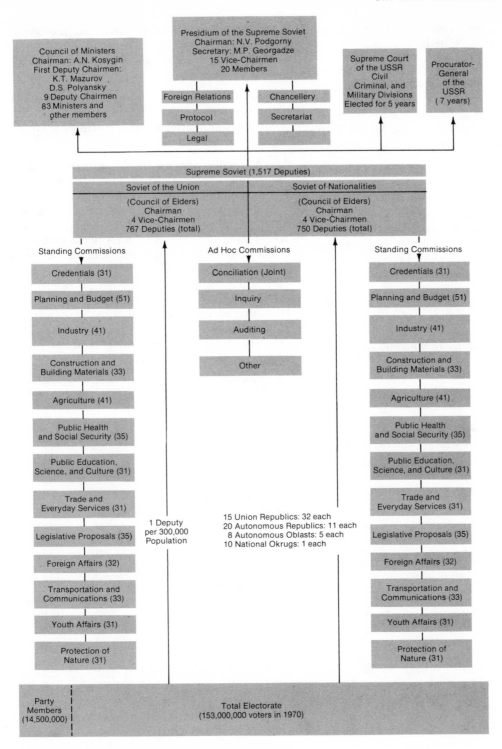

FIG. 8-2. *Constitutional structure of the Soviet state.*

must share authority with the Presidium in the following important spheres:

Foreign Affairs and National Security—representation of the USSR in international relations; conclusion, ratification, and renunciation of treaties; questions of war and peace; organization of national defense and security; direction of foreign trade on the basis of a state monopoly.

Constitutions—control over the observance of the constitution and insuring the conformity of the union republic constitutions with the all-union document; admission of new republics; confirmation of boundary changes between union republics and other administrative-territorial boundary alterations.

Economics—determination of the national economic plan; approval of the consolidated state budget; allocations of taxes and revenue between union and local budgets; determination of land tenure and use of natural resources; administration, organization, and/or direction of banks and other financial, credit, and mone-

tary institutions; administration of economic enterprises, transport, communications, state insurance, and the organization of a uniform system of national economic statistics.

Education and Welfare—determination of the "basic principles" of education and public health; determination of the principles of labor legislation.

Normally, sessions of the Supreme Soviet are not devoted to passing "laws" (zakons) but to confirming executive orders (ukazes) of the Presidium, and this it can do quickly. Thus, on a single day—April 26, 1954—the Supreme Soviet managed to ratify forty ukazes of the Presidium, most of which had altered the constitution. This was accomplished with neither debate nor extensive "discussion." Aside from those statutes which merely confirmed the decrees of the Presidium and introduced minor constitutional alterations of an administrative character, the Supreme Soviet between 1938 and 1956 enacted less than 25 zakons.[10]

[10] *Sbornik Zakonov S.S.S.R. i Ukazov Prezidiuma Verkbovnovo Soveta S.S.S.R., 1938–1956* (Moscow, 1956).

TABLE 8-2. *Social Composition of the Supreme Soviet of the USSR, 1958–70*

	SN	SU	1958 Total	Percentage	SN	SU	1962 Total	Percentage
Intelligentsia	419	504	923	67.0%	426	487	913	63.3%
Party apparatus	106	167	273	19.8	113	170	283	19.6
State apparatus	106	94	200	14.5	125	101	226	15.7
Managerial-Technical	112	135	247	17.9	82	104	186	12.9
Cultural-Scientific	72	77	149	10.8	82	80	162	11.2
Armed forces	23	31	54	3.9	24	32	56	3.9
Workers	134	153	287	20.8	144	205	349	24.2
Collective farmers	81	74	155	11.2	82	93	175	12.1
Others	6	7	13	0.9	0	6	6	0.4
Totals	640	738	1,378	100.0%	652	791	1,443	100.0%
Women				26.6%	175	215	390	27.0%
Party membership	488	599	1,047	76.0	490	604	1,094	75.8
Elected for 1st time	—	—	—	—	473	534	1,007	69.8
Higher Ed. (complete & incomplete)	—	—	—	48.7	340	421	761	52.7
Secondary Ed. (G & S)	—	—	—	11.8	110	129	239	16.6
Over 40 years of age	—	—	—	70.5	358	471	829	57.4

The Supreme Soviet, although an impotent body, represents primarily the privileged elites of Soviet society and largely duplicates the social membership and even the personnel of the hierarchies in the party, state, economic, and military establishments. For this reason, it should not be surprising that the policies of the party are adopted by the Supreme Soviet with neither questions nor criticisms. Over 79% (1,200) of the deputies were elected to the Twenty-third Party Congress in 1966 and nearly 85% (1,284) were elected delegates to the Twenty-fourth Party Congress in 1971.

The social configuration of the Supreme Soviet (Table 8-2) during the post-Stalin period betrays a remarkable uniformity from one soviet to the other. Although the proportion of the intelligentsia has been steadily diminishing, the distribution of the elites within the intelligentsia has been relatively constant, with the managerial-technical group showing the greatest decrease in representation in favor of more "workers." Males consistently account for slightly less than 75% of the membership, and party membership seems to hold at slightly above that proportion. The turnover in membership is unusually high, with about two-thirds of each Supreme Soviet being made up of new deputies. The continuity is represented at the core by the leadership of the regime, which is carried over from one session to the next. Well over half the membership of each Supreme Soviet is consistently over 40 years old, while the proportion of deputies with some higher education now consistently holds to more than 50%. In the organization of the Supreme Soviet, virtually every formal officer of the body, including the chairmen of nineteen of the twenty-six standing commissions, is a member of the party's Central Committee, and most of the "debate" and "discussion" is thus carried on by deputies who are also members of the Central Committee. Thus, the Supreme Soviet in some respects represents a selected audience of citizens before which the decisions of the Central Committee are trans-

	SN	SU	1966 Total	Percentage	SN	SU	1970 Total	Percentage
Intelligentsia	453	460	913	60.2%	403	432	839	55.5%
Party apparatus	129	160	289	19.1	109	152	261 *	17.2
State apparatus	131	98	229	15.1	115	102	217	14.3
Managerial-Technical	83	104	187	12.3	63	91	154 †	10.1
Cultural-Scientific	84	68	152	10.0	89	57	146	9.6
Armed forces	26	30	56	3.7	27	30	57	3.8
Workers	181	225	406	26.8	228	253	481	31.7
Collective farmers	105	72	177	11.7	119	82	201	13.3
Others	11	10	21	1.4	—	—	—	—
Totals	750	767	1,517	100.0%	750	767	1,517	100.0%
Women	203	222	425	28.0%	231	230	463	30.5%
Party membership	568	573	1,141	75.2	534	562	1,096	72.3
Elected for 1st time	533	482	1,015	66.9	442	404	846	55.8
Higher Ed. (complete & incomplete)	406	402	808	53.3	372	408	800	51.4
Secondary Ed. (G & S)	134	141	275	18.1	224	224	448	29.5
Over 40 years of age	425	476	901	59.4	413	474	882	58.5

SOURCES: For 1962 figures—*Pravda,* April 25, 1962; for 1966 figures—*Pravda,* August 4, 1966; for 1970 figures—*Verkhovny Sovet SSSR, Vosmovo Sozyva* (Statisticheskii Sbornik) Moscow, 1970.

NOTE: SN = Soviet of Nationalities; SU = Soviet of the Union.

* Includes twenty trade union and Komsomol officials.

† Includes eighty-one kolkhoz chairmen.

muted into legal acts of state, and before which some of the differences in the Central Committee are given a public (though esoteric) airing.

Since about one-fifth of the Supreme Soviet is made up of Central Committee members, there are bound to be some interesting similarities in the social composition of the Central Committee and the country's highest legislative organ. But the differences are even more remarkable. Like the Central Committee, the Supreme Soviet is predominantly male, but whereas the Central Committee is nearly a male monopoly (95%), the usual practice is to elect one-fourth of the deputies in the Supreme Soviet from the fairer sex. The age structure of the Central Committee is older than that of the Supreme Soviet, with 70% of its membership in 1966 being over 50 years old. The turnover rate in the Central Committee betrays wide variation and fluctuates in accordance with factional fortunes (in 1966, it was only 15% for full members and somewhat higher for candidates), whereas the Supreme Soviet registers an even turnover rate of about two-thirds each time. Only 2.8% of the Central Committee is made up of "workers and peasants" whereas in the Supreme Soviet they now make up over 40%. This suggests once again that the proportion of women and workers and peasants in any Soviet institution, organization, or association is a fairly reliable guide to its real power, influence, and status in the Soviet system.

The Supreme Soviet "at Work"

The Supreme Soviet is composed of two chambers, constitutionally of equal power: the Soviet of the Union and the Soviet of Nationalities. By custom, however, the Soviet of the Union carries the higher prestige and ranks in protocol over the Soviet of Nationalities. The Soviet of the Union is composed of deputies elected from single-member districts, in the ratio of one deputy per 300,000 population. As a general rule, the Soviet of the Union includes among its deputies a larger proportion of high party and state officials than does the Soviet of Nationalities.

The Soviet of Nationalities is elected on the basis of nationality units; identical national

units have equal representation, irrespective of geographical or demographic size. Each union republic since 1966 is entitled to thirty-two deputies; each autonomous republic is assigned eleven deputies, while autonomous oblasts are allotted five deputies each, and national okrugs one apiece. The Soviet of Nationalities is thus both federal and multinational. The Supreme Soviet is one of the largest elected legislative bodies in the world; in 1970, it consisted of 1,517 deputies, of which 767 were members of the Soviet of the Union and 750 members of the Soviet of Nationalities, whereas in the 1962 Supreme Soviet of 1,443 deputies, 791 were in the Soviet of Union and only 652 in the Soviet of Nationalities. The numerical size of the two chambers was equalized by adding seven new deputies to the delegations from each of the fifteen union republics.

Each chamber has a Council of Elders (*Sovet Stareishin*), which is an informal and quasi-secret body made up of senior deputies that makes the preliminary arrangements for the organization and procedure of each chamber, prepares the agenda for the opening session, and seems always to be consulted in moments of crisis. Constitutionally, each chamber is provided with a chairman and four vice-chairmen, who constitute the presidium of each house (not to be confused with either the former Presidium of the party *or* of the Supreme Soviet) and preside over its meetings. While the chambers may sit jointly or separately, sessions of both chambers begin and terminate simultaneously and virtually all sessions are held jointly.[11]

[11] Even the agendas of the two chambers are identical. Thus, at the opening session of the Supreme Soviet elected in March 1962, a spokesman for each chamber, "speaking on behalf of the Council of Elders," introduced the following agenda for each house (from *Pravda,* April 24, 1962): "(1) election of the Credentials Committee; (2) selection of standing committees; (3) ratification of decrees of the Presidium of the USSR Supreme Soviet; (4) selection of the Presidium of the USSR Supreme Soviet; (5) report on negotiations in Geneva; (6) formation of the USSR government and the USSR Council of Ministers; (7) selection of the USSR Supreme Court; and (8) working out of the draft of the new USSR constitution." Identical Agendas for both chambers were adopted at the opening sessions of the Supreme Soviets selected in 1966 and 1970.

According to the constitution, the Supreme Soviet is convoked into regular session by its Presidium and can be convened into special session at the direction of the Presidium or upon the demand of one of the union republics. In actual practice, until 1955 the Supreme Soviet was normally convened only once a year, and the character and duration of its sessions were extraordinary by any standard. Between 1946 and 1954, this "highest organ of state power" sat for a total of forty-five days, with the longest session lasting seven days and the shortest exactly 67 minutes (to confirm the changes made after Stalin's death). Since 1955, a determined effort has been made to use this body more often, and although its sessions still last for only four to seven days, they have taken place at the regular intervals required by the constitution.

The Supreme Soviet is not a deliberative body; the deliberations take place elsewhere. Nor is it a debating assembly; debates, too, are held elsewhere, if at all. Neither does it formulate policy. It functions essentially as a listening assembly, and most of its "working" time is preoccupied with hearing reports from government ministers. It listens attentively and with conditioned enthusiasm; if requested, it enacts legislation with rare dispatch, whether the subject be fundamental or trivial. "Debate" is ritualized; proposals and comments from the floor are prearranged with consummate precision. Panegyrics are delivered by a dozen or more carefully selected deputies; the appropriate personalities and actions of the past are roundly condemned, while the wisdom and correctness of the government is widely praised. During the entire existence of the Supreme Soviet, there has never been a single negative vote (or abstention) cast in either chamber, and no disagreement between the two bodies has ever occurred.

Since 1955, when Malenkov announced his resignation before the Supreme Soviet, calculated efforts have been made to enhance its prestige and to give it a more conspicuous role in the policy process. Meetings of the Supreme Soviet have been more frequent, and it is employed more often as a sounding board for policies which require dramatization and public dissemination.

The possibility, no matter how remote it may appear at the moment, that ritual and ceremony may some day be replaced with substance should not be ignored. Lifeless legal bodies playing a ritualistic role sometimes come to life under certain conditions and circumstances. Increasingly, Soviet scholars and even party officials (largely from the non-Russian republics) are suggesting that the Supreme Soviet be allowed to behave more like an authentic legislative body. The chairman of the Presidium of the Armenian Republic even had the audacity to suggest that more than one candidate (nominated, however, through the single Communist party) be offered in some districts to give Soviet citizens a personal choice between two equally deserving candidates.

In some areas of legislative concern, such as education, economic reorganization, health and welfare, judicial procedures, and criminal codes, discussion in the Supreme Soviet has been lively—even gingerly contentious—and has approximated genuine legislative debate. It is too early to make reliable predictions concerning possible changes in the powers and function of the Supreme Soviet, but one important clue will be the role it is assigned in any new constitution which may be forthcoming.

"Strengthening the Supreme Soviet": The Party Apparatus and the Supreme Soviet

In recent years, beginning with the Twenty-third Party Congress in 1966, members of the Secretariat and other high party officials, from Brezhnev on down, have shown remarkable solicitude and zeal in calling for the "strengthening" of the Supreme Soviet and an expansion of its duties, powers, and responsibilities. Initially, this appeared to be a part of the routine rhetorical obeisance paid to the "highest organ of state power." It now appears evident, however, that this campaign has been accompanied by an increased flurry of activity on the part of the Secretariat and party apparatus within the Supreme Soviet, of which many are deputies. And if the Supreme Soviet is to be converted into an authentic legislative body, what could be more natural than the party apparatus assuming the leadership of the legislative branch of the state as it seeks to preserve and strengthen its control and audit functions over the increasingly recalcitrant Council of Ministers and state bureaucracy?

The party apparatus, whose authority and legitimacy have no standing under law, is chronically in danger of having its ideological and political lines of control and audit going to the Council of Ministers short-circuited by the constitutional and judicial lines of responsibility and accountability coming from the Council of Ministers to the Supreme Soviet and its Presidium. Under conditions of factional conflict, the organs of executive and administrative power might at some point defy the party apparatus and insist on a higher accountability to the Supreme Soviet as a strategy designed to jettison onerous party apparatus controls and interferences.[12] To circumvent this possibility, the party apparatus appears to have divised a novel strategy of its own: to take over the Supreme Soviet and flesh out its constitutional authority with the power of the apparatus and thus convert it into an institutional, constitutional power base of its own. In this way, not only would the apparatus find a social function sanctioned by law, constitution, and legality, but it would retain custody of the credentials of legitimacy and, more importantly, would transform a furtive party-state squabble into a respectable and decent struggle between executive and legislative authority and power. And thus, if the Council of Ministers should attempt to short-circuit the party apparatus by appealing to the higher authority of the Supreme Soviet, the party apparatus could be ready to accommodate them.

Recent legislation regulating the composition of the Council of Ministers, the Presidium, and the standing commissions of the Supreme Soviet, as well as certain aspects of behavior on the part of Brezhnev and other high party officials, give credence to these developments.

As noted earlier, in the past general secretaries have always felt it necessary to buttress their purely ideological authority with constitutional sanction, and the route has always been for them to assume the posts of general secretary and premier simultaneously. In all past cases, however, once this happens, the former general secretary becomes essentially a personal symbol of the state and tends to allow the party apparatus to atrophy. What the party apparatus needs, therefore, is a more durable institutional affirmation of its legitimacy, one which can survive the passage of personalities.

In 1966, a significant step was taken in this direction with the expansion of the Supreme Soviet's infrastructure of subinstitutions and of the power of the party apparatus within it. The Supreme Soviet's nine feeble permanent standing commissions (four in the Soviet of the Union and five in the Soviet of Nationalities) were expanded to ten for each chamber, for a total of twenty. In the following year, the commissions were further reorganized and expanded to thirteen for each chamber, with a total of 912 members (see Fig. 8-2). Even more significantly, the Supreme Soviet adopted a statute (*zakon*) governing the composition, powers, responsibilities, and status of the commissions. According to this law, adopted on October 12, 1967, the standing commissions of the Supreme Soviet were converted from bodies whose legal existence was based upon the internal acts of the Supreme Soviet and each of its chambers into organs "having the force of law." According to the report of M. S. Solomentsev, chairman of the Legislative Proposals Commission of the Soviet of the Union, this law serves not only to establish "the rights and obligations of the chambers' commissions, but [is] also a law regulating the interrelations of the standing commissions and other state bodies."[13]

Under the new law, several relationships which had hitherto been governed by custom were now defined legally. Thus, article 5 of the law stipulates that

the following people cannot be elected to standing commissions: the chairmen of the chambers; their

---

[12] Thus, Khrushchev, when confronted with a demand to resign, may have countered that, since he was accountable only to the Supreme Soviet as premier, that body should be convened, but constitutional niceties were swept away as his colleagues refused to provide him with a forum to override their decision.

[13] Quoted in *Izvestia*, October 13, 1967.

vice-chairmen; deputies who are members of the Presidium of the Supreme Soviet, the U.S.S.R. Council of Ministers, the U.S.S.R. Supreme Court; and the U.S.S.R. procurator general.

What does this mean? It means that virtually the only deputies who can be appointed to these commissions are ordinary citizen deputies (who provide all the votes), local government officials, and *full-time party functionaries.* The new law, in effect, clears the way for the party apparatus to take over the Supreme Soviet by seizing the commanding heights of the standing commissions—namely, their chairmanships and vice-chairmanships—and in this way continue to assert their supervisory and auditing functions over the Council of Ministers in their institutional capacity as the cadre of the Supreme Soviet.

When the law on the commissions is examined, it is remarkable how closely the powers and duties of the party apparatus are duplicated and paralleled by those of the commissions, which article 2 defines as follows:

1. the "elaboration of [legislative] proposals for examination by the appropriate chamber or by the Presidium of the U.S.S.R. Supreme Soviet"—i.e., the initiation and drafting of legislation;

2. the "preparation of conclusions on questions submitted for examination by the U.S.S.R. Supreme Soviet and its Presidium";

3. the provision of "assistance to state bodies and organizations . . . in their work of implementing the decisions of the U.S.S.R. Supreme Soviet and its Presidium"; and

4. the exercise of *"control over the activity of U.S.S.R. Ministers and departments,* all other All-Union organizations and republic and local bodies and organizations in executing the U.S.S.R. Constitution, the laws of the U.S.S.R. and other decisions of the U.S.S.R. Supreme Soviet and its Presidium." (italics supplied)

Furthermore, article 2 specifies that the "standing commissions . . . are called upon to promote, in all their activities during U.S.S.R.

Supreme Soviet sessions and in the period between sessions, uninterrupted and effective work by the Supreme Soviet as the highest representative body of state authority in the U.S.S.R." Article 6 then provides for the continuous functioning of the commissions in periods when the Supreme Soviet is not in session (which is most of the time) by stating that its work during this period will be coordinated by the Presidium of the Supreme Soviet.

The law on the commissions thus creates an entirely new line of supervisory control over the Council of Ministers, which is already legally accountable to the Supreme Soviet and its Presidium and ideologically accountable to the Secretariat of the Central Committee. Increasingly, however, the Presidium of the Supreme Soviet, the party apparatus, and the commissions of the Supreme Soviet converge not only in terms of authority over the Council of Ministers but in composition as well.

The Presidium of the Supreme Soviet elected in 1970, for example, numbers among its ordinary members seven members of the Politburo, including General Secretary Brezhnev. Since membership in the Presidium is incompatible with membership in the Council of Ministers, the only Politburo members eligible for membership in the Presidium are party functionaries. Thus, Grishin, Kunayev, Shelest, Rashidov, and Masherov are all republic or powerful local first secretaries. This group undoubtedly constitutes the decisive core of the Presidium.

When we look at the other end of the Supreme Soviet, at the commissions, we find a similar situation with respect to chairmanships and vice-chairmanships of important commissions. Thus, the long-time chairman of the Foreign Affairs Commission of the Soviet of the Union is Suslov, a Secretariat and Politburo member, while another Secretariat member, Katushev, is vice-chairman. In the counterpart commission of the Council of Nationalities, the chairman is Secretariat member Ponomarev, while the vice-chairman is the first secretary of the Lithuanian party, Shniechkus. The chairman of the Legislative Proposals Commission in the Council of the Union is another Secretariat member, Solomentsev, while his vice-chairman is Kospanov, a full member of the Central Committee. In the parallel commission in the other chamber the chairman is Kebin, first secretary of the Estonian party, while his vice-chairman is also a full member of the Central Committee. Altogether, nineteen of the twenty-six standing-commission chairmen are full members or candidate members of the Central Committee. And the expansion of the standing commissions increasingly makes them parallel the departments of the party's Central Committee apparatus itself.

The demand that the Supreme Soviet's responsibilities and powers be further strengthened was renewed with even greater force at the Twenty-fourth Party Congress in 1971 by Brezhnev:

Let me remind you that the necessity of enhancing the role of the Soviets was emphasized in the decisions of the 23rd CPSU Congress. In the past few years a good deal has been done in this direction. . . . The USSR Supreme Soviet and the Union-Republic Supreme Soviets have intensified their control over the work of ministries and departments and over the state of affairs in the basic sector of economic and cultural construction. The increased number of standing committees and the more systematic organization of their activity enable the deputies to display more initiative, to delve more deeply into the work of executive agencies, and to take a more active part in the preparation of draft laws.[14]

Since the 1967 law on the standing commissions of the Supreme Soviet not only expands their powers and strengthens their constitutional status, but also gives the party apparatus a de facto monopoly over their composition, strengthening the powers, duties, and responsibilities of the Supreme Soviet and its standing commissions essentially strengthened the power and status of the party apparatus over the executive and administrative organs of the state. The party apparatus, in this way, acquires constitutional sanction and validity as it desperately

seeks to find a new function and to reassert its dominance in the political system. What could be more logical than taking over the "highest organ of state power" in the Soviet Union?

THE PRESIDIUM OF THE SUPREME SOVIET

The Presidium of the Supreme Soviet is defined in the constitution as one of the "higher organs of state power" and is vested with a wide and impressive range of both ceremonial and substantive powers, combining executive, legislative, diplomatic, military, and judicial functions. It functions as the collegial or plural chief of state of the Soviet Union, whose closest counterpart in the West is the Swiss Federal Council; otherwise, it is distinctively Soviet in character and is an expression of the party principle of collective leadership and responsibility. The chairman of the Presidium acts as the ceremonial head of the Soviet Union.

The Presidium is elected by the Supreme Soviet in joint session at the first meeting after new elections, and its tenure is identical with that of the Supreme Soviet which elected it. It is now composed of thirty-seven members: a chairman, fifteen vice-chairmen, a secretary, and twenty additional members. Since December 1958, each republic is entitled to a vice-chairman. Before 1958, the allocation of a vice-chairman to each republic was customarily accomplished by electing the chairman of a republic Presidium as vice-chairman of the all-union Presidium, and this is still governed by custom. An examination of the composition of the Presidium since its establishment in 1938 reveals that among the ordinary members are to be found high-ranking military officials, representatives of autonomous republics, high party officials of republic organizations, and from four to six full or candidate members of the party Politburo.[15] As a rule, the general

---

[14] *Pravda,* March 30, 1971. For authoritative Soviet commentary on these themes, see L. T. Krivenko, "The Standing Committees and the Ministries," *Sovetskoye Gosudarstvo i Pravo,* January (No. 1), 1970; G. A. Kuzmicheva, "Interpolation By Deputies," *Ibid.,* March (No. 3), 1970; and P. F. Pigalev, "Improving the Functioning of the Soviets of Working People's Deputies," *Ibid.,* April (No. 4), 1970.

[15] According to *Izvestia,* June 16, 1970, the composition of the Presidium aside from its chairman, Podgorny, consisted of six ordinary members who were full or candidate members of the party Politburo; Brezhnev was the only member with simultaneous membership in the party Politburo and Secretariat. Of the remaining members, sixteen were also full or candidate members of the Central Committee.

secretary of the party is elected as an ordinary member of the Presidium when he does not occupy an executive or administrative position in the government. Thus, both Stalin and Khrushchev were ordinary members of the Presidium during the period when they held no other government office—as is the case with Brezhnev since Khrushchev's ouster. This practice invests the party leaders with a high official status which can be held in reserve and employed when demanded by protocol.

The chairman of the Presidium is its most conspicuous member, but not necessarily the most powerful one. Only six individuals have occupied this position. The first was the veteran Bolshevik and long-time Politburo member, Mikhail Kalinin, who served as the ceremonial chief of state from 1919 until his death in 1946. His successor, Nikolai Shvernik, was a relatively low-ranking member of the party hierarchy (a candidate member of the Politburo) and was picked by Stalin, no doubt, because of his apparent passion for anonymity. He was replaced after Stalin's death by Marshal Voroshilov, a popular military-political leader. Marshal Voroshilov announced his retirement in 1960, but apparently he was forced out because of his complicity in the plot to unseat Khrushchev in June 1957. His successor was the present general secretary, Leonid Breshnev, then a veteran party functionary and loyal Khruschev supporter who, like Voroshilov and Kalinin, was a full member of the party's highest body at the time of his appointment. Brezhnev yielded to Anastas Mikoyan in 1964, who retired in favor of N. V. Podgorny in 1965.[16]

The chairman of the Presidium is frequently, but incorrectly, referred to as the "President of the Soviet Union." Under the constitution, his powers are no greater than those of other members. Normally, the chairman performs all the symbolic and ceremonial acts in the name of the Presidium, and enjoys the prestige and prerogatives normally enjoyed by a titular chief of state. He presides over sessions of the Supreme Soviet, signs the decrees

and other acts issued by the Presidium, and formally promulgates laws of the Supreme Soviet with his signature. He dispatches ambassadors and ministers, receives the credentials of foreign emissaries, and issues acts of pardon and amnesty.

The powers of the Presidium under article 49 of the constitution are very broad, but they are even broader in actual practice. As a "higher organ of state power," the Presidium is, in effect, a working legislature and to all intents and purposes exercises the entire spectrum of state power during intervals between sessions of the Supreme Soviet. It is, in the words of one Soviet authority, "the *highest permanently functioning organ of state power of the Soviet Union.*" [17] It issues decrees (ukazes) which have the force of law throughout the union, although in theory these decrees must be based on laws enacted by the Supreme Soviet.

Just as it shares legislative authority with the Supreme Soviet, its executive powers overlap those of the Council of Ministers. In its executive capacity, the Presidium convenes and dissolves the Supreme Soviet, annuls decisions and orders of the councils of ministers of the USSR and of the union republics (if they do not conform to law), institutes and awards decorations and titles of honor, and, during intervals between sessions of its parent body, releases and appoints ministers of the USSR on the recommendation of the Council of Ministers, subject always to subsequent confirmation by the Supreme Soviet.

The Presidium's diplomatic and military powers are very extensive. It can order general or partial mobilization; proclaim martial law in separate localities or throughout the union; create military titles, diplomatic ranks, and other special titles; appoint and remove the high command of the armed forces; and, in between sessions of the Supreme Soviet, is empowered to declare a state of war in the event of military attack or to fulfill treaty obligations.

The role and function of the Presidium in practice and its relationship to the Supreme Soviet are precisely the reverse of theory. Since both the Supreme Soviet and its Presidium are

---

[16] Mikoyan now sits as an ordinary member of the Presidium. Before the recent deaths of Shvernik and Voroshilov, who also served as ordinary members, Podgorny presided over a Presidium containing no less than four ex-chairmen.

[17] V. Karpinsky, *The Social and State Structure of the U.S.S.R.* (Moscow, 1951), p. 122.

creatures of the party, the relationship between the two bodies depends on the requirements and conveniences of the party. As is the case with the Supreme Soviet, the Presidium is the captive of the party. It is the chief legalizing instrument of the party, since its membership overlaps that of the party Politburo and Secretariat.

Party policies and decisions can be almost instantaneously promulgated as decrees of the Presidium. Thus, Khrushchev's ouster was promptly legalized on October 15, 1964, when his alleged request to be relieved of his duties was accepted by the Presidium of the Supreme Soviet one day after his reputed indictment by the Central Committee plenum. In the complex maneuvering which preceded Khrushchev's fall, Brezhnev gave up the chairmanship of the Presidium of the Supreme Soviet in July 1964 in order to devote full time to work in the Secretariat, and was succeeded by Mikoyan. After Khrushchev's displacement in October 1964, the influence and power of Podgorny experienced a rise, and it became necessary to award him a post commensurate with his new political eminence. This position is rapidly emerging as the third most prestigious post in the country (after general secretary and premier).

THE COUNCIL OF MINISTERS

The Council of Ministers is described by the constitution (article 64) as "the highest executive and administrative organ of state power" in the USSR. The Council of Ministers, also called the "government," is invested with the principal responsibility for the execution and administration of policy, as distinct from its formulation, which is, of course, the province of the party summit. The Council of Ministers is nominally accountable to the Supreme Soviet and its Presidium, but in fact is more nearly an administrative arm of the party Politburo with which its membership overlaps. The head of the Council of Ministers is formally called Chairman of the Council of Ministers, but also called "Premier" informally.

The lines of accountability, responsibility, control, and audit to which the Council of Ministers is now subject is becoming exceedingly complex and bewildering, even for Soviet ministers and administrators. As a body which juridically resembles a cabinet in a Western parliamentary system, the council is constitutionally subordinate to the Supreme Soviet, which formally "appoints" it in joint session (article 56). It is also constitutionally "responsible and accountable" to the Presidium of the Supreme Soviet when the latter is not in session, which, of course, means about 350 days out of the year. At the same time, the council is politically and ideologically responsible and accountable to the Politburo—superficially in the manner that a Western premier is responsible politically to his party or his party's executive board, except that there is only one party in the Soviet system. This, more or less, exhausts the lines of "responsibility and accountability."

At the same time, the Council of Ministers is subject to lines of "control and audit," which while distinguishable from "responsibility and accountability" in the abstract are much more difficult to delineate in actuality. The Politburo is responsible for formulating policy; the Council of Ministers is charged with its administration and execution; while the Secretariat checks and monitors its faithful, efficient and prompt fulfillment. The main "control and audit" institutions have been the party Secretariat, whose jurisdiction is political rather than legal, and the party Control Committee, whose precise functions are obscure. Under the 1967 law on the standing commissions of the Supreme Soviet, the standing commissions also now enjoy "control" functions over the Council of Ministers which have the force of law. As noted earlier, since the standing commissions are largely dominated by representatives of the party apparatus, party and legislative control jurisdictions tend to merge at this point. And because the Central Committee is the parent body to both the Politburo and the Secretariat, the Council of Ministers is politically and ideologically accountable to it as well.

This, of course, often results in contradictory directives, crossed lines, confusion, maladministration, and inefficiency, but it also serves to keep the administrators on their toes. In actuality, the relationship between the Politburo and the Council of Ministers in the decision-making process depends more on the degree of common memberships in the two organs than on constitutional norms (see Table 8-3). The same is true for ordinary ministers as well.

In the 1970 Council of Ministers, Kosygin and his two first deputy premiers, Mazurov and Polyansky, were full members of the Politburo, while Voronov and Shcherbitsky, ex officio members of the Council of Ministers (as premiers of the Russian SFSR and the Ukraine), were also Politburo members. The only other Politburo member on the Council of Ministers was Andropov (candidate member), who has been chairman of the Committee on State Security since 1967. Kosygin's nine deputy chairmen and nearly thirty of his ministers and ex officio colleagues on the Council of Ministers are now full members of the Central Committee. Another 35–40 ministers and ex officio members of the council are candidate members of the Central Committee, while a handful serve on the Central Auditing Commission. Thus, virtually all of the Council of Ministers of 95–97 members were elected as full or candidate members of the Central Committee.

Under Stalin, particularly after he became chairman of the Council of Ministers in 1941, interlocking membership between the council and the party's Central Committee was virtually complete and was designed to ensure maximum harmony and coordination between party policy and state administration. Distinctions between formulation and execution of policy were blurred and rendered irrelevant, since the Politburo of the party and the Presidium of the Council of Ministers had almost identical memberships. Stalin, by a simple motion, could transform the same group of individuals from one body to another, since he was the head of both.

Between 1924 and 1941, Stalin chose to rule from his post in the Secretariat of the party, and was thus completely separated from the formal organs of the state and the administration. Shortly before Germany attacked the Soviet Union in 1941, Stalin, sensing imminent crisis, suddenly assumed chairmanship of the Council of Ministers (called Council of People's Commissars until 1946), relegating Molotov—chairman since 1930—to full-time duty as commissar of foreign affairs. Once a secondary institution, the chairmanship was immediately invested with an authority that it had possessed only under Lenin. But Stalin also retained his post as general secretary. Thus, as head of both party and government, he made policy in one capacity and executed it in the other!

The separation of the general secretaryship from the premiership after Stalin's death once again drove a wedge between the organs of the state and the party. But Khrushchev's assumption of the chairmanship of the Council of Ministers in March 1958, while still retaining his post of first secretary, signified that the functions of policy formulation and administration could once again be united in a single person. The conflict between the organs of policy formulation (the party) and state administration (the government) was reduced to a minimum, with Khrushchev standing at the apex of both structures; but with his abrupt removal, the two positions were sundered and the stage set for a possible resumption of rivalry and conflict.

One should not rule out the possibility that Brezhnev covets the post of premier and would like to combine it with his party post. As general secretary, Brezhnev enjoys formal and ceremonial priority only at home and in the world of Communist states and parties. Under international law, he possesses no status, in spite of his immense power and prestige at home. Brezhnev's call for more party audit and control over administrative bodies and officials, as well as his reputed insistence at being present at meetings of the Council of Ministers and even addressing them, suggests that he has more than a passing interest in assuming direct responsibility for administration and government; furthermore, being the premier of a great power catapults one into the limelight of international celebration and publicity, as Khrushchev quickly discovered when he became premier in 1958.

Executive authority in the Soviet government is formally distributed between the Presidium and the Council of Ministers, with the former exercising appointive, ceremonial, and

TABLE 8-3. *Interlocking of Government and Party Institutions and Personnel in the Soviet Union, 1971*

First Secretaries of Republics	Members of the Secretariat	Members of the Politburo	Presidium of the Council of Ministers
	Brezhnev *(Gen'l Sec'y)*	Brezhnev	
		Kosygin	Kosygin *(Chairman)*
	Suslov	Suslov	
		Podgorny	
	Kirilenko	Kirilenko	
		Polyansky	Polyansky *(First Deputy)*
		Voronov	Voronov (ex officio) *
		Shelepin	
Shelest *(Ukraine)*		Shelest	
Pelshe *(Latvia)*		Pelshe	
		Mazurov	Mazurov *(First Deputy)*
		Grishin	
Kunayev *(Kazakh)*		Kunayev	
		Shcherbitsky	Shcherbitsky (ex officio)
	Kulakov	Kulakov	
Mzhavanadze *(Georgia)*		Mzhavanadze	
Rashidov *(Uzbek)*		Rashidov	
	Demichev	Demichev	
	Ustinov	Ustinov	
Masherov *(Byelorussia)*		Masherov	
		Andropov	
	Ponomarev		
	Solomentsev *		
	Kapitonov		
	Rudakov		
	Katushev		

* Solomentsev replaced Voronov as RSFSR Premier in November 1971 and was appointed a candidate member of the Politburo.

titular functions and the latter being charged with the actual execution of the law. Administrative power, however, is vested exclusively in the council, and although it is formally accountable and responsible to the Supreme Soviet and/or its Presidium, the council is in reality independent of both organs in the exercise of its authority. Only lip service is paid to the fiction of accountability to the Supreme Soviet.

Under article 68 of the constitution, the Council of Ministers is empowered to coordinate the work of ministries and other organs of administration under its jurisdiction; direct the work of economic organizations through central and union republic institutions; execute economic plans; administer the budget, credit, and monetary system; adopt measures for the maintenance of public order, state security, and the rights of citizens; exercise general guidance

Presidium of the Supreme Soviet	Premiers of Republics	Chairmen of Supreme Soviet Commissions	Other Positions
Brezhnev			
		Suslov	
Podgorny *(Chairman)*			
	Voronov *(RSFSR)*		
Shelest			Shelepin *(Trade Union Chairman)* Pelshe *(Party Control Commission)*
			Grishin *(Moscow Party Secretary)*
Grishin Kunayev			
	Shcherbitsky *(Ukraine)*		
Rashidov			
Masherov			Andropov *(State Security)*
		Ponomarev Solomentsev*	

in foreign relations; and fix the annual contingents to be conscripted into the armed forces and direct the general organization of the military forces. It is also empowered to establish special committees and central administrative organs under its jurisdiction for economic, cultural, and defense matters.

The functions and powers of the Council of Ministers so modestly outlined in the constitution are, in fact, only a small part of what the council actually does. The magnitude of its responsibilities is like that which the president of the United States and his cabinet would have if they had responsibility not only for federal administration but for the duties now per-

formed by the states and also by private businesses and trade unions.

The Council of Ministers is thus the most important organ of the Soviet state and is the chief administrative instrument of the party summit. Under the constitution, it is empowered to issue decrees and orders in carrying out its functions, but these must be in conformity with laws in operation. It is charged with checking the execution of its own acts, but both the Supreme Soviet and the Presidium are authorized to annul decrees and orders of the council if they are in conflict with existing law, or for any reason whatsoever, although no decree or order of the council has ever been overruled in the entire history of the Soviet system. The decrees and orders of the council, which are binding throughout the union, constitute the overwhelming bulk of legislation in the Soviet Union. Although the Council of Ministers, constitutionally, is not a legislative body, it is the chief source of law in the Soviet state.

The composition, but not the operational structure, of the Council of Ministers is established by the constitution, and these provisions of the constitution have been subject to more emendations, perhaps, than any other. The council is directed by a smaller decision-making body called the Presidium of the Council of Ministers (not to be confused with either the Presidium of the Supreme Soviet or the former Presidium of the party) and consists of the chairman and his deputies, which, as of 1971, included *two* first deputy chairmen and nine deputies of lesser party rank. The 98-member Council of Ministers appointed in July 1970 was made up of the following categories: [18]

1. *Presidium:* One chairman, two first deputy chairmen; nine deputy chairmen.

2. *Fifty-six Ministries:*

   25 ALL-UNION MINISTRIES: Aviation Industry; Automobile Industry; Foreign Trade; Gas Industry; Civil Aviation; Machine Building for Light Industry, Food Industry, and Household Appliances; Medical Industry; Merchant Marine; Defense Industry; General Machine Building; Instrument-Making and Means of Automation and Control Systems; Transportation; Radio Industry; Medium Machine-Building; Machine Tool and Tool Industry; Machine Building for Construction, Road Building, and Civil Engineering; Shipbuilding Industry; Tractor and Farm-Machine Building; Transport Construction; Heavy Power and Transport Machine-Building; Pulp and Paper Industry; Chemical and Petroleum Machine-Building; Electronics Industry; Electrical Equipment Industry

   31 UNION REPUBLIC MINISTRIES: Geology; Public Health; Higher and Specialized Secondary Education; Foreign Affairs; Culture; Light Industry; Lumber and Wood-Processing Industry; Land Reclamation and Water Resources; Installation and Specialized Construction Work; Meat and Dairy Industry; Petroleum Extracting Industry; Oil Refining and Petrochemical Industry; Defense; Internal Affairs; Food Industry; Industrial Construction; Building Materials Industry; Public Education; Fishing Industry; Communications; Rural Construction; Agriculture; Construction; Heavy-Industry Construction; Trade; Coal Industry; Finance; Chemical Industry; Nonferrous Metallurgy; Ferrous Metallurgy; Power and Electrification

3. *Eleven State Committees:* Foreign Economic Relations; Prices; State Security; State Planning; Material and Technical Supply; Science and Technology; Construction Affairs; Labor and Wages; Vocational and Technical Education; Procurements; Forestry

4. *Four Specialized Agencies:* Central Statistical Administration; State Bank; All-Union Farm Machinery, Fuel, and Fertilizers; People's Control Committee

5. *Ex officio:* The fifteen republic premiers.

The enormous size of the Council of Ministers has been accompanied by a corresponding decrease in its power and significance as a deliberative organ. In fact, the council rarely meets as a body and, when it does, betrays little more animation than listening to and applauding various reports. The decision-making functions of the council have been preempted by the Presidium of the Council of Ministers.

The Chairman and Presidium of the Council of Ministers

The Presidium of the Council of Ministers is the principal administrative decision-making organ of the Soviet government. It presides over the ministries and other administrative organs of the government, supervises their work, coordinates their activities, settles jurisdictional conflicts, and decides questions of a general administrative character. Decrees (*postanovleniya*) of the council of a general character are issued

18 *Pravda,* July 16, 1970.

by the Presidium in the name of the council and signed by the chairman or first deputy and countersigned by the administrator of affairs, who is in charge of the drafting and other housekeeping agencies of the council. Orders (*rasporyazheniya*) of the council, which are decisions more operational and current in character, can be signed by the chairman, first deputy, or a deputy. Individual ministers are empowered to issue instructions and regulations that are administratively binding within the agencies under their jurisdiction.

The most influential member in the Council of Ministers is its chairman, who has always been in the highest rank of the party hierarchy. This office has been occupied by only eight men since its establishment on the day after the Revolution: Lenin (1917–24); Rykov (1924–30); Molotov (1930–41); Stalin (1941–53); Malenkov (1953–55); Bulganin (1955–58); Khrushchev (1958–64); and Kosygin (1964–   ). Of these, all but Lenin, Rykov, Stalin and Khrushchev are still alive; except for Lenin, all of the past occupants of this post, whether dead or alive, are in varying degrees of disgrace. Rykov was executed in 1938 after the last of the notorious purge trials; Stalin's corpse has been banished from Lenin's mausoleum and his memory defiled; Molotov, Malenkov, and Bulganin have been explicitly denounced as "antiparty"; while Khrushchev was disgraced as a "nonperson."

The size and composition of the membership of the Presidium has varied in response to the vagaries of factional politics. Under Stalin, the council's Presidium consisted of a dozen or more members, most of whom did not carry ministerial portfolios after 1949. Apparently, Stalin operated through an even smaller body, the "Bureau" of the Presidium, whose existence, but not composition, was revealed only after Stalin's death. Immediately after Stalin's death, the secret "Bureau" was abolished, the Presidium was reduced in size, and first deputies were restored to various consolidated portfolios, as were other members of the party Presidium in the government. In the first post-Stalin government, the council Presidium consisted of the chairman (Malenkov), four first deputies (Beria, Molotov, Kaganovich, Bulganin), and one dep-

uty (Mikoyan)—all of whom were full members of the party Presidium. The size of the council Presidium increased and reached a peak after February 1955, when Bulganin displaced Malenkov as premier. Bulganin's council Presidium in 1956 consisted of five first deputies (all members of the party Presidium) and eight deputies (including the disgraced Malenkov, who remained a full member of the party Presidium), and the council itself expanded to include more than fifty ministries.

In the following year, however, after the economic reorganization acts of May 1957, the abolition of twenty-five economic ministries and other ministerial reorganizations reduced the number of ministries to less than twenty. By 1964, the ministries had been reduced to eleven, but the size of the council expanded to more than seventy members because of the admission of other agencies and organs.

After Khrushchev's ouster, the elaborate structure of state committees erected by Khrushchev was progressively dismantled and the ministry was restored as the principal administrative unit of the council. By 1970, the government once again included over sixty ministries, while the number of state committees dwindled to eleven, thus restoring the pre-Khrushchev equilibrium between these two administrative forms.

MINISTRIES AND OTHER DEPARTMENTS

Ministries in the central government are of two types: all-union and union republic. The all-union ministries, of which there were twenty-five in 1970, are administrative agencies which are completely centralized in the federal government and are limited to matters which are incapable of being decentralized, such as foreign trade, merchant marine, etc. The union republic ministries (thirty-one in 1970) are departments dealing with matters in which jurisdiction is shared between the center and the circumference. According to Soviet constitutional doctrine and administrative practice, the union republic ministries are governed by a system of dual subordination. The ministry exists at two levels; in Moscow and in each of the fifteen union republics. Constitutionally, each union republic ministry is responsible to its corresponding supreme organ of state authority, but, administratively, the union republic ministries in the republics are subordinated to their counterparts in the central government.

The union republic ministries are primarily functional in character and include what are normally considered to be the most important departments of government: foreign affairs and defense. The union republic ministries are useful devices for decentralizing administration and responsibility, without, at the same time, relinquishing control of policy from the center. Thus whereas the union republic minister in Moscow is appointed by the all-union Supreme Soviet and the union republic ministers in the republics are appointed by their respective supreme soviets, article 76 of the constitution specifies that the Moscow ministries direct the activities of the union republic ministries in the republics. In the case of foreign affairs, this division of authority is only a matter of form, and in the case of defense does not go beyond the printed words of the constitution. For the Ministries of Culture, Health, Higher Education, and Agriculture, however, genuine deconcentration of administrative personnel and responsibility can be usefully and constructively introduced.

The state committees are organized much like the ministries, and are also of two types: all-union and union republic. The main difference is that the department is directed by a committee rather than by a minister, although in some cases the chairman may carry the title of minister. With one or two exceptions (notably the Committee for State Security), the committees which have been retained deal with matters which cut across various departments and agencies and thus require coordination, such as Science and Technology. The conversion of the Ministry of State Security (the secret police) into a state committee was calculatedly designed to dismantle the dangerous apparatus built by Beria and to insure that it could not again become an instrument of a single individual.

THE NATIONAL ECONOMIC COUNCILS (SOVNARKHOZ)

In May 1957, virtually the entire network of economic ministries was set aside and their powers redistributed among more than one hundred regional economic councils, with complete authority over all industrial enterprises within their territorial jurisdiction.

All the councils were established within the boundaries of union republics, in order not to offend local sensitivities, although this created problems of an economic character. Large republics were divided into several regions, while the smaller republics constituted a single sovnarkhoz. In order to overcome the drawbacks of drawing economic regions to correspond with political divisions, the one hundred or so economic regions were grouped together into seventeen main economic regions.

The sovnarkhoz system failed to survive the ouster of Khrushchev, with whom it was intimately associated. While it served the purpose of decentralizing economic power, and thereby effectively destroyed the power base of the heavy industrial managers, many of whom resisted Khrushchev's economic innovations, it was far from a success from the standpoint of productive efficiency. It stimulated localism, and in some cases infused the republics with a sense of economic nationalism as localities were impelled to produce more in response to local needs, demands, and interests, than to those of the center. Beginning in March 1965, a sweeping reorganization was inaugurated as the sovnarkhoz system was dismantled and the economic state committees once again transformed into ministries. The Supreme Council of the National Economy, the All-Union Council of the National Economy, and the republic councils of the national economy and the economic regions were all scrapped, while the State Planning Committee once again was restored as the top planning body of the Soviet Union. Anxiety that the old defects of the restored system might be revived as well was reflected in Brezhnev's caveat at the Twenty-third Party Congress:

We would like to caution Ministry workers against attempts to revive a narrow departmental approach to matters, a fault of which the former ministries were frequently guilty.[19]

HOW "NEW" GOVERNMENTS ARE FORMED

Since the Soviet governmental machinery is organized along pseudo-parliamentary lines, it is not surprising that the relationship between the Council of Ministers and the Supreme Soviet imitates those of authentic parliamentary systems. In the Soviet system, there are four formal occasions when a "new" government is required: (1) after the election of a new Supreme Soviet (regularly every four years); (2) when the chairman of the Council of Ministers resigns; (3) when the chairman dies or becomes incapacitated; (4) when the chairman loses the confidence of the Supreme Soviet.

The last occasion has never materialized, but it remains a possibility. From 1941, when Stalin replaced Molotov as the head of the government, until Stalin's death in March 1953, only the first occasion arose. At the initial meeting of a newly elected Supreme Soviet, Stalin would submit a written statement "surrendering" the powers of his government to the Supreme Soviet, meeting in joint session, which would be accepted. Almost simultaneously, the Supreme Soviet would then commission Stalin to submit proposals for a "new" government. At the "next" joint sitting (the following afternoon or day), the chairman of the Presidium would announce the "new" government proposed by Stalin. The announcement would be greeted with a prearranged outburst of odes to Stalin delivered by selected deputies, whereupon Stalin's "new" government "was then voted upon as a whole and unanimously adopted amidst loud applause passing into an ovation in honor of Comrade Stalin, who was elected

Chairman of the Council of Ministers of the USSR." [20]

Stalin's sudden death in March 1953 confronted his successors with the problem of devising a formula for organizing a "new" government for the first time since Lenin and Stalin had ceased dominating the scene. The crisis clearly required supraconstitutional procedures, whose only counterpart elsewhere is the *coup d'état*. In other words, the vacuum created by Stalin's death could only be filled outside the constitution, because it was a question of power and not a question of law. On March 7, 1953, an extraordinary joint decree was issued over the names of the party's Central Committee, the Council of Ministers, and the Presidium of the Supreme Soviet, which cleverly embraced every conceivable instrument of legitimacy and legality in the Soviet system and included all possible contenders for power.

The Presidium of the Supreme Soviet received a new chairman and secretary (although the constitution specifies that the members of the Presidium can only be elected by the Supreme Soviet). Malenkov was advanced to Stalin's vacated post of premier, and other members of the party Presidium were appointed first deputies, deputies, and ordinary ministers. One week later, on March 15, 1953, the Supreme Soviet, in a breathless session of 67 minutes, approved the *fait accompli,* and the bare bones of constitutional procedure were thus preserved.

"New" governments following resignations of the chairman have been nominated three times, the first time on February 8, 1955, when a statement was read by the chairman of the Council of Union on behalf of Malenkov before the Supreme Soviet at one o'clock in the afternoon, in which he submitted his resignation on grounds of administrative inexperience and incompetence. The premier of the Russian SFSR moved that the resignation be accepted, which was unanimously approved, and in less than 10 minutes the session was adjourned. At 4:00 P.M., the Supreme Soviet was reconvened,

---

[19] *Pravda*, March 30, 1966.

[20] Karpinsky, *Social and State Structure of the U.S.S.R.*, pp. 123–24.

and Khrushchev, the first speaker, proceeded to nominate Nikolai Bulganin as Malenkov's successor. Five minutes after the session started, Bulganin was unanimously approved as the new chairman. The next day, Bulganin delivered his acceptance speech and submitted his list of proposed ministers.

The second resignation took place in March 1958, when Bulganin submitted his resignation, which was accepted unanimously. Khrushchev's name was placed in nomination by Marshal Voroshilov, the chairman of the Presidium of the Supreme Soviet. The first secretary was approved as the new premier unanimously by acclamation, and the "new" government was in business less than 24 hours after the convocation of the Supreme Soviet.

The third resignation allegedly took place at the October 14, 1964 plenum of the Central Committee. No deliberations of this plenum have ever been published, and serious doubts about its actual convocation are widespread. Khrushchev was removed abruptly in a carefully planned *coup* while he was vacationing on the Black Sea. According to the official version of events, Khrushchev requested of the Central Committee (not of the Supreme Soviet) that "he be released from the duties of First Secretary of the Central Committee of the CPSU, member of the Presidium of the Central Committee of the CPSU, and Chairman of the USSR Council of Ministers, in view of his advanced age and deterioration in the state of his health." [21] The request was promptly granted, and on the next day he was formally relieved of his post by the Presidium of the Supreme Soviet, which then proceeded to unanimously appoint Kosygin in his place. Khrushchev's removal and Kosygin's appointment were then duly ratified by the Supreme Soviet several months later— on December 9, 1964.[22]

[21] *Pravda,* October 16, 1964.
[22] *Pravda,* December 10, 1964.

It should be noted that the procedure employed in Khrushchev's resignation departed significantly from the Malenkov and Bulganin resignation scenarios. Khrushchev did not publicly ask to be relieved; nor did he even appear before the Supreme Soviet or its Presidium, to which he was constitutionally responsible, to make a statement. In fact, Khrushchev never made a public statement concerning any aspect of his alleged resignation, and furthermore, he did not indulge in any public confession of error, incompetence, or disloyalty, as was the case with his two predecessors. Another important deviation is that the Central Committee was the first to announce his resignation, not the Presidium of the Supreme Soviet. And no account was given of how Kosygin was recommended to the Presidium for appointment, although in December 1964, Brezhnev formally nominated Kosygin at the ratification session of the Supreme Soviet.

The precision and rapidity with which the Supreme Soviet accepted resignations and approved "new" governments, with neither advance notice nor deliberation, is sufficiently eloquent by itself to demonstrate the nature of the responsibility and accountability of the Council of Ministers to the Supreme Soviet. Needless to say, the smoothness of the changeovers simply reflects the fact that all the basic questions were decided in the party Politburo and were then simply formalized in the presence of the Supreme Soviet. In a strictly technical sense, the procedure seems to resemble the manner in which governments are chosen by party caucuses or executive committees in democratic countries, which are then ratified by parliaments, with the very significant exception that the party Politburo is, as we have seen, the only "party caucus" tolerated in the Soviet system. In the case of Khrushchev's removal, however, the regime came perilously close to violating its own party procedures and constitutional norms which it has so sedulously sought to observe since Stalin's death.

Although the Soviet system is now more than a half-century old, any attempt to determine with precision its definitive contours would still be premature. Soviet society has been subjected to a continuous process of social and political convulsions that have been engineered from the top in an attempt to achieve the ideological goals of the party leadership. Still, Soviet society today remains an unfinished social order. From the standpoint of the party leadership, current Soviet society represents simply another way-station on the road to communism. Changes, radical and trivial, will continue to be initiated from above, following the needs of the moment, although what in fact emerges will continue to represent a balance between the imperatives of ideology and the resistance of internal and external forces to change.

In the evolution of Soviet society, significant groups with an interest in arresting further social transformations have continuously emerged, and the present state of affairs is no different except that the social groups which today have a vested interest in maintaining the status quo are more differentiated, more influential, and more firmly rooted than those of previous periods. It would be a mistake, however, to assume that they will necessarily be any more successful in arresting further social transformations. External impediments, in the form of differently perceived interests by various Communist states, particularly China, and the successful resistance of the non-Communist world to the expansion of the Communist sphere are just as likely to force a reshaping of the ideological goals of Soviet society as are internal forces. Soviet society thus remains in a condition of flux.

Certain features of the Soviet system have achieved a degree of permanence because they not only satisfy the requirements of ideology, but have won genuine popular acceptance: the public ownership of the means of production, natural resources, and financial institutions, and state control of communications, information, health, education, welfare, and culture are two examples. The collective-farm system, on the other hand, seems to be universally disliked and represents an unwelcome burden on agriculture and the peasantry. The one-party system

NINE

the

Soviet Union

today . . .

and tomorrow

finds wide acceptance, although the people would prefer more flexibility in nominations and elections and would like more than one candidate to stand for political office. It might also be noted that some nationalities, particularly the three Baltic countries, would prefer to be outside the Soviet community altogether, and tensions continue to arise over the Communist failure to reconcile completely the conflicts between national dignity and Soviet patriotism, between local national pride and Great Russian nationalism.

PROBLEMS AHEAD

The dilemmas of the Soviet system thus derive from the failure of social realities to correspond with desirable ideological goals which were promised or are claimed (democracy, freedom, etc.), and from the state's efforts to impose undesirable ideological goals (collectivized agriculture, for example) or to transform existing institutions and processes which are acceptable into unacceptable patterns. These dilemmas and problems can be grouped into four general categories: (1) problems arising out of the necessity to falsify or rationalize reality (ideological distortion or false perception); (2) problems arising from the failure to legitimize or legalize the transfer of power; (3) problems of social equilibrium and stabilization; (4) problems arising from the utilization of economic resources and production. Implicit also is the fundamental problem arising from the conflict between the requirements of internal stability and the ideological goals of foreign policy.

Ideological Distortions

The Soviet system continues to be plagued by the agonies of what we might call false perception resulting from ideological distortions of reality. While many of these problems appear esoteric, they are of crucial significance in a society in which a systematically articulated ideology is officially enshrined. In some instances, Soviet leaders and citizens appear to believe many things to be true which are in fact false, and this results in a condition known as "false consciousness," an aberration which infects all societies, but one to which Soviet society is especially prone.

Soviet society is described as "free," "democratic," and without class hostility, although this is patently untrue. It is asserted that the Communist party represents the monolithic will of all classes, whose interests are unified and harmonious, whereas in fact social groups in Soviet society perceive their interests differently, and the Communist party articulates the will of the elites rather than that of all social classes. Formulating policy and social behavior in accordance with beliefs which are out of focus with reality results in distorted perceptions of problems and situations and gives rise to misdirected or inappropriate solutions and responses. Problems which in fact exist remain unnoticed and without solutions, while problems which do not exist appear as real and are met with artificial solutions.

Legitimacy and Succession

A perennial and still unresolved problem in the Soviet system is that of the institutionalization and legitimization of political power. Theoretically, the problem does not exist, and, in official doctrine, Soviet leaders and citizens must behave as if the problem is nonexistent. Theoretically, power is lodged in the party and is then delegated to the central organs of the party, which exercise this power in a collective or institutional rather than personal capacity. Power, however, cannot be exercised impersonally, but must be possessed and exercised by individuals, who may be members of bodies or groups.

At any given time in the Soviet system, the institutional seat of power can be defined, but the particular personalities who hold the reins of power cannot. Thus, while Stalin was alive, power theoretically rested in the party Politburo, but in fact was vested in Stalin as a person. When Stalin died, theoretically no power vacuum existed, since the Politburo as a body continued to function. In fact, a profound vacuum resulted because no orderly process had been devised for transferring power. The official ideology refused to recognize the existence of such a problem. In the absence of a legal or predetermined succession procedure, the problem was resolved informally by a struggle for supremacy among various personalities, cliques, and groups, although the existence of such a struggle was itself repeatedly denied. The composition of various party and state organs changed with each phase of the struggle, but no actual transfer of power in the party hierarchy was officially recognized, since, theoretically, the power of the party is always lodged in its central organs.

Although certain unwritten ground rules seem to be developing governing the struggle for power, these do not enjoy official recognition, nor are they explicitly articulated; and unless an orderly system for transferring power is devised, a dangerous vacuum will continue to exist at the very apex of the Soviet system.

Another closely related problem of power is the precise relationship that exists between the party and the state. Again, in theory, no problem is supposed to exist; the party devises policy and transmits it to the state for execution and implementation as law. In fact, however, tensions appear between the two not only because this functional division of labor is impossible to sustain in a meaningful sense, but also because each inevitably becomes the instrument of power of those who control it. This tension, in practice, is resolved only when both institutions are under the control of a single center of power, reflected usually in the unification of the highest post in the government and the highest post in the party in a single person. Thus, as did Lenin throughout his lifetime and Stalin from 1941 to 1953, Khrushchev between 1958 and 1964 held the position of party leader and premier of the government. The fact that the two posts were once again separated after Khrushchev's removal demonstrates that the problem still has not been resolved. As long as the problems of power and succession are not dealt with in their realistic—as opposed to their ideologically distorted—dimension, the Soviet system will continue to be threatened with instability at the very pinnacle of power,

and each succession crisis will carry with it the potential for disaster.

Social Stratification and the Party

The Communist party is being increasingly transformed into an arena in which the various Soviet elites make known their demands on one another, articulate their special interests, and try to impose their desires as the unified will of society as a whole. It is clear that one of the most substantial problems of the Soviet social order is how to reduce the inevitable tensions between the desire of a privileged group, the Soviet intelligentsia, to preserve its special status and the ideological imperative of a classless society to which the party leadership is committed. While theoretically the intelligentsia as an entity is committed to a classless society, in actual fact only the party apparatus appears to have an enduring interest in it. The very function of the party apparatus is to preserve the purity and integrity of the Communist doctrine. Besides, the apparatus's political power is not likely to be undermined by the implementation of Communist egalitarian principles. On the contrary, it would probably be enhanced, since egalitarian reforms would tend to undermine the position of privileged nonparty groups.

According to Soviet doctrine, the intelligentsia is destined to dissolve into the society as a whole. Hence, the idea of recognizing distinct groups within the intelligentsia—although they exist in actuality—is in flagrant conflict with Marxism-Leninism. But since future Communist development will be determined by both the ideological commitment of the party and the attitude of social groups, the study of social structure and social stratification is extremely important. There is no question but that the several elites which have crystallized within the Soviet intelligentsia have, on the whole, a vested interest in preserving largely intact the social order which exists in the Soviet Union today. They would like nothing better than to receive official recognition guaranteeing the status quo. While quasi-autonomous interest groups flourish within the intelligentsia, they enjoy neither legal nor ideological recognition, and hence the fiction must be preserved that they do not exist. Only the intelligentsia as a whole enjoys ideological acceptance—as a "stratum" of the working class. Thus, a constant friction and conflict between the upper social groups in the intelligentsia and the party apparatus is likely to be the rule in Soviet society for some time to come. The party leaders will attempt to undermine the vested interests of the intelligentsia, while the latter will try to buttress its social position either by constitutional reform or by capturing the very citadel of political power, the leadership of the party.

Some Soviet scholars are therefore calling for the recognition of "intraclass" differences based upon social function and the division of labor—which, they concede, give rise to divergent social attitudes and interests. They make a sharp distinction between *class* structure, which is slated for extinction, and *social* structure (and thus *social* stratification), which they argue is an inevitable and ineradicable feature of any organized society. Although the new bourgeoning Soviet field of "complex sociological research" is designed to facilitate the transition to Communist society, it is more likely to rationalize the existing social system; and what one Soviet observer maintains is the function of "bourgeois" sociologists appears more accurately to be an esoteric justification for the new Soviet science of "complex sociology":

Sociologists in the bourgeois world cope perfectly well with the role of "social engineers." Their specific recommendations and forecasts are devoted, as a rule, to improving the existing structures and institutions, to eliminating individual conflicts and contradictions. To put it simply, they devise the lubricants that enable a rusting mechanism to function normally. They boldly disclose contradictions of social organization, but only in order to strengthen its foundations, to heal its ulcers, and prolong its life.[1]

The regime clearly recognizes the existence of the tensions between the desire of social elites to maintain their privileges and the ideo-

logical imperative of a classless society. The ideological key to the resolution of this dilemma is to raise the level of productivity to the point where it meets total social demand, which then automatically renders superfluous all necessity for establishing priorities in the distribution of rewards. The economic transformation of society, according to the Soviets, will bring about the necessary psychological transformation of man so that "it will become a habit to work to the best of one's ability, not only as a duty, but also as an inner urge," and then both the material and psychological prerequisites for a classless society will have been met. In Soviet jargon, this means that distinctions between physical and "mental" labor and between rural and urban life must be eliminated so that "the activity of all workers of Communist society will be a combination of physical and mental work."

It can be safely assumed, therefore, that existing social distinctions and differentials in rewards and status will persist for some time and that privileged elites will endeavor to maintain their privileges; but it can also be expected that the regime will take periodic measures to curb these tendencies so that social mobility in Soviet society will remain relatively high. The intelligentsia will continue to expand in numbers and occupations. It seems hardly credible that privileged elites will disappear voluntarily in Soviet society. Yet the ultimate goal is precisely that. "With the victory of Communism," writes one authority, "there will be no intelligentsia as a separate social stratum."

Raising the Standard of Living

Raising the standard of living in the Soviet Union has crucial ideological significance, since Communist society requires an economy of abundance to provide the material basis for the psychological and moral transformation of man. The tremendous effort devoted to enhancing the productive forces of the country, however, are not all directed to raising the standard of living, for the regime is still determined to enhance Soviet military power and promote

---

[1] *Komsomolskaya, Pravda,* June 2, 1967.

the ideological goal of world communism, albeit with diminishing enthusiasm. Consequently, the major Soviet economic effort is directed toward three fields, which results in a certain amount of conflict, since the Soviet economy is not capable of satisfying the needs of all three simultaneously. The three fields are: (1) heavy industry—the goal is to maintain a high rate of industrial growth for prestige purposes and to accomplish foreign policy objectives; (2) military power—again for purposes of prestige as well as national security and for the promotion of ideological objectives, in part through military assistance to various foreign countries; and (3) consumer goods and food production.

Production for the consumer has always received the lowest priority in the Soviet Union, particularly in agriculture, and one of the basic tensions of contemporary Soviet society stems from the desire of the people for a more rapid improvement in their standard of living, as opposed to the regime's insistence on assigning priority to heavy industry and military power. Since Stalin's death, greater attention has been devoted to raising the standard of living, and substantial progress has been made, but this has merely whetted the public's appetite rather than satisfied it. Furthermore, the Soviet people are now more aware that the standard of living could be even higher if less effort and investment were channeled into the production of heavy industry and rockets.

Agricultural production, particularly, has always lagged far behind industrial growth. While industrial goals are consistently achieved and sometimes exceeded, agricultural production almost always falls short of planned targets. This has created a serious imbalance in the Soviet economy, and, while the Soviet public is not undernourished or on the verge of a subsistence diet, the agricultural sector of the Soviet economy remains a jerry-built structure which can crumble in the face of a serious crisis.

The inefficiency of agricultural production in the Soviet Union stems from two causes: the low priority it receives in terms of investment and effort, and the collective-farm system. Admittedly, food production could be significantly increased if the state funneled greater resources in that direction, but this would be at the expense of heavy industry and armament. Early in 1962, Khrushchev publicly rejected this alternative in favor of boosting prices for meat and dairy products by 25–30% as an inducement to the farmers to produce more in exchange for greater profits.[2] This served only to raise slightly the peasant's standard of living at the relatively greater expense of the urban standard of living, thus was not an effective solution.

Altering the structure of Soviet agriculture could also result in greater food production, but again at the expense of redistributing income between town and country. Incentives for greater production within the collective-farm system have just about reached their maximum point, and the regime is now confronted with the major decision of whether to accept stagnation in agriculture or to stimulate further growth—either by greater investment at the expense of industry and armaments or by radically revising the collective-farm system to give the peasant greater incentives for greater effort. Khrushchev's successors have put more money into agriculture, and this, combined with better efficiency and more incentives for the peasant, has been rewarded with two extraordinary bumper harvests (in 1966 and 1967).

One of the great anomalies of the Soviet system is the vast disparity between its low material standard of living and its high level of culture and education. This imbalance produces psychological tensions which cannot be sustained over a long period of time. As the intelligentsia becomes acutely aware of the imbalances and incongruities of the Soviet system, particularly as it gains knowledge of how its social counterparts in other industrial societies live, it may begin thinking in terms of solutions outside the framework of official doctrine, especially if the further implementation of doctrinal goals would have an adverse effect on its station in society. Already there are important signs which indicate that the educated elite of the coming generation will be less inclined to accept at face value the ideological goals of the regime and will be even less predisposed to

---

2 At the November 1962 plenum of the Central Committee, Khrushchev announced a 30% increase in agricultural investment.

accept the frequently disingenuous rationalizations and explanations which are advanced to justify existing policies and conditions. While the satisfactions, on the whole, outweigh the tensions in Soviet society, and violent internal upheavals against the regime are not likely, the possibility of a silent revolution transforming both the internal and external goals of the Soviet system in the direction of greater social stability, greater freedom, and more attention to concrete and material (rather than ideological) problems is a real one.

CHAPTER 2

BERDYAEV, NICOLAS, *The Origins of Russian Communism* (London: Geoffrey Bles, 1948).

———, *The Russian Idea* (New York: Macmillan, 1948).

BILLINGTON, JAMES, *The Icon and the Axe* (New York: Knopf, 1966).

BLACK, C. E. (ed.), *The Transformation of Russian Society: Aspects of Social Change since 1861* (Cambridge: Harvard University Press, 1960).

CARR, E. H., *A History of Soviet Russia: The Bolshevik Revolution, 1917–1923,* 3 vols. (New York: Macmillan, 1951–1953).

CHAMBERLIN, W. H., *The Russian Revolution, 1917–1921,* 2 vols. (New York: Macmillan, 1935).

FLORINSKY, M. T., *Russia: A History and an Interpretation* (New York: Macmillan, 1953).

KARPOVICH, M., *Imperial Russia, 1801–1917* (New York: Macmillan, 1932).

KENNAN, G. F., *Russia Leaves the War: Soviet American Relations, 1917–1920* (Princeton: Princeton University Press, 1956).

KERENSKY, ALEXANDER, *Russia and History's Turning Point* (New York: Duell, Sloan & Pearce, 1965).

MAYNARD, JOHN, *Russia in Flux* (New York: Macmillan, 1948).

PARES, SIR BERNARD, *A History of Russia,* 5th ed. (New York: Knopf, 1947).

PIPES, R., *The Formation of the Soviet Union* (Cambridge: Harvard University Press, 1954).

SCHUMAN, F. L., *Russia since 1917* (New York: Knopf, 1957).

SETON-WATSON, HUGH, *The Decline of Imperial Russia* (New York: Praeger, 1952).

SUKHANOV, N. N., *The Russian Revolution, 1917: A Personal Record* (New York: Oxford University Press, 1955).

TROTSKY, LEON, *The History of the Russian Revolution,* 3 vols. (New York: Simon & Schuster, 1936).

CHAPTER 3

BALZAK, S. S.; V. F. VASYUTIN; AND Y. G. FEIGIN, *Economic Geography of the U.S.S.R.* (New York: Macmillan, 1949).

bibliography

BARGHOORN, F. C., *Soviet Russian Nationalism* (New York: Oxford University Press, 1956).

BEREDAY, G. Z. F., AND J. PENNAR (eds.), *The Politics of Soviet Education* (New York: Praeger, 1960).

BERGSON, ABRAM, AND SIMON KUZNETS, *Economic Trends in the Soviet Union* (Cambridge: Harvard University Press, 1963).

CAMPBELL, R., *Soviet Economic Power* (Boston: Houghton Mifflin, 1960).

COLE, J. P., *Geography of the U.S.S.R.* (Baltimore: Md.: Penguin Books, 1967).

Comparisons of the United States and Soviet Economics, Parts 1–5 (Washington, D.C.: Govt. Printing Office, 1966).

DEWITT, N., *Education and Professional Employment in the U.S.S.R.* (Washington, D.C.: National Science Foundation, 1961).

INKELES, A., *Public Opinion in Soviet Russia* (Cambridge: Harvard University Press, 1949).

KOLARZ, W., *Russia and Her Colonies* (New York: Praeger, 1952).

NOVE, ALEC, *Economic Rationality and Soviet Politics* (New York: Praeger, 1964).

———, *The Soviet Economy*, rev. ed. (New York: Praeger, 1966).

SCHWARTZ, HARRY, *The Soviet Economy since Stalin* (Philadelphia: Lippincott, 1965).

SHABAD, T., *Geography of the U.S.S.R.* (New York: Macmillan, 1951).

CHAPTER 4

ASPATURIAN, V. V., "The Contemporary Doctrine of the Soviet State and its Philosophical Foundations," *American Political Science Review* (December, 1954).

DANIELS, R. W. (ed.), *A Documentary History of Communism* (New York: Random House, 1960).

DEGEORGE, RICHARD T., *The New Marxism* (New York: Pegasus, 1968).

GRULIOW, LEON (ed.), *Current Soviet Policies,* Vols. 1–4 (New York: Praeger, 1953, 1957, 1960, 1962).

HAIMSON, L. H., *The Russian Marxists and the Origins of Bolshevism* (Cambridge: Harvard University Press, 1955).

HOOK, SIDNEY, *From Hegel to Marx* (New York: The Humanities Press, 1950).

HUNT, R. N. C., *The Theory and Practice of Communism,* 5th ed. (New York: Macmillan, 1957).

JAWORKSKY, MICHAEL, *Soviet Political Thought: An Anthology* (Baltimore: The Johns Hopkins Press, 1967).

LEITES, N., *A Study of Bolshevism* (Glencoe, Ill.: The Free Press, 1953).

MARCUSE, H., *Soviet Marxism* (New York: Columbia University Press, 1958).

MEYER, ALFRED G., *Communism* (New York: Vintage, 1966).

———, *Leninism* (Cambridge: Harvard University Press, 1957).

———, *Marxism: The Unity of Theory and Practice* (Cambridge: Harvard University Press, 1954).

PLAMENATZ, J., *German Marxism and Russian Communism* (London: Longmans, Green, 1954).

SIMMONS, E., *Continuity and Change in Russian and Soviet Thought* (Cambridge: Harvard University Press, 1955).

WILSON, E., *To the Finland Station* (New York: Harcourt, Brace, 1940).

WOLFE, B., *Three Who Made a Revolution* (New York: Dial Press, 1948).

ULAM, ADAM B., *The Unfinished Revolution* (New York: Random House, 1959).

CHAPTER 5

ALLILUYEVA, SVETLANA, *Twenty Letters to a Friend* (New York: Harper and Row, 1967).

BAUER, R., *The New Man in Soviet Psychology* (Cambridge: Harvard University Press, 1952).

BERLINER, JOSEPH S., *Factory and Manager in the U.S.S.R.* (Cambridge: Harvard University Press, 1957).

BROWN, EMILY C., *Soviet Trade Unions and Labor Relations* (Cambridge: Harvard University Press, 1966).

DINERSTEIN, H. S., *Communism and the Russian Peasant* (Glencoe, Ill.: The Free Press, 1955).

DJILAS, M., *The New Class* (New York: Praeger, 1957).

GRANICK, D., *The Red Executive* (Garden City, N.Y.: Doubleday, 1960).

INKELES, A., AND R. BAUER, *The Soviet Citizen* (Cambridge: Harvard University Press, 1959).

INKELES, A., R. BAUER, AND C. KLUCKHOHN, *How the Soviet System Works* (Cambridge: Harvard University Press, 1956).

INKELES, ALEX, *Social Change in Soviet Russia* (Cambridge: Harvard University Press, 1968).

———, AND K. GEIGER, *Soviet Society* (Boston: Houghton Mifflin, 1961).

JASNY, N., *The Socialized Agriculture of the U.S.S.R.* (Stanford, Calif.: Stanford University Press, 1949).

KASSOF, ALAN (ed.), *Prospects for Soviet Society* (New York: Praeger, 1968).

KOLARZ, WALTER, *Religion in the Soviet Union* (London: St. Martin's Press, 1961).

LAIRD, ROY D., *Collective Farming in Russia* (Lawrence, Kansas: University of Kansas Publications, 1958).

LAQUEUR, W., AND L. LABEDZ (eds.), *The Future of Communist Society* (New York: Praeger, 1962).

MOORE, B., *Terror and Progress: U.S.S.R.* (Cambridge: Harvard University Press, 1954).

NICOLAEVSKY, BORIS I., *Power and the Soviet Elite* (London: Pall Mall Press, 1965).

PIPES, R. (ed.), *The Russian Intelligentsia* (New York: Columbia University Press, 1960).

VUCINICH, A., *Soviet Economic Institutions* (Stanford, Calif.: Stanford University Press, 1952).

CHAPTER 6

BRZEZINSKI, Z., *The Permanent Purge* (Cambridge: Harvard University Press, 1956).

CARR, E. H., *The Interregnum* (New York: Macmillan, 1954).

———, *Socialism in One Country*, Vols. 1 and 2 (New York: Macmillan, 1958, 1960).

DEUTSCHER, I., *The Prophet Armed: Trotsky, 1879–1921* (New York: Oxford University Press, 1954).

———, *The Prophet Unarmed: Trotsky, 1922–1929* (New York: Oxford University Press, 1959).

GEHLEN, MICHAEL P., *The Communist Party of the Soviet Union* (Bloomington, Indiana: Indiana University Press, 1969).

JACOBS, DAN N. (ed.), *The New Communist Manifesto and Related Documents*, 2nd ed. (Evanston, Ill.: Row, Peterson, 1962).

LEITES, N., AND E. BERNAUT, *The Ritual of Liquidation* (Glencoe, Ill.: The Free Press, 1954).

RESHETAR, J., *A Concise History of the Communist Party of the Soviet Union* (New York: Praeger, 1959).

SCHAPIRO, L., *The Communist Party of the Soviet Union* (New York: Random House, 1959).

———, *The Origin of the Communist Autocracy* (Cambridge: Harvard University Press, 1955).

STALIN, J. V., *History of the Communist Party of the Soviet Union* (New York: International Publishers, 1938).

TREADGOLD, D., *Lenin and His Rivals* (New York: Praeger, 1960).

TRISKA, JAN (ed.), *Soviet Communism: Program and Rules* (San Francisco: Chandler, 1962).

WOLIN, S., AND R. SLUSSER (eds.), *The Soviet Secret Police* (New York: Praeger, 1957).

CHAPTER 7

ARENDT, H., *The Origins of Totalitarianism* (New York: Harcourt, Brace, 1951).

ARMSTRONG, JOHN A., *The Soviet Bureaucratic Elite* (New York: Praeger, 1959).

———, *The Politics of Soviet Totalitarianism* (New York: Random House, 1961).

AZRAEL, JEREMY, *Managerial Power and Soviet Politics* (Cambridge: Harvard University Press, 1966).

BARGHORN, FREDERICK L., *Politics in the U.S.S.R.* (Boston: Little, Brown, 1966).

BIALER, SEWERYN (ed.), *Stalin and his Generals* (New York: Pegasus, 1969).

BRUMBERG, A., *Russia under Khrushchev* (New York: Praeger, 1962).

BRZEZINSKI, ZBIGNIEW, AND SAMUEL HUNTINGTON, *Political Power: U.S.A./U.S.S.R.* (New York: Viking Press, 1964).

CONQUEST, ROBERT, *The Great Terror* (New York: Macmillan, 1968).

———, *Power and Policy in the U.S.S.R.* (New York: St. Martin's Press, 1961).

———, *Russia after Khrushchev* (New York: Praeger, 1965).

DALLIN, ALEXANDER, AND BRESLAUER, GEORGE W., *Political Terror in Communist Systems* (Stanford: Stanford University Press, 1970).

DEUTSCHER, I., *Stalin* (New York: Oxford University Press, 1948).

FAINSOD, M., *Smolensk under Soviet Rule* (Cambridge: Harvard University Press, 1958).

———, *How Russia Is Ruled*, 2nd ed. (Cambridge: Harvard University Press, 1963).

FLERON, FREDERIC J. (ed.), *Communist Studies and the Social Sciences* (New York: Rand-McNally, 1969).

FRIEDRICH, C., AND Z. BRZEZINSKI, *Totalitarian Dictatorship and Autocracy* (Cambridge: Harvard University Press, 1956).

HYLAND, W., AND SHRYOCK, R. W., *The Fall of Khrushchev* (New York: Funk and Wagnalls, 1968).

JOHNSON, CHALMERS (ed.), *Change in Communist Systems* (Stanford: Stanford University Press, 1970).

KOLKOWICZ, ROMAN, *The Soviet Military and the Communist Party* (Princeton: Princeton University Press, 1967).

KULSKI, W. W., *The Soviet Regime,* 4th ed. (Syracuse, N.Y.: Syracuse University Press, 1963).

LINDEN, CARL, *Khrushchev and the Soviet Leadership, 1957–1964* (Baltimore: Johns Hopkins Press, 1966).

LODGE, MILTON C., *Soviet Elite Attitudes Since Stalin* (Columbus, Ohio: Chas. E. Merrill Co., 1969).

MEAD, M., *Soviet Attitudes toward Authority* (New York: McGraw-Hill, 1951).

MOORE, BARRINGTON, *Soviet Politics—The Dilemma of Power* (Cambridge: Harvard University Press, 1948).

PLOSS, SIDNEY, *Conflict and Decision-Making in Soviet Russia* (Princeton: Princeton University Press, 1965).

—— (ed.), *The Soviet Political Process* (Waltham, Mass.: Ginn and Co., 1971).

RUSH, MYRON, *Political Succession in the U.S.S.R.* (New York: Columbia University Press, 1965).

SKILLING, GORDON, AND GRIFFITHS, F. (eds.), *Interest Groups in Soviet Politics* (Princeton: Princeton University Press, 1970).

SWEARER, HOWARD, *The Politics of Succession in the U.S.S.R.* (Boston: Little, Brown, 1964).

TATU, MICHEL, *Power in the Kremlin: From Khrushchev to Kosygin* (New York: Viking, 1967).

WOLFE, B. D., *Khrushchev and Stalin's Ghost* (New York: Praeger, 1957).

CHAPTER 8

ANDREWS, WILLIAM G. (ed.), *Soviet Institutions and Policies, Inside Views* (Princeton: Van Nostrand, 1966).

ASPATURIAN, V. V., *The Union Republics and Soviet Diplomacy* (Geneva, Switz.: Libraire Droz, 1960).

BERMAN, H. J., *Justice in Russia* (Cambridge: Harvard University Press, 1950).

CARSON, G. B., JR., *Electoral Practices in the U.S.S.R.* (New York: Praeger, 1956).

CORNELL, RICHARD (ed.), *The Soviet Political Systems* (Englewood Cliffs, N.J.: Prentice-Hall, 1970).

HAZARD, J. N., *The Soviet System of Government,* rev. ed. (Chicago: University of Chicago Press, 1960).

KELSEN, H., *The Communist Theory of Law* (New York: Praeger, 1955).

MEISEL, J. H., AND E. KOZERA (eds.), *Materials for the Study of the Soviet System* (Ann Arbor, Mich.: George Wahr, 1953).

MEYER, ALFRED G., *The Soviet Political System* (New York: Knopf, 1965).

MORGAN, GLENN G., *Soviet Administrative Legality* (Stanford: Stanford University Press, 1962).

National Policy Machinery in the Soviet Union (Washington, D.C.: Govt. Printing Office, 1960).

SALISBURY, HARRISON E., *The Soviet Union: The Fifty Years* (New York: Harcourt, Brace & Co., 1967).

SCOTT, DEREK, J. R., *Russian Political Institutions* (New York: Praeger, 1961).

TOWSTER, J., *Political Power in the U.S.S.R., 1917–1947* (New York: Oxford University Press, 1948).

TURNER, J., AND H. McCLOSKEY, *The Soviet Dictatorship* (New York: McGraw-Hill, 1960).

VYSHINSKY, A. Y. (ed.), *The Law of the Soviet State* (New York: Macmillan, 1948).

WERTH, A., *Russia under Khrushchev* (New York: Crest Books, 1962).

ALFORD, ROBERT R., *Party and Society: The Anglo-American Democracy* (Chicago: Rand McNally, 1963).

ALMOND, GABRIEL A., AND JAMES S. COLEMAN, *Politics of the Developing Areas* (Princeton: Princeton University Press, 1960).

————, AND G. B. POWELL, *Comparative Politics: A Developmental Approach* (Boston: Little, Brown, 1965).

————, AND SIDNEY VERBA, *The Civic Culture* (Princeton: Princeton University Press, 1964).

ASHER, ROBERT E., *Development of the Emerging Countries* (Washington, D.C.: Brookings Institution, 1962).

BEER, SAMUEL H., *British Politics in the Collectivist Age* (New York: Knopf, 1965).

————, AND ADAM B. ULAM (eds.), *Patterns of Government: The Major Political Systems of Europe,* rev. ed. (New York: Random House, 1962).

BLACK, MAX (ed.), *The Social Theories of Talcott Parsons* (Englewood Cliffs, N.J.: Prentice-Hall, 1961).

BRAIBANTI, RALPH, AND JOSEPH J. SPENGLER (eds.), *Tradition, Values and Socio-economic Development* (Durham: Duke University Press, 1961).

BRINTON, CRANE, *The Anatomy of Revolution,* rev. ed. (Englewood Cliffs, N.J.: Prentice-Hall, 1952).

CATLIN, GEORGE E. G., *Systematic Politics* (Toronto: Toronto University Press, 1962).

DAHL, ROBERT A., *Modern Political Analysis* (Englewood Cliffs, N.J.: Prentice-Hall, 1970).

————, "A Critique of the Ruling Elite Model," *American Political Science Review* (June 1958).

DEAN, VERA M., *The Nature of the Non-Western World* (New York: New American Library, 1957).

DEUTSCH, KARL W., *Nationalism and Social Communication: An Inquiry into the Foundations of Nationality* (New York: Wiley, 1953).

————, LEWIS J. EDINGER, ROY C. MACRIDIS, AND RICHARD L. MERRITT, *France, Germany and the Western Alliance: A Study of Elite Attitudes on European Integration and World Politics* (New York: Scribners, 1967).

DUIJKER, H. L. J., AND N. H. FRIJDA, *National Character and National Stereotypes* (Amsterdam: North Holland Publishing Co., 1960).

DUVERGER, MAURICE, *Political Parties: Their Organization and Activity in the Modern State,* translated by Barbara and Robert North (New York: Wiley, 1954).

selected bibliography

COMPARATIVE ANALYSIS
AND
POLITICAL SYSTEMS

————, *Sociologie Politique* (Paris: Presses Universitaires de France, 1966).

EASTON, DAVID, *A Framework of Political Analysis* (Englewood Cliffs, N.J.: Prentice-Hall, 1965).

————, *The Political System: An Inquiry into the State of Political Science* (New York: Knopf, 1953).

————, *A Systems Analysis of Political Life* (New York: Wiley, 1965).

ECKSTEIN, HARRY, *Pressure Group Politics: The Case of the British Medical Association* (Stanford: Stanford University Press, 1960).

————, AND DAVID APTER (eds.), *Comparative Politics: A Reader* (Glencoe, Ill.: The Free Press, 1963).

EHRMANN, HENRY W. (ed.), *Interest Groups in Four Continents* (Pittsburgh: Pittsburgh University Press, 1958).

EMERSON, RUPERT, *From Empire to Nation: The Rise to Self-assertion of Asian and African Peoples* (Cambridge: Harvard University Press, 1960).

ETZIONI, AMITAI, *A Comparative Analysis of Complex Organizations* (Glencoe, Ill.: The Free Press, 1961).

FESTINGER, LEON, AND DANIEL KATZ (eds.), *Research Methods in the Behavioral Sciences* (New York: Holt, Rinehart and Winston, 1966).

FINER, HERMAN, *The Theory and Practice of Modern Government,* rev. ed. (New York: Holt, 1949).

FORTES, MEYER, AND E. E. EVANS-PRITCHARD (eds.), *African Political Systems* (London: Oxford University Press, 1940).

FREEMAN, EDWARD A., *Comparative Politics* (London: Macmillan, 1873).

FRIEDRICH, CARL J., *Constitutional Government and Democracy: Theory and Practice in Europe and America,* rev. ed. (Boston: Ginn, 1950).

————, AND Z. K. BRZEZINSKI, *Totalitarian Dictatorship and Autocracy* (Cambridge: Harvard University Press, 1956) (New York: Praeger, 1961).

FROHOCK, FRED M., *The Nature of Political Inquiry* (Homewood, Ill.: Dorsey Press, 1967).

GALBRAITH, JOHN K., *Economic Development in Perspective* (Cambridge: Harvard University Press, 1962).

GOLEMBIEWSKI, G., "The Group Basis of Politics," *American Political Science Review* (December 1960).

HARGROVE, E., "Political Leadership in Anglo-American Democracies" in Lewis J. Edinger, *Political Leadership in Industrialized Societies* (New York: Wiley, 1967).

HECKSHER, GUNNAR, *Comparative Politics and Government* (London: Allen & Unwin, 1957).

HOSELITZ, BERT F. (ed.), *The Progress of Underdeveloped Areas* (Chicago: Chicago University Press, 1952).

HUNTINGTON, SAMUEL P., *Political Order in Changing Societies* (New Haven: Yale University Press, 1968).

HYMAN, HERBERT, *Political Socialization: A Study in the Psychology of Political Behavior* (Glencoe, Ill.: The Free Press, 1959).

JOHNSON, JOHN J. (ed.), *The Role of the Military in Underdeveloped Countries* (Princeton: Princeton University Press, 1962).

KAPLAN, MORTON A., *The Revolution in World Politics* (New York: Wiley, 1962).

KAUTSKY, JOHN, *Political Change in Underdeveloped Countries* (New York: Wiley, 1962).

KERLINGER, FRED N., *Foundations of Behavioral Research: Educational and Psychological Inquiry* (New York: Holt, 1967).

LANDAU, M., "On the Use of Functional Analysis in American Political Science," *Social Research* (Spring 1968).

LaPALOMBRA, JOSEPH, "Macrotheories and Microapplications in Comparative Politics: A Widening Chasm," *Comparative Politics* (October 1968).

———— (ed.), *Bureaucracy and Political Development* (Princeton: Princeton University Press, 1963).

————, AND MYRON WEINER (eds.), *Political Parties and Political Development* (Princeton: Princeton University Press, 1966).

LAQUEUR, WALTER Z. (ed.), *The Middle East in Transition* (New York: Praeger, 1958).

LASSWELL, HAROLD D., AND ABRAHAM KAPLAN, *Power and Society: A Framework for Political Inquiry* (New Haven: Yale University Press, 1950).

————, AND DANIEL LERNER (eds.), *World Revolutionary Elites: Studies in Coercive Ideological Movements* (Massachusetts: M.I.T. Press, 1970).

LASSWELL, HAROLD D., DANIEL LERNER, AND C. EASTON ROTHWELL, *The Comparative Study of Elites: An Introduction and Bibliography* (Stanford: Stanford University Press, 1952).

LATHAM, EARL, *The Group Basis of Politics* (New York: Octagon, 1965).

LERNER, DANIEL, *The Passing of Traditional Society: Modernizing the Middle East* (Glencoe, Ill.: The Free Press, 1958).

LEVY, MARION J., JR., *The Structure of Society* (Princeton: Princeton University Press, 1952).

LIPSET, SEYMOUR M., *Political Man: The Social Bases of Politics* (Garden City, N.Y.: Doubleday, 1960).

LIPSET, SEYMOUR M., *The First Nation* (New York: Basic Books, 1963).

MACKENZIE, WILLIAM J., *Politics and Social Science* (Baltimore: Penguin, 1967).

MACRIDIS, ROY C., "Comparative Politics and the Study of Government," *Comparative Politics* (October 1968).

——— (ed.), *Foreign Policy in World Politics* (Englewood Cliffs, N.J.: Prentice-Hall, 1972).

——— (ed.), *Political Parties: Contemporary Trends and Ideas* (New York: Harper Torchbooks, 1967).

———, *The Study of Comparative Government* (Garden City, N.Y.: Doubleday, 1955).

———, AND BERNARD E. BROWN, *Comparative Politics: Notes and Readings* (Homewood, Ill.: The Dorsey Press, 1961).

MARX, FRITZ MORSTEIN, *The Administrative State: An Introduction to Bureaucracy* (Chicago: Chicago University Press, 1957).

MACIVER, ROBERT M., *The Web of Government* (New York: Macmillan, 1947).

MCCLELLAND, DAVID C., *The Achieving Society* (Princeton, N.J.: Van Nostrand, 1961).

MEEHAN, EUGENE J., *Theory in Method of Political Analysis* (Homewood, Ill.: Dorsey Press, 1965).

———, *Contemporary Political Thought: A Critical Study* (Homewood, Ill.: Dorsey Press, 1967).

MERKL, PETER H., *Modern Comparative Politics* (New York: Holt, 1970).

MERRITT, RICHARD L., AND STEIN ROKKAN, *Comparing Nations: The Use of Quantitative Data for Cross-National Research* (New Haven: Yale University Press, 1966).

MERTON, ROBERT K., *Social Theory and Social Structure* (Glencoe, Ill.: The Free Press, 1949).

MICHELS, ROBERT, *Political Parties* (New York: Dover, 1959).

MILLIKAN, MAX F., AND DONALD L. M. BLACKMER (eds.), *The Emerging Nations* (Boston: Little, Brown, 1961).

MITCHELL, WILLIAM, *Sociological Analysis and Politics: The Theories of Talcott Parsons* (Englewood Cliffs, N.J.: Prentice-Hall, 1967).

MOORE, BARRINGTON, JR., *Political Power and Social Theory* (Cambridge: Harvard University Press, 1958).

MOORE, B., JR., *The Social Origins of Democracy and Dictatorship* (Boston: Beacon, 1966).

NEUMANN, SIGMUND, "Comparative Politics: A Half Century Appraisal," *Journal of Politics* (August, 1957).

——— (ed.), *Modern Political Parties: Approaches to Comparative Politics* (Chicago: University of Chicago Press, 1956).

PARSONS, TALCOTT, *Essays in Sociological Theory: Pure and Applied* (Glencoe, Ill.: The Free Press, 1949).

———, *The Social System* (Glencoe, Ill.: The Free Press, 1951).

———, AND EDWARD A. SHILS, *Toward a General Theory of Action* (Cambridge: Harvard University Press, 1951).

PYE, LUCIAN, *Politics, Personality and Nation Building—Burma's Search for Identity* (New Haven: Yale University Press, 1962).

ROKKAN, STEIN (ed.), "Citizen Participation in Political Life," *International Social Science Journal,* Vol. XII, No. 1 (1961).

ROSTOW, WALT W., *The Stages of Economic Growth, A Non-Communist Manifesto* (Cambridge: Cambridge University Press, 1960).

RUNCIMAN, WALTER G., *Social Sciences and Political Theory* (Cambridge: Cambridge University Press, 1963).

RUSSETT, BRUCE, et al., *Handbook of World Indicators* (New Haven: Yale University Press, 1964).

RUSTOW, DANKWART A., *A World of Nations: Problems of Political Modernization* (Washington, D.C.: Brookings, 1967).

———, *Politics and Westernization in the Near East* (Princeton: Princeton University, Center of International Studies, 1956).

SELLIN, THORSTEIN, AND RICHARD D. LAMBERT (eds.), "Asia and the Future of World Leadership," special issue of the *Annals of the American Academy of Political and Social Sciences,* Vol. 318 (July, 1958).

SHONFIELD, ANDREW, *Modern Capitalism* (London: Oxford University Press, 1966).

SIFFIN, WILLIAM J. (ed.), *Toward a Comparative Study of Public Administration* (Bloomington: University of Indiana Press, 1957).

STALEY, EUGENE, *The Future of Underdeveloped Countries: Political Implications of Economic Development,* rev. ed. (New York: Praeger, 1961).

STINCHCOMBE, ARTHUR L., *Constructing Social Theories* (New York: Harcourt, 1970).

ULAM, ADAM B., *The Unfinished Revolution* (New York: Random House, 1960).

VERBA, SIDNEY, "Conclusion: Comparative Political Culture," in Lucian Pye and Sidney Verba (eds.) *Political Culture and Political Development* (Princeton: Princeton University Press, 1970).

————, "Some Dilemmas in Comparative Research," *World Politics* (October 1967).

WHEARE, KENNETH D., *Modern Constitutions* (New York: Oxford University Press, 1951).

WISEMAN, H. VICTOR, *Political Systems: Some Sociological Approaches* (New York: Praeger, 1966).

index

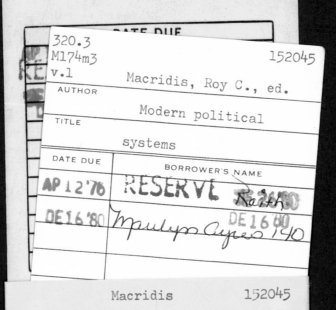